Oxford University Press
Digital Learning
Resources

*Patterns of
World History
with Sources*

Volume One to 1600

FOURTH EDITION

Peter von Sivers
Charles A. Desnoyers
George B. Stow

Carefully scratch off the
silver coating to see your
personal redemption code.

OXFORD
UNIVERSITY PRESS

Directions for access

Oxford Insight Study Guide and Additional Digital Course Materials

Patterns of World History comes with a wealth of
powerful tools to help you succeed in your course.

Follow these steps to access your resources:

Visit oup.com/he/vonsivers4e

Select the edition you are using, then select student
resources for that edition

Follow the on-screen instructions, entering your personal
redemption code when prompted

For assistance with code redemption or
registration, please contact customer support at
learninglinkdirect.support@oup.com.
or 855-281-8749.

About the Cover

This pictorial map of the Yellow River is both an artistic masterpiece and a source of scientific information. Ordered by the founding emperor of the Ming dynasty, the Hongwu Emperor Zhu Yuanzhang (r. 1368–1398), the map is executed in true proportions and was used to assess the impact of the frequently flooded Yellow River. The houses in the map indicate the population of towns and villages, with each house representing 100 families.

Patterns of
World History

Patterns of World History

VOLUME ONE to 1600

Fourth Edition

Peter von Sivers
University of Utah

Charles A. Desnoyers
La Salle University

George B. Stow
La Salle University

New York   Oxford
OXFORD UNIVERSITY PRESS

Oxford University Press is a department of the University of Oxford.
It furthers the University's objective of excellence in research, scholarship,
and education by publishing worldwide. Oxford is a registered trade mark of
Oxford University Press in the UK and certain other countries.

Published in the United States of America by Oxford University Press
198 Madison Avenue, New York, NY 10016, United States of America.

For titles covered by Section 112 of the US Higher Education
Opportunity Act, please visit www.oup.com/us/he for the latest
information about pricing and alternate formats.

Library of Congress Control Number: 2020030201

Printing number: 9 8 7 6 5 4 3 2
Printed in Mexico by Quad/Mexico

Coniugi Judithae dilectissimae

—PETER VON SIVERS

To all my students over the years,
who have taught me at least as much as I've taught them;
and most of all to my wife, Jacki, beloved in all things,
but especially in her infinite patience and fortitude
in seeing me through the writing of this book.

—CHARLES A. DESNOYERS

For Susan and our children, Meredith and Jonathan.

—GEORGE B. STOW

—I hear and I forget; I see and I remember; I do and I understand
(Chinese proverb) 我听见我忘记;我看见我记住;我做我了解

Brief Contents

MAPS xix

STUDYING WITH MAPS xxi

PREFACE xxii

**NOTE ON DATES
AND SPELLINGS** xxx

ABOUT THE AUTHORS xxxi

WORLD PERIOD ONE

From Human Origins to Early Agricultural Centers

Prehistory to 600 BCE 2

1. The African Origins of Humanity, Prehistory–10,000 BCE
   2

2. Agrarian–Urban Centers of the Middle East and Eastern Mediterranean, 11,500–600 BCE
   26

3. Shifting Agrarian Centers in India, 3000–600 BCE
   54

4. Agrarian Centers and the Mandate of Heaven in Ancient China, 5000–481 BCE
   76

5. Origins Apart: The Americas and Oceania, 14,500–600 BCE
   100

WORLD PERIOD TWO

The Age of Empires and Visionaries

600 BCE–600 CE 124

6. Chiefdoms and Early States in Africa and the Americas, 600 BCE–600 CE
   124

7. Interaction and Adaptation in Western Eurasia: Persia, Greece, and Rome, 550 BCE–600 CE
   148

8. Empires and Visionaries in India, 600 BCE–600 CE
   174

9. China: Imperial Unification and Perfecting the Moral Order, 722 BCE–618 CE
   196

WORLD PERIOD THREE

The Formation of Religious Civilizations
600–1450 CE   220

10. Islamic Civilization and Byzantium, 600–1300 CE
    220
11. Innovation and Adaptation in the Western Christian World, 600–1450 CE
    252
12. Contrasting Patterns in Eurasia, 600–1600 CE
    280
13. Religious Civilizations Interacting: Korea, Japan, and Vietnam, 550–1500 CE
    304
14. Patterns of State Formation in Africa, 600–1450 CE
    328
15. The Rise of Empires in the Americas, 600–1550 CE
    350

WORLD PERIOD FOUR

Interactions across the Globe
1450–1750   370

16. Western Christian Overseas Expansion and the Ottoman–Habsburg Struggle, 1450–1650
    370
17. The Renaissance, New Sciences, and Religious Wars in Europe, 1450–1750
    394
18. New Patterns in New Worlds: Colonialism and Indigenous Responses in the Americas, 1500–1800
    422

FURTHER RESOURCES   R-1
CREDITS   C-1
SOURCE INDEX   SI-1
SUBJECT INDEX   I-1

Contents

MAPS   xix

STUDYING WITH MAPS   xxi

PREFACE   xxii

NOTE ON DATES AND SPELLINGS   xxx

ABOUT THE AUTHORS   xxxi

WORLD PERIOD ONE

From Human Origins to Early Agricultural Centers

PREHISTORY TO 600 BCE   2

Chapter 1
Prehistory–10,000 BCE

The African Origins of Humanity   2

The Origins of Humanity   3

    Hominins: No Longer Apes, but Not Yet Human   4

Human Adaptations: From Africa to Eurasia and Australia   7

    The African Origins of Human Culture   7

    Migration from South Asia to Australia   10

    Migration from Asia to Europe   14

The Ice Age Crisis and Human Migration to the Americas   17

    The Ice Age   17

Putting It All Together   23

Features:

Patterns Up Close:
The Disappearance of the
Neanderthals   20

Against the Grain:
The Hobbits of Flores
Island   24

▶ PATTERNS OF EVIDENCE: **Sources for Chapter 1**

1.1—Shell bead jewelry from the Grotte des Pigeons, Taforalt, Morocco •
1.2—Python-shaped ornamented rock found in the Rhino Cave, Botswana •
1.3—Pottery's diverse origins in East Asia • 1.4—Flax fibers found at the
Dzudzuana Cave, Republic of Georgia, Caucasus Mountains

Chapter 2
11,500–600 BCE

Agrarian–Urban Centers of the Middle East and Eastern Mediterranean   26

Agrarian Origins in the Fertile Crescent, ca. 11,500–1500 BCE   27

    Sedentary Foragers and Foraging Farmers   28

    The Origin of Urban Centers
in Mesopotamia and Egypt   31

Interactions among Multiethnic and Multireligious Empires,
ca. 1500–600 BCE   41

    The Hittite and Assyrian Empires, 1600–600 BCE   41

    Small Kingdoms on the Imperial Margins,
1600–600 BCE   44

Religious Experience and Cultural Achievements   47

Features:

Patterns Up Close:
Babylonian Law Codes   36

Against the Grain:
Akhenaten the
Transgressor   52

Putting It All Together   50

▶ PATTERNS OF EVIDENCE: **Sources for Chapter 2**

2.1—Law Code of Hammurabi • 2.2—Three spinal injury cases documented in the Edwin Smith Papyrus • 2.3— Advice from a royal scribe to his apprentice, Middle Kingdom Egypt, Twelfth Dynasty • 2.4— Sketch of the palace complex at Knossos, Minoan Crete • 2.5— The Great Hymn to the Aten

Chapter 3 3000–600 BCE	**Shifting Agrarian Centers in India**	54
	The Vanished Origins of Harappa, 3000–1500 BCE	56
	The Region and People	56
	Adapting to Urban Life in the Indus Valley	59
	The Collapse of the Cities	62
	Interactions in Northern India, 1500–600 BCE	63
	The Vedic World, 1750–800 BCE	64
	Statecraft and the Ideology of Power, 800–600 BCE	66
	Indian Society, Culture, and Religion, 1500–600 BCE	68
	Society and Family in Ancient India	68
	Cultural Interactions to 600 BCE	70

Features:

Patterns Up Close:
The Caste System   70

Against the Grain:
A Merchants' Empire?   74

Putting It All Together   73

▶ PATTERNS OF EVIDENCE: **Sources for Chapter 3**

3.1—The Bhagavad Gita • 3.2—Prayer to Varuna • 3.3—The Brihadaranyaka Upanishad • 3.4—*The Code of Manu*

Chapter 4 5000–481 BCE	**Agrarian Centers and the Mandate of Heaven in Ancient China**	76
	The Origins of Yellow River Cultures, 5000–1766 BCE	78
	Geography and Climate	78
	The Origins of Neolithic Cultures	80
	The Age of Myth and the Xia Dynasty, 2852–1766 BCE	82
	The Interactions of Shang and Zhou History and Politics, 1766–481 BCE	84
	The Shang Dynasty, 1766–1122 BCE	84
	The Mandate of Heaven: The Zhou Dynasty to 481 BCE	87
	Economy, Society, and Family Adaptation in Ancient China	89
	Shang Society	89
	Interactions of Zhou Economy and Society	90
	Gender and the Family	91
	Interactions of Religion, Culture, and Intellectual Life in Ancient China	92

Oracle Bones and Early Chinese Writing 93
Adaptations of Zhou Religion, Technology, and Culture 95

Putting It All Together 96

▶ PATTERNS OF EVIDENCE: **Sources for Chapter 4**
4.1—Excerpts from *The Book of Odes (Shijing)* • 4.2—The Announcement of the Duke
of Shao • 4.3—*The Book of Lord Shang (Shangjun Shu)* • 4.4—Iron sword with jade
handle, earliest cast-iron object (Western Zhou), from Henan Museum, Guo state,
Sanmenxia city

Chapter 5
14,500–600 BCE

Origins Apart: The Americas and Oceania 100

Adapting to the Americas 102
The Environment 102
Foragers 105

Agriculture, Villages, and Urban Life 107
The Neolithic Revolution in the New World 108
The Origins of Urban Centers 109
The First Mesoamerican Settlements 112

The Origins of Pacific Island Migrations 117
Lapita and Cultural Expansion 118
Creating Polynesia 119

Putting It All Together 119

▶ PATTERNS OF EVIDENCE: **Sources for Chapter 5**
5.1—Quipu from the Caral-Supe culture, Peru • 5.2—Textile fragment from
Chavín de Huántar, Peru • 5.3—New DNA results show Kennewick Man was Native
American • 5.4—Lapita pot shards, found in Vanuatu, western Pacific

Features:

Patterns Up Close:
The Chinese Writing
System   94

Against the Grain:
Women's Voices   98

Features:

Patterns Up Close:
The Origin of Corn   112

Against the Grain:
Rapa Nui: Catastrophe or
Continuity?   122

WORLD
PERIOD
TWO

The Age of Empires and Visionaries
600 BCE TO 600 CE

Chapter 6
600 BCE–600 CE

**Chiefdoms and Early States in Africa
and the Americas** 124

Agriculture and Early African Kingdoms 125
Saharan Villages, Towns, and Kingdoms 126
The Kingdom of Aksum 128

The Spread of Villages in Sub-Saharan Africa 130
West African Savanna and Rain-Forest Agriculture 130

The Spread of Village Life to East and South Africa 131
Patterns of African History, 600 BCE–600 CE 134

Early States in Mesoamerica: Maya Kingdoms and Teotihuacán 134
The Maya Kingdoms in Southern Mesoamerica 135
The Kingdom of Teotihuacán in the Mexican Basin 140

The Andes: Moche   141

    The Moche in Northern Peru   142

Paracas and the Nasca in Southern Peru   143

Putting It All Together   144

▶ PATTERNS OF EVIDENCE: **Sources for Chapter 6**

    6.1—Africa's earliest bananas • 6.2—Relief sculpture from Meroë, Sudan •

    6.3—The Inland Niger Delta • 6.4—Lady K'atun, Queen of Piedras Negras •

    6.5—Cosmas Indicopleustes (Cosmas the India-Voyager), *Christian Topography*

Chapter 7
550 BCE–600 CE

Interaction and Adaptation in Western Eurasia: Persia, Greece, and Rome   148

Early Persia and Greece   150

    The Origins of the Achaemenid Persian Empire   150

    Greek City-States in the Persian Shadow   152

    Alexander's Empire and Its Successor Kingdoms   155

Interactions between the Persian and Roman Empires   155

    Parthian Persia and Rome   156

    The Sasanid Persian and Late Roman Empires   159

Adaptations to Monotheism and Monism in the Middle East   163

    Challenge to Polytheism: The Origins of Judaism, Zoroastrianism, and
Greek Philosophy   163

    Toward Religious Communities and Philosophical Schools   165

The Beginnings of Science and the Cultures of Kings and Citizens   167

    The Sciences at the Library of Alexandria   168

    Royal Persian Culture and Arts   168

    Greek and Roman Civic Culture and Arts   169

Putting It All Together   171

▶ PATTERNS OF EVIDENCE: **Sources for Chapter 7**

    7.1—The Cyrus Cylinder • 7.2—Herodotus, *Histories* • 7.3—Hippocrates, *On
the Sacred Disease* • 7.4—1 Maccabees • 7.5—Graffiti from the walls of Pompeii •
7.6—The murder of the philosopher Hypatia, Alexandria, Egypt

Chapter 8
600 BCE–600 CE

Empires and Visionaries in India   174

Patterns of State Formation in India: Republics, Kingdoms, and Empires   176

    The Road to Empire: The Mauryas   176

    The Classical Age: The Gupta Empire   180

    The Southern Kingdoms, ca. 300–600 CE   180

The Vedic Tradition and Its Visionary Reformers   182

    Reforming the Vedic Tradition   182

    The Maturity of Hinduism: From the Abstract to the Devotional   185

Features:

Patterns Up Close:
The Mayan Ball Game   138

Against the Grain:
Nasca Lines: Speculation and
Explanation   146

Features:

Patterns Up Close:
The Plague of Justinian 160

Against the Grain:
Women in Democratic
Athens   173

Stability amid Disorder: Economy, Family, and Society   188
    Tax and Spend: Economy and Society   188
    Caste, Family Life, and Gender   189

Strength in Numbers: Art, Literature, and Science   192

Putting It All Together   193

▶ PATTERNS OF EVIDENCE: **Sources for Chapter 8**
    8.1—The Seven Pillar Edicts of King Ashoka • 8.2—*The Questions of King Milinda
(The Milindapanha)* • 8.3—Fa Xian, Excerpt from *A Record of Buddhistic Kingdoms* •
8.4—Kalidasa, *The Cloud Messenger*

Features:

Patterns Up Close:
The Global Trade of Indian
Pepper   190

Against the Grain:
India's Ancient
Republics   194

Chapter 9
722 BCE–618 CE

China: Imperial Unification and Perfecting the Moral Order   196

Visionaries and Empire   198
    Confucianism, Legalism, and Daoism   198
    The Qin Dynasty   201
    The Han Dynasty   203

The Domestic Economy: Society, Family, and Gender   207
    Industry and Commerce   208
    Gender Roles   211

Intellectual Trends, Aesthetics, Science, and Technology   211
    Confucianism, Education, and History during the Han   212
    Buddhism in China   214
    Intellectual Life   215

Putting It All Together   216

▶ PATTERNS OF EVIDENCE: **Sources for Chapter 9**
    9.1—*Analects (Lunyu)* of Confucius • 9.2—*Book of Mencius* (Mengzi) • 9.3—Li Si,
"Memorial on the Burning of Books," from the *Shiji* • 9.4—Ban Zhao, *Admonitions for
Women (Nüjie)*

Features:

Patterns Up Close:
The Stirrup   206

Against the Grain:
Individualism and Universal
Love: Yang Zhu
and Mo Di   218

WORLD PERIOD THREE

The Formation of Religious Civilizations

600–1450 CE

Chapter 10
600–1300 CE

Islamic Civilization and Byzantium   220

The Formation of Islamic Religious Civilization   222
    The Beginnings of Islam   222
    Islamic Theology, Law, and Politics   225

Eastern Christian Civilization in Byzantium   229
    Byzantium's Difficult Beginnings   229
    The Seljuk Invasion and the Crusades   233

Islamic and Eastern Christian Civilizations at Their Height 237
    State and Society in Mamluk Egypt   238

Byzantine Provincial and Central Organization   239
Commercial Relations from the Atlantic
to the South China Sea   241

Religion, Sciences, and the Arts in Two Religious Civilizations   243
Islamic Culture: Intellectual and Scientific Expressions   243
Artistic Expressions in Islamic Civilization   244
Learning and the Arts in Byzantium   245

Putting It All Together   248

▶ PATTERNS OF EVIDENCE: **Sources for Chapter 10**
10.1—Al-Jahiz: The Story of the Judge and the Fly • 10.2—Documents related to the
iconoclasm controversy • 10.3—Memoirs of Usama Ibn Munqidh • 10.4—A Jewish
engagement contract from Fustat (Old Cairo) • 10.5—An Islamic mystic's highest
meditative state

Chapter 11
600–1450 CE

**Innovation and Adaptation in
the Western Christian World**   252

The Formation of Christian Europe, 600–1000   254
Frankish Gaul and Latin Christianity   254

Recovery, Reform, and Innovation, 1000–1300   259
The Political Recovery of Europe   259
The Economic and Social Recovery of Europe   260
Religious Reform and Expansion   264
Intellectual and Cultural Developments   267

Crisis and Creativity, 1300–1415   270
The Calamitous Fourteenth Century   270
Signs of a New Era in the Fifteenth Century   274

Putting It All Together   276

▶ PATTERNS OF EVIDENCE: **Sources for Chapter 11**
11.1—Einhard's *Life of Charlemagne* • 11.2—Adelard of Bath, *Questiones naturales* •
11.3—Feudal contracts and the swearing of fealty • 11.4—Peter Abelard, *The Story of
My Misfortunes* • 11.5—Giovanni Boccaccio, *The Decameron*, "Putting the Devil Back
in Hell" • 11.6—Flagellants attempt to ward off the Black Death in Germany and in
England

Chapter 12
600–1600 CE

Contrasting Patterns in Eurasia   280

India: The Clash of Cultures   282
Buddhist and Hindu India after the Guptas   282
Islam in India, 711–1398   283
Toward the Mughal Era, 1398–1450   285

Interactions and Adaptations: From Buddhism to Neo-Confucian Synthesis
in China   287
Creating a Religious Civilization under the Tang   287
The Song and Yuan Dynasties, 960–1368   290

The Ming to 1450: The Quest for Stability   296

Society, Family, and Gender   297

Perceptions of Perfection: Intellectual, Scientific, and Cultural Life   298

Putting It All Together   300

▶ PATTERNS OF EVIDENCE: **Sources for Chapter 12**

12.1—The *Chachnamah* • 12.2—Poetry of the Tang Dynasty • 12.3—Model of a
Ming ship in the flotilla of Zheng He • 12.4—Genghis Khan Strikes West

Features:

Patterns Up Close:
Gunpowder   292

Against the Grain:
Empress Wu   302

Chapter 13
550–1500 CE

Religious Civilizations Interacting: Korea, Japan, and Vietnam   304

Korea to 1450: Innovation from Above   306

People and Place: The Korean Environment   306

Conquest and Competition: History
and Politics to 1450   307

Economy, Society, and Family   310

Religion, Culture, and Intellectual Life   312

Japan to 1450: Selective Interaction and Adaptation   313

The Island Refuge   313

Adaptation at Arm's Length: History and Politics   313

Economy, Society, and Family   317

Religion, Culture, and Intellectual Life   319

Vietnam: Human Agency and State Building   321

The Setting and Neolithic Cultures   321

Economy, Society, and Family   323

Religion, Culture, and Intellectual Life   324

Putting It All Together   325

▶ PATTERNS OF EVIDENCE: **Sources for Chapter 13**

13.1—Murasaki Shikibu, *The Tale of Genji* • 13.2—*Nihongi (Chronicles of Japan)* •
13.3—*Haedong kosŭng chŏn*, on Buddhism in Korea • 13.4—Copper head of
Bodhisattva Avalokiteshvara, Vietnam

Features:

Patterns Up Close:
Printing   310

Against the Grain:
Zen and Bushido   327

Chapter 14
600–1450 CE

Patterns of State Formation in Africa   328

Christians and Muslims in the Northeast   330

Nubia in the Middle Nile Valley   330

Ethiopia in the Eastern Highlands   333

Adaptation to Islam: City-States and Kingdoms in East and Southern Africa   335

The Swahili City-States on the East African Coast   335

Traditional Kingdoms in Southern and Central Africa   337

Central African Chiefdoms and Kingdoms   340

Cultural Encounters: West African Traditions and Islam   341

The Kingdom of Ancient Ghana   341

The Empire of Mali   342

Rain-Forest Kingdoms   346

Features:

Patterns Up Close:
The Sculptures of Ife   344

Against the Grain:
Sundiata's Rise to
Power   348

Putting It All Together   346

▶ PATTERNS OF EVIDENCE: **Sources for Chapter 14**

14.1—*The Fetha Nagast,* Ethiopia • 14.2—Ibn Battuta: Journey to the East African
Coast • 14.3—'Abd al-'Azīz al-Bakrī, Description of West Africa • 14.4—Walls and
moats at Sungbo's Eredo, Nigeria

Chapter 15   **The Rise of Empires in the Americas**   350
600–1550 CE

The Legacy of Teotihuacán and the Toltecs in Mesoamerica   352
   Militarism in the Mexican Basin   352
   Late Maya States in Yucatán   354

The Legacy of Tiwanaku and Wari in the Andes   355
   The Expanding State of Tiwanaku   355
   The Expanding City-State of Wari   357

American Empires: Aztec and Inca Origins and Dominance   358
   The Aztec Empire of Mesoamerica   358
   The Inca Empire of the Andes   360

Imperial Society and Culture   363
   Imperial Capitals: Tenochtitlán and Cuzco   364
   Power and Its Cultural Expressions   365

Putting It All Together   367

▶ PATTERNS OF EVIDENCE: **Sources for Chapter 15**

15.1—Skeletons in a Wari royal tomb site, El Castillo de Huarmey, Peru •
15.2—Ahuitzotl, Eighth King (*Tlatloani*) of the Aztec Empire • 15.3—Bernal Díaz,
The Conquest of New Spain • 15.4—Pedro Cieza de León on Incan roads

Features:

Patterns Up Close:
Human Sacrifice   366

Against the Grain:
Amazon Rain-Forest
Civilizations   369

WORLD PERIOD FOUR

Interactions across the Globe

1450–1750

Chapter 16   **Western Christian Overseas Expansion and the Ottoman–**
1450–1650   **Habsburg Struggle**   370

The Muslim–Christian Competition in the East and West, 1450–1600   372
   Iberian Christian Expansion, 1415–1498   372
   Rise of the Ottomans and Struggle with the Habsburgs for Dominance, 1300–1609   376

The Centralizing State: Origins and Interactions   384
   State Transformation, Money, and Firearms   384

Imperial Courts, Urban Festivities, and the Arts   387
   The Ottoman Empire: Palaces, Festivities, and the Arts   387
   The Spanish Habsburg Empire: Popular Festivities and the Arts   389

Putting It All Together   391

▶ PATTERNS OF EVIDENCE: **Sources for Chapter 16**

16.1—Columbus reports on his first voyage, 1493 • 16.2—Christopher Columbus,
The Book of Prophecies • 16.3—Thomas the Eparch and Joshua Diplovatatzes,

Features:

Patterns Up Close:
Shipbuilding   378

Against the Grain:
Tilting at Windmills   392

"The Fall of Constantinople" • 16.4—Evliya Çelebi, "A Procession of Artisans at Istanbul" • 16.5—Ogier Ghiselin de Busbecq, "The Court of Suleiman the Magnificent" • 16.6—Janissary musket

Chapter 17
1450–1750

The Renaissance, New Sciences, and Religious Wars in Europe 394

Cultural Transformations: Renaissance, Baroque, and New Sciences   396

The Renaissance and Baroque Arts   396

The New Sciences   398

The New Sciences and Their Social Impact   401

The New Sciences: Philosophical Interpretations   404

Centralizing States and Religious Upheavals   405

The Rise of Centralized Kingdoms   405

The Protestant Reformation, State Churches, and Independent Congregations   407

Religious Wars and Political Restoration   411

Putting It All Together   419

▶ PATTERNS OF EVIDENCE: **Sources for Chapter 17**

17.1—Examination of Lady Jane Grey, London • 17.2—Emilie du Châtelet, *Discourse on Happiness* • 17.3—Sebastian Castellio, *Concerning Whether Heretics Should Be Persecuted* • 17.4—Duc de Saint-Simon, "The Daily Habits of Louis XIV at Versailles" • 17.5—Giorgio Vasari, *The Life of Michelangelo Buonarroti* • 17.6—Galileo Galilei, Letter to the Grand Duchess Christina de' Medici

Chapter 18
1500–1800

New Patterns in New Worlds : Colonialism and Indigenous Responses in the Americas 422

The Colonial Americas: Europe's Warm-Weather Extension   424

The Conquest of Mexico and Peru   424

The Establishment of Colonial Institutions   428

The Making of American Societies: Origins and Transformations   438

Exploitation of Mineral and Tropical Resources   438

Social Strata, Castes, and Ethnic Groups   440

The Adaptation of the Americas to European Culture   443

Putting It All Together   446

▶ PATTERNS OF EVIDENCE: **Sources for Chapter 18**

18.1—Scandal at the Church: José de Álfaro Accuses Doña Theresa Bravo and others of insulting and beating his Castiza wife, Joséfa Cadena •

18.2—Marina de San Miguel's Confessions before the Inquisition, Mexico City •

18.3—Nahuatl Land Sale Documents, Mexico • 18.4—*The Jesuit Relations*, French North America

FURTHER RESOURCES   R-1

CREDITS   C-1

SOURCE INDEX   SI-1

SUBJECT INDEX   I-1

Features:

Patterns Up Close:
Mapping the World   406

Against the Grain:
The Digger Movement   420

Features:

Patterns Up Close:
The Columbian Exchange   436

Against the Grain:
Juana Inés de la Cruz   448

Maps

Map 1.1   Early Human Origins to 3 Million Years Ago   6
Map 1.2   Human Migration Out of Africa   11
Map 1.3   The Ice Age   18
Map 1.4   Human Migration to the Americas   22
Map 2.1   Farming and Settlement in the Ancient Middle East and Eastern Mediterranean   29
Map 2.2   Urban Centers in Mesopotamia and Egypt, 5500–3500 BCE   32
Map 2.3a   The Akkadian Kingdom   35
Map 2.3b   Kingdom of Babylonia   35
Map 2.4   Old Kingdom Egypt, ca. 2613–2160 BCE   40
Map 3.1   India: Physical Features and the Monsoon Cycle   57
Map 3.2   Harappan Civilization, ca. 2300 BCE   59
Map 3.3   Mohenjo-Daro   60
Map 3.4   Northern India, ca. 600 BCE   68
Map 4.1   Early China: Geography and Climate   79
Map 4.2   Shang China   85
Map 4.3   Zhou China   87
Map 5.1   The Environment of the Americas   104
Map 5.2   Early Urban Centers in the Andes   110
Map 5.3   Major Corn-Producing Regions of the World   113
Map 5.4   Adena and Hopewell Cultures   116
Map 5.5   The Colonization of the Pacific   117
Map 6.1   The Kingdoms of Meroë and Aksum, ca. 650 BCE–600 CE   128
Map 6.2   Villages and Settlements in Sub-Saharan Africa, 600 BCE–600 CE   132
Map 6.3   Mayan Civilization, ca. 200 BCE–800 CE   135
Map 6.4   Teotihuacán, ca. 100 CE–500 CE   142
Map 6.5   Andean Centers, 600 BCE–600 CE   144
Map 7.1   Achaemenid Persian Empire   151
Map 7.2   Greece in the Sixth Century BCE   153
Map 7.3a,b   Alexander's Empire (a) and Successor Kingdoms after the Breakup of Alexander's Empire (b)   157
Map 7.4   The Plague of Justinian   160
Map 7.5   Nomadic Invasions and Barbarian Migrations into the Roman Empire, 375–450 CE   162
Map 8.1   Northern India, ca. 400 BCE   177
Map 8.2   The Mauryan Empire under Ashoka, 273–231 BCE   178
Map 8.3   The Gupta Empire   181
Map 8.4   The Spread of Buddhism to 600 CE   187
Map 8.5   Asian Trade Routes, ca. 100 CE   191
Map 9.1   The Qin Empire   201
Map 9.2   The Han Empire   204
Map 9.3   China in 589 CE   206
Map 9.4   Industry and Commerce under the Han   209
Map 9.5   The Silk Road, ca. 150 CE   212
Map 10.1   Arab Conquests to 750   224

Map 10.2   The Islamic Commonwealth, ca. 1022 CE   228
Map 10.3   The Byzantine Empire, ca. 1025 CE   231
Map 10.4   The Crusader Kingdoms, ca. 1140 CE   236
Map 10.5   The Afro-Eurasian World Commercial System, ca. 1300   242
Map 11.1   The Empire of Charlemagne   256
Map 11.2   Mediterranean Trade in the Twelfth and Thirteenth Centuries   262
Map 11.3   The First Crusade, 1095–1099   266
Map 11.4   The Spread of the Black Death in Europe   272
Map 11.5   The Great Western Schism, 1378–1417   274
Map 12.1   Harsha's Empire, ca. 645 CE   283
Map 12.2   Eurasian Trade Routes, ca. 1000 CE   285
Map 12.3   India under the Sultanate of Delhi   286
Map 12.4   East and Central Asia, 618–960   288
Map 12.5   The Mongol Empire   295
Map 13.1   Korea: Topography and Precipitation   308
Map 13.2   Korea under the Koryo, 936–1392   309
Map 13.3   Japan: Topography and Climate   314
Map 13.4   Heian Japan   316
Map 13.5   Southeast Asia: The Physical Setting   322
Map 14.1   Long-Distance Trade in Northeast Africa and the Middle East, 800–1200   332
Map 14.2   The Ethiopian Highlands, ca. 1450   335
Map 14.3   Swahili City-States, ca. 1400   338
Map 14.4   The Luba Kingdom, ca. 1400   340
Map 14.5   West African States, 600–1450   343
Map 15.1   North America and Mesoamerica, ca. 1100   353
Map 15.2   Tiwanaku and Wari, ca. 1000   357
Map 15.3   The Aztec Empire, ca. 1520   359
Map 15.4   The Inca Empire, ca. 1525   361
Map 15.5   Tenochtitlán and the Mexican Basin   365
Map 16.1   Africa, the Mediterranean, and the Indian Ocean, 1415–1498   373
Map 16.2   The Ottoman Empire, 1307–1683   380
Map 16.3   Europe and the Mediterranean, ca. 1560   381
Map 16.4   Ottoman–Portuguese Competition in the Indian Ocean, 1536–1580   383
Map 17.1   Centers of Learning in Europe, 1500–1770   402
Map 17.2   European Warfare, 1450–1750   408
Map 17.3   The Protestant Reformation, ca. 1580   410
Map 17.4   Europe in 1648   415
Map 17.5   The Expansion of Russia, 1462–1795   417
Map 18.1   The European Exploration of the Americas, 1519–1542   427
Map 18.2   The Colonization of Central and South America to 1750   430
Map 18.3   The Colonization of North America to 1763   434
Map 18.4   The Columbian Exchange   437

Studying with Maps

MAPS

World history cannot be fully understood without a clear comprehension of the chronologies and parameters within which different empires, states, and peoples have changed over time. Maps facilitate this understanding by illuminating the significance of time, space, and geography in shaping the patterns of world history.

Global Locator

Many of the maps in *Patterns of World History* include *global locators* that show the area being depicted in a larger context.

Projection

A map *projection* portrays all or part of the earth, which is spherical, on a flat surface. All maps, therefore, include some distortion. The projections in *Patterns of World History* show the earth at global, continental, regional, and local scales.

Topography

Many maps in *Patterns of World History* show *relief*—the contours of the land. Topography is an important element in studying maps because the physical terrain has played a critical role in shaping human history.

Scale Bar

Every map in *Patterns of World History* includes a *scale* that shows distances in both miles and kilometers, and in some instances in feet as well.

Map Key

Maps use symbols to show the location of features and to convey information. Each symbol is explained in the map's *key*.

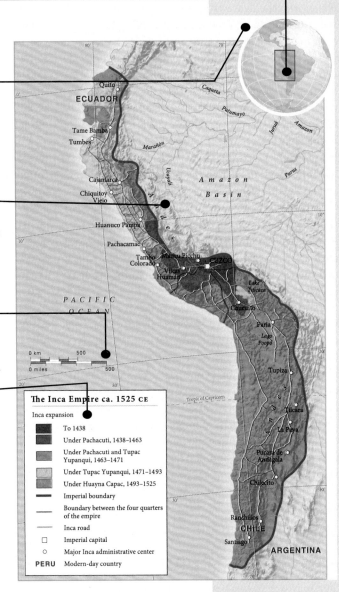

The Inca Empire ca. 1525 CE

Inca expansion

- To 1438
- Under Pachacuti, 1438–1463
- Under Pachacuti and Tupac Yupanqui, 1463–1471
- Under Tupac Yupanqui, 1471–1493
- Under Huayna Capac, 1493–1525
- Imperial boundary
- Boundary between the four quarters of the empire
- Inca road
- □ Imperial capital
- ○ Major Inca administrative center
- **PERU** Modern-day country

Preface

The response to the first three editions of *Patterns of World History* has been extraordinarily gratifying to those of us involved in its development. The diversity of schools that have adopted the book—community colleges as well as state universities; small liberal arts schools as well as large private universities—suggests to us that its central premise of exploring *patterns* in world history is both adaptable to a variety of pedagogical environments and congenial to a wide body of instructors. Indeed, from the responses to the book we have received thus far, we expect that the level of writing, timeliness and completeness of the material, and analytical approach will serve it well as the discipline of world history continues to mature. These key strengths are enhanced in the fourth edition of *Patterns* by constructive, dynamic suggestions from the broad range of students and instructors who are using the book.

It is widely agreed that world history is more than simply the sum of all national histories. Likewise, *Patterns of World History*, Fourth Edition, is more than an unbroken sequence of dates, battles, rulers, and their activities, and it is more than the study of isolated stories of change over time. Rather, in this textbook we endeavor to present in a clear and engaging way how world history "works." Instead of merely offering a narrative history of the appearance of this or that innovation, we present an analysis of the process by which an innovation in one part of the world is diffused and carried to the rest of the globe. Instead of focusing on the memorization of people, places, and events, we strive to present important facts in context and draw meaningful connections, analyzing whatever patterns we find and drawing conclusions where we can. In short, we seek to examine the interlocking mechanisms and animating forces of world history, without neglecting the human agency behind them.

The *Patterns* Approach

Our approach in this book is, as the title suggests, to look for patterns in world history. We should say at the outset that we do not mean to select certain categories into which we attempt to stuff the historical events we choose to emphasize, nor do we claim that all world history is reducible to such patterns, nor do we mean to suggest that the nature of the patterns determines the outcome of historical events. We see them instead as broad, flexible organizational frameworks around which to build the structure of a world history in such a way that the enormous sweep and content of the past can be viewed in a comprehensible narrative, with sound analysis and ample scope for debate and discussion. In this sense, we view them much like the armatures in clay sculptures, giving support and structure to the final figure but not necessarily preordaining its ultimate shape.

From its origins, human culture grew through interactions and adaptations on all the continents except Antarctica. A voluminous scholarship on all regions of the world has been accumulated, which those working in the field have to attempt to master if their explanations and arguments are to sound even remotely persuasive. The sheer volume and complexity of the sources, however, mean that even the knowledge and expertise of the best scholars are going to be incomplete. Moreover, the humility with which all historians must approach their material contains within it the realization that no historical explanation is ever fully satisfactory or final; as a driving force in the historical process, creative human agency moves events in directions that are never fully predictable, even if they follow broad patterns. Learning to discern patterns in this process not only helps novice historians to appreciate the complex challenges (and rewards) of historical inquiry; it also develops critical thinking abilities in all students.

As we move into the third decade of the twenty-first century, world historians have long since left behind the "West plus the rest" approach that marked the field's early years, together with economic and geographical reductionism, in the search for a new balance between comprehensive cultural and institutional examinations on the one hand and those highlighting human agency on the other. All too often, however, this is reflected in texts that seek broad coverage at the expense of analysis, thus resulting in a kind of "world history lite." Our aim is to simplify the study of the world—to make it accessible to the student—without making world history itself simplistic.

Patterns of World History, Fourth Edition, proposes the teaching of world history from the perspective of the relationship between continuity and change. What we advocate in this book is a distinct intellectual framework for this relationship and the role of innovation and historical change through patterns of origins, interactions, and adaptations. Each small or large technical or cultural innovation originated in one geographical center or independently in several different centers. As people in the centers interacted with their neighbors, the neighbors adapted to, and in many cases were transformed by, the innovations. For us, "adaptation" includes the entire spectrum of human responses, ranging from outright rejection to creative borrowing and, at times, forced acceptance.

Small technical innovations often went through the pattern of origin, interaction, and adaptation across the world without arousing much attention, even though they had major consequences. For example, the horse collar, which originated in the last centuries BCE in China and allowed for the replacement of oxen with stronger horses, gradually improved the productivity of agriculture in eleventh-century western Europe. More sweeping intellectual–cultural innovations, by contrast, such as the spread of universal religions like Buddhism, Christianity, and Islam and the rise of science, have obviously had profound consequences—in some cases leading to conflicts lasting centuries—and affect us even today.

Sometimes change was effected by commodities that to us seem rather ordinary. Take sugar, for example. It originated in Southeast Asia and was traded and grown in the Mediterranean, where its cultivation on plantations created the model for expansion into the vast slave system of the Atlantic basin from the fifteenth through the nineteenth centuries, forever altering the histories of four continents. What would our diets look like today without sugar? Its history continues to unfold as we debate its merits and health risks and it supports huge multinational agribusinesses.

Or take a less ordinary commodity: opium. Opium had been used medicinally for centuries in regions all over the world. But the advent of tobacco traded from the Americas to the Philippines to China, and the encouragement of Dutch traders in the region, created an environment in which the drug was smoked for the first time. Enterprising rogue British merchants, eager to find a way to crack closed Chinese markets for other goods, began to smuggle it in from India. The market grew, the price went down, addiction spread, and Britain and China ultimately went to war over China's attempts to eliminate the traffic. Here, we have an example of an item generating interactions on a worldwide scale, with impacts on everything from politics to economics, culture, and even the environment. The legacies of the trade still weigh heavily on two of the rising powers of the recent decades: China and India. And opium and its derivatives, like morphine and heroin, continue to bring relief as well as suffering on a colossal scale to hundreds of millions of people.

What, then, do we gain by studying world history through the use of such patterns? First, if we consider innovation to be a driving force of history, it helps to satisfy an intrinsic human curiosity about origins—our own and others'. Perhaps more importantly, seeing patterns of various kinds in historical development brings to light connections and linkages among peoples, cultures, and regions—as in the aforementioned examples—that might not otherwise present themselves.

Second, such patterns can also reveal similarities and differences among cultures that other approaches to world history tend to neglect. For example, the differences between the civilizations of the Eastern and Western Hemispheres are generally highlighted in world history texts, but the broad commonalities of human groups creating agriculturally based cities and states in widely separated areas also show deep parallels in their patterns of origins, interactions, and adaptations. Such comparisons are at the center of our approach.

Third, this kind of analysis offers insights into how an individual innovation was subsequently developed and diffused across space and time—that is, the patterns by which the new eventually becomes a necessity in our daily lives. Through all of this we gain a deeper appreciation of the unfolding of global history from its origins in small, isolated areas to the vast networks of global interconnectedness in our present world.

Finally, our use of a broad-based understanding of continuity, change, and innovation allows us to restore culture in all its individual and institutionalized aspects—spiritual, artistic, intellectual, scientific— to its rightful place alongside technology, environment, politics, and socioeconomic conditions. That is, understanding innovation in this way allows this text to help illuminate the full range of human ingenuity over time and space in a comprehensive, even-handed, and open-ended fashion.

Options for Teaching with *Patterns of World History*, Fourth Edition

Patterns of World History is available in two versions designed to offer instructors flexible teaching options:

1) *Patterns of World History with Sources*, which includes approximately four textual and visual sources after every chapter. This section, called "Patterns of Evidence," enhances student engagement with key chapter patterns through contemporaneous voices and perspectives. Each source is accompanied by a concise introduction to provide chronological and geographical context; "Working with Sources" questions after each selection prompt students to make critical connections between the source and the main chapter narrative.
2) *Patterns of World History, Brief Edition,* which provides the same organization and narrative as *Patterns of World History with Sources,* but does not include source material at the end of each chapter.

For the convenience of instructors teaching a course over two 15-week semesters, both versions of *Patterns* are limited to 31 chapters. For the sake of continuity and to accommodate the many different ways schools divide the midpoint of their world history sequence, Chapters 15–18 overlap in both volumes; in Volume 2, Chapter 15 is given as a "prelude" to Part Four. Those using a trimester system will also find divisions made in convenient places, with Chapter 10 coming at the beginning of Part Two and Chapter 22 at the beginning of Part Five.

Patterns of Change and Six Periods of World History

Similarly, *Patterns* is adaptable to both chronological and thematic styles of instruction. We divide the history of the world into six major time periods and recognize for each period one or two main patterns of innovation, their spread through interaction, and their adoption by others. Obviously, lesser patterns are identified as well, many of which are of more limited regional interactive and adaptive impact. We wish to stress again that these are broad categories of analysis and that there is nothing reductive or deterministic in our aims or choices. Nevertheless, we believe the patterns we have chosen help to make the historical process more intelligible, providing a series of lenses that can help to focus the otherwise confusing facts and disparate details that comprise world history.

World Period One (Prehistory–600 BCE): **Origins of human civilization—tool making and symbol creating—in Africa as well as the origins of agriculture, urbanism, and state formation in the three agrarian centers of the Middle East, India, and China.**

World Period Two (600 BCE–600 CE): **Emergence of the Axial Age thinkers and their visions of a transcendent god or first principle in Eurasia; elevation of these visions to the status of state religions in empires and kingdoms, in the process forming multiethnic and multilinguistic polities.**

World Period Three (600–1450): **Disintegration of classical empires and formation of religious civilizations in Eurasia, with the emergence of religiously unified regions divided by commonwealths of multiple states.**

World Period Four (1450–1750): **Rise of new empires; interaction, both hostile and peaceful, among the religious civilizations and new empires across all continents of the world. Origins of the New Science in Europe, based on the use of mathematics for the investigation of nature.**

World Period Five (1750–1900): **Origins of scientific–industrial "modernity," simultaneous with the emergence of constitutional and ethnic nation-states, in the West (Europe and North America); interaction of the West with Asia and Africa, resulting in complex adaptations, both coerced and voluntary, on the part of the latter.**

World Period Six (1900–Present): **Division of early Western modernity into three competing** visions: communism, supremacist nationalism, and capitalism. After two horrific world wars and the triumph of nation-state formation across the world, capitalism remains as the last surviving version of modernity. Capitalism is then reinvigorated by the increasing use of social networking tools, which popularizes both "traditional" religious and cultural ideas and constitutionalism in authoritarian states.

Chapter Organization and Structure

Each world period addresses the role of change and innovation on a broad scale in a particular time and/or region, and each chapter contains different levels of exploration to examine the principal features of particular cultural or national areas and how each affects, and is affected by, the patterns of origins, interactions, and adaptations:

- *Geography and the Environment*: The relationship between human beings and the geography and environment of the places they inhabit is among the most basic factors in understanding human societies. In this chapter segment, therefore, the topics under investigation involve the natural environment of a particular region and the general conditions affecting change and innovation. Climatic conditions, earthquakes, tsunamis, volcanic eruptions, outbreaks of disease, and so forth all have obvious effects on how humans react to the challenge of survival. The initial portions of chapters introducing new regions for study therefore include environmental and geographical overviews, which are revisited and expanded in later chapters as necessary. The larger issues of how decisive the impact of geography on the development of human societies is—as in the commonly asked question "Is geography destiny?"—are also examined here.
- *Political Developments:* In this segment, we ponder such questions as how rulers and their supporters wield political and military power. How do different political traditions develop in different areas? How do states expand, and why? How do different political arrangements attempt to strike a balance between the rulers and the ruled? How and

why are political innovations transmitted to other societies? Why do societies accept or reject such innovations from the outside? Are there discernible patterns in the development of kingdoms or empires or nation-states?
- *Economic and Social Developments*: The relationship between economics and the structures and workings of societies has long been regarded as crucial by historians and social scientists. But what patterns, if any, emerge in how these relationships develop and function among different cultures? This segment explores such questions as the following: What role does economics play in the dynamics of change and continuity? What, for example, happens in agrarian societies when merchant classes develop? How does the accumulation of wealth lead to social hierarchy? What forms do these hierarchies take? How do societies formally and informally try to regulate wealth and poverty? How are economic conditions reflected in family life and gender relations? Are there patterns that reflect the varying social positions of men and women that are characteristic of certain economic and social institutions? How are these in turn affected by different cultural practices?
- *Intellectual, Religious, and Cultural Aspects*: Finally, we consider it vital to include an examination dealing in some depth with the way people understood their existence and life during each period. Clearly, intellectual innovation—the generation of new ideas—lies at the heart of the changes we have singled out as pivotal in the patterns of origins, interactions, and adaptations that form the heart of this text. Beyond this, those areas concerned with the search for and construction of meaning—particularly religion, the arts, philosophy, and science—not only reflect shifting perspectives but also, in many cases, play a leading role in determining the course of events within each form of society. All of these facets of intellectual life are in turn manifested in new perspectives and representations in the cultural life of a society.

Features

- **Seeing Patterns/Thinking Through Patterns:** "Seeing Patterns" and "Thinking Through Patterns" use a question–discussion format in each chapter to pose several broad questions ("Seeing Patterns") as advance organizers for key themes, which are then matched up with short essays at the end ("Thinking Through Patterns") that examine these same questions in a sophisticated yet student-friendly fashion.

- **Patterns Up Close:** Since students frequently apprehend macro-level patterns better when they see their contours brought into sharper relief, "Patterns Up Close" essays in each chapter highlight a particular innovation that demonstrates origins, interactions, and adaptations in action. Spanning technological, social, political, intellectual, economic, and environmental developments, the "Patterns Up Close" essays combine text, visuals, and graphics to consider everything from the pepper trade to the guillotine.
- **Against the Grain:** These brief essays consider counterpoints to the main patterns examined in each chapter. Topics range from visionaries who challenged dominant religious patterns, to women who resisted various forms of patriarchy, to agitators who fought for social and economic justice.
- **Marginal Glossary:** To avoid the necessity of having to flip pages back and forth, definitions of key terms are set directly in the margin at the point where they are first introduced.

Today, more than ever, students and instructors are confronted by a vast welter of information on every conceivable subject. Beyond the ever-expanding print media, the Internet and the Web have opened hitherto unimaginable amounts of data to us. Despite such unprecedented access, however, all of us are too frequently overwhelmed by this undifferentiated—and too often indigestible—mass. Nowhere is this truer than in world history, by definition the field within the historical profession with the broadest scope. Therefore, we think that an effort at synthesis—narrative and analysis structured around a clear, accessible, widely applicable theme—is needed, an effort that seeks to explain critical patterns of the world's past behind the billions of bits of information accessible at the stroke of a key on a computer keyboard. We hope this text, in tracing the lines of transformative ideas and things that left their patterns deeply imprinted into the canvas of world history, will provide such a synthesis.

Changes to the Fourth Edition

- **New Feature: Integrated World Period and Chapter Overviews** We have eliminated the separate world period introductions in favor of including their key points on the opening left-hand page of each chapter, with their relationship to specific origins, interactions, and adaptations highlighted, as well as the uniqueness and similarities these share with the other chapters in that World Period. We believe this specificity and recursiveness will enhance the pedagogical possibilities of the text.
- We have continued to tighten the narrative, focusing even more on key concepts and (with the guidance of reviewers) discarding inessential historical details. We are profoundly grateful to the reviewers who pointed out errors and conceptual shortcomings.
- **Updated scholarship** All chapters were revised and updated in accordance with recent developments and new scholarship. Here is a chapter-by-chapter overview that highlights the changes we made in the fourth edition:
- **World Period One** Chapter 1 was largely rewritten to reflect the results of recent research on early hominins, Neanderthals, cave paintings, and the settling of the Americas. Chapter 2 contains new paragraphs on the collapse of the Bronze Age and Sea People, as well as the Göbekli archaeological site, incorporating new information. Chapter 3 updates the material on ancient India and Harappans and employs the latest scholarship on the interaction of Indo-Europeans with peoples of northern India. Chapter 4 includes updated material on the Tarim Basin mummies, and Chapter 5 contains new sections on the weather/climate phenomena El Niño and Younger Dryas.
- **World Period Two** In Chapter 6, the account of Aksum, Himyar, and Yemen in the sixth century CE was rewritten, as was the feature "Against the Grain" on the Nasca lines in ancient South America. Chapter 7 begins with a new vignette on Queen Shirin (ca. 575–628) in the Sasanid Persian Empire, followed by added segments concerning the status of women in Greek and Roman society and Aristotle's role in Greek philosophy, along with a rewritten "Patterns Up Close Essay" on the Plague of Justinian. Chapter 8 contains a

revised section on Jainism and additional material on Buddhism, and Chapter 9 adds a survey of the contemporary debate about the "Han Synthesis."

- **World Period Three** In Chapter 10 the text has been shortened, streamlining the discussion of Islamic theology and law. Chapter 11 conveys references to St. Hilda, abbess of the monastery of Whitby, along with a revised segment on feudalism. Chapter 12 has been renamed "Contrasting Patterns in Eurasia" to better reflect the full range of material contained within it; it focuses more strongly on the Mongol interval and adds specificity to the discussion of Neo-Confucian philosophy. The coverage of the Mongols has been increased in Chapter 13, and the new chapter title, "Religious Civilizations Interacting," reflects these changes.
- **World Period Four** In Chapter 15, the feature "Patterns Up Close" was rewritten to reflect the recent archaeological discovery of the Templo Mayor skull racks. The account in Chapter 16 of the Ottoman conquest of 1453 has been rewritten, along with revised segments concerning Apocalyptic Expectations and Charles V.
- **World Period Five** In Chapter 22 the discussion of the Haitian Revolution has been revised. Chapter 23 has a new "Patterns Up Close" feature on the uprising of the town of Canudos in Brazil, 1895–1898. Chapter 25 offers revised discussions of Abdülhamit II's accession to the throne of the Ottoman Empire in 1876 and of serfdom in Russia. A new section on agriculture in Russia during the first half of the nineteenth century has been added to enhance the understanding of the empire's economy and society in the early part of the century. Chapter 26 has new discussions of the weapons revolution and modernism in music.
- **World Period Six** Chapter 28 includes rewritten discussions of the founding of the Weimar Republic, along with a relocated section on the republican revolution in China. In Chapter 29 several segments, including Cold War origins, postwar Eastern Europe, and partition on the Indian subcontinent, have been rewritten. In Chapter 30 we revised the discussion of "To Get Rich is Glorious": China's Four Modernizations; Zimbabwe and Angola: The Revolution Continued; and South Africa: From Apartheid

to "Rainbow Nation," including reference to the Soweto uprising. Chapter 31 updates world events to the beginning of 2020.

Ensuring Learning Success

Oxford University Press offers instructors and students a comprehensive ancillary package for qualified adopters.

Enhanced eBook

Every new copy of the fourth edition comes with an access code that provides students with resources designed to enhance their engagement with world history, including an eBook enhanced with these learning tools:

- "Closer Look" videos that analyze selected artworks, accompanied by narration and self-assessment
- interactive maps
- interactive timelines
- flashcards
- chapter quizzes
- matching activities
- primary sources
- note-taking guides

Oxford Insight Study Guide

The Adaptive Digital Study Guide increases student understanding of core course material by engaging students in the process of actively reading, validating their understanding, and delivering tailored practice. The study guide delivers a custom-built adaptive practice session based on the student's demonstrated performance within each learning objective. In-depth data on student performance powers a rich suite of reporting tools that inform instructors on their students' proficiency across learning objectives.

Oxford Learning Link

Instructors who adopt the Fourth Edition have access to an instructor's resource manual, a computerized test-item file, videos from the Oxford University Press World History Video and Image Libraries, and PowerPoint slides of all the images, maps, charts, and figures in the text. All of these items, and much more, are available to adopters at the Oxford Learning Link.

For those instructors who wish to integrate Oxford's instructor and student learning resources directly into their campus learning management system, an interoperable course cartridge can be installed. Contact your OUP representative to learn more about the interoperable course cartridge for *Patterns of World History*.

Additional Learning Resources

Uncovering World History
Make history meaningful and memorable for students by teaching them the skills to "Do History." Oxford University Press is proud to develop and support innovative learning experiences for today's students. "Uncovering World History" offers students and instructors a rich and rewarding learning experience in their World History course. Embracing this model of "uncovering," and focusing on major transcultural and transnational events and experiences, the units develop student's historical thinking skills. To learn more about "Uncovering World History," please go to https://www.oxfordpresents.com/ms/getz/.

- *Mapping Patterns of World History*, Volume 1: To 1600: Includes approximately 50 full-color maps, each accompanied by a brief headnote, as well as blank outline maps and Concept Map exercises.
- *Mapping Patterns of World History*, Volume 2: Since 1400: Includes approximately 50 full-color maps, each accompanied by a brief headnote, as well as blank outline maps and Concept Map exercises.

FORMATS
Offering choices for both students and instructors, Oxford University Press makes *Patterns of World History* available in different formats:

- paperback
- eBook (available from several vendors, including RedShelf, Vital Source, and Chegg)
- loose-leaf
- inclusive access

Packaging Options
Patterns of World History can be bundled at a significant discount with any of the titles in the popular Very Short Introductions, World in a Life, or Oxford World's Classics series, as well as other titles from the Higher Education division world history catalog (www.oup.com/us/catalog/he). Please contact your OUP representative for details.

Acknowledgments
Throughout the course of writing, revising, and preparing *Patterns of World History* for publication we have benefited from the guidance and professionalism accorded us by all levels of the staff at Oxford University Press. John Challice, vice president and publisher, had faith in the inherent worth of our project from the outset and provided the initial impetus to move forward. Katie Tunkavige carried out the thankless task of assembling the manuscript and did so with generosity and good cheer, helping us with many details in the final manuscript. Keith Faivre steered us through the intricacies of production with the stoicism of a saint.

Most of all, we owe a special debt of gratitude to Charles Cavaliere, our editor. Charles took on the daunting task of directing this literary enterprise at a critical point in the book's career. He pushed this project to its successful completion, accelerated its schedule, and used a combination of flattery and hard-nosed tactics to make sure we stayed the course. His greatest contribution, however, is in the way he refined our original vision for the book with several important adjustments that clarified its latent possibilities. From the maps to the photos to the special features, Charles's high standards and concern for detail are evident on every page.

Developing a book like *Patterns of World History* is an ambitious project, a collaborative venture in which authors and editors benefit from the feedback provided by a team of outside readers and consultants. We gratefully acknowledge the advice that the many reviewers, focus group participants, and class testers (including their students) shared with us along the way. We tried to implement all of their excellent suggestions. We owe a special debt of thanks to Evan R. Ward, who provided invaluable guidance for the revision of the coverage of Latin America and the Caribbean in World Period Five. Of course, any errors of fact or interpretation that remain are solely our own.

Reviewers of the Fourth Edition

Beau Bowers, Central Piedmont Community College

Mark Z. Christensen, Brigham Young University

James S. Day, University of Montevallo

Caroline Hasenyager, Virginia State University

Randi Howell, Central Piedmont Community College

Andrey Ivanov, University of Wisconsin at Platteville

Sean Kane, Central Piedmont Community College

Rose Mary Sheldon, Virginia Military Institute

Joshua Shiver, Auburn University

Arlene Sindelar, University of British Columbia

Jean Skidmore-Hess, Georgia Southern University

Ryan H. Wilkinson, Ambrose University

Please let us know your experiences with *Patterns of World History* so that we may improve it in future editions. We welcome your comments and suggestions.

Peter von Sivers

pv4910@xmission.com

Charles A. Desnoyers

desnoyer@lasalle.edu

George B. Stow

gbsgeorge@aol.com

Note on Dates and Spellings

In keeping with widespread practice among world historians, we use "BCE" and "CE" to date events and the phrase "years ago" to describe developments from the remote past.

The transliteration of Middle Eastern words has been adjusted as much as possible to the English alphabet. Therefore, long vowels are not marked. The consonants specific to Arabic (alif, dhal, ha, sad, dad, ta, za, `ayn, ghayn, and qaf) are either not indicated or rendered with common English letters. A similar procedure is followed for Farsi. Turkish words follow the alphabet reform of 1929, which adds the following letters to the Western alphabet or modifies their pronunciation: c (pronounced "j"), ç (pronounced "tsh"), ğ (not pronounced but lengthening the preceding vowel), ı ("i" without dot, pronunciation close to short e), i/İ ("i" with dot, including in caps), ö (no English equivalent), ş ("sh"), and ü (no English equivalent). The spelling of common contemporary Middle Eastern and Islamic terms follows daily press usage (which, however, is not completely uniform). Examples are "al-Qaeda," "Quran," and "Sharia."

The system used in rendering the sounds of Mandarin Chinese—the northern Chinese dialect that has become in effect the national spoken language in China and Taiwan—into English in this book is *hanyu pinyin*, usually given as simply pinyin. This is the official romanization system of the People's Republic of China and has also become the standard outside of Taiwan (the Republic of China). Most syllables are pronounced as they would be in English, with the exception of the letter *q*, which has a palatal "ch" sound (pronounced at the very front of the mouth); ch itself has a non-palatal "ch" sound (pronounced further back, as in English). *Zh* is a non-palatal "j" and *j* a palatal "j." Some syllables also are pronounced—particularly in the regions around Beijing—with a retroflex r so that the syllable *shi*, for example, carries a pronunciation closer to "shir." Finally, the letter r in the *pinyin* system has no direct English equivalent, but an approximation may be had by combining the sounds of "r" and "j."

Japanese terms have been romanized according to a modification of the Hepburn system. The letter *g* is always hard; vowels are handled as they are in Italian—*e*, for example, carries a sound like "ay." We have not, however, included diacritical markings to indicate long vowel sounds for *u* or *o*. Where necessary, these have been indicated in the pronunciation guides.

For Korean terms, we have used a variation of the McCune-Reischauer system, which remains the standard romanization scheme for Korean words used in English academic writing, but eliminated any diacritical markings. Here again, the vowel sounds are pronounced more or less like those of Italian and the consonants like those of English.

For Vietnamese words, we have used standard renditions based on the modern Quoc Ngu ("national language") system in use in Vietnam today. The system was developed by Jesuit missionaries and is partly based on the Portuguese alphabet. Once more, we have avoided diacritical marks, and the reader should follow the pronunciation guides for approximations of Vietnamese terms.

Latin American terms (Spanish, Nahuatl, or Quechua) generally follow local usage, including accents, except where they are Anglicized, per the *Oxford English Dictionary*. The now commonly used form "Tiwanaku" is preferred to the traditional Spanish spelling "Tiahuanaco."

We use the terms "Native American" and "Indian" interchangeably to refer to the peoples of the Americas in the pre-Columbian period and "Amerindian" in our coverage of Latin America since independence.

In keeping with widely recognized practice among paleontologists and other scholars of the deep past, we use the term "hominins" in Chapter 1 to emphasize their greater remoteness from apes and proximity to modern humans.

Phonetic spellings often follow the first appearance of a non-English word whose pronunciation may be unclear to the reader. We have followed the rules for capitalization per *The Chicago Manual of Style*.

About the Authors

Peter von Sivers is associate professor emeritus of Middle Eastern history at the University of Utah. He has previously taught at UCLA, Northwestern University, the University of Paris VII (Vincennes), and the University of Munich. He has also served as chair of the Joint Committee of the Near and Middle East, Social Science Research Council, New York, 1982–1985; editor of the *International Journal of Middle East Studies*, 1985–1989; member of the board of directors of the Middle East Studies Association of North America, 1987–1990; and chair of the SAT II World History Test Development Community of the Educational Testing Service, Princeton, NJ, 1991–1994. His publications include *Caliphate, Kingdom, and Decline: The Political Theory of Ibn Khaldun* (1968), several edited books, and three dozen peer-reviewed chapters and articles on Middle Eastern and North African history, as well as world history. He received his Dr. phil. from the University of Munich.

Charles A. Desnoyers is professor of history at La Salle University in Philadelphia. He has previously taught at Temple University, Villanova University, and Pennsylvania State University. In addition to serving as History Department chair from 1999 to 2007, he was a founder and long-time director of the Greater Philadelphia Asian Studies Consortium, and president (2011–2012) of the Mid-Atlantic Region Association for Asian Studies. He has served as a reader, table leader, and question writer for the AP European and World History exams. He served as co-editor of the World History Association's *Bulletin* from 1995 to 2001. In addition to numerous articles in peer-reviewed and general publications, his work includes *Patterns of East Asian History* (2019, Oxford University Press), *Patterns of Modern Chinese History* (2016, Oxford University Press), and *A Journey to the East: Li Gui's "A New Account of a Trip Around the Globe"* (2004, University of Michigan Press). He received his PhD from Temple University.

George B. Stow is professor of ancient and medieval history and director of the graduate program in history at La Salle University, Philadelphia. His teaching experience embraces a variety of undergraduate and graduate courses in ancient Greece and Rome, medieval England, and world history, and he has been awarded the Lindback Distinguished Teaching Award. Professor Stow is a member of the Medieval Academy of America and a Fellow of the Royal Historical Society. He is the recipient of a National Defense Education Act Title IV Fellowship, a Woodrow Wilson Foundation Fellowship, and research grants from the American Philosophical Society and La Salle University. His publications include a critical edition of a fourteenth-century monastic chronicle, *Historia Vitae et Regni Ricardi Secundi* (University of Pennsylvania Press, 1977), as well as numerous articles and reviews in scholarly journals including *Speculum*, *The English Historical Review*, the *Journal of Medieval History*, the *American Historical Review*, and several others. He received his PhD from the University of Illinois.

Patterns of
World History

World Period One

From Human Origins to Early Agricultural Centers, Prehistory to 600 BCE

Humans appeared late in the evolution of the world. While the earth is 4.5 billion years old, the first human-like beings only appeared about 6 million years ago, and modern humans did not appear in East Africa until about 100,000 years ago. These humans migrated from there to Eurasia and Australia 80,000–60,000 years ago and to the Americas 17,500–14,600 years ago.

As people became more numerous, human culture became more differentiated. The triad of origins-interactions-adaptations as the fundamental pattern in world history took shape. Human ingenuity and interaction with the environment in the Middle East, Asia, Europe, Australia, and the Americas led to vastly different adaptations. Foraging originated in Africa. Farming, urbanization, and state formation originated in the Middle East. In the Americas, humans fashioned similarly differentiated livelihoods and political structures. Australia's poorer natural environment slowed its differentiation process.

Chapter 1

The African Origins of Humanity

Prehistory–10,000 BCE

CHAPTER ONE PATTERNS

Origins, Interactions, Adaptations The rise of modern humanity in Africa was not predictable and did not proceed in a straight line. Many hominin species came and went, and how the species of anatomically and intellectually modern humans originated is still obscure. Nevertheless, in the course of their existence these species contributed step by step to the fashioning of stone tools and hunting weapons, the domestication of fire, the creation of objects of symbolic expression, and funerary customs. Networks of trade appeared.

Uniqueness and Similarities The humans who migrated from Africa to the rest of the world some 70,000 years ago were foragers, living off plants, hunted animals, and fish. Wherever they settled in camps with temporary dwellings, they banded together in more or less egalitarian clans and lineages under elders. While the livelihoods of these early humans resembled each other closely, their cultural expressions displayed unique characteristics. The Cro-Magnon rock art of southwestern France and northern Spain shines with its abundant animal depictions, the Aborigine rock art of Australia and the Amerindian rock art of the Americas delight with their human figures. With its diversity and sophistication, prehistoric humanity still impresses us today.

O n November 30, 1974, Donald Johanson and Tom Gray left their campsite in the Afar desert of Ethiopia in northeastern Africa to search for fossils of human predecessors. Members of the expedition had so far found only animal bones.

After two hours, Johanson glimpsed something out of place and called out, "That's a bit of a hominid [now called "hominin"] arm." He and Gray began to locate other bones nearby. "An unbelievable, impermissible thought flickered through my mind," Johanson remembered. "Suppose all these fitted together? Could they be parts of a single, extremely primitive skeleton? No such skeleton had ever been found—anywhere." The two raced back to the camp, sharing their excitement with the other scientists and local Afar workers. That night, a tape recorder was playing the Beatles' song "Lucy in the Sky with Diamonds," so fossil Hadar AL 288-1, dated to 3.2 million years ago, became known ever after as "Lucy."

Today, while Lucy is neither the oldest nor the most significant fossil ever found, she remains the most famous. For many people, Lucy—the petite female buried for 3.2 million years—is all they know about human origins.

CHAPTER OUTLINE

The Origins of Humanity

Human Adaptations: From Africa to Eurasia and Australia

The Ice Age Crisis and Human Migration to the Americas

Putting It All Together

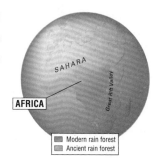

The Origins of Humanity

The story of Lucy introduces our study of the origins and evolution of humankind. In the course of millions of years, splits among hominin lineages produced lines of early humans who could fashion stone tools. From among lineages other than that of Lucy evolved the line of the anatomically and intellectually modern human (*Homo sapiens*), who fashioned cultural artifacts such as jewelry, geometric figures cut into stone, and rock drawings. Modern humans left Africa and spread to Eurasia, Australia, and the Americas. These first modern humans were *cultural*

ABOVE: Satellite View Southward Across the African Rift Valley.

Seeing Patterns

❯ What made it possible for *Homo sapiens* to survive in a dangerous environment? Why is it difficult to imagine life as a prehistoric forager?

❯ Where did humans go when they left Africa, and what kinds of lives did they establish for themselves in the areas where they settled? Which were the most important social patterns that evolved, and how were humans impacted by the worsening Ice Age?

❯ Why did early humans create cave paintings and figurines? Do these show patterns that can be interpreted?

Hominins: Forerunners of humans after genetically splitting from the chimpanzees.

Bipedalism: The ability to walk upright on hind legs; a defining characteristic of hominins and, later, humans.

beings, by means of which they had acquired a measure of freedom from evolution. Instead of nature writing their history, they could create their own human history.

Hominins: No Longer Apes, but Not Yet Human

Modern humans are the descendants of early human-like primates called **hominins**. It is assumed that the line of hominins split from that of the chimpanzees around 7–5 million years ago in Africa. The parentage among the 20 or so known species of hominins coming thereafter is unclear. The fog begins to lift only around 1.8 million years ago, with the emergence of *Homo erectus*, the first hominin that left Africa and was adaptable to many new environments in Eurasia.

Many historians view the *pre*history of humans as a field belonging to archaeologists and anthropologists. For these historians, *history* begins only with the rise of the first cities in Mesopotamia around 3500 BCE, in which scribes created written documents. This view is unfortunate, since historians routinely consider the findings of scholars in other disciplines, such as archaeology, anthropology, climatology, geography, medicine, and sociology, when they write histories on topics after about 3500 BCE. Furthermore, since written records can be unreliable, historians turn to the findings of other disciplines wherever they can. Indeed, in the twenty-first century some historians have argued for eliminating the artificial distinction between prehistory and history, speaking instead of the "deep history" of humanity.

Who Are Our Ancestors?   The specific environmental and genetic interactions favorable for the split between the chimpanzee and hominin lines are complex. Climate change, reflected in the earth's rain forests advancing and retreating, played a part. It took about 1 million years, from 5 to 4 million years ago according to the genetic clock, and a fairly large population of 50,000–70,000 animals for the split between the chimpanzees and the first hominins to begin and be completed.

The genetic clock, however, is not beyond controversy; it is also not synchronic with the three oldest known fossil fragments (as of 2019), which seem to fall into the time right after the split but are too fragmentary to allow for a full determination: the Saharan Toumaï skull (7–6 million years old), East African Orrorin femurs (6.1–5.7 million years), and East African *Ardipithecus kaddaba* teeth (5.8–5.4 million years). But this time is now questionable as a result of a more complete fossil find published in 2019. The 11.6-million-year-old arm and leg bones of two creatures discovered in a clay pit in southwestern Germany appear to indicate some form of **bipedalism**. This astoundingly early appearance of the human characteristic of bipedalism is difficult to square with the genetic clock or the ages of the hitherto three earliest fossil fragments, and thus the question of the beginning of the hominin line has become even less answerable than before.

Firmer ground is reached with Ardi (*Ardipithecus ramidus*, 4.5–4.3 million years ago), a descendant of *A. kaddaba* who was definitively a hominin. In their home in the tropical rain forests and savannas of East Africa, the members of this species were able to engage in straight-limbed tree-walking. They could climb down and step out of the rain forest, walking upright into the savanna. Thereby, they increased their adaptability, especially during dry periods when the rain forest shrank. Knuckle-walking apes, by contrast, stayed in the rain forest.

The Ardi species was not able yet to venture very far into drier environments. After 200,000 years, it was replaced by a different species, the **australopiths** (scientific name *Australopithecus*). These hominins date to 3.9–1.8 million years ago and were widespread (see Map 1.1). We are fairly certain of these date ranges and regional distributions because of a couple of key paleoanthropological finds: (1) a set of fossilized footprints uncovered in Kenya and (2) "Lucy," the almost complete skeleton found in Ethiopia. The footprints reveal how much improved the australopiths were as walkers on the ground, but they were still also very much at home in the rain forest.

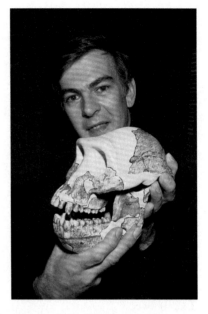

Donald Johanson with Lucy

Environmental Adaptability   Improved upright walking became a key evolutionary advantage to hominins. Walking on two feet frees the arms to do something else. Being upright exposes a smaller body surface to the sun, a factor important for venturing out from the rain forest into the **savanna** and steppe. The plant resources available in these environments made the diet of hominins more flexible than that of the apes, which were limited to their rain-forest habitat. It was in the savanna environment, today the Kenyan Turkana steppe basin, that hominins around 3.3 million years ago fashioned the first stone tools, that is, rocks split in such a way that the broken pieces had sharp edges. The discovery of these tools, made in 2011, dethrones the 2.5-million-year-old Oldowan tools, unearthed in 1936 also in the Turkana basin, from their place as the oldest tools. It now appears that the first evidence of awakening intelligence has to be located in the earliest hominins rather than their successors.

On the Threshold of Humanity   The making of tools became more refined and widespread about 2.5 million years ago in the hands of australopith successor lineages. These younger flaked stones are called **Oldowan** tools (after the Olduvai region in the Tanzanian Great Rift Valley); they enabled the hominins to broaden their diet from vegetarian foods to more or less regular meals of meat. Hominins became omnivores, partaking of a broader range of nutrition available in nature.

Australopiths: Hominin species of the genus *Australopithecus* that existed before those classed under the genus *Homo*.

Savanna: Grassland with more or less extensive stands of trees.

Oldowan toolmaking: Early stone-carving technique, which consisted of splitting a stone into two, thereby producing sharp edges on both fragments. See also **Acheulian** and **Levallois toolmaking**.

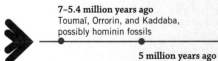

7–5.4 million years ago
Toumaï, Orrorin, and Kaddaba, possibly hominin fossils

5 million years ago
Split of the chimpanzee–hominin lines, as indicated by the genetic clock

4.5 million years ago
Ardi hominins, first assumed human ancestor line

4.2–1.8 million years ago
Multiple lines of australopith hominins

1.8 million years ago
Homo erectus, present in Asia and Africa

300,000 years ago
Homo sapiens, or Modern Human, emerges in East Africa

80,000–60,000 years ago
Modern humans migrate from East Africa to Asia

60,000–50,000 years ago
Modern humans migrate to Australia

35,000 years ago
Earliest evidence of modern humans in Europe and Siberia

13,500–13,000 years ago
Traditional assumption of human arrival in the Americas

9,400–9,300 years ago
"Spirit Cave Mummy" and "Kennewick Man" in the North American West

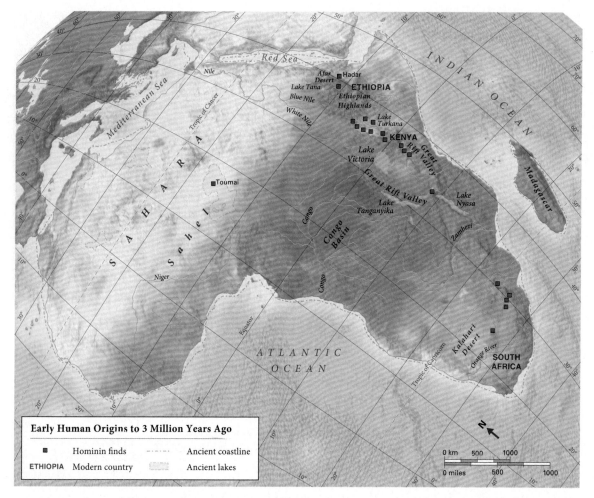

MAP 1.1 **Early Human Origins to 3 million years ago**

Paleolithic: Old Stone Age, 2.5 million–11,500 years ago.

The making of stone tools marks the beginning of the **Paleolithic**, or Old Stone Age, which lasted until about 11,500 years ago.

A cool, dry spell of the climate about 1.8 million years ago made mobility again very important. New hominin lines evolved which no longer climbed trees, whose members were fully stabilized on their feet and could walk long distances. They could deal equally with rain forest, savanna, grasslands, and now also steppe habitats, and mastered control of fire in caves one million years ago, as announced in 2004 on the basis of finds in South Africa. Small groups of hominins, so scholars assume, formed camp groups, huddling around fires at cave entrances or under rock overhangs. Although their brain sizes were about half of those of fully evolved modern humans, these new lines of hominins were the first to adopt skills that we can recognize as human.

One of the new hominin lines was that of *Homo erectus*. In a study published in 2020, this line is assumed to have emerged in South Africa around 2 million years ago. Members of this group migrated to Eurasia 1.8 million ago, as finds in Dmanisi Cave in Georgia, published in 2013, suggest. The cave contained five sets of fully preserved skulls and bones with anatomies widely differing from one another. Had they been found individually in dispersed caves, researchers would have viewed them as belonging to five different lines of hominins. Instead, it is now believed that they all belonged to the same line of *Homo erectus*, a "polymorphous species" whose members could look very different from each other. They disappeared eventually after about 1 million years from their wide-ranging habitat in Africa-Eurasia.

H. erectus created improved stone tools in most places where the line lived. Instead of continuing to use the simple Oldowan stones with sharp edges, it created the new **Acheulian** [ah-SHOO-lee-yan] stone technology, around 1.8–1.6 million years ago. (This technology was named after Saint-Acheul, a suburb of Amiens in northern France where the first finds were made in the nineteenth century.) Acheulian tools were oval or pear-shaped hand axes cut with the help of hammer stones from larger cores, or they were one or more flakes split from cores. When the edges of these hand axes became dull, *H. erectus* split smaller flakes away to resharpen the edges. A simple visual comparison of Oldowan and Acheulian tools reveals how much the manual skills of early humans advanced in about a million years.

Human Adaptations: From Africa to Eurasia and Australia

Oldest Stone Tools to Date. These tools, discovered in Kenya at the Lomekwi 3 archaeological site in the Turkana Basin, are 3.3 million years old.

Acheulian toolmaking: A technique which consisted of flaking a hard piece of rock (especially flint, chert, or obsidian) on both sides into a triangle-shaped hand axe, with cutting edges, a hand-held side, and a point.

H. erectus was probably the ancestor of *H. sapiens* (Latin for 'wise human,' called "modern human" in this chapter), the species of humans to which we belong. Scholars are far from agreed, however, as to how many intermediate lineages existed between then and now. When anatomically modern *H. sapiens* emerged in Africa about 300,000 years ago, two characteristics distinguished this human being from its forerunners: *technical skills* and *cultural creativity*. These two characteristics represent a fundamental transformation of hominins.

The African Origins of Human Culture

The oldest specimen of an anatomically modern *H. sapiens* found so far is a jawbone with teeth recovered from the site of Jebel Irhoud in Morocco. It was dated in 2017 to 312,000 years ago. The archaeological record documenting modern humans in Africa is still spotty, but the 17 sites containing bone and skull remnants of *H. sapiens*, as well as a half-dozen sites with human artifacts, demonstrate that this species, in a process of gradual development in Africa, became physically and intellectually fully human and capable of culture. While humans remained subject to the interaction between environment and genes, requiring constant adaptation, culture gave them the freedom to accept or reject—a completely new dimension largely independent from nature.

Levallois toolmaking:
A stone technique whereby stone workers first shaped a hard rock into a cylinder or cone.

Livelihood   Early hominins were scavengers, not hunters. They may have purposely followed predators and chased them away after the kill. Stone scrapers, once invented, facilitated the separation of meat from carcasses. An elusive post–*H. erectus* line introduced spears in the form of sharpened sticks some 400,000 years ago and thus allowed the transition from scavenging to hunting. Really effective spears had to await *H. sapiens* as the creator of the much-refined new stone working technique, the **Levallois** [le-val-WAH], derived from the name of a suburb of Paris, France, where in the nineteenth century the first spear points were found. With this technique, a craftsperson chipped off small flakes from the edges of a prepared stone core and then hammered a larger flake—flat on the bottom, domed on the top, and sharpened by the small flakes around the edge—from the center, leaving a deep indentation in the spent core. These center flakes could be as large as hand axes and meat cutters or as small as spear points. The appearance of spear points and increasingly large numbers of animal bones in the archaeological sites indicates that *H. sapiens* was emerging as an efficient hunter. The hunt tended to be the province of males and remained a prestige occupation for much of human history. But it provided no more than a supplement to *H. sapiens'* nutrition, which remained plant-based.

The combination of the male-dominated hunt with the communal gathering of plant foods defines "forager society." Foraging, sometimes called "hunting and gathering," was the dominant pattern of human history for several hundred thousand years. It is also the least documented period, requiring for its understanding a combination of archaeology with the anthropological insights gained from observation of surviving foraging societies. Thus, descriptions of such societies are unavoidably somewhat speculative.

H. sapiens continued to live in sheltered places provided by cave entrances and rock overhangs. But there were also campsites with hut-like shelters made from branches. Clothing consisted of skins and furs acquired through hunting. Hearths, in which modern humans could build fires, served as places for cooking and warmth. Anthropological studies suggest that extended families congregated around the hearths for comfort and companionship. In the vicinity of the campsite, a total of a dozen dispersed families formed a clan, among which sexual partners were chosen.

Around 120,000 years ago, food gathering and preparation appear to have become considerably more varied. Groups of *H. sapiens* began to include fish and shellfish in their diet, using tools carved from bone, such as hooks and barbed points mounted on spears. With the help of grindstones, men and women pulverized hard seeds for consumption or storage. Plaster-lined storage pits appeared in the camps, as did separate refuse dumps. As the settlements became more numerous, trade networks sprang up, providing toolmakers with obsidian mined as far as

200 miles away. Obsidian is a glass-like hard rock found near volcanoes and therefore relatively rare, so it was much sought after. This initial period of trademarks the beginning of increasing human *interaction*—a process vital to the transferring of cultural and technological innovation among human groups.

Gender Relations   A central element in human culture is the relationship between men and women. Unfortunately, archaeology is unable to reveal much about this relationship in Paleolithic forager society. Obviously, the roles of men and women were less specialized among foragers than in **agrarian–urban society**: males and females spent most of their time collecting and preparing plant foods together, and the male-dominated hunt was a supplemental occupation. But how much these occupations furthered a male–female balance or allowed for one of the two genders to become dominant is not easy to determine.

Agrarian–urban society: Population living in villages, towns, and cities and engaged in farming, handicrafts, local trade, and perhaps also long-distance luxury trade.

With the rise of feminism in academia, scholars revived the idea, popular in the nineteenth century, of an early female-centered society. This society, it has been asserted, was egalitarian, peaceful, and goddess-oriented. It was agrarian but is assumed to have had deep roots in the preceding forager stage of human life. In this view, warlike male dominance came about only with the rise of horseback-riding herders from the Eurasian steppes.

Other anthropologists assumed that male dominance began at about the same time that warring kingdoms emerged in the Middle East. War captives became slaves, and hierarchies emerged in which women found themselves relegated to inferior positions. However the origins of patriarchy are explained, there is little controversy over its connection with agrarian–urban life. What came before, however, and was prevalent during the Paleolithic forager period of human history, is impossible to determine one way or the other.

Creation of Symbols   Activity in the camps of *H. sapiens* expanded from the craftsmanship of tools to creating nonutilitarian objects. This expansion was perhaps the decisive step with which anatomically modern *H. sapiens* became fully modern. Around 135,000 years ago, humans in what is today Morocco, in northwest Africa, perforated seashells and fragments of ostrich eggshell and strung them on leather strips as pendants and necklaces. The significance of this step cannot be overemphasized. By themselves, seashells and ostrich eggshells are natural objects of no particular distinction, but as jewelry they have the unique meaning of beauty for their wearer. They are *symbols*, which are mental concepts distinct from shells found as objects in nature.

Anatomically and intellectually modern *H. sapiens* was the first and (as far as we know) only being that did not think only in the concrete, practical terms of toolmaking but also in *abstract* symbolic terms by using something to express something else, such as jewelry for the concept of beauty. This transformation may be seen as the foundation of art, religion, philosophy, science, and all other intellectual pursuits.

Archaeological examples for the emergence of abstract symbolic thinking in Africa are not yet very numerous. But taken together, they powerfully suggest an intellectual modernity emerging to match the earlier anatomical modernity of African *H. sapiens*. From about 90,000 years ago, for example, we begin to see gravesites—indicators of reflection on the significance of life, death, ancestral

Apollo 11 Cave, Namibia. An animal depicted on a stone slab, from about 25,000 years ago. Together with the Blombos Cave flake and ochre, this artwork is evidence of early humans' ability to create symbols.

dignity, and generational continuity. Humans added jewelry as the preferred grave gift, suggesting the contemplation of an afterlife.

Even more recognizably abstract are the early symbols, appearing on a 73,000-year-old ochre-painted stone flake and a 70,000-year-old piece of ochre, excavated in 2018 and 1991 respectively, in Blombos Cave and on 60,000-year-old ostrich eggshell fragments excavated in 1996 in Diepkloof Rock Shelter, both in South Africa. They display geometrically arranged lines, the meaning of which is unknown. Ochre is a soft, reddish form of rock easily turned into a powder or paste and as such often found as a gift in prehistoric graves, perhaps symbolizing blood with its power of life. Ostrich eggshells served as containers that could be adorned with engravings. Finally, a small stone plaque from the Apollo 11 Cave in Namibia, featuring the image of an animal, is of particular importance for the appreciation of the African origin of *H. sapiens*: It is estimated to be 25,000 years old.

Collectively, the above examples can be taken as a confirmation of *H. sapiens* not only as a technically versatile toolmaker but also as the one animal capable of creating symbols that signify something beyond the materials from which they were made.

Migration from Africa   Once the *H. sapiens* lineage was fully equipped with practical skills and the foundations of culture, there was no way of holding it back in Africa. In 2018, archaeologists examining a fossil finger bone found in Saudi Arabia concluded that it belonged to an 85,000-year-old *H. sapiens* specimen. This bone is currently the earliest piece of a fossil of *H. sapiens* outside Africa and the Levant.

Many scholars assume that these groups left Africa for Asia by crossing the straits between Ethiopia and Yemen and between Oman and Iran. The members of this group, it is thought, moved along the coast, arriving in India, Malaysia, and Indonesia about 77,000 years ago. Some of their descendants seem to have reached China about 70,000 years ago, sailing to Australia sometime after 60,000 years ago, and crossing from Korea over a then existing land bridge to Japan about 30,000 years ago. Eventually, modern humans from south Asia migrated northwestward to Europe and northeastward to Siberia, where they arrived around 44,000 years ago. The Siberian groups then made their way to Alaska in North America 25,000 years ago, completing the journey around the world in 60,000 years (see Map 1.2).

Migration from South Asia to Australia

Australia was the only large world region where foraging remained dominant until the modern scientific–industrial age and, therefore, could be studied until quite recently. Largely isolated from the rest of the world until the eighteenth century, the Australian foragers developed a distinct culture of their own. But since they shared the same *H. sapiens* genes as their hunter-gatherer relatives on the

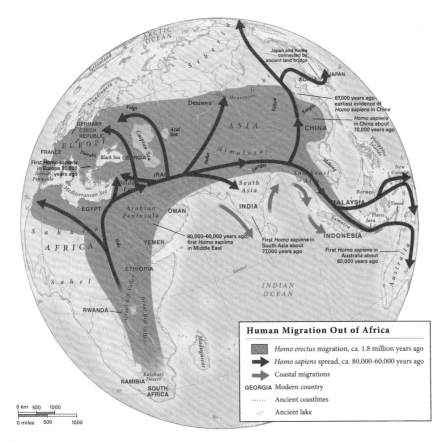

MAP 1.2 Human Migration Out of Africa

Afro-Eurasian continent, the life patterns of both remained fundamentally similar, in terms of foraging, social organization, and symbolical expression.

Geography and Migration   Although it is the smallest of the earth's continents, Australia extends across a variety of geographical zones. In the north, rain forests became dominant. In eastern Australia, various mixtures of forest, savanna, and steppe evolved. The center and most of the west of the continent developed a mixture of steppes, deserts, and lakes. The south (today's southeastern Australia and Tasmania) became temperate, with an almost South African or Mediterranean climate. Small pockets of mountain vegetation came into existence only in what are today the central parts of eastern Australia and southern Tasmania. These geographical environments became the homes to modern humans, who came originally from Africa and had adapted to life in south Asia.

During an ice age 70,000–60,000 years ago, south Asia and most of the northern islands of Indonesia were connected by land bridges. Farther south, island chains where one could travel by raft without losing sight of land encouraged farther travel. Inevitably, the mariners reached a point where land was no longer visible on the horizon. About 60,000 years ago, the distance from the island of Timor to Australia was 65 miles. Scholars have speculated that smoke rising from lightning-produced brush fires in the south could have suggested to some enterprising mariners that there was land beyond the horizon. Whatever motivated them to take to the sea, they evidently succeeded in crossing it.

Settlement of the Continent   *H. sapiens* groups arrived on the Australian continent and slowly fanned out. The descendants of the original settlers became known in our own time as **Aboriginals**. Bringing their African and south Asian foraging customs with them, the settlers hunted the Australian animals and gathered edible plants. Unlike in Africa and Eurasia, with their profusion of dangerous animals, there were few predator species to threaten these first humans. The largest animals went extinct after the end of the ice age about 16,000 years ago, finding it difficult to adjust to warmer temperatures. After that time, humans had to make do with medium and small animals to hunt, such as kangaroos and wombats.

Aboriginals: The original settlers of Australia, who arrived some 60,000–50,000 years before the arrival of European settlers at the end of the eighteenth century CE.

As elsewhere in foraging societies, men were the hunters. They used spears and spear throwers—short sticks with a curve or hook on the end to extend the length of the thrower's arm and give additional power to the flight of the spear. Once the large animals were gone, hunting became a highly diversified set of activities for the Aboriginals.

Women, and secondarily men, were responsible for gathering plant foods. The basic staples were wild millet and rice. The main fruits and vegetables were the solanum [sow-LAH-num], a tomato-like fruit; the yam daisy, a sweet, milky tuber; and the quandong [KWAN-dong] fruit. Women used grindstones to prepare vegetables and hard seeds, such as pine nuts, flax, and acacia seeds, as well as bracken (a large fern) and bindweed (a family of vines).

Eucalyptus, a native of Australia found nearly everywhere on the continent, served for firewood in stone-built hearths. People also used fire as a hunting tool and to promote revegetation. Controlled fires drove animals to where strategically positioned hunting parties could slaughter them. Forest fires were used to synchronize more closely the production and collection of nuts and fruits on trees. Over time, the Aboriginals developed a keen sense of how to efficiently exploit as well as preserve nature.

Australia was less rich in grasses suitable for grain cultivation than Eurasia. Australia had only two types of edible grass seeds; in Eurasia, there were around 40 types. Thus, foraging remained the dominant mode of subsistence, even if people stayed in their camps for long periods of time before moving. Only in the south, where eel trapping was the main form of livelihood, did permanent villages appear, similar to their counterparts in late forager Africa, Europe, North America, and Japan. Aboriginals thus remained closely adapted to the basic patterns of forager livelihood until the first English settlers arrived at the end of the eighteenth century CE.

Social Structures and Cultural Expressions   Since modern-day Aboriginals remained faithful to their traditional forms of life, a great deal about their social structures and organization is known. Australian anthropologists have collected a wealth of data, observing forager culture as it existed in the nineteenth and early twentieth centuries.

According to this literature, in the traditional Aboriginal society of the nineteenth century or earlier, marriages were predominantly *monogamous*. Some men who not only were successful hunters but also became wealthy through trade could acquire additional wives. Families that camped together formed *clans*, units in which all families considered themselves descendants of a common ancestor. Groups of clans formed lineages of between 500 and 1,500 members. Generally, lineages were too large to camp or move about together. They were, rather, loose associations of clans living miles apart from which individuals selected their marriage partners. Marriages took place among members of one group of clans and members of another group. Lineages met collectively once a year at one of the sacred places of their land for rituals and ceremonies.

The Dreamtime   Despite this loose social organization, lineage members considered themselves trustees of clearly marked parcels of ancestral land. Typical markers were identifiable features of the landscape, such as rocks, rivers, or trees. Taboos—forbidden things or practices—and myths surrounded both land and markers. People venerated them through myths and rituals presided over by respected elders. The most esteemed elders possessed a deep knowledge of the clan's past in the **Dreamtime**, the name given by English-speaking anthropologists to the ancient period in which the lineage's past was embedded.

The Dreamtime consisted of the stories, customs, and laws that defined the lineage in its assumed original, perfect state at the time of creation. Elders acquired access to this time through trance states, requiring many years of initiation, training, and practice. Their knowledge of the Dreamtime, it was believed, gave them access to creation's hidden forces. Elders, however, did not possess a monopoly on this knowledge. All members of the clan had access to its sacred heritage and hidden forces.

Aboriginal elders were never able to wield political power through armed forces within their own lineages. Since there was no agriculture and, therefore, no agricultural surplus, and since trade did not evolve beyond the exchange of obsidian, tools, and weapons, elders could not acquire enough wealth to pay fighters. On the continent's northern coast, there was a modest trade in local pearls for goods from Timor, but it was insufficient to support the rise of powerful chiefdoms. Aboriginal society thus remained "stateless" in the sense of possessing no administrative institutions.

Australian Rock Art   How much the Dreamtime involved rock paintings is unfortunately not known. Contemporary Aboriginals are unable to interpret the meaning of early rock paintings. Changing climatic conditions leading to different migration patterns are presumably responsible for modern Aboriginals losing their familiarity with the meanings of ancient Australian rock art.

The best-known Australian rock images are the so-called Bradshaw paintings (also called "Gwion Gwion") in the Kimberley Region of northwest Australia, which probably date to a period 30,000–17,000 years ago. Scholars divide the

Dreamtime: In the Australian Dreamtime (a term based on the word *alcheringa* in the Aranda language), the elder constructs an imaginary reality of the lineage's origins and roots, going back to the time when the world was created and the creator devised all customs, rituals, and myths.

Australian Shamans in a Trance. These "Bradshaw" figures are usually interpreted as showing movements and communication with the spirits of animated cosmic nature.

Bradshaw paintings into two major stylistic periods, beginning with (1) indentations, grooves, and animals and followed by (2) elongated human figures with tassels or sashes, fruits and vegetables resembling human figures, and clothespin and stick figures.

The two periods are very difficult to date, since so far none of the places where they have been found have yielded any material that could be reliably carbon-dated. So far, only one Bradshaw painting has been dated, to some 17,500 years ago, thanks to an overlaid wasp nest. Scholars generally assume that the proliferation of Bradshaws was roughly contemporary with the flourishing of prehistoric rock art in Europe.

The striking parallelism between Australian and Eurasian rock art demonstrates that humans did not have to interact to express themselves culturally in similar ways. Similar forager patterns could evolve without mutual contact. The fact that a proliferation of rock paintings occurred more or less simultaneously in Australia and Eurasia suggests that none of the human groups migrating away from Africa was privileged over any other. This cultural parity among foragers needs to be kept in mind as we turn to African *H. sapiens* migrating to Europe.

Migration from Asia to Europe

There was a gap of at least 20,000 years between groups of modern humans leaving Africa (80,000–60,000 years ago) and migrating to Europe (42,000 years ago). Scholars assume that these humans settled first in Central Asia before their descendants fanned out to East Asia and Europe. By that time, *H. sapiens* was well adapted to the climate of the savannas and steppes. Little is known about the migratory path these descendants chose as they walked across the Asian interior to Europe (see Map 1.2).

Neanderthals and Other Lines   When *H. sapiens* arrived in Europe, this region was already settled by another human line, that of the **Neanderthals** [nee-AN-der-thawl or nay-AN-der-tall, after a valley in northwest Germany where the first specimen was found in the nineteenth century]. This line and the line of the Denisovans—relatives discovered in 2008 in Siberia and in 2019 in China, Indonesia, and Papua New Guinea—are assumed to have descended from a successor to *H. erectus* 300,000 years ago, although the exact descent is unclear. In fact, scholars now speak of several successor lineages, including that of the diminutive *H. florensis* in Indonesia, coexisting and interbreeding with *H. erectus* in Europe and Asia.

In their forager livelihood, the Neanderthal and modern human species were very similar. Neanderthals, however, were smaller and more heavily boned than modern humans. Neanderthals probably were able to talk, as a 2013 computer modeling of the function of a fossilized hyoid bone (supporting the tongue in the throat) established. They also buried their dead, even though without grave gifts. The stone and bone toolkits of the two were alike, but whether Neanderthals progressed from drawing symbols (lines, dots, or squares) to drawing animals or humans is not certain. Currently the oldest example of a symbolic drawing is a red square executed with red mineral paint in the cave of La Pasiega in Cantabria, in northern Spain. Thanks to the dating of mineral outcroppings on top of the drawing, it could be dated in 2018 to 64,000 years ago (although the method was disputed in 2019).

Most intriguing is the discovery, publicized in 2016, of the cave of Bruniquel in southwestern France. At a distance of 1,100 feet from the entrance, some 176,000 years ago Neanderthals broke off stalagmites from the floor and arranged them in one large and one incomplete small circle. Burned bones testify to the use of fire (for cooking and lighting?) in the cave. Slowly, we are beginning to receive a more detailed idea of the depth of Neanderthal life and culture in Europe and Asia prior to the arrival of modern humans.

The Neanderthal and modern human lineages overlapped for about 2,000 years in Europe. During this time, they mingled with each other, but without merging. For reasons still heavily disputed, the Neanderthals died out by around 40,000 years ago and only the modern humans survived (see "Patterns Up Close"). The Denisovans survived in Central and Southeast Asia for another 10,000 years and perhaps even longer.

Rock Paintings and Figurines   As the modern humans settled into Asia and Europe, they began their career with an extraordinary cultural outburst. Some 1,000 caves with rock paintings and engravings, as well as aboveground sites with small figurines, attest to its creativity. Currently, the oldest known artifacts are the paintings of Leang Bulu' Sipong 4 cave on the island of Sulawesi in Indonesia and El Castillo cave in Cantabria in northern Spain, both dated to 44,000–40,000 years ago, and a small ivory figurine of a mammoth dating to 35,000 years ago and found in 2007 in the Hohlenstein-Stadel cave in southwestern Germany.

The find in Indonesia is particularly important because it documents that the artistic outburst of *H. sapiens*, if it did not already occur in Africa, definitely happened during the Ice Age all over Europe-Asia-Australia and not merely in Western Europe. Similarly widespread are a number (32 at the last count) of figurative and nonfigurative signs/symbols, such as chevrons, crosshatchings, and ladders, found alongside the rock paintings, interpreted by some as possible precursors of scripts.

Several thousand years later, an entire class of female figurines called "Venuses" appeared all over western Europe. These figurines were made of stone or bone, and one of them, unearthed in the Czech Republic, was formed of fired clay ca. 26,000 years ago. The creation of the first ceramic pieces was thus a Paleolithic invention, even though the regular production of pottery appeared only some 17,000 years later, in agrarian society. All figurines were small and transportable. Some Venuses have been interpreted as fertility goddesses, indicating an early matriarchy, but this interpretation is questionable given the variety of female and male figurines of the Venus type. Other scholars view these figurines as dolls for children in the camps or as representatives of relatives or ancestors in camp rituals.

The great majority of rock paintings in Europe show animals, either alone or in herds, at rest or in motion, chasing or fleeing other beasts or locked in conflict with each other. The oldest paintings found so far are of steppe animals—reindeer, horses, cattle, aurochs, bison, mammoths, or rhinoceroses—with which modern humans, migrating from the Russian steppes into central and western Europe, were familiar. Dating to 30,000 years ago, they were discovered in 1994 in Chauvet [show-VAY] Cave in southern France.

26,000-Year-Old Venus Figurine. This is the oldest known figurine made of fired clay. It was excavated at Dolní Věstonice, Czech Republic, in 1925. Many more broken figurines were found near the kiln. They perhaps represented family members during rituals and, as bearers of their spirits, had to be destroyed at the end of the rituals so as to end their influence.

A number of drawings and figurines show therianthropes, that is, human–animal figures. A well-known example, at Lascaux [lass-COE] in southwestern France and dated to 17,000 years ago, is that of a prostrate human figure with a bird's head and an erect penis. Another example is the small figurine of the lion-man, found in the Hohlenstein-Stadel cave in Germany, 35,000 years old. One could tentatively conclude from these and a half dozen other examples that modern humans give us traces here of beginning reflections on the deeper levels of relations among things in nature, something that could be called "nature religiosity."

Modern chemical analyses have shown that the rock painters knew how to grind and mix minerals to make different colors. They used protrusions in the rock walls to enhance three-dimensionality. In a number of images, frontal and lateral views are combined. One image depicts a bison with six legs, evidently imitating its swift motion. Thus, the thematic diversity of images had its complement in technical versatility.

The main places with rock art are halls and domes deep inside often miles-long caves. The complete darkness inside was illuminated with torches and grease-filled bowls with wicks. Flutes, made of swan bones, and stalagmites, probably tapped as percussion instruments, testify to the presence not only of painters but also of musicians. To judge by the extant footprints, teenagers as well as adults, men as well as women assembled inside the caves. Modern scholars speculate that the caves were places for rituals, perhaps even shamanic assemblies, in which elders, in trance, entered a spiritual world shared with other living beings. It is possible to recognize in the Paleolithic artifacts the beginnings of religious thought, specifically the idea of a spiritual nature connecting humans, animals, and plants with each other.

Lascaux Cave. This 17,000-year-old image of a birdman could be interpreted as depicting the scene of a mortally wounded, angry bison attacking a defenseless human. Alternatively, it might also depict a human in deep sleep or trance (with an erect penis) in the presence of one of the most common steppe animals, also with an enlarged sexual organ. The interest in human–animal interchange and in sexuality might represent a growing awareness not only of a common spirituality in humans, animals, and plants, but also of a common vitality animating the world.

The Ice Age Crisis and Human Migration to the Americas

Modern humans experienced two ice ages. The first one, 70,000–60,000 years ago, created land bridges that enabled humans to cross much of the Indonesian archipelago on foot and travel the rest of the distance by boat to Australia. This ice age was comparatively mild and brief, in contrast to the last ice age of the world's history, 33,000–17,000 years ago, which severely altered the flora and fauna on all continents. Humans, although suffering through it, exploited it for one major achievement: their migration to the Americas, probably beginning 17,000 years ago.

The Ice Age

The end of the Paleolithic era occurred during one of the climatically most inhospitable periods in world history, the Ice Age. Large parts of the world either descended into a deep freeze or became bone-dry. The northern zone of Eurasia, from England to Siberia, turned into a desolate steppe wasteland, partially covered with gigantic ice sheets. Most of North America, from Canada to the Midwest, was covered by the giant Cordilleran ice sheet. The central zone, from southern France to Mongolia, consisted of semiarid steppe lands. The southern zone, from Iberia to southern China, was temperate but semidry, with grasslands and pockets of woodlands.

In Africa and Australia, the rain forest was reduced to a few areas in central Africa and the northern tip of Australia, leaving the rest of those continents largely exposed to drought. The northern Sahara and southern Kalahari in Africa as well as the interior of Australia transformed what were once rich savannas and rain forests into deserts. Life for modern humans in Eurasia, Africa, and Australia during this ice age was an arduous struggle for daily survival (see Map 1.3).

Living Conditions   Nevertheless, the modern humans possessed the technological and mental resources to survive in the harsh Ice Age environment. They had a variety of implements for catching fish, snaring birds, and hunting animals, including harpoons, fishhooks, darts made of bone, fishnets, and bird traps. Boomerangs, invented independently in Europe and Australia, were used for hunting larger fowl. Wooden handles attached to large stone axe heads increased the efficiency of cutting meat or wood. In a situation of increasingly scarce large animals, *H. sapiens* became efficient at hunting small animals.

Human mobility increased substantially. Canoes took the form of dugouts or were constructed of bone and wood frames covered with skins. As a result of innovations like the canoe, the range for trading expanded. Baltic amber (fossilized tree resin prized for making jewelry) has been found 600 miles away from its origin in southern Europe, and Mediterranean shells in Ukraine, 800 miles to the northeast.

Ice Age humans dressed themselves warmly, wearing hooded fur coats stitched together with bone needles, using thin leather strips, as evidenced by figurines discovered in Siberia. An imprint left on kiln-fired clay, found in the Czech Republic, indicates that humans also began to weave woolen cloth on looms. No doubt, *H. sapiens* groups were decimated by the impact of the Ice Age, but survivors were still hanging on when the world finally began to warm up again around 19,000 years ago.

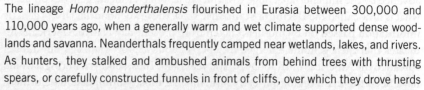

Patterns Up Close | The Disappearance of the Neanderthals

Deer in Hunting Scene, discovered 2017 in the cave Liang Bulu Sipong 4, on the island of Sulawesi, Indonesia. It was carbon-dated to 44,000 years ago and thus predates the animal scenes found in French and Spanish caves.

The lineage *Homo neanderthalensis* flourished in Eurasia between 300,000 and 110,000 years ago, when a generally warm and wet climate supported dense woodlands and savanna. Neanderthals frequently camped near wetlands, lakes, and rivers. As hunters, they stalked and ambushed animals from behind trees with thrusting spears, or carefully constructed funnels in front of cliffs, over which they drove herds of animals for slaughter. They often roamed over considerable distances, placing caches of spears and points at various intervals in order to replenish their hunting weapons.

Beginning about 110,000 years ago, the climate gradually changed from warm and wet to cold and dry, bringing about an increase in steppe and open grasslands. This change, however, often reversed for periods of varying length. During times of greater fluctuation, sometimes within three or four generations, Neanderthals had to adjust their hunting style to open landscapes where larger hunting parties and throwing spears were required. During a time of respite about 75,000–44,000 years ago, the climate and environment stabilized at a relatively warm and wet level, and Neanderthals resumed their accustomed forms of livelihood.

When they were in contact with modern humans 42,000-40,000 years ago in Europe, however, the situation changed dramatically, and the Neanderthals died out. What exactly happened is still highly controversial. An older theory assumed

the Yucatán peninsula. The teeth were from an almost perfectly preserved skeleton of a 15- or 16-year-old girl, named Naia (from Gr. *naias*, water nymph) by her discoverers, who had fallen into the sinkhole. According to the study, published in 2014, Naia's skeleton dates to 13,000–12,000 years ago. Her mitochondrial DNA—as well as that of the "Anzick-1" fossil of the same age found in Montana, also published in 2014—is closely related to that of the groups of Siberian *H. sapiens* that had migrated to Beringia during the Ice Age.

It appears, therefore, that members from one single, genetically uniform population in Beringia populated the Americas from at least ca. 16,500 years ago, that is, if one accepts the pre-Clovis archaeological record. Two papers published in 2016 confirm the assumption of a genetically uniform population of first settlers coming from Beringia. This population is related to Siberians but has small DNA admixtures (1–2 percent) pointing to people from the Andaman Islands (west of Malaysia), New Guinea, and Australia. The two papers agree that these admixtures happened prior to the arrival of the above population in the Americas but differ on how early and directly these admixtures took place.

increasingly lethal hostilities between the two lineages, pitting the allegedly less technically advanced Neanderthals against the allegedly more modern humans. This theory received its death knell in 2010, when the Swedish-born paleogeneticist Svante Pääbo and his team based in Leipzig, Germany, completed an analysis of Neanderthal DNA (from bones from Croatian Neanderthals) and found that there was interbreeding with modern humans: the genome of modern humans contains some 1–4 percent of Neanderthal genes. At the time, Pääbo's findings were sensational, although today, with DNA sequencing available to the general public, the existence of admixtures to the human genome is no longer surprising.

Another culprit was asserted to have been the onset of the Ice Age, which the warm-weather Neanderthals were unable to withstand: step by step, they retreated from northern Europe to southern Spain, where they had their last stand on Gibraltar. But the Neanderthals were long gone when the Ice Age began 33,000 years ago; a new dating of Neanderthal fossils from Bajondillo Cave near Málaga, published in 2019, suggests Neanderthal's disappearance by 40,000 years ago.

A 2019 theory, finally, advances the idea of differential "disease burdens" carried by the two lineages: modern humans found it easier to adjust to northern Neanderthal diseases than Neanderthals to acquire immunity against (more numerous or lethal?) tropical diseases. Whether this disease theory will withstand the rigors of scientific research is open to question, and at present the extinction of the Neanderthal species of humans remains a mystery.

Questions

- Before reading this essay, what misconceptions did you have about Neanderthals?
- Is it important for world historians to study the history of Neanderthals? If yes, for which reasons?

Native Americans or Amerindians   In 1996 a skull was discovered on the banks of the Columbia River near Kennewick, Washington. Subsequently, the archaeologist James Chatters found most of the bones belonging to the skull nearby and dubbed the fossil "Kennewick Man." A California lab dated them to about 9,000 years ago.

According to US law, ancient remains found on federal land (which is the case in Kennewick) belong to the Native American tribe that can prove parentage. An Oregon tribe claimed the bones, and a lengthy lawsuit ensued between several tribes, backed by the US government, and a number of archaeologists concerned to have scientific access to the fossil. The lawsuit was settled in 2004 in favor of the archaeologists, who claimed that the cranial features of Kennewick Man pointed more to a person of Ainu descent in Japan than to Native American parentage. New DNA tests in 2015, however, determined that Kennewick Man is definitely Native American, even if his skull seems to be different. Accordingly, five Native American or Amerindian Columbia Plateau tribes buried Kennewick Man on February 17, 2017, on their grounds.

It is thus clear today that the original settlers of the Americas are descendants of a single population that had moved from Siberia to Beringia some 25,000

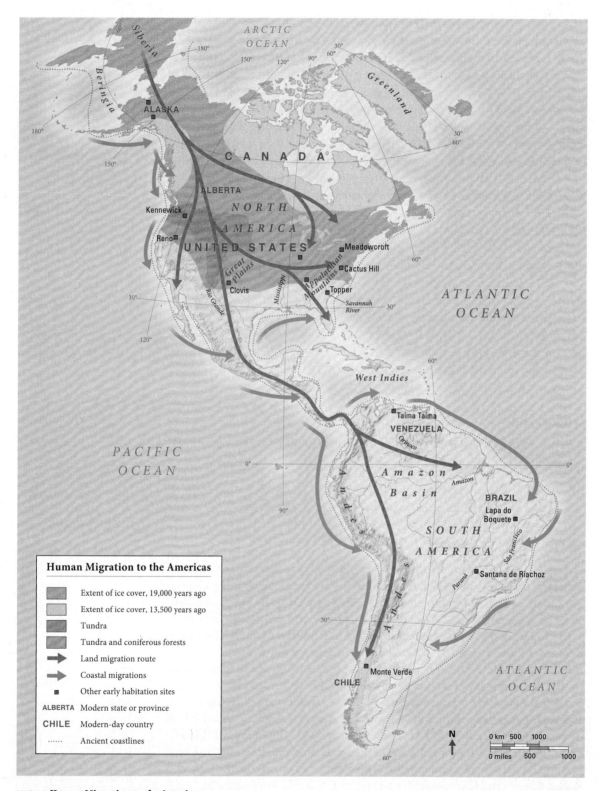

MAP 1.4 Human Migration to the Americas

years ago. During various stages of the thaw after the Ice Age (16,500–13,500 years ago), groups from among this population traveled by boat or on foot to the Americas, where they dispersed rapidly and diversified genetically. We call these settlers today Native Americans or Amerindians.

Putting It All Together

The time it took from Ardi to the first modern humans in East Africa was slightly less than 7 million years. Another 100,000 years elapsed before modern humans peopled the earth, down to Clovis and the transition to agriculture in the Fertile Crescent of the Middle East. From there, in another 10,000 years we reached our own time. The time proportions are staggering: the history from Clovis and the Fertile Crescent to the present is a mere 0.02 percent of the time from Ardi to the present and 4 percent of that from the first *H. sapiens* fossil to the present. Practically the entire time we needed to become genetically human is buried in the "deep history" mentioned at the beginning of this chapter.

Nearly as deeply buried is the process during which we began to carve out the space for culture. Realizing how long these genetic and cultural time spans of prehistory are is what matters for us today; the 10,000 years of history from the shift of forager to agrarian–urban and eventually scientific–industrial society represent a breathtakingly short, yet overwhelmingly complex, time of development. When we consider the much slower deep history of humanity, we become aware that, had it not been for this slow incubation, we would never have been able to sustain the speed of the later history of which we are the current product.

The principal reason for the slow pace of deep history was the conscious effort of foragers to limit population growth. Women as well as men, constantly on the move in search for food, had a strong interest in having few children. Of course, Paleolithic populations grew over the course of the millennia; otherwise, there would not have been a pattern shift from foraging to agrarian–urban life. Thus, even though the culture of foraging sought to inhibit population growth, this culture was not so rigid that people under climatologically and environmentally benign circumstances were not open to material and cultural change. It was under these circumstances at the end of the Ice Age, 13,500 years ago, that humans in some parts of the world gradually abandoned foraging and began adapting to agriculture.

Review and Relate

Thinking Through Patterns

Examine the ways historians approach the big questions of this chapter.

We are twice removed from the world of foragers: After foraging came farming, which is also difficult to understand, because today's pattern of life is part of scientific–industrial civilization. *H. sapiens* foragers in prehistory relied on their stone

> What made it possible for *H. sapiens* to survive in a dangerous environment? Why is it difficult to imagine life as a prehistoric forager?

tools, bows and arrows, rock shelters, clan members, and unsurpassed knowledge of animals, berry bushes, fruit and nut trees, mushroom patches, and grass fields to guide them through their daily lives. Collecting vegetables, catching fish, and killing the occasional animal did not take as much of an effort as farming later did, and foragers had more leisure time than farmers engaged in the annual agricultural cycle.

> **Where did humans go when they left Africa, and how did they establish themselves in the areas where they settled? How did they adapt to the worsening Ice Age?**

After modern humans left East Africa, probably in several waves between 80,000 and 60,000 years ago, in all likelihood they first went to northern India, before fanning out in all directions to Australia, Siberia, and Europe. They encountered *H. erectus* and successors, such as Neanderthals, and interbred with the latter. The modern humans who settled in Australia remained foragers, because the Australian flora did not include grasses that could be cultivated through selective breeding into grains. From the complex lineage societies into which they evolved, we can see that forager life could acquire a differentiated culture, expressed in the so-called Dreamtime. However, when the Ice Age hit, forager clans and lineages had to adapt to harsh environmental conditions and retreat southward. Foremost among the adaptations were the abilities to make protective woolen clothing and build boats with which to travel to more favorable places.

> **Why did early humans create cave paintings and figurines? Do they show patterns that can be interpreted?**

The existence of tens of thousands of prehistoric cave paintings and figurines found on all continents attests to the great importance *H. sapiens* gave to the representation of humans, animals, plants, and hybrid figures with which they shared the natural world. The attention they paid to these beings—at rest or in motion, alone or in groups, in outline or full detail—shows how important it was to them to identify the inhabitants of their world accurately and to teach the young how to recognize them in nature. Yet, as important as it was to have an accurate knowledge of visible things, these early humans also conceived of an invisible world in which identities could be exchanged, shared, or merged. In this sense, prehistoric art can be seen as the first expression of spiritual experience, in which humans expressed awareness not only of the visible world in all its diversity but also of an invisible world of other identities.

- The story of *H. floresiensis* is a story of overlapping species. Which other examples of species overlapping each other are there?

- Improved measurement technologies require constant revisions. Which cases of revision, in addition to that of *H. floresiensis*, come to mind?

Against the Grain

Consider this as a counterpoint to the main patterns examined in this chapter.

The Hobbits of Flores Island

In 2003, an Australian–Indonesian team unearthed the partial fossils of 13 hominins in a cave on the island of Flores in the southern archipelago of Indonesia. The fossils were of beings that measured only 3–4 feet high and had brains no larger than those of chimpanzees or some australopiths. Layers of earth in which the fossils were discovered seemed to date to fairly recent times, and accordingly their owners were declared to have lived as late as 18,000 years ago. Their closest relatives seemed to be members of the species *H. erectus*, and to the astonishment of the scholarly world, this diminutive new type of hominin, dubbed *H. floresiensis*, appeared to have survived well into the period of modern humans, even if isolated from mainland Asia.

The hominins of the island entered popular imagination as the "hobbits of Flores," on account of their seeming similarities with the diminutive characters in J. R. R. Tolkien's *Lord of the Rings* novels. Did these hobbits perhaps survive even later than 18,000 years ago? Researchers cited oral history among the modern inhabitants of Flores, recorded by ethnologists, which included stories about small creatures in remote parts of the island stealing food and snatching children around the time of the Portuguese arrival in the sixteenth century. It looked like evolution had reversed itself.

In 2016, however, new and improved radiocarbon measurements of the layers of soil surrounding the fossils revealed that the hobbit finds were much older than originally calculated; the hominins actually lived on the island between 100,000 and 60,000 years ago. Nevertheless, even if—disappointingly—hobbit islanders and *H. sapiens* on the way to Australia did not meet, the long survival of *H. erectus* still remains remarkable indeed.

Key Terms

Aboriginals   12
Acheulian toolmaking   7
Agrarian–urban society   9
Beringia Standstill   19
Australopiths   5

Bipedalism   4
Dreamtime   13
Hominins   4
Levallois toolmaking   8
Oldowan toolmaking   5

Paleolithic   6
Savanna   5
Tundra   18

Learn more with this chapter's digital tools, including the Oxford Insight Study Guide, at http://www.oup.com/he/vonsivers4e. Please see the Further Resources section at the back of the book for additional readings and suggested websites.

Sources for Chapter 1

Shell bead jewelry from the Grotte des Pigeons, Taforalt, Morocco

ca. 82,000–75,000 BCE

The discovery of 13 shells in a cave in eastern Morocco in 2007 has led to a discussion about the oldest known form of human ornamentation. Because each shell contains a pierced hole and traces of red ochre (a pigment derived from a type of rock), archaeologists concluded that the shells had been strung together as necklaces or bracelets. Another important detail is that the shell is from a genus of marine snail called *Nassarius*. The closest this snail is found to the site (at least today) is an island off the coast of Tunisia, more than 800 miles away.

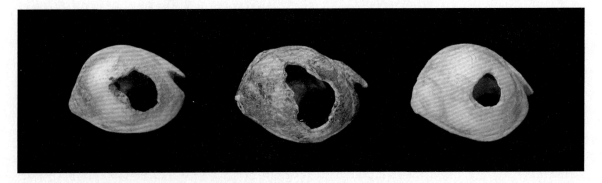

▶ **Working with Sources**

1. Why is the creation of jewelry a significant step in the development of human society?

2. What might this find indicate about trade patterns and networks in northern Africa around 80,000 years ago?

Source: *Smithsonian Institution, National Museum of Natural History*, http://humanorigins.si.edu/evidence/behavior/art-music/jewelry/ancient-shell-beads

| SOURCE 1.2 | Python-shaped ornamented rock found in the Rhino Cave, Botswana |

ca. 70,000 BCE

Archaeologists working in the Tsodilo Hills of Botswana in 2006 may have found the oldest evidence of a form of human ritual behavior. One cavern contains a large rock, roughly 20 feet long and 6.5 feet wide, that resembles a giant python, with the natural features of the stone forming its eye and mouth. While its resemblance to a reptile may be natural, there are also several hundred man-made grooves along its side, indicating an attempt to replicate scales with fashioned tools. Spearheads were also found at the site, and similar ones in the area have been dated to 77,000 years ago. Researchers have concluded that this was a worship site for the inhabitants of the region in this period.

▶ **Working with Sources**

1. What symbolic connections might early humans have attributed to snakes, and why might snakes have been depicted and worshipped?

2. What does the growth of "abstract symbolic thinking" suggest about the development of early *H. sapiens* societies?

Source: http://www.nbcnews.com/id/15970442/ns/technology_and_science-science/t/scientists-find-first-known -human-ritual/#.XoJ4VohKiM8

SOURCE 1.3   Pottery's diverse origins in East Asia

ca. 20,000–10,000 BCE

The controlled use of fire originated with *Homo erectus* and the use of fire in hearths was introduced by *Homo sapiens*. As is now known from archaeological research in the first two decades of the twenty-first century, the transition from hearths to kilns for the firing of clay pots and figurines occurred during the Ice Age (ca. 22,000–9500 BCE)—much earlier than was hitherto assumed. In other words, foragers ("hunter-gatherers" in the document), not farmers and early urban dwellers, discovered the art of firing clay.

Pottery making may not have emerged in one Big Bang–like event. Instead, it was more like a cluster of ceramic eruptions among ancient East Asian hunter-gatherer groups as the last ice age waned, a new study suggests.

East Asian hunter-gatherer populations living about 700 kilometers apart made and used cooking pots in contrasting ways between around 16,200 and 10,200 years ago, says a team led by Shinya Shoda, an archaeologist currently based at the University of York in England. Each of those

Source: Adapted from Bruce Bower, "Food Residues Offer a Taste of Pottery's Diverse Origins in East Asia," *ScienceNews*, February 10, 2020, https://www.sciencenews.org/article/food-residues-offer-taste-pottery-diverse-origins-east-asia

groups probably invented its own distinctive pottery-making techniques, the scientists suspect.

"Our results indicate that there was greater variability in the development and use of early pottery than has been appreciated," Shoda says.

Pieces of ceramic cooking pots from one group preserved chemical markers of fish, including salmon, Shoda's group reports in the Feb. 1, 2020, *Quaternary Science Reviews*. Early pottery making by those hunter-gatherers accompanied seasonal harvests of migrating fish, the researchers say.

Fatty acids extracted from remnants of a second group's pots came from hoofed animals such as sheep or goats. Those vessels were used to render grease from animals' bones, the team suggests.

Each group appears to have had its own pottery-making style. Members of the Osipovka culture, who lived along the Lower Amur River in what's now the Russian Far East, crafted cone-shaped vessels with flat bottoms and thick walls. Clay paste was mixed with gravel and other material. Inside and sometimes outside surfaces of pots were scraped with tools like combs.

At sites of the Gromatukha culture, situated on the banks of the Amur River and its tributaries northwest of Osipovka sites, researchers found slightly curved pots that rested on either flat or round bases. Clay was typically mixed with grass, especially in the oldest pots. Cord marks and zigzag patterns cover many vessels.

Other researchers have reported that the earliest known pottery, from Xianrendong Cave in southern China, dates to roughly 20,000 years ago (*ScienceNews: 6/28/12*). Although there has been debate about the accuracy of that age estimate, "it is certain that the world's oldest pottery gradually emerged in East and Northeast Asia from 20,000 to 10,000 years ago," says archaeologist Hiroyuki Sato of the University of Tokyo. That timing corresponds with the end of the Pleistocene Ice Age, which lasted from roughly 2.6 million to 11,700 years ago.

Chemical residue findings for the Gromatukha pottery challenge a currently popular view among researchers that the earliest pottery was used only for cooking fish and shellfish, says Sato, who did not participate in the new study. Shoda's group provides the first chemical evidence of land animals being cooked in some of the world's earliest clay pots.

The researchers analyzed chemical residues on 23 pot shards from three Osipovka sites and five pot shards from one Gromatukha site. Signs of fish having been cooked in Osipovka pots came as no surprise, Shoda says. More than 100 freshwater fish species currently inhabit the Amur River, as well as fish such as salmon that return to the river to spawn from late spring to early fall.

Past excavations of at least 15 sites indicate that Osipovka pottery was produced in large quantities only after around 13,700 years ago. Osipovka people probably started out using ceramic pots to prepare fish for special events or ceremonies, not daily meals, the researchers speculate.

Only three Gromatukha sites have been excavated, so less is known about pottery making in that culture. But chemical residues indicate that the Gromatukha menu leaned heavily on land animals, Shoda says.

In a 2016 paper, Shoda and his colleagues reported chemical evidence of what they now regard as a third, comparably old pottery-making tradition that arose in Japan. Distinctive pots of Japan's Jōmon culture, unearthed at one well-preserved site, were used to cook fish and mollusks from around 14,000 years ago until as late as 5,000 years ago, the scientists found.

▶ Working with Sources

1. In which ways do the discoveries of early pottery making in East Asia change the traditional conception of how foragers ("hunter-gatherers") lived?

2. What were the advantages of pottery for cooking during the prehistoric Ice Age?

SOURCE 1.4   Flax fibers found at the Dzudzuana Cave, Republic of Georgia, Caucasus Mountains

ca. 30,000 BCE

A 2009 paper in *Science* announced the identification of at least 488 fibers of flax attached to clay samples found in a cave in Georgia, in the Caucasus Mountains. Some of these fibers had been spun and dyed, and one of the threads (no. 8 in the figure) had been twisted. The applied colors, ranging from black to gray to turquoise, may indicate that the inhabitants of the cave were engaged in producing colorful textiles. The presence of spores in the cave indicates that fungus was probably already growing on the clothes and progressively breaking them down.

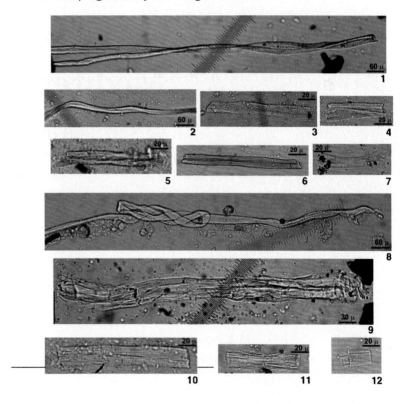

▶ **Working with Sources**

1. What does the manufacture of clothing suggest about the sophistication of Upper Paleolithic human societies?

2. Can the manufacture of textiles in this period be compared to other forms of handcraft in the same era?

Source: *Science Magazine*, September 11, 2009, http://www.sciencemag.org/content/325/5946/1359.full#xref-ref-2-1

World Period One

From Human Origins to Early Agricultural Centers, Prehistory to 600 BCE

Humans appeared late in the evolution of the world. While the earth is 4.5 billion years old, the first human-like beings only appeared about 6 million years ago, and modern humans did not appear in East Africa until about 100,000 years ago. These humans migrated from there to Eurasia and Australia 80,000–60,000 years ago and to the Americas 17,500–14,600 years ago.

As people became more numerous, human culture became more differentiated. The triad of origins-interactions-adaptations as the fundamental pattern in world history took shape. Human ingenuity and interaction with the environment in the Middle East, Asia, Europe, Australia, and the Americas led to vastly different adaptations. Foraging originated in Africa. Farming, urbanization, and state formation originated in the Middle East. In the Americas, humans fashioned similarly differentiated livelihoods and political structures. Australia's poorer natural environment slowed its differentiation process.

Chapter 2

Agrarian–Urban Centers of the Middle East and Eastern Mediterranean

11,500–600 BCE

CHAPTER TWO PATTERNS

Origins, Interactions, Adaptations The transition from foraging to agriculture was neither preprogrammed nor necessary. At the end of the Ice Age in the Middle East, propitious climatic circumstances helped in the selected breeding of early variations of wheat and the domestication of farm animals. Increasingly dry weather around 7000 BCE, however, induced some farmers to pioneer irrigated agriculture in villages along the Tigris, Euphrates, and Nile. Irrigated agriculture led to vastly improved surpluses and as a result, around 5400 BCE, to a transition from villages to cities.

Uniqueness and Similarities Some cities became city-states or territorial kingdoms with rulers, palaces, temples, bureaucracies, soldiers, craftsmen, and merchants. Patriarchy and class structures emerged, requiring elaborate legal codes for regulation. Conquering kings created empires—regional states with vassal kings, multiple temples with their own gods, and inhabitants speaking a variety of languages. Between ca. 3100–2300 BCE, Early Dynastic Egypt and the empire of Akkad emerged, unifying the Nile Valley and Mesopotamia/Syria, respectively. Subsequently, Egypt evolved into a religiously, ethnically, and linguistically unified state while Akkad gave way to a sequence of empires characterized by multiple ethnicities, languages, and religions.

The high priestess Enheduanna [en-hay-doo-AN-nah] lived at the end of the third millennium BCE and was a daughter of Sargon of Akkad, ruler of Mesopotamia's first recorded kingdom. She is the first writer in world history we know by name. Her best-known poem, "The Exaltation of Inanna," was written after a rebel leader had deposed her as high priestess. In the poem Enheduanna sadly wonders why Inanna (also later known as Ishtar), the goddess of love, fertility, and war, has abandoned her, and she pleads to the goddess to take her back into her favor.

After reciting prayerful poems night and day, Enheduanna finally succeeded: Inanna accepted her priestess's appeals and the rightful ruler returned Enheduanna to her temple position.

By the end of the third millennium BCE, **agrarian–urban society** had become well established in several different areas. Foragers had pioneered agriculture and village settlements during a long period of 5,000 years in the Fertile Crescent of the Middle East. Once these early inhabitants had become farmers, they began interacting with foragers in the marshes of the Mesopotamian river delta. This combined population founded cities in which craftspeople, priests and priestesses, merchants, kings, and rebels mingled, creating the fundamentals of the urban amenities of contemporary civilization. This chapter will trace the origins of farming, villages, cities, kingdoms, and empires in the Middle East, the first of the agrarian–urban centers in world history.

Agrarian Origins in the Fertile Crescent, ca. 11,500–1500 BCE

The movement from foraging to agriculture took several millennia. During this time, farmers built villages, in which they worked small garden-like plots and depended on annual rains for the growth of their crops. Farming gathered

CHAPTER OUTLINE

Agrarian Origins in the Fertile Crescent, ca. 11,500–1500 BCE

Interactions among Multiethnic and Multireligious Empires, ca. 1500–600 BCE

Religious Experience and Cultural Achievements

Putting It All Together

Agrarian–urban society: A society characterized by intensive agriculture and people living in cities, towns, and villages.

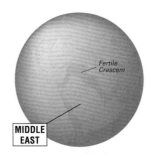

ABOVE: Standard of Ur (ca. 2500 BCE) in Mesopotamia, showing the so-called Peace/Banquet Scene, with the king (top row, third from the left) observing a variety of urban and rural activities.

Seeing Patterns

❯ What are the main factors that enabled the transition from foraging to farming?

❯ Where did the pattern of agricultural life first emerge and why?

❯ How did the creation of agrarian–urban society— what we commonly call "civilization"—make for an entirely new pattern in world history?

momentum as people mastered methods of irrigation. Farmers began to settle in the two great river valleys of the Tigris–Euphrates [you-FRAY-teez], in present-day Turkey, Syria, and Iraq, and the Nile in Egypt. In these valleys, irrigation using river water allowed for larger plots and bigger harvests. Nutrient-rich river silt from the regular floods made the fields more fertile and provided for surpluses of grain. These surpluses allowed populations to build cities and states with ruling institutions composed of kings, advisors, armies, and bureaucracies.

Sedentary Foragers and Foraging Farmers

The Middle East and the eastern Mediterranean region stretch over portions of three continents—eastern Europe, southwestern Asia, and northeastern Africa. This region has always formed a single geographical unit within which there was circulation of goods and ideas, although it did not constitute a single cultural zone. After the rise of the political institution of the empire, from about 1100 BCE, areas in the Middle East and the eastern Mediterranean were often also in competition with each other.

Geography and Environment   The western half of the region includes Thrace and Greece in the north, together with numerous islands in the Aegean Sea. The terrain on the mainland as well as the islands is mostly mountainous and forested. To the east lies Anatolia, which comprises most of modern Turkey. Anatolia is a peninsula consisting of a central high plain ringed by mountain chains and traversed by rivers.

South of Anatolia and lying on the eastern shore of the Mediterranean Sea is the Levant, encompassing modern Syria, Lebanon, Israel, and Palestine. Along the coastline is a mountain chain reaching from Mount Lebanon in the north to the hill country of Palestine in the south. The Levant, the Taurus Mountains of southeastern Anatolia, and the Zagros Mountains of southwestern Iran are often referred to collectively as the "Fertile Crescent"—the birthplace of agriculture (Map 2.1).

To the east of the mountain chain extends the Syrian steppe, which gives way on the south to the Arabian Desert. South of the Levant on the African continent are Egypt and Nubia (today's northern Sudan) on both sides of the Nile River. Both are largely covered by desert but bisected by the fertile Nile valley. The Middle East also includes three smaller regions:

- Persia (modern-day Iran), stretching from the Caspian Sea southward to the Persian Gulf
- Mesopotamia, "the land between the rivers," namely the Euphrates and Tigris in present-day Iraq and Kuwait
- the Arabian Peninsula, consisting of modern Saudi Arabia, the United Arab Emirates, Qatar, Oman, and Yemen.

Recent historical climate research has established that between the end of the Ice Age (around 11,500 BCE) and 4000 BCE, monsoon rain patterns extended farther west than they do today. When the monsoon still covered the Middle East, from the Mediterranean coast to the Persian Gulf, vegetation covered land that is desert today. At present, only the highlands of Yemen and mountain rings around the central salt desert of Iran receive enough rain to sustain agriculture. At the eastern end of the Middle East is Afghanistan, a country with steppe plains and high mountains bordering on India. It was also a center of early **agrarian society**.

Agriculture first appeared in the Fertile Crescent for several reasons: its moderate climate, its fertile soil, and its access to abundant water sources for irrigation. Other advantages of this region included large areas of wild grains as well as a variety of domesticated animals. Finally, because of its central location, agricultural advances were easily transmitted from the Fertile Crescent to Egypt in the West and to India and China in the East.

Agrarian society: At a minimum, people engaged in farming cereal grains on rainfed or irrigated fields and breeding sheep and cattle.

Hamlets   The richness of the Fertile Crescent in plants and animals during the early centuries after the end of the Ice Age seems to have encouraged settlement. Semipermanent hamlets, forming the Natufian culture (11,500–9500 BCE), arose in the Jordan and upper Euphrates valleys.

Each hamlet of the Natufians, consisting of about 60 inhabitants, contained a few semicircular pit houses. The Natufians buried their dead underneath the floors of abandoned houses or along the edges of settlements. Some graves contained ornaments, and at least two persons were found buried with their dogs. Later Natufians often removed the skulls of their ancestors—whether before or after the burial of the body is unknown—and venerated them in altar niches in their houses. Thus began an important ancestral cult that spread across the Middle East and lasted for several millennia.

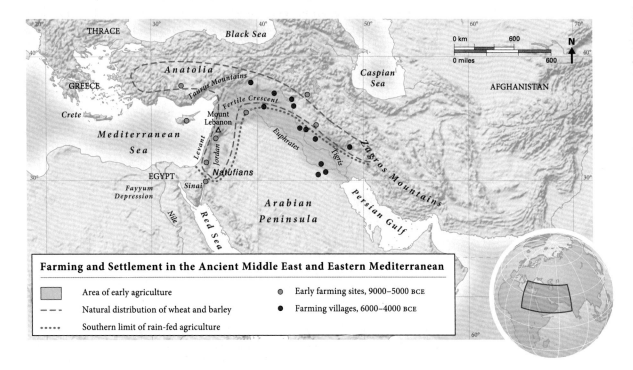

MAP 2.1 **Farming and Settlement in the Ancient Middle East and Eastern Mediterranean**

The Natufians went out into the woods with baskets and obsidian-bladed sickles to gather wild cereal grains. Back in the hamlets, the grain was ground with pestles on grindstones. Storage seems to have been minimal, limited to portable containers, such as baskets. The abundant food supply, however, did not last. A near-glacial cold and dry period from 10,800 to 9500 BCE, called the "Younger Dryas," caused wild cereal stands to wither and game animals to leave. Most of the sedentary foragers deserted their hamlets and returned to a fully migratory life of foraging. The short-lived, semisettled culture of the Natufians withered away.

In the few hamlets that survived, people turned to storing grain in plastered pits or stone silos to get through the harsher winters. In spring, they planted some of their stored grain. When a warmer and more humid climate returned, a new era began: the **Neolithic**, or New Stone Age. Scholars use this designation for the period from about 9600 to 4500 BCE in the Middle East because it was characterized by innovations such as polished stone implements (spades and sickles); the introduction of agriculture; animal domestication; and sun-dried bricks, plaster, and pottery.

Neolithic Age: Period from ca. 9600 to 4500 BCE when stone tools were adapted to the requirements of agriculture, through the making of sickles and spades.

Selective Breeding of Grain and Domestic Animals   In the early Neolithic Age, summer temperatures increased by an extraordinary 7 degrees in just a few generations. For another 2,000 years, temperatures continued to rise at a more modest rate. In this balmy climate, hamlets expanded into villages of around 300–500 inhabitants. People continued to collect grain but also began to plant fields. Through selective breeding, they gradually weeded out early-ripening varieties and began harvesting fields in which all grain ripened at the same time. By about 7000 BCE, farmers in the Middle East were breeding the large-grained wheat and barley of today.

Parallel to the selective breeding of grain, farmers also domesticated pulses (the edible seeds of pod-bearing plants), beginning with chickpeas and lentils. Pulses helped to refertilize grain fields, as the pods, stalks, and roots contain the nitrogen needed by all plants to grow. Farmers continued to hunt, but they also captured young wild goats and sheep and through selective breeding accustomed them to live with humans in their houses and in pens—the first domestication of livestock.

The original agriculture—the cultivation of grain and pulses and the domestication of goats and sheep—relied on annual rains in the Fertile Crescent

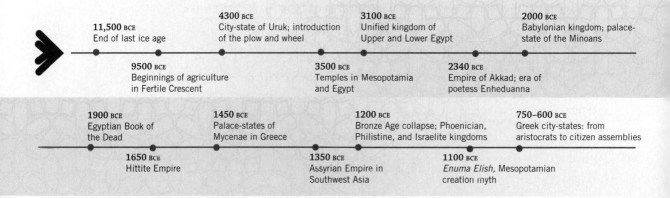

11,500 BCE
End of last ice age

4300 BCE
City-state of Uruk; introduction of the plow and wheel

3100 BCE
Unified kingdom of Upper and Lower Egypt

2000 BCE
Babylonian kingdom; palace-state of the Minoans

9500 BCE
Beginnings of agriculture in Fertile Crescent

3500 BCE
Temples in Mesopotamia and Egypt

2340 BCE
Empire of Akkad; era of poetess Enheduanna

1900 BCE
Egyptian Book of the Dead

1450 BCE
Palace-states of Mycenae in Greece

1200 BCE
Bronze Age collapse; Phoenician, Philistine, and Israelite kingdoms

750–600 BCE
Greek city-states: from aristocrats to citizen assemblies

1650 BCE
Hittite Empire

1350 BCE
Assyrian Empire in Southwest Asia

1100 BCE
Enuma Elish, Mesopotamian creation myth

and became more widespread when farmers tapped creeks for irrigation during dry months. Inhabitants of this region discovered the benefits of rotating their crops and driving goats and sheep over the stubble of harvested grain fields, using the animals' droppings for refertilization and leaving the fields fallow for a year. Around 6500 BCE, these peoples added cattle, pigs, donkeys, and pottery to their farms. The epic transition from foraging to farming had been completed.

The Origin of Urban Centers in Mesopotamia and Egypt

During the fifth millennium BCE, the climate of the Middle East and eastern Mediterranean changed from one with monsoon rains falling during the summer to one with wet winters and dry summers prevailing in the west and north and general dryness in the east and south. Most of the Arabian Peninsula began to dry up. In lower Mesopotamia, drier conditions forced settlers to pay closer attention to irrigation. All of these changes would contribute to the rise of the first agrarian–urban centers founded along rivers—in the Middle East, Egypt, the Indus valley in the Indian subcontinent, and later the Yellow River valley in China.

FIRST AGRARIAN–URBAN CENTERS

Euphrates and Nile Floods   The swift Tigris River in eastern Mesopotamia did not lend itself easily to the construction of irrigation canals. The slower Euphrates River in western Mesopotamia, however, provided favorable conditions for irrigated farming. At its lower end, in present-day Iraq, the Euphrates united with the Tigris and dispersed out into swampland, lagoons, and marshes, which supported a rich plant and animal life. It was here that the first farmers of the Fertile Crescent settled, establishing the Ubaid culture (6000–4000 BCE).

The annual snowmelt in the mountains of northeastern Anatolia caused the Euphrates and Tigris to flood the plains below. The floods arrived in early spring just as the first grain was ready for harvest, forcing the farmers into heroic efforts to keep the ripening grain fields from being inundated by water. And yet the spring floods helped prepare the fields for the growing of smaller crops. The floods also softened hardened soils and sometimes leached them of salt deposits. Thus, in spite of some drawbacks, irrigated farming in lower Mesopotamia, with its more predictable water supplies, was more productive than the more irregular rain-fed agriculture to the north.

The Egyptian Nile originates in East Africa, where the rains hit during the early summer. Much of this rain is collected in Lake Victoria, from which the White Nile flows northward. In the Sudan it unites with the Blue Nile from Ethiopia, which carries water and fertile silt. The Nile usually begins to swell in July, crests in August–September, and recedes during October. For the Neolithic inhabitants of Egypt, these late-summer and fall floods created conditions quite different from those of lower Mesopotamia, which depended on the spring floods.

In Egypt, the floods coincided with the growing season of winter barley and wheat. Silt carried by the Nile fertilized the fields every year prior to planting. The first agricultural settlements appeared in the Fayyum [fay-YOOM], a swampy depression off the Nile southwest of modern Cairo, around 5200 BCE. By about 3500 BCE, agriculture had spread south along the Nile and north into the delta.

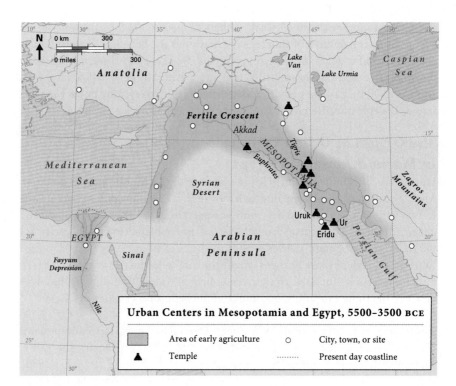

MAP 2.2 **Urban Centers in Mesopotamia and Egypt, 5500–3500 BCE**

Assembly: Gathering of either all inhabitants or the most influential persons in a town; later, in cities, assemblies and kings made communal decisions on important fiscal or juridical matters.

Sharecroppers: Farmers who received seed, animals, and tools from landowners in exchange for up to two-thirds of their harvest and access to land.

Nomads: People whose livelihood was based on the herding of animals, such as sheep, goats, and cattle; later also horses and camels. They moved with their animals from pasture to pasture according to the seasons, living in tent camps.

Early Towns   Between 5500 and 3500 BCE, villages in lower Mesopotamia and Upper Egypt developed into towns. They were composed of a few thousand inhabitants, with markets where farmers exchanged surplus food staples and traders offered goods not produced locally. The Mesopotamian towns administered themselves through local **assemblies**, in which male adults decided on communal matters. For nearly two millennia, towns in this region regulated their irrigated agriculture through communal cooperation (see Map 2.2).

Irrigation made it possible for townspeople in Mesopotamia and Egypt to accumulate agricultural surpluses to protect themselves against famine and allowed for population increases. Some people accumulated more grain than others, and the first social distinctions along the lines of wealth appeared. Gradually, wealthy families became owners of land beyond their family properties. **Sharecroppers** who worked these lands paid rent (in the form of grain) to the new landowners. Other landless farmers left agriculture altogether and became **nomads**, breeding onagers (ancestors of donkeys), sheep, and goats on steppe lands. Wealthy landowners appropriated the places of ritual and sacrifice in the villages and towns and constructed temples, mansions, workshops, and granaries.

Eventually, the landowning priestly families turned the production of such goods as tools, pottery, cloth, and leatherwork over to specialized craftspeople, paying them with grain rations. The landowners employed traders who traveled to other areas with crafts (pottery, cloth, leather goods), trading them for raw materials. Mesopotamian merchants traveled with cloth and tools to villages and towns in the Zagros Mountains and returned with timber, stone, obsidian, and copper. Egyptian villagers traded textiles with villagers in the Sinai Peninsula in return for copper and with Nubian villagers in return for gold.

Around 4300 BCE, some mountain people in the region had mastered the crafts of mining and smelting copper. This metal was too soft to replace obsidian, but the many other uses to which it was put have led scholars to mark the middle of the fifth millennium BCE as the moment when the Neolithic, or New Stone Age, of polished stone tools came to an end and the Chalcolithic, or Copper Age, began.

Temples   In the course of the fifth millennium BCE, wealthy landowners gained control over the communal grain stores and clan shrines and enlarged these into town shrines. Adjacent to the early temples were kilns, granaries, workshops, breweries, and administrative buildings. The wealthy landowners, presiding over the temples as priests, were responsible for the administration of all aspects of cult ritual in the temples, as well as the provision of labor in the temple fields.

In Upper Egypt, landowner-priests presided over the construction of the first temples around 3500 BCE, together with elegantly embellished tombs for themselves. One such tomb painting shows a leader carrying out an expedition on the Nile upstream to Nubia, returning with gold and ebony to create ornaments for his temple and tomb. Unfortunately, the sparse archaeological record in Egypt at this point presents few details concerning the transition from village to town.

The World's First Cities   In contrast to a town, a **city** (or **city-state**, if the surrounding villages are included) is defined as a place with a population of more than 5,000, including a number of nonfarming inhabitants, such as craftspeople, merchants, and administrators. The latter lived on the food they received in exchange for their own handiwork. To keep order, the dominant landowner-priest created a personal entourage of armed men. The first place in Mesopotamia to fit the definition of a city was Uruk, founded near Eridu (southwest of Nasiriya in modern Iraq) around 4300 BCE. Within a millennium, it was a city of 50,000–80,000 inhabitants, a mixture of palaces, multistory administrative buildings, workshops, residences, and palace estates; villages clustered around the city, with both large and small individual farms. It was in what is called the land of Sumer (now southern Iraq).

The people of Uruk were pioneers of technical and intellectual innovations. It was here that the first known plow was found. Plowing and controlled sowing allowed for much larger harvests. Uruk craftspeople introduced the potter's wheel, which accelerated and made more precise the manufacture of earthenware and ceramics. The sizes of jars, pots, and bowls gradually became standardized, simplifying the storage of grain and its distribution in the cities.

At the same time, two-and four-wheeled carts pulled by oxen expedited the transportation of large quantities of grain from the fields to the city. The grain was made into bread and beer. By some estimates, more than 40 percent of Mesopotamia's grain was committed to beer production.

Another important invention was bronze. Bronze is an alloy of copper and arsenic or tin; its strength makes it useful for tools and weapons. During the

City, city-state: A place with a population of more than 5,000, with nonfarming inhabitants (craftspeople, merchants, administrators), markets, and a city leader capable of compelling obedience to his decisions by force.

Cuneiform Script. Scribes impressed the syllables on the wet clay with a wedge-shaped reed stylus.

following centuries, bronze replaced stone and copper implements for all but a few purposes in the Middle East and eastern Mediterranean, leading historians to refer to this as the Bronze Age (in the Middle East, from 3300 to 1200 BCE).

Cuneiform Writing   The administrators in the bureaucracy, who were responsible for the accounting and distribution of grain, animals, ceramics, textiles, and imported raw materials, greatly simplified their tasks around 3450 BCE by inventing a form of writing. Scribes wrote Sumerian in cuneiform [kyoo-NEE-uh-form] (from Latin *cuneus* "wedgeshaped") script on clay tablets, using signs denoting objects and sounds from the spoken language. For the first time, scribes could not only write down the language they spoke but also clarify for future generations the meaning of the sculpted and painted artifacts that would otherwise have been mute witnesses of history. With the advent of writing, record-keeping, communication, increasingly abstract thought, and, for the first time, history could all be recorded.

Kingdoms in Mesopotamia, Egypt, and Crete   With the introduction of the plow, city leaders greatly expanded their landholdings. They employed large groups of laborers to cut canals through riverbanks, making vast new areas of lowlands available for farming. Portions of this land served as overflow basins for floodwaters, to protect the ripening grain fields. Craftspeople invented devices to channel water from the canals into small fields or gardens. As a result of this field and irrigation expansion, the grain surpluses of both temples and villages increased enormously.

Kingship in Mesopotamia   A consequence of the expansion of agriculture was the rise of nearly two dozen cities in lower and central Mesopotamia. As cities expanded and multiplied, the uncultivated buffer lands that had formerly separated them disappeared. People drew borders and fought over access to water and the ownership of wandering livestock.

When wars broke out, city dwellers built walls and recruited military forces from among their young population. The commanders, often of modest origins, used their military positions to acquire wealth and demanded to be recognized as leaders. They challenged the authority of the priests, who had been the traditional heads of villages and towns. Depending on circumstances, the Mesopotamian city assemblies chose their leaders from either the self-made or the priestly leaders, calling the former "great men" (sing. *lugal*) and the latter "kings" (sing. *en*).

Once in power, a leader sought to impose dynastic or family rule on the city. To set himself apart from his assembly colleagues, he claimed divine or sacred sanction for his kingship. The King List of 2125 BCE, in which the reigns of all early kings in lower Mesopotamia were coordinated, begins: "After the kingship descended from heaven, the kingship was in Eridu." In other words, the kings argued that as divinely ordained rulers, neither they nor their sons and grandsons needed the consensus of the assemblies for their power. The earliest king known by name and attested in the archaeological record was Enmebaragesi [en-me-ba-ra-GAY-see] of Kish, who reigned around 2500 BCE.

Akkad and Babylonia During the 2000s BCE, Mesopotamian cities began competing for military supremacy. The first royal dynasty to bring them together in a unified territorial state or polity was that of Akkad (ca. 2340–2150 BCE), to the north of Sumer, whose language, Akkadian, belongs to the Semitic family. Sargon ("The Great"), the first major king (r. 2334–2279 BCE), commanded several thousand foot soldiers. At its height, Sargon's Akkadian empire—the world's first—stretched from Mesopotamia into Asia Minor and Syria. Sargon's grandson, Naram-Sin, added the Zagros Mountains and Syria to the Akkadian kingdom and claimed to be the "king of the four (world) shores." He was the first king to conceive of the unification of the ethnically, linguistically, and religiously diverse peoples of the Middle East, with or without their consent. However, he did not yet possess the military means to embark on large-scale conquests and **empire** building (see Map 2.3).

> **Empire:** Large multiethnic, multilinguistic, multireligious state consisting of a conquering kingdom and several defeated kingdoms.

A later major Mesopotamian kingdom was Babylonia, centered in what had been Akkad and speaking Akkadian. Its best-known king was Hammurabi (r. 1792–1750 BCE), who ordered the engraving of the entire code of Babylonian law onto a 7-foot slab of basalt. Hammurabi saw himself as the executor of a divinely sanctioned law that punished evildoers and rewarded the righteous. By today's standards, Hammurabi's laws were harsh, threatening severe punishments for crimes against property, land, and commerce. The law of Mesopotamia was no longer the customary law of villages and towns but the royal writ, divinely ordained and backed by military force (see "Patterns Up Close").

Patriarchy and Gender The development of society in the Middle East and beyond gave rise to another pattern: the patriarchal structure of society. The wars among the city-states and kingdoms were important events in the creation of new patterns of gender relations. War captives provided cheap labor as slaves in temple households and wealthy residences, giving the priestly and self-made kings an edge in the restructuring of agrarian–urban society. A ruling class emerged, composed of dynastic families who collaborated with other landowning and priestly families. One rank below the ruling class were the merchants and craftspeople, who formed a hierarchy among themselves. At the bottom of this increasingly hierarchical society were slaves and other marginal urban groups, such as day laborers and prostitutes.

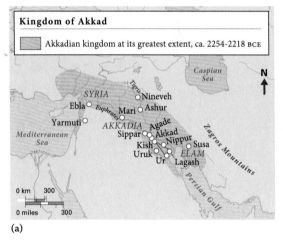

(a)

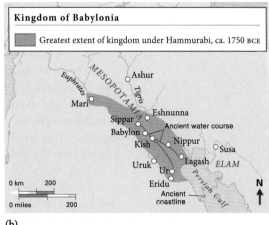

(b)

MAP 2.3 **(a) The Akkadian Kingdom. (b) Kingdom of Babylonia**

Babylonian Law Codes

The Old Babylonians in lower Mesopotamia produced the earliest known collections of written laws. Because of their formal, written nature, these law codes differed from earlier oral and customary law, common in all early cultures. When did these laws originate, how did they develop across time, and what was their influence on later ages?

The origin and evolution of the legal tradition are intertwined with developments associated with the complexity of urban life. Intricate systems of irrigation and drainage canals, along with dikes and dams, necessitated not only extensive planning and maintenance but also the allotment of plots of land. The emergence of complex political, economic, and social relationships called for the establishment of a set of centrally administered rules and regulations in order to provide for conflict resolution as well as retribution for wrongdoing.

Across a span of nearly 500 years, from the earliest codification of King Urukagina of Lagash in ca. 2350 BCE to the monumental code of Hammurabi in 1750 BCE, law developed through a successive series of increasingly comprehensive and refined legal codes consistent with the developing complexities of urban expansion. Consequently, evolving law codes address correspondingly wider audiences, they cover a broader spectrum of social classes, and they present more complex examples of potential infractions as well as more nuanced resolutions. Most of these legal codes open with a prologue, which is followed by a body of laws, and close with an epilogue. In terms of format, Sumerian laws follow the format of "if this, then that" regarding violations and ensuing punishments, and punishments are meted out with reference to social status. Finally, they pay growing attention to the importance of irrigation, with more and more references to the maintenance of river dikes and irrigation canals, along with harsh consequences for neglecting this.

The transition from agrarian societies to urban civilizations had several implications for gender roles. In more egalitarian agricultural societies, there was little room for gender distinctions. This changed with the growth of urban centers. New arrangements were required to accommodate the political, economic, military, and religious changes brought about by urban life. Each of these spheres was dominated by males. Men developed and administered military affairs, and fighting forces were restricted to males. Men also emerged as rulers and high-ranking administrators, regulated commercial and trading matters, and formed the ranks of scribes, priests, and other functionaries.

Another factor of urban life was the emergence of wealth and property rights, which gave rise to the need to ensure inheritance of private property through male descent. Because this required both establishing and maintaining the legitimacy of the male line, sexual activities of women were restricted. As a result, women's roles were confined to household functions, thereby subordinating their social status.

The law code of Hammurabi, king of Babylon (r. 1792–1750 BCE), represents the first complete written and well-organized code of law. Like earlier models, the code acknowledges distinctions in social categories along with inequalities among them but goes beyond them in addressing more social classes and grouping the classes according to relative wealth and social standing. Also, like previous collections, the code is broken down into several categories, including issues related to property and family law, but here again, it covers many more possible scenarios in an effort to close previous loopholes.

The code departs significantly from its Sumerian predecessors when it comes to retribution in that it calls for more extreme punishments according to the principle of *lex talionis* (from Latin *talio* 'compensation in kind'). Thus, "If a man put out the eye of another man, his eye shall be put out." Further, the importance of maintaining irrigation systems is consistent with earlier themes but expressed in more nuanced terms: "If anyone open his ditches to water his crop, but is careless, and the water flood the field of his neighbor, then he shall pay his neighbor [grain] for his loss."

The long-term influence of Sumerian and Babylonian legal codes—particularly Hammurabi's code—extends far beyond ancient Mesopotamia. Instances of its influence appear in the development of biblical law, and some of its principles found their way into Roman law, especially the codification of civil cases.

Questions

• What do the first law codes tell us about ancient Sumerian and Babylonian societies?

• Are the legacies of these first law codes still evident in modern Western legal practice today? If yes, in which ways?

Stele with Hammurabi's Code

The formation of hierarchical social structures did not stop with the rise of social classes. As we shall see in later chapters, men assumed legal power over women on all levels of society in nearly every agrarian–urban culture. As attested in the law code of Hammurabi, married women enjoyed some legal rights, including the right to sue for divorce if they could prove mistreatment. In general, however, wives were in many ways considered the property of their husbands, who could divorce their wives in cases of neglect of the household without returning dowries, and who could engage in sexual relations with mistresses and prostitutes—while wives caught in adultery were thrown into the river along with their lovers.

Women in Egyptian society fared better in some ways than their Mesopotamian counterparts. Although they also existed in a male-dominated society, women were accorded more respect in marriage, and they had more legal rights; they could own and transfer property, and they could sue for divorce. A few women in Egyptian royalty were considered nearly equal to men. In

Egyptian Hieroglyphs. These hieroglyphs found in Luxor, Valley of the Kings, were carved into the wall and colored.

New Kingdom Egypt (1550–1070 BCE), princesses were considered to be of divine descent just as princes were. Sisters and brothers or half-brothers sometimes married each other, reinforcing the concept that their lineage was divine and pure.

In later millennia, after empires formed, noblewomen disappeared from their male-dependent public positions and lived in secluded areas of the palaces. Men tightened the law, relegating women to inferior family positions. Patriarchy was thus a product not of agrarian but of urban society in the city-states and kingdoms of Mesopotamia and, a little later, Egypt.

Egyptian Kingdoms   In Egypt, the first city was Hierakonpolis [high-er-a-KON-po-lis], founded around 3000 BCE in Upper (i.e., southern) Egypt. As in Mesopotamia, the rulers of cities began to develop into small-scale kings. Whoever among these was the first king, he unified all Egyptian lands and established the first dynasty of Egypt's Early Dynastic Period (ca. 3100–2613 BCE), choosing Memphis, near modern Cairo, as his capital. At first, lesser rulers continued their reigns in the other cities. They even rebelled against the king from time to time. Therefore, the early policies of the Egyptian kings were focused almost exclusively on the unification of Egypt.

The first king claimed divine birth from Egypt's founder god, Horus, the falcon-headed deity. As god on earth, the king upheld the divine order. Inhabitants of his kingdom were no more than humble servants whose duty was to pay the king taxes and construct a palace and tomb for him. Of course, in practice this royal supremacy was far from complete. Even during times of strong centralization there were always some powerful figures, such as provincial landowners and governors, who held title to their properties and collected rents from the farmers working on these properties. As in Mesopotamia, the claim of the kings to divinity did not keep rivals from bidding for supreme power.

Hieroglyphs, Bureaucracy, and Pyramids   As with cuneiform in Mesopotamia, the Egyptian kings were greatly aided in the process of unification by the introduction of a system of accounting and writing. Around 3500–3200 BCE, administrators and scribes developed hieroglyphic writing in Egypt. In this system, formalized pictures symbolizing objects and syllables were used to represent words; such writing was used for royal inscriptions, often on stone. The writing material normally used in Egypt was papyrus (though clay, metal, and other materials were used as well), which was more expensive but less cumbersome than the Mesopotamian clay tablets. The Egyptian language, which evolved into the modern Coptic (a liturgical language), is distantly related to the Semitic family.

In addition to aiding in communication, writing lent itself to a larger and more efficient bureaucracy in Egypt. At the beginning of the Old Kingdom (ca. 2613–2181 BCE), the royal palace and temple became hierarchical organizations in which everything was minutely regulated. Using arithmetic manuals, scribes calculated the quantities of bread, beer, and meat rations to be distributed; of timber for the shipyards; and of flax for the linen-weaving workshops. In its complexity, the Egyptian bureaucratic system of the Old Kingdom easily surpassed that of lower Mesopotamia during the contemporaneous Akkadian period (see Map 2.4).

The most astounding bureaucratic achievement of the Old Kingdom was the construction by Khufu (r. 2589–2566 BCE) of a pyramid near modern Cairo as a funerary monument for himself. Along with two other pyramids, Khufu's Great Pyramid makes up the famous Giza pyramids, which served as tombs for the bodies of later kings. By the orders of Khufu, stone workers quarried local limestone from cliffs along the Nile for the central portion of each of the pyramids. Finer, less brittle casing stones came from quarries upstream on the Nile. Ramparts of chipped stone and other debris, as well as sledges, rollers, and heavy levers made of timber, helped laborers move the stone blocks into place, as much as 479 feet high. After the completion of the pyramid, the construction machinery was dismantled, and today sand covers what were once the workers' camps.

Great Pyramid of Giza and Sphinx. The pyramid of Khafre, one of the three pyramids at Giza, was constructed during the Old Kingdom (ca. 2500 BCE). The Sphinx, shown in the foreground, has the body of a lion and the face of a man, perhaps that of Khafre.

The workforce, perhaps as many as 10,000 laborers, consisted of farmers who were working off their annual one-month labor service owed to the king. A special labor office made sure that regular field labor was disrupted as little as possible. Although the workers were strictly supervised, we know that they also occasionally went on strike. Labor unrest, however, could easily be suppressed by the Egyptian army.

The kings of the Middle Kingdom (ca. 2040–1750 BCE) focused on agricultural projects, mining, and trade. During Amenemhet III's long reign (r. ca. 1843–1796 BCE), Egypt reached the peak of its internal development. Workers transferred from Syria drained the Fayyum Depression and created irrigated fields. Merchants developed close relations with other merchants in the Levant, from where they imported cedar wood for ships, roofs, and coffins. Egyptian exports consisted of objects made of gold. By the end of Amenemhet's reign, the kingdom numbered about 1 million inhabitants and was a formidable power.

The Minoan Kingdom   After farming had spread from the Levant to Anatolia, seafaring Anatolians carried the practice westward around 6500 BCE to mainland Greece and the Aegean islands. They settled first on the islands of Crete and Cyprus. Crete is about 170 miles long and 35 miles wide at its widest point. Over the millennia, some of the early villages of Crete grew into towns, and by around 2000 BCE small states with kings, spacious palaces, and surrounding villages were flourishing. The dominant **palace-state** was that of the Minoans (named after its mythical founder, King Minos), with as many as 12,000 inhabitants in the sprawling palace at Knossos and a few villages outside.

Palace-state: A city or fortified palace with surrounding villages.

The Minoan kingdom was centered on a vast palace. Among the palace personnel were scribes who used a pictorial-syllabic script on clay tablets similar to the writing and recording systems of Mesopotamia. Unfortunately, this script, called

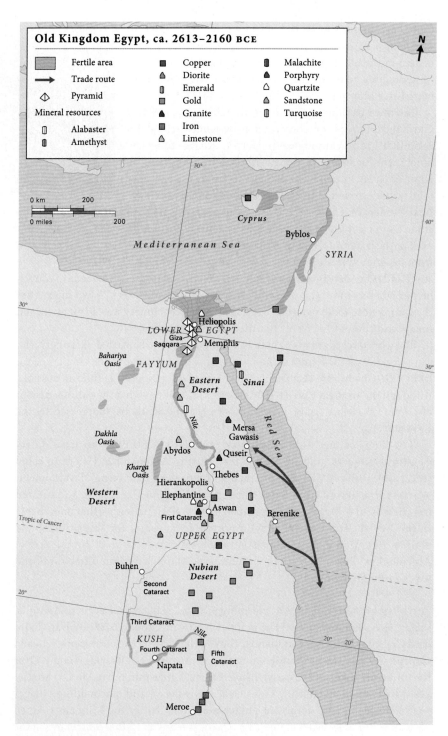

Old Kingdom Egypt, ca. 2613–2160 BCE

Fertile area	Copper	Malachite
Trade route	Diorite	Porphyry
Pyramid	Emerald	Quartzite
Mineral resources	Gold	Sandstone
Alabaster	Granite	Turquoise
Amethyst	Iron	
	Limestone	

MAP 2.4 **Old Kingdom Egypt, ca. 2613–2160 BCE**

Linear A by scholars, has thus far not been deciphered. In the villages, farmers produced grain, olive oil, wine, and honey. Royal merchants traded these products for obsidian, copper, and tin from mainland Greece, Anatolia, and Cyprus. Craftspeople made pottery, bronze vessels, and jewelry for the palace as well as for export to Egypt, Syria, and Mesopotamia. Minoans were skilled boat builders who constructed oceangoing vessels. While Minoan Crete borrowed creatively from its older neighbors, it also created its own independent trade and seafaring traditions.

Interactions among Multiethnic and Multireligious Empires, ca. 1500–600 BCE

From around 1700 to 1000 BCE, society in the Middle East and the Mediterranean changed in important ways. Chariot warfare, iron tools, and iron weapons were developed and refined. Agriculture spread from the original core of Syria, Mesopotamia, and Egypt to the periphery in Greece, central Anatolia, central Asia, and Arabia. Conquerors built large empires in which a small, ethnically defined ruling class ruled over collections of other ethnic groups, speaking a multiplicity of languages and sacrificing to a multiplicity of gods.

The Hittite and Assyrian Empires, 1600–600 BCE

Agriculture spread from the Middle East to foragers in western Europe and central Asia. Villagers in central Asia, who are thought to have spoken the language reconstructed as Proto-Indo-European (the ancestor of most of the languages of Europe today), domesticated the horse and used it for pulling chariots. Later, they migrated with their horses and chariots to the Middle East, India, and western Europe, where they settled as ruling classes among the indigenous villagers.

Horses and Chariots from Central Asia   The spread of agriculture into Europe and central Asia had major consequences for the Middle East and the eastern Mediterranean. Shortly after 3000 BCE, in the region around the Ural Mountains, villagers who probably spoke Proto-Indo-European domesticated the horse. Around 2000 BCE, town leaders in the southern Ural Mountains emerged who were equipped with horse-drawn chariots as well as with composite bows made of a combination of grooved wood and horn carefully glued together. This bow was much more powerful than the simpler bows dating back to the Paleolithic. A chariot could accommodate two or three warriors, one to guide the horses and the others to shoot arrows. Around 1700 BCE, both the chariot and the composite bow made their entry into the Middle East and eastern Mediterranean. They contributed to a major transformation of kingdoms that had hitherto relied solely on foot soldiers.

The Hittite Empire   The first rulers in the Middle East to make use of chariots and composite bows for their military were the Hittites (1650–1182 BCE), speakers of an Indo-European language who had settled in central Anatolia. This area, one of the richest mining regions in the Middle East, had large iron deposits. By around 1500 BCE, smiths in Anatolia had fully mastered the art of ironmaking. The Hittites incorporated iron into the equipment of their chariot armies, in the form of swords, helmets, and protective armor. The combination of these military elements gave the Hittites an early advantage, which they used to greatly enlarge the scope of conquests, creating an empire consisting of many different peoples, languages, and temple religions. At its peak, the Hittite Empire stretched from Anatolia to northern Syria, comprising peoples of many languages and religions.

To distinguish themselves from ordinary kings, the Hittite kings called themselves "great kings." When they conquered rival kingdoms, they left the lesser, conquered kings in place as provincial rulers. The core of Hittite armies consisted of a nobility of highly trained, disciplined, and mobile chariot warriors. In the conquered lands, the "great kings" placed nobles in strategic garrisons to keep the local, non-Hittite rulers in check. Since the imperial warehouses held limited amounts of foodstuffs, the nobility received land grants, using the rents they extracted from the towns and villages for their livelihood. This Hittite system of employing both its nobility and local rulers was to become the model of organization for all subsequent Middle Eastern and eastern Mediterranean empires.

Imperial Egypt During the New Kingdom (ca. 1550–1070 BCE), the Egyptians vigorously pushed their border with the Hittites as far north as possible. The Egyptians eventually clashed with the Hittites at Qadesh [KAH-desh] in northern Syria (1274 BCE), where they engaged in the largest chariot battle ever fought in the Middle East. Neither side prevailed, and in the earliest known peace treaty—the Treaty of Kadesh—the two empires decided to curb their imperialism and coexist diplomatically with each other, with Syria divided between them.

Bronze Age collapse: Around 1200 BCE, this was the result of the collapse of the Hittite Empire and the weakening of the Egyptian New Kingdom; chariot warfare had become unsustainable in these early kingdoms.

Iron Age: Beginning around 1500–1200 BCE, smiths were able to produce sufficiently high temperatures to smelt iron bloom, a mixture of iron and a variety of impurities.

A short time later, this coexistence was shattered by invasions of the "Sea Peoples," who probably came from southern Europe (northern Greece or southern Italy), as genetic research published in 2019 suggests. Originally a mixture of farmers and herders displaced by local warfare, these people had raided the Mycenaean [my-sen-EE-yan] kingdoms of southern Greece, as we discuss later in this chapter. Joined by survivors of the collapsing kingdoms, they took to the sea (hence their name "Sea Peoples") and sailed to the wealthy kingdoms of the Levant. One group of Sea Peoples, presumably remnants of one of the Mycenaean kingdoms, destroyed the Hittite Empire in 1207 BCE. The Egyptian Empire lost southern Syria to another set of seafaring invaders, the Philistines (called Peleset [PE-le-set] by the Egyptians), and retreated to Sinai, abandoning its imperial ambitions. It was from the skeletons of ten Peleset individuals unearthed in Ashkelon, Israel, that the new genetic determination of origins was made.

The invasions by Sea People triggered the so-called **Bronze Age collapse** of ca. 1200 BCE with which the **Iron Age** in the Middle East and eastern Mediterranean began. The collapse is explained as a crisis in which the overextended early empires of the Hittites and Egyptians were unable to sustain the enormous expenses required for chariot warfare.

Tutankhamen Hunting. Detail from a painted chest found in the king's tomb, Thebes, ca. 1340 BCE.

The Assyrians   Emerging after the Bronze Age collapse, the Assyrians (ca. 1350–607 BCE) founded a new empire, which, like the Hittite Empire, was based on rain-fed agriculture. Its capital was Assur, a city founded in upper Mesopotamia around 2000 BCE on an island in the Tigris River (west of today's Kirkuk). Originally, Assur's farming base was too limited to support territorial conquests. Instead, its inhabitants enriched themselves through trade. They built trading outposts as far away as central Anatolia and exchanged textiles for timber, copper, tin, and silver, much of which they sold to the Babylonians in the south. In the fourteenth century BCE, the Assyrian kings began to use Assur's commercial riches to finance their first large-scale conquests.

The Assyrians expanded into both the Zagros Mountains and Syria, reaching the borders of the Hittite Empire and claiming equal status with them. Stopped at the Hittite borders, Assyrian troops turned southeastward and expanded into lower Mesopotamia. Here, they occupied Babylon for a short period, humiliating it by carrying away the statue of the city god.

After some severe military setbacks, during which Assyria was reduced to its upper Mesopotamian center, ambitious kings renewed Assyrian expansion, creating the Neo-Assyrian Empire, which lasted from 934 to 607 BCE. They systematically and ruthlessly conquered the lands around them. In fact, the Assyrians were among the most brutal campaigners in recorded history. They destroyed temples, razed cities, and forcibly deported the defeated inhabitants of entire provinces to other parts of the empire. Scholars have estimated that hundreds of thousands of deportees had to walk hundreds of miles through the countryside before being settled in new villages. At the peak of their conquests (745–609 BCE), the Assyrian rulers became the first to unify all of the Middle East, a dream first expressed by King Naram-Sin of Akkad centuries earlier. This same accomplishment of unification would be repeated several more times in the years to come.

Small Kingdoms on the Imperial Margins, 1600–600 BCE

Syria was a region between the Hittite (or, later, Assyrian) Empire in the north and the Egyptian Empire in the south. The dominant form of political organization there was the city-state under a royal dynasty. In northern Syria, the city-states were those of the Phoenicians; in southern Syria, they were those of the Philistines on the coast and the Israelites in the hills. In the eastern Mediterranean, outside the military reach of the Hittite and Assyrian Empires but in commercial contact with them, were the Mycenaean palace-states and early Greek city-states.

The Phoenicians The people known to the Greeks as Phoenicians and to the Egyptians as Canaanites held the city-states of Byblos, Sidon, and Tyre (ca. 1600–300 BCE), each with a population of several tens of thousands. The Phoenicians also controlled the slopes of Mount Lebanon with its famous cedars, which were much sought after in the Middle East and eastern Mediterranean as construction material. No less important was a species of sea snail collected on the beaches, from which a highly valued purple textile dye was extracted. Urban craftspeople made ceramics, textiles, leather goods, jewelry, and metal ware with distinctive Phoenician designs, destined for sale abroad. More than any other territorial states in the Middle East, the Phoenician city-states were engaged in trade.

Phoenicians as traders appear in the historical record from 2500 BCE onward. During ca. 1600–1200 BCE, the Phoenicians and Mycenaeans shared the sea trade of the eastern Mediterranean. On land, they preferred paying tribute to, and occasionally putting their fleets at the service of, Hittite or Egyptian imperial overlords. When the Mycenaean kingdoms and Hittite Empire collapsed and the Egyptians withdrew around 1200 BCE under the onslaught of the Sea Peoples, the Phoenicians seized their chance. Systematically expanding their reach in the Mediterranean, they established trade outposts on islands and along the Mediterranean coast as far west as modern Morocco and Spain.

In addition to founding numerous ports and outposts around theMediterranean, the Phoenicians introduced the alphabet. From rock inscriptions discovered in 1998 in Egypt, it appears that Phoenician (or Syrian) merchants began experimenting around 1900–1800 BCE with a writing system in which letters replaced the traditional signs and syllables, with each letter standing for a spoken consonant. The Phoenician alphabet of ca. 1200 BCE was the most widely used, becoming the ancestor of all alphabetical scripts.

Phoenician, Greek, and Roman Alphabets. This illustration reveals similarities among the Phoenician, Greek, and Roman alphabets. Phoenician traders carried the alphabet across the Mediterranean, where it was adopted by Greeks. Subsequent interactions among Greeks, Etruscans, and Romans resulted in the transition to Roman letter forms, which in turn ultimately provided the foundation for English characters.

The Philistines and Israelites During its imperial phase (ca. 1550–1200 BCE), Egypt controlled the Palestinian towns of Gaza, Ashkelon, Ashdod, Gath, and Ekron. Occasionally, the Egyptian kings aided their governors in these towns by carrying out punitive campaigns. After one such campaign, a defeated people in southern Syria was "stripped bare, wholly lacking seed," as an Egyptian inscription of 1207 BCE recorded. The name used in the inscription for this people was "Israel," the first time this name appeared in the records. "Israel" seemed to refer to some sort of tribal alliance among Canaanite villagers and herders in the hills.

A short time after the Philistines, known to Egyptians as Peleset, took over southern Syria and Egypt withdrew, agriculture and trade recovered from Egyptian taxation. The coastal Philistines established garrisons among the Israelites in order to secure trade routes. In response, as is recorded in the Hebrew Bible (the Old Testament in Christian usage), a military leader named Saul and a number of tribal leaders recruited a military force that began a war of liberation against the Philistines. According to this scripture, Saul was killed during the early stages of the war, and his successor, David, completed the liberation, establishing himself as king in Jerusalem shortly after 1000 BCE.

According to the Hebrew Bible, Jerusalem was a town on top of a mountain spur in southern Syria. To date, archaeologists have found few traces of the early city. Moreover, they have not even been able to confirm the rise of Jerusalem from village to city level. For historians, therefore, the biblical account, like those of many ancient texts, is perhaps best understood not as history but as a religious foundation story.

According to the Hebrew Bible, the two states that emerged after Solomon, Israel in the north (930–722 BCE) and Judah in the south (930–587 BCE), enjoyed only short periods of independence after liberating themselves from the coastal Philistines. The empire of Assyria and its successor, Neo-Babylonia (626–539 BCE), conquered the two kingdoms in the eighth to seventh centuries BCE. The kingdoms' elites had to resettle in other parts of Syria or in Mesopotamia. The Philistines, together with people in the Syrian steppes (collectively called "Arabs"), suffered similar defeat. In their place, Anatolian and Iranian populations settled in Syria. The final wave of Israelite deportations, under the Neo-Babylonians in 597–582 BCE, became the "Babylonian captivity" mourned by prophets in the Hebrew Bible.

The Mycenaeans and Early Greeks   Parallel to the Phoenicians, Philistines, and Israelites in Syria, the Mycenaeans arose in Greece and the eastern Mediterranean during the middle of the second millennium BCE. After the adaptation to farming, demand for agricultural products among the villages had advanced sufficiently to result in the emergence of towns and cities which traded in these goods as well as in copper and bronze wares. Around 1700 BCE, in Attica and the Peloponnesus, leaders built forts as refuges in times of war. The best known among these forts were Mycenae, Tiryns, Pylos, Sparta, and Athens.

Two centuries later, the forts evolved into palaces with warrior lords and kings, as well as administrative offices, surrounded by clusters of villages. In these palace-states, scribes introduced a new, cuneiform-derived script, called Linear B, which has been identified as Greek, and unlike the Linear A of the Minoans has been deciphered. This script provides us with invaluable information for understanding early Greek culture. About 1450 BCE, Mycenaean warriors equipped with chariots and bronze weapons sailed to Minoan Crete and conquered the island. The Mycenaeans were a major seafaring power in the eastern Mediterranean, establishing trading outposts in competition with the Phoenicians.

The Mycenaean palace-states were short-lived. When an earthquake hit, around 1250 BCE, the walls of many palaces collapsed. Branches of the Sea Peoples, discussed above, raided the weakened Mycenaean palace-states. The descendants of the kings, however, managed to salvage some wealth, as evidenced by their tombs. Iron swords and jewelry found in these tombs were of Phoenician origin and indicate that some sea trade continued even after the destruction of the Mycenaean states.

A general recovery in Greece began during the eighth century BCE. Trade in agricultural goods was revived. The Anatolian craft of ironworking spread to Greece. Literacy returned as the Greeks adapted the Phoenician alphabet for their own language. The population increased rapidly. After 750 BCE, many Greeks emigrated to the Anatolian west coast and as far as Italy and the Black Sea to colonize the land and establish new cities. As they developed into city-states of their own, the settlement region on the Anatolian coast became known as "Ionia."

Instead of a palace, a sacred precinct in a city's center served as an open space for general assemblies. Contained within this space were a temple and administrative buildings. Farmers in villages outside the city walls produced foodstuffs for the urban dwellers. A city with surrounding villages formed a city-state, or *polis* (plural *poleis*). Each of these new city-states administered its own internal and external affairs, although they also formed alliances or pursued hostilities with each other.

Initially, kings from among large landowning families (the aristocracy) were responsible for the administration of the city-states. During the period 750–600 BCE, conflict often broke out between the aristocracy and the common folk over the distribution of land. Some aristocrats exploited these conflicts and allied themselves with groups of commoners. Once allied, these aristocrats assumed power as tyrants (which simply meant "absolute rulers," with no implication of cruelty), who attempted to create family dynasties.

Other aristocrats opposed the tyrants and agreed to power sharing with the commoners. Through trade, many commoners were becoming wealthier than the aristocrats. Both aristocrats and commoners served as foot soldiers in the city-states' defense forces. These forces relied not on charioteers but on foot soldiers, who were heavily armed with shields, lances, and swords.

In the narrow valleys and defiles of Greece and Ionia, these disciplined regiments were nearly impossible to break if each man held his position and the men in the back moved up to take the place of those who fell. It was not individual aristocratic valor that counted but the courageous willingness of each citizen-soldier to support and protect each other. Thus, as many ordinary city dwellers became the military equals of the aristocracy in the crucible of battle, they began to demand an equal share of political power in times of peace.

Political reformers in the sixth century BCE gave commoners their first political rights. The best-known reforms were those introduced in Athens and Sparta. In Athens, aristocratic rule was replaced with political rights distributed according to levels of property ownership. The poorest class had the right to participate in the citizen assembly, cast votes, and sit on juries; members of the wealthier classes could run for a variety of leadership and temple offices. In Greece, and later Rome, these traditions would evolve into the ancestral forms of many of the political institutions we live under today, particularly **republican** and **democratic** offices.

In Sparta, the traditional rule by two coequal kings was held in check through a board of five officers elected annually from among the popular assembly. These officers were responsible for the administration of day-to-day affairs in Sparta. The assembly was made up of all landowners wealthy enough to live in town because of the revenue they collected from their legally indentured (unfree) tenant farmers in the surrounding villages. These political reforms, however, did not prevent new tyrants from rising up in periodic takeover attempts. Thus, in the middle of the first millennium BCE, Greeks were still struggling to find a consistent direction for their political development.

Religious Experience and Cultural Achievements

By around 5500 BCE, when agriculture had replaced foraging, many human groups began to move from naturalism to polytheism as their new form of religion. In *naturalism*, people revere the forces of the natural world. However, there is no indication in the available archaeological record that people personified these forces, making them particular deities. With the rise of cities and the development of writing, these forces received personal names. *Polytheism* is the general term used to denote religions of personified forces in nature. Since many of the religious and cultural achievements were expressed in writing, we can evaluate them today with far better understanding than we can the cultures of the foragers and early farmers.

Toward Polytheism   The creators of the Paleolithic rock paintings in Africa, Europe, and Australia (discussed in Chapter 1) have left us few hints of their spiritual preoccupations in their world full of dangerous animals. In the Neolithic transition period from foraging to agriculture, the principal change was the transfer of images and ritual from caves to aboveground sanctuaries and towns.

An example of the transfer of imagery to a sanctuary was Göbekli Tepe in southern Anatolia, a place where foragers came together for rituals during 9000–6000 BCE. Images of animals, mostly in the form of reliefs, have been unearthed since 1996 when excavations began. These images show that naturalism was still in force, even if the venue was no longer a cave. Human skulls with incisions, discovered in 2017, are interpreted as indicators of a Neolithic ancestor cult, also present in the later agricultural settlements of the Natufians (see below). The oldest place documenting the transfer of ritual from the cave to the surface is the town of Çatal Hüyük [cha-TAHL hoo-YOOK] (7500–5700 BCE) in southern Anatolia. At its height, the town had 5,000 inhabitants, who lived in densely packed houses accessible only from the top with ladders. The inhabitants farmed outside of town and hunted extensively. Large rooms in town, probably communal, contained a concentration of artifacts, among which Venus-type figurines and reliefs and wall paintings of animals are prominent. The imagery is reminiscent of that of the Paleolithic foragers, but the emergence of urban places of

Republicanism: A system of government in which, in the place of kings, the people are sovereign, often electing representatives to executive and legislative offices.

Democracy: A system of government in which most or all of the people elect representatives and in some cases decide on important issues themselves.

ritual indicates that humans were far along in the transition from naturalism to polytheism.

During the Ubaid period in Mesopotamia (6000–4000 BCE), urban places of ritual evolved into temples. Urban dwellers then took the decisive steps of transition from naturalism to polytheism in the period 3500–2500 BCE, when forces of nature began to lose influence in daily life. With the advent of a partnership with nature in the production of food supplies instead of hunting and gathering, as well as kings and the appearance of writing, the transition from natural spirituality to polytheism was begun. This connection between writing, kingship, and gods is crucial for an understanding of polytheism and religion in general. Prior to 3500 BCE, religion tended to be an impersonal and nameless naturalism; thereafter, it was the polytheism of gods and kings, often with colorful personalities, told in myths and epics.

In polytheistic empires, rulers were very tolerant toward the phenomenon of multiple gods, even though they had a personal relationship with only one god, their patron deity, and the priesthood of their deity's temple. Even strong rulers never had the power to force the many temple priesthoods of their empires to give up their gods. Egyptian kings, however, unified Egypt more thoroughly than their Mesopotamian counterparts, who never overcame the long city-state tradition of their region. Under royal influence, therefore, Egyptian priesthoods devised a hierarchically organized pantheon of all gods, along with elaborate stories about these gods.

During the New Kingdom period (ca. 1550–1070 BCE), kings and priests came into close contact with other empires of the Middle East. They developed an understanding that all gods taken together were really only a few deities, or even only one, with many different manifestations. One king, Akhenaten (1353–1336 BCE), went even further, conceiving of the Sun as the only god, to whom all Egyptians were henceforth to pray. The new Sun religion was too radical to survive Akhenaten. But its brief appearance demonstrates the full range of meaning which polytheism as a religion could acquire. (See "Against the Grain.")

Akhenaten and His Family. This wall painting shows Akhenaten, the 18th Dynasty (New Kingdom) Egyptian pharaoh, and his family worshiping Aten. Images like these were designed to broadcast Akhenaten's devotion to the solar disc among his subjects.

Mesopotamian and Egyptian Literature

Among the earliest writings in the world exploring religious themes are the *Epic of Gilgamesh* and the myth known as *Enuma Elish*, which had their origins in third-millennium BCE Mesopotamia. The first is the story of Gilgamesh, a mythical king in early Sumer. Gilgamesh, according to the epic, ruled Uruk and built its walls. He fought many battles and performed heroic deeds but failed in his quest to find immortality. In the end, Gilgamesh could not escape the fate of all mortals and had to suffer death too.

Flood stories featured prominently in these early texts; and there are several similarities between those conveyed in the Epic of Gilgamesh and Genesis, the first book of the Hebrew Bible. In each, the gods (or God) unleash a gigantic flood as punishment for sinful behavior, whereupon a righteous figure is directed to build a boat and to fill it with select humans and animals in order to escape the deluge. After they land on a mountaintop, sacrifices are offered, which appease the Creator's wrath.

The myth of *Enuma Elish* (named after its first line, which means "when on high . . .") tells the story of creation, beginning with a time when nothing existed but Father Abzu (the Depth or Abyss) and Mother Tiamat (Ocean) and their numerous children, who were the city gods of Mesopotamia. The raucous behavior of his children enraged Abzu. He tried to kill them but was instead murdered by one of them. Tiamat [tee-ya-MAT] and her second husband continued the violent domestic battle, finally driving the children away. Marduk [MAR-dook] alone among the children eventually returned and slaughtered both his mother and stepfather. He split Tiamat's body into halves, which became heaven and earth. From the blood of the stepfather he made humankind, whom he predestined to serve the gods. One senses how the unknown authors of this text struggle with the question of the divine, which comes before everything else, as well as power in nature—at times benevolent and at times violent, always unpredictable, even as people sacrifice to please it.

The Egyptian version of the creation myth begins with an original ocean. In the Egyptian telling, an island arose from the depth of the ocean. The ruler of this island was the self-created god Atum, who contained all the qualities of nature in himself. He created things in pairs, one after the other, beginning with air and water and finishing his handiwork with the male and female of the human race. This Egyptian creation myth does not begin with a primordial god, as in Mesopotamia, but an original chaotic ocean, out of which well-ordered creation emerged. It is also less violent, a reflection of the more harmonious growth of the Egyptian kingdom and empire. By comparing the two myths one can see how their authors were struggling to come to grips with such basic existential questions as chaos and order, as well as infinity and finitude.

Sculptures and Paintings   Early Mesopotamian kings had massive statues made of themselves, showing them posed in prayer. In Egypt, compact, block-like royals stand freely or sit impassively on their thrones. On many high-relief sculptures carved into stone, larger-than-life-size kings trample victoriously over diminutive enemies. In all these sculptures, the primary objective of the artists was not photographic realism but a rendering of the gulf between gods and kings on one hand and subjects on the other.

Wall paintings were highly popular among Mesopotamians, Egyptians, and Minoans. Paintings filled the interior of tombs, illustrating scenes from their owners' lives. Faces, arms, and legs were painted in profile; eyes, shoulders, and the upper body appear frontally; the waist is half frontal but turned to reveal the navel. Later, as more nonroyal people built tombs for themselves, the complex multiangled royal perspective gave way to a simpler, single-angle realism.

The Greek arts began in the Minoan and Mycenaean city-states. Minoan wall paintings, stylistically related to those of the Egyptian New Kingdom (1550–1070 BCE), show realistic scenes with vegetation, birds, dolphins, and bulls. The art of Mycenae is known to us mostly from small sculptures, masks, drinking vessels, and jewelry found in the tombs of royal warriors. Through their close contact with the Assyrians, the Greeks in their growing city-states (during the period of ca. 750–600 BCE) learned about their arts. Winged and fighting animals, as well as muscular gods and heroes, appear in vase paintings. Egypt was the inspiration for the development of sculptures, which initially were block-like, wide-eyed, and stylized. Gradually, however, with the decline of the aristocracy, stylized representation was replaced by realism.

Scientific Beginnings   In both Mesopotamia and Egypt, we get the first glimpses of humans constructing abstract ideas, without recourse to the senses—for example, in mathematics. Mathematical calculations, such as addition and subtraction, began in Mesopotamia even before the first writing system was introduced.

Subsequently, scribes developed tables for multiplication and division, squares, cubes, square roots, cube roots, and reciprocal and exponential functions. They calculated numerical approximations for the square roots of 2 and 3. Babylonian mathematical interests also focused on the roots of algebra. Other scribes laid the foundations for geometry and astronomy by devising the system of 60 degrees for arcs, angles, and time—all still in use today.

In Egypt, the *Rhind Mathematical Papyrus* (ca. 1550 BCE), an early handbook of geometric and algebraic questions, was typically used by scribes and administrators. It teaches the apprentice scribe how to calculate the volume of rectangles, triangles, and pyramids and how to measure the slopes of angles. As in Mesopotamia, Egyptian mathematics implicitly employed important mathematical principles without yet stating them explicitly.

The *Kahun* (ca. 1825 BCE) and *Edwin Smith* (ca. 1534 BCE) *Papyri* are the best-known texts on the applied science of medicine. They cover diagnosis, prescriptions, and surgery. A few examples illustrate ancient Egyptian medical standards. Headache is diagnosed as "half head," which the Greeks translated as "*hemikrania*," from which our English word "migraine" is derived. Remedies for treating stiffness of limbs, pregnancy, birth complications, and childhood diseases, as well as advice on birth control and abortion, include mixtures of homeopathic herbs and elements. Surgeons received advice on how to use copper knives for male and female circumcision and needles for stitching up wounds. During their work, physicians were encouraged to repeat magic formulas that encouraged patients to use their own self-healing powers.

Putting It All Together

The beginning of the agrarian age in the Middle East and eastern Mediterranean was marked by agricultural surpluses, especially in irrigated areas. Depending on the size of the surplus, a pattern of state formation became visible along which city-states, kingdoms, and empires emerged in the various areas of the region. The central concern of the rulers in these small and large states was establishing and maintaining their authority, which included the use of military force— something not always easy to justify, especially when trade and ruling-class cooperation were also important. Therefore, the rulers appealed to gods—that is, personalized forces in nature stronger than rulers. The will of these forces was conceived as being expressed in the law code of each state. Gods were lawgivers, and their law possessed divine authority; thus, rulers became the executers of the god-given law.

Although "divine," the rulers' mandate was never absolute. Popular or aristocratic assemblies from preroyal times of tribal or clan organization survived stubbornly or were revived in the Greek *poleis*. Although the Hittite and Assyrian kings succeeded in marginalizing these assemblies during periods of empire building, the divine mandate was not exclusively theirs, and they had to share power, if only to a limited degree. It is important to note that this tradition of assemblies, which we often associate solely with Greece, was widespread in the Middle East. This awareness is necessary to understand the period after 600 BCE, when individuals arose with messages of personal salvation stating that it was not simply fate or misfortune to live and die under these often harsh imperial powers. Instead, they insisted that the destiny of humanity *transcended* these all-too-human institutions.

Review and Relate

| Thinking Through Patterns

Examine the ways historians approach the big questions of this chapter.

One crucial factor in this pattern was the environment of the Fertile Crescent. Adequate rainfall, abundant edible plants suitable for domestication, and several animals that proved useful and easy to domesticate characterized the region. But had it not been for human beings mastering irrigation, such a transition might have remained confined to small microclimatic regions. Populations in the great riverine agricultural areas in Mesopotamia and Egypt (and, as we will see in the following chapters, India and China) took as their task the mastery of the fertility of river valleys and the use of reliable river water for irrigation, rather than relying on rainfall. Here was a system adaptable to a variety of climates, as witnessed by the fact that these four early agricultural civilizations arose in dry climates watered by large river systems.

> **What are the main factors that enabled the transition from foraging to farming?**

While scholars still debate the origins of the domestication of plants and animals, most are in agreement that the Fertile Crescent was central to this process.

> **Where did the pattern of agrarian life first emerge and why?**

Here, experimentation with local grains, leaf plants, and pulses during the Neolithic helped humans develop more reliable crops, which were then traded locally and further afield. Animals like sheep, goats, and cattle were similarly found over wide areas and were easy to trade, which led to the sharing of information about raising livestock. Another important factor was that as populations grew as a result of the stability of food production by agriculture, groups split off and started their own communities, carrying the new techniques with them. Thus, by about 5000 BCE, the basic techniques and species of Eurasian and North African domestication were well established.

> **How did the creation of agrarian–urban society—what we commonly call "civilization"—make for an entirely new pattern of world history?**

The ability of humans to create large food surpluses encouraged a considerable degree of settlement. Such stability enabled the nonproducing part of the population to occupy themselves with creating nonagricultural things. As these elements of villages and towns grew and became more complex, they allowed the cumulative knowledge and production of human beings to expand. In short, cities created an entirely new kind of society with elaborate class hierarchies. Rivalry and competition among cities required ever more powerful defenses. From this period, the patterns of urban life and of state formation were established, patterns we readily recognize today as our own.

- Why was Akhenaten's revolt against prevailing religious practices considered so revolutionary?

- Are there any possible similarities between Akhenaten's approach to monotheism and later examples found in either early Judaism or Zoroastrianism?

| Against the Grain

Consider this as a counterpoint to the main patterns examined in this chapter.

Akhenaten the Transgressor

As early as the Old Kingdom (ca. 2686–2181 BCE) Re (or Ra), the sun god, was well established as the supreme deity (sometimes referred to as the "Father of the Gods") in the Egyptian polytheistic pantheon. Re was closely associated with kings, who were often depicted as his sons. During the Middle Kingdom, Amenhotep III ("Amun is satisfied") (1386–1349 BCE) promoted the worship of Amun-Re as the focus of Egyptian religion. It was therefore assumed that Amenhotep's son and successor, Amenhotep IV (1353–1336 BCE), would follow in his father's footsteps.

For reasons that are not altogether clear, Amenhotep IV repudiated the cult of Amun-Re in favor of a new object of devotion, that of the Aten (the solar disc). To drive home the point, early in his reign **Amen**hotep IV ("God Amun is satisfied") changed his name to Akhen**aten** ("devoted adherent of God Aten"). Thus, in place of Amun as the *supreme* god among all the gods, Aten was now designated as the *sole* god for all Egyptians.

After closing down all temples of Amun, Akhenaten constructed a new capital at Akhetaten (now Amarna), hundreds of miles north of Thebes, the center of the priestly cult attending Amun-Re. Here, the new temples to Aten were designed as sun temples, facing east in order to admit the light of the rising sun into the interior. Moreover, in various forms the Aten was depicted as a solar disc, whose rays of light were directed to the hands of Akhenaten and his queen, Nefertiti (see page 48).

Akhenaten's experiment at overturning existing orthodoxy was short-lived. His successor (possibly his own son), given the name Tutenkh**aten**, quickly reverted to the previous cult of Amun-Re, taking the name Tutenkh**amen** (1336–1327 BCE). Nevertheless, Akhenaten's revolution generated considerable scholarly conjecture. Among explanations for his motives, it has been thought that his intention was to undermine the growing political power of the priests of Amun-Re. Alternatively, perhaps Akhenaten was determined to replace the former polytheism with a quasi-monotheistic religion devoted primarily to himself and only tangentially to the solar disc. A third theory suggests that Akhenaten was interested in opening up religion to wider participation by all Egyptians. Perhaps the most provocative of speculations concerns whether Akhenaten was the forebear of later monotheistic worship in the ancient Near East.

Key Terms

Agrarian society 29
Agrarian–urban society 27
Assembly 32
Bronze Age collapse 42
City, city-state 33

Democracy 47
Empire 35
Iron Age 42
Neolithic Age 30
Nomads 32

Palace-state 39
Republicanism 47
Sharecroppers 32

Learn more with this chapter's digital tools, including the Oxford Insight Study Guide, at http://www.oup.com/he/vonsivers4e. Please see the Further Resources section at the back of the book for additional readings and suggested websites.

Sources for Chapter 2

Law Code of Hammurabi

ca. 1772 BCE

In order to "cause justice to prevail in the land" and to "further the welfare of the people," the Amorite King Hammurabi (ca. 1792–1750 BCE), having made Babylon his capital and having conquered Mesopotamia, issued a comprehensive code of laws. He caused them to be inscribed on stones that were erected at crossroads and in marketplaces throughout his kingdom, so that all his subjects would understand the penalties that their actions might incur. This document survives on one of these stones, topped by an illustration showing Hammurabi receiving the order to write as directed by the sun god Shamash. The stone was discovered by French archaeologists in 1901–1902, and it remains one of the treasures of the Louvre Museum in Paris.

1. If a man accuse a man, and charge him with murder, but cannot convict him, the accuser shall be put to death.

3. If a man in a case before the court offer testimony concerning deeds of violence, and do not establish the testimony he has given . . . the man shall be put to death.

53. If a man neglect to strengthen his dike, and do not strengthen his dike, and a break be made in his dike and he let the water carry away farmland, then the man in whose dike the break has been made shall restore the grain which he has damaged.

54. If he be not able to restore the grain, they shall sell him and his goods, and the farmers whose grain the water has carried away shall divide the results of the sale.

104. If a merchant give an agent grain, wood, oil, or goods of any kind with which to trade, the agent shall write down the money received and return it to the merchant. The agent shall take a sealed receipt for the money which he gives to the merchant.

105. If the agent be careless and do not take a receipt for the money which he has given to the merchant, the money not receipted for shall not be placed to his account.

Source: Nels M. Bailkey and Richard Lim, eds., *Readings in Ancient History: Thought and Experience from Gilgamesh to St. Augustine*, 6th ed. (Boston: Houghton Mifflin, 2002), 28–36.

196. If a man destroy the eye of another man, they shall destroy his eye.

197. If he break a man's bone, they shall break his bone.

198. If he destroy the eye of a common man or break a bone of a common man, he shall pay one *mina* of silver.

199. If he destroy the eye of a man's slave or break a bone of a man's slave, he shall pay one-half his price.

206. If a man strike another man in a quarrel and wound him, that man shall swear, "I did not strike him intentionally," and he shall be responsible for the physician.

207. If he die as a result of the blow, he shall swear as above, and if it were the son of a gentleman, he shall pay one-third *mina* of silver.

228. If a builder erect a house for a man and complete it, he shall give him two shekels of silver per *sar* of house as his wage.

229. If a builder erect a house for a man and do not make its construction firm and the house which he built collapse and cause the death of the owner of the house, that builder shall be put to death.

233. If a builder erect a house for a man and do not surround it with walls of proper construction, and a wall fall in, that builder shall strengthen that wall at his own expense.

253. If a man hire a man to oversee his farm and furnish him the seed-grain and entrust him with oxen and contract with him to cultivate the field, and that man steal either the seed or the crop and it be found in his possession, they shall cut off his fingers.

From the Epilogue:

The great gods proclaimed me, and I am the guardian shepherd whose scepter is righteous and whose beneficent shadow is spread over my city. In my bosom I carried the people of the land of Sumer and Akkad; under my protection I brought their brethren into security; in my wisdom I sheltered them.

That the strong might not oppress the weak, and that they should give justice to the orphan and the widow. . . .

▶ **Working with Sources**

1. When are financial and capital punishments applied in the code, and is there a consistent principle at work here?

2. Why is Hammurabi concerned with the regulation of business transactions, and particularly when they have to do with agriculture?

Three spinal injury cases documented in the Edwin Smith Papyrus

ca. 1550 BCE

The following is an excerpt from a contemporary (2010), medically based translation of the Edwin Smith Papyrus, the oldest extant text on medicine, which originated in Egypt ca. 1550 BCE. The translators' notes emphasize how clinically accurate ancient Egyptian physicians and surgeons were with their examinations, diagnoses, and—in large part—treatment of traumatic injuries. The treatment with alum, honey, and a layer of fresh meat under bandages is well-known in medicine for the moisturizing, antibacterial, and coagulating benefits it provides.

Case #29: Cervical stab wound, perforating a vertebra

Title Treatment instructions concerning a knife wound in a vertebra in the back of his neck.

Examination If you should examine a man with a flesh wound because of a knife slash in a vertebra in the back of his neck, penetrating to the bone and perforating the bone of a vertebra of the back of his neck: if when you clean out that oozing wound, take note: the shuddering/wincing because of it is great! He has found he is unable to look at both his shoulders and his chest.

Diagnosis Then you are to say about it: "A wound of the flesh in the back of his neck, penetrating to the bone and perforating the bone of a vertebra in the back of his neck, and one who suffers from rigidity in the back of his neck: (this is) a medical condition I intend to fight with."

Treatment You should bind it over fresh meat the first day. Afterward, lay (him) down on his resting place/camp bed, until the critical period of his affliction passes.

Case #32: Cervical vertebral compression fracture

Title Treatment instructions for a subsidence in a vertebra in the back of his neck.

Examination If you should examine a man for a subsidence in a vertebra in the back of his neck and his face is fixed and he cannot turn his neck, you must say to him: "Look to the front of your chest and to your two shoulder joints." Then he finds he is unable to turn his face. He can look to neither the front of his chest nor his two shoulder joints.

Source: Excerpted and adapted from Joost J. van Middendorp, Gonzalo M. Sanchez, and Alwyn L. Burridge, "The Edwin Smith Papyrus: A Clinical Reappraisal of the Oldest Known Document on Spinal Injuries," *European Spine Journal* 19,11 (2010): 1815–1823, https://www.ncbi.nlm.nih.gov/pmc/articles/PMC2989268/#CR9

The above article is based on *The Edwin Smith Papyrus: Updated Translation of the Trauma Treatise and Modern Medical Commentaries*, tr. Edmund S. Meltzer and Gonzalo M. Sanchez (Atlanta, GA: Lockwood Press, 2012).

Diagnosis Then you are to say about him: "One who has a subsidence in a vertebra in the back of his neck (this is) a medical condition I can heal."

Treatment You have to bind it over fresh meat the first day. You have to loosen his bandages, and you then apply ointment to his head as far as the back of his neck. You have to bandage it over alum and you should treat him afterward with honey every day. It means his treatment protocol is 'sitting upright' until he recovers.

Explanation As for 'a subsidence in a vertebra of the back of his neck,' he says, concerning the depressing of a vertebra of the back of his neck: "The inside of the back of his neck is like a foot sinking into cultivated soil; it is a compressing/collapsing downwards."

Case #33: Cervical burst fracture with spinal cord injury and brain contusion [bruise]

Title Treatment instructions concerning a crushed vertebra of the back of his neck.

Examination If you should examine a man having a crushed vertebra in the back of neck and you find him with one vertebra fallen into its counterpart, and now he is stuporous and he does not speak. It is his fall head downward which caused a vertebra to crush into its counterpart and you find he is unaware of both his arms and his legs because of it.

Diagnosis Then you are to say about him: "One who has a crushed vertebra in the back of his neck, and he is unaware of both his arms and legs and is stuporous (this is) a medical condition that cannot be healed".

Explanation A As for 'a crushed vertebra in the back of his neck,' he says concerning the falling of one vertebra of the back of his neck into its counterpart, "it is one entering into the other one without moving back and forth."

Explanation B As for 'it is his fall head downward, that is what caused one vertebra to crush into its counterpart,' it means, his falling head downward, upon the vault of his head, forcibly drives one vertebra of the back neck into its counterpart.

▶ **Working with Sources**

1. What does the ancient physician include in his examination? What would a modern practitioner add or eliminate?

2. What critical technical aids were unavailable to the ancient practitioner but are used routinely today in medical treatment?

SOURCE 2.3

Advice from a royal scribe to his apprentice, Middle Kingdom Egypt, Twelfth Dynasty

ca. 1878–1839 BCE

The Papyrus Lansing is a letter of instruction from the royal scribe (and "chief overseer of the cattle of Amun-Re, King of Gods") Nebmare-nakht to his apprentice Wenemdiamun. It seems to date from the reign of the pharaoh Senusret III (Sesostris III). The letter conveys a great deal of practical advice to an up-and-coming scribe—as well as warnings about what temptations he must avoid to be successful. While Nebmare-nakht is clearly proud of the status his work has earned him, he also illuminates the specific duties and responsibilities of a royal official in this period.

The scribe of the army and commander of the cattle of the house of Amun, Nebmare-nakht, speaks to the scribe Wenemdiamun, as follows. Be a scribe! Your body will be sleek; your hand will be soft. You will not flicker like a flame, like one whose body is feeble. For there is not the bone of a man in you. You are tall and thin. If you lifted a load to carry it, you would stagger, your legs would tremble. You are lacking in strength; you are weak in all your limbs; you are poor in body.

Set your sight on being a scribe: a fine profession that suits you. You call for one; a thousand answer you. You stride freely on the road. You will not die like a hired ox. You are in front of others.

I spend the day instructing you. You do not listen! Your heart is like an empty room. My teachings are not in it. Take their meaning to yourself!

The marsh thicket is before you each day, as a nestling is after its mother. You follow the path of pleasure; you make friends with revelers. You have made your home in the brewery, as one who thirsts for beer. You sit in the parlor with an idler. You hold the writings in contempt. You visit the prostitute. Do not do these things! What are they for? They are of no use. Take note of it!

Furthermore. Look, I instruct you to make you sound; to make you hold the palette freely. To make you become one whom the king trusts; to make you gain entrance to treasury and granary. To make you receive the ship-load at the gate of the granary. To make you issue the offerings on feast days. You are dressed in fine clothes; you own horses. Your boat is on the river; you are supplied with attendants. You stride about inspecting. A mansion is built in

Source: Translated by A. M. Blackman and T. E. Peet, *Journal of Egyptian Archaeology* 11 (1925): 284–298, as quoted by Miriam Lichtheim, *Ancient Egyptian Literature* (Berkeley and Los Angeles: University of California Press, 1973), vol. 2, 171–172.

your town. You have a powerful office, given you by the king. Male and female slaves are about you. Those who are in the fields grasp your hand, on plots that you have made. Look, I make you into a staff of life! Put the writings in your heart, and you will be protected from all kinds of toil. You will become a worthy official.

Do you not recall the fate of the unskilled man? His name is not known. He is ever burdened [like an ass carrying] in front of the scribe who knows what he is about.

Come, let me tell you the woes of the soldier, and how many are his superiors: the general, the troop-commander, the officer who leads, the standard-bearer, the lieutenant, the scribe, the commander of fifty, and the garrison-captain. They go in and out in the halls of the palace, saying, "Get laborers!". . . .

His march is uphill through mountains. He drinks water every third day; it is smelly and tastes of salt. His body is ravaged by illness. The enemy comes, surrounds him with missiles, and life recedes from him. He is told: "Quick, forward, valiant soldier! Win for yourself a good name!" He does not know what he is about. His body is weak, his legs fail him. When victory is won, the captives are handed over to his majesty, to be taken to Egypt. The foreign woman faints on the march; she hangs herself on the soldier's neck. His knapsack drops, another grabs it while he is burdened with the woman. . . .

Be a scribe, and be spared from soldiering! You call and one says: "Here I am." You are safe from torments. Every man seeks to raise himself up. Take note of it!

▶ **Working with Sources**

1. How does Nebmare-nakht attempt to make the life of a diligent scribe attractive to his apprentice? How does he use negative examples to steer Wenemdiamun in the right direction?

2. Why is the position of scribe so prominent in Middle Kingdom Egypt? What role does a scribe play in relation to the Pharaoh?

SOURCE 2.4

Sketch of the palace complex at Knossos, Minoan Crete

ca. 1700–1400 BCE

In 1900, Sir Arthur Evans discovered the remains of a vast palace complex on the island of Crete in the southern Aegean Sea. Christening the civilization "Minoan" after the legendary King Minos of Crete, Evans continued to excavate at Knossos and at other sites around the island. The palace

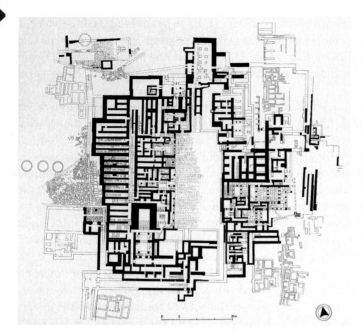

at Knossos seems to have contained hundreds of rooms, including a throne room and storage spaces for food and cisterns for the collection of water. The legacy of Evans's work can be viewed at the visual archive held at the Ashmolean Museum in Oxford, England. There is a virtual tour of the site: http://www.steveflanagan.co.uk/media/tours/knossospalace/Knossos.html

▶ **Working with Sources**

1. Can the palace complex at Knossos be compared with palace sites in Mesopotamia and Egypt in the second millennium BCE? In what respects?

2. What do you think the palace complex suggests about the structure of Minoan society?

SOURCE 2.5

The Great Hymn to the Aten

ca. 1353–1336 BCE

This hymn to the Egyptian sun god Aten has been attributed to King Akhenaten ("the devoted adherent of Aten"), the pharaoh formerly known as Amenhotep IV. While Akhenaten's experiment in monotheism was short-lived, the poem reflects the connections this revolutionary religious thinker attempted to forge between himself and an all-powerful deity. Note that he also solicits the blessings of Aten for himself, as leader of the Egyptian people, and for his wife, the famous Nefertiti.

Splendid you rise in heaven's
   lightland,
O living Aten, creator of life!

When you have dawned in eastern
   lightland,
You fill every land with your beauty.

Source: Translated by J. A. Wilson, as quoted by Miriam Lichtheim, *Ancient Egyptian Literature*, vol. 2, 96–99.

Neferkheprure, Only-one-of-Re: Akhenaten

You are beauteous, great, radiant,
High over every land;
Your rays embrace the lands,
To the limit of all that you made.

. . .

When you set in western lightland,
Earth is in darkness as if in death;
One sleeps in chambers, heads
    covered,
One eye does not see another.
Were they robbed of their goods,
That are under their heads,
People would not remark it.
Every lion comes from its den,
All the serpents bite;
Darkness hovers, earth is silent,
As their maker rests in lightland.

. . .

Ships fare north, fare south as well,
Roads lie open when you rise;
The fish in the river dart before you,
Your rays are in the midst of the sea.
Who makes seed grow in women,
Who creates people from sperm;

Maat: balance, law, justice

Who feeds the son in his mother's
    womb,
Who soothes him to still his tears.
Nurse in the womb,
Giver of breath,
To nourish all that he has made.

. . .

You are in my heart,

There is no other who knows you,
Only your son, *Neferkheprure,
    Only-one-of-Re*,
Whom you have taught your ways
    and your might.
[Those on] earth come from your
    hand as you made them,
When you have dawned they live,
When you set they die;
You yourself are lifetime, one lives
    by you.
All eyes are on your beauty until you
    set.
All labor ceases when you rest in the
    west;
When you rise you stir [everyone] for
    the King,
Every leg is on the move since you
    founded the earth.
You rouse them for your son who
    came from your body,
The King who lives by Maat, the
    Lord of the Two Lands,
Neferkheprure, Only-one-of-Re,
The Son of Re who lives by **Maat**, the
    Lord of crowns,
Akhenaten, great in his lifetime;
And the great Queen whom he loves,
    the Lady of the Two Lands,
Nefer-nefru-Aten Nefertiti, living
    forever.

▶ **Working
with Sources**

1. **How does the hymn reflect on the practical advantages provided by the
   sun?**

2. **How does the hymn reinforce the power of Aten in political terms?**

World Period One

From Human Origins to Early Agricultural Centers, Prehistory to 600 BCE

Humans appeared late in the evolution of the world. While the earth is 4.5 billion years old, the first human-like beings only appeared about 6 million years ago, and modern humans did not appear in East Africa until about 100,000 years ago. These humans migrated from there to Eurasia and Australia 80,000–60,000 years ago and to the Americas 17,500–14,600 years ago.

As people became more numerous, human culture became more differentiated. The triad of origins-interactions-adaptations as the fundamental pattern in world history took shape. Human ingenuity and interaction with the environment in the Middle East, Asia, Europe, Australia, and the Americas led to vastly different adaptations. Foraging originated in Africa. Farming, urbanization, and state formation originated in the Middle East. In the Americas, humans fashioned similarly differentiated livelihoods and political structures. Australia's poorer natural environment slowed its differentiation process.

Chapter 3

Shifting Agrarian Centers in India

3000–600 BCE

CHAPTER THREE PATTERNS

Origins, Interactions and Adaptations The first civilization of India was that of the Harappans. By the nineteenth century BCE, a collection of large cities, towns, and villages were located throughout the Indus Valley watershed. Their interactions with Mesopotamia and surrounding regions were extensive, and their adaptations to their environment, were considerable. Yet their writing remains undeciphered, and why their civilization vanished is unknown.

The peoples who displaced them ultimately regenerated urban life in India, but this time centered on the Ganges Plain. Their religious beliefs formed the basis of Hinduism and their written language became Sanskrit.

Uniqueness and Similarities Harappan civilization was in many ways unique. The mysteries surrounding its religion, political organization, and writing system—as well as why it declined—reinforce this singularity. Its architecture and urban layouts suggest at least a cultural unity over the largest area of its time.

Like the other great riverine civilizations of the ancient world, the Harappans had to ensure the fertility of their lands as well as guard against floods, which suggests a high degree of organization. In like manner, the Indo-European-speaking migrants that followed tended to set up similar kinds of agrarian-urban societies wherever they settled.

The inscriptions on the ancient seals were unlike anything General Alexander Cunningham had seen before in India. Some years previously, in 1856, British engineers working on an extension of the East India Railway had found ancient mounds stuffed with fire-baked bricks. They looted the bricks to use as ballast for the railroad tracks. Fortunately, the men noticed that some of the bricks contained these puzzling signs and sent them to Cunningham, who was known for his archaeological work at Indian Buddhist sites. Intrigued by their antiquity, Cunningham had the sites placed under protection. The tracks of the railroad, it turned out, were being supported by the remains of one of the world's most ancient cities! Identifying the civilization that created it, however, would prove to be one of archaeology's greatest challenges.

The railroad workers had stumbled upon the "lost city" of Harappa—the center of one of the world's oldest societies. Although archaeologists have been working at Harappa since the 1920s, basic questions about this society remain to be answered. For example, how did their writing system—composed of the symbols carved on the seals first brought to Cunningham—work? Why did Harappan society vanish almost entirely after just 600 years? And while scholars believe that Harappan village life set many of the patterns for later Indian rural society, what were the fundamental patterns that marked these founding cultures, and how did these patterns change the lives of the peoples in the region and come to be adopted and adapted by them?

One important pattern marking the history of northern India, like that of Mesopotamia, lies in regular migration and invasion. Although all of India did not experience rule by a single regime until the nineteenth century CE, cultural and religious unity had already been created thousands of years earlier under the influence of newly emerging states along the Ganges River.

CHAPTER OUTLINE

The Vanished Origins of Harappa, 3000–1500 BCE

Interactions in Northern India, 1500–600 BCE

Indian Society, Culture, and Religion, 1500–600 BCE

Putting It All Together

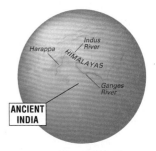

ABOVE: Buffalo figurines from the Indus Valley, ca. 2500 BCE

Seeing Patterns

❯ Who were the Harappans? Where did they come from? What evidence exists for their origins?

❯ What explanations have been offered for the collapse of Harappan society?

❯ How well do the rival theories hold up, given what scholars and archaeologists have discovered?

❯ How can we know about the newcomers to northern India? What sources exist for historians to examine?

❯ What patterns can we see evolving in the Ganges River states that will mark the subsequent development of Indian civilization?

Maintaining this cultural continuity while managing innovation from outside has marked India to the present day. Among their most significant achievements, these early Ganges states gave rise to some of the world's most important religions: Hinduism, Jainism, and Buddhism.

The Vanished Origins of Harappa, 3000–1500 BCE

Unlike Egypt or Mesopotamia, the cities of the Indus Valley flourished for less than 1,000 years—from about 2500–1700 BCE—before vanishing. Anchored by two major cities—Harappa [hah-RAP-uh] in the north and Mohenjo-Daro [moe-hen-joe DAH-roe] in the southwest—and extending from the upper Ganges River to the Arabian Sea, a network of small cities, towns, and villages marked by a consistency of architecture and artifacts occupied the largest cultural area of the third millennium BCE. Trade with southwest Asia and Egypt extended Harappan influence even farther.

Although the sophistication of this "Harappan" or "Indus Valley" culture's urban planning, the standardization of weights and measures, and the attention to cleanliness and comfort all suggest a high level of social organization, we know virtually nothing of its arrangement. Scholars have not yet deciphered most of the Harappan pictographic symbols. The fundamental question remains: Why, as the new mode of urban society gathered momentum elsewhere, did the inhabitants of the Indus Valley abandon their cities and disappear from the historical record?

The Region and People

The subcontinent that includes the modern states of India, Pakistan, and Bangladesh is attached to the Eurasian landmass, but is almost completely cut off from it by forbidding physical barriers. The lower two-thirds of India form a peninsula surrounded on three sides by the Arabian Sea, the Indian Ocean, and the Bay of Bengal. To the north of the bay, extending from Bangladesh through the Indian province of Assam to the north and east and deep into Myanmar (formerly Burma), are continuous ranges of mountainous rainforests. Some of the world's highest annual rainfall totals—over 100 inches—are recorded here.

Forming the northeastern border of the subcontinent above the rain belt are the Himalaya Mountains. These meet another range, the Hindu Kush, which extends into Pakistan and, with the Sulaiman and Kirthar ranges, marks the northwestern border of the region. Access to the Indian peninsula by land is thus limited to a handful of mountain passes through the Himalayas and the more easily crossed Khyber and Bolan Passes of the northwest. Historically, these have been avenues of trade, migration, and invasion (see Map 3.1).

The Monsoon System   Surrounded by water and framed by high mountains, India's internal **topography** also influences its climate. The Deccan Plateau, Vindhya Range, and other internal highland areas tend to both trap tropical moisture against the west coast and funnel it toward the region drained by the Ganges River in the northeast. The moisture itself comes from the summer winds of the monsoon system. The winds, which carry moisture generated from the heat of

Topography: The physical features—mountains, rivers, deserts, swamps, etc.—of a region.

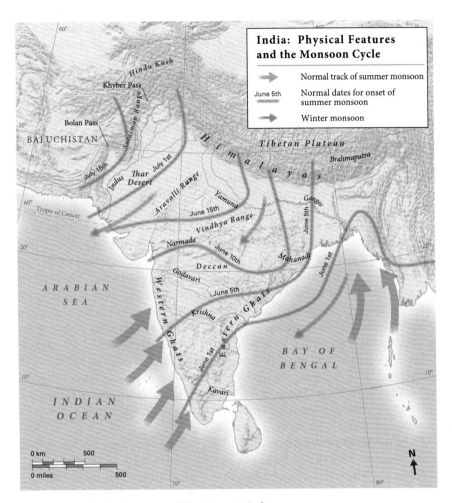

MAP 3.1 **India: Physical Features and the Monsoon Cycle**

central and southern Africa as they flow southwest to northeast over the Indian Ocean from June through October, govern the climatic cycles of southeastern Asia, Indonesia, and southern China as well as India. In the winter months, the winds reverse direction and pull hot, dry air down from Central Asia. During this dry season, rainfall is scant or nonexistent over large areas of South Asia.

The monsoon cycle exerts a powerful influence on Asian agriculture. In India, where the monsoon rainfall amounts differ widely from region to region, even minor variations in the timing of the cycle or the volume of rain may spell potential flood or famine. Generally speaking, the subcontinent becomes drier as one moves farther north and west until one reaches the Thar [TAAR] or Great Indian, Desert and the plain of Sind. It is this arid region bordered by mountains and watered by the Indus River system that saw the rise of the first Indian cities.

Harappan civilization depended on the Indus. This vast river system has a slow, meandering course that for millennia has left behind rich deposits of fertile soil. Moreover, like the Yellow River in China, the constant buildup of silt in the riverbed periodically caused the water to overflow its banks and change course—dangerous for those living close by but an effective means of spreading soil over a wide area.

Mehrgarh Culture The peopling of the Indian subcontinent has been the subject of intense research over the last several decades. The advent of advanced dating techniques and the refinement of DNA analysis and genetic testing have yielded a complex picture of the region's historical demography. Groups of people in India's extreme south still chant prayers so ancient that the meaning of the words has long been lost. Recent testing has suggested that they may be genetically linked to some of the earliest migrants out of Africa.

More recent peoples, perhaps speakers of a parent language belonging to a hypothetical "Elamo-Dravidian" family (supposed to include both ancient Elamite, spoken in southwestern Iran, and the modern Dravidian languages), are believed to have moved into the region near the Indus. They may have been part of a wave of early agriculturalists emerging from the area of the Fertile Crescent. Researchers have found a number of Neolithic sites near the river, one of the most productive being Mehrgarh [MARE-gar], located near a strategic mountain pass in Baluchistan. Scholars have dated the Mehrgarh culture to about 6000 BCE, making it perhaps the oldest on the Indian subcontinent for which we have a reliable archaeological record. Like the inhabitants of the Fertile Crescent, villagers in Neolithic Baluchistan raised wheat and barley and domesticated sheep, goats, and cattle. As long ago as 5500 BCE, pottery was being produced in the area. Also dating from this period are the crafting and trading of fine lapis lazuli beadware, later a coveted item among Harappan luxury goods. Significantly, even the earliest Baluchistani dwellings are made of mud brick, a material that became a hallmark of the Harappan cityscape. For all of these reasons, some archaeologists have viewed Mehrgarh culture as a possible precursor to Harappa.

Scholars agree that by about 3000 BCE a culture of villages and towns with trade networks, pottery, and domesticated plants and animals had long been established in the hills of Baluchistan adjacent to the Indus and its western tributaries. Attracted by the ease of growing crops in the fertile river valleys, the inhabitants of these hill sites extended their settlements eastward sometime before 2600 BCE, culminating in the region's first cities.

6500–3000 BCE
Mehrgarh Neolithic culture in
areas west of the Indus River

1700–1300 BCE
Late Harappan period

1400–800 BCE
Composition of the Vedas by
the Indo-European migrants

2500–1700 BCE
Mature Harappan period

1500–1200 BCE
Indo-European migrations
enter northern India

600–500 BCE
Development of the written
language of Sanskrit

800–500 BCE
Reemergence of urban life, now
centered along the Ganges

600–400 BCE
Composition of the
Upanishads

ca. 600 BCE
Essential structures of *varna* and *jati*
(caste) social systems in place

Adapting to Urban Life in the Indus Valley

By about 2300 BCE, the two major cities of Harappa and Mohenjo-Daro anchored a system of small cities, towns, and villages encompassing between 650,000 and 850,000 square miles (see Map 3.2). At its height, the city of Harappa had a population of over 40,000, comparable to that of the largest Mesopotamian cities of the period. Located on a floodplain, these cities were built on artificial hills to protect them from flood damage. Mohenjo-Daro, for example, was built on two 40-foot mounds separated by a channel 200 yards wide for easy access to the Indus.

Harappan Uniformity   While the cities of Mesopotamia and Egypt contained architectural features specific to their respective cultures, Harappan cities seem almost to have been designed by the same hand. Harappa and Mohenjo-Daro, as well as several smaller cities and numerous towns, are laid out according to a planned grid, with squares, public buildings, and markets at regular locations. The larger streets are straight and paved with brick. They are laid out according to standard widths, with drains and gutters connected to a sewer system (see Map 3.3). The bricks themselves were produced according to a uniform formula. Moreover,

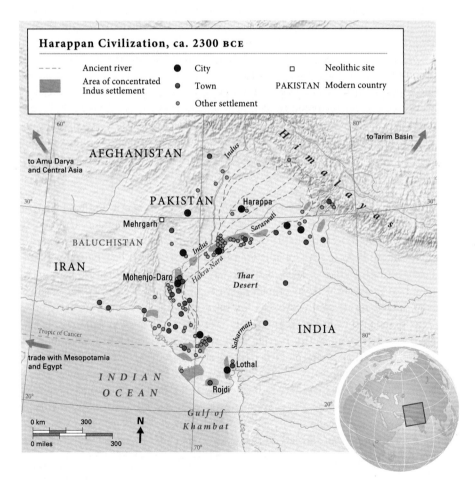

MAP 3.2 **Harappan Civilization, ca. 2300 BCE**

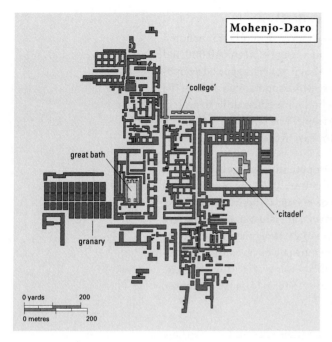

Mohenjo-Daro

'college'

great bath

'citadel'

granary

0 yards 200

0 metres 200

MAP 3.3 **Mohenjo-Daro**

Cesspits: Deep holes or trenches used to deposit human waste and refuse; in the case of Harappa, they were flushed with water into city sewers and drains, ultimately leading to the adjacent river.

the Harappans developed perhaps the world's first decimal system and used it in designing highly refined scales of weights and measures.

This uniformity extended to individual buildings. Houses of several stories were made of brick and plastered with gypsum, their floor plans similar even at widely separated sites. Many had brick-lined indoor wells and toilets emptying into terra-cotta **cesspits** whose overflow connected to the city's drains and sewers. Nearly all dwellings had a bathing room with a waterproof floor and drain system to direct the water into channels in the street. Wheel-turned, mass-produced clay pots, jars, cooking vessels, copper- and bronzeware, and even toys have been found at various sites.

The Harappan Diet   The rich soil of the region supported the staple crops of wheat and barley as well as peas, melons, figs, and sesame. Recent work has uncovered sophisticated irrigation systems designed to conserve water during dry periods. Cattle appear to have been the chief domestic animals, and large herds may have been signs of wealth. It is not clear, however, whether they were used principally for food and milk or as work animals, as were water buffaloes. Whatever the case, some scholars see in their importance at this early time the origins of the later centrality of the cow in Indian culture and religion. Sheep and pigs also appear to have been an important part of the Harappan diet. Seal carvings and figurines suggest that the Harappans were sophisticated dog breeders.

Harappan Identity and Government   Evidence concerning the identity of the Harappans is obscure and contradictory. Everyday items and statuary offer few clues. Symbols found on what are believed to be merchant seals are seen by some to hold tenuous links to the Dravidian family to which belong the languages of most modern south Indian peoples. Scholars have also suggested that the Harappans may have been an eastern branch of a people called "Proto-Mediterraneans," who ranged across southwest Asia. More recently, scholars have suggested that their predecessors in the region may have been "Elamo-Dravidian" speakers from the area around the Fertile Crescent/Zagros Mountains. Complicating the matter further, archaeologists have identified an urban society designated as the "Bactria-Margiana Archaeological Complex" (BMAC) to the northwest of the Indus Valley culture that shared some technological features with the Harappans. However, the uniqueness of Harappan urban life argues against any theory of simple cultural diffusion.

As with other early urban cultures, there appears to have been a close relationship among the religious, political, and social spheres of Harappan society. Nevertheless, the clues again yield little that is definitive. For example, the replication of city plans and architecture throughout such a wide area might indicate the kind of strong central authority and bureaucratic control typically found in a kingdom or empire. Yet we know virtually nothing of how it might have been organized. Indeed, there seems to be an absence of the kind of monumental architecture of palaces and temples so characteristic of other wealthy, centralized states. Moreover, some departures from the uniformity of previous sites found in recent work at Rojdi [ROEJ-dee] have led scholars to amend this picture in favor of one of overall unity marked by discernible regional styles. This modified view, along with findings that suggest that remnants of Harappan culture survived the collapse of the cities, would seem to work against theories of highly centralized control.

Harappan Trade   The ability to mass-produce a vast array of articles and the existence of elaborate port facilities imply an occupation-based class system as well as a merchant class with overseas connections. Sumerian records from about 2300 BCE tell of a people called "Meluhha," now believed by many scholars to be the Harappans, who carried on seaborne trade and maintained colonies of merchants in several Mesopotamian cities. There is evidence of Harappan merchandise being traded as far away as Egypt and central Asia.

Because of the apparent occupational specialization of the Harappans, some scholars have theorized that they may have belonged to guilds, organizations whose members all pursue the same trade or craft. However, the uniformity of Harappan dwellings, in contrast to their amenities—generous living quarters, indoor plumbing, and so forth—defy any easy generalizations about class structure.

The Harappans appear to have maintained complex trade networks both within their cultural sphere and outside of it. Fortified border settlements, evidently trading posts, extended their influence to the borders of modern Iran and as far north as the Amu Darya River (the ancient Oxus), the region of the BMAC. Curiously, however, we see virtually no evidence of foreign trade goods such as handicrafts in the Indus cities, perhaps suggesting tight government control over outside influences.

In addition to bulk foodstuffs, the Mesopotamian records mentioning the Meluhha note that their merchants dealt in beadwork, lapis lazuli, pearls, rare woods, cotton cloth, and dog and cat figurines. Due in part to our inability to decipher the Harappan symbols, we know much less about their imports. The network of cities along the Indus also seems to have been pivotal in the long-distance trade of copper from Baluchistan and in the exchange of gold, silver, semiprecious stones, shells, and timber throughout an extensive area north and west into Afghanistan and east to central Asia.

Harappan Bronze Bull Figurine. Cattle figured prominently in Harappan culture but most likely as work animals and providers of milk products as in India today. Harappans were also skilled metallurgists and left a wide variety of bronze artifacts. This figurine, believed to be a toy, is emblematic of the importance of cattle to the Indus civilization.

Lothal   Located several miles up the Sabarmati River from the Gulf of Khambhat (Cambay), Lothal [LOW-tal] was a large Harappan seaport. Recent work has shown it to be not only a vital link in Harappan maritime trade in the Arabian Sea and points west but an important manufacturing center, as well.

Lothal's central structure is an enormous basin that was once connected to an inlet of the river. Most researchers believe that this was a dock for oceangoing ships, though some contend instead that it was a reservoir for water storage. Nearby are a number of structures believed to have been warehouses, each marked with what appear to be the stamps and seals of merchants.

Lothal was also a regional craft center, with microbeads used for decorative craft items and jewelry as its chief product for internal trade and export. The city's site may have been chosen because of its proximity to sources of stones for bead making. The site, with the city planning and water systems typical of Harappan cities, is also notable for its pottery kilns and bead factories, complete with worker housing. Yet, for all this wealth of artifacts, answers to such questions as who the merchants or workers were, how they were organized and governed, what levels of mobility there might have been among different classes, and even precisely what those classes might have been remain elusive.

Harappan Religion   Clues about Harappan religion are equally tantalizing. The swastika, a symbol associated with the cyclical nature of life in Indian and Buddhist art long before its appropriation by the Nazis in the twentieth century, is first found in the cities of the Indus. Some scholars suggest that the Harappan system of symbols, generally assumed to be a form of writing, may instead be understood as a form of religious shorthand for use in the multiethnic and multilingual Indus society. Figurines depicting real as well as mythical animals have been found, which, along with female figurines and **phallic stones**, may connote a type of fertility religion. Like many Neolithic and agrarian–urban cultures, the Harappans interred their dead with ornaments, pottery, and perhaps food, and may have believed in an afterlife. Such finds suggest continuities with later Hindu practices. However, for the moment, the nature of Harappan religion remains an open question.

Phallic stones: Stones in the shape of, or meant to evoke, the male sex organ; Indian religions use a host of phallic images, or lingams, in shrines, rituals, and festivals to symbolize the male, or active, forces of both natural and supernatural creation.

The Collapse of the Cities

Around 1900 BCE the major cities of Harappan society appear to have been in decline. By 1700 BCE the great cities seem to have been abandoned; their people moved out to smaller outlying towns and villages, many returning to farming or becoming herders.

Some recent interpretations of Harappan urban decline attribute it to ecological collapse. The surrounding land had perhaps reached the limits of its capacity to support large cities. Weather-related problems may have stretched these limits even further. One theory holds that a prolonged regional drought occurred around 2200 BCE, resulting in a drying up of vital branches of the Indus watershed. Increasing salt levels in the Indus may have played a role, perhaps as the result of diverting too much of its water for irrigation and supplying the cities; another study places part of the blame on earthquakes, which may have partially diverted the river's flow around 1800 BCE. We do know that the Hakra-Nara River was abruptly shunted, possibly by an earthquake, into the Indus by the early eighteenth century BCE, resulting in a progressive drying up of its old watershed and increased flooding on the lower Indus.

By about 1500 BCE remnants of the Indus civilization were found only within isolated regional cultures that blended Harappan influences with those of

Dockyard at Lothal. While some scholars maintain that this structure was a holding tank or reservoir for the local irrigation system, the current consensus is that it was in fact a technologically advanced area for loading and unloading oceangoing ships. A sophisticated system of channels kept it flooded to the proper level, prevented overflow, and, with locks and gates, allowed access to the river and sea.

neighboring peoples. The expansion of Harappan village agriculture to the east and south, however, continued. Indeed, the hallmarks of Harappan urban life—the cultivation of regionally appropriate staple crops and domesticated animals by people organized in villages—might justly be called the foundation of Indian social history. It would be centuries, however, before India again saw the rise of cities.

Interactions in Northern India, 1500–600 BCE

The "villains" of the Harappan collapse were long considered to be Indo-European-language-speaking migrants from the north who called themselves "Aryans" (Sanskrit, "the noble ones")—a term which, through a series of twisted associations and garbled history, Adolf Hitler and the Nazis later identified with Germans. The identification of the **Indo-European family of languages** with the peoples of northern Europe in the nineteenth century prompted the Nazi appropriation of the term "Aryan" for those of Germanic ethnicity in the 1930s and 1940s. The traditions associated with the "Aryans" recount their movement south and east through the Khyber Pass and across the Punjab, probably between 1700 and 1400 BCE. Their accounts of epic battles were formerly assumed to refer to their conquest of the Harappans. The earliest of their religious texts, the *Rig-Veda* [rig VAY-duh], refers to a short, dark-skinned people whom the Aryans contemptuously called *dasas*, or "the others." It also mentions conflicts with sedentary phallus-worshipping people who lived in cities, which would seem to describe the Harappans.

These works, however, were not written down until centuries after the events may have occurred, and whether their references date from the mid-second millennium BCE or were added later is still not resolved. Moreover, while battles undoubtedly

Indo-European family of languages: A large language family of western Eurasia that comprises most of the languages of Europe together with those of northern India and Iran.

did occur, periods of peaceful migration and settlement also appear to have existed. Perhaps the most significant problem, however, is that the Harappan cities appear to have already been largely abandoned by the time the newcomers arrived.

In addition, the relative lack of Aryan artifacts; conflicts of interpretation among archaeologists, classical scholars, and linguists; and a growing body of scholarship by Indian researchers have challenged the role of Aryan migration. Indeed, some Indian nationalist scholars have suggested that long-held assumptions about the Aryans grew out of nineteenth-century beliefs of European superiority supported by the British occupation of India. Their contention is that the roots of Vedic society came not with invaders from the north but from peoples—perhaps the remnant of the Harappans themselves—already long established in Punjab and, later, along the Ganges River. This interpretation, however, has been rejected by most scholars on several grounds. The society depicted in the Vedas—male-centered, aristocratic, centralized—appears to bear little resemblance to the urban, egalitarian-appearing, Harappans. The importance of the horse to later Vedic society also suggests a close connection to the Indo-Europeans, the people who appear to have domesticated the horse. At present, DNA evidence has yielded nothing definitive, while linguistic scholars and many archaeologists argue in favor of considerable Indo-European interaction in the region. Moreover, the introduction of iron implements in the first millennium BCE is associated with Indo-European groups in other places, including China. While the weight of evidence strongly favors the Indo-European migration argument, the debate will most likely remain unresolved for some time.

The Vedic World, 1750–800 BCE

Most scholars at present assign a prominent role to the "Aryan" migrants. While, as we have seen, their exact homeland is unknown, many scholars believe it to be in the area around the Caspian Sea. Nomadic peoples speaking a set of languages descended from Proto-Indo-European appear to have migrated into Asia Minor, the eastern Mediterranean, Iran, and deep into central Asia. They spread such technologies as ironworking and the use of the horse and chariot.

Indo-European Origins   Their ancestors had already introduced items and ideas throughout Eurasia long before the Aryans arrived in India; their presence may have even predated the Neolithic settlement of the continent. More recently, branches are believed to have migrated east and west across the continent from perhaps 4000 to 2500 BCE. They are believed to have introduced the domestication of the wild horses of the central Asian steppes, along with such items as bridles and weapons for use on horseback. Similarly, it seems likely that they spread the technology of the chariot from the Mediterranean to China.

Scholars have reconstructed the Proto-Indo-European language ancestral to those spoken by these groups; it is the parent tongue of a family of languages that comprises (among others) Greek, Latin, the Germanic languages (including English), the Celtic and Slavic language families, and the Indo-Iranian languages, including what became the Indian literary language, Sanskrit. A number of words with common roots for certain basic objects or concepts may be found among these languages. Examples include *pater* (Latin), *Vater* (German), and *pitar* (Sanskrit) for "father"; *septem* (Latin), *sieben* (German), and *sapta* (Sanskrit) for "seven"; and *est* (Latin), *ist* (German), and *asti* (Sanskrit) for "is."

The Vedas Around 2000 BCE a linguistic group designated "Indo-Aryans" had already split off from the Indo-Iranian subgroup and began moving toward northern India. However, this history is extraordinarily difficult to unravel. Some scholars see the Indo-Aryans as emerging from the BMAC culture east of the Caspian Sea; others see them as engaging in wars within the BMAC against the indigenous settled inhabitants; still others see them as migrating into the Punjab long after the Harappan cities declined. In this context, they view their accounts of great "battles" and storming "citadels" as in reality cattle raids and attacks on village corrals.

In any case, the migrants had an oral tradition of epic poetry, hymns, prayers, and allegorical myth and history that would be preserved until it was committed to writing after 600 BCE. The core works, composed from around 1400 to 800 BCE, are the religious hymns known as the **Vedas** ("knowledge" or "truths").

The *Rig-Veda*, the earliest of the Vedas, is currently believed to have been composed between about 1400 and 900 BCE. Its verses were memorized and passed down orally from generation to generation by priests and their successors until written down ca. 300 BCE. Some of the oldest recorded poetry in any Indo-European language, the *Rig-Veda* provides an allegorical vision of a society led by warrior chieftains and priests, and composed of herders, cultivators, artisans, and servants. These groups became the prototypes of the four early social divisions, or *varnas*—priests, warriors, merchants, and commoners (see "Patterns Up Close"). Material wealth and skill in battle were the most valued attributes of Vedic culture. This emphasis on struggle and daring is seen as evidence of a strongly patriarchal, hierarchical society based on kinship and prowess.

Vedas: The most ancient Hindu scriptures, written in early Sanskrit and including hymns, philosophy, and guidance on priestly ritual.

Early North Indian Society and Economy The Indo-European-speakers benefited from the diffusion of earlier Bronze Age crafts and distributed these crafts throughout Eurasia. Their bronze spear tips, arrowheads, and blades, in addition to their chariots and horse-borne warriors, gave them an advantage over the village communities they encountered. After the beginning of the first millennium BCE, they also helped spread the use of iron.

The Vedic peoples made extensive use of horse-drawn wagons and chariots in battle. The earliest migrants may have introduced the horse to northern India, and it is likely that they first brought the chariot to late Xia or early Shang China. Bridles, yokes, harnesses and other items related to the use of horses have been found at a number of sites. The horse was so potent a symbol of power in Vedic culture and religion that its sacrifice became the most sacred of all ceremonies.

Ranging across vast stretches of grassland, the early Vedic peoples carried much of their food supply with them in the form of domestic animals. As with the Harappans, cattle were the chief measure of wealth, thus continuing the centrality of the "sacred cow" to the Indian religious experience. Sheep and goats were also mainstays of their livestock, while milk and butter, particularly the clarified butter called "ghee" [GEE, with a hard "g"], occupied a prominent place in their religious symbolism.

The Settlement of Northern India While the Vedas provide a literary account of Indo-European society and religion, the history of the settlement of northern India is more obscure. Evidence suggests a prolonged period of migration and settlement in the northwest of the subcontinent marked by a gradual transition of the Vedic peoples from a nomadic and pastoral life to a settled and agricultural one. Evidence of large towns in the area around present-day Delhi dates to as early as 1000 BCE. An important catalyst in the reemergence of large cities was the beginning of widespread rice cultivation in the newly opened lands to the east.

First domesticated in Neolithic Southeast Asia and south-central China, rice proved well suited to the climate of the Ganges basin once the forests had been cleared. The introduction of iron tools such as plows and axes was instrumental in preparing the land. High yields and a climate warm enough to permit two crops per year helped ensure the surpluses necessary to support a network of villages, towns, and cities, sometimes called by archaeologists India's "second urbanization."

However, the labor required at every stage of the rice plant's growth cycle needed many hands for its successful cultivation. Hence, the infrastructure of rice culture—the dikes, drainage ditches, terraces, raised paths, and other items related to water control—demanded sophisticated social organization. From roughly 800 BCE, strong agrarian-based states called *janapadas* ("populated territories" or "clan [*jana*] territories") emerged in northern and northeastern India.

Statecraft and the Ideology of Power, 800–600 BCE

By the sixth century BCE the *janapadas* were close to a cultural, if not a military, conquest of the subcontinent. Supported by the agricultural wealth and trade of the region, their religion spread steadily east and south. Sixteen large states, or *mahajanapadas*, now dominated northern India from the Bay of Bengal to the foothills of the Himalayas. The largest of these, along the Ganges, grew increasingly contentious. Buoyed by large revenues and supported by belief in kingship as divine, their respective quests for domination grew as they absorbed their weaker neighbors. In this respect, as we shall see in Chapter 4, these states shared much in common with their contemporaries, the states of Zhou China.

Centralization and Power among the Ganges States   The growing power and prosperity of the larger states led to increasing centralization. The two wealthiest *mahajanapadas*, Magadha and Kosala, found the route to consolidation through centralized kingdoms supported by the Brahmans, or priests. By the sixth century BCE this combination of state power and religion had produced kings, or *maharajas* who wielded power that was seen as both secular and divine.

Other large states retained systems of government in which power was more diffuse. Scholars sometimes refer to these states, ruled by councils as opposed to kings, as "republics." The most powerful of the republics, the Vajjian (or Vrijian) Confederacy, was ruled by a chief whose authority was derived from a council of representatives of the principal clans. The council members were in turn responsible to local assemblies of clan elders and notables.

Growing economic prosperity coupled with fierce competition among all the states required ever greater efficiency in collecting revenue and spending for defense and pushed them toward either monarchy or absorption. The Vajjian Confederacy, for example, was eventually absorbed by Magadha during its drive for empire in northern India.

Thus, by the sixth century BCE, these states, like the Greek poleis and the states of late Zhou China, were in continual political crisis. Attempts to create a balance of power repeatedly failed as the largest states relentlessly vied for control.

Increasing sophistication in strategy, tactics, and military technology put a premium on manpower and revenue, thus giving the larger states further advantages. By the late fourth century BCE, when these armies faced the threat of invasion by the forces of Alexander the Great and his successor Seleucus, they would number in the hundreds of thousands of men.

The Ideology of Rulership   Warfare conducted by kings with godlike status raised ethical and practical questions about the nature of kingship, the responsibilities of rulers to their subjects, and their role as agents of a universal order. How should the ideal ruler comport himself for the good of his kingdom, subjects, and himself in accordance with his divine mission?

The growing size, wealth, and power of the Ganges states made such questions increasingly important. By 600 BCE all the Gangetic rulers were in the situation later described by the political strategist Kautilya [kaw-TEEL-yuh] of Magadha in his political treatise, the *Arthashastra* [ar-tuh-SHAS-truh]. In this constant war of all against all, says Kautilya, the wise ruler understands that those who encircle him on all sides and "prevail in the territory adjacent to his are. . . known as the enemy." On the other hand, those who control the territory "that is separated from the conqueror's territory by one [namely, the enemy's territory] is the constituent known as friend." Hence, one's policy toward neighboring states should be opportunistic: Attack the weak, seek allies against the strong, bide one's time with equals, and practice duplicity wherever and whenever necessary. As we shall see, there are many parallels with late Zhou Chinese treatises such as Sun Zi's *Art of War*. The prime purpose of such action, however, must always be the welfare of one's subjects by means of the survival and prosperity of the state.

This grim vision of statecraft was tempered by the themes of the epics, composed during the Vedic period. The two most famous epics are the Mahabharata [muh-hah-BAH-ruh-tuh] and the Ramayana [ruh-MAH-yuh-nuh], which were committed to writing only in the third century BCE. The Mahabharata describes the struggles among the descendants of the king Bharat, and the conflicting obligations imposed on the individual by state, society, and religion. The sixth book, the Bhagavad Gita [BUH-guh-vud GEE-tuh] (Song of the Lord), has been called the "Indian gospel" because of its concentration on the balance of ethics and action.

On the eve of a battle in which the enemy army includes his relatives and former companions, Arjuna, the protagonist, agonizes over fighting against his family and friends. His charioteer—the god Krishna in disguise—reminds him of the need to fulfill his duty according to *dharma* [DAR-muh] (literally "that which is firm"). Krishna tells Arjuna that the higher law of dharma demands that he put aside his personal reservations and fulfill his larger obligation to fight and win. If Arjuna forces himself to do his duty because it must be done, abandoning his attachment to the result—whatever it may be—then, according to Krishna, he is acting wisely and advancing the course of the universe.

Illustration from the Mahabharata. The stories of the Mahabharata continue to be among the most popular forms of entertainment in India today. In this 1598 CE painting, Arjuna confronts his relatives on the battlefield.

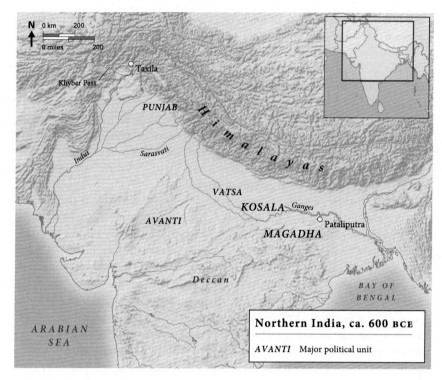

MAP 3.4 **Northern India, ca. 600 BCE**

By about 600 BCE, the largest of the northern Indian states were attempting both to expand southward and to absorb their neighbors along the Ganges. In this volatile political environment, they developed ideologies of kingship and power based on a common understanding of the Vedas and a realistic appraisal of their respective political environments. At once supported and trapped by the idea of dharma as it relates to kingship, they would struggle for the next several centuries until the state of Magadha incorporated the northern third of the subcontinent into an empire (see Map 3.4).

Indian Society, Culture, and Religion, 1500–600 BCE

The first chronicles of Indian history do not make their appearance until well after the beginning of the Common Era. The documentary evidence we have about social history is found in religious and literary texts, law codes, and the collections of folktales and genealogies called the *Puranas* [poor-AH-nuhs] ("legends"), which date from about 500 BCE.

Society and Family in Ancient India

While part of Indian religious thought was increasingly concerned with the nature of the Absolute and ways to connect with it (see Chapter 8), much of the rest dealt with the arrangement of society, law, and duty; the role of the family and its individual members; and relationships between men and women.

Dharma and Social Class   The Bhagavad Gita illustrates the dilemmas of following one's dharma: duty in accordance with one's capabilities and the requirements of one's place in society. Krishna outlines these duties succinctly to Arjuna in Bhagavad Gita passages that closely echo the *varnas*: "Tranquility, control, penance, purity, patience, and honesty, knowledge, judgment, and piety are intrinsic to the action of a priest," he notes, while "heroism, fiery energy, resolve, skill, refusal to retreat in battle, charity, and majesty in conduct are intrinsic to the action of the warrior." The activities that support the subsistence of society such as farming, herding cattle, and commerce "are intrinsic to the action of a commoner," while "action that is essentially service is intrinsic to the servant."

The great majority of Indians fell into Krishna's last two categories. Although one of the distinctive developments in the rise of the Gangetic states had been the rebirth of urban life in India, the village remained the center of the social world for most of the subcontinent's inhabitants. Villagers were organized by clan and *jati*, or **caste** (see "Patterns Up Close").

Rigidly hierarchical, the social system based on *jati* ("to be born into") functioned as a kind of extended family, each with its own clans, villages, local dialects, gods, laws, advisory councils, and craft and work specializations. Thus, as the organization of society became more complex, the ritual importance of the four *varnas* of the Vedas was giving way to the occupational emphasis of *jati*.

As the system expanded south, it incorporated local leaders, clan elders, and other notables into the higher castes. Sometimes entire villages were accorded their own castes on the basis of lineage or occupational specialty. At its peak, the number of castes and subcastes may have exceeded 3,000. As the various peoples of the subcontinent were brought into the structure, the older ritual divisions of the early Vedic era were broken down even further, though their traces remain even to the present.

The force of dharma extended into the personal realm as well. Behavior in village society and the family, and even the possibilities for religious fulfillment, hinged upon carrying out the demands of dharma. These demands varied according to an individual's social standing, gender, and place in the family.

Caste: A system in which people's places in society—how they live, the work they do, and whom they marry—are ascribed by heredity rather than achieved by merit.

Gender Roles: Men and Women in Society   The importance of family life in India is evident in religious scriptures and the law codes, or *smriti* [SMER-tee]. By 600 BCE, *artha* [AHR-tuh], the pursuit of subsistence and prosperity, was recognized as a moral course of action necessary to sustain family position and harmony. For example, the male householder of the upper castes was expected to habitually subordinate his own needs to those of his family and dependents.

The position of women in the Indian family and in Indian society is more difficult to determine. Unswerving loyalty and devotion on the part of wives and daughters was demanded and highly prized. In household matters a wife should be engaged "in the collection and expenditure of. . . (the husband's) wealth, in cleanliness, in dharma, in cooking food for the family, and in looking after the necessities of the household." The position of women in this context, the code says, is "deserving of worship." The reciprocal aspect of the demand for loyalty and devotion, as the Code of Manu advises, is that, "regarding this as the highest dharma of all four classes, husbands. . . must strive to protect their wives."

Women's sexuality was seen as simultaneously compelling and threatening. The idea of *kama*, as encapsulated in the later *Kama Sutra*, included the enjoyment

The Caste System

The *janapadas* developed an interlocking social order based on ethnicity and occupation. As the Vedic peoples settled into northern India, their nomadic society became firmly defined by ritual position and occupational status. There were four *varnas* ("form, shape"; it can also mean "color"): the first three for priests, warriors, and commoners, and a fourth that included both servants and laborers. The origin of the *varnas*, according to the *Rig-Veda*, lay in the seminal sacrifice of the cosmic being Purusha [POO-roo-sha], which gave form to the universe: his mouth became the Brahmans, or priests; his arms became the *kshatriyas* [k(uh)-SHA-tree-yuhs]—kings and warriors; his two thighs the *vaishyas* [VIE-sh(ee)-yuhs], or merchants; and from his two feet came the *shudra*, or peasants, servants, and laborers.

The newcomers' task of establishing themselves as an elite class over the indigenous peoples meant that the system had to accommodate everyone, but with tight restrictions placed on social mobility. Thus, it appears that intermarriage was forbidden between the new elites and the *dasas*, the term used for non-Aryans, and the latter were incorporated into the peasant/laborer/servant *varna*. By the sixth century BCE divisions between Aryans and non-Aryans originally based on ethnicity or locale were giving way to ones based on occupation. An elaborate *jati*, or caste, system was already developing.

Based on the original divisions of the four *varnas*, each caste included a huge number of subcastes according to hereditary occupations. A new category of "excluded" castes—the so-called untouchables (today called Dalits)—was added, comprising people whose occupations were considered ritually unclean. The excluded castes also came to include "outcastes," people who for various offenses had "lost caste" and were therefore placed on the fringes of society. In what was perhaps a

of sex by men and women as part of a balanced social and religious life. In contrast, the material world in general, and sexuality in particular as its most enticing aspect, was also understood to divert a person from fulfilling his or her dharma and to pose a threat to the social and natural order if not properly controlled. The close relationship between society and religion in this regard allowed men to explore ways of going "beyond" the material and sexual world by engaging in solitary, often celibate, religious practices.

On the other hand, it also bolstered the idea that a woman without the protection of a husband or family was a danger to herself and a source of temptation to others. For both men and women, independence from the social system of family, clan, or caste—unless channeled into an approved religious or social practice—was subject to severe sanction. But due to the concept that the family was the foundation of society as a whole and the place of women was at the center of family life, the burdens of supporting the system and the penalties for failing to do so fell far more heavily on women than on men.

Cultural Interactions to 600 BCE

The social system of *varna* and *jati* held together as the religion of the Vedas expanded into the diverse body of beliefs, practices, and philosophy that would later be referred to by outsiders as "Hinduism." The term is derived from the Persian

lingering vestige of early Vedic attempts at ethnic separation, stringent prohibitions were imposed on sexual relations between *shudras* and members of the castes within the first three *varnas*.

The evolving *jati* system expanded southward as the Ganges River states pushed farther into these areas. Eventually, it incorporated villages, clans, and sometimes even entire tribal groups into their own *jatis.* Though highly restrictive in terms of social mobility, these arrangements guaranteed a prescribed place for everyone in society. Moreover, the idea of movement between castes became part of Indian religious traditions through the doctrines of continual rebirth and the transmigration of souls. Thus, the Indian response to the problem of incorporating a multiplicity of ethnic, linguistic, and religious groups into its expanding culture was to create a space in society for each, while ensuring stability by restricting social mobility and encouraging good behavior through the hope of a higher place in the next life. The fact that the system continues today despite its dissolution by the Indian government is testimony to its tenacious cultural roots and long-standing social utility.

Brahmans. At the top of the varna and caste system were the priestly class of Brahmans. Note the sacred thread worn diagonally across the chests of these Brahman men in this 1913 photo. The thread indicates their "twice-born" status.

Questions

- How is the caste system a cultural adaptation?
- How does the persistence of the caste system today demonstrate its social utility?

word *hindu,* taken from the Sanskrit *sindhu,* or "river," in reference to the inhabitants of the Indus Valley.

As the members of the most important *varna,* the prestige of the Brahmans (priests) grew as they monopolized the performance of rituals and sacrifices. The priests maintained the oral tradition of the Vedas, preserving the exact formulas of the old rituals while also creating new ones centered on the needs of a more sedentary, agrarian people. The growing emphasis on the precise details of various rituals spurred the development of education among the men of the upper castes. By the sixth century BCE, the major works of the Vedic and Brahmanic oral tradition were being committed to writing in Sanskrit, from this time forward the sacred language of Indian scriptures (until the Buddhist scriptures in Pali).

Toward New Religious Directions   At the same time, this trend contributed to an increasing belief within the Vedic-Brahmanic tradition that only the precise observance of all the proper forms of ritual behavior could ensure their effectiveness. Since the formulas for these rituals were for the most part accessible only to the upper *varnas* and were considered the special province of the Brahmans, there was considerable social and religious exclusiveness attached to the tradition as well. Indeed, the punishment prescribed for those in lower *varnas* caught overhearing the inner secrets of Brahmanic ritual was to have molten lead poured into their ears.

Asceticism. For millennia great respect has been accorded those who withdraw from the lure of the material world and seek the unchanging within. Here, a modern "world renouncer," or *sannyasi*, is shown.

A movement away from this restrictive view was already apparent by 600 BCE. Instead of appeasing the gods through the precise performance of ritual, some in the upper *varnas* began seeking the forces behind that order and trying to achieve communion with them. Two paths within the Vedic-Brahmanic tradition emerged.

One path was **asceticism**, full or partial renunciation of the material world. The Vedic tradition revered hermits and those who fled society in order to purify themselves. The many schools of ascetic practice held that the distractions of making a living, raising a family, and even the body itself hindered the quest for one's spiritual essence. These schools developed strategies for uncovering the unchanging, and thus real, "self," removed from a world where everything is impermanent and illusory.

The practices of certain schools of *yoga* ("discipline"), for example, were based on the belief that mastery of the body allowed the adept to achieve communion with this inner self. Since the body, as part of the physical world, is subject to constant change, the discipline of postures, breathing, and meditation allows the practitioner to go beyond its limitations and find that which is unchanging within.

The other emerging path to a deeper spiritual reality was scriptural. Between the seventh and fifth centuries—though perhaps from as early as 800 BCE—a group of writings called the Upanishads [uh-PAHN-i-shahds] ("secret knowledge") marked a new direction within the Vedic tradition. The Upanishads represented the Vedanta, the "fulfillment" of the Vedas, in which the hidden symbolism was revealed and inconsistencies were reconciled.

The material world was increasingly regarded as extraneous as well. The individual "self" (*atman*) was ultimately to become identified with the cosmic "essence" (*brahman*—note that this usage is different from the same term used to describe the priestly *varna*).

Karma-Samsara   Such speculation about the nature of individual and universal "essence" was beginning to be reflected in culture and society. Caste, and its accompanying obligations, led to the idea of **karma-samsara**, the transmigration of souls and reincarnation. By the sixth century BCE, the two ideas appear to have been widely accepted. The concept of a nonmaterial essence or "soul" carrying with it the residue of one's deeds—*karma*—is coupled with the idea of the rebirth of the soul into a new body—*samsara*. Successful pursuit of dharma within the context of the caste system ensures an advance in caste

Bathing in the Ganges at Varanasi. The sacred character of rivers in the Indian religious experience may go back all the way to the Harappans. As the multiple religious traditions we know as Hinduism developed in the Ganges valley, that river assumed a position of central importance in terms of ritual purification. Here, bathers are shown on the ghats—steps built on the riverbank—of the city of Varanasi, also known as Benares, site of some of Hinduism's holiest shrines.

in the next life. Ultimately, one achieves *moksha*—release from the karmic cycle—when one is fully able to grasp the principles of *atman: brahman* and *dharma*.

Putting It All Together

In the Indus Valley, as in Egypt and Mesopotamia, the factors required for the transition to agrarian-based cities emerged around 2500 BCE. Yet many questions remain unanswered about how Harappan society worked and why it fell.

Invasion by nomads was formerly seen as the cause. The pattern of struggle between the settled and the nomadic did indeed play out in various parts of the world for thousands of years. However, recent scholarship suggests that for the Harappans, the coming of the nomadic Indo-Europeans may not have had much of an impact, making the questions of interaction and adaptation that much more intriguing.

In India, the interruption in urban life lasted nearly 1,000 years. When cities again arose, they were centered hundreds of miles from the old, now forgotten Harappan sites. Instead of the apparent uniformity of the earlier society, the new one was to be marked by the struggle of individual states for supremacy. Yet, although these Gangetic states lacked political unity, their cultural and religious similarity remained an important factor throughout Indian history. The *jati* system allowed Indian society to adapt to increasing complexity.

Not surprisingly, this unsettled period of interaction and adaptation within the Gangetic societies was marked by widespread questioning of social, political, and religious arrangements. In the India of 600 BCE, the Vedic tradition was steered in new directions through the speculations of the earliest Upanishads. Moreover, amid the diversity of ascetic religious experience, some visionaries were shortly to map the direction of entirely new religious paths. One of these, Buddhism, may be seen as the beginning of a vitally important new pattern of world history.

Asceticism: The full or partial renunciation of the material world.

Karma-samsara: The concept of a nonmaterial essence or "soul" carrying with it the residue of one's deeds—*karma*—coupled with the idea of the rebirth of the soul into a new body—*samsara*.

Review and Relate

Thinking Through Patterns

Examine the ways historians approach the big questions of this chapter.

The mystery of the origins of the Harappans remains unsolved. Most scholars believe their ancestors had been in the Indus region or nearby Baluchistan for millennia. Some also see them as perhaps related to extremely ancient peoples inhabiting the region around modern Kerala. While carbon-14 dating, linguistic tracking, DNA surveys, and sedimentary analysis of ruins have all enhanced our understanding, our inability to decipher the Harappan script means that a key tool for understanding any civilization, the literary record, remains elusive.

❯ Who were the Harappans? Where did they come from? What evidence exists for their origins?

> What explanations have been offered for the collapse of Harappan society? How well do the rival theories hold up, given what scholars and archaeologists have discovered?

Collapse can come from predictable causes—war, famine, ecological degradation—or random ones like earthquakes or volcanic eruptions. The literary record of the Aryans long suggested that they had conquered the Harappans, but this record seems in conflict with more recent discoveries about the flooding patterns of the Indus, the sedimentary analysis of built and rebuilt structures, and salinization levels at various points in the river. As is most often the case, historians generally expect to find no single *sufficient cause*—one that by itself led to the collapse—but rather a number of *necessary causes*—ones that contributed but were not capable of causing the collapse all by themselves.

> How can we know about the newcomers to northern India? What sources exist for historians to examine?

Another ongoing debate revolves around the identity and nature of the newcomers into northern India. Here, as noted in the previous discussion, the literary record of the Vedas, particularly the oldest, the *Rig-Veda*, appears in conflict with much of the archaeological evidence. While the Vedas are clear about where the newcomers ended up, they are vague about where they originated. Indo-European-speaking peoples ranged across Eurasia, which we can tell from the spread of their languages, the technologies associated with them, and as we shall see in the following chapter, their mummified remains at sites in the Tarim Basin in China's extreme west. But because they left little in the way of archaeological sites, piecing together their story from their material culture is extremely challenging.

> What patterns can we see evolving in the Ganges River states that will mark the subsequent development of Indian civilization?

Not all of the early north Indian states were monarchies, but the religious aura of the monarchs and its relationship to the first stirrings of what will become Hinduism is striking. The permeation of society by religion is a pattern that continues to this day, as is the desire for transcending the bounds of the material world through ascetic or scholarly methods. The most pervasive pattern lies in the development of the caste system as the basic social structure of society, which endures even today in the face of a constitutional ban.

Against the Grain

Consider this as a counterpoint to the main patterns examined in this chapter.

A Merchants' Empire?

• What similarities and differences do you see among the Harappans and other river-based agrarian–urban societies?

Patterns of development among the land-based agrarian–urban civilizations of the Mesopotamians, the Egyptians, the Gangetic states, and (as we will see in Chapter 4) the states arising in ancient China depended on rivers for the fertility of their soil, for irrigation, and for transport. Such riverine societies, which need large-scale public works projects to control the rivers on which they depend, develop powerful central governments capable of directing their enormous undertakings. Such governments control vast labor resources and tend to display their power by means of monumental architecture and other visible signs of state and religious unity and harmony.

The exception to this pattern appears to be the Harappan system of cities in the Indus Valley. Although the Indus cities were at least as reliant on the river as the cities of these other agrarian–urban civilizations, we see practically no evidence of a central government of any kind, aside from the striking uniformity of buildings and materials. We see no monumental palaces or tombs. Apart from what may be modest temples and baths, we see little in the way of any kind of state religion or cult, though religious objects themselves are quite numerous. There is little to suggest a large state presence of any kind as reflected in the categories of artifacts found in, say, Egypt or Mesopotamia.

So how did things function? One intriguing (if still unproven) theory suggests that, rather than having a powerful central government and bureaucracy to marshal the resources of the state, the Harappan cities were part of a well-integrated merchants' empire. This possibility is supported in part by the vast amount of trade articles recovered in the Indus region; the many apparent craft workshops and warehouses; the harbor and docking facilities; and by the theory that Harappan writing may in fact be a sophisticated shorthand script used principally by merchants.

If this is indeed the case, it goes "against the grain" not only of the early patterns of riverine civilization but of the trends of world history in general. One thinks of the Republic of Venice, three thousand years later, as another trading empire, run by a merchant aristocracy for the benefit of its traders. It may well have been that the Harappan system was organized and run along similar lines. If so, its size and influence make it unique in its mode of operation—as it appears to have been in so many other ways.

- Based on your reading of this chapter, is there evidence that works against the theory of a "merchants' empire" to explain the apparent differences between the Indus Valley and other early river civilizations?

Key Terms

Ascetism   72
Caste   69
Cesspits   60

Indo-European family of
   languages   63
Karma-samsara   72

Phallic stones   62
Topography   56
Vedas   65

Learn more with this chapter's digital tools, including the Oxford Insight Study Guide, at http://www.oup.com/he/vonsivers4e. Please see the Further Resources section at the back of the book for additional readings and suggested websites.

Sources for Chapter 3

| SOURCE 3.1 | ## The Bhagavad Gita |

ca. 1750–800 BCE, written down in the third century BCE

The Bhagavad Gita comprises the sixth book, and is the central component, of the Mahabharata. Because it centers on the struggles between kings and princes, the Mahabharata can be read as a reflection of the ideological components of rulership in ancient India. At its center is a power struggle between the descendants of two brothers, culminating in a comprehensive war that ends in the victory of one branch of the family over the other. Elements of philosophy, religion, and moral behavior appear throughout the poem, and the concepts of *dharma* (natural law, correct behavior) and chaos are introduced by Krishna, the wise sage who appears at critical moments to explain the wider implications of what seems a simple battle narrative. The speakers in the following excerpt are Dhritarâshtra, a blind king in the midst of a succession crisis; Sañgaya, the visionary narrator of the battle; and Arjuna, one of the five sons of Pandu, the Pandava.

BHAGAVADGÎTÂ. CHAPTER I.

Dh*r*itarâsh*t*ra said:
    What did my (people) and the Pâ*n*davas do, O Sañgaya! when they assembled together on the holy field of Kurukshetra, desirous to do battle?

           . . .

Sañgaya said:
    Thus addressed by Gudâkesa, O descendant of Bharata! Hrishîkesa stationed that excellent chariot between the two armies, in front of Bhîshma and Dro*n*a and of all the kings of the earth, and said, O son of Prithâ! Look at these assembled Kauravas.' There the son of Prithâ saw in both armies, fathers, and grandfathers, preceptors, maternal uncles, brothers, sons, grandsons, companions, fathers-in-law, as well as friends. And seeing all those kinsmen standing (there), the son of Kuntî [Arjuna] was overcome by excessive pity and spake thus despondingly.

Source: *The Bhagavadgita, with the Sanatsugatiya and the Anugita*, trans. Kashinath Trimbak Telang (Oxford: Clarendon, 1882), 37, 39–41, 42, 73–75, 87–88, and 91.

Arjuna said:

Seeing these kinsmen, O Krishna! standing (here) desirous to engage in battle, my limbs droop down; my mouth is quite dried up; a tremor comes on my body; and my hairs stand on end; the Gândîva (bow) slips from my hand; my skin burns intensely. I am unable, too, to stand up; my mind whirls round, as it were; O Kesava! I see adverse omens and I do not perceive any good (to accrue) after killing (my) kinsmen in the battle. I do not wish for victory, O Krishna! nor sovereignty, nor pleasures: what is sovereignty to us, O Govinda! what enjoyments, and even life? Even those, for whose sake we desire sovereignty, enjoyments, and pleasures, are standing here for battle, abandoning life and wealth-preceptors, fathers, sons as well as grandfathers, maternal uncles, fathers-in-law, grandsons, brothers-in-law, as also (other) relatives. These I do not wish to kill, though they kill (me), O destroyer of Madhu! Even for the sake of sovereignty over the three worlds, how much less then for this earth (alone)?

· · ·

Sañgaya said:

Having spoken thus, Arjuna cast aside his bow together with the arrows, on the battle-field, and sat down in (his) chariot, with a mind agitated by grief.

CHAPTER VII.

The Deity said:

O son of Prithâ! now hear how you can without doubt know me fully, fixing your mind on me, and resting in me, and practicing devotion. I will now tell you exhaustively about knowledge together with experience; that being known, there is nothing further left in this world to know. Among thousands of men, only some work for perfection; and even of those who have reached perfection, and who are assiduous, only some know me truly. . . .

There is nothing else, O Dhanañgaya! higher than myself; all this is woven upon me, like numbers of pearls upon a thread. I am the taste in water, O son of Kuntî! I am the light of the sun and moon. I am 'Om' in all the Vedas, sound in space, and manliness in human beings; I am the fragrant smell in the earth, refulgence in the fire; I am life in all beings, and penance in those who perform penance. Know me, O son of Prithâ! to be the eternal seed of all beings; I am the discernment of the discerning ones, and I the glory of the glorious. I am also the strength, unaccompanied by fondness or desire, of the strong. And, O chief of the descendants of Bharata! I am love unopposed to piety among all beings. And all entities which are of the quality of goodness, and those which are of the quality of passion and of darkness, know that they are, indeed, all from me; I am not in them, but they are in me. The whole universe deluded by these three states of mind, developed from the qualities, does not know me, who am beyond them and inexhaustible; for this delusion of mine, developed from the qualities, is divine and difficult to transcend. Those cross beyond this delusion who resort to me alone. Wicked men, doers of evil (acts), who are deluded, who are deprived of their knowledge by (this) delusion, and who incline to the demoniac state of mind, do not resort to me. But, O Arjuna! doers of good (acts) of four classes worship me: one who is distressed, one who is seeking after knowledge, one who wants wealth, and one, O chief of the descendants of Bharata! who is possessed of knowledge. Of these, he who is possessed of knowledge, who is always devoted, and whose worship is (addressed) to one (Being) only, is esteemed highest.

. . .

CHAPTER X.

. . .

Arjuna said:

You are the supreme Brahman, the supreme goal, the holiest of the holy. All sages, as well as the divine sages Nârada, Asita, Devala, and Vyâsa, call you the eternal being, divine, the first god, the unborn, the all-pervading. And so, too, you tell me yourself, O Kesava! I believe all this that you tell me (to be) true; for, O lord! neither the gods nor demons understand your manifestation. You only know yourself by yourself. O best of beings! creator of all things! lord of all things! god of gods! lord of the universe! be pleased to declare without, exception your divine emanations, by which emanations you stand pervading all these worlds. How shall I know you, O you of mystic power! always meditating on you? And in what various entities, O lord! should I meditate on you? Again, O Ganârdana! do you yourself declare your powers and emanations; because hearing this nectar, I (still) feel no satiety.

The Deity said:

. . . I am the rod of those that restrain, and the policy of those that desire victory. I am silence respecting secrets. I am the knowledge of those that have knowledge And, O Arjuna! I am also that which is the seed of all things. There is nothing movable or immovable which can exist without me. O terror of your foes! there is no end to my divine emanations. Here I have declared the extent of (those) emanations only in part. Whatever thing (there is) of power, or glorious, or splendid, know all that to be produced from portions of my energy.

▶ Working with Sources

1. **Why does Arjuna feel compelled to act, despite the competing claims of family ties?**

2. **How does the text develop the theme of supreme knowledge and its power?**

SOURCE 3.2 Prayer to Varuna

Varuna, who seldom appears in Indian religious literature after the Vedic period, was the regulator of the cosmos. It is he who guides the sun and moon and determines the weather—a vital function in a place so dependent on the monsoon cycle. The writer here begs Varuna for forgiveness for an unknown offense and seeks his protection.

Wise are the races [of gods and men] through the greatness of him who propped apart the two wide worlds. He pressed forth the high, lofty vault of heaven and, likewise, the stars. And he spread out the earth [beneath].

In my own person, I speak this together [with him]: "When shall I be in [obedience to] Varuna? Might he take pleasure in my oblation, becoming free of anger? When shall I contentedly look upon his mercy?"

I ask about that trouble, Varuna, desiring to understand; I approach those who know to ask [about it]. The knowing say the same thing to me: "Varuna is now angry with you."

Was the offense so great, Varuna, that you want to crush your friend and praiser? O you who are impossible to deceive, wholly self-sustaining, you will explain this to me. I would swiftly humble myself before you with reverence to be free of guilt.

Release from us the deceits of our ancestors and those that we have done ourselves. Release Vasishtha, O King, like a cattle-stealing thief [from his bondage] or a calf from its rope.

This mistake was not my intention: it was liquor, pride, dice, ignorance. The elder is [caught] in the offense of the younger. Even sleep does not ward off untruth.

Like a slave, I shall serve my master; I, without offending, [shall serve] the angry one. The civilizing god has enlightened those without understanding. The more knowing man hastens to the clever one for riches.

This praise is for you, Varuna, the self-sustaining: may it repose in your heart. May prosperity in peace be ours, prosperity also in war. Protect us always with well-being.

▶ **Working with Sources**

1. Why would the supplicant offering the prayer make the request so personal?

2. How does the nature of the request to Varuna differ from the concepts embodied in the Brihadaranyaka Upanishad below?

Source: Ainslie T. Embree, *Sources of Indian Tradition*, 2nd ed., vol. 1 (New York: Columbia University Press, 1988), 11.

SOURCE 3.3

The Brihadaranyaka Upanishad

ca. 600 BCE

A diverse set of writings, the Upanishads were thought to convey secret knowledge and serve as the *vedanta*, or fulfillment, of the Vedic tradition. Among these documents are the Aranyakas ("forest books"), which may have been recited originally by hermits who had retreated to forests. Throughout the Upanishads one can see the full development of the principle of the joining of the individual self (*atman*, or "soul") with the *brahman*, or "world soul"/"soul essence."

SECOND ADHYÂYA. FIRST BRÂHMAṆA.

1. There was formerly the proud Gârgya Bâlâki, a man of great reading. He said to Agâtasatru of Kâsi, 'Shall I tell you Brahman?' Agâtasatru said: 'We give a thousand (cows) for that speech (of yours), for verily all people run away, saying, Ganaka (the king of Mithilâ) is our father (patron).'

2. Gârgya said: 'The person that is in the sun, that I adore as Brahman.' Agâtasatru said to him: 'No, no! Do not speak to me on this. I adore him verily as the supreme, the head of all beings, the king. Whoso adores him thus, becomes Supreme, the head of all beings, a king.'

3. Gârgya said: 'The person that is in the moon (and in the mind), that I adore as Brahman.' Agâtasatru said to him: 'No, no! Do not speak to me on this. I adore him verily as the great, clad in white raiment, as Soma, the king.' Whoso adores him thus, Soma is poured out and poured forth for him day by day, and his food does not fail.

4. Gârgya said: 'The person that is in the lightning (and in the heart), that I adore as Brahman.' Agâtasatru said to him: 'No, no! Do not speak to me on this. I adore him verily as the luminous.' Whoso adores him thus, becomes luminous, and his offspring becomes luminous.

· · ·

13. Gârgya said: 'The person that is in the body, that I adore as Brahman.' Agâtasatru said to him: 'No, no! Do not speak to me on this. I adore him verily as embodied.' Whoso adores him thus, becomes embodied, and his offspring becomes embodied. Then Gârgya became silent.

14. Agâtasatru said: 'Thus far only?' 'Thus far only,' he replied. Agâtasatru said: 'This does not suffice to know it (the true Brahman).' Gârgya replied: 'Then let me come to you, as a pupil.'

Kshatriya: Second highest of the four *varnas* (castes) in Hindu society.

15. Agâtasatru said: 'Verily, it is unnatural that a Brâhmaṇa should come to a **Kshatriya**, hoping that he should tell him the Brahman. However, I shall make you know him clearly,' thus saying he took him by the hand and rose.

Source: *The Upanishads*, vol. 2, trans. F. Max Müller (Oxford: Clarendon, 1884), 100–101 and 103–105.

And the two together came to a person who was asleep. He called him by these names, 'Thou, great one, clad in white raiment, Soma, King.' He did not rise. Then rubbing him with his hand, he woke him, and he arose.

16. Agâtasatru said: 'When this man was thus asleep, where was then the person (purusha), the intelligent? And from whence did he thus come back?' Gârgya did not know this?

17. Agâtasatru said: 'When this man was thus asleep, then the intelligent person (purusha), having through the intelligence of the senses (prânas) absorbed within himself all intelligence, lies in the ether, which is in the heart. When he takes in these different kinds of intelligence, then it is said that the man sleeps (svapiti). Then the breath is kept in, speech is kept in, the ear is kept in, the eye is kept in, the mind is kept in.

18. But when he moves about in sleep (and dream), then these are his worlds. He is, as it were, a great king; he is, as it were, a great Brâhmana; he rises, as it were, and he falls. And as a great king might keep in his own subjects, and move about, according to his pleasure, within his own domain, thus does that person (who is endowed with intelligence) keep in the various senses (prânas) and move about, according to his pleasure, within his own body (while dreaming).

19. Next, when he is in profound sleep, and knows nothing, there are the seventy-two thousand arteries called Hita, which from the heart spread through the body. Through them he moves forth and rests in the surrounding body. And as a young man, or a great king, or a great Brâhmana, having reached the summit of happiness, might rest, so does he then rest.

20. As the spider comes out with its thread, or as small sparks come forth from fire, thus do all senses, all worlds, all Devas, all beings come forth from that Self. The Upanishad (the true name and doctrine) of that Self is 'the True of the True.' Verily the senses are the true, and he is the true of the true.

▶ Working with Sources

1. How does the text develop the principles of brahman and soma addressed in Chapter 3?

2. What is the responsibility of the king with respect to knowledge?

SOURCE 3.4   *The Code of Manu*

ca. 100–300 CE

The *Code of Manu* deals with many different features of Hindu life, such as the proper behavior of different castes and methods for ritual purification. The "Manu" referred to in the title is the legendary "first man" of Hindu culture, also recognized as the first lawgiver. Thus, the *Code of Manu* is thought of within Hinduism as a text based on human traditions (*smriti*), but it is also believed to be consistent with the values included in texts that are divinely revealed (*shruti*), such as the "Purusha Hymn." As a result, it restates and reaffirms traditional values and structures, but it does so on the basis of religious authority.

The responsibilities described for women in the *Code of Manu* need to be understood within the context of Hinduism. As was discussed in Chapter 3, a central component of Hinduism is the concept of *dharma* ("that which is firm"). Hindus believe that by living up to the religious and social responsibilities attached to one's social position (caste and gender), one sustains the proper order of the universe and gains good *karma*, moving up the scale of reincarnation toward unity with the *brahman*, or World Soul. Composed following a period of unrest, the *Code of Manu* represents a vigorous attempt to reestablish order within the Hindu world.

Hear now the duties of women.

By a girl, by a young woman, or even by an aged one, nothing must be done independently, even in her own house.

Her lord is dead to her sons; a woman must never be independent.

She must not seek to separate herself from her father, husband, or sons; by leaving them she would make both (her own and her husband's) families contemptible.

She must always be cheerful, clever in (the management of her) household affairs, careful in cleaning her utensils, and economical in expenditure.

Him to whom her father may give her, or her brother with the father's permission, she shall obey as long as he lives, and when he is dead, she must not insult (his memory)....

[B]etrothal (by the father or guardian) is the cause of (the husband's) dominion (over his wife).

The husband who wedded her with sacred texts, always gives happiness to his wife, both in season and out of season, in this world and in the next.

Though destitute of virtue, or seeking pleasure (elsewhere), or devoid of good qualities, (yet) a husband must be constantly worshipped as a god by a faithful wife.

No sacrifice, no vow, no fast must be performed by women apart (from their husbands); if a wife obeys her husband, she will for that (reason alone) be exalted in heaven.

Source: *The Law of Manu*, in *The Sacred Books of the East*, vol. 25, trans. G. Bühler (Oxford: Clarendon, 1886), 194–197, 328–330, 332, 335, 344–345.

A faithful wife, who desires to dwell (after death) with her husband, must never do anything that might displease him who took her hand, whether he be alive or dead. . . . [L]et her emaciate her body by (living on) pure flowers, roots, and fruit; but she must never even mention the name of another man after her husband has died.

Until death let her be patient (of hardships), self-controlled, and chaste, and strive (to fulfill) that most excellent duty which (is prescribed) for wives who have one husband only. A virtuous wife who after the death of her husband constantly remains chaste, reaches heaven, though she have no son, just like those chaste men.

By violating her duty towards her husband, a wife is disgraced in this world, (after death) she enters the womb of a jackal, and is tormented by diseases (the punishment of) her sin. . . .

[A] female who controls her thoughts, speech, and actions, gains in this (life) highest renown, and in the next (world) a place near her husband.

Women must particularly be guarded against evil inclinations, however trifling (they may appear); for, if they are not guarded, they will bring sorrow on two families. . . . No man can completely guard women by force; but they can be guarded by the . . . (following) expedients: Let the (husband) employ his (wife) in the collection and expenditure of his wealth, in keeping (everything) clean, in (the fulfillment of) religious duties, in the preparation of his food, and in looking after the household utensils. Women, confined in the house under trustworthy and obedient servants, are not (well) guarded; but those who of their own accord keep guard over themselves, are well guarded. . . .

Through their passion for men, through their mutable temper, through their natural heartlessness, they become disloyal towards their husbands, however carefully they may be guarded in this (world).

(When creating them) Manu allotted to women (a love of their) bed, (of their) seat and (of) ornament, impure desires, wrath, dishonesty, malice, and bad conduct. . . . The production of children, the nurture of those born, and the daily life of men, (of these matters) woman is visibly the cause.

Offspring, (the due performance of) religious rites, faithful service, highest conjugal happiness and heavenly bliss for the ancestors and oneself, depend on one's wife alone.

He only is a perfect man who consists (of three persons united), his wife, himself, and his offspring; thus (says the Veda), and (learned) Brahmanas propound this (maxim) likewise, "The husband is declared to be one with the wife." . . .

The husband receives his wife from the gods, (he does not wed her) according to his own will; doing what is agreeable to the gods, he must always support her (while she is) faithful.

"Let mutual fidelity continue until death," this may be considered as the summary of the highest law for husband and wife.

▶ Working with Sources

1. According to the code, how should men relate to women? In what ways are men asked, in their relationships with women, to keep order?

2. How are women rewarded for behaving the way the code instructs them to? How are the rewards connected with the Hindu belief in reincarnation and karma?

World Period One

From Human Origins to Early Agricultural Centers, Prehistory to 600 BCE

Humans appeared late in the evolution of the world. While the earth is 4.5 billion years old, the first human-like beings only appeared about 6 million years ago, and modern humans did not appear in East Africa until about 100,000 years ago. These humans migrated from there to Eurasia and Australia 80,000–60,000 years ago and to the Americas 17,500–14,600 years ago.

As people became more numerous, human culture became more differentiated. The triad of origins-interactions-adaptations as the fundamental pattern in world history took shape. Human ingenuity and interaction with the environment in the Middle East, Asia, Europe, Australia, and the Americas led to vastly different adaptations. Foraging originated in Africa. Farming, urbanization, and state formation originated in the Middle East. In the Americas, humans fashioned similarly differentiated livelihoods and political structures. Australia's poorer natural environment slowed its differentiation process.

Chapter 4

Agrarian Centers and the Mandate of Heaven in Ancient China

5000–481 BCE

CHAPTER FOUR PATTERNS

Origins, Interactions, and Adaptations While Neolithic cultures arose in several areas in China, the most studied of these have been along the Yellow River plain. Here the Yangshao and Longshan cultures arose, ultimately giving rise to China's first agrarian–urban societies. The first written records tell of three dynasties, Xia, Shang, and Zhou, each supplanting the other and justifying their conquests by claiming the Mandate of Heaven. Though interactions with outside peoples were limited, contacts with nomads brought horse and chariot technologies. As in other riverine societies, the Yellow River cultures continually battled its propensity to flood.

Uniqueness and Similarities China's comparative isolation allowed its cultures to be largely self-fashioning. In architecture, city planning, bronze and jade work, and writing, they are unique among the early riverine civilizations. Except for the cultures within China and the sporadic contacts with nomads, there was little diffusion and acculturation from outside.

Despite this relative isolation, early Chinese states expanded their territories and their culture; by 600 BCE they were beginning to influence peoples on their periphery. The demands of flood control encouraged state-sponsored projects, and the introduction of wet rice agriculture brought rapid population growth.

The twenty-first Shang king, Wu Ding, prepared to commune with his ancestors about his wife's pregnancy. Fu (Lady) Hao was his favorite (and most powerful) wife. Well educated and highly capable as an administrator, Fu Hao had even on occasion led Shang armies in the field. Now she was entrusted with what Wu Ding and his court considered to be the most important duty of all: continuing the line of Shang kings. These kings believed that the past, present, and future rulers of their line formed an unbroken continuum, with the deceased existing in a spirit realm accessible to the living by ritual divination. Therefore, Wu Ding, whose concern for Fu Hao and her unborn child was paramount, sought the advice of the ancestors about her condition and that of her child to come. Wu Ding and his chief diviner, Que [chway], intoned their questions and held a cleaned and dried shoulder blade of an ox over heat. The diviner then tapped it carefully with a bronze rod and attempted to read the meaning of the cracks as they appeared in the hot bone. As a final step, they incised Que's name as diviner, the date, the question, and the ancestors' response into the bone as a permanent record of the inquiry.

Que's reading of the cracks was: "It is bad; it will be a girl." Although this was considered disappointing because of the desire for a male heir, Fu Hao remained Wu Ding's most beloved wife until her death, after which the king continued to seek her advice through oracle bones. Her tomb, one of the most completely preserved from the Shang era, tells us a great deal about society and gender, economics and trade, and the origins and interactions of Chinese states among themselves and with neighboring peoples.

Like Harappa along the Indus, the Shang state also developed along a river, China's Yellow River. But while Harappa and the other cities of the Indus all but disappeared, the Shang and subsequent dynasties developing in China's Yellow River valley have profoundly influenced East and

CHAPTER OUTLINE

The Origins of Yellow River Cultures, 5000–1766 BCE

The Interactions of Shang and Zhou History and Politics, 1766–481 BCE

Economy, Society, and Family Adaptation in Ancient China

Interactions of Religion, Culture, and Intellectual Life in Ancient China

Putting It All Together

ABOVE: Bronze bells, such as these examples from the fifth century BCE, were used as musical accompaniments in Zhou religious ceremonies.

Seeing Patterns

❯ How did the interplay of environment and climate help to influence the earliest patterns of Chinese civilization? How do historians address the question of whether "geography is destiny" in this case?

❯ What can the remains of Neolithic Chinese settlements tell us about the continuities and disruptions of Chinese history?

❯ How did the Zhou concept of the Mandate of Heaven operate?

Southeast Asia to the present day. Unlike the history of India, the political and cultural experience of China was marked by relatively little outside influence and thousands of years of centralized rule. Moreover, for the great majority of its history, China would be perhaps the world's greatest exporter of ideas and goods.

The Origins of Yellow River Cultures, 5000–1766 BCE

Over the centuries, the origins and development of some of China's first Neolithic cultures took place along the Yellow River and the Wei River. China's most famous Neolithic village lies at Banpo on the Wei, and the area where the Yellow and Wei converge features burial mounds from China's early village and town cultures. Nearby is the modern city of Xi'an [SHE-ahn], the capital of no fewer than 13 Chinese regimes during its long history. Here, too, is the famous tomb complex of China's first emperor, Qin Shi Huangdi [CHEEN shuhr HWANG-dee], packed with thousands of life-sized terra-cotta soldiers.

Geography and Climate

China's natural boundaries have had a profound effect on its history and society. As with India, the Himalayas and Pamirs along the southern border of Tibet mark one natural barrier. River systems have also represented past borders, though not impermeable ones. In addition, the northern and western deserts—the Gobi, Ordos, and Taklamakan—have served as natural boundaries.

These geographical features have limited the principal avenues of outside interaction to the narrow corridor running west of Xi'an, south of Mongolia, and north of the modern province of Qinghai [CHING-high], spanning the routes of the famous Silk Road. Like the Khyber Pass in India, this opening has historically been the main avenue into China; unlike the Khyber, however, it has seldom been an invasion route for outsiders. While the origins and early development of ancient China were more isolated than those of the other Eurasian centers of civilization, the relative absence of interaction with outside competitors facilitated both cultural and political unification.

China's climate is more varied than that of India. The area south of the Qin [cheen] Mountains marks the northern boundary of the region regulated by the monsoon, with warm temperatures and abundant summer rainfall. The suitability of the southern regions for rice cultivation resulted in rapid growth and high population density there, as in the Gangetic societies of India. Above the monsoon line, temperatures and rainfall amounts are influenced more by the weather systems of the Eurasian interior. Thus, northern China is subject to blistering summers and frigid winters with low precipitation.

As a result, China's population has historically been concentrated in the plains along the major river valleys and along the coast. Three main river systems—the Pearl River (Zhujiang) in the south, the Yangzi [YAHNG-zuh] River (at 3,988 miles, the third longest in the world), and the Yellow River (Huanghe)—where the most influential early Chinese societies developed, have remained the primary avenues of agriculture and commerce (see Map 4.1).

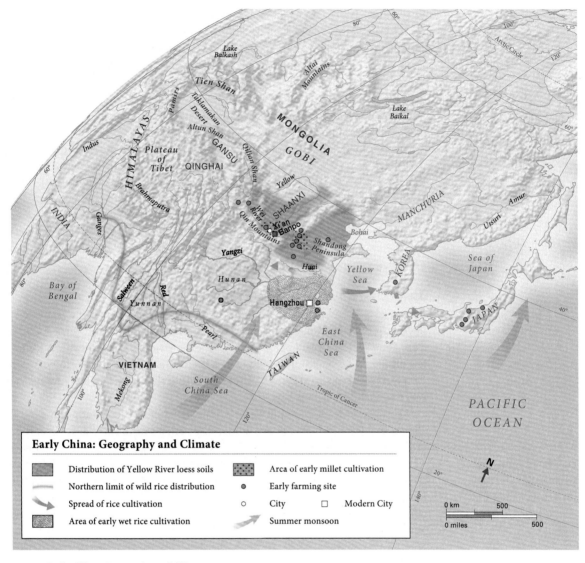

Early China: Geography and Climate

▬ Distribution of Yellow River loess soils	▨ Arca of early millet cultivation
╱ Northern limit of wild rice distribution	● Early farming site
➤ Spread of rice cultivation	○ City □ Modern City
▨ Area of early wet rice cultivation	➤ Summer monsoon

MAP 4.1 Early China: Geography and Climate

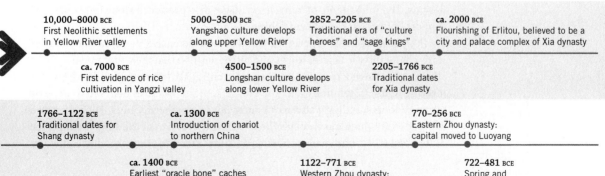

10,000–8000 BCE
First Neolithic settlements
in Yellow River valley

ca. 7000 BCE
First evidence of rice
cultivation in Yangzi valley

5000–3500 BCE
Yangshao culture develops
along upper Yellow River

4500–1500 BCE
Longshan culture develops
along lower Yellow River

2852–2205 BCE
Traditional era of "culture
heroes" and "sage kings"

2205–1766 BCE
Traditional dates
for Xia dynasty

ca. 2000 BCE
Flourishing of Erlitou, believed to be a
city and palace complex of Xia dynasty

1766–1122 BCE
Traditional dates for
Shang dynasty

ca. 1300 BCE
Introduction of chariot
to northern China

770–256 BCE
Eastern Zhou dynasty:
capital moved to Luoyang

ca. 1400 BCE
Earliest "oracle bone" caches
with archaic Chinese writing

1122–771 BCE
Western Zhou dynasty:
capital located at Xi'an

722–481 BCE
Spring and
Autumn period

The Yellow River   Rising in the highlands of Gansu and flowing north to the Ordos Desert, the Yellow River then turns south and east out of Inner Mongolia for 500 miles before making its bend to the east and the sea, a total distance of about 3,000 miles. The mineral-rich soil it picks up as it flows gives it a yellowish tint, hence its name. As with the Nile in Egypt, the rich soil carried by the river has brought abundantly productive agriculture to arid northern China, but as with the Indus, the constant buildup of silt in the riverbed also causes it to overflow its banks and devastate fields and villages in its path.

This building up and bursting of natural levees, along with earthquakes and occasional human actions, have caused the Yellow River to change course 26 times over the last 3,000 years. Efforts to control the river have a prominent place in the mythology, history, and political and social organization of the region. For example, Yu, the supposed founder of the Xia dynasty, was said to have labored for decades to control the river's rampages. Thus, despite its gift of fertility over the course of thousands of years, the Yellow River's unpredictable nature has prompted writers to sometimes refer to it as "China's sorrow."

The Origins of Neolithic Cultures

Between 70,000 and 20,000 years ago, modern *Homo sapiens* became established in eastern Eurasia. Human communities ranged across north and central China from about 30,000 years ago, marking an extensive foraging culture. Within a few millennia of the last glacial retreat, settlements began to appear in northern China containing the first traces in the region of the transition from forager to agrarian society.

Millet: A species of grass cultivated for its edible white seeds and as hay for animal feed.

Agriculture developed quickly in China. Sites of rice cultivation in central China, dating to 7000 BCE, are among the earliest in the world. Even earlier, **millet** was being grown in the north. Recent work suggests that early strains of wheat and barley, perhaps spreading from areas around the Fertile Crescent, may also have been grown. Chickens, pigs, sheep, cattle, and dogs were also widely raised. Areas along the Yellow River contain some of the earliest agricultural villages in China, and several prototypical cultures emerged here and along the North China Plain over the next several thousand years.

Banpo Village   Perhaps the most studied of the thousands of Neolithic sites across China is Banpo Village, located on the outskirts of Xi'an. Banpo Village is representative of Yangshao [yahng-shaow], or "painted pottery," culture, which flourished from 5000 to 3500 BCE. Although the potter's wheel had not yet been introduced from western Eurasia, Yangshao communities like Banpo had sophisticated kilns that fired a variety of clay vessels painted with animal and geometric designs. The inhabitants of Yangshao villages also produced stone implements to support hunting, farming, and fishing.

The perimeter of Banpo is surrounded by a defensive ditch, rather than the walls characteristic of later towns and cities, with 40 thatched-roof homes of mud and straw arranged around a rectangular central structure believed to be a clan meeting house or religious site. The village contains features believed to be early forms of long-standing patterns of rural life in northern China, such as raised clay beds with flues laid through them—an early version of the *kang* [kahng], the heated bed still found in older northern Chinese farming homes today. Silkworm cocoons and crude needles suggest the early development of silk weaving. Especially interesting are the pot shards bearing stylized pictures of animals and geometric markings that some Chinese scholars have speculated may be ancestral forms of the Chinese written language.

Longshan Culture   Settled life in villages and towns appears to have expanded during the Longshan period from about 4000 to 2000 BCE. The earliest distinct Longshan artifacts have now been dated from as far back as 4500 BCE. A later branch of Longshan culture based in what is now Henan [heh-nahn] Province is also believed to have arisen around 2000 BCE, lasting until about 1500 BCE, when it was absorbed by the Shang dynasty.

Like their Yangshao counterparts, Longshan potters were highly skilled. The black-colored pottery associated with Longshan culture is particularly refined. The introduction of the potter's wheel from the west in the mid-third millennium BCE—one of the earliest indications of late Neolithic Chinese interactions with other peoples—permitted unprecedented precision, while improved kilns and experimentation with kaolin clays began a process of ceramic innovation that ultimately resulted in the first porcelain thousands of years later.

After 2000 BCE, the Longshan and other late Neolithic cultures began a transition to a society marked by large towns and small cities supported by agriculture. Towns of several thousand inhabitants have been uncovered, and a number of sites contain elaborate altars. The use of gold, copper, bronze, and jade in jewelry is also increasingly evident. Craft specialization and emerging social classes are detectable.

Beyond the North China Plain   In the regions below the Yangzi River basin in central China, the most extensive distinctive culture is that of Dapenkeng, which flourished from 5000 to 2500 BCE. Artifacts including pot shards, arrowheads, and polished tools and axes indicate a sophisticated coastal and riverine society along a corridor from the borders of modern Vietnam along the south China coast to Fujian Province and across the Taiwan Strait to the western coast of that island.

The extent of Dapenkeng culture and the similarity of its artifacts over a wide area suggest interaction with peoples throughout the region. The origins of this culture appear to be quite different from those of the north. Linguists generally agree that this area was part of a Proto-Austronesian-speaking region, one whose parent language was distinct from the Sino-Tibetan language group that contains the various Chinese dialects and that had strong links to the Austronesian speakers on modern Taiwan. Scholars studying the origins of the Polynesian language family—which is part of the Austronesian group—are searching for links with these people on Taiwan and along the China coast.

Painted Pottery, or Yangshao, Earthenware Basin Found at Banpo Site. Contrast and compare this piece with the one from Longshan (p. 82). What similarities and differences can you spot?

Dawenkou Longshan Black Pottery Stemcups, ca. 2500 BCE. Note the elegant shaping and fine detail that made these early vessels widely imitated in centuries to come.

Origins of Rice Cultivation   The most far-reaching innovation in the regions south of the North China Plain was the development of widespread rice cultivation, which likely originated in Southeast Asia and the area extending from China's modern province of Hunan to the coastal reaches of the Yangzi River. Southeast Asia remained an important source of new rice strains that allowed China's food production to keep pace with its population until well into the nineteenth century. Other food sources domesticated elsewhere making their appearance in Neolithic south China include chickens and cattle, especially the water buffalo. Cattle were raised primarily for farm work rather than consumption.

Toward a Chinese Culture   While it was long believed that Chinese civilization originated in and expanded outward from the Yellow River valley cultures, scholars now suggest that around 3000 BCE the area approximating modern China consisted of a collection of agrarian communities that remained distinct in their own right but whose interactions with each other resulted in cultural elements that ultimately became identified as "Chinese." Though scholars have filled in much of the picture of these ancient cultures, the precise time and duration of their transition to one marked by cities is still debated. Chinese chroniclers, however, drawing upon the world's largest and longest literary record, have long given pride of place in this regard to their first three dynasties: the Xia, Shang, and Zhou.

The Age of Myth and the Xia Dynasty, 2852–1766 BCE

The Chinese are a historically minded people. For thousands of years, the use of writing for purposes of record keeping has been of paramount importance, and the written word itself was considered to have a kind of inner power. For millennia, the careful study and writing of history have been vital elements of individual self-cultivation as well as key mechanisms for political and social control (see "Patterns Up Close").

Among the earliest collections of Chinese writings we have are those of the *Shujing* [SHOO-jing]. Also known as the *Book of History* or *Classic of Documents*, the *Shujing,* a compilation of material purportedly from 2357 to 631 BCE, is a principal documentary source for information about China's first three dynasties: the Xia [shee-AH], Shang [shahng], and Zhou [joe].

Culture Heroes and Sage Kings   According to Chinese legend, mythical culture heroes and sage kings reigned from 2852 to 2205 BCE and introduced many of China's basic elements and institutions. Among the contributions attributed to the first culture heroes were medicine, divination, writing, agriculture, fire, and silkworm cultivation. The three sage kings—Yao, Shun, and Yu—whose reigns followed the culture heroes set the example for strong moral leadership. They are credited with passing the role of leadership on to the most worthy men instead of to their own family members.

Between Myth and History   The *Shujing* acclaims Yu, the last sage king, as the tamer of the Yellow River. He is also traditionally considered to be the founder of the Xia dynasty in 2205 BCE. Because of the difficulty in establishing a clear archaeological record, however, Yu and his successors have largely remained suspended between myth and history.

Moreover, as the sole literary account we have of the period, the *Shujing* has assumed a dominant and, most likely, misleading role as the master narrative of ancient Chinese history. Some scholars have even argued that the Xia were an invention of the Zhou. More recently, some have suggested that their rule was in fact a kind of Shang mythology. On the other hand, some, notably a group of Chinese archaeologists, have noted that the relative accuracy of the dates given in the *Shujing* for events in the Shang dynasty suggests a similar level of reliability for its accounts of the earlier Xia.

Recent archaeological work has moved closer to confirming the historical existence of a widespread culture, if not yet a state, corresponding to the literary accounts of the Xia. Artifacts, particularly early bronze ritual vessels, appear throughout regions described in the *Shujing* as belonging to the Xia and, in some cases, considerably beyond it.

Xia Society   Much of what is known about the Xia is based on the premise that the Xia was a transitional society, building on the material culture of the late Longshan and Yangshao cultural periods. Of particular note in this transition are the growing importance of bronze casting, the increasingly complex symbols on pottery, and the widespread evidence of large-scale efforts at flood control.

As we have seen, the Yangshao and Longshan cultures stretched across a continuum from small hunting, fishing, and farming villages to substantial agriculturally supported towns. The Xia, however, appear to have reached the tipping point at which most of the hallmarks of urban society began to appear. For example, excavation at the Erlitou [AR-lee-toe] site in southern Shaanxi Province, dated to perhaps 2000 BCE, reveals a walled city of moderate size containing what is believed to be the foundation of China's first palace.

Literary evidence suggests that Xia leaders exercised a strong family- or clan-based rule, and the archaeological evidence seems to support this. Evidence indicating the role of the elites as mediators with the spirit world, and particularly with the ancestors of Xia rulers, is also found at Erlitou. China's first bronze ritual vessels, as well as jade figurines, turquoise jewelry, the world's earliest lacquered wood items, and cowry shells (a medium of exchange monopolized by the Xia rulers) all testify to their leaders' religious and social roles. As with a number of Longshan sites, cemeteries outside the city suggest the development of social classes in the number and kind of burial artifacts and the position and richness of elite plots.

Though the boundaries of Chinese history have been pushed back considerably by such work, the Xia remain, like their contemporaries the Harappans, an elusive—if perhaps not a "lost"—civilization. For at least one leading scholar, however, the findings at Erlitou represent not merely a regional variation among many ancient cultures, but "an early form of Chinese civilization" (Sarah Allen, "Erlitou and the Formation of Chinese Civilization," *Journal of Asian Studies*, 66:2 [May, 2007]: 490).

The Interactions of Shang and Zhou History and Politics, 1766–481 BCE

The Shang dynasty represents the first genuine flowering of urban society in East Asia, featuring the attributes of such cultures elsewhere: metallurgy, a varied agricultural base, an increasingly centralized political and religious system, growing **social stratification**, a written language, and cities. In all of these areas the Shang made considerable contributions; in some, they were startlingly original.

Social stratification: A hierarchical arrangement of groups or classes within a society—for example, peasants, merchants, officials, ministers, rulers.

The Shang Dynasty, 1766–1122 BCE

Unlike the idealized rule of the sage kings depicted in the *Shujing*, Shang social and political organization was kinship-based, with an emphasis on military power and efficiency of command. As in Mesopotamia, the advent of cities required rulers to wield greater power for defense and internal regulation, while appealing to an authority beyond human power for legitimacy. Thus, loyalty was pledged to the Shang king and his family. Members of the king's extended family controlled political and religious power, with more distant relatives acting as court officials.

Among the Shang kings mentioned in literary records, rulership often passed from uncle to nephew, though sometimes it went from elder brother to younger. Unlike in the Aryan system of *varna*, there was no rigidly defined priestly class, though spirit mediums and diviners were widely used by Shang rulers. Local leaders who controlled walled cities and towns and their surrounding lands were employed by the ruling families as regional officials, as were specially designated Shang allies. Though small compared to the forces commanded by their successors, the armies fielded by Shang rulers were the most powerful in East Asia in their day (see Map 4.2).

The Introduction of the Chariot   One of the most exciting finds of the last several decades has been the complete mummified remains of a number of men and women believed to be speakers of Tocharian, an Indo-European language, in western China's Tarim Basin. Among them are men with brown hair, tattoos, wearing trousers and garments with tartan plaid patterns; and women with red hair and assorted ornaments of a type found in widely scattered areas of Eurasia. Some of the mummies have been dated to 2000 BCE. Though no chariots have been found with them, their garments and artifacts suggest the use of horses.

The chariot was possibly introduced to China through interaction with these people, around 1300 to 1200 BCE. Chariots were shortly preceded by the introduction of the horse from the west, an innovation that had already revolutionized transport and warfare through much of Eurasia. The small Mongolian ponies native to the northern reaches of Shang lands were not useful as transport or draft animals, but the larger and faster steeds of central

Shang Weapon. A bronze ceremonial axe head with intricate decorative markings, from the thirteenth to the eleventh century BCE.

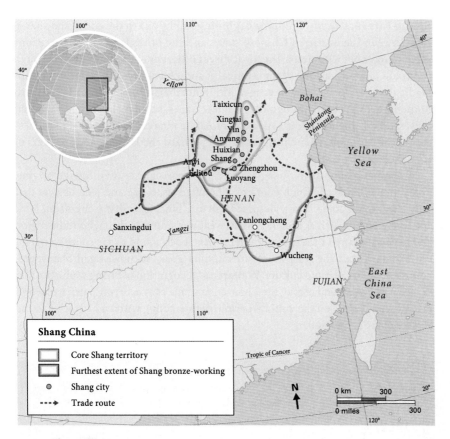

MAP 4.2 **Shang China**

and western Eurasia were to remain important items of trade for the Chinese for thousands of years.

Shang chariots were pulled by two horses and generally held three men. Detachable wheels held by linchpins permitted easy storage and repair. Both charioteers and infantry wielded large composite bows that curved away from the archer in their unstrung state for additional power. As with other ancient peoples, the combination of archers with the chariot gave Shang forces considerable striking power, especially when employed against infantry formations.

Shang Politics and Foreign Relations   Because their prestige depended on their military power and harmony with their ancestors, the Shang rulers constantly mounted campaigns for sacrificial victims—both material and human. Archaeological evidence and oracle bone inscriptions suggest that the greater part of Shang foreign relations with **client states** and allies consisted of enforcing tribute and labor service. Shang kings, especially Wu Ding, led expeditions against settled peoples to the west, the most prominent of whom, the Zhou, based around modern Xi'an, were ultimately enlisted as allies and clients. Wu Ding's successors met with less success, however, and over time shifting coalitions of former allies and client states began to encroach on Shang lands.

Client states: States that are dependent on or partially controlled by more powerful ones.

Shang Interactions   From the beginnings of the Xia to the end of the Shang, ties between the northern Chinese states and the other Eurasian civilizations seem to have been tenuous. The most direct links appear to have been through the trade and migrations of an ethnically and culturally diverse group of no-madic–pastoral peoples who ranged along northern Eurasia from Ukraine to Manchuria in the east. Though they left few traces, scholars have theorized that these nomads included both speakers of Altaic languages—the distant ances-tors of the Mongols, Manchus, Turks, and perhaps the Huns—and speakers of Indo-European ones.

A number of objects in Shang tombs carry clear signs of their foreign origins. For example, Fu Hao's tomb contains a number of bronze and jade objects that only later would come into widespread use in China. The Shang circulated local and foreign items such as bronze vessels, weapons, and jade throughout the region and beyond. Many of these foreign items have been found as far south as north-ern Vietnam, and the peoples of surrounding areas acknowledged Shang pre-dominance in wealth and culture. Widespread recognition of Shang sophistication marks, with the ascendancy of the Zhou, an example of a recurring pattern of world history: conquerors on the cultural periphery interacting with and adapting to the culture of the conquered.

Shang Chariot. Whether used for battle or state functions, Shang-era chariots were distinctive in their wide stance, roominess, and portability. The photograph shows a careful reconstruction of a Shang chariot with authentic bronze decorations and lacquered finish. Note the linchpins holding the wheels to the axles. These could be quickly removed for ease in changing wheels or breaking down the chariot in order to carry its parts separately.

The Mandate of Heaven: The Zhou Dynasty to 481 BCE

Unlike the Xia and Shang dynasties, the nearly nine centuries of Zhou rule are extensively documented in literary works. Like the *Shujing*, these other Zhou records contain much of uncertain origin. Nevertheless, they suggest both an ongoing quest for social, political, and moral order and institutional and intellectual experimentation. They also provide us, in the closing date of the *Spring and Autumn Chronicles* (481 BCE), with an important transition point with which to end this chapter. As we will see in Chapter 9, out of the increasingly fierce competition among the Zhou states for expansion and survival in the succeeding Warring States period came China's ultimate unification into an empire that would last, with brief interruptions, for over 2,000 years.

The Mandate of Heaven   By the twelfth century BCE, the size of the Shang state had shrunk considerably due to encroachment by peoples to the north and west. Oracle bones also suggest an increased concentration of power in the hands of the last Shang kings, a situation coinciding with their dissolution and corruption. Against this backdrop, the state of Zhou to the west—which had become a Shang dependency—took military action. The *Shujing* tells of the Zhou kings pushing their holdings eastward from 1122 BCE, taking much of the Shang territory under their control. Sometime around 1045 BCE, Zhou forces captured and burned the last Shang capital and stronghold near Anyang. The Zhou sought to portray their conquest as morally justified by Shang decadence (see Map 4.3).

Conquest by one of the three earliest Zhou dynasties, as depicted in the literary record, did not mean exile, extinction, or enslavement for those defeated. On the contrary, the conquerors were shown as presenting their victories as acts of moral renewal by ridding the conquered of oppressive or degenerate rulers and restoring leadership to the worthy. The idealized speeches of the new rulers in the *Shujing* attempt to justify their actions and seek the cooperation of all classes in the new order.

As the compilers of this literary record, the Zhou sought to place themselves firmly within it. While it is unknown whether the practices they recorded had been widespread or were newly invented by the conquerors, they provided the backdrop for one of China's most enduring historical and philosophical concepts: the **Mandate of Heaven**.

According to this idea, a dynasty's right to rule depends on the moral correctness of its rulers. Over time, dynasties grow weaker and

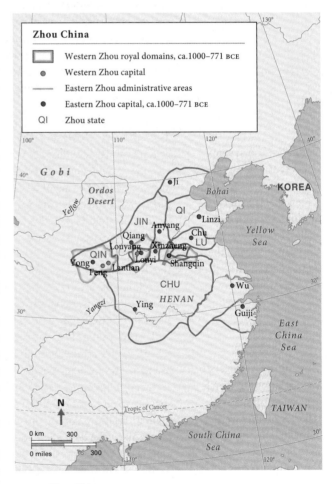

Zhou China

▭ Western Zhou royal domains, ca.1000–771 BCE

● Western Zhou capital

— Eastern Zhou administrative areas

● Eastern Zhou capital, ca.1000–771 BCE

QI Zhou state

MAP 4.3 **Zhou China**

Mandate of Heaven:
Philosophical concept
that developed in China
in which a dynasty's
right to rule depends on
the moral correctness of
its rulers.

tend to become corrupt. Under such conditions, rebellion from within or conquest by outside forces becomes morally justified. The success of such actions is then seen as proof that heaven's approval or "mandate" has been taken from the old rulers and bestowed on the insurgents, who may then legitimately found a new dynasty. Ultimately, however, the new dynasty, too, will decline. The idea of such a "dynastic cycle" operating as the driving force of history was later codified by court historians during the Han dynasty (202 BCE–220 CE).

Throughout Chinese history, these concepts not only allowed political renewal to take place internally but framed a remarkably durable system within which the Chinese and outside conquerors could maintain governmental and societal continuity.

Western Zhou and Eastern Zhou   By the end of the eleventh century BCE, nearly all of northern China had come under Zhou rule, marking the beginning of the Western Zhou era, which lasted until 771 BCE. Zhou rulers placed family, distinguished subjects, allies, and even some defeated Shang notables in leadership positions of these territories. By the eighth century BCE, however, the more powerful of these territories had begun to consolidate their holdings into states of their own. Though the states would continue to pledge their loyalty to the Zhou court, this resulted in a weakening of Zhou political power. A half century of war among court factions for ultimate rule, border struggles with nomadic peoples to the west and north, and a devastating earthquake further weakened Zhou power, resulting in the court being driven from its capital at Xi'an in 771 BCE and relocating to the east in Luoyang. This forced move began the Eastern Zhou period (770–256 BCE).

The Zhou in Decline   The Zhou system of decentralized government called *fengjian* [fung-jien], usually rendered as "**feudalism**," gave autonomy to its local rulers and thus contributed to the weakening of the Zhou central government and the strengthening of its dependent states. As these dependent states grew in power, local rulers became less loyal to the Zhou leadership.

Feudalism: A system
of decentralized
government in
which rule is held by
landowners who owe
obligations of loyalty and
military service to their
superiors and protection
to those under them.

The prestige of the Zhou court was further weakened after its flight to the relatively isolated Luoyang in 770 BCE. Continuing border problems with nomadic–pastoral peoples to the north and west around the Zhou home state and the isolation of its new capital drastically cut the flow of revenue from the dependent domains. This isolation was important, since these states were in a period of economic expansion. Within a few generations of the inauguration of the Eastern Zhou in 770 BCE, Zhou power had significantly weakened.

During the mid-seventh century, the most important of these states was Qi [chee], which dominated northeast China and much of Shandong. Through diplomacy and military power, Qi became the first "senior," or *ba* [bah], state in a system of **hegemony** in which the lesser Zhou states deferred to the *ba* state. The successive *ba* states mounted alliances against non-Zhou states and attempted to regulate relations among those within the system. Qi was succeeded by Jin, which reorganized the *ba* system and, in 579 BCE, sponsored a truce and disarmament among the Zhou states.

Hegemony: A system of
state relations in which
less powerful states
directly or implicitly
agree to defer to the lead
of the most powerful
state, which is, thus, the
hegemon.

By the latter part of the sixth century, a rough balance of power among the four leading states of Jin, Chu [Choo], Qi, and Qin held sway. While this system functioned for several decades, new powers on the peripheries, expansion into non-Zhou lands, and civil war in Jin led to the partition of Jin in 403 BCE, marking the formal opening of the Warring States period. By its close, Zhou itself had been absorbed by the combatants (in 256 BCE), and Qin would emerge as the creator of a unified empire in 221 BCE.

Economy, Society, and Family Adaptation in Ancient China

From Neolithic times, the Chinese economy has been based on agriculture. It was only in early 2012 that China's urban population outstripped its rural one. Still, as late as 2015 approximately 44 percent of China's people were involved in agricultural pursuits. Both the Yellow River states and those in the south of China outside of the control of the Shang and Zhou dynasties relied on a peasant subsistence economy based on family and clan landownership, with much of the local political power diffused to the villages. While the problems of land-centered social relationships long occupied Chinese rulers, China, unlike some other agriculturally based societies, never developed an extensive system of slave labor.

Family life played a dominant role among all members of ancient Chinese society. Here, as in other agrarian kingdoms, the position of women in power among the elite eroded over time. By the late Zhou period, the hierarchy of patriarchy and the growing influence of notions of filial piety—a behavioral model based on relationships among members of a family headed by the father—were becoming established.

Shang Society

Though Shang leaders frequently moved their headquarters, nearly all of their newly established capitals were comparable in scale to those developing in India and the Mediterranean.

Erligang   The capital city at Erligang [AR-lee-gahng] was characteristic of the late Xia or early Shang period. It had a defensive wall enclosing an urban center. The area within the walls was the province of the rulers, related families, diviners, and craftspeople who served the elites. Merchants and craftspeople involved in the manufacture of non-elite items lived outside the city walls, as did peasants and slaves.

Life in Erligang for the non-elite centered on communal agriculture. They tilled the soil with small plows, stone-tipped hoes, and assorted wooden implements. They grew millet and vegetables and raised water buffalo, sheep, chickens, and pigs. The pig had been domesticated since at least Yangshao times. Even today, the written character for "family" or "household" (家, *jia*) is represented by a stylized depiction of a pig under a roof.

Social Class and Labor   Outside the larger cities, a more differentiated social structure, with artisans of various trades organized according to lineage, emerged. Craft guilds and other organizations came to be dominated by family groups, as was the case later in imperial China. The constant warfare of Shang rulers and their increasing interest in monumental projects, such as flood control along the Yellow River and its tributaries, all boosted the need for labor. Professional soldiers and local militia satisfied Shang military needs. Conscript labor, however, constituted an increasingly important part of the workforce.

Interactions of Zhou Economy and Society

The large size of the territory claimed by the Zhou dynasty, and the enhanced trade that this expansion entailed, added to the wealth and power of all the rulers of its dependencies. The expansion of these dependencies to the Yangzi River basin brought much of East Asia's most productive farmland under some form of Zhou control and increased interaction with the region's inhabitants.

Innovation and Adaptation in Agriculture   In the north, the introduction of the soybean from Manchuria boosted crop yields and pushed growers to cultivate more marginal lands. The rotation of wheat and millet allowed for more intensive farming. The use of more efficient ox-drawn plows and, from the fourth century BCE, iron-tipped tools, as well as irrigation and water-conservancy efforts, pushed yields even further. In the south, the Zhou dependencies developed as rice cultivation facilitated population growth, and the economic and demographic center of China moved steadily southward. By the middle of the sixth century BCE, the Zhou kingdoms taken together constituted the world's most populous, and perhaps richest, agriculturally based urban society.

Zhou Rural Society   The Zhou rulers devised a system of ranks for governing their dependencies based on the size of landholdings. Members of the aristocracy were responsible for collecting taxes from their dependents, and commoners were required to provide military service to those of higher rank in return for protection. Peasants worked their own lands, with the lands of the aristocracy often scattered in plots among those of the commoners.

The Well-Field System   The Zhou were the first to attempt a uniform system of land tenure in China. This method of land division, called the well-field system, was said to have been devised by the Duke of Zhou. In this arrangement, each square *li* (one *li* is about one-third of a mile), consisting of 900 *mou* (one *mou* is about one-sixth of an acre), was divided into a grid of nine plots. Individual families would each work one of the eight outside plots, while the middle one would be farmed in common for the taxes and rents owed the landowner or local officials. The term "well-field" comes from the Chinese character for "[water] well" (井, *jing*), which resembles a grid. Whether the system was ever widely practiced is a matter of debate, yet it remained the benchmark against which all subsequent attempts at land reform were measured.

By the late 500s BCE, the need of individual Zhou governments to use the wealth of their states to support their militaries and bureaucracies prompted them to institute land taxes based on crop yields and, in some cases, to commute labor obligations to direct taxes payable in kind to the state. Then, as now, the taxes tended to affect the poor the most.

The New Classes: Merchants and Shi   Further evidence for the decline of the Zhou agrarian-based feudal system is the rise of new classes. The growing power of the new merchant class began a struggle with governments for control of vital commodities. It also introduced the perception of merchants as *usurpers,* whose drive for profit from trafficking in the goods of others endangered the stability of Zhou social institutions. Accompanying the rise of a merchant class was the advance of a cash economy and the coining of money.

Though viewed with distaste by the landed aristocracy, merchants were increasingly seen as useful resources. Their rise to economic prominence, however, meant that their social position lay outside the traditional structures of agrarian life. Their independence and mobility, along with the growth of cities as centers of trade, helped spur centralization as Zhou rulers attempted to create more inclusive systems of administration. Direct taxation by the state, uniform law codes, and administrative restructuring altered the old arrangement of mutual obligation between aristocratic landowners and dependent peasant farmers. Here, members of the new *shi* class, drawn from the lower aristocracy and wealthier commoners, took on the role of bureaucrats and advisors. From the ranks of the *shi* would rise many of China's most famous thinkers, starting with Confucius.

Central Asian Interactions   The growing wealth of north and central China spurred an increase in trade outside of the Zhou realm as well as among its constituent states, particularly in the south and along well-established routes into central Asia. In this interchange, Zhou traders were increasingly helped by the carriers of the central Asian exchange.

By the sixth century BCE, a series of loosely related cultures along this northern front can be discerned. These peoples appear to have taken Zhou goods much farther than originally thought, and scholars are only now beginning to realize the extent of their trade relations. What goods may have been involved in such exchanges remains unknown, however, until a period of better-recorded trade along the Silk Road began in the second century BCE.

Gender and the Family

Serious study of gender roles in ancient China is difficult because of the scarcity of records from earlier times. However, the development of women's instructional literature from roughly the first century BCE to the first century CE allows scholars to chart a shift in perspectives of female "virtue" and proper behavior in the home and in public.

Elite Women of the Shang   In marked contrast to later Chinese court life, with its seclusion of wives and concubines, elite women of the Shang often participated in political, and even military, affairs. As we saw in the opening of this chapter, one of the most complete Shang burial sites is that of Fu Hao, who was buried with hundreds of artifacts—as well as the sacrificial skeletons of sixteen people and six dogs. The 1975 discovery of her tomb helped bring to life a woman whose existence, though well established in written records, had otherwise been elusive.

The artifacts also shed light on Shang technology and material culture, court life, and especially the position of women among the aristocracy. For example, inscriptions on oracle bones in Fu Hao's tomb indicate that she wielded considerable power and influence even before becoming Wu Ding's principal wife. Prior to coming to court at the Shang capital of Yin sometime in the late thirteenth century BCE, she owned and managed a family estate and was apparently well educated. She both supervised and conducted religious rituals at court and during military expeditions. As Wu Ding's chief confidant she advised him on political and military strategy and diplomacy. She even conducted her own military campaigns against Shang adversaries.

Women's Status in Transition   Elite women like Fu Hao appear to have shared a comparatively equal status with male rulers, even to the point of leading armies and practicing divination, though it should also be mentioned that their tombs tend to be smaller and less elaborate than males of comparable rank. In the literature of the early Zhou era, women were depicted as occupying important positions as mentors and advisors. Women's crafts such as spinning and weaving were highly regarded. The *Poetry Classic* (Book of Odes), in depicting the lives of ordinary people, suggests a far more egalitarian relationship between men and women than would be the case during the imperial period.

The wives and concubines of rulers in many instances had their own sets of records and genealogies as well, an important asset among the powerful in this family-conscious society. Even by the late Zhou period, a woman like Lady Ji of the state of Lu was able to instruct her son, the high official Wen Bo (Earl Wen), in the arts of government. In this role of advisor, she was much praised for her virtue by subsequent thinkers.

Although late Zhou women might be well educated and highly capable, they seldom ruled in their own right. In fact, during the Spring and Autumn period (722–481 BCE), women were frequently barred from involvement in state affairs. The same general trend may be glimpsed at other levels of society as well. The web of family, clan, village, and class associations of the Zhou era reflects considerable respect for the wisdom and work of women, but these skills were increasingly seen as best exercised in the home instead of in the public sphere. The later development of state-sponsored Confucianism, with its emphasis on filial piety, ushered in a markedly secondary role for women.

Interactions of Religion, Culture, and Intellectual Life in Ancient China

Like the gods of the early Mesopotamians, the first Chinese gods were local deities that inhabited a spirit world presided over by a ruling god. In China, the rulers' ancestors occupied the highest rungs of the spirit world, and worship largely consisted of communication with them. Religion was not separate from everyday life, but permeated all aspects of it.

While it creatively adapted and adopted many other aspects of Shang culture, the Zhou era marked a turn toward a more abstract concept of religion. As an illustration of this, Shangdi, the chief Shang deity, and other beings with superhuman powers but human-like personalities began to give way to the more distant Zhou concept of "heaven" (*tian*) as the animating force of the universe. By the late Zhou era, this concept of heaven as the guiding cosmic force had become central to nearly every major Chinese religious and philosophical tradition.

Oracle Bones and Early Chinese Writing

As we saw earlier with Wu Ding, seekers of guidance would consult the diviner, who would ask questions of the ancestors. The bones were then heated, tapped with a rod, the resulting cracks interpreted as answers, and the information incised in the bone. Several thousand distinct symbols have been identified, and many are clearly ancient versions of modern Chinese characters. Chinese characters became increasingly stylized and, after the Qin era (221–202 BCE), put into standard forms. But in most cases, these retained enough of their earlier character to be recognizable to later readers. Moreover, the political and religious significance of Shang and Zhou ritual vessels, which, in many cases, contained inscriptions in archaic characters, ensured that some knowledge of them would be preserved.

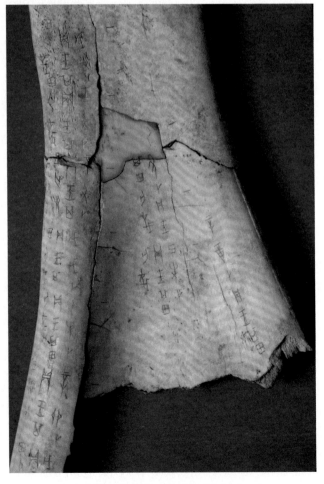

Shang Bronzes Although some of the early bronze articles and weapons found at late Longshan sites may have come by way of trade routes from western Asia, bronze-casting techniques used in China quite likely diffused northward from Southeast Asia at about the same time. The best evidence for this is that the technique favored by Shang and Zhou casters is unique to China and radically different from the method of the peoples of western Eurasia. Shang and early Zhou ritual vessels themselves, with their richly stylized reliefs of real and mythical animals incorporated into the design, are unlike anything outside of East Asia.

Shang Religion The use of elaborately decorated bronze vessels was important to elite Shang religious ceremonies, where offerings of meats,

Shang Oracle Bone Inscription on Shoulder Blade of an Ox

Patterns Up Close | The Chinese Writing System

The Three Excellences. Poetry, painting and calligraphy are still considered among the highest arts in China and those areas of Asia influenced by Chinese culture. The character being painted here is *fu*, or "blessing," one of the most commonly used in expressions of well-wishing or celebration.

Of all the innovations associated with China, perhaps the one with the longest-lasting impact is its writing system. Like those of the Egyptians, the Harappans, and the Mayans, it was originally a system based on pictures. As with these other systems, the pictures became simplified and standardized for ease of interpretation.

The association of the written language with early Chinese religious practices, court ceremonial functions, and self-cultivation and character development imbued it over the centuries with a spiritual dimension. The discipline demanded by learning the thousands of characters necessary for advanced literacy and the artistic possibilities embodied in the brush and ink traditionally used to write them placed calligraphy at the top of Chinese aesthetic values. Thus, wherever written Chinese is used, skill in the three interrelated "excellences" of painting, poetry, and calligraphy is esteemed.

The Chinese written language had a tremendous impact on the course of Asian history. While it requires extensive memorization, it is remarkably adaptable as a writing system because the meaning of the characters is

grains, and wine were made. Although we know little about the religious practices of Shang commoners, the number of artifacts and oracle bones found at the gravesites of elites and at the remains of royal palaces has clarified the belief system of the rulers.

The principal deity, Di or Shangdi, presided over the spirit world and governed both natural and human affairs. Shangdi was joined by the major ancestors of the dynastic line, deities believed to influence or control natural phenomena, and local gods appropriated from various Shang territories. The religious function of the Shang ruler, as it appears to have been for the Xia and would be for subsequent Chinese dynasties, was to act as the intermediary between the world of the spirits and that of humanity. Hence, rituals appear to have consisted largely of sacrifices to ancestors to ensure their benevolence toward the living. As we have seen, the Shang sought the guidance of their ancestral spirits through divination on a wide variety of human affairs as well as on natural phenomena.

As the Shang state grew more powerful, the size of the sacrifices also increased. Like the Xia, the Shang practiced human sacrifice. Excavations at both Erligang and later capitals have yielded numerous sites containing headless skeletons. The evidence suggests that the death of a ruler was accompanied by the slaughter of hundreds of slaves, servants, and war captives, perhaps to serve the deceased in the spirit world.

independent of their pronunciation. Thus, speakers of non-Chinese languages could attach their own pronunciations to the characters and, as long as they understood their structure and grammar, could use them to communicate. This versatility enabled Chinese to serve as the first written language not only for speakers of the Chinese family of dialects and languages on the Asian mainland but also for the Koreans, Japanese, and Vietnamese, whose spoken languages are totally unrelated to Chinese. The pattern of interaction and adaptation prompted by the acquisition of the written language allowed the vast body of Chinese literature, philosophy, religion, history, and political theory to tie the literate elites of these states together within a common cultural sphere. In this respect, it functioned in much the same way as Latin among the educated of Europe. Even today, in all these countries, the ability to read classical Chinese is considered to be a mark of superior education. Moreover, the cultural heritage transmitted by Chinese characters continues to inform the worldviews of these societies.

Questions

- How did the pattern of interaction and adaptation that characterized the development of the Chinese writing system bring people together into a common cultural sphere?

- How does the impact of the Chinese writing system compare to the impact other writing systems have had in other parts of the world?

Adaptations of Zhou Religion, Technology, and Culture

The Zhou sought to legitimize their reign by adopting many of the forms of art and ritual practiced by the defeated Shang. As before, the ruler maintained his place as mediator between the human and divine worlds. But the Zhou also appear to have followed the trend toward more abstract religious ideas we have observed in other early civilizations.

Heaven The Zhou introduced the concept of *tian*, "heaven," as an impersonal controlling force of the universe. It replaced the more human-like Shangdi. It was this more abstract heaven whose mandate gave the right to rule to all subsequent Chinese dynasties. Thus, throughout the history of imperial China, the emperor retained the title of *Tianzi*, "son of heaven," as a symbol of his obligation to fulfill heaven's mandate as a son serves his father.

Iron Casting The use of iron was introduced during the Zhou period. Some late Shang and western Zhou tombs

Ritual Vessel with Taotie Design Pattern

❯ How did the Zhou concept of the Mandate of Heaven operate?

The Mandate of Heaven was a way for the Zhou to retrospectively legitimize their conquests and to create a precedent for future moral renewal. As part of a dynastic cycle, it set the pattern for the Chinese view of history. The rule of a particular dynasty was expected to advance in reform and expansion in its early stages, reach a comfortable point of harmony in its middle stages, and go into moral and material decline in its final stages. From that point, revolt breaks out and heaven transfers its mandate to a new dynasty—*if that revolt succeeds*. This pattern of dynastic cycle and heavenly mandate made China's historical experience—conveniently fitted to the theory—not only comprehensible but also predictable. Alert rulers searched for signs that the mandate was in danger; the people speculated about portents presaging dynastic change. Even China's modern rulers are heirs to this pattern; during human-made and natural disasters, the Communist Party is even more alert to possible signs that the people are expecting a "dynastic" change.

| Against the Grain

Consider this as a counterpoint to the main patterns examined in this chapter.

Women's Voices

- It often seems as if women had somewhat greater freedom among the earliest civilizations we have encountered than they would in the period after 600 BCE. Do you think this is a fair observation? If so, which of these societies seemed to offer the most agency to women?

- Why did China become increasingly patriarchal over time? Does the development of urban–agrarian society necessarily lead to patriarchy?

Although scholars debate whether Neolithic villages like Banpo may have been matrilineal or matriarchal, there is agreement that by the time of the first three dynasties, the northern Chinese states and their successors were a rigorously patriarchal society and culture. As we shall see in Chapter 9, this would be reinforced by Confucian values. Yet women were not without influence in ancient China; indeed, male Confucian writers noted the exploits of outstanding women of the past, even those who went beyond what came to be seen as the filial, domestic ideals celebrated in manuals of female deportment.

Long before this period, however, the *Shijing* (Book of Songs), in its collections of sung poems from the common people, contained a number of compositions that, although the individual authors are unknown, show strong evidence of having been either composed by women or in the persona of women. In them we may have a few glimpses of the authentic voices of ancient Chinese women. Consider this lament from a young woman facing the challenges of family expectations for marriage:

> My mind is not a mirror;
> It cannot [equally] receive [all impressions]
> I, indeed, have brothers,
> But I cannot depend on them.

I meet with their anger ...

Silently I think of my case,

And, starting as from sleep, I beat my breast. (Number 26; "Cypress Boat")

In an almost visceral way, the speaker gives voice to the frustration of the independent mind and heart in conflict with family and social convention. Her song was to be a familiar one over the intervening centuries.

Key Terms

Client states 85	Hegemony 88	Millet 80
Feudalism 88	Mandate of Heaven 88	Social stratification 84

Learn more with this chapter's digital tools, including the Oxford Insight Study Guide, at http://www.oup.com/he/vonsivers4e. Please see the Further Resources section at the back of the book for additional readings and suggested websites.

Sources for Chapter 4

SOURCE 4.1

Excerpts from *The Book of Odes* (*Shijing*)

ca. 2852–481 BCE

Over 300 poems of various lengths were anthologized and transmitted by Confucius in the early fifth century BCE. Philosophers of the Confucian school (see Chapter 9) cherished the Odes and cited them frequently, and they have continued to entrance readers with their naturalistic imagery and personal voices. Only two samples are given here, but this rich tradition of poetry should be sampled at length.

Wild and Windy

Wild and windy was the day;
You looked at me and laughed,
But the jest was cruel, and the laughter mocking.
My heart within is sore.

There was a great sandstorm that day;
Kindly you made as though to come,
Yet neither came nor went away.
Long, long my thoughts.

A great wind and darkness;
Day after day it is dark.
I lie awake, cannot sleep,
And gasp with longing.

Dreary, dreary the gloom;
The thunder growls.
I lie awake, cannot sleep,
And am destroyed with longing.

I Beg of You, Zhong Zi

I beg of you, Zhong Zi,
Do not climb into our homestead,
Do not break the willows we have planted.
Not that I mind about the willows,
But I am afraid of my father and mother.
Zhong Zi I dearly love;
But of what my father and mother say
Indeed I am afraid.
I beg of you, Zhong Zi,
Do not climb over the wall,
Do not break the mulberry-trees we have planted.
Not that I mind about the mulberry-trees,
But I am afraid of my brothers.

Source: Arthur Waley, trans., *The Book of Songs*, edited with additional translations by Joseph R. Allen (New York: Grove, 1996), 27 and 65.

Zhong Zi I dearly love;
But of what my brothers say
Indeed I am afraid.

I beg of you, Zhong Zi,
Do not climb into our garden,
Do not break the hard-wood we have
    planted.

Not that I mind about the
    hard-wood,
But I am afraid of what people will
    say.
Zhong Zi I dearly love;
But of all that people will say
Indeed I am afraid.

▶ Working
with Sources

1. **How do the poems deal with the theme of love, whether reciprocated or not?**

2. **What do they suggest about gender relations in ancient China?**

SOURCE 4.2   The Announcement of the Duke of Shao

One of the key concepts of Chinese philosophies of rulership is that of the Mandate of Heaven: Heaven gives permission to rule to the ruler and dynasty that is most morally worthy. In this excerpt from the earliest Chinese historical record, the *Shujing* (Book of History or Classic of Documents), the Duke of Shao, believed to be one of King Wen of the Zhou Dynasty's ten sons, here tells the conquered people of Yin (the Shang) of his king's intent to embody the virtues of the founders of the previous dynasties, Xia and Shang, that allowed them Heaven's favor.

"Oh! God dwelling in the great heavens has changed his decree respecting his great son and the great dynasty of Yin. Our king has received that decree. Unbounded is the happiness connected with it, and unbounded is the anxiety. Oh! how can he be other than reverent?

"When Heaven rejected and made an end of the decree in favor of the great dynasty of Yin, there were many of its former wise kings in Heaven. The king, however, who had succeeded to them, the last of his race, from the time of his entering into their appointment, proceeded in such a way as to keep the wise in obscurity and the vicious in office. The poor people in such a case, carrying their children and leading their wives, made their moan to Heaven. They even fled, but were apprehended again. Oh! Heaven had compassion on the people

Source: Clae Waltham, trans., *Shu Ching: Book of History* (Chicago: Gateway Edition, 1971) 162–166.

of the four quarters; its favoring decree lighted on our earnest founders. Let the king sedulously cultivate the virtue of reverence.

"Examining the men of antiquity, there was Yü, founder of the Hsia dynasty. Heaven guided his mind, allowed his descendants to succeed him, and protected them. He acquainted himself with Heaven, and was obedient to it. But in process of time the decree in his favor fell to the ground. So also is it now when we examine the case of Yin. There was the same guiding of its founder T'ang, who corrected the errors of Hsia, and whose descendants enjoyed the protection of Heaven. He also acquainted himself with Heaven, and was obedient to it. But now the decree in favor of him has fallen to the ground. Our king has now come to the throne in his youth. Let him not slight the aged and experienced, for it may be said of them that they have studied the virtuous conduct of the ancients and have matured their counsels in the sight of Heaven.

"Oh! although the king is young, yet he is the eldest son of Heaven. Let him effect a great harmony with the lower people and that will be the blessing of the present time. Let not the king presume to be remiss in this but continually regard and stand in awe of the perilous uncertainty of the people's attachment.

"Let the king come here as the vice-regent of God and undertake the duties of government in this center of the land. Tan said, 'Now that this great city has been built, from henceforth he may be the mate of great Heaven, and reverently sacrifice to the spirits above and below; henceforth he may from this central spot administer successful government.' Thus shall the king enjoy the favoring regard of Heaven all complete, and the government of the people will now be prosperous.

"Let the king first bring under his influence those who were the managers of affairs under Yin, associating them with the managers of affairs for our Chou. This will regulate their perverse natures and they will make daily advancement. Let the king make reverence the resting place of his mind; he must maintain the virtue of reverence.

"We should by all means survey the dynasties of Hsia and Yin. I do not presume to know and say, 'The dynasty of Hsia was to enjoy the favoring decree of Heaven just for so many years,' nor do I presume to know and say, 'It could not continue longer.' The fact was simply that, for want of the virtue of reverence, the decree in its favor prematurely fell to the ground. Similarly, I do not presume to know and say, 'The dynasty of Yin was to enjoy the favoring decree of Heaven just for so many years,' nor do I presume to know and say, 'It could not continue longer.' The fact simply was that, for want of the virtue of reverence, the decree in its favor fell prematurely to the ground. The king has now inherited the decree—the same decree, I consider, which belonged to those two dynasties. Let him seek to inherit the virtues of their meritorious sovereigns; let him do this especially at this commencement of his duties."

▶ Working with Sources:

1. Why did the Duke feel it necessary to convince the conquered Yin of his king's rectitude when the Zhou had already defeated them and now ruled?

2. How does the Duke explain how the king intends to bring just government to the new domains?

<table><tr><td>SOURCE 4.3</td></tr></table>

The Book of Lord Shang (Shangjun Shu)

ca. 338 BCE

This collection of sayings and reports attributed to Lord Shang (d. 338 BCE) may have been compiled by later officials, but its vision of a centralized bureaucracy was emulated at many points in China's turbulent history. The work is composed of 25 or more brief sections, some of which are lost, but the remainder address the necessity of good and competent government.

The guiding principles of the people are base and they are not consistent in what they value. As the conditions in the world change, different principles are practiced. Therefore it is said that there is a fixed standard in a king's principles. Indeed, a king's principles represent one viewpoint and those of a minister another. The principles each follows are different but are one in both representing a fixed standard. Therefore, it is said: "When the people are stupid, by knowledge one may rise to supremacy; when the world is wise, by force one may rise to supremacy." That means that when people are stupid, there are plenty of strong men but not enough wise, and when the world is wise, there are plenty of clever men, but not enough strong. It is the nature of people, when they have no knowledge, to study, and when they have no strength, to submit.

...

A sage-prince understands what is essential in affairs, and therefore in his administration of the people, there is that which is most essential. For the fact that uniformity in the manipulating of rewards and punishments supports moral virtue is connected with human psychology. A sage-prince, by his ruling of men, is certain to win their hearts; consequently he is able to use force. Force produces strength, strength produces prestige, prestige produces virtue, and so virtue has its origin in force, which a sage-prince alone possesses, and therefore he is able to transmit benevolence and righteousness to the empire.

...

Source: Sebastian De Grazia, ed., *Masters of Chinese Political Thought: From the Beginnings to the Han Dynasty* (New York: Viking, 1973), 339–343.

Of old, the one who could regulate the empire was he who regarded as his first task the regulating of his own people; the one who could conquer a strong enemy was he who regarded as his first task the conquering of his own people. For the way in which the conquering of the people is based upon the regulating of the people, is like the effect of smelting in regard to metal or the work of the potter in regard to clay; if the basis is not solid, then people are like flying birds or like animals. Who can regulate these? The basis of the people is the law. Therefore, a good ruler obstructed the people by means of the law, and so his reputation and his territory flourished.

▶ Working with Sources

1. Why does Lord Shang assume there will be an antagonistic relationship between a ruler and the ruled?

2. Would he think it preferable for a leader to appear virtuous rather than to actually be virtuous?

SOURCE 4.4

Iron sword with jade handle, earliest cast-iron object (Western Zhou), from Henan Museum, Guo state, Sanmenxia city

ca. 1046–771 BCE

When this sword was discovered in 1990, it challenged conventional wisdom about when and under what circumstances Chinese people made the first cast-iron object. The dating of the object to the Western Zhou period pushed back the earliest date of this kind of manufacture by over 200 years. The sword consists of an iron blade, a bronze handle core, and a jade handle. Embedded turquoises were also found at the joint of the blade and the handle.

Source: http://www.ourtravelpics.com/photo/zhengzhou_2/62/

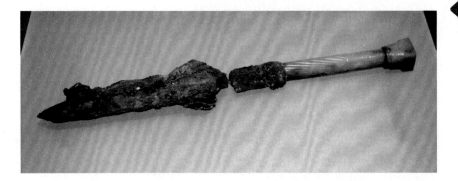

▶ Working
with Sources

1. What does this object suggest about the casting technology and metal-working prowess of workers in the Zhou dynasty?

2. Why would a cast-iron sword have been an especially effective weapon in this era?

World Period One

From Human Origins to Early Agricultural Centers, Prehistory to 600 BCE

Humans appeared late in the evolution of the world. While the earth is 4.5 billion years old, the first human-like beings only appeared about 6 million years ago, and modern humans did not appear in East Africa until about 100,000 years ago. These humans migrated from there to Eurasia and Australia 80,000–60,000 years ago and to the Americas 17,500–14,600 years ago.

As people became more numerous, human culture became more differentiated. The triad of origins-interactions-adaptations as the fundamental pattern in world history took shape. Human ingenuity and interaction with the environment in the Middle East, Asia, Europe, Australia, and the Americas led to vastly different adaptations. Foraging originated in Africa. Farming, urbanization, and state formation originated in the Middle East. In the Americas, humans fashioned similarly differentiated livelihoods and political structures. Australia's poorer natural environment slowed its differentiation process.

Chapter 5

Origins Apart: The Americas and Oceania

14,500–600 BCE

CHAPTER FIVE PATTERNS

Origins, Interactions, Adaptations Parallel to, but independent from, Eurasia-Africa, people in the Americas also shifted from foraging to agriculture during this period. The first region was the Peruvian west coast, where the Caral-Supe agrarian–urban culture emerged, beginning ca. 3600 BCE, nearly simultaneously with Mesopotamia and Egypt. In the absence of working animals from the Americas, however, neither plow nor wheel could make its appearance and agriculture was limited to manual labor. In Oceania, distance and the small size of the islands impeded the spread of agrarian–urban culture. Nevertheless, the Lapita people, originally from Taiwan, colonized most islands of the Pacific, beginning ca. 1600 BCE and settling as farmers of yams, taro, chickens, and pigs.

Uniqueness and Similarities The parts of the Americas where agrarian–urban culture emerged shared many of the characteristics of their Eurasian counterparts. Although we know little about the rulers, the temples testify to the existence of social stratification, with priests, laborers, craftsmen, and merchants. Writing had not yet developed, although quipus (sets of knotted cotton strings) might have been used for record keeping. Overall, agrarian–urban development in the Americas testifies not only to universal human ingenuity but also to the ubiquity of the same social forces.

In 2001, anthropological archaeologists announced a stunning discovery in the archaeology of the Americas. The scientists had conducted radiocarbon dating tests on plant fibers taken from site excavations of Caral [kah-RAHL], in the Supe [soo-PAY] valley in Peru. The site had stirred interest because of its immense size, monumental pyramids, and evidence of early urban living. The test results, however, now demanded a complete retelling of the history of civilization in the Americas.

Because earlier evidence had suggested a relatively late arrival for modern humans in the Americas, and because of the scarcity of domesticable grain plants, the earliest known American civilizations had been assumed to be much more recent than their earliest Eurasian and African counterparts—until now, that is.

But the Caral-Supe results put the date of the materials tested at 2627 BCE, making the city as old as the pyramids of Egypt and the ancient Mesopotamian cities. Indeed, work at nearby sites showed that they had been occupied by substantial villages for far longer, that the entire area was supported by irrigation works, and that Caral-Supe is just one of 18 similar urban sites in the Supe valley (often referred to as forming the Chico Norte Civilization).

CHAPTER OUTLINE

Adapting to the Americas

Agriculture, Villages, and Urban Life

The Origins of Pacific Island Migrations

Putting It All Together

THE AMERICAS AND OCEANIA

The fact that Caral-Supe was an agrarian–urban center in the Americas roughly contemporaneous with similar centers in the Middle East, India, and China demonstrates that a continent with no contact to Eurasia-Africa until 1492 CE nevertheless displayed similar patterns of origin, interaction, and adaptation. By 1492 its evolution had even reached the moment of imperial political organization which typified Eurasia at that time. Although history is neither uniform nor predetermined, it nevertheless seems to display comparable patterns of origin, interaction, and adaptation regardless of whether the continents were connected or isolated. Beginning with their common heritage of forage culture, adaptable to nearly all parts of the world, humans evidently

ABOVE: Cut from copper, this bird was made by villagers of the early American Hopewell culture (ca. 200 BCE–500 CE).

engaged in comparable economic activities, social customs, political institutions, and intellectual-spiritual experiences. This chapter is devoted to the exploration of the early history of two world regions, the Americas and Oceania, which evolved in separation from Eurasia-Africa prior to early modernity.

Adapting to the Americas

As discussed in Chapter 1, humans arrived in the lower Americas around 14,500 BCE, according to the carbon dating of tools and lithic artifacts at the Cooper's Ferry site. Since a split between the Cordilleran and Laurentide ice sheets in Canada began to appear only around 12,000 BCE in various places to allow for a passable corridor, the settlers of Cooper's Ferry cannot have come by land. They must have been traveling by boat along the coast to the Columbia River and upstream to the Snake and Salmon Rivers.

The Environment

Next to Eurasia, the two parts comprising the American continent encompass the largest landmass on earth and form the Western Hemisphere. Located north and south of the equator, the Americas share somewhat similar types of landscape and climate (see Map 5.1).

The Americas' most prominent geographical feature is a contiguous spine of mountain ranges, or **cordilleras** [cor-dil-YEH-ras], near or along the entire western coast. Known as the Rocky Mountains in the north, these ranges become the Sierra Madre in the center and the Andes in the south. Water from these mountains feeds nearly all river systems on the continents. Both continents also share low mountain systems along their eastern coasts. North and South America meet in Mesoamerica near the equator, with North America then reaching northward to the North Pole and South America extending southward almost to Antarctica. Thus, the climatic zones of both South and North America range from extreme cold to subtropical and tropical warmth.

Geographical Regions   North America consists of four main geographical regions:

- The Mountain West
- The Canadian Shield, which stretches from today's Canada to Greenland
- The Great Plains and central lowlands in the center of today's United States
- The Appalachian Mountains in the east and the broad coastal plain along the Atlantic Ocean.

The four regions vary considerably in precipitation and temperature. Historically, they have produced widely differing modes of subsistence and society among their inhabitants.

Mesoamerica and South America form six distinct geographical regions:

- The Central American mainland and the Caribbean islands
- The Andes Mountain region along the west coast
- The Guyana Shield, a rocky plateau that separates the Amazon River and basin in the south from the Orinoco River

- The Brazilian Shield, a rocky crust in the east jutting into the South Atlantic Ocean
- The Gran Chaco in the east between the Andes and the Paraguay River
- The Patagonian Shield, in the center of the continent's southern tip.

Here, the size of the mountains and the extent of the rain forests dictated even greater regional separation than in North America until recent times.

During winters in North America, freezing winds from the Arctic blow south across the Canadian Shield into the central plains, or American Midwest. By contrast, at the southern tip of South America, air currents are predominantly westerly and more moderate and do not push winter frost very far northward. Thus, apart from the southern tip at Cape Horn and Tierra del Fuego, snow and frost are mostly limited to the Andes. In North America, winter and summer temperatures vary greatly, as do precipitation levels. Generally, the eastern and midwestern regions of North America receive regular rainfall throughout the year, while the western regions and lower Pacific coast tend to be drier.

In Mesoamerica, the Caribbean, and the northern two-thirds of South America, temperatures and humidity levels tend to be high. Large steppe and desert areas cover the western third of North America, while in South America deserts and steppes are mostly found along the northwestern coast and in the interior of the south. Prior to modern times, large forests covered the eastern two-thirds of North America and the northern half of South America.

Trade Winds and Ocean Currents   Like the monsoon system that influences the agriculture of India, China, the Indian Ocean, and western Pacific regions, large-scale weather events governed at least in part by the actions of continental weather systems and ocean currents have played historical roles in South America. Their cycles are still only partially understood.

Running roughly parallel to the eastern coasts of northern South America and nearly all of North America, the Gulf Stream current of the Atlantic Ocean moves warm water from the south Atlantic along the eastern seaboard of the United States. Driven by west-east trade winds, the Gulf Stream then heads northeast toward the European coast. In the Americas, the Gulf Stream's interactions with wind patterns in fall and winter in eastern North America frequently result in large storms called northeasters or "nor'easters."

More destructive is the frequency with which the Gulf Stream guides hurricanes into the Caribbean Sea and along the North American coast. The immense

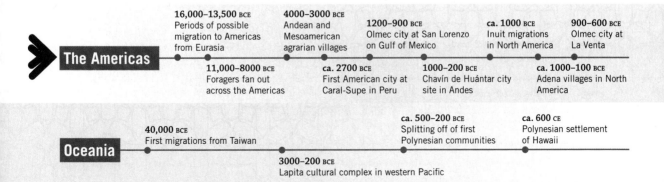

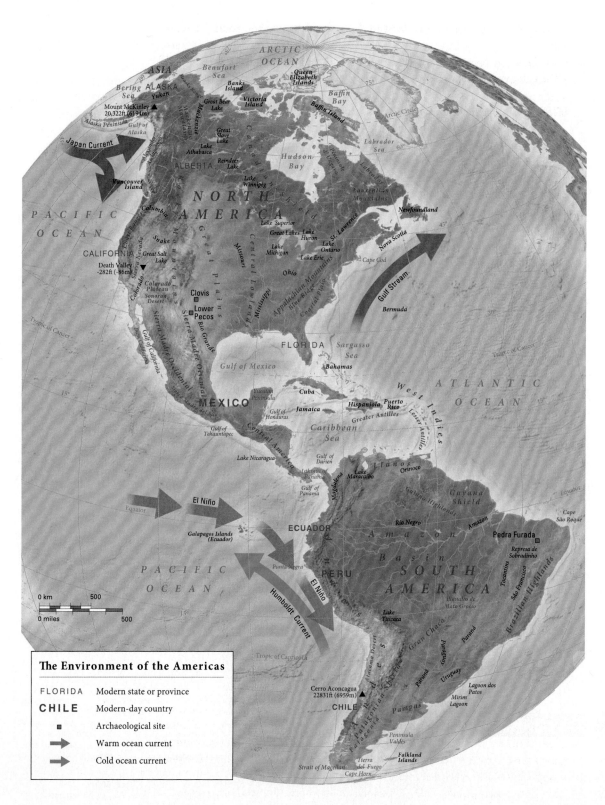

MAP 5.1 The Environment of the Americas

"heat pump" of the African interior and Sahara Desert spawns tropical disturbances in the southeastern Atlantic, which gain strength over the warm waters there and the Caribbean as they move westward. Historically, the east–west trade winds north of the equator that drive the tropical disturbances played a vital role in fostering the first European voyages to the Western Hemisphere as well as the trans-Atlantic slave trade by making navigation swift and predictable (Chapters 16 and 19). In the case of hurricanes, however, the storms are often picked up by the Gulf Stream, fed by its warm waters, and directed north from Cuba along the North American coast, where, in modern times, they have caused immense destruction.

In the Pacific, the Kuroshio and North Pacific currents work in a similar fashion. Warm waters of the western Pacific move northeastward past Japan toward Alaska, gradually cooling down. They turn then southeastward along the Pacific coast of Canada and the United States. This flow has a moderating effect on climate, particularly along the coasts from Alaska to California. The waters are generally cool and provide important fish and marine mammal habitats. For millennia, they supplied the peoples of the west coast with ample sustenance.

El Niño   The Pacific region is the home of the **El Niño** phenomenon, which plays a major role during the South American summer (Christmastime, hence "El Niño"). In cycles that vary from three to eight years, southeast-northwest trade winds off the coast weaken and fail to drive the warm surface water off the coasts of Peru and Chile. This water would normally flow along the equator to the other side of the Pacific. As a result, the abundance of fish in front of Peru and Chile is reduced, due to the lower amount of nutrients in warmer water. On the coast, abundant rainfall can cause inundations and landslides, making El Niño a potentially calamitous weather phenomenon.

El Niño: A periodic slowing of the flow of currents in the Pacific, greatly altering water temperatures and weather patterns on the west coast of South America.

Foragers

As we saw in Chapter 1 and above, genetic studies published in 2015–2016 suggest that the first Americans were ancient North Eurasians in Siberia who migrated first to Beringia and then to North and South America. They were foragers, living off plants, hunted animals, and seafood, as they found it along the Pacific coast of North America. As they settled, they became the ancestors of the peoples we call today Native Americans or Americans.

Spear Points   At present, there are about three dozen sites in North and South America dating to the period of 14,500–11,390 BCE, that is, from the earliest migration to the rise of the so-called Clovis people. The lithic finds at these sites— spear points, blades, scrapers, hand axes, blanks, and tools—show similarities with finds around the Pacific Rim at the same time period. Spear points are typically stemmed, that is, they consist of triangular or leaflike ("foliate") points with stems that were hafted with leather strips onto the thrusting spear. Overall, the number of lithics recovered so far is still low in comparison with the subsequent prolific style of points, that of Clovis (after a town in New Mexico close to where they were first discovered in 1929).

The Clovis points are perhaps the technically most advanced and elegantly shaped spear points found in Stone Age archaeological sites. They date to the period 11,390–10,850 BCE and had fishtails instead of stems at their base, with concave grooves ("flutes") in the center of the fishtails. Tests carried out in 2017 at Kent State University revealed that the fluted Clovis points were more difficult to knap but more robust in penetrating the fur and skin of animals without breaking. There are altogether some 1,500 sites all over North America and northern South America where Clovis spear points were found. The chert required for knapping the points was often quarried in faraway places and required negotiations with the bands in control of these places. In South America, south of today's Venezuela, the influence of the Clovis style resulted in the development of stemmed but fluted spear points. Notwithstanding its wide geographical distribution, the Clovis style was short-lived; after a little more than 500 years, the foragers supporting it disappeared from North America.

Climate Changes and Asteroids   The probable reason for their disappearance was the onset of the **Younger Dryas** (YD, 10,400–9500 BCE), a sudden 800-year cold spell in the northern hemisphere interrupting the general warming trend after the Ice Age. The Clovis people likely moved southwards, merging with the stem-fishtail people of South America. In this case, they left an empty landscape behind that filled up again only after the end of the YD, as it did with the Folsom foragers (9500–8000 BCE). Folsom spear points are characteristically full-fluted, from base to point. By contrast, in the Middle East the contemporary semisettled Natufians (see Chapter 2), relying largely on collecting wild grains, were unable to sustain themselves in place during the YD and withered away, fortunately leaving archaeological traces behind.

> **Younger Dryas:** Cold period with near Ice Age temperatures; name derived from a white blooming plant flourishing during the period, itself named for a Greek mythological nymph.

As for the causes of the onset of the YD, there has been a vigorous debate among scientists since 2007, when the so-called asteroid impact theory was first proposed. According to the latest refinement of this theory in 2019, one or several asteroids (or one asteroid breaking up) hit the earth in some 50 places, from Greenland to southern Chile. The impact was allegedly so devastating that melting ice water changed ocean currents, firestorms incinerated entire landscapes with forests and savannas, and huge amounts of dust were blown into the atmosphere, darkening the sun and causing a centuries-long-impact winter and ice age temperatures. Initially ridiculed, the Younger Dryas Impact Theory is now seriously discussed, although still far from approaching a scientific consensus.

In this respect, the theory is at a stage where the so-called "Clovis First" debate was in 1997 when archaeologists for the first time entertained the notion that the first settlers of the Americas antedated the Clovis foragers. The lesson for students of world history is that they need to be aware of scientific theories impinging on history, but at the same time be cautious in accepting them prior to an emerging consensus.

Toward Settlements   When the climate improved again around 9500 BCE, foragers had to contend with the disappearance of large game, such as elephants, mammoths, mastodons, glyptodons, camels, and horses. To be sure, the foragers had always also hunted small animals and quite a few species of those also suffered extinction. But why the North American megafauna disappeared so massively, in contrast to Eurasia, where horses and camels survived, is still poorly understood. Overhunting by foragers might be one factor, as seems to be the case for the mammoth. But other species, such as the elephant, giraffe, or rhinoceros in Africa, survived the human hunt. Perhaps the most convincing explanation comes from a 2016 article in *Science*, which looked at the survival of species during the last 55,000 years. In this time of generally cold temperatures there were 15 so-called "interstadials" when average temperatures rose quickly for short periods from 39 to 61 degrees Fahrenheit, each time wiping out a number of megafauna species. It is thus clear that species disappeared in all warming periods, not merely after the last ice age, although humans might have helped on that occasion.

As larger game became scarce, people in coastal areas began relying more on fish and shellfish, and those in inland regions increased their collection of seeds and nuts. Hunters began to make greater use of the **atlatl** or spear thrower, originally brought over from Eurasia. Bone was used for spears, fishhooks, awls, needles, combs, and spatulas. Humans continued to live in rock shelters and caves, but also constructed huts covered with skins. More permanent wooden structures appeared along the seacoasts, the Great Lakes, and rivers, where there were plentiful resources of fish, shellfish, and waterfowl. As bands of hunters and gatherers acquired more household goods and hunting instruments, they became less inclined to move large distances. As in Eurasia and Africa, they increasingly tended to stay close to long-term food sources and centers of ceremonial life.

Early Ceremonial Life   Sedentary foragers began to bury their dead in cemeteries, which soon became territorial centers. They buried their dead with gifts to help them in the life after death. Leaders of forager bands were often shamans, elders with spiritual powers. These shamans fell into trances, during which they experienced merging with powerful animals or other people, charming animals into submission, exorcising evils from humans, or healing afflictions. In their territorial centers, leaders and elders formed councils for the administration of their settlements and hunting grounds.

Shaman-led ceremonies often took place in caves or under overhangs, where people painted animals and humans on the rock walls. Probably the oldest paintings are those of Pedra Furada [PAY-drah foo-RAH-dah] in northeastern Brazil, dating to about 8000 BCE. One of the most distinctive ceremonial paintings is the "white shaman" at Lower Pecos in Texas, dating to 2000 BCE. He is depicted in a trance; his feet are feline, his arms are feathered, and he is surrounded by animals and humans, both dead (upside down) and alive (upright).

Agriculture, Villages, and Urban Life

One major change associated with the pattern of transition from foraging to agriculture is the ability to support large populations. Another change is the

Atlatl (Aztec, "water thrower"): Handheld narrow board or rail with a hook used to hurl darts or small spears overhand at targets.

The White Shaman, Lower Pecos, Texas, ca. 2000 BCE. The practice of shamanism—the belief in the ability of certain individuals to communicate with or inhabit animals or people—appears to be a common feature of many widely diverse peoples, including peoples in Siberia and other areas in northern Eurasia. Many scholars believe that migrants from Asia carried these religious forms with them to the Americas.

creation of the potential for conflict and destruction on an unprecedented scale. In the Americas, this pattern of world history appears to have begun somewhat later than in many areas of Eurasia and Africa.

The Neolithic Revolution in the New World

The first steps toward agriculture occurred in central and southern Mexico in Mesoamerica and in Peru and Ecuador in the Andes. Foragers shortened their annual migrations and extended existing patches of wild potatoes, beans, and **teosinte** [tay-oh-SIN-tay] in the period between 8000 and 6000 BCE. Careful harvesting and replanting led to early domesticated varieties of these plants. Potatoes, beans, and cotton were domesticated first in Peru, and corn at the same time in southern Mexico. By about 3500 BCE, foragers in these regions had completed their transformation into farmers (see "Patterns Up Close").

Teosinte: A wild grass native to Mesoamerica, believed to be ancestral to maize (corn).

Plants and Animals   In addition to potatoes, beans and corn, early farmers in Mesoamerica also domesticated squash, manioc, avocado, and chili pepper; in the Andes, quinoa, amaranth, and tomatoes. In time, many of these plants were exchanged between the two regions. The domestication of animals in the Americas was more modest. As most large mammals had died out after the last Ice Age, there were few animals left of the right size for use as draft, pack, or riding animals (see Figure 5.1). The Americas had no horses or cattle until they were brought by the Spanish in the sixteenth century CE. The development of the wheel, so intimately connected with draft animals, never took place in the Americas, though some of the world's best roads were built through the Andes. The llama was the only animal in pre-Columbian America to provide even modest transportation services as a pack animal. The wool of the alpaca became an important textile fiber in the Andes. In the relative absence of domesticated animals raised for meat, hunting and fishing remained important methods of obtaining food (see Figure 5.1).

Early Settlements   Early agricultural settlements ranged in size from a few extended families to as many as 1,000 inhabitants. As in Neolithic China, the typical dwelling was a round wooden house with a sunken floor, stone foundation, and thatched roof. Some early American agrarian peoples mummified their dead, while others buried their dead in **midden** piles on the outskirts of their villages or in the sand dunes along the beaches. Funerary gifts were modest. In contrast to more transient hunter–gatherer settlements, agrarian villages became settled communities of the living and the dead.

Between 3500 and 2000 BCE, villagers in the lowlands along the Andes coast of Peru built rafts of balsa wood, which enabled them to fish farther from shore.

Midden: A refuse pile. Archaeologists treasure such piles because a great deal can be learned about the material culture of a society by what people threw out over long periods of time.

Comparative Timeline for Domestication of Animals

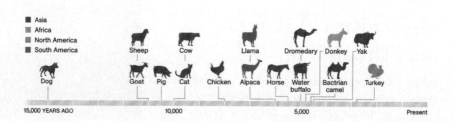

They also pioneered the use of irrigation in the dozens of river deltas along the coast for the growth of cotton (for fishnets and textiles) and food staples (beans and corn). With the fish catches and crop yields boosted by irrigation, the population of the villages increased, and the first signs of social stratification appeared. Scholars have speculated that upstream families had more water and thus accumulated greater food reserves than downstream families. Under the leadership of upstream elders, inhabitants of several villages pooled their labor and built monumental plazas, platforms, and terraces.

As had other societies making the agrarian transition, Mesoamerican and Andean societies also began producing pottery. The earliest known pottery dates to about 3300–3200 BCE on the northern Andean coast; by 1800 BCE pottery making had spread throughout central and southern Mexico. Patterned cotton textiles dating to about 3000 BCE have been found along the coasts of Ecuador and Peru. Condors, double-headed snakes, felines, and human figures were typical motifs on the textiles.

The Origins of Urban Centers

Caral-Supe is one of at least 18 sites of a culture that flourished in the valleys descending from the Andes to the coast. It features monumental stone architecture, including pyramid-shaped temples, plazas, dwellings of different sizes, and a large amphitheater. In 2001, carbon dating revealed the artifacts at the site to be from 2627 BCE, making this by far the oldest city in the Americas and contemporary with the early Mesopotamian cities and the Great Pyramid of Egypt.

Urban Life   Scholars now theorize that this city, like the similarly mysterious sites along the Indus, was part of a civilization supported by agriculture and fishing, with trading networks and a class system. They have linked the Caral-Supe culture to that of Áspero nearby, of the same age. The varied climate, ranging from the coast through lowland plains and river valleys up to mountain highlands, produced pumpkins, squash, sweet potatoes, corn, chilies, beans, and cotton, while the rivers and sea yielded a variety of edible aquatic life. The agriculture of the valley was supported by a sophisticated irrigation system (see Map 5.2).

Farmers were the largest social class, with merchants, administrators, and priests also in evidence, although class hierarchy remains unclear. Varying sizes of houses suggest disparities of wealth, and the proximity of some of the houses to pyramids seems to indicate a religious or bureaucratic connection. The uses to which the amphitheater was put can only be guessed.

Perhaps the most intriguing artifact is an intact quipu, a device of knotted ropes tied together in patterns that form a system of communication. Since the quipu was also used by the Incas over 4,000 years later, it represents not only a direct connection between these two societies but one of the world's first, and oldest, systems of record keeping in continuous use.

Other Andean Cultures   Of smaller scale and a somewhat later period are the structures at El Paraíso, Peru, which date from about 2000 BCE. Villagers built large rectangles of locally quarried rock and mud mortar. They filled the interior of the rectangle with rock rubble encased in large mesh bags, which may have been used to measure the amount of labor each villager contributed. Multichambered

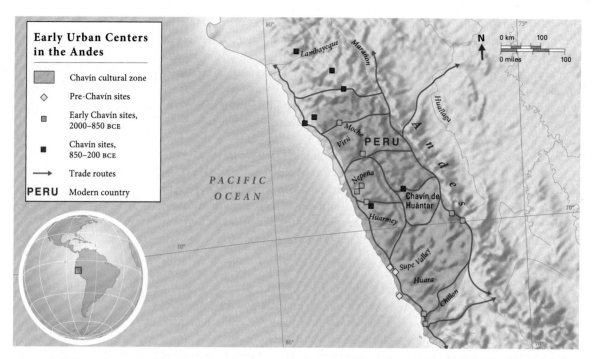

MAP 5.2 **Early Urban Centers in the Andes**

and multistoried buildings made of stone occupied some of the platforms. Steep staircases led from the lower plazas up to these buildings, which were plastered and painted. Wooden beams supported the roofs.

Charcoal-filled pits in the building chambers indicate that some form of sacrifice took place there. The chambers were small, allowing access to no more than a few prominent villagers or shamans. The rest of the villagers assembled on upper and lower platforms, according to their social status, to participate in religious functions and share communal feasts. Early sculptures dating to 1519 BCE suggest that villagers might also have assembled for military displays.

Farmers in the Andean highlands also built ceremonial centers in their villages. As in the lowlands, these centers contained firepits for sacrificial offerings. Highlanders, in addition to farming, engaged in trade, exchanging obsidian and cotton for lowland pottery. Sometime around 1500 BCE, highlanders developed skills in metallurgy, laying the foundation for the development of exquisitely crafted metalwork.

Chavín de Huántar   Work on the small highland city of Chavín de Huántar [cha-VEEN de WAN-tar] (ca. 1000–200 BCE) has yielded important insights into Andean cultural patterns. Situated in a valley high in the Andes Mountains on both banks of a tributary to the Marañón River, Chavín carried on long-distance trade, built and graded roads protected with retaining walls, and cleared mountain paths. Residents of Chavín imported obsidian and metals and exported textiles, pottery, and gold and silver artifacts.

Early Chavín was a small place of some 300 inhabitants, most of whom—including priest-rulers and craftspeople—were detached from agriculture.

Another 700 full-time farmers and herders lived in outlying hamlets. Farmers grew potatoes, quinoa, and some corn on the slopes and valley floor, supplementing the sparse rainfall with irrigation. Corn was used for bread and for brewing a type of beer called *chicha*. On the higher grasslands, herders bred llamas and alpacas for dried meat and wool. Llamas also served as pack animals.

Chavín's ceremonial center consisted of U-shaped ramparts built on a plaza and lined with cut and polished stone. The walls enclosed partially interconnected underground complexes. Within the U was a round, sunken court accessible via staircase. A cross-shaped, centrally located chamber contained a stone sculpture of what is assumed to have been the center's main deity: a fanged, snarling feline creature, standing upright like a human, with one clawed paw extended upward and the other hanging down. The sculpture might have had a shamanic significance, symbolizing the priest's ability to assume the powers of a wild animal.

Other underground chambers were used for sacrificial offerings, possibly human as well as animal. Canals guided water through the underground chambers. Priest-rulers and the assembled villagers used the temple complex to offer sacrifices, observe open-air rituals, celebrate feasts, dance, and perform music.

By around 500 BCE, the population had grown to about 3,000 inhabitants. Artisans living in the town began to specialize in particular crafts. Whether these craftspeople had given up agricultural labor completely is not known. Homes for the wealthy were built of stone, while those of the less-well-off were made of adobe. The rich dined on the meat of young llamas; poorer residents subsisted on the meat of decommissioned pack animals. Around the town, there must have been a number of villages with farmers producing enough food to feed the urban dwellers.

The increased population meant larger assemblies, which in turn required bigger platforms and a larger temple for more sacrifices. By 400 BCE, Chavín had become the culturally dominant center of the region. Travelers, traders, and pilgrims visited the temple, offering seashells, coca leaves, and textiles to the priests in return for receiving temple blessings. Residents of Chavín provided services for the visitors, such as lodging and meals. Craftspeople produced clothing, wall hangings, banners, and pottery in what were identifiable Chavín patterns, motifs, and styles.

Chavín de Huántar, New Temple. Chavín is one of the best-studied sites and over the years has yielded considerable information about town and small-city life in the ancient Americas.

Inhabitants of Chavín pioneered new techniques in the making of textiles and in metallurgy. Goldsmiths devised new methods of soldering and alloying gold and silver to make large ornamental objects. Small objects, such as golden headbands, ear spools, beads, and pins, signified prestige and wealth. Gold artifacts found in the graves of the wealthy attest the high value residents of Chavín appear to have placed on gold.

Chavín came to a gradual end, perhaps declining as other centers began producing equivalent goods and competing in trade. In any event, sometime after 500

Patterns Up Close | The Origin of Corn

The teosinte grass does not seem to be a likely productive food crop, or even edible. Yet when some bold people first began to cultivate it, they launched one of the most momentous revolutions in world history: a completely independent chapter in the transition from foraging to agriculture and, ultimately, to agrarian-based urban civilization. The ultimate result of their work—maize, or corn—ultimately became the world's most versatile and widely grown food crop (see Map 5.3). Indeed, ancient Mayans believed that humans themselves were made from corn.

Various Types of Corn

The origin of corn is believed to be in what is now southern Mexico. According to a 2018 genetic paper, some 9,000 years ago foragers began the process of cultivating the unpromising teosinte grass into the grain that would eventually sustain vast numbers of people. For a long time, plant geneticists were not in agreement as to how the domestication process took place. Recently, however, a number of enticing clues about the process have emerged.

In a 2016 study by researchers from the Natural History Museum of Denmark, a 5,310-year-old maize cob from the Teotihuacán Valley was subjected to DNA testing. The analysis established that this was maize in an intermediate stage of domestication. That is, a number of key genes had already been altered by the process of humans selecting the seeds of promising plants. Among the most significant of these are the elimination of a hard seed coat—for softer, more edible kernels—and changes in the plants' flowering time. Changes still to come included raising the sugar content in the kernels, multiplying their number, and controlling the plants' seed dispersal time to make harvesting easier and more uniform. The researchers theorize that this intermediate maize was not yet a staple, but rather a supplement in the diets of small, mobile, seasonally foraging clans.

BCE, archaeologists note a decisive trend toward militarization, with the emergence of fortified villages and forts in the region. Chavín may have succumbed to military attack. Sometime around 200 BCE, it appears that squatters invaded the largely deserted city, which subsequently fell into ruin.

The First Mesoamerican Settlements

In Mesoamerica, the first permanent villages appear to date from around 1800 BCE. The first ceremonial centers appeared along the Pacific coast of southern Mexico and Guatemala around 1500 BCE. As in the Andes, the ceremonial centers consisted of plazas, platforms, and terraces. Metallurgy, however, did not develop here for another millennium; instead of metals, craftspeople used jade for ornaments. By around 1200 BCE, agrarian society throughout the Andes and

Regarding the other changes leading to staple maize, promising results were presented by plant geneticist Mary Eubanks in 2004, who attempted to experimentally trace the origins of corn. Her experiments showed convincingly that teosinte was, in fact, an ancestor plant of modern corn but that it had at some point been bred with gamagrass, which contains key genes for multiplying and enlarging the kernels on each ear. Moreover, her work supported other recent research that suggested that the plant had developed rapidly into a usable staple, though it would seem that it spent a considerable time in its intermediate stage as a supplemental crop, before it resembled, a thousand years ago, the corn we have today.

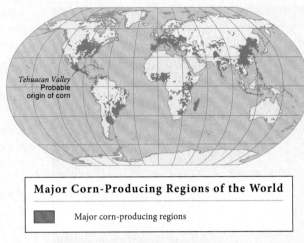

Major Corn-Producing Regions of the World

■ Major corn-producing regions

MAP 5.3 **Major Corn-Producing Regions of the World**

We have to assume that this momentous feat was accomplished by plan and experimentation, given its complexity. The result permanently altered the agricultural patterns of world history, particularly over the last 300 years. Corn's versatility allows it to be cultivated on every habitable continent, often on land too marginal to support any other staple crop. It is widely used as human and animal food and helped to sustain population expansions in North America, Asia, and Europe. It spawned huge industries in such modern foodstuffs as corn syrup and oil and older ones like whiskey and beer. Most recently, and controversially, it has been touted as a biofuel. In short, this American innovation's uses are still unfolding.

Questions

- Why is the innovation of corn a "momentous revolution in world history"?
- How does the fact that this example of bioengineering occurred 6,000–7,000 years ago put today's debate on genetically modified foods into a new perspective?

Mesoamerica was characterized by ceremonial centers centrally located among several villages, monumental structures of plazas and platforms, and the production of sacred ornaments.

The Olmec The first important Mesoamerican center was that of the Olmecs at San Lorenzo (1200–900 BCE), located on the Gulf of Mexico in forested coastal lowlands. Farmers in these lowlands had to cut down and burn the dense tropical rain forest before they could plant corn. Once the riverbanks had been cleared, the silt deposited by floods during the rainy season and the rich soil created favorable agricultural conditions. As in Mesopotamia, Egypt, India, and China, the rivers here proved productive. The high yield from corn harvests allowed for the rise of wealthy ruling families, who assumed dominant positions over small farmers.

Olmec Jade Mask. Like the Chinese, Mesoamerican peoples appear to have worked jade from very ancient times.

The ceremonial center of San Lorenzo was located on a plateau, on which archaeologists have unearthed some 60 terraced platforms, 20 ponds, countless basalt-lined drainage troughs, and the foundations of dwellings for 1,000 inhabitants. The dense concentration of dwellings suggests that San Lorenzo was an urban center inhabited by priests, administrators, and craftspeople. Based on estimates of crop yields in the area and the number of dwellings at the site, scholars believe that some 10,000 small farmers lived around the center, producing the surplus food needed by the urban center.

The priest-rulers of San Lorenzo engaged thousands of farmers as laborers to construct the plateau and its terraced platforms. Laborers quarried blocks of basalt from a mountain range 70 miles to the northwest of San Lorenzo. Large groups of workers shouldered beams from which the basalt blocks, weighing 18 tons on average, hung in slings. They carried these blocks to the coast and shipped them to San Lorenzo on rafts. There, sculptors fashioned the blocks into fierce-looking, helmeted heads, kneeling or sitting figures, and animal statues. It is unknown whether these figures represented priest-rulers, gods, or divine beings.

Olmec priest-rulers also commissioned sculptors to craft figurines and masks from jade and serpentine. Since jade and serpentine could be obtained only from areas some 200 miles away, San Lorenzo appears to have been not an isolated urban center but a place with far-reaching trade connections.

Around 900 BCE, a mysterious event took place that destroyed San Lorenzo. Whatever occurred, the event left San Lorenzo's large stone sculptures mutilated and buried in carefully prepared graves, along with the sculptors' tools used in creating the images. Following the fall of San Lorenzo, La Venta, 50 miles to the northeast, became the leading Olmec center. The first settlers at La Venta cleared the rain forest from a ridge on a swampy river island in the lowlands and then graded the ridge to create a plateau. On the plateau they erected terraced platforms and a 100-foot-high earthen mound to establish an urban center. Burial sites at La Venta contained axes and figurines made of serpentine and jade as well as mirrors ground from iron-bearing ores. Rulers' regalia included mirrors, but what significance these might have had is unknown.

About 600 BCE, La Venta ended under circumstances as mysterious as those that destroyed San Lorenzo. The next Olmec center was at Tres Zapotes, a more modest complex 70 miles to the northwest. Tres Zapotes endured from about 500 to 1 BCE, when it was eclipsed by new ceremonial centers in the highlands west of the Olmec lowlands.

Through their long-distance trade, the Olmecs left a cultural imprint throughout Mesoamerica. Olmec traders obtained obsidian in Guatemala and jade from mines south of the Mexican Basin and in Guatemala and Costa Rica. In exchange for these raw materials, the Olmecs exported cacao beans, pottery, textiles, and jewelry. Along their trade routes, the Olmecs maintained settler outposts to supply the traders.

Olmec Writing?   A fist-sized clay seal displaying a bird relief was discovered in 2002 in a dump at La Venta. The seal, dating to 650 BCE, shows the bird with what appears to be a speech bubble, pronouncing the two symbols "3 Ajaw" and "Ajaw." The symbol means "lord," and "3 Lord" could be the name of an Olmec king. The seal was used to stain textiles for the royal family. Unfortunately, no further texts have been found, with the exception of the Cascajal [kahs-ka-HAHL] stone in Veracruz, found in 2006 and dated to 1100–900 BCE. The stone's authenticity, however, is still controversial, and in any event, the sum of one seal and one inscribed stone slab are still insufficient for the deciphering of what is assumed to be the Olmec script.

Foraging and Farming Societies Outside the Andes and Mesoamerica

After 2000 BCE, many foragers in North and South America had adopted agriculture as a full or partial mode of subsistence. Foraging groups continued to persist, however, in some places down to the present. Using stone tools, they hunted whales in the extreme north, cleared some of the forests of east and midwest North America, irrigated and farmed arid areas of the southwest, and foraged and farmed in the Amazon basin of South America.

The Inuit   The Inuit [INN-ooh-it] arrived from Siberia in the far northern tundra of North America around 2000 BCE. For a long period, they remained traditional hunter–gatherers. Much later, during the first millennium CE, they began hunting whales. As many as 20 sailors with paddles manned a boat built of walrus ribs and skin. In the summer, boats traveled the coastal seas for weeks at a time. A whale carcass could feed a hamlet for an entire winter.

The Inuit lived in pit houses framed by whale ribs, covered with walrus skin, and piled over with sod. The entrances were long, dipped tunnels that trapped the cold air below the floor of the house. On winter hunts, people built snow houses, or igloos, from ice blocks. During the summer, the Inuit moved from the pit houses to tents. Women used caribou sinew and seal and caribou pelts to make warm and watertight clothing. For transportation on snow and ice, the Inuit used dog teams to pull sleds. They traded mammal teeth and carved bone artifacts for timber and earthenware from the south. By 1000 CE the Inuit had expanded from the North American Arctic eastward to Greenland.

Adena and Hopewell   Agricultural villages appeared in the cleared forest areas of the central and northern parts of North America by the first millennium BCE. The villagers of the Adena (1000–100 BCE) and Hopewell (200 BCE–500 CE) cultures in the center and east pooled their labor to build ridges and mounds used in ceremonies and rituals. The phenomenon of mound building seems to have been widespread. A small Adena mound covering a child's grave in Labrador is estimated to be some 7,500 years old. Others, much larger and more recent (about 4,500 years old), have been found in the lower Mississippi valley. At Hopewell, large square and circular enclosures contained multiple mounds encompassing dozens of acres of land. Research suggests that some of the Hopewell settlements were connected by roads up to 60 miles long, perhaps serving communal purposes such as official visits and gift exchanges (see Map 5.4).

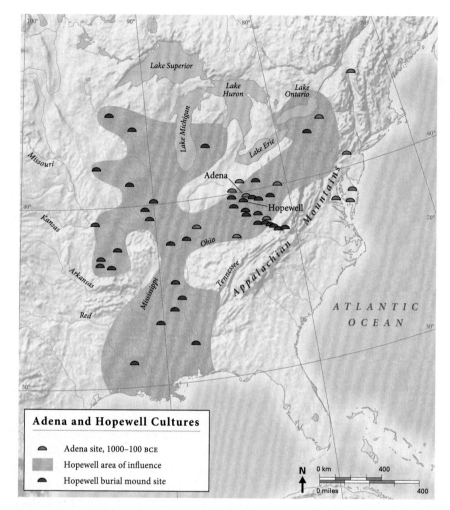

MAP 5.4 **Adena and Hopewell Cultures**

Amazonian Peoples   In the floodplains of the Amazonian rain forest in South America, agricultural villages also date to the first millennium BCE. The best-explored culture is that of Marajó [mah-rah-ZHO], on a large island in the mouth of the Amazon. At its height in ca. 500 BCE, the Marajó built large funeral mounds. The cultures of the floodplains in the upper Amazon drainage are still largely unexplored. For example, at an unknown date, the Baures culture in today's Bolivia established a complex of canals, raised fields, moat-enclosed villages, and causeways connecting the villages. The complexity of this culture left a strong impression on the Spanish missionaries who visited the area in the sixteenth century CE.

The Islands of the Caribbean   The earliest hunter–gatherer settlements in the rain forests of the Caribbean islands date to the fourth millennium BCE, but from where on the mainland these first settlers came is unknown. The first agricultural settlements appeared between 500 BCE and 500 CE, when migrants from the Orinoco River region in the northeast of South America colonized the eastern Caribbean as far west as today's Dominican Republic and Haiti. These people built villages and terraces, and their ceramics suggest a shamanic religion. Beginning in eastern Hispaniola around 500 CE, villagers supported the emergence of the Taíno [ta-EE-no] chieftain society that by ca. 1500 comprised nearly the entire Caribbean. Influenced by Mayan culture (see Chapter 6), some Taíno chiefs built ball courts and causeways. In their villages, the chiefs employed specialized craftspeople. Sailors using canoes traveled extensively to the mainland and among the islands in search of salt, jade, and metals. These travels connected the Taíno chiefdom society with Mesoamerican societies on the mainland.

The Origins of Pacific Island Migrations

The peopling of the islands of Oceania may be seen as an extreme case of one of the great patterns of world history—interactions between cultures separated by great expanses of ocean. In prehistoric times, Asians traveled not only to the Americas but also to the islands of the Pacific and Indian Oceans (see Map 5.5).

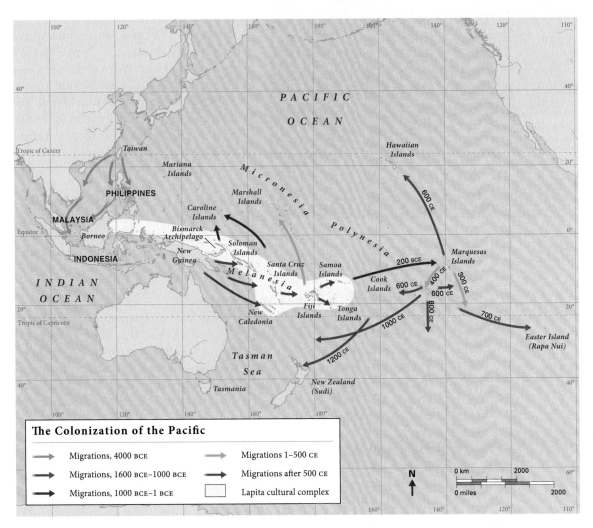

MAP 5.5 The Colonization of the Pacific

Bwaimas, Papua New Guinea. Some of the earliest known human attempts at agriculture took place in the highlands of Papua New Guinea perhaps 9,000–7,000 years ago. The introduction of yams several millennia later created an enduring staple crop, and their portability allowed their spread as they sustained seafarers throughout the Pacific. Bwaimas are storehouses for yams.

The populating of Oceania must rank as one of humankind's greatest feats. Vast amounts of open ocean had to be crossed between many of the island groups in the Pacific in order to settle them. Nevertheless, early seafaring people settled island after island, traveling until they had discovered nearly every island of Oceania. Using linguistic analysis, scholars theorize that the people of Oceania are at least partially related to Taiwan's aboriginal population. About 6,000 years ago, the first seafaring people left Taiwan and, together with subsequent waves of emigrants, spread out in westerly and easterly directions. They settled in the Philippines, Indonesia, and the Malay Peninsula, bestowing their languages and ethnic identities on the aboriginal peoples of these lands.

Descendants of these settlers later spread farther into the Indian and Pacific Oceans. In the Indian Ocean, they sailed as far west as Madagascar, an island off the east coast of Africa, where they arrived around 200 CE and founded a number of chiefdoms. In the Pacific Ocean, they sailed to the Bismarck Archipelago, off the eastern coast of New Guinea. It was on this archipelago that settlers created the Lapita culture around 1600 BCE, which was the homeland for the colonization of Oceania— that is, the islands of Polynesia, Micronesia, and parts of Melanesia. On the map, Oceania forms a huge triangle comprising Polynesia, Hawaii, New Zealand, and Easter Island, with Micronesia and Melanesia to the west.

Lapita and Cultural Expansion

By the fourth millennium BCE, a sophisticated system known as the Lapita [la-PEE-ta] cultural complex had become established. Named for a site on the island of New Caledonia, the Lapita culture was a system of kinship-based exchanges among the inhabitants of thousands of islands. Of particular importance was obsidian, which was highly prized as a material for tools and weapons in the absence of workable metals. Another item in demand was pottery decorated with stamped patterns now called Lapita ware, after shards located at that site.

Environment and Long-Distance Navigation   By about 1600 BCE, decisive innovations in long-distance navigation over hundreds of miles of open sea as well as the systematic colonization of otherwise uninhabitable islands had emerged. Large, sophisticated sail- and paddle-driven oceangoing canoes provided reliable craft for such journeys. An orally transmitted storehouse of navigational information enabled sailors to set their courses by the sun and stars, retain mental maps of islands, read winds and currents, and take advantage of seasonal reverses in prevailing wind directions.

Perhaps the most important development centered on supplying such voyages. The cultivation of storable root crops, especially yams and taro, proved invaluable in sustaining long voyages. Among other staples circulated among the colonized islands were breadfruit, coconuts, and bananas, as well as such domesticated animals as pigs, chickens, and dogs. From 1600 to 100 BCE, Lapita sailors moved eastward and settled the islands of Vanuatu, Tonga, Fiji, and Samoa. Archaeologists believe that Fiji may be the source of the culture that sparked the next outward migration, that of the Polynesians.

Creating Polynesia

As populations grew, the primary mode of governmental and economic organization, the kinship-based chiefdom, became increasingly elaborated. On Tonga, the Society Islands, the Marquesas, and later the Hawaiian Islands, the power of centralizing chiefs extended over several islands.

Interaction and Expansion   The effect of centralization and intensified agriculture in the more productive islands on their inhabitants is uncertain. Up to a point, they may have made these societies more efficient as food producers. But the difficulties we have seen in other societies of sustaining large populations on limited amounts of land were undoubtedly intensified in island societies. Environmental problems related to overpopulation may have developed in the Cook Islands and the Marquesas around 900–1000 CE and again in 1200–1300 CE. Political disputes arising from struggles between centralizing and decentralizing factions may have played a role as well. In any case, there seems to have been a break around 1200 CE that resulted in the longest period of migration yet: to Rapa Nui (Easter Island) around 1200 CE, to Hawaii between 1219 and 1266 CE, and New Zealand between 1200 and 1300 CE.

Later Interactions   By the time of the first European contact in the early sixteenth century, nearly every habitable island in the Pacific had been settled, and some had populations of many hundreds of thousands. As we shall see in subsequent chapters, however, this vast achievement of Polynesian exploration and colonization would soon be threatened by disease and a new breed of conquerors and colonists. The next three and a half centuries of European exploration of the Pacific would carry with them disastrously unforeseen consequences.

Putting It All Together

Though separated from each other by thousands of miles of ocean, the Americas and Oceania share common patterns with each other as well as with the cultures of Eurasia and Africa. The first pattern is that even in such widely separated areas, human foraging communities at roughly the same time independently began a process toward the development of agriculture and animal domestication. While domestication of the first plants and animals and gathering

- hey

into more settled village life began shortly after the last retreat of the glaciers in Eurasia, it came somewhat later in the Americas, perhaps because human groups were still few in number and could be sustained by large-game hunting. It is also the case that the plant that ultimately became a chief staple of the American societies, corn, required extensive experimentation before becoming domesticated. Thus, it is only around 4000 BCE that we see the beginning of its extensive cultivation.

The second pattern is growth and sophistication of social structures and the development of the city and of monumental architecture for religious and political purposes. In some cases, the types of structures—pyramids, terraces, and obelisks, for example—seem to follow an almost universal pattern. Recent finds at the Caral-Supe sites show how rapidly the development of large cities took place once the threshold of plant and animal domestication was crossed. Like those of the Indus Valley, the accomplishments of the society that created Caral survived in the local practices of Andean peoples long after the cities themselves were abandoned. The settlements of the Olmecs, though coming somewhat later, were equally imposing in their architecture, the efficacy of their farming and irrigation, the sophistication of their social structures, and their development of writing.

In the case of Oceania, the peopling of the islands of the Pacific was inseparable from trade and cultural connections. Colonizing uninhabited islands could take place only when the plants and animals required could be brought along and provision could be made to trade for unavailable items. Thus, in terms of square mileage, the Lapita and Polynesian cultures extended over one of the world's largest regions, including thousands of islands. Yet, the very size of this region meant that once it was colonized, the islanders found it difficult to maintain contact with each other. Gradually, a variety of island cultures grew up in isolation from each other. Furthermore, the island surfaces available to agriculture impeded the growth of villages beyond subsistence and the development of the agrarian–urban pattern. It is, therefore, all the more remarkable that people on Rapa Nui devised a glyphic writing system, called rongorongo, which, unfortunately, remains undeciphered. Despite its handicaps, Oceanic culture impresses with its achievements.

Review and Relate

Thinking Through Patterns

Examine the ways historians approach the big questions of this chapter.

> What do historians see as the advantages and disadvantages of the separate evolution of the Americas?

This question is often debated. For one thing, we can ask instead why we should consider the Americas as "isolated," rather than Eurasia and Africa. But it is true that the societies were not as large or diverse as their Eurasian counterparts.

Historically, too, scholars still often view the two sets of continents as "old" and "new," and from that perspective they view the Americas as "isolated." How one interprets the question also revolves around how one sees the roles of invasion, infusion of innovation, and cultural competition. Some scholars have argued that the very shape of Eurasia allowed for the dissemination of innovation along areas similarly situated in latitude and therefore climate. The Americas, however, were more longitudinally oriented, making such diffusion more difficult. Some argue that the separateness of the Americas allowed them to cultivate distinctive cultural traits among their populations. Yet others argue that constant mixing of peoples and ideas accelerates innovation and, hence, "progress." One distinct disadvantage of separation is that peoples become susceptible to diseases suddenly inflicted on them. Thus, from the sixteenth to the early eighteenth centuries, virulent epidemics of Eurasian and African diseases like smallpox devastated the peoples of the Americas when introduced.

While the Pacific Islanders had abundant access to food, the islands themselves were generally too small to allow the accumulation of enough surplus food to free up the numbers of nonfarmers necessary to build and maintain a city. In addition, the islands themselves contained limited amounts of building materials and fresh water, while their isolation helped guard them against attack. Culturally, the islanders also had grown to *expect* that if their numbers outran the food supply, they could simply find another island to which the excess population could migrate.

> Why did no cities develop on the larger Pacific Islands?

Historians look at this question in one of two ways: culturally or practically. Some cultural scholars see a lack of deep-seated affinities for circular motion in the belief systems of the American peoples as helping to prevent them from relating to the motion of the wheel in the way that Eurasian and African peoples did. Yet American societies were not unaware of the concept of circular motion. Scholars favoring a practical approach argue that the environment of the mountains close by seacoasts, rain forests, and dry, hilly regions was not conducive to bulk transport by wheeled vehicles and that the peoples there simply were never forced to look for more efficient means of transport.

> The wheel is often cited as the most basic human invention, yet large and sophisticated civilizations were able to flourish without this signal innovation. Why do you think it did not develop in the Americas?

| **Against the Grain**

Rapa Nui: Catastrophe or Continuity?

Consider this as a counterpoint to the main patterns examined in this chapter.

- Confronted with two very different accounts, one generally accepted and the other still struggling to become known, what reasons would you give to justify your choice?

- Why do responsible historians usually wait before they discard an older theory and embrace a new revisionist one, even if the new one is more convincing?

In his highly popular book *Catastrophe* (2005), the physiologist Jared Diamond advanced the theory of "ecocide" perpetrated by the Polynesians who settled the island ca. 900 CE. According to the book, the settlers grew to more than 15,000 and in the process completely deforested the island, using the timber for the transportation of the *moai*, the famous gigantic stone sculptures of gods, which the chiefs used to "impress the masses" and extract taxes from them. Rats contributed to the deforestation as well, eating the palm seeds. As erosion on the denuded land progressed, entire animal species hunted for food died out, and agriculture on the depleted soil declined. People began to doubt the chiefs and in a civil war around 1680 overturned the sculptures, decimated each other, and even descended into cannibalism. The few survivors, so Diamond concludes, carved out a meager life in dire poverty.

Moai on the Island of Rapa Nui (Easter Island). Polynesian settlers around 1200 or later created these sculptures, which are believed to be images of ancestors responsible for guarding the fields on the island. Maoi ("statues") could be as tall as 33 feet and weigh up to ten tons.

Against the grain of this still generally accepted catastrophist account, used as a warning against unrestrained environmental destruction, a few archaeologists (notably Terry Hunt and Carl Lipo) present Rapa Nui as the story of how a small group of people worked together under challenging circumstances. They write that when the first settlers arrived around 1200 CE, much of the island was covered with palm groves. With the expansion of agriculture the groves shrank, and by 1400 only small stands remained. But the story does not end there. Repeated droughts during ca. 1500–1700 reduced the island's aquifers, most of which flowed out to the surrounding ocean. It was from holes on the beaches that the villages provided themselves with fresh water, which became the most valuable resource. Some 288 moai statues are close to these aquifer outlets and are interpreted as embodiments of ancestors guaranteeing access to their respective lineages of descendants. Displaying incredible innovation and determination, teams of villagers dragged the moai (average weight 14 tons) with ropes from the quarries to the beaches. Despite the difficult environment, the islanders managed to maintain cohesion.

The first Western explorers arrived on Rapa Nui in the early 1700s, bringing diseases with them that severely reduced indigenous population numbers, from perhaps 7,500 in 1600 to 111 in the 1860s. Peruvian slave raids further decimated the population. Today, the about 8,000 inhabitants of Rapa Nui live as part of a "special territory" administered by Chile.

Key Terms

Atlatl 107	El Niño 105	Teosinte 108
Cordilleras 102	Midden 108	Younger Dryas 106

Learn more with this chapter's digital tools, including the Oxford Insight Study Guide, at http://www.oup.com/he/vonsivers4e. Please see the Further Resources section at the back of the book for additional readings and suggested websites.

Sources for Chapter 5

Quipu from the Caral-Supe culture, Peru

2600–2000 BCE

Recent archaeological discoveries in the Caral-Supe valley have pushed back the timeline of cultural development in the Andes by several millennia. A fixture of later Incan culture, the quipu was an elaborate series of knotted ropes that seemed to serve as a coded system of communication. Its presence in Caral-Supe demonstrates that the quipu was used in the region as much as 3,000 years before its earliest previous attestation. Moreover, this quipu was apparently left as an offering on the stairway of a public building when another building was built on top. Below is the image of a much later quipu dating to the Inca Empire.

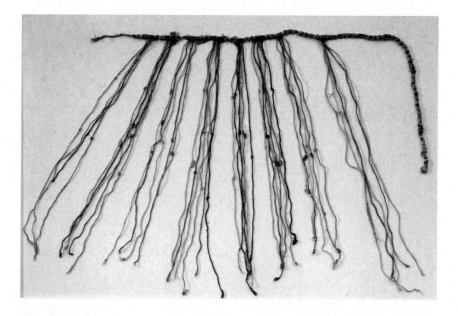

▶ **Working with Sources**

1. What does this object suggest about the continuities among various Andean cultures over several thousand years?

2. What does the existence of an object used for accounting suggest about this culture's administrative and bureaucratic sophistication?

Source: © President and Fellows of Harvard College, Peabody Museum of Archaeology and Ethnology, Harvard University, PM# 2004.24.35177 (digital file# 153390016)

SOURCE 5.2   # Textile fragment from Chavín de Huántar, Peru

ca. 500–200 BCE

Now housed in the Metropolitan Museum of Art in New York City, this section of an elaborately crafted and painted piece of textile attests to the manufacturing prowess of the Chavín people. In the image, a central fanged figure grasps and may be controlling a four-eyed monster. The snake-like elements of this figure have led to the conclusion that he is an ancestor of the *khipucamayuc*, the Inca name for the keeper of a quipu.

▶ **Working with Sources**

1. What does the sophistication of this object indicate about the division of labor in Chavín society at its peak?

2. What were the likely connections between textile manufacture and the operation of quipu in the period?

SOURCE 5.3

New DNA results show Kennewick Man was Native American

ca. 6500 BCE

Nothing was ordinary about the events surrounding the remains of Kennewick Man. The two students who discovered his remains on the banks of the Columbia River in 1996 were trying to sneak into a concert. Native Americans who demanded the remains for reburial were rebuffed by scientists insisting that the bones were only distantly related to those of today's tribes. An appeals court in 2004 ruled that the remains were too old to allow for a direct cultural link and allowed for scientific research to continue. A decade later, a genetic study concluded that Kennewick Man's remains were indeed the ancestral bones of a Native American. Finally, in 2017, this modern Odyssean journey ended with Kennewick Man's ceremonial reburial in the Columbia River Basin.

In July 1996, two college students were wading in the shallows of the Columbia River near the town of Kennewick, Wash., when they stumbled across a human skull. At first the police treated the case as a possible murder. But once a nearly complete skeleton emerged from the riverbed and was examined, it became clear that the bones were extremely old — ca. 8,500 years old, it would later turn out.

The skeleton, which came to be known as Kennewick Man, or the Ancient One, is one of the oldest and perhaps the most important — and controversial — ever found in North America. Native American tribes said that the bones were the remains of an ancestor and moved to reclaim them in order to provide a ritual burial. But a group of scientists filed a lawsuit to stop them, arguing that Kennewick Man could not be linked to living Native Americans. Adding to the controversy was the claim from some scientists that Kennewick Man's skull had unusual "Caucasoid" features. Speculation flew that Kennewick Man was European.

Danish scientists published an analysis of DNA obtained from the skeleton. Kennewick Man's genome clearly does not belong to a European, the scientists said. "It's very clear that Kennewick Man is most closely related to contemporary Native Americans," said Eske Willerslev, a geneticist at the University of

Source: Adapted from Carl Zimmer, "New DNA Results Show Kennewick Man Was Native American," *New York Times*, June 18, 2015.

Copenhagen and lead author of the study, which was published in the journal Nature. "In my view, it's bone-solid." . . .

The scientific study of Kennewick Man began in 2005, after eight years of litigation seeking to prevent repatriation of Kennewick Man to the Native American tribes. A group of scientists led by Douglas W. Owsley, division head of physical anthropology at the Smithsonian Institution, gained permission to study the bones. [In 2014], they published a 670-page book laying out their findings. Kennewick Man stood about 5 foot 7 inches, they reported, and died at about the age of 40. He was probably a right-handed spear-thrower, judging from the oversized bones in his right arm and leg. . . .

In 2013, one of the scientists examining the skeleton, Thomas W. Stafford of the University of Aarhus in Denmark, provided Dr. Willerslev and his colleagues with part of a hand bone. Dr. Willerslev and other researchers have developed powerful methods for gathering ancient DNA. Once they had assembled the DNA into its original sequence, the scientists compared it with genomes from a number of individuals selected from around the world. They also examined genomes from living New World people, as well as the genome Dr. Willerslev and his colleagues found in a 12,600-year-old skeleton in Montana known as the Anzick child. This analysis clearly established that Kennewick Man's DNA is Native American. . . .

After determining that Kennewick Man was a Native American, Dr. Willerslev approached the five tribes that had fought in court to repatriate the skeleton. He asked if they would be interested in joining the study. "We were hesitant," said Mr. Joel Boyd, of the Colville Tribes. "Science hasn't been good to us." Eventually, the Colville agreed to join the study; the other four tribes [of the area in Washington State] did not.

The Colville Tribes and the scientists worked out an arrangement that suited them all. Dr. Willerslev and his colleagues sent equipment for collecting saliva to the reservation. Colville tribe members gathered samples and sent them back. In exchange for permission to sequence the DNA, Dr. Willerslev and his colleagues agreed that they would share the data with other scientists only for confirmation of the findings in the Nature study. Dr. Willerslev also invited representatives of the five tribes to Copenhagen, where they observed the research in his lab. They donned body suits to enter a clean room in the lab in order to perform a ceremony in honor of the Ancient One. Dr. Kim M. TallBear, a cultural anthropologist at the University of Texas, praised the way the scientists worked with the Native Americans. "There's progress there, and I'm happy about that," she said.

When Dr. Willerslev and his colleagues looked at the Colville DNA, they found that it was the closest match to Kennewick Man among all the samples from Native Americans in the study. But other scientists stressed that the new study didn't have enough data to establish a tight link between Kennewick Man and any of the tribes in the region where he was found. Unlike in Canada or Latin America, scientists in the United States do not have many genomes of Native Americans. Dr. TallBear saw this gap as a legacy of the distrust between Native Americans and [many] scientists.

In addition to the conflict over Kennewick Man, the Havasupai Indians of Arizona won a court case in 2010 to take back blood samples that they argued were being used for genetic tests to which they didn't consent. Some scientists may be reluctant to get into a similar conflict. "People are scared post-Havasupai," Dr. TallBear said. . . .

Postscript (PVS, CAD, GBS): The US Congress passed a resolution in September 2016 to return the bones and skull of Kennewick Man to the five Native American tribes of the Columbia River region for burial. On February 18, 2017, 200 members of the tribes attended the burial ceremony.

▶ **Working with Sources**

1. Why was it so important for the scientific community to establish the ancestry of Kennewick Man?

2. Do you agree with the compromise reached between Dr. Willersley and the Colville Tribe concerning the genetic investigation of Kennewick? Do you think there are better solutions?

SOURCE 5.4

Lapita pot shards, found in Vanuatu, western Pacific

ca. fourth millennium BCE

Named for a site in the archipelago of New Caledonia, the Lapita culture was a system of kinship-based exchanges among the inhabitants of thousands of islands in the western Pacific. Elements of "Lapita ware," decorated with stamped patterns, were in high demand, and pots were exchanged among the inhabitants of the islands.

▶ **Working with Sources**

1. What do the elaborate designs imprinted on this pot suggest about the sophistication of Lapita culture?

2. How can the pot be connected with the themes of navigation and gift exchange in the wider Polynesian culture?

Source: © Philippe Métois

World Period Two

The Age of Empires and Visionaries, 600 BCE–600 CE

In the middle of the first millennium BCE, two major transformations changed the course of world history.

- **Empires in Eurasia** Two types of conquering kingdoms or empires formed, after Akkad had pioneered this form of polity during the first world period. The first type, in the Middle East, Mediterranean, and India, was that of multiethnic and multireligious empires, which followed each other in sequence. The second type consisted of the ethnically and religiously more uniform empires of Egypt and China.

- **Visionaries and the Adoption of State Religions** Around 700–500 BCE, visionaries arose who proclaimed the idea of personal salvation. They anchored this idea in the higher, absolute standard of monotheism or monism, which was not bound to any state on Earth. Followers of the visionaries formed communities and schools based on texts that expounded monotheistic or monist teachings. Eventually, rulers adopted these teachings and turned them into state religions.

Chapter 6

Chiefdoms and Early States in Africa and the Americas

600 BCE–600 CE

CHAPTER SIX PATTERNS

Origins, Interactions, Adaptations Africans in the Sahara interacted with the Middle East early on. In World Period One they adapted to agriculture, village life, urbanism, and kingdom formation (Nubia and Kush along the Nile). After 300 CE, the kingdom of Aksum in the Ethiopian highlands of East Africa adopted Christian monotheism, while Africans farther south shifted from foraging to agriculture, villages, and chiefdoms and remained faithful to African spirituality. By 600 CE, urbanism had spread to West Africa and foraging had retreated into the interior of the continent. In the Americas, state formation continued with the emergence of the Maya kingdoms, in which the adoption of a script for monuments testified to a high degree of urban culture.

Uniqueness and Similarities The kingdom of Meroë [MEH-ro-wee] and its successor Aksum provided important links for early commercial interaction among West Africa, the Mediterranean, and India. As such, they provide examples of the mutual adaptation of material culture across continents.

In the Americas, the Maya kingdoms and Teotihuacán demonstrate how humans were able to construct complex temples, artistically expressive murals, and imposing stadiums with limited technical means (no work animals, plows, and wheels).

A humble stone carving in Oaxaca, in southern Mexico, carbon-dated to about 600 BCE, is the earliest documentation for the existence of a 260-day divinatory calendar in Mesoamerica, which later played a central part in Mayan time reckoning and divination. This calendar system is still in use by people in southern Mexico, making it among the world's longest-lived methods of reckoning time. Similarly, an astronomical observatory in Kenya, carbon-dated to 300 BCE, is the earliest example of the so-called Borana lunar calendar of 354 days. It is still in use today among the Kushite herders of East Africa. The two calendars are reminders of the ubiquity and diversity of calendar systems.

During the period 600 BCE–600 CE, the Americas and sub-Saharan Africa shared patterns of agricultural development, spread of villages, emergence of chiefdoms, and early rise of kingdoms. These institutions evolved more slowly than in the more populated Eurasia. Since there was little contact between Eurasia on one hand and the Americas and much of sub-Saharan Africa on the other, it is remarkable that the patterns of agriculture and life in villages, chiefdoms, and kingdoms were fairly consistent *within* world regions as much as *across* world regions. Nevertheless, as we saw in Chapter 5, the isolated world regions, through their own internal interactions, adapted to a transition from foraging to agriculture.

CHAPTER OUTLINE

Agriculture and Early African Kingdoms

The Spread of Villages in Sub-Saharan Africa

Early States in Mesoamerica: Maya Kingdoms and Teotihuacán

The Andes: Moche

Paracas and the Nasca in Southern Peru

Putting It All Together

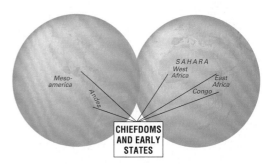

Agriculture and Early African Kingdoms

Sub-Saharan Africa transitioned from forager to agrarian–urban society less rapidly and less completely than Eurasia. However, north of the Sahara, Africans interacted with the Middle East and adapted to its agrarian patterns early on.

ABOVE: The ruins of Meroitic pyramids at Jebel Barkal in modern Sudan

Seeing Patterns

❯ How does comparing and contrasting sub-Saharan Africa with the Americas during 600 BCE–600 CE help in understanding the agrarian–urban patterns of social and political development across the world?

❯ Where did chiefdoms, cities, and kingdoms arise in sub-Saharan Africa and why? On which forms of agriculture, urbanization, and trade were they based?

❯ Which areas in the Americas saw the development of a corn-and potato-based agriculture that did not depend on the plow, the wheel, and ironmaking?

Chiefdom: An agricultural village or town of up to 1,000 inhabitants, in which people know each other, requiring a person of authority (an elder or the head of a large family) to keep order as a respected chief, without using military force.

They adopted village life, built cities, and created kingdoms (such as Kush and Nubia along the Nile) well before the period of 600 BCE–600 CE. After 600 CE, the kingdoms of Meroë in the Nile valley and Aksum in the Ethiopian highlands flourished, while Africans farther south shifted from foraging to agriculture, villages, and chiefdoms. By 600 CE, urbanism had spread to West Africa and foraging had shrunk across the continent.

Saharan Villages, Towns, and Kingdoms

For many millennia, the Sahara was hospitable, furthering the pattern shift from foraging to agriculture. But around 5000–3000 BCE, the desert expanded, and savannas and steppes retreated southward. Agrarian life relocated to oases and the Nile River valley. In the northeast, the kingdom of Meroë established a capital of the same name in the middle Nile basin, supported by an agricultural surplus, which was produced with the help of annual Nile floods and irrigation.

Saharan Chiefdoms and Kingdoms   The earliest evidence of Africans shifting from foraging to agriculture comes from around Khartoum, the capital of modern Sudan. Archaeological sites reveal a culture of raising cattle, cultivating sorghum, and shaping distinctive pottery. By the period between 4000 BCE and the first written records in Egypt in 3100 BCE, a substantial **chiefdom** had emerged in northern Sudan, then called Nubia. This chiefdom was based on farming, livestock raising, and trading of gold as well as rain-forest ivory and timber from farther south. Archaeologists have noted that tombs in Nubia contained objects rivaling those of the Egyptians, including objects from southwest Asia and beyond. Nubian military prowess emerged in Egyptian records, with archers especially sought after as mercenaries.

After 2500 BCE, the kings of Nubia built a palace, large tombs, temples, and a wall around their capital city of Kerma, the first African city outside Egypt. During 1850–1400 BCE Kerma and Egypt were rivals for the control of Nile trade, until Egypt eventually destroyed Kerma and colonized Nubia for about half a millennium. Nubia regained autonomy early in the first millennium BCE, in a state centered around the city of Napata. Later, the Napatan kings liberated themselves from Egyptian control and even assumed the throne of their northern neighbor as the twenty-fifth dynasty (ca. 780–686 BCE). But when Assyria, the first empire to unify all of the Middle East, conquered Egypt, the defeated king relocated himself farther upstream at Meroë.

The Villages of Tichitt and Oualata   Contemporaneously with the Nubian kingdoms, villages emerged in today's Mauretania. As in Nubia, the climate in the western Sahara had changed during 5000–3000 BCE. As the monsoon patterns moved eastward, foragers retreated to shallow lakes and oases. During 3000–2000 BCE, these foragers domesticated pearl millet, which required less water to grow.

Archaeological evidence points to the emergence of sizable villages at Tichitt [tee-SHEET] and Oualata [wa-LAH-ta] in Mauretania around 2000 BCE, which flourished until 600 BCE. There were corrals for cattle and granaries for millet, as well as evidence of craftspeople smelting copper. Tomb mounds, perhaps for the chiefs in the villages, held beads and copper jewelry. The social structure may have been based on wealth in livestock, but how society was regulated, its religion, and the form of chiefly authority are unclear. One theory holds that as these people eventually retreated farther south as the Sahara dried out, they may have been the founders of the **kingdom** of ancient Ghana (see Chapter 14).

Meroë on the Middle Nile   The kings of Meroë were successors of the twenty-fifth Nubia-descended dynasty of Egypt, who, under Assyrian pressure, withdrew to the steppes of the middle Nile. Here they built their capital, Meroë. At that time, the floodplain to the south of the capital still received sufficient monsoon rainfall to support agriculture. In addition, the kings built large water reservoirs to supply its farmers. Presumably, the kingdom financed itself with the agricultural surplus.

At its height, from the sixth through fourth centuries BCE, the city of Meroë encompassed 20,000 inhabitants. The kingdom was largely decentralized. The provinces downstream and upstream along the Nile were autonomous, ruled by their own town chiefs. Outside the agricultural area, cattle nomads grazed their herds.

The difference in power between the kings and the chiefs was defined by the royal control over trade. Miners in the desert north of the capital produced iron ore, and farmers south of the capital grew cotton. Smiths and weavers in Meroë produced weapons, hoes, utensils, and cloth, both for local consumption and for trade beyond the kingdom. Hunters in the south acquired ivory from elephants and feathers from ostriches. Traders carried these down the Nile to Egypt or across the Red Sea to Yemen by boat, returning with olive oil and wine from Egypt and frankincense and myrrh from Yemen (see Map 6.1).

From the seventh century BCE, people in Meroë mined, smelted, and forged iron—perhaps the first to do so in sub-Saharan Africa. However, the origin of smelting and forging iron in sub-Saharan Africa is disputed. It is generally agreed that the craft of iron smelting evolved in Hittite Anatolia during several centuries after 1500 BCE (see Chapter 2). While the possible spread of ironworking from the Middle East to Africa has not been proven, the independent origin of early ironworking in Africa (among the Nok in West Africa) has not been demonstrated conclusively either.

Meroë's Cultural Achievements   In Meroë, the kings adapted their Nubian–Egyptian heritage to the steppe and savanna south of the Sahara. Their monuments acquired a distinct style. Although the main temple was devoted mainly to the Egyptian pantheon, the priests also added native deities, such as the lion god Apedemek. The inherited Egyptian hieroglyphics seem to have evolved into an alphabetic script, although it is still undeciphered.

Kingdom: A city-state or territorial state of at least several thousand inhabitants in which a ruler, claiming a divine mandate and supported by a military force, keeps order and provides for defense against outside attacks.

AFRICA, SHOWING SITES IN MAURETANIA 2000 BCE–600 BCE

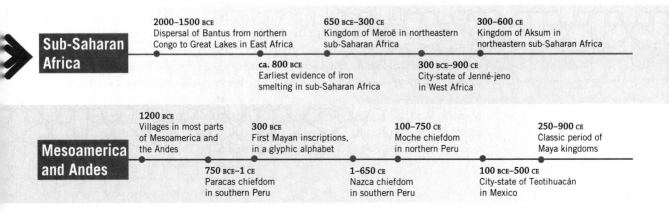

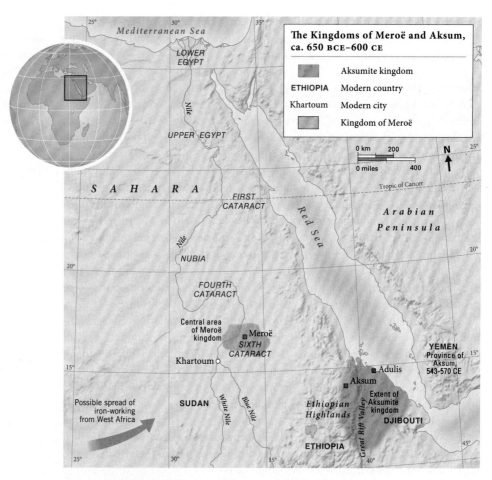

MAP 6.1 **The Kingdoms of Meroë and Aksum, ca. 650 BCE–600 CE**

Meroë was well known to the outside world. Mediterranean travelers visited it frequently. In the early first century CE, the kings of Meroë skirmished with Rome over border issues. As much as Meroë provided a physical network for regional travelers, it also provided an intellectual link between Eurasia and Africa—a link the people of Meroë facilitated through their adaptations.

The Kingdom of Aksum

Meroitic trade with the Red Sea crossed the Ethiopian highlands, and highlanders gradually acculturated to Meroë as well as Yemen. In the early first century CE, a king replaced the chiefdoms of the highlands and established the kingdom of Aksum (300–600 CE). Based on agriculture, this kingdom assumed control of the trade from Meroë. Aksum became the major supplier of African goods to the Roman Empire, from where it accepted Christianity in the early 300s.

Meroë's Decline and Aksum's Rise   Three factors contributed to Meroë's decline in the third century CE. First, the iron industry required charcoal, which is made by burning wood; when all the forests had been burned, the industry was doomed. Second, beginning in the late 200s BCE, camel nomads from the deserts east of the Nile raided northern Meroë. Third, the eastern neighbor, Ethiopia, acculturated to Meroë and became a participant in its trade; eventually, chiefs in the high plain of Aksum took it over. Aksum was located close to the coast and Red Sea ports. Agricultural and commercial wealth enabled the chiefs of Aksum to assume the succession of Meroë.

Agriculture in the Ethiopian highlands was of considerable age. In the lower elevations, farmers used ox-driven plows for the cultivation of wheat and barley. In higher elevations, farmers grew teff, a high-yielding small-sized grain. Abundant grasslands supported cattle breeding. The Red Sea coast supported only a few ports dependent on their hinterland. Because of its elevation, Ethiopia was a largely self-contained region in Africa, remaining outside the large population movements and cultural assimilation characteristic of West and East Africa.

Aksum's Splendor   Aksum (also spelled Axum), founded around 100 CE, came into its own around 300 CE. Its king, Ezana (ca. 303–350 CE), adopted Christianity as the state religion in 333 CE. Like the later Roman emperors, Ezana replaced tolerance for polytheistic religions with the requirement of conversion to a single faith (see Chapter 7). When the Roman emperors embraced what would become the Roman Catholic interpretation of Christianity, Aksum opted for Coptic Christianity, which was dominant in Egypt. It did not break with the Roman Empire, however, and even sided with it in the 500s CE against the Sasanid Persians, but it kept its distance.

Another centralizing policy of Aksum was the use of a gold-based currency through which taxation was facilitated. The kings of Aksum acquired their gold by sending merchants to the southern highlands outside the kingdom, where the gold was mined. The merchants paid with salt, iron, and cattle. Finally, a small central administration of tax collectors, tax farmers, and provincial tribute collectors ensured delivery of agricultural surplus to granaries in the towns and the capital. Even though more centralized than Meroë, Aksum was well below the level of administrative coherence of a typical Middle Eastern or Mediterranean kingdom or empire.

Aksumite Stela, pre-400s CE. This is the largest of hundreds of stone monoliths, some with tombs and altars, attesting to the architectural sophistication of the kingdom. Workmen transported them from quarries three miles away, where they had cut the stelae with iron tools. Some of the stelae, like the one above, have false windows and doors, looking like modern Art Deco buildings.

Imperialism and Crisis   When Aksum became Christian, the kings of Himyar in Yemen, on the other side of the Red Sea, chose Judaism as their faith. Himyar, however, possessed a considerable number of Christian subjects and it was inevitable that Aksum and Himyar would come to blows over their fate. In 520, Aksum invaded Himyar to come to the aid of the allegedly persecuted Christians and established a viceroyalty. After a period of political instability, Aksum made Yemen a regular province (543–570 CE).

But Aksum eventually lost the province when the Sasanid Persians invaded in 570 CE and annexed it to their empire. The Sasanids had recovered earlier than the Romans from nomadic invasions in the earlier 500s on their northern borders—invasions which had lessened their competition over Arabia and the Indian spice trade. The Sasanids were determined to take control of this trade from the Romans and their Aksumite allies. After 570 CE, Aksumite trade in the Red Sea declined precipitously. The capital city shrank, and over time provincial rulers in the highlands farther south rose to prominence. Although Ethiopia did not disintegrate as Meroë had done, after 600 CE its regional role was modest.

The Spread of Villages in Sub-Saharan Africa

By about 600 BCE, agriculture and pastoralism were common in East Africa and West Africa. Both emerged when people retreated from the increasingly dry Sahara, following the gradual southward shift of West Africa's three ecological zones. The first and northernmost zone was the steppe, or **Sahel** (Arabic *sahil*, or "coast" of the "sea" of the Sahara Desert). The second zone was the savanna. The third zone was a belt of rain forest along the coast from Guinea to Cameroon. By 600 BCE villages were most numerous in the savanna, where farming was most productive.

Sahel: An area of steppe or semidesert bordering the Sahara.

West African Savanna and Rain-Forest Agriculture

The village of Jenné-jeno [JEN-nay JEN-no] in the inland delta of the Niger and middle Senegal Rivers developed into a major urban center during 300–900 CE. It was a chiefdom with a regional trade for raw materials and luxury goods. In the rain forest, the so-called Bantu dispersal, with its combination of yam, taro, banana, and oil palm village agriculture, was well established.

Seated Figure, Jenné-jeno, Terra-Cotta, Thirteenth Century; New York, Metropolitan Museum. This convoluted figure, sculpted with exquisite refinement, shows a person in an apparently intense meditative pose.

Inland Delta Urbanism   The river Niger originates in the far west of the West African rain forest. Midway along its northeastern leg, it forms the 250-mile-long and 50-mile-wide inland delta. In the first millennium BCE, the delta was located entirely in the savanna, forming a huge area of swamps, islands, and canals. Over time, a dense network of villages developed. After 300 BCE one village, increasing to town size, became the center of satellite villages. This is how Jenné-jeno, at the southern end of the delta, originated. By 900 CE Jenné-jeno was a city of between 5,000 and 13,000 inhabitants. A prominent craft was pottery, with some potters specializing in the creation of small terra-cotta figurines, such as horsemen, archers, and humans in convoluted poses. The city was surrounded by 25 villages. Other towns with satellite villages developed farther downstream, making the delta the most populated area in West Africa.

Little is known about the social stratification and power structure of Jenné-jeno. It is clear that this urban–rural center had a line of chiefs, some basic administrative offices, and craftspeople. A gold ring and objects made of copper and bronze dated to 850–900 CE have been found. Copper and iron ore had to be carried in from mines in the desert and savanna to be smelted and manufactured into weapons and implements. Two glass beads, dated to the pre-600

CE period, seem to have come from overseas. Thus, trans-Saharan trade seems to have been in existence, supporting an urban demand for luxuries.

Rain-Forest Settlements   Evidence for rain-forest agriculture comes from the Kintampo complex of 2250–750 BCE, located in today's Ghana. Archaeologists have found traces of wood and mud huts, domesticated livestock, pottery, terracotta figurines, and polished stone implements. The assumption is that the villagers practiced slash-and-burn farming, growing yams and oil palms.

Early Plant Domestication?   In 1996 at Nkang in the Cameroons, archaeologists were able to date banana **phytoliths** to about 500 BCE. Phytoliths are silica from soil sediments deposited in bananas. Their dating caused unrest among Africanists who believed that the banana had arrived with Indonesian sailors on the East African coast sometime between 200 and 500 CE. Evidently, Indian Ocean connections between Southeast Asia and East Africa are of greater antiquity than hitherto assumed. Did bananas, yams, sugarcane stalks, and rice travel westward with intrepid Polynesian sailors thousands of years ago?

Village Farming   West African slash-and-burn farming consisted of clearing small areas of rain forest for villages of up to 500 inhabitants. Virgin rain forest was relatively easy to cut, even with stone tools, prior to the arrival of iron axes in the 800s BCE. Each clearing was large enough for a village of a few hundred farmers, family fields, communal fallow land, and cattle and goats.

If a village grew beyond its population capacity, a group had to depart and select a new site in the rain forest for clearing. Yam fields had to lie fallow for 10–15 years, during which the rain forest grew back. This secondary rain forest had few tall trees and a proliferation of medium vegetation. After millennia of slash-and-burn cultivation, nearly all virgin African rain forests were replaced by secondary forest. As in so many other places in the world, what many might perceive as pristine "jungle" was in fact the creation of human hands.

Phytoliths: Many plants pick up silica from the soil. After these plants decay, the silica returns to the soil in the form of phytoliths, which can be analyzed microscopically. Carbon dating of soil layers provides approximate dates.

The Spread of Village Life to East and South Africa

Groups of yam, banana, and oil palm farmers of southeast Nigeria, at the eastern end of the West African rain-forest belt, exhausted their area for clearings around 2000 BCE. They were fortunate in their search for new spaces to clear, because they had the nearby equatorial rain forest of the Congo at their disposal. Once there, a northerly group began to disperse around 1500 BCE eastward into the savanna of the Great Lakes in East Africa. On their way, they adapted to the cereal agriculture and iron crafting of the savanna villagers. They spoke closely related languages belonging to a family given the name Bantu by a nineteenth-century German linguist based on a reconstructed word meaning "people" (compare Zulu *abantu*). Under the impact of these newcomers, from 600 BCE–600 CE, nearly all foragers in eastern and southern Africa became either villagers or cattle nomads and adopted Bantu languages and culture (see Map 6.2).

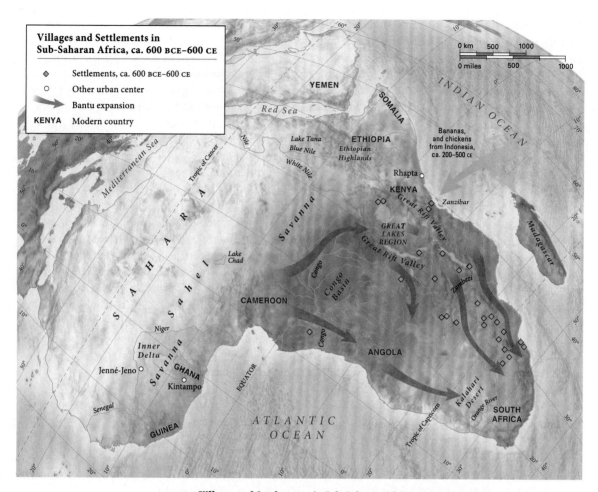

MAP 6.2 Villages and Settlements in Sub-Saharan Africa, 600 BCE–600 CE

Tsetse Fly: This insect can carry the virus that causes sleeping sickness, causing extreme fatigue and eventual death in humans and domesticated animals. Some animal species were able to adapt as dwarf variations, notably horses, cattle, and goats. The fly thrives in low elevations in rain forests, along rivers, and around lakes.

Inland Villagers and Nomads   When the northern Bantu arrived around 600 BCE, much of the land around the Great Lakes was forested savanna. As villagers cleared the forest, the threat of the **tsetse fly** diminished, and nomads from the north were able to expand southward. As in the Middle East, these nomads had a symbiotic relationship with the villagers, from whom they acquired grain. In the meantime, the southern migrants of the original Bantu dispersal of 2000 BCE had settled the Congo equatorial rain forest and, under the impact of their northern and eastern cousins, had complemented their yam and oil palm agriculture with millet and sorghum, as well as ironworking. Only small pockets of the original Paleolithic foragers of the virgin rain forest, commonly known as pygmies since the nineteenth century (the people so designated, however, prefer to be referred to by the name of their tribal groups), continued their traditional lifestyle, although they adopted Bantu languages as well.

The conversion of the foragers to farming was the work of both eastern Great Lakes and western Congo branches of Bantu descendants. The foragers either retreated before the farmers or adapted voluntarily to farming and speaking a Bantu language. Some savanna foragers, speaking Khoisan-family languages, retreated into the Kalahari Desert and steppe in western and central South Africa and remained hunter–gatherers. The process from Bantu origins and Bantu interaction with the nomads and foragers of East and South Africa to the mutual adaptations was still incomplete in 600 CE.

African Traditional Rituals   An analysis of Bantu linguistic roots and of early Iron Age (350–900 CE) sites in South Africa provides a glimpse into traditional **African spirituality**. Bantus distinguished between the daily cycles of renewal and disintegration in village households and the fields on one hand and the calendar movements of heaven on the other. Rituals and observance of taboos and omens kept the village and field cycles on their regular paths.

Ancestor and nature spirits had to be given their due respect through sacrifices, lest they disrupt the cycles of renewal and disintegration. Charms, mixed from herbs, protected against unintended insults of the spirits. Male or female witches in the villages could, out of envy, vengeance, or malice, severely harm or even kill their victims. Village diviners or healers were able to enter the spirit world, recognize bewitchment, and stop it through **witchcraft**. In the early African Iron Age, the adoption of rituals involving the human and field cycles—and, in some places, the calendar cycle, as evidenced by the Borana calendar—represented the main changes in African patterns of reality conceptualizations.

African spirituality:
Perception of reality based on the concept of nature in all its manifestations (planets and stars, landscapes, trees and plants, animals and humans), pervaded by spirits and influencing each other.

Witchcraft: A belief in which an evil person (male or female) can harm an innocent victim at a distance and cause the victim to become possessed, with attendant illnesses.

Indonesian Contacts   In 200–500 CE, Indonesian sailors brought new species of bananas and chickens to East Africa. These sailors were descended from Austronesian farmers who had dispersed to the islands of the Pacific, Philippines, and Indonesia, beginning around 4000 BCE, and who may have also traveled to East Africa, as discussed earlier in the chapter. The mariners of 200–500 CE sailed on large outriggers with canted square sails, which made it possible to sail at an angle from the headwind. Prevailing wind patterns in the southern Indian Ocean would otherwise have made sailing westward from Indonesia to Africa difficult. Where on the African coast the Indonesians landed is unknown, although they definitely settled the still-uninhabited tropical island of Madagascar.

Stone Relief of a Large Outrigger Merchant Ship, Buddhist Temple of Borobudur, on the Indonesian Island of Java, ca. 800 CE. This type of ship traveled regularly from Java to East Africa on the cinnamon trade route, with its merchants exchanging spices for ivory, wild animal skins, and slaves during the early centuries of the first millennium.

Incipient Urbanism on the East Coast   East Africans also benefited from trade with the Middle East. Archaeological evidence points to the inclusion of the northern East African coast into the Yemeni commercial network in the last centuries BCE, which connected Meroë, Egypt, Persia, India, Sri Lanka, and (indirectly) Indonesia and China.

By the mid-first century CE, a Hellenistic Greek source mentions Yemenis intermarrying with locals in the town of Rhapta along the Kenyan coast. Although no archaeological remnants of Rhapta have been located, Roman glass beads and shards found on Zanzibar and the Tanzanian coast suggest regular journeys beginning around 200 CE. The beads and ceramics were presumably exchanged for ivory, rock crystal, ostrich feathers, and hardwood. If this account is true, the later Swahili cities antedated the spread of Islam by several centuries—just as in the case of Jenné-jeno in West Africa before the rise of Islamic Saharan kingdoms.

Patterns of African History, 600 BCE–600 CE

Sub-Saharan Africa evolved along two basic patterns in the period 600 BCE–600 CE. First, in the northeast, Meroë and Aksum adapted themselves to Middle Eastern agriculture, with its plow, wheat, and barley. In addition, both African-domesticated sorghum and millet—and in Aksum teff—were grown. Irrigated farming and long-distance trade allowed chiefs to build kingdoms, which lasted as long as the urban infrastructure could be supported. The exhaustion of timber ended the royal pattern of social and political evolution in the sub-Saharan northeast.

Second, in the northwest of sub-Saharan Africa, inhabitants pioneered the agricultures of the steppe, savanna, and rain forest. Millet was productive enough to support the rise of villages. In the inland delta of the Niger, the irrigated farming of millet and rice allowed for the rise of a city, Jenné-jeno. With its long-distance trade, this city foreshadowed the post-600 CE rise of Saharan kingdoms. Farther south, in the rain forest, the farming of yam, banana, and oil palm supported the emergence of small and widely dispersed villages. The expansion of the Bantus and their agriculture brought village life as well as iron smelting to all parts of sub-Saharan Africa.

Africa and the Americas   The Americas displayed similarities to the internal sub-Saharan interactions and adaptations. The latter, as we have seen, were responsible for patterns of village, city, and kingdom formation. In Mesoamerica as well as in the Peruvian Andes, internal processes of interaction and adaptation also supported a pattern of village, city-state, and kingdom development from 600 BCE to 600 CE.

The principal difference, however, was that in sub-Saharan Africa this evolution gradually expanded also to the central and southern regions, whereas in the Americas no such expansion took place until after 600 CE. Social and political formation patterns spread to North America only after 600 CE, as represented by the Pueblo and Cahokia cultures.

Early States in Mesoamerica: Maya Kingdoms and Teotihuacán

In Chapter 5 we saw that the chiefdoms of Caral-Supe (2600–2000 BCE) and Chavín de Huántar (1000–200 BCE) in the Andes as well as those of the Olmecs (1200–600 BCE) in Mesoamerica represent the development from agriculture and villages to urbanization, chiefdoms, and kingdoms. In the period of 600 BCE–600 CE, in the southern Yucatán Peninsula of Mexico and the Mexican Basin in south-central Mexico, chiefdoms evolved into kingdoms. In the Andes, urban centers formed under chiefly rule, although in Teotihuacán and Moche the urban culture was nearly as diversified as in the Mesoamerican kingdoms.

The Maya Kingdoms in Southern Mesoamerica

By creating clear-cuts, elevated fields, and terraces on hill slopes, Mayan villagers in the Yucatán Peninsula established agriculture based on squash, beans, and corn. Around 600 BCE, towns evolved into cities, where chieftains transformed themselves into kings. By organizing the farmers during the winter, they created city-states with temple pyramids and palaces, surrounded by outlying villages. Among these city-states, the most powerful during the period 600 BCE–600 CE were Tikal and Calakmul (see Map 6.3).

The Mayas on the Yucatán Peninsula   The climate of the Yucatán Peninsula is subtropical, with a rainy season from May to September. The base of the Yucatán Peninsula consisted of rain-forest lowlands and swamps, traversed by rivers. To the south were rain-forest highlands, sloping from mountains that descended toward the lowlands in the north and the Pacific coast in the south. The northern region consisted of dry and riverless lowlands. Maya culture began in the center and south and later radiated into the southern mountains and northern lowlands. Limestone quarries in the northern lowland areas provided stone for construction. The volcanic south was quarried for its lava stone and was also rich in obsidian and jade.

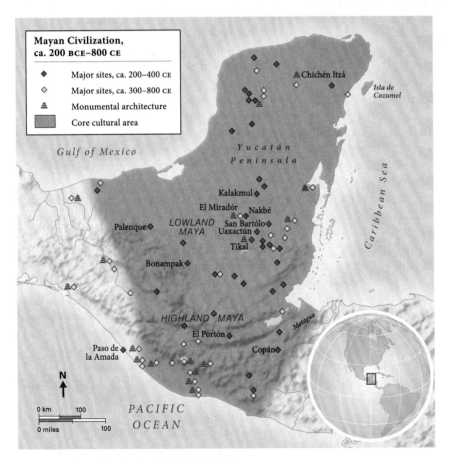

MAP 6.3 **Mayan Civilization, ca. 200 BCE–800 CE**

El Mirador, La Danta Temple, 600 BCE–150 CE. By height (236 feet), volume, and footprint, this pyramid was the largest of all Maya sacred structures and one of the largest buildings of the premodern world. At present, the site is only partially excavated, and archaeological work is still ongoing. The temple visible atop the pyramid is surmounted by a rooster-like roof comb, once covered by stucco figurines of Maya deities.

The early Mayas cut down the rain forest in order to clear fields, drain swamps, and build villages on low stone platforms near water sources. By around 1000 BCE, some villages had evolved into towns. Elite lineages under chieftains resided in the towns and controlled the best lands, while more humble lineages in the surrounding villages were on less productive soils. Although society was organized by familial descent, social stratification by wealth began to differentiate the lineages.

Early Kingdoms   As in the agrarian centers of Eurasia, debt dependence was probably the earliest lever of power in the hands of the Mayan chieftains. Rich farmers had larger families, built bigger homes, and had more domestic workers producing pottery and textiles. Thus, in the period 1000–600 BCE, these wealthy farmers transformed themselves into chieftains, exerting family rule for extended periods over a central town surrounded by satellite villages.

Beginning in the seventh century BCE, chieftains in some agriculturally rich areas increased their wealth so that they could claim to be kings. Kings surrounded themselves with military forces. They began to collect taxes, enlarge their towns into cities, and conquer other villages. During slack times in the agricultural cycle, these kings commanded farmers to construct ceremonial monuments. Nakbé (700 BCE–150 CE), a city in the north of the central lowlands, was the site of the first temple pyramids on ceremonial platforms. These pyramids were stepped stone structures, as high as 200 feet, with staircases to the temples on top where kings conducted sacrifices to the gods of the emerging divine pantheon.

A nearby town, El Mirador (600 BCE–150 CE), became a city with surrounding villages about a century after Nakbé. With about 100,000 inhabitants, hundreds of ceremonial and palatial structures on its platforms, and a 236-foot pyramid built around 300 BCE, this Mayan city was the largest early center of what ultimately were more than 4,400 Mayan urban and rural sites. Only the later Tikal (200–600 CE) reached a similar size. To the surprise of archaeologists, the El Mirador site has turned out to be already as fully Mayan, with its temple pyramids, elite structures, stelae, ball courts, sweat houses, and commoner quarters, as the later and better-known classical centers. Maya culture at its peak has to be considered—as it is in this chapter—within a much longer time horizon than previously assumed.

Progress made in deciphering the Maya glyphic script has revealed that the Maya region consisted of some 15–17 dominant kingdoms in the central lowlands during the Early Classic Period, each with a capital and one or more secondary cities. Marriage alliances among the royal lineages of the capitals and secondary cities maintained the cohesion of the kingdom. Frequent wars in the region were either intra-kingdom rebellions or wars among secondary cities in different kingdoms. Direct military competition between the kingdoms of Tikal and Calakmul, however, endured for many centuries.

Spirituality and Polytheism   Kings and their households lived in palaces adjacent to the temple pyramids. Kings often assumed the names of animals combined with human-made objects—for example, "Spear Thrower Owl," "Shield Jaguar," and "Smoke Squirrel." On wall paintings, earthenware vessels, and stelae, kings were recognizable by their richly decorated headdresses and clothing. When sons of kings were still minors, their mothers assumed the roles of regents. Occasionally, women ruled as queens. After death, kings were buried in pyramids or in separate tombs and were assumed to have taken their places among the gods.

    Polytheism emerged alongside traditional nature spirituality around 2500 BCE. Nature spirituality was shared by all, commoners and chiefs. The gods of polytheism were more powerful than the spirits of ancestors. They were the embodiments of forces of nature whose favor the kings—more powerful than chiefs—had to curry if rich harvests were to occur and the kingdoms were to flourish.

    Mayan kings considered themselves servants of the gods that populated the divine pantheon by the time of the Olmecs in the eleventh century BCE and continued to grow during the Maya period. The kings made daily sacrifices to these gods in rituals in the temples atop the pyramids. The main sacrifice was the gift of blood—a heritage from traditional spirituality: blood as the force of life—which Mayan kings drew from their ear lobes, tongues, and penises. During times of war, captured enemies were also sacrificed. Through their blood, the kings nourished nature and supported the human and divine worlds.

Polytheism: Personification of the forces of nature and the performance of rituals and sacrifices to ensure the benevolence of the gods and goddesses.

The Ruling Classes   Kings and officials assembled for the administration of justice, the collection of rents and tributes, commercial exchanges, and diplomatic relations. Many of these functions required expert knowledge of the annual calendar. Other functions, such as military action, required divination to discover the most favorable star constellations under which to proceed. The tracking of these units of times fell to calendar specialists, mathematicians, and astronomers.

    The Mayans used four calendars. One calendar was the 260-day, or 9-month, divinatory calendar, which scholars interpret as being related to the human gestation period. A second calendar, based on the solar year of 365 days and important for agriculture, was nearly as old. A third calendar, the Mayan Calendar Round, commenced every 52 years when the divinatory and solar calendars began on the same day. The Mayas believed that this calendar inaugurated cycles of calamitous as well as fortuitous times. The fourth calendar in use among the Mayas was the Long Count Calendar, which counted the days elapsed since the mythical origin of the universe. Sophisticated mathematics were required to coordinate these four calendars.

    Other activities of the royal family and court consisted of daily processions, feasts, and ball games played in stadiums on the temple-palace grounds. These ritualized, refined pastimes were far beyond the reach of common farmers and craftspeople. A stratified social hierarchy typified the Maya kingdoms (see "Patterns Up Close").

The Commoners   The commoners, whose taxes supported the royal courts, lived in compounds of thatched huts around courtyards on stone platforms, safe from the floodwaters of the rainy season from May to September. In these houses, women were in charge of cooking, weaving, pottery making, the growing of garden vegetables and fruits, and the rearing of domestic animals. Women and men fabricated tools from chert, bone, and wood. In larger Maya kingdoms, some households seem to have specialized in tool manufacturing and weaving, with both women and men participating.

Patterns Up Close | The Mayan Ball Game

Although it shares its ancient age with similar games in China, the Persian Middle East, and the Greek and Roman Mediterranean, only in Mesoamerica was the team ball game played according to formal rules in stadiums constructed specifically for this purpose. In Mesoamerica, the oldest stadium to date, from 1400 BCE, was found in the ruins of Paso de la Amada in the far southeast of today's Mexico. Adjacent to the palace of the chief, this ball court measures 260 by 23 feet, with two 7-foot-high spectator platforms on both long sides. Later, during the Maya period, these platforms usually rose theater-style on both sides, for better viewing from farther away. Given the proximity of the ball court to the chief's residence, it is possible that other chiefdoms in the area engaged in what we would call today "league tournaments."

The solid-rubber ball was around 2 feet in diameter and weighed 8 pounds. Players often wore protective gear around their hips and helmets on their heads, as shown in murals and on ceramics.

Under the Maya, who called the game *pitz* and built about 1,500

The Mayan Ball Game. Note the strong body protection around the midsection of the players as well as the elaborate headdresses, symbolizing animals.

Men grew corn in fields that were cut into the rain forest through slash-and-burn techniques. Fields near rivers and in swamps were raised, rectangular islands on which the mud from adjacent canals had been heaped. Slopes along river valleys were terraced in order to retain rain or irrigation water. Cotton, cacao, and tobacco fields formed special plantations requiring intensive labor. Hunting and fishing were important occupations among both royals and commoners.

The hard agricultural labor of the commoners produced an agricultural surplus, which supported ruling dynastic families as well as craftspeople in the cities. In addition, they were employed for building the temple-palace compounds. Craftspeople worked for the embellishments of the royal palaces, creating reliefs, wall paintings, pottery, and inscriptions.

Glyphic script: The Maya developed a script of some 800 images. Some are pictograms standing for words; others are syllables to be combined with other syllables to form words.

Mayan Writing   Mayan writing is a **glyphic** as well as a syllabic script, numbering some 800 signs. It is structurally similar to Sumerian cuneiform and Egyptian hieroglyphics. In their basic form, glyphs are *pictograms*, one-word images of the most essential features of what is to be depicted. But glyphs were also used as syllables, consisting of one, two, or three signs combining consonants and vowels. Combinations of multiple syllabic glyphs, or syllabograms, are pronounced as a series of syllables. Given the immense number of possible combinations of pictograms and syllabograms, the complexity of Mayan writing long resisted all efforts to decipher it.

A breakthrough came when scholars interpreted stelae monuments as records of royal births, accessions to the throne, and deaths. First, scholars realized that

courts, the rules became more formalized. Teams had from one to seven players. A basic rule was that the ball had to be hit with the hip, but in variations, players struck the ball with forearms, bats, or hand stones. The team that dropped the ball most often lost.

The significance of the Mayan ball game fits into the larger pattern of agrarian–urban society with its chiefdoms and kingdoms whose polytheism required elaborate rituals and sacrificial practices. Although the archaeological record is debatable, it appears that ball games took place during chiefly or royal festivities and fertility rituals, and perhaps also human sacrifices. The apparent but also disputed role of some players as human sacrifices on a number of murals was a late Mayan phenomenon. Today, these religious roots of games are largely forgotten. Instead, modern sports have rituals of their own, such as flag-waving, parading, tailgating, and hooliganism. Whether religious or secular, rituals are permanent fixtures that follow their own patterns, parallel to those of society at large.

Questions

- How did the ball game serve as a microcosm for larger patterns in Mayan society?

- What function could the ball game have played in relations among the various Mayan chiefdoms?

Mayan writing had the above-mentioned syllabic component; then, the architect and Maya specialist Tatiana Proskouriakoff discovered that the inscriptions on many royal stelae contained information on dynastic dates and events. The final breakthrough came at the Maya site of Palenque in 1973 when scholars recognized the syllables *k'inich* as referring to the Mayan sun god as well as to individual kings. Since then, scholars have assembled a dictionary of as many as 1,000 words, and it has become possible to chronicle the dynasties of Maya kingdoms.

The Crisis of the Kingdoms   Spectacular building activities characterized the Maya region during ca. 400–600 CE. Ruling classes must have grown considerably, and farmers in some kingdoms may no longer have been willing to produce food as well as provide labor for temples and palaces. Destruction identified in some archaeological sites could be the result of revolts. In other places, overexploitation of the soil, loss of topsoil on terraces, or salinization of lowland fields as the result of neglected drainage might have increased the imbalance between the peasants and ruling classes. Frequent wars among the kings might have reduced the size of the ruling class, with negative consequences for the farmers.

The destructive interplay among the ruling class, farmers, and the environment produced a crisis from the late 500s CE through the mid-600s CE. It led to the collapse of many older Mayan kingdoms and endangered the survival of the strongest newer ones in the southern lowlands. When the crisis ended, Maya power shifted to the northern lowlands of the Yucatán Peninsula.

The Kingdom of Teotihuacán in the Mexican Basin

The subtropical climate of Yucatán extended northward into the highlands, in which the Mexican Basin was the largest agricultural region. The region supported the growing of beans, squash, and corn. The northern part of the basin developed village life later than the south, but its closeness to obsidian quarries gave these villages commercial advantages. Militarily and economically, the town of Teotihuacán in the north developed into a city-state that became politically and culturally dominant across all of what is today Mexico.

The Mexican Basin   The Mexican Basin is a large, 7,400-foot-high bowl without river outlets in southern Mexico. In the center of the bowl was Lake Texcoco [tes-CO-co], nourished by rivers flowing down from mountain chains on the eastern and western sides. As in the Maya region, the basin enjoyed a rainy season during the summer. River water, channeled through irrigation canals to terraces and the flatlands around the central lake, as well as numerous bays, supported a moderately productive agriculture.

During the period of village expansion (1200–600 BCE), many of the slopes surrounding this bowl were forested, providing firewood, timber, and game. Fish in the lake near the rivers were another food source. Clay deposits in the flatlands and obsidian quarries on the slopes of the northeastern mountains provided resources for the manufacture of ceramics, tools, and weapons. However, the high elevation and temperature differences between winter and summer did not allow for cultivation of cotton, cacao, vanilla, and other tropical products of lowland Maya agriculture. These latter products had to be acquired by trade.

The principal plant fiber for the weaving of clothes came from the *maguey* [ma-GAY] plant, a cactus that grows in poor soil and does not need much water. The juice of this plant was fermented and consumed as an alcoholic drink called pulque [PULL-kay; Nahuatl *octli*]. If people wished to manufacture clothes from cotton or acquire cacao, vanilla, jade, or quetzal feathers, they had to trade their obsidian. Commercial exchange was necessary for village expansion and the subsequent pattern of kingdom formation.

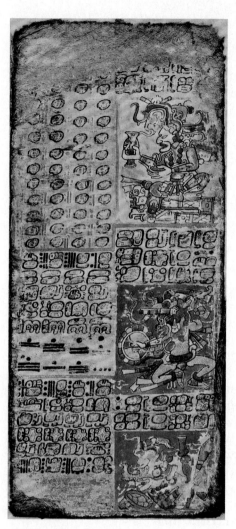

Mayan Glyphs. Beginning in the fourth century BCE, scribes in the Maya kingdoms developed a written language composed of pictograms and syllables, eventually numbering about 800 signs. This language allowed communication among educated people in the different Maya kingdoms, who spoke often mutually unintelligible local languages. Because of the double meaning of each glyph as pictogram and syllable, it took most of the twentieth century for scholars to decipher the Mayan language. The example shown here is from the Dresden Codex.

Teotihuacán   In a valley to the northeast of Lake Texcoco, villagers in the early centuries of the Common Era dug a large canal system with raised fields similar to those of the Maya. Villages around this canal network eventually formed the city of Teotihuacán. We do not know when the transition from chieftains to chiefly dynasties and kings occurred. The iconic writing system, less developed than that of the Mayas, does not allow for identification of any rulers or lineages. Teotihuacán was a city-state with an anonymous dynasty. In its physical appearance it was even more imposing than most of the Maya kingdoms (see Map 6.4).

In the first century CE, the rulers of Teotihuacán laid out an urban grid along a north–south axis that included two densely constructed city quarters of some 2,200 housing units. Near the central avenue, adobe houses lined both sides of the alleyways. Some 600 houses had the appearance of workshops, primarily for the making of tools. The workshops indicate a degree of nonagricultural crafts specialization, which one would expect from a city. Farther away, houses and fields were interspersed. Canals, reservoirs, and a drainage system facilitated the transportation of food, the provision of drinking water, and the elimination of waste. By around 300 CE, Teotihuacán had grown to as many as 100,000 inhabitants.

Teotihuacán's temple pyramids, palaces, markets, and city quarters were built on a vast scale. The Temples of the Moon and the Sun, built at the northern end of the city, were ceremonial centers that attracted pilgrims from the Mexican Basin and beyond. Archaeologists interpret the Temple of the Sun as a construction on top of a cave symbolizing the entrance to the nether world. In the third century CE, the temple of the god of the feathered serpent (called by the Nahuatl name Quetzalcoatl [ket-sal-COA]) was built, probably in honor of the then reigning dynasty. The founding king sacrificed some 260 humans, probably war captives, to garner the goodwill of the god. After what appears to have been an internal uprising in the 400s CE, new rulers destroyed the temple's façade. Wall paintings and pottery, depicting rulers, priests, gods, and mythical figures in processions, rituals, and dances, attest to a highly developed aesthetic culture.

The Decline of the City   As in the case of the Maya kingdoms, the balance among the peasantry, urban inhabitants, rulers, and construction workers was not always easy to maintain. Hints of an internal upheaval point to the balance being lost for the first time around 400 CE. Another such upheaval occurred in the late 500s. Thereafter, the population of the central city quarters declined. The outlying quarters reverted back to the village level as farming communities for centuries to come. The mid-500s saw prolonged periods of cooler weather and droughts and were generally a more difficult time for farming in the Americas. In contrast to the agriculturally richer Maya kingdoms, the Mexican Basin found a return to urbanism and kingdoms more difficult.

At its height, Teotihuacán exerted an influence considerably greater than the Maya kingdoms. Its trade reached deep into the Maya region and beyond, to the Isthmus of Panama. Teotihuacán exchanged its obsidian for cotton, rubber, cacao, jade, and quetzal feathers from the subtropical lowlands. Its gods, especially the deity of the feathered serpent, were sacrificed to everywhere in Mesoamerica. Similarly, Teotihuacán was instrumental in spreading its architectural style (inward-sloping platforms, surmounted by temples) from the Basin of Mexico to the Yucatán Peninsula. In the later 300s CE and throughout the 400s, Maya rulers of Tikal, Uaxactún [wa-shahk-TOON], and other kingdoms claimed descent from rulers of Teotihuacán, evidently seeking to benefit from the city's prestige as a ceremonial center.

The Andes: Moche

In Andean South America, a pattern of chiefdom formation evolved between 3000 and 2000 BCE, a millennium earlier than in Mesoamerica. Because of the absence of large plains and the enormous differences in elevation within short distances, however, relatively small chiefdoms remained the dominant social formation in the Andes.

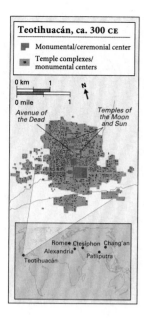

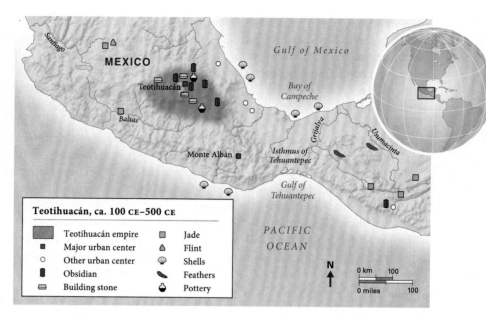

MAP 6.4 **Teotihuacán, ca. 100 CE–500 CE**

The Moche in Northern Peru

The Moche Valley was the place of the two largest ceremonial centers in the Andes, the Temple Pyramids of the Sun and the Moon. The power of its main chiefdom must have been impressive, since large numbers of farmers had to be mobilized for the construction of these pyramids. But it remained a federation of village chiefdoms clustered around an urbanized temple center with a dominant chiefly lineage.

Moche Origins   The Moche Valley was at the center of nine coastal valleys in what is today northern Peru. It had a subtropical climate with moderately wet winters and dry summers. It supported an irrigated agriculture of corn, pulses, cotton, and potatoes; llamas and alpacas from the highlands were domesticated for wool and light transportation. Here, the earliest evidence of the emergence of the Moche chiefdoms (100–750 CE) is the tomb of the "Lord of Sipán," dated to 50 CE. The tomb contained the chief's mummy, clad in warrior clothing and richly decorated with gold and silver jewelry. Eight people, including his wife, and a dog were buried with him. This chieftain was wealthy and powerful indeed.

A Federated Chiefdom   Half a century later, Moche chieftains began the construction of the two Temple Pyramids of the Sun and the Moon. About 100 village teams participated in the construction, which lasted intermittently for centuries. At the feet of the two temples was a city that included administrative offices and workshops. Lesser chieftain lineages ruled in the more remote valleys.

None of the participating villages appears to have grown beyond the moderately large units at the mouth of valleys, and it seems that they coexisted peacefully. When the generally cooler and drier climate of the sixth century CE arrived, it had a greater negative impact on the agriculture of the central chiefdom in Moche, closer to the coast and at the end of the river streams, than on the chiefdoms upstream in the valleys. In the Moche Valley, with its two huge temples, the balance between chiefly elites and farmers was more difficult to maintain than in the farther valleys with smaller elites and comparatively larger peasantries. Eventually, in the early 600s CE, the Moche elite dissolved, while smaller elites in nearby valleys carried on and eventually disappeared also, sometime around 750 (see Map 6.5).

Paracas and the Nasca in Southern Peru

Southern Peru was much drier, and its agrarian population density lagged behind that of the north. Nevertheless, Paracas [pah-RAH-kas] and Nasca (also spelled "Nazca") possess considerable cultural significance.

Teotihuacán, Temple of the Feathered Serpent God Quetzalcóatl. This sculpture of a serpent's head with its exposed, menacing fangs and the collar made of feathers is one of many along the front wall of this temple. The hybrid deity (quetzal bird and snake [*cóatl*]), bringer of rain in the summer, bridged the fertile Earth and the planet Venus.

Paracas Chiefs   Desert conditions on the southern Peruvian coast and dependence on runoff water from Andean snowmelt required more elaborate irrigation works than on the northern coast. The patterns of social formation from foraging to villages and chiefdoms were correspondingly slower and more modest. Shamans and chiefs on the Paracas peninsula and the Ica valley set the pattern in motion when they unified a number of hamlets. Subsequently, other Paracas chiefdoms appeared in neighboring valleys, forming a loose confederation (750 BCE–1 CE).

A necropolis on the peninsula contained hundreds of mummies of chieftains, wrapped in the colorful wool and cotton mantles still characteristic of southern Peru today. The icons woven into the mantles and painted on pottery allowed scholars to identify the Paracas chiefs. These icons included figures holding weapons, plants, or skulls; other icons were felines, birds, or whales, often with humanlike features. Although contemporary with the Maya kingdoms in Mesoamerica, the Paracas chiefdoms in the Andes remained culturally compact, without evolution toward urbanization.

The Nasca Ceremonial Center   The transition from pottery painted after firing to predecorated (slipware) ceramics defines the shift from the Paracas to the Nasca chiefdoms (1–650 CE). Nasca chiefs built ceremonial centers, modest adobe structures that covered preexisting mounds. Cahuachi [ka-WAH-chee], the main pilgrimage center, contained 40 such structures, assumed to represent the contributing chiefdoms.

During the extended cold weather and drought periods of the sixth century CE, Nasca chiefs mobilized villagers for the construction of a tunnel network for irrigation. Workers tapped underground water in the mountains and guided it onto the slopes of the valleys and into reservoirs. These sophisticated constructions, with intermittent shafts and manholes for cleaning and repair, were built so sturdily that many of them are still in operation today.

The Nasca Geoglyphs   Another Nasca innovation consisted of the so-called Nasca **geoglyphs**, large geometric and animal figures laid out in the dry highlands

Geoglyphs: Long geometric lines and figures as well as outlines of animals formed in the desert by removing darker stones and exposing the lighter sand underneath.

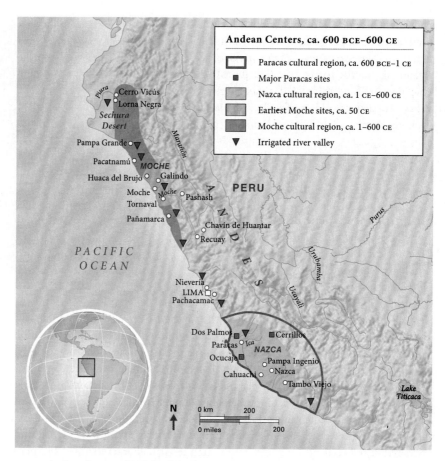

MAP 6.5 **Andean Centers, 600 BCE–600 CE**

and on the valley slopes of the chiefdoms. Villagers constructed lines, triangles, and trapezoids, as well as images of animals, by removing dark-colored rocks and exposing the lighter sand underneath. These geoglyphs are unique to the Andes, and the closest parallel was not created until nearly a millennium later when the Incas arranged sacred objects outside their capital, Cuzco, in straight lines.

Eventually, the Nasca came under the influence of the highland state of Wari (or Huari), a later city-state in the Andes (see Chapter 15). This state expanded its political and cultural influence toward the southern Peruvian coast in the first half of the 700s CE and gradually transformed the identity of the Nasca chiefdoms.

Putting It All Together

In the period 600 BCE–600 CE, agriculture and life in villages became nearly universal. Only Australia remained outside this development from foraging to agrarian settlements. While remnants of foraging societies survived, notably in sub-Saharan Africa and in the Americas, humans in those two places developed in the same direction as those in Eurasia—toward cities, kingdoms, and long-distance luxury trade.

Agrarian-based urban culture, however, was a fragile achievement in Eurasia, sub-Saharan Africa, Mesoamerica, and the Andes. Irregularities of the weather and the slow improvement of food plant productivity meant that agriculture was a tenuous enterprise. Corncobs, especially, evolved only slowly toward greater length and were still quite short during the Maya period. Not until the time of the Aztecs did selective breeding produce corn of modern proportions. Dynastic cities regularly outstripped the natural resources of their local environments, as was the case in Meroë, Aksum, the Maya cities, and Teotihuacán. However, sooner or later, new city-based states arose.

The primary royal urban achievements were monumental architecture, sophisticated metal and textile craftsmanship, and forms of intellectual expression. In cities these crafts became the refined products of specialized workers who did not participate in farming.

Similarly, precocious intellectual achievements appeared both in nomadic contexts, as witnessed by the Borana calendar of the Kushite nomads in Kenya, and in small-town agricultural chiefdoms, as seen in the geoglyphs created in the desert landscape by the Nasca of Peru. The intellectual accomplishments in royal cities were even more sophisticated, as exemplified by the Mayan writing system and calendars.

Altogether, evolving largely on their own, both sub-Saharan Africa and the Americas made long strides in the period 600 BCE–600 CE toward expressing the same depth of humanity that was already on display in Eurasia. They did not yet have empires or possess the literary breadth that favored the rise of the visionaries of transcendence, hallmarks of the Middle East, India, and China during 600 BCE–600 CE. But their more compact cultures were not lacking in any of the overall patterns that characterized Eurasia.

Review and Relate

| Thinking Through Patterns

Examine the ways historians approach the big questions of this chapter.

Innovations in world history usually originated in one specific place and then radiated outward to new populations through interactions among different peoples. Through adaptation, the new populations incorporated innovations into their own cultures. Given their (relative) separation from Eurasia, sub-Saharan Africa and the Americas were partially or entirely limited to their own internal patterns of innovation. Encountering the same experiences and challenges as humans in Eurasia, their responses were remarkably comparable. Thus, the history of the world was not merely the history of peoples coming into more and more intensive contact with each other. It was also the history of peoples experiencing similar local challenges without transcontinental interaction.

❯ How does comparing and contrasting sub-Saharan Africa with the Americas during 600 BCE–600 CE help in understanding the agrarian–urban patterns of social and political development across the world?

❯ Where did chief-
doms, cities, and
kingdoms arise in
sub-Saharan Africa and
why? On which forms
of agriculture, urban-
ization, and trade were
they based?

Agrarian sub-Saharan Africa during 600 BCE–600 CE is an example where inter-action with the Middle East—as well as, in some periods, the absence of inter-action—formed the background for comparable processes of economic, social, and political developments. The middle Nile Valley and the highlands of Ethiopia gave rise to the plow-based agrarian kingdoms of Meroë and Aksum, both receiving their origi-nal plows and grain from the Middle East and maintaining a lively trade for luxury goods with that region. By contrast, the West African inland Niger delta grew into the urbanized chiefdom of Jenné-jeno, with limited external interactions. Through inter-action and adaptation, forms of farming as well as iron smelting (the latter perhaps received from the Middle East) traveled south in sub-Saharan Africa, together with the Bantu expansion.

❯ Which areas in the
Americas saw the
development of a
corn- and potato-based
agriculture that did
not depend on the
plow, the wheel, and
ironmaking?

Three regions in the Americas were favorable for the development of densely settled villages, some of which subsequently evolved into cities and kingdoms: Yucatán, with its Maya kingdoms; the Mexican Basin, with the city-state of Teotihuacán; and Peru, with the Moche and Nasca chiefdoms.

| Against the Grain

Consider this as a counterpoint to the main patterns examined in this chapter.

Nasca Lines: Speculation and Explanation

• Is it important to be
aware of purely specula-
tive theories of world
history? For what reasons?

• What are some other
feats of ancient engi-
neering, architecture,
or craft that seem to
inspire speculative (or
even fantastic) theories?
Do historians have a

Peruvian archaeologist Toribio Mejia Xesspe was the first scholar to describe the Nasca geoglyphs, which he viewed in 1927 from adjacent hills. The true extent of the glyphs, however, became known only once seen from the air. The pioneer of the aerial mapping of the site was Paul Kosok, an American historian who crisscrossed the area by plane during the 1940s. Further mapping was carried out by his assistant, Ma-ria Reiche, a trained mathematician from Germany who devoted her life to recording and protecting the Nasca lines. Over the years, new lines have been discovered, some as recently as 2018, including some which predate the Nasca culture.

Based on the discovery that a number of lines converged at the winter and sum-mer solstices, Reiche published her theory that the Nasca geoglyphs were elements of a complex astronomical calendar and observatory. Her theory did not find much sup-port among later scholars, who demonstrated that only 20 percent of the glyphs had an astronomical significance. Reiche's theory, however, inspired popular writers to engage in frequently outlandish speculation about the site. These speculations have fostered much pseudoscience, ranging from theories about premodern GPS technology and electromagnetic beams to extraterrestrials.

A more sober explanation, advanced in a 2017 book and subsequent articles, focuses on the systematic exploration of underground aqueducts called *puquios* (from a Quechua word) tapping into aquifers that carried water from mountain snowmelts. In various places (outlined by Nasca lines?), these puquios were accessible through pits, fortified by rock walls. The pits described points in what the Paracas and Nasca people believed to have been sacred landscapes (known by the Quechua word *huaca*, also spelled *wak'a*), pervaded by animal spirits (hence the animal geoglyphs). As mentioned above (and discussed again in Chapter 15), the Incas also considered their landscapes, covered with shrines, to be sacred. The connection between the scarce water resources and Nasca lines had been suspected already by Xesspe and a few later explorers, but it was only with more systematic research that the puquio-huaca connection has become evident.

particular responsibility to engage with or dispute "fringe" theories?

Key Terms

African spirituality   133
Chiefdom   126
Geoglyphs   143
Glyphic script   138

Kingdom   127
Phytoliths   131
Polytheism   137
Sahel   130

Tsetse fly   132
Witchcraft   133

Learn more with this chapter's digital tools, including the Oxford Insight Study Guide, at http://www.oup.com/he/vonsivers4e. Please see the Further Resources section at the back of the book for additional readings and suggested websites.

Sources for Chapter 6

| SOURCE 6.1 | Africa's earliest bananas |

The banana is botanically a berry, and the banana tree is actually a large herb. The word "banana" is probably of West African origin, perhaps from Wolof *banaana*; it entered English from Spanish or Portuguese. Originally, the banana came from Southeast Asia, where it was one of the earliest domesticated fruits, ca. 8000–6000 BCE. The following text discusses Professor Robertshaw's recent archaeological research on the banana in Africa.

Many years ago, my wife and I bought our daughter a stuffed toy gorilla that was clutching a banana in its hand. Now, almost anyone would assume that gorillas have been eating bananas for as long as there have been gorillas. Like most archaeologists who work in Africa, however, I doubted that bananas were an important part of a gorilla's diet because I was taught that bananas had been introduced to Africa from Southeast Asia only within the last 2,000 years. As a result of a recent project in Uganda, however, now I am not so sure. When did the banana cross the Indian Ocean to Africa? As you might have predicted, the answer is slippery.

I have spent many years investigating the rise and fall of Bunyoro, a precolonial kingdom that ruled in the wet, tropical region of western Uganda during the last millennium. While I was doing my work in one part of Uganda, David Taylor, now professor of geography at Trinity College, Dublin, was drilling cores in highland swamps in the Rukiga Highlands, a corner of Uganda famous, as it happens, for its gorillas. David was identifying pollen in his cores to reconstruct climate and vegetation history. Eventually we met and ended up writing several papers together—though not in the pub—exploring the relationships between climate change, political economic history, and vegetation shifts in Uganda. Then we persuaded the National Geographic Society to give us a grant to collect sediment cores from papyrus swamps adjacent to the archaeological sites I had been investigating. And so the summer of 2001 found David and me, as well as Julius Lejju, David's Ugandan doctoral student (now teaching at Mbarara University), standing at the edge of a small, papyrus-choked swamp at the site of Munsa, where deep ditches a couple of miles in length were originally dug about 500 years ago.

Direct evidence of ancient agriculture usually takes the form of charred seeds and other plant remains. But that is no use when it comes to bananas

Source: Peter Robertshaw, "Africa's Earliest Bananas," *Archaeology* 59,5 (September/October 2006), https://archive.archaeology.org/0609/abstracts/bananas.html, accessed 2-12-2020

because nobody ever broke a tooth on a seed in a banana milkshake. This is where phytoliths enter the picture. Phytoliths (literally "plant-stones") are microscopic silica bodies found in the stems and leaves of plants. Whereas the plant dies and decays, phytoliths are virtually indestructible and so become incorporated into sediment cores. Happily, different families, and sometimes even species, of plants produce phytoliths of distinctly different shapes.

When Julius told David that he had found some banana phytoliths in our cores, we were pleased but not surprised since bananas are grown at Munsa today. The earliest documentary reference to bananas in Africa is from the sixth century A.D. Historians and archaeologists often thought that bananas were probably introduced to Africa via Madagascar, which was colonized by people from Southeast Asia in the first millennium A.D. This idea, however, was thrown into doubt some years ago on the basis of linguistic, botanical, and geographical evidence, all of which suggested that bananas might well have been introduced much earlier. There was no way to prove this, though, a few years ago a team of Belgian scientists had caused a commotion of their own by reporting that they had discovered banana phytoliths dated to 500 B.C. in Cameroon, thereby pushing back the date for the first appearance of bananas in Africa by about a thousand years.

Then Julius unleashed a bombshell: He had identified several banana phytoliths toward the bottom of one of the cores, in sediments that accumulated more than 5,000 years ago! Now here we were with bananas that were well over 2,500 years older still. Were they really banana phytoliths? And if they were that old, how could they have reached the middle of Africa so long ago? All of a sudden, we were not only challenging the assumption that bananas only reached Africa in the last 2,000 years, but that African connections to the Indian Ocean world may be more ancient than we previously supposed.

▶ **Working with Sources**

1. **The document above reveals interesting interconnections between science and history. How would you summarize these interconnections in the case of the banana?**

2. **Bananas are among the most satiating and nutritious fruits. If you explore Google, which list of major nutritional benefits can you identify?**

SOURCE 6.2

Relief sculpture from Meroë, Sudan

ca. 600–300 BCE

The kings of Meroë, successors of the Nubia-descended twenty-fifth dynasty of Egypt, established their capital on the Middle Nile about 100 miles north of Khartoum, Sudan. At its height, the city was home to more than 20,000 people. Its surviving buildings have qualified it as a UNESCO World Heritage Site.

Source: ©Unesco/Ron Van Oers.

▶ Working with Sources

1. **How does the relief reflect the ongoing influence of ancient Egyptian iconography and symbolism?**

2. **What was the extent of the empire around Meroë, and what was the source of its influence?**

SOURCE 6.3 The Inland Niger Delta

The United States Geological Survey, from which the following text on the Inland Niger Delta is taken, provides up-to-date scientific research concerning "the natural hazards that threaten lives and livelihoods, the water, energy, minerals, and other natural resources we rely on, the health of our ecosystems and environment, and the impacts of climate and land-use change." It is a branch of the Department of the Interior and was established in 1879. Since that time it has been sought out by students and teachers alike for its "natural science expertise and its vast earth and biological data holdings."

Source: United States Geological Survey, West Africa: Land Use and Land Cover Dynamics https://eros.usgs.gov/westafrica/case-study/landscape-diversity-and-dynamics-inland-niger-delta, accessed 2-12-2020

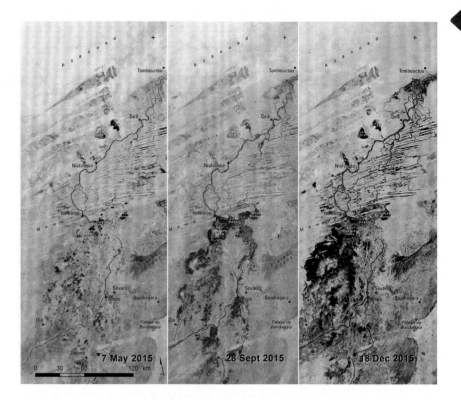

The Inland Niger Delta is the largest wetland in West Africa. It is spectacular in both its landscape diversity and dynamics. Water from the Niger River, which originates 900 km upstream in the Guinean Highlands, spreads out into a wide floodplain about 380 km long in central Mali. It has a very gentle gradient, dropping only 8 m over its entire length. The floodplain is a highly dynamic complex of wetlands, channels, islands and lakes that provides important habitat for fish, water birds, and other wildlife. The seasonal flooding also supports pasture and rice farming. The delta has provided livelihoods for people for millennia. Today, over 1 million people depend on the resources of the delta. About a quarter of the Delta's population lives in cities like Djenné, Mopti, Niafounké, and Timbuktu.

In the recent geologic past, the Inland Delta area was once a huge lake, fed by the Upper Niger River. At some point in that wet period, the lake overflowed to the east through a breach. The interior lake was drained, although a number of small relic lakes remain.

The three Landsat images capture the dynamics of natural flooding as seen in May, September, and December 2015. The May image shows the extreme dryness of the land at the peak of the hot, dry season. The semi-permanent water bodies (dark blue and green) of the Delta stand out. Several major lakes have dried out since the early 1970s, most notably Lake Faguibine, whose arrowhead-shaped lakebed is clearly seen in the north. The low flood levels of the drier years are insufficient to reach many lakes and depressions. Flooding begins when the Niger and the Bani Rivers begin to rise. Starting in July, the Niger River rises about 4 m in 100 days. Peak level may even reach 6 m in the years of high rainfall (Zwarts and others, 2009). As the center image shows (above), by late September the natural flooding of the Inland Delta is well underway. Acting like a giant sponge, vast wetlands come to life. The southern Delta swells and greens first, while the northern Delta area experiences a two- to three-month delay in flooding. In the December image, the annual high water level has finally reached the northern Delta, while the southern Delta has already been drained of much of its water. Between the southern and northern floodplain, flooding permeates a total area of about 40,000 sq km. Numerous ephemeral lakes, along with the more permanent ones, like grapes on a vine, receive and store the floodwaters, releasing them gradually as the river level subsides.

Vast floating meadows of vegetation occupy the areas of deeper water, dominated by an aquatic grass species known locally as bourgou. During the flooding, bourgou, along with wild rice and other species, produce a considerable amount of habitat for fish and water birds and nutritious fodder for cattle during the dry season. As the water subsides in the dry season, the floodplain vegetation provides green pasture for the millions of cattle, sheep, and goats. Farmers cultivate rice, mainly in the southern Delta. They use a West African rice variety that grows well as the water rises. It is then harvested when the waters recede. This floodplain rice is more extensive than irrigated rice fields, which can also be found in the Inland Delta.

Flood forecasts will become increasingly important as the population grows and pressure on water resources increases. Water level measurements and satellite images help predict the onset of seasonal floods and help achieve food security. An early warning system will help predict drought and monitor food security. Data from both on the ground and satellites help manage water resources.

▶ **Working with Sources**

1. **Which factors would have contributed to the Inland Niger Delta having been the cradle of the oldest city in West Africa, Jenné-jeno?**

2. **Why did the Inland Niger Delta, in spite of its size and population density, never possess a kingdom of its own but was always part of the surrounding steppe kingdoms and empires?**

SOURCE 6.4

Lady K'atun, Queen of Piedras Negras

This image of Lady K'atun, surrounded by a Mayan Glyph text, comes from Stela 1 at Piedras Negras. The kingdom of Piedras Negras (seventh century BCE–850 CE) was a major Mayan polity located in northeastern Guatemala. Its ruins today contain a particularly rich treasure of stelae

Source: Mark Pitts, "Lady K'atun – Queen of Piedras Negras," in Mark Pitts, *A Brief History of Piedras Negras as Told by the Ancient Maya: History Revealed in Maya Glyphs* (The Aid and Education Project, Inc.), ch. 11, 77–84, http://www.famsi.org/research/pitts/pitts_piedras_negras_history.pdf, accessed 2-13-2020

and altars with inscriptions. At its height, the kingdom had a population of some 50,000 inhabitants. In 686 CE it incorporated the neighboring polity of Namaan, of which K'atun was the queen. Stela 1 records her marriage to King K'inich Yo'nal Ahk II (687–729 CE) of Piedras Negras.

Rough Translation of the Glyphs

"On [Mayan calendar] 9.12.02.00.16, 5, Kib 14 Yaxk'in [July 4, 674 CE] Lady K'atun, Lordess of Namaan, was born.

   "On [Mayan calendar] 9.12.14.10.11, 9 Chuwen 9 K'ank'in [November 13, 686] she was "enclosed" [as part of marriage ceremony] and 5 days later on 1 Kib 14 K'ank'in she was "revealed /adorned" [betrothed]...

▶ Working
with Sources

1. Generally, only Maya kings were commemorated on stelae. Why, do you think, was Queen K'atun given her own stela for commemoration?

2. On the stela, Queen K'atun is perhaps depicted in the so-called hieratic style of art, described at the end of Chapter 7 in this book. If you agree, what would be the elements of this art in the Meso-American context?

| SOURCE 6.5 | # Cosmas Indicopleustes (Cosmas the India-Voyager), *Christian Topography* |

ca. 550 CE

This remarkable account of a merchant's travels throughout Eastern Africa, the Arabian Peninsula, and India resulted from the singular obsession of a monk in retirement. Determined to prove that a proper understanding of earth's geography would confirm God's creation—and that the earth was a flat, oblong table surrounded by the ocean—the monk Cosmas reflected back on his extensive voyages, which had probably been undertaken to further a spice-import business. Cosmas commented on the trading practices of the Aksumites and on their wealthy culture, providing one of the few available outsider glimpses of Aksum.

The region that produces frankincense is situated at the projecting parts of Ethiopia, and lies inland, but is washed by the ocean on the other side. Hence the inhabitants of Barbaria, being near at hand, go up into the interior and, engaging in traffic with the natives, bring back from them many kinds of spices, frankincense, cassia, calamus, and many other articles of merchandise, which they afterwards send by sea to Agau, to the country of the Homerites [Yemen], to Further India, and to Persia.

This very fact you will find mentioned in the Book of Kings, where it is recorded that the Queen of Sheba, that is, of the Homerite country, whom afterwards our Lord in the Gospels calls the Queen of the South, brought to Solomon spices from this very Barbaria, which lay near Sheba on the other side of the sea, together with bars of ebony, and apes and gold from Ethiopia which, though separated from Sheba by the Arabian Gulf, lay in its vicinity. We can see again from the words of the Lord that he calls these places the ends of the earth, saying: *The Queen of the South shall rise up in judgment with this generation and shall condemn it, for she came from the ends of the earth to hear the wisdom of Solomon* (Matthew 12:42). For the Homerites are not far distant from Barbaria, as the sea which lies between them can be crossed in a couple of

Source: Cosmas Indicopleustes, *Christianike Topographia*, Book 3, trans. and ed. Christopher Haas, Villanova University; available online: http://www29.homepage.villanova.edu/christopher.haas/cosmas_indicopleustes.htm

days, and then beyond Barbaria is the ocean, which is there called Zingion. The country known as that of Sasu is itself near the ocean, just as the ocean is near the frankincense country, in which there are many gold mines.

The King of the Aksumites, accordingly, every other year, through the governor of Agau, sends thither special agents to bargain for the gold, and these are accompanied by many other traders—upwards, say, of five hundred—bound on the same errand as themselves. They take along with them to the mining district oxen, lumps of salt, and iron, and when they reach its neighborhood they make a halt at a certain spot and form an encampment, which they fence round with a great hedge of thorns. Within this they live, and having slaughtered the oxen, cut them in pieces, and lay the pieces on the top of the thorns, along with the lumps of salt and the iron. Then come the natives bringing gold in nuggets like peas, called *tancharas,* and lay one or two or more of these upon what pleases them—the pieces of flesh or the salt or the iron, and then they retire to some distance off. Then the owner of the meat approaches, and if he is satisfied he takes the gold away, and upon seeing this, its owner comes and takes the flesh or the salt or the iron. If, however, he is not satisfied, he leaves the gold. When the native, seeing that he has not taken it comes and either puts down more gold, or takes up what he had laid down, and goes away.

Such is the mode in which business is transacted with the people of that country, because their language is different and interpreters are hardly to be found. The time they stay in that country is five days more or less, according as the natives more or less readily coming forward buy up all their wares. On the journey homeward they all agree to travel well-armed, since some of the tribes through whose country they must pass might threaten to attack them from a desire to rob them of their gold. The space of six months is taken up with this trading expedition, including both the going and the returning. In going they march very slowly, chiefly because of the cattle, but in returning they quicken their pace lest on the way they should be overtaken by winter and its rains.

For the sources of the river Nile lie somewhere in these parts, and in winter, on account of the heavy rains, the numerous rivers which they generate obstruct the path of the traveler. The people there have their winter at the time we have our summer. It begins in the month *Epiphi* of the Egyptians and continues till *Thoth,* and during the three months the rain falls in torrents, and makes a multitude of rivers all of which flow into the Nile.

▶ **Working with Sources**

1. **How does Cosmas characterize the Aksumites, and to what other peoples does he compare them?**

2. **How and why does Cosmas allude to Old and New Testament accounts in his analysis of cultures adjoining the Red Sea?**

World Period Two

The Age of Empires and Visionaries, 600 BCE–600 CE

In the middle of the first millennium BCE, two major transformations changed the course of world history.

- **Empires in Eurasia** Two types of conquering kingdoms or empires formed, after Akkad had pioneered this form of polity during the first world period. The first type, in the Middle East, Mediterranean, and India, was that of multiethnic and multireligious empires, which followed each other in sequence. The second type consisted of the ethnically and religiously more uniform empires of Egypt and China.

- **Visionaries and the Adoption of State Religions** Around 700–500 BCE, visionaries arose who proclaimed the idea of personal salvation. They anchored this idea in the higher, absolute standard of monotheism or monism, which was not bound to any state on Earth. Followers of the visionaries formed communities and schools based on texts that expounded monotheistic or monist teachings. Eventually, rulers adopted these teachings and turned them into state religions.

Chapter 7

Interaction and Adaptation in Western Eurasia

PERSIA, GREECE, AND ROME, 550 BCE–600 CE

CHAPTER SEVEN PATTERNS

Origins, Interactions, and Adaptations During the period 550 BCE to 600 CE, the western Eurasian world initially experienced the emergence of successive Persian regimes in the Middle East, the expansion of the Roman Empire across the Mediterranean world, and the development of city-states in Greece. Over time, however, rivalries among them, combined with internal weaknesses and external intrusions, culminated in the transition from the western Roman Empire to Germanic successor states. At the same time, the eastern Roman and Sasanid Persian Empires competed for dominance in the Middle East.

Uniqueness and Similarities The most important development in the empires and kingdoms of the Middle East was the emergence of visionaries who opened the perspective of personal salvation through faith in a single deity (monotheism). For Jews, it was the vision of Yahweh and his 10 commandments; for Zoroastrians, it was the vision of the apocalypse and a savior at the end of the world that appeared as new elements in world history. In combination, these visions laid the foundations for Judaism, Christianity, and Islam. Among the Greeks, philosophers replaced polytheistic thought with monism: the concept of an ultimate truth as the path to personal salvation in place of the many truths of polytheism.

During the period 550 BCE–600 CE, the Middle East and the Mediterranean formed one unitary arena of world history. The interactions and adaptations in this arena, therefore, warrant treatment in a single chapter, as is done here, in order to avoid essentializing any one of its components, that is, Persia, Greece, or Rome, in isolation. The vignette chosen for this chapter—Shirin, queen of the Sasanid Persians—symbolizes for one last moment this Middle Eastern–Mediterranean unity before it broke apart politically into an Eastern Christian Byzantine/Islamic region in the Middle East and a Western Christian region in western Europe.

Shirin (ca. 580–628) was an East Syriac Christian said to have been of Aramaic origin from the Mesopotamian province of Khuzistan (today southwestern Iran). We do not know how Emperor (Persian *shahanshah*, "king of kings") Khosrow II (also known by his Greek name Chosroes; r. 590–628), a Zoroastrian, encountered her originally. All we are told is that he was passionately in love with her, his favorite queen. Apparently, Shirin had trouble conceiving and so Khosrow enlisted the miracle powers of two Christian saintly figures for the successful birth of what appear to have been daughters. After the intervention of a court physician, Shirin also gave birth to two sons, one of whom became Khosrow's successor for a short period. In collaboration with this physician, Shirin rose subsequently to the position of power behind the throne. Her main focus was the empire's religious policy during the two decades when the empire reigned supreme after conquering much of the Roman Empire in the last and most cataclysmic war between the two perennial enemies (602–628).

To execute this religious policy, first Shirin and her physician changed their allegiance from the struggling East Syriac church to that of the rapidly expanding monophysite church now known as the Syriac Orthodox Church. Then, during the period of Sasanid supremacy, the two banked on the monophysites to also overtake the Orthodox (Chalcedonian) church of

CHAPTER OUTLINE

Interactions between Persia and Greece

Interactions between the Persian and Roman Empires

Adaptations to Monotheism and Monism in the Middle East

The Beginnings of Science and the Cultures of Kings and Citizens

Putting It All Together

PERSIA, GREECE, AND ROME

Mediterranean Sea

ABOVE: Detail from the Ara Pacis Augustae (Altar of Augustan Peace), commissioned by the Roman Senate in 13 BCE and consecrated in 9 BCE.

Seeing Patterns

❯ Why should the Middle East and Mediterranean Europe during the period 600 BCE–600 CE be studied as a single unit?

❯ What is transcendence, and why is it important to understand its importance in world history?

❯ Which elements characterize the institutions that grew out of the Middle Eastern monotheisms of Judaism and Christianity and the monism of Greek philosophy and science?

the Roman Empire. At this time, Khosrow captured what was believed to be the cross to which Jesus had been nailed in Jerusalem and turned this precious relic over to Shirin for safekeeping in her palace. One is tempted to speculate whether she wanted it to be a bargaining chip for the final dominance of her monophysite branch of Christianity.

In a spectacular reversal of fortune, however, the Romans regained the initiative under the new emperor Heraclius (610–641), who was the son of the governor of the province of Africa (which included all Byzantine possessions in the Western Mediterranean). The emperor proclaimed an Orthodox Christian liberation war against the Zoroastrian Sasanids in 622 and advanced as far as northern Mesopotamia six years later. Khosrow's regime collapsed amidst a palace coup, in which Khosrow, Shirin, her firstborn son and brief heir, as well as more than a dozen children by Khosrow and women in his harem of allegedly 10,000 were killed. In contrast to their physical deaths, however, the two passionate lovers lived on in subsequent cycles of Persian and Arabic stories and, in translation, in the Romantic era of modern European culture.

Early Persia and Greece

The Achaemenid Persian conquest of the Middle East, from Anatolia and Egypt in the west to northwestern India in the east, was relatively easy compared to the conquest of Greece, whose inhabitants resisted fiercely. Although Persia subjugated the Greek city-states of the Anatolian coast, it was unable to conquer the Greek mainland. A century and a half later, Alexander the Great unified Greece and led it to victory over Persia, establishing a short-lived Macedonian–Greek Empire. Alexander's generals divided the empire into three successor kingdoms under which politics stabilized until the Persians, under the Parthians and Sasanids, renewed the Persian imperial tradition.

The Origins of the Achaemenid Persian Empire

The Persians originated as agrarian villagers and nomadic horse and sheep breeders during the Bronze Age in central Asia south of the Ural Mountains. Toward the end of the third millennium BCE, groups of nomads migrated from the Urals southward to the Aral Sea region. The Persians were a branch that migrated sometime before the 800s BCE farther into the southwestern Iranian province of Fars, from which the name "Persia" is derived.

Persian Conquests   The first speakers of a Persian language to appear in the historical record were the Medes, who had arrived from central Asia in southwest Iran at the end of the Bronze Age. In the middle of the sixth century, they shared the region with a number of other small groups, among which were the Achaemenids. The head of the Achaemenids, Cyrus II the Great (r. ca. 550–530

BCE), incorporated the Medes and embarked on a series of imperial conquests. Outlined in a text on a clay cylinder, Cyrus describes himself as the representative of the high god Marduk on earth and his rule as that of peace and justice everywhere. He first expanded into Anatolia (modern-day Turkey), where he conquered the kingdom of Lydia [LIH-dee-ya]. Next, Cyrus turned to the neighboring Greek city-states of Ionia on the southwestern Anatolian coast. His generals besieged these cities until their inhabitants either surrendered or returned to the Greek mainland.

Cyrus himself was busy with the conquest of the Iranian interior and north, as far as Afghanistan. In 540 BCE he began his campaign against Neo-Babylonia in Mesopotamia, capturing the capital of Babylon a year later. The Phoenician city-states in Syria submitted voluntarily in the following years. Within a little more than a decade, Cyrus unified all of the Middle East except Egypt, which the empire conquered in 525 BCE (see Map 7.1). In Jerusalem, Cyrus permitted the rebuilding of the Temple by Jews returning from Mesopotamia in 538, where their ancestors had been deported a century and a half earlier (see Chapter 2).

Persian Arms   The Achaemenid Persians achieved their conquests with the help of armed, mobile mounted archers as well as **cataphracts**—horsemen with heavy armor. The archers fought with composite bows, and the cataphracts with lances. Infantry soldiers armed with bows, arrows, shields, and javelins provided support for the cavalry.

Persian kings supplemented their armies with heavily armored infantry recruited from among the Anatolian Greeks. These foot soldiers, called **hoplites**, fought in ranks in mass formations called phalanxes. They were equipped with spears, iron swords, shields, helmets, and protective armor. In close quarters, hoplite phalanxes were nearly invincible. The Persian navy comprised as many as 1,200 galleys during its peak in the fifth century BCE. Apart from fighting naval battles against the Greeks, the navy also explored the western Mediterranean and the coast of Africa. Altogether, the Persian military was a formidable fighting machine.

Cataphracts: Heavily armed and protected cavalry soldiers, riding the powerful Nisean breed of horses and recorded for the first time in Iran, ca. 600 BCE.

Hoplites: Greek foot soldiers who fought in closed ranks.

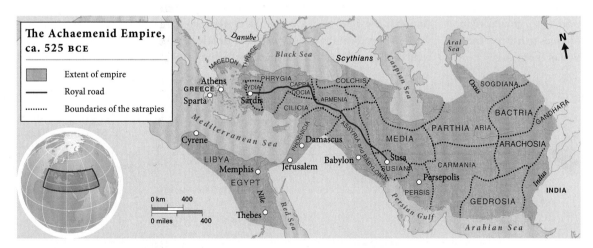

MAP 7.1 **Achaemenid Persian Empire**

Persian Administration   The Achaemenid Persian Empire encompassed Mesopotamia and Egypt as well as the Indus Valley and had an estimated 15 million inhabitants. The empire consisted of some 70 ethnic groups across 30 provinces, which were granted considerable autonomy. Most kings prayed to the god Ahuramazda (a-hoo-ra-MAZ-da) of the Zoroastrians, but others selected other deities from the Persian pantheon.

Around 500 BCE, the kings replaced indigenous rulers with their own governors from the Persian aristocracy. These provincial governors, or satraps, were powerful rulers. They administered Persian law and collected tributes and taxes. When called upon by the kings, the governors contributed their provincial troops to the royal army. Officially, the Achaemenid king called himself "king of kings" (**shahanshah** [shaw-an-shaw])—that is, emperor.

Shahanshah: "King of kings," the title of Persian rulers.

The shahanshahs maintained their central administration from the palace at Persepolis [per-SEH-poh-lis]. The language used for administrative purposes was Aramaic, a Semitic language that was commonly spoken in the Middle East of the period. Clay tablets were used as writing material in Mesopotamia, but Persian scribes preferred parchment or papyrus scrolls. A basic principle of the empire's financial administration was the hoarding of all incoming silver and gold. Trade was not yet fully monetized, and the kings minted only small amounts of coins. As elsewhere in Asia, villagers continued to pay taxes or rents in kind, and local markets functioned on the basis of barter.

To maintain communications and order across the empire, the Persians created "royal roads," perhaps the first such highways in the world, which connected Persia with Anatolia and Mesopotamia. Governors provided distance markers, inns and depots, and police and army posts. The roads were intended primarily for quick troop movements, although traders used them as well.

Greek City-States in the Persian Shadow

In the sixth century BCE, while Persia evolved into an empire, hundreds of city-states (singular *polis*; plural *poleis*) dotted Anatolia, Greece, and Italy. The most populous of these poleis were Athens and Sparta, which competed for dominance. Their rivalry eventually benefited Persia in its attempt to assume power over Greece.

Oracles: Priests or priestesses consulted in temples to learn of the will of the gods.

Athens and Sparta   Most of the Greek city-states ruled themselves independently. Two common bonds were the **oracles** and the Olympic Games. Greeks went to the oracles to settle disputes or to divine their future. The Olympic Games,

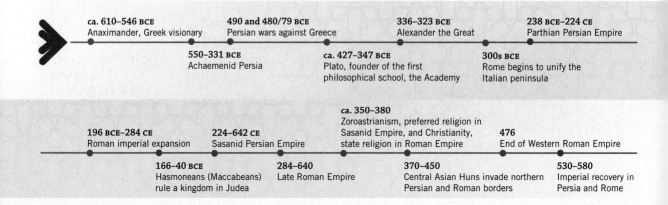

| ca. 610–546 BCE Anaximander, Greek visionary | 490 and 480/79 BCE Persian wars against Greece | 336–323 BCE Alexander the Great | 238 BCE–224 CE Parthian Persian Empire |
| 550–331 BCE Achaemenid Persia | ca. 427–347 BCE Plato, founder of the first philosophical school, the Academy | 300s BCE Rome begins to unify the Italian peninsula | |

| 196 BCE–284 CE Roman imperial expansion | 224–642 CE Sasanid Persian Empire | ca. 350–380 Zoroastrianism, preferred religion in Sasanid Empire, and Christianity, state religion in Roman Empire | 476 End of Western Roman Empire |
| 166–40 BCE Hasmoneans (Maccabeans) rule a kingdom in Judea | 284–640 Late Roman Empire | 370–450 Central Asian Huns invade northern Persian and Roman borders | 530–580 Imperial recovery in Persia and Rome |

MAP 7.2 Greece in the Sixth Century BCE

in the sanctuary site of Olympia, brought together the Greek youth for athletic competitions. Athens, with 200,000 inhabitants, and Sparta, with 140,000 inhabitants, were the largest city-states (see Map 7.2).

Athens is located on the peninsula of Attica in southeastern Greece. Its limited agricultural resources forced inhabitants to specialize in the production of cash crops, which they traded for grain and metals from Italy, the Black Sea region, and Egypt. The focus on trade helped in the emergence of mercantile interests among the landowning citizenry. In 508 BCE, Cleisthenes, a prominent landowner, forged an alliance between merchant landowners and smallholders to bring about new constitutional reforms (building on earlier ones by Solon in 594). He expanded the rights of citizens to sit on juries and participate in the legislative assembly. Proposals adopted by the assembly were to be ratified by the citizenry, and executive power was vested in boards of elected magistrates. Such reforms were the first steps toward the creation of Athenian democracy in the middle of the next century.

Sparta was Athens's principal rival. It was located in the Peloponnesus [peh-lo-po-NEE-sus] Peninsula southwest of Athens. Unlike land-poor Athens, Sparta had room to enlarge its agricultural base before eventually turning to maritime trade. Its constitutional organization preceded that of Athens by a century and, therefore, embodies more traditional traits. Citizenship was based on landownership, and Spartan citizens were entitled to stand for participation in the Council of

Elders and the Board of Overseers, the decisions of which were ratified by the assembly of owners of medium-sized properties. Executive power was in the hands of two hereditary kings. Army service was of crucial importance in Sparta, and even women received vigorous physical training.

The village farmers in Sparta and the other Greek city-states were noncitizens of unfree status, in contrast to the free farmers in the Middle East. In Athens, small free farmers were at the center of early reform efforts. In Sparta, however, the farmers, called "helots," were the descendants of surrounding peoples conquered by Sparta during its years of expansion.

Since, in addition to villagers, women were excluded from political participation, constitutional rule benefited only some in the Greek city-states. This was true even in the mid-fifth century BCE, when the final round of Athenian reforms under Pericles extended voting and office rights to all male citizens. Athens' "golden age" of democracy was in fact restricted to no more than one-third of the population at its height. In retrospect, Greece was not the only pioneer of constitutional rule; it shared this role with other early societies in Mesopotamia and India, although each adopted rule by assemblies independently and not as a result of interaction.

Women in Greek society were considered citizens, but they were unable to vote. Spartan women enjoyed more rights than their Athenian counterparts, who were primarily responsible for management of the household (*oikonomia*, from which the word *economics* is derived) as well as the nurturing and raising of children. Well-educated women served as *hetairai*, "companions," for men at symposia (dinner and drinking parties). The most exalted status available to Greek women was that of priestesses delivering prophecies at oracles, of which the most renowned was the Temple of Apollo at Delphi.

Greece and Persia   Their maritime commercial wealth made the Greek city-states irresistible targets of Persian imperialism. When Athens supported the Ionian revolt of the Greek city-states in 499–494 BCE, the Persian monarchy found its justification to wage war against the Greeks. They suppressed the revolt and organized two invasions of the Greek mainland (492–490 and 480–479 BCE). To meet the invasion, the Greek city-states on the mainland united under the joint leadership of Athens and Sparta. In two battles, on land at Marathon (490 BCE) and on the sea at Salamis (480 BCE), the united Greeks repelled both Persian invasions. Greece managed to preserve its liberty and escape Persian imperial dominance.

Soon, however, the Greek world was plunged into devastating internal conflict. After the repulsion of the Persian invasions, Athenian–Spartan unity fell apart. As a substitute, Athens formed a league with as many as 200 poleis around the Aegean and Black Seas. When Athens diverted a portion of the league's membership contributions to the reconstruction of its war-damaged citadel, the Acropolis, anger against this perceived self-service erupted into the Peloponnesian War (431–404 BCE). During this war, Sparta made itself the champion of liberation from what many Greek cities viewed as an Athenian empire. After depleting Athens' land forces, Sparta—with Persian financial support—built a navy, which won a brilliant victory over Athens, forcing the latter to sue for peace in 404 BCE.

Once involved again in Greek politics, the Achaemenid Persians stoked fears of Spartan dominance. During yet another round of hostilities, a coalition of city-states led by Athens and backed by Persia defeated Sparta. In the King's Peace of 386 BCE, the Persians granted the Greeks in Anatolia autonomy, provided they recognized Persia's dominance. Persian imperial hegemony over Anatolian Greece would last for about half a century.

Alexander's Empire and Its Successor Kingdoms

The one Greek area that remained outside Persian control was Macedonia, on the northern periphery of the Greek city-states. In the middle of the 300s BCE, a king, Philip II (359–336 BCE), unified Macedonia. He conquered the Greek city-states to the south, and his son Alexander continued the expansion with the conquest of Persia.

East Meets West. A turbaned man stands next to a Corinthian capital in the Hellenistic city of Ai-Khanoum, founded in what is today northern Afghanistan—ancient Bactria—in the fourth century BCE, after Alexander's conquests. Ai-Khanoum was one of the focal points of Hellenism in the East. Archaeological excavations in the 1970s revealed a flourishing city, with a Greek-style theater, a huge palace, a citadel, a gymnasium, and various temples.

Alexander and His Successors In 337 BCE, Philip declared war on the Persian Empire. Just as Philip was getting ready to invade Anatolia, he was assassinated in a court intrigue. Philip's son Alexander took over both throne and campaign, setting off for Persia in 334 BCE. In three battles (334–330 BCE), Alexander defeated the Persian defenders. The Persian forces retreated into what is today Afghanistan. Alexander occupied the Persian royal towns and confiscated the Persian treasury. During a drunken revelry in the palace town of Persepolis, the imperial palace burned down, perhaps a final act of vengeance for the destruction of the Acropolis by the Persians.

Alexander next invaded India, but monsoon rains and exhausted troops forced him to retreat. As he left, he appointed governors over northwest India. Under these governors, Greek culture entered the subcontinent (see Chapter 8). Alexander returned to the Middle East, where he died of a fever at the age of 33 (323 BCE). In just 11 years, he had turned the mighty Persian Empire into a Macedonian–Greek one (see Map 7.3).

Alexander's generals divided the empire among themselves, founding kingdoms, among which Antigonid Greece (276–167 BCE), Ptolemaic Egypt (305–30 BCE), and Seleucid southwest Asia (305–64 BCE) were the most important. About 1 million Greeks emigrated during the 200s BCE to the Middle East, imprinting their **Hellenistic** (Greek-influenced) culture on urban life. Thus, even though the Macedonian–Greek Empire failed politically, its cultural legacy lasted for centuries.

Hellenistic culture: Refers to Greek culture during the period from 323 BCE to 31 BCE.

Interactions between the Persian and Roman Empires

A century after Alexander's conquests, a resurgent Persia—based in the northeastern province of Parthia—emerged on the periphery of the Seleucid kingdom. This coincided with Rome's expansion after the unification of Italy. On the periphery of the successor kingdoms of Alexander's Macedonian–Greek Empire, both Parthia and Rome pressed against the Antigonids, Seleucids, and Ptolemies. After conquering these kingdoms, Rome and Parthia eventually met in Anatolia and Syria in the early second century BCE. Neither, however, succeeded in eliminating the other. As a result, the Middle East and the Mediterranean remained politically divided.

Parthian Persia and Rome

Parthia was originally part of the Seleucid kingdom. In the 240s BCE an Eastern Iranian people, distant relatives of the Persians, migrated from central Asia to Parthia, where they defeated the Seleucid governor. The Parthians expanded their power and in 141 BCE conquered Iran and Mesopotamia. In 109 BCE, Mithridates II the Great (r. ca. 123–88 BCE) formally renewed the Persian Empire in his capital Ctesiphon (across the Tigris from the Seleucid capital of Seleucia, near modern Baghdad) by assuming the title "king of kings" and taking over the traditional Iranian pantheon of gods.

Parthian Diplomacy   Parthian Persia was a major diplomatic power. In 115, Wudi [woo-DEE] (r. ca. 140–87 BCE), the emperor of Han China, sent a diplomatic mission to Mithridates II, part of Wudi's ongoing efforts to secure his northern border against Turkic nomadic invaders and find allies among the nomads in Bactria. Although no alliance between Persia and China came to be, this first diplomatic contact opened up the Silk Road, which, for many centuries to come, was the main central Asian trade route.

At the other end of this empire, on the upper Euphrates River, the Parthian Persians established first contacts with Rome. Early efforts at diplomacy failed, however, and Rome and Persia soon came to blows.

Roman Republican Origins   The western Mediterranean became part of the Middle Eastern and eastern Mediterranean agrarian centers in the course of the first millennium BCE. Phoenicians from the eastern Mediterranean established ports, the most important of which was Carthage, in today's Tunisia. Later on, Greeks established city-states in southern Italy and Sicily. In north-central Italy was the kingdom of the Etruscans, a people who originally came from Anatolia and the Levant and settled in Italy ca. 2000 BCE. The kingdom included Rome, founded around 1000 BCE.

Around 500 BCE, the Romans overthrew their kings and created a republic (from Latin *res publica*, "public matter"), electing leaders and forming a constitutional government. Around 450 BCE, the Romans adopted the Twelve Tablets, a set of laws. A chief priest was responsible for administering the cult of the patron god, Jupiter, and fixing the calendar. The later polytheistic religious practices of the Romans resembled those of the Greeks and Persians.

Legionaries: Roman foot soldiers who fought in semi-closed ranks.

Expansion of the Republic   In the 300s BCE, when Rome began to unify the peninsula, it organized its citizen army into legions. The infantry of **legionaries** consisted of landed citizens able to pay for their weapons and armor. Wealthy Romans also manned the cavalry, including cataphracts, while small landholders made up the light infantry of skirmishers. With the help of these legionaries, Rome completed the unification of Italy and in three wars (246–146 BCE) conquered its strongest rival, Carthage.

In the middle of these wars, around 200 BCE, Carthage sought to protect itself against Rome through an alliance with the kingdom of Antigonid Greece. In a first expansion east, the Romans defeated the Antigonids and, in 196 BCE, issued the Isthmus Declaration, according to which the Greeks of Greece, Anatolia, and farther east were to be "free" of Antigonid overlordship and governed by their

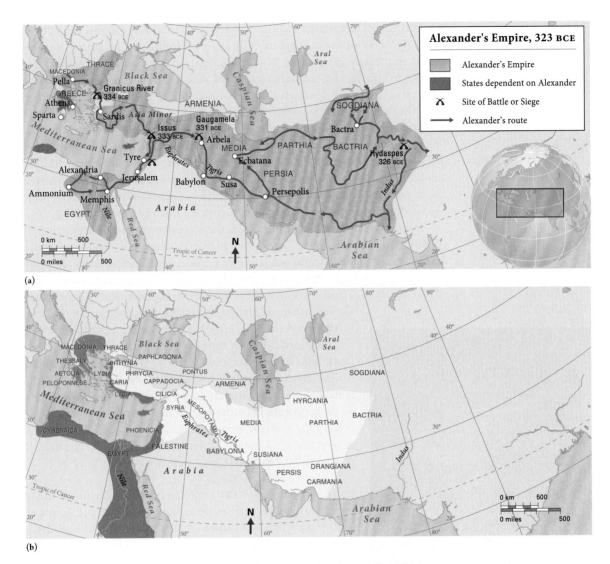

MAP 7.3 **Alexander's Empire (a) and Successor Kingdoms after the Breakup of Alexander's Empire (b)**

own laws. When the Greeks rebelled in the middle of the second century BCE, they were ruthlessly repressed by the Romans, who eventually reduced Greece to provincial status.

With the Isthmus Declaration, Rome became an empire, in fact if not in name. (Historians usually date the official beginning of the Roman Empire to 27 BCE, when the Senate bestowed the title "Augustus" on Octavian.) In the wake of Rome's expansion into North Africa, Greece, and Anatolia during the second and first centuries BCE, a new ruling class of wealthy landowners emerged. These consisted of Italian aristocrats who had appropriated the land of smallholders absent for extended periods during their service as legionaries, turning these lands into large estates worked by tenant farmers or slaves. Ruling-class members also acquired conquered lands overseas, where they established estates worked by enslaved war captives.

Discharged legionaries and dispossessed farmers crowded Rome, while rebellious slaves on estates in southern Italy and Sicily rebelled. The most dangerous revolt was that of Spartacus in 73–71 BCE. Spartacus was an army deserter from Thrace in Greece who had been recaptured, enslaved, and trained as a gladiator. Spartacus' followers devastated estates throughout Italy and held the Roman army in check for three years before it succeeded in defeating them.

Efforts by social reformers at improving the lot of the poor failed against the fierce resistance of the landowners. One reform that succeeded was that of Marius, who was senator from 107 to 85 BCE. He opened the army ranks to the landless and enlisted them for up to 20 years of service. Upon retirement, soldiers received plots of land in conquered provinces. This reform benefited imperial expansion, but it also encouraged generals to use the army for their own ambitions.

In the middle of the first century BCE, three ambitious generals were vying for control of the empire. Julius Caesar (100–44 BCE), a magistrate, was from a prominent family and a successful conqueror of northwestern Europe. After returning from his conquests, in 48 BCE he defeated his last remaining rival, Pompey (106–48 BCE), also a consul and leader of the empire's strongest military forces. When Caesar then in addition to his consulate assumed several titles traditionally held by other magistrates, including that of "dictator for life," he provoked much opposition. In the Senate, several assassins killed Caesar, and a "triumvirate" of generals assumed power.

The triumvirate did not last. Civil war broke out, and the ultimate victor was Octavian (r. 31 BCE–14 CE). Octavian created a new constitutional order with himself as leader, always maintaining the pretense of being merely the first of the citizenry. In practice he possessed unlimited powers under the title of Augustus ("the Revered One"), bestowed on him in 27 BCE.

Augustus. The famous Augustus of Prima Porta, dated to 15 CE, is probably a copy of a bronze original commissioned by Octavian at some date after he was honored with the title "Augustus" in 27 BCE. Intended as a representation of the power and authority of Rome's first emperor, the statue depicts Augustus as barefooted, a symbolic image of gods and heroes.

The Augustan Age   To consolidate his power, Augustus limited imperial expansion in the north to France, England, and Germany, west of the Rhine and Danube Rivers. He ordered the construction of a wall linking the two rivers to keep the Germanic tribes on the other side at bay. In the east, a series of wars (56 BCE–1 CE) with the Persian Parthian Empire ended inconclusively. Egypt, Syria, and Judea came under direct Roman rule; Armenia became a Roman client state; Upper Mesopotamia east of the Euphrates remained Parthian; and peace reigned between Rome and Parthia for two generations.

All 44 Roman provinces outside Italy had to pay poll and agricultural taxes, primarily to support a standing army, which Augustus reduced by half to the size of the earlier civil war armies. Tax money also supported the building and upkeep of roads and ports, as well as wheat subsidies and circuses for the inhabitants of Rome and other large cities. In contrast to the huge military, the number of civilian Roman administrators in the provinces was small. The Roman Peace (*pax romana*) rested more on the projection of military might than on a civilian administration, as in Han China.

Women in Roman society, although unable to vote, were afforded more freedom than those in Greek society. Restricted under guardianship during the

Republic, women in the Augustan age and later, especially those among the upper class, openly engaged in public entertainments at the games and the theater. In fact, a few women actively involved themselves in political affairs; e.g., Livia (58 BCE–29 CE), the wife of Augustus, and Agrippina the Younger (15–59 CE), Nero's mother, both acting as counselors to their husbands with the imperial title of *augusta*. As in ancient Greece, a few selected young girls served as high priestesses in sacred religious rituals.

The Sasanid Persian and Late Roman Empires

Parthia challenged Rome twice more (161–166 CE and 193–198 CE). It lost both times and had to give up the province of Upper Mesopotamia and much of its economic wealth. Divisions in the ruling class of the Parthians began to appear. In the early 200s, a priestly family in Fars assumed provincial leadership functions in opposition to the dynasty. Ardashir, a descendant of this priestly family, finally ended Parthian rule in 224 and declared himself king of kings, establishing the Sasanid Persian Empire (224–642 CE).

Roman Crisis   Just when Persian imperial power was rejuvenated through a new dynasty, the Roman Empire fell into a political and economic crisis that lasted half a century (234–285 CE). Some two dozen emperors followed each other in rapid succession on the throne, and for a while the empire even fragmented into three pieces.

In addition to the internal conflicts, Germanic tribes broke through the northern defenses and during 260–276 pillaged as far south as northern Italy. At the same time, both Rome and Persia were afflicted by an outbreak of mass disease in 251–266, foreshadowing the plague of 541 (see "Patterns Up Close"). At the end of the 200s, it appeared that Rome was at its end.

Emperor Diocletian (r. 285–305), however, salvaged the empire. He divided it into an eastern and a western half, doubled the number of provinces and civil administrators, and created military districts. He regularized tax collection, increased the number of legions, and created a mobile field army. Civil peace returned to the empire, albeit at the price of increased militarization.

Adoption of Monotheism   The early Sasanids were too busy consolidating their enormous territory to exploit the Roman crisis to the fullest. Although they invaded Roman territories in Syria and Anatolia, the Romans always regained control. Diocletian, after his reforms, was even able to push the border eastward to the Tigris River.

In the first half of the 300s, while Rome and Persia continued their inconclusive wars, both empires underwent religious transformation. They began to shift away from polytheism and toward the elevation of monotheism to the status of state religion. During the previous polytheist millennia in the Middle East and the Mediterranean, kings and emperors had supported imperial temple priesthoods in their capitals in return for the justification of their rule. But when the Romans and Persians suffered internal crises, rulers became aware of the need for a unifying single religious bond.

At the beginning of the reign of Emperor Constantine I the Great (r. 306–337 CE), Christianity's adherents represented a small percentage of the Roman population,

Patterns Up Close

The Plague of Justinian

At the end of the 500s, neither the Roman nor the Sasanid Empire was as populous and wealthy as before the nomadic invasions from the north. In addition, for the first time (in 541), a mass epidemic, the bubonic plague, hit the world from China to Roman England. It was recorded most vividly in the Roman Empire, where it became the "Plague of Justinian"—it sickened the emperor himself for several weeks—dramatically reducing population levels everywhere. The plague probably originated in northwestern China and reached the Mediterranean through caravans traveling along the Silk Road via the Sasanid Empire.

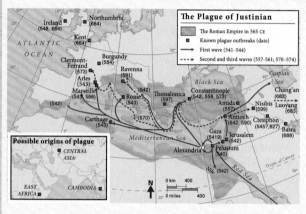

MAP 7.4 **The Plague of Justinian**

Historians know now that for the plague to become a pandemic, average temperatures must have declined. Fleas are most likely to jump from infected rodents, like rats, to humans at 59–68 degrees Fahrenheit. Such a temperature decline might have occurred a few years prior to 541, with the eruption of the volcano Krakatau in Indonesia in 535, the ashes of which obscured the sun for years. Although the climate returned to normal a few years later, recurrent cycles of the plague every decade or two until well into the 700s prevented population levels from recovering.

Observers in various cities of the Roman Empire have left vivid accounts. People infected by the

comprised primarily of the lower classes. Christianity had begun three centuries earlier with the preaching of Jesus of Nazareth. Since Christians refused to recognize the pantheon of Roman gods, however, they were periodically persecuted. But their numbers recovered, and by the early 300s the Christian Church was well developed. Thus, their existence in the Empire had become visible enough for contenders to the imperial throne to take Christianity seriously as a potential source of support and imperial unity.

General Constantine appealed to this support when he fought his way in 312 to power in Rome. A year later, as emperor, he issued an edict of toleration, and in 325 he presided over the Council of Nicaea (now Iznik in Turkey), which issued the **Nicene Creed** as the common doctrinal platform among Christians. Baptized shortly before his death, Constantine can be considered the first Christian Roman emperor. Several pagan emperors succeeded Constantine before Christianity became the sole state religion with the closing of the Temple of Jupiter in Rome in 380.

In Persia, under the sponsorship of Shapur II (r. ca. 307–379), Zoroastrian priests began to write down the Yasht, the oldest holy scripture of Zoroastrianism. The shahinshahs, with large Jewish and Christian minorities in Mesopotamia, made Zoroastrianism the preferential religion in ca. 350, with Christianity and Judaism accorded a protected status. Thus, both empires sought to strengthen internal unity through the adoption of a single monotheistic faith in the course of the fourth century.

Nicene Creed: Basic Christian doctrine defining faith as belief in God, the Father; Jesus Christ, his son of the same substance; and the Holy Ghost.

plague bacillus developed a high fever, followed by swelling of the lymph nodes in the groin, the armpits, and the neck. Most people died within days. Although quarantine was practiced, there was no known medicine against the plague. Many clerical observers at the time were convinced that sinfulness was what had attracted God's wrath. For us modern observers, the most important lesson of the Plague of Justinian is the evidence it provides of how interconnected the various parts of Eurasia and Africa were toward the middle of the 500s CE (see Map 7.4).

The Plague of Justinian shows us also how climate and disease followed their own natural patterns in world history. By killing up to one-third of the population and keeping population levels low for at least a century, the Plague of Justinian severely impacted city-state, kingdom, and empire patterns. The reduced population levels led to increased labor costs and food shortages; it also made survivors wealthier. Plagues hit states and societies with impartial ferocity. Justinian's plague favored neither Rome nor Persia and thus in the end had a more quantitative than lasting qualitative effect on the process of world history.

Questions

- What does Justinian's plague tell us about the interconnectedness of Afro-Eurasia at this time?

- How does understanding the impact of disease and climate on human societies add a new dimension to the patterns of world history?

Nomadic Invasions   The Roman and Sasanid Empires experienced severe disruptions from the migrations of peoples across Eurasia. The migrations began in the mid-300s when the western branch of the Huns—nomads in the steppes of central Asia east of the Ural Mountains—moved westward and southward on the Silk Road. During their journey westward, the Huns grew into a federation of nomads, farmers, and town dwellers of mixed ethnic and linguistic composition.

As the Huns entered the plains north of the Black Sea, they encountered local Germanic farming populations, whom they defeated. Other Germanic peoples, such as the Visigoths, fled from the Huns and negotiated their entry into the Roman Empire. In the early 400s CE, both Hunnish and Germanic peoples overcame the defenses of the Romans, poured into the western half of the Roman Empire, and eventually ended the western line of emperors, an event remembered as the fall of Rome in 476 (see Map 7.5).

The emperors in the eastern half of the empire withstood the migrants' threat, in part because of Constantinople's strategic location, allowing for a rapid deployment of troops to the threatened provinces. The Sasanids, however, succumbed to invasions in 483–485 and were forced to pay tribute for a number of years. A third branch of Huns invaded the Gupta Empire of India toward the end of the 400s. In the mid-500s, the Sasanids eventually recovered from the invasions, but the Guptas did not. Further compounding matters, plague struck the Middle East and Europe in 541 (see "Patterns Up Close").

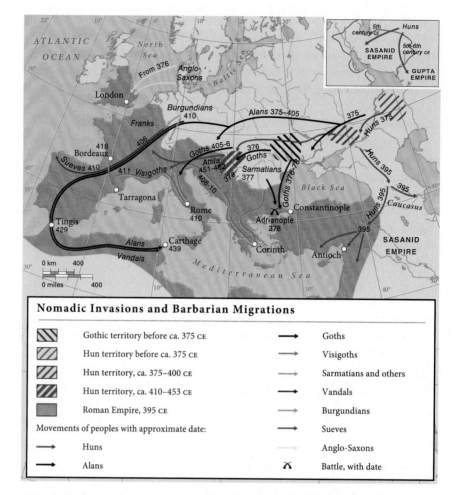

MAP 7.5 Nomadic Invasions and Barbarian Migrations into the Roman Empire, 375–450 CE

Roman and Persian Recovery   The architect of the reconstruction of the Roman Empire was Justinian I the Great (r. 527–565 CE). Justinian's generals reconquered most of the western Mediterranean and Italy from the Germanic invaders. As the empire stabilized, prosperity returned. With improved tax revenues, Justinian was able to finance reform measures, including a reorganization of the legal system. Justinian's *Codex Justinianus* became the legal foundation for the Roman Empire's successor, the Byzantine Empire (610–1453), as well as the Islamic empire of the Abbasids (750–1258), together with Persian law.

Justinian also oversaw the construction of Hagia Sophia ("Holy Wisdom"), until the construction of Saint Peter's in Rome the largest Christian church. Begun in 532, Hagia Sophia combines Roman features with new elements. It was designed to provide for a large open space, capped by a huge dome surrounded by windows.

In Persia, Khosrow I (r. 531–579) rebuilt the Sasanid Empire. He began his rule in the aftermath of a civil war that pitted Mazdak, a renegade Zoroastrian priest and social reformer, and the dynasty against the Zoroastrian priesthood and the ruling class. In this war, the dynasty confiscated landed estates from the ruling class and distributed its lands to small military landowners (*dihqans*). Khosrow, scion of the dynasty but siding with the ruling class, seized power and had Mazdak executed, ending the social reforms. But he maintained the military reforms in favor of the *dihqans*, thereby distancing himself from the traditional ruling class.

Like Justinian, Khosrow also pursued military expansion. In 530, Khosrow reopened hostilities against the Romans. In the north, Khosrow defeated European and Turkic tribes, expanding the border eastward to Turkistan. A plea from the king of Yemen in southwestern Arabia to aid him in his efforts to repel a Roman-backed Ethiopian invasion brought Khosrow's fleet to southern Arabia in 575–577, and Arab vassal kings established Persian control over much of the rest of Arabia. In contrast to Rome, the reach of Persia was much expanded at the end of the sixth century.

Adaptations to Monotheism and Monism in the Middle East

Rome and Sasanid Persia were strong unitary empires at the end of the 500s CE. Both were religiously unified through the adoption of the monotheisms of Christianity and Zoroastrianism. The adoption of these religions came at the end of a lengthy process that originated at the beginning of the Achaemenid Persian Empire (550–330 BCE). Visionaries of religious monotheism and philosophical monism emerged at that time but had only small numbers of followers. It took many centuries before followers of each faith achieved imperial sanction as the preferred or obligatory state religion.

Challenge to Polytheism: The Origins of Judaism, Zoroastrianism, and Greek Philosophy

Religious visionaries of the sixth century BCE arose in a polytheistic environment. All polytheisms had one basic characteristic in common: the gods all descended from something unnamable that existed prior to creation and remained in a state of **transcendence**. Unity preceded and transcended multiplicity, and even though perceived reality consisted of both, in thought they could be separated from each other.

Transcendence: Realm of reality above and beyond the limits of sensory experience.

Judaism   Concepts of transcendence appeared more or less simultaneously during the 600s BCE in Mesopotamia, Iran, and Anatolia. The historically most influential case was that of an anonymous Jewish visionary, whom scholars have dubbed "Deutero-Isaiah" or "Second Isaiah" (fl. ca. 560 BCE) in Mesopotamia. After their deportation by the Neo-Babylonians from Palestine (597–582 BCE), as we saw in Chapter 2, many Israelites lived in Babylonian exile. After the establishment of the Achaemenid Persian Empire and its subsequent conquest of Babylonia and Syria, including Palestine, Israelite scribes began to compile their religious traditions from Palestine. They became the founders of what is called today "Judaism," and one of them, Deutero-Isaiah, was the first to declare Yahweh [YAH-way], or God, to be the only god of the Jews. In Deutero-Isaiah's words, there are no gods but Yahweh, who is the single, invisible creator and sustainer of the world. He is transcendent—a conceptual reality beyond the sensory or empirical reality of this world.

Some of Deutero-Isaiah's followers petitioned the Persian king to allow them to leave for Jerusalem and restore the temple destroyed by the Neo-Babylonians. The Persian king issued the permit in 538 BCE, and a group of monotheists returned to Jerusalem to construct the Second Temple (completed in 515 BCE). A new priesthood took up residence in the Temple and administered the emerging monotheistic faith of Judaism.

Zoroastrianism   Zoroastrians attribute their origin to Zoroaster (also called Zarathustra), who is supposed to have lived sometime in the centuries around 1200 BCE, long before the rise of monotheism. The earliest recorded references to Zoroaster's teachings, however, date only to the rise of the Achaemenid Persian Empire in 550 BCE. These teachings were handed down orally by a priestly class, the magi. The main text is the Avesta; its language, called Avestan, is closely related to Old Persian.

In the Avesta, the earliest section is called the Yasht. It speaks of the glories of Ahura Mazda (the creator god), the last of which, bestowed on humankind at the end of history, is that of the savior who will restore the world. Other sections of the Avesta describe a time of trial and tribulation just prior to the arrival of the savior. This period of devastation was later called the "apocalypse" (Greek *apokalypsis*, "uncovering" or "revelation"). These themes—Savior and apocalypse—are trademarks of Zoroastrianism. In later centuries they became central in Judaism, Christianity, and Islam. They replaced the polytheistic notion of a shadowy afterlife in the underworld with salvation of the righteous in God's transcendent kingdom.

Zoroastrian Fire Temple. Consisting of a cube with a superimposed dome, this Zoroastrian temple, one of the best preserved, is located outside Baku in present-day Azerbaijan. Zoroastrianism was prevalent in the Caucasus region until the arrival of Christianity, and then Islam.

It appears that under the Parthians the magi introduced traditional Iranian and Anatolian cults of fire, maintained in fire temples, into Zoroastrianism. How far the fire temples evolved into congregational places for priests and laity, however, is still a matter of conjecture.

Greek Philosophy   *Philosophy* is from a Greek word meaning "love of wisdom." The first Greek philosophers known to us are Thales, Heraclitus, and Thales's pupil Anaximander, who lived during the first half of the 500s BCE in the city of Miletus on the Anatolian coast. Of these, Thales of Miletus is usually credited with beginning the Greek philosophical tradition of divorcing scientific explanations of natural phenomena from mythical forces. In contrast to Judaism and Zoroastrianism, Anaximander formulated the impersonal, or monist, "principle of the infinite" as the invisible unitary cause underlying the world (Greek *kosmos*). A debate over principles ensued after Anaximander and his successors proposed several other cosmic principles. This debate became the basis for the rise of the mathematical and physical sciences.

Aristotle. A leading figure in the development of Western science and philosophy, Aristotle is well known for his contributions to cosmology, biology, and physics—particularly the relationship of mechanics to theories of motion.

The Athenian Plato (ca. 427–347 BCE) extended the debate from principles in nature to a principle common to all areas of reality, calling it Being (*ousia*). In his thinking, Being is embodied in the transcendent forms of Truth, Justice, and Beauty. These forms, so Plato argued, represent final standards against which all earthly assertions about truth, justice, and beauty in daily life are to be measured. Anaximander's monism thus led via Plato to science and philosophy.

Plato's student, Aristotle (384–322 BCE), contributed a wide range of essays and treatises on philosophy and the sciences. Unlike Plato, Aristotle's concept of empirical truth was obtainable through observation of the empirical world rather than through transcendent forms, although he had to admit to Plato that the ultimate or unmoved mover of the world is transcendent and cannot be observed. Aristotle's reduced version of transcendence resonated throughout subsequent eras; medieval scholastics considered him "the Master of them that know."

The Break from Polytheism to Monotheism   The common thread linking the three visions of transcendence is that they all involve transcendent symbols, such as God or Being, which can only be thought by the mind, not experienced by the senses. Polytheist reality, however, is undivided, with gods and humans sharing a natural world in which everything is felt by the senses. Given this contrast, it is not surprising that over time monotheism became incompatible with polytheism. Gradually, polytheism disappeared from the Middle East and Mediterranean.

Toward Religious Communities and Philosophical Schools

The small Jewish community that built the Second Temple in Jerusalem grew more rapidly than the Zoroastrian fire temple communities and Greek philosophical schools. Eventually, it spawned a Jewish reform movement, Christianity, which in turn changed the Roman Empire from polytheism to monotheism.

Judaism in Palestine   The Achaemenid Persian kings allowed the Jews, who had moved from Mesopotamia to Palestine and had founded the Second Temple in Jerusalem, a large degree of autonomy. Under their successors, the Ptolemaic and Seleucid kings in the states after Alexander the Great, this autonomy declined. These kings introduced Hellenistic institutions and culture into Palestine, forcing the Jews to allow polytheism and philosophy in their midst. The Jews successfully rebelled, establishing the autonomous Hasmonean (also called "Maccabean") kingdom (140–37 BCE), which sought to limit the Hellenization of society.

However, educated Jews learned Greek and read the writings of the Greek philosophers. Scribes translated Jewish scriptures into Greek, and in the second half of the 200s BCE, prayer houses, called "**synagogues**," emerged in cities and towns. The monotheism of Yahweh continued to be exclusively administered by priests. But preachers in the synagogues, called "Pharisees," made this monotheism increasingly popular among ordinary Jews.

In the first century BCE, the Herodians replaced the Hasmoneans in Palestine and the Romans and Persian Parthians replaced the Seleucids as overlords in the Middle East. The Herodian Jews interacted not only with the culture of Hellenism but also with the culture of the Romans and their Parthian neighbors to the east. Many Jews adapted to the Roman philosophical school of the Stoics (who advocated an ethics in harmony with the laws of nature) and to the Persian Zoroastrian-inspired apocalypse. Elements of philosophy and the apocalypse, coming together in the teachings of the Pharisees in the synagogues, found widespread followers in the Jewish population. Palestine was a cauldron of cultural influences—some monotheistic, others monist, some clashing with polytheism.

The Origins of Christianity   It was from this cauldron that the Jewish reform movement of Christianity arose in the first century CE. The earliest scriptures of the Christians, contained in the New Testament, describe the founding figure, Jesus of Nazareth, as a preacher and healer in Galilee in northern Palestine. After he was baptized by John, Jesus is reported to have deemphasized the Mosaic as well as the Pharisaic law and to have preached what he expressed as the "law of love" (Mark 12:29–30). Only if one loved God and one's neighbor as one loved oneself would one acquire the proper understanding of Mosaic and Pharisaic law and be prepared for the apocalypse and salvation in the heavenly kingdom soon to come.

When Jesus is reported to have gone to Jerusalem to preach during the Jewish Passover, he attracted the attention of the Roman governor of Judea, Pontius Pilate. Concerned about a repetition of the religious revolt of Judah Gamala in 6 CE against the Roman census, he had Jesus arrested, tried, and condemned to death on the cross. The New Testament is contradictory as to the degree of Jewish participation in Pilate's actions

Again according to the New Testament, shortly after Jesus's death, miraculous resurrection, and ascension to the right side of God, the Pharisee Paul of Tarsus converted to Jesus's law of love. Paul retained the concept of the apocalypse but also argued that salvation had already begun and would soon be completed with Jesus's return at the head of the heavenly kingdom. Paul traveled and preached to Christian communities which formed in the Roman Empire during the middle of the first century CE.

The Christian Church   Missionaries preached Christianity in the Roman Empire from scriptures that evolved in the first three centuries CE. During this

Synagogues: Jewish meeting places for prayer and legal consultation.

time, the first canon of accepted writings, the New Testament, was assembled. A hierarchy of bishops and priests preached from these scriptures to laypeople, Jewish or pagan. From early on, however, Christians were divided on how to understand the New Testament. The philosophically educated tended to interpret it figuratively—that is, by reading their philosophical concepts into scripture. Others, opposed to Greek philosophy, preferred a literal interpretation. A struggle over the integration of scripture and philosophy into a single Christian civilization ensued.

Mural from Dura-Europos on the Euphrates. The city, founded in 303 BCE, was home to a sizable Jewish community whose synagogue was adorned with murals in the Parthian-Hellenistic style. Shown here is a depiction of the infant Moses being rescued from the Nile.

Principal figures in the struggle were theologians, called "Church Fathers." One of the most important was Augustine (354–430). His two main works are the *Confessions*, in which he describes his conversion to Christianity and reflections on spirituality, and *The City of God*, in which he defends Christianity against the accusation by many Romans that its adoption as the state religion in 380 contributed to the decline of the empire. Thanks to the Church Fathers, the church was set on a path of merging monotheism and philosophy as the basis for a Christian civilization.

As a result of the Church Fathers' theological works and debates in church councils during the period of ca. 400–600, three main Christian denominations evolved. The Orthodox Catholic Church, supported by the Roman emperors, the patriarchs of Constantinople, and the pope in Rome adopted a Christology that defined Jesus Christ as being simultaneously fully human and fully divine. The Eastern Syriac Church, under the Catholicos (Patriarch), adhered to a similar Christology but was subject to the Sasanid shahanshahs. The Coptic Church in Egypt and Jacobite Church in Syria, by contrast, defined Christ as possessing only a single, divine nature from birth (and thus are called monophysite). Both Copts and Jacobites, subject to the Roman emperors but bitterly opposed to the two-nature Christology of the Orthodox-Catholic and Eastern Syriac Churches, represented a general tendency in early Christianity toward the divinization of Jesus. This tendency was cut short, however, in the 600s with the emergence of Islam, in which Jesus is viewed as entirely human (see Chapter 10).

The Beginnings of Science and the Cultures of Kings and Citizens

Monotheism and philosophy entered society early on during the Jewish Second Temple kingdom in Palestine. In the Persian and Roman Empires this incorporation, in the form of preferred or state religions, took longer. Greek science became important in Ptolemaic Egypt (305–30 BCE). The Ptolemies provided state support for the development of mathematics, physics, astronomy, and the applied science of mechanics. The other inherited forms of cultural expression—painting, sculpture, architecture, and literature—remained within traditional polytheistic confines.

Nevertheless, in Greece and Rome these latter cultural forms underwent substantial innovation, influenced by Hellenism as well as Parthian and Sasanid Persia.

The Sciences at the Library of Alexandria

The Ptolemies and their Roman successors sponsored a new type of institution of Greek learning, the institute for advanced study. Centers of research, principally libraries and museums, flourished at Pergamon, Alexandria, and elsewhere. The Library of Alexandria (280 BCE–ca. 400 CE) was devoted primarily to research in the mathematical and natural sciences. The Library featured holdings of half a million scrolls, laboratories for anatomical dissection, an astronomical observatory, and botanical gardens.

The most developed branch of the sciences at the Library was geometry. Euclid (fl. ca. 300 BCE), one of the founders of the Library, provided geometry with its basic definitions and proofs in his *Elements*. In addition to geometry, mathematicians laid the foundations for algebra. In the absence of a practical Greek number system, however, algebra had to await the Muslims and the Arabic numeral system (originally devised in India) to evolve fully.

Alexandrian geographers and astronomers calculated the earth's circumference and tilt and formulated the first heliocentric astronomical theory, according to which the earth spins around the sun. As it happened, this theory was rejected on the basis of Aristotelian empiricism, and the opposite unobservable theory, which placed the earth at the center of the planetary system, became dominant. Claudius Ptolemy (ca. 87–170 CE), therefore, devised a geometric system of the planets' observable movements around the earth which dominated until the work of Copernicus in the sixteenth century. In addition to astronomy, physics also flourished at the Library, exemplified by the work of Archimedes (287–212 BCE), who investigated the behavior of floating bodies in the new science of hydrostatics.

The Library came to its end under unknown circumstances at the beginning of the 400s CE. Its legacy, however, was such that later Islamic rulers resumed the tradition of sponsoring institutes for advanced study.

Royal Persian Culture and Arts

As heirs of both Achaemenid Persian and Greek traditions, the Parthians forged a new synthesis between inherited styles and Hellenistic elements, while maintaining a palace culture of their own. For example, courtiers listened to bards who recited the exploits of Greek heroes. Other bards and minstrels traveled among aristocratic families, composing stories of their masters' courtly loves and intrigues or their exploits in battles against nomadic invaders from central Asia. After the end of the Parthian dynasty, these stories grew in both length and complexity. They exist today in a modern Persian version, called the *Book of Kings* (*Shahname* [sha-na-MAY]), compiled by the poet Firdosi [feer-dow-SEE] in the eleventh century CE.

The Sasanids were major transmitters of Indian texts to the Middle East and the Mediterranean. Examples include collections of animal fables, instruction manuals on chess, and medical texts complete with discussions of anatomy, diseases, and herbs. All these texts, which were both useful and entertaining, played important roles at the Sasanid court.

In architecture, the characteristic features of Sasanid palaces were the monumental dome and the barrel vault. The central audience hall of the palace in the capital, Ctesiphon, built ca. 250 CE, had a barrel vault 118 feet high. Other palaces had squinched domes of up to 45 feet across, covering square audience and banquet halls. Squinches are curved triangular transition spaces between the dome and the corners of the halls. In order to counter the outward thrust of the dome's weight, buttresses supported the walls on the outside. The techniques of both barrel vaulting and the dome were transmitted from Sasanid Persia to Christian Armenia, Rome, and ultimately western Europe, where they appeared in church architecture.

Greek and Roman Civic Culture and Arts

With the disappearance of kings and aristocracies in the Greek city-states during the sixth century BCE, wealthy citizens began to patronize artists and even created works of literature, sculpture, painting, and architecture themselves. Greeks began to experiment with individual shapes, types, and models, seeking realistic representation in their art.

As in Mesopotamia and Egypt, seasonal festivals were of great importance in Greece. In contrast to Mesopotamia and Egypt, however, Greek city culture encouraged personal artistic expression, and festivals became occasions for the composition of songs and poems whose authors were remembered by name. Both culture and arts are called "civic" because they were sustained by individual citizens as well as by the state, in contrast to the court-centered Parthian and Sasanid Persians.

Greek Literature and Art   The earliest Greek literature dates to the eighth century BCE. The period 750–600 BCE was a time of close cultural contact between the rising Greek city-states and the Neo-Assyrian Empire, which dominated Syria

Monumental Barrel Vault of the Sasanid Royal Reception Hall, Ctesiphon.

and Anatolia. Assyrian versions of the Mesopotamian epic and creation myths, *Gilgamesh* and *Enuma Elish*, made their way to the Greeks, where they were doubtless incorporated into Greek culture.

This incorporation was the work of two writers, Homer (fl. ca. 730 BCE) and Hesiod (fl. ca. 700 BCE), both from Greek city-states in Anatolia, and both familiar with Mesopotamian themes. Homer composed two epics in the form of extended poems, the tragedy *Iliad* and the narrative legend *Odyssey*. Hesiod's *Theogony* begins with "Chaos, the Abyss," out of which the earth, or Gaia, came into being. The rest of the *Theogony* is devoted to telling the stories of some 300 divinities descended from Chaos and Gaia. Three of the first four generations of deities destroyed each other violently. The fourth, the Olympians, became the present polytheistic pantheon of gods, with Zeus as the patriarch. A famous representative of early lyric poetry was Sappho (ca. 620–550 BCE) of Lesbos, an Aegean island. Her few surviving poems express passionate and romantic emotions devoted primarily to her love for women. The Greek theater emerged around 500–480 BCE out of the rituals of the Dionysiac cult. During the annual Dionysiac processions, groups of citizens competed for the presentation of the best tragedy or comedy. These competing groups, or choruses, performed through declamation and dance. Tragedy developed out of Dionysiac myths and comedy from the Dionysiac processions.

Among the most important writers who composed for the early Greek stage were the tragedians Aeschylus, Sophocles, and Euripides, as well as the comedian Aristophanes. In *The Persians*, Aeschylus developed the theme of the Greeks defending their freedom from Persian tyranny, a theme which in the course of time changed into the Europeans defining their culture as superior to that of the Other, the inferior Orient. In this chapter, which focuses on Persia, Greece, and Rome as equal partners in a single, undivided region of the Middle East and the Mediterranean Sea, we seek to overcome the otherization of the Orient. In other respects as well, all four authors, and many of their successors, continue to exercise a profound influence on the evolution of culture today.

In the fifth century BCE, Greek sculptors abandoned the traditional Middle Eastern symbolic royal style that required figures to project dignity and solemnity. Instead, sculptors began to explore physical movement and emotion. In terms of themes, poses, and individuality, Greek vase paintings and sculptures achieved a remarkably wide range, from athletes exerting themselves to serene models of human beauty. Faithful to their democratic polis culture, Greek sculptors and painters turned from a symbolic to a realistic style of representation.

Roman Literature and Art   Greece influenced Roman culture early on. By the middle of the third century BCE, Romans had translated Greek plays and poetry into Latin, and prose writings on political and historical themes, also modeled on Greek precursors, appeared. In his epic poem *The Aeneid*, Virgil (70–19 BCE) played down the influence of Greece by positing the origins of Rome in Troy, the rival of Greece. In his *Odes*, Horace (65–8 BCE) glorified courage, patriotism, piety, justice, and a respect for tradition, which he regarded as uniquely Roman virtues. These writers viewed Rome as the culmination of civilization.

Roman sculpture followed the Greek style. Among the earliest sculptures were marble busts which aristocratic Romans had made of their patriarchs.

These busts, kept in family shrines, were a central part of aristocratic life in the republic. On columns and triumphal arches, reliefs celebrated military victories, and civic Romans adorned their cities with monumental structures that provided their empire with greater visibility.

Roman pictorial art existed in the form of wood panels, wall paintings, and floor mosaics. In the fifth century CE, what was possibly the first illustrated book appeared, depicting scenes from Virgil's *Aeneid*. Nearly all panel paintings have perished, but wall paintings have survived in larger numbers, accidentally due to their preservation in Pompeii and other places buried by the eruption of Mount Vesuvius in 79 CE. The paintings demonstrate Roman art at a remarkably skilled level.

Rome's architecture was initially closely modeled on the Greek and Etruscan heritage in Italy. In the imperial age, when the desire for monumental architecture developed, the Romans—shortly after the Parthians—adopted the elements of arch and dome for large buildings. An example is the Pantheon in Rome, built in 118–126 CE. This building, a temple dedicated to all the Roman gods, consists of a dome placed on top of a drum and lit by a round open skylight at its apex (diameter and height both 142 feet). The circular foundation wall made squinches unnecessary.

Beginning with the first Christian emperor, Constantine, in the early fourth century CE, there was a return from realistic to symbolical representation in the arts. The rich variety of literature was reduced to religious poetry and hymns. The representational style of pagan Greece and Rome changed into the hieratic style of art, in which the sanctity of the human figure is emphasized. Christian artists began to emphasize what they considered essential for sacredness and drew from Middle Eastern models, which retained connections to symbolism. Religious uniformity came to dominate culture in the Roman and Sasanid Persian Empires, as it dominated their politics in the form of state religion.

Scene from the *Aeneid*. According to Virgil's *Aeneid*, on his journey from Troy, Aeneas landed in North Africa and fell madly in love with Dido, the queen of Carthage. One day, as they were hunting, a storm forced the two to seek shelter in a cave. Destiny, however, demanded that Aeneas travel on to Italy and found Rome. In her grief at his departure, Dido committed suicide. The cave episode is illustrated here in a manuscript of the fifth century CE.

Putting It All Together

This chapter on world empires began with Alexander's bold quest to unite the Mediterranean, Middle East, and India. For Alexander it was still possible to think in terms of one supreme god in heaven and one empire on earth. But after the introduction of monotheism, the situation changed. For the Persians and Romans, the one single God anywhere and nowhere disapproves of all imperial projects on earth and prefers a commonwealth of multiple kingdoms. It is this reevaluation of politics and history that the visionaries of ca. 600 BCE can be seen as having contributed to world history.

Review and Relate

Thinking Through Patterns

Examine the ways historians approach the big questions of this chapter.

> Why should the Middle East and Mediterranean Europe during the period 600 BCE–600 CE be studied as a single unit?

The sharp division between Europe and the Middle East that exists today is a recent phenomenon. During the period of late multireligious and early monotheistic empires, from 600 BCE to 600 CE, the two regions were intertwined and are accordingly treated in a single chapter. Initially, the sequence of the multireligious Persian and Macedonian Empires dominated the Middle East and eastern Mediterranean. Later, the competition between the subsequent two empires, Rome and Persia, inaugurated a pattern of urbanization, a deepening gulf between the wealthy and the poor, and the immigration of tribal people from central Asia.

> What is transcendence, and why is it important to understand its role in world history?

The awareness of transcendence exists constantly, even if it remains for the most part unexpressed and little thought about. You do not know from where you came and what the origin of your consciousness is; nor did people in the past. The great visionaries of 700–500 BCE abstracted a separate, transcendent God or first principle from the world to explain its origin. In polytheism, there had been a single world in which the high god, plus all the other gods and goddesses in heaven, intermingled with humans on earth. Following the visionaries, thinkers explored new, abstract dimensions of justice and thought in the new intellectual disciplines of science, philosophy, and theology.

> Which elements characterize the institutions that grew out of the Middle Eastern monotheisms of Judaism–Christianity and monism of Greek philosophy-science?

In the Middle East and eastern Mediterranean, visionaries created bodies of transcendent thought that evolved into the Zoroastrian and Jewish religions as well as Greek philosophy and science. The scriptures of these visionaries and their early followers expounded the nature of God or the first principle. The visionaries and their successors attracted communities of like-minded followers. Zoroastrianism, Judaism, and Christianity were religions of salvation: firm believers in the power of God's forgiveness would be saved in a transcendent kingdom of heaven. For Zoroastrians, Jews, and Christians—cogs in the giant, brutal, and meaningless multireligious machines of the Persian and Roman empires—this religious promise of salvation was the only way of making sense out of life. Eventually the emperors themselves converted, making monotheism the religion of their states.

| Against the Grain

Consider this as a counterpoint to the main patterns examined in this chapter.

Women in Democratic Athens

Even though democratic rule in Athens is usually cited as a model of egalitarian rule, the status of women in Athenian society reflects a glaring contradiction.

Several indicators point to policies of marked gender inequality. Athenian women could neither vote nor own property. Their marriages were often arranged, primarily for monetary gain; once married, women could not sue for divorce. A married woman was under the constant control of a guardian, either her husband or her nearest male relatives. Women were required to bring dowries into the marriage, which were immediately assigned to the husband's control.

For the most part, women's roles consisted of bearing and raising children, inculcating in them the values of the polis, and managing the household. Because women were believed to be more emotional and driven by sexual passion than men, they were seen to pose a threat to stability. Thus, Athenian women were largely confined to the home, although older ones frequented the marketplace and civic center and occasionally attended festivals. Women also participated in funerals, weddings, and religious rituals, and some were priestesses. Educated women routinely accompanied men as companions to plays and dinner parties. At the bottom of the social ladder were slave women and prostitutes.

Why were Athenian women relegated to second-class citizenship? In a patriarchal society like Athens, men determined cultural norms, which reflected negative views of women. For example, in Euripides' *Medea* the protagonist laments "If only children could be got by some other way without the female sex. . . If women didn't exist, human life would be rid of all its miseries." And in his *Politics* Aristotle observes that "the male is by nature superior, and the female inferior; and the one rules, and the other is ruled; this principle, of necessity, extends to all mankind."

- How does the inferior status of Athenian women represent a contradiction to the prevailing view of Athenian democracy?

- In what ways does this image of women in Athens compare and contrast with women's status in other ancient civilizations?

Key Terms

Cataphracts   151
Hellenistic Culture   155
Hoplites   151

Legionaries   156
Nicene Creed   160
Oracles   152

Shahanshah   152
Synagogues   166
Transcendence   163

Learn more with this chapter's digital tools, including the Oxford Insight Study Guide, at http://www.oup.com/he/vonsivers4e. Please see the Further Resources section at the back of the book for additional readings and suggested websites.

Sources for Chapter 7

The Cyrus Cylinder

539 BCE

Founder of the Achaemenid Persian Empire, Cyrus the Great rose to the throne of a small kingdom in 559 BCE; by the time of his death in 529, he had brought virtually the entire Near East under his control. In 539, he conquered Babylon and drove out Nabonidus, the last of the Neo-Babylonian kings. However, he was hailed as a liberator by the priests of the Babylonian god Marduk, and he issued a remarkable document in which he praised himself for the restoration of all temples, priesthoods, and cults in his vast empire. The text, which was publicized in Akkadian, an ancient Mesopotamian language, is preserved on a clay cylinder, today called the Cyrus Cylinder and housed in the British Museum.

...

On account of their complaints, the lords of the gods became furiously angry and left their [the Babylonians'] land; the gods, who dwelt among them, left their homes. . . . In all lands everywhere [the god Marduk] searched; he looked through them and sought a righteous prince after his own heart, whom he took by the hand. He called Cyrus, king of Anshan, by name; he appointed him to lordship over the whole world.

The land of Qutu, all the Umman-manda, he cast down at his feet. The black-headed people, whom he gave his hands to conquer, he took them in justice and righteousness. Marduk, the great lord, looked joyously on the caring for his people, on his pious works and his righteous heart. To his city, Babylon, he caused [Cyrus] to go; he made him take the road to Babylon, going as a friend and companion at his side. His numerous troops, in unknown numbers, like the waters of a river, marched armed at his side. Without battle and conflict, he permitted him to enter Babylon. He spared his city, Babylon, a calamity. Nabonidus, the king, who did not fear him, he delivered into his hand.

...

When I [Cyrus] made my triumphal entrance into Babylon, I took up my lordly residence in the royal palace with joy and rejoicing; Marduk, the great

---

Source: Rogers, Robert W., ed. and trans., *Cuneiform Parallels to the Old Testament* (1912; repr. Eugene, OR: Wipf & Stock, 2005), 380–384. Available at http://www.kchanson.com/ANCDOCS/meso/cyrus.html, accessed April 6, 2020.

lord, moved the noble heart of the residents of Babylon to me, while I gave daily attention to his worship. My numerous troops marched peacefully into Babylon. In all Sumer and Akkad I permitted no enemy to enter.

The needs of Babylon and of all its cities I gladly attended to. The people of Babylon [and . . .], and the shameful yoke was removed from them. Their dwellings, which had fallen, I restored. I cleared out their ruins. Marduk, the great lord, rejoiced in my pious deeds, and graciously blessed me, Cyrus, the king who worships him, and Cambyses, my own son, and all my troops, while we, before him, joyously praised his exalted godhead.

...

And the gods of Sumer and Akkad—whom Nabonidus, to the anger of the lord of the gods, had brought into Babylon—by the command of Marduk, the great lord, I caused them to take up their dwelling in residences that gladdened the heart. May all the gods, whom I brought into their cities, pray daily before Bel and Nabu for long life for me, and may they speak a gracious word for me and say to Marduk, my lord, "May Cyrus, the king who worships you, and Cambyses his son, their [. . .] I permitted all to dwell in peace [. . .]."

▶ Working with Sources

1. How and why did Cyrus incorporate local deities into his public image after subjugating Babylon?

2. How does this document compare with other texts on peace and justice in Mesopotamia?

SOURCE 7.2   # Herodotus, *Histories*

ca. 420s BCE

Having failed to defeat the Athenians in their first attempt in 490 BCE, the Persians launched a massive invasion of the entire Greek peninsula in 480, under the leadership of Darius's successor, Xerxes. Thirty-one Greek cities agreed to band together to resist this force of (according to Herodotus) 1,700,000 Persian soldiers, in addition to a sizable naval contingent. Herodotus envisions a conversation between Xerxes and the Spartan defector Demaratus shortly before the first major confrontation between Persia and the Greeks at Thermopylae. In answer to the king's question, Demaratus claims that the Greeks will prove more difficult to defeat than Xerxes expects.

Source: Herodotus, *The Histories*, trans. Aubrey de Sélincourt (Harmondsworth, UK: Penguin, 1954), 403–405.

Having sailed from one end to the other of the line of anchored ships, Xerxes went ashore again and sent for Demaratus, the son of Ariston, who was accompanying him in the march to Greece. "Demaratus," he said, "it would give me pleasure at this point to put to you a few questions. You are a Greek, and a native, moreover, of by no means the meanest or weakest city in that country—as I learn not only from yourself but from the other Greeks I have spoken with. Tell me, then—will the Greeks dare to lift a hand against me? My own belief is that all the Greeks and all the other western peoples gathered together would be insufficient to withstand the attack of my army—and still more so if they are not united. But it is your opinion upon this subject that I should like to hear."

...

"I think highly," [Demaratus said,] "of all Greeks of the Dorian lands, but what I am about to say will apply not to all Dorians, but to the Spartans only. First then, they will not under any circumstances accept terms from you which would mean slavery for Greece; secondly, they will fight you even if the rest of Greece submits. Moreover, there is no use in asking if their numbers are adequate to enable them to do this; suppose a thousand of them take the field—then that thousand will fight you; and so will any number, greater than this or less."

Xerxes laughed. "Demaratus," he exclaimed, "what an extraordinary thing to say! Do you really suppose a thousand men would fight an army like mine?"

...

"King," Demaratus answered, "I knew before I began that if I spoke the truth you would not like it. But, as you demanded the plain truth and nothing less, I told you how things are with the Spartans. Yet you are well aware that I now feel but little affection for my countrymen, who robbed me of my hereditary power and privileges and made me a fugitive without a home—whereas your father welcomed me at his court and gave me the means of livelihood and somewhere to live. Surely it is unreasonable to reject kindness; any sensible man will cherish it. Personally I do not claim to be able to fight ten men—or two; indeed I should prefer not even to fight with one. But should it be necessary—should there be some great cause to urge me on—then nothing would give me more pleasure than to stand up to one of those men of yours who claim to be a match for three Greeks. So it is with the Spartans; fighting singly, they are as good as any, but fighting together they are the best soldiers in the world. They are free—yes—but not entirely free; for they have a master, and that master is Law, which they fear much more than your subjects fear you. Whatever this master commands, they do; and his command never varies: it is never to retreat in battle, however great the odds, but always to remain in formation, and to conquer or die. If, my lord, you think that what I have said is nonsense—very well; I am willing henceforward to hold my tongue. This time I spoke because you forced me to speak. In any case, I pray that all may turn out as you desire."

Xerxes burst out laughing at Demaratus' answer, and good-humoredly let him go.

▶ **Working with Sources**

1. **For what reasons does Demaratus think the Spartans will fight so hard to resist Xerxes?**

2. **What does the passage reveal concerning Herodotus' attitude toward the Greeks—and the Persians?**

SOURCE 7.3

Hippocrates, *On the Sacred Disease*

Hippocrates of Cos (ca. 460–377 BCE), considered the founding father of the medical profession—manifested in the Hippocratic Oath—is associated with the Hippocratic Corpus, a large collection of treatises on a variety of physical, mental, and other medical issues. Prior to the emergence of natural and rational sciences among pre-Socratic Greek philosophers in the sixth century BCE, diseases and illnesses were attributed to divine forces, with the result that their treatment was feckless. A prime example is epilepsy, which appears suddenly and without any prior symptoms. In *On the Sacred Disease*, however, the author refutes divine causation, emphasizing instead a combination of natural factors, which can be treated through reason and observation.

It is thus with regard to the disease called Sacred: it appears to me to be nowise more divine nor more sacred than other diseases, but has a natural cause like other affections. Men regard its nature and cause as divine from ignorance and wonder, because it is not at all like to other diseases. And this notion of its divinity is kept up by their inability to comprehend it, and the simplicity of the mode by which it is cured, for men are freed from it by purifications and incantations. But if it is reckoned divine because it is wonderful, instead of one there are many diseases which would be sacred; for, as I will show, there are others no less wonderful and prodigious, which nobody imagines to be sacred. The quotidian, tertian, and quartan fevers, seem to me no less sacred and divine in their origin than this disease, although they are not reckoned so wonderful. And I see men become mad and demented from no manifest cause, and at the same time doing many things out of place; and I have known many persons in sleep groaning and crying out, some in a state of suffocation, some jumping up and fleeing out of doors, and deprived of their reason until they awaken, and afterward becoming well and rational as before, although they be pale and weak; and this will happen not once but frequently. And there are many and various things of the like kind, which it would be tedious to state particularly.

Source: Hippocrates, *On the Sacred Disease*, trans. Francis Adams, http://classics.mit.edu/Hippocrates/sacred.html

They who first referred this malady to the gods appear to me to have been just such persons as the conjurors, purificators, mountebanks, and charlatans now are, who give themselves out for being excessively religious, and as knowing more than other people. Such persons, then, using the divinity as a pretext and screen of their own inability to of their own inability to afford any assistance, have given out that the disease is sacred, adding suitable reasons for this opinion, they have instituted a mode of treatment which is safe for themselves, namely, by applying purifications and incantations, and enforcing abstinence from baths and many articles of food which are unwholesome to men in diseases. Of sea substances, the surmullet, the blacktail, the mullet, and the eel; for these are the fishes most to be guarded against. And of fleshes, those of the goat, the stag, the sow, and the dog: for these are the kinds of flesh which are apt to disorder the bowels. Of fowls, the cock, the turtle, and the bustard, and such others as are reckoned to be particularly strong. And of potherbs, mint, garlic, and onions; for what is acrid does not agree with a weak person. And they forbid to have a black robe, because black is expressive of death; and to sleep on a goat's skin, or to wear it, and to put one foot upon another, or one hand upon another; for all these things are held to be hindrances to the cure. All these they enjoin with reference to its divinity, as if possessed of more knowledge, and announcing beforehand other causes so that if the person should recover, theirs would be the honor and credit; and if he should die, they would have a certain defense, as if the gods, and not they, were to blame, seeing they had administered nothing either to eat or drink as medicines, nor had overheated him with baths, so as to prove the cause of what had happened. But I am of opinion that (if this were true) none of the Libyans, who live in the interior, would be free from this disease, since they all sleep on goats' skins, and live upon goats' flesh; neither have they couch, robe, nor shoe that is not made of goat's skin, for they have no other herds but goats and oxen. But if these things, when administered in food, aggravate the disease, and if it be cured by abstinence from them, godhead is not the cause at all; nor will purifications be of any avail, but it is the food which is beneficial and prejudicial, and the influence of the divinity vanishes.

Thus, they who try to cure these maladies in this way, appear to me neither to reckon them sacred nor divine. For when they are removed by such purifications, and this method of cure, what is to prevent them from being brought upon men and induced by other devices similar to these? So that the cause is no longer divine, but human. For whoever is able, by purifications conjurations, to drive away such an affection, will be able, by other practices, to excite it; and, according to this view, its divine nature is entirely done away with. By such sayings and doings, they profess to be possessed of superior knowledge, and deceive mankind by enjoining lustrations and purifications upon them, while their discourse turns upon the divinity and the godhead. And yet it would appear to me that their discourse savors not of piety, as they suppose, but rather of impiety, and as if there were no gods, and that what they hold to be holy and divine, were impious and unholy. This I will now explain.

For, if they profess to know how to bring down the moon, darken the sun, induce storms and fine weather, and rains and droughts, and make the sea and land unproductive, and so forth, whether they arrogate this power as being derived from mysteries or any other knowledge or consideration, they appear to me to practice impiety, and either to fancy that there are no gods, or, if there are, that they have no ability to ward off any of the greatest evils. How, then, are they not enemies to the gods? For if a man by magical arts and sacrifices will bring down the moon, and darken the sun, and induce storms, or fine weather, I should not believe that there was anything divine, but human, in these things, provided the power of the divine were overpowered by human knowledge and subjected to it. But perhaps it will be said, these things are not so, but, not withstanding, men being in want of the means of life, invent many and various things, and devise many contrivances for all other things, and for this disease, in every phase of the disease, assigning the cause to a god. Nor do they remember the same things once, but frequently. For, if they imitate a goat, or grind their teeth, or if their right side be convulsed, they say that the mother of the gods is the cause. But if they speak in a sharper and more intense tone, they resemble this state to a horse, and say that Poseidon is the cause. Or if any excrement be passed, which is often the case, owing to the violence of the disease, the appellation of Enodia is adhibited; or, if it be passed in smaller and denser masses, like bird's, it is said to be from Apollo Nomius. But if foam be emitted by the mouth, and the patient kick with his feet, Ares then gets the blame. But terrors which happen during the night, and fevers, and delirium, and jumpings out of bed, and frightful apparitions, and fleeing away,-all these they hold to be the plots of Hecate, and the invasions and use purifications and incantations, and, as appears to me, make the divinity to be most wicked and most impious. For they purify those laboring under this disease, with the same sorts of blood and the other means that are used in the case of those who are stained with crimes, and of malefactors, or who have been enchanted by men, or who have done any wicked act; who ought to do the very reverse, namely, sacrifice and pray, and, bringing gifts to the temples, supplicate the gods. But now they do none of these things, but purify; and some of the purifications they conceal in the earth, and some they throw into the sea, and some they carry to the mountains where no one can touch or tread upon them. But these they ought to take to the temples and present to the god, if a god be the cause of the disease. Neither truly do I count it a worthy opinion to hold that the body of man is polluted by god, the most impure by the most holy; for were it defiled, or did it suffer from any other thing, it would be like to be purified and sanctified rather than polluted by god. For it is the divinity which purifies and sanctifies the greatest of offenses and the most wicked, and which proves our protection from them. And we mark out the boundaries of the temples and the groves of the gods, so that no one may pass them unless he be pure, and when we enter them we are sprinkled with holy water, not as being polluted, but as laying aside any other pollution which we formerly had. And thus it appears to me to hold, with regard to purifications.

But this disease seems to me to be no more divine than others; but it has its nature such as other diseases have, and a cause whence it originates, and its nature and cause are divine only just as much as all others are, and it is curable no less than the others, unless when, from of time it is confirmed, and has become stronger than the remedies applied. Its origin is hereditary, like that of other diseases. For if a phlegmatic person be born of a phlegmatic, and a bilious of a bilious, and a phthisical of a phthisical, and one having spleen disease, of another having disease of the spleen, what is to hinder it from happening that where the father and mother were subject to this disease, certain of their offspring should be so affected also? As the semen comes from all parts of the body, healthy particles will come from healthy parts, and unhealthy from unhealthy parts. And another great proof that it is in nothing more divine than other diseases is, that it occurs in those who are of a phlegmatic constitution, but does not attack the bilious. Yet, if it were more divine than the others, this disease ought to befall all alike, and make no distinction between the bilious and phlegmatic.

▶ **Working with Sources**

1. **What examples of divine causes of epilepsy are presented in this treatise; and why were they previously accepted as such?**
2. **What remedies does the author recommend for the treatment of epilepsy?**

SOURCE 7.4

1 Maccabees

ca. 134 BCE

Just before his death in Babylon in June 323 BCE, Alexander the Great was the unrivaled conqueror of an enormous portion of the known world, counting modern Greece, Egypt, the Middle East, Iran, and Afghanistan among his possessions. However, when he died, leaving his kingdom "to the strongest," conflicts immediately broke out among his Macedonian successors to determine who that strongest man was. A part of the military and political struggle that followed was an attempt to Hellenize, with varying levels of success, the older and more entrenched cultures Alexander had defeated as he raced through Africa and Asia. This process continued for the next three centuries. In the mid-second century BCE, one of these successor kings, Antiochus IV Epiphanes, attempted a brutal imposition of Greek cultural values on the Jews in Jerusalem. This effort, and the revolt it triggered, is described in the apocryphal (i.e., not part of the standard canon) Jewish book of 1 Maccabees. Notice that the Hellenistic era did not appear to everyone to have been a fortuitous blending of disparate cultures.

Source: *The Apocrypha: Revised Standard Version of the Old Testament* (New York: Thomas Nelson & Sons, 1957), 190–192.

1 After Alexander son of Philip, the Macedonian, who came from the land of Kittim, had defeated King Darius of the Persians and the Medes, he succeeded him as king. (He had previously become king of Greece.) **2** He fought many battles, conquered strongholds, and put to death the kings of the earth. **3** He advanced to the ends of the earth, and plundered many nations. When the earth became quiet before him, he was exalted, and his heart was lifted up. **4** He gathered a very strong army and ruled over countries, nations, and princes, and they became tributary to him. **5** After this he fell sick and perceived that he was dying. **6** So he summoned his most honored officers, who had been brought up with him from youth, and divided his kingdom among them while he was still alive. **7** And after Alexander had reigned twelve years, he died. **8** Then his officers began to rule, each in his own place. **9** They all put on crowns after his death, and so did their descendants after them for many years; and they caused many evils on the earth.

10 From them came forth a sinful root, Antiochus Epiphanes, son of King Antiochus; he had been a hostage in Rome. He began to reign in the one hundred thirty-seventh year of the kingdom of the Greeks. **11** In those days certain renegades came out from Israel and misled many, saying, "Let us go and make a covenant with the Gentiles around us, for since we separated from them many disasters have come upon us." **12** This proposal pleased them, **13** and some of the people eagerly went to the king, who authorized them to observe the ordinances of the Gentiles. **14** So they built a gymnasium in Jerusalem, according to Gentile custom, **15** and removed the marks of circumcision, and abandoned the holy covenant. They joined with the Gentiles and sold themselves to do evil. **16** When Antiochus saw that his kingdom was established, he determined to become king of the land of Egypt, in order that he might reign over both kingdoms. **17** So he invaded Egypt with a strong force, with chariots and elephants and cavalry and with a large fleet. **18** He engaged King Ptolemy of Egypt in battle, and Ptolemy turned and fled before him, and many were wounded and fell. **19** They captured the fortified cities in the land of Egypt, and he plundered the land of Egypt.

20 After subduing Egypt, Antiochus returned in the one hundred forty-third year. He went up against Israel and came to Jerusalem with a strong force. **21** He arrogantly entered the sanctuary and took the golden altar, the lampstand for the light, and all its utensils. **22** He took also the table for the bread of the Presence, the cups for drink offerings, the bowls, the golden censers, the curtain, the crowns, and the gold decoration on the front of the temple; he stripped it all off. **23** He took the silver and the gold, and the costly vessels; he took also the hidden treasures that he found. **24** Taking them all, he went into his own land. He shed much blood, and spoke with great arrogance. **25** Israel mourned deeply in every community, **26** rulers and elders groaned, young women and young men became faint, the beauty of the women faded. **27** Every bridegroom took up the lament; she who sat in the bridal chamber was mourning. **28** Even the land trembled for its inhabitants, and all the house of Jacob was clothed with shame. **29** Two years later the king sent to the cities of Judah a chief collector of tribute, and he came to Jerusalem with a large force. **30** Deceitfully he spoke peaceable words to them, and they believed him; but he suddenly fell upon the city, dealt it a severe blow, and destroyed many people of Israel. **31** He plundered the city, burned it with fire, and tore down its houses and its surrounding walls. **32** They took captive the women and children, and seized the livestock. **33** Then they fortified the city of David with a great strong wall and strong towers, and it became their citadel.

...

44 And the king sent letters by messengers to Jerusalem and the towns of Judah; he directed them to follow customs strange to the land, **45** to forbid burnt offerings and sacrifices and drink offerings in the sanctuary, to profane sabbaths and festivals, **46** to defile the sanctuary and the priests, **47** to build altars and sacred precincts and shrines for idols, to sacrifice swine and other unclean animals, **48** and to leave their sons uncircumcised. They were to make themselves abominable by everything unclean and profane, **49** so that they would forget the law and change all the ordinances. **50** He added, "And whoever does not obey the command of the king shall die." **51** In such words he wrote to his whole kingdom. He appointed inspectors over all the people and commanded the towns of Judah to offer sacrifice, town by town. **52** Many of the people, everyone who forsook the law, joined them, and they did evil in the land; **53** they drove Israel into hiding in every place of refuge they had. **54** Now on the fifteenth day of Chislev, in the one hundred forty-fifth year, they erected a desolating sacrilege on the altar of burnt offering. They also built altars in the surrounding towns of Judah, **55** and offered incense at the doors of the houses and in the streets. **56** The books of the law that they found they tore to pieces and burned with fire. **57** Anyone found possessing the book of the covenant, or anyone who adhered to the law, was condemned to death by decree of the king. **58** They kept using violence against Israel, against those who were found month after month in the towns. **59** On the twenty-fifth day of the month they offered sacrifice on the altar that was on top of the altar of burnt offering. **60** According to the decree, they put to death the women who had their children circumcised, **61** and their families and those who circumcised them; and they hung the infants from their mothers' necks. **62** But many in Israel stood firm and were resolved in their hearts not to eat unclean food. **63** They chose to die rather than to be defiled by food or to profane the holy covenant; and they did die.

▶ Working with Sources

1. To what specific innovations does the writer of this document object? Why?

2. What evidence is contained in this document of cultural misunderstanding?

SOURCE 7.5   Graffiti from the walls of Pompeii

ca. 79 CE

This is a small sample of the array of painted, scratched, and scribbled graffiti archaeologists have discovered on the walls of the city of Pompeii, which was sealed in ash after the eruption of Mount Vesuvius in 79 CE.

I

Twenty pairs of gladiators of Decimus Lucretius Satrius Valens, life-time flamen [priest] of Nero son of Caesar Augustus [Claudius], and ten pairs of gladiators of Decimus Lucretius Valens, his son, will fight at Pompeii on April 8, 9, 10, 11, and 12. There will be a full card of wild beast combats, and awnings [for the spectators]. Aemilius Celer [painted this sign], all alone in the moonlight.

II

Market days: Saturday in Pompeii, Sunday in Nuceria, Monday in Atella, Tuesday in Nola, Wednesday in Cumae, Thursday in Puteoli, Friday in Rome.

III

6th: cheese 1, bread 8, oil 3, wine 3 [expenses in food, in coins called *asses*]
7th: bread 8, oil 5, onions 5, bowl 1, bread for the slave [?] 2, wine 2
8th: bread 8, bread for the slave [?] 4, grits 3
9th: wine for the winner 1 *denarius* [a higher denomination of coin], bread 8, wine 2, cheese 2
10th: [. . .] 1 *denarius*, bread 2, for women 8, wheat 1 *denarius*, cucumber 1, dates 1, incense 1, cheese 2, sausage 1, soft cheese 4, oil 7

IV

Pleasure says: "You can get a drink here for an as, a better drink for two, Falernian [fine quality wine] for four."

V

A copper pot is missing from this shop. 65 sesterces reward if anybody brings it back, 20 sesterces if he reveals the thief so we can get our property back.

VI

The weaver Successus loves the innkeeper's slave girl, Iris by name. She doesn't care for him, but he begs her to take pity on him. Written by his rival. So long.
    [Answer by the rival:] Just because you're bursting with envy, don't pick on a handsomer man, a lady-killer and a gallant.

Source: Naphtali Lewis and Meyer Reinhold, eds., *Roman Civilization: Selected Readings*, vol. 2 (New York: Columbia University Press, 1990), 276–278.

[Answer by the first writer:] There's nothing more to say or write. You love Iris, and she doesn't care for you.

VII

Take your lewd looks and flirting eyes off another man's wife, and show some decency on your face!

VIII

Anybody in love, come here. I want to break Venus' ribs with a club and cripple the goddess' loins. If she can pierce my tender breast, why can't I break her head with a club?

IX

I write at Love's dictation and Cupid's instruction;
   But damn it! I don't want to be a god without you.

X

[A prostitute's sign:] I am yours for 2 *asses* cash.

▶ **Working with Sources**

1. Are you surprised by what these graffiti reveal about daily life in Pompeii?

2. How could this material be used to assess the relative standing of women in Roman society? Should it be used in this way?

SOURCE 7.6	The murder of the philosopher Hypatia, Alexandria, Egypt

ca. 415 CE

Born around 360 CE and instructed by her father, Theon, a mathematician and the last librarian of the famous Library of Alexandria, Hypatia directed the Platonic school in the city, teaching students who were of mixed religious commitments but were, presumably, all men. The few sources that mention her agree that she was abducted, stripped of her clothes, and stoned to death with roof tiles by a fanatical group of Christians, but the precise sequence of events that led to this atrocity has always been controversial.

Because all of these sources were composed by Christians—with the exception of her own correspondence with a former student, the bishop Synesius of Cyrene—the lynching of Hypatia may be interpreted as an instance of fanaticism attempting to destroy reason, or as the elimination of a dangerous pagan influence in the midst of a Christianizing Egypt. The latter approach has, unfortunately, been more common, given Christian influence—and misogyny—in Western societies and the installation of her main opponent, Bishop Cyril of Alexandria, as one of the "fathers of the church."

There was a woman in Alexandria named Hypatia. She was the daughter of the philosopher Theon. She had progressed so far in her education that she surpassed by far the philosophers of her time, and took over the Neoplatonic school that derived from Plotinus, and set forth every philosophical approach to those who wanted to learn them. Accordingly people from all over who wanted to study philosophy rushed to her side. Because of the dignified reputation that derived from her education, she began (with due modesty) to address even the rulers. And she had no hesitation about being in the company of men, since they all respected her more because of her extraordinary chastity.

Source: Socrates, *Ecclesiastical History* 7.15, available in Maureen B. Fant and Mary R. Lefkowitz, trans., *Women's Life in Greece and Rome: A Source Book in Translation*, 4th ed. (London, Oxford, New York, New Delhi, and Sydney: Bloomsbury Academic, 2016), 415–416.

Then she became the subject of envy. Because she was frequently in the company of Orestes, people in the church began to slander her, as if that were what was preventing Orestes from making friends with the bishop. Some hot-headed men who agreed with this, who were led by a certain Peter the Reader, were on the lookout for the woman when she returned to her house from wherever she had been. They threw her out of her carriage, and dragged her to the church known as Caesarion. They tore off her clothing, and killed her with potsherds. When they had torn her apart limb from limb, they took the pieces of her body to the place called Cinaron, and burned them.

This act did no small amount of damage to Cyril and to the Church at Alexandria. For murder and fighting, and everything of that sort, are totally alien to those who believe in Christ. These events took place after Cyril had been bishop for four years, and Theodosius for ten [ca. 415 CE], in the month of March, during Lent.

...

About Hypatia the philosopher. An illustration of how disorderly the Alexandrians are. She was born and raised and educated in Alexandria. She inherited her father's extraordinarily distinguished nature, and was not satisfied with the training in mathematics that she received from her father, but turned to other learning also in a distinguished way. Although she was a woman she put on a man's cloak and made her way into the center of the city and gave to those who wanted to listen public lectures about Plato or Aristotle or about some other philosophers. In addition to her teaching she also excelled in the practical arts, being just and chaste, she remained a virgin, though she was so beautiful to look at that one of her pupils fell in love with her. When he was no longer able to control his passion, he let her know how he felt about her. The uneducated stories have it that Hypatia told him to cure his disease through the study of the arts. But the truth is that he had long since given up on culture; instead, she brought in one of those women's rags and threw it at him, revealing her unclean nature, and said to him, "This is what you are in love with, young man, and not with the Beautiful," and in shame and wonder at this ugly display his soul was converted and he became more chaste.

That (according to this account) is what Hypatia was like, skilled in debate and dialectic, intelligent in her conduct and politically adept. The other citizens understandably were fond of her and accorded her the greatest respect, and the current magistrates of the town always went first to her, as used to happen also in Athens. For even though the practice had died out, the name of philosophy still seemed distinguished and impressive to the people who had primary charge of the city. It then happened that the man in charge of the opposing sect, Cyril, passed by Hypatia's house and saw a large crowd in front of the door, consisting of men and horses, some arriving, some leaving, and some waiting there. He asked what the gathering was, and why there was commotion in front of the house, and learned from his followers that the philosopher Hypatia was giving a lecture and that this was her house. And when he learned this he was very upset and soon planned her murder, the most unholy of all murders. As she was going out to lecture, as was her custom, a group of bestial men attacked her, true ruffians, who had no respect for God and no concern for men's indignation; they killed the philosopher and brought the greatest pollution and disgrace on their fatherland.

▶ Working
with Sources

1. Was Hypatia killed principally because she was a female philosopher or because she was a non-Christian philosopher?

2. How did Hypatia both refer to and transcend the boundaries placed upon women in ancient Greco-Roman society?

World Period Two

The Age of Empires and Visionaries, 600 BCE–600 CE

In the middle of the first millennium BCE, two major transformations changed the course of world history.

- **Empires in Eurasia** Two types of conquering kingdoms or empires formed, after Akkad had pioneered this form of polity during the first world period. The first type, in the Middle East, Mediterranean, and India, was that of multiethnic and multireligious empires, which followed each other in sequence. The second type consisted of the ethnically and religiously more uniform empires of Egypt and China.

- **Visionaries and the Adoption of State Religions** Around 700–500 BCE, visionaries arose who proclaimed the idea of personal salvation. They anchored this idea in the higher, absolute standard of monotheism or monism, which was not bound to any state on Earth. Followers of the visionaries formed communities and schools based on texts that expounded monotheistic or monist teachings. Eventually, rulers adopted these teachings and turned them into state religions.

Chapter 8

Empires and Visionaries in India

600 BCE–600 CE

CHAPTER EIGHT PATTERNS

Origins, Interactions, and Adaptations By the end of the fourth century BCE the many states of the Gangetic Plain had been consolidated into an empire that embraced nearly all of the Indian subcontinent. The Mauryans and succeeding states and empires interacted intensively with the Persians and Hellenistic Greeks, Romans, Indian-influenced kingdoms in Southeast Asia, and as far afield as China, Vietnam, Korea, and Japan.

Uniqueness and Similarities By 600 CE, India was one of the most religiously and ethnically diverse areas in the world. The vast variety of religious experience that made up "Hinduism" was unique to India and the areas in Southeast Asia influenced by Indian culture. An outgrowth of India's religious and cultural heritage was the caste system and the concept of reincarnation. India's position made it the center not only for Indian Ocean trade, but also with the Silk Road.

Like China and Persia, empire had become firmly established in India, but like the Hellenistic and Roman worlds, internal strife and outside invaders prevented any of its empires from completely subjugating the subcontinent. In the cultural sphere, India produced two important religions: Buddhism and Hinduism. Its status as home of the Buddha placed it at the heart of a religious and cultural sphere that extended throughout Central and East Asia.

It was one of the most intriguing meetings of the ancient world, though no one could have foreseen its significance. By the age of 30, Alexander the Great had already become the most successful military leader the world had ever seen. However, the conquest of northern India had so far eluded him. As Alexander prepared to invade the most powerful Indian state, Magadha [MUG-a-duh], he retreated to the northern city of Taxila [TAX-i-la], near the modern capital of Islamabad in Pakistan, to replenish his forces and rethink his situation.

While in Taxila, Alexander met with a man identified by his biographers simply as "Sandrokottos," who had recently fled the Magadhan court after a failed attempt to overthrow its government. Though we can only speculate about their meeting, Alexander's use of local politics in his past military campaigns suggests that he sought to take advantage of Sandrokottos's knowledge of Magadha in planning his attack. The intelligence Alexander obtained must have been discouraging, for he soon abandoned his plans to invade India and, facing the possibility of mutiny among his men, withdrew to the safer confines of Babylon, where he died in 323 BCE. Following Alexander's death, one of his commanders, Seleucus Nikator [si-LOO-kus ni-KAY-tor], gained control of the eastern reaches of his empire. By 321 BCE, however, Seleucus found his territory around the Indus River threatened by a powerful new Indian state created by none other than Alexander's former ally, Sandrokottos. It was not until the end of the eighteenth century CE that the shadowy "Sandrokottos" was identified by English Sanskrit scholars as Chandragupta Maurya [chun-dra-GOOP-ta MOWR-yah], the founder of India's first and largest indigenous empire.

The meeting between Alexander and Chandragupta thus symbolized a key future pattern of Indian history: intensifying exchanges of ideas and goods between peoples of vastly different cultures and beliefs.

CHAPTER OUTLINE

Patterns of State Formation in India: Republics, Kingdoms, and Empires

The Vedic Tradition and Its Visionary Reformers

Stability amid Disorder: Economy, Family, and Society

Strength in Numbers: Art, Literature, and Science

Putting It All Together

INDIA, 800 BCE–800 CE

ABOVE: Pilgrims walk in procession around the stupa at Sarnath in northern India, where the Buddha gave his first sermon after attaining enlightenment.

Seeing Patterns

❯ Think about the reasons for the spread of Buddhism inside and outside of India. How have historians seen the decline of Buddhism in India?

❯ What do you consider to be the most influential patterns in Indian history to this point? Why?

❯ Do you think some of Ashoka's ideas could be implemented by governments today? Why or why not?

Indian visionaries and innovators have made profound contributions to various patterns of world history. In turn, India's place as a crossroads of trade and invasion continually brought innovation from outside. Many centuries later, the lore of India's wealth and culture would fire the imaginations of Europeans and drive them to seek out the connection first established by Alexander and Chandragupta.

Patterns of State Formation in India: Republics, Kingdoms, and Empires

By 1900 BCE, people were abandoning the agrarian–urban centers of the Indus valley and migrating eastward to the Punjab and Ganges valley, where they drew on their past experience building new agrarian–urban centers in northern India. State formation proceeded rapidly. The earliest traces of villages date to about 1200 BCE. Thereafter, polities emerged quickly, in the form of warrior republics and kingdoms, both of which flourished in the early first millennium BCE.

A gradual consolidation process set in from about 800 BCE onward, with a few kingdoms emerging as the strongest states, while the warrior republics disappeared. The process of state formation reached a first peak with the Mauryan Empire, which united northern and central India and experimented with Buddhism. State and religion were firmly united in the Hindu Gupta Empire (320–550 CE), which, along with its contemporary, Christian Rome, became the first states in world history to lay the foundation for a religious civilization.

The Road to Empire: The Mauryas

In the early first millennium BCE, the emerging states along the Ganges River valley developed political systems ranging from republics to centralized monarchies whose rulers were accorded godlike status. The agricultural advances made in these areas, particularly the dikes, ponds, flooded fields, and drainage systems necessary for growing rice, resulted in the emergence of wealthy, centralized states led by Magadha and Kosala [KOH-sa-la], along with the lesser states of Vatsya and Avanti farther west (see Map 8.1).

During the half century before Alexander attempted to expand his empire into northern India, Mahapadma Nanda [muh-HAH-pud-ma NAHN-da], a member of the *shudra* (or lowest) *varna*, seized power in Magadha and conquered Vatsya and Avanti. By the 330s BCE, the taxes imposed by the Nandas brought unprecedented wealth to the Magadhan capital of Pataliputra [pah-ta-lee-POO-tra]. The Nandas, however, were not alone in their aspirations for universal empire.

Chandragupta Maurya   Little is known of Chandragupta's early life. It is believed that he was taught by the philosopher Kautilya, whose *Arthashastra* became the most influential political treatise in Indian history (see Chapter 3). Kautilya was instrumental in the young Chandragupta's first attempt to seize power from the ruling Nandas. When the revolt was unsuccessful, the two fled to Taxila, a dominant trade crossroads strategically located near the Khyber Pass, where they encountered Alexander.

Alexander's role in building Chandragupta's empire is less obvious. The disruptions caused by Alexander's attempted invasions allowed Chandragupta to secure

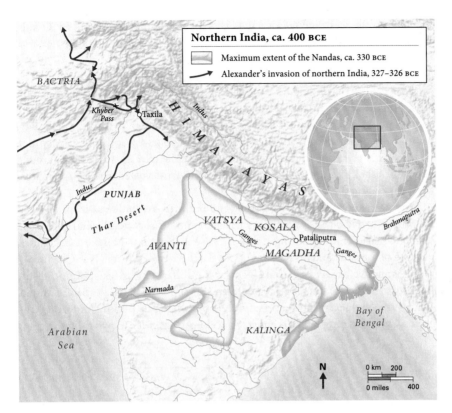

MAP 8.1 Northern India, ca. 400 BCE

the most vulnerable of the Nandas' client states while methodically surrounding and ultimately conquering Magadha. By 321 BCE Chandragupta had secured the capital, and he embarked on a campaign to enlarge his empire. Following a series of battles with Alexander's successor, Seleucus Nikator, the Greeks surrendered their north Indian and Indus territories to Chandragupta. Seleucus and his successors maintained relations with the Mauryas through the Greek ambassador Megasthenes [me-GAS-the-neez], posted to the Mauryan capital of Pataliputra. Megasthenes's accounts of the enormous wealth of the capital and the efficiency of Mauryan government formed the basis of classical and medieval European understanding of India.

Chandragupta stepped down from his throne around 297 BCE and joined an ascetic religious order, the Jains, formed on the basis of the teachings of the visionary Mahavira (see below). Chandragupta's son continued to expand the Mauryan

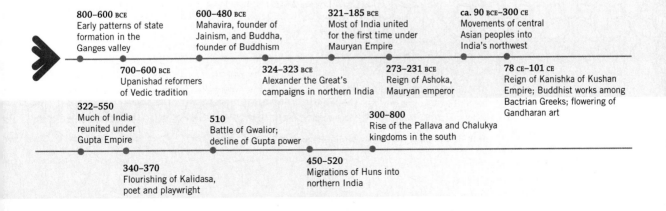

800–600 BCE
Early patterns of state formation in the Ganges valley

700–600 BCE
Upanishad reformers of Vedic tradition

322–550
Much of India reunited under Gupta Empire

340–370
Flourishing of Kalidasa, poet and playwright

600–480 BCE
Mahavira, founder of Jainism, and Buddha, founder of Buddhism

324–323 BCE
Alexander the Great's campaigns in northern India

510
Battle of Gwalior; decline of Gupta power

450–520
Migrations of Huns into northern India

321–185 BCE
Most of India united for the first time under Mauryan Empire

273–231 BCE
Reign of Ashoka, Mauryan emperor

300–800
Rise of the Pallava and Chalukya kingdoms in the south

ca. 90 BCE–300 CE
Movements of central Asian peoples into India's northwest

78 CE–101 CE
Reign of Kanishka of Kushan Empire; Buddhist works among Bactrian Greeks; flowering of Gandharan art

domains to the west and south, but it was his grandson Ashoka [ah-SHO-kah] (r. ca. 273–231 BCE) who emerged as perhaps India's most dominant ruler until the nineteenth century CE.

Ashoka   Born around 304 BCE, Ashoka may have seized the throne from his father. Like his predecessors, he drove the Mauryan Empire deeper into the south (see Map 8.2). The climax of his efforts was a war he fought with the kingdom of Kalinga. By Ashoka's own admission, 100,000 people were killed in the conflict. At the height of his power but deeply moved by the carnage in Kalinga, around 260 BCE Ashoka abruptly converted to Buddhism and vowed to rule his kingdom by "right conduct" alone.

Ashoka told much of his own story and outlined his Buddhist-inspired ideas for proper behavior on inscriptions in caves and on rocks and pillars set up in strategic places throughout his empire. These inscriptions present a fascinating glimpse of the ruler and his personal vision of the idea of dharma (see Chapter 3). One distinctive aspect of Ashoka's support of dharma was his adoption of the Buddhist concept of *ahimsa*, or nonviolence. Ashoka declared dozens of animal species to be under his protection, forbade the wholesale burning of forests, and even warned his people not to burn grain husks, in order to avoid injuring any

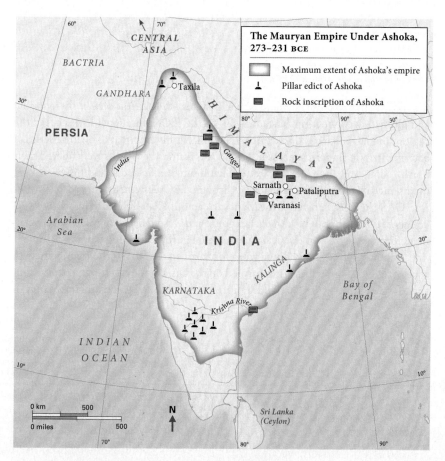

MAP 8.2 **The Mauryan Empire under Ashoka, 273–231 BCE**

creatures living within them. Ashoka's devotion to dharma even extended to sending his sons to Sri Lanka as Buddhist missionaries.

Although Ashoka advocated the peaceful principles of dharma, the records of his reign also indicate that his empire was a kind of police state. While allowing the practice of religions other than Buddhism, Ashoka kept a tight rein on his subjects through a network of spies and informers, a practice begun by his grandfather Chandragupta. All government officials were also subject to periodic review of their adherence to dharma. Thus, the governmental apparatus was geared toward uplifting the people's morality and supervising their happiness.

Ashoka also encouraged a unified system of commercial law, standardization of weights and measures, and uniform coinage—innovations that facilitated commerce. A majority of state revenues came from taxes on harvests of grain plus those on internal and external trade. Under the Mauryans, India was the major crossroads in the exchange of gold and silver sought by the Hellenistic kingdoms and for the expanding maritime trade accompanying the advance of Buddhism into Southeast Asia. In the north, Taxila and the cities and towns along the caravan routes from China to the west grew wealthy from the exchange of luxury goods.

The immense wealth and power flowing into Ashoka's court in Pataliputra made that city of half a million perhaps the richest in the ancient world. The wealth at Ashoka's command and his devotion to dharma allowed the government to spend lavishly in sponsoring public works as well as temples and shrines for various religious groups.

Ashoka's regime represents an attempt to construct a moral order, a pattern of world history that emerged repeatedly as states seeking to become world empires turned to religious and philosophical systems that proclaimed universal truths. The ultimate end of this process, which we will explore in detail in Part 3, was the development of religious civilizations.

The Nomadic Kingdoms of the North   With the end of the Mauryan Empire around 185 BCE, northern India was transformed into regional kingdoms run by local rulers. Greek-speaking peoples from Bactria—descendants of troops and colonists who had followed Alexander the Great—controlled some of these territories. Their most famous ruler, Menander, achieved immortality in Buddhist literature as "King Milinda."

By the first years of the Common Era, Greek rule in northern India was ended by new nomadic groups from central Asia, known by their Chinese names as the Xiongnu [SHIUNG-noo] (believed by some to be related to the Huns) and the Yuezhi [YOO-eh-jih]. As they moved into northern India sometime around 25 CE, the Yuezhi became known as the Kushans. Under its most famous ruler, Kanishka (r. ca. 78–101 CE), the Kushan Empire expanded into not only northern India but also much of modern Pakistan and Afghanistan. Kanishka, like Menander, adopted Buddhism. Through his efforts, the new religion expanded along the caravan routes of central Asia.

Although the arrival of new groups expanded the cultural resources of northern India and aided the spread of Buddhism, it also prevented the development of stable states in the region. As migrations ebbed by the end of the third century, however, a new and aggressive line of rulers, the Guptas, established power in the Ganges valley. Under their rule would come India's great classical age.

Capital of Ashoka Pillar of Sarnath. The lion motif atop the chakravartin wheel, symbolizing universal kingship, tops one of Ashoka's famous pillars. The one from which this capital was taken had been set up to commemorate the Buddha's first sermon in Sarnath's deer park.

MOVEMENT OF NOMADIC PEOPLES, 300 BCE–100 CE

The Classical Age: The Gupta Empire

Scholars agree that the Gupta line, like the Mauryans, originated somewhere near Magadha. The first major ruler of the dynasty was Chandragupta I (r. ca. 320–335 CE; no relation to the Chandragupta of the Mauryan Empire), whose new state occupied much of old Magadha and Kosala. His successor, Samudragupta [sa-MOO-dra-goop-ta] (r. ca. 335–380 CE), expanded the borders of the empire even farther.

Under Samudragupta, the Gupta dominion extended far up the Ganges River to the borders of the Kushans south of Taxila and down the coast deep into the territory of the Pallavas [PUH-la-vas] in the south. Like Chandragupta I, he forged ties to regions outside of Gupta control, whose populations in turn pledged their loyalty to him. Samudragupta's son Chandragupta II (r. ca. 380–413 CE) continued to expand the empire, adding the southern and western Gujarati territories of the Shakas. The cumulative effect of these conquests was that, once again, the Indian subcontinent stood on the threshold of unity (see Map 8.3).

Hinduism: A convenient shorthand term for the vast multiplicity of religious practices derived from the Vedic, Brahmanic, Upanishadic, and later traditions in India and those places influenced by Indian culture.

Court and Culture   During the reign of the Guptas, the collection of religious traditions called **Hinduism** flourished. Indeed, the Guptas actively used the gods and practices of Hinduism, particularly in their devotion to Vishnu and Shiva, to extend their legitimacy not just as kings but as universal rulers. Although the Guptas made Hinduism the privileged religion in the state, they permitted the practice of other faiths, including both Jainism and Buddhism. Under their influence, the first distinctly "Hindu" art included a staggering profusion of temples and shrines built to honor a variety of deities. Literary culture flourished, from classical treatises on political and social behavior to poetry and plays.

The Waning of Gupta Power   Gupta power began to fade under the reigns of Chandragupta II's son and grandson. A new wave of central Asian nomads, the Hunas, defeated the Guptas in 510 CE and established themselves as the dominant force in northwest India. By 515 CE, the eastern tributary states of the Guptas had broken away.

The Southern Kingdoms, ca. 300–600 CE

The southern regimes of the Pallavas, Pandyas, Cholas, and Chalukyas of peninsular India enjoyed a comparatively stable period from the decline of the Guptas until the installation of the Muslim sultanates of the north. One reason was the absence of a powerful empire pushing south. Freed from the need to defend themselves, the southern kingdoms could pursue the pacification of their own realms. In addition, their ruling classes shared to some degree a common culture.

Devotional: In the context of this chapter, belonging to a branch of Hinduism in which one dedicates oneself to practices that venerate, honor, or adore a particular god or divinity. The largest of these branches are dedicated to Vishnu and Shiva.

The development of Hinduism among the Tamils, the region's chief ethnic group, included the rise of **devotional** branches of Hinduism and an outpouring of spectacular religious art. The southern kingdoms' most tangible remains are the Hindu temple complexes. The Pallavas, for example, under Mahendra Varman I (r. 590–630 CE), carved the Mandapa Temple from solid rock. His descendant Narasimha Varman II (r. 695–728 CE) sponsored the seven rock pagodas of Mahabali Puram. Perhaps most spectacular of all was the eighth-century CE Rashtakuta complex of Krishna I at Kailasanatha, again carved from solid rock.

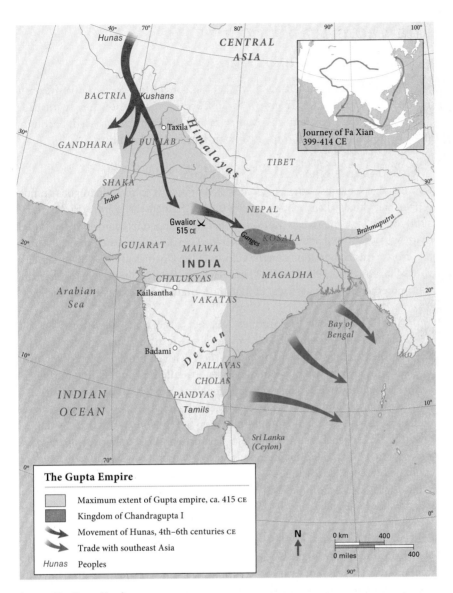

MAP 8.3 **The Gupta Empire**

The power and wealth of the region was enhanced by the promotion of trade, especially with the Indianized enclaves of Southeast Asia and the Indonesian archipelago. As a result, Indian religions, culture, and economics dominated Indian Ocean trade until it was gradually taken over by the Muslims after the thirteenth century CE.

Regional Struggles   South of the Ganges, the systems of *varna* and *jati* (see Chapter 3) tended to revolve more around where one lived than they did in the north. A major division also existed among the local leaders, who were generally members of the upper *varnas,* and their subjects. Within these divisions, rulers tended to be predatory in their efforts to enrich their kingdoms. The rise of the Chalukya state on the western side of the peninsula in the mid-sixth century CE, along with that of the Vakatakas of the Deccan Plateau and the Rashtakutas in the early eighth century CE, resumed the struggle for wealth and territory among the older southern kingdoms.

The Vedic Tradition and Its Visionary Reformers

Beginning around 700 BCE, visionaries sought to reform the Vedic tradition. As we noted in Chapter 3, the first of these men created the Upanishads. In the next two centuries, Mahavira and the Buddha followed, becoming the founding figures, respectively, of Jainism and Buddhism.

Reforming the Vedic Tradition

As we saw in Chapter 3, the Vedas consisted of hymns to the Hindu gods and described the rituals these deities required. They framed the culture of the period 1200–600 BCE, a time when warrior republics and kingdoms competed against each other for wealth and power in the Punjab and Ganges valley. It was against the backdrop of this competition that the authors of the Upanishads (ca. 700–300 BCE), Mahavira (trad. 599–527 BCE), and Gautama, the Buddha, sought to reform the polytheistic Vedic heritage through the formulation of a single first principle.

The Upanishad Visionaries   Many authors of the more than 100 Upanishads were Brahmanic priests whose principal objective was a vision of cosmic unity. This Upanishadic vision, with its proclamation of monism, was similar to those propounded in the Middle East and China during the same time: They insisted on a transcendent first principle as universal truth.

The Indian visionaries were hermit teachers whose disciples sought to merge their personal selves (*atman*) into the universal self (*brahman*) and thereby achieve salvation. These teachers led their disciples through brief aphorisms, paradoxes, and negations into deep meditation, through which they considered salvation could be achieved. In the highest state of understanding of atman–brahman, one could attain release from the cycles of death and rebirth and thus enter into transcendence, or *moksha*.

Criticism of the Vedic Rituals and Sacrifices   Although they were advocates of monism, the authors of the Upanishads remained faithful to the Vedic rituals, sacrifices, and doctrines. However, as strong kingdoms emerged in the 500s BCE, criticism of religious ritual grew. Urbanization and trade created new classes to whom rituals and sacrifices meant less than they did to the kings and the priestly class. These new classes viewed the rituals and sacrifices as formalistic and wasteful. For the kings and priests, these religious practices were essential to legitimize their power. The Vedic doctrine that eventually divided the priests and their strongest critics, however, was that of the cycle of karma–samsara (see Chapter 3), death and rebirth.

The Ascetic Break: Jainism   The founder of the Jains, Nigantha Nataputta [nee-GAN-ta nah-ta-POO-ta], was born around 540 BCE. At the age of 30 he left home and gave up all his worldly possessions to become an ascetic, and after 12 years he found meditative enlightenment. He was given the titles *jina* ("conqueror") and Mahavira ("great hero"), and his followers became known as **Jains**. For the next 40 years, he wandered throughout India without clothes or possessions, spreading the new sect's principles and practices. Finally, demonstrating the movement's ideal of not taking the life of any being, Mahavira refused all food and died near Pataliputra.

Coins of the Northwest Kingdoms, Second Century BCE and Late First Century CE. The complex history of the area encompassed by modern Afghanistan and Pakistan has been understood principally through the coins minted by the many rulers of frequently shifting territories. The silver coin (above) was minted by a Bactrian Greek king, probably in the second century BCE. The gold coin (below) with the Greek inscription was the product of the reign of the famous Buddhist king Kanishka (78–101 CE) of the Kushans and depicts the king himself.

Jains: Followers of Mahavira who believe that the aim of life is to liberate the soul by acquiring as little karma as possible.

The Kailasantha Temple. Hewn from a single, solid rock, the Kailasantha Temple, part of an elaborate complex in east-central India, is considered the world's most monumental sculpture. Strongly influenced by south Indian architectural traditions, the temple complex dazzles the visitor with carvings of innumerable deities, mythic figures, and erotic imagery. The work is so detailed and painstakingly done that it was said to have moved its master builder to cry, "Oh! How did I do this?"

Schism: A division; when used in a religious context it usually refers to the splitting of members of a certain religion into two or more camps over matters of doctrine, ritual, etc.

Jain doctrine begins with a universe in which all things possess *jiva*, a kind of "soul" that yearns to be free from the material world. Jains believe that even inanimate objects possess *jiva*, though at different levels or "senses." These "souls" are governed by the degree to which a thing's past karma stands between it and its release from material bondage. For humans, karma builds up according to the injuries one does to others, intentionally or not. The way to enlightenment, therefore, is to act so that one acquires as little karma as possible, while performing actions of suffering and self-sacrifice to reduce the karma one already has. As karma dissipates, the soul lightens and ultimately rises to freedom.

Ahimsa   Jain monks try to prevent injury to any object, especially living things. There has been a **schism** between those who insist on complete nakedness—to avoid injuring creatures that might be trapped in one's clothing—and those who wear a simple white robe. Some wear gauze masks to prevent breathing in invisible organisms; others carry brooms to sweep small creatures out of one's path. Monks live by begging food from others. The most dedicated ritually fasted to death in resolute refusal to harm living things; this was seen as the ultimate act of ahimsa, or nonviolence.

The strict practices of the Jains did not appeal to most people. Nonetheless, the patronage of kings, including Chandragupta Maurya, and a laity of supporters helped ensure the sect's vitality. Modern Jains practice a modified form of the earlier traditions, engaging in vegetarianism or veganism, though often wearing

Statue of the Jain Saint Gomateshwara at Karnataka. The world's largest statue cut from a single stone, this figure was built at the site of the famous Jain monastery where, it was said, Chandragupta Maurya entered the order and fasted to death, following the example of the sect's founder, Mahavira.

clothes indistinguishable from those of other traditions. Some also still participate in certain ceremonies in the nude or with their traditional white garments. The religion's most distinctive element, however, is that it is rigorously **atheistic**, choosing not to worship any god but insisting instead on meditatively merging into a unity that is both universal and transcendent.

Atheistic: Not believing in a god or supreme being.

The Middle Way: Buddhism   Buddhism began in part as a reaction against such extreme ascetic practices as Jainism. Siddhartha Gautama, whose title of "Buddha" means "the Enlightened One," is believed to have been born a prince in the Sakya republic in the Himalayan foothills, for which he is also known as Sakyamuni. His traditional birth date is given as 563 BCE, though recent accounts have moved it to at least the mid-400s BCE. At the age of 29, Gautama left his world of privilege and followed various Vedic paths. At one point, following a discipline of extreme asceticism, his path of self-deprivation led him to fast nearly to death.

During his travels, Gautama was exposed to human suffering. His shock and compassion drove him to try to understand the continual round of death and rebirth. According to Buddhist accounts, after deep meditation he achieved enlightenment under a bodhi tree (a kind of fig) on the outskirts of the modern city of Bodh Gaya. Shortly afterward, he went to a deer park in Sarnath, near the city of Varanasi (Benares), where he found five former disciples and preached to them what became known as the Middle Way.

The Four Noble Truths, the Noble Eightfold Path, and Nirvana   Gautama believed that the nature of the universe is change. All beings suffer because they attach themselves to what they will ultimately lose. Although they crave permanence, they rely only on their senses, which provide the illusion of stability but actually obscure the true nature of things. In pursuit of their desires, they commit evil deeds and accumulate karma. Over many lifetimes, the karma stays with them, building up with each life and keeping them from breaking free of the cycle of death and rebirth. Gautama distilled these insights into the Four Noble Truths:

1. All life is suffering.
2. Suffering arises from craving.
3. To stop suffering, one must stop craving.
4. One stops craving by following the Noble Eightfold Path of right views, right resolve, right speech, right conduct, right livelihood, right effort, right mindfulness, and right concentration.

Later sermons and commentaries further described the Eightfold Path. The path represents a course of life in which one avoids extreme behaviors, adheres to a code of conduct that favors **altruism** and nonviolence, and respects the life of all living beings. Through meditation and "right mindfulness" one then reaches a state of calm nonattachment with an uncluttered mind able to grasp the universal truth. This final stage is known by the Sanskrit word *nirvana*, or nothingness. In Buddhism, this nothingness is a version of the *moksha*—transcendence—first explored in the Upanishads.

Altruism: The practice of acting in an unselfish manner for the good of others.

After the Buddha's death, disputes arose about the correct interpretations of his teachings and questions about how followers should conduct themselves. Over the following two centuries, several Buddhist councils were held, and during one of these meetings, one group separated from the main body of adherents. The now-separate group became known as Theravada [ter-ra-VAH-dah], "the teachings of the elders." Under Ashoka's influence, Theravada Buddhism became the approved sect, with the first complete surviving texts dating from this time.

Buddhist Texts   The Pali Canon, written in Pali, the sacred language of Buddhism (closely related to Sanskrit), is a collection of texts that forms the foundation of Theravada Buddhism and nearly all Buddhist schools. The collection is also called by the Sanskrit name *Tripitaka* [tree-PIT-a-ka] , or "Three Baskets"; it consists of the *Vinaya* [vee-NAI-yah] *Pitaka*, treatises on conduct and rules of discipline for monks; the *Sutra* [SOO-truh] *Pitaka*, consisting of sutras, or "discourses," most of them believed to have originated with the Buddha; and the *Abhidharma* [a-bee-DAR-ma] *Pitaka*, doctrines of philosophy and metaphysics.

As Theravada Buddhism spread, it became more accessible. Stories of the Buddha's last days implied that he would save everyone who followed his path. Coupled with this was a developing tradition of the Buddha as one in a long line of past and future buddhas, suggesting the potential for a devotional component. Finally, the concept of the *bodhisattva* [boh-dee-SUHT-vuh] describes one who, having achieved enlightenment, does not proceed to nirvana but instead helps the suffering achieve their own enlightenment.

Theravada and Mahayana   During the first century CE, the largest branch of Buddhism, Mahayana [ma-hah-YAH-na], the "greater vehicle," emerged. Mahayana spread along the trade routes into central Asia, into the borderlands of the Parthian Persians, and ultimately to China, Korea, Japan, and Tibet (see Map 8.4). As it spread, its schools divided into *esoteric* branches—those seeking enlightenment through scriptural or other kinds of deep knowledge—and devotional branches. Of the devotional schools, that of Amitabha [a-mee-TAH-ba], the Heavenly Buddha of the Western Paradise, is today the most popular Buddhist sect in both China and Japan, where he is called Amida (see Chapters 9 and 13).

As Buddhism spread across Asia, its decline had already begun in India. With the revitalization and consolidation of the older Vedic and Brahmanic traditions into Hinduism, Buddhism faced competition for converts and noble patronage (see below).

The Maturity of Hinduism: From the Abstract to the Devotional

During the period from the Mauryans to the rise of the Guptas, the continuing push of state formation to the south meant that local deities were incorporated into the older Vedic and Upanishadic traditions. From these southern areas emerged devotional cults, especially those of Vishnu and Shiva, culminating in the *bhakti* movements beginning in the seventh century CE.

On the other hand, the growth of new religions like Buddhism and Jainism challenged such cultural mainstays as the caste system, the inevitability of the karmic cycle, and the domination of society and salvation by the traditional ruling classes. As a result of these challenges and through the popularity of the grand epics of the Mahabharata and Ramayana, the spreading of the classical texts of the

Great Buddhist Stupa at Sanchi. The need for commemorative burial mounds and reliquaries for the Buddha's relics spawned a characteristic structure called a stupa, meaning "gathered" or "heap." Brimming with symbolic motifs representing the stages of enlightenment, the structures changed considerably from this example—built in the first century BCE over an earlier one from the Mauryan period—as they spread through East Asia, where they assumed the shape of the pagoda.

first and second centuries, and Gupta patronage, a rejuvenated brand of religious experience, Hinduism, is distinctly recognizable by the fourth century CE.

Avatars, Shakti, and Tantra   Hindu beliefs hold that the subcontinent was a single land united by faith. Another belief is a full continuum of religious experience, ranging from the highly abstract to the emotional and mystical, springing from devotion to a particular god. Perhaps due to the influence of Buddhism and Jainism, salvation was increasingly seen as accessible to all.

The most important Hindu gods were Brahma, Vishnu, and Shiva. Of these, the main divisions of devotion emerged between Vishnu, the beneficent preserver, and Shiva, the powerful, fertile giver and destroyer of life, the "Lord of the Dance" of the universe. Both Vishnu and Shiva can manifest themselves through avatars or incarnations, the most popular of which is Krishna, an incarnation of Vishnu, who plays a central role in the Bhagavad Gita. The appeal of the new devotional traditions of Hinduism to all castes made the religion increasingly popular. Hinduism allowed that one could achieve salvation according to one's

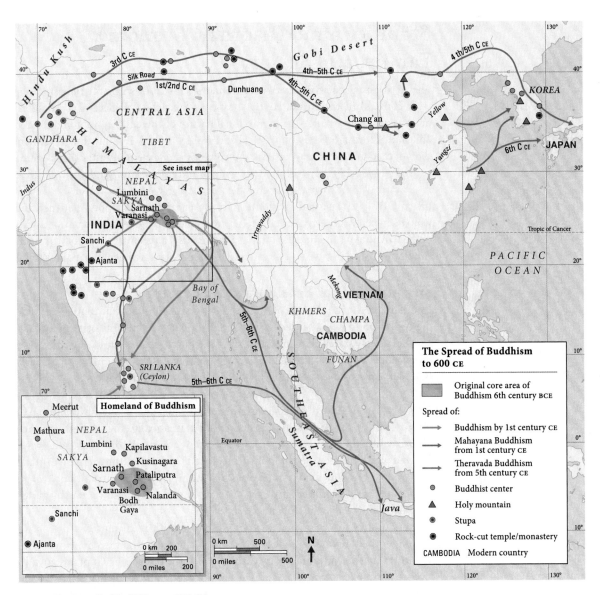

MAP 8.4 The Spread of Buddhism to 600 CE

caste and ability. By the seventh century CE, religious poets were carrying the message of devotional Hinduism to all believers in vernacular languages and creating some of the most passionate and beautiful religious poetry ever recorded.

A related development was that of Shakti, literally "power," sometimes called "tantra." Shakti practitioners probed the darker edges of the multiple natures of the gods—especially Shiva and his consort Kali, or Durga—associated with death and destruction. To this end they purposely violated social norms, with the objective of proving their mastery over attachment to the acts themselves and to push beyond the ordinary dualities of good and evil. The idea of transcending norms also passed into Buddhism at about the same time, in the fourth and fifth centuries CE. Here it was also referred to as "tantra," and its mysticism formed important elements of Tibetan Buddhism.

Stability amid Disorder: Economy, Family, and Society

The agrarian-based economy of India remained for 2,000 years the richest (along with China's) in the world. As the economy flourished, society as a whole remained relatively stable. The hierarchical nature of the caste system maintained continuity through times of political turmoil. Although Buddhism and Jainism did not recognize the caste system, they did not fundamentally alter that system.

The relationships between men and women and among family members outlined in Chapter 3 grew increasingly complex, particularly from the age of the Guptas onward. Despite the trend in Buddhism toward greater equality between men and women, beliefs such as the strictly delineated spheres of husband and wife, the idea of the female as a fundamental force of the universe, and a male vision of women as simultaneously desirable and threatening became more prevalent during this time.

Tax and Spend: Economy and Society

By 600 BCE, the inhabitants of the emerging Gangetic states had long since made the transition to being settled agriculturalists. With the vast majority of inhabitants of the new states being peasants from the lowest *shudra varna*, the chief form of revenue was harvest taxes. The average tax levied on the people of these early states appears to have been around one-sixth of their annual harvest.

Accelerating Taxes   With the expansion of Magadha in the fifth and fourth centuries BCE, the agricultural tax increased dramatically. The accelerating pace of urban life, the explosion of trade, and the increasingly differentiated castes allowed whole new classes of items to be taxed. Moreover, the increase in trade had led to a growing commercial class expanding beyond the traditional *vaisya* (merchant) *varna*, while the growing need for capital and credit was met by guilds of bankers and traders in precious metals.

Tariffs: Taxes levied on imports.

Agricultural taxes of about one-quarter to one-third of the harvest continued under the Guptas. As under the Mauryans, bankers and merchants were frequently tapped by rulers for ready cash. Despite low **tariffs**, the Guptas enjoyed a favorable balance of trade. Indeed, the empire's self-sufficiency in nearly all commercial items meant that foreign traders had to pay for their goods in gold or silver.

Trade and Expansion   By the time of Persia's invasion in the late sixth century BCE, the reputation of the wealth of northern India was already well established among the Greeks. In the wake of the conquests of Alexander, interactions with the expanding Hellenistic world extended the reach of Indian trade through the eastern Mediterranean and the newly acquired Roman domains.

With the decline of the Mauryans and the adoption of Buddhism by peoples of the northwest, the region around Taxila became the hub of a caravan trade that from the third century BCE to the third century CE linked nearly all of Eurasia from Roman Britain to Han China and beyond through the Silk Road (see Chapter 9). In addition, Buddhist, Jain, and Brahmanic religious elements all spread westward to enrich the intellectual climate of the Parthians, Greeks, and Romans.

Indians also dominated the region's maritime trade until they were gradually displaced by Muslims from the ninth to the fifteenth centuries CE and by

Europeans shortly thereafter. Colonies of Greek, Roman, Persian, and Arab traders clustered in the western port cities of Broach (now Bharuch) and Kalliena (now Kalyan). A testament to the importance of trade in the Greco-Roman world was the first-century guide to the Indian Ocean, the *Periplus* (marine atlas) *of the Erythrean Sea* (see "Patterns Up Close").

Indian Influence beyond India   By the first century CE, this expanding trade region had established outposts in Southeast Asia and the Indonesian archipelago. In the second century CE, small settlements of Indians on the Malay Peninsula led to the first Indianized kingdom in the area, known by the Chinese name Funan, in the Mekong delta of Southeast Asia, ruled by the brahmin Kaudinya. The spread of both Buddhism and the Indian system of "god-kings" soon reached the nearby Khmers [k-MARES] (Cambodians) and the state of Champa (along the coast of modern Vietnam). By the seventh and eighth centuries CE, these areas became important trade centers connecting the Indian states with Tang China and Heian Japan.

The appeal of Buddhism enhanced the Indian economy by both increasing the volume of trade on the subcontinent and providing a uniform structure for its expansion abroad. Pilgrims and monks were natural candidates to assist in the circulation of goods and ideas. Monasteries served as way stations along well-traveled routes; commercial centers grew up around larger complexes along branches of the Silk Road. The international character of Buddhism linked India to an emerging cultural sphere that soon spanned Eurasia. By the fourth century CE, trade ties had been established with the Romans, the Sasanid Persians, the remnant states of Han China, and the Buddhist and Indianizing territories of Southeast Asia (see Map 8.5).

Caste, Family Life, and Gender

The basic patterns of Indian society were already being forged by the seventh century BCE. Thereafter, the fusion of Vedic traditions into a distinct form of Hindu culture, drawn heavily from Brahmanic religious and social practices, proceeded apace. In the Gupta Empire, Hinduism evolved into a religious civilization.

Maturation of the Caste System   Perhaps the most distinctive marker of Hinduism as a religious civilization is the caste (*jati*) system. One of the caste system's chief functions was to absorb and acculturate peoples of divergent languages, ethnicities, and religious practices into an integrated social whole. Within the framework of caste, all people had reciprocal, if not equal, rights and responsibilities. Even those at the bottom levels had a necessary, if disagreeable, societal function.

During the Mauryan era, Ashoka's advocacy of dharma reinforced older notions of duty according to social position, while such treatises as the *Code of Manu* (written down by 200 CE) helped solidify concepts of model conduct among the various classes. By the Gupta period, renewed interest in societal stability after nearly five centuries of disorder prompted increased attention to stricter boundaries for acceptable behaviors within the different *jatis*. Along with this, the idea of **ritual pollution** resulting from unsanctioned contact with lower castes becomes increasingly common.

Yet the caste system had strengths that contributed to its longevity. Like religious organizations and guilds in medieval Europe, *jati* membership gave each person a recognized and valued place in society. In some areas, especially in the south, entire villages or clans were incorporated into their own *jatis*; in others,

Ritual pollution: The act of someone or something becoming "unclean" in terms of religious taboos or prohibitions.

Patterns Up Close

The Global Trade of Indian Pepper

Pepper was perhaps the world's most sought-after commodity for thousands of years. Indeed, its importance ultimately drove European adventurers to Africa and the Americas as they sought a direct all-water route to its source in India.

The black pepper plant (*Piper nigrum*) is a vine native to the Malabar Coast of India in the modern state of Kerala. As far back as the thirteenth century BCE, Egyptian records show black pepper being used in mummifications. By the third century BCE, pepper had become a mainstay of south India's burgeoning Indian Ocean trade, with annual cargoes going to China, Southeast Asia, and Egypt. The Hellenistic cultural exchange conducted through Ptolemaic Egypt spread the use of pepper throughout the Mediterranean world. By the first century BCE, traders from Egypt, coastal Arabia, and northeast Africa made annual voyages to the Malabar ports for pepper. But it was after the Roman acquisition of Egypt that pepper became the subject of a kind of mania throughout their empire. Contemporary Romans like Pliny the Elder regularly complained of the amount of gold required to keep the empire adequately spiced, and the export of gold to India was ultimately curtailed.

How does one account for pepper's popularity? Initially, part of pepper's attraction may have been its exotic quality. But it had also long been used for medicinal purposes in India, and from Roman times through the European Middle Ages it was hailed in European and Arab treatises as healthful. Moreover, although pepper's effectiveness as a preservative is questionable, it was nonetheless useful as a flavor enhancer in a variety of preserved foods.

Pepper Pot. The earliest records of pepper being imported into Britain are from the first century. Discovered in 1992, this exquisite pepper pot—a special container intended to hold this expensive spice—is designed in the shape of an empress and dates to the fifth century CE. Made of gold and silver, it testifies to the high value placed on such a precious commodity, especially in a remote place like Britain.

ethnicity or occupation might be the determining criteria. Although the upper castes dominated the political structure of rural society, social power was in fact more diffuse. For example, the members of various caste and guild councils were customarily represented at state functions. Some castes became associated with special feasts and their sponsoring deities, giving them a degree of informal power.

Jainism, Buddhism, and Caste   Jainism and Buddhism influenced the caste system as well, offering powerful alternative traditions to the acceptance of *varna* and *jati*. Moreover, their potential for anyone, regardless of social position, to break free of the cycle of death and rebirth undermined the hierarchical order of the caste system and made Jain and Buddhist practitioners equals in a society of believers. Their alternative institutions, self-sufficiency, good works, and commercial expertise also gave them considerable material power, particularly when patronized by nobles or monarchs.

Family Life and Hindu Culture   As we saw in Chapter 3, the role of women in Indian society was perhaps more complex than in other agrarian-based cultures. The idea of female "dependence" was central to the Hindu conception of the family. Obedience and loyalty to senior female and male authority within the

The Arab occupation of the prime transshipment areas of the eastern Mediterranean and the termini of the Silk Road and, by the fourteenth century, their domination of Indian Ocean trade caused the price of Indian commodities to soar in Europe. The urge to break the Islamic monopoly of the spice trade ultimately drove the Portuguese to sail around Africa and Columbus to sail into the Atlantic, hoping to go directly to the Malabar Coast. The commercial network built on pepper and other spices was now positioned to drive what would grow into the world's first global trading system.

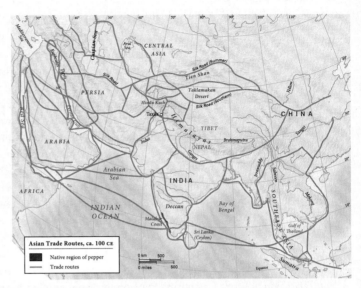

MAP 8.5 **Asian Trade Routes, ca. 100 CE**

Questions

- How does the global trade in Indian pepper show the connectedness of Eurasia in this period in world history?

- What are the origins of the pepper trade? How did it change over time through interactions? What adaptations, if any, resulted from these interactions?

hierarchy of the family was a woman's dharma, her duty regardless of her position in the caste system.

Although in the Tamil areas of the south families remained matrilineal, female property rights were limited. Yet wives customarily controlled the household accounts and supervised servants and hired help. Women of higher classes were expected to have knowledge of poetry, literature, and conversational skills. And the vast majority of men and women were united through marriages arranged by their families after careful negotiation and often betrothed before adolescence.

A number of texts described the "four stages of life" for men: student, householder, hermit, and wanderer. In the first stage, that of the student, boys of the "twice-born" upper castes were taken into the household of a *guru*, or teacher, to study the works of the Vedic–Brahmanic–Upanishadic tradition. At the second stage (householder), a man was expected to make a good marriage, establish a prosperous household, and continue his religious duties. As old age approached, he entered the third stage (hermit) and was expected to retreat to the forest and work to master the self in preparation for the end. In the final (wanderer) stage, he would move beyond desire for life or death, wandering without home or possessions and, ideally, attaining moksha (release from the cycle of death and rebirth).

Balancing Male and Female Roles   Although women were, for the most part, treated as subservient members of a patriarchal society, they were also seen by men both as complementary opposites and as potential impediments to moksha. Women in literature, like Sita in the Ramayana, were often depicted as heroic and resourceful. Moreover, from the Gupta period on, devotees appealed to a number of goddesses. Fertility, sexuality, and growth, largely associated with femaleness, were all celebrated in Hindu literature, statuary, and religious symbolism. The depictions of sexuality in Hindu temples are among the most erotic forms of art in the world. In contrast with this celebration of sexuality, however, was the perception of women as temptresses who anchored men to the sensual world, potentially delaying their release from the karmic cycle.

These contradictions are illustrated in the *Kama Sutra*, or *Aphorisms of Love*, written perhaps sometime in the first or second century CE by Vatsyayana [vaht-s-YAH-ya-na]. Although best known in the West for its descriptions of sexual practices, it is more properly understood as a guide to the everyday worship of living. The majority of the text deals not with sex but rather with how to become a person of culture. For women, the *Kama Sutra* details such activities as singing, dancing, and cooking—but also chemistry, metallurgy, and even driving horses and elephants.

Strength in Numbers: Art, Literature, and Science

The vast number of cultural contributions from India makes it impossible to do more than hint at their richness here. One area worth noting, however, is Gandharan art. During the time of the Kushan Empire, the influences of the old empire of Alexander the Great met the new religious movements within Buddhism to create this new style.

Early representations of the Buddha had been symbolic: the "wheel of dharma," an empty throne, or a footprint. Around the beginning of the Common Era, the tradition of depicting the Greek gods as realistically human merged with the new Buddhist sensibilities to create the first images of the Buddha, which looked remarkably like some Greek depictions of the god Apollo. This Gandharan approach spread across northern India. Over time, however, the style declined as less realistic and more symbolic representations became standard throughout the Mahayana religious sphere. Perhaps the most important Buddhist thinker of this time was Nagarjuna [nah-GAR-joo-na] (ca. 150–250 CE). A leading exponent of Mahayana Buddhism, he championed the concept of the Bodhisattva, as well as a complex logic called *catuskoti* ("four corners"). The idea is that there are four possibilities regarding a statement: it can be true; false; both true and false; or neither true nor false. For Nagarjuna, we are limited in perception by language, but there is a deeper level of indescribable or ineffable reality that may be directly experienced by certain kinds of meditation.

Gandharan Buddhas. One of the most stunning syntheses of artistic and religious traditions occurred in the wake of the decline of the Seleucid states and the invasion of the Kushans. In the area centered around Gandhara (in modern northeast Afghanistan and northwest Pakistan), Hellenistic artistic techniques of realistic human representation fused with the developing practices of Mahayana Buddhism to create sculptures like the head pictured here, from the second or third century CE, believed to be that of a bodhisattva, or perhaps of Siddhartha Gautama.

Science and Mathematics   In addition to Buddhism, the most profound intellectual influences from India on the surrounding regions were in science and mathematics. From the second century BCE until the second century CE, India was an importer of scientific and mathematical concepts from the Greco-Roman and Persian spheres. Greek geometry, for example, made its way into northern India during this time.

In exchange, however, concepts of Indian health regimens—some involving yoga discipline—along with the vast body of Indian medicine, with its extensive knowledge of herbal remedies, seem to have moved west. The second-century CE medical text *Charaka Samhita*, for example, like its counterparts in the Mediterranean and later European world, taught a health regimen based on the balance of humors.

In the area of mathematics and astronomy, an important synthesis of ideas took place from the time of the Mauryans through the twelfth and thirteenth centuries CE. During the Hellenistic period, Indians adopted the calendar of the eastern Mediterranean and southwest Asia, which had a 7-day week, a 24-hour day, and a 365-day solar year—along with the 12 zodiacal signs of the Greco-Roman world. Indian thinkers refined these imported concepts to levels unsurpassed in the ancient world. The subtleties of some of the philosophical schools had already required intervals of time and numbers that still stagger the imagination today. For example, cycles of time marking eternity in some philosophical schools were measured in intervals larger than current estimates of the age of the universe. Philosophical discussion on the nature of matter in infinitesimal space among some schools anticipated key arguments of modern physicists regarding the principle of indeterminacy.

Like the Chinese, Indian mathematicians and astronomers during the Gupta period had already developed a decimal system; however, they now employed the first use of the zero, initially marked by a dot, as a placeholder, and developed a system of positive and negative numbers. Their work with the geometry of the Greeks enabled them to calculate pi to four decimal places as well as to develop methods for the solving of certain kinds of algebraic equations. By the eleventh and twelfth centuries CE, the acquisition of these techniques by the Arabs and their transmittal of them to the new universities of Christian Europe gave us the system we still use today, known by the somewhat misleading name of "Arabic numerals."

Putting It All Together

Over the course of roughly a millennium, a number of important patterns of world history emerged in India. The political, cultural, social, religious, and economic systems of the states along the Ganges River were diffused to all parts of the Indian subcontinent. With the maturing of these patterns came the tendency to see the subcontinent as a unified entity in nearly every way except in politics. Here, despite the accomplishments of the Mauryans and Guptas, unity would prove elusive—in some respects even to the present day. This would prove particularly true, as we will see in later chapters, with the coming of Islam.

In terms of its regional influence and beyond, India's impact was disproportionately large. By at least the time of Ashoka, the population of the subcontinent was second only to that of China. Within it was contained one of the world's most active sources of religious traditions. The influence of Hinduism spread to Indonesia and Southeast Asia; Buddhism through this period was the world's largest religious system, as well as the first "universal" one.

Paradoxically, many of the factors that allowed for this tremendous richness of religious, cultural, and intellectual traditions also contributed to the subcontinent's political instability, particularly in the north. Here, continual migrations of outside peoples cross-fertilized the cultural resources of the region but also impeded political unification.

Review and Relate

Thinking Through Patterns

Examine the ways historians approach the big questions of this chapter.

> **Think about the reasons for the spread of Buddhism inside and outside of India. How have historians seen the decline of Buddhism in India?**

An important historical pattern is that of individuals we call "visionaries." In this chapter, we place the Buddha in this category as a man who sought to go beyond the Hindu bounds of death and rebirth. Like the other visionaries we examine, however, the Buddha's fundamental message of transcendence and enlightenment can be adapted to any belief system. As his message moved outward from India, it adapted to local customs by borrowing bits of indigenous religious mythology and belief while keeping the fundamental message intact. Local people in turn adapted it to their own beliefs and made it their own. In East Asia, it received a boost from the translation of Buddhist scriptures into literary Chinese and the circulation of Buddhist practitioners, monks, merchants, and pilgrims throughout the Buddhist cultural sphere. Its decline in the place of its birth appears to have been due in part to the shift of its cultural center to China and Japan and the official support of the Guptas for Hinduism.

> **What do you consider to be the most influential patterns in Indian history to this point? Why?**

How do historians establish criteria of "importance"? One measure of this is to assess the influence of certain patterns and practices on a culture or society over time. Change over time (or the lack of it) is an important indicator of the prevalence and kind of innovation taking place in a society. So some influential patterns in Indian history might include the permeation of religion into all aspects of Indian life, the search for transcendence of the material world, the caste system as the social fabric of the subcontinent, and the prominence of India as a crossroads astride the trade routes of the Indian Ocean and the great land routes across Eurasia.

> **Do you think some of Ashoka's concepts could be implemented by governments today? Why or why not?**

Ashoka's ideas seem quite modern in many ways, and his decrees regarding the protection of animals and ecological matters might certainly have some current application. Yet it must also be remembered that he is still far removed in time and culture from the modern world. His ideas of dharma as duty might not carry exactly the same import as today. Historians are routinely conscious of the pitfalls of identifying too closely with peoples in very different cultures in the remote past. "The past is a foreign country," it is often said (quoting the novelist L. P. Hartley), "They do things differently there."

Against the Grain

Consider this as a counterpoint to the main patterns examined in this chapter.

• What difficulties did all republics that sprang from agrarian–urban society face? Were they in the end insurmountable? Why?

India's Ancient Republics

In addition to kingdoms, the ancient Gangetic states also included republics (*ganas*). Accustomed as we are to thinking of such political institutions as exclusive to the Mediterranean world, representative forms of government have appeared in nearly all human societies. Yet until very recent times, as scientific-industrial society and the nation-state have come to dominate global politics and economics, republics had proved problematic to sustain. In Greece and Rome, for example, popular-based governments seemed inevitably to descend into factionalism, demanding a strong ruler to restore order.

The early Indian republics of the late Vedic period were also seen by contemporaries to be models of power sharing in some respects but were as vulnerable to internal dissension and factionalism as their counterparts elsewhere. For states moving toward a unified conception of concentrated power and religious unity, the instability of power sharing seemed increasingly unattractive, even dangerous. Moreover, the requirements of economic stability in agrarian societies and the growing rigidity of caste also militated against the viability of republics.

And yet this form of social organization was discussed a number of times in the Mahabharata, in the accounts of Alexander's expeditions into India, and in a number of Buddhist accounts of northern Indian states as late as the second century CE. Detailed descriptions of their workings occur in the political treatises of Kautilya, and Arrian, the historian of Alexander, notes that republics such as Malla offered the Greek armies some of the fiercest resistance they encountered. Perhaps here lies a clue to what contemporaries viewed as their true strengths and vulnerabilities: All commentators insist that no form of government works better when the people are unified and have a stake in the existing order; but factionalism and division are in the end fatal. As Indian society as a whole became more complex and differentiated, the drive for political unity, so it was believed, would become that much stronger. With the creation of empires by the Mauryans and Guptas, the age of the republics in India was to pass—until 1947. Today, with its constitution and representative government, India prides itself on being the world's largest democracy.

> • Do you think Indian republics were more vulnerable than those elsewhere to problems of disunity and factionalism? What role do you think religion played in sustaining or undermining them?

Key Terms

Altruism   184

Atheistic   184

Devotional   180

Hinduism   180

Jains   182

Ritual pollution   189

Schism   183

Tariffs   188

OXFORD
insight study guide
Active Engagement, Deeper Understanding

Learn more with this chapter's digital tools, including the Oxford Insight Study Guide, at http://www.oup.com/he/vonsivers4e. Please see the Further Resources section at the back of the book for additional readings and suggested websites.

Sources for Chapter 8

The Seven Pillar Edicts of King Ashoka

ca. 247–246 BCE

The third of the Mauryan kings, Ashoka ruled a vast empire throughout the Indian subcontinent in the period 273–231 BCE. His abrupt conversion to Buddhism in 260 led him to govern according to Buddhist principles—at least as he understood them. His new policies with respect to "righteous" governance were posted in a series of edicts that were engraved on rocks and pillars at strategic spots in his empire. A sample of these contains both very specific injunctions—imposed upon himself and upon his subordinates—and general principles, which could presumably be adapted to changing real-world circumstances.

1. Beloved-of-the-Gods speaks thus: This Dharma edict was written twenty-six years after my coronation. Happiness in this world and the next is difficult to obtain without much love for the Dharma, much self-examination, much respect, much fear (of evil), and much enthusiasm. But through my instruction this regard for Dharma and love of Dharma has grown day by day, and will continue to grow. And my officers of high, low and middle rank are practicing and conforming to Dharma, and are capable of inspiring others to do the same. Mahamatras in border areas are doing the same. And these are my instructions: to protect with Dharma, to make happiness through Dharma and to guard with Dharma.

. . .

4. Beloved-of-the-Gods speaks thus: This Dharma edict was written twenty-six years after my coronation. My Rajjukas are working among the people, among many hundreds of thousands of people. The hearing of petitions and the administration of justice has been left to them so that they can do their duties confidently and fearlessly and so that they can work for the welfare, happiness and benefit of the people in the country. But they should remember what causes happiness and sorrow, and being themselves devoted to Dharma, they should encourage the people in the country (to do the same), that they may attain happiness in this world and the next. These Rajjukas are eager to serve me. They also obey other officers who know my desires, who instruct

Source: Ven. S. Dhammika, trans. DharmaNet, 1994, http://www.cs.colostate.edu/~malaiya/ashoka.html#PILLAR

the Rajjukas so that they can please me. Just as a person feels confident having entrusted his child to an expert nurse thinking: "The nurse will keep my child well," even so, the Rajjukas have been appointed by me for the welfare and happiness of the people in the country.

The hearing of petitions and the administration of justice have been left to the Rajjukas so that they can do their duties unperturbed, fearlessly and confidently. It is my desire that there should be uniformity in law and uniformity in sentencing. I even go this far, to grant a three-day stay for those in prison who have been tried and sentenced to death. During this time their relatives can make appeals to have the prisoners' lives spared. If there is none to appeal on their behalf, the prisoners can give gifts in order to make merit for the next world, or observe fasts. Indeed, it is my wish that in this way, even if a prisoner's time is limited, he can prepare for the next world, and that people's Dharma practice, self-control and generosity may grow.

Krosas: Unit of land measure.

7. Beloved-of-the-Gods, King Piyadasi, says: Along roads I have had banyan trees planted so that they can give shade to animals and men, and I have had mango groves planted. At intervals of eight **krosas**, I have had wells dug, rest-houses built, and in various places, I have had watering-places made for the use of animals and men. But these are but minor achievements. Such things to make the people happy have been done by former kings. I have done these things for this purpose, that the people might practice the Dharma.

Beloved-of-the-Gods, King Piyadasi, speaks thus: My Dharma Mahamatras too are occupied with various good works among the ascetics and householders of all religions. I have ordered that they should be occupied with the affairs of the Sangha. I have also ordered that they should be occupied with the affairs of the Brahmans and the Ajivikas. I have ordered that they be occupied with the Niganthas. In fact, I have ordered that different Mahamatras be occupied with the particular affairs of all different religions. And my Dharma Mahamatras likewise are occupied with these and other religions.

Beloved-of-the-Gods, King Piyadasi, speaks thus: These and other principal officers are occupied with the distribution of gifts, mine as well as those of the queens. In my women's quarters, they organize various charitable activities here and in the provinces. I have also ordered my sons and the sons of other queens to distribute gifts so that noble deeds of Dharma and the practice of Dharma may be promoted. And noble deeds of Dharma and the practice of Dharma consist of having kindness, generosity, truthfulness, purity, gentleness and goodness increase among the people.

Beloved-of-the-Gods, King Piyadasi, speaks thus: Whatever good deeds have been done by me, those the people accept and those they follow. Therefore they have progressed and will continue to progress by being respectful to mother and father, respectful to elders, by courtesy to the aged and proper behavior towards Brahmans and ascetics, towards the poor and distressed, and even towards servants and employees.

Beloved-of-the-Gods, King Piyadasi, speaks thus: This progress among the people through Dharma has been done by two means, by Dharma regulations and by persuasion. Of these, Dharma regulation is of little effect, while persuasion has much more effect. The Dharma regulations I have given are that various animals must be protected. And I have given many other Dharma regulations also. But it is by persuasion that progress among the people through Dharma has had a greater effect in respect of harmlessness to living beings and non-killing of living beings.

▶ Working with Sources

1. **To what extent did Ashoka claim to be occupying a paternal role in relationship to his people? Is it likely his specific instructions were actually carried out?**

2. **Are there indications here that Ashoka really aimed at creating what we might perceive as a kind of police state? In what respects?**

SOURCE 8.2   *The Questions of King Milinda (The Milindapanha)*

ca. 100 BCE

A series of Greek rulers attempted to maintain the Hellenizing goals of Alexander the Great in Bactria (modern Afghanistan), long after his death in 323 BCE. The most famous ruler in this line was Menander I (ca. 160–130 BCE), who achieved immortality in Buddhist literature by engaging in a debate with the Buddhist sage Nagasena. Their talks, set out as a series of dilemmas to be posed and (if possible) resolved, became an important exposition of Buddhist ideas and supposedly led to the conversion of Menander ("King Milinda") to Buddhism. In any event, *The Milindapanha* reflects the fusion of Greek and Indian traditions of philosophy, in the fascinating cauldron of world contact that existed in central and South Asia.

DILEMMA THE FORTY-SECOND. MODERATION IN FOOD.

4. 'Venerable Nâgasena, the Blessed One said:
"Be not remiss as to (the rules to be observed) when standing up (to beg for food). Be restrained in (matters relating to) the stomach."

Source: T. W. Rhys Davids, trans., *The Questions of King Milinda*, vol. 2 (Oxford: Clarendon, 1894), 4–7 and 20–22.

But on the other hand he said:

"Now there were several days, Udâyin, on which I ate out of this bowl when it was full to the brim, and ate even more."

"Now if the first rule be true, then the second statement must be false. But if the statement be true, then the rule first quoted must be wrong.

This too is a double-edged problem, now put to you, which you have to solve."

5. 'He who has no self-control as regards the stomach, O king, will destroy living creatures, will take possession of what has not been given to him, will be unchaste, will speak lies, will drink strong drink, will put his mother or his father to death, will slay an Arahat, will create a schism in the Order, will even with malice aforethought wound a Tathâgata. Was it not, O king, when without restraint as to his stomach, that Devadatta by breaking up the Order, heaped up for himself karma that would endure for a kalpa? It was on calling to mind this, O king, and many other things of the same kind, that the Blessed One declared:

"Be not remiss as to (the rules to be observed) when standing up (to beg for food). Be restrained in (matters relating to) the stomach."

6. 'And he who has self-control as regards the stomach gains a clear insight into the Four Truths, realizes the Four Fruits of the life of renunciation, and attains to mastery over the Four Discriminations, the Eight Attainments, and the Six Modes of Higher Knowledge, and fulfils all that goes to constitute the life of the recluse. Did not the parrot fledgling, O king, by self-restraint as to his stomach, cause the very heaven of the great Thirty-Three to shake, and bring down Sakka, the king of the gods, to wait upon him? It was on calling to mind this, O king, and many other things of a similar kind, that the Blessed One declared:

"Be not remiss as to (the rules to be observed) when standing up (to beg for food). Be restrained in (matters relating to) the stomach."

7. 'But when, O king, the Blessed One said: "Now there were several days, Udâyi, on which I ate out of this bowl when it was full to the brim, and ate even more," that was said by him who had completed his task, who had finished all that he had to do, who had accomplished the end he set before him, who had overcome every obstruction, by the self-dependent Tathâgata himself about himself.

Just, O king, as it is desirable that a sick man to whom an emetic, or a purge, or a clyster has been administered, should be treated with a tonic; just so, O king, should the man who is full of evil, and who has not perceived the Four Truths, adopt the practice of restraint in the matter of eating. But just, O king, as there is no necessity of polishing, and rubbing down, and purifying a diamond gem of great brilliancy, of the finest water, and of natural purity; just so, O king, is there no restraint as to what actions he should perform, on the

Tathâgata, on him who hath attained to perfection in all that lies within the scope of a Buddha.'

'Very good, Nâgasena! That is so, and I accept it as you say.'

DILEMMA THE FORTY-SIXTH. THE MOCKING OF THE BUDDHA.

19. 'Venerable Nâgasena, it was said by the Blessed One of Six-tusks, the elephant king,

> "When he sought to slay him, and had reached him with his trunk,
> He perceived the yellow robe, the badge of a recluse,
> Then, though smarting with the pain, the thought possessed his heart,—
> 'He who wears the outward garb the Arahats wear
> Must be scatheless held, and sacred, by the good.'"

'But on the other hand it is said:

"When he was Gotipâla, the young Brahman, he reviled and abused Kassapa the Blessed One, the Arahat, the Buddha supreme, with vile and bitter words, calling him a shaveling and a good-for-nothing monk."

'Now if, Nâgasena, the Bodisat, even when he was an animal, respected the yellow robe, then the statement that as Gotipâla, a Brahman, he reviled and abused the Blessed One of that time, must be false. But if as a Brahman, he reviled and abused the Blessed One, the statement that when he was Six-tusks, the elephant king, he respected the yellow robe, must be false. If when the Bodisat was an animal, though he was suffering severe and cruel and bitter pain, he respected the yellow robe which the hunter had put on, how was it that when he was a man, a man arrived at discretion, with all his knowledge mature, he did not pay reverence, on seeing him, to Kassapa the Blessed One, the Arahat, the Buddha supreme, one endowed with the ten powers, the leader of the world, the highest of the high, round whom effulgence spread a fathom on every side, and who was clad in most excellent and precious and delicate Benares cloth made into yellow robes? This too is a double-edged problem, now put to you, which you have to solve.'

20. 'The verse you have quoted, O king, was spoken by the Blessed One. And Kassapa the Blessed One, the Arahat, the Buddha supreme, was abused and reviled by Gotipâla the young Brahman with vile and bitter words, with the epithets of shaveling and good-for-nothing monk. But that was owing to his birth and family surroundings. For Gotipâla, O king, was descended from a family of unbelievers, men void of faith. His mother and father, his sisters and brothers, the bondswomen and bondsmen, the hired servants and dependents in the house, were worshippers of Brahmâ, reverers of Brahmâ; and harboring the idea that Brahmans were the highest and most honorable among men, they reviled and loathed those others who had renounced the world. It was through hearing what they said that Gotipâla, when invited by Ghatîkâra the potter to visit the teacher, replied: "What's the good to you of visiting that shaveling, that good-for-nothing monk?"

21. 'Just, O king, as even nectar when mixed with poison will turn sour, just as the coolest water in contact with fire will become warm, so was it that Gotipâla, the young Brahman, having been born and brought up in a family of unbelievers, men void of faith, thus reviled and abused the Tathâgata after the manner of his kind. And just, O king, as a flaming and burning mighty fire, if, even when at the height of its glory, it should come into contact with water, would cool down, with its splendor and glory spoilt, and turn to cinders, black as rotten blighted fruits—just so, O king, Gotipâla, full as he was of merit and faith, mighty as was the glory of his knowledge, yet when reborn into a family of unbelievers, of men void of faith, he became, as it were, blind, and reviled and abused the Tathâgata. But when he had gone to him, and had come to know the virtues of the Buddhas which he had, then did he become as his hired servant; and having renounced the world and entered the Order under the system of the Conqueror, he gained the fivefold power of insight, and the eightfold power of ecstatic meditation, and became assured of rebirth into the Brahmâ heaven.'

'Very good, Nâgasena! That is so, and I accept it as you say.'

▶ Working
with Sources

1. To what extent does this dialogue reflect elements of the Greek philosophical tradition, explored in Chapter 7?

2. How do both speakers deploy real-world examples, in order to enhance their philosophical arguments?

SOURCE 8.3 Fa Xian, excerpt from *A Record of Buddhistic Kingdoms*

The difficulties of translating and interpreting Buddhist scriptures (sutras) in the early centuries of Chinese Buddhism prompted pilgrims and travelers to seek them at their source. One of the earliest of these, Fa Xian, journeyed to India and Sri Lanka from 399 to 414 CE and left us one of the few descriptions of Buddhism in India from that time. Here he describes the vital influence of the earlier rule of Ashoka in his description of Pataliputra, the modern city of Patna.

PÂṬALIPUTTRA OR PATNA, IN MAGADHA. KING AŚOKA'S SPIRIT-BUILT PALACE AND HALLS. THE BUDDHIST BRAHMAN, RÂDHA-SÂMI. DISPENSARIES AND HOSPITALS.

Having crossed the river, and descended south for a yojana, [the travellers] came to the town of Pâṭaliputtra, in the kingdom of Magadha, the city where king Aśoka ruled. The royal palace and halls in the midst of the city, which exist now as of old, were all made by spirits which he employed, and which piled up the stones, reared the walls and gates, and executed the elegant carving and inlaid sculpture-work,—in a way which no human hands of this world could accomplish.

King Aśoka had a younger brother who had attained to be an Arhat, and resided on Gṛidhra-kûṭa hill, finding his delight in solitude and quiet. The king, who sincerely reverenced him, wished and begged him [to come and live] in his family, where he could supply all his wants. The other, however, through his delight in the stillness of the mountain, was unwilling to accept the invitation, on which the king said to him, "Only accept my invitation, and I will make a hill for you inside the city." Accordingly, he provided the materials of a feast, called to him the spirits, and announced to them, "To-morrow you will all receive my invitation; but as there are no mats for you to sit on, let each one bring [his own seat]." Next day the spirits came, each one bringing with him a great rock, [like] a wall, four or five paces square, [for a seat]. When their sitting was over, the king made them form a hill with the large stones piled on one another, and also at the foot of the hill, with five large square stones, to make an apartment, which might be more than thirty cubits long, twenty cubits wide, and more than ten cubits high.

In this city there had resided a great Brahman, named Râdha-sâmi, a professor of the mahâyâna, of clear discernment and much wisdom, who understood everything, living by himself in spotless purity. The king of the country honoured and reverenced him, and served him as his teacher. If he went to

Source: James Legge, trans., *A Record of Buddhistic Kingdoms* (New York: Dover, 1965), 77–78.

inquire for and greet him, the king did not presume to sit down alongside of him; and if, in his love and reverence, he took hold of his hand, as soon as he let it go, the Brahman made haste to pour water on it and wash it. He might be more than fifty years old, and all the kingdom looked up to him. By means of this one man, the Law of Buddha was widely made known, and the followers of other doctrines did not find it in their power to persecute the body of monks in any way.

By the side of the tope of Aśoka, there has been made a mahâyâna monastery, very grand and beautiful; there is also a hînayâna one; the two together containing six hundred or seven hundred monks. The rules of demeanour and the scholastic arrangements in them are worthy of observation.

▶ **Working with Sources:**

1. What features of the region does Fa Xian find most striking?
2. Given that this period is generally seen as the "classical" period of Hinduism in India, how does Fa Xian appear to see the status of Buddhism?

SOURCE 8.4 Kalidasa, *The Cloud Messenger*

ca. fourth–fifth centuries CE

Sometimes described as the "Shakespeare of India," Kalidasa mastered various literary genres in his lifetime and continued to thrive, even in Western translations, into modern times. He composed three plays, two epic poems, and a series of shorter poems. Among these is *The Cloud Messenger*, in which a man asks a passing cloud to carry a message to his beloved wife, who is awaiting him in the Himalayas. Translated from the Sanskrit into English in the early nineteenth century, *The Cloud Messenger* served as the inspiration for composer Gustav Holst's 1910–1912 choral work *The Cloud Messenger*.

Yaksha: A demigod attendant to the god of wealth.

A certain **yaksha** who had been negligent in the execution of his own duties, on account of a curse from his master which was to be endured for a year and which was onerous as it separated him from his beloved, made his residence among the hermitages of Ramagiri, whose waters were blessed by the bathing of the daughter of Janaka and whose shade trees grew in profusion.

That lover, separated from his beloved, whose gold armlet had slipped from his bare forearm, having dwelt on that mountain for some months, on the first day of the month of Asadha, saw a cloud embracing the summit, which resembled a mature elephant playfully butting a bank.

Source: The Cloud Messenger - Part 01, http://allpoetry.com/poem/8526541-The-Cloud-Messenger---Part-01-by-Kalidasa

Managing with difficulty to stand up in front of that cloud which was the cause of the renewal of his enthusiasm, that attendant of the king of kings, pondered while holding back his tears. Even the mind of a happy person is excited at the sight of a cloud. How much more so, when the one who longs to cling to his neck is far away?

As the month of Nabhas was close at hand, having as his goal the sustaining of the life of his beloved and wishing to cause the tidings of his own welfare to be carried by the cloud, the delighted being spoke kind words of welcome to the cloud to which offerings of fresh kutaja flowers had been made.

Owing to his impatience, not considering the incompatibility between a cloud consisting of vapor, light, water and wind and the contents of his message best delivered by a person of normal faculties, the yaksha made this request to the cloud, for among sentient and non-sentient things, those afflicted by desire are naturally miserable:

Without doubt, your path unimpeded, you will see your brother's wife, intent on counting the days, faithful and living on. The bond of hope generally sustains the quickly sinking hearts of women who are alone, and which wilt like flowers.

Just as the favorable wind drives you slowly onward, this cataka cuckoo, your kinsman, calls sweetly on the left. Knowing the season for fertilization, cranes, like threaded garlands in the sky, lovely to the eye, will serve you.

Siddhas: Experts in spiritual matters.

Your steady passage observed by charming female **siddhas** who in trepidation wonder 'Has the summit been carried off the mountain by the wind?,' you who are heading north, fly up into the sky from this place where the nicula trees flourish, avoiding on the way the blows of the trunks of the elephants of the four quarters of the sky....

Even though the route would be circuitous for one who, like you, is northward-bound, do not turn your back on the love on the palace roofs in Ujjayini. If you do not enjoy the eyes with flickering eyelids of the women startled by bolts of lightning there, then you have been deceived!

On the way, after you have ascended to the Nirvandhya River, whose girdles are flocks of birds calling on account of the turbulence of her waves, whose gliding motion is rendered delightful with stumbling steps, and whose exposed navel is her eddies, fill yourself with water, for amorous distraction is a woman's first expression of love for their beloved.

When you have passed that, you should duly adopt the means by which the Sindhu River may cast off her emaciation—she whose waters have become like a single braid of hair, whose complexion is made pale by the old leaves falling from the trees on her banks, and who shows you goodwill because she has been separated from you, O fortunate one.

...

Even if you arrive at Mahakala at some other time, O cloud, you should wait until the sun passes from the range of the eye. Playing the honorable role of drum at the evening offering to Shiva, you will receive the full reward for your deep thunder.

There, their girdles jingling to their footsteps, and their hands tired from the pretty waving of fly-whisks whose handles are brilliant with the sparkle of jewels, having received from you raindrops at the onset of the rainy season that soothe the scratches made by fingernails, the courtesans cast you lingering sidelong glances that resemble rows of honey-bees.

Then, settled above the forests whose trees are like uplifted arms, being round in shape, producing an evening light, red as a fresh China-rose, at the start of Shiva's dance, remove his desire for a fresh elephant skin—you whose devotion is beheld by Parvati, her agitation stilled and her gaze transfixed.

▶ Working with Sources

1. How do the places seen by the cloud on its journey relate to the husband's feeling of longing for his wife?

2. How are the outer and inner worlds connected in this poem?

World Period Two

The Age of Empires and Visionaries, 600 BCE–600 CE

In the middle of the first millennium BCE, two major transformations changed the course of world history.

- **Empires in Eurasia** Two types of conquering kingdoms or empires formed, after Akkad had pioneered this form of polity during the first world period. The first type, in the Middle East, Mediterranean, and India, was that of multiethnic and multireligious empires, which followed each other in sequence. The second type consisted of the ethnically and religiously more uniform empires of Egypt and China.

- **Visionaries and the Adoption of State Religions** Around 700–500 BCE, visionaries arose who proclaimed the idea of personal salvation. They anchored this idea in the higher, absolute standard of monotheism or monism, which was not bound to any state on Earth. Followers of the visionaries formed communities and schools based on texts that expounded monotheistic or monist teachings. Eventually, rulers adopted these teachings and turned them into state religions.

Chapter 9

China

Imperial Unification and Perfecting the Moral Order, 722 BCE–618 CE

CHAPTER NINE PATTERNS

Origins, Interactions, and Adaptations The Warring States Period (403–221 BCE) culminated in China's first empire, the Qin. Its successor, the Han Dynasty, became China's longest-lived dynasty and the model for those to come. Its interactions included trading and warring with nomadic peoples, pushing west to control the Silk Road, diplomatic and trade relations with Rome, and the invasion of Korea and Vietnam. After a 350-year interruption, the empire was reunified in 589. The systems of government and Confucian ideology developed by the Han and subsequently refined would dominate Chinese empires until 1912.

Uniqueness and Similarities China's emperor-centered, bureaucratically run dynasties would help it achieve stability for over 2,000 years. Two of China's "Three Beliefs"—Confucianism and Daoism—are the products of the "Hundred Schools of Thought" that arose during China's Warring States Period. Confucianism would go on to dominate the governmental systems of much of East Asia.

China contributed two key figures to the list of Axial Age visionaries: Confucius and Laozi. Buddhism, the third of the Three Beliefs, arrived in the first century CE, developing multiple schools in China, and becoming a vehicle through which the full spectrum of Chinese culture spread to Central Asia, East Asia, and Vietnam. As with India, it connected China to a Buddhist sphere of pilgrimage and trade that peaked between 600–1000 CE.

"**V**enerable sir, since you have not considered a thousand *li* too far to come, may I presume that you bring something that may profit my kingdom?" Even today one can sense the air of challenge, however polite, in the question. The speaker, King Hui of Liang, had seen his kingdom steadily eroded by powerful surrounding states at the height of China's Warring States period (403–221 BCE).

The "venerable sir" to whom he addressed his question, however, was in no mood to banter. Warming to his topic, the Confucian sage Mencius laid out his rebuttal:

> Why must your Majesty use that word "profit?" What I am provided with, are counsels to benevolence and righteousness, and these are my only topics. If Your Majesty say, "What is to be done to profit my kingdom?" the great officers will say, "What is to be done to profit our families?" and the inferior officers and the common people will say, "What is to be done to profit our persons?" Superiors and inferiors will try to snatch this profit the one from the other, and the kingdom will be endangered . . . There never has been a benevolent man who neglected his parents. There never has been a righteous man who made his sovereign an after consideration.

> —James Legge, trans., *The Works of Mencius*
> (New York: Dover Reprint, 1970, pp. 125–126)

Chastened but intrigued, King Hui and his son and successor, Xiang, finally said to Mencius, "I wish quietly to receive your instructions."

This story from the opening pages of the fourth-century BCE *Book of Mencius* illustrates the ultimate direction of Chinese political thought, the way Chinese ideas would influence nearby peoples, and, more generally, the larger pattern of empires and states adopting the ideas of visionary thinkers. As we shall see, starting with Confucius—from whom Mencius drew his ideas—Chinese thinkers suggested ways of looking at the world,

CHAPTER OUTLINE

Visionaries and Empire

The Domestic Economy: Society, Family, and Gender

Intellectual Trends, Aesthetics, Science, and Technology

Putting It All Together

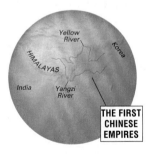

ABOVE: One of the world's most recognized structures, this section of the Great Wall near Beijing was upgraded in the early fifteenth century CE.

Seeing Patterns

❯ Was the First Emperor's ruthlessness justified by his accomplishments in his empire?

❯ How would you compare the values expressed by Confucius and Mencius to those of contemporary society?

❯ How have historians viewed the role of women in early imperial China?

how to behave in it, and how to govern it that ranged from radically abstract to firmly practical, from collective to individualistic, and from an absence of active government to near totalitarianism.

Visionaries and Empire

The period from the eighth century BCE until the first unification of China under the Qin in 221 BCE is regarded as China's most fertile period of intellectual exploration. The foundations of nearly every important school of Chinese philosophy were laid during this era. Of these various systems, those that had the greatest impact were Confucianism, Legalism, and Daoism.

Confucianism, Legalism, and Daoism

The historical Confucius is an elusive figure. According to traditional accounts, he was born in 551 BCE to a family named Kong. In Confucian texts he is referred to as "the Master" (*zi* or *fuzi*) or "Master Kong" (*Kong fuzi*) [kong FOO-zuh], and European Roman Catholic missionaries in China during the seventeenth century rendered *Kong fuzi* into Latin as "Confucius." As a member of the growing *shi* class (see Chapter 4), Confucius sought a position as political adviser to the courts of Zhou states in northern China. However, like the visionaries of India, he spent most of his life as an itinerant teacher, spreading his ideas about ethics and politics to a growing group of followers.

Confucian Doctrine   Confucius has been called "China's first great moralist." His teachings—as presented in the *Lunyu*, or *Analects*, the central Confucian text—see human beings as inclined toward ethical behavior and human society as a perfectible moral order. According to Confucius, there are certain fundamental patterns that are manifestations of the *Dao* ("Way") of the universal order.

One of these fundamental patterns is the relationship between parent and offspring. People develop their moral character to reflect well upon their parents and serve those in higher social or political stations as they serve their own parents. This example of human society as a kind of extended family applies at every level; indeed, drawing on the idea of the Mandate of Heaven (see Chapter 4), Confucius makes the ruler himself responsible to heaven for his country. Emperors in later regimes would habitually refer to themselves as the "sons of heaven," to emphasize this filial duty.

For Confucius, mutual obligations serve as checks on the arbitrary exercise of power. Hence, when asked to sum up his thinking in one word, Confucius answered, "**Reciprocity**: Do not do unto others what you would not have them do to you." Confucius believed that individuals should strive for the qualities of *ren* (a comprehensive understanding of and practice of humane action) by practicing *li* (usually translated as "ritual": the observance of rules of decorum as guides to appropriate behavior toward others). People who did so would not only perfect their own character but also set an example for the rest of society.

Reciprocity: Mutual exchange of things, ideas, etc.

Confucian Government   Confucius lived during a time of social and political disorder. His teachings center on ways to restore order and make government and society more humane. But because Confucian doctrine emphasizes personal responsibility, the structure of government is far less important than the ethical fitness of the ruler and the people. Good government, according to Confucius, begins with educated leaders and officials of strong moral character. To describe this ideal of behavior, Confucius introduced the concept of the **junzi** ("the superior man" or "gentleman"). Those who attain these ideals comprise a kind of aristocracy of merit, while rulers with these qualities set an example for their subjects.

Just as the *junzi* cultivated his personal ethics and morals, a state run by *junzi* would spread these values to society by fostering ritual and social institutions that encouraged proper behavior. The observance of *li* (ritual) would make appropriate behavior routine and help people to develop a sense of right and wrong, thus acquiring a stake in the social order.

Confucius died in 479 BCE. Two later students of Confucian doctrine, Mencius and Xunzi [SHYOON-zuh], continued to spread his teachings, with their own contributions. Despite challenges from competing philosophical schools, Confucian ideals ultimately became the standard for Chinese politics and scholarship.

Junzi: According to Confucius, the "superior man" or "gentleman" who behaves according to an ethical and moral ideal. A society run by *junzi* will foster social institutions that encourage proper behavior.

Mencius   By Mencius's time, in the fourth century BCE, the continual warfare among the Zhou states had led many thinkers to question assumptions about the private and the social good. Their answers varied from radical individualism to universal love and altruism.

Mencius (*Mengzi*, or Master Meng; ca. 385–312 BCE), like Confucius, believed that people were fundamentally good and that individuals must continually work to refine this goodness in order to avoid being led astray by negative influences. He concluded that the way to proper behavior is through cultivating the Confucian virtues as a bulwark against negative forces.

The *Mengzi*, or *Book of Mencius*, is written in more of a narrative form than the *Analects*. Its most powerful sections deal with the obligations of rulers to their subjects. A ruler's primary duty for Mencius is to maintain the "people's livelihood" and uphold the "righteousness" of the state. A state ruled by righteousness and humanity ensured that the people would be prosperous and orderly. A ruler who abused or neglected his subjects upset the social order and the natural tendency of people toward good. In such a case, the people had the right and the obligation to invoke the Mandate of Heaven and depose him. In the end, said Mencius, the people, not the ruler, are the foundation of the state.

Xunzi   As states grew increasingly powerful and warfare more deadly, Mencius's optimistic view of human nature seemed less practical to many. Like Mencius, Xunzi (trad. ca. 310–219? BCE) was also a student of Confucian philosophy but had a much

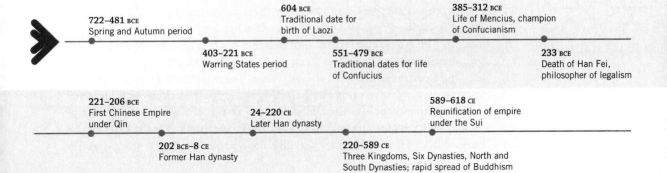

722–481 BCE
Spring and Autumn period

604 BCE
Traditional date for
birth of Laozi

385–312 BCE
Life of Mencius, champion
of Confucianism

403–221 BCE
Warring States period

551–479 BCE
Traditional dates for life
of Confucius

233 BCE
Death of Han Fei,
philosopher of legalism

221–206 BCE
First Chinese Empire
under Qin

24–220 CE
Later Han dynasty

589–618 CE
Reunification of empire
under the Sui

202 BCE–8 CE
Former Han dynasty

220–589 CE
Three Kingdoms, Six Dynasties, North and
South Dynasties; rapid spread of Buddhism

darker view of human nature. During the Warring States period, Xunzi came to believe that individuals were self-involved creatures capable of regulating themselves only through immense effort. Only by enforcing the restraints of civilization could individuals approach the Confucian ideals of virtue and humanity. Thus, by the end of the third century BCE, Confucian thinkers had come to radically opposed conclusions about the nature of human beings. Xunzi's pessimism formed the basis of the Legalist school that finally restored order and created the first Chinese empire.

Legalism   For Legalists, building a strong state was of the utmost importance. Out of Xunzi's view of humans as inclined toward evil, his students Han Fei (d. 233 BCE) and Li Si (d. 208 BCE) developed laws and practices based on the absolute will of the ruler. Order in a state, they claimed, could be implemented only through the institution of strict laws imposed on all subjects. Since Legalists believed that compliance on small matters led to compliance on larger ones, they imposed harsh punishments for even tiny infractions. The Legalists argued that all subjects must serve the state through productive activities, especially agriculture and military service. Other occupations were discouraged, and idlers were put to work by force. Only government-approved history and literature were tolerated. Although **Legalism** had many critics, it was its strict practices, not the more moderate ideals of Confucianism or Daoism, that imposed order on China.

Legalism: School of thought first articulated by Xunzi (310–219 BCE) that saw humans as greedy and selfish and urged leaders to adopt strict rules to prevent their subjects from doing evil.

Daoism   While most Chinese philosophical schools accepted the Dao as the ordering principle of the universe, they differed as to the means of achieving harmony with it. For Confucians, study and self-cultivation put the individual in tune with the Dao. For followers of the Daoist tradition, attributed to Laozi (Lao Tzu), however, the Confucian path prevented genuine understanding of and harmony with the Dao. The historical Laozi is even more obscure than Confucius. In fact, many scholars believe Laozi to be a mythical figure. Chinese tradition cites his birth date as 604 BCE and gives his name as Li Er.

For Daoists the **Dao** was not the ordering force *within* the universe but the transcendent first principle *beyond* the universe. The Confucian Dao can be named; the Daoist Dao, like the relationship in Hinduism between atman and brahman, cannot be named. The Dao is beyond all dualities and unifies them in a great whole. Since the Dao transcends the world, including all such opposites as "good" and "evil," no single path of action would lead an individual to union with it. To choose the good, as the Confucians do, is therefore to follow only a limited part of the universal Dao. Instead, the Daoists taught that only through self-reflection and contemplation of paradoxes might an individual come to know the Dao.

Dao: The transcendent first principle beyond the universe. Daoists teach that only through self-reflection and contemplation of paradoxes can an individual come to know the Dao.

Daoism and Government   Daoist political theory held that the best government was that which governed least. Here, the key idea is one from the most famous Daoist work, the *Daode Jing* (*The Classic of the Way and Virtue*, often spelled *Tao Te Ching*): "By non-action there is nothing that is not done." The ruler should not push specific policies but rather let all things take their natural course, for even as they run to extremes they will always reverse. The ruler's understanding of these universal cycles leads to union with the Dao and keeps the world in equilibrium.

These three schools of thought were all to play a role in the development of China's political and cultural life. Confucianism would provide the basis for the bureaucracy of China's empires and ideals of a perfectible moral order; Daoism would provide the mystical dimension of Chinese culture; finally, Legalism would unify the last of the warring states into a single structure under the Qin [chin].

The Qin Dynasty

The Qin state ultimately claimed victory over its opponents and established centralized rule throughout China. Qin had several powerful advantages over its competitors. Its position on the western fringe of the Zhou world meant that it was free to expand its economic base by promising land to peasant cultivators as the state seized territory on its western frontier.

Qin and Zhou   The agricultural surplus that resulted from these land grants led to increased prosperity for the state. Qin's location was also a benefit when it came to military preparedness. Many of the warring states were in close proximity to each other, and the constant battles among them depleted their economic and military resources. Qin, on the other hand, was not surrounded by powerful hostile states and so could participate in limited military campaigns, mostly against nomadic groups, which strengthened their fighting skills but did not upset their economy or weaken their army. By 350 BCE, Qin rulers reorganized the state by eliminating the last of the old Zhou institutions and replacing them with a centralized system that anticipated a number of later Legalist principles. In 256 BCE, the Qin conquered Zhou itself (see Map 9.1).

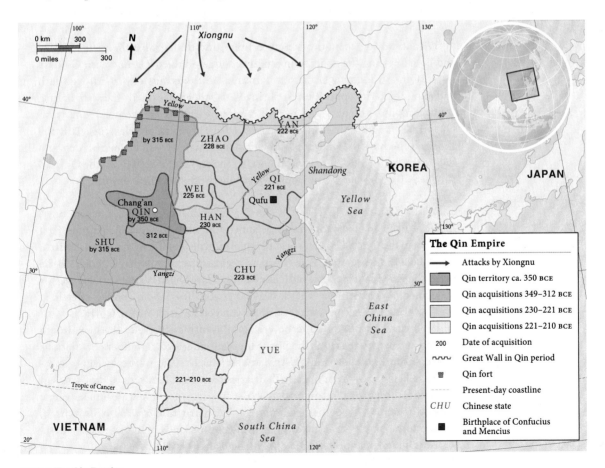

MAP 9.1 The Qin Empire

Terra-Cotta Warriors at the First Emperor's Tomb. One of the most important archaeological finds of the twentieth century, the Qin burial complex, was discovered in 1974 by a local farmer digging a well. Over 5,000 figures have been unearthed so far, all with individualized features. The dig has been enclosed and a museum built on site. Along with the Great Wall, it is one of China's most popular tourist destinations.

With its strong economy, expert military, and the Legalist theorists Han Fei and Li Si advising the court, Qin rapidly conquered the other northern Chinese states. Qin armies, now swollen to hundreds of thousands of men, drove south and eliminated the opposition of the many tribal peoples below the state of Yue, continuing into the northern part of modern Vietnam. In the north and west, Qin armies fought a series of campaigns to drive nomadic peoples, especially the Xiongnu (perhaps the ancestors of the Huns), from newly established borders and secure the trade routes into central Asia. By the end of the 220s BCE, the Qin had subdued all of the states that would constitute the first Chinese empire.

The First Emperor   In 221 BCE, the Qin ruler Cheng (r. 246–221 as Qin ruler; 221–209 BCE as First Emperor) proclaimed himself Qin Shi Huangdi, the First Emperor of the Qin, and with Li Si as his chief minister instituted the Legalist system throughout the new empire. As a safeguard against attacks by nomadic peoples in the north, the First Emperor deployed tens of thousands of forced laborers to join together the numerous defensive walls of the old Zhou states. This massive project stretching over 1,400 miles would become the first iteration of the Great Wall of China.

With virtually unlimited resources and the ruthless drive of the Legalists to expand and fortify the state, the First Emperor undertook a number of ambitious projects. The Chinese writing system was standardized, as were all weights, measures, and coinage—even the length of axles on carts. Hundreds of thousands of conscript laborers worked on roads, canals, and irrigation and water conservancy projects. The First Emperor also ordered the construction of a tomb for himself, a mammoth complex that included an army of thousands of life-sized terra-cotta warriors intended to protect Qin Shi Huangdi after his death.

From his palace in Chang'an, the site of modern Xi'an, the First Emperor tightened his control. Scholars, particularly Confucians, who objected to government policies were buried alive. Any literature not officially sanctioned by the government was destroyed. Writers of the following Han dynasty have left accounts of mass executions of dissenting scholars.

When Qin Shi Huangdi died, his exhausted subjects erupted in rebellion. Minister Li Si provoked additional discontent by conspiring to keep the First Emperor's death a secret in order to rule as regent for the monarch's son. He was captured attempting to flee the rebellion and executed in 208 BCE; after mutilating him his captors systematically dismembered him in accordance with Qin law. After a brief civil war, a general named Liu Bang restored order to the region. He proclaimed himself emperor in 202 BCE and called his new dynasty the Han.

The Han Dynasty

If the Qin constructed the Chinese empire, the Han perfected it. Like the Roman Empire with which it is frequently compared, the Han developed a centralized political system of rule that blended the administrative structures of the Qin with more moderate Confucian ideals of government as a moral agent. This model of rule endured—with some interruptions and modifications—for over 2,000 years.

Unlike earlier rulers who came from aristocratic families, Liu Bang, who had taken the reign name Gaozu (r. 202–195 BCE), had been a peasant. Perhaps because of this background, he had little interest in restoring the decentralized system of the Zhou, which favored the aristocratic classes. Instead, he left intact the Qin structure of centralized ministries and regional **commanderies**. Han rulers reduced taxes and labor obligations and rescinded the most severe punishments imposed under the Qin. Han rulers altered the Qin system of leveling social classes by instituting uniform rules for different segments of society—aristocrats as well as commoners. Under the Han, the upper ranks of society were taxed at lighter rates and exempted from most forms of corporal punishment.

Commanderies: Districts under the control of a military commander.

As the Han Empire expanded, so did its bureaucracy. Officials were divided into graded ranks ranging from the heads of imperial ministries to district magistrates. Below these officials were clan leaders and village **headmen**. Landowners were to collect and remit the taxes for themselves and their tenants, while the lower officials recorded the rates and amounts, kept track of the labor obligations of the district, and mobilized the people during emergencies.

Headmen: Local leaders; these were usually chosen by the people of the village, clan, district, etc., rather than appointed by the government.

Wudi, the Martial Emperor   Like both his predecessors and successors, Wudi, whose reign name means "Martial Emperor" (r. ca. 140–87 BCE), faced the problem of defending the empire's northern and western boundaries from nomadic peoples, especially the Xiongnu. He extended the Great Wall begun by the Qin to provide greater protection. Hoping that a strong Chinese presence would discourage invaders, Wudi encouraged people to move to areas along the northern and western borders of the empire (see Map 9.2).

Wudi worked to suppress Xiongnu raids on central Asian trade routes, especially the Silk Road. He made diplomatic efforts, offering the Xiongnu supplies, but when those efforts failed, he mounted military campaigns against them. The Han also adopted the practice of "**sinicizing**" the nomadic peoples, which involved encouraging nomadic peoples to assimilate themselves to Chinese

Sinicizing: The pattern by which newcomers to areas dominated by Chinese culture were encouraged to adopt that culture for themselves.

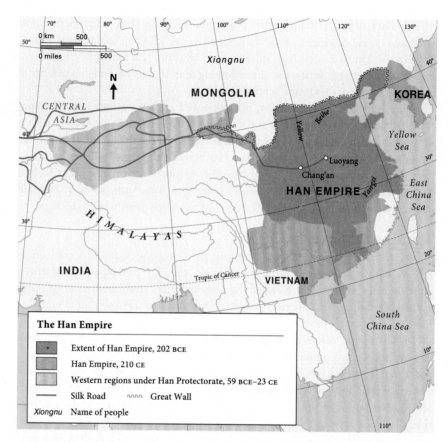

MAP 9.2 **The Han Empire**

culture and identity. Once they had been assimilated, the threat of nomadic invasion would be lessened. Wudi drove his armies into central Asia, northern Vietnam and Korea, extending Han rule into those areas. Along with the imposition of Han rule came the Chinese writing system and Confucian ideology and practices.

Wang Mang and the Red Eyebrow Revolt   The Han era has traditionally been divided into the Former, or Western, Han (202 BCE–8 CE) and the Latter, or Eastern, Han (24–220 CE). During the brief interval between 8 and 24 CE, Han rule was temporarily interrupted when a relative of the royal family, Wang Mang (45 BCE–23 CE), seized power. Wang Mang attempted to reform land distribution in an effort to reduce the huge disparity between rich landowners and peasants and tenant farmers. Wang Mang's proposed reforms provoked a revolt led by a Daoist secret society called the Red Eyebrows who killed Wang Mang and sacked the capital of Chang'an. An imperial relative restored the Han dynasty in 24 CE but moved the capital east to Luoyang, where the empire continued in somewhat reduced size. Wang Mang's attempts at land reform and the Red Eyebrow revolt hastened the collapse of the last of the old aristocratic landholdings. Together with the sense of renewal accompanying the restoration of the Han dynasty, these events temporarily masked the empire's growing weakness.

Han Decline   By the late second century CE, the Han dynasty was showing signs of strain. Ambitious infrastructural improvements ordered by Han emperors were carried out by peasant labor required by the government as a form of taxation. This made it difficult for peasants to farm, and agricultural productivity declined. Furthermore, the loss of some borderland territory reduced the tax base just when the empire required more revenue to maintain the Great Wall and military outposts protecting the empire from nomadic invasions. Battles within the royal family, aggravated by increasing regional power falling into the hands of Han generals and a Daoist revolt after 184 CE, finally brought the Han dynasty to an end in 220 CE.

Between Empires   After the collapse of the Han, China experienced its most chaotic post-imperial political period. This interlude of turmoil is traditionally divided into the era of the Three Kingdoms (220–280 CE), the overlapping Six Dynasties period (222–589 CE), and the also overlapping period of the North and South Dynasties (317–589 CE).

From the initial Three Kingdoms period through the numerous short-lived "dynasties" that followed, the aim of reconstituting the empire was always present. Parallels with the problems besetting the Roman Empire at the same time were striking: The growing power of landed elites, the increasing weakness of the bureaucracy, and the defense problems of the north and west all persisted. In the absence of effective centralized administration, the infrastructure fell into disrepair, the internal economy grew more regionalized, external trade declined, and warfare, famine, and banditry haunted the land.

Unlike the fall of the Roman Empire in the west, however, by the fifth century CE the rebuilding process had begun, when an eastern Turkic people whom the Chinese called the Toba established the state of Northern Wei in northern China. Taking advantage of the new military tactics growing from the development of the stirrup, Northern Wei established itself as a dominant power in the region. By the beginning of the sixth century, the Toba had a formal policy of assimilating into Chinese culture—taking Chinese names, marrying into leading families, reviving old imperial rites, and carrying out limited land reform. In organizing land redistribution to the peasants, they helped pave the way for the return of centralized administration, military service, and tax collection. A Toba general named Yang Jian succeeded in uniting most of the old Han lands in 589 CE and called the reunified dynasty the Sui (589–618 CE) (see Map 9.3).

The Empire Reclaimed   The Sui pursuit of empire building—particularly an ill-conceived invasion of the Korean peninsula after 589 CE—prompted unrest. The Sui used forced labor for construction projects, including palaces, roads, and the Grand Canal. Linking the Yangzi River with the Yellow River, the Grand Canal facilitated shipment of food crops from the south to the capital at Chang'an. The Grand Canal, still in operation today, proved vital as northern capitals increasingly depended on food supplies shipped from the south.

Patterns Up Close | The Stirrup

The stirrup joins the long list of familiar Chinese path-breaking technologies such as paper, the compass, printing, the horse collar, and gunpowder. The stirrup has been recognized by historians as being of major importance. It not only completely changed the way humans used horses but also ushered in a new type of warfare that altered the structure of societies and dominated military strategy for 1,000 years.

Although the horse had been employed in Eurasian warfare for over 2,000 years, its utility had been limited to pulling chariots and supporting mounted archers and riders with light spears. With the introduction of the large, powerful Nisean horse to the forces of the Persian Empire around 430 BCE, militaries began to deploy *cataphracts*, heavily armored cavalry. The central problem, however, of using such horses in pitched battles was the difficulty of mounting a horse when one was weighed down with armor and weapons and the ease with which one could be unhorsed, especially in close combat.

Around the beginning of the Common Era, the first attempts at saddles with straps for supporting a rider's feet began to appear in northern India. But these employed only a simple toe loop, and the saddle concentrated the rider's weight on a small area of the horse's back, tiring the animal. This idea for the stirrup appears to have spread via the Silk Road, and by the early 300s CE a recognizably modern iron stirrup with a flat bottom and semicircular top began to be used in north and central China; the earliest remains discovered so far date to 302 CE. At about the same time, saddles with a rigid frame to distribute the rider's weight more evenly and better padding to cushion its effects on the horse began to be employed.

Jin Dynasty Iron Stirrups. Widespread use of the stirrup not only brought the use of horses back to the forefront of warfare, it also led to a resurgence in power of Eurasian mounted nomadic peoples. The ornate stirrups pictured here helped the nomadic Jurchen people displace the Northern Song dynasty (see Chapter 12) and set up their own Jin dynasty, which lasted from 1127 to 1234. Their downfall was brought about by another mounted nomadic people—the Mongols—who not only displaced the Jurchens but went on to conquer the Southern Song in 1279 and incorporate their new Yuan dynasty into the short-lived Mongol super-empire spanning Eurasia in the late thirteenth and early fourteenth centuries.

The outbreak of rebellion following the death of the second Sui emperor, Yangdi, brought the 16-year-old commander Li Shimin to power. Li had the Sui emperor killed, placed his own father on the throne, and announced the founding of the Tang dynasty in 618 CE. In less than a decade, he forced his father to abdicate and took power in his own right in 627 CE.

As we will see in the next part, the reconstitution of the Chinese empire under the Sui and its expansion and consolidation under the Tang placed China among the world's regions marked by the ascendancy of religious civilizations. Like Christianity in the late Roman Empire, Buddhism made inroads in China following the collapse of the Han. Indeed, through the work of Chinese missionary monks it had also become established in Korea

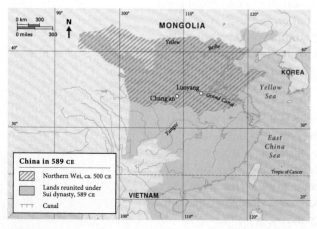

MAP 9.3 **China in 589 CE**

The effects of these changes were soon apparent in a China now dominated by feuding states and marauding nomads in the post-Han era. With his legs secured to his mount and a high saddleback to cushion him in combat, a mounted warrior could use a long lance to charge directly into enemy formations without fear of being immediately unhorsed. Furthermore, both he and his horse could wear heavier armor than before. The stirrup proved so effective that by the fifth century CE the armies of all the states in China had adopted and refined the technology. In China, it helped pave the way for the Sui reunification in 589.

It was in western Eurasia, however, that the new technology saw its greatest impact after its arrival in the seventh century CE. The politically fractured eras of post-Roman and post-Carolingian Europe meant that local elites and regional strongmen had to mount their own defenses. The stirrup and related military innovations allowed them to do this without heavily equipped armies, while the expenses necessary to adopt the new technology ensured that it would remain a monopoly of the rich and powerful. Thus the relationships comprising feudalism matured as peasants placed themselves in the service of their mounted protectors. The rough parity and independence of this widely dispersed warrior elite proved a powerful obstacle to the patterns of centralized state formation and empire building. Ironically, it would be another Chinese invention that would ultimately end this way of warfare many centuries later: gunpowder.

Questions

- How does the stirrup show that a technological innovation can lead to broader cultural and societal adaptations?
- Which environmental and geographical conditions facilitated the impact of the stirrup across Eurasia in ways not possible in the Americas?

and Japan. The Tang would see the completion of this process. Buddhism permeated Tang China to an extent never surpassed in later dynasties. For a period in the late seventh and early eighth centuries CE, it even became the established Chinese state religion. In this regard, China became not only part of a regional religious and cultural sphere during the Tang but also an important part of a new world pattern that would encompass Islamic civilization, orthodox Christianity in the Eastern Roman (Byzantine) Empire and much of eastern Europe, and the Western Christian civilizations of Roman Catholicism and Protestantism.

The Domestic Economy: Society, Family, and Gender

Throughout Chinese history, agriculture was the basis of the domestic economy. Yet from the Han dynasty on, China exported far more in luxury goods and technology than it imported. Unlike regimes in India, which actively fostered trade, the Confucian view of the pursuit of profit as corrupting meant that Chinese governments preferred to adopt a passive, but controlling, role in trade. Although merchants were held in low esteem, the state recognized that trade was indispensable to the financial health of the empire.

Industry and Commerce

By the first century CE, Chinese manufacturers were making paper using a method still considered to make the highest-quality product for painting or literary work. Artists were also producing "proto-porcelain" that, with additional refinements, would one day become the true porcelain known as "china." Earthenware figurines produced in Tang China are among the most coveted in the world today. In other arts, the use of lacquer was also well established. By the second century CE, the Chinese had perfected silk production and had become world leaders in textile weaving. Both treadle- and water-powered looms were in widespread use, and silk with standardized designs was produced for export. Chinese silks were much in demand from Persia and Rome. But much of the most important domestic production centered on bulk textiles.

Iron and Salt   By the Han period, the Chinese were producing cast iron in huge foundries, and the mining industry may have employed as many as 100,000 people. The foundries produced ingots of standardized sizes and weights. Salt mines used complex gearing, bamboo piping, and evaporators fired by natural gas. Because of the enormous productivity of the iron-making and salt-mining industries, the government sought ways to regulate them. The government also sponsored programs aimed at improving the empire's infrastructure. The unpredictable flow of China's rivers required constant attention to dikes, dredging, reservoirs, and canals to ease transportation (see Map 9.4).

Papermaking. Among the most momentous inventions of the Han era was papermaking. The process involved mashing plant fibers in a treadle-powered mortar and pestle, immersing the mash in water so the fibers would form a suspension, and then filtering the mixture with a fine mesh screen, which when allowed to dry produced a sheet of paper.

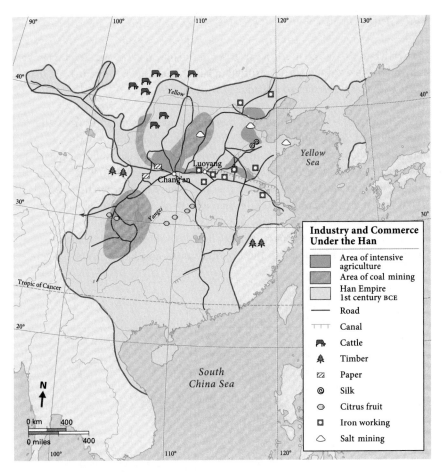

Industry and Commerce Under the Han

- Area of intensive agriculture
- Area of coal mining
- Han Empire 1st century BCE
- Road
- Canal
- Cattle
- Timber
- Paper
- Silk
- Citrus fruit
- Iron working
- Salt mining

MAP 9.4 Industry and Commerce under the Han

Land Reform   By the time of the late Han, the top of the social hierarchy was assumed by the scholar-gentry—the educated large landholders who constituted the Confucian bureaucracy. Since the upper ranks of the landowners and bureaucrats either were exempt from taxes or paid reduced amounts, the tax burden fell increasingly on tenants and owners of small parcels of land. Poor harvests made the situation even worse for those already heavily taxed. Because the north, despite its irrigation works, was more prone to crop failure than the south, it was also proportionally more heavily taxed.

Such problems made land reform and redistribution an ongoing concern. The Tang, for example, continued the policy of land redistribution begun during the brief Sui dynasty. Although the Tang land redistribution policy promoted prosperity, it also contributed to absentee landlordism and tenancy, as wealthier landlords near large cities often maintained households there. Usury grew as well, particularly during times of economic stress. The continual problem of land tenure and attempts at reform and redistribution is even today a concern in China.

Agricultural Productivity   Technical and systemic innovations increased agricultural productivity. In addition to such staples as wheat, millet, and barley in the north and rice in the south, a variety of semitropical fruits and vegetables were cultivated. New strains of rice resulted in larger harvests on more marginal land. Trade with Central Asia had introduced wine grapes.

The Silk Road   The expansion of maritime and caravan trade from the seventh century CE on spread Chinese technology abroad and brought new products into the Chinese empire. Early examples of silk appear to have reached the Mediterranean and North Africa as early as the first millennium BCE. By the first century BCE, artifacts clearly identifiable as Chinese had turned up in Egypt; by the fourth and fifth centuries CE, Indian and Persian middlemen extended the Chinese trade to the African kingdoms of Kush and Aksum.

The principal routes connecting the Chinese to the various trading centers of central Asia, and ultimately to the Mediterranean and Rome, were collectively

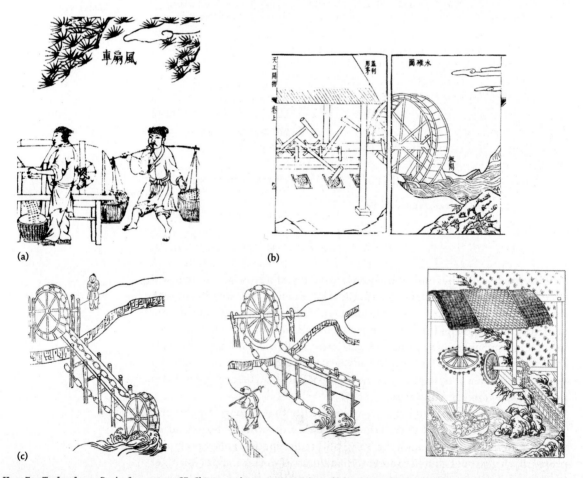

Han-Era Technology. By the first century CE, Chinese sophistication in crafts and labor-saving devices could be seen in a number of areas. While the illustrations here are from the famous seventeenth-century compendium of technology *Tiangong kaiwu* (The Works of Nature and Man), all of them illustrate techniques in use during the Han period: (*a*) *fengche* winnowing machine; (*b*) undershot waterwheel driving hammers in a pounding mill; (*c*) vertical and horizontal waterwheels driving chain-bucket "dragon pumps" for irrigation.

later known as the **Silk Road** (see Map 9.5). Although the Chinese tried to guard the secrets of its production, the demand for silk was so high that many peoples along the caravan routes were soon engaged in making silk themselves. Competition among producers and merchants in western Eurasia became so keen that the Roman emperor Justinian allied with the African kingdom of Aksum in the sixth century CE in part to contest the growing Persian dominance of the trade in fine silks. In the process, the Romans sought to create their own silk monopoly to service the western trade.

Silk Road: Overland trade routes that connected eastern and western Eurasia, beginning at the end of the fourth century BCE.

Gender Roles

Women in imperial China were subordinate to men. Although early Confucian works were relatively flexible about the position of women, the Han period saw a more hierarchical, patriarchal model of women's behavior develop. At the same time, the emphasis on sons as carriers of the ancestral line and their potential to enter state service led to a devaluing of daughters. In times of severe economic stress on families, young girls were the first to suffer. Families, especially in rural areas, would sometimes sell their daughters into prostitution or kill female infants.

Although some elite women achieved prominence in intellectual pursuits, like the historian Ban Zhao (48–116 CE), women's education centered on domestic virtues and crafts such as tending to silkworms, supervising family-scale silk production, spinning, and weaving. Daughters were either married off or placed with other families through adoption or servitude. Yet, in theory at least, there was always supposed to be an element of complementarity and reciprocity between men and women, especially husband and wife, as there was in theories of *yin* and *yang*.

From the fifth century CE on, the popularity of monastic Buddhism created attractive alternatives for those fleeing family pressures, especially women. Women enrolled in Buddhist schools could become highly educated, and the communities themselves, like Christian monasteries in Europe, often owned large tracts of land and wielded considerable local influence. At the same time, the strictness of regulations on sexual and family life varied, particularly among officials and the commercial classes. Foreign influences also affected behavior, particularly in places engaged in international trade. Tantric Buddhist (see Chapter 8) and Daoist sexual practices contributed to a more relaxed approach to relations between men and women during the Tang as well.

Intellectual Trends, Aesthetics, Science, and Technology

The period from the sixth century BCE until the first unification of China under the Qin in 221 BCE is regarded as China's most fertile period of intellectual exploration. Long-term contacts with the East Asian Buddhist sphere from the end of the Han through the Tang era resulted in a number of new Buddhist schools spreading throughout East Asia.

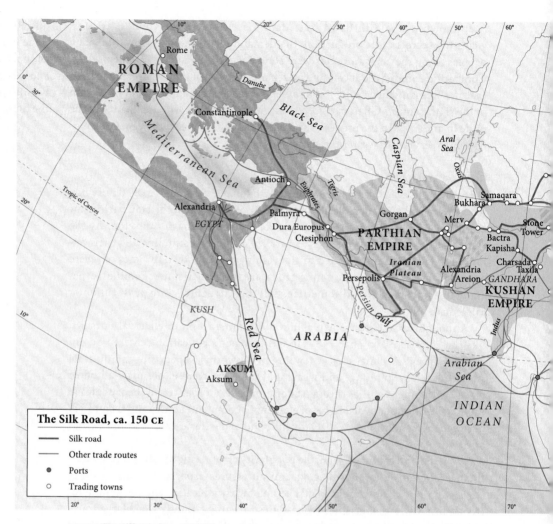

MAP 9.5 **The Silk Road, ca. 150 CE**

Confucianism, Education, and History during the Han

While the first Han rulers favored a philosophical system that combined Legalism with aspects of other schools, over time a form of Confucianism became the preferred governmental doctrine. Confucian emphasis on the ethical correctness of officials, caring for the people, filial piety, and the study of history were a good fit for Han administrators. By the second century CE, the growing popularity of Confucian academies led to their subsidization by the state, in effect placing all official education in the hands of these academies. This made knowledge of Confucianism the principal test for entrance into the bureaucracy. This practice of merit-based service would remain in force until the opening years of the twentieth century. A form of it would be adopted by Korea, Japan, and Vietnam (see Chapter 13).

The Han Confucian Synthesis?   Although Confucianism served as the foundation for Han education, Confucian doctrine had changed from the early

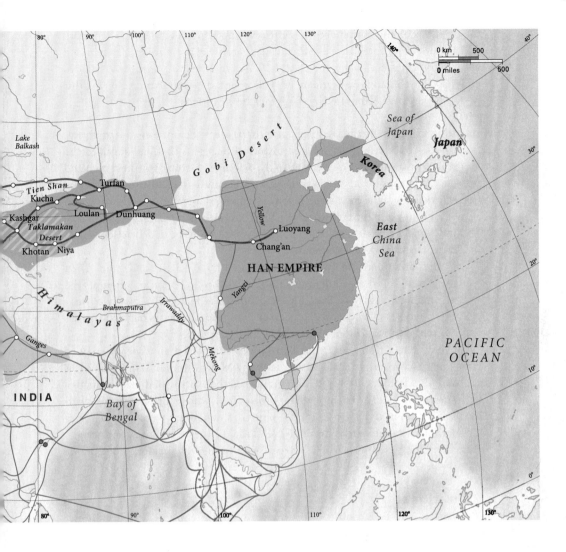

teachings. During the Warring States period and the era of Qin rule, much Confucian thought had been altered, and many texts had been lost. Thus, the Confucianism that finally received state approval reflected the new realities of the Han dynasty. So many other elements from the fragments of philosophical tradition that had survived the Qin period went into government theory and practice that scholars have come to question the long-accepted perception of a straightforward "Han Synthesis" of Confucianism and imperial government.

This diverse blending of political, ethical, and cosmological thought is evident in the era's chief treatise on government, the *Huainan zi*. In this document, the Confucian ideals of humane, righteous, and filial behavior by the powerful are linked with Daoist ideas of the ruler as divorced from day-to-day administration and Legalist notions on the role of officials. As the intermediary between heaven, humankind, and earth, the emperor occupied a position of cosmological significance. For continuity's sake, a dynasty had to be hereditary—in contradiction to Confucius's ideas. Hence, acceptance of a hereditary imperial line strengthened the emphasis on the notion of filial piety as a central virtue. Indeed, a short work that achieved widespread use as a first reader because of its basic ideas and limited vocabulary was the *Xiaojing*, the *Classic of Filial Piety*. At the same time, the idea of dynastic cycles and the Mandate of Heaven became even stronger during this period as they were elaborated by the great Han historians.

Han Historians   By the Han period, with the ideal of empire encouraging cultural unity, court historians collated historical materials that had survived the Qin purges in an attempt to systematize the writing of history. For these men and women, the purpose of history writing was the accurate transmission of information and analysis of the events portrayed in terms of a larger vision of the direction and purpose of human history. For the Han historians, history was cyclical, and moral lessons learned from human events were to be tied to actions taken at various stages of these cycles.

The father-and-son team of Sima Tan (d. 110 BCE) and Sima Qian (145–86 BCE), whose *Shiji* (*The Records of the Grand Historian*) attempts the first complete history of the Chinese people, also included a survey of non-Chinese peoples in that work. Hence, the Han records give us our first written accounts of Japan and other places on the Chinese periphery.

Several generations later, the Ban family comprised another dynasty of Han court historians. Writing after the Wang Mang interval, Ban Biao (3–54 CE) and his son Ban Gu (32–92 CE) pioneered the writing of dynastic history with their *Hanshu* (*The History of the Former Han*), whose format was followed by all subsequent dynastic histories. Ban Gu's daughters were also scholars and writers, and his sister Ban Zhao (48–116 CE) carried on the family tradition of history writing as well as a treatise on women's behavior, *Admonitions for Women*.

Buddhism in China

By the mid-first century CE, when it is first mentioned in Chinese accounts, Buddhism had already split into the major divisions of Theravada (Hinayana), which had established itself in southern India and Sri Lanka, and Mahayana, which would be established in China.

The introduction of Mahayana Buddhism into China presents a number of interesting parallels with that of Christianity into Rome. Both religions emphasized personal enlightenment or salvation. Both were initially seen as "foreign" systems and subjected to official resistance or persecution before emerging triumphant. Finally, while both challenged existing hierarchies, the institutions of both were also adopted by rulers who wanted to expand their power.

Language and Scripture   The incompatibility of the Chinese written language with Sanskrit and Pali scriptures complicated the introduction of Buddhism to China. The earliest Buddhist missionaries had to borrow from Daoist terminology and invent a new vocabulary of Chinese terms. This eclecticism resulted in a proliferation of sects and a growing need on the part of Chinese converts to travel to India for study and guidance. The famous pilgrim Xuan Zang (596–664 CE)

Bodhisattva Guanyin, Sixth Century CE. Originally incorporating aspects of both genders, Guanyin came to be depicted as female as Buddhism became firmly established in China. For Pure Land adherents, she was the bodhisattva invoked in times of extreme peril, and "the miracles of Guanyin" (*Kannon* in Japan) was a favorite theme of both Chinese and Japanese artists.

went to India in 623 CE and brought back the collection of scriptures still housed in the monastery he founded just outside Xi'an.

Buddhist Schools   The period between the dissolution of the Han and the ascendancy of the Tang saw the founding of many important schools of East Asian Buddhism. By the fifth century, the school of popular devotion to Amida (Sanskrit Amitabha; see Chapter 8), the Buddha of the Pure Land, was spreading rapidly in China. For Pure Land followers, merely invoking Amida's name is sufficient for salvation. Even today, it remains the most popular Buddhist sect in both China and Japan. Amida is often pictured with the bodhisattva Guanyin (Kannon in Japan; Sanskrit Avalokitesvara), the Goddess of Mercy, who is frequently invoked during times of peril.

Another influential Buddhist school was Tiantai, centered on the scripture of the *Lotus Sutra*. Tiantai emphasized contemplation of the sutras (Buddhist scriptures) as the vehicle to enlightenment and later inspired schools of esoteric (see Chapter 8) paths to enlightenment.

A third school was Chan Buddhism, better known by its Japanese name, Zen. As outlined in its central text, *The Platform of the Sixth Patriarch*, by Hui Neng (638–713 CE), the path to enlightenment is through meditation and the example of a master. While limited in its influence in China, the emphasis on discipline and obedience made Zen the preferred Buddhist school of Japan's warrior aristocracy after the twelfth century CE.

Aesthetics: The study of the beautiful; the branches of learning dealing with categorizing and analyzing beauty.

Intellectual Life

Chinese concepts of **aesthetics** that developed during the first millennium CE came to influence the arts throughout East Asia. The most important developments during this period were the maturation of poetry, painting, and calligraphy. Central to each is the idea of spontaneous creation as a reflection of the inner state of the artist. The artist in each of these media seeks to connect with the Dao by indirectly suggesting some aspect of it in the work itself.

The Sciences   Because the imperial establishment relied on the prediction of comets, eclipses, and other omens to monitor the will of heaven, astronomy and mathematics were especially important. Chinese mathematicians had worked out formulas and proofs to figure the areas of most standard geometric forms. They had also calculated pi to four places and were able to solve simultaneous algebraic equations. The astronomers Zhang Heng (78–139 CE)

Earthquake Detector. One of the more ingenious pieces of high technology to come out of the Han period was a working earthquake detector created by Zhang Heng (78–139 CE) in 134 CE. In the model illustrated here, carefully balanced balls were placed inside the large vessel. A tremor coming from a particular direction would jar the ball closest to the direction of the quake and send it down a track where it would fly from the mouth of one of the dragons on the outside of the "vessel" and fall into the yawning mouth of the frog underneath. Thus, anyone checking the device could tell at a glance that a quake had occurred and from what direction by seeing which frog held a ball.

and Wang Chong (27–100) each championed theories of a universe governed by natural forces. Zhang built a water-powered armillary sphere—a hollow globe surrounded by bronze bands, representing the paths of the sun, stars, and planets—and, in 134, devised what was perhaps the world's first practical earthquake detector.

Printing and Proto-Porcelain   One of the signal innovations of Eurasia was printing. While woodblock prints of popular Buddhist works had become available in major Chinese cities by the eighth century CE, by the end of the Tang and the beginning of the Song dynasties, presses employing both carved block and movable copper type were in regular use in China, Korea, and Japan. The innovation of printing dramatically raised literacy rates, and by the beginning of the Song era China had some of the highest preindustrial literacy rates achieved in human history.

Though there is debate about when the breakthroughs resulting in true porcelain first occurred, by the Tang period distinctive brown and green glazed figures, often depicting the peoples and animals of the caravan trade, were widely exchanged. By the Song, delicate white, crackled glaze and sea-green celadon ware were produced and sought by connoisseurs as the height of aesthetic refinement. Today, such pieces are considered to be among the world's great art treasures.

Putting It All Together

The political and social turmoil of the late Zhou era was also an innovative period in Chinese intellectual and cultural history. During this era the most important schools of Chinese thought and philosophy developed: Confucianism, Daoism, and Legalism. While Confucianism ultimately triumphed as the ideology of imperial China, it was the Legalist state of Qin that created the empire itself.

When the Qin dynasty fell in 206 BCE, much of the infrastructure of the early empire, including the Great Wall, was in place. The Han dynasty, from 202 BCE to 220 CE, retained the administrative structure of the Qin but softened the harsh laws and punishments of the Legalists. Eventually, the form of Confucianism practiced by the empire's administrators became the imperial ideology. By the end of the Han, China had created a solid alliance between the state and this all-encompassing ethical and legal system.

The 400 years of unity under the Qin and the Han had conditioned the Chinese to believe that empire was the natural goal of the patterns of political formation in China and that any interruptions in these patterns would be brief. Thus, Chinese history has been marked by rhythms of inner- and outer-directedness. Along with these rhythms came a belief, reinforced by dynastic historians, that human society and the cosmos were knit together in a moral order, made perfectible by the power of the empire and the dedication of a bureaucracy selected for its understanding of ethics in human affairs. Thus, throughout the imperial era—and even in our own time—Chinese students and scholars have both guided and remonstrated with those in power.

Review and Relate

| Thinking Through Patterns

Examine the ways historians approach the big questions of this chapter.

I n ancient times, most people studied history for the moral lessons it offered and to avoid making the same mistakes their ancestors did. The Chinese studied it in hopes of grasping its basic patterns so as to understand the present and antici-pate the future. For most of the twentieth century, Western historians have sought to avoid making moral judgments about the past, instead seeing their job as being detectives rather than judges. For them, to judge history by the standards of the present is to be "presentist," and thus to see the past as always inferior to the pres-ent. But how does one deal with such things as genocide, extreme cruelty, or slavery? One way out of this dilemma might be to weigh the actions of the First Emperor against the standards of morality current in *his* day. Yet here, too, we encounter a problem: There were so many new schools of thought emerging in China then that no single one dominated; moreover, the First Emperor himself created his own system of morality based on Legalism. Perhaps, then, the best that we can do is to note that he set the fundamental pattern for Chinese imperial government for the next 2,000 years—but at considerable cost.

» **Was the First Emperor's ruthless-ness justified by his accomplishments in his empire?**

P erhaps the biggest difference between Confucian society and modern American society is in the way both see the ideal forms of societal relations. Americans see the individual, the rule of law, democracy, and equality as funda-mental to a good society. The purpose of government is to allow people to do as they wish while stipulating the limits within which they can do so. Confucian concepts of government and society put a premium on hierarchy and harmony. People are not seen as mere individuals but as part of larger patterns: family, clan, village, society, state. These in turn are seen as part of a hierarchy that stretches from the poorest peasant to the emperor himself. Reciprocal rights and responsibilities are present at every level for protection of the weak, but equality is not seen as important. The role of government itself is seen as providing a moral example to the people. If it teaches them well through regulations, customs, and ritual, then the people aspire to be good.

» **How would you compare the values expressed by Confucius and Mencius to those of contemporary society?**

O ne of the most unattractive things about imperial China to the majority of us today is that it often appears that women were held in low regard, abused, denied basic human rights, and even tortured for fashion's sake, as with foot binding. The Confucian emphasis on hierarchy within society and the family tends to reinforce this impression. But scholars have in recent years shown the picture to be much more complex. While historians agree that in some respects women's roles deteriorated,

» **How have histori-ans viewed the role of women in early impe-rial China?**

the evidence suggests that there were also times, such as during the Tang and early Song periods, when they exercised considerable freedom and influence. The pattern of "inner" and "outer" as it governed the traditional Chinese family is still discernible in many Chinese households today: While husbands go off to work, women definitely hold sway within the "inner" realm of the house.

|Against the Grain

Consider this as a counterpoint to the main patterns examined in this chapter.

Individualism and Universal Love: Yang Zhu and Mo Di

- The appearance of visionary thinkers seems around 600 BCE to have been an extraordinarily widespread phenomenon. Why were the times of great turmoil in these societies such fertile ones for new ideas?

- What ideas in other cultures seem to be like those of Yang and Mo? How do they also differ? Do they spring from similar conditions?

The period of the "hundred schools" of thought ranges from the deceptively passive mysticism of the Daoists to the totalitarian ambitions of the Legalists. At its height, however, during the time of the Confucian thinker Mencius (385–312), the two schools of thought that he and his disciples considered most influential and dangerous were an exercise in extremes: the radical individualism of Yang Zhu and the advocacy of universal love of Mo Di (or Mozi).

Yang Zhu taught that since life was short and death inevitable, people should take what enjoyment they can. After all, he said, the four great sages (including Confucius) "during their life had not a single day's joy. Since their death they have had grand fame that will last through the ages. . . . [but] their fame is no more to them than the trunk of a tree or a clod of earth." Moreover, the most infamous villains who enjoyed vast wealth and pleasures went smiling to their graves, caring not at all in death about their ill fame.

Mo Di, on the other hand, taught that the only truly humane way to approach the world was to love all people equally. To do otherwise is to be overly partisan in one's duties to society. The followers of Mo put these ideas into action during the Warring States period by volunteering to help the inhabitants of besieged cities defend themselves.

In the end, the extremes of both systems would undoubtedly have made them unworkable. That of Confucius, with its emphasis on family relationships and duties at the micro and macro levels, was ultimately more in harmony with Chinese society—so much so that it continues to shape that society even today.

Key Terms

Aesthetics   215
Commanderies   203
Dao   200

Headmen   203
Junzi   199
Legalism   200

Reciprocity   198
Silk Road   211
Sinicizing   203

Learn more with this chapter's digital tools, including the Oxford Insight Study Guide, at http://www.oup.com/he/vonsivers4e. Please see the Further Resources section at the back of the book for additional readings and suggested websites.

Sources for Chapter 9

Analects (Lunyu) of Confucius

ca. 500–479 BCE

The details of Confucius's life are murky, especially given the chaos surrounding the declining Zhou period in the 490s and 480s BCE. It is important to take into account the impact of interstate conflict on Confucius's philosophical insights. A commoner who was effectively shut out of power by the three noble clans of Lu, Confucius was eventually driven out and forced to wander among the other states, because of the resentment of this traditional aristocracy. Despite the resistance of warring aristocrats, Confucius advocated a new approach to government, in which respect for the weak, poor, and defenseless would form the basis for civil society.

[12.7] Zigong asked about government. The Master [Confucius] said, "Sufficient food, sufficient arms, and popular trust [in the ruler]."

Zigong said, "If this were impossible, and we would have to dispense with one of these three, which should come first?"

[Confucius] said, "Dispense with arms."

Zigong said, "If this were impossible, and we would have to dispense with one of these two, which should come first?"

[Confucius] said, "Dispense with food. Since antiquity, there has always been death. But people without trust have no standing."

[12.11] Lord Jing of Qi asked Confucius about government. Confucius answered, "The lord acts as a lord, the minister as a minister, the father as a father, the son as a son."

The lord said, "Excellent! Surely, if the lord does not act as a lord, nor the minister as a minister, nor the father as a father, nor the son as a son, then although I might have grain, would I be able to eat it?"

[12.13] The Master said, "In hearing litigation, I am like other people. What is necessary is to cause there to be no litigation."

[12.17] Ji Kangzi asked Confucius about government. Confucius answered, "To govern is to correct. If you lead with rectitude, who will dare not be correct?"

[12.18] Ji Kangzi was vexed at the thieving [in his state] and asked Confucius about it. Confucius answered, "If you, sir, were not covetous, then even if you were to reward them for it, they would not steal."

Source: Victor H. Mair, Nancy Shatzman Steinhardt, and Paul R. Goldin, eds., *Hawai'i Reader in Traditional Chinese Culture* (Honolulu: University of Hawai'i Press, 2005), 48–49.

[13.3] Zilu said, "The Lord of Wei is waiting for you to effect government. What will you do first?"

The Master said, "What is necessary is to rectify names!"

Zilu said, "Is there such a thing? Master, you are wide of the mark. Why such rectification?"

The Master said, "You, you are uncouth. A noble man should appear more re-served about what he does not know. If names are not rectified, then speech does not flow properly. If speech does not flow properly, then affairs are not completed. If affairs are not completed, then ritual and music do not flourish. If ritual and music do not flourish, then punishments and penalties do not hit the mark. If pun-ishments and penalties do not hit the mark, the people have no way to move hand or foot. Thus, for the noble man, names must be able to be spoken, and what he speaks must be able to be carried out. With regard to his speech, the noble man's [concern] is simply that there be nothing that is careless."

[13.10] The Master said, "If there were one [among the princes] who would make use of me, within no more than twelve months, [the government] would be ac-ceptable. Within three years there would be success."

▶ **Working with Sources**

1. **To what extent did Confucius expect to be consulted by the leaders of the various states?**

2. **What does he seem to have envisioned as the ultimate basis of proper government?**

SOURCE 9.2

Book of Mencius (Mengzi)

The Confucian thinker Mencius had a difficult intellectual environment in which to defend the Sage's ideas. During the Hundred Schools period of the late Zhou the followers of Yang Zhu and Mo Di (see "Against the Grain") proved to be among his most consistent opponents. In the following pas-sages Mencius mounts his arguments against Yizhi (I Chih)'s espousal of Mo Di; in the second he condemns both Mo and Yang's extremes.

Source 9.2a

Mencius Corrects Yizhi

CHAP. V. 1. The Mohist, Î Chih, sought, through Hsü Pî, to see Mencius. Men-cius said, "I indeed wish to see him, but at present I am still unwell. When I am better, I will myself go and see him. He need not come here *again*."

2. Next day, Î *Chih* again sought to see Mencius. Mencius said, "To-day I am able to see him. But if I do not correct his errors, the *true* principles will not be fully evident. Let me first correct him. I have heard that this Î is a Mohist. Now Mo considers that in the regulation of funeral matters a spare simplicity should be the rule. Î thinks with *Mo's doctrines* to change *the customs of* the kingdom;—how does he regard them as if they were wrong, and not honour

Source: James Legge, trans., *The Works of Mencius* (New York: Dover, 1970), 257–260.

them? Notwithstanding his views, Î buried his parents in a sumptuous manner, and so he served them in the way which *his doctrines* discountenance."

3. The disciple Hsü informed Î of these remarks. Î said, "*Even according to* the principles of the learned, we find that the ancients *acted towards the people* 'as if they were watching over an infant.' What does this expression mean? To me it sounds that we are to love *all* without difference of degree; but the manifestation *of love* must begin with our parents." Hsü reported this reply to Mencius, who said, "Now, does Î really think that a man's affection for the child of his brother is *merely* like his affection for the infant of a neighbour? What is to be approved in that *expression* is simply this:—that if an infant crawling about is likely to fall into a well, it is no crime in the infant. Moreover, Heaven gives birth to creatures in such a way that they have one root, and Î makes them to have two roots. This is the cause *of his error.*"

Source 9.2b

Mencius Outlines His Opposition to Yang and Mo

9. "*Once more,* sage sovereigns cease to arise, and the princes of the States give the reins to their lusts. Unemployed scholars indulge in unreasonable discussions. The words of Yang Chû and Mo Tî fill the country. *If you listen to* people's discourses throughout it, *you will find that* they have adopted the views either of Yang or of Mo. *Now,* Yang's principle is—'each one for himself,' which does not acknowledge *the claims of* the sovereign. Mo's principle is—'to love all equally,' which does not acknowledge *the peculiar affection due to* a father. But to acknowledge neither king nor father is to be in the state of a beast. Kungming Î said, 'In their kitchens, there is fat meat. In their stables, there are fat horses. But their people have the look of hunger, and on the wilds there are those who have died of famine. This is leading on beasts to devour men.' "

▶ Working
with Sources:

1. **What are Mencius's principal arguments against Yizhi?**

2. **Why does Mencius defend Confucius's partiality against universal love?**

SOURCE 9.3

Li Si, "Memorial on the Burning of Books," from the *Shiji*

ca. 100 BCE

Virtually no records have survived from the period between the unification of China in 221 BCE and the collapse of the Qin Empire 15 years later. Accordingly, historians are forced to rely on documents composed

Source (9.2b): Ibid., 282–284.

Source: *Shih chi* 87:6b–7a, in de Bary, Chan, and Watson, comps., *Sources of Chinese Tradition,* vol. 1 (New York: Columbia University Press, 1960), 140–141.

during the Han dynasty for relevant information. Nevertheless, one of the stories passed along, concerning the advice of Li Si to the emperor, is a stark reminder of how fragile learning can be, even in a temporarily successful polity. The *Records of the Grand Historian* (*Shiji*), a lengthy history of China compiled by Sima Qian (ca. 145–86 BCE), also includes a detailed biography of Li Si.

In earlier times the empire disintegrated and fell into disorder, and no one was capable of unifying it. Thereupon the various feudal lords rose to power. In their discourses they all praised the past in order to disparage the present and embellished empty words to confuse the truth. Everyone cherished his own favorite school of learning and criticized what had been instituted by the authorities. But at present Your Majesty possesses a unified empire, has regulated the distinctions of black and white, and has firmly established for yourself a position of sole supremacy. And yet these independent schools, joining with each other, criticize the codes of laws and instructions. Hearing of the promulgation of a decree, they criticize it, each from the standpoint of his own school. At home they disapprove of it in their hearts; going out they criticize it in the thoroughfare. They seek a reputation by discrediting their sovereign; they appear superior by expressing contrary views; and they lead the lowly multitude in the spreading of slander. If such license is not prohibited, the sovereign power will decline above and partisan factions will form below. It would be well to prohibit this.

Your servant suggests that all books in the imperial archives, save the memoirs of Qin, be burned. All persons in the empire, except members of the Academy of Learned Scholars, in possession of the *Book of Odes*, the *Book of History*, and discourses of the hundred philosophers should take them to the local governors and have them indiscriminately burned. Those who dare to talk to each other about the *Book of Odes* and the *Book of History* should be executed and their bodies exposed in the market place. Anyone referring to the past to criticize the present should, together with all the members of his family, be put to death. Officials who fail to report cases that have come under their attention are equally guilty. After thirty days from the time of issuing the decree, those who have not destroyed their books are to be branded and sent to build the Great Wall. Books not to be destroyed will be those on medicine and pharmacy, divination by the tortoise and milfoil, and agriculture and arboriculture. People wishing to pursue learning should take the officials as their teachers.

▶ **Working with Sources**

1. Li Si's advice may seem extreme, but is there a logical element to his reasoning?

2. Why was he advocating the destruction of these specific books?

Ban Zhao, *Admonitions for Women (Nüjie)*

ca. 80 CE

Ban Zhao (45–ca. 116 CE) was by far the most educated woman of her day, and she trained many important male scholars. The *Han Shu* (the continuation of Sima Qian's *Shiji*) was originally undertaken by her father, Ban Biao (3–54 CE), and continued by her brother Ban Gu (32–92). Ban Zhao is credited with giving the *Han Shu* its present shape after the deaths of her father and brother, but she is most famous today for her advice book, directed toward young women.

I, the unworthy writer, am unsophisticated, unenlightened, and by nature unintelligent, but I am fortunate both to have received not a little favor from my scholarly Father, and to have had a cultured mother and instructresses upon whom to rely for a literary education as well as for training in good manners. More than forty years have passed since at the age of fourteen I took up the dustpan and the broom in the Cao family [the family into which she married]. During this time with trembling heart I feared constantly that I might disgrace my parents, and that I might multiply difficulties for both the women and the men of my husband's family. Day and night I was distressed in heart, but I labored without confessing weariness. Now and hereafter, however, I know how to escape from such fears.

Being careless, and by nature stupid, I taught and trained my children without system. Consequently I fear that my son Gu may bring disgrace upon the Imperial Dynasty by whose Holy Grace he has unprecedentedly received the extraordinary privilege of wearing the Gold and the Purple, a privilege for the attainment of which by my son, I a humble subject never even hoped. Nevertheless, now that he is a man and able to plan his own life, I need not again have concern for him. But I do grieve that you, my daughters, just now at the age for marriage, have not at this time had gradual training and advice; that you still have not learned the proper customs for married women. I fear that by failure in good manners in other families you will humiliate both your ancestors and your clan. I am now seriously ill, life is uncertain. As I have thought of you all in so untrained a state, I have been uneasy many a time for you. At hours of leisure I have composed . . . these instructions under the title, "Lessons for Women." In order that you may have something wherewith to benefit your persons, I wish every one of you, my daughters each to write out a copy for yourself.

From this time on every one of you strive to practice these lessons.

HUMILITY

On the third day after the birth of a girl the ancients observed three customs: first to place the baby below the bed; second to give her a potsherd [a piece of broken pottery] with which to play; and third to announce her birth to her ancestors

---

Source: Nancy Lee Swann, *Pan Chao: Foremost Woman Scholar of China* (New York: London Century, 1932), 82–90.

by an offering. Now to lay the baby below the bed plainly indicated that she is lowly and weak, and should regard it as her primary duty to humble herself before others. To give her potsherds with which to play indubitably signified that she should practice labor and consider it her primary duty to be industrious. To announce her birth before her ancestors clearly meant that she ought to esteem as her primary duty the continuation of the observance of worship in the home.

These three ancient customs epitomize woman's ordinary way of life and the teachings of the traditional ceremonial rites and regulations. Let a woman modestly yield to others; let her respect others; let her put others first, herself last. Should she do something good, let her not mention it; should she do something bad let her not deny it. Let her bear disgrace; let her even endure when others speak or do evil to her. Always let her seem to tremble and to fear. When a woman follows such maxims as these then she may be said to humble herself before others.

Let a woman retire late to bed, but rise early to duties; let her not dread tasks by day or by night. Let her not refuse to perform domestic duties whether easy or difficult. That which must be done, let her finish completely, tidily, and systematically. When a woman follows such rules as these, then she may be said to be industrious.

Let a woman be correct in manner and upright in character in order to serve her husband. Let her live in purity and quietness of spirit, and attend to her own affairs. Let her love not gossip and silly laughter. Let her cleanse and purify and arrange in order the wine and the food for the offerings to the ancestors. When a woman observes such principles as these, then she may be said to continue ancestral worship.

No woman who observes these three fundamentals of life has ever had a bad reputation or has fallen into disgrace. If a woman fail to observe them, how can her name be honored; how can she but bring disgrace upon herself?

. . .

IMPLICIT OBEDIENCE

Whenever the mother-in-law says, "Do not do that," and if what she says is right, unquestionably the daughter-in-law obeys. Whenever the mother-in-law says, "Do that," even if what she says is wrong, still the daughter-in-law submits unfailingly to the command. Let a woman not act contrary to the wishes and the opinions of parents-in-law about right and wrong; let her not dispute with them what is straight and what is crooked. Such docility may be called obedience which sacrifices personal opinion. Therefore the ancient book, "A Pattern for Women," says: "If a daughter-in-law who follows the wishes of her parents-in-law is like an echo and shadow, how could she not be praised?"

▶ Working with Sources

1. What does Ban Zhao tell us about the status of daughters-in-law in her culture? Are these fates capable of being avoided?

2. What should be the central and perennial activities of a woman's life, in the opinion of Ban Zhao? Did she conduct her own life differently?

World Period Three

The Formation of Religious Civilizations, 600–1450 CE

The rise of religious civilizations on the continents of Asia, Europe, and Africa is a striking phenomenon that unifies the period of 600–1450 in world history. It can be considered as a continuation of the intellectual and institutional transformations that began with the emphasis on monotheism and monism by the visionaries of the mid-first millennium BCE.

The religious civilizations were not monolithic and displayed many regional variations. Internal diversity notwithstanding, they shared a number of common characteristics:

- Religious civilizations formed in regions which were larger than any single state within them: They superseded empires as the largest units of human unification.

- The civilizations were *scriptural*—that is, based on canonical (commonly agreed on) texts inherited in most cases from earlier periods. Members of educated elites (clergy, scholars, sages) taught and interpreted the scriptures to the laypeople.

- Despite hostilities among the religious civilizations, merchants, missionaries, pilgrims, and travelers visited each other's areas. They fostered a lively exchange of technical and cultural innovations from one end of Eurasia and Africa to the other.

Chapter 10

Islamic Civilization and Byzantium

600–1300 CE

CHAPTER TEN PATTERNS

Origins, Interactions, Adaptations Islamic civilization and Byzantium originated in the wake of the ruinous war of annihilation between the Roman and Sasanid empires. Islamic civilization arose in lands conquered from the Romans and Sasanids. Byzantium rallied around Eastern Christianity and recovered from its initial territorial losses to Arab invaders. During a time of intensive interaction, Muslims adopted much of the philosophical and scientific heritage from ancient Greece. At the height of their civilizational achievements, both Muslims and eastern Christians gave up their initial imperial structures and organized their polities as commonwealths: large territories with a multiplicity of independent regional rulers under a single religion.

Uniqueness and Similarities As Islamic civilization and Eastern Christian Byzantium evolved from imperial origins into commonwealths, their port cities and inland urban centers functioned as hubs of intensive cultural and mercantile interaction. Islamic scholars and merchants traveled extensively between Spain, Africa, Central Asia, India, and beyond, while their Byzantine counterparts traversed the region between the Balkans, Muscovy, and Anatolia. Over time, innumerable ethnic groups from the periphery adapted to Islam and Eastern Christianity to form multiethnic religious civilizations.

Safra, a wife whose husband left her for another woman in twelfth-century Cairo, describes her anguish in letters to her estranged husband Khidr. She is offended that Khidr denigrates her as unattractive and reveals secrets to his new lover, who is also married. In Safra's words, his "repulsive, shameless talk" causes her deep suffering. Were she not a good Muslim, she says, she would curse him both privately and in public.

The letters also reveal that she was independently wealthy, while her husband was not. Since he could not pay her the obligatory portion of the "bride wealth" at the time of the wedding, she let it stand as a loan. Not only did he not make payments; he did not even feed and clothe her or pay their rent. When he began his affair, she retreated to the countryside. But he insisted she return and promised to leave his mistress. As soon as she returned to Cairo, however, he went back to his lover. He slipped into Safra's house at night and stole most of the household furnishings, ultimately leaving her with an empty house.

Safra's story provides a glimpse into the legal side of Islamic civilization. Islamic law afforded women considerable protections. Safra was a woman of property, holding personal title to possessions as well as to debts payable to her. She could go to court, where she had standing as a complainant, and could initiate divorce proceedings. Even though Islamic civilization was as patriarchal as the other religious civilizations of the time, women exercised considerably more rights than in the Persian and Roman Empires.

CHAPTER OUTLINE

The Formation of Islamic Religious Civilization

Eastern Christian Civilization in Byzantium

Islamic and Eastern Christian Civilizations at Their Height

Religion, Sciences, and the Arts in Two Religious Civilizations

Putting It All Together

Byzantium

Islamic Civilization

BYZANTIUM AND THE ISLAMIC WORLD, ca. 1000 CE

ABOVE: Detail of an early Quran (Surah 48: 27–28) written in Kufic script during the eighth or ninth century.

Seeing Patterns

> Why can the period 600–1450 be described as the age of religious civilizations? How do Eastern Christian and Islamic civilizations fit this description?

> Which cultural traditions combined to form Islamic religious civilization during its formative period? What were the most characteristic patterns?

> How did Eastern Christian or Byzantine civilization evolve over time? On which institutions was this civilization based, and how did it evolve, wedged between Islamic and Western Christian civilizations?

Commonwealth: A large territory with a multiplicity of independent regional rulers under a single religion.

The Formation of Islamic Religious Civilization

Arab conquests and the rise of Islam were foundational events during the period 600–900. In the 600s, the Arabs carved out a kingdom by exploiting the preoccupation of the eastern Roman and Sasanid Persian Empires with their destructive wars of conquest in 602–628. Two Arab dynasties, the Umayyads and then the Abbasids, built an empire stretching thousands of miles east and west. Given the enormous distances, the Abbasids granted autonomy to outlying provinces. In the process, their empire changed into a **commonwealth** of many states sharing a single Islamic religion. The pattern that Islamic religious civilization followed during its formative period was a variation of what happened in the other parts of Asia and Europe in the first millennium CE: regions of religious civilizations grew much larger than the political units within them, resulting in the appearance of commonwealths (Middle East, Europe, India) or periodic unity and disunity (China).

The Beginnings of Islam

At the beginning of the 600s, the Sasanid Persian and Roman Empires battled each other in a lengthy war, which left their Arab subjects in Syria and Mesopotamia (Iraq) to their own devices. The Arabs had been nomadic inhabitants of the Syrian-Arabian desert since they began to use the camel as a pack animal around 1000 BCE (domesticated ca. 2500 BCE). They founded kingdoms and city-states on the Arabian Peninsula in the early centuries CE. By the early 600s, nearly all Arabs on the peninsula had been Christianized. In the mid-600s Arab leaders conquered Sasanid Iraq and Roman Syria, captured Egypt from the Romans, and destroyed the Sasanid Persian Empire. The first evidence of Islam as a religion separate from Christianity appeared among the Arabs. Through further conquests, the Arab realm became an empire, stretching by the mid-eighth century from Iberia in the west to the Indus River in the east.

The Final Roman–Persian War   The Roman–Persian rivalry reached a climax during the first three decades of the 600s. In 602, King of Kings Khosrow II (r. 590–628) invaded the Roman Empire to avenge the murder of the emperor in a palace coup. Within a little more than a decade, Khosrow's generals had conquered Syria, Egypt, and Anatolia, and the Romans were hard pressed to defend themselves in their capital. The empire was eventually saved by Heraclius (r. 610–641), the son of a provincial governor of the province of Africa who seized power in Constantinople (now Istanbul in Turkey) in 610. He reorganized the military and was able to drive the Sasanids back to Iraq. In 628 Khosrow was murdered by rivals, and the Sasanids were forced to make peace.

After his victory, Heraclius restored the prewar administrative structures in the province of Syria. He subsidized Arab leaders, reintroduced locally re-cruited garrisons and bishops in cities, and reduced the size of the army. To simplify the central administration, he replaced Latin with Greek as the language of the bureaucracy and the multiple Latin titles of the emperor (*imperator, caesar, augustus*) with the single Greek title of king (*basileus*), Christ's representative on earth. Thus it was under Heraclius that the Roman Empire became the Byzantine Empire, or Byzantium for short.

The Arab Empire of the Umayyads The victory of Heraclius over the Sasanid Persians in 628 encouraged the Arabs to begin incursions from the north Arabian desert into neighboring regions. In a series of raids in 628–636, they invaded Persian Iraq. The Persians, racked by a dynastic war in the wake of Khosrow II's defeat by Heraclius and his murder by a family member, found it difficult to stop the Arabs. The early successes of the eastern Arabs against the Persians encouraged the Arabs in the west to begin raids in 632 against the Byzantines in Palestine. Heraclius had reestablished Byzantine rule in Syria and Palestine after 628, but the exorbitant costs of the war against the Sasanid Persians had led him to concentrate his limited military forces in the north on the Persian frontier. His inability to defend the south with full force cost him dearly: in a series of battles in 634–638 he lost Palestine and Syria to the Arabs and was forced to retreat to Anatolia. Subsequently, the Arabs conquered Byzantine Egypt (639–642) and ended the last resistance of the Sasanids in Persia in 651. An Arab empire rose in Palestine, Syria, Egypt, and Persia, which the strongman Muawiya (r. 661–680) consolidated under the dynastic rule of the Umayyads.

Umayyad Religious Developments Under the third Umayyad ruler, Abd al-Malik (685–705), signs emerged of a religious orientation in the Arab Empire. Arabic inscriptions in and on the Dome of the Rock, dating to 691/692, refer to the prophet Muhammad and biblical predecessors, including Jesus the Messiah, as servants of God. Polemical verses oppose the Christian theology of Jesus as son of God, while other verses describe **Muslims** as believers in the "concordance" (*islam*) among all prophetic messages of the past. By implication this means that following God's commands in this concordance will bring salvation on the Day of Judgment.

The Dome of the Rock on Jerusalem's Temple Mount can be viewed as Abd al-Malik's counter-monument to the Church of the Holy Sepulcher on the other side of Jerusalem, built on the site of Jesus's tomb. Presumably he saw himself as the true "representative of God" (Arabic *khalifa*, borrowed into English as **caliph**) vis-à-vis the Byzantine emperor. Similarly, the emerging Islamic faith of the One God, Allah, which he was shaping as the state religion of the Umayyad Empire, was offered as a faith superior to **Trinitarian** Byzantine Christianity. To buttress this anti-Trinitarian state religion, Abd al-Malik created a strong central administration and army, with Arabic as the bureaucratic language.

Umayyad Conquests in West and East Abd al-Malik's successors continued the Umayyad efforts to take over Byzantium. Armies composed of Arabs and Berbers conquered Byzantine North Africa in 686–698. In 711, dissident Visigothic nobles invited Berber and Arab troops into the Iberian Peninsula to help them oust the reigning Visigothic king. The Berbers, Arabs, and Visigothic allies then divided Iberia among themselves. In the same year, the Umayyads expanded their rule into central Asia and the Indus Valley.

Muslim: Initially: believer in the concordance among all prophetic messages from Abraham to Jesus. Later on: believer who submits to the will of God (Arabic *Allah*).

Caliph: Representative of God, and later successor of Muhammad, on earth.

Trinitarianism: Christianity based on the doctrine of God the Father, Son, and Holy Spirit.

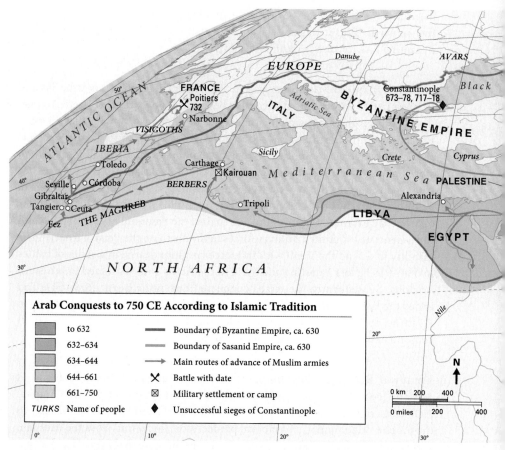

MAP 10.1 Arab Conquests to 750

Two decades later, the Iberian Berbers and Arabs pushed into France. One of these raids was commemorated in Western Christianity as the Battle of Tours in central France (732 or 733). Here, Charles Martel (r. 714–741), the forerunner of the Western Christian Carolingian empire, beat back the invading raiders. Similarly, Arab campaigns in the Caucasus failed around 740. It became evidently impossible to dispatch cavalry armies during summer campaigns from the capital of Damascus any farther than the Pyrenees, Hindu Kush, and Caucasus Mountains (see Map 10.1).

From the Umayyads to the Abbasids   The end of expansion and the need to shift from conquest to consolidation created a religio-political crisis in the empire. In Iran, the crisis exploded into revolution, as Persian military lords and Arab settlers expected a "rightly guided" leader (*Mahdi*, or Messiah) to arrive. This Mahdi would establish a realm of justice on earth at the end of time before God's Judgment. The revolutionaries overthrew the Umayyads in 750, but instead of the Mahdi and his realm of justice, the new dynasty of the Abbasids emerged. After moving the capital of the empire to Baghdad in Iraq, the Abbasids built the same kind of top-heavy central administration and army that had characterized the Umayyads.

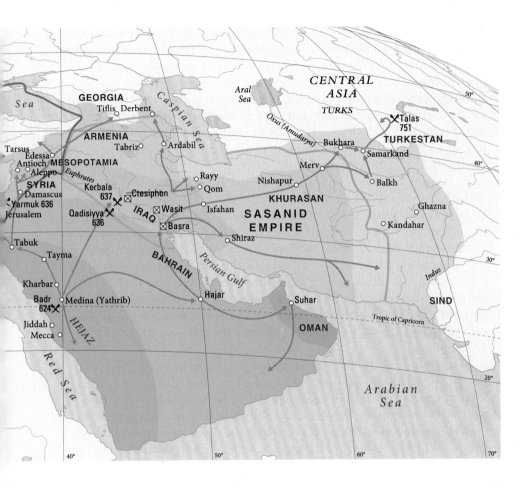

Islamic Theology, Law, and Politics

In Iraq, the Abbasids completed what the Umayyads had begun in Syria. They enlarged and systematized the state religion of Islam, and sponsored the translation of scientific, philosophical, legal, and literary works from Syriac and Persian into Arabic. Schools and libraries spread from Baghdad to cities from Iberia to northwest India. Many of these cities became cultural and political centers of their own, under autonomous dynasties that recognized the Abbasid caliphs in Baghdad but were basically independent. By around 950, an Islamic religious civilization organized into a commonwealth under ethnically diverse dynasties had emerged.

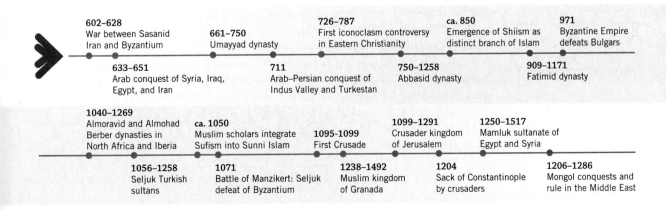

602–628
War between Sasanid
Iran and Byzantium

661–750
Umayyad dynasty

726–787
First iconoclasm controversy
in Eastern Christianity

ca. 850
Emergence of Shiism as
distinct branch of Islam

971
Byzantine Empire
defeats Bulgars

633–651
Arab conquest of Syria, Iraq,
Egypt, and Iran

711
Arab–Persian conquest of
Indus Valley and Turkestan

750–1258
Abbasid dynasty

909–1171
Fatimid dynasty

1040–1269
Almoravid and Almohad
Berber dynasties in
North Africa and Iberia

ca. 1050
Muslim scholars integrate
Sufism into Sunni Islam

1095-1099
First Crusade

1099–1291
Crusader kingdom
of Jerusalem

1250–1517
Mamluk sultanate of
Egypt and Syria

1056–1258
Seljuk Turkish
sultans

1071
Battle of Manzikert: Seljuk
defeat of Byzantium

1238–1492
Muslim kingdom
of Granada

1204
Sack of Constantinople
by crusaders

1206–1286
Mongol conquests and
rule in the Middle East

Sunna: The paradigmatic "path" of Muhammad's traditions, which, if trodden by believers, will lead to salvation.

Shaping Islamic Theology   In the 800s, scholars, judges, and bureaucrats in the Abbasid Empire completed the compilation of the Quran, the beginnings of which date back to the late 600s. Since it is God's word, the Prophet Muhammad himself appears only a few times in the Quran. Therefore, after the compilation of the Quran, traditions (*ahadith*, plural of *hadith*) about Muhammad's life were gathered into encyclopedic collections as well as a biography (*sira*). Together, these traditions and the biography of the Prophet acquired the status of scripture, under the name of **Sunna**, although in contrast to the Quran, they are not revelations.

Today, after more than a generation of extensive research, a scholarly consensus is beginning to emerge, according to which neither the traditions nor the biography of Muhammad are sufficient to serve as a history of Islamic origins. Being removed by at least 150 years from the events they describe as having taken place in western Arabian Mecca and Medina, they are too far away in time to be reliable accounts. Scholars have so far been unable to trace any traditions further back than ca. 720, that is, roughly to the time of the sons of Abd al-Malik, who was discussed above as the ruler under whom the first signs of an emerging Islam appeared. In other words, there is no Islamic documentation for the events of the early 600s; the first Muslim accounts apart from the Quran we have date to the 800s and 900s.

This is not to say that the traditions and the biography of the Prophet are devoid of kernels of historical truth. Present-day scholars of Islamic origins merely argue that it is not possible to identify any of these kernels clearly and unambiguously as historically true. They are embedded in the religious preoccupations of the Abbasids and their scholars and are therefore theology more than history. Parallels to the gap between the literature on origins and the assumed earlier origins in Islam can be found also in Ancient Israel, Zoroastrianism, Christianity, Hinduism, Buddhism, Confucianism, and Daoism, as reflected in the corresponding chapters of this book.

Umma: Community of all who believe in one God, with Muhammad as his prophet, and reject pagan idolatry (*jahiliyya*, "ignorance") or associationism (*shirk*), such as the Christian doctrine of Trinity.

The intention in this Abbasid theology of Islamic origins is clear; the caliphs and their scholars sought to further a new monotheistic religion that had left any Christian roots behind and centered on what one may call Islam's triple Arabness: the Arab Muhammad preached an Arabic Quran to the Arabs of Arabia, thereby ending an assumed paganism on the peninsula. Instead of developing the early community (***umma***) into yet another soon-to-be-forgotten Christian sect in the Middle East, like others that had arisen in previous centuries, the Abbasids turned it into its own separate religion. For this religion they claimed superiority: thanks to their zeal for holy war (***jihad***), the Muslims had conquered the Persians and had reduced the Byzantines to Anatolia and the Balkans.

Jihad: Literally "struggle" (for the path of God—*fi sabil Allah*). This can range from personal struggle for faith to war in the name of Islam.

Five religious duties identify a Muslim: the profession of faith, prayer, fasting, almsgiving, and pilgrimage to Mecca. The profession of faith is summed up in the formula "There is no God but God, and Muhammad is his messenger." Prayer is performed five times daily; on Fridays the noon prayer is carried out in the congregational mosque. Fasting means a month-long abstinence during Ramadan from food, drink, and sex during the daylight hours. Almsgiving is a donation or tax to benefit the poor, and the pilgrimage (*hajj*) is a journey to Mecca made at least once in one's life.

Creating Islamic Law   The five religious duties are part of the body of moral–legal duties, the **Sharia**. The Abbasids had inherited a judicial system from the Umayyads that was based on the legal traditions of Roman Syria and Sasanid Persia. In the late 700s, the dynasty sponsored the translations of digests of the Justinian Roman law codex in order to create a unified legal system. Since Muslims were at the same time compiling the Quran, it is not surprising that the creation of the Sharia became part of the same unification process. When it was completed in the late 900s, the Sharia encompassed the legal verses of the Quran, the prophetic Sunna, and legal commentaries.

Sharia: The combined body of the legal verses of the Quran, the prophetic Sunna, and the legal commentaries of the 800s and 900s, covering law as well as morality.

The Separation of State and Religion   The shaping of Islamic theology and law became controversial toward the middle of the 800s. If all theology and law had to be based on the Quran and Sunna, sooner or later every possible moral or legal matter would be unchangeably grounded in God's authority. Nothing could be added to the Sharia or changed in it, and one could only interpret. To preserve their freedom to shape the Sharia, the caliphs instituted a loyalty oath from 833 to 849, which required all judges and jurists to support the policy of continued caliphal legislation.

A minority refused the oath and found support among the urban craftsmen and traders who believed that God's law should be above human manipulation. After riots, the Abbasids enacted a compromise whereby the religious scholars (*ulama*) became the guardians of the Sharia and the caliphs its executors. This compromise resulted in a separation of religion and state, with the ulama responsible for the judicial system and the state executing the law according to its own interests.

Shiite Islam   From about 950 onward, Islam under the guardianship of the ulama is known as Sunni Islam. It expresses the Sunna of the Prophet and the consensus of the religious community represented by the ulama and laid down in the Sharia. Sunni Islam has always encompassed the majority of Muslims (about 90 percent today). Followers of Shiite [SHEE-ite] Islam make up about 10 percent of Muslims worldwide, although they are the majority in contemporary Iran, Iraq, and Lebanon.

The origin of Shiite Islam as a religio-political movement dates to the end of the Umayyads, when revolutionaries proclaimed the imminent arrival of the Mahdi. Tradition places the Shiite beginnings in the period of the first four caliphs, when Caliph Ali lost his throne and Ali's grandson Husayn lost his bid for the caliphate against the Umayyads. According to tradition, Ali was a cousin of the Prophet; the husband of one of his daughters, Fatima; and the founder of the Alid family, whose eldest male in direct descent was entitled to the leadership of the Muslim community in place of the Umayyads.

The main differences between Sunnism and Shiism concern the roles of tradition and authority. The tradition of Husayn's martyrdom near Karbala in Iraq at the hands of the Sunni Umayyads is central for all Shiites and is commemorated during Ashura, the tenth day of the month Muharram. The authority of the Alid descendants in the past, and today of the leaders of the Shiite clergy, is absolute and infallible. Sunnis, by contrast, reject the Karbala tradition. For them the consensus of the community separate from rulers and the absence of a scholarly hierarchy among the ulama are supreme. Shiite–Sunni differences have flared up throughout history to the present day.

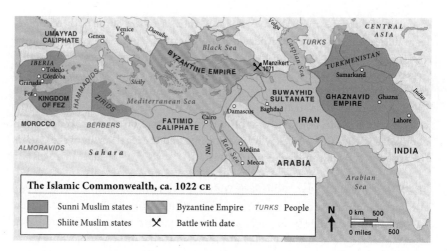

MAP 10.2 **The Islamic Commonwealth, ca. 1022 CE**

When the Abbasids squashed the apocalyptical expectation of God's king-dom at the end of time, apocalypticism went underground. It resurfaced in 874 when the twelfth-generation descendant of Ali was reported to have died with-out a visible successor. A radical group formed in Syria around the doctrine that a descendant of the seventh-generation leader would appear soon as the Mahdi. A dispute concerning the legitimate successor in the seventh generation divided the Shiites. Those who accepted the twelfth-generation descendant remained nonrevolutionary.

The radical group of "Seveners" fomented armed rebellions around 900 in outlying provinces of the Islamic commonwealth. The most successful rebel-lion was that of the Fatimids in 909 in eastern Algeria and Tunisia. The Fatimids (909–1171) went on to found a counter caliphate to that of the Abbasids, extend-ing from North Africa to Egypt, western Arabia, and parts of Syria. Until their end they claimed to represent God's kingdom on earth through a higher form of justice than that of the Abbasids.

The Abbasids in Crisis   In the second half of the 800s, the Abbasids were hit by severe financial problems. The Sasanid Persian expansion of agriculture be-tween the Euphrates and Tigris Rivers, continued by the Abbasids, had reached the limits of its potential. Agricultural tax revenue shrank. As a result, the admin-istration found it difficult to maintain its palace culture and bureaucracy. Palace guards, no longer paid, took over still-fertile tax districts directly as personal as-signments in place of direct salaries.

By the early eleventh century, a majority of the soldiers in the guards were Turks, recruited as slaves and manumitted as adults. From 861 to 945, Turkic slave com-manders wielded power in Baghdad while retaining the caliphs as titular heads of the government. The main function of the generals was the control of fiscal affairs in Iraq, but they also continued the Umayyad holy war against Byzantium. The only other active jihad activity was the Muslim conquest of Byzantine Sicily by an autonomous dynasty in Tunisia, completed by the Fatimids (827–902). For all practical purposes, the conquest period had ended.

Eastern Christian Civilization in Byzantium

Under siege by the Umayyads and Abbasids, Byzantium retreated to Anatolia and parts of the Balkans. Byzantium survived because its emperors reconstituted the state on a military and religious basis: locally organized border defenses and redefinition of Christian doctrine. Similar to the Abbasid Empire, Byzantium evolved into the center of a commonwealth of Eastern Christian states.

Byzantium's Difficult Beginnings

The Roman transition to the Byzantine Eastern Christian civilization was gradual. Nevertheless, the switch in emphasis from the pagan title of emperor to that of Christian king (*basileus*), the Umayyad military pressure, the organization of the Anatolian defense, and (after some doctrinal experimentation) renewed affirmation of Eastern Christian orthodoxy amounted to a new civilizational identity. Once this new identity and the recovery from the Muslim (and, in the Balkans, Slavic) onslaughts were achieved, Byzantium followed a pattern similar to that of the Muslims. Eastern Christianity became a commonwealth, with autonomous realms in the Balkans and what are now Ukraine and western Russia, and evolved into a top-heavy centralized state relying on palace guards.

Survival Strategies   Under constant Arab pressure in eastern Anatolia, northern Africa, and Sicily (636–863), the Byzantine Empire shrank to an Anatolian–Balkan realm. Between 653 and 833, both the Umayyad and Abbasid caliphs attacked Constantinople seven times. The empire survived the attacks only by withdrawing from much of the Balkans and concentrating on Anatolia. Around 580, Slavs migrated southward to settle in the Balkans. Here, they gradually became the linguistically dominant population, assimilating speakers of other languages, such as groups of Bulgars from the Volga region whose language was related to Turkish. The Bulgars had migrated in the 500s to the Byzantine lower Danube, where they were influenced by Slavic culture and asserted their independence from Byzantium in 681. As the Byzantines were fighting for survival against the Arabs in Anatolia, the Bulgars became a major power in the Balkans.

Focusing initially almost entirely on Anatolia, the emperors created new, stationary troops based in districts known as "themes" (Greek *themata*) and recruited from among volunteer foot soldiers in the interior Byzantine provinces. Themes were made up of small plots from imperial estates in the exposed provinces of Anatolia (and later also against the Slavs in the Balkans); the troops were also given cash and food provisions, which were collected as taxes from large landowner estates and free farmers. Their main task was to harass the invading Arabs. Southern Anatolia suffered harshly from constant Arab raids. Provincial life in Anatolia became increasingly poor for its Christian inhabitants, and even Constantinople declined in wealth.

Iconoclasm   Throughout this period the Byzantine emperors actively shaped religious doctrine and law, similar to the caliphs in the Islamic empire. One religious dispute taken up by the emperors was **iconoclasm** (726–787 and 814–842),

Iconoclasm: Removal of all religious images from churches and monasteries during a period in the Byzantine Empire, under orders of the emperors.

that is, the destruction of religious images in accordance with Exodus 20:40 in the Hebrew Bible. As the Christian church had evolved in the first six centuries CE, church fathers and theologians who stressed the divinity of Jesus and the role of his mother Mary as the "God bearer" gained prominence, especially in Egypt and Syria. Churchmen who, by contrast, sought to hold on to the human status of Jesus and Mary became marginalized or were declared heretical. The rise of Islam reversed this trend, with its radical emphasis on all prophets, including Jesus, being mere humans. In the 720s, when Byzantium was no longer burdened with the Churches of Egypt and Syria, the return to a more even-handed view of Jesus as both divine and human became attractive again in the eyes of bishops and emperors. Accordingly, the latter viewed divine images (or images of divine figures) with disdain.

Under orders by emperors, the destruction or plastering over of images gathered speed in the 750s, although it was by no means uniform or intense in all parts of the empire. Since the production of art was expensive and the state was strapped for resources at a time of still-dangerous Muslim incursions, the emperors were relieved to be able to reduce their patronage. But in the 800s, the Muslim danger abated, and resistance in the ordinary population, still deeply committed to the trend of the previous centuries toward the divinization of Jesus, made it increasingly difficult for the emperors to remain committed to iconoclasm. Monks, who were much closer to the population than bishops, patriarchs, and emperors, had a particular interest in images; many monasteries contained the tombs of saints and their images, and both functioned for pilgrims in the same way as Jesus and Mary did—they were intercessors to God.

By 842 the emperors had given up their opposition to images, and thereafter they withdrew from imposing doctrines on the Church. Like the caliphs in the Abbasid Empire, the Byzantine emperors left religion to the religious institution. As we will see in Chapter 11, a similar disengagement between politics and religion occurred in Western Christianity after the investiture controversy two centuries later. In this respect, the religious civilizations of Islam, Byzantium, and Western Christianity followed similar patterns of development.

Transformation into a Commonwealth   In the mid-800s, the strategy of using troops based in themes to defend Anatolia finally paid off. Exploiting the fiscal crisis of the Abbasids after ca. 850, theme commanders raided

The Byzantine Commonwealth. Characteristic of eastern Christianity are the many churches dedicated to Hagia Sophia, "Holy Wisdom," which can be found throughout the Byzantine commonwealth, from the Balkans to the Caucasus. Though each region developed its own architectural style, they all organized sacred space in similar ways. A masterpiece of design and engineering based in part on the theories of the third-century BCE mathematician Archimedes, the Hagia Sophia in Constantinople was dedicated in 537 by the emperor Justinian on the foundations of an earlier structure (a). Its massive dome was often compared to the great dome of heaven itself, and the church would become the prototype for many others throughout the commonwealth in subsequent centuries, including the Cathedral of Saint Sophia in Kiev (today Kyiv), whose foundations were laid early in the eleventh century (b). While it exhibits a distinctly Kievan style of church architecture, including over a dozen cupolas, the cathedral nonetheless embodies an unmistakable Byzantine tradition whose roots extend deep into the past.

Muslim settlements in eastern Anatolia and northern Iraq with increasing frequency. By 965, Byzantium had regained all of Anatolia, and in 969 it retook the northern Syrian gateway of Antioch. The emperors now turned to the Balkans. Here, the Bulgars had converted to Eastern Christianity in 864 and, under their own emperors, had forced Byzantium to pay tribute in the early 900s. But in 971, the Byzantines crushed the Bulgars and reintegrated their realm into the empire. By the middle of the eleventh century, Byzantium's territory extended again from Belgrade and the Balkans southeast to Antioch in northern Syria.

The reintegration of the Balkans into the empire formed the background for the transformation of Byzantium into a commonwealth of Eastern Christianity. In the late 700s or early 800s what is today Kiev (also "Kyiv," today in Ukraine) was an outpost of the mixed Jewish, Christian, and Muslim Khazar realm northeast of the Black Sea, but in the late 800s fell to Norman merchants from Scandinavia known as Varangians, who had pushed south from the Baltic Sea and were eager to

MAP 10.3 **The Byzantine Empire, ca. 1025 CE**

establish a trading route to Byzantium. The Varangian princes in the lands under their control were known as "Rus" (from which "Russia" is derived), probably a name of Scandinavian origin. By the 800s, most Varangians had intermarried with Slavs and had become culturally Slavic. In addition to trading, the Rus repeatedly raided Byzantium, thereby adding to the difficulties of the empire during the 800s and early 900s. By the mid-900s, Rus trading and raiding had made Kiev a regional power.

In 988, Grand Prince Vladimir I of Kiev (r. 980–1015) decreed the conversion of his subjects to Christianity. With this conversion of Rus, Eastern Christianity expanded beyond the Byzantine Empire into the lands north of the Black Sea. An Eastern Christian commonwealth of states emerged in this region similar to that of Islam in the Middle East and the Mediterranean.

Military Changes   The Kievan troops in the service of the Byzantine Empire, called the Varangian Guard, formed the nucleus of foreign palace guards and fulfilled functions similar to those of the Turkic slave guards among the Abbasids. In Byzantium, they were added to balance older Armenian or indigenous regiments recruited to protect the emperors from rivals for the throne. These rivals were often from provincial landowning families, which formed an aristocracy that remained prominent until the end of Byzantium in 1453.

In the later 900s, when the empire had recovered, the emperors embarked on a recentralization of the empire, unifying military and civil control over the themes in order to weaken the aristocracy. The effect of these changes in the military was a rising dependency of the emperors on palace guards and a weakening of the border defenses. The Byzantine Empire experienced the same phenomenon of a top-heavy state and a power-hungry palace military that had already plagued the Abbasids for two centuries.

The first province where the beginning military weakness of Byzantium had consequences was southern Italy. In this restless place, the emperor had no choice in 1051 but to appoint a local lord to the governorship. Western Norsemen, or Normans, had entered the service of regional lords who were fighting both the Byzantines and Muslim raiders from Sicily. Initially, Byzantium and the papacy in Rome cooperated against the Normans, even though the pope was at loggerheads with the patriarch of Constantinople over clerical jurisdiction in southern Italy. At one point, in 1053, the Normans achieved a military victory over the pope, but since they submitted to his authority soon thereafter, the latter was now free to pursue his jurisdictional claims more forcefully. Striving for jurisdictional supremacy over both Western and Eastern Christianities, the pope, Leo IX (in office 1049–1054), dispatched an embassy to Constantinople to assert his claim.

Unfortunately for the lead ambassador, the patriarch of Constantinople, Michael I Cerularius (in office 1043–1059), was also a man of elevated views about his role. For him, the pope was at best a first among equals and he even viewed himself as the arbiter of the Byzantine imperial order, deciding among claimants to the imperial throne. He refused to meet with the ambassador for months, even though the emperor still favored continued cooperation with the pope. The two churches had not been in communion for about half a century, disagreeing over a variety of liturgical and monastic practices (among others, the *filioque* in the **Creed**, the bread of the **Eucharist**, and **celibacy**). The central dispute was about

Creed: "... [A]nd the Holy Spirit, the Lord, the giver of life, who proceeds from the Father and the Son [*filioque*], who with the Father and the Son is adored and glorified" (partial quote). The *filioque* was inserted into the Creed in Spain at the end of the 500s to combat Arianism, which denied the divinity of Jesus, but it was never ratified in Eastern Christianity.

Eucharist: The partaking of bread and wine in commemoration of Jesus Christ's last supper. Byzantium accused Rome of serving unleavened bread, which it denounced as "Jewish."

Celibacy: Abstinence from sexual relations and/or marriage. Eastern Christianity allows clerical marriage.

Byzantine Woman Defending Her Virtue. Conscious of their privileged status, the Varangian Guards often mistreated ordinary people in the population. Like the Turkish slave guards at the Abbasid court, they had the reputation of being thieves, murderers, and rapists. In this image, Ioannes Skylitzes (ca. 1040–1101), a historian and illustrator, delighted in depicting the story of a woman who not only defended her virtue successfully by killing her attacker but also had the stunned surviving Varangians turn over the clothes of their dead comrade to her.

the jurisdictional authority of the pope as laid down in the *Donation of Constantine*, a document forged in Rome in the 700s that gave the pope supremacy over the patriarchs of Constantinople, Alexandria, Antioch, and Jerusalem. Although taken at face value in the eleventh century, the *Donation* was interpreted differently in west and east. Only in the Renaissance, as explained in Chapter 17, did scholars unmask the document as a fake.

Eventually, in July 1054, the ambassador placed a letter on the altar of Hagia Sophia, excommunicating Michael from the Church. Michael responded with an excommunication of the embassy. In order to pacify the popular unrest that was forming in the streets, both patriarch and emperor blamed the events on a conspiracy by the governor of southern Italy, alleged to be a secret Catholic, who had sent a false embassy pretending to be from Rome. Thus, in 1054 the first formal step was taken to ratify what had been in existence already for several centuries, that is, the existence of two separate Christianities, an Eastern Orthodox Christianity and a Western Catholic Christianity.

The Seljuk Invasion and the Crusades

The decline of Byzantine power in Italy had an equally fatal parallel in the east of the Byzantine Empire, in Asia Minor or Anatolia. Islamized Seljuk [sel-JOOK] Turks had migrated in the early eleventh century southwestward from central Asia. They conquered the shrunken Abbasid realm and inflicted heavy land losses on the Byzantines in Anatolia. To beat back the Seljuks, the emperors called on the pope for help, the recent church split in 1054 notwithstanding. The pope responded by sending the First Crusaders, who conquered Jerusalem in 1099. The subsequent crusader kingdom of Jerusalem was of some help to Byzantium in regaining land lost to the Seljuks in Anatolia, but a century later Western Christians sacked Constantinople in the Fourth Crusade and established a Latin empire in Byzantium for nearly two generations (1204–1261). The crusader kingdom survived until 1291, when the Muslim Mamluks of Egypt and Syria captured Jerusalem.

The Seljuk Invasion   As discussed earlier, Turks formed part of the ethnic mix of Islamic civilization from the early 800s onward. Technically, they had the status of military slaves (*mamalik*, pl. of *mamluk*) in the service of Arab and Persian dynasties as elite troops. Once converted to Islam, however, they were free men, and as such, some Turks even founded dynasties. To replenish the ranks of Turkish elite troops, the rulers sent raiding parties into the grazing grounds of central Asia inhabited by pagan nomadic Turkish clans and federations. Gradually, however, nomadic Turkish leaders benefiting from trade developed an interest in urbanized Islamic civilization. This interest was similar to that of the Rus of Kiev seeking to adopt Eastern Christianity, as we saw above. It was in this context that the Seljuk Turks east of the Volga River converted to Islam and began their migration into the Islamic commonwealth.

Seljuk leaders believed that Muslims had grown lax with their holy war against the Byzantines. Furthermore, they considered Shiism a heresy. In Baghdad, freeborn non-revolutionary "Twelver" Shiites had partially replaced the Turkish slaves in the palace guards. In Egypt and parts of Syria, the revolutionary "Sevener" Fatimids still sought to overthrow the Abbasids in Iraq. Assuming the exalted title "sultan" (from Arabic for "authority, power"), the Seljuk leaders devoted themselves to jihad and began their first raids against the Byzantines in the 1040s. By 1059 they were in control of Baghdad, from which they conducted their holy war against Byzantium and the Fatimids.

The Defeat of Manzikert   The Byzantine emperors did not have time to rebuild an army that could stop the Seljuk conquest. An effort in 1071 to drive the Seljuks from eastern Anatolia failed. The assortment of remaining theme soldiers and central regiments, as well as palace guards and other mercenaries, was unable to hold together at Manzikert (now Malazgird) in eastern Anatolia. In the end, the emperor Romanus Diogenes (r. 1068-1071) found himself a prisoner of the Seljuk sultan.

The consequences of the defeat were severe. In the following decade and a half, the Seljuks occupied most of Anatolia, leaving the Byzantines in command of only a few coastal cities and islands. In the mid-1000s, Normans carved out realms for themselves from Byzantine southern Italy and Greece. From there they invaded Greece and became a real threat for the empire in the second half of the eleventh century.

The situation improved only in 1092, when the reigning sultan died and the Seljuk Empire broke apart into competing successor states. By this time, a reform-minded emperor, Alexius I Comnenus (r. 1081–1118), had driven out the Normans from Greece. Alexius turned his attention to his most dangerous Muslim neighbor, the Rum Sultanate of the Seljuks in Nicaea, 60 miles from Constantinople. However, he needed more troops than he was able to pay for in the Varangian

Guard, his only reliable military force. Relations with Western Christianity had improved, and when Alexius sent an embassy in the spring of 1095 to Rome, he found a sympathetic ear.

The Crusades   Alexius received more from the pope than he had bargained for. At the Council of Clermont in 1095, Pope Urban II (r. 1088–1099) called for an armed pilgrimage to aid Byzantium and liberate the church from the Seljuks. Well-equipped knights as well as poorer folk responded enthusiastically (for more on the Crusades, see Chapter 11). For Alexius, the crusade was an embarrassment. It included Normans who had battled him in Greece. Even if he were able to control them, how much land in Anatolia would the victorious crusaders turn over to him? And even if considerable territory were ceded, how would he be able to defend it by himself? At first, Alexius did indeed receive what he wanted; with the help of the Byzantine navy, the crusaders conquered Nicaea and grudgingly turned it over to him.

In the period thereafter, however, Alexius was under no illusion about the willingness of the crusaders to conquer Anatolia and Syria for him. Even though

Battle of Manzikert. The battle was not only a bitter defeat for the Byzantine army at the hands of the Seljuks; it was also a personal humiliation for Emperor Romanus IV (see image), who had done his best to prepare for battle. This humiliation had such repercussions even in Western Christianity that Maître de Rohan, the artist of this miniature, in the early fifteenth century still found it worthy of commemoration. Rohan, in the service of members of the French aristocracy, was a major manuscript illustrator of his time.

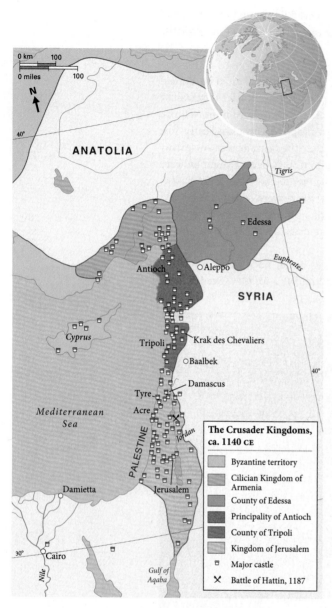

MAP 10.4 The Crusader Kingdoms, ca. 1140 CE

the emperor sent aid to the crusaders during their siege of Antioch (1097–1098), he did not receive the city after the crusaders' victory. Nor did he obtain Jerusalem, which the crusaders conquered from the Fatimids in 1099. Instead, in 1100 the crusaders made Jerusalem the capital of an independent crusader kingdom.

For Muslim historians in the early 1100s, the crusades were delayed Christian jihads in revenge for Arab expansion under the Umayyads. They dated the beginning of this revenge to the Norman invasion of Muslim Sicily in 1061 and the Castilian capture of Toledo in 1085. The fall of Jerusalem in 1099 exposed, they felt, an alarming laxness of Muslim religious zeal.

The loss of Sicily, Toledo, and Jerusalem was substantial. The Emirate of Sicily had flourished for a century and a half. The Emirate of Toledo had been part of a nearly three-century-old Islamic culture in Iberia whose power derived from its gold trade with West Africa and palace guards manned by Slavic slave soldiers. The losses of Sicily and Toledo effectively ended Muslim dominance in the Mediterranean.

Muslim Recovery and Byzantine–Crusader Cooperation Imad al-Din Zengi (r. 1127–1146) was a Turkish-descended leader from Upper Iraq who took the admonitions of the historians to heart. He, and later his sons, made steady progress against the crusader kingdom. He had weathered the Second Crusade of 1147–1149, mounted in response to his sack of Edessa, but could not prevent the crusaders from repairing relations with Byzantium. After submitting Antioch to Byzantine overlordship, they received naval support in return. The king of Jerusalem married a Byzantine princess in 1158, and the emperor himself married a princess from Antioch in 1160. Constantinople and Jerusalem forged a powerful alliance.

The alliance paid off in 1169, when a Byzantine fleet carried crusaders to an invasion of Fatimid Egypt. The Fatimids had never recovered from the loss of the Palestinian–Syrian coast after 1099 to the crusaders. Unfortunately for the Byzantium–crusader alliance, however, the Muslims also coveted Egypt and drove out the Byzantines. By 1171 Muslims had established a formidable anti crusader realm.

Jerusalem and Constantinople Lost   The Sunni Muslim conquest of Shiite Egypt was a turning point for both the crusaders and Byzantium. The Kurdish-descended emir Saladin (Salah al-Din Yusuf ibn Ayyub, r. 1174–1193), leader of the anti-crusader realm, parlayed the agricultural wealth of Egypt into a formidable war machine that wore down the crusaders. In 1187, his victory in the Battle of Hattin, near the Sea of Galilee, enabled Saladin to reconquer Jerusalem and nearly wipe out the kingdom.

The Third Crusade of 1189–1192, in response to the losses after Hattin, saved the rump kingdom from destruction. Its failure to regain Jerusalem, however, set the stage for the Fourth Crusade in 1204, planned as a mass campaign to take the holy city. But the crusade became instead a Venetian conquest of Byzantium with the sack of Constantinople in 1204. The concentrated urban wealth of Constantinople in Byzantium was too tempting to be resisted, even if Eastern Christians were brethren in the faith and Muslims the enemy.

Precarious Crusader Survival   Having established a fragile Latin regime (1204–1257), western Europeans became obsessed with conquering wealthy Egypt as a prelude for saving the crusader kingdom. Five more crusades (1191–1291) were launched for the benefit of the kingdom, whose capital was now at Acre. Only one of them landed in Acre; all others sailed to, or toward, Egypt without ever achieving permanent conquest.

Beginning in the mid-1200s, however, the crusader kingdom became the victim of new political forces arising in the Middle East. In 1250 the Mamluks—Turkish military slaves from the Russian steppes and dominant in the armies of Saladin's successors—established their own regime in Egypt (1250–1517). In 1260 the Mamluks had to face the pagan Mongols, who had emerged in the previous half-century under Genghis Khan (r. 1206–1227) and his descendants as a major power (see Chapter 13). The Mongols were tough competition for the Mamluks.

In 1255 the Mongols conquered Iran and Iraq, ended what remained of the Abbasid caliphate in Baghdad in 1258, and advanced into Syria. The Mamluks, however, defeated the Mongols at Ain Jalut in Galilee in 1260 and in other battles in the following decades, and pushed them from Syria back into Iraq and Iran. Under the name of Ilkhanids, the Mongols converted to Islam and became linguistically Persian. Close to being free of the Mongol threat, the Mamluks terminated the crusader state in 1291 with the conquest of Acre.

Islamic and Eastern Christian Civilizations at Their Height

By 1300, the borders between Western and Eastern Christianity as well as Islam were again clearly drawn. The most important Islamic state was the Mamluk Sultanate in Egypt, Palestine, and Syria. Victorious against the crusaders and the Mongols, this rich and powerful state endured for nearly three centuries (1250–1517) and represented Middle Eastern Islamic civilization at its peak. Byzantium had been rebuilt as a small realm located mostly in the Balkans (1261–1453). Both the Mamluk Sultanate and Byzantium were eventually

THE MAMLUK EMPIRE, ca. 1300

Divorce Court. Husband and wife arguing about a divorce before a judge; scene from al-Hariri, *Maqamat* (ms. dated 1222). Hariri's stories, among the most popular during the classical period, involve a poor but eloquent storyteller traveling from town to town in different disguises but being recognized each time by the fictional author. The stories include occurrences of everyday life, like this divorce.

emperors settled free foot soldiers and horsemen on plots of land, they also collected taxes in money and distributed them in the form of stipends among the soldiers. Furthermore, plenty of small freeholders and large landlords who owned property inherited from the late Roman period coexisted with the soldiers settled on themes.

In the mid-700s, during the difficult years of defense, the emperors and their central administration were unable to prevent the rise of the landed aristocracy. Landlords acquired small farms and reserved the positions of generals for their families; they became a hereditary aristocracy. Free farmers turned increasingly into tenant farmers. Like the Mamluk emirs a little later, the aristocratic landlords were the wealthiest segment of imperial society.

The Recentralization of the Empire   Generals from the aristocracy were the main competitors for the office of emperor in Constantinople. But when the empire recovered from the 900s onward, high officials of the central administration developed their own ambitions hostile to those of the aristocracy. In the eleventh and twelfth centuries, the emperors were torn between the interests of the aristocracy and the administrators. In the eleventh century, few emperors were up to the task of long-term reforms, such as ensuring regular training of soldiers and prohibiting the acquisition of land by the aristocracy.

The easy way out was to hire mercenaries, beginning with the Varangian Guard. Competent emperors, as from the Komnenos (also Comnenus) dynasty (1081–1185), however, realized that the state could not finance more than small numbers of mercenaries. Instead, they made use of the land assignment institution (*pronoia*), which allowed an assignee to collect all taxes from a parcel of land in return for military service. This institution became the backbone of a patronage system in Constantinople.

After the hiatus of 1204–1261, with its Latin crusader regime, the Byzantine court and its top families were largely gone. What was left were the aristocratic families in the reconstituted provinces. Their reluctance to submit permanently to the new Palaiologos (also Palaeologus) imperial family of post-1261 eventually doomed Byzantium when the Ottomans made their final attack in 1453.

Commercial Relations from the Atlantic to the South China Sea

The Persians and Romans had pioneered the trade of gold and silver for luxuries during the period 600 BCE–600 CE. This trade expanded during the Fatimid and Mamluk periods in Egypt, facilitated by the cultural unity of Islamic civilization. In addition, Byzantium during its heyday (950–1050) and western Europe after the First Crusade (1099) were integrated into the luxury trade. An Afro-Eurasian commercial world system, extending from West Africa to China, linked the Islamic, Eastern Christian, and Western Christian civilizations to the Indian and Chinese civilizations (see Map 10.5).

Trade Routes and Commerce   To understand the West Africa–China world trade, we begin with West Africa. Villagers mined gold in the rain forest on the upper Niger and Senegal Rivers and traded with African merchants from kingdoms located along the middle Niger (see Chapter 14). The kings sent raiding parties to other regions in the rain forest to capture slaves. Merchants and kings then sold the gold and surplus of slaves to visiting Muslim merchants from North Africa and Iberia.

The visitors from the north paid with North African and Iberian manufactures and with salt from mines in the Sahara. In the Mediterranean basin, Muslims, Jews, and Western and Eastern Christians shared the trade of West African gold and European timber for Indian and Indonesian spices, dyestuffs, ointments, and cottons as well as Chinese silks, porcelain, and lacquerware. The Mamluks allowed only Muslims and Jews to travel beyond the Mediterranean, and thus Christians remained limited to the Mediterranean.

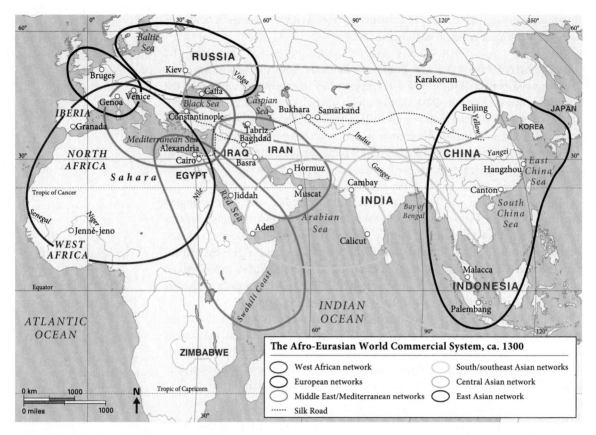

MAP 10.5 The Afro-Eurasian World Commercial System, ca. 1300

There were three secondary trade routes. First, there was the overland Silk Road with its gold-for-luxuries trade that connected Iran with China via central Asia, active particularly during the Mongol period. Second, there was the maritime East African trade route, where merchants exchanged manufactures for ivory, gold, and slaves. And third, there was the Volga route, where Rus merchants traded gold, silver, spices, ivory, silk, wine, and fur, connecting the Middle East with western Europe via the Baltic Sea. Both primary and secondary trade routes yielded the Mamluks immense supplementary tax revenues.

Islamic and Jewish merchants in the Egyptian center of this network were for the most part wholesalers for whom the import and distribution of eastern luxuries formed only a part of their overall commercial activities. They also organized the regional production and distribution of raw materials and contracted with craftspeople for the production of various goods. Merchants who were also **tax farmers** maintained grain stores, with employees responsible for collecting, shipping, brokering, and marketing the grain. Others farmed the taxes from ports or public auction houses. Diversification was the preferred path to consistent profitability in the merchant class.

Tax farming: A system for collecting taxes and rents from the population, where the state grants the right of collection to private individuals.

The Black Death   Extensive travel, however, yielded unforeseen risks. The more densely people lived together and the more frequently they traveled, the more often they incurred the risk of spreading disease. The Black Death of 1347 was, scholars surmise, set off by the Mongol invasion of Vietnam. Southeast Asia was one of the permanent breeding grounds for the pandemic among rodent fleas. From here, the Mongols dispersed the bacillus via China and the Silk Road to the Black Sea area. Genoese merchants carried the virulent disease to the Mediterranean and north-west Europe (see Chapter 11). Egyptian sources indicate that the plague recurred for another century and a half. Not until the 1500s did Middle Eastern population levels recover to pre-1347 levels.

Religion, Sciences, and the Arts in Two Religious Civilizations

Despite the impact of the Black Death, Mamluk Egypt and reconstituted Byzantium during the 1300s and 1400s were active cultural centers. Scholars and artists developed their respective cultures within traditional boundaries. In Islamic civilization, the most important new cultural phenomenon was mystical (Sufi) Islam, and in Eastern Christianity it was a revival of Platonism.

Islamic Culture: Intellectual and Scientific Expressions

Mystical Islam, or **Sufism**, developed from the Christian, Zoroastrian, and Greek philosophical heritages interacting within the Muslim world. Around 1050 Muslim scholars integrated Sufism into the Sunni-dominated Islamic civilization, and around 1200 Sunni mystics adapted Sufism to popular practice in the form of congregational broth-erhoods in lodges. Educated Muslims were conversant in phi-losophy and the sciences, both of which flourished in the period 1050–1300.

Sufism: Meditative devotion to faith, expressed in the form of prayer, ecstasy, chanting, or dancing.

Sunni–Sufi Islam   Sufism involved a form of meditative practice in pursuit of a pure (and personal) experience of the internal and infinite divine. The practice went beyond the prayers prescribed in Islam. Since this experience took place within themselves, early Sufis in the 900s were often accused of violating the Islamic doc-trine of God's external transcendence. It was only in the second half of the eleventh century during the Seljuk-sponsored religious revival that a compromise was reached: As long as Sufis subscribed to the Sharia, they could practice Sufism.

In the 1200s, teachers of Sufism founded lodges in which they provided training in meditative practice for Muslims. With time, these lodges branched out to urban centers as well as villages and even among nomadic tribes. Sunni Muslims of all walks of life joined. By around 1450, Islamic civilization was a commonwealth

Maritime Trade. This image, an illustration in Hariri's *Maqamat* (ms. dated 1236), depicts a stylized oceangoing sailing ship used in trade between Arabia and India.

not only of competing states but also of competing Sufi brotherhoods. The Sunni–Sufi compromise dominated in Islamic civilization until ca. 1900.

Philosophy and Sciences   As in the case of Sufism, philosophers also encountered opposition from among the proponents of Sunnism and did so for the same reason of violating the transcendence doctrine. Greek philosophical writings had attracted Muslim thinkers well before the emergence of mature Sunnism. A central concern of the Muslim philosophers was the reconciliation of Platonic-Aristotelian thought with Islam. Leading philosophers, such as Ibn Sina (Avicenna, ca. 980–1037) and Ibn Rushd (Averroës, 1126–1198), achieved this reconciliation by viewing philosophy as the discipline of logical concepts and religion its equivalent in stories. Ibn Khaldun (1332–1406), a philosopher of history and political theorist, on the other hand, found philosophy and speculative (that is, philosophically inspired) theology incompatible with religion. In his conclusion, which carried the day, philosophy and speculative theology were inferior forms of thought, while Sharia-inspired Sufism was superior. As in Western Christianity, thinkers struggled with the question of compatibility between thought and faith.

As with philosophy, scientific texts were also available in Arabic translation. Islamic scientists made major contributions beyond the discoveries of the Greeks. The Greeks had developed geometry into a mathematical science, but they had left algebra undeveloped until the Alexandrian period of Hellenism. The Persian Muhammad ibn Musa al-Khwarizmi (ca. 780–850) laid the foundations for the conversion of algebra into a mathematical science.

After Khwarizmi, mathematicians developed decimal fractions, raised numbers to high powers, extracted roots from large numbers, and investigated the properties of complex equations with roots and higher-degree powers. Persian and Arab astronomers refined the work of the Alexandrian astronomer Ptolemy (d. ca. 168 CE). Physicists elaborated on Archimedes's investigations into the physics of balances and weights and developed the impetus theory of motion.

Medicine was based on comprehensive handbooks, and specialized medical fields included ophthalmology, obstetrics and pediatrics, and pharmacology. The discovery in the 1200s of the pulmonary circulation system of the body anticipated similar European medical discoveries by several centuries. In general, prior to ca. 1500, the sciences in Islamic civilization were well ahead of those of the Western Christians. It was thanks to stimulation by the Muslims that the Western Christians eventually caught up.

Artistic Expressions in Islamic Civilization

During the formative period of Islamic civilization (800–950), secular poetry and prose flourished. As Sunni–Sufi Islam fully evolved (1050–1200), religion was interwoven with the telling of stories, the painting of miniatures, and the building of mosques and palaces. Persian artistic traditions reemerged from pre-Islamic times, and Turkish central Asian steppe traditions entered Islamic culture.

Islamic Literature   The first extant poems in Arabic celebrate the clan ethos of courage, trust, generosity, and hospitality in Arabia (800s). They follow the quest theme common to many folktales and myths. In the cosmopolitan culture of Baghdad, new forms of literature evolved, with urban themes such as the pleasures of sensual abandonment, seduction, and homosexual love. Essays expressing refined taste, elegance, and wit circulated widely. Popular collections of short stories included the *Maqamat,* about an impersonator telling tall stories to gullible listeners, and the *Arabian Nights,* first written down in Mamluk Damascus during the 1300s.

Persian and Turkish Muslims preserved their pre-Islamic pasts in epics celebrating the heroic deeds of their ancestral leaders in central Asia. The poet Firdosi (940–1020) collected the traditions of the Persians into the *Book of Kings* (*Shahnameh*). The anonymous epic *Dede Korkut* originated among the central Asian Turks at the time of the Arab conquests and was written down in the 1300s. Both ethnic groups also produced outstanding poets, among whom the Sufi Jalal al-Din Rumi (1207–1273), born in Balkh (now in Afghanistan) but living most of his life under the Seljuk Sultanate of Rum (hence "Rumi"), acquired worldwide popularity. Although Arabic remained the basic literary language, Persian gained increasingly in popularity.

Painting and Architecture in Islam   In the visual arts, Arabs and early Muslims followed the hybrid realistic-hieratic style that had become common in the Mediterranean and Middle East during the 300s. However, since Islamic law contains prohibitions against painting and sculpting, the visual arts disappeared entirely from public spaces and retreated to the domestic sphere of the courts of rulers.

By contrast, the architecture of mosques and palaces was intended for public use. Mosques followed the architectural style of the Arab open courtyard and covered prayer hall or Persian open courtyard with surrounding half domes and galleries. Among the surviving palaces, the best preserved is the Alhambra of Granada (ca. 1350–1450), with its honeycomb-style decorations. Religious and palace architectures were perhaps the most direct forms in which the identity of Islamic culture was expressed.

Learning and the Arts in Byzantium

In contrast to Islamic civilization, the Eastern Christianity of Byzantium was a fully formed religious civilization from its beginning in 640. The principal institutions of higher learning were the secular Magnaura and the theological Hagia Sophia, which offered the study of the liberal arts and theology. During its difficult struggle for survival against the Arabs, Slavs, Bulgars, and Rus, Constantinople declined in both wealth and sponsorship of knowledge and the arts.

In the arts, Byzantine iconoclasm during the 700s and 800s caused the destruction of icons and mosaics. It also disrupted the transmission of artistic techniques. When the public display and veneration of images became the officially sanctioned doctrine again in the mid-800s, it took a while for the arts to recover.

Byzantine Icons and Islamic Miniatures

One prominent result of the interactions between the Mediterranean and the Middle East in the early centuries CE was a merging of their respective realistic and hieratic artistic styles. Artists now focused on hieratic significance (that is, characteristic features in images aiding in immediate recognition). While the main subject or object remained realistic, symbolic elements highlighted its significance. Background details appeared in nonrealistic fashion, especially in miniature painting.

The halo is an example of the realistic–hieratic style. The halo, a traditional Mesopotamian motif, was associated with gods, heroes, and kings. The three Persian dynasties (Achaemenids, Parthians, and Sasanids) adopted this Mesopotamian tradition, as did the imperial Romans.

In the fourth century, the halo was transferred from the gods, heroes, and kings to depictions of Jesus. Thus, the pagan symbol of glory ultimately became the sign of holiness in Christianity. The halo similarly continued in Islamic miniatures where Prophet Muhammad, prophets of the Hebrew Bible, and angels are surrounded by flaming halos. In contrast to Western art, both Byzantine Christians and Muslims retained the halo for rulers.

In Byzantium, icons became devotional paintings, predominantly on wooden panels, but also on other media, such as mosaics and textiles. They functioned as vehicles through which their owners transferred their veneration to the persons depicted. Icon painters also incorporated gold, silver, enamel, and gemstones on their icons. Portable or affixed to altars and walls, they became ubiquitous in Byzantium and later in Russia.

In the period of 900–1200, icons became not only increasingly important fixtures in churches and monasteries but also major elements in the church liturgy. Long rows of icons on church walls marked the days of the church year. Priests and monks carried double-sided icons during processions. Ironically, the largest production of icons for churches and monasteries occurred after the hiatus of the Latin Empire (1261–1453), during a time when Byzantium was a small and impoverished realm.

In contrast to the public role of church-commissioned icons in Byzantium, Islamic figurative art was private and entirely limited to the courts of rulers as the only patrons of artists. Scholars assume that the Muslims developed their aniconism

Revival of Learning   The period ca. 950–1200 saw an explosion in the production of icons, mosaics, and frescoes, as well as the building of new churches and monasteries. Byzantine mosaic craftspeople and painters were sought after by the caliphs in Iberia, who avoided hiring artists from their Abbasid and Fatimid rivals. Byzantine craftspeople were also popular with the princes of Kiev, who, after

(opposition to figurative images) parallel to the Byzantine periods of iconoclasm. This attitude is represented in the Islamic tradition, where the Quranic warnings against idolatry (e.g., 21:57–59) are interpreted as prohibitions against figurative art. While the church hierarchy in Byzantium eventually overcame iconoclasm, however, there was no such hierarchy in Islam, and so aniconism remained in force.

The continuation of figurative art on palace walls or as miniatures in books attests to the power of the Mesopotamian hieratic traditions over which the Islamic religious scholars had no influence. This art became wide-ranging in its subjects, leaving the production of strictly hieratic representations of rulers in their glory far behind. It began with the Umayyad, Abbasid, and Fatimid palace frescoes, reliefs, sculptures, ceramics, and metal wares of ca. 700–1200. Illustrations in the medical literature dating to the 1110s show similarities with Byzantine icons. In the 1100s and early 1200s, courts in Iraq sponsored miniaturists for drawings of mechanical devices (al-Jazari, d. 1206) as well as urban and rural scenes in storybooks. After 1250, the Mamluk sultans commissioned miniaturists to illustrate their military exercise manuals and the kings of Granada hired painters to create frescoes. In later years, miniature-painting proliferated under the Ottoman, Safavid, and Mughal rulers (see Chapters 16 and 20). Some miniaturists became famous for the illustration of Persian and Indian literary classics or the battles won by their benefactors. Similarly famous were the illustrated lives of Prophet Muhammad and the prophets of the Muslim tradition, as if aniconism had never existed in Islamic civilization.

Questions

- Is it difficult to relate to the hieratic style in art, as exemplified by Byzantine icons, today? If yes, why?

- Why was pictorial art so important to Muslim rulers—so much so that they defied their religious scholars?

Christ Pantocrator. This is the oldest Christ icon, dating to the sixth century. It is kept together with a large collection of icons at the Monastery of Saint Catherine on the Sinai Peninsula in Egypt. Like most icons in this collection, it is encaustic—that is, painted with a mixture of heated beeswax and pigments. Later painters used egg yolk in the place of beeswax. The Greek word *pantocrator* means "Almighty" and refers to Jesus's majesty as the king of the kingdom to come. But Jesus was also the crucified human; the left side of his face is accordingly depicted—in a very subtle way—as more human than the right.

their conversion, carried the Byzantine arts into the commonwealth of Eastern Christian states.

Higher learning also revived after 950. The state built public schools of law and philosophy in the middle of the 1000s, followed by a church school for theology at the end of the century. Philosophers revived the tradition of commenting on Plato, Aristotle, and the Neoplatonic synthesis inherited from Hellenistic antiquity. This revival aroused among churchmen the same suspicions as among the Muslim religious scholars and led to the condemnation of some philosophers.

Byzantine Renaissance   The disruption of 1204–1261 by the Fourth Crusade and Latin Empire saw a tremendous loss of Byzantine art as well as manuscripts, this time to Venetian pillage during the Fourth Crusade. When Byzantium was restored, Plato scholars initiated a recovery of philosophy, which resulted in a return of Western Christians, this time peacefully, to that city in search of Platonic writings. The Academy of Florence, a leading institution of the Italian Renaissance (see Chapter 17), invited Byzantine Plato scholars to help in the recovery of the texts of this philosopher. Further scholars emigrated to Italy after the fall of Constantinople to the Ottomans in 1453. Thus, Western Christianity renewed its adaptation to stimuli from a neighboring civilization, in contrast to Eastern Christianity and Islamic civilization, which continued within their existing traditions.

Putting It All Together

Both Islamic and Eastern Christian civilizations were based on a synthesis of religious revelation and Greek philosophy and science. This synthesis had begun in the Roman and Sasanid Persian Empires. Muslims accomplished their cultural synthesis after the period of Arab conquest, roughly during 800–950. Eastern Christians completed their synthesis in the period 950–1050, after their recovery from the Arab, Slav, Bulgar, and Rus onslaughts. Both refined their internal civilizational achievements well into the 1400s. Thereafter, they did not absorb substantial new cultural stimuli from the outside until about 1700, when the Muslim Ottoman sultans invited western Europeans to reform their empire.

Islamic civilization was an outgrowth of the Arab conquests in the Middle East, central Asia, northern Africa, and Europe in the 600s and early 700s. It emerged as an adaptation of the Arabs to the heritages of the Jews, Christians, Greeks, Romans, and Persians. Its core was the monotheism of Allah, and its cultural adaptations were to Greek philosophy and science, Roman law, and Persian statecraft, as well as artistic and architectural traditions of the Middle East and Mediterranean. At its height, during 950–1450, a commonwealth of competing Islamic states represented Islamic civilization. This ethnically diverse commonwealth with Arab, Turkish, Persian, and Berber rulers and states shared a number of common characteristics, among which were the same canon of scriptures (the Quran and the Sunna), moral norms and laws (Sharia), and religious institutions (separate state and religious authorities as well as Sunni–Sufi brotherhoods). These characteristics endured to 1300 and beyond.

The Roman Empire evolved into what we call the Byzantine Empire around 640, when the emperors, under attack by the Arabs, reorganized their military forces and redefined the inherited Christian theology. Byzantium recovered politically and culturally in the mid-900s, and the empire changed into a commonwealth when the Kievan Rus converted to Eastern Christianity.

The recovery lasted only a century. The Seljuk Muslim Turks conquered most Anatolian provinces of Byzantium (1071–1176), and the Venetians conquered Constantinople in the Fourth Crusade and established the Latin Empire (1204–1261). Byzantium recovered thereafter for another two and a half centuries, but after 1453 Eastern Christian civilization shifted to Muscovy (which grew into Russia).

Review and Relate

Thinking Through Patterns

Examine the ways historians approach the big questions of this chapter.

The adoption of Christianity and Zoroastrianism as state religions in the Roman and Sasanid empires did not prevent these empires from eventual collapse. But both empires helped launch the period of religious civilizations. New empires arose in this period, beginning around 600. Byzantium was Christian from its inception. The Arab empire adopted Islam early on, initially under the Umayyads and fully in the Abbasid-led commonwealth of states. Eastern Christian and Islamic civilizations were characteristic of religious civilizations because both embraced basic religious scriptures, upheld a form of separation of state and religion, and adapted to inherited cultural traditions.

The pattern of Islamic civilization included revealed scripture, a religiously interpreted history, the separation of state and religion, the fusion of revealed religion and Greek philosophy, and the adaptation to the scientific and artistic heritage from Rome and Persia. The pattern was completed early, by about 950, with the emergence of Sunni Islam, but continued to evolve internally through Sufi Islam. The result was an Islamic civilization around 1300 that was composed of many states and even more autonomous religious congregations existing alongside the mosques.

The late Roman Empire achieved a close integration of Christianity, Hellenistic philosophy and science, and Roman law, but it was hard-pressed for survival by the conquering Arabs. When the eastern Roman, or Byzantine, Empire recovered, it elevated Eastern Greek Orthodox Christianity to a supreme position. A powerful recentralization effort strengthened the empire, especially in the

> Why can the period 600–1450 be described as the age of religious civilizations? How do Eastern Christian and Islamic civilizations fit this description?

> Which cultural traditions combined to form Islamic religious civilization? What were the most characteristic patterns?

> How did Eastern Christian or Byzantine civilization evolve over time? On which institutions was this civilization based, and how did it evolve, wedged between Islamic and Western Christian civilizations?

Balkans. But in the wake of the Seljuk invasions and Western Christian crusades, the empire weakened again, surviving in a much-diminished form until it was conquered by the Ottoman Muslims in 1453. Eastern Christianity survived as a state religion in Russia.

| Against the Grain

Consider this as a counterpoint to the main patterns examined in this chapter.

Ibn Taymiyya as a Dissenter from the Sunni–Sufi Consensus

- Was Ibn Taymiyya right in standing up against the Muslims of his time and in preaching jihad against Mongols who had converted to Islam? If yes, for which reasons?

- Are contemporary Islamists correct in claiming that their present situation in Islamic countries closely resembles that of Ibn Taymiyya facing the Mongols? If yes, are rulers in contemporary Islamic countries similar to the Mongols?

Born in Harran, in northern Iraq, Taqi al-Din ibn Taymiyya (1263–1328) became a refugee as a child when his family fled from the pagan Mongols, fulfilling their Sharia duty to live in a Muslim-governed country. Ibn Taymiyya grew up in Damascus, then ruled by the Egyptian Mamluks, and became a prominent religious scholar in the Hanbali legal school.

Among the four legal schools, the Hanbali school was the one most devoted to the study of the Quran and prophetic traditions. Ibn Taymiyya invoked these traditions when he dedicated his scholarly career to combating the form of popular brotherhood and saintly Islam dominant in the Islamic world at the time. He did not condemn, however, Sunnis engaging in spiritual Sufi practices as individuals—a point often overlooked by modern reformist Muslims, for whom he is a hero.

Most of Ibn Taymiyya's contemporaries would have shrugged off his rantings against brotherhood members had he not shown exemplary courage during a time of continuing Mongol attacks. Since 1260 the Mongols had tried to conquer Mamluk Syria and Egypt, and in 1299–1303 they succeeded in occupying parts of Syria. At one point during the occupation, the Mamluks sent a mission of religious scholars, including Ibn Taymiyya, to the Mongols to implore their ruler Ghazan (r. 1295–1304) to end his attacks. Ghazan had officially converted to Islam in 1295 but continued to adhere to Mongol law rather than the Islamic Sharia. Only Ibn Taymiyya had the courage to stand before the Mongol ruler and accuse him of being an infidel. This feat of courage earned Ibn Taymiyya both admiration and resentment from scholars of the other religious schools.

Ibn Taymiyya apparently had both an aura of self-importance and a short temper. It was this arrogance that Ibn Taymiyya's detractors confronted, attacking him on his own ground of legalism. They accused him of violating the Islamic unity doctrine in his teachings and misinterpreting the doctrine of fighting the infidels as a religious duty.

As a result of these accusations, the Mamluks imprisoned Ibn Taymiyya. In the end, Ibn Taymiyya died in jail, a lone dissenter during a time when the majority of Muslims adhered to a different form of Islam. His teachings were revived, however, in the twentieth century when Islamists reclaimed him as the preacher of an Islamic revolution against their own "Mongol" rulers and Islamic laxity in general.

Key Terms

Caliph 223	Iconoclasm 229	Sunna 226
Celibacy 232	Jihad 226	Tax farming 242
Commonwealth 222	Muslim 223	Trinitarianism 223
Creed 232	Sharia 227	Umma 226
Eucharist 232	Sufism 243	

Learn more with this chapter's digital tools, including the Oxford Insight Study Guide, at http://www.oup.com/he/vonsivers4e.
Please see the Further Resources section at the back of the book for additional readings and suggested websites.

PATTERNS OF EVIDENCE |
Sources for Chapter 10

SOURCE 10.1	## Al-Jahiz: The Story of the Judge and the Fly

ca. 776–868

A l-Jahiz ("Goggle Eyed," actual name Abu Uthman Amr ibn Bahr al-Kinani) was one of the most important writers during the beginning of the classical cultural blossoming of the Abbasid Empire. Of East African ancestry, he grew up in poverty in Basra (in southern Iraq). Here he acquired a broad education in theology, philology, lexicography, poetry, history, and politics. His book on the caliphate attracted the attention of Caliph al-Ma'mun, and it was under al-Ma'mun's patronage that Jahiz wrote over 200 books and essays on a wide range of secular and religious topics. Many of these texts contain anecdotes and asides like the following amusing but edifying story.

We had a qadi in Basra called Abd Allah ibn Sawwar. People had never seen a judge as grave, as imperturbable, as dignified, or as mild-tempered as he, or anyone as self-controlled and in command of his every movement as he was. He used to perform the morning prayer in his house (he lived near his mosque). Then he would come and hold session, sitting with his robe wrapped around his drawn-up knees and without leaning against anything.

He always sat upright, without moving a limb, not turning, not untying his knee wrap, keeping his feet together, and not supporting himself on either side, so that he looked like a building made of stone, or erect like a rock. He would remain like this, until he would get up to perform the noon prayer. Then he would return to his seat and stay there until he would get up to perform the afternoon prayer. Then he would go back and sit down, remaining like that until he would get up for the sunset prayer. He would sometimes return to his place, but it often happened that he still had something to read such as deeds, contracts, or documents. He would then perform the last evening prayer and go home.

Truth be told: during the entire time that he was thus engaged he did not once get up to perform his ablutions, nor had he any need to do so. Nor did he drink water or any other drink. This was his routine, whether the days were

Source: Al-Jahiz, *Kitab Al-Hayawan*, ed. Abd al-Salam Muhammad Harun, 8 vols. (Cairo: Mustafa al-Babi al-Halabi, 1965–1969), III:298–402. Adapted from Geert Jan Van Gelder, trans., *Classical Arabic Literature: A Library of Arabic Literature Anthology* (New York: New York University Press, 2012), 184–186. http://ebookcentral.proquest.com/lib /utah/detail.action?docID=1109598

long or short, in summer and winter. In addition to this he never so much as moved his hand or gestured by moving his head.

He only spoke, and concisely at that, conveying much with few words. One day, when he was sitting in this way, with his assessors and the public seated around him and in two rows in front of him, a fly landed on his nose and lingered there a long while. Then it moved toward the inside corner of his eye. He wanted to endure when it got into the corner of his eye and bit it with its piercing proboscis, just as he had endured it when it landed on his nose, without twitching the tip of his nose or wrinkling his face or whisking it away with his finger.

When the fly had troubled him for some time, hurting him and stinging him, and intending to move on to a spot where it could no longer be ignored, the qadi brought his eyelids together, closing his eye. But it did not move. This induced him to continue closing and opening his eye, but the fly would merely move aside until his eyelid had stopped moving, and then applied itself again to the corner of the eye with a vengeance, worse than before, plunging its proboscis in the same spot where it had injured him before.

This time the qadi was even less able to bear and endure it than before. He blinked his eyelids, opening his eyes with ever increasing force, alternately opening and shutting them. The fly would move aside until the movement stopped and would then return to its place, pestering him until it had exhausted his endurance and had done its utmost. At that point the qadi could not refrain from whisking it away with his hand, which he did with the eyes of the people on him, though they pretended not to see him.

The fly moved away until he had lowered his hand and had stopped moving, then returned to its place. This caused the qadi to fall back on driving it away with the hem of his sleeve, and to do so repeatedly. He was aware that his every movement was being witnessed by his assessors and the others who were present. As they looked at him he said, "I swear that flies are more persistent than a black beetle and more conceited than a crow! May God forgive me! So many have been pleased with themselves whereupon God, the Mighty and Sublime, wished to make them aware of their own weakness that was hidden from them! I knew that I had a reputation as one of the gravest of people, but now God's feeblest creature has got the better of me and has shamed me." Then he recited God's word: "And if a fly should rob them of anything, they would never rescue that from it. Feeble indeed are the seeker and the sought!" [Quran 22:73]

▶ Working with Sources

1. Why is it that one wants both to laugh at Judge Ibn Sawwar's encounter with the fly but also feels sympathy for him?

2. What is the ideal image of a judge in Islamic society (according to Ibn Sawwar) and how would you compare it to our ideal in contemporary Western society?

Documents related to the iconoclasm controversy

Seventh–ninth centuries CE

The Byzantine Empire was racked by a series of religious disputes that pulled in emperors as well as priests. One of the most significant of these was an ongoing difference of opinion concerning "graven images" of Jesus and other prominent figures in Christian narratives. Was it proper to create and display images of God, and, if so, should existing "icons" be destroyed in order to protect the faithful? These documents represent the two major perspectives on this debate, between the poles of the "iconodule" (pro-icon) position and the "iconoclastic" (anti-icon) position.

ICONODULE POSITION:
1. Quinsextum Council (in Trullo), 692 CE, ruling by Justinian II (685–695; 705–711):

"Now, in order that perfection be represented before the eyes of all people, even in paintings, we ordain that from now on Christ our God, the Lamb who took upon Himself the sins of the world, be set up, even in images according to His human character, instead of the ancient Lamb. Through this figure we realize the height of the humiliation of God the Word and are led to remember His life in the flesh, His suffering, and His saving death, and the redemption ensuing from it for the world."

2. John of Damascus (675–749), Oration (*Patrologia orientalis* 94, cols. 1258C-D)

"When we set up an image of Christ in any place, we appeal to the senses, and indeed we sanctify the sense of sight, which is the highest among the perceptive senses, just as by sacred speech we sanctify the sense of hearing. An image is, after all, a reminder; it is to the illiterate what a book is to the literate, and what the word is to the hearing, the image is to sight. We remember that God ordered that a vessel be made from wood that would not rot, gilded inside and out, and that the tables of the law should be placed in it and the staff and the golden vessel containing the manna—all this for a reminder of what had taken place, and a foreshadowing of what was to come. What was this but a visual image, more compelling than any sermon? And this sacred thing was not placed in some obscure corner of the tabernacle; it was displayed in full view of the people, so that whenever they looked at it they would give honor and worship to the God Who had through its contents made known His design to them. They were of course not worshipping the things themselves; they were

Source: Excerpts from Anthony Bryer and Judith Herrin, eds., *Iconoclasm: Papers Given at the Ninth Spring Symposium of Byzantine Studies, University of Birmingham, March 1975* (Birmingham, UK: Centre for Byzantine Studies, University of Birmingham, 1977).

being led through them to recall the wonderful works of God, and to adore Him Whose words they had witnessed."

3. *Horos* (Definition of Faith) at the Seventh Ecumenical Council, Nicaea, 787 CE:

"We define with accuracy and care that the venerable and holy icons be set up like the form of the venerable and life-giving Cross, inasmuch as the matter consisting of colors and pebbles and other matter is appropriate in the holy church of God, on sacred vessels and vestments, walls and panels, in houses and on the roads, as well as the images of our Lord and God and Savior Jesus Christ, of our undefiled Lady of the Holy Mother of God, of the angels worthy of honor, and of all the holy and pious men. For the more frequently they are seen by means of pictorial representation the more those who behold them are aroused to remember and desire the prototypes and to give them greeting and worship of honor—but not the true worship of our faith which befits only the divine nature—but to offer them both incense and candles, in the same way as to the form and the venerable and life-giving Cross and the holy Gospel and to the other sacred objects, as was the custom even of the ancients."

ICONOCLASTIC POSITION:
1. The *Horos* (Definition of Faith) at the Council of Hieria, 754 CE:

"The divine nature is completely uncircumscribable and cannot be depicted or represented in any medium whatsoever. The word Christ means both God and Man, and an icon of Christ would therefore have to be an image of God in the flesh of the Son of God. But this is impossible. The artist would fall either into the heresy which claims that the divine and human natures of Christ are separate or into that which holds that there is only one nature of Christ."

2. The *Horos* (Definition of Faith) at Iconoclastic Council of 815 CE:

"Wherefore, taking to heart the correct doctrine, we banish from the Catholic Church the unwarranted manufacture of the spurious icons that has been so audaciously proclaimed, impelled as we are by a judicious judgment; nay, by passing a righteous judgment upon the veneration of icons that has been injudiciously proclaimed by Tarasius [Patriarch, 784–802] and so refuting it, we declare his assembly [i.e., Seventh Ecumenical Council in 787] invalid in that it bestowed exaggerated honor to painting, namely, as has already been said, the lighting of candles and lamps and the offering of incense, these marks of veneration being those of worship. We gladly accept, on the other hand, the pious council that was held at Blachernae, in the church of the all-pure Virgin, under the pious Emperors Constantine V and Leo IV [in 754] that was fortified by the doctrine of the Fathers, and in preserving without alteration what was expressed by it, we decree that the manufacture of icons is unfit for veneration and useless. We refrain, however, from calling them idols since there is a distinction between different kinds of evil."

▶ **Working with Sources**

1. Do you find one of the positions in this theological debate more convincing than the other? Why?

2. Was it necessary for the Byzantine emperors to intervene in this controversy? Why or why not?

SOURCE 10.3

Memoirs of Usama Ibn Munqidh

ca. 1180s

A scholar, a gentleman, and a warrior, Usama (1095–1187) had ample opportunity to meet crusader forces in person on the battlefield and in civilian life. After a distinguished military career, he became a consultant and advisor to Saladin in 1174. Basking in Saladin's favor, Usama became the center of attention in Damascus. He began a memoir describing the various peoples whom he had encountered during his long and adventurous life. His observations are often humorous, sometimes baffling, but always imbued with curiosity about people whose customs are strange—and intriguing.

Among the Frankish [i.e., Crusaders, known to Arabs as "al-Ifranj"] captives who were carried into my father's home was an aged woman accompanied by her daughter—a young woman of great beauty—and a robust son. The son accepted Islam, and his conversion was genuine, judging by what he showed in the practice of prayer and fasting. He learned the art of working marble from a stonecutter who had paved the home of my father. After staying for a long time with us my father gave him as wife a woman who belonged to a pious family, and paid all necessary expenses for his wedding and home. His wife bore him two sons. The boys grew up. When they were five or six years old, their father, young Rā'ūl, who was very happy at having them, took them with their mother and everything that his house contained and on the second morning joined the Franks in Afāmiyah, where he and his children became Christians after having practiced Islam with its prayers and faith. May Allah, therefore, purify the world from such people!

Mysterious are the works of the Creator, the author of all things! When one comes to recount cases regarding the Franks, he cannot but glorify Allah

Source: Philip K. Hitti, trans., *An Arab-Syrian Gentleman and Warrior in the Period of the Crusades: Memoirs of Usāmah ibn-Munqidh* (Princeton, NJ: Princeton University Press, 1987), 160–161, 162–163, and 164–165.

(exalted is he!) and sanctify him, for he sees them as animals possessing the virtues of courage and fighting, but nothing else; just as animals have only the virtues of strength and carrying loads. I shall now give some instances of their doings and their curious mentality.

. . .

The king of the Franks [Fulk of Anjou, king of Jerusalem] had for treasurer a knight named Bernard, who (may Allah's curse be upon him!) was one of the most accursed and wicked among the Franks. A horse kicked him in the leg, which was subsequently infected and which opened in fourteen different places. Every time one of these cuts would close in one place, another would open in another place. All this happened while I was praying for his perdition. Then came to him a Frankish physician and removed from the leg all the ointments which were on it and began to wash it with very strong vinegar. By this treatment all the cuts were healed and the man became well again. He was up again like a devil.

Another case illustrating their curious medicine is the following:

In Shayzar we had an artisan named abu-al-Fath, who had a boy whose neck was afflicted with scrofula. Every time a part of it would close, another part would open. This man happened to go to Antioch on business of his, accompanied by his son. A Frank noticed the boy and asked his father about him, "Wilt thou swear by thy religion that if I prescribe to thee a medicine which will cure thy boy, thou wilt charge nobody fees for prescribing it thyself? In that case, I shall prescribe to thee a medicine which will cure the boy." The man took the oath and the Frank said:

"Take uncrushed leaves of glasswort, burn them, then soak the ashes in olive oil and sharp vinegar. Treat the scrofula with them until the spot on which it is growing is eaten up. Then take burnt lead, soak it in ghee butter and treat him with it. That will cure him."

The father treated the boy accordingly, and the boy was cured. The sores closed and the boy returned to his normal condition of health.

I have myself treated with this medicine many who were afflicted with such disease, and the treatment was successful in removing the cause of the complaint.

. . .

Here is an illustration which I myself witnessed:

When I used to visit Nāblus, I always took lodging with a man named Mu'izz, whose home was a lodging house for the Moslems. The house had windows which opened to the road, and there stood opposite to it on the other side of the road a house belonging to a Frank who sold wine for the merchants. He would take some wine in a bottle and go around announcing it by shouting, "So and so, the merchant, has just opened a cask full of this wine. He who wants to buy some of it will find it in such and such a place." The Frank's pay for the announcement made would be the wine in that bottle. One day this Frank went home and found a man with his wife in the same bed. He asked him, "What could have made thee enter into my wife's room?" The man replied, "I was tired, so I went in to rest." "But how," asked he, "didst thou get into my bed?" The other replied, "I found a bed that was spread, so I slept in it." "But," said he, "my wife was sleeping together with thee!" The other replied,

"Well, the bed is hers. How could I therefore have prevented her from using her own bed?" "By the truth of my religion," said the husband, "if thou shouldst do it again, thou and I would have a quarrel." Such was for the Frank the entire expression of his disapproval and the limit of his jealousy.

▶ **Working with Sources**

1. **What proof does Usama offer of the uncivilized nature of the Christian invaders of the Middle East?**

2. **How does he demonstrate Islamic cultural, if not always military, superiority in his account?**

SOURCE 10.4

A Jewish engagement contract from Fustat (Old Cairo)

11 November 1146

A treasure trove of letters, contracts, legal instruments, etc., known as the Cairo Geniza, attests to the lives of both prominent and average Jewish people, especially in the eleventh and twelfth centuries. Due to their *dhimmi* status (that is, officially recognized religious minorities in a predominantly Muslim state), Jews experienced occasional persecution in the Middle East and North Africa (much less than in Europe). In the Fatimid Empire (909–1171), they engaged in normal business and personal activities, and these documents provide a welcome window into their daily life.

This is a copy of the engagement contract of Abū Mansūr Semah, son of Rabbānā Japheth [known as] the elder Abū ʿAlī, the perfumer, to Sitt al-Khāssa, the daughter of the elder Abu 'l-Barakāt Ibn al-Lebdī.

On Monday, the fifth day of the month of Kislev of the year 1458 of the era of the documents, in Fustat, Egypt, which is situated on the Nile River and which is under the jurisdiction of our lord Samuel, the great Nagrid—may his name be forever—M. Semah, the young man, son of M. and R. Japheth the elder, son of M. and R. Tiqvā, the elder, the Friend of the yeshiva—may he rest in Eden—concluded a match with Sitt al-Khāssa, his fiancée, a virgin, the daughter of M. and R. Berakhōt, the elder—may he rest in Eden.

His obligation is a first installment of 40 certified dinars, to be given as a gift at the time of the wedding, and a final installment of 100 certified dinars. Abū Mansūr Semah, the fiancé, presented the 40 dinars of the first installment, and the elder Abū'l-ʿAlā' Musallam, the perfumer, son of Sahl, received them from

Source: Shlomo D. Goitein, *A Mediterranean Society: The Jewish Communities of the Arab World as Portrayed in the Documents of the Cairo Geniza*, vol. 4 (Berkeley: University of California Press, 1983), 317–319.

him. The wedding is set for the month of Kislev of the coming year—may we be destined for life in it—which is the coming year 1459 [1147].

Semah assumed these obligations toward Sitt al-Khāssa: She will be regarded as trustworthy in all that concerns food and drink in the house, no suspicion may be cast upon her, nor can he demand from her an oath concerning any of these things, not even a supplementary oath. He may not marry another woman, nor retain a maidservant whom she dislikes. Should he do any of these things, the final installment is hers, and he must release her [from the marriage bond by divorce]. In the case that there are no children, half of what remains of the dowry returns to her family. She may choose the place and the domicile where she wishes to live. The rent of her properties is hers, she may spend it for whatever purpose she prefers; he has no say in the matter.

Should he nullify this engagement contract and not marry her during the said Kislev, she will receive 20 dinars. This is a debt and an obligation, binding [as from now]. We made the symbolic purchase from M. Semah, the young man, for Sitt al-Khāssa, the fiancée, according to all that is recorded above, a purchase which is definite and strict, made with the proper object for such a transaction.

We also made the symbolic purchase from Sitt al-Sāda, the daughter of the elder Abū Nasr, the physician, the mother of Sitt al-Khāssa, the fiancée, in the most rigorous terms, binding as from now: Should her daughter Sitt al-Khāssa nullify the engagement contract and refuse to marry the fiancé during the said month of Kislev, she would owe the fiancé 20 [dinars]. . . . This has taken place after the verification of her identity.

Signatures: Mevōrākh b. Solomon [of] b[lessed] m[emory]. Sadaqa b———.

▶ **Working with Sources**

1. Are the parties to this contract eager to demonstrate, particularly to Muslim officials, that they understand business affairs and can conduct them sensibly among themselves?

2. What differences are reflected in this document between the roles of women and men with respect to marriage?

SOURCE 10.5

An Islamic mystic's highest meditative state

Twelfth Century

The most famous representative of Sunni mysticism, or Sufism (see the end of Chapter 6), is Abu Hamid al-Ghazali (ca. 1058–1111). The excerpt below is perhaps the clearest exposition of the climactic moment of Divine experience ever formulated within the context of revealed religion. Its metaphorical language requires patient, step-by-step contemplation. Note particularly Ghazali's skillful handling of the images of the clear glass filled with red wine and the red glass filled with clear water as symbols for the experience of the Divine.

(45) The Gnostics [or mystics, *'ārifūn*], after having ascended to the heaven of reality, agree that they see nothing in existence save the One, the Real. Some of them possess this state as a cognitive gnosis [mystical insight, *'irfān*]. Others, however, attain this through a state of tasting. Plurality is totally banished from them, and they become immersed in sheer singularity. Their rational faculties become so satiated that in this state they are, as it were, stunned. No room remains in them for the remembrance of any other than God, nor the remembrance of themselves. Nothing is with them but God. They become intoxicated with such an intoxication that the ruling author of their rational faculty is overthrown. Hence, one of them says, "I am the Real!" another, "Glory be to me, how great is my station!" and another, "There is nothing in my robe but God!"

(46) The speech of lovers in the state of intoxication should be concealed and not spread about. When this intoxication subsides, the ruling authority of the rational faculty—which is God's balance in His earth—is given back to them. They come to know that what they experience was not the reality of unification but that it was similar to unification. It was like the words of the lover during a state of extreme passionate love:

> I am He whom I love,
>
> and He whom I love is I!

(47) It is not unlikely that a person could look into a mirror in an unexpected place and not see the mirror at all. He supposes that the form he sees is the mirror's form and that it is united with the mirror. Likewise, he could see wine in a glass and suppose that the wine is the glass' color. When the situation

Source: Adapted from Al-Ghazali, *The Niche of Lights*, trans. David Buchman (Provo, UT: Brigham Young University Press, 1998), 17–18.

becomes familiar to him and his foot becomes firmly established within it, he asks for forgiveness from God and says:

> The glass is clear, the wine is clear,
>
> the two are similar, the affair confused,
>
> As if there is wine and no glass,
>
> or glass and no wine.

There is a difference between saying "The wine is the cup" and "It is *as if* the wine is the cup."

(48) When this state gets the upper hand, it is called "extinction" in relation to the one who possesses it. Or, rather, it is called "extinction from extinction," since the possessor of the state is extinct from himself and from his own extinction. For he is conscious neither of himself in that state, nor of his own unconsciousness of himself. If he were conscious of his own unconsciousness, then he would [still] be conscious of himself. In relation to the one immersed in it, this state is called "unification," according to the language of metaphor, or is called "declaring God's unity," according to the language of reality. And behind these realities there are also mysteries, but it would take too long to delve into them.

▶ **Working with Sources**

1. Ghazali draws a clear line between himself and the "intoxicated" Sufis who identify themselves with God ("in their robe"). Why does he think these Sufis are mistaken?

2. Why—according to Ghazali—are mystics in their highest state of meditation unaware of both their consciousness and unconsciousness?

World Period Three

The Formation of Religious Civilizations, 600–1450 CE

The rise of religious civilizations on the continents of Asia, Europe, and Africa is a striking phenomenon that unifies the period of 600–1450 in world history. It can be considered as a continuation of the intellectual and institutional transformations that began with the emphasis on monotheism and monism by the visionaries of the mid-first millennium BCE.

The religious civilizations were not monolithic and displayed many regional variations. Internal diversity notwithstanding, they shared a number of common characteristics:

- Religious civilizations formed in regions which were larger than any single state within them: They superseded empires as the largest units of human unification.

- The civilizations were *scriptural*—that is, based on canonical (commonly agreed on) texts inherited in most cases from earlier periods. Members of educated elites (clergy, scholars, sages) taught and interpreted the scriptures to the laypeople.

- Despite hostilities among the religious civilizations, merchants, missionaries, pilgrims, and travelers visited each other's areas. They fostered a lively exchange of technical and cultural innovations from one end of Eurasia and Africa to the other.

Chapter 11

Innovation and Adaptation in the Western Christian World

600–1450 CE

CHAPTER ELEVEN PATTERNS

Origins, Interactions, and Adaptations Following the disintegration of the western Roman Empire, the Catholic Church emerged as the only unifying force. However, the overwhelmingly rural and Germanic kingdoms had little connections to the Roman-Mediterranean cultural heritage. The foundations of a Western Christian civilization slowly formed through interactions with both Islamic civilization and Eastern Christian religious civilization. Additional exchanges with Byzantium led to the Renaissance, which made Western Christianity a highly diverse, heterogeneous civilization in contrast to the other, more homogeneous and unified religious civilizations of the Middle East, India, and China.

Uniqueness and Similarities The process of acculturation created a unique mosaic of competing religious and political institutions in Europe. The competition led to the formation of a centralized Church as well as centralized national monarchies with considerable degrees of similarities among each other. Centralization, however, was only partially successful, and participatory politics inherited from earlier centuries evolved powerfully in some monarchies through the institutions of estates general and parliaments.

Around 575 a casual encounter took place in Rome that had enormous implications for the future of Western Europe. A monk from the Monastery of St. Andrew came upon several boys for sale in the slave market. Struck by their fair skin and light hair, he asked about their ethnic origin. He was informed that the youths were from the far-off island of Britain and were called "Angles." The monk replied that because of their angelic appearance they should instead be called "angels." He then asked whether the inhabitants of Britain were Christians. When told that they still clung to pagan beliefs, he remarked that it was a pity that such beautiful young persons were not blessed with Christian faith.

In the year 596, the monk, now elevated to the papacy as Pope Gregory I (r. 590–604), dispatched a group of monks to Britain, led by Augustine (later named the first archbishop of Canterbury), on a missionary campaign of conversion among the Anglo-Saxons of southern England. Throughout the seventh century, Roman Christianity spread into Anglo-Saxon England, eventually eclipsing the already established Celtic form of the faith brought over from Ireland in the fifth century. During the first half of the eighth century, English missionary monks, most notably St. Boniface (680–754), carried Christianity to the continent.

The papal reign of Gregory I represents a new era in the history of Western Europe. By encouraging the conversion of Germanic kings to Christianity in return for the sanction of the church, Gregory advanced the role of the papacy throughout Europe and made the Roman papacy a significant power.

CHAPTER OUTLINE

The Formation of
Christian Europe,
600–1000

Recovery, Reform, and
Innovation, 1000–1300

Crisis and Creativity,
1300–1415

Putting It All Together

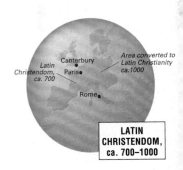

LATIN
CHRISTENDOM,
ca. 700–1000

ABOVE: A Flemish tapestry from ca. 1440 shows a lady courted by two gentlemen in a rose garden.

Seeing Patterns

❯ How did the Merovingians and Carolingians construct a new Christian European civilization during the seventh and eighth centuries?

❯ What were key factors in the political, economic, and social recovery of Europe during the eleventh and twelfth centuries?

❯ What were some of the cultural and intellectual developments during the "twelfth-century renaissance," and how did they contribute to medieval civilization?

❯ How did the church influence political developments in Europe during the twelfth and thirteenth centuries?

❯ What events made fourteenth-century Europe so dismal? How did these combine to spell the gradual demise of medieval institutions and perspectives?

Latin Christendom: Those countries professing Christian beliefs under the primacy of the pope.

In addition, Gregory's efforts led to the independence of **Latin Christendom** from the Eastern Greek Church at Constantinople. Moreover, Gregory established an institutional structure and organized a hierarchy that furthered the rise of a unified Christian religious civilization in Europe that would endure until around 1450, when the Renaissance ushered in a new phase in European history.

The Formation of Christian Europe, 600–1000

During the fifth century, Roman provincial rule in the west collapsed and a new post-Roman period of cross-cultural interactions began, combining Greco-Roman and Germanic traditions, as well as Christian values. The Roman administrative practice of grouping provinces into dioceses formed the foundation of the diocesan system of the early church. A distinctively Christian European civilization gradually emerged. An important feature of this new civilization was the dominance of the church, whose alliance with Frankish kings—particularly Charlemagne—initiated a new church–state relationship in the West. This civilization nearly dissolved during the civil wars among Charlemagne's successors and the ninth-century invasions by non-Christians. During the later tenth century, however, the restoration of order was under way in post-Carolingian Europe. Despite the turbulence of the ninth and tenth centuries, a new cultural and religious cohesiveness provided a sense of optimism; Latin Christendom had survived.

Frankish Gaul and Latin Christianity

Amid the confusion caused by Germanic invasions and the breakdown of Roman rule during the fifth century, the first attempt to restore political order appeared in Frankish Gaul. Although Merovingian kings relied on force to unite the kingdom, they also recognized the importance of the church as a unifying force. After a period of political turmoil, a new line of Frankish kings, the Carolingians, emerged during the eighth century. At the same time, the Christian Church played a role in the shaping of Frankish Gaul and early medieval European civilization. The concept of Christendom as a common identity through the practice of Western Christianity began to take shape.

The Merovingians   Unlike most other Germans, the Franks became Western Christians, and as a result they were not rejected as heretics by native Gallo-Romans. For these reasons, Frankish Gaul was ideally suited to lay the foundation for a Christian state in post-Roman Europe.

The first Frankish dynasty, the Merovingians [mer-oh-VIN-gee-anz], was established by the Frankish king Clovis (r. 481–511). Clovis adopted Christianity, which gave him the backing of Christian bishops in Gaul. As a result, Clovis had powerful allies in his attempt to control a unified Christian kingdom. However, because of the Merovingian practice of dividing inheritances among surviving heirs, soon after his death Clovis's kingdom was split up into Austrasia in the east, Neustria in the west, and Burgundy in the southeast.

The Carolingians   During the eighth century one aristocratic family, the Carolingians, rose to power in Austrasia and eventually took control of all of the Frankish lands. Carolingian leader Charles Martel ("the Hammer") (ca. 714–741) increased the authority of the Carolingians by promoting his ties with the church. His defeat of advancing Muslim armies at the Battle of Tours in 732 or 733 made him the leader of the most powerful force in Latin Christendom.

Martel's son, Pepin III ("the Short") (751–768), succeeded his father as mayor of the palace in 741, and enhanced ties with the church in two ways. First, in 751 he was crowned by the reigning pope as the king of the Franks, thereby replacing the former Merovingian line of kings with a new Carolingian dynasty. Second, the **coronation** established a new Franco-papal alliance. This affinity between Rome and Frankish Gaul allowed Europe to develop independently of the Byzantine Empire in the East. In addition, the pope included the ceremony of **unction** in the coronation ceremony, introducing into western European history the concept of sacred kingship "by the grace of God."

Coronation: The act or ceremony of crowning a sovereign.

Unction: The act of anointing with oil as a rite of consecration.

The Early Medieval Church   The church contributed to the development of a new era in Western history. The secular (from Latin *saeculum,* or "worldly") clergy included bishops—among them bishops of Rome, who later became popes—and urban priests. The regular (from *regula,* or "rule") clergy were monks and nuns who lived in rural monasteries. Each of these monasteries made distinctive contributions to early medieval culture.

The model for monastic life was established by St. Benedict (ca. 480–543) in his *Holy Rule.* The daily lives of Benedictine monks were devoted to prayer and manual labor and were regulated by a series of "offices," or times of the day given over to specific tasks. In economic terms, Benedictine monasteries helped to revitalize rural agricultural production. Most monasteries had a watermill and a forge, and their large landholdings produced significant quantities of grain and wine. In addition, Benedictine monks expanded arable lands.

Monasteries also preserved classical and early Christian culture. The limited education available during the early medieval period took place mostly in monasteries. Monks copied and studied the works of the Church Fathers, along with texts from the Bible and papal decrees, thus laying the foundation for a new, Christian civilization for medieval Europe. Education and learning were also provided by monasteries; St. Hilda, abbess of the monastery of Whitby, was known for her contributions to learning.

The Papacy   While monks lived in rural monasteries, bishops of the church resided in urban centers. Although major cities throughout the Roman Empire had bishops, the bishop of Rome emerged as spiritual head of the Christian Church in western Europe. The most important of the early medieval popes was Gregory I (see vignette at the beginning of this chapter).

Gregory was responsible for making the Roman papacy a power in the West. His letters to Childebert II (r. 575–595), king of the Franks, laid the foundation for the Franco-papal alliance that came to fruition in the eighth century. Gregory also enhanced the prestige of the Roman papacy in Italy, which gave rise to the Papal States and the separation of the Roman and Eastern Roman Church. Finally, Gregory facilitated the conversion of pagans to Christianity.

The Age of Charlemagne   Following the death of Pepin III in 768, his son Charlemagne ("Charles the Great") (r. 768–814) inherited the Frankish crown. Charlemagne represents the first full synthesis of Roman, Germanic, and Christian elements to forge a unified Christian empire. Because Charlemagne raised the status of western Europe to rival the civilizations of Byzantium and Islam, the Mediterranean was no longer the center of civilization in the West.

Through military campaigns and effective rule, Charlemagne administered the largest empire in Europe since the collapse of Roman rule in 476 (see Map 11.1). From a palace at Aachen, Charlemagne ruled over a centralized empire composed of different ethnic and linguistic groups. Charlemagne also reformed legal practices by

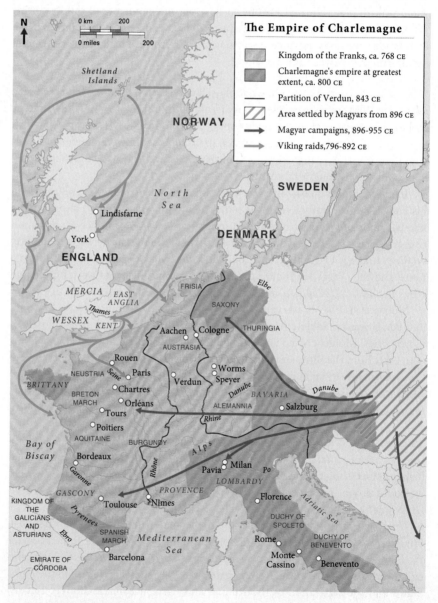

MAP 11.1 The Empire of Charlemagne

instituting the Frankish inquest, a forerunner of the jury system, which was carried to England at the time of the Norman Conquest.

Charlemagne's reign made intellectual contributions to medieval Europe, including educational reform. Monks were instructed to make copies of both Roman and Christian texts, including the Bible and the *Rule* of St. Benedict, preserving and disseminating many classical authors and texts.

Like his forebears, Charlemagne took an active interest in affairs of the church. Not only did he promote the interests of Christianity throughout his kingdom, but he also intervened in papal affairs in Rome. In 774 Charlemagne journeyed to Rome to offer protection against the Lombards, and in 800 he gave assistance to Pope Leo III (r. 795–816), who was attacked by rivals. While attending Mass at St. Peter's on Christmas Day, Charlemagne was crowned "emperor of the Romans" by a grateful Leo III.

The creation of a new Roman emperor in the West announced the independence of western Europe from the Byzantine East, and it signaled a shift in the center of power away from the Mediterranean and toward Europe north of the Alps. Charlemagne's new imperial status was recognized (reluctantly) not only by the Byzantine court but also by the Abbasid caliph in Baghdad, Harun al-Rashid (r. 786–809).

Charlemagne's Throne. Charlemagne frequently traveled throughout his realm, and one place where he stopped several times was Ravenna on the Adriatic coast of Italy, where he would admire the magnificent sixth-century church of San Vitale. Inspired by its harmonious proportions and stunning mosaics, Charlemagne determined to build a replica at Aachen. The Palatine Chapel, the only surviving component of his palace, combines Byzantine and Carolingian architectural styles.

Post-Carolingian Europe   Shortly after his death in 814, Charlemagne's empire was torn apart. Charlemagne's eldest son, Louis the Pious (r. 814–840), divided the empire among his three sons, who then squabbled over their respective shares. By the terms of the Treaty of Verdun in 843, the empire was divided into eastern, western, and central portions. At the same time, devastating raids by Vikings from the north and Muslim pirates from the south further disturbed the situation. Magyar horsemen from the plains of Hungary terrorized East Frankland in the same period, although they were more inclined to settle onto farmlands than to plunder (see Map 11.1).

The Feudal Age   The name traditionally given to the form of governance that arose in West Frankland during the ninth through the eleventh centuries is **feudalism**. Historians have never fully agreed on a precise definition of the term; feudalism was based on no formal theory, and it was nowhere uniform, consistent, or a system. Yet, amid the turmoil of the ninth and tenth centuries, feudalism

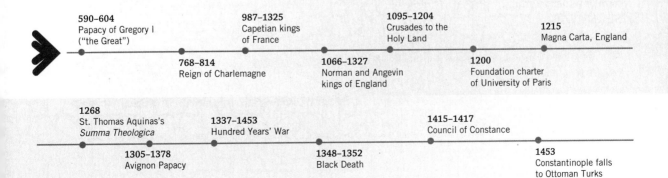

590–604
Papacy of Gregory I
("the Great")

768–814
Reign of Charlemagne

987–1325
Capetian kings
of France

1066–1327
Norman and Angevin
kings of England

1095–1204
Crusades to the
Holy Land

1200
Foundation charter
of University of Paris

1215
Magna Carta, England

1268
St. Thomas Aquinas's
Summa Theologica

1305–1378
Avignon Papacy

1337–1453
Hundred Years' War

1348–1352
Black Death

1415–1417
Council of Constance

1453
Constantinople falls
to Ottoman Turks

King Henry II. Henry II is generally considered the most important of English medieval kings, primarily because of his establishment of royal justice as predominant over baronial and ecclesiastical courts, along with the institution of trial by jury, his dynamic increase in the royal treasury, and the expansion of the Angevin empire in France.

provided security at the local level in the absence of central government. Put in other terms, feudalism consisted of public power in private hands.

Feudalism consisted of powerful landed aristocrats (lords) who assembled small private armies consisting of dependents (vassals). Since wealth and power were now measured in terms of landholdings, vassals were rewarded for their services with grants of land, known as *fiefs* (Latin *feuda*, sing. *feudum*).

Lord–vassal relationships and institutions marked a turning point in European history that led to the later formation of centralized kingdoms. Most important was the concept of loyalty to someone higher in the feudal hierarchy. Even though in practice the local aristocratic lords were sometimes stronger than royal figures, in theory all land and power were possessed by kings, who stood at the apex of the feudal hierarchy. By using these and other elements of feudal relationships to his advantage, a royal figure could convert the feudal relationships to royal control of his realm, either peacefully through legal procedures or by military action.

Whereas feudalism refers to the political and governmental aspects of life in the ninth and tenth centuries, **manorialism** refers to social and economic affairs of the time. Large manorial estates in rural areas constituted self-sustaining agricultural communities. The manorial estate consisted of several buildings: the castle or manor house, the church, the barn, and the mill (see Figure 11.1).

Peasants lived in small cottages in a confined area of the estate, surrounded by fields for crops, stands of timber for building and fuel, and a fishpond. Peasants had to provide free labor, called "boon work," on the lord's fields. The physical pattern of such manors may still be seen in many areas of France.

Feudalism: An arrangement in which vassals were protected and maintained by their lords, usually through the granting of fiefs, and required to serve under them in war.

Manorialism: The medieval European system of self-sustaining agricultural estates.

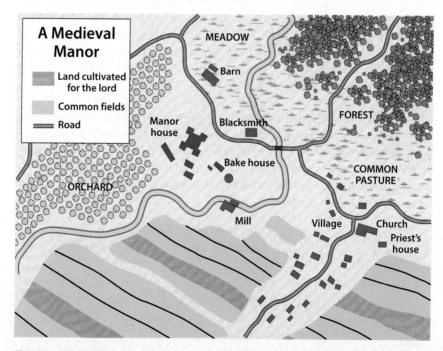

Figure 11.1 A Medieval Manor. This illustration shows the layout of a typical manor, with the manor and its satellite buildings next to a village surrounded by fields for planting and common (waste) land.

Recovery, Reform, and Innovation, 1000–1300

From about 1000 to 1300, Europe experienced revitalization, expansion, and cultural creativity and innovation. The period began with the appearance of competing, politically centralizing kingdoms and with advancements in agriculture, commerce, and trade. Reforms in the church provided a framework for a unified western European Christian religious civilization, culminating in papal supremacy over Europe around the beginning of the thirteenth century. During the so-called twelfth-century renaissance, extending from ca. 1050 to 1250, a cultural revolution in universities produced new philosophical and scientific perspectives that, along with interaction with the Islamic world, came to distinguish western Europe from other world civilizations.

The Political Recovery of Europe

Europe in the middle of the ninth century was plagued by internal civil wars and external invasions. All signs of central government had disappeared as a result of the collapse of the Carolingian Empire. By around 1300, however, most of western Europe was governed by centralized administrations headed by kings, who restored both political and fiscal health to their realms.

France and England   The French nobility elected Hugh Capet (r. 987–996) as their king in 987 CE, establishing a new royal dynasty, the Capetians, in place of the former Carolingians. The king's court was where all disputes among his vassals were resolved, and the location of Hugh's royal **demesne** [de-MAIN] in the lands around Paris meant that he was at the strategic and commercial center of France. Like the Carolingians, the Capetians enjoyed the support of the church. Not only did they have control over dozens of bishoprics and monasteries, they alone were anointed with holy oil (unction) as a part of the coronation ceremony.

> **Demesne:** All territories controlled directly by the king.

Over the next 300 years, Capetian kings extended royal control in France through success in minor wars against the nobles and marriages between Capetian heirs and members of the nobility. Determined to make France the most powerful country in Europe, Philip IV (r. 1285–1314) established a representative assembly in France, the **Estates-General**, in order to raise revenues. Composed of the three social "estates"—the clergy, the nobility, and the townspeople—this body laid the foundation for the French parliament and played an important role in later events leading up to the French Revolution.

> **Estates-General:** The French representative assembly composed of the three social "estates" in France, first convened by Philip IV.

Compared to the slow process of building a centralized monarchy in Capetian France, the establishment of centralized rule in England took a much shorter period of time. After William, Duke of Normandy, defeated an Anglo-Saxon army at the Battle of Hastings in 1066, he was proclaimed king of England as King William I (r. 1066–1087; known as "William the Conqueror"). William then seized control of all lands in the realm, distributing them to his followers. To secure his claim to the throne, he built castles throughout the country.

William's successors continued his practice of centralizing authority. Henry II (r. 1154–1189), the first of the Plantagenet kings of England, reformed the judicial

Baron: A term borrowed from French designating feudal vassals who held lands in return for service and loyalty to the king.

Writ: A written order issued by a court, commanding the party to whom it is addressed to perform or cease performing a specified act.

Parliament: A representative assembly in England that, by the fourteenth century, was composed of great lords (both lay and ecclesiastical) and representatives from two other groups: shire knights and town burgesses.

system by making royal courts the final courts of appeal, thereby overriding the authority of **baronial** courts. Moreover, Henry established a uniform code of justice (known as English common law), which replaced the complex jurisdictions of baronial and local courts. Even more effective was Henry's use of royal **writs** and the jury system, which provided justice for all disputants.

Henry's son John (r. 1199–1216), however, alienated the baronage of England, who forced John to sign Magna Carta ("the Great Charter") in 1215. Magna Carta established several important principles: the king must rule in accordance with established feudal practices, he must consult with the barons before levying taxes, and all free men have the right to trial by jury if charged with a crime. Many of these concepts also contributed to a new institution known as **Parliament**.

During the thirteenth century, the English Parliament increased its power. In order to raise money for an anticipated French attack against England, Edward I (r. 1272–1307) convened in 1295 the so-called Model Parliament, composed of an upper house of nobles and a lower house of "knights of the shires and burgesses of the towns." This precedent established the origin of Parliament's House of Lords and House of Commons, which still exist today.

Germany   Events in East Frankland, or Germany, took a different turn. One setback to centralized rule was the division of the eastern portion of Charlemagne's realm into five regional groupings, or duchies, each under the control of a powerful duke. This made it difficult for kings to centralize royal authority.

Imperial involvement in papal affairs in Italy also made centralization difficult. When Otto I of Saxony (r. 936–973) took power as king of the Germans, he extended Germanic influence in Italy in order to reestablish Charlemagne's protection of the papacy. In 962, Otto put down political disturbances and protests against the church. In gratitude, Pope John XII (r. 955–964) proclaimed Otto "emperor of the Romans," forming the basis of what has been termed the "Holy Roman Empire."

In ensuing years Otto's successors extended German control south of the Alps into Italy. Frederick I (1152–1190), the first to bear the title Holy Roman Emperor, greatly expanded German holdings in Italy in the north, and in 1155 he was named king of Italy. After his defeat at the hands of a coalition of northern Italian cities in 1176, however, Frederick was forced to grant them quasi-independence, in return for their support against papal interests in the Italian peninsula. Frederick next turned his attention to Sicily. By marrying his son, the future Henry VI (r. 1190–1197), to Constance of Sicily, daughter of the Norman king of Sicily, Frederick added the Kingdom of Sicily to the lands controlled by the Holy Roman Empire.

The Economic and Social Recovery of Europe

Europe also recovered economically during this period. At the year 1000 agriculture was still the mainstay of the economy, there was little commerce, and the few cities were underpopulated. By 1300, however, trade and commerce were flourishing, urban life was expanding, and a new social class of merchants had emerged.

The Agricultural Revolution   Developments in agriculture contributed to Europe's economic revival. One important factor was the heavy-wheeled plow, fitted with an iron blade and a moldboard (a curved iron blade to cut through, lift, and turn the newly dug soil). The use of animal manure fertilizers and the transition from a two-field to a three-field system also increased crop production. In the three-field system, one field was planted in the spring for a fall harvest, another was planted in the winter for a spring harvest, and the third remained fallow to enable its soil to regenerate nutrients.

The agricultural revolution in Europe was largely due to innovations from elsewhere in Eurasia (perhaps from China), which were transmitted to Europe through cross-cultural interactions (mostly via the Silk Road trade network). Among these innovations were the use of horses with collar harnesses (instead of slower-moving oxen); iron horseshoes; the tandem harness, allowing horses to work in pairs; the vertical waterwheel; and the single-wheeled barrow.

Moreover, new forms of mechanical energy—also of Asian origin—were introduced to Europe through interactions with the Islamic world. As early as 1050, watermills were in wide use. Windmills, which were borrowed from Islamic Iran during the twelfth century, converted the power of water or wind into pounding and grinding motions used for the production of cloth goods, beer, and grain products. Even the first deep-drilled water well, introduced in the twelfth century, was of Chinese origin. Finally, through Muslim Spain the Europeans benefited from Islamic advances in agriculture.

These innovations meant an increase in both the quantity of agricultural production and the quality and variety of food. Improvements to the European diet resulted in an increase in population: in 1000, the population stood at about 36 million; by 1100 it had jumped to 44 million, and by 1200 to 58 million. By 1300 the European population reached about 80 million.

Commerce and Trade   The revolution in agricultural production sparked a rejuvenation of commerce and trade in urban centers. As Europe's population grew, so did the demand for consumer goods. The expansion of mercantile elites in urban centers also provoked a demand for luxury goods from beyond Europe.

One focal point of the revival of trade and commerce developed in northern Europe, where Flemish weavers began a flourishing exchange with wool-producing centers in England, particularly with monasteries in the north of the island, in the twelfth century. Another productive source of the commercial trade revival in northern Europe was the importation of French wines into England beginning in the later eleventh century, occasioned by the Norman Conquest in 1066.

Far more vital, however, was the revival of European commerce and trade across the Mediterranean. When the Umayyad rulers were displaced by the Abbasids, maritime contacts between Islamic and Christian merchants resumed. In addition, the Norman conquest of Islamic southern Italy and Sicily (1046–1091) afforded the northern Italian maritime cities of Pisa, Genoa, and Venice the opportunity to collaborate with Islamic merchants in Alexandria and the Levant. By the end of the eleventh century, Italian traders had established commercial ties with Constantinople, Syria, and Cairo.

The most momentous change in European trade and commerce took place near the close of the thirteenth century. Around 1275, first Genoese and then Venetian maritime traders sailed westward across the Mediterranean, through the Strait of Gibraltar, and then out into the Atlantic. In 1309 Ferdinand IV (r. 1295–1312), king of Castile and León in Spain, claimed control of Gibraltar from the Muslims, ensuring full access to the Atlantic. Before these developments, trading patterns were primarily of a one-way nature: European merchants imported modest quantities of goods, mostly spices, from China and India. Thanks to economic advances in the West, however, European merchants now had products, such as textiles, to export to the East (see Map 11.2).

Cross-Mediterranean trade and commerce were facilitated by navigational innovations, some of which were assimilated as a result of interactions with Islamic and Byzantine merchants. Navigation was improved by advances in European ship design, especially the incorporation of the sternpost rudder. The principal advantage of the stern-mounted rudder was that it allowed for the construction of larger ships, which in turn increased the volume of transported goods. Another improvement was the adoption from Muslim sailors of the lateen sail, a front-mounted triangular sail that allowed for tacking into the wind. It was largely owing to this navigational device that Italian ships were able to sail into the westerly winds that had previously prevented their sailing through the Strait of Gibraltar into the Atlantic. Most important was the introduction of the magnetic compass. Whether of independent invention or derived from China, where it was used on Chinese ships as early as around 1090, the magnetic compass first appeared in Europe in 1190. Use of the compass greatly facilitated maritime travel beyond the sight of land.

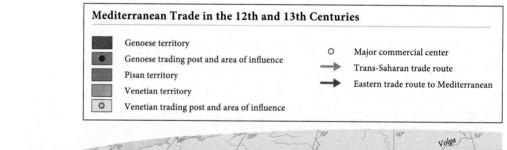

Mediterranean Trade in the 12th and 13th Centuries

- ▬ Genoese territory
- ⊙ Genoese trading post and area of influence
- ▬ Pisan territory
- ▬ Venetian territory
- ⊙ Venetian trading post and area of influence
- ○ Major commercial center
- → Trans-Saharan trade route
- → Eastern trade route to Mediterranean

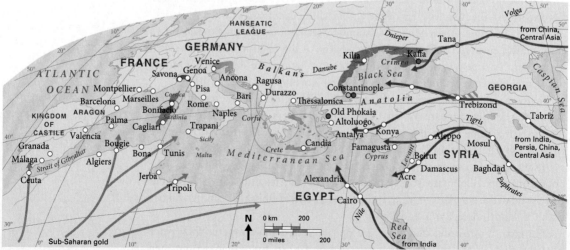

MAP 11.2 **Mediterranean Trade in the Twelfth and Thirteenth Centuries.**

Early Capitalism and a Cash Economy   This renewed trans-Mediterranean commercial activity sparked innovations in commerce and monetary exchange that contributed to the development of European **capitalism**. Increasing commercial transactions prompted a need for coined money. Meanwhile, medieval fairs created new business procedures like record-keeping and accounting practices, along with bills of exchange (the forerunner of the modern bank check) to replace transport of large amounts of coins. These transactions were facilitated by the use of paper, invented in China, then adopted by Islamic merchants, and subsequently transmitted to Europe in the eleventh century through Muslim Spain. Other financial and legal instruments were devised to promote long-distance trade.

Capitalism: An economic system characterized by private or corporate ownership of capital goods, by investments that are determined by private decision, and by prices, production, and the distribution of goods that are determined mainly by competition in a free market.

Urban Growth   The revitalization of trade and commerce contributed to the rejuvenation of urban life in eleventh-century Europe. Artisans and merchants were drawn to vibrant urban centers, along with craftspeople and laborers, many of whom fled rural manors in order to begin new lives in cities. These cities were small by today's standards. Most numbered around 5,000 people, although London and Bruges each held about 40,000 inhabitants, while cities like Venice and Genoa in northern Italy boasted populations of around 100,000.

Social Patterns   Social patterns within the revitalized urban centers of the eleventh and twelfth centuries evolved for several reasons. Of primary importance was the cash economy, which resulted in the appearance of a new social class: the hired military. Cities benefited from the cash contributions of wealthy businessmen in order to build cathedrals and large town halls. Finally, cities produced a new class of people, the **bourgeoisie** [boor-zhwa-ZEE]. Composed of merchants and artisans who lived in "burghs" (cities), the bourgeoisie produced and sold goods for commercial exchange. This new "middle class" of people would greatly influence the development of medieval representative governments.

Bourgeoisie: The urban-based middle class between the wealthy aristocracy and the working class.

Urban women were employed as butchers, candle makers, metal crafters, silk weavers, and bookbinders. However, women were rarely admitted as full members to craft **guilds**. For the majority of working women, better opportunities were available in what were known as "bye industries," or home-based enterprises, like spinning cloth and brewing ale. In some cases, widows took over their late husband's trade and worked as single women.

Guilds: Associations of artisans and merchants intended to protect and promote affairs of common interest.

Comprising a small but distinct minority of the European population in the eleventh century, Jews were spread in communities around the Mediterranean world. Through their travels, Jews developed both geographical knowledge and the command of multiple languages. They served as diplomats and engaged in moneylending and banking.

As the eleventh century unfolded, however, tolerance toward Jews began to wane. Jews were increasingly vilified as murderers of Christ, a sentiment fanned by the First Crusade in 1096. In many cases Jews were forced to live together in walled-off, gated ghettos in towns, which frequently held charters of liberty separate from those of the towns. Several countries expelled Jews—England in 1290, France in 1306, and a number of continental cities in the early 1400s—resulting in their dispersal throughout eastern Europe.

Religious Reform and Expansion

From 1000 to 1300, the clerical establishment of medieval Europe underwent dramatic reform. The reform movement in the church began in monasteries, then spread to the ecclesiastical hierarchy in cities, and eventually resulted in a new age of religious enthusiasm throughout Europe.

Monastic Reform   The effort at monastic reform began in France in a monastery founded at Cluny in 910 by Duke William I (875–918) of Aquitaine. Cluny was established as a monastery free of obligations to either feudal lords or local ecclesiastical control and committed to the Benedictine rule. The number of reformed monasteries increased during the eleventh and twelfth centuries. The most successful of new monastic orders was the Cistercians, founded in 1098 in a remote area of eastern France at Citeaux. The appeal of the Cistercian order lay in its austerity; Cistercians were enjoined to devote their total beings to "God's work" (*opus Dei*).

Papal Reform and the Investiture Controversy   The papacy underwent similar reform. The church sought independence from secular influence, particularly the practice by which lay rulers appointed and invested bishops, abbots, and popes with their spiritual authority. Popes, however, believed it was the exclusive right of the clergy to make such appointments. The creation of the College of Cardinals, inaugurated by the Papal Election Decree in 1059, ensured that only the College of Cardinals was empowered to elect the pontiff of the Holy Catholic Church. The result was the elimination of the role of the Holy Roman (German) emperor in the appointment of popes.

This conflict led to the "Investiture Controversy." Pope Gregory VII (r. 1073–1085) insisted that appointment of the clergy was to be controlled solely by the church. When the German emperor Henry IV (1056–1106) openly challenged Gregory's proclamation, the pope excommunicated him. The struggle between popes and emperors continued until 1122, when an agreement known as the Concordat of Worms was reached. This agreement stipulated that German bishops must be elected by church officials.

The investiture controversy was a victory for the church and a loss for the empire. Gregory's actions proved that popes could force emperors to acknowledge papal authority, and Henry IV's struggle with the church proved disastrous for his successors. Later German emperors never fully recovered from the distraction of attempting to control matters in both Germany and Italy. The five Germanic principalities reasserted their independence from royal control, and Germany remained disunited until the later nineteenth century.

Popular Piety and a Religious Society   As early as the eleventh century, ordinary Europeans took a more active interest in religion. This movement was caused by several factors. One was the reform movement in the church, which resulted in both higher standards of conduct among clergy and the increased authority of the pope. Another factor was the construction of shrines dedicated to Christian saints, whose relics were considered powerful aids in the quest for personal salvation.

Another factor was new ways of depicting Jesus and Mary, the mother of Jesus. Whereas in the earliest years of the church the crucifixion of Jesus was rarely

(a)

(b)

Changing Views of Christ. The Crucifixion scene from the door of the basilica of Santa Sabina, Rome, ca. 430, is formal and stylized: Christ is remote (a). In contrast, the Crucifixion commissioned by the archbishop of Cologne, Germany, just before 1000, shows a suffering Christ—a human being in agony and sorrow, hanging from a cross (b).

represented, by the tenth century the Crucifixion was portrayed as a reminder of his sacrifice for the redemption of humanity's sins.

The popularization of Christian piety was further encouraged by new concepts of time. One concept derives from the biblical book of Genesis, where the creation of the earth took six days, leaving the seventh as a day of rest. Another concept, the numbering of years in accordance with the Christian era, was introduced in 532 by Dionysius Exiguus (ca. 470–544), a Roman monk. For Dionysius, historical time began with the birth of Christ, hence his designation of *Anno Domini* ("in the year of the Lord") to denote a new dating system.

These concepts of time had several implications for Europeans. Two Christian feast days now became standard: the birth of Christ was celebrated on December 25 (Christmas) and his resurrection on a movable date called **Easter**. Saints' days became major events. Finally, the ringing of church bells announced the hours of the day, which provided for regulation of daily routines.

One alarming aspect of popular piety was the appearance of heretical movements within the church (see "Against the Grain" below). In an effort to rechannel the devotion of the faithful, Pope Innocent III (r. 1198–1216) licensed two new religious orders, the Franciscans and the Dominicans. Founded by St. Francis of Assisi (1181/2–1226), the Franciscan order, by living simply and aiding the poor and the sick, inspired a new dedication to Christianity. The Dominicans, founded by St. Dominic (1170–1221) in 1216, believed that the best way to combat heresy was to teach the doctrines of the church. The Dominican order included many famous medieval theologians in its ranks, such as St. Thomas Aquinas (ca. 1225–1274).

Easter: Christian celebration of the Resurrection of Christ; celebrated on the Sunday following the first full moon after the vernal equinox.

The Crusades   Like the reform movement of the church, the Crusades were in part inspired by the new wave of religious enthusiasm sweeping Europe. But another factor was the so-called *Reconquista*, or reconquest, of formerly Christian lands that had been taken over by Muslims.

Small groups of Spanish Christians had retreated in the 700s into the far northwest of the Iberian Peninsula, while the Muslims controlled most of the lands from their capital in Córdoba. In 1031, however, squabbling among Muslim factions, which ended the Umayyad caliphate, led to a loosening of Muslim control throughout Spain, which in turn prompted two kings of Christian territories to launch an offensive. The breakthrough occurred in 1085 when Toledo was liberated from Muslim control, resulting in almost half of Spain returning to Christian control.

A similar effort by Norman knights to retake Christian territory from Muslim control took place in southern Italy and Sicily between 1061 and 1090, resulting in a Norman kingdom in Sicily allied with the papacy. In return for their protection of the papacy, the kings were given total control over all the higher clergy in their realm.

These successes against the Muslims in the western Mediterranean occurred simultaneously with alarming developments in the eastern Mediterranean. As we have seen in Chapter 10, by the 1080s Seljuk Turks had seized control of substantial territories in the Middle East, prompting Pope Urban II to call for the launching of a crusade to the Holy Land in 1095 (see Map 11.3). Urban called on the barons of Europe to assemble their feudal armies and march to the east to liberate Jerusalem from Muslim control. Europe's feudal nobility most likely saw in this expedition the promise of new lands and a chance to use their military training for a good cause.

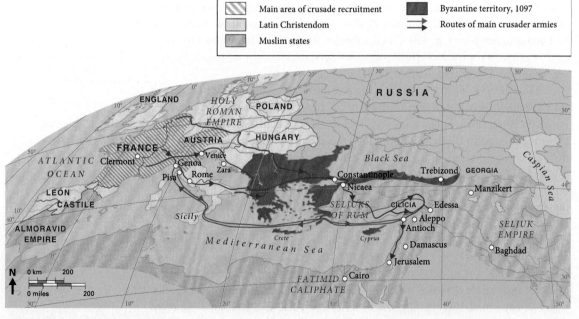

MAP 11.3 **The First Crusade, 1095–1099**

In 1096–1097, the baronial forces assembled in Constantinople, and in June 1097 they took Nicaea from the Turks. Two years later, in the summer of 1099, Jerusalem was finally freed from Muslim control—but at a horrific cost in human life.

Other crusades followed throughout the twelfth century. In 1144 the fall of the crusader state of Edessa (in present-day Turkey) to a resurgence of Islamic militancy caused renewed interest in a second crusade. Led by King Louis VII of France and Holy Roman Emperor Conrad III, this crusade failed to reach Jerusalem. The taking of Jerusalem by the Muslim leader Saladin in 1187 ignited the Third Crusade, led by kings Frederick I of Germany, Philip II of France, and Richard I of England. Although the crusaders captured Acre from the Muslims in 1191, dissension between Philip II and Richard I resulted in Philip's hasty return to France.

The Fourth Crusade was instigated by Pope Innocent III and launched in 1201. The crusading army contracted with the Venetians for passage by ship to the east. The Venetians, taking advantage of transporting a crusading army, attacked the Adriatic port city of Zara, their commercial rival. Outraged by an attack on a Christian city, Innocent III excommunicated the crusaders, most of whom ignored the papal ban. From Zara the Venetians transported the army to Constantinople in 1204, where they plundered the city, slaughtering innocent Christians in the process. In the long run, the Fourth Crusade not only weakened the authority of subsequent Byzantine rulers but also deepened animosities between the Roman and Eastern Orthodox Churches.

Although the crusading movement failed to keep Jerusalem out of Muslim hands and resulted in heavy casualties, the Crusades produced some positive achievements for Europeans. The ability of popes to organize European knights into armies enhanced their prestige in both the west and the east. The Crusades also helped to establish Western Christian dominance of sea traffic in the Mediterranean. In addition, the retaking of Christian territories in southern Italy, Sicily, and Spain gave European scholars access to new sources of Greco-Arabic scientific advances, and it resulted in the transmission of Islamic architecture to Western Europe (see "Patterns Up Close").

Intellectual and Cultural Developments

The High Middle Ages (ca. 1000–1300) saw new directions in the intellectual and cultural expressions of Western Christian religious civilization. Two symbols of this civilization—the Gothic cathedral and the university—were born during the "twelfth-century renaissance."

Universities Monastic schools in rural areas gave way to cathedral schools in urban centers, which offered instruction in the skills required by the commercial world of the twelfth century. Creative thinkers and the students they attracted flocked to cathedral schools in the larger cities of Europe. In time, groups of students and teachers formed the first universities at Salerno, Bologna, and Paris.

Particularly in Paris, the university curriculum began to focus on the philosophy of Aristotle, whose rediscovery was owing to the efforts of Gerbert of Aurillac (ca. 946–1003), later named Pope Sylvester II (r. 999–1003). As a young man Gerbert had studied mathematics, astronomy, and Aristotelian logic in Islamic Spain. Later, as deacon of the cathedral school at Reims, Gerbert introduced both

The Gothic Cathedral

Although the Gothic cathedral is the iconic symbol of medieval European Christianity, its origins can be traced back to late imperial Rome. Following Constantine's Edict of Milan in 313, Christians no longer had to worship in secret, and church leaders sought a public building that could accommodate larger congregations. The Roman basilica, a civic hall traditionally used for public functions, was ideal for early Christian worship. Its design was assimilated by the church and transformed from pagan to Christian usage. The basilica style featured a long central aisle (or nave), roofed over with timber, ending with an intersecting transept and an arched passage into a semicircular apse with a raised platform.

During the post-Roman early medieval period, other earlier Roman and Christian architectural styles were adapted to European circumstances. The result was the Romanesque style of church architecture, which appeared from ca. 800 to 1000. A key feature of Romanesque architecture was the replacement of the basilica's low timber roofs with stone barrel vaults, which required massive stone piers and exterior walls to support the weight. In addition, the apse was expanded beyond the transept by the addition of a circular walkway (the ambulatory) to allow pilgrims to view Christian relics. Finally, the focal point of the exterior was now the western façade, flanked by two towers. During the tenth and eleventh centuries, further changes in Romanesque churches included the enlargement of interiors, the increased height of the nave, and the addition of a clerestory with rounded arches above the nave to admit more light into the interior.

Nave of the Abbey Church of St. Denis

The revitalization of urban life and lay piety in the eleventh and twelfth centuries led architects to assimilate some features of the Romanesque into a new design. The first attempt to open up gloomy Romanesque interiors—and an early expression

the sciences and Aristotelian logic to his students, many of whom in turn helped spread the new learning throughout cathedral schools in Europe.

During the eleventh and twelfth centuries, two important developments in universities resulted from the popularity of Aristotelian logic. One of these was a method of pursuing philosophical and theological truth by use of Aristotelian logic, known as **scholasticism**. The problem was that Aristotle posed a serious threat to church authority, since a better understanding of his ideas revealed just how incompatible his thinking was with religious doctrine.

What emerged was a fundamental disagreement between those who placed the truths of faith before the truths of reason in attempting to gain knowledge of God's existence and those who placed reason first. The most famous advocates of these opposing schools of thought were St. Anselm (ca. 1034–1109) and Peter Abelard (1079–1142). Anselm argued that faith must precede reason ("I believe in order that I might understand"). Abelard, the most popular teacher at the cathedral school of Notre Dame in Paris during these years, disagreed, arguing,

Scholasticism: A medieval method of determining theological and philosophical truth by using Aristotelian logic.

of the new Gothic style—was made in 1144 at the abbey church of St. Denis in Paris under the direction of Abbot Suger (1085–1151). To enlarge the space and provide more light, Suger turned to solutions already in practice in late Romanesque churches: the pointed arch, the ribbed vault, and flying buttresses.

Pointed arches allowed for higher vertical thrusts in weight distribution, resulting in soaring naves. The pointed arch, widely used as early as the eighth century in Islamic architecture, was most likely transmitted to Europe from Sicily.

Ribbed vaults were improvements over earlier Romanesque groin vaults in that they provided for elevated vaults while at the same time directing the vertical thrust downward through more slender columns, thus providing greater interior space. Ribbed vaults also allowed for thinner outer walls, which could accommodate large glass windows that allowed in more light. There is considerable conjecture over whether the technique of ribbed vaults may have originated in earlier Islamic architecture. It has been argued, however, that the earlier Islamic models were primarily used in domes instead of the nave, and in any event were designed for different purposes.

Flying buttresses—perhaps the most innovative feature of the Gothic style—were then used to support the thinner outer walls, distributing the thrust of the ribbed vaults and pointed arches away from the outer wall and down toward the ground. Another innovation at St. Denis was the incorporation of stained-glass panels (frequently depicting stories from the Bible) in the outer walls, which provided dazzling arrays of color and light in the interior.

Questions

- How does the Gothic cathedral demonstrate the origins–interactions–adaptations process in action?

- What types of cultural adaptations are evident in houses of worship built in modern times?

"I understand in order that I might believe." Abelard's apparent favoring of reason over faith tipped the balance in favor of those who were inclined to question traditional Christian doctrine.

So popular was Aristotle by the middle of the thirteenth century that in addition to the earlier division between those who advocated either the truths of faith or reason, a third perspective was offered by those who took a middle path. It was to this latest camp that St. Thomas Aquinas (ca. 1224–1274) belonged. In his *Summa Theologica*, Aquinas argued that, instead of considering the truths of reason as being totally irreconcilable with the truths of faith, it was possible to consider a compromise, or a synthesis of the two, that would in the end lead to a knowledge of God's existence and, thus, to personal salvation.

Law and Medicine   In the twelfth century, universities began to offer training in law and medicine. Scholars at Bologna discovered the Roman legal tradition preserved in Justinian's *Corpus Iuris Civilis*. It was at Bologna around 1140 that

Canon law: The law of the church.

the *Corpus* inspired a monk named Gratian to compile a compendium of ecclesiastical law known as the *Decretum*. Gratian's student Peter Lombard's *Book of Sentences*, produced in 1150, served along with the *Decretum* as the foundation for the development of **canon law**, utilized by the papacy in its struggles to contest secular power.

Medical studies were taught at Salerno in the late eleventh century. Located in Sicily, Salerno was able to assimilate Islamic and Byzantine medical advances. Serving as the nucleus of medical studies at Salerno were the works of the Roman physician Galen and the *Canon of Medicine* compiled by the Islamic scholar Ibn Sina (or Avicenna, 980–1037). These works formed the foundation of medical studies throughout medieval European universities.

Medieval Science Medieval scholars were fascinated by scientific texts of the ancient Greeks. This interest was sparked not only by Gerbert of Aurillac but also by Christian advances into Spain and southern Italy in the late eleventh century. The Christian conquest of Toledo in 1085, followed by the retaking of Sicily in 1090, provided European scholars access to Islamic scientific learning. Adelard of Bath (ca. 1080–1152), who translated Greek scientific texts from Arabic into Latin, served as a bridge between the Islamic and Western Christian worlds.

Perhaps the most important of Adelard's successors in England was Robert Grosseteste (ca. 1175–1253), a bishop of Lincoln and a dabbler in the new scientific studies of natural phenomena. Grosseteste recognized the value of mathematics. He was also among the earliest scholastics to question the scientific authority of Aristotle. Grosseteste's arguments were developed by his student Roger Bacon (ca. 1214–1294), whose principal contribution to the development of Western science was to emphasize the role of mathematics and experimentation.

During the early years of the fourteenth century, another "school" of natural scientists, the so-called Oxford Calculators, advanced scientific studies. They challenged many of Aristotle's shortcomings regarding natural science. Perhaps the best known of the Calculators' contributions is the mean speed theorem, which anticipates Galileo's law of falling bodies (objects of different weights fall with uniform rates of acceleration in a vacuum).

Crisis and Creativity, 1300–1415

The fourteenth century, generally considered an era of calamities, marks the transition from the Middle Ages to the Renaissance. The early part of the century witnessed a series of economic reversals. Near mid-century a devastating plague originating in Southeast Asia ravaged Europe. A long, drawn-out period of war between England and France began in 1337 and ended in 1453. In addition, the authority of the papacy was both challenged from without and weakened from within. As bleak as things were, however, signs of new creative forces appeared as early as the middle of the century.

The Calamitous Fourteenth Century

Fourteenth-century Europeans suffered deeply. At the beginning of the century a dramatic climatic change, termed the "Little Ice Age," accompanied by heavy rains, resulted in reversals in the economic and social realms, a prolonged period of poor harvests followed by famine, and a disastrous plague added to the misery of daily life.

Famine   From 1315 to 1322 Europe was hit by famine. One cause was a sudden disparity between an expanding population and its available food supply. No new advances were made in agricultural technology, and after centuries of expansion and clearing of lands there was no new space available for increased agricultural production. To make matters worse, the average annual temperature dropped during this period, creating the "Little Ice Age," with catastrophic consequences for agriculture.

Plague   Near mid-century, Europe's already weakened populations suffered a horrific outbreak of plague. The disease originated in Asia and was transmitted in goods transported by Mongol traders in the 1330s. It spread westward along trade routes to the Black Sea and was introduced to the West when grain-carrying Genoese merchant ships, infested with rats, sailed from the Crimea to ports in Sicily and northern Italy in 1346–1347. Within a year, the plague had spread into northern Europe via trade routes, carried by infected rats and fleas, fanning out across Europe north of the Alps. People with infected lungs inadvertently spread the disease by close contact with others and by frequent coughing.

The disease took its name "Black Death" from the appearance of blackened body sores called buboes (hence the name "bubonic plague"). Once the sores appeared, infected people suffered with high fevers, swollen lymph nodes, and painfully aching joints and usually died within three days. The plague ravaged Europe from 1348 to 1352 and returned sporadically in the 1360s, 1370s, and 1390s.

The highly contagious disease was next to impossible to contain. Europe's population was weakened as a consequence of famine, and overcrowded and unsanitary European cities created ideal conditions for the rapid spread of the disease. Moreover, medieval medicine was lacking when it came to the treatment of illnesses and diseases.

It has been estimated that England alone may have lost nearly 1 million from a total population of around 4 million. Urban areas were the hardest hit; Florence suffered losses amounting to around 50,000 out of a total population of 85,000. An estimate of the number of people who died throughout Europe as a result of the first wave of the plague puts the total loss at about one-third of the entire population (see Map 11.4).

There was economic and social fallout from the Black Death across Europe. It was widely believed that the plague was provoked by a wrathful God who punished Christians for their sins. A more sinister response was a wave of anti-Semitism, which targeted Jews as scapegoats and accused them of poisoning wells—an ominous foreshadowing of the Spanish Inquisition (see Chapter 16). The decline of Europe's population caused a downturn in commerce and trade, and in rural areas a decline in the production of grain. The reduction in the number of agricultural workers made their labor more sought-after than before the plague. The result of these increasing tensions between the well-off and those

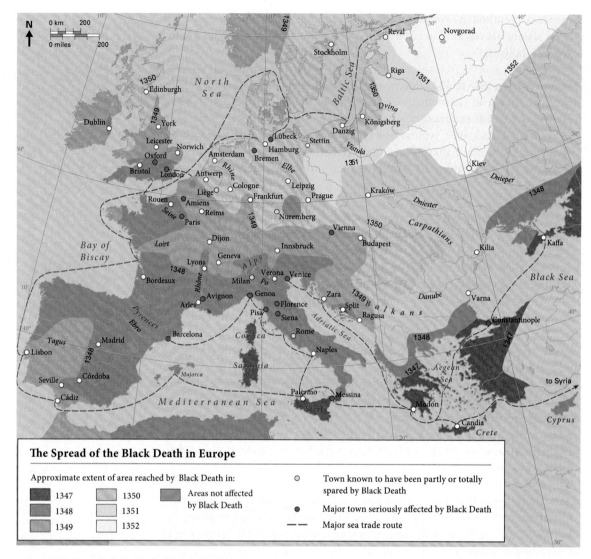

MAP 11.4 The Spread of the Black Death in Europe

less well-off was a series of social uprisings throughout Europe. The most serious social revolt occurred in London in 1381. Known as the Peasants' Revolt, the uprising included wealthy country residents as well as participants from the ranks of the urban working classes.

The Hundred Years' War   From the mid-fourteenth to the mid-fifteenth century, Europe was embroiled in a disastrous conflict dubbed the "Hundred Years' War" by nineteenth-century historians. At issue was a dispute over English landholdings in France, retained after the Norman Conquest in 1066. When the English king Edward III (r. 1327–1377) laid claim to the vacant French throne in 1328, his claim was rejected in favor of Charles IV (r. 1322–1328), the first of the Valois rulers. These issues came to a head in 1337 when Philip VI (r. 1328–1350) seized control of Gascony and fighting erupted between the two countries.

The conflict was fought in three phases. Early on, English forces triumphed at the Battle of Crécy in 1346, the Battle of Poitiers in 1356, and the Battle of Agincourt in 1415. Just as it seemed that English forces were on the verge of declaring victory, a 17-year-old peasant girl, Joan of Arc (ca. 1412–1431), encouraged the uncrowned Charles VII (r. 1422–1461) to relieve the siege of Orléans in 1429, where English forces were routed. The victory at Orléans inspired the French to continued victories. The conflict finally came to an end in 1453, when the English conceded a French victory in terms agreed to in the Treaty of Paris, leaving the English in possession of only the port of Calais.

The economic consequences of the war were serious. The war—fought entirely on French soil—destroyed both crops and small farms. In both England and France, financing the war meant new and increased taxes, especially for the peasantry. The war even affected the religious realm. It prevented the resolution of the **Western Schism** as rival popes sought the support of contending French and English kings and their subjects.

Western Schism: The period 1378–1417, marked by divided papal allegiances in Latin Christendom.

Crises in the Church   Troubles began during the papacy of Pope Boniface VIII (r. 1294–1303), who clashed with Philip IV (r. 1285–1314) of France. Philip levied a tax on the French clergy. In response, Boniface excommunicated Philip; the latter retaliated in 1303 by ordering the imprisonment of the pope, who subsequently died. Boniface's successor, Clement V (r. 1305–1314), left Rome and took up residence in Avignon, on the French border. Clement appointed a number of French clergymen to the College of Cardinals. From 1305 to 1378 successive French popes continued to reside at Avignon, a period known as the Avignon Papacy.

In 1378 Pope Gregory XI (r. 1370–1378) returned to Rome, but he died shortly after his arrival there. Perhaps in response to pressure from a Roman mob to elect

Burial of Plague Victims. With up to 50 percent of the people in some places in Europe dying of the plague, burial scenes, such as this one depicted in a Flemish manuscript, were common throughout the middle and late fourteenth century.

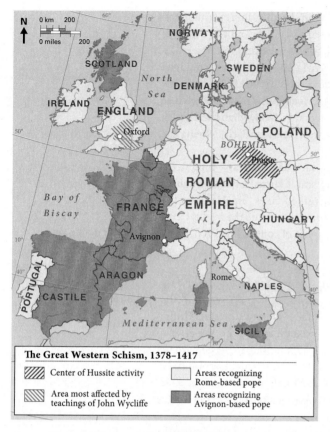

The Great Western Schism, 1378–1417

- ▨ Center of Hussite activity
- ▧ Area most affected by teachings of John Wycliffe
- ☐ Areas recognizing Rome-based pope
- ■ Areas recognizing Avignon-based pope

MAP 11.5 **The Great Western Schism, 1378–1417**

Sacrament: An outward and physical sign of an inward and spiritual grace.

either a Roman or an Italian as the next pope, the predominantly French College of Cardinals elected an Italian archbishop, Urban VI (r. 1378–1389). The cardinals, regretting their selection of Urban, returned to Avignon and elected a Frenchman as the new pope, Clement VII (r. 1378–1394). The Council of Pisa in 1409 deposed both reigning popes and named a new one, Alexander V (r. 1409–1410). However, the two reigning popes refused to step down, with the result that the church had not one or two but *three* popes.

Adding to the church's problems were outspoken critics, including John Wycliffe (ca. 1330–1384), an Oxford theologian. Wycliffe railed against the wealth and abuses of the clergy, denied the power of priests to act as intermediaries between believers and God, and disputed the validity of many **sacraments**. Wycliffe also oversaw the translation of the Bible into Middle English. Wycliffe's teachings reached Bohemia in central Europe when the English king Richard II (r. 1377–1399) married the princess Anne of Bohemia. John Huss (Anglicized form of Jan Hus; 1370–1415), a radical religious reformer at Prague, enthusiastically supported Wycliffe's ideas (see Map 11.5).

Signs of a New Era in the Fifteenth Century

The dire circumstances of the fourteenth century prompted adaptations and subsequent transformations in the succeeding century that prefigured the transition to the Renaissance. We can observe these adjustments in political, economic, and cultural aspects of fifteenth-century Europe.

Political Reorganization in France and England   After the Hundred Years' War, new conceptions of royal authority arose in both England and France. In France, fifteenth-century rulers utilized warfare as an opportunity to centralize their authority. One outcome was to enhance the efficiency and power of the royal bureaucracy. Another was the raising of new taxes without consulting the Estates-General.

The state of politics in England was similarly affected by the course of the Hundred Years' War. Throughout the course of the war, English monarchs were repeatedly forced to convene Parliament in order to gain access to funds to prosecute the war effort. Before granting monies to the crown, however, the House of Commons, consisting of merchants and lesser nobility, insisted on "redress of grievances before consent to taxation." As a result, the House of Commons eventually gained the right to introduce all important tax legislation in Parliament.

European Commerce and Trade   When France regained control of Flanders during the course of the Hundred Years' War, England—then at war with the French—was forced to abandon its profitable wool trade with Flemish merchants. As a result, England developed a far more lucrative trade in manufactured cloth products, of which by 1500 it had become a leading exporter.

When the Hundred Years' War disrupted trade in France, new lanes of commerce opened up across Europe. Germanic towns in northern Europe had formed a trading alliance, known as the **Hanseatic League** (from Old German *hansa* "troop; convoy; merchant association"), as early as the thirteenth century. The league reached its peak of influence during the later fourteenth and fifteenth centuries. A new commercial axis extended from the cities of the Hanseatic League in the north southward to the northern Italian cities of Venice and Genoa.

Hanseatic League: A trade network of allied ports along the North Sea and Baltic coasts, founded in 1256.

Of crucial importance for the future of European trade was the collapse of the so-called Pax Mongolica in 1368. Following the expansion of the Mongol Empire during the thirteenth and fourteenth centuries, travel and trade networks flourished between China and the West across the Silk Road. Thus, the Mongols facilitated the transfer of technological innovations from China to Europe. When, however, Mongol rule in China dissolved and was replaced by the Ming dynasty, travel on the Silk Road was no longer profitable. European merchants were forced to resort to southern maritime routes, in use already from the 750s onward.

Innovations in Business Techniques   Several innovative economic practices contributed to a revitalization of Europe's economy during the fifteenth century. Smaller markets brought on increased competition among merchants, who sought new business methods in order to remain solvent. New accounting procedures increased the efficiency of record keeping. In addition, the introduction of maritime insurance, which protected investments in seaborne trade, fueled an increase in trans-Mediterranean trade and commerce, while at the same time increasing profits for individual investors.

New banking procedures also facilitated the expansion of Europe's economy by providing loans to merchants and manufacturers. Florence emerged as the center of huge banking partnerships such as the Medici Bank; the Medici family went on to dominate Florentine civic affairs by 1450.

Developments in the Church   As a consequence of the disintegration of papal leadership during the fourteenth century, the church was controlled by councils of bishops in the early fifteenth century. In order to resolve the crises of the fourteenth century, the Council of Constance (1414–1417) was convened by the Holy Roman emperor. Its first order of business was to depose the three reigning popes and to restore papal authority to a single pontiff, who took the name Martin V (r. 1417–1431). Second, to put an end to heretical movements, principally the teachings of John Wycliffe, the council convicted John Huss of heresy and burned him at the stake. The execution of Huss had momentous implications for the future of the church, especially in Germany. Finally, to improve the management of the church, the council declared that councils of bishops would meet frequently in order to keep popes under their strict control.

The popes resisted the increasing power of the bishops but had to make concessions to secular rulers to gain their support. The result was the further weakening of the Roman Church and the creation of national churches, independent of control from Rome.

Literature   Literary expression flourished, in large part due to the growing popularity of cultural expression in **vernacular** languages instead of Latin. Education in the vernacular was especially popular in the city-states of northern Italy, where the emphasis was on educating students for productive careers in the secular world, rather than training them to become priests.

Vernacular: The native, common spoken language of a particular region.

A number of Italian authors chose to write in the vernacular rather than in Latin. Noteworthy examples include the poet Dante Alighieri (1265–1321), author of *The Divine Comedy*, a long epic poem written in Italian and completed in 1321; Francesco Petrarca, called Petrarch in English (1304–1374), known as the "father of Renaissance humanism," who wrote a series of love sonnets to his beloved Laura; and Giovanni Boccaccio (1313–1375), whose *Decameron* draws its inspiration from the first-century CE Roman author Petronius.

English and French writers of the fourteenth century also produced works in their native languages. *Piers Plowman*, composed in Middle English by William Langland (ca. 1332–1400), presents a series of complaints and laments about the aristocracy and the clergy in late-fourteenth-century England. Geoffrey Chaucer (ca. 1340–1400), a friend and contemporary of Langland's, also satirized abuses in contemporary society, most famously in his *Canterbury Tales*. Christine de Pizan (ca. 1364–1430) of France composed both poetry and prose; she was primarily concerned with advancing the status of women, and for her criticisms of male behavior is often considered the first feminist writer.

Philosophy   The era's philosophy challenged basic medieval theological beliefs. In place of Aquinas's attempt to reconcile differences between the truths of faith and reason, the intellectuals of the time turned toward the latter, especially toward Aristotle. The earliest philosopher to take this approach was the Oxford Franciscan John Duns Scotus (ca. 1266–1308), who argued for the separation of reason from theology. William of Ockham (ca. 1285–1349), another Oxford Franciscan, carried the assault on the Aquinas synthesis even further. He was an extreme nominalist, arguing that concrete things alone are real and general concepts exist only in the mind.

Putting It All Together

Following the collapse of the Mediterranean Roman Empire, a new Christian religious civilization developed in western Europe during the period ca. 600–1400. The Germanic invasions that brought down Roman rule in the western provinces destroyed imperial unity in the West and created in Europe a series of smaller political entities. After a brief period of centralized imperial rule during the reign of Charlemagne in the later eighth century, medieval Europe fell back in the ninth and tenth centuries into a feudal pattern of decentralized political entities. Feudalism prevented the reassertion of a single European empire and prepared Europe for the appearance of several highly centralized, competing kingdoms.

In terms of cultural developments, the Germanic invasions and subsequent destruction of Roman rule in the West were immensely disruptive, forcing the formation of a new, distinctly European culture based on Roman legacies, Germanic customs, and Christian institutions. Of these, the Christian Church would prove the most important in shaping a new European religious civilization.

During the fourteenth century, Europe experienced several transforming events. The horrors of famine and plague, accompanied by over a century of warfare between England and France, led Europeans to question traditional medieval values. In addition, internal problems in the church resulted in a lessening of its authority and prestige. At the same time, however, several developments—particularly in the cultural sphere—prepared Europe for the transition to Renaissance secularism and humanism.

Review and Relate

Thinking Through Patterns

Examine the ways historians approach the big questions of this chapter.

The Merovingians and Carolingians constructed a new Western Christian civilization during the seventh and eighth centuries by utilizing the support of the Christian Church. Through their conversion to Christianity, as well as their support and encouragement of monastic expansion, they earned the support of bishops, priests, and monks. In addition, the creation of the Franco-papal alliance during the eighth century, followed by Charlemagne's personal involvement in church affairs, ensured the emergence of a new Christian foundation for Europe.

> How did the Merovingians and Carolingians construct a new Christian European civilization during the seventh and eighth centuries CE?

Some key factors in the political, economic, and social recovery of Europe during the eleventh and twelfth centuries included the emergence of centralized kingdoms in France and England. The expansion of agricultural advances and the development of commerce and trade produced a population surge, which in turn resulted in urbanization and the emergence of a new bourgeois middle class of merchants and traders.

> What were key factors in the political, economic, and social recovery of Europe during the eleventh and twelfth centuries?

During the "twelfth-century renaissance," urban cathedral schools developed into universities in Europe. In order to serve the needs of an expanding urban and commercial economy, more practical disciplines like law and medicine were studied. Aristotelian logic and science, assimilated from contacts in Spain and Sicily, resulted in a debate between the truths of reason and the truths of faith. Although temporarily resolved by Aquinas in the late thirteenth century, Aristotelian thought dominated philosophy and theology in the fourteenth century. Another result of the fascination with

> What were some cultural and intellectual developments during the "twelfth-century renaissance," and how did they contribute to medieval civilization?

Aristotle was the development of natural science at Oxford and Paris, which during the later thirteenth and early fourteenth centuries began to uncover flaws in Aristotelian scientific conceptions.

As a result of a series of ecclesiastical reforms in both the monastic and episcopal arms of the church, a series of increasingly powerful popes began to assert papal primacy over secular rulers, and, indeed, over all European institutions. Pope Gregory VII humbled the German emperor Henry IV in the eleventh century, and Pope Innocent III did the same with King John of England in the beginning of the thirteenth century.

The fourteenth century witnessed several calamitous setbacks that, taken together, signaled the end of the medieval era and the early stages of the Renaissance era. Among these events were the Black Death, the Hundred Years' War, and the Avignon papacy, followed by the Western Schism, which eventually produced three competing popes. At the same time philosophers as well as theologians began to challenge earlier assertions of papal authority, resulting in the Council of Constance (1414–1417), which ultimately replaced papal control of the church with councils of bishops during the fifteenth century.

> **What events made fourteenth-century Europe so dismal? How did these combine to spell the gradual demise of medieval institutions and perspectives?**

| Against the Grain

Consider this as a counterpoint to the main patterns examined in this chapter.

The Cathar Heresy

- In what ways does Catharism represent a contrast to the patterns of development of medieval Europe?

- How were the religious and political authorities able to end the Cathar threat?

In 1144, the dedication of the Gothic abbey church at St. Denis illustrated the power and glory of Roman Christianity in European Christendom. And yet, only one year earlier—in 1143—a heretical cult posed the most dangerous challenge to Catholic Christianity in its history.

Known as Cathars (from the Greek *katharoi*, "pure ones"), or Albigensians (from Albi, a city in southwestern France), this heretical movement reflected anticlerical sentiments emanating from educated urbanites and rural laity alike, dismayed by the materialism, corruption, and worldliness of the clerical establishment. It probably came from the Byzantine Empire and may have been influenced by a combination of Persian Zoroastrianism and Manichaeism, dualistic religions in which forces of good and light (represented by God and the spiritual world) struggle against forces of evil and darkness (represented by Satan) for dominance. Cathars believed that the only way to escape from Satan's grasp was to forego all material things of this world, including marriage, sex, and certain foods. And because Christ was, in part, of the material world, Cathars rejected major elements of Orthodox Christianity.

Alarmed at its growing influence, Pope Innocent III moved to suppress Catharism. He ordered the Albigensian crusade (1209–1229), which resulted in the brutal suppression of the movement. When a force of French knights stormed the center of Cathar resistance at Beziers, they were ordered by the presiding bishop to slaughter all of its inhabitants, both Catholic and Cathar. Further efforts to eliminate Catharism included an Inquisition in 1234, and the movement finally dissolved in 1329, when the last of the Cathars were burned at the stake.

Key Terms

Baron 260

Bourgeoisie 263

Canon law 270

Capitalism 263

Coronation 255

Demesne 259

Easter 265

Estates-General 259

Feudalism 257

Guilds 263

Hanseatic League 275

Latin Christendom 254

Manorialism 258

Parliament 260

Sacrament 274

Scholasticism 268

Unction 255

Vernacular 276

Western Schism 273

Writ 260

OXFORD
insight study guide
Active Engagement, Deeper Understanding

Learn more with this chapter's digital tools, including the Oxford Insight Study Guide, at http://www.oup.com/he/vonsivers4e. Please see the Further Resources section at the back of the book for additional readings and suggested websites.

Sources for Chapter 11

SOURCE 11.1   Einhard's *Life of Charlemagne*

ca. 830 CE

The model for Einhard's *Vita Caroli Magni* was Suetonius's biographies of the first 12 Roman emperors, and particularly of Augustus, composed in the second century CE. The biography is thus an example of the general attempt to revive interest in and appreciation for pre-Christian Roman antiquity in the midst of the "Carolingian Renaissance," of which Einhard was both a product and a driving force. Educated at the Palace School at Aachen (Charlemagne's capital), Einhard established a close personal and professional connection with the man himself. Due to his intimate knowledge of Charlemagne's behavior, habits, and outlook, Einhard was ideally placed to write his biography, which was composed after Charlemagne's death but contained pointed advice to the man's successors.

§24. . . His main meal of the day was served in four courses, in addition to the roast meat which his hunters used to bring in on spits and which he enjoyed more than any other food. During his meal he would listen to a public reading or some other entertainment. Stories would be recited for him, or the doings of the ancients told again. He took great pleasure in the books of Saint Augustine and especially in those which are called *The City of God*.

. . .

§25 He spoke easily and fluently, and could express with great clarity whatever he had to say. He was not content with his own mother tongue, but took the trouble to learn foreign languages. He learnt Latin so well that he spoke it as fluently as his own tongue; but he understood Greek better than he could speak it. He was eloquent to the point of sometimes seeming almost garrulous.

He paid the greatest attention to the liberal arts; and he had great respect for men who taught them, bestowing high honours upon them. When he was learning the rules of grammar he received tuition from Peter the Deacon of Pisa, who by then was an old man, but for all other subjects he was taught by Alcuin, surnamed Albinus, another Deacon, a man of the Saxon race who came from Britain and was the most learned man anywhere to be found. Under him the Emperor spent much time and effort in studying rhetoric, dialectic

Source: Einhard and Notker the Stammerer, *Two Lives of Charlemagne*, trans. Lewis Thorpe (Harmondsworth, UK: Penguin, 1969), 78–80.

and especially astrology. He applied himself to mathematics and traced the course of the stars with great attention and care. He also tried to learn to write. With this object in view he used to keep writing-tablets and notebooks under the pillows on his bed, so that he could try his hand at forming letters during his leisure moments; but, although he tried very hard, he had begun too late in life and he made little progress.

§26 Charlemagne practised the Christian religion with great devotion and piety, for he had been brought up in this faith since earliest childhood. . . . He donated so many sacred vessels made of gold and silver, and so many priestly vestments, that when service time came even those who opened and closed the doors, surely the humblest of all church dignitaries, had no need to perform their duties in their everyday clothes. He made careful reforms in the way in which the psalms were chanted and the lessons read. He was himself quite an expert at both of these exercises, but he never read the lesson in public and he would sing only with the rest of the congregation and then in a low voice.

▶ **Working with Sources**

1. **How does this passage reflect the attempt to re-create the ancient past during the Carolingian Renaissance?**

2. **Did Charlemagne separate his private life from his public image? Why?**

SOURCE 11.2   Adelard of Bath, *Questiones naturales*

During the eleventh and twelfth centuries, scores of European scholars traveled to Arabic lands in order to indulge their interest in learning more about the scientific writings of the ancient Greeks, particularly those of Aristotle. Known as the "Latin Translators," their combined efforts through the course of the twelfth and thirteenth centuries introduced scores of Greco-Arabic scientific texts into European institutions of learning. Among these figures was an English scholar, Adelard of Bath (ca. 1080–1150), whose teaching expressed his fascination with Muslim science first in France, and ultimately in England during his tenure in the court of Henry I (ca. 1068–1135). Adelard is remembered especially for his most renowned work, *Questiones naturales* (*Natural Questions,* ca. 1125), consisting of 76 chapters in which he addresses aspects of natural science. In the following chapter, cast in the form of a dialogue with his nephew, who reflects an attitude of skepticism, Adelard throughout expresses his indebtedness to Islamic scholars. The following is taken from the preface and a later discussion.

Source: From Adelard of Bath, *Dodi Ve-Nechdi*, ed. and trans. H. Gollancz (London: Oxford University Press, 1920), 91–92, 98–99, 137–138.

ADELARD: You will remember, Nephew, how seven years ago when you were almost a child in the learning of the French, and I sent you along with the rest of my hearers to study with a man of high reputation, it was agreed between us that I should devote myself to the best of my ability to the study of Arabic, while you on your part were to acquire the inconsistencies of French ideas.

NEPHEW: I remember, and all the more because, when departing, you bound me under a solemn promise to be a diligent student of philosophy.

The result was that I applied myself with great diligence to this study. Whether what I have said is correct, the present occasion will give you an opportunity of discovering; since when you have often set them forth, 1, as hearer only, have marked the opinions of the Saracens, and many of them seem to me quite absurd; I shall, therefore, for a time cease to exercise this patience, and when you utter these views, shall attack them where it seems good to me to do so.

To me it seems that you go too far in your praise of the Arabs, and show prejudice in your disparagement of the learning of our philosophers. Our reward will be that you will have gained some fruit of your toil; if you give good answers, and I make a good showing as your opponent, you will see that my promise has been well kept.

ADELARD: You perhaps take a little more on you than you ought; but as this arrangement will be profitable not only to you but to many others, I will pardon your forwardness, making however this one stipulation, that when I adduce something unfamiliar, people are to think not that I am putting forward an idea of my own, but am giving the views of the Arabs. If anything I say displeases the less educated, I do not want them to be displeased with me also: I know too well what is the fate which attends upon the teachers of the truth with the common herd, and consequently shall plead the case of the Arabs, not my own.

NEPHEW: Let it be as you will, provided nothing causes you to hold your peace.

ADELARD: I think then that we should begin with lighter matters, and if here I fail to give you a reasonable account, you will know what to expect in more important subjects. Let us begin then at the bottom, and so proceed upwards. . . .

ADELARD: It is a little difficult for you and me to argue about animals. I, with reason for my guide, have learned one thing from my Arab teachers, you, something different; dazzled by the outward show of authority you wear a head-stall. For what else should we call authority but a head-stall? Just as brute animals are led by the head-stall where one pleases, without seeing why or where they are being led, and only follow the halter by which they are held, so many of you, bound and fettered as you are by a low credulity, are led into danger by the authority of writers. Hence, certain people arrogating to themselves the title of authorities have employed an unbounded licence in writing, and this to such an extent that they have not hesitated to insinuate into men of low intellect the false instead of the true. Why should you not fill sheets of paper, aye, fill them on both sides, when to-day you can get readers who require no proof of sound judgment from you, and are satisfied merely with the name of a time-worn title? They do not understand that reason has been given to individuals that, with it as chief judge, distinction may be drawn between the true and the false. Unless reason were appointed to be the chief judge, to no purpose would she have been given to us individually: it would have been enough for the writing of laws to have been entrusted to one, or at most to a few, and the rest would have been satisfied with their ordinances and authority. Further, the very people who are called authorities first gained the confidence of their inferiors only because they followed reason; and those who are ignorant of reason, or neglect it, justly desire to be called blind. However, I will not pursue this subject any further, though I regard authority as matter for contempt. This one thing, however, I will say. We must first search after reason, and when it has been found, and not until then, authority if added to it, may be received. Authority by itself can inspire no confidence in the philosopher, nor ought it to be used for such a purpose. Hence logicians have agreed in treating the argument from authority not as necessary, but probable only. If, therefore, you want to bear anything from me, you must both give and take reason. I am not the man whom the semblance of an object can possibly satisfy; and the fact is, that the mere word is a loose wanton abandoning herself now to this man, now to that.

▶ **Discussion Questions**

1. Why does Adelard's nephew have doubts about Arabic learning?

2. How does Adelard explain and support his respect for what Arabs had taught him?

SOURCE 11.3

Feudal contracts and the swearing of fealty

1127 and 1219

In the catastrophe brought on by the assaults on all their borders, some European Christians were forced to devise new means of self-protection. Into this vacuum of governmental authority came new "feudal" relationships between lords and vassals. Over time, these contractual relationships became increasingly regularized. The terms of these relationships can be reconstructed through documents describing the ceremonial and formulaic aspects of feudal obligations.

How the Count of Flanders received the homage of his vassals (1127):

Enfeoffed: Invested with an estate, or "fief."

Through the whole remaining part of the day those who had been previously **enfeoffed** by the most pious Count Charles did homage to the [new] count, taking up now again their fiefs and offices and whatever they had before

Source: James Harvey Robinson, *Readings in European History*, vol. 1 (Boston: Ginn & Company, 1904), 178–180.

rightfully and legitimately obtained. On Thursday, the seventh of April, homages were again made to the count, being completed in the following order of faith and security.

First they did their homage thus. The count asked the vassal if he were willing to become completely his man, and the other replied, "I am willing"; and with hands clasped, placed between the hands of the count, they were bound together by a kiss. Secondly, he who had done homage gave his fealty to the representative of the count in these words, "I promise on my faith that I will in future be faithful to Count William, and will observe my homage to him completely against all persons, in good faith and without deceit." And, thirdly, he took his oath to this upon the relics of the saints. Afterward the count, with a little rod which he held in his hand, gave investitures to all who by this agreement had given their security and accompanying oath.

Pons of Mont-Saint-Jean becomes the man of the Countess of Champagne (1219):

I, Pons of Mont-Saint-Jean, make known to all, both present and future, that since I have long been the man of my beloved Lady Blanche, countess of Champagne, for twenty pounds assigned to the fair at Bar, and since later both the countess and my dear lord have added other twenty pounds assigned to the same fair and gave me three hundred pounds in cash,—I swore by the saints that I would in good faith aid them and their heirs with my people and fortifications. If necessary I will fight especially against Erard of Brienne and Philippa his wife, and against Adelaide, queen of Cyprus, and her heirs, and against all who would aid them; except that should the said countess or count or their people be against Milo of Noyers, my sister's husband, in his castle of Noyers or elsewhere in his lands, neither I nor my people shall be held to go thither. If, however, the said Milo or his people set upon the countess or the count or their people, we shall be held to defend them and their lands with all our might.

It is also to be known that my heir who shall hold Charniacum shall also have the fief above mentioned of forty pounds.

That all this shall be held valid, I corroborate what has here been written with the impression of my seal. Done in the year of grace 1219, in the month of June.

▶ **Working with Sources**

1. **Why are religious terms invoked so often in these documents in order to solidify the relationships between lords and vassals?**

2. **Did feudal contracts with women differ from those with men?**

SOURCE 11.4   Peter Abelard, *The Story of My Misfortunes*

ca. 1132

One of the most brilliant professors and theologians of the European Middle Ages, Peter Abelard (1079–1142) became a star performer in the academic art of "dialectic." His abilities also earned him many enemies. When he turned his attention to the thorny subject of the Trinity, one of the principal elements of Christian belief, Abelard incurred the wrath of powerful members of the institutional church, of which he, as a professor, was also a part. In his autobiography, *The Story of My Misfortunes*, Abelard detailed the episodes of envy, backbiting, and stupidity that dogged him throughout his life. He also recalled his affair with Heloise (d. 1163), his former pupil and intellectual equal. The letters they exchanged survive as some of the most passionate and beautiful documents of the period.

It so happened that at the outset I devoted myself to analysing the basis of our faith through illustrations based on human understanding, and I wrote for my students a certain tract on the unity and trinity of God. This I did because they were always seeking for rational and philosophical explanations, asking rather for reasons they could understand than for mere words, saying that it was futile to utter words which the intellect could not possibly follow, that nothing could be believed unless it could first be understood, and that it was absurd for any one to preach to others a thing which neither he himself nor those whom he sought to teach could comprehend. Our Lord Himself maintained this same thing when He said: "They are blind leaders of the blind" (Matthew, xv, 14).

Now, a great many people saw and read this tract, and it became exceedingly popular, its clearness appealing particularly to all who sought information on this subject. And since the questions involved are generally considered the most difficult of all, their complexity is taken as the measure of the subtlety of him who succeeds in answering them. As a result, my rivals became furiously angry, and summoned a council to take action against me, the chief instigators therein being my two intriguing enemies of former days, Alberic and Lotulphe.

. . .

On one occasion Alberic, accompanied by some of his students, came to me for the purpose of intimidating me, and, after a few bland words, said that he was amazed at something he had found in my book, to the effect that, although God had begotten God, I denied that God had begotten Himself, since there was only one God. I answered unhesitatingly: "I can give you an explanation of this if you wish it." "Nay," he replied, "I care nothing for human explanation or reasoning in such matters, but only for the words of authority." "Very well," I said; "turn the pages of my book and you will find the authority likewise." The book was at hand, for he had brought it with him. I turned to the passage I had

Source: Henry Adams Bellows, trans., *The Story of My Misfortunes: The Autobiography of Peter Abélard* (New York: Macmillan, 1922), 36–44.

in mind, which he had either not discovered or else passed over as containing nothing injurious to me. And it was God's will that I quickly found what I sought. This was the following sentence, under the heading "Augustine, On the Trinity, Book I": "Whosoever believes that it is within the power of God to beget Himself is sorely in error; this power is not in God, neither is it in any created thing, spiritual or corporeal. For there is nothing that can give birth to itself."

When those of his followers who were present heard this, they were amazed and much embarrassed.

. . .

Straightway upon my summons I went to the council, and there, without further examination or debate, did they compel me with my own hand to cast that memorable book of mine into the flames.

▶ **Working with Sources**

1. **Explain the positions of Abelard and Alberic concerning "logic" and "faith" in this regard.**

2. **How does Abelard turn the tables on Alberic in his line of reasoning?**

SOURCE 11.5

Giovanni Boccaccio, *The Decameron*, "Putting the Devil Back in Hell"

ca. 1350

A Latin scholar, poet, and biographer, Boccaccio (1313–1375) is most famous today as the author of the *Decameron*. This compilation of 100 tales, by turns serious, bawdy, and irreverent, purports to be a rendition of the stories told over the course of 10 days by 10 young men and women who had fled Florence to escape the Black Death. Many of the tales are based on older legends, and they frequently reflect the humor of the common people of the era, often at the expense of their spiritual and social betters. Religious authorities were frequent targets of this sort of satire, reflecting their ubiquitous presence in the lives of medieval Europeans, as well as, perhaps, a deep undercurrent of resentment regarding their privileges.

. . . And so, coming to the facts, I say that in the city of Gafsa in Tunisia there was once a very rich man who, among other children, had a beautiful and genteel daughter named Alibec. She, not being a Christian, but hearing many

Source: Giovanni Boccaccio, "Putting the Devil Back in Hell" (3.10), from *The Decameron: Selected Tales / Decameron: Novelle scelte*, trans. Stanley Appelbaum (Mineola, NY: Dover, 2000), 87–93.

Christians who lived in the city praising the Christian religion and the service of God, asked one of them one day how God could be served in the easiest way. This man replied that God was best served by those who fled worldly things, like those men who had gone into the lonely deserts of the Thebaid.

[Alibec goes into the desert, seeking out a willing hermit, and finally arrives at the door of a man who is willing to help her.]

. . . She reached the cell of a young hermit, a very devout and kind person named Rustico, and asked him the same thing she had asked the others.

. . .

First feeling his way with certain questions, he learned that she had never slept with a man and was just as naïve as she looked. And so he planned a way to have her submit to his pleasure under the pretext of serving God. First he told her at length that the devil was the enemy of God; then he gave her to understand that the service most pleasing to God was putting the devil back in hell, to which place God had condemned him.

The girl asked him how that was done, and Rustico replied: "You'll soon know; to make it happen, do what you see me doing." And he began to take off the few garments he was wearing until he was stark naked; and the girl did the same. Then he knelt down as if he were going to pray, and he made her do the same, facing him.

As they knelt there, Rustico's desire flared up more than ever at the sight of her great beauty, and there ensued the resurrection of the flesh. Seeing that and wondering at it, Alibec said: "Rustico, what's that thing I see on you sticking out like that? I don't have one."

"My daughter," said Rustico, "that's the devil I told you about. And now look: he's giving me terrible discomfort, so that I can hardly stand it."

Then the girl said: "Praised be God, for I see that I'm better off than you, because I don't have that devil!"

Rustico said: "It's true, but you have something else that I don't have, and you have it in place of this."

Alibec said: "What is it?"

Rustico replied: "You have hell, and, believe me, I think God has sent you here to save my soul, because, whenever this devil causes me this distress, if you want to take pity on me and let me put him back in hell, you will give me the greatest relief, and you're doing God the greatest pleasure and service—if you've really come to this area for that purpose, as you say."

The girl replied in good faith: "Oh, Father, since I have hell, let it be whenever you like."

Then Rustico said: "Bless you, daughter! Let's go put him back so he'll leave me in peace."

Saying that, he led the girl to one of their pallets and taught her how to position herself to imprison that being who was accursed of God.

. . .

After a fire destroys much of Gafsa, Alibec is the only surviving heir to her father's property, and she is married to a young man named Neerbal.

But, being asked by the ladies what she had done to serve God in the desert—this was before Neerbal had slept with her—she replied that she had served Him by putting the devil back in hell, and that Neerbal had committed a great sin by taking her away from that service. The ladies asked: "How is the devil put back in hell?"

Partly with words and partly with gestures, the girl showed them how. They laughed so loud at this that they're still laughing, and they said: "Don't fret, youngster, no, because that's done here, too; Neerbal and you will do God good service that way."

▶ Working with Sources

1. **Is Alibec's naïveté designed to convey a warning to the reader?**

2. **Does this tale reflect a mocking attitude toward all forms of religiosity?**

SOURCE 11.6 | # Flagellants attempt to ward off the Black Death in Germany and in England

1348 and 1349

Although flagellation (beating oneself with a whip) had been practiced as a means of spiritual discipline by monks long before, it did not emerge as a public group activity until the thirteenth century. While Europe was besieged by the Black Death (1348–1352), the Brotherhood of Flagellants (which also included women) resorted to ever more spectacular public flagellation. The movement probably originated in eastern Europe and took root most deeply in German-speaking areas, as the following account demonstrates. As we see from the subsequent report of Robert of Avesbury, however, they had also crossed into England, offering some sort of solution to the plague crisis.

In 1348 a race without a head aroused universal wonder by their sudden appearance in huge numbers. They suddenly sprang up in all parts of Germany, calling themselves cross bearers or flagellants.

. . .

They were called flagellants because of the whips [*flagella*] which they used in performing public penance. Each whip consisted of a stick with three knotted thongs hanging from the end. Two pieces of needle-sharp metal were run through the centre of the knots from both sides, forming a cross, the ends of which extended beyond the knots for the length of a grain of wheat or less. Using these whips they beat and whipped their bare skin until their bodies were

---

Source: "52. The Flagellants," from the *Chronicon Henrici de Hervordia and from the Concerning the Miraculous Deeds of King Edward III* by Robert of Avesbury, in Rosemary Horrox, *The Black Death* (Manchester, UK: Manchester University Press, 1994), 150–154.

bruised and swollen and blood rained down, spattering the walls nearby. I have seen, when they whipped themselves, how sometimes those bits of metal penetrated the flesh so deeply that it took more than two attempts to pull them out.

Flocking together from every region, perhaps even from every city, they overran the whole land. In open country they straggled along behind the cross in no particular order, but when they came to cities, towns and villages they formed themselves into a procession, with hoods or hats pulled down over their foreheads, and sad and downcast eyes, they went through the streets singing a sweet hymn. In this fashion they entered the church and shut themselves in while they stripped off their clothes and left them with a guard.

. . .

After this, one of them would strike the first with a whip, saying, "May God grant you remission of all your sins. Arise." And he would get up, and do the same to the second, and all the others in turn did the same. When they were all on their feet, and arranged two by two in procession, two of them in the middle of the column would begin singing a hymn in a high voice, with a sweet melody.

From Robert of Avesbury:

In that same year of 1349, about Michaelmas [29 September], more than 120 men, for the most part from Zeeland or Holland, arrived in London from Flanders. These went barefoot in procession twice a day in the sight of the people, sometimes in St Paul's church and sometimes elsewhere in the city, their bodies naked except for a linen cloth from loins to ankle. Each wore a hood painted with a red cross at front and back and carried in his right hand a whip with three thongs. Each thong had a knot in it, with something sharp, like a needle, stuck through the middle of the knot so that it stuck out on each side, and as they walked one after the other they struck themselves with these whips on their naked, bloody bodies; four of them singing in their own tongue and the rest answering in the manner of the Christian litany. Three times in each procession they would all prostrate themselves on the ground, with their arms outstretched in the shape of a cross. Still singing, and beginning with the man at the end, each in turn would step over the others, lashing the man beneath him once with his whip, until all of those lying down had gone through the same ritual. Then each one put on his usual clothes and, always with their hoods on their heads and carrying their whips, they departed to their lodgings. It was said that they performed a similar penance every night.

▶ Working with Sources

1. **What did the flagellants think was the source and cause of the plague?**

2. **How might their behavior have made matters worse for the observers?**

World Period Three

The Formation of Religious Civilizations, 600–1450 CE

The rise of religious civilizations on the continents of Asia, Europe, and Africa is a striking phenomenon that unifies the period of 600–1450. It can be considered as a continuation of the intellectual and institutional transformations that began with the visionaries of the mid-first millennium BCE.

The religious civilizations displayed many regional variations. Internal diversity notwithstanding, they shared a number of common characteristics:

- Religious civilizations formed in regions which were larger than any single state within them: They superseded empires as the largest units of human unification.

- The civilizations were scriptural—that is, based on canonical (commonly agreed on) texts inherited from earlier periods. Members of educated elites taught and interpreted the scriptures to laypeople.

- Despite hostilities, merchants, missionaries, and pilgrims traveled from one area to another, fostering a lively exchange of technical and cultural innovations across Afro-Eurasia

Chapter 12

Contrasting Patterns in Eurasia

600–1600 CE

CHAPTER TWELVE PATTERNS

Origins, Interactions, and Adaptations While the scriptural core was formed early in the development of Buddhism, Hinduism, and Islam, each religion contained different schools of interpretation that spurred the rise of offshoot sects and esoteric branches. Within each system, movements arose that sought to uncover the original intent of the founders.

The interaction of Islamic and Hindu states in India resulted in efforts to coexist. In the Chinese sphere, Buddhism competed with Confucian ideals; along with Daoism, its influence on Confucianism led to the creation of Neo-Confucianism.

Uniqueness and Similarities The key developments in Asia during this period involve the rise of civilizations that adopted the philosophies and religions of early visionaries as state ideologies.

There were regional variations:

Hinduism now found itself in competition with Islam in India; Buddhism found itself in competition with both Islam and Hinduism in Southeast Asia; and Confucianism became firmly established not only in China but in Korea, Japan, and Vietnam as well.

All of these belief systems were scriptural, and their core texts were carried and interpreted by elites. In addition, they all had missionary features.

All of these systems and their respective cultural spheres interacted with each other extensively. In the case of the Mongols, they interacted within the largest political land entity ever created.

In the mid-seventh century CE, Arab armies described northwest India as a desert waste with a hostile populace. Every attempt they made to invade the northwest Indian region of Sind was defeated. Following these failed attempts, a more ambitious invasion was mounted by Muhammad Ibn Qasim, a cousin of the governor of Iraq who was responsible for the conquest of eastern lands.

Ibn Qasim's army brutally pursued the move into India. Wearing coats of chain-mail armor and equipped with siege machinery, they decimated the major cities, executed most of the defenders, and extracted plunder and slaves before completely occupying the area in 711. Though Ibn Qasim's rule in the wake of his violent conquest was considered relatively moderate, he met his death through the duplicity of his new subjects.

When the daughters of Dihar, the ruler of the conquered city of Dehal (Karachi in modern Pakistan), were taken back to the governor of Iraq as tribute, they accused Ibn Qasim of making sexual advances toward them. The governor immediately ordered his cousin Ibn Qasim to be sewn up in a raw leather sheath and transported home. This was meant to inflict maximal suffering, and, indeed, Ibn Qasim died two days into the journey. When his putrefied body was shown to the women who had accused him, they proudly admitted to their deception and revenge on their conqueror.

The clash of cultures and religions has marked the history of the Indian sub-continent. In this contested area, the Hindu vision of Islam has remained one of ruthless conquest. Muslims, on the other hand, have tended to view Hindus as treacherous infidels. Such competing visions have created a pattern of fragile *syncretic* social and political formation (a pattern in which attempts are made to reconcile two different traditions with little or no common ground). In this case, the two cultures actually coexist with considerable hostility toward

CHAPTER OUTLINE

India: The Clash of Cultures

Interactions and Adaptations: From Buddhism to Neo-Confucian Synthesis in China

Putting It All Together

ABOVE: This painting from the first half of the fourteenth century shows astronomers at work in Tabriz, the capital of the Ilkhan khanate in northwestern Iran. Tabriz became a flourishing, cosmopolitan center of learning under the Ilkhans.

Seeing Patterns

❯ How did interactions between Muslims and Hindus in India lead to attempts at religious syncretism?

❯ What steps were taken by Hindus and Muslims to lessen the conflicts between the two rival religious traditions?

❯ How was the Tang dynasty in China different from its predecessors and successors?

❯ How effectively did the religious and philosophical traditions of Buddhism, Confucianism, and Daoism blend together in creating Neo-Confucianism? Where did they clash?

❯ How were the Mongols able to defeat numerically and technologically superior peoples and create their enormous empire? What were their strengths and weaknesses as rulers?

one another. The dominant pattern has been that each has used the differences of the other to define its own religious civilization more distinctly.

The case of China provides a useful contrast. Here, despite the belief of officials and scholars of the Song dynasty (960–1279) that the fall of the previous dynasty, the Tang, was partly due to the "foreign" influence of Buddhism, there were no persecutions or forced conversions. Song Confucian scholars borrowed from Buddhist cosmological perspectives and Daoist beliefs to create a pattern of *synthetic* social and political formation (a pattern in which the most durable opposing elements merge together into a compatible whole). The result, notwithstanding the brief Mongol interval, was a coherent Chinese religious civilization for the next 1,000 years. The Mongol period, however brief, represents an important break point for much of Eurasia. Because we examine its impact in several regions covered in separate chapters, we have elected to examine that impact in the context of those chapters rather than devoting a complete chapter to the Mongols' extraordinary feats.

India: The Clash of Cultures

The early centuries of the Common Era saw the maturing of two divisions among the religious and cultural experiences of India. The first was the spread of Buddhism out of northern India into Central Asia, China, and ultimately to Korea, Japan, and Vietnam. More important for Indian history, however, was the maturation from the fourth to the sixth centuries of the religious practices that we know as "Hinduism." For it was Hinduism, rather than Buddhism, that would dominate Indian life until Islam ultimately established itself in the north. India was transformed from a Hindu religious civilization into a frontier between the competing religious civilizations of Islam and Hinduism.

Buddhist and Hindu India after the Guptas

By the 500s CE, the last Gupta monarchs were pressured on their borders by Central Asian Huns. Moving through the Khyber Pass into northern India, the Huns established themselves in the Punjab and adjacent regions, creating new states as the Gupta lands disappeared.

Harsha Vardhana   One stable regime in the north following the Guptas was that of Harsha Vardhana (r. 606–647). Harsha's life and reign are known to us via the *Life of Harsha*, by the poet Bana, and the account of the famous Chinese Buddhist pilgrim Xuan Zang (see Chapter 9).

Xuan Zang met Harsha and discovered that the ruler was a devout Buddhist. Xuan Zang notes that Buddhism had once permeated the land, despite the favoritism shown by the Guptas earlier toward Hinduism. However, Buddhism was in decline due in part to the popularity of the new devotional strains of Hinduism rapidly gaining adherents.

Xuan Zang found Harsha's kingdom in many ways a model state. The state, however, barely outlived its ruler. The middle years of Harsha's reign saw the Arabs probing the borders of Sind in advance of their full conquest in 711. Meanwhile, following Harsha's reign, northern India was once again divided into regional kingdoms (see Map 12.1).

The Hindu States of the South   The political center of the subcontinent shifted south. By the latter part of the ninth century, a Chola [CHO-luh] state based in Tanjore [tan-JORE] captured Kanchipuram [kahn-CHEE-poor-um], advanced south into the Pandya kingdom, and captured their capital at Madurai. In the next century, the Cholas conquered Kerala, invaded Sri Lanka, and expanded their control of the trade with Southeast Asia. The Cholas then advanced northward, allying themselves with the eastern Chalukyas in 1030. In the west, however, the revived western Chalukyas fought the Cholas to a standstill.

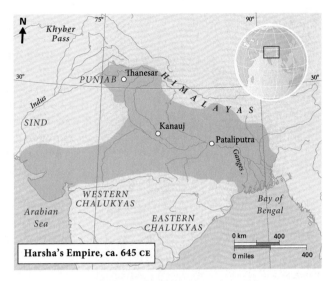

MAP 12.1 **Harsha's Empire, ca. 645 CE**

The clove trade of the Molucca Islands (in what is now Indonesia) increased the strategic value of that area, which the Indian-influenced Sumatran state of Srivijaya exploited in the tenth and eleventh centuries. In response to the threats Srivijaya posed, the Cholas sent a maritime expedition in 1025 that temporarily reduced its power. In this context, the coming of the Arabs to northern India resulted in a broadening of the subcontinent's position in the world economy. Arab merchants continued their trade in the western ports of India, and despite the religious antagonisms, caravan traffic also continued. India now became part of a triangle of trade that spanned Eurasia (see Map 12.2).

Vijayanagar   A new Hindu state emerged in 1336 with the founding of the city of Vijayanagar ("City of Victory"). Its rulers presided over a political arrangement that, like the Gupta Empire, some scholars have described as feudal, as it absorbed the remnants of the older southern kingdoms. Local leaders collected taxes and provided men and provisions for the army, while retaining considerable autonomy. For more than 200 years, the state of Vijayanagar resisted the Islamic sultanates of the north. In 1564, however, their armies were decimated by a regional coalition of northern Muslim sultanates equipped with the newest technologies—cannon and small arms. The city was then abandoned.

Islam in India, 711–1398

While conquering Arabs incorporated much of modern Afghanistan, Pakistan, and some parts of northwest India into their empire during the early 700s, the rest of India experienced contact with Islam more peacefully through maritime trade with Muslim merchants. In Central Asia, Arab armies moving eastward along the caravan routes advanced through conquest, settling in the cities of Turkestan and raiding into the territories of Turkic nomadic tribes.

Rajarajeshwara Temple, Tanjore, India. This early-eleventh-century Hindu temple is the largest in all of India and one of the most beautiful. It was richly endowed with spoils taken from Chola conquests.

The Career of Mahmud of Ghazna   The Persian rulers in Iran and Central Asia enrolled Turkic slaves in their palace guards and converted them to Islam. The son of one of these slave officers was Sultan Mahmud of Ghazna, who declared himself independent of his Persian overlord. In 997 Mahmud embarked on a career of expansion lasting until his death in 1030. Early in his career, Mahmud conquered territory comprising part of Iran, as well as Afghanistan and Turkestan. Later expeditions moved into the old Ganges River states.

The Northern Sultanates   Mahmud and his successors, the Ghaznavids, ruled for nearly two centuries. But their empire was too large to hold together, and a Persian ruler subject to the Ghaznavids, Muhammad of Ghur, declared his independence and conquered most Ghaznavid lands. In 1192, he defeated the Rajputs, considered Hindu India's most ferocious warriors. Striking deep into northern India, Muhammad set up a Muslim state at Delhi, which endured (1181–1526) under the name of the Sultanate of Delhi. The founders of this state were Turkic generals of slave origin. Their successors were Turkic and Afghan dynasties which ruled until the invasion of Babur, the Mongol-descended founder of the Mughal Empire of India in 1526 (see Map 12.3).

Among the more colorful rulers of the Delhi Sultanate was the female sultan Raziya (r. 1236–1240), who seized the throne from her brother and wore male attire on the battlefield. During her short reign, she pressed south and east to Bengal and settled Muslim refugees from Mongol-controlled lands within her own domains.

The renewed Mongol expansion which led to the destruction of the Abbasid caliphate in 1258 was accompanied by raids along the Delhi Sultanate's borders. Out of this period came the reign of Balban from 1266 through 1287. Balban's suppression of rivals resulted in a succession struggle at his death, and a new set

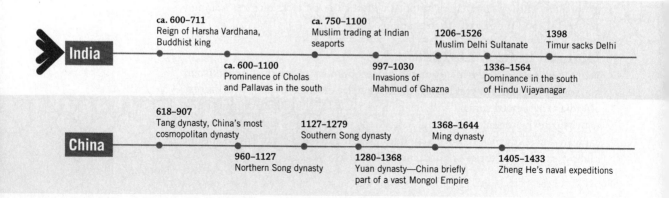

India

ca. 600–711
Reign of Harsha Vardhana, Buddhist king

ca. 600–1100
Prominence of Cholas and Pallavas in the south

ca. 750–1100
Muslim trading at Indian seaports

997–1030
Invasions of Mahmud of Ghazna

1206–1526
Muslim Delhi Sultanate

1336–1564
Dominance in the south of Hindu Vijayanagar

1398
Timur sacks Delhi

China

618–907
Tang dynasty, China's most cosmopolitan dynasty

960–1127
Northern Song dynasty

1127–1279
Southern Song dynasty

1280–1368
Yuan dynasty—China briefly part of a vast Mongol Empire

1368–1644
Ming dynasty

1405–1433
Zheng He's naval expeditions

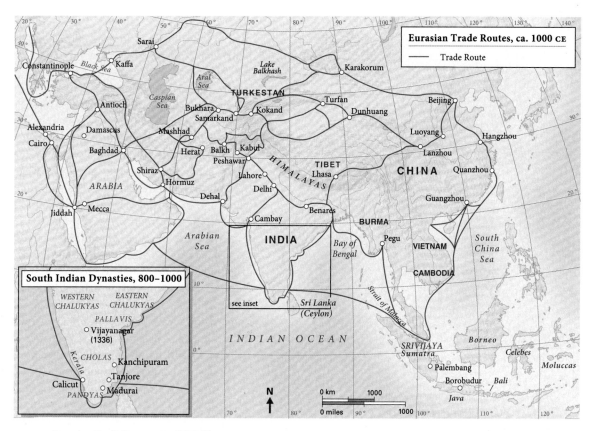

MAP 12.2 Eurasian Trade Routes, ca. 1000 CE

of sultans, the Khaljis, came to power in 1290. The Khaljis soon expanded into southern India.

After a period of turmoil the Tughluq rulers rose in 1320 and held power until 1413. Perhaps the most controversial ruler of the line was Muhammad ibn Tughluq (d. 1351), named by his detractors "Muhammad the Bloody." Discontent over high taxes, debased coinage, famine, and ruthless atrocities against his enemies was prevalent during his reign. Within a few decades of his death, powerful forces from the north brought an end to Tughluq rule and altered the region's politics for generations to come.

Toward the Mughal Era, 1398–1450

In 1398, the Central Asian nomad Timur (often called Tamerlane; r. 1370–1405) descended on northern India and Southwest Asia (see Chapter 20). Though himself a Muslim, Timur did not spare the Muslim capital of Delhi. His invasion broke the power of the Tughluqs. Two smaller sultanates, those of the Sayyids (1414–1451) and the Lodis (1451–1526), then held the area around Delhi. The coming of the Mughals in 1526, however, would usher in both stability and imperial aspirations.

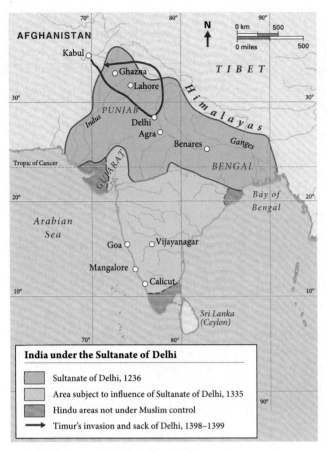

MAP 12.3 **India under the Sultanate of Delhi**

The Economy of Islamic India   India's wealth continually attracted invasions by outsiders. The turnover of goods acquired by Turkic and Arab incursions financed the emerging northern Muslim sultanates. Even after these states became financially stable, the attraction of the wealth of the southern states resulted in frequent expeditions against them.

The northern sultanates also supported their economies through heavy taxation. Ala-ud-din Khalji embarked on an ambitious campaign to institute wage and price controls in order to keep food prices low and urban granaries full. In this, Ala-ud-din was surpassed in zeal by Muhammad "the Bloody" Tughluq. Muhammad also instituted price controls and attempted to stabilize the currency. Despite the sultans' constant need for money, however, Muslim prohibitions against usury kept banking and capital in the hands of Hindus, Buddhists, and Parsees (descendants of Zoroastrian emigrants from Persia).

Muslims and Caste   Islam appealed to those most discontented with the caste system. Islam's minority status in India, however, meant that it was never possible to carve out an Islamic-majority state within the sultanates.

Over time, cross-cultural compromise was reluctantly granted by both sides. Nearly all Hindu and Muslim sects were eventually allowed to practice to some degree. Muslim repugnance toward some Hindu customs gradually became less overt. At the same time, Hindus in some areas adopted the Muslim practice of veiling women.

The Sikhs   By the fifteenth century the unique position of the Muslim sultanates of northern India as havens for refugees from the ravages of the Mongols, as well as for Sufis (practitioners of Islamic mysticism) and Muslim dissidents, provided a rare opportunity for interchange between Muslim and Hindu sects.

Sikhism: Indian religion founded by Guru Nanak that combines elements of Hindu and Muslim traditions.

The climax of this movement came with the guru ("teacher") Nanak (1469–1539), who founded the faith of **Sikhism**. Combining elements of Hinduism and Islam, the Sikhs, due to religious persecution in the seventeenth century, eventually became more of a fighting faith.

While Sikhism appeared to be a step toward reconciliation between Islam and Hinduism, in fact both Hindus and Muslims opposed the Sikhs, and they were persecuted a number of times under the Mughals. India thus remained a tenuously syncretic religious and cultural society among the world's religious civilizations.

Interactions and Adaptations: From Buddhism to Neo-Confucian Synthesis in China

The Tang dynasty (618–907) marked the completion of the reconstitution of the Chinese empire begun under the Sui. The influence of Buddhism at the imperial court made China a Buddhist empire. Since the Han, China's ideology had been based on the ethics of Confucianism and some elements of Daoism combined with the imperial structure inherited from the Qin (see Chapter 9). By the mid-600s this ideology of statehood had fused with Mahayana Buddhism to give China an overtly religious civilization. China thus joined the ranks of Hindu India (soon to be split by Islam), the Islamic caliphates, the Christian eastern Roman Empire, and the developing states of Western Christian Europe as polities dominated by a universal religion.

The Tang were succeeded by the Song dynasty (960–1279), which has been seen as the beginning of China's early modern period. The political system that marked China from this period until the twentieth century was a departure from Buddhism, which was blamed for the downfall of the Tang. Instead, the new synthesis of official beliefs blended elements of three ethical-religious schools—Confucianism, Daoism, and Buddhism—to create a system called "Neo-Confucianism."

Creating a Religious Civilization under the Tang

Determined to complete the consolidation begun under the Sui, the Tang led military expeditions into Central Asia. The Tang reestablished rule in Korea and opened diplomatic relations with Japan, which in 645 adopted Tang imperial institutions, Buddhism, and Confucian bureaucracy.

Expansion and Consolidation   The Tang Empire's position as the eastern terminus of the Silk Road; its maritime trade with India, Japan, Southeast Asia, the Middle East, and Africa; and its integration of Buddhist culture led to China's first extensive encounter with the major agrarian–urban societies to the west. During the seventh century, Muslim conquests in Southwest Asia brought China into contact with the Arab Empire. In 674, members of the Sasanid Persian royal house fled the Arabs to the Tang capital at Chang'an, introducing the Tang elites to Arab, Persian, and Central Asian goods and cultural forms.

With the Tang Empire expanding, the capital of Chang'an (the present city of Xi'an) grew into perhaps the largest city in the world, with as many as 2 million people in its metropolitan area. It became the model for urban planning throughout eastern Asia (see Map 12.4).

Qutb Minar, Delhi. The sense of the northern Indian sultanates being a sanctuary for Muslims from other locales translated into efforts on the part of rulers to outperform their counterparts. The wealth of the area allowed them the resources with which to build a number of spectacular structures. The Qutb Minar, built next to Delhi's first mosque, is said to still be the world's largest minaret, requiring the efforts of two rulers before being finished by the Tughluq sultan Feroz Shah (d. 1388).

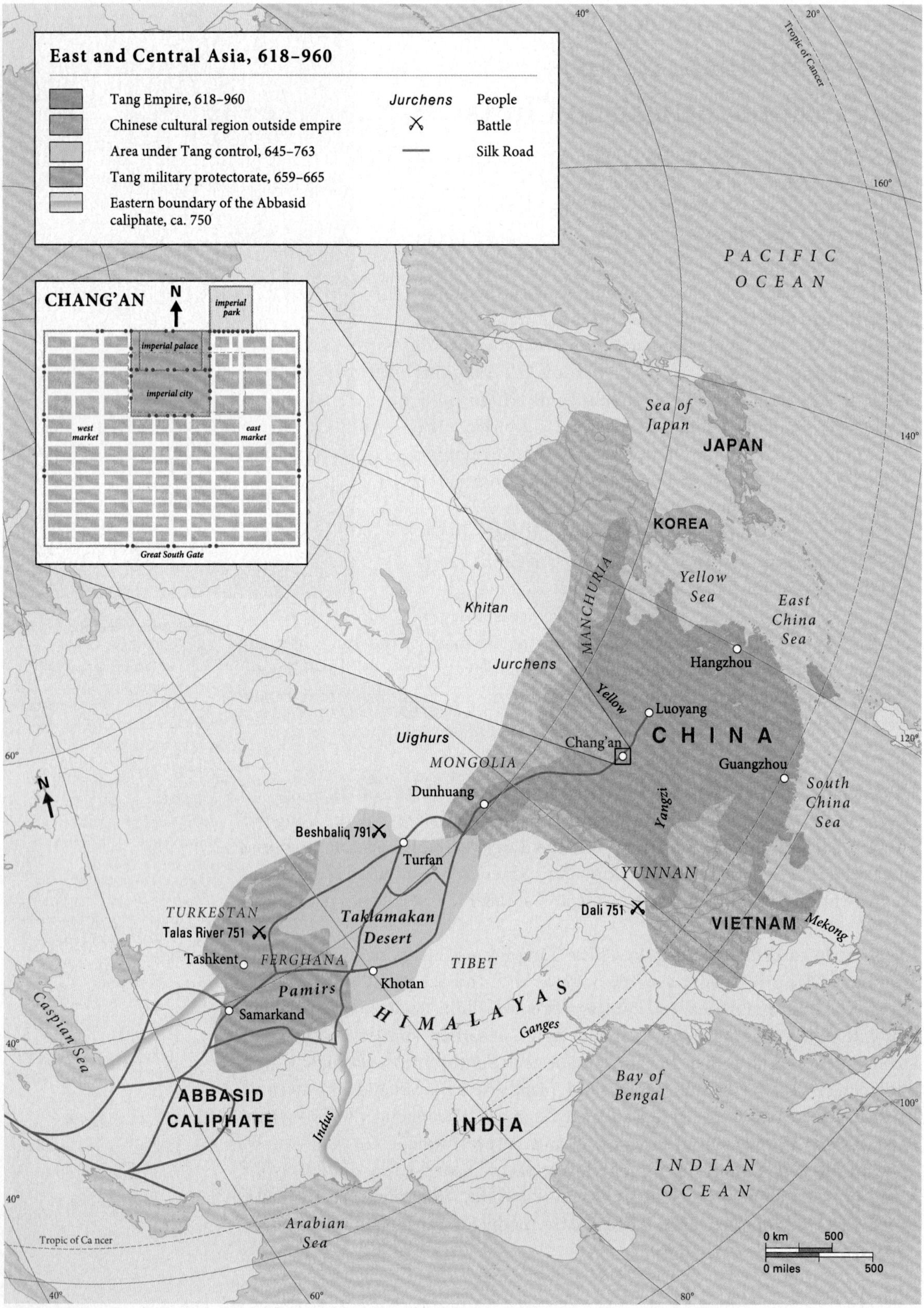
East and Central Asia, 618–960
Tang Empire, 618–960
Chinese cultural region outside empire
Area under Tang control, 645–763
Tang military protectorate, 659–665
Eastern boundary of the Abbasid caliphate, ca. 750
Jurchens People
Battle
Silk Road
CHANG'AN
N
imperial park
imperial palace
imperial city
west market
east market
Great South Gate
PACIFIC OCEAN
Sea of Japan
JAPAN
KOREA
Yellow Sea
East China Sea
Hangzhou
MANCHURIA
Khitan
Jurchens
Yellow
Luoyang
CHINA
Uighurs
Chang'an
MONGOLIA
Guangzhou
South China Sea
Dunhuang
Yangzi
Beshbaliq 791
Turfan
YUNNAN
TURKESTAN
Talas River 751
Taklamakan Desert
Dali 751
VIETNAM
Mekong
Tashkent
FERGHANA
TIBET
Khotan
Pamirs
HIMALAYAS
Samarkand
Ganges
Caspian Sea
ABBASID CALIPHATE
Indus
INDIA
Bay of Bengal
INDIAN OCEAN
Arabian Sea
Tropic of Cancer
0 km 500
0 miles 500
40°
20°
160°
140°
120°
100°
80°
60°

MAP 12.4 East and Central Asia, 618–960

The Examination System   The Tang refined Han bureaucracy into a form that survived into the twentieth century. The Tang bureaucratic structure introduced an examination system for entry into government service. Because the exams were open to a large portion of the male population, state service ensured a degree of social mobility based on merit rather than birth. The initial tests were open to men of all classes except merchants, artisans, and convicted criminals. Those who passed the initial tests could sit for provincial exams and, if successful, would be eligible for minor posts. Individuals who passed the metropolitan tests were eligible for national service. Other Tang reforms included the establishment of a board of censors to check behavior among officials, the obligation of lower officials to report the infractions of those above them, and the rotation of official posts to prevent individuals from developing local power bases.

Prosperity and Its Discontents   As the Tang dynasty prospered, many of the problems that had plagued the Han dynasty reasserted themselves. For example, as the center of population moved south, the northern regions languished while the capital grew economically isolated. Moreover, as maritime trade grew, the infrastructure of roads, courier stations, and especially canals required ever more investment. This was a problem in the case of the capital of Chang'an, which had ballooned to a size that was now unsustainable without constant grain shipments from the south, while its isolation made it vulnerable to attack.

Tang efforts to control military outposts along the Silk Road led to conflict with Arab expansion by the early eighth century. A series of setbacks at the hands of the Tibetans, border uprisings in Manchuria, Korea, and Yunnan, and a decisive defeat by Arab forces at Talas in 751 helped spark a general revolt. From 755 to 762 a rebellion initiated by the Tang commander An Lushan (703–757) devastated large sections of the empire. As with the later Han, the dynasty was now in a downward spiral.

For the next century and a half the problems of rebuilding and revenue loss persisted. Confucians questioned a number of the premises of the regime. They criticized Buddhism for being patronized and subsidized by the Tang court and were critical of Buddhism's "foreign" ideas and practices that contradicted Confucian standards. At the same time, Buddhist monasteries, which paid no taxes, were tempting targets for a cash-strapped government. In 845, despite Tang sponsorship of Buddhism, the government seized all Buddhist holdings, although followers were allowed to continue their religious practices. Sporadic civil war continued for the remainder of the century, leading to the collapse of the Tang dynasty in 906. Following this collapse, China again entered a period of disunity until the emergence of the Song in 960.

Camel with Musicians. Music played an important role in Tang China and was enjoyed privately as well as on public occasions. This brightly colored glazed earthenware sculpture, dated to 723 CE, shows three musicians riding a Bactrian (two-humped) camel. Their long coats, facial hair, and hats indicate that they are from Central Asia; indeed, the lute held by one of the figures is an instrument that was introduced to China from Central Asia in the second century CE.

Cosmopolitan Commerce   From Chang'an, merchants and others traveled along the Silk Road, while Chinese, Indian, and Arab ships ventured as far as Africa. The compass, a Chinese invention, guided ships throughout the Indian Ocean and Southeast Asia. Drawn by lucrative opportunities, colonies of Chinese merchants could be found throughout the Indian Ocean and Southeast Asia.

Among the export items most coveted by foreign merchants were tea and silk. Tea was the beverage of choice during the Tang and vied with silk for supremacy as a cash crop during the Song. With its medicinal properties—and the requirement of boiling the water to make it—tea had a profound effect on the overall health of the population in China, Vietnam, Korea, Japan, and Central Asia, and for hundreds of years tea remained China's most lucrative export item.

The influence of foreigners in arts and culture marks a radical departure from the Chinese styles that came before and after. Indeed, the period saw controversial trends regarding the role and deportment of women. As exemplified in the person of the famous Empress Wu (r. 690–705), China's first **empress dowager**, women occasionally exercised considerable authority in political affairs during this time (see below, "Against the Grain").

Empress dowager: In monarchical or imperial systems in which succession is normally through the male line, the widow of the ruler.

Tang Poetry   Tang poetry attempts to suggest powerful emotions or themes in minimalist fashion. For example, the Confucian sensibilities of the Tang poet Du Fu (ca. 721–770) are often detectable in his poems such as "Mourning Chen Tao." His friend Li Bai (or Li Bo, 701–762)—carefree, witty, and a lover of wine and women—was in many ways his opposite. Li Bai's poetry evokes happier moments, but frequently conveys them as fleeting and bittersweet.

The Song and Yuan Dynasties, 960–1368

During the Song dynasty (Northern Song: 960–1127; Southern Song: 1127–1279), China achieved great sophistication in terms of material culture, technology, ideas, economics, and urban living. Its incorporation into the Mongol empire opened the country to influence from neighboring peoples and helped to spread Chinese influence westward. Finally, the new synthesis of Neo-Confucianism as a secular philosophy with religious overtones would carry China into the twentieth century.

Empress Wu. Wife of Emperor Gaozong, Wu Zetian declared herself empress dowager after his death in 684 and founded a new Zhou dynasty in 690. She is the only woman in Chinese history until Empress Dowager Cixi at the turn of the twentieth century to have exercised so much power.

Reforms of Wang Anshi   The Song, like the Tang, instituted a government based on merit rather than heredity. The Song, however, broadened the eligibility of those seeking to take the civil service exams, and an increasingly large and unwieldy bureaucratic system emerged. The need for administrative reform spurred the official Wang Anshi ([wahng ahn-SHIr] 1021–1086) to propose initiatives to increase state control over the economy and reduce the power of local interests. He also urged cutting the number of bureaucratic positions in order to lessen the power of local officials and clan heads. Opposition to these proposed reforms, however, forced Wang from office in 1076.

The Northern Song also faced external problems. Because the Tang had lost much of northern China to nomadic groups, the Song lands were substantially smaller than those of the Tang. Although the Song maintained a professional army as well as a formidable navy, this massive force was ineffective against the swift militaries of invading nomadic groups. The Song also tried diplomacy and bribery to maintain China's dominance. Such efforts, however, were unable to keep the northern part of the empire from falling to the nomadic Jurchens, who conquered the capital at Kaifeng in 1127.

The decreased size of what historians call the Southern Song Empire resulted in a more southern-oriented and urbanized economy, with a new capital at Hangzhou [hahng-jo]. Despite the bureaucracy's disdain for the merchant and artisan classes, the state had always recognized the potential of commerce to generate revenue. Thus, while attempting to bring the largest enterprises under state control, the government pursued measures to facilitate trade. These practices, combined with excellent roads and canals, fostered the development of a vigorous internal Chinese market along with continued lively overseas trade.

The Mongol Conquest: Creating the Super-Empire   Commercial success, however, could not save the Song from invasion by nomadic peoples. For centuries, disparate groups of Turkic-speaking nomadic peoples had lived in scattered tribes and clans in eastern Central Asia. There was no real push to unite these groups until the rise to power of the Mongol leader Temujin (ca. 1162–1227), who united them into one confederation in 1206. Temujin gave himself the title Genghis Khan ("Universal Ruler") of this now unified Mongol entity.

Following confederation, the Mongols launched a half-century of steady encroachment on the Jurchen's Jin Dynasty (the former Northern Song) in northern China. Genghis Khan's grandson Khubilai (or Kublai) Khan (1215–1294) resumed the Mongol offensive in southern China. In 1267 he moved his capital from Karakorum to Khanbaligh (or Khanbaliq), called by the Chinese Dadu—the future city of Beijing. Hangzhou, the Southern Song capital, fell to the Mongols in 1276; the death of the Song emperor in 1279, as he attempted to flee, brought the dynasty to an end.

The Yuan Dynasty   In 1280 Khubilai Khan proclaimed the Yuan dynasty, taking the reign name of Shizu. This dynasty pulled China into an empire spanning all of Eurasia from Korea to the interior of Poland and probing as far as Hungary, Java, and Japan. In a way, however, the acquisition of China also signaled a significant change in Mongol fortunes. On one hand, many of the world's richest, most populous, and commercially vibrant areas were now under the control of what was nominally a unified empire. In terms of all the constituent khans encouraging trade, building infrastructure along land routes, and sponsoring and protecting caravans—including pioneering innovations in insuring them and in limiting liability for investors and traders—it represented a prototypical free trade zone.

Politically, however, it became increasingly fragmented. By the time of Khubilai's death in 1294, what had been one empire was now essentially four squabbling **khanates**: the Ilkhans in Persia and the Middle East, whose advance

Khanate: A political entity, common to the Eurasian steppe. A khanate is ruled by either a khan (man) or a khatun (woman).

Gunpowder

Perhaps the most momentous invention to emerge from the Song era was gunpowder. The substance, a mixture of saltpeter (nitrates), sulfur, and charcoal, was originally used as a medicine for skin irritations until its propensity to burn rapidly was established. The early Chinese term for gunpowder, *huoyao* ("fire medicine"), preserves this sense of its use.

It is unclear when the first weapons employing gunpowder were used. By the Southern Song, however, the Chinese army and navy had weapons that utilized gunpowder both as a propellant and as an explosive. The use of "fire arrows"—rockets mounted to arrow shafts—was recorded during a battle with the Mongols in 1232. The Song navy launched missiles and even employed ships with detachable sections filled with explosives with which to ram other ships. By the end of the century, primitive bronze cannon were also employed as well as gunpowder satchels to blow open city gates and fortifications.

The use of gunpowder weapons by the Song against the Mongols caused the invaders to adopt them for themselves. Indeed, toward the end of the war, the Mongols increasingly employed explosives in their siege operations against Chinese walled cities. They also used

Song Era Bronze Cannon. Discovered in 1980, the Wuwei bronze cannon has been dated to ca. 1214-1227, making it one of the earliest large gunpowder artillery weapons. The gun is over three feet in length with a bore diameter of about five inches.

had been halted by the Mamluks of Egypt; the Golden Horde, occupying a vast stretch of territory in what is now Ukraine and Russia; the khanate of Chagatai, centered at Samarkand and occupying a pivotal position along the Silk Road in Central Asia; and the Yuan Dynasty of Khubilai Khan, stretching from Mongolia into Korea, through most of China, and down into Tibet and Vietnam.

The necessity of adopting and inhabiting the institutions they now commanded required adaptation on an unprecedented scale in order to make them function in an orderly way. This was especially true for the Mongols, because their tiny population of about a million had to rule as many as one hundred times that number of people. Moreover, the brilliant governmental improvisations of Genghis Khan in conquering his empire now came up against institutions that in some cases had functioned for over a thousand years and were based on philosophical and ethical systems even older. Thus, the Mongols, like the Manchus who came after them, found themselves reluctantly adapting to Chinese culture to keep the existing systems in operation while struggling to maintain the culture, mores, and belief systems of the steppes.

them in the 1270s and 1290s during their failed invasions of Japan. The need for these weapons pushed their dispersion throughout the Mongol holdings and beyond. By the beginning of the Mongol Yuan Dynasty, the first iron cannons were being produced.

It is difficult to overestimate the importance of gunpowder in human affairs. The Ottomans, Safavids, and Mughals made its use in warfare so central to their efforts that historians often refer to them as "the gunpowder empires." But it was among the states of Europe that these weapons were to achieve their highest levels of development. Incessant warfare among the European states and against the Ottomans fueled the development of bigger and deadlier cannon and lighter and more accurate small arms. The use of these weapons brought on the age of the infantry armed with muskets. By the end of the eighteenth century, even though muskets and artillery were technologically similar the world over, a high degree of drill among bayonet-equipped infantry with flintlock muskets gave European armies an edge against the Ottomans, Mughals, and Africans.

Questions

- How do gunpowder's origins as a medicine complicate the way we typically view technological and cultural adaptations?

- What would have been the consequence for world history if the military uses of gunpowder had never been discovered?

Mongol toleration of religious traditions left them free to experiment with foreign faiths. To a considerable extent, the fragmentation of the Mongol Empire broke down the idea of Genghis Khan that the leadership should not adopt any one of the existing systems of religious, cultural, and political traditions because none of them could be satisfactorily stretched to fit the needs of universal empire. Thus, the Ilkhans in Southwest Asia now converted to Islam, married into the local population, and eventually disappeared as a distinct ethnicity. Likewise, the descendants of Chagatai converted to Islam and, though their line did not stay intact, attempted to maintain their genealogy. For their part, some of the Mongols in Yuan territories (as well as Han Chinese and members of other minority groups) also converted to Islam. Others converted to Buddhism, with the Tibetan varieties, such as the Yellow Hat sect later headed by the Dalai Lama, proving especially attractive.

Administrative Adjustments   In the Yuan territories, administrative needs ultimately trumped Mongol practices of circulating officials of different nationalities throughout the entire empire. Initially, a number of senior Chinese officials were purged and others resigned in protest against the new order. These changes even spawned a new genre of Chinese landscape painting, which featured a solitary figure in official's robes sitting in exile in his mountain fastness. The practice of bringing in officials and advisors from other regions in the empire had proved only partially successful and caused widespread consternation among the remaining Chinese officials and aspiring scholar-gentry. Ultimately, the examination system was reinstated in 1315, and continued until 1905.

Commerce Without Borders   While contemporary source material on the rise of the Mongols under Genghis Khan is scarce—the Persian accounts were written later, and even the *Secret History of the Mongols* was composed around 1240, long after Genghis Khan had died—a number of accounts make their appearance from the second half of the thirteenth century on. Though the four large khanates competed for prestige and resisted Khubilai's claim to the title of Great Khan, the relative ease of travel and enhanced commerce continued. China was open on an unprecedented scale to a variety of foreign goods, ideas, and travelers, while Chinese goods like paper money, gunpowder, coal, the compass, and dozens of other innovations circulated in greater variety and profusion than ever before. Emissaries and missionaries from the developing states of Europe for the first time now traveled east to the capital city of Khanbaligh.

The two most famous travel accounts of the era, those of the Venetian Marco Polo (1254–1324) and Ibn Battuta of Tangier (1304–1369), who both lived and traveled throughout the Mongol Empire, are testaments to the powerful impact of Mongol rule in facilitating travel over such a vast area. Indeed, it was during the brief rule of the Mongols that the European image of China as a fairyland of exotica, fabulous wealth, and wondrous inventions was firmly set (see Map 12.5).

The End of the Khans   The Yuan period, however, is almost universally regarded by the Chinese as one of imperial China's darkest times. Although the Mongols quickly restored order and allowed a relative tolerance of religious practice and expression, the period was seen as an oppressive time of large standing armies, withdrawal from service of many Chinese officials, ineffective administration, forced labor, and heavy taxes, especially on the peasants.

Compounding the intensity of the tensions between Mongols and their subjects was perhaps the single worst disaster of the fourteenth century, the bubonic plague—known in Europe as the Black Death. While scholars have only recently begun to examine Chinese mortality rates resulting from the plague, Chinese accounts suggest that they were in all likelihood similar to those of Europe in some areas, with perhaps one-third of the population of about 100 million being carried off from the 1340s until the end of the century. One thing that seems clear, however, was that by facilitating travel and commerce, the Mongol regimes unknowingly opened the door for the disease to go from being a regional disaster to a continent-wide pandemic.

Over the following decades, the power of the Mongols continued to decline, both at the center and one by one in the peripheral states as well. The first and most dramatic event was the overthrow of the Yuan in China and the restoration of Chinese rule under the Ming Dynasty. This was accompanied by an exodus of refugee officials and Mongol civilians, though many Mongols who had settled in China decided to take their chances and stay. As mentioned above, many had also converted to Islam. By mid-century, all of these factors contributed to outbreaks of rebellion in China. In 1368, a coalition led by a soldier–Buddhist monk named Zhu Yuanzhang [joo yuwen-jahng] (1328–1398) drove the Mongols from the capital at Khanbaligh and proclaimed a new dynastic line, the Ming.

How should we assess the Mongol era as a whole? Although it was once considered a byword for barbarism on a stupendous scale, recent scholars have recalibrated their views considerably. Mongol emphasis on destroying feudal aristocracies, elevating artisans and merchants, facilitating trade, and tolerating multiple religions have all been cited as paving the way for the early modern era.

Yet it is undeniable that the creation of the empire and repeated wars among the later khans were accompanied by unprecedented death and destruction. Though we have no reliable figures for the region as a whole, rough estimates put the population of the areas touched by the Mongols at perhaps 150 million, of which perhaps 18 to 30 million may have died, excluding those killed during the bubonic plague. Thus, while many modern historians have come to see the Mongol era as a key—perhaps *the* key—to the transition from the medieval to the early modern world, the cost was for many unacceptably high.

Khubilai Khan as the First Yuan Emperor, Shizu (Shih-tzu)

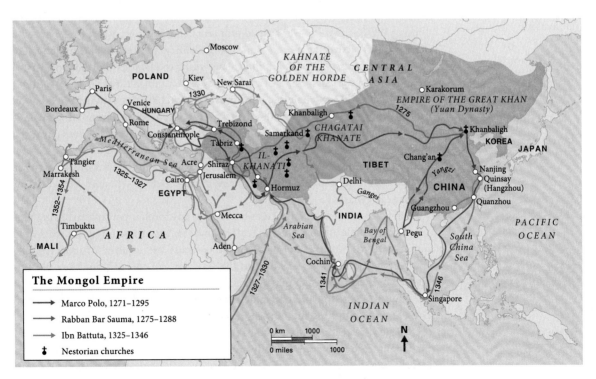

The Mongol Empire

→ Marco Polo, 1271–1295

→ Rabban Bar Sauma, 1275–1288

→ Ibn Battuta, 1325–1346

† Nestorian churches

MAP 12.5 **The Mongol Empire**

The Ming to 1450: The Quest for Stability

Zhu took the reign name of Hongwu. Under his leadership, Chinese politics and customs were restored and a centralized government was established. This new imperial state would, with minor modifications, see China into the twentieth century.

The Grand Secretariat   Hongwu streamlined this bureaucracy by concentrating power around the emperor. He created the Grand Secretariat, a group of senior officials who served as an advisory board for the emperor; it remained at the apex of imperial Chinese power into the twentieth century. Ming emperors now had a base from which to take measures to protect the empire from incursions by nomadic groups in the north. One step to protect against invasion was taken in 1421, when the capital of the empire was moved from Nanjing ("Southern Capital") to Khanbaligh, now renamed Beijing ("Northern Capital"), so that a strong Chinese presence in the region would discourage invasion. Further safeguards against invasion included upgrading the Great Wall and building new fortifications.

Population Recovery   While the country fortified its borders and reinstated political systems dismantled by the Mongols, it also contended with a drop in population. A population estimated at perhaps 100 million in 1100 may have been reduced to around 60 million by 1400. The population rebound, however, did not assume significant proportions until it was aided by new food crops introduced through the expanding global trade of the sixteenth and seventeenth centuries.

The Interlude of Naval Power   Thanks to the foundation laid by Hongwu [hoong-WOO], the dynasty's third emperor, Yongle [young-LUH], inherited a state in 1403 recovering its economic dynamism. In addition to building much of the infrastructure of imperial Beijing—including the famous "Forbidden City"—he ordered China's first and last great naval expeditions. These voyages, sent out from 1405 to 1433, were perhaps the most remarkable feats of maritime technology and power of their day. The fleets were composed of dozens of enormous ships, some over 400 feet long, equipped with cannon, watertight compartments, sternpost rudders, compasses and accurate gridded maps. Led by Yongle's childhood companion, the Muslim palace eunuch Zheng He, and carrying as many as 20,000 crew and soldiers, the fleets were unmatched anywhere in the world for hundreds of years.

The first voyages were aimed at overawing any foreign powers harboring pretenders to Yongle's throne. As the realization set in that these foreign threats were nonexistent, the voyages became focused on trade and exploration, covering the Indian Ocean, the Persian Gulf, and the East African coast. Along the way they planted or reestablished contact with Chinese merchants in South and Southeast Asia. Even today, stone markers in Chinese may be found along the East African coast testifying to the wide-ranging scope of these expeditions.

Yongle's successors put an end to the expeditions. The reasons for this abrupt turnabout were both political and strategic. By the 1430s the Mongols were again threatening the northern frontiers. The expense of the voyages and the realization that there were no significant naval rivals were reasons to discontinue them in the face of the Mongol threat. In addition, the Confucian officials argued that maritime trade was not essential to the overall welfare of the empire.

Toward the Ming Decline   The activist style of Hongwu and Yongle proved to be the exception rather than the rule during the Ming period. Through most of the sixteenth century, a succession of weak emperors would erode the stability of the reformed Ming imperial system. To compensate for the weakness at the center, power was increasingly diffused throughout the system. Over time, much of it was acquired by the grand secretaries and provincial governors, while at the village level, magistrates and village headmen assumed the bulk of power and responsibility.

Society, Family, and Gender

With the refinement of the examination system and the elaboration of the bureaucracy during the Song, which was renewed during the Ming, the key point of intersection between the people and the government was the district magistrate.

The Magistrate   The position of magistrate brought with it enormous responsibility. Assisted by clerks and secretaries, messengers, and constables, he supervised all aspects of local government. He presided over all official ceremonies, conducted the local Confucian examinations, and set a moral example for his constituents.

The Scholar-Gentry and Rural Society   While China boasted some of the world's largest cities, more than 85 percent of the country remained rural during the period from the Song to the Ming. At the top of the local structures of power and influence were the **scholar-gentry**, who were the educated and included all ranks of degree holders and their families.

 Scholar-gentry membership seldom exceeded 1–2 percent of the population. The chief qualification was attainment of at least the lowest official degree. The demands of memorizing the classical canon, however, were such that the wealthy had a distinct advantage. Still, there were enough poor boys who succeeded, often with the financial support of their home villages and extended families, to provide a degree of mobility within the system.

 Their position as community leaders and their Confucian ethics often placed the scholar-gentry in tension with the official bureaucracy. Along with the district magistrate, they presided over ceremonies at temples and led all clan ceremonies. In addition, the scholar-gentry mingled with the official authorities as social equals; sometimes they actually outranked the local magistrate.

 Local government thus relied on the cooperation of the gentry and people with the magistrates. The gentry represented a consistent network of people to carry out the day-to-day work of government. They took seriously the Confucian injunction to remonstrate with officials and could rally the people to subvert the policies of unpopular magistrates. Moreover, as influential men themselves, they could even bring about changes in regional or imperial policy.

Village and Family Life   The tendency toward greater centralization under the Ming also influenced Chinese village life. While life among the peasants still

Scholar-gentry:
Chinese civil servants who attained their positions through merit, and who served the local population as arbitrators of Confucian ethics and morality.

revolved around family, clan, and lineage, institutions perfected under the Ming lasted into the twentieth century.

Originally conceived during the Song dynasty, the *baojia* system of village organization called for families to register all members and be grouped into clusters of 10. One family in each cluster was then assigned responsibility for the others. Each group of responsible families would then be grouped into 10, and a member would be selected from them to be responsible for the group of 100 households, and so on up to the 1,000-household level. The system allowed the authorities to bypass gentry resistance to government directives and guaranteed a rural network of informers.

Peasant Women's Lives   The patterns of work and peasant life changed little from the Song through the Ming. The simple, efficient tools available to farmers had remained fundamentally unchanged from the preceding centuries.

Tensions in village life continued to be magnified in the lives of women and girls. The brief Mongol period of political domination had virtually no impact on Chinese social institutions. Mongol patterns of more egalitarian gender and class relations that had prevailed on the steppe thus remained limited to the Mongols themselves. For the Chinese, on the one hand, the education of upper-class women made them more marriageable. Study of proper Confucian etiquette occupied most of their curriculum. The custom of painful **foot binding** originated during the Song, gained ground during the Ming, and continued until it was banned by the People's Republic of China after 1949. **Female infanticide** also rose in rural areas during times of social stress. As in previous periods, rural girls were frequently sold into servitude by financially pressed families.

Foot binding: The practice of tightly wrapping the feet of young girls in order to break and reset the bones to compress the feet to about one-third of their normal size. Mothers generally did this to their daughters to make them more marriageable, since tiny feet were considered the epitome of female beauty.

Female infanticide: The killing of girl babies.

Perceptions of Perfection: Intellectual, Scientific, and Cultural Life

The period from the Tang to the Ming was marked by technological prowess that appears to have subsided after 1500. One possible answer as to why it suddenly subsided after this time may be that the Chinese felt that they had achieved such a high degree of technological sophistication and perfection in government and social organization that there was simply no need to advance them further.

The Neo-Confucian Synthesis   The intermingling of Confucianism with Buddhist, Daoist, and other traditions of thought forced its reformulation by the Song period. During the twelfth century, this reformulation matured into Neo-Confucianism, which combined the moral core of Confucian ethics with an emphasis on speculative philosophy borrowed from Buddhism and Daoism. Though the impetus no doubt came in part from these other two systems, Neo-Confucian thinkers were careful to insist that all their key concepts could be found in the ideas of Confucius and Mencius and in the Classics.

Neo-Confucianism holds that one cannot sit passively and wait for enlightenment, as the Buddhists were alleged to do, but must actively "seek truth through facts" in order to understand the relationships of form or "essence" (*li*—not to be confused with the word for ritual, which is also pronounced *li*) and *qi* [chee], the dynamic force from which things and events are produced as they govern the constitution of the totality of the universe. Like yin and yang, *li* and *qi* are seen as complementary opposites but, as in many formulations in Chinese philosophy, one (*li*, the essence) has priority over the other (*qi*). Thus, the ethical self and the epistemological self spring from the same source and are different manifestations of the same unity. Exploration of the physical universe undertaken in this spirit is thus the ultimate act of Confucian self-cultivation, in that one apprehends the Way (*Dao*) on every level. The steps involved in this process are explored in one of the Four Books of Confucianism emphasized by the Neo-Confucians, the *Great Learning* (the others being the *Analects*, *Mencius*, and the *Doctrine of the Mean*). Indeed, this method came to be called *daoxue*, "the study of the way (*dao*)." This vision of Neo-Confucianism was perfected by Zhu Xi [joo shee] (ca. 1129–1200).

Zhu Xi's speculative Neo-Confucianism faded during a Buddhist revival in the Ming era, which favored the more direct ethical action favored by Wang Yangming [wahng yahng-ming] (1472–1529). For Wang, as for Zhu Xi, truth was unitary. He believed that all people carry within them an intuitive sense of the fundamental order of the universe. It is out of this instinct toward the right that one investigates the universe in order to refine one's conclusions. Wang's other area of emphasis was the unity of knowledge and action. The sage, he argued, must take action in the world, both to be a moral example to others and to complete his own self-cultivation.

Technological Peaks   The notion of perfectibility woven through Song and Ming philosophy can also be seen in the scientific and technical realms. While a number of previous innovations were refined, in other cases high points had been achieved early and continued unchanged. For example, Zheng He's innovative ships of the fifteenth century remained unsurpassed triumphs of Chinese naval architecture until the mid-nineteenth century. And while new firearms were introduced in the seventeenth and eighteenth centuries, they remained essentially unchanged until the 1840s.

From the Tang through the Southern Song, China produced technological innovations that would have a profound effect inside and outside the empire, including the horse collar, moldboard plow, wheelbarrow, compass, gunpowder, porcelain, paper, and advanced iron casting. By the height of the Song period, China dominated production and distribution of tea, sugar, silk, porcelain, paper, and cotton cloth. An infrastructure of commercial credit, printed paper money, and insurance supported China's network of industry and trade.

Porcelain and Literature   Many of the advances in technology, such as the production of true porcelain, revolved around luxury items. Following centuries of experimentation, Song craftspeople hit upon the formula for creating the world's most celebrated ceramics. Surviving examples of elegant white and celadon (a shade of green) Song porcelain vessels are among the world's most precious art treasures. Techniques for using blue cobalt oxide pigments were originally introduced from Iraq in the ninth century and were being utilized by Song and Ming potters to brighten their porcelain ware. Kilns sponsored and run by the government allowed for unprecedented volume and quality control.

Song Porcelain. Porcelain reached its full maturity during the Song dynasty, and objects from that period are highly coveted even today. This celadon (sea-green, sometimes with a delicate crackle glaze) ewer with a double phoenix head and peony decorations dates from the Northern Song (960–1127).

The growing wealth, leisure, and literacy of the scholar-gentry and urban classes also created a demand for popular literature. The novel as a literary genre first made its appearance in China during the Yuan period but emerged as a form of mass entertainment only in the sixteenth century. These novels, written in a combination of classical and colloquial language, captured the imaginations of seventeenth- and eighteenth-century readers.

Putting It All Together

The experiences of India and China during the period from the seventh through the fifteenth centuries provide us with important areas of comparison. In the realm of political continuity, India was subject to a succession of governments set up by invaders from the north and west, while the kingdoms to the south jockeyed for power among themselves and over the Indian-influenced states of Southeast Asia. While there was cultural and religious continuity in the south, the north was dominated alternately by Hinduism and Buddhism, and ultimately by Islam. In the end, none of these claimed full dominance, though Islam remained the religion of the rulers after the twelfth century.

In the case of China, despite the Mongol invasion during the fourteenth century, the basic political structure reemerged with greater centralization than ever during the Ming dynasty. Culturally, the Mongols' influence on China was negligible; moreover, the Mongols made themselves culturally Chinese in order to rule, despite their efforts to maintain their ethnic autonomy. Chinese leadership in technical innovation kept up its former pace, and the brief incorporation into the Mongol Empire facilitated other cultures' interaction with Chinese advances.

The most dramatic difference, however, came in the realm of religion. India, from the time of Mahmud of Ghazna, never completely adapted itself to Islam. Northern India became an uneasily *syncretic* area where Hindus and Muslims attempted to coexist with each other. Even attempts to bridge the gulf between Hindus and Muslims, such as Sikhism, were not successful in attaining widespread acceptance.

In China, however, the dominant political structures of empire and the cultural assumptions of Confucianism not only resisted Mongol attempts to circumvent them but in the end were largely adopted by the conquerors. Unlike the Muslim conquerors in India, the Mongols proved receptive to several of the religious traditions they encountered in their conquests. Tensions between Buddhism and Confucianism in China resulted not in persecution of the Buddhists but in Confucian thinkers borrowing Buddhist approaches to speculative philosophy and creating an expanded synthetic ideology, Neo-Confucianism.

Review and Relate

| Thinking Through Patterns

Examine the ways historians approach the big questions of this chapter.

In contemplating this question, we must consider the fundamental beliefs of these two religious traditions and what kinds of changes take place as religions interact with other long-established beliefs. Hinduism encompasses many different religious assumptions and has long tried to fit newly arrived belief systems into its own traditions. This is where the clash with Islam is most evident. Islam teaches that there is no God but God (Allah); Hinduism would place Allah next to its other gods, which Muslims find intolerable. This fundamental clash of views makes any compromise difficult. As Muslim leaders find that they cannot force their Hindu subjects, who vastly outnumber them, to accept the new religion, they must therefore find ways to lessen its impact while holding true to Islam. Thus, some leniency must be given, or rule becomes impossible, but each side keeps its distance from the other in an uneasy coexistence.

Some compromises were made to lessen conflict between the major traditions. Muslim rulers routinely suspended their insistence on governing by Islamic law and let the Hindu majority govern itself according to its own traditions. In some cases,

> How did interactions between Muslims and Hindus in India lead to religious syncretism?

> What steps were taken by Hindus and Muslims to lessen the conflicts between the two rival religious traditions?

Hindu women even adopted the veil, like their Muslim counterparts. The most spectacular steps were the founding of new religious traditions incorporating both Hindu and Muslim elements—Sikhism, for example, and, as we will see in Chapter 20, the Mughal ruler Akbar's attempt at a synthetic religion.

> **How was the Tang dynasty in China different from its predecessors and successors?**

The Tang was China's most cosmopolitan dynasty, which made it quite different from its predecessors. This cosmopolitanism largely resulted from the widespread practice of Buddhism. China was now integrated into a Buddhist cultural sphere that allowed circulation of ideas and goods. Thus, China's rulers knew more about their neighbors, and through Buddhism, shared a community of religious interest with them. The reaction to Buddhism as a "foreign" faith in the Song period made China turn more inward; consequently, its larger ties with the Buddhist world deteriorated, never to reach Tang-level connections again.

> **How effectively did the religious and philosophical traditions of Buddhism, Confucianism, and Daoism blend together in creating Neo-Confucianism? Where did they clash?**

The longevity and diversity of Neo-Confucianism over time suggest that the blending was quite effective. The synthesis of Confucian, humanist-based morality coupled with the speculative ventures of Daoists and Buddhists created a complete, self-sustaining system.

> **How were the Mongols able to defeat numerically and technologically superior peoples and create their enormous empire? What were their strengths and weaknesses as rulers?**

The extraordinary mobility of Mongol horsemen was certainly an important factor in their success as was their adaptability in using the technologies they encountered in their conquests. Their approach to war as akin to a hunt, rather than as a field to establish one's reputation is also a factor. As rulers, their initial success came in large part from Genghis Khan's flexibility in using local rulers he subjugated and in commissioning his daughters to rule areas through marriage. Their weaknesses, however, perhaps stemmed from trying to adapt the ad hoc techniques of the steppes to sedentary civilizations with long-established and sophisticated modes of government. Their innovations, so many of which strike us as deceptively "modern," were often deeply resented by those they ruled.

| Against the Grain

Consider this as a counterpoint to the main patterns examined in this chapter.

Empress Wu

- In what ways does Empress Wu appear as a classic nonconformist?
- In what ways does Empress Wu resemble other ambitious women in history?

The Tang ruler Wu Zetian, or Empress Wu (r. 690–705), exemplified her era's contradictory trends toward both greater restrictiveness and wider latitude in personal behavior, particularly in the case of women. The daughter of a public works official, she spent a brief period at court as a servant to the empress. Disillusioned by life in the capital and drawn to the austerities of Buddhism, she joined a women's monastery, only to return to the palace when her beauty piqued the interest of an imperial prince. She deftly exploited the opportunity.

Hostile chroniclers in subsequent dynasties attributed much of her success, like that of Cleopatra in Egypt, to her sexual exploits, though the records also note that she was well educated, shrewd in her dealings with ministers, and a practiced hand at employing imperial spectacle. In 684, after the death of her husband, who had become the emperor, she ruled as empress dowager and as regent for her son. In reality, however, she held all the actual power. A devout Buddhist, she declared Buddhism the state religion. In 690, she inaugurated the new Zhou dynasty, and in 693 she took the Buddhist title Divine Empress Who Rules the Universe.

Though she was an able ruler according to the Tang official histories, the act of creating her own dynasty and new titles for herself—including an insistence on the "male" title of "emperor"—was considered usurpation by many of her subjects, and a resistance soon followed. To many Tang leaders, Wu's empowering of Buddhists and Daoists over Confucians was deplorable. As a result, scurrilous accusations were laid against her, including allegations of sexual depravity, the torture and execution of her opponents, and even the murder of her own child in her quest to achieve political power. However, she was able to stifle revolts and to preserve the continuity of the dynasty, succumbing to natural causes in 705.

Following the Confucian backlash of the Song era, no woman in imperial China would wield this kind of power again until the reign of the empress dowager Cixi in the late nineteenth and early twentieth centuries. Even today, however, Wu remains a controversial figure; while she is celebrated in China as an early feminist role model, she is also seen as an ambitious, cruel, and self-serving schemer.

Key Terms

Empress dowager   290
Female infanticide   298
Foot binding   298
Khanate   291
Scholar-gentry   297
Sikhism   286

Learn more with this chapter's digital tools, including the Oxford Insight Study Guide, at http://www.oup.com/he/vonsivers4e. Please see the Further Resources section at the back of the book for additional readings and suggested websites.

Sources for Chapter 12

The *Chachnamah*

ca. 1200

Composed in Arabic and translated into Persian in the twelfth and thirteenth centuries, the *Chachnamah* details the Arab conquest of Sind (a province corresponding to northwest India and Pakistan) in the eighth century. The work details the campaign led by Muhammad Ibn Qasim, which was the most successful of the many attempts by Muslims to conquer the region. In this history of the campaign, Ibn Qasim is both a conquering hero and a defender of Islam, subduing non-Muslims and imposing new religious values in his wake.

A description of the battle

Hazlí states that, in that army of the Arabs there was a brave soldier by name Háris son of Marrah. He was at the head of a column of one thousand fully armed warriors. He had three brave slaves with him, one of whom he retained to bear his arms, and the other two he appointed as officers in the army, each being made the leader of 500 men. When they arrived at Makrán the news was carried to Kíkánán, where the people prepared for battle and commenced fighting. They were about 20,000 men.

[Nevertheless] the army of Islám attacked them and overpowered them, and seeing no other help, the natives retreated to the gates of the town. But when the Arab army left the battle-field and marched after the residents of Kíkánán, the latter came down to obstruct their progress. The Arab army made an onset, with their war cry of "Alláhu Akbar" [God is great] and from the left and the right the cliffs echoed the cry of "Alláhu Akbar." When the infidels of Kíkánán heard those cries they were much frightened, and some of them surrendered and accepted Islám and the rest fled away, and from that time up to our day, on the anniversary of that battle, cries of "Alláhu Akbar" are heard from the mountain.

They had already completed this victory when they received the sad news of the martyrdom of His Highness the Commander of the Faithful, Alí son of Abí Tálib, (on whom be peace). They, therefore, turned back, and when they arrived at Makrán, they learnt that Muáwiyeh son of Abísafiyán had become the Khalífah.

· · ·

Source: *The Chachnamah: An Ancient History of Sind*. Translated by Mirza Kalichbeg Fredunbeg. Commissioner's Press, 1900. Reprinted by Rana Saad, Maryland, 2004. pp. 63–66.

A tradition

It is related by Abul Hasan, who heard it from Hazlí, and Hazlí from Muslim son of Muhárib son of Muslim son of Ziyád, that when Muáwiyeh despatched the expedition of 4,000 men under Abdulláh son of Sawád, no one had to kindle fire in his camp, as they had carried abundant provisions for the journey, ready made for use. It was only on a single night that fire-light was perceived in the camp, and, on enquiry being made, it was found that a pregnant woman had been confined and fire was urgently required. Abdulláh gave her permission and she gave a merry banquet, and for three days continually entertained the whole army (with fresh-cooked food).

When Abdulláh arrived at Kíkánán, the enemy made an assault on him, but the army of Islám routed them, and secured plenty of booty. The people of Kíkánán assembled in large numbers, and occupied the mountain passes. The battle now raged furiously and Abdulláh son of Sawád found it necessary to keep his men in their ranks, by making a stand himself with a party of selected men, fully armed; and he appealed to the hearts of others in the following words: "O children of the Prophet's companions, do not turn your faces from the infidels, so that your faith may remain free from any flaw and you acquire the honour of martyrdom." Hearing these words his men assembled round the standard of Abdulláh, and one of these men, who belonged to the family of Abdul Kais, came out with a challenge to a single fight. Instantly the chief of the enemy's forces engaged with him. The example of this hero was followed by another Yásar son of Sawád. The chief was killed, but the army of Kíkánán made a general assault, by which the army of Islám was ultimately put to flight. The whole mountainous region now became alive with fighting men and the Musalmans beat a (hasty) retreat, and came back to Makrán.

A tradition

Abul Hasan relates that he heard Hátim son of Kutai-bíah Sahlí say: "That day I myself was in the army when the son of Sawád fought with his youthful adversary, and his friends advanced in the same manner, and killed many men of the enemy's side. After a hard fight they at last fell martyrs and I stripped the dead bodies of the enemy, and found a hundred signet rings."

. . .

Safyán son of U'r Hindí appointed to carry on the religious war in Hind

It is related by Hazlí who heard it from Tibuí son of Músá, who again heard it from his father, that on Abdulláh son of Sawád being martyred, he appointed Sinán son of Salmah as his successor. Soon afterwards Muáwiyeh wrote to Ziyád, (the then governor of Irák) to select a proper person for the holy wars in Hind. When he received the letter, Ziyád nominated Ahnaf son of Kais, who was liked by all, and was the pride of the Faithful. Ahnaf forthwith went to Makrán, where he remained for a period of two years, and after two years and one month he was removed from that post.

▶ Working
with Sources

1. **To what extent is this conflict envisioned as a "religious war"?**
2. **Why does the document concern itself with successions of political power?**

SOURCE 12.2 — Poetry of the Tang Dynasty

ca. 750 CE

The Tang period (618–907) witnessed a renaissance of poetry, often-times compressing vivid natural imagery and poignant emotion into short pieces of only a few verses. The poetry of Li Bai (or Li Bo, 701–762) was particularly influential in the West when his verses on drinking and the pleasures of life were rendered in translation. However, there is also a strong current of pacifism and social criticism in Tang poetry, particularly in the work of Li's friend Du Fu (721–770).

Du Fu, "A Drawing of a Horse by General Cao at Secretary Wei Feng's House"

Throughout this dynasty no one had painted horses
Like the master-spirit, Prince Jiangdu—
And then to General Cao through his thirty years of fame
The world's gaze turned, for royal steeds.
He painted the late Emperor's luminous white horse.
For ten days the thunder flew over Dragon Lake,
And a pink-agate plate was sent him from the palace—
The talk of the court-ladies, the marvel of all eyes.
The General danced, receiving it in his honoured home
After this rare gift, followed rapidly fine silks
From many of the nobles, requesting that his art
Lend a new lustre to their screens.
. . . First came the curly-maned horse of Emperor Taizong,

Source: "A Drawing of a Horse by General Cao at Secretary Wei Feng's House," trans. Witter Bynner; adapted from http://www.shigeku.com/xlib/lingshidao/hanshi/dufu.htm; Li Bo poem translated by Hugh Grigg; https://eastasiastudent.net/china/classical/li-bai-jiang-jin-jiu/

Then, for the Guos, a lion-spotted horse....
But now in this painting I see two horses,
A sobering sight for whosoever knew them.
They are war-horses. Either could face ten thousand.
They make the white silk stretch away into a vast desert.
And the seven others with them are almost as noble.
Mist and snow are moving across a cold sky,
And hoofs are cleaving snow-drifts under great trees—
With here a group of officers and there a group of servants.
See how these nine horses all vie with one another—
The high clear glance, the deep firm breath.
... Who understands distinction? Who really cares for art?
You, Wei Feng, have followed Cao; Zhidun preceded him.
... I remember when the late Emperor came toward his Summer Palace,
The procession, in green-feathered rows, swept from the eastern sky—
Thirty thousand horses, prancing, galloping,
Fashioned, every one of them, like the horses in this picture....
But now the Imperial Ghost receives secret jade from the River God,
For the Emperor hunts crocodiles no longer by the streams.
Where you see his Great Gold Tomb, you may hear among the pines
A bird grieving in the wind that the Emperor's horses are gone.

Li Bo: "Bring in the Wine!"

Have you not seen -
that the waters of the Yellow River come from upon Heaven,
surging into the ocean, never to return again;
Have you not seen -
in great halls' bright mirrors, they grieve over white hair,
at dawn like black threads, by evening becoming snow.
In human life, accomplishment must bring total joy,
do not allow an empty goblet to face the moon.
Heaven made me - my abilities must have a purpose;
I spend a thousand gold pieces completely, but they'll come back again.
Boil a lamb, butcher an ox - now we shall be joyous;
we must drink three hundred cups all at once!
Master Cen,
Dan Qiusheng,
bring in the wine! -
the cups must not stop!

I'll sing you a song -

I ask that you lend me your ears.

Bells, drums, delicacies, jade - they are not fine enough;

I only wish to be forever drunk and never sober again.

Since ancient times, sages have all been solitary;

only a drinker can leave his name behind!

The Prince of Chen, in times past, held feasts at Pingle;

ten thousand cups of wine - abandon restraint and be merry!

Why would a host speak of having little money? -

you must go straight and buy it - I'll drink it with you!

my furs worth a thousand gold pieces,

call the boy and have him take them to be swapped for fine wine,

and together with you I'll wipe out the cares of ten thousand ages.

▶ **Working with Sources**

1. **How does Du's poem reflect on the preservation of historical memory?**

2. **What moods do Li's poem suggest to the reader?**

SOURCE 12.3 Model of a Ming ship in the flotilla of Zheng He

ca. 1420

Between 1405 and 1433, a series of naval expeditions were sent out by Yongle, the third emperor of the Ming dynasty, under the command of the remarkable Zheng He (1371–1435). The largest of Zheng's ships were over 400 feet long and were thus more than four times the length of Christopher Columbus's *Santa Maria*. His voyages took Zheng to the coasts of Southeast Asia, Indonesia, India, Arabia, and East Africa. In 2010, marine archaeologists attempted to find remains of one of Zheng's ships off the coast of Kenya, near Malindi, a site Zheng visited in 1418. This photograph shows a model of one of Zheng's ships, compared with a model of the *Santa Maria*. The model is displayed in a shopping mall in Dubai, United Arab Emirates.

Source: © Liu Liqun/Chinastock.

▶ **Working with Sources**

1. What does the greater size of Zheng He's ships compared to the ones Columbus used say about the imperial ambitions of Ming China in the fifteenth century?

2. Why might this ship be of interest to shoppers in Dubai?

SOURCE 12.4 Genghis Khan Strikes West

ca. 1228 CE

The tactics of Genghis Khan and the Mongols in taking cities and towns evolved from their experiences of hunts on the steppes. In battle these frequently involved a small force feigning retreat to draw the enemy away from their fortifications and then overwhelming and enveloping them with the main force, which had used the local topography for concealment. Here, as he did repeatedly, he successfully uses these tactics on Sultan Jalal al-Din.

Source: *The Secret History of the Mongols*, adaptation by Paul Kahn (Boston: Cheng and Tsui, 1998), 157–158.

In the Year of the Hare

Chingis Khan went to war with the Moslems,

riding off past the settlement of Alai.

He took the Merkid, Khulan Khatun, from his wives as companion

and left his brother Odchigin in command of the Great Camp.

The first army he sent out was commanded by Jebe,

behind them he sent another led by Subetei,

and behind them a third under Tokhuchar.

Sending off these three commanders he told them:

"Ride off to the outside of the Sultan's armies

and wait there until I arrive.

Then you'll attack them from your side when I strike from mine."

Jebe rode out past the cities ruled by Amin al-Mulk without touching them.

Subetei's forces also passed them unharmed,

but behind them Tokhuchar robbed these frontier towns

and stole many animals from their herds.

Amin al-Mulk cried:

"They're robbing my cities!"

and he took all his forces to join the Moslem Sultan, Jalal al-Din.

When Amin al-Mulk and Jalal al-Din joined together

they sent an army out to attack Chingis Khan.

In front of Chingis Khan's army were troops led by Shigi Khutukhu.

Jalal al-Din defeated Shigi Khutukhu's troops

and drove them back toward Chingis Khan's camp.

Then from behind appeared the armies of Jebe, Subetei, and Tokhuchar,

who fell on the Moslem armies,

killing many and breaking their ranks,

keeping them from reforming at the cities of Bukhara, Samarkand, or Otrar,

driving them back to the banks of the Indus,

so that they were forced to throw themselves into the waters

and many Moslems drowned in the river.

Jalal al-Din and Amin al-Mulk swam the river,

saving their lives,

while Chingis Khan led his forces along the Indus

where they made their camp on the Parwan Plain.

Later Chingis Khan sent Bala of the Jalayir clan

off to pursue Jalal al-Din across the Indus into Punjab.

He rewarded Jebe and Subetei for what they'd done, saying:

"Jebe, you had a different name when you fought us as one of the Tayichigud, but now you've become my Jebe, my weapon.

As for you, Tokhuchar,

you willfully disobeyed me and attacked the cities on the frontier.

This caused Amin al-Mulk to join forces with Jalal al-Din against us.

For having done that I'll have your head cut off."

But after saying that he did not kill Tokhuchar.

Instead he lectured him about his disobedience

and removed him from the command of the army.

▶ Working
with Sources

1. Given that Mongol armies used these battlefield tactics over a long period of time, why would their opponents not find more effective ways of countering them?

2. What observations can you make about Genghis Khan's qualities as a commander from the above excerpt?

World Period Three

The Formation of Religious Civilizations, 600–1450 CE

The rise of religious civilizations on the continents of Asia, Europe, and Africa is a striking phenomenon that unifies the period of 600–1450 in world history. It can be considered as a continuation of the intellectual and institutional transformations that began with the emphasis on monotheism and monism by the visionaries of the mid-first millennium BCE.

The religious civilizations were not monolithic and displayed many regional variations. Internal diversity notwithstanding, they shared a number of common characteristics:

- Religious civilizations formed in regions which were larger than any single state within them: They superseded empires as the largest units of human unification.

- The civilizations were *scriptural*—that is, based on canonical (commonly agreed on) texts inherited in most cases from earlier periods. Members of educated elites (clergy, scholars, sages) taught and interpreted the scriptures to the laypeople.

- Despite hostilities among the religious civilizations, merchants, missionaries, pilgrims, and travelers visited each other's areas. They fostered a lively exchange of technical and cultural innovations from one end of Eurasia and Africa to the other.

Chapter 13

Religious Civilizations Interacting

Korea, Japan, and Vietnam, 550–1500 CE

CHAPTER THIRTEEN PATTERNS

Origins, Interactions, and Adaptations While Buddhism faced early competition from Japan's indigenous religion of Shinto, it soon proved remarkably able to adapt. Buddhist missionary work, monasticism, and networks of shrines and pilgrimage sites anchored Korea, Japan, and Vietnam, along with China and Southeast Asia, in a greater Buddhist cultural sphere. Confucianism, however, was a more difficult fit. In all three societies, Confucian concepts were adopted by elites but proved less successful in displacing older social norms.

Two important waves of intrusion challenged the Buddhist sphere. From the eighth century on, Islam spread into Northern India and Central Asia and made important inroads into China. The rise of the Mongols also provided a severe challenge. While many Mongols converted to Islam, some also converted to Buddhism.

Uniqueness and Similarities The world period in this section represents the rise and furthest extent of the religious civilization of Buddhism. In all of the areas covered in this chapter, Buddhism coexisted peacefully with indigenous religious and philosophical systems and adopted a number of local beliefs and practices. In Korea, Japan, and Vietnam, Buddhism came with the entire panoply of Chinese culture, including the writing system, Confucianism, law, and government. While many of these influences became a permanent part of the local culture, each of these societies developed variations suited to local needs and tastes, and all three struggled to achieve and retain political independence from China.

The brushstrokes flowed across the paper, as they had since she began practicing them as a young girl. For Murasaki Shikibu (ca. 973–1025), the daughter of a minor noble in the court at Heian-Kyo in central Japan, the words had become her refuge from palace life, where a woman's every move was carefully prescribed. The court women of Heian Japan (794–1185 CE), in their thick, stiff winter kimonos, their teeth blackened and faces powdered white to enhance their beauty, were monitored by palace chamberlains and commented on by court gossips. Murasaki's older contemporary Sei Shonagon had responded to this restricted life by skewering its pretentions in her scandalous *Pillow Book*.

Murasaki's literary interests, however, were different. Though she was trained in kanji, the literary Chinese that functioned as Japan's first written language, her private writings were written in the simpler kana script based on a **syllabary** of sounds in the Japanese spoken language. Like Sei Shonagon's, her work centered on court life. But her subject was the adventures of a fictional prince named Genji. Scholars have recognized her *Genji Monogatari*, the *Tale of Genji* (ca. 1000), as the world's first novel. It remains even today Japan's most popular work of fiction and one of the world's great literary masterpieces.

In the sixth century CE, Chinese writing, culture, thought, and Buddhism were adopted by the ambitious Japanese state of Yamato. Sensing that power and prestige would grow from adapting China's centralized imperial institutions, Yamato leaders remade their state along these lines over the next two centuries. But the suitability of these institutions to Japan's clan-based society was at best uneven.

The tensions in state formation created by this situation were noticeable as well in Korea and Vietnam, which also adapted Chinese institutions. Like the Japanese, the Koreans and Vietnamese would create their own writing systems while retaining Chinese as a literary language. They would also struggle, like the

CHAPTER OUTLINE

Korea to 1450: Innovation from Above

Japan to 1450: Selective Interaction and Adaptation

Vietnam: Human Agency and State Building

Putting It All Together

Syllabary: A system of written symbols representing the sounds of syllables, rather than individual consonants and vowels.

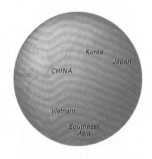

ABOVE: Detail from twelfth-century Japanese scroll depicting *The Tale of Genji*.

Seeing Patterns

> How was the history of Korea affected by its relations with China? With Japan?

> Which important elements of Chinese culture were adapted by the Japanese for their own purposes? What advantages did Japan have over Korea and Vietnam in this regard?

> Which Japanese adaptations of Chinese institutions did not work well in Japan? Why?

> In what ways was the experience of Vietnam similar to that of Japan and Korea? How was it different?

Altaic: In linguistics, a hypothetical family of languages descended from that spoken by inhabitants of the region of the Altai Mountains in Central Asia. Proposed examples include the Turkic languages, Mongolian, and Manchu; attempts to include Japanese and Korean are controversial.

Striated: Having thin lines or bands.

Japanese and Chinese, to balance Buddhism with a Confucian government. The dynamism within these tensions would allow each to make imported Chinese culture their own as they followed distinct courses of state formation—Korea and Vietnam often struggling under China's political shadow, and Japan clinging fiercely to its independence.

Korea to 1450: Innovation from Above

The influence of imperial China spread throughout East, Northeast, and Southeast Asia. Chinese writing, literature, law, government, and thought, as well as imported religions such as Buddhism, all shaped local customs and practices. But as these imports were often imposed from the top down, they met frequent resistance at the village and clan levels. Thus, tensions between elites and locals in the assorted Korean kingdoms emerged against a backdrop of invasion and collaboration. From the beginning, these societies asserted their political independence from the Chinese. However, their position on or near the Chinese border, their role as havens for refugees, and the pressures of potential invasion provided a conduit for the spread of Chinese innovations. For the Koreans themselves, shifting relations with China shaped the struggles of their different kingdoms for dominance.

People and Place: The Korean Environment

The terrain of the Korean peninsula resembles that of the adjacent region of Manchuria to the north. The Amnokkang (Yalu) River and the Kangnam (Gangnam) Mountains form the present dividing line with Manchuria, but Korean kingdoms have at times extended beyond them into modern China's northeast. The areas south of the modern city of Seoul are somewhat flatter. Agriculture has historically been concentrated in the river floodplains and coastal alluvial flats.

Climate and Agriculture   The climate of Korea is continental in the north but influenced by the monsoon system in the south. As in northern China, summer and winter temperatures are extreme, with distinct rainy (summer) and dry (winter) seasons. Annual rainfall amounts differ widely: from average lows of 30 inches in the northeast to 60–70 inches in the southwest. Like the western side of the Japanese islands, Korea is largely blocked by Japanese mountain ranges from the moderating effects of the Japan Current.

The difficulties of the terrain and the possibility of drought pose challenges similar to those facing agriculturalists in northern China, with crops such as millet and wheat dominating and rice farming catching on only much later in the south, where rainfall and the terracing of hillsides made it feasible (see Map 13.1).

Ethnic Origins   The ethnic origins of the Koreans are obscure, though some evidence points to a Central Asian homeland and links to the **Altaic**-speaking peoples. East and northeast Asia was home to some of the world's first pottery, though the potter's wheel did not arrive in the area for millennia. On the Korean peninsula, pot shards dating from 4000 BCE have been uncovered in **striated** styles not unlike the Jomon wares of Japan, which some scholars have suggested points to early interaction or perhaps a common ancestry.

Conquest and Competition: History and Politics to 1450

The first Korean state predated any Chinese influence. Zhou Chinese annals contain apparent references to the kingdom of Choson—"The Land of the Morning Calm." Choson seems to have extended into southern Manchuria, with its capital located on the site of the modern city of Pyongyang. It is believed to have been founded after 1000 BCE. No indigenous records exist of its early years.

The Three Kingdoms   The first attempt by the Chinese at invasion was under the Qin (221–206 BCE). By 108 BCE, their successors, the Han, briefly brought much of the peninsula under their sway. It is from this period that the first written records of the Koreans, Japanese, and Vietnamese appear in Han histories. As related in Sima Qian's *Records of the Grand Historian*, the Han conquest of Chaoxian (Choson) was rife with chaos. Long before this, however, Chinese agricultural techniques, methods of bronze and iron smelting, and other technologies found their way to Choson and beyond. Early contacts between Choson and the Zhou Chinese states from the ninth century BCE on saw the arrival of bronze tools, coins, and weapons. By the fifth century BCE, the technology of iron smelting was also established on the Korean peninsula.

Following the Han conquests, a more systematic Chinese transformation was attempted. The Han incorporated most of the peninsula into their empire, with Pyongyang as their regional capital. They encouraged Chinese settlement in the newly acquired territories. An indirect effect of the conquest was a stream of refugees into the unoccupied regions of the south and to Japan, facilitating cultural exchanges and trade. Koreans were important actors in early Japanese history, and with the founding of the small Japanese holding of Kaya (Gaya) in 42 CE, Japanese territorial claims were established on the peninsula.

At the same time, the foundations had been laid for the so-called Three Kingdoms of Korea: Koguryo [go-GUR-yo] (37 BCE–668 CE), Paekche [BAAK-chih] (18 BCE–660 CE), and Silla [SI-lah] (57 BCE–935 CE). By the fourth century CE, the dissolution of the Han Empire encouraged the Koreans to push the

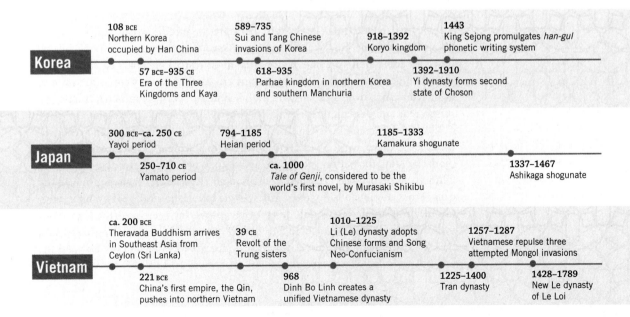

Korea

| 108 BCE Northern Korea occupied by Han China | 589–735 Sui and Tang Chinese invasions of Korea | 918–1392 Koryo kingdom | 1443 King Sejong promulgates *han-gul* phonetic writing system |

| 57 BCE–935 CE Era of the Three Kingdoms and Kaya | 618–935 Parhae kingdom in northern Korea and southern Manchuria | 1392–1910 Yi dynasty forms second state of Choson |

Japan

| 300 BCE–ca. 250 CE Yayoi period | 794–1185 Heian period | 1185–1333 Kamakura shogunate |

| 250–710 CE Yamato period | ca. 1000 *Tale of Genji*, considered to be the world's first novel, by Murasaki Shikibu | 1337–1467 Ashikaga shogunate |

Vietnam

| ca. 200 BCE Theravada Buddhism arrives in Southeast Asia from Ceylon (Sri Lanka) | 39 CE Revolt of the Trung sisters | 1010–1225 Li (Le) dynasty adopts Chinese forms and Song Neo-Confucianism | 1257–1287 Vietnamese repulse three attempted Mongol invasions |

| 221 BCE China's first empire, the Qin, pushes into northern Vietnam | 968 Dinh Bo Linh creates a unified Vietnamese dynasty | 1225–1400 Tran dynasty | 1428–1789 New Le dynasty of Le Loi |

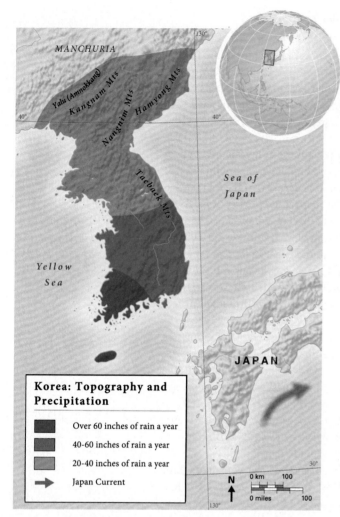

Korea: Topography and Precipitation

Over 60 inches of rain a year

40-60 inches of rain a year

20-40 inches of rain a year

Japan Current

N

0 km   100

0 miles   100

MAP 13.1 **Korea: Topography and Precipitation**

Chinese out of the peninsula. In the wake of their retreat, the three rival kingdoms began a struggle for dominance. Koguryo, in the extreme north, formed the largest state. In the south, the areas that had never been under Chinese control had a history of ties to Japan and, consequently, tended to be more outward-looking.

In 372 the Chinese state of Jin sent Buddhist missionaries to Koguryo. With them came Chinese writing and Confucian thought. In 427, Koguryo remade itself along Chinese lines with a central Confucian bureaucracy, examinations, a reconstituted land tax, and a conscription system. Meanwhile, the two southern kingdoms continually fought off domination by their northern rival. Paekche's maritime contacts with south China and its wars with Koguryo aided the spread of Buddhism there from 364 to 371. While Buddhism had also come to Silla, its clan-based monarchy adopted a Chinese-style bureaucracy that left power largely in the hands of warrior aristocrats.

The reunification of China under the Sui dynasty in 589 soon resulted in another invasion of the north. After several Tang campaigns were repulsed, the Chinese concluded an alliance with Silla in 660, spelling the immediate end of Paekche. Threatened along two fronts, Koguryo itself finally submitted in 668. Silla was ultimately recognized by the Chinese as a client state controlling all of Korea south of Pyongyang in 735.

Korea to the Mid-Fifteenth Century   By the middle of the eighth century, Silla was in decline. In 780 the king was assassinated, and revolts threatened stability for some time to come. Among the most restive members of Silla society were the merchants, who, like their counterparts in China, were both aware of their economic power and sensitive to the contempt of the Confucian-influenced aristocracy and bureaucrats.

One such merchant, Wong Kon (d. 943), subdued the kingdom and reconstituted it as Koryo—from which comes the name "Korea." The Chinese imperial model of state formation proved attractive to Wong, who, after the practice of Chinese emperors, was accorded a posthumous reign name, Taejo. He moved the capital to Kaesong and adopted Chinese-style bureaucratic and tax systems, with military and labor conscription. Koryo even built its own version of the Great Wall near the Yalu River as a barrier to the nomadic peoples to the north (see Map 13.2).

By the middle of the thirteenth century, Koryo, like much of the rest of Asia, had begun to feel the power of Mongol expansion. In 1231, Mongol forces laid

Pulguksa Temple. Buddhism put down strong roots in Silla after its introduction in the fourth century. The Pulguksa temple was first built in Kyongjiu, the Silla capital, in 535 as part of the state Buddhist school. The stone pagodas were built in the ninth century under the auspices of the new Son school, better known by its Japanese name, Zen.

siege to Kaesong. The fall of the city inaugurated four decades of irregular warfare and forced the withdrawal of the government to the south. The Mongols deported perhaps 250,000 Koreans as slave laborers to other parts of the Mongol Empire. The Koryo court finally capitulated in 1259. As in most of the occupied areas of Eurasia, the advantages brought by Mongol unity were eclipsed in Korea by the cruelty of the conquest itself.

In 1368, the Mongol Yuan dynasty in China was overthrown by Zhu Yuanzhang, who inaugurated the Ming dynasty (1368–1644). As had nearly every previous dynasty, the Ming planned to invade Korea. In 1388 the Korean leader Yi Song-gye made the strategic decision not to resist the Ming, but moved against the Korean court instead, founding the Yi dynasty in 1392 and resurrecting the name of Choson for the new state. The Yi concluded a diplomatic/commercial agreement with China that formed the basis for what is often referred to as the Ming "tribute system" (see Chapter 21).

Meanwhile, the Yi polity adapted to Chinese-style institutions. The centralized government of the Ming was echoed in Choson, and the adoption of Neo-Confucianism drove out older local customs. A new capital was established, and the state was divided into eight provinces following the

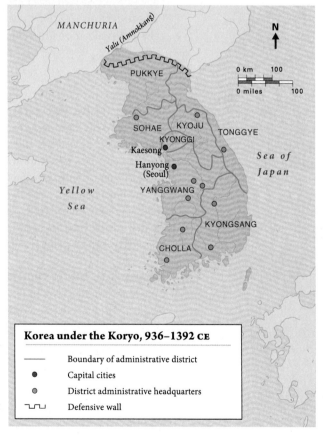

Korea under the Koryo, 936–1392 CE

——	Boundary of administrative district
●	Capital cities
○	District administrative headquarters
⊓⊔	Defensive wall

MAP 13.2 **Korea under the Koryo, 936–1392**

Patterns Up Close | Printing

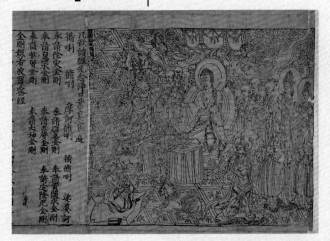

Woodblock Printing. Although the Chinese, Japanese, and Koreans all developed versions of movable type presses, the huge number of characters in literary Chinese made their use problematic. Mass production of printed material was much easier to manage with carved woodblocks, as with the page pictured here. The illustration is from the Buddhist *Diamond Sutra*, believed to be the world's oldest dated printed work, published in 868.

Seven centuries before the invention of the printing press and movable type revolutionized the intellectual life of early modern Europe, these developments in East Asia had a similar effect. In many respects, the consequences of these innovations were different, because of the languages and the technical media with which printers in China, Korea, Japan, and Vietnam worked, and the cultural patterns of handwriting and calligraphy as artistic skills cultivated by elites slowed the spread of printing. Yet by the fourteenth century, the societies of East Asia achieved the highest preindustrial literacy rates in the world. These would be unmatched in Europe for centuries.

The earliest extant examples of woodblock printing date to the fall of the Han dynasty in 220 CE. Printers carved blocks of text on book-sized boards, inked them, and pressed the cloth or paper pages on them to get copies. The boards could then be shaved down and carved again as needed. By the eighth century the Chinese had also begun to experiment with copper movable type inserted vertically into standardized rows in a system very much like the one Gutenberg devised

Chinese model of prefectures and districts. A uniform law code was promulgated in 1485, and the Confucian exam structure was broadened to include a two-tiered official class, the *yongban* and *chungin*.

The new class structure was not without problems. To stabilize the *yongban* class, Yi rulers made large land grants to the great officials of the kingdom. These landholders, however, used their grants to amass local power. Unlike Chinese officials, who were moved from place to place to avoid just this, they tended to remain in their own territories and resisted attempts from the throne to rein in their excesses. Over time, many became like regional rulers.

Economy, Society, and Family

Like their counterparts in China, rulers in the Korean kingdoms were preoccupied with problems of landlordism and tenancy, land reform, maintenance of local infrastructures, and alleviating want during times of shortage.

Land Reform   Rulers under Chinese influence proposed schemes of land redistribution based on the Chinese "well-field" model (see Chapter 4). More ambitious was the *chongjon* system of Silla, begun in 722. This system mandated a government-sponsored distribution of land, with taxes paid in kind. Additionally, peasants were instructed to develop specialized cash crops or engage in small-craft manufacture. A prime example was sericulture—the

centuries later. But, ironically, these presses remained more curiosities than practical devices. The obstacle was the Chinese written language—and, at this time, the written languages of Korea, Japan, and Vietnam as well. Unlike the English alphabet with its 26 letters, literary Chinese has thousands of different characters. It was simply impractical for typesetters to cast adequate supplies of characters, organize them, and sort through them to compose the text to be copied. It was far less work to just carve the text blocks from scratch.

One catalyst for printing was the growing popularity of Buddhism throughout East Asia. As would be the case centuries later with the spread of religious tracts during the Protestant Reformation, the desire of Buddhists to read scriptures proved a stimulus to literacy, though in practical terms only those with considerable leisure could master the literary Chinese of the scriptures. Still, the establishment of woodblock printing as a major industry in East Asia by the fourteenth century has been seen by a variety of scholars as one of the hallmarks of early modernity centuries before that term is applied to Europe.

Questions

- How did the innovation of woodblock printing facilitate the spread of Buddhism throughout East Asia?
- What does the use of printing say about the relationship between literacy and state formation?

planting of mulberry trees as food for silkworms, the raising of silkworms, and the production of silk.

The Yi dynasty of Choson prioritized the implanting of Neo-Confucian values in the countryside as well as among elites. A new system of land tenure was made part of a more general stabilizing of all classes. Peasant rents were fixed at half the crop, and, as in the Chinese system, a hierarchy of village headmen, bureaucrats, and magistrates was set up to collect taxes, settle disputes, and dispense justice.

The institution of Chinese systems in Korea attracted the elites more than the peasant and artisan classes. This aggravated societal tensions, despite the governmental efficiencies they created. One factor was the bureaucracy's attempt to enhance its power at the expense of the merchant and artisan classes. In the countryside, power remained in the hands of the landholder aristocracy, which meant conditions for peasants resembled the serfdom of their European contemporaries.

Neo-Confucian Influence   Particularly in the cities, Song Chinese–influenced material culture was evident by the eleventh and twelfth centuries. Interregional trade was brisk, and Korea's position at the center of the East Asian Buddhist world made it a trade and pilgrimage crossroads. Korean artisans became proficient in porcelain making and book printing; many of the oldest Chinese, Korean, and Japanese works extant were printed by Korean publishers.

Under the Yi, the Confucian exams became more open, though the new social arrangements called for two official classes, the *yongban*, or scholar-gentry, and the *chungin*, or minor officials. Below these were the *yangmin*, commoners of different professions as well as peasants and serfs, while the lowest group, the *chonmin*, consisted of bond slaves, laborers, and prostitutes.

Though the Confucian exams theoretically allowed for some degree of social mobility, they were monopolized by the *yongban*. The institution of hereditary classes, intended to create a stable and harmonious social structure, instead concentrated wealth in the hands of the rural gentry. In many places, the older patterns of aristocratic local power continued. Thus, by the end of the fifteenth century, the divide between the wealthy, educated, sophisticated capital and large provincial cities and the tradition-bound countryside was increasing.

Women and Society   Until the arrival of Confucian institutions in the Korean countryside, local village life, as in Vietnam and Japan, tended toward more equality between men and women than would later be the case. In Korea, this egalitarianism persisted despite Neo-Confucian precepts. Until the sixteenth and seventeenth centuries, for example, bilateral and **matrilocal** marriage patterns tended to be the norm. As in Japan and Vietnam, the communal nature of rice agriculture made women and girls more equal partners in local rural society. Women's property and inheritance rights, far more expansive than in Confucian China, also reflected this.

> **Matrilocal:** Living with the family of the bride.

Under the Neo-Confucian reforms of the Yi, these practices changed. Strictly delineated gender roles, long a staple among the urban elites and official classes, became a cornerstone of moral training in rural academies and in the home.

Religion, Culture, and Intellectual Life

Early Korean religion appears to have been nature-spiritual. One could appeal to the spirits through shamans or animals believed to have certain powers. Like Shinto in Japan, these beliefs continued at the local level long after the introduction of more formalized systems. The invasion of the Han brought the Chinese concepts of heaven, earth, and humankind along with imperial rituals. Most importantly, Buddhism was introduced to the Three Kingdoms during the fourth century CE.

Buddhism, Printing, and Literacy   All the Korean kings seized the combination of Buddhism, Han Confucianism, and their institutions as a way to enhance their states. In Silla, the court pursued a course of striving for Buddhist "perfection." It built the 210-foot Hwang Nyonsu temple in 645. Others sponsored the publication of Buddhist works: Koryo produced a version of the *Tripitaka* printed on 80,000 hand-carved wood blocks. This contributed to the high level of functional literacy in written Chinese among Korean elites. Due to the demand for Buddhist works, twelfth-century Korea developed into one of the world's early centers of publishing (see "Patterns Up Close").

Korea's literacy received a further boost during the reign of King Sejong (r. 1418–1450). Here, the development of the Korean phonetic script *hangul*, like the use of kana in Japan, made the introduction of writing much simpler than literary Chinese. Yet, like kana in Japan, it also created a two-tiered system of literacy:

> **Hangul:** Korean phonetic script, introduced in the middle of the fifteenth century.

Chinese remained the written medium of choice among the elites, while hangul became the written language of the commoners and, increasingly, women. Such divisions notwithstanding, the explosion of vernacular literature contributed to Korea attaining, with Japan, some of the highest levels of functional literacy in the preindustrial world.

Japan to 1450: Selective Interaction and Adaptation

The case of Japan raises exciting questions about the effects of isolation. Like Britain, Japan's geographical position allowed it to selectively interact with and adapt to continental innovations. Acculturation in Japan—a country which never experienced a successful invasion—was almost completely voluntary, a characteristic unique among the societies of Eurasia.

The Island Refuge

Japan's four main islands, Honshu, Hokkaido, Kyushu, and Shikoku, are varied in climate. The northernmost island of Hokkaido has cold winters and cool summers; the central island of Honshu, bisected north to south by mountain ranges, has a temperate to subtropical climate on the eastern side, where it is moderated by the Japan Current, and a colder, more continental climate on the western side, which faces Korea and northeastern China. The small southern island of Shikoku and the southernmost island of Kyushu have warm, moist weather governed by the Pacific monsoon system (see Map 13.3).

The Limitations of the Land   Only about one-fifth of the territory of Japan's islands is arable. In the narrow plains and valleys, the majority of which are on the temperate Pacific side of the mountains, the soil is mineral-rich and the rainfall abundant. But islanders face the limitations of the land in supporting a growing population. Like the Korean peninsula, the ruggedness of the land forced its people to live in politically isolated, culturally united communities. Communication by water was often most convenient, both among the Japanese home islands and across the strait to Korea.

Adaptation at Arm's Length: History and Politics

The origins of the Japanese are obscure. Two groups appear to have migrated to the islands from the Asian mainland via Ice Age land bridges, perhaps 10,000–20,000 years ago. Their descendants, the Utari or Ainu, are today regarded as Japan's aboriginal peoples. Details of their religious practices and recent DNA typing have led some anthropologists to link them to the peoples of Central Asia, Siberia, and the Americas.

The later inhabitants may have originally come from the peoples who migrated into Southeast Asia, Indonesia, and eventually the central Pacific. They may also have been descended from Polynesian travelers and migrants from the Asian mainland. Linguistic evidence suggests a very tenuous connection to Korean and perhaps even to the Altaic language family.

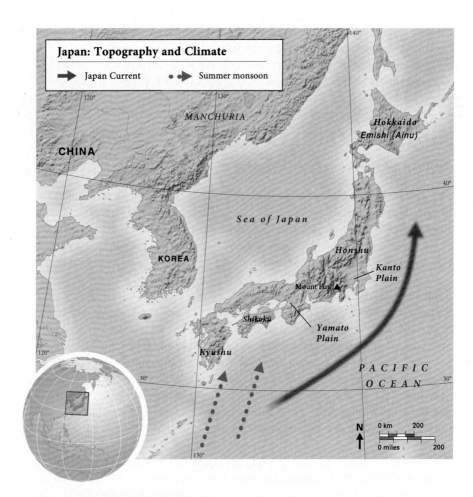

Japan: Topography and Climate

Japan Current   Summer monsoon

MANCHURIA

CHINA

Hokkaido
Emishi (Ainu)

Sea of Japan

Honshu

Kanto
Plain

KOREA

Mount Fuji

Shikoku

Yamato
Plain

Kyushu

PACIFIC
OCEAN

N

0 km   200
0 miles   200

MAP 13.3 Japan: Topography and Climate

Microlith: A very small blade made of flaked stone and used as a spearpoint, especially in the Mesolithic era.

Matriarchal: A social system in which the mother is head of the family.

Matrilineal: Relating to, based on, or tracing ancestral descent through the maternal line.

Jomon and Yayoi   Japan's prehistory (ca. 13,000–300 BCE) has been designated by archaeologists as the Jomon period. Artifacts of this period include lightly fired clay vessels and **microlith** items: arrowheads, spear points, tools made of bone and antler, and nets and fishhooks. **Matriarchal** and **matrilineal** clans appear to have dominated society, clustered mostly near the sea or slightly inland. Fishing and harvesting seaweed were the major forms of subsistence. As among the American peoples of the Pacific Northwest, the bounty of the sea and forests enabled village life to develop in the absence of an early agricultural revolution.

During the final half-millennium before the Common Era, increased intercommunication among Japanese, Koreans, and the Late Zhou Chinese coastal states laid the groundwork not only for the introduction of agriculture to the Japanese islands but for an almost simultaneous Bronze Age as well. During the last centuries of the Jomon period, it appears that some of the grain crops of northern Asia found their way to the islands. During a 600-year period designated Yayoi (300 BCE–300 CE), imported and domestically manufactured bronze and iron articles appeared. Southern Honshu and Kyushu also saw the cultivation of rice.

These changes were introduced by the dislocations resulting from the creation of China's first empire in 221 BCE and the influx of Korean refugees after the initial Chinese invasion of Korea.

As elsewhere in Asia, the rice revolution allowed for population growth in Japan. The movement away from fishing and gathering combined with the efficiency of metal tools and weapons also fostered state formation among the larger and more powerful clans, or *uji*. Thus, sometime after 250 CE, Japan's first fully evolved state, Yamato, emerged on the Kanto Plain near modern Tokyo. Japan's first monumental architecture, enormous burial mounds called *kofun*, date from this period.

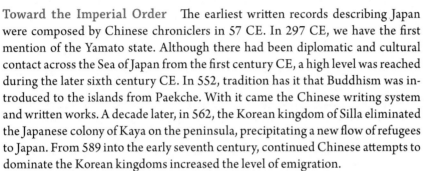

Jomon Jar and Yamato Sharinseki Disk. The distinctive herringbone pattern and flared top mark this pottery as Middle Jomon, perhaps 5,000–6,000 years old. The disk made of finely worked steatite was taken from a third-century CE kofun burial mound in central Japan. It may be related as a religious object to similar kinds of ornaments found in China.

Toward the Imperial Order   The earliest written records describing Japan were composed by Chinese chroniclers in 57 CE. In 297 CE, we have the first mention of the Yamato state. Although there had been diplomatic and cultural contact across the Sea of Japan from the first century CE, a high level was reached during the later sixth century CE. In 552, tradition has it that Buddhism was introduced to the islands from Paekche. With it came the Chinese writing system and written works. A decade later, in 562, the Korean kingdom of Silla eliminated the Japanese colony of Kaya on the peninsula, precipitating a new flow of refugees to Japan. From 589 into the early seventh century, continued Chinese attempts to dominate the Korean kingdoms increased the level of emigration.

The growing power of China and Silla prompted the Soga *uji*'s Empress Suiko (r. 592–628) and her nephew, Prince Shotoku (ca. 573–621), to connect Yamato to mainland conceptions of politics, culture, literature, and, ultimately, the imperial system itself. Yamato adoptions included Buddhism as a state religion (594), the Chinese lunar calendar for state record keeping (604), and the prince's constitution, modeled on Confucian and Buddhist precepts (604).

The most far-reaching changes came later in the century, with the *Taika*, or Great Reform, of 645. The remaking of the Yamato regime along Chinese lines in the wake of the *Taika* marks the beginning of the imperial Japanese state. Soga clan control of the court was overturned, and Fujiwara no Kamatari, an adviser to the new emperor, Tenchi, ushered in a connection between his family and the imperial court that continued into the twentieth century.

In less than a century, the first Chinese-style imperial histories were composed; the concept of the Mandate of Heaven was adopted to justify the overthrow of the Sogas; the emperor as the center of a hierarchical system of government was institutionalized; and a census, uniform taxation, and conscription and labor service were enacted. The edicts mandating these changes were promulgated as the Taiho Code of 702, which remained the basis of Japanese law until the late nineteenth century.

Yamato's spiritual roots in Shinto, with its connection to nature, had dictated that the seat of the state be frequently moved. Because of the requirements of a far larger system of government, however, it was decided that a permanent capital should be built. The first site selected, at Nara, saw the creation in 710 of a close replica of the Tang capital at Chang'an. In 794, a larger capital was completed nearby along the same lines called Heian-kyo, the future city of Kyoto. The era of imperial rule from this capital, which lasted until 1185, is referred to as the Heian period (see Map 13.4).

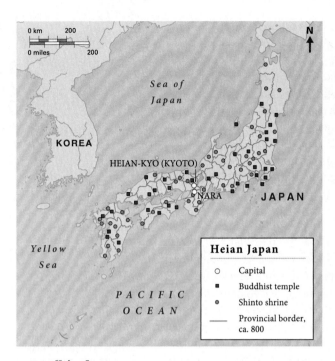

0 km   200

0 miles   200

N

*Sea of
Japan*

KOREA

HEIAN-KYŌ (KYOTO)

NARA   JAPAN

*Yellow
Sea*

PACIFIC
OCEAN

Heian Japan

○   Capital

■   Buddhist temple

●   Shinto shrine

——   Provincial border,
ca. 800

MAP 13.4 **Heian Japan**

Heian Japan   As the imperial order penetrated all the Japanese home islands except Hokkaido and the adoption of Buddhist culture connected Japan to an interconnected Asian sphere, Heian Japan became a land of contrasts, with local rumblings of discontent. The elites of the capital and provincial administrative centers saw themselves as part of a cosmopolitan world, as fashions in poetry, literature, fine arts, calligraphy, music, and clothing all found their way to court and beyond.

For the members of the new classes into which the majority of Japan's people had been placed (peasants, artisans, merchants, and Buddhist monks), many of the changes had been disruptive. Power and military strength were diffusing from the court and capital out into the countryside. This was particularly true in more remote regions, where the most aggressive *uji* had assembled forces. The bureaucracy became weaker as the local *uji* began to reassert power and especially in the wake of a smallpox epidemic (735–737) that reduced the population by as much as one-third.

Despite court attempts to create a Chinese-style "well-field" system, tenancy became a chronic problem. Clan estates were given tax-exempt status because of their military contributions, and the estates of Buddhist monasteries were similarly exempt. By the late eleventh century, perhaps half of the land in the empire had become exempt from taxes. As the countryside became more self-sufficient, the capital became more isolated—and more reliant on local military cooperation.

The court was often divided by factional disputes. Three decades of civil war between factions supporting the claims of the Taira clan and those pledged to the Minamoto, or Genji, finally ended in 1185 with the defeat of the Taira. Shortly thereafter, Minamoto Yoritomo was given the title Sei-i-tai **Shogun**, and the period of the **Shogunates** was inaugurated, lasting until 1867.

Shogun: The chief military official of Japan. The office was hereditary under the Tokugawa family from 1603 until 1867.

Shogunate: The government, rule, or office of a shogun.

Japan under the Shoguns   Though the emperor at Kyoto theoretically remained in charge with the shogun as his deputy, the arrangement in fact hastened the drain of power from the capital. In order to restore order, Yoritomo set up his headquarters at Kamakura in 1192, several hundred miles from Kyoto near present-day Tokyo. Thus began an interval known as the Kamakura shogunate, which officially lasted till 1333. The court itself remained the center of religious and ceremonial life, but the real center of power was the shogun's headquarters. Meanwhile, in 1274, the Mongols launched the first of two major attempts to invade Japan. Their first armada was defeated, while in 1281 their fleet was smashed by a typhoon, known ever after by the Japanese as *kamikaze*, the "divine wind."

Emperors occasionally led unsuccessful attempts to reassert their own power. The most ambitious of these was the revolt by Emperor Go-Daigo in 1333. Securing the support of the powerful leader Ashikaga Takauji [ah-shee-KAH-gah

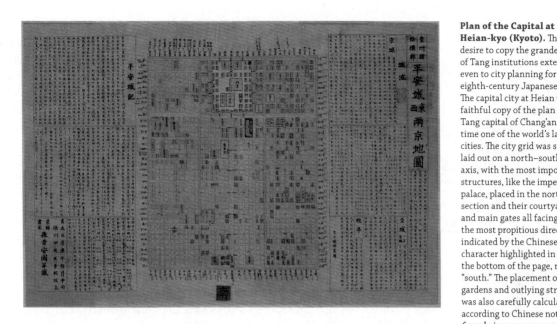

Plan of the Capital at Heian-kyo (Kyoto). The desire to copy the grandeur of Tang institutions extended even to city planning for the eighth-century Japanese court. The capital city at Heian was a faithful copy of the plan of the Tang capital of Chang'an, at the time one of the world's largest cities. The city grid was strictly laid out on a north–south axis, with the most important structures, like the imperial palace, placed in the northern section and their courtyards and main gates all facing south, the most propitious direction, indicated by the Chinese character highlighted in red at the bottom of the page, meaning "south." The placement of gardens and outlying structures was also carefully calculated according to Chinese notions of *feng shui* geomancy regarding trees, hills, and water.

tah-kah-OO-jee], Go-Daigo's faction was crippled when the opportunistic Ashikaga switched sides twice during the conflict. Ashikaga finally placed his own candidate on the throne, drove Go-Daigo into exile, and moved his headquarters to Kyoto. For the first time in nearly 200 years, the seats of political and cultural influence were reunited in the same city, and the refinements of court life were now available to the warrior classes. There thus was born the "dual way" of the sword and writing brush. The patronage of the *daimyo*, or regional lords, and their retainers, the **samurai**, ensured development of the Chinese-inspired arts of painting, poetry, and calligraphy. Zen and tea, introduced in the twelfth century, forged an armature of discipline in both the martial and courtly arts.

Samurai: A Japanese warrior who was a member of the feudal military aristocracy.

Daimyo and samurai prided themselves on a strict system of loyalty and honor—*bushido*, the "Way of the Warrior." Indeed, the tradition of *seppuku* or *hara-kiri*—ritual suicide—developed originally as a way to show one's "sincerity" and disdain for death and capture on the battlefield. One was also expected to show honor and respect to one's opponents.

By the fifteenth century, however, armies were increasingly dominated by massed ranks of infantry. By the middle of the following century, the adoption of firearms and advances in fortification made Japan perhaps the most heavily armed country on earth. The fluidity of the military situation had social consequences, and by the middle of the sixteenth century it was increasingly possible for commoners to rise through the ranks and become commanders and even *daimyo*.

One important reason for these conditions was the instability of the Ashikaga Shogunate. In 1467, factional struggles would finally erupt into all-out war for 10 years, the effects of which would last more than a century.

Economy, Society, and Family

The diversification of Japan's economy began with the Yayoi period, around 300 BCE. Wet rice and vegetable agriculture allowed early Japanese communities to

Japanese *Daimyo* Armor.
This extraordinarily well-preserved torso armor and helmet is believed to date from the fourteenth century and may have belonged to the shogun Ashikaga Takauji (r. 1338–1358). The helmet is bronzed iron, while the cuirass is made of thousands of overlapping iron and lacquered leather scales held together in horizontal rows by means of rivets. The combination made for effective protection against swords and arrows while allowing considerable freedom of movement.

sustain the sedentary population necessary for assimilating new technologies and concentrating power for state formation. The limited amount of arable land also meant that the populations of large open areas (like the Kanto Plain) were in an advantageous position to subdue their neighbors. By the high point of the Yamato period, Chinese accounts describe an economy with the majority of inhabitants engaged in agriculture and with emerging merchant and artisan classes.

The New Economy   By the sixth century, nearly every domesticated plant and animal from the mainland suitable to the environment had been introduced to Japan. Like their counterparts on the mainland, the Yamato court and its successors regulated economic activity in the form of land and produce taxes, taxes on trade, monopolies on strategic commodities, and requisitions of labor for infrastructural projects.

Yet these efforts at centralization were only partially effective. The larger *uji*, whose power had theoretically been reduced by the creation of a state bureaucracy, got around the problem by supplying many of the officials for the new body. They took advantage of government incentives to reclaim land. By such means the large *shoen* holdings and monastery estates with their tax exemptions acquired regional political and military power.

The period from 1250 to 1450 saw cycles of expansion in overseas commerce, with colonies of Japanese merchants operating in the Philippines, Java, and Malacca, as well as in Korea and China. Through their wares, the *daimyo* and samurai became sophisticated connoisseurs of luxury goods. As the early ports and towns grew, Japanese craftspeople imitated and refined Chinese crafts. Moreover, a diverse middle class organized into trade guilds were also consumers of luxury items. Their increased demand for capital spurred a monetization of the economy and the beginnings of banking and credit systems.

Advances in Agriculture   The period from 1250 to 1600 saw an increase in both cultivation of Japan's arable land and the introduction of new crops. As it had throughout East Asia, the use of fast-ripening rice strains from Southeast Asia vastly enhanced stocks of this staple. In some areas, the wet paddy fields it required allowed dry raised beds for vegetables to be made from the soil taken out of the paddies. The introduction of the Chinese "dragon pump" (see Chapter 9) facilitated irrigation. Finally, a triple-cropping system with vegetables grown on the raised beds in between fields allowed families to subsist on only a few acres of land. With this enhanced productivity, the population of about 5 million in 1100 doubled, perhaps as early as 1300; by 1450 it was on its way to doubling again.

Family Structure   As in Korea, the earliest social structures of Japan appear to have been matrilocal and, most likely, matriarchal. *Uji* before the sixth century were organized around female lineages. This was to change with the coming of Chinese institutions. During the sixth and seventh centuries, women at the top, like Empress Suiko of the Soga clan, could still wield considerable political power. By the height of the power of the Heian court, Confucian patriarchal institutions had greater influence but were moderated by Buddhism and Shinto. Aristocratic women controlled property, though they increasingly tended to wield political power through men. They were sequestered at court and forced into a highly refined ritual life, yet they created their own influential cultural world.

Outside the court, the moderating institution for commoners, and particularly women, was the Buddhist monastery. As in China and Korea, the monasteries provided havens for women and men who did not marry or had fled bad marriages. They provided education, thus helping to increase literacy. They also provided avenues of political power.

The family life of commoners was governed by a mix of Confucian filial piety, local clan relations, and the desire to improve the family's position through marriage. As in China, girls came to be considered expendable because they would move in with their husband's family. Arranged marriages were the norm, and by way of forcing such issues, rape, kidnapping, and family vendettas were all too common. Under the Tokugawa shogunate, strictly regulated Neo-Confucian family codes were enforced by the shogun's local officials.

Religion, Culture, and Intellectual Life

The foundations of Japan's original religion, **Shinto**, go back into remote antiquity. Scholars have used the word "vitalism" to describe Shinto belief in the power of *kami*—spirits of divinities, beings living and departed, nature as a whole, and even inanimate objects like mountains and streams. Reverence for these forces extended to fertility and earthly vitality.

Shinto: Japan's indigenous religion, which emphasizes reverence for nature and the importance of "vitality."

The importance of vitality was reinforced by an emphasis on ritual purity. On the other hand, death and corruption were things to be separated from as much as possible.

The Way of the Gods   Shinto means "the way of the gods," and Japanese mythology recognized an array of deities. Chief among these were Izanagi and Izanami, whose initial sexual act created the Japanese home islands, as well as Amaterasu, the sun goddess, considered the ancestor of Japan's emperors, purportedly starting with Jimmu in 660 BCE. Until the emperor Hirohito renounced his divinity at the end of World War II, every Japanese emperor was considered a god in the Shinto pantheon by believers.

Although it had undoubtedly arrived some time before, the customary dating of the introduction of Buddhism to Japan is 552 CE, when the king of Paekche sent a collection of Buddhist scriptures as a present to Yamato. The new religion soon became well established among Japanese elites, and Buddhism became the state religion of Yamato in 594. Buddhism and Shinto were ultimately able to coexist. The ability of Buddhism to adapt the cosmologies of other traditions to its core beliefs made it an easy fit for Shinto. For their part, Shinto believers could add Buddhist entities to the list of *kami*. Such accommodations facilitated the spread of the religion.

Most of the schools of Buddhism established in Japan had first become popular in China. The first to establish itself at Nara was the Hosso school, based on texts brought back from India. This was shortly displaced by the Tendai school and the Shingon sect, which dominated the imperial court for most of the Heian period.

As noted in Chapter 9, for Tendai followers, the most important scripture was the Lotus Sutra, which includes the key revelation that all beings possess the potential for salvation. Esoteric Buddhism, on the other hand, placed more emphasis on scriptural study and aesthetics. The popular devotional schools of Buddhism also came to Japan during the eighth and ninth centuries. Their simplicity and optimism ensured widespread adherence.

The Miracles of Kannon. Amida Buddhism was the most popular school throughout East Asia, and the most popular figure of the many bodhisattvas was Kannon (Guanyin in China). On this long handscroll dated to 1257, Kannon saves her followers from assorted tribulations; here, she appears to two men set upon by soldiers or brigands.

Zen: School of Buddhism in which adherents follow an experienced master and seek to achieve *satori*, a flash of enlightenment signaling the recovery of one's Buddha nature.

Though neither achieved widespread popularity, two other Buddhist schools deserve mention because of their influence. The first is a wholly Japanese development. Nichiren (1222–1282) advocated a Japan-centered, patriotic form of Buddhism. Perhaps more influential was the practice of **Zen**. Arriving in Japan from China in the twelfth century, it spread among the *daimyo* and samurai, who had the discipline to pursue its rigors. Zen seeks to achieve *satori*, a flash of enlightenment signaling the recovery of one's Buddha nature. Zen adherents follow the instructions of an experienced master rather than engage in prolonged scriptural study. Practitioners seek to open themselves to enlightenment by lowly, repetitive tasks, contemplating paradoxes and sitting in meditation. All of these practices can be useful to a warrior.

One final area in which Zen permeated the life of the warrior classes was in the use of tea. Introduced from China by the Zen monk Eisai (1141–1215), tea drinking in Japan spread as an aid to discipline and meditation among monks in the twelfth century. Soon, it became popular among the upper classes. Its presentation was refined by the sixteenth-century tea master Sen-no Rikyu (1522–1591), whose ritual of the tea ceremony became a popular preparation for battle among *daimyo* and samurai.

Forging a Japanese Culture The Chinese influence on Japan included an understanding of the importance of histories and record keeping. The first

Chinese-influenced Japanese histories, the *Nihongi* (*Chronicles of Japan*) and *Kojiki* (*Records of Ancient Matters*), made their appearance during the early eighth century. At about the same time, the first collection of Japanese poetry published in Chinese, the *Man'yoshu* (*The Ten Thousand Leaves*) appeared. It illustrated the problems inherent in using Chinese characters as a method of rendering Japanese sounds.

The *Man'yoshu* uses one-syllable Chinese characters picked for their similarity to Japanese sounds and strings them together into Japanese words. If one can follow the *sounds* of the words, one can grasp the meaning of the poems; if, however, one attempts to read them based on the *meaning* of the characters, they become gibberish. This problem was solved by devising the *kana* syllabary, a system of 50 symbols that form the building blocks of Japanese words. By the late ninth century, a social divide had arisen between predominantly male, Buddhist, elite users of literary Chinese and literate women and members of the lower elites who favored the *kana* system. As in China and Korea, the technology of printing spurred the circulation of these works and pushed functional literacy to some of the highest premodern levels in the world.

The most important literary developments to come from the use of *kana* were the novel and the prose diary. The former is credited to Murasaki Shikibu, whose *Tale of Genji* is often considered the world's first novel. Seclusion for court women fostered self-analysis, and Murasaki's writing illuminates the tension between Buddhist ideas and the requirements of the court.

Vietnam: Human Agency and State Building

Modern scholars of Southeast Asia emphasize the similarities of the lived experience of the common people on both sides of the cultural divide between areas influenced by India and those influenced by China. This approach considers the agency of people: their taking of the initiative in deciding matters of acculturation, political systems, and so forth. Here, we explore the agency of people in their acceptance and rejection of certain influences and innovations.

The Setting and Neolithic Cultures

Southeast Asia stretches from the borders of Assam in India to the Mekong delta in the south of what is now Vietnam. The region is divided into watersheds separated by mountain ranges running generally parallel to them. Even today much of the region is heavily forested, with abundant rainfall supplied by the summer monsoon, which acts as the region's principal climatic regulator. The river valleys and coastal plains are believed to have supplied the wild ancestors of the first rice plants (see Map 13.5).

The Neolithic revolution appears to have taken place in Southeast Asia at about the same time as it did in Southwest Asia. The origins of these peoples are obscure, with speculation centering on a homeland perhaps in southern China. Out of the fertile subtropical and tropical regions in which they settled, it is believed that the basics of wet rice agriculture and the domestication of chickens and pigs may well have diffused north into China and perhaps west to northern India.

Village Society and Buddhism   The earliest records of the peoples and states in the region are likewise fragmentary. Late Zhou Chinese references frequently

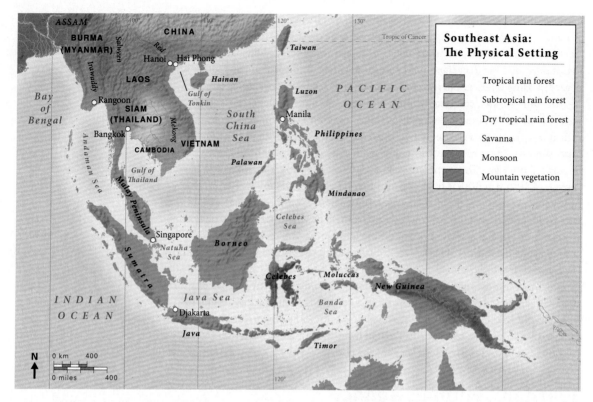

MAP 13.5 **Southeast Asia: The Physical Setting**

Bride-price: Amount negotiated between the family of the groom and the family of the bride to be paid by the former to the latter in some marriage traditions, as compensation for the loss of her labor.

mention the state of Yue, but its southern borders appear to have been fluid. The social structure suggests a village-based agricultural system in which women enjoyed far more equality than would later be the case. Villages and clans were often bilateral or matrilineal and matrilocal. Men paid a **bride-price** to the families of their wives, and divorce for either spouse appears to have been relatively easy. As in other places in East Asia during the first millennium BCE, women occupied roles as officials, diplomats, merchants, and small-business operators. The area also became one of the first outposts of Buddhism, which would come to be the majority religion in the region for the next 2,000 years.

Nam Viet: History and Politics to 1450 With the unification of China under the Qin in 221 BCE, Yue was incorporated into the First Emperor's new state. Thus began a period of Chinese occupation and local resistance in the area lasting over 1,000 years. As in Korea, the occupation brought with it Chinese culture, including writing, political ideas, and cultural preferences. Like their counterparts in Korea and Japan, the new Vietnamese literate elites were incorporated into the world of Chinese civilization and the Buddhist cultural and religious sphere. Southeast Asia's geographical position in the center of the maritime portion of this sphere encouraged openness to outside influences.

Sinicization and Resistance Repeated invasions from the north also encouraged the formation of a Vietnamese ethnic identity. The collapse of the Qin in the period 206–202 BCE encouraged a rebellion against the local Chinese officials of *Nam Viet*—the Vietnamese equivalent of Chinese *Nanyue* ("Southern Yue"), as the

Qin had called their new southern province. The Han emperor Wudi reoccupied northern Vietnam in 111 BCE and reimposed Chinese institutions on the region.

Han attempts at sinicization raised tensions between the new Chinese-influenced elites and those who retained their cultural independence. In 39 CE a rebellion began that to this day is commemorated as helping to form the modern Vietnamese national identity. Trung Trac, the widow of a local leader executed by the Chinese, and her sister Trung Nhi (both ca. 12–43 CE) led their local militia and defeated the Han garrison, sparking a general revolt. The Chinese, however, soon overpowered the forces of the Trung sisters, who according to some Vietnamese accounts drowned themselves rather than be taken alive. For the next millennium, northern Vietnam would remain within the imperial Chinese orbit.

In the three and a half centuries following the breakup of the Han Empire in 220 CE, the region gained some political autonomy, but the power of Vietnam's sinicized elites continued to ensure their loyalty to China. With the reunification of China under the Sui and Tang, the drive for Chinese political control of the Vietnam region as well as Korea was taken up again, and the north was soon fully reincorporated into imperial China. During the political chaos following the fall of the Tang, however, the long-awaited opportunity for independence arrived again.

Independence   Dinh Bo Linh, the first emperor of Vietnam, solidified his control of the region in 968. Though politically independent of China, Vietnam's new Li dynasty (1010–1225), long immersed in Chinese notions of Confucianism and statecraft, instituted Song-style institutions and created its own bureaucracy. Continuing a pattern of expansion, the Li pushed south during the dynasty's two centuries of control.

With the fall of the Li dynasty, the Tran dynasty (1225–1400) soon faced the threat of the Mongols, who in 1280 would subdue the southern Song in China and form the Yuan dynasty. The Mongols made three attempts at invasion, but the unsuitability of Mongol strategy and tactics and the resistance of the Vietnamese ultimately prevented further Mongol expansion and allowed the Tran to keep the dynasty intact.

Cultural and Political Conflict   Even during the height of the Mongol threat, the Tran continued to push southward. Much of this drive was aimed at the state of Champa, which itself had ambitions to achieve regional dominance. Centuries before, the Vietnamese had expanded at the expense of Champa. Champa and the Khmers (Cambodians), influenced by India, had briefly united to subdue another Indian-influenced state, the trading kingdom of Funan, in the 600s. A reconstituted Champa now represented not just a strong political threat but—as a Sanskrit, Hindu, and Theravada Buddhist state—a cultural rival, as well. In the resulting war, the new Le dynasty of Dai Viet ("Great Viet"), founded in 1428 by Le Loi, decisively broke the power of the Champa in 1471. The remnants of their state were incorporated into Vietnam in 1720.

Economy, Society, and Family

Since the Neolithic domestication of rice, Vietnam has been one of the world centers of wet rice cultivation. In the eighteenth century, roughly 90 percent of the people were engaged in agriculture, a figure consistent with other East Asian agrarian-based societies. As in those societies, the rhythms of the agricultural year were governed by the monsoon cycle. During the long rainy season of the summer, rice, vegetables, and commercial crops would be cultivated.

As in southern China and Japan, families could be sustained on relatively small amounts of land and required few complex tools. Along with draft animals like water buffalo, these would often be held communally by clans within the village. Villages consisted of raised, thatch-roofed dwellings, surrounded by a bamboo fence and centered on a shrine to the ancestral spirits.

Politics, Labor, and Trade   Two key political institutions kept order. The village headman was elected, but had to be approved by the imperial court, which, like its Chinese counterpart, ruled through a Confucian bureaucracy of provincial governors, prefects, and magistrates. The headman collected the taxes and dues and sat with a council of notables. His powers, however, were checked by the council itself, which consisted of members of a scholar-gentry class. Thus, there was a balanced tension between the power of the central government and local interests.

One legacy of the Chinese occupation was the use of conscription and corvée (unpaid, forced) labor by Vietnamese dynasties. Peasants were required to serve in the army four months per year—indefinitely during national emergencies. They could also be sentenced to slave labor for various offenses. In many cases, they would be sent to open up virgin land for agriculture, which would be theirs to keep upon the expiration of their sentences.

Changing Position of Women   One pattern of history the Vietnamese shared with the other societies we have examined in this chapter is that of changes in the status of women over time. The nature of the agricultural work undertaken was communal, and men and women worked in the fields together. As in Korea and Japan, kinship lines were bilateral—traced through either spouse—or matrilineal. Chinese influence and Neo-Confucian emphasis on filial piety, hierarchy, and separate roles for men and women eroded this equality, though less markedly in Vietnam than in Korea or Japan. In villages, ports, and market cities, women were merchants, entrepreneurs, and craftspeople. This was reinforced by the prominence of the different Mahayana schools of Buddhism. Buddhist nuns and abbesses wielded considerable power, though their positions were often at odds with the Confucian precepts of the elites. Still, women's rights to divorce and property ownership were upheld in the Neo-Confucian law code of 1460.

Religion, Culture, and Intellectual Life

As they struggled to maintain their political independence, the Vietnamese developed their own cultural distinctiveness. While the porous border region with southern China and geographical and ethnic ties to other Southeast Asian peoples ensured a flow of influences, not all were readily absorbed.

Mahayana and Theravada Buddhism in Vietnam   Whether the practice of ancestor veneration arrived with the Chinese or whether it was present before is as yet unsettled. Nearly all villages had a shrine for a founding ancestor where periodic ceremonies honoring him would take place. As in Korea, the coming of the Han emperor Wudi's armies in the second century BCE brought the imperial system of the Son of Heaven as intermediary between heaven and earth. At about the same time, however, Theravada Buddhism was being established in the Indianized ports of Southeast Asia. Although the Han retreat from the north allowed for the emergence of Mahayana Buddhism in the area, it was Indian-influenced Theravada that would dominate the religious and cultural life of Vietnam for centuries to come.

Later, the Tang occupation brought an infusion of Mahayana influence as well as the entire spectrum of Confucian and Daoist ideas. While Mahayana became the dominant division from this time on, the Vietnamese at the local level tended to pursue a synthesis of all of these systems in their beliefs. Similarly, the Vietnamese court sought to reconcile the differences among the systems by promulgating edicts on their compatibility. Indeed, some emperors sought to take a leading role in developing a unique strain of Vietnamese Buddhism.

Chu Nom   During the fifteenth-century consolidation of Dai Viet, the Le dynasty undertook a sinicization of the country, adopting Chinese law codes and dress. As in Korea and Japan, Chinese-style histories were compiled and court-sponsored literary projects commissioned. Here again, the literary language favored by the court for such projects continued to be the Chinese of the elites. As in Korea and Japan, an attempt was made during the tenth century to develop a vernacular writing system. Called *chu nom* ("southern characters"), the new script combined existing Chinese characters picked for the similarity of their sounds to Vietnamese words with newly invented Chinese-style characters for meaning. In theory, it would be easier to use as a tool for literacy. However, because it retained much of the complexity of Chinese characters, it never had the widespread circulation of hangul or kana in Korea or Japan.

Putting It All Together

While there are commonalities among the patterns of state formation and religious interaction along the outer ring of Chinese influence, each state responded to that influence in its own way. From the beginning, each state sought to maintain its political independence, though all acculturated to some degree to Chinese models. The attractiveness of those models was related to their usefulness in state building. That is, while the Koreans and Vietnamese struggled to throw off the Chinese political yoke, the systems and values of the invaders also gave tools to the invaded, allowing them to organize their new regimes after they had won independence. The invaders also came with moderating institutions like Mahayana Buddhism. They were therefore equipped with a wide range of options to adopt or discard, as the situation demanded. In that sense, the cultural intrusion was far more successful than the political one.

In the case of Japan, since the early Yamato state did not have Chinese traditions imposed on it from the outside, its leaders could afford to be more selective in what to adopt. However, the wholesale adoption of Chinese institutions proceeded even more quickly in Japan than on the mainland. Part of this may be attributed to the power that such institutions could provide to a government; part of it may also have been a sense on the part of the Japanese that states on the mainland based on these institutions were a potential threat.

By the end of the fifteenth century, all three of these states were in the process of consolidating civilizations based on Chinese models and prominently including Neo-Confucianism and Buddhism among their governing traditions. They may therefore be considered part of the dominant trend toward the formation of religious civilizations, a pattern we have emphasized in Part 3 of this volume. However, given the specific adaptations to local conditions, the three states were quite different from each other and from China. Yet faced with varying degrees of dislocation, foreign intrusion, or rebellion, all would seek similar solutions to these problems.

Review and Relate

| Thinking Through Patterns

Examine the ways historians approach the big questions of this chapter.

> **How was the history of Korea affected by its relations with China? With Japan?**

The various Korean kingdoms were affected by China through conquest. Chinese culture and institutions were planted in Korea during the Qin, Han, Sui, and Tang eras. This also prompted the Korean kingdoms to assert their political independence and to be discriminating about which Chinese institutions to adopt. Thus, Neo-Confucianism was adopted because of its use as a state-supporting ideology. Chinese writing, though useful as the means of acquiring the literature of China, ultimately yielded to the hangul system as more convenient.

> **Which important elements of Chinese culture were adapted by the Japanese for their own purposes? What advantages did Vietnam have over Korea and Japan in this regard?**

Korea served as both a cultural intermediary between Japan and China and as a mainland target for conquest. Thus, Korea's status as a buffer between the two regional powers made its position precarious.

In addition to the Bronze Age elements of wet rice cultivation and bronze implements, cultural elements, beginning with the Chinese writing system, were the most influential. With the writing system came ideas of government, ethics, philosophy, literature, and Buddhism. Unlike Korea and Vietnam, Japan acquired all of these more or less voluntarily and had the leisure to adopt them according to its own needs, rather than have them imposed by conquest.

> **Which Japanese adaptations of Chinese institutions did not work well in Japan? Why?**

While the Chinese writing system gave Japan a ready-made literature, the language itself was not well suited to the Japanese vernacular. Thus, by the 800–900s it had to be supplemented with the kana system. More serious was the less-than-perfect fit of the Chinese governmental structures with Japan's clan-based society. Cleavages developing during the Heian period would cause the social breakdown that resulted in the era of the shoguns, which lasted until 1867.

> **In what ways was the experience of Vietnam similar to that of Japan and Korea? How was it different?**

Like Japan and Korea, much of Vietnam was influenced by the importation of Chinese culture, including Buddhism, the imperial system, and Confucianism. Like Korea, and unlike Japan, Vietnam suffered centuries of Chinese invasion and occupation. But Vietnam, positioned on the border with the Indianized states of Southeast Asia, also was influenced by Indian culture in its southern and western areas, causing interactions and adaptations that did not take place in the other states inside the Chinese sphere of cultural and political influence.

| **Against the Grain**

Consider this as a counterpoint to the main patterns examined in this chapter.

Zen and Bushido

One seemingly counterintuitive development in the political and religious history of Japan is the marriage of a sect of Buddhism—a pacifistic belief system—to the warrior nobility of Japan, the *daimyo*, and their retainers, the samurai. Zen Buddhism became the central religious practice of the warrior classes. The adoption by warriors of a pacifistic creed is not unique to Japan—one need only consider the history of Christianity to see some broad parallels. But Christianity, as the state religion of Rome and its successor empires and kingdoms, was the only approved religion for all classes. Zen was one of many competing variants of Buddhism available to Japanese warriors. So how does one account for its appeal?

Perhaps we may view it this way: While Buddhism teaches respect for all sentient beings, the duties of a warrior might induce one to extend the ideal of "nonattachment" to a state of indifference toward one's own life or death—and by extension to that of others. Moreover, the rigors of Zen practice are not unlike those of military training: breaking down the ego by performing humbling tasks, being remade by strict discipline and constant repetition, and finally achieving a new "self." There is also an element of elitism in becoming one of the few who achieve the highest levels, though those who do reach them are expected to be humble in their bearing. Zen thus provides a balance of opposites—the strict discipline to fight without regard for one's own safety on the battlefield, and in the process to transcend the self, reaching a state that brings the flash of enlightenment—*satori*. This condition of disciplined mindfulness extended to poetry, painting, and calligraphy, providing the basis for yet another unity of opposites: the dual way of the sword and the writing brush unique to Japan.

- Are there other religions in Japan (such as Shinto) that might work equally well for warriors? Why?

- Is Japan unique in adapting a pacifistic religion for use by warrior classes? Can you think of ways that, for example, Christian warriors adapted their beliefs to support their profession?

Key Terms

Altaic   306
Bride-price   322
Hangul   312
Matriarchal   314
Matrilineal   314

Matrilocal   312
Microlith   314
Samurai   317
Shinto   319
Shogun   316

Shogunate   316
Striated   306
Syllabary   305
Zen   320

OXFORD
insight study guide
Active Engagement, Deeper Understanding

Learn more with this chapter's digital tools, including the Oxford Insight Study Guide, at http://www.oup.com/he/vonsivers4e. Please see the Further Resources section at the back of the book for additional readings and suggested websites.

Sources for Chapter 13

| SOURCE 13.1 | Murasaki Shikibu, *The Tale of Genji* |

ca. 1000

The daughter of a minor noble in the court at Heian-Kyo in central Japan, Murasaki Shikibu (ca. 973–1025) created Japan's most popular work of fiction and one of the world's great literary masterpieces. *The Tale of Genji* (*Genji Monagatari*) is composed of acute observations of the subtleties of court life, and Murasaki focused particularly on the lives of women at court. Although the tale is fictional, it reflects the era in which it was written, as the novelist strove to make the action in it plausible to the reader. In the process, she also crafted a compelling and compulsively readable story.

When he [Genji] returned to His Excellency's residence, sleep eluded him. Images of her [the Rokujō Haven, his love interest] as he had known her down the years ran through his mind, and he wondered in vain regret why she had taken such offense at each of his casual diversions, undertaken while he complacently assumed that she would eventually change her mind about him, and why she had persisted to the end in disliking him so. It seemed like a dream now to be wearing gray, and the thought that her gray would have been still darker if she had outlived him prompted,

> I may do no more, and the mourning I now wear is a shallow gray,
>
> but my tears upon my sleeves have gathered in deep pools.

Lord Fugen: A bodhisattva closely associated with the Lotus Sutra.

He went on to call the Buddha's Name, looking more beautiful than ever, and his discreet chanting of the scripture passage, "O **Lord Fugen** who seest all the manifest universe," outdid the most practiced monk's. The sight of his little son would start fresh tears for "the grasses of remembering" and yet without this reminder of her. . . . The thought gave him some comfort.

. . .

He now held the world and its ways, so distasteful already, in unqualified aversion, and he thought that without this fresh tie he would certainly assume the guise to which he aspired, except that every time his mind took this turn,

Source: Murasaki Shikibu, *The Tale of Genji*, trans. Royall Tyler (Harmondsworth, UK: Penguin, 2001), "Heart-to-Heart" (Aoi), 178–179.

he would straightaway start thinking how much his young lady in the west wing must miss him. He still felt a void beside him, however closely his women might gather around him while he lay at night alone in his curtained bed. Often he lay wakeful, murmuring, "Is autumn the time to lose one's love?" and listening, sick at heart, to the priests, whom he had chosen for their voices, calling the name of the Buddha Amida.

Oh, how sadly the wind moans as autumn passes! he thought as for once he lay alone and sleepless into a foggy dawn, but then a letter arrived on deep blue-gray paper, tied to chrysanthemums just now beginning to open and placed beside him by a messenger who left without a word. The delightful effect pleased him, and he noted that the writing was the Haven's.

> "Have you understood my silence? The sad news I hear, that a life can pass so soon, brings tears to my eyes, but my thoughts go first of all to the sleeves of the bereaved. My heart is so full, you know, beneath this sky."

Her writing is more beautiful than ever! He could hardly put it down, but her pretense of innocence repelled him. Still, he had not the heart to withhold an answer, and he hated to imagine the damage to her name if he should do so. Perhaps the lady he had lost had indeed been destined somehow to meet this end, but why should he have seen and heard the cause so clearly? Yes, he was bitter, and despite himself he did not think that he could ever feel the same about the Haven again.

After long hesitation, since the Ise Priestess's purification might well present another difficulty, he decided that it would be cruel not to answer a letter so pointedly sent, and he wrote on mauve-gray paper, "My own silence has indeed lasted too long, but although I have thought of you, I knew that in this time of mourning you would understand."

▶ Working with Sources

1. What view of Japanese court life in the Heian period is revealed in this passage? How do the requirements of place, name, reputation, and hierarchy create tension for Genji?

2. What does the passage suggest about the religious beliefs and syncretism of Japanese society in this period?

SOURCE 13.2 *Nihongi (Chronicles of Japan)*

The early years of the Common Era saw the first descriptions in official Chinese histories of foreign territories like Vietnam, Korea, and as above, Japan. These areas are generally depicted as exotic, un- or semi-civilized places, with an emphasis on how their societies differ from that of China. As Chinese culture spread to the peripheral areas, all of them adopted Chinese forms of historical writing, though the subject matter often departed from stock Chinese themes. In this excerpt from Japan's first official history, the *Nihongi*, the creation of the Japanese islands themselves is addressed.

From the History of the Kingdom of Wei (ca. 597 CE)

The people of Wa [Japan] dwell in the middle of the ocean on the mountainous islands southeast of [the prefecture of] Daifang. They formerly comprised more than one hundred communities. During the Han dynasty, [Wa] envoys appeared at the court; today, thirty of their communities maintain intercourse with us through envoys and scribes. . . .

The land of Wa is warm and mild. In winter as in summer the people live on raw vegetables and go about barefooted. They have [or live in] houses; father and mother, elder and younger, sleep separately. They smear their bodies with pink and scarlet, just as the Chinese use powder. They serve food on bamboo and wooden trays, helping themselves with their fingers. When a person dies, they prepare a single coffin, without an outer one. They cover the graves with earth to make a mound. When death occurs, mourning is observed for more than ten days, during which period they do not eat meat. The head mourners wail and lament, while friends sing, dance, and drink liquor. When the funeral is over, all members of the family go into the water to cleanse themselves in a bath of purification.

When they go on voyages across the sea to visit China, they always select a man who does not comb his hair, does not rid himself of fleas, lets his clothing get as dirty as it will, does not eat meat, and does not lie with women. This man behaves like a mourner and is known as the "mourning keeper." When the voyage meets with good fortune, they all lavish on him slaves and other valuables. In case there is disease or mishap, they kill him, saying that he was not scrupulous in observing the taboos. . . .

Whenever they undertake an enterprise or a journey and discussion arises, they bake bones and divine in order to tell whether fortune will be good or bad. First they announce the object of divination, using the same manner of speech as in tortoise shell divination; then they examine the cracks made by fire and tell what is to come to pass.

In their meetings and in their deportment, there is no distinction between father and son or between men and women. They are fond of liquor. In their

Source: Wm. Theodore de Bary, ed., *Sources of East Asian Tradition*, vol. 1 (New York: Columbia University Press, 2008), 624–626; 628, 629.

worship, men of importance simply clap their hands instead of kneeling or bowing. The people live long, some to one hundred and others to eighty or ninety years. Ordinarily, men of importance have four or five wives; the lesser ones, two or three. Women are not loose in morals or jealous. There is no theft, and litigation is infrequent. In case of violations of the law, the light offender loses his wife and children by confiscation; as for the grave offender, the members of his household and also his kinsmen are exterminated. There are class distinctions among the people, and some men are vassals of others. Taxes are collected. There are granaries as well as markets in each province, where necessaries are exchanged under the supervision of the Wa officials. . . .

When the lowly meet men of importance on the road, they stop and withdraw to the roadside. In conveying messages to them or addressing them, they either squat or kneel, with both hands on the ground. This is the way they show respect. When responding, they say "ah," which corresponds to the affirmative "yes."

The country formerly had a man as ruler. For some seventy or eighty years after that there were disturbances and warfare. Thereupon the people agreed upon a woman for their ruler. Her name was Pimiko. She occupied herself with magic and sorcery, bewitching the people. Though mature in age, she remained unmarried. She had a younger brother who assisted her in ruling the country. After she became the ruler, there were few who saw her. She had one thousand women as attendants, but only one man. He served her food and drink and acted as a medium of communication. She resided in a palace surrounded by towers and stockades, with armed guards in a state of constant vigilance. . . .

From the Nihongi, The Birth of the Land (early 8th century CE)

Before the land was created, there were twelve deities, whose "forms were not visible." Izanami and Izanagi were the last of these, not the first, but they were directed by the other deities in concert to solidify the drifting flotsam and jetsam on the sea to shape the land. In the subsequent profusion of creativity, many islands and regions were formed, each reflecting the Japanese people's strong sense of place and pluralism.

Izanagi and Izanami stood on the floating bridge of Heaven and held counsel together, saying, "Is there not a country beneath?" Thereupon they thrust down the jewel-spear of Heaven and, groping about therewith, found the ocean. The brine which dripped from the point of the spear coagulated and became an island which received the name of Ono-goro-jima.

The two deities thereupon descended and dwelt in this island. Accordingly they wished to become husband and wife together, and to produce countries.

So they made Ono-goro-jima the pillar of the center of the land.

Now the male deity turning by the left and the female deity by the right, they went round the pillar of the land separately. When they met together on one side, the female deity spoke first and said, "How delightful! I have met with a lovely youth." The male deity was displeased and said, "I am a man, and by right should have spoken first. How is it that on the contrary thou, a woman, shouldst have been the first to speak? This was unlucky. Let us go round again." Upon this the two deities went back, and having met anew, this time the male deity spoke first and said, "How delightful! I have met a lovely maiden."

Then he inquired of the female deity, saying, "In the body is there aught formed?"

She answered and said, "In my body there is a place which is the source of femininity." The male deity said, "In my body again there is a place which is the source of masculinity. I wish to unite this source-place of my body to the source-place of thy body." Hereupon the male and female first became united as husband and wife.

Now when the time of birth arrived, first of all the island of Ahaji was reckoned as the placenta, and their minds took no pleasure in it. Therefore it received the name of Ahaji no Shima.

Next there was produced the island of Ō-yamato no Toyo-aki-tsu-shima. (Here and elsewhere [the characters for Nippon] are to be read Yamato.)

Next they produced the island of Iyo no futa-na and next the island of Tsu-kushi. Next the islands of Oki and Sado were born as twins. This is the prototype of the twin-births which sometimes take place among mankind.

Next was born the island of Koshi, then the island of Ō-shima, then the island of Kibi no Ko.

Hence first arose the designation of the Great Eight-Island Country.

Then the islands of Tsushima and Iki, with the small islands in various parts, were produced by the coagulation of the foam of the salt-water.

▶ **Working with Sources:**

1. **What similarities in the form of the Chinese and Japanese accounts do you see?**

2. **Why would the *Nihongi* start with the role of the gods in the creation of the land?**

SOURCE 13.3   *Haedong kosŭng chŏn*, on Buddhism in Korea

ca. 1215

The *Lives of Eminent Korean Monks* is a compilation of biographies of Buddhist monks from the Three Kingdoms period of Korean history (first century BCE through tenth century CE). It promotes Buddhist piety by stressing the (often supernatural) deeds of these monks, and it is also a valuable source for Korean history. In spite of its importance, the work was

Source: "Púpkong Declares Buddhism the National Faith," in Peter H. Lee, ed. *Sourcebook of Korean Civilization*, vol. 1, *From Early Times to the Sixteenth Century* (New York: Columbia University Press, 1993), 75–77.

long thought lost until portions of it were found at a Buddhist temple in the early twentieth century. This passage of the *Lives* deals with the introduction of Buddhism as the national faith of the Silla Kingdom in 527 CE, under King Pŏpkong.

The monk Pŏpkong was the twenty-third king of Silla, Pŏphŭng [514–540]. His secular name was Wŏnjong; he was the first son of King Chijŭng [500–514] and Lady Yŏnje. He was seven feet tall. Generous, he loved the people, and they in turn regarded him as a saint or a sage. Millions of people, therefore, placed confidence in him. In the third year [516] a dragon appeared in the Willow Well. In the fourth year [517] the Ministry of War was established, and in the seventh year [520] laws and statutes were promulgated together with the official vestments. After his enthronement, whenever the king attempted to spread Buddhism his ministers opposed him with much dispute. He felt frustrated, but, remembering Ado's devout vow, he summoned all his officials and said to them: "Our august ancestor, King Mich'u, together with Ado, propagated Buddhism, but he died before great merits were accumulated. That the knowledge of the wonderful transformation of Śākyamuni should be prevented from spreading makes me very sad. We think we ought to erect monasteries and recast images to continue our ancestor's fervor. What do you think?" Minister Kongal and others remonstrated with the king, saying, "In recent years the crops have been scarce, and the people are restless. Besides, because of frequent border raids from the neighboring state, our soldiers are still engaged in battle. How can we exhort our people to erect a useless building at this time?" The king, depressed at the lack of faith among his subordinates, sighed, saying, "We, lacking moral power, are unworthy of succeeding to the throne. The yin and the yang are disharmonious and the people ill at ease; therefore you opposed my idea and did not want to follow. Who can enlighten the strayed people by the wonderful dharma?" For some time no one answered.

In the fourteenth year [527] the Grand Secretary Pak Yŏmch'ok (Ich'adon or Kŏch'adon), then twenty-six years old, was an upright man. With a heart that was sincere and deep, he advanced resolutely for the righteous cause. Out of willingness to help the king fulfill his noble vow, he secretly memorialized the throne: "If Your Majesty desires to establish Buddhism, may I ask Your Majesty to pass a false decree to this officer that the king desires to initiate Buddhist activities? Once the ministers learn of this, they will undoubtedly remonstrate. Your Majesty, declaring that no such decree has been given, will then ask who has forged the royal order. They will ask Your Majesty to punish my crime, and if their request is granted, they will submit to Your Majesty's will."

The king said, "Since they are bigoted and haughty, we fear they will not be satisfied even with your execution." Yŏmch'ok replied, "Even the deities venerate the religion of the Great Sage. If an officer as unworthy as myself is killed for its cause, miracles must happen between heaven and earth. If so, who then will dare to remain bigoted and haughty?" The king answered, "Our basic wish is to further the advantageous and remove the disadvantageous. But now we have to injure a loyal subject. Is this not sorrowful?" Yŏmch'ok replied, "Sacrificing his life in order to accomplish goodness is the great principle of the official. Moreover, if it means the eternal brightness of the Buddha Sun and the perpetual solidarity of the kingdom, the day of my death will be the year of my birth." The king, greatly moved, praised Yŏmch'ok and said, "Though you are a commoner, your mind harbors thoughts worthy of brocaded and embroidered robes." Thereupon the king and Yŏmch'ok vowed to be true to each other.

Afterward a royal decree was issued, ordering the erection of a monastery in the Forest of the Heavenly Mirror, and officials in charge began construction. The court officials, as expected, denounced it and expostulated with the king. The king remarked, "We did not issue such an order." Thereupon Yŏmch'ok spoke out, "Indeed, I did this purposely, for if we practice Buddhism the whole country will become prosperous and peaceful. As long as it is good for the administration of the realm, what wrong can there be in forging a decree?" Thereupon, the king called a meeting and asked the opinion of the officials. All of them remarked, "These days monks bare their heads and wear strange garments. Their discourses are wrong and in violation of the Norm. If we unthinkingly follow their proposals, there may be cause for regret. We dare not obey Your Majesty's order, even if we are threatened with death." Yŏmch'ok spoke with indignation, saying, "All of you are wrong, for there must be an unusual personage before there can be an unusual undertaking. I have heard that the teaching of Buddhism is profound and arcane. We must practice it. How can a sparrow know the great ambition of a swan?" The king said, "The will of the majority is firm and unalterable. You are the only one who takes a different view. I cannot follow two recommendations at the same time." He then ordered the execution of Yŏmch'ok.

▶ **Working with Sources**

1. What does Yŏmch'ok's plan reveal about resistance to Buddhism in Korea in the sixth century—and about the role of an advisor to the Korean king in the period?

2. What seems to have been the role of self-sacrifice in the establishment of Buddhism in Korea?

| SOURCE 13.4 | Copper head of Bodhisattva Avalokiteshvara, Vietnam |

eighth–ninth century CE

This head, crafted from copper alloy, is all that remains of an impressive image found in central Vietnam. It depicts the Avalokiteshvara, the embodiment of Buddhist compassion, and the Amitabha Buddha is perched on the crown. It points to the emergence of a pan–Southeast Asian bodhisattva type in the eighth and ninth centuries, as well as to the superb metal-casting skills of artisans in the Cham territories of Vietnam.

▶ Working with Sources

1. How does the image reveal the phenomenon of "religious civilizations interacting" and the emergence of an international Buddhist culture in Southeast Asia?

2. What does the head suggest about the social structure of Vietnam in this period?

Source: Thierry Ollivier. © RMN-Grand Palais/Art Resource, NY.

World Period Three

The Formation of Religious Civilizations, 600–1450 CE

The rise of religious civilizations on the continents of Asia, Europe, and Africa is a striking phenomenon that unifies the period of 600–1450 in world history. It can be considered as a continuation of the intellectual and institutional transformations that began with the emphasis on monotheism and monism by the visionaries of the mid-first millennium BCE as ways to understand the world in which they lived.

The religious civilizations were not monolithic and displayed many regional variations. Internal diversity notwithstanding, they shared a number of common characteristics:

- Religious civilizations formed in regions which were larger than any single state within them: They superseded empires as the largest units of human unification.

- The civilizations were *scriptural*—that is, based on canonical (commonly agreed on) texts inherited in most cases from earlier periods. Members of educated elites (clergy, scholars, sages) taught and interpreted the scriptures to the laypeople.

- Despite hostilities among the religious civilizations, merchants, missionaries, pilgrims, and travelers visited each other's areas. They fostered a lively exchange of technical and cultural innovations from one end of Eurasia and Africa to the other.

Chapter 14

Patterns of State Formation in Africa

600–1450 CE

CHAPTER FOURTEEN PATTERNS

Origins, Interactions, Adaptations Intensified patterns of interactions and adaptations developed in Sub-Saharan Africa during the period 600–1450. Egyptian-Syrian Coptic Christianity was adopted by the Nubian and Ethiopian kingdoms. At the same time, Muslim merchants from Iraq and Iran created a string of independent city-states along the East African coast. In West Africa, pagan kings, and later, conquering emperors who had converted to Islam, founded states stretching from the Sahara to the edge of the rain forest in association with Muslim merchants from North Africa. In all these areas, adaptation processes produced distinctly African variations of Christianity and Islam, as well as uniquely African forms of cultural expression.

Uniqueness and Similarities In the interior of Africa, political and cultural transformation was considerably slower. Here, as in many areas of the Americas, the specific climatic, soil, and health conditions were less conducive to population growth, urbanization, and social stratification. Generally, clan and village societies prevailed, although increased commercial relations with the north accelerated the growth of kingdoms and palace towns along the coasts of West Africa and Southeast Africa. In strong interaction with its neighbors, Sub-Saharan Africa adapted to their influences in its own specific ways.

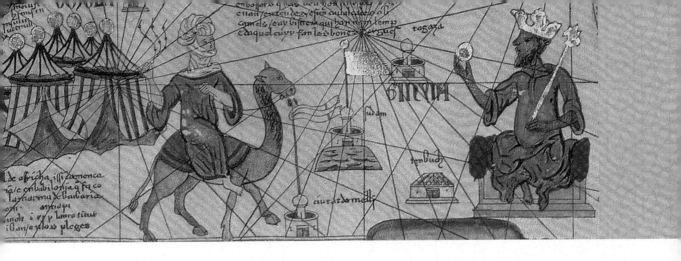

According to local tradition, the founder of the gold-trading kingdom of ancient Ghana (ca. 400–1200) in West Africa was Dinga. He was said to be a descendant of Bilal, the Ethiopian whom, according to tradition, the Prophet Muhammad chose as the first muezzin, the person who calls the Muslim faithful to prayer. When Dinga arrived from Arabia to the Sahel, south of the Sahara Desert in West Africa, he asked a many-headed snake at a well for water. The snake refused, and Dinga subdued her through magic to receive his drink. After marrying the snake's three daughters, he fathered three sons, the eldest of whom was a half-human, half-serpent being who went to live underground. The two younger sons were still growing when their father returned to Arabia.

The second son grew into an inconsiderate man who mistreated his father's old servant. The third son turned into a much kinder person, giving the same servant his leftover meals. Years later, Dinga felt his end coming and summoned his two sons to give them their respective inheritances. The elderly servant, who had never forgotten the kindness of the younger son, persuaded this son to go first, disguised as his older brother, to receive the lion's share of Dinga's estate. The father bestowed his power of magic as well as the kingdom on the youngest son, while the older son received the more modest power of rain making.

The two sons struck a deal whereby Ghana would receive enough rain and gold as long as its people would sacrifice a virgin and a colt every year. After many years of sacrifices, a Wagadu man and admirer of a virgin about to be sacrificed slew the snake brother. As he was dying, the snake brother cursed the people of Wagadu, which lost its abundance of rain and gold. A parched and impoverished Ghana fell to its enemies.

This story gives us a glimpse of a main pattern underlying the history of sub-Saharan Africa between 600 and 1450: adaptation of African spirituality to Islam. The pattern displays itself particularly in West and East

CHAPTER OUTLINE

Christians and Muslims in the Northeast

Adaptation to Islam: City-States and Kingdoms in East and Southern Africa

Cultural Encounters: West African Traditions and Islam

Putting It All Together

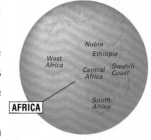

ABOVE: Detail from the Catalan Atlas (1375), showing Mansa Musa, the king of Mali, on his throne.

329

Seeing Patterns

> What patterns of adaptation did the Christian kingdoms of northeast Africa demonstrate in their interactions with the civilizations of the Middle East and eastern Mediterranean?

> What were the responses of Africans to Muslim merchants who connected them with the trading zone of the Indian Ocean and Mediterranean? As these Africans adapted to Islam, which forms of political organization did they adopt?

> In what ways did the economic and political transformations on the East African coast and West Africa affect developments in the interior?

Africa, whose rulers converted to Islam and incorporated Islamic beliefs and practices into their traditional African spirituality. In the northeast, Coptic Eastern Christianity prevailed in Ethiopia, although in adjacent Nubia it was replaced by Islam.

Christians and Muslims in the Northeast

Between 600 and 1250, Nubia was a Christian kingdom along the middle Nile in the Sahara and sub-Saharan steppe, built on agriculture and trade. Ethiopia, Nubia's neighbor in the highlands to the southeast, was similarly Christian but, unlike Nubia, was a collection of decentralized chiefdoms until one of the chiefs centralized rule in 1137. Both Nubia and Ethiopia were cases of the adaptation of sub-Saharan polities to the patterns of state formation of the Middle East.

Nubia in the Middle Nile Valley

About a century after the end of the kingdom of Meroë (see Chapter 6), small Nubian successor states dominated the middle Nile valley. In the course of the mid-500s, these states converted to Coptic Christianity and united into a single kingdom. Open to trade with the empire of the Arab Umayyads, Arab merchants came to dominate Nubian commerce. The position of these merchants led to Muslim political control: in 1276, the Egyptian Mamluks defeated the Christian king of Nubia and installed a puppet regime. By around 1450, Christianity in Nubia had largely given way to Islam.

The Rise of Christian Kingdoms in Nubia   In the early centuries of the Common Era, the use of the camel created a transportation revolution in the Sahara and opened up new routes for commerce and invasion. As a result, a new ruling class of Nubians arose in the middle Nile valley during the 400s. Nubian chiefs and their followers established three small kingdoms along the middle Nile that prospered in large part as the result of the rapid spread of the animal-driven waterwheel invented in Egypt in the first century CE.

In the 500s, Egyptian missionaries converted the Nubians to Christianity. New churches and monasteries were built, and kings and members of the ruling class sponsored these Christian institutions. As was the case among their contemporaries in the Mediterranean and Middle East, the Nubian rulers appreciated the unifying effect of a single state religion over the multiplicity of local cults.

Barely Christianized, Nubia now had to withstand an invasion of Arabs from Egypt. After the establishment of the Arab emirate of Syria, Iraq, and Egypt (see Chapter 10), the new governors in Egypt organized military campaigns into neighboring countries. In 652, one of these campaigns penetrated deep into Nubia. But an army of Nubian archers defeated the Arabs, forcing them to retreat. In a subsequent agreement, the two sides formally recognized each other. Later Muslim historians reinterpreted this pact, ignoring the defeat and presenting it as a treaty of submission to Islamic hegemony. Nevertheless, the pact endured and blocked the advance of Islam into East Africa for 600 years.

Royal Power and Governance   In the 700s, the three Nubian kingdoms were unified by a "great king." Power remained largely decentralized, however, with an official called an "eparch" who governed the northern subkingdom. The **Coptic** patriarch of Alexandria appointed the bishops, who were independent from the kings, in contrast to bishops in Catholic Europe at the same time (see Chapter 11).

In terms of financial administration, vassal rulers were probably powerful landlords who sent presents to the great king. As in Europe, abbots of monasteries were also landlords to whom peasant farmers paid rent. Most likely, in the vicinity of the great king's residence some basic fiscal mechanisms existed whereby village headmen delivered taxes in kind. Another source of income for the kings and eparchs was long-distance trade. In this respect, the Christian great kings of Nubia were similar to their Islamic counterparts in eastern and western Africa.

Agriculture   The farmland of the Nubian villages consisted of arable land on the fertile banks of the Nile. The annual summer floods between June and September left this land covered with rich sediment. Palm orchards helped to anchor the silt, and stone walls and jetties built into the Nile captured additional amounts of alluvial soil. As the floods receded in fall, villagers grew sorghum, millet, barley, wheat, and cotton.

Higher fields away from the banks required waterwheels for irrigation and were planted during the winter. In the spring, farmers planted second crops on the banks and at higher elevations. Vineyards and wine making became more important as the kingdoms evolved. Farmers also kept cattle, donkeys, sheep, goats, and pigs.

Long-Distance Trade   The pact of 652 between the Arabs and Nubia included clauses concerning the trade of Egyptian goods for ivory and slaves. The latter two items came from the tropical territories on the White Nile, and the kings taxed the merchant caravans at various resting places along the way.

In the period between 800 and 1200, long-distance trade attracted Muslim merchants and craftspeople to the northern province of the Nubian kingdom. A money economy emerged, based on Islamic gold dinars. Muslim merchants also settled along the Red Sea coast, especially once the North African Fatimid caliphs had conquered Egypt in 969. To compete with the Iraqi Abbasid caliphs on the Persian Gulf, the Fatimids developed maritime trade with India through the Red Sea (see Map 14.1).

From Christian to Islamic Nubia   In the mid-1000s, the Fatimids (see Chapter 10) resettled unruly nomadic migrants from Arabia to Upper Egypt. These migrants and their neighbors began raiding Nubia in the early 1100s. The local rulers in northern Nubia, principal defenders against the raids, gained in power vis-à-vis the Nubian kings. Dynastic rivalries broke out, and in the 1200s both usurpers and pretenders to the throne appealed to Egypt for support. The Mamluks, who governed Egypt at this time (1250–1517, see Chapter 10), responded by including Nubia in their anti-Christian holy war efforts. They reinterpreted the pact of 652 as a treaty requiring regular tributes, particularly slaves, from Nubia. In 1276, they conquered Nubia, installed a Christian vassal king, and levied the *jizya* head tax, which non-Muslims in Islamic lands had to pay. The

Coptic Christianity: A branch of Christianity centered in Egypt that stresses the divine, monophysitic nature of Jesus, in contrast to Catholic Western and Orthodox Eastern Christianities, in which his human as well as divine nature are emphasized.

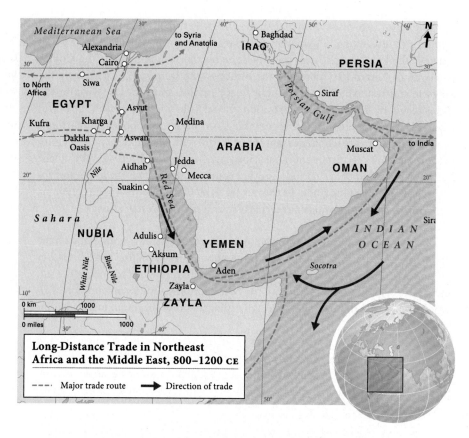

MAP 14.1 **Long-Distance Trade in Northeast Africa and the Middle East, 800–1200**

Christian dynasty eventually gave way to Muslim rulers, and by 1365 the Nubian kingdom had ceased to exist altogether.

Viewed in retrospect, the Nubian pattern of political formation resembled the feudal practices (see Chapter 11) of many other places around the world. In this pattern, kings acting as representatives of God on earth relied on the support of federated chiefs, who functioned much like vassals.

In addition, the patriarch of Alexandria never lost control over the appointment of Nubian bishops—unlike the pope in his struggles during the high Middle Ages with the Holy Roman emperors over lay investiture—and Nubian churches

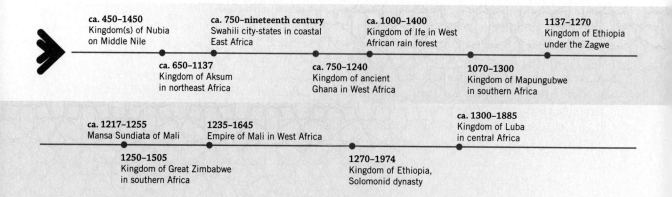

were outposts of the Egyptian Coptic Church. Had the Nubian Church been a "national church" like the churches in Europe (see Chapter 17), it might have been in a better position to resist Islamization once Muslim rulers took over.

Ethiopia in the Eastern Highlands

Although the Christian kingdom of Aksum had diminished to a chiefdom by the 600s, it continued (in cooperation with the Coptic Church) to represent the church's mission to convert the southern highland Africans. Eventually, new dynasties revived the mission, among which the Solomonids and their Christian Crusades were the most successful. In Ethiopia, the adaptation to Christianity was more thorough than in Nubia. The Ethiopians embarked on a pattern of forming an African Christian civilization.

Christianity in the Highlands   The kings of Aksum and the patriarch of the Coptic Church abandoned their capital by the mid-600s. They continued to trade ivory, ostrich feathers, musk, and myrrh for linen and cotton textiles and spices on the Red Sea, but no longer issued coins. When Muslim rulers in Egypt in the late 800s occupied ports on the west coast of the Red Sea and expanded trade with India and East Africa, Aksum became a partner in this trade and sold slaves captured in raids to the south. The Aksum kings campaigned southward, taking priests and settlers with them to convert the highland Africans. Reduced as it was, Aksum continued to be a factor in highland politics.

However, in the 970s the Africans subjected to conversion struck back. A queen, Gudit (Judith), led destructive campaigns in which churches and monasteries were burned, towns destroyed, and thousands of people killed or enslaved. After her reign of terror of a purported 40 years, a remnant of the Aksumite kingdom recovered and survived modestly for another century, but little is known about it.

State and Church under the Zagwe Kings   Political stability returned to the highlands with the Zagwe dynasty (1137–1270), some 300 miles south of Aksum. To its neighbors, the Zagwe kingdom was known as Ethiopia or Abyssinia, names rooted in the Hebrew and Christian Bibles. The Zagwe continued the Aksumite tradition of church sponsorship and missionary work in the south.

One king in the mid-twelfth century attempted to create an Ethiopian Church independent of the patriarch of Alexandria, but the Egyptian sultan refused the split. The Muslims were not about to relinquish the indirect leverage they possessed in Ethiopia through their political control over the patriarchs in Egypt. Had Ethiopia succeeded, the development of a "national church" would have occurred—the opposite of the situation in Europe at that time (see Chapter 11).

Church sponsorship expressed itself in the construction of 11 churches carved from subterranean rock during the early 1200s, called the Lalibela churches. The churches were arranged in two groups, separated by a stream named the Yordanos, after the biblical Jordan River. The policy of the Zagwe dynasty was the re-creation of Zion, perhaps in succession to Jerusalem, which the Muslims reconquered in 1187 from the western European crusaders. Accordingly, the dynasty used these churches during Holy Week for elaborate masses and processions.

Church of St. George, Lalibela, Ethiopia. Stonemasons cut this church and its interior from the surrounding rock formation. This and 10 other churches, built in the early 1200s, are part of a pilgrimage center created in the image of the Holy Land in Palestine.

Under the Zagwe kings, the conversion of the peoples in the central and southern highlands to Christianity resumed, and Christian settlers from the north were encouraged to colonize those lands. The central and southern highlands offered opportunities for the establishment of new villages, fields, and pastures. With its fertile volcanic soil, southern Ethiopia became one of the most productive agricultural regions of sub-Saharan Africa.

The political system that emerged in the center and south was an extension of what Aksum had pioneered in the north. Under a king ruling by divine right, Ethiopia was a confederation of provincial lords who lived in villages among their farmers and collected rents. Legally, ownership of the land was vested in families and had the status of inalienable property, with the family lords holding the right to collect rents.

The Solomonid Dynasty   Christians from the north now shifted their missionary efforts southward. In 1270, a new dynasty of kings, the Solomonids, emerged some 300 miles south of Aksum, in the region of today's capital of Ethiopia, Addis Ababa. These new kings claimed descent from a union between the queen of Sheba and the Israelite king Solomon. They also claimed to have inherited the Israelite Ark of the Covenant after the destruction of the First Temple by the Neo-Babylonians. The religious heritage of the Solomonids still lives on in Ethiopia. Outside Africa, this heritage has been embraced by the Rastafarians—Afrocentric Christians who form a small minority in Jamaica.

Ethiopian Christians and Coastal Muslims   During the 1300s and most of the 1400s, Ethiopia was a powerful kingdom. The kings commanded a sizable mercenary army, with which they extended their authority over small principalities of Christians, traditional Africans, and Muslims in the southern highlands and Rift Valley, as well as Muslim sultanates along the Red Sea coast. This extension began with the conquests of King Amda Seyon (r. 1314–1344). A century after the Mamluks had eradicated the crusader kingdom of Jerusalem in the Middle East (1291), Solomonid Ethiopia was carrying on the Christian holy war in sub-Saharan Africa (see Map 14.2).

The Muslim sultanates along the Red Sea coast relied principally on trade, linking East Africa via the Rift Valley with the India–Mediterranean sea lane. Farther away from the coast, the lands were too dry to support more than populations of camel nomads. Urban dwellers, nomads, and pastoralists had converted to Islam in the centuries after 800 when autonomous Muslim rulers in Egypt began the expansion of trade via the Red Sea with India and East Africa.

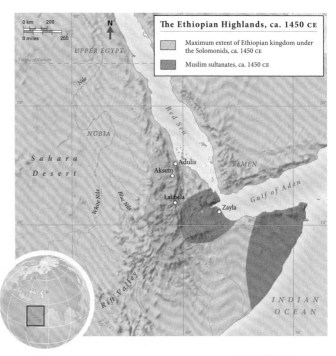

MAP 14.2 **The Ethiopian Highlands, ca. 1450**

Initially, the Ethiopian kings were ruthless in their efforts to subdue the sultans. But the kings were also pragmatic enough to exempt Muslim merchants and pastoralists from the church's missionary efforts in the south of the kingdoms. Similarly, in the end, the kings had little choice but to tolerate the sultans as Muslim vassals. Ethiopia became a multiethnic, multilinguistic, and multireligious empire in which the kings limited the church's conversion efforts.

Adaptation to Islam: City-States and Kingdoms in East and Southern Africa

During the period 600–1450, the Swahili people emerged as an indigenous African population of Muslims. They were divided into dozens of city-states along a 2,000-mile stretch of the African east coast, from today's Somalia in the north to Mozambique in the south. Swahili merchants were middlemen between the interior of East Africa and the Middle East as well as India. In the interior, increasing agricultural resources and trade with the Swahilis encouraged the expansion of chiefdoms but not yet the rise of kingdoms, except in the far south, in the middle Limpopo valley, and on the Zimbabwean plateau, where local people mined gold. Here, beginning around 1075, towns, cities, and kingdoms arose, the best known of which was Great Zimbabwe (ca. 1250–1505).

The Swahili City-States on the East African Coast
Arabs first established trade contacts in the 700s with Bantu-speaking villagers in coastal East Africa. In the following centuries, these villagers adapted themselves to long-distance trade and Islamic civilization. They evolved into an urban society

Patrician: Term used in this chapter to denote Muslims in Swahili society claiming Middle Eastern descent and, by virtue of profiting from long-distance trade with the countries around the Indian Ocean, either ascending to the throne of their cities as kings or governing their cities in councils, together with other patricians.

of kings, **patricians**, religious scholars, sailors, fishermen, and farmers based in small port cities. The kings and patricians were consumers of luxury goods brought to them by Middle Eastern and Indian merchants. The patricians acquired goods from the interior, which the Muslim merchants from overseas took back home.

Swahili Beginnings   The East African coast has few bays and natural harbors. Many small rivers open into the Indian Ocean, and their estuaries provide some room for anchorage. Only the Zambezi River in the south was large enough to allow longer-range water traffic and the building of inland towns. Islands, reefs, and mangrove swamps were numerous and favored the use of small vessels among the Swahilis for communication along the coast. Monsoons blowing from the southwest from April to September bring the northern half of the East African coast most of its annual rain. These monsoon winds facilitated sea voyages between Africa, the Middle East and India. The southern half of the coast has no reliable seasonal winds, making sailing conditions less predictable.

The majority of people in the interior of sub-Saharan Africa spoke Bantu languages and possessed a diversified agriculture and iron implements. In the mid-700s CE, a cultural differentiation between the Bantu-speakers of the interior and the east coast began to emerge as the coastal population adapted to Islam, while traditional African spirituality persisted in the hinterland. The earliest Muslim merchants in East Africa were Khariji dissidents from the Middle East. They had opposed the caliphs shaping the emergent Islamic state religion. The caliphs pushed the dissidents into political insignificance in distant provinces with limited agriculture. Given the challenges of these regions, the Kharijis took to trade.

Early on, the Kharijis were mostly interested in slaves, who were in great demand for rural labor in the Islamic empire. After a slave revolt from 868 to 883 disrupted the Abbasid Empire's trade through the Persian Gulf, large-scale rural slavery in the region ended. Black slave imports from East as well as West Africa continued on a smaller scale, however.

Adaptation to Islam   After the Kharijis lost their trade advantage, Muslim merchants from the heartland of the Islamic empire traveled to East Africa to purchase luxury goods such as ivory, hardwoods, and skins. One of the heartland cities was Shiraz, the capital of the Shiite dynasty of the Buyids (945–1055) in Iran. Wealthy Swahili merchant families associated themselves with them, claiming Shirazi descent. Members of these families migrated southward and founded new trading centers as far away as the Comoros Islands.

After 1050, mainstream Islam rose in prestige. Sharifian descent—that is, the possession of a genealogy going back to the Prophet Muhammad—began to rival Shirazi descent. Islamic families claiming Shirazi or Sharifian descent thus assumed dominant positions in the Swahili cities.

Urbanism   Swahili urbanism along the East African coast encompassed several hundred towns and about two dozen city-states of up to 10,000 inhabitants, either on the mainland or on islands off the coast (see Map 14.3). Many cities featured a central open space containing the Friday mosque for the congregational noon prayer, the main city well, and tombs of Islamic saints. Around the mosque were the inner cities of the patricians. Craftspeople lived in the less densely settled outskirts.

Separate commoner towns housed fishermen, boat builders, and sailors. Further inland lived non-Muslim client populations who traded meat and food staples to the cities. Cities, towns, and inland people thus formed loosely organized city-states under the leadership of the patricians.

Governance   In the period 600–1450, the Swahili city-states were governed by kings and/or councils of patrician elders. Mainland cities were more vulnerable and therefore more dependent on inland alliances than cities located on islands. Both hinterland and inland populations were trade partners whom the Swahili patrician merchants visited but among whom they did not settle. The merchants did not establish mosques in the interior, and the interior population did not convert to Islam.

The office of chieftainship as the traditional African institution binding lineage federations together served to express the communality of the cities and surrounding rural peoples. The mainland kings were Muslims, but in dealings with their non-Muslim allies they acted more like traditional chiefs. By contrast, the patrician councils in the island cities had no inland allies and at times even dispensed with kings.

The Swahili city-states and port states were considerably smaller than the Christian or Islamic kingdoms of Nubia, Ethiopia, and southern, central, and western Africa. Nevertheless, the patricians' regalia clearly expressed royal aspirations. The most important royal prerogative was the minting of coins. Given, however, that power on the Swahili coast was based on commercial, and not landed, wealth from which to collect taxes, in administrative practice the kings were never more than firsts among equals in the patriciate.

One prominent visitor was Zheng He, the admiral whom the Ming emperors entrusted with an Indian Ocean expedition and who in 1405 explored among other areas the Swahili coast (see Chapter 12). Even though his journey was principally for the purpose of displaying Ming power after the Mongol interlude, it can be seen as falling within the pattern of routine merchant journeys across the Indian Ocean and the South China Sea.

Traditional Kingdoms in Southern and Central Africa
The first region in the interior with a pattern of increasing wealth and population density during the period 600–1505 was southern Africa, on and around the Zimbabwean plateau. Here, the original foragers of the grasslands were adapting to the Bantu-speaking culture arriving from the north (see Chapter 6). Chiefs became powerful on the basis of large herds of cattle. Later, by trading with coastal Swahili merchants, the chiefs initiated a pattern of political formation, building cities and kingdoms, such as Mapungubwe and Great Zimbabwe.

The Kingdom of Mapungubwe   Khariji Swahili merchants from the north had founded the coastal town of Chibuene for the purpose of buying ivory. This trade added to the wealth accumulated by chiefs and marked the incorporation of the southern African hinterland into Swahili long-distance trade.

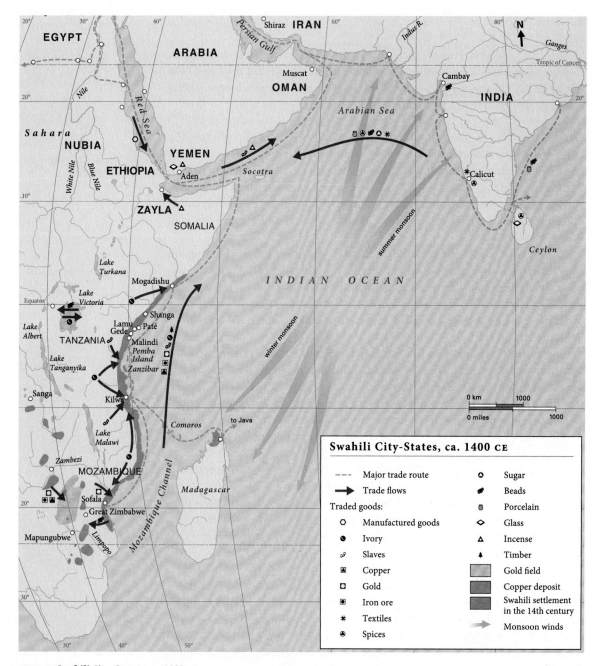

MAP 14.3 Swahili City-States, ca. 1400

When chiefs acquired cattle and imported goods from the coast, the first towns arose in the interior. Larger towns followed, culminating with Mapungubwe [mah-poon-GOOB-way], the capital of the first kingdom (1070–1300). Gold began to be mined in the early 900s and for the next four centuries was the major export item from Swahili cities to the Middle East and India. When Mapungubwe arose as an urban-centered kingdom, the southern African interior developed an urban craftspeople class who did not practice agriculture and cattle herding.

Gift of a Lion by a Swahili Merchant. This painting, which dates from the Ming Dynasty (1368–1648), depicts the exchanges between East Africa and the Ming court in China.

Excavations in Mapungubwe and ethnographic studies have yielded important insights into the institution of southern African kingship. The king resided on a hill that had previously been used for rainmaking ceremonies. He and his family were in ritual seclusion from the commoners, who lived in the town at the foot of the hill. The hill also contained residences for a few senior wives. Many female members of the royal family resided in villages outside Mapungubwe, where they were married to allies and clients of the kings.

The king was in charge of rainmaking ceremonies and harvest feasts, but the actual rituals were conducted by the diviner, an expert in spirituality. Although royal power was associated with spiritual authority, there was an institutional division between the king's power over life and death and the diviner's authority to summon the spirits. Thus, African kingship shared the pattern of rulership development encountered also in Eurasia and the Americas: royal power was legitimate only if combined with spiritual or divine authority.

Golden Rhinoceros. This golden rhinoceros was found among the items of the royal dynasty of Mapungubwe, signifying the power and magic of the kings. The kingdom was organized around the mining and trading of gold with the Swahili cities and, from there, with the Islamic Middle East.

The Kingdom of Great Zimbabwe   The kingdom of Great Zimbabwe (1250–1505) represents the culmination of the southern African kingdoms. Initially a tributary state of Mapungubwe, Great Zimbabwe emerged as a kingdom in its own right when the cooling and drying trend in the climate made agriculture in the Limpopo valley more difficult. Inhabitants abandoned Mapungubwe in the

Great Zimbabwe, Passageway. The person in the center, visible at the end of the curve, provides an idea of the scale of the massive urban structures erected under the kings. The stonemasons were highly specialized craftspeople, who constructed walls that outlasted the demise of the Zimbabwe kingdom in the middle of the fifteenth century.

second half of the 1200s, with evidence of some royalty migrating north to Great Zimbabwe.

Great Zimbabwe was located at the southern end of the Zimbabwean plateau, where gold was found. Granite for the construction of stone walls could be quarried easily, using heat from fires to split off layers of rock. At its height, the capital was the seat of a kingdom extending northward across the Zimbabwean plateau. Most settlements in the kingdom were dedicated to gold mining and trading, but the primary sources of income were cattle and grain.

Today, the best-known structure remaining of the capital is the so-called Great Enclosure within the Western Enclosure complex, an imposing 36-foot-high circular wall built of granite. The royal palace precinct contained buildings similar to those in Mapungubwe. All enclosures were once densely packed with houses, presumably occupied by the kings and/or the ruling classes. Commoners lived in simple thatched huts built outside the enclosures with timber and plastered with clay.

The kingdom of Great Zimbabwe ended around 1505 when Swahili merchants replaced the initial southern Limpopo trade route with the shorter northern Zambezi route.

Central African Chiefdoms and Kingdoms

The central African rain forest and savanna participated in the general pattern of increased agricultural production and population expansion between 600 and 1450. In the Congo Basin, relatively favorable agricultural conditions supported the formation of kingdoms. One savanna site, the Lake Upemba depression in the south of today's Democratic Republic of the Congo, was the home of the Luba people, who founded a kingdom sometime in the period between 1000 and 1300 (see Map 14.4).

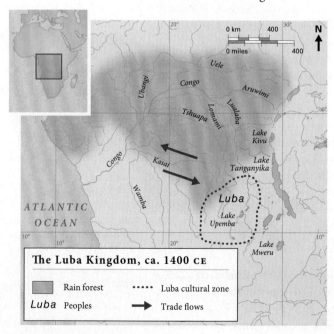

The Luba Kingdom, ca. 1400 CE

- Rain forest
- *Luba* Peoples
- ••••• Luba cultural zone
- → Trade flows

MAP 14.4 **The Luba Kingdom, ca. 1400**

Luba Origins Archaeologists date the earliest evidence for the existence of permanent agricultural and fishing settlements around Lake Upemba to the period around 800. Villagers relied on fish, sorghum, millet, chickens, goats, and sheep. Locally produced iron and salt added to the resources. Hunting groups formed the nucleus, around 1000, for the emergence of chiefs.

Similar to the kings of Mapungubwe and Zimbabwe, Luba kings possessed magic powers, which entitled only the descendants from their bloodline to succeed to the throne. The chieftains of other clans were excluded from the succession. A stable balance was established between the king and the chieftains, making Luba the model for subsequent kingdoms in the savanna of central Africa. The Luba kingdom itself survived until the beginning of Belgian colonialism at the end of the nineteenth century.

Cultural Encounters: West African Traditions and Islam

A pattern of regional trade, urbanization, and chiefdom formation was also characteristic for West Africa from the middle of the first millennium CE onward. Around 600, chiefs became kings when they unified their clans, conquered some neighbors from whom they collected tributes, and arranged alliances with others. Like their later African colleagues in the eastern half of Africa, they claimed to possess magic powers and adopted royal customs of seclusion. Two kingdoms, ancient Ghana and Mali, followed each other in the period 600–1450. Their royal–military ruling clans gradually converted to Islam, while the general population remained faithful to its African religious traditions.

The Kingdom of Ancient Ghana

Ancient Ghana emerged in the 600s and advanced to the status of a kingdom after 750, when it became the center for trade across the Sahara with the North African Islamic states. In the 1100s, however, drought and provincial unrest weakened Ghana. The kingdom gave way in 1240 to Mali, an empire which began its rise in the upper Niger rain forest and savanna.

Formation of Ancient Ghana   A period of progressive desertification (3000–300 BCE) had driven the inhabitants of the southern Sahara southward into what became the Sahel, a belt of steppe, grassland, and marginal agriculture. During the period 600 BCE–600 CE, the climate stabilized, and village formation expanded across the Sahel and northern savanna from Lake Chad in the east to the Senegal valley in the west. The city of Jenné-jeno emerged around 300 and was a center of regional trade of urban manufactures in exchange for iron and gold from the upper Niger and Senegal valleys and copper from the Sahara.

After 300, the regional trade became a long-distance trade. With the arrival of the Arabian camel, it became possible to travel through the desert. Long-distance merchants from the cities of Roman North Africa contacted Soninke merchants in the Sahel and exchanged Roman manufactures as well as Saharan copper and salt for gold. Cowrie shells, imported by Rome from the Indian Ocean and exported to West Africa, attest to trade connections even farther than the Mediterranean.

It took some time for the trans-Saharan exchanges to become regular. Only after the loss of their gold mines in northwestern Iberia to Germanic migrants did the Romans regularize the trans-Saharan trade, beginning in the mid-500s. The regularization had a profound effect in the Sahel. In the 600s, Soninke chiefs, enriched by the Saharan trade, equipped their followers with swords and lances and subjugated more distantly related Soninke groups in the Sahel between the Niger and Senegal valleys. In the mid-700s, one of the chiefs proclaimed himself king in Wagadu, a city in the Sahel northwest of the inland delta, and founded the kingdom of ancient Ghana (as distinguished from the modern state of Ghana).

Ancient Ghana lasted through the wet period of the first millennium (300–1100) and eventually succumbed to the successor state of Mali, when it could not adapt in the Sahel to the emerging dry period (1100–1500).

From Roman to Islamic Trade   Ancient Ghana received its gold from Bambuk, a region in the rain forest at the western edge of the kingdom. The Bambuk gold fields occupied a no-man's-land between the kingdom of ancient Ghana and the chiefdom of Takrur on the lower Senegal. Soninke merchants went no farther than nearby towns, from which they conducted their trading activities with the gold-mining villagers.

Romanized Berbers gave way to Islamized Berbers in the trans-Saharan trade after about 750. As was the case in Swahili East Africa, Khariji merchants pushed by the emerging Islamic empire into the outer provinces were the first Muslims to travel to the African interior. According to an eleventh-century Arabic source, Wagadu was a twin city, with its merchant and royal halves several miles apart. In contrast to their Swahili colleagues, the kings of Ghana avoided a combination of traditional kingship with Islam. Even though they benefited from including Muslims in their administration, they were not about to surrender their exalted, magical royal authority over life and death to the supremacy of Islamic law.

From African Spirituality to Islam in the Ruling Class   While the kings of Ghana retained traditional African spirituality, the Soninke merchants converted to Islam, which made business with the North African and Middle Eastern merchants easier to transact. By the early 1000s, the merchants in the trading towns near the Bambuk villages were Muslims, and the adjacent state of Takrur had also become Islamic. The sectarian Khariji Islam gave way to mainstream Sunnism.

In the early 1100s the kings of Ghana followed their merchants by also converting to Islam. The Sahel and savanna villagers, however, retained their African spirituality. As a result, Ghana now resembled the states on the Swahili coast and their hinterlands, where only the rulers and merchants were Muslim. In addition to the villagers, a number of allied Soninke chiefs remained faithful to traditional spirituality; and during the second half of the 1100s the cohesion of the kingdom began to weaken. In 1180, the founding clan of ancient Ghana ceded power to another clan, which established a new dynasty in Wagadu and adopted a policy of conquest of the southern savanna. For the next half century Ghana was an imperial power, trading gold not only from the Senegal River in the west but also from the newly conquered upper Niger and Black Volta Rivers in the south (see Map 14.5).

The Empire of Mali

The opening of new gold sources exposed hitherto marginal peoples to the influence of long-distance trade, royal rule, and Islam. One of these peoples, the Malinke, built the empire of Mali, a polity of many ethnic, linguistic, and religious groups. At its height, Mali stretched from the Atlantic to the Niger bend and from the Sahara to the rain forest.

Increased Trade   Mali was the beneficiary of the demand for gold in the Islamic realms on the other side of the Sahara. In addition to the existing Islamic mints, Christian mints in Europe began to stamp gold coins. In response to the

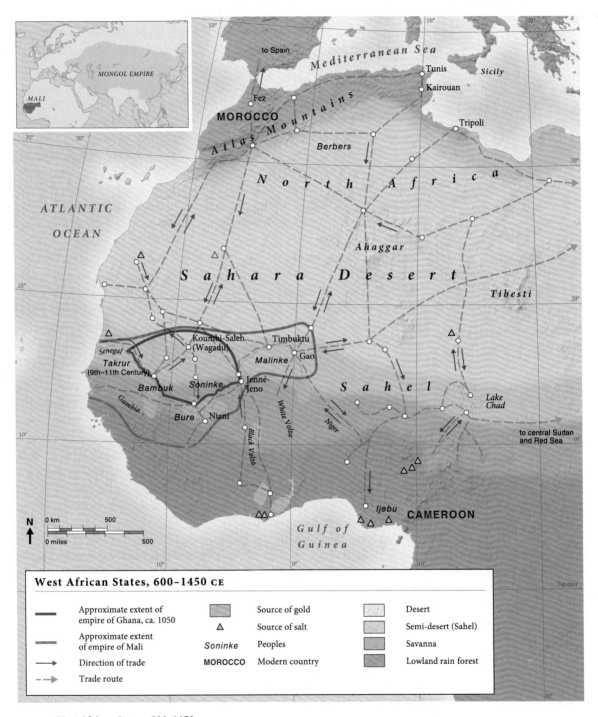

MAP 14.5 **West African States, 600–1450**

increased demand for gold, merchants encouraged the opening of new gold fields in the upper Niger and its tributaries.

The people in this region were Malinke villagers who spoke a language related to that of the Soninke in the north, but who were ethnically distinct. In the

The Sculptures of Ife

Forager, villager, and pastoral societies developing in the direction of chiefdoms, but not yet kingdoms, preserved traditional ancestor cults within their African spirituality. The sculptures, figures, and figurines of Africa played a role in that preservation.

As lineages evolved, generations of ancestors became an anonymous collective. The spirits of the ancestors in the invisible world, therefore, were conceived as being collectively present, to be consulted and nourished through sacrifices. One could "trap" them in sculptures, figures, and figurines, which emphasized the head, believed to be the seat of the spirit, at the expense of the torso and limbs, which were indicated in rudimentary fashion. The heads were generally fashioned in abstract ways, corresponding to the collective nature of the ancestors. These artifacts, therefore, were not "primitive;" their style was generic because the collective of the ancestors was generic.

When societies reached the level of kingdoms, kings became exceptional persons, endowed with ancestral magic (in Africa) or a transcendent divine mandate (in Eurasia) to exercise power, not merely chiefly authority. Generic ancestor "traps" would not do; artists had to apply the techniques of naturalistic representation so that the kings would recognize themselves in them. Of course, after a while sculptures turned into generic likenesses again (left), as they did in Mesopotamia and Egypt, since kingship became an ordinary institution with undistinguished kings not worth remembering.

Guardian Figure, Bakota Area, Gabon, Nineteenth–Twentieth Century. The abstract Bakota figure, above, with its generic geometric elements, represents the collective lineage spirit; the much more realistic Nigerian figure on the next page represents royalty who wished to be remembered individually.

course of the 1000s, these villagers had acculturated to ancient Ghana, which they recognized as overlord. When the new dynasty of Ghana conquered much of the Malinke lands at the end of the 1100s, resistance against the new rulers rose quickly. In a rebellion in 1230–1235, the Malinke not only liberated themselves but went on to conquer ancient Ghana.

The leader of the conquest was the inspiring hero Sundiata (ca. 1217–1255). He and his adventures were at the center of an **oral tradition**, with stories handed down from generation to generation. In the nineteenth and twentieth centuries, anthropologists recorded and translated these traditions. According to this tradition, Sundiata defeated ancient Ghana in 1235 and founded the empire of Mali, with its capital, Niani, on an upper Niger tributary in modern Guinea.

Oral traditions: Myths, tales, and stories (e.g., the foundation myth of Wagadu) handed down from generation to generation. In the absence of other sources, oral traditions should not be equated with history.

The Malian Empire   Mali was the first enduring empire in sub-Saharan Africa (1235–1645). At its height in the early 1300s, the territory of Mali was surpassed only by that of the contemporary Mongol Empire. At the core of the empire were Malinke clans whose kings and chiefs met in an assembly under the emperors and assumed the title of *mansa*. Oral tradition records the laws, customs, and traditions of which the assembly was the guardian and according to which the empire was governed.

As in ancient Ghana, Mali's power rested on a large, horse-borne army recruited from the Soninke clans. And like their royal predecessors in ancient

The Ife terra-cotta, copper, and bronze royal heads stem from that innovative time period of about 200 years (1100–1300) when kingship was new in Ife. The naturalism of these figures is striking, especially when one takes into consideration that Christian and Muslim figurative art during the same period was still nonrepresentative, in the sense of being hieratic—that is, it typically represented standardized ideas about how biblical and prophetic figures should look, so that their God-pleasing nature was immediately recognizable. The stripes on the faces of some Ife figures (right) are believed to represent scarifications, or the making of scars marking the passage from youth to adulthood or distinguishing one lineage from another, as practiced in parts of Africa.

Questions

- How does the history of African sculptures, such as those from Ife, provide evidence for studying the patterns of state building in this period?

- Why does material culture represent such an important dimension in understanding the African past?

Ghana, the Malian emperors relied on a small central administration run by Muslims as well as by slaves. The empire financed itself with tributes from vassal kingdoms in the Sahel and river chiefdoms with villagers and fishermen, as well as taxes on commerce of goods and manufactures. Since the new gold fields and the capital of Niani were located on a tributary of the Niger, the rulers relied on water transport downriver to the cities of Jenné-jeno, Timbuktu (founded in ca. 1100), and Gao. In the mid-1300s, these three cities replaced Wagadu as the main transshipment centers of goods for the Saharan caravans.

In 1324, the Malian ruler Mansa Musa (r. ca. 1312–1337) annexed the city of Timbuktu from its Tuareg Berber founders. There he founded a college and a library, part of the Sankoré Mosque. Timbuktu became a center of learning, focused on Islamic law but also offering ancillary fields of study which judges and independent scholars were required to know. The independent scholars were often members of merchant families who kept private libraries in their residences. In the mid-1400s, with some 100,000 inhabitants, the commercial and scholarly hub of Timbuktu was one of the larger cities in the world.

The Decentralization of Mali   Timbuktu flourished even while its imperial overlord, Mali, unraveled in the later 1300s. Dynastic disputes broke out, and outsiders, including rain-forest groups and Tuareg nomads, attacked from the south and north. As a result, some of the Sahel provinces broke away and established

The Sankoré Mosque of Timbuktu, Mali. The mosque evolved in the fourteenth century into a large university with a library housing hundreds of thousands of manuscripts. A preservation program under UN auspices seeks to restore and preserve these manuscripts today.

independent kingdoms. Deepening drought conditions eventually caught up with Mali, and by 1450, Mali had shrunk to a kingdom in the savanna.

Rain-Forest Kingdoms

The West African rain forest stretches from modern Guinea above the southwestern corner of West Africa to Cameroon on the bend to central Africa, where it transitions to the Congo rain forest. In the earlier period of 600 BCE to 600 CE, savanna peoples with iron implements had entered the rain forest and founded villages in clearings. As elsewhere in Africa, the region saw a pattern of political formation that included village clusters, chiefdoms, and kingdoms with urban centers and sophisticated crafts, such as bronze casting in Nigeria.

The Kingdom of Ife   The earliest village cluster to urbanize was that of Ife [EE-fay], the spiritual center of the Yoruba ethnic group and its oral traditions. By 1000 it was a kingdom with a walled capital with a palace, shrines, houses, and craft workshops. One highly developed art was sculpting, in terra-cotta, copper, or bronze.

Sungbo's Eredo   Ife set the example for other chiefdoms to develop as kingdoms between 1000 and 1450. Oyo, which expanded from the rain forest northward, arose as a trade center, trading with first Ghanaian and then Malian merchants. In the other chiefdoms evolving into a kingdom, leaders mobilized villagers for the construction of earthworks. One of these chiefdoms, Ijebu, encompassed a capital and villages on a territory of 22 square miles, surrounded by a combined moat and rampart up to 70 feet deep/high and 100 miles long, the Sungbo's Eridu. In nearby Benin, smaller earthworks around villages became the nucleus for an important kingdom in 1440. In both Ijebu and Benin, the moats and ramparts required centuries of hard labor with nothing more than iron shovels.

Scholars are still undecided over the purpose of these constructions: protection, boundary markers, toll collection, or perhaps all three? Equally difficult is an explanation for the collective labor: how were chiefs or kings able to motivate workers? As in the Americas and Pacific, where followers built huge temples or transported heavy stone sculptures across distances, authority buttressed by ancestral pedigree and spirituality can be seen as a powerful motivator.

Putting It All Together

Africa in the period 600–1450 displayed patterns of political and cultural development that included the creative adaptation of African spirituality to Christianity and Islam and indigenous kingdom formation. Adaptation depended on regional conditions and the degree of integration into Eurasian long-distance trade. The Nile valley and northeastern highlands incorporated Christianity into their local traditions. They adopted the Christian institutional division between kingship and church, in which kingship was a sacred office but subject to Christian law and ethics. The church, for its part, was an autonomous, hierarchical body. As in post-1000 Christian western Europe, the Nubian and Ethiopian churches were subject to a distant religious authority.

Coastal East and West Africa adopted Islam, which arrived through merchants. In eastern Africa, Islam took root among the coastal people and did not penetrate inland. In western Africa, merchants and kings converted, while the rural population of farmers and herders remained devoted to African spirituality.

In the same period, African kingship was a new institution with roots in the traditions of chieftainship in villages and village clusters. The kings emphasized their royal powers over life and death but also continued to claim the traditional chiefly powers of spirituality and magic. It is important to emphasize that Africa needed neither Christianity nor Islam to embark on its own distinctive pattern of kingdom formation.

Between 600 and 1450, however, this pattern clearly remained an exception amid the sub-Saharan population, the majority of whom remained stateless. They possessed chiefs but did not unite into larger polities or trade farther away than within their regions. The silent presence of this unrecorded majority of stateless Africans should be kept in mind, alongside the kingdoms and empires, in seeking to understand Africa's significance in world history during this period.

Review and Relate

Thinking Through Patterns

Examine the ways historians approach the big questions of this chapter.

In the period 600–1450, the northeast of sub-Saharan Africa was drawn into the orbit of Eastern Christian and Islamic civilizations without fully adopting their formative patterns. Perhaps the most extensive adaptation occurred in the sphere of trade. Beginning in 1250 in Nubia, the expansionist regime of the Muslim Mamluks in Egypt put the African Christians on the defensive. By 1450 the middle Nile region was Islamized. In contrast, an expansionist Christian Ethiopia put Muslims on the coast of the Red Sea on the defensive and Christianized the pagan southern highlands.

> What patterns of adaptation did the Christian kingdoms of northeast Africa demonstrate in their interactions with the civilizations of the Middle East and eastern Mediterranean?

❯ **What were the responses of Africans to Muslim merchants who connected them with the trading zone of the Indian Ocean and Mediterranean? As these Africans adapted to Islam, which forms of political organization did they adopt?**

❯ **In what ways did the economic and political transformations on the East African coast and in West Africa affect developments in the interior?**

The inclusion of the East African coast and sub-Saharan West Africa into the Muslim Indian Ocean and Mediterranean trading zone resulted in the rise of small coastal Swahili states and two large West African polities: the kingdom of ancient Ghana and the empire of Mali. Muslim mariners and merchants interacted with Islamized local African rulers and merchants to exchange Middle Eastern manufactures for African luxury commodities as well as slaves. Adaptation to Islamic religious civilization was a phenomenon limited to the ruling classes and associated merchant circles.

The adaptation of coastal East Africa to Islamic religious civilization had an indirect effect on the interior of southern Africa. Here, chiefs in Zimbabwe used the wealth from the Swahili trade network for the transformation of their chiefdoms into kingdoms. The East and West African expansion of trade under the impact of Islam may have also indirectly led to a population increase in the interior of Africa. Such an increase became noticeable toward the 1300s, especially in the Congo basin, where the Luba kingdom was the first to emerge.

| Against the Grain

Consider this as a counterpoint to the main patterns examined in this chapter.

Sundiata's Rise to Power

- What are the similarities and differences between the epics of Sundiata and Homer (Chapter 7)?

- Compare the messages of the Epic of Sundiata and Machiavelli's *The Prince* (Chapter 17). In what ways are they comparable, even if separated by time and region?

The Sundiata epic is the story of a disadvantaged hero who emerges triumphant. It begins with a king's sister: insulted by not receiving her fair share of a meal during a royal feast, she turns herself into a forest buffalo and devastates the fields of the kingdom's villages. Hunters from the neighboring kingdom of the Malinke slay her. The king rewards them with an ugly hunchback woman, heir of the buffalo spirit's forest powers. The reward is in fulfillment of a prophecy according to which the Malinke king has to find an ugly hunchback to give him a successor. But a jealous co-wife casts a spell, and Sundiata, the successor, is born a cripple. During puberty, thanks to the inheritance of his mother's forest powers, Sundiata stands up, uproots a tree, and becomes a physically superior hunter.

But the king's co-wife forces Sundiata into exile. Her own son, succeeding to the throne, is unable to withstand conquest by a neighboring king. A former blacksmith, this king is endowed with forest powers and tyrannizes the Malinke. In despair, the Malinke recall Sundiata from exile. Sundiata prevails in the end because his beautiful sister sacrifices her honor. During a one-night stand in the tyrant's chamber she discovers his dark secret: a cock's spur attached to an arrow can break his invulnerability. Shooting one such arrow, Sundiata achieves his final victory and creates the empire of Mali.

Traditional West African spirituality is built on the conceptualization of a world created by a remote god, in which civilization and nature mingle. Accordingly, existence is embedded in pairs of opposing but complementary elements. These opposing pairs are skillfully woven into the epic, suggesting that figures marginal to village life, such as hunters or blacksmiths, can cut across the established social order with its jealousies and intrigues to tap into the forces of nature, and found new kingdoms and empires.

Key Terms

Coptic Christianity   331   Patrician   336
Oral traditions   344

OXFORD
insight study guide
Active Engagement, Deeper Understanding

Learn more with this chapter's digital tools, including the Oxford Insight Study Guide, at http://www.oup.com/he/vonsivers4e. Please see the Further Resources section at the back of the book for additional readings and suggested websites.

Sources for Chapter 14

| SOURCE 14.1 | *The Fetha Nagast*, Ethiopia |

Fifteenth century

In the classical period Ethiopia was a multiethnic, multilingual, and multi-religious state in which the kings limited the Church's conversion efforts. Nevertheless, the kings continued to emphasize their Christian identity, and this factor is reflected in their adoption and endorsement of the Fetha Nagast, or Law of the Kings, in the mid-fifteenth century. This legal code had originally been written in Arabic by a Coptic Christian in Egypt, probably in the mid-thirteenth century. While living under Muslim rule, the Copts were allowed to adopt portions of Justinian's law code and the resolutions of church councils for their own governance. Translated from Greek, and with many biblical passages added, the code connected Egyptian Christians to their Byzantine, Roman, and Judeo-Christian heritage, founding the basis of law squarely in that tradition. The Ethiopian monarchs had the Arabic source translated into Ge'ez (the state language of Ethiopia at the time), and the translator added a section on kingship, a portion of which is subsequently offered. The Law of the Kings remained the law in Ethiopia until 1930, when Emperor Haile Selassie I issued the country's first modern constitution.

CHAPTER XLIV

KINGS

Section I.

TH. The king you appoint must be one of your brethren. It is not proper for you to appoint over yourself an alien and an infidel, lest he multiply horses, women, gold and silver [to himself]. And when he sits on the throne of his kingdom, some priests shall write for him the Divine Book, so that he may keep it by his side and read it throughout his life, in order to learn the fear of God, his Creator, to observe his commandments, and to practice them, lest his heart become proud [and feel contempt] for his brethren. He must never swerve either to the right or to the left from what has been laid down in the Law, so that

Source: Excerpt from *The Fetha Nagast*, trans. Paulos Tzadua, ed. Peter L. Strauss (Durham, NC: Carolina Academica, 2009), 271–273.

his days and his sons' days may be prolonged in his kingdom [Deuteronomy 17:15f], and his faith in God may be perfect. **EB 9**. Because of faith the walls of Jericho were pulled down, when the sons of Israel marched around them for seven days. Because of faith, Gideon and Barak and Samson and Jephtha and David defeated the kings, served the cause of justice, found what they hoped for, were victors in war, and defeated the army of the enemy [Hebrews 11:30, 32f]. **RSTA 54**. And if the king becomes a heretic, from that moment he is no longer a king, but a rebel.

Section II.

Our Lord said in the Gospel: "Give to the king what is the king's and to God what is God's [Matthew 22:21]." And Apostle Paul said in his letter to the Romans: "Every one of you must be submissive to the authority of your ruler, since a ruler is appointed only by God. And God has appointed all these rulers...." [Romans 13:1f].

    St. John Chrysostom, in his explanation of this passage, has said: The Apostle had already shown [this] in his other letters, commanding the [lesser] chiefs to give due obedience to the higher chiefs, as the servant must obey the master. This the Apostle did, showing that Our Lord did not abrogate all the laws by His precepts, but confirmed them. And his saying: "Every soul" is because every man must conform himself to this; and his saying: "A ruler is appointed only by God," means that God has provided for the appointment of judges and rulers to take place, so that the world may become beautifully calm. And for that reason He has established the ruler, since equality of forces causes many wars. And God in His wisdom has established many kinds of authority, such as that of a man in respect to woman, the father in respect to the son, the old in respect to the young, the master in respect to the slave, the teacher in respect to the disciple, and, more so, the chief in respect to the one who is placed under him. The Lord acted in the same manner with the body, [creating] the head and placing the other parts under it; he also did thus with other animals, such as bees, **raza**, ants, antelopes, eagles, buffaloes, and all kinds of fish—every one has its chief, and when there is no authority there is confusion and lack of order. And his words: "Since he is God's minister calling thee to good and beautiful things," mean that he will lead you daily in your obedience to God. His punishments will be directed against those who rebel against God, murderers, fornicators, thieves, and wrong-doers; but his favors go to the obedient, who obey the Highest—Whose name be praised!—to those who despite the world and to those who do works of perfection and are righteous.

        . . .

Section III.

MAK 37. Let the king give honor to the order of the clergy, as Constantine, elected, faithful, and righteous king, and those who were after him did. Let him give from his wealth to each of them, according to their rank. First of all he shall give to the bishops, then to the priests, next, to the deacons, and then to those who are below them. He shall exempt them from tribute, presents, and the other things to be given to the rulers. Let him assign something to the churches for the maintenance of widows, orphans, and the poor, so that they

Raza: A type of bird.

may entreat God to strengthen the true faith with belief in the Holy Trinity, so that the day of the Christians' king may be long.

. . .

Section IV.

The king shall judge with equity in the middle of his people. He shall not be partial, either toward himself or toward the others, toward his son, his relatives, his friends, or the alien in any way which brings about injustice. And it is written in reference to kings: "The honored king loves justice, but the unjust king loves evil and injustice, to the ruin of his soul." And Solomon the wise has said: "To increase justice and save the oppressed is better than the offering and sacrifices" [Proverbs 21:3].

Do not take the wealth of anyone by violence; do not buy from him by force, either openly or by trick, in order not to be afflicted by God in this world and in the future. In this world, as befell the King Ahab and his wife Jezebel, when Naboth refused to sell him his vineyard and Jezebel schemed to kill him and took the vineyard; God smote Ahab and made his race perish; and next to him he smote Jezebel, and the dogs ate her in the aforesaid vineyard [2 Kings 21]. As for the future world, the Apostle said: "Wrong-doers and apostates shall not inherit God's Kingdom" [1 Corinthians 6:9].

▶ **Working with Sources**

1. **How does the author of this portion of** *The Fetha Nagast* **use biblical passages and historical comparisons to accentuate his points? Why?**

2. **What is the king's primary obligation to his people? Under what conditions could he lose his power?**

SOURCE 14.2 # Ibn Battuta: Journey to the East African Coast

ca. 1304–1369

Shams al-Din Ibn Battuta, a judge from Tangiers, Morocco, traveled the entire then-known world of Eurasia and Africa, with the exception of Western Christian Europe. He visited East Africa probably in 1331/2 but remained on the coast, in contrast to West Africa, where he traveled in the interior for more than a year. As brief as his East Africa travelogue is, his observations are extremely valuable, in that they provide us with descriptions of the spiritual life of the Islamic Berbera, Swahili, and Sofala people living

Source: Adapted from *Ibn Battúta Travels in Asia and Africa, 1325–1354*, trans. Hamilton A.R. Gibb (London and Boston: Routledge & Kegan Paul, 1929), 110–113.

along the coast, in distinction to those of the people of the African interior who adhered to their traditional ancestor spirituality.

. . . I took ship at Aden, and after four days at sea reached Zayla' [Zeila, today in Somalia], the town of the Berbera, who are a negro people. Their land is a desert extending for two months' journey from Zayla' to Maqdashaw [Mogadishu, today in Somalia]. Zayla' is a large city with a great bazaar, but it is the dirtiest, most abominable, and most stinking town in the world. The reason for the stench is the quantity of its fish and the blood of the camels that they slaughter in the streets. When we got there, we chose to spend the night at sea, in spite of its extreme roughness, rather than in the town, because of its filth.

On leaving Zayla' we sailed for fifteen days and came to Maqdashaw, which is an enormous town. Its inhabitants are merchants and have many camels, of which they slaughter hundreds every day. . . . When a vessel reaches the port, it is met by *sumbuqs*, which are small boats, in each of which are a number of young men, each carrying a covered dish containing food. He presents this to one of the merchants on the ship saying "This is my guest," and all the others do the same. Each merchant on disembarking goes only to the house of the young man who is his host, except those who have made frequent journeys to the town and know its people well; these live where they please. The host then sells his goods for him and buys for him, and if anyone buys anything from him at too low a price or sells to him in the absence of his host, the sale is regarded by them as invalid. This practice is of great advantage to them.

When these young men came on board our vessel, one of them approached me. My companions said "This man is not a merchant, but a theologian," whereupon the young man called out to his friends "This is the qadi's [judge's] guest." Amongst them was one of the qadi's men, who went to tell him of this, so he came down to the beach with a number of students and sent one of them to me. When I disembarked with my party, I saluted him and his party, and he said "In the name of God, let us go and salute the Shaykh." Thereupon I said "And who is this Shaykh?" He answered "The Sultan," for they call the sultan 'the Shaykh.' I said to him "When I have settled down I shall go to him, and he replied "It is the custom that whenever a theologian, or Sharif [descendant of Prophet Muhammad], or man of religion comes here, he must see the sultan before taking his lodging." So I went to him as they asked.

The Sultan, whose name is Abu Bakr, is of Berbera origin, and he talks in the Maqdishi language, though he knows Arabic. When we reached the palace and news of my arrival was sent in, a eunuch came out with a plate containing betel leaves and areca [betel] nuts. He gave me ten leaves and a few nuts, the same to the qadi, and the rest to my companions and the qadi's students, and then said "Our master commands that he be lodged in the students' house." Later on the same eunuch brought food from the Shaykh's palace. With him came one of the wazirs [ministers], whose duty it was to look after the guests, and who said "Our master greets you and bids you welcome." We stayed there three days, food being brought to us three times a day, and on the fourth, a Friday, the qadi and one of the wazirs brought me a set of garments. We then went to the mosque and prayed behind the screen [enclosed section, for protection of the ruler]. When the 'Shaykh' came out I greeted him and he bade me welcome. He put on his sandals, ordering the qadi and myself to do the same, and set out for his palace on foot. All the other people walked barefooted. Over his head were carried four canopies of coloured silk, each surmounted by a golden bird. After the palace ceremonies were over, all those present saluted and retired.

I embarked at Maqdashaw for the Sawahil [Swahili] country, with the object of visiting the town of Kulwa [Kilwa, in today's Tanzania], in the land of the Zanj [East African blacks]. We came to Mambasa [Mombasa, in today's Kenya], a large island two days' journey by sea from the Sawahil country. It possesses no territory on the mainland. They have fruit trees on the island, but no cereals, which have to be brought to them from the Sawahil. Their food consists chiefly of bananas and fish. The inhabitants are pious, honourable, and upright, and they have well-built wooden mosques.

We stayed one night in this island, and then pursued our journey to Kulwa, which is a large town on the coast. The majority of its inhabitants are Zanj, jet-black in colour, and with tattoomarks on their faces. I was told by a merchant that the town of Sufala [in today's Mozambique] lies a fortnight's journey [south] from Kulwa, and that gold dust is brought to Sufala from Yufi in the country of the Umis [in today's Zimbabwe], which is a month's journey distant from it.

Kulwa is a very fine and substantially built town, and all its buildings are of wood. Its inhabitants are constantly engaged in military expeditions, for their country is contiguous to the heathen Zanj [raided and sold into Middle Eastern slavery]. The sultan at the time of my visit was Abu'l-Muzaffar Hasan, who was noted for his gifts and generosity. He used to devote the fifth part of the booty made on his expeditions to pious and charitable purposes, as is prescribed in the Koran, and I have seen him give the clothes off his back to a mendicant who asked him for them. When this liberal and virtuous sultan died, he was succeeded by his brother Dawud, who was at the opposite pole from him in this respect. Whenever a petitioner came to him, he would say " He who gave is dead, and left nothing behind him to be given." Visitors would stay at his court for months on end, and finally he would make them some small gift, so that at last people gave up going to his gate.

▶ Working with Sources

1. **What were the principal differences among the three regions of land and people along the East African coast?**

2. **Why was Ibn Battuta a privileged traveler, in contrast to merchants, and why did the African rulers treat him with great courtesy?**

SOURCE 14.3   'Abd al-'Azīz al-Bakrī, Description of West Africa

1068

A l-Bakrī was born in Spain, and it appears that he never left that country. However, he collected information from people he met who had traveled to the Sahara and the Sudan, and he published his findings in a work called *The Book of Routes and Realms* (*Kitāb al-masālik wa-'l-mamālik*). Al-Bakrī, who died in 1094, was famous for his curiosity about the geography, languages, and natural landscape of places he had not himself visited. The greater part of his major book is still unpublished, but the following section provides insight into the changing religious landscape in Ghana in the early eleventh century.

GHĀNA AND THE CUSTOMS OF ITS INHABITANTS

Ghāna is a title given to their kings; the name of the region is Awkār, and their king today, namely in the year 460/1067–8, is Tunkā Manīn. He ascended the throne in 455/1063. The name of his predecessor was Basī and he became their ruler at the age of 85. He led a praiseworthy life on account of his love of justice and friendship for the Muslims. At the end of his life he became blind, but he concealed this from his subjects and pretended that he could see. When something was put before him he said: "This is good" or "This is bad." His ministers deceived the people by indicating to the king in cryptic words what he should say, so that the commoners could not understand.

. . .

The city of Ghāna consists of two towns situated on a plain. One of these towns, which is inhabited by Muslims, is large and possesses twelve mosques, in one of which they assemble for the Friday prayer. There are salaried imams and muezzins, as well as jurists and scholars. In the environs are wells with sweet water, from which they drink and with which they grow vegetables. The king's town is six miles distant from this one and bears the name of Al-Ghāba. Between these two towns there are continuous habitations. The houses of the inhabitants are of stone and acacia (*sunt*) wood. The king has a palace and a number of domed dwellings all surrounded with an enclosure like a city wall (*sūr*). In the king's town, and not far from his court of justice, is a mosque where the Muslims who arrive at his court (*yafid 'alayh*) pray. Around the king's town are domed buildings and groves and thickets where the sorcerers of these people, men in charge of the religious cult, live. In them too are their idols and the tombs of their kings. These woods are guarded and none may enter them and

Source: 'Abd al-'Azīz al-Bakrī, "Ghāna and the Customs of Its Inhabitants," trans. J. F. P. Hopkins, in N. Levtzion and J. F. P. Hopkins, *Corpus of Early Arabic Sources for West African History* (Cambridge, UK: Cambridge University Press, 1981), 79–81.

know what is there. In them also are the king's prisons. If somebody is imprisoned there no news of him is ever heard. The king's interpreters, the official in charge of his treasury and the majority of his ministers are Muslims. Among the people who follow the king's religion only he and his heir apparent (who is the son of his sister) may wear sewn clothes. All other people wear robes of cotton, silk, or brocade, according to their means. All of them shave their beards, and women shave their heads.

. . .

When the people who profess the same religion as the king approach him they fall on their knees and sprinkle dust on their heads, for this is their way of greeting him. As for the Muslims, they greet him only by clapping their hands.

Their religion is paganism and the worship of idols (*dakākīr*). When their king dies they construct over the place where his tomb will be an enormous dome of *sāj* [acacia?] wood. Then they bring him on a bed covered with a few carpets and cushions and place him beside the dome. At his side they place his ornaments, his weapons, and the vessels from which he used to eat and drink, filled with various kinds of food and beverages. They place there too the men who used to serve his meals. They close the door of the dome and cover it with mats and furnishings. Then the people assemble, who heap earth upon it until it becomes like a big hillock and dig a ditch around it until the mound can be reached at only one place.

▶ **Working with Sources**

1. **Is there anything surprising, at least in al-Bakrī's description, in the reinforcement of royal authority in Ghana?**

2. **How was the religious balance between Muslims and non-Muslims maintained in this kingdom, and why?**

SOURCE 14.4 ## Walls and moats at Sungbo's Eredo, Nigeria

ca. 1000–1450

The chiefdom of Ijebu encompassed a capital and villages on a territory of 22 square miles, surrounded by a deep moat and towering rampart almost 100 miles long. The iron-saturated soil would have made the construction process very difficult, especially since the labor was achieved with nothing more than iron shovels. This drawing illustrates what archaeologists believe to have been the arrangement of a typical cross section of this structure. It is named for Bilikisu Sungbo, a mythical priestess-queen who was credited with ordering the construction of the moat and rampart.

Source: P. J. Darling, "Sungbo's Eredo, Southern Nigeria," *Nyame Akuma* 48 (1998), 55–61.

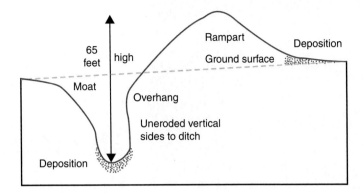

▶ Working
with Sources

1. Was this moat and rampart constructed for defensive purposes, or for some other reason? How do the size and extent of walls and moats of Ijebu compare with defensive structures created by other civilizations in the period before 1500 CE?

2. What does the existence of this edifice reveal about the use of collective labor in Ijebu in this period?

World Period Three

Religious Civilizations, 600–1450 CE

The rise of religious civilizations on the continents of Asia, Europe, and Africa is a striking phenomenon that unifies the period of 600–1450 in world history. It can be considered as a continuation of the intellectual and institutional transformations that began with the emphasis on monotheism and monism by the visionaries of the mid-first millennium BCE as ways to understand the world in which they lived.

The religious civilizations were not monolithic and displayed many regional variations. Internal diversity notwithstanding, they shared a number of common characteristics:

- Religious civilizations formed in regions which were larger than any single state within them: They superseded empires as the largest units of human unification.

- The civilizations were *scriptural*—that is, based on canonical (commonly agreed on) texts inherited in most cases from earlier periods. Members of educated elites (clergy, scholars, sages) taught and interpreted the scriptures to the laypeople.

- Despite hostilities among the religious civilizations, merchants, missionaries, pilgrims, and travelers visited each other's areas. They fostered a lively exchange of technical and cultural innovations from one end of Eurasia and Africa to the other.

Chapter 15

The Rise of Empires in the Americas

600–1550 CE

CHAPTER FIFTEEN PATTERNS

Origins, Interactions, Adaptations In the three agrarian–urban zones of the Americas, state building continued unabated in the period after 600 CE. In the south, it moved from the Andean coast to inland valleys and highlands. Here, the states of Wari and Tiwanaku, based on corn and potatoes, respectively, dominated until around 1050. In Mesoamerica, the Maya were able to overcome a severe drought and survive until ca. 1200 in the climatically different Chichén Itzá city-state. In the Mexican basin and adjacent obsidian-carrying mountains, the Toltecs dominated (900–1200). State-building in the Americas peaked with the creation of the Aztec (1427–1521) and Inca (1438–1533) empires, both of which were cut short by the Spanish conquest.

Uniqueness and Similarities The agrarian–urban states of the Americas, evolving into empires parallel to those in Eurasia and Africa, were sophisticated organizations. They all had to reckon with the technical limitations (no work animals, plows, and wheeled transportation) prevalent in the Americas. Nevertheless, the Aztecs and the Incas created remarkably large-sized states with impressive military and administrative structures.

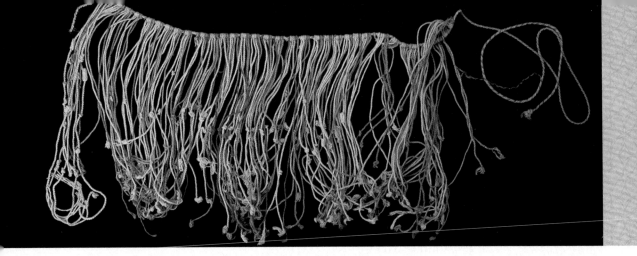

J ust outside Lima lies the shantytown of Túpac Amaru, named after the last Inca ruler, who died in 1572. People fleeing the Maoist Shining Path guerillas southeast of Lima settled here during the 1980s. Archaeologists knew that the site was an ancient burial place called Puruchuco (Quechua, "Feathered Helmet") but could not prevent the influx of settlers. By the late 1990s, the temporary shantytown had become an established settlement. However, residents realized that archaeologists had to be consulted before the shantytown could be officially recognized.

During excavations from 1999 to 2001, archaeologists unearthed one of the most astounding treasures in the history of American archaeology. The team discovered some 2,200 mummies, most of them bundled up in blankets and perfectly preserved. Many bundles also contained burial gifts of food and jewelry.

Scholars hope that when all of the mummies have been unwrapped, more will be learned about the social characteristics of the buried people, as so much about the Inca Empire that ruled the Andes from 1438 to 1533 remains unknown.

T he Inca Empire and the Aztec Empire (1427–1521) grew from patterns that began to form around 600 CE in Mesoamerica and the Andes (see Chapter 5). After 600, kingdom formation spread across Mesoamerica and arose for the first time in the Andes. These kingdoms were states with military ruling classes that could conquer larger territories than was possible prior to the 600s. Military competition prepared the way for the origin of empires. Even though empires arrived later in the Americas than in Eurasia, they demonstrate that humans, once they had adopted agriculture, followed similar patterns of social and political formation across the world.

CHAPTER OUTLINE

The Legacy of
Teotihuacán and the
Toltecs in Mesoamerica

The Legacy of Tiwanaku
and Wari in the Andes

American Empires: Aztec
and Inca Origins and
Dominance

Imperial Society and
Culture

Putting It All Together

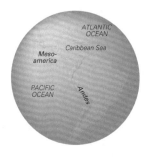

ABOVE: This kind of knotted string assembly (a *quipu*) was used in the Andes from ca. 2500 BCE onward for the recording of taxes, population figures, calendar dates, troop numbers, and other data.

351

Seeing Patterns

❯ Within the patterns of state formation basic to the Americas, which types of states emerged in Mesoamerica and the Andes during the period 600–1550? What characterized these states?

❯ Why did the Tiwanaku and Wari states have ruling classes but no dynasties and central bureaucracies? How were these patterns expressed in the territorial organization of these states?

❯ What patterns of urban life characterized the cities of Tenochtitlán and Cuzco, the capitals of the Aztec and Inca Empires? In which ways were these cities similar to those of Eurasia and Africa?

The Legacy of Teotihuacán and the Toltecs in Mesoamerica

The city-state of Teotihuacán had dominated northern Mesoamerica from 200 BCE to the late 500s CE (see Chapter 6). After its collapse, the surrounding towns and villages perpetuated the cultural legacy of Teotihuacán. Employing this legacy, the conquering state of the Toltecs unified part of the region from 900 to 1180. At the same time, after an internal crisis, the southern Maya kingdoms on the Yucatán Peninsula reached their late flowering, together with the northern state of Chichén Itzá.

Militarism in the Mexican Basin

After the ruling class of Teotihuacán disintegrated at the end of the sixth century, the newly independent small successor states of Mesoamerica continued Teotihuacán's cultural heritage. The Toltecs, migrants from the north, militarized the Teotihuacán legacy and transformed it into a program of conquest.

Ceremonial Centers and Chiefdoms   In the three centuries after the end of Teotihuacán, the local population declined from some 200,000 to about 30,000. However, other places around the Mexican Basin and beyond rose in importance. The region to the northwest of the valley had an extensive mining industry that produced a variety of gemstones. Independent after 600, inhabitants built small states and traded their gemstones to their neighbors.

To the north were the Pueblo cultures in today's southwestern United States. These cultures, which flourished between 700 and 1500, were based on irrigated farming systems and are known for their painted pottery styles. These cultures might have been in contact with the Mississippi cultures, of which the city of Cahokia (650–1400) near modern St. Louis is the best-known site (see Map 15.1).

To the south, in western Mesoamerica, chiefdoms flourished on the basis of metallurgy (especially copper), which arrived with Ecuadoran seaborne merchants ca. 600–800. Copper, too soft for agricultural implements or military weapons, was used mostly in household objects and as jewelry.

The Toltec Conquering State   Soon after the collapse of Teotihuacán, craftspeople and farmers migrated north to Tula. They founded a ceremonial center and town with workshops known for tools fabricated from the local Pachuca obsidian. Around 900, new migrants arrived from northwest Mexico as well as the Gulf Coast. The northerners spoke Nahuatl [NAH-wat], the language of the later Aztecs, and after taking possession of Tula, they made it their ancestral city.

The integration of the new arrivals resulted in the abandonment of the temple and the departure of a defeated party of Tulans.

The new Tula of 900 developed quickly into a large city with a new temple. It later became the capital of the conquering state of the Toltecs, whose warrior culture influenced Mesoamerica from around 900 to 1180 (see Map 15.1).

The Toltecs introduced two innovations in weaponry that improved the effectiveness of hand-to-hand combat: a short sword made of hardwood with inlaid obsidian edges that could slash as well as crush, and obsidian daggers with wooden

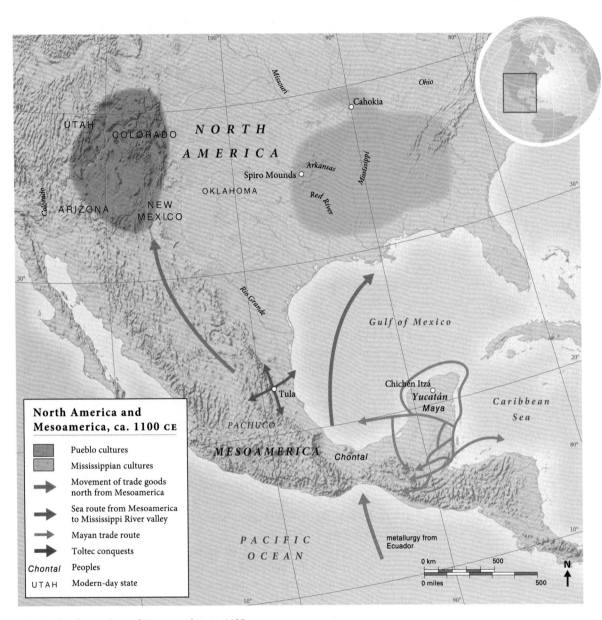

MAP 15.1 **North America and Mesoamerica, ca. 1100**

handles worn inside a band on the left arm. Traditional dart throwers and slings
for stone projectiles completed the offensive armament of the warriors.

The Toltec army was sufficiently large to engage in battles of conquest within
four days' march from Tula. Any target beyond this range was beyond their capabilities, given the logistics—and, of course, Toltecs did not have the benefit of

600	600–900	850–1000	1427–1521
End of city-state of Teotihuacán in Mexican Basin	Late Maya kingdoms in Yucatán Peninsula	City-state of Chichén Itzá in northern Yucatán Peninsula	Aztec Empire in Mesoamerica

600–1100	700–1000	900–1170	1438–1533
Conquering state of Tiwanaku in Andes (southern Peru/Bolivia)	Conquering state of Wari in Andes (central Bolivia)	Toltec conquering state, north of Mexican Basin	Inca Empire in Andes

wheeled vehicles. Thus, the only way of projecting power beyond the four-day range was to establish colonies and to have troops accompany traders. As a result, the Toltec state projected its power through the prestige of its large military, rather than through an administrative imposition of governors, tributes, and taxes.

Trade   The Toltecs established a large trade network based on Tula's obsidian. Merchants moved southward into the cacao, vanilla, and bird-feather production centers of Chiapas and Guatemala, to the north into gemstone mining regions, and westward into centers of metal mining. Metallurgy advanced around 1200 with the development of the technology of bronze casting. Bronze was preferable to copper for axes and bells; both were prized by the elites in Tula.

The Late Toltec Era   Toltec military power declined in the twelfth century when the taxable grain yield around the city diminished. Sometime around 1180, foraging peoples from the northwest invaded, attacking Toltec communication lines. The disruptions caused an internal revolt, which brought down the ceremonial center and its palaces. By 1200, Mesoamerica relapsed into a period of small-state coexistence.

Late Maya States in Yucatán

Teotihuacán's demise at the end of the sixth century was paralleled by a realignment of the balance of power among the Maya kingdoms in the southern Yucatán lowlands of Mesoamerica. This realignment was resolved by around 650. A period of late flowering spanned the next two centuries, followed by a shift of power from the southern to the northern part of the peninsula.

The Southern Kingdoms   At its height during the fourth and fifth centuries, Teotihuacán had interjected itself into the balance of power among the Maya kingdoms of southern Yucatán. Alliances shifted, and wars racked the lowlands, destroying several older states. A dozen new kingdoms emerged and established a new balance of power among themselves. After a lengthy hiatus, Maya culture entered its final period (650–900).

The final period in the southern, rain forest–covered lowlands and adjacent highlands was marked by agricultural expansion and ceremonial monument construction. The rain forest on hillsides was cut down and terraces were built for soil retention. The largest kingdoms grew to 50,000–60,000 inhabitants and reached astounding rural population densities of about 1,000 persons per square mile. They were administratively the most centralized polities ever created in indigenous American history.

The late Maya states did not last long. Torrential downpours washed the topsoil from the newly built hillside terraces. Malnutrition resulting from the shrinking agricultural surface began to reduce the labor force. In the end, even the ruling classes suffered, with members killing each other for what remained of agricultural surpluses. By about 900, the Maya kingdoms in southern Yucatán had shriveled.

Chichén Itzá in the North   A few small Maya states on the periphery survived. The most prominent among them was Chichén Itzá [chee-CHEN eet-SAH], which flourished from about 850 to 1000. The region would appear to be inhospitable, as the climate was very dry and the surface was rocky or covered with thin topsoil. There were no rivers, but many sinkholes in the porous limestone underneath the soil held water. Cisterns to hold additional amounts of water for year-round use were cut into the limestone; this water, carried in jars to the surface, supported a productive garden agriculture.

Chichén Itzá was founded during the phase of renewed urbanization in 650. The population was composed of local Maya as well as the Maya-speaking Chontal from the Gulf Coast farther west. Groups among these people engaged in long-distance trade, both overland and in boats along the coast. Since trade in the most lucrative goods required contact with people outside even the farthest political reach of either Teotihuacán or Tula, merchants traveled in armed caravans.

Chontal traders adopted Toltec culture, and in Chichén Itzá around 850 they superimposed their adopted culture over that of the original Maya. At the very end of the period of Teotihuacán, Maya, and Toltec cultural expansion, the three cultures finally merged on the Yucatán Peninsula. This merger did not last long: Already around 1000 the ruling-class factions left the city-state for unknown reasons, and it diminished in size and power.

Chacmool (Offering Table) at the Entrance to the Temple of Warriors, Chichén Itzá. Chacmools originated here and spread to numerous places in Mesoamerica, as far north as Tenochtitlán and Tula. Offerings to the gods included food, tobacco, feathers, and incense. Offerings might have included also human sacrifices. The table in the form of a prostrate human figure is in itself symbolic of sacrifice.

The Legacy of Tiwanaku and Wari in the Andes

Mesoamerica and the Andes shared the tradition of regional temple pilgrimages. In the Andes, the chiefdoms remained mostly coastal. Around 600 CE, the two conquering states of Tiwanaku in the highlands of what are today southern Peru and Bolivia and Wari in central Peru emerged. Both states represented a major step in the formation of larger, militarily organized polities.

The Expanding State of Tiwanaku

Tiwanaku was a political and cultural power in the south-central Andes during the period 600–1100. It began as a ceremonial center and developed into a state dominating the region around Lake Titicaca. At its apogee it planted colonies in regions far from the lake and conveyed its culture through trade to peoples even farther away.

Agriculture on the High Plain   The Andes consist of two parallel mountain chains along the west coast of South America. In southeastern Peru and western Bolivia, an intermountain plain, 12,500 feet above sea level, extends as wide as 125 miles. At its northern end lies Lake Titicaca, which has one outlet at its southern

Tiwanaku, Kalassaya Gate. Within the Temple of the Sun, this gate is aligned with the sun's equinoxes and was used for festive rituals. Note the precise stonework, which the Incas later developed further.

Reciprocity: In its basic form, an informal agreement among people according to which a gift or an invitation has to be returned after a reasonable amount of time; in the pre-Columbian Americas, an arrangement of feasts instead of taxes shared by ruling classes and subjects in a state.

end, a river flowing into Lake Poopó [po-PO], a salt lake 150 miles south. The Lake Titicaca region receives winter rains sufficient for agriculture and grazing.

The region around Lake Titicaca offered nearly everything necessary for an advanced urbanization process. The lake's freshwater supported fish and resources such as reeds from the swamps, which served for the construction of boats and roofs. The food staples were potatoes and quinoa. The grasslands of the upper hills served as pastures for llama and alpaca herds. Llamas were used as transportation animals, and alpacas provided wool; the meat of both animals was a major protein source.

Farmers grew their crops on hillside terraces or on raised fields close to the lake. The raised-field system, which farmers adopted from peoples of the Maya lowlands, consisted of a grid of narrow strips of earth, separated from each other by channels. Mud from the channels, heaped onto the strips, replenished their fertility. By 700, the city of Tiwanaku had 20,000 inhabitants.

Ceremonial feasts brought together elite lineages and clients, or ordinary craftspeople and villagers. Elites and clients cohered through **reciprocity**—that is, communal labor by clients rewarded by the elites with feasting. Forced labor through conscription or taxation did not appear until shortly before the collapse of the state.

Expansion and Colonization The region around southern Lake Titicaca housed related but competing elite–client hierarchies. Ruling clans and ordinary farmers comprised a state capable of imposing military power beyond the center. Counterbalancing clans at the head of similar hierarchies prevented the rise of permanent, unified central administrations and military forces.

The hallmark of Tiwanaku authority was the prestige of its ceremonial center rather than military might. Tiwanaku feasting ceremonies could be considered expressions of Tiwanaku authority—and pilgrims who partook in the feasts came into its orbit.

Yet military force did play a role in the western valleys of the Andes. Merchants accompanied by warriors traveled hundreds of miles. Settler colonies were additional forms of power projection, especially those established in the Moquegua [mow-KAY-gwah] valley to the west. Here, Tiwanaku emigrants established villages, which sent some of their corn or beer to the capital in return for salt and obsidian tools. Although overall less militarily inclined than the Mesoamerican states of the same time period, Tiwanaku wielded a visible influence over southern Peru (see Map 15.2).

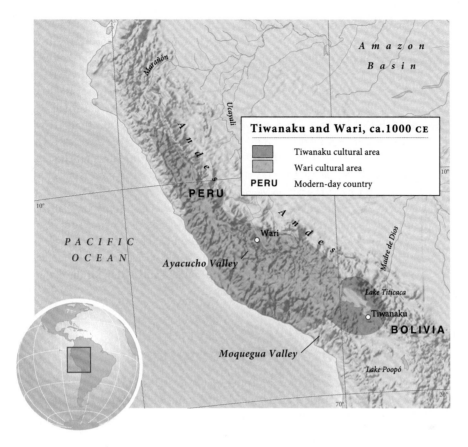

MAP 15.2 **Tiwanaku and Wari, ca. 1000**

The Expanding City-State of Wari

Little is known about early settlements in central Peru. The state of Wari emerged around 600, and expansion to the south put Wari into direct contact with Tiwanaku. The two states came to some form of mutual accommodation, and it appears that neither embarked on an outright conquest of the other. Their military postures remained limited to their regional spheres of influence.

Origins and Expansion   Wari was centered on the Ayacucho valley, a narrow 9,000-foot-high plain in northern Peru. The land is mountainous, interspersed with valleys and rivers. Farmers grew potatoes, corn and cotton. In the seventh century, Wari grew to 30,000 inhabitants and brought neighboring cities under its control. It also expanded terrace farming. Like Tiwanaku, Wari became the center of a developed urbanism and a diversified agriculture.

In addition to maintaining control over the cities in its vicinity, Wari constructed new towns with plazas, housing for laborers, and halls for feasting. Outside the core area, Wari elites established colonies. It appears that Wari exercised much stronger political control over the chiefs of its core region than Tiwanaku and was more active in founding colonies.

The Wari–Tiwanaku Frontier   Wari established a colony upstream in the Moquegua valley with extensive terraces, canals, and protective walls. This building activity coincided with the establishment by Tiwanaku of downstream farming colonies. It is possible that there was tension with Tiwanaku during the initial period (650–800), but during 800–1000 the two agricultural communities developed closer ties. Very likely, the Moquegua valley was politically so far on the periphery of both states that neither had the means to impose itself on the other.

Wari, like Tiwanaku, was an expanding state. Both were governed by elite clans which benefited from reciprocal patron–client organizations. However, there is evidence of increased internal tension after 950 in the two states. Groups defaced sculptures, destroyed portals, and burned down edifices. Scholars have argued that it was perhaps the fragility of power based on an increasingly unequal sharing that caused the rift between elites and subjects.

Why would elites allow reciprocity to be weakened? Some suggest that climatic change made large feasts no longer possible. A more convincing explanation suggests environmental degradation as the result of agricultural expansion. As in the late Maya kingdoms, the exhausted land could perhaps no longer sustain an increasing population. Unfortunately, an ultimate explanation for the disintegration of Tiwanaku and Wari remains elusive.

American Empires: Aztec and Inca Origins and Dominance

Building on the traditions of the Toltec and Wari states, in the early fifteenth century centralized multireligious, multiethnic, and multilinguistic polities arose. They were the empires of the Aztecs and Incas.

The Aztec Empire of Mesoamerica

The ancestors of the Aztecs (also called Mexica [me-SHEE-ka]) left Tula and arrived at the Mexican Basin at an unknown time. They eventually conquered the Mexican Basin, the site of today's Mexico City. In the fifteenth century, they conquered an empire that encompassed Mesoamerica from the Pacific to the Gulf of Mexico and from the middle of modern northern Mexico to the Isthmus of Panama.

Settlement in the Mexican Valley   According to the Aztecs' founding myth, the first Aztec was born on an island in a lake or in a mountain cave northwest of the Mexican Basin. This Aztec ancestor and his descendants migrated south, guided by their hunter–warrior patron god Huitzilopochtli [weet-see-lo-POCHT-lee] to a land of plenty. When the ancestors arrived at the Mexican Basin, an eagle perched on a cactus commanded the Aztecs to settle and build a temple to their god. In this temple they were to sacrifice to the god the blood of humans captured in war.

The historical record in the Mexican Basin becomes clearer in the fourteenth century, during which the Aztecs appeared as clients of two Toltec-descended overlords in city-states on the southwestern shore. Here they created two islands, founded a city with a ceremonial center, and rendered military service to their overlords. Aztec leaders married into the elites of the neighboring city-states and gained the right to have their own ruler presiding over a council of the elite and priests.

The Rise of the Empire   After the successful rebellion in 1428 of a triple alliance among the Aztec city-state and two other vassal states against the reigning city-state in the Mexican Basin, the Aztec leader Itzcóatl [its-CO-at(l)] (r. 1428–1440) emerged as the dominant figure. Tenochtitlán, the Aztec city on one of the islands, became the capital of an empire that consisted of a set of six "inner provinces" in the Mexican Basin. Local elites were required to attend ceremonies in Tenochtitlán, bring and receive gifts, leave their sons as hostages, and intermarry with the elites of the triple alliance. Farmers had to provide tribute, making the imperial core self-sufficient.

After further conquests by the middle of the fifteenth century, the triple alliance created an imperial polity from the Pacific to the Gulf (see Map 15.3). This state was more centralized than the Teotihuacán and Toltec city-states. In this empire, local ruling families were generally left in place, but commoners had to produce tributes of foodstuffs and manufactures. In some provinces, Aztec governors replaced the rulers; in others, Aztec tribute collectors (supported by troops) held local rulers in check and supervised the transportation of the tributes. Although reciprocity

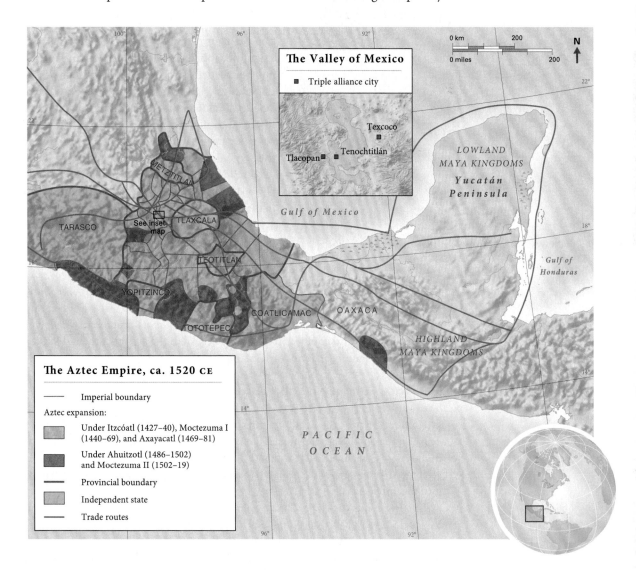

MAP 15.3 **The Aztec Empire, ca. 1520**

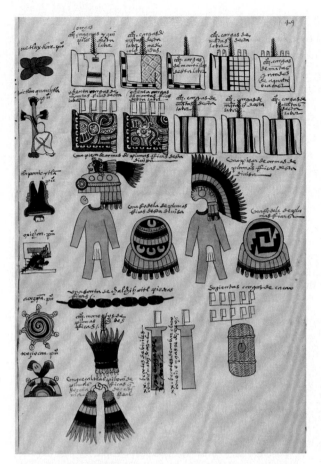

List of Tributes Owed to the Aztecs. The list includes quantities of cotton and wool textiles, clothes, headgear with feathers, and basketry. The Aztecs did not continue the complex syllabic script of the Maya, but used instead images, including persons with speech bubbles, for communication. Spanish administrators and monks who copied the Aztec manuscripts added their own explanations to keep track of Native American tributes.

continued, it was now clearly subordinate to military considerations. The resulting multiethnic, multireligious, and multilinguistic empire was still developing in the early sixteenth century when the Spanish arrived. The state of Tlaxcala [tlash-KAH-la], held out in opposition, together with enemy states on the periphery. Although the triple alliance did everything to expand, pockets of anti-Aztec states survived and eventually became allies of the Spanish. The key policy of continued expansion of Aztec central control was the threat of warfare. This fear-inducing tactic was an integral innovation in the imperialism of the Aztecs.

The Military Forces The triple alliance ruled 1.5 million inhabitants in the Mexican Basin. This number yielded up to a quarter of a million potential soldiers. Initially, the army was recruited from among the elite of the Aztecs and their allies. But toward the middle of the fifteenth century, Aztec rulers set up separate military school systems for the sons of the elite as well as the commoners. After graduation, soldiers rose in the army hierarchy on the basis of merit, particularly their success in the capture of enemies for future sacrifice.

The Aztecs inherited the weaponry and armor of the Toltecs, including the bow and arrow, as well as the obsidian-spiked broadsword, derived from the Toltec short sword. Clubs, maces, and axes functioned as secondary weapons. Body armor, consisting of quilted, sleeveless cotton shirts, thick cotton helmets, and round wooden or cane shields, was also adopted from the Toltecs. With the arrival of the Aztecs, the Americas had acquired the heaviest infantry weaponry in their history.

The Inca Empire of the Andes

The southern Peruvian city-state of Cuzco, with its Inca elite, emerged in the early fifteenth century at the head of a militaristic conquering polity. Within another century, the Incas had established an empire, called Tawantinsuyu [ta-wan-tin-SOO-yoo] (Quechua, "Four Regions"), symbolizing its geographical expanse. It stretched from Ecuador in the north to central Chile in the south, with extensions into the upper Amazon and western Argentina (see Map 15.4).

The Incas, like the Aztecs, had a founding myth. In one version, the creator god Viracocha [vee-ra-KO-cha] summoned four brothers and four sisters, pairing them as couples and promising them a land of plenty. They would find this land when a golden rod would get stuck in the soil. Alternatively, the sun god Inti [IN-tee] did the pairing of the couples before sending them with the golden rod to their promised land. In Cuzco, where the rod plunged into fertile soil, the Incas drove out the existing farmers.

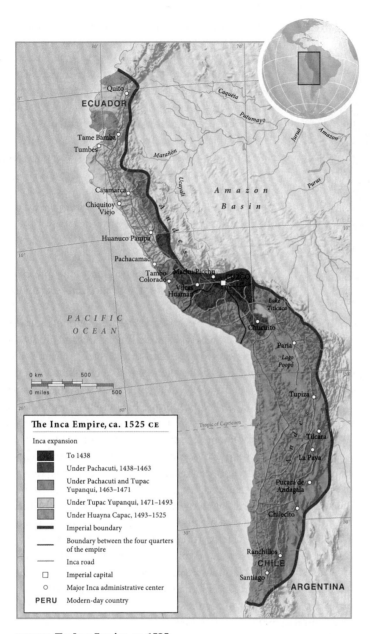

MAP 15.4 The Inca Empire, ca. 1525

In the fourteenth century, Cuzco became a serious contender in the regional city-state competition. Eight rulers are said to have succeeded each other in the consolidation of Cuzco as a local power, although little is known about them. Firm historical terrain is reached with the ninth ruler, Pachacuti (r. 1438–1471). The history of the Incas from 1438 onward is known much better, primarily because of the records of the Spanish conquerors.

Imperial Expansion The system of reciprocity that characterized earlier Mesoamerican and Andean history continued under the Incas. *Ayllu* [AY-yoo], the Quechua term for a household with an ancestral lineage, implied mutual

Aztec Weapons. Aztec weapons were well-crafted hardwood implements with serrated obsidian edges, capable of cutting through metal, including iron. As slashing weapons they were highly effective in close combat.

Mit'a: Innovation of the Incas in which subjects were obligated to deliver a portion of their harvests, animal products, and domestically produced goods to nearby storehouses for use by Inca officials and troops. The *mit'a* also provided laborers for construction projects as well as workers on state farms or mines.

Quipu: Knotted string assembly, used in the Andes from ca. 2500 BCE onward for the recording of taxes, population figures, calendar dates, troop numbers, and other data.

obligations among groups of households, neighborhoods, villages, and city-states. The most important social expression of reciprocity remained the feast. In the Incan Empire, the state collected more from the *ayllus* than Tiwanaku and Wari had done, but whether it returned comparable amounts through feasts and celebrations was a matter of contention, often leading to armed rebellion.

The earliest conquests under Pachacuti were around Lake Titicaca, as well as the north of the former Wari state. The Incas then expanded 1,300 miles northward to southern Ecuador and 1,500 miles southward to Chile. The final provinces, added in the early sixteenth century, were in northern Ecuador as well as on the eastern slopes of the Andes. The capital, Cuzco, with some 100,000 inhabitants in the early sixteenth century, was laid out in a grid of four streets. Symbolically, the capital reached out to the four regions of the empire—coast, north, south, and Amazon rain forest.

Administration   Ethnic Inca governors administered the four regions, which were subdivided into provinces, each with an Inca subgovernor. Most provinces were composites of former city-states, which remained under their local elites. A system of population organization was imposed by the Inca rulers. According to this system, members of the local elites commanded 10,000, 1,000, 100, and 10 household heads for the *mit'a* [MIT-ah] (Quechua, "turn," in reference to service obligations rotating among the subject lineages). The services were owed by subjects to the empire as a form of taxes.

The *mit'a* was an important innovation the Incas contributed to the history of the Americas. In contrast to the Aztecs, who shipped taxes in kind to their capital by boat, the Incas had no efficient means of transportation for long distances. The only way to make use of the taxes in kind was to store them locally. The Incas built storehouses and required subjects to deliver a portion of their goods and harvests under *mit'a* obligations to the nearest storehouse. These supplies enabled the Incas to conduct military campaigns far from Cuzco. In addition, it was through the *mit'a* that laborers were assembled for construction projects, often far from the urban center. Finally, *mit'a* provided laborers for mines, quarries, farms, and colonies.

To keep track of *mit'a* obligations, officials used bundles of knotted cord (*quipu*, or *khipu* [KEE-poo], "knot"). The numbers of knots on each cord in the bundles contained information on population figures and service obligations. The use of quipus was widespread in the Andes long before the Inca. Although some 700 have been preserved, attempts to decipher them have so far failed (see Chapter 5).

Military Organization   Under the *mit'a* system of the Inca Empire, men were required to serve in the military. As in the Aztec Empire, administrators made sure that enough laborers remained in the villages to take care of their other obligations of farming, herding, transporting, and manufacturing. Intermediate commanders came from the local and regional elites, and the top commanders were members of the two upper and lower Inca ruling elites.

Inca weaponry was comparable to that of the Aztecs, consisting of bows and arrows, dart throwers, slings, clubs with spiked bronze heads, wooden

Inca Roads. Inca roads were paths reserved for runners and the military. They were built on beds of rocks and rubble and connected strategic points in the most direct line possible.

broadswords, bronze axes, and bronze-tipped javelins. The Incas also used a snare to entangle the enemy's legs. Protective armor consisted of quilted cotton shirts, copper breastplates, wooden helmets, and shields.

During the second half of the fifteenth century, the Incas turned from conquest to consolidation. Faced with rebellions, they deemphasized the draft and recruited longer-serving troops from a smaller number of trusted peoples. These troops garrisoned forts throughout the empire and were part of the settler colonies in rebellious provinces and border regions. Personal guards recruited from non-Inca populations accompanied leading ruling-class members. The professionalization of the Inca army, however, lagged behind that of the Aztecs, since the Incas did not have military academies open to their subjects.

Communications The Incas created an excellent imperial communication and logistics structure. They improved on the road network that they inherited from Tiwanaku, Wari, and other states. Roads extended from Cuzco nearly the entire length of the empire. The roads often required extensive grounding, paving, staircasing, and tunneling. In many places, the 25,000-mile road network still exists today.

The roads were reserved for troops, officials, and runners carrying messages. For their convenience, every 15 miles, or at the end of a slow one-day journey, an inn provided accommodation. Armies stopped at barracks or pitched tents. Despite the fact that they did not have wheeled transport, the Incas were aware of how crucial paved and well-supplied roads were for infantry soldiers.

Imperial Society and Culture

As Mesoamerica and the Andes entered their imperial age, cosmopolitan capitals with monumental ceremonial centers and palaces emerged. Ceremonies and rituals impressed on enemies and subjects alike the irresistible might of the empires.

Aqueduct from the Western Hills to Tenochtitlán. This aqueduct, still standing today, provided fresh water to the palace and mansions of the center of the island, to be used as drinking water and for washing.

Imperial Capitals: Tenochtitlán and Cuzco

In the fifteenth century, the Aztec and Inca capitals were among the largest cities of the world, encompassing between 100,000 and 200,000 inhabitants. Although their monumental architecture followed different artistic traditions, both emphasized platforms and sanctuaries atop large pyramid-like structures as symbols of elevated power as well as closeness to the gods.

Tenochtitlán as an Urban Metropolis
More than half of the approximately 1.5 million people living during the fifteenth century in the Mexican Basin were urban dwellers. Such an extraordinary concentration of urban citizens was unique in the agrarian world prior to the industrialization of Europe, when cities usually held no more than 10 percent of the total population (see Map 15.5).

The center of Tenochtitlán, on the southern island, was a large platform. In an enclosure on this platform were the main pyramid, with temples to the Aztec gods on top, and smaller ceremonial centers. Also on the platform were a food market, palaces of the ruling elite, courts of law, workshops, a prison, and councils for teachers and the military. Aztecs and visitors assembled each day to pay respect to the ruler and to trade in the market.

In 1473, the southern island was merged with the northern island. At the center of the northern island was the principal market of the combined islands, which attracted as many as 40,000 people each day. The sophistication of the market was comparable to that of any market in Eurasia during the fifteenth century.

Causeways linked the capital with the lakeshore, and people traveled inside the city on a system of canals. Dikes with sluices regulated both the water level and the salinity of the lake. Potable water arrived from the shore via an aqueduct on one of the western causeways. Professional water carriers took fresh water from the aqueduct to commoners in the city; professional waste removers collected human waste from urban residences and took it to farmers for fertilizer.

The two city centers—the pyramid and palaces in the south and the market in the north—were surrounded by residential quarters, many of which were inhabited by craftspeople of a shared profession. The rooms of the houses surrounded a central patio—an architectural preference common to Mesoamerica and the Andes, as well as the Middle East and Mediterranean.

Chinampas: Small, artificial islands in Lake Texcoco created by farmers for raising agricultural crops.

Residents of quarters farther away from the center were farmers. Here, a grid of canals encased small, rectangular islands devoted to housing compounds and/or farming. A raised-field system prevailed, whereby farmers dredged the canals and heaped the fertile mud on top of the rectangular islands, called **chinampas**. In contrast to the luxurious palaces of the elite, housing for farmers consisted of humble plastered huts. As in all agrarian societies, farmers—subject to high taxes or rents—were among the poorest folk.

On the surface of the *chinampas*, farmers grew seed plants as well as maguey [mag-AY], a large succulent agave. This evergreen plant has a large root system, which stabilizes the ground, and produces fiber for weaving and pulp for making pulque [POOL-kay], a fermented drink.

Ownership of the *chinampas* was vested in clans, which, under neighborhood leaders, were responsible for the allocation of land and adjudication of disputes as well as the payment of taxes in kind to the elite. There were also members of the elite who possessed estates and employed managers to collect rents from the farmers. Whether there was a trend from taxes to rents is unknown.

Cuzco as a Ceremonial-Administrative City

The site of the Inca city of Cuzco was a triangle formed by the confluence of two rivers. At one end was a hill on which were built the imperial armory and a temple dedicated to the sun god. Enormous stone walls followed the contours of the hill.

Below, the city was laid out in a grid pattern. The residents of the city, all belonging to the Inca ruling class, lived in adobe houses arranged in a block-and-courtyard pattern similar to that of Wari. Squares and temples served as ceremonial centers. The Coricancha [ko-ri-KAHN-cha], the city's main temple, stood near the confluence of the rivers. This temple was a walled compound set around a court-

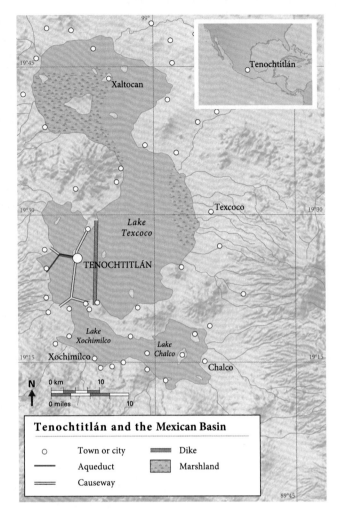

MAP 15.5 **Tenochtitlán and the Mexican Basin**

yard. Each year, priests of the empire's ceremonial centers sent a sacred object to the Coricancha to demonstrate their obedience to the central Inca temple.

Across the rivers were settlements for commoners with markets and storehouses. In the fields, interspersed stone pillars and shrines were aligned on sight lines radiating from the Coricancha, tying the countryside closely to the urban center. They bore a similarity to the Nasca lines in southern Peru (see Chapter 5). Farther away were imperial estates with unfree laborers from outside the *mit'a* system. In contrast to the Aztec elite, which allowed meritorious generals to rise in the hierarchy, the Inca elite remained exclusionary, allowing no commoners to reside in Cuzco.

Power and Its Cultural Expressions

Ruling elites emphasized the display of power during the period 600–1500. This was particularly true with the Aztecs and Incas during the fifteenth century.

Inca Ruling-Class Gender Relations

The greatest honor for Inca girls in Cuzco and provincial colonies was to enter at age 10–12 into the service of a

Human Sacrifice

In the first millennium CE, Mesoamerica and the Andes evolved from their early nature spirituality to polytheism. The earlier heritage, however, remained a strong undercurrent, as seen in human as well as animal and agricultural sacrifices. Rulers appeased the gods also through a form of self-sacrifice, the piercing of tongue and penis. The feathered serpent god Quetzalcóatl was the Mesoamerican deity of self-sacrifice, revered in the city-states of Teotihuacán (200 BCE–570 CE) and Tula (ca. 900 CE). Under the Toltecs and the Aztecs, this god receded in favor of warrior gods such as Tezcatlipoca and Huitzilopochtli. The survival of traditional blood rituals and human sacrifices within polytheism was a pattern that distinguished the early American empires from their contemporary Eurasian counterparts.

In 2015, Mexican archaeologists discovered the remnants of what once was the huge skull rack (*tzompantli*) in front of the main temple. Here, expert sacrificers first cut out the hearts of the victims, most of whom were captured warriors. Then they

52.

Human Sacrifice. Human sacrifice among the pre-Columbian Mesoamericans and Andeans was based on the concept of a shared life spirit or mind, symbolized by the life substance of blood. In the American spiritual-polytheistic conceptualization, the gods sacrificed their blood, or themselves altogether, during creation; rulers pierced their earlobes, tongues, or penises for blood sacrifices; and war captives lost their lives when their hearts were sacrificed to sustain the gods.

"House of Chosen Women." An inspector from Cuzco visited villages to select attractive young girls for the service. These houses had female instructors who provided the girls with an education in cooking, beer making, weaving, and officiating in the ceremonies of the Inca religion. After their graduation, the young women became virgin temple priestesses, were given in marriage to non-Incas honored for service to the ruler, or became servants or concubines of the Inca elite. The collection of this girl tribute was separate from the reciprocity system.

The form of agriculture in Mesoamerica and the Andes gave males fewer opportunities to accumulate wealth and power than plow agriculture did in Eurasia. Nevertheless, the gradual agrarian–urban diversification of society, even if it was slower in the Americas than in Eurasia, proceeded along similar paths of increasing male power concentration. An emphasis on gender differences, therefore, should be viewed as a characteristic phenomenon arising in imperial contexts.

Inca Mummy Veneration   Other houses in Cuzco were ghostly residences in which servants catered to the needs of deceased, mummified Inca emperors and their principal wives. During the mummification process, attendants removed the cadaver's internal organs, placed them in special containers, and desiccated the bodies until they were completely mummified. Servants dressed the mummies in their finest clothing and placed them back into their residences amid their possessions, as if they had never died. The mummies received daily meals and were carried around by their retinues for visits to their mummified relatives. On special occasions, mummies were lined up according to rank on Cuzco's main plaza to participate in ceremonies and processions. In this way, they remained fully integrated in the daily life of the elite.

severed the heads, cleaned them of their flesh, cut holes into the temples, and lined up the skulls on the bars of a rack 118 feet long and 16 feet high. Years later, the remains were taken off and cemented into two five-foot-high towers in front of the rack. The number of skulls is estimated to be in the thousands.

It is possible that the *tzompantli* was a heritage from earlier American societies. A few skulls with holes in the temples were found, for example, in Chichén Itzá. But it was Aztec society where the divine blood ritual reached its apogee in importance—evidently in conjunction with their empire being the most populated and expansive.

Questions

- In examining the question of whether empires such as the Inca and the Aztec employed human sacrifice for prestige purposes, can this practice be considered an adaptation that evolved out of earlier rituals, such as royal bloodletting?

- If the Aztec and the Inca did indeed employ human sacrifice for prestige purposes, what does this say about the ability of these two empires to use cultural and religious practices to consolidate their power?

In Andean society, mummies were crucial ingredients in the religious heritage, in which strong nature-spiritual elements survived underneath the polytheistic overlay of astral gods. In the spiritual tradition, a dead person's spirit, while no longer in the body, remains nearby and needs daily nourishment in order not to be driven away. Hence, even though non-Incan Andean societies removed the dead from their daily living spaces, descendants had to visit tombs regularly with food and beer. The tradition survives today in the Catholic Días de Muertos customs on November 1 and 2.

The expenses for the upkeep of the mummy households were the responsibility of the deceased emperor's bloodline, headed by a surviving brother. As heirs of the emperor's estate, the members of the bloodline formed a powerful clan within the ruling class. The new emperor was excluded from this estate and had to acquire his own new one in the course of his rule. In the early sixteenth century, however, this mechanism of keeping the upper and lower rungs of the ruling class united became counterproductive. Emperors lacking resources had to contend with brothers richly endowed with inherited wealth and ready to engage in dynastic warfare—as actually occurred shortly before the arrival of the Spanish (1529–1532).

Putting It All Together

The Aztec and Inca Empires unleashed extraordinary creative energies. Sculptors, painters, and (after the arrival of the Spanish) writers recorded the traditions as well as the innovations of the fifteenth century. Aztec painters produced codices, or illustrated manuscripts, that present the cultural and administrative activities of their societies in exquisite detail. Today, a handful of these codices survive, preserved in Mexican and European libraries.

The Aztec and Inca Empires were polities that illustrate how humans not in contact with the rest of the world developed patterns of innovation that were remarkably similar. On the basis of an agriculture that produced ample surpluses, humans made the same choices as their cousins in Eurasia and Africa. Specifically, in the period 600–1500, they created temple-centered city-states, just like their Sumerian and Hindu counterparts. Their military states were not unlike the Chinese warring states. And, finally, their empires were comparable to those of the New Kingdom Egyptians or the Assyrians. The Americas had their own unique variations of these larger historical patterns, but they nevertheless displayed the same humanity as found elsewhere.

Review and Relate

> Within the patterns of state formation basic to the Americas, which types of states emerged in Mesoamerica and the Andes during the period 600–1550? What characterized these states?

> Why did the Tiwanaku and Wari states have ruling classes but no dynasties and central bureaucracies? How were these patterns expressed in the territorial organization of these states?

> What patterns of urban life characterized the cities of Tenochtitlán and Cuzco, the capitals of the Aztec and Inca Empires? In which ways were these cities similar to those of Eurasia and Africa?

Thinking Through Patterns

Examine the ways historians approach the big questions of this chapter.

The basic pattern of state formation in the Americas was similar to that of Eurasia and Africa. Historically, it began with the transition from foraging to agriculture and settled village life. As the population increased, villages became chiefdoms, which in turn became city-states. American city-states often became conquering states, beginning with the Maya kingdoms and Teotihuacán. Military states in which ruling classes sought to expand territories, such as Tula and Tiwanaku and Wari, were characteristic of the early part of the period 600–1550. Their successors—the Aztec and Inca Empires—were multiethnic, multilinguistic, and multireligious polities that dominated Mesoamerica and the Andes before the Spanish conquest brought them to a premature end.

The states of Tiwanaku and Wari had cohesive ruling classes but no dynasties or centralized bureaucracies. These ruling classes and their subjects were integrated through systems of reciprocity. Over time, tensions arose, either between stronger and weaker branches of the ruling classes or between rulers and subjects over questions of obligations and justice. When these tensions erupted into internal warfare, the states disintegrated, often in conjunction with environmental degradation and climate change.

Tenochtitlán and Cuzco, the capitals of the Aztec and Inca Empires, were urban centers organized around temples and associated residences of the ruling dynasties and their priestly classes. They also contained quarters inhabited by craftspeople, and large central markets. Armed caravans of merchants and porters transported luxury goods across hundreds of miles. Tenochtitlán had an aqueduct for the supply of drinking water, and Cuzco was traversed by a river. Both capitals had agricultural suburbs in which farmers used irrigation for their crops.

Against the Grain

Consider this as a counterpoint to the main patterns examined in this chapter.

Amazon Rain-Forest Civilizations

For years, scholarly opinion held that the Amazonian river basin, covered by rain forest, was too inhospitable to allow for more than small numbers of widely dispersed foragers. Even farmers, living in populated villages, could not possibly have founded complex societies. Slash-and-burn agriculture prevented the advance of urban life: After exhausting the soil, whole villages had to pack up and move.

However, scholars now realize that this belief was erroneous. Modern farmers, encroaching on the rain forest, noticed two hitherto neglected features. First, these farmers found in stretches of forest and savanna a black soil so fertile that it did not require fertilizers. Second, as they slashed and burned the rain forest and savanna with their modern tools, the farmers exposed monumental earthworks that had previously escaped attention. The two features were connected. The black soil was the result of centuries of soil enrichment by indigenous people who also built the earthworks. Instead of slashing and burning, these people had engaged in "slashing and charring"—that is, turning the trees into nutrient-rich charcoal rather than quickly depleted ash.

Scholars have now documented large-scale settlements in areas along the southern tributaries to the Amazon. In the Purus region, for example, researchers employing aerial photography revealed a huge area home to perhaps 60,000 inhabitants during a period around the late thirteenth century. This area is adjacent to the farthest northeastern extension of the Inca Empire into the Amazon. Thus, when the Incas expanded into the rain forest, they clearly did so to incorporate advanced societies into their empire. Thanks to scholars who challenged the orthodoxy of the "empty rain forest," we are rediscovering the Amazonian past.

- Which is more important: to save the rain forest or uncover its archaeological past? Can the two objectives be combined?
- Compare the Amazonian earthworks to those of Benin in Africa during the same period (Chapter 14). Which similarities and differences can you discover?

Key Terms

Chinampas   364
Mit'a   362
Quipu   362
Reciprocity   356

Learn more with this chapter's digital tools, including the Oxford Insight Study Guide, at http://www.oup.com/he/vonsivers4e. Please see the Further Resources section at the back of the book for additional readings and suggested websites.

PATTERNS OF EVIDENCE |
Sources for Chapter 15

SOURCE 15.1

Skeletons in a Wari royal tomb site, El Castillo de Huarmey, Peru

ca. 600–1000 CE

In 2013, 63 skeletons were discovered in a tomb at El Castillo de Huarmey, about 175 miles north of Lima, in what would seem to be the first imperial tomb of the Wari culture discovered in modern times. Most of the bodies were female, and wrapped in bundles in the seated position typical of Wari burials. Three of the women appear to have been Wari queens, as they were buried with gold and silver jewelry and brilliantly painted ceramics.

Source: REUTERS/Enrique Castro-Mendivil.

However, six of the skeletons were not wrapped in the textiles, but instead positioned on top of the burials. Archaeologists have concluded that these people may have been sacrificed for the benefit of the others.

> ▶ **Working with Sources**
>
> 1. **How do the burial practices of Wari culture compare with those of other civilizations in Mesoamerica and the Andes?**
> 2. **What might this tomb suggest about the roles and expectations of women in Wari culture?**

SOURCE 15.2

Ahuitzotl, Eighth King (*Tlatloani*) of the Aztec Empire

Ruled 1486–1502

Ahuitzotl was a celebrated military leader, whose fame rested on his successes in war. The Spanish chronicler Fray Diego Durán collected a number of orations from the time of his reign, among which three are reproduced below in English translation. The first is a prayer by the women of the Aztec Empire for Ahuitzotl's victory in the war against the province of Tecuantepec, the second is Ahuitzotl's victory address to the Aztecs' patron god Huitzilopochtli, and the third is the funerary speech by the king of one of the Aztecs' allies at the occasion of Ahuitzotl's unexpected death.

Prayer of the Aztec Women during the War of the Triple Alliance (Aztecs, Tezcoco, and Tlacopán) under Ahuitzotl against Tecuantepec

Oh great Lord of All Created Things, remember your servant who has gone to exalt your honor and the greatness of your name. He has gone to offer his blood in that sacrifice which is war, to serve you. Behold, Lord, that he did not go out to work for me or for his children! Nor did he go to his usual labors to support his home, with tumpline on his head, or with a digging stick in his hand. He went for your sake, in your name, to obtain glory for you. Therefore, oh Lord, let your pious heart have pity on him who with great labor and affliction now goes through the mountains and valleys, hills and precipices, offering you the moisture, the sweat, from his brow. Grant him victory in this war so that he may return to rest in his home, and so my children and I may see his countenance again, may feel his presence.

Ahuitzotl: Victory Address to the Patron God Huitzilopochtli

Oh almighty, powerful Lord of All Created Things, You for whom we live, whose vassals and slaves we are, Lord of the Day and of the Night, of the Wind and the Water, whose strength keeps us alive! I offer You thanks for the help You

Source: Adapted from Fray Diego Durán, *The History of New Spain*, trans. Doris Heyden (Norman, OK: University of Oklahoma Press, 1994), 351, 357, and 384.

have given me, for having brought me back to Your city with the victory You granted me. I have returned to this great city of Mexico-Tenochtitlán where our ancestors, the Chichimecs and Aztecs, with great pains and the sweat of their brows discovered the blissful eagle seated upon the prickly pear cactus. There the eagle ate and rested, next to the springs of blue and red waters, which were filled with flying fish and with white snakes and white frogs. This wondrous thing appeared because You wanted to show us the greatness of Your power and Your will. You made us masters of the wealth we now possess, and I give You infinite thanks, Oh Lord, for not frowning upon my extreme youth—for I am still a boy—or my lack of strength or the weakness of my chest.

You have subjected those remote and barbarous nations to my power, to my control. You have won all these things, all is Yours! All has been won to give You honor and praise! Therefore, Oh powerful and heroic Huitzilopochtli, in order to honor You and to be successful in war, You have brought us to this place that was only water before, which our ancestors filled in and upon it built our city under Your orders. In thanks for these favors I offer You part of the spoils that have been won by the strength of our chests and arms and aided by You, Oh Lord!

Death of Ahuitzotl: Funerary Address by Nezahualpilli, King of Tezcoco and Member of the Triple Alliance (Aztecs, Texcoco, and Tlacopan)

Oh my son, valorous youth, lord and powerful king, be at ease, let rest and tranquility be with you. Now, Lord, you have left the difficult task of ruling Mexico-Tenochtitlán and the hardship of that work, where you were obliged to receive and attend all those who came before the grandeur of the god Huitzilopochtli and this illustrious city. You have left as unprotected orphans the lords and great men in your kingdom, you have left the old men, the old women, the widows and orphans and all the poor people who looked to you to remedy their poverty. You have gone to rest with your fathers and grandfathers but you have abandoned the loved ones who helped you bear the work of governing this world: they are your brothers, your cousins, your uncles, your close relatives. Your sons and daughters have become orphans, your wives are forsaken.

This city has been steeped in darkness since the sun has gone down, the sun has been hiding since your death. The royal seat is without light because your majesty and grandeur illuminated it, threw light upon it. The place, the chamber, of the omnipotent god is now full of dust, of refuse, the chamber that you ordered swept and kept clean, for you were the image of this god and you governed his state, pulling out the weeds and thorns that appeared in it. Now you have been freed from performing this servile and confining task. The ties with which you were bound have now been broken, those ties that held you to them with the care and sense of responsibility that you always exercised in making decisions about this, about that. Rest then, my son, rest in peace. Here I bring you these creatures of God, your servants, so they will go before you and serve you there in the place of rest.

▶ **Working with Sources**

1. **What do the sources say about the role of war in the Aztec Empire? How was war justified?**

2. **Who was Ahuitzotl? Describe his personality, both in terms of his own self-view and those of the Aztec women and Nezahualpilli.**

SOURCE 15.3

Bernal Díaz, *The Conquest of New Spain*

ca. 1568

In the course of the fifteenth century, the Aztecs established an empire centered in the Mexican Basin (surrounding present-day Mexico City, after the drainage of most of the valley) but encompassing Mesoamerica from the Pacific to the Gulf of Mexico. The resulting state, far more centralized than the preceding Teotihuacán and Toltec city-states, commanded a large extent of territory and thrived on the trade in raw materials that were brought in from both coasts of their empire. Bernal Díaz, born in 1492 in Spain, would join the Spaniards in the conquest of Mexico, but he also left behind vivid eyewitness accounts of occupied Aztec society in the sixteenth century. Among them is this description of the market in Tlatelolco, one of the central cities at the heart of Aztec imperial power.

Caciques: Nobles.

Our Captain and those of us who had horses went to Tlatelolco mounted, and the majority of our men were fully equipped. On reaching the market-place, escorted by the many *Caciques* whom Montezuma had assigned to us, we were astounded at the great number of people and the quantities of merchandise, and at the orderliness and good arrangements that prevailed, for we had never seen such a thing before. The chieftains who accompanied us pointed everything out. Every kind of merchandise was kept separate and had its fixed place marked for it.

Let us begin with the dealers in gold, silver, and precious stones, feathers, cloaks, and embroidered goods, and male and female slaves who are also sold there. They bring as many slaves to be sold in that market as the Portuguese bring Negroes from Guinea. Some are brought there attached to long poles by means of collars round their necks to prevent them from escaping, but others are left loose. Next there were those who sold coarser cloth, and cotton goods and fabrics made of twisted thread, and there were chocolate merchants with their chocolate. In this way you could see every kind of merchandise to be found anywhere in New Spain, laid out in the same way as goods are laid out in my own district of Medina del Campo, a centre for fairs, where each line of stalls has its own particular sort. So it was in this great market. There were those who sold sisal cloth and ropes and the sandals they wear on their feet, which are made from the same plant. All these were kept in one part of the market, in the place assigned to them, and in another part were skins of tigers and lions, otters, jackals, and deer, badgers, mountain cats, and other wild animals, some tanned and some untanned, and other classes of merchandise.

. . .

Then there were the sellers of pitch-pine for torches, and other things of that kind, and I must also mention, with all apologies, that they sold many canoe-loads of human excrement, which they keep in the creeks near the market. This was for the manufacture of salt and the curing of skins, which they say cannot be done without it. I know that many gentlemen will laugh at this, but I assure them it is true. I may add that on all the roads they have shelters made of reeds or straw

Source: Bernal Díaz del Castillo, *The Conquest of New Spain*, trans. J. M. Cohen (Baltimore: Penguin, 1963), 232–234.

or grass so that they can retire when they wish to do so, and purge their bowels unseen by passers-by, and also in order that their excrement shall not be lost.

But why waste so many words on the goods in their great market? If I describe everything in detail I shall never be done. Paper, which in Mexico they call *amal*, and some reeds that smell of liquid amber, and are full of tobacco, and yellow ointments and other such things, are sold in a separate part. Much cochineal is for sale too, under the arcades of that market, and there are many sellers of herbs and other such things. They have a building there also in which three judges sit, and there are officials like constables who examine the merchandise. I am forgetting the sellers of salt and the makers of flint knives, and how they split them off the stone itself, and the fisherwomen and the men who sell small cakes made from a sort of weed which they get out of the great lake, which curdles and forms a kind of bread which tastes rather like cheese. They sell axes too, made of bronze and copper and tin, and gourds and brightly painted wooden jars.

Cue: Temple.

We went on to the great **cue**, and as we approached its wide courts, before leaving the market-place itself, we saw many more merchants who, so I was told, brought gold to sell in grains, just as they extract it from the mines. This gold is placed in the thin quills of the large geese of that country, which are so white as to be transparent. They used to reckon their accounts with one another by the length and thickness of these little quills, how much so many cloaks or so many gourds of chocolate or so many slaves were worth, or anything else they were bartering.

▶ **Working with Sources**

1. **How and why does Díaz use comparisons from other markets while describing the one in Tlatelolco?**

2. **What do the specific elements of this market suggest about the importance of trade and commerce in pre-Columbian Mexico?**

SOURCE 15.4

Pedro Cieza de León on Incan roads

1541–1547

The Incas created an imperial communications and logistics infrastructure that was unparalleled in the Americas, with two highways extending to the north and south from Cuzco nearly the entire length of the empire. The roads, which were up to 12 feet wide, crossed the terrain as directly as possible, which clearly required a tremendous labor force to create. In many places, even today, the 25,000-mile road network still exists. Pedro Cieza de León was born in Spain in 1520 and undoubtedly traveled along the extensive, and still functional, Roman road system of his native land as a child. When he arrived in the New World at the age of 13, he was captivated and impressed by the civilizations that the Spanish were supplanting. In 1541, he began writing his account of the Incas, tracing their heritage and government for the benefit of those who would never see the territory he did—or travel the roads that made his observations possible.

Source: Pedro Cieza de León, *The Incas*, trans. Harriet de Onis, ed. Victor Wolfgang von Hagen (Norman: University of Oklahoma Press, 1959), 135–137.

CHAPTER 42 (ii.xv)

Of how the buildings for the Lord-Incas were constructed, and the highways to travel through the kingdom [of Peru].

One of the things that most took my attention when I was observing and setting down the things of this kingdom was how and in what way the great, splendid highways we see throughout it could be built, and the number of men that must have been required, and what tools and instruments they used to level the mountains and cut through the rock to make them as broad and good as they are. For it seems to me that if the Emperor were to desire another highway built like the one from Quito to Cuzco, or that which goes from Cuzco to Chile, truly I do not believe he could do it, with all his power and the men at his disposal, unless he followed the method the Incas employed. For if it were a question of a road fifty leagues long, or a hundred, or two hundred, we can assume that, however rough the land, it would not be too difficult, working hard, to do it. But these were so long, one of them more than 1100 leagues, over mountains so rough and dismaying that in certain places one could not see bottom, and some of the sierras so sheer and barren that the road had to be cut through the living rock to keep it level and the right width. All this they did with fire and picks.

. . .

When a Lord-Inca had decided on the building of one of these famous highways, no great provisioning or levies or anything else was needed except for the Lord-Inca to say, let this be done. The inspectors then went through the provinces, laying out the route and assigning Indians from one end to the other to the building of the road. In this way, from one boundary of the province to the other, at its expense and with its Indians, it was built as laid out, in a short time; and the others did the same, and, if necessary, a great stretch of the road was built at the same time, or all of it. When they came to the barren places, the Indians of the lands nearest by came with victuals and tools to do the work, and all was done with little effort and joyfully, because they were not oppressed in any way, nor did the Incas put overseers to watch them.

Aside from these, great fine highways were built, like that which runs through the valley of Xaquixahuana, and comes out of the city of Cuzco and goes by the town of Muhina. There were many of these highways all over the kingdom, both in the highlands and the plains. Of all, four are considered the main highways, and they are those which start from the city of Cuzco, at the square, like a crossroads, and go to the different provinces of the kingdom. As these monarchs held such a high opinion of themselves, when they set out on one of these roads, the royal person with the necessary guard took one [road], and the rest of the people another. So great was their pride that when one of them died, his heir, if he had to travel to a distant place, built his road larger and broader than that of his predecessor, but this was only if this Lord-Inca set out on some conquest, or [performed] some act so noteworthy that it could be said the road built for him was longer.

▶ **Working with Sources**

1. **How were the Incas' roads a manifestation of royal power, at least in Cieza de León's estimation?**

2. **What technical challenges faced the Incan road builders, and how did they overcome them?**

World Period Four

Interactions across the Globe, 1450–1750

The fifteenth century saw a renewal of the imperial impulse in the religious civilizations of the world. A forerunner had been the Mongol empire, which however did not last long; in less than 100 years it was replaced in China by the Ming. The founders of the subsequent new empires were the Mughals in India; the Ottomans, Safavids, and Songhay in the Middle East and Islamic Africa; the Habsburgs in Europe; and the seaborne empires of Portugal and Spain. One byproduct of this new imperial impulse was the discovery of the Americas, which in turn inspired the formulation of the heliocentric universe. The rediscovery of Greek literature in Europe had already set into motion the Renaissance, a broad new approach to understanding the world that provided the spark for the New Science.

China and India, by far the wealthiest and most populous agrarian–urban empires, enjoyed leading positions in the world because they produced everything they needed and wanted. Europe, however, acquired warm-weather crops and minerals through overseas colonial expansion, which would help it to challenge the traditional order.

Chapter 16

Western Christian Overseas Expansion and the Ottoman–Habsburg Struggle

1450–1650

CHAPTER SIXTEEN PATTERNS

Origins, Interactions, Adaptations In 600 CE, Western Christian civilization was the poorest and least diversified religious civilization in Eurasia. In contrast to the other religious civilizations, which continued to undergo refinements instead of diversification, Western Christianity acculturated through interaction and adaptation by absorbing outside stimuli from its Islamic and Eastern Christian neighbors. This process of absorption resulted in a heterogeneous rather than uniform culture by the time of the Renaissance in Europe (ca. 1450).

Uniqueness and Similarities Western Christian civilization is unique among the religious civilizations for its high degree of political, social, and cultural diversity. Islamic civilization, heir of deep and differentiated traditions, continued to undergo adaptations under the Ottoman Empire, but it did not break with the past. By contrast, Western Christianity evolved with often increasing internal tensions that were political (competing monarchies), social (religious divisions), and cultural (New Science and Enlightenment). Out of these tensions, the West eventually broke with its agrarian–urban past through what we call "modernity"—a decisive break that presented a unique challenge for the world's peoples.

Al-Hasan ibn Muhammad al-Wazzan (ca. 1494–1550) was born in Muslim Granada soon after the Christian conquest of this kingdom in southern Iberia in 1492. Unwilling to convert to Christianity, Hasan's family emigrated to Muslim Morocco around 1499–1500. Here, Hasan received a good education and entered the administration of the Moroccan sultan, traveling to sub-Saharan Africa and the Middle East on diplomatic missions.

In 1517, as he was returning home from a mission to Constantinople, Christian **corsairs** kidnapped him. Like their Muslim counterparts, these corsairs roamed the Mediterranean to capture travelers, whom they then held for ransom or sold into slavery. For a handsome sum of money, they turned Hasan over to Pope Leo X (1513–1521), who ordered Hasan to convert to Christianity and baptized him with his own family name, Giovanni Leone di Medici. Hasan became known in Rome as Leo Africanus ("Leo the African"). He stayed for 10 years in Italy, initially at the papal court and later as a scholar in Rome. During this time, he taught Arabic to Roman clergymen and compiled an Arabic–Hebrew–Latin dictionary. His most enduring work was a travelogue, *Description of Africa*, which was for years the sole source of information about sub-Saharan Africa in the Western Christian world.

In 1527 Charles V (r. 1516–1558), king of Spain and emperor of the Holy Roman Empire of Germany, invaded Italy and sacked Rome. Hasan survived but probably departed for Tunis sometime after 1531, seeking a better life in Muslim North Africa. Unfortunately, all traces of Hasan after his departure from Rome are lost. It is possible that he perished in 1535 when Charles V attacked and occupied Tunis (1535–1574), although it is generally assumed that he lived there until around 1550.

CHAPTER OUTLINE

The Muslim–Christian Competition in the East and West, 1450–1600

The Centralizing State: Origins and Interactions

Imperial Courts, Urban Festivities, and the Arts

Putting It All Together

ABOVE: This 1630 map by João Teixeira Albernaz the Elder (late 1500s–ca. 1662), member of a prominent family of Portuguese mapmakers, shows Arabia, India, and China.

Seeing Patterns

> What patterns characterized Christian and Muslim competition in the period 1300–1600? Which elements distinguished them from each other, and which elements were similar? How did the pattern change over time?

> How did centralizing states in the Middle East and Europe function in the period 1450–1600? How did economics, military power, and imperial objectives interact to create the centralizing state?

> Which patterns did cultural expressions follow in the Habsburg and Ottoman Empires? Why did the ruling classes of these empires sponsor these expressions?

Corsairs: In the context of this chapter, Muslim or Christian pirates who boarded ships, confiscated the cargoes, and held the crews and travelers for ransom; they were nominally under the authority of the Ottoman sultan or the pope in Rome, but operated independently.

The world in which Hasan lived was a Muslim–Christian world composed of the Middle East, North Africa, and Europe. Although Muslims and Christians traveled with relative freedom in much of this world, the two religious civilizations were locked in a pattern of fierce competition.

By the fifteenth century, the Christians sought to rebuild the crusader kingdom of Jerusalem, which had been lost to the Muslims in 1291. Searching for a route that would take them around Africa, they hoped to defeat the Muslims in Jerusalem with an attack from the east. In the process, the Christians discovered the Americas. For their part, the Muslims under the Ottoman sultans conquered eastern and central Europe while defending North Africa and driving the Portuguese out of the Indian Ocean.

The Muslim–Christian Competition in the East and West, 1450–1600

In the second half of the fifteenth century, the Western Christian kings resumed the *Reconquista* of Iberia. During the same period, the Muslim principality of the Ottomans conquered lands in both Anatolia and the Balkans. After the Muslim conquest of Constantinople in 1453 and the Western Christian conquest of Granada in 1492, the Ottoman and Habsburg Empires emerged and evolved into the main Muslim-Christian rivals of the seventeenth century.

Iberian Christian Expansion, 1415–1498

Portugal resumed its *Reconquista* policies by expanding to North Africa in 1415. Looking to circumnavigate the Muslims, collect West African gold, and reach the Indian spice coast, the Portuguese established fortified harbors along the African coastline. Castile and Aragon conquered Granada in 1492, occupied ports in North Africa, and sent Columbus to discover an alternate route to India. Columbus's discovery of America instead delivered the prospect of a new continent to the rulers of Castile and Aragon (see Map 16.1).

Maritime Explorations   In 1277–1281, mariners of the Italian city-state of Genoa resumed commerce by sea between the Mediterranean and the economically emerging northwestern Europe. In Lisbon, Portuguese shipwrights and their Genoese teachers developed ships suited for Atlantic seas. In the early fifteenth century they developed the caravel, a ship with upward-extending fore and aft sides, a stern rudder, and square as well as triangular lateen sails. The Portuguese became important traders between Mediterranean, Flemish, and English ports. The sea trade stimulated an exploration of the eastern Atlantic. By the early fifteenth century, the Portuguese had discovered the Azores and Madeira, while the Castilians began a conquest of the Canary Islands. Here, the indigenous inhabitants, the Guanches, put up a fierce resistance. But settlers carved out colonies on conquered parcels of land, enslaving the Guanches to work in sugarcane plantations. They thus introduced the sugarcane plantation system from the eastern Mediterranean, where it had Byzantine and Crusader roots on the island of Cyprus, to the Atlantic.

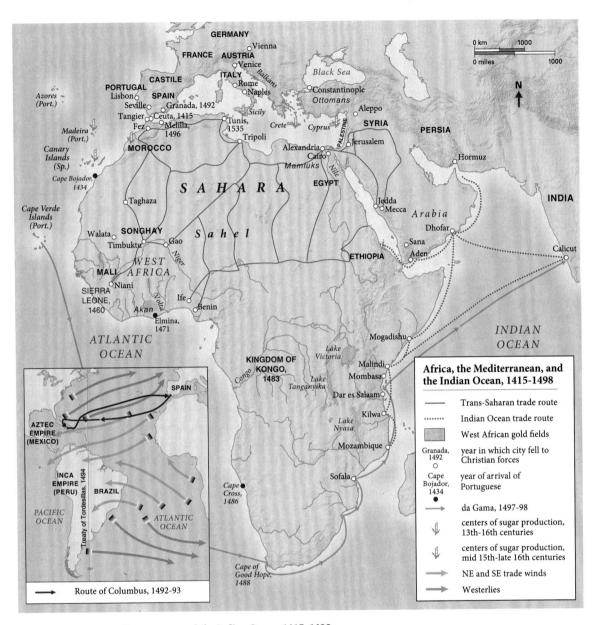

MAP 16.1 **Africa, the Mediterranean, and the Indian Ocean, 1415–1498**

Apocalyptic Expectations   The loss of the crusader kingdom in Palestine to the Muslim Mamluks in 1291 had stirred deep feelings of guilt among Western Christians. Efforts to reconquer Jerusalem failed, in part because rulers in Europe were warring against each other for territorial gain. The failure did not dampen periodic spiritual revivals, however, especially in the Franciscan and **military orders** of Iberia. These monks, often well connected with the Iberian royal courts, were believers in apocalypse—that is, the imminent end of the world and the Second Coming of Christ.

Military orders: Ever since the early 1100s, the papacy encouraged the formation of monastic fighting orders, such as the Hospitalers and Templars, to combat the Muslims in the crusader kingdom of Jerusalem; similar *Reconquista* orders, such as the Order of Christ (successor of the Templars) and Order of Santiago, emerged in Iberia to eliminate Muslim rule.

According to the **Apocalypse**, Christ's return could happen only in Jerusalem. This made it urgent for the Christians to reconquer the city. Christians as well as Muslims saw no contradiction between religion and military conquest. A providential God, so they believed, justified the conquest of lands and the enslavement of the conquered. The religious justification of military action, therefore, was a declaration by believers that God was on their side to help them to conquer and convert.

In Portugal, political claims in the guise of apocalyptic expectations guided the military orders in "reconquering" Ceuta, a northern port city of the Moroccan sultans that had once been in Visigothic hands. Accordingly, a fleet under Henry the Navigator (1394–1460) took Ceuta in 1415, capturing a stock of West African gold. Henry, a brother of the ruling Portuguese king and grand master of the Order of Christ, was searching for the West African source of Muslim gold. By the middle of the fifteenth century, Portuguese mariners had reached the "gold coast" of West Africa, where local rulers imported gold from the interior Akan fields.

Apocalypse: In Greek, "uncovering" or "revelation"—that is, the unveiling of events at the end of history, before God's judgment; during the 1400s, expectation of the imminence of Christ's Second Coming, with precursors paving the way.

Reforms in Castile

The Portuguese renewal of the *Reconquista* stimulated a similar revival in Castile, which occurred after the dynastic union of Castile and Aragon–Catalonia under their respective monarchs, Queen Isabella (r. 1474–1504) and King Ferdinand II (r. 1479–1516). The two monarchs used the reconquest ideology to speed up political and religious reforms.

Among the political reforms was the recruitment of urban militias and judges to check the military and judicial powers of the aristocracy. Religious reform focused on education for the clergy and enforcement of Christian doctrine among the population. The institution entrusted with the latter was the Spanish Inquisition, a body of clergy appointed in 1481 to discover and punish those deemed to be in violation of Christian theology and church law. These reforms laid the foundations for increased state power.

The Conquest of Granada

The *Reconquista* culminated in a 10-year campaign (1482–1492) that resulted in Granada falling into Christian hands. The last emir of Granada negotiated terms for an honorable surrender. According to these terms, Muslims who stayed as subjects of the Castilian crown were permitted to worship in their mosques.

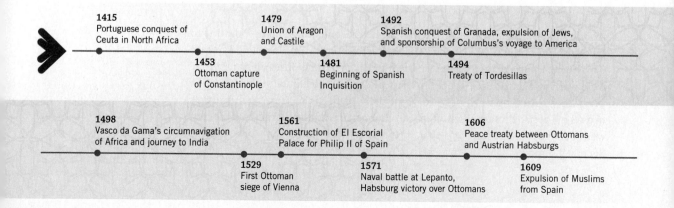

1415
Portuguese conquest of Ceuta in North Africa

1453
Ottoman capture of Constantinople

1479
Union of Aragon and Castile

1481
Beginning of Spanish Inquisition

1492
Spanish conquest of Granada, expulsion of Jews, and sponsorship of Columbus's voyage to America

1494
Treaty of Tordesillas

1498
Vasco da Gama's circumnavigation of Africa and journey to India

1529
First Ottoman siege of Vienna

1561
Construction of El Escorial Palace for Philip II of Spain

1571
Naval battle at Lepanto, Habsburg victory over Ottomans

1606
Peace treaty between Ottomans and Austrian Habsburgs

1609
Expulsion of Muslims from Spain

The treaty did not apply to the Jews of Granada, however, who were forced to either convert to Christianity or emigrate. Many emigrated in 1492 to Portugal and the Ottoman Empire. Portugal adopted its own expulsion decree in 1497. This ended the nearly millennium-and-a-half-long Jewish presence in Sefarad, as Spain was called in Hebrew.

After the expulsion of the Jews, it did not take long for the Christians to violate the Muslim treaty of surrender. The church forced conversions, burned Arabic books, and transformed mosques into churches. In 1499 the Muslims of Granada rebelled. Christian troops crushed the uprising, and Isabella and Ferdinand abrogated the treaty of surrender. During the early sixteenth century, Muslims were forced to convert, disperse to other provinces, or emigrate.

Columbus's Journey to the Caribbean   In early 1492, Isabella and Ferdinand authorized the mariner Christopher Columbus (1451–1506) to build two caravels and a larger carrack and sail across the Atlantic. Columbus promised to reach India ahead of the Portuguese. Money for the construction of ships came from Castilian and Aragonese crusade levies on the Muslims.

In September, Columbus and his mariners departed from the Castilian Canary Islands, catching the favorable South Atlantic easterlies. After a voyage of a little over a month, Columbus landed on one of the Bahaman islands, mistakenly assuming that he was close to the Indian subcontinent. After three months, he left a colony of settlers behind and returned to Iberia with seven captured Caribbean islanders and some gold.

Although disappointed by the meager returns of Columbus's first and subsequent voyages, Isabella and Ferdinand were delighted to have acquired new islands in the Caribbean, in addition to the Canaries. In one blow they had drawn even with Portugal.

Vasco da Gama's Journey to India   Portugal continued to search for a way to India around Africa. In 1498, the king appointed a member of the crusading Order of Santiago, Vasco da Gama (ca. 1469–1524), to command four caravels for the journey to India. After six months, the ships arrived in Calicut, the main spice trade center on the Indian west coast.

The first Portuguese mariner sent ashore by da Gama in Calicut encountered two North African Muslims, who addressed him in Castilian Spanish and Genoese Italian: "The Devil take you! What brought you here?" The mariner replied: "We came to seek Christians and spices." The Muslim and Hindu merchants were uninterested in the goods designed for the African market offered by da Gama and demanded gold or silver, which the Portuguese had only in small amounts. As rumors spread about a Muslim and Hindu plot against him, da Gama prudently sailed home.

However, Portugal soon mastered the India trade. The Portuguese crown organized regular journeys around Africa, and when Portuguese mariners ventured in the other direction to northeast Brazil, they claimed it for their expanding commercial network. During the early sixteenth century, as the Portuguese India fleets brought considerable amounts of spices from India back to Portugal, the project of retaking Jerusalem receded into the background.

Christopher Columbus. Because there is no known contemporary portrait of Columbus, considerable conjecture attends his real appearance. Apart from scattered descriptions presented by a few who knew him, scholars consider this portrait painted by Lorenzo Lotto in 1512 as perhaps the most accurate depiction.

Rise of the Ottomans and Struggle with the Habsburgs for Dominance, 1300–1609

While Muslim rule was disappearing from the Iberian Peninsula in the late fifteenth century, the opposite was happening in the Balkans. Here, the Ottoman Turks expanded Islamic rule over Christians. By the late sixteenth century, when conflict between the Habsburgs and Ottomans reached its peak, entire generations of Croats, Germans, and Italians feared a Muslim conquest of all of Western Christian Europe.

Late Byzantium and Ottoman Origins   The rise of the Ottomans was related to the decline of Byzantium. The emperors of Byzantium had reclaimed their "empire" in 1261 from its Latin rulers and Venetian troops. This empire was a midsize kingdom with modest agricultural resources. But it was still a valuable trading hub, given Constantinople's strategic position. Thanks to its commercial wealth, Byzantium experienced a cultural revival that influenced the Western Renaissance in Italy.

Both Balkan Slavs and Anatolian Turks appropriated Byzantine provinces in the late thirteenth century, further reducing the empire. One of the lost provinces was Bithynia, where, in 1299, the Turkish warlord Osman (1299–1326) declared himself an independent ruler. Osman and other Turkish lords in the region were nominally subject to the Seljuks, the Turkish dynasty that had conquered Anatolia from the Byzantines two centuries earlier but by the early 1300s was disintegrating.

During the first half of the fourteenth century, Osman and his successors conquered further Anatolian provinces from Byzantium. In 1354, the Ottomans gained their first European foothold on a peninsula about 100 miles southwest of Constantinople. Thereafter, it seemed only a matter of time before the Ottomans would conquer Constantinople.

Through skillful mixture of defense and diplomacy, however, the Byzantine emperors salvaged their rule for another century. They were also helped by Timur the Great (also known as Tamerlane; r. 1370–1405), a Turkish-descended ruler from central Asia who sought to rebuild the Mongol Empire. He defeated the Ottomans in 1402. Timur and his successors were unsuccessful with their dream of Mongol world rule; the Ottomans needed nearly two decades (1402–1421) to reconstitute their empire in the Balkans and Anatolia. Under Mehmet II, "the Conqueror" (r. 1451–1481), they finally laid siege to the Byzantine capital.

From Constantinople to the Adriatic Sea   Mehmet's siege and conquest of Constantinople (April 5–May 29, 1453) is one of the stirring events of world history. Using their superiority in troop strength, the Ottomans bombarded Constantinople's walls with heavy cannons. Unable to cut the heavy chain blocking the entrance to the harbor in the Golden Horn, Mehmet circumvented it by having troops drag ships on rollers over the Galata hill on the opposite side into the harbor. The soldiers massed on these ships assaulted the harbor walls with the help of ladders. When cannon fire succeeded in breaching a relatively weak wall section in the north, the Ottoman besiegers stormed the city. The last Byzantine emperor, Constantine XI, perished in the massacre that followed the Ottoman occupation of the city.

Mehmet repopulated Constantinople and appointed a new patriarch at the head of the Eastern Christians, to whom he promised full protection as his subjects. He ordered the construction of the Topkapı Palace (1459), the transfer of the administration to the city, and the resumption of expansion in the Balkans, where he forced the majority of rulers into submitting to vassal status.

Mehmet's Balkan conquests brought him to the Adriatic Sea, from where the Ottomans were poised to launch a full-scale invasion of Italy. When the sultan died unexpectedly, his successor turned back, preferring instead to consolidate the Ottoman Empire in the Balkans.

Imperial Apogee   In 1514, they defeated the Persian Safavids in Iran, who had risen in 1501 to form a rival Shiite empire in opposition to the Sunni Ottomans. In the southern Middle East, tensions between the Ottomans and the Mamluk Turks erupted in war in 1517. The Ottomans defeated the Mamluks and took control of western Arabia, including the holy pilgrimage city of Mecca. A year later, in 1518, the future Sultan Süleyman I, "the Magnificent" (r. 1520–1566), drove the Spanish from much of North Africa, which the latter had conquered in the name of the *Reconquista* in the 1490s and early 1500s.

In the Balkans, the Ottomans completed their conquests of Serbia and Hungary with the annexation of Belgrade and Buda (now part of Budapest) as well as a brief siege of Vienna in 1529. By the second half of the sixteenth century, the Ottoman Empire was a vast multiethnic and multireligious state of some 15 million inhabitants extending from Algeria in the Maghreb to Yemen in Arabia and from Upper Egypt to the Balkans and the northern shores of the Black Sea (see Map 16.2).

Morocco and Persia   In the period 1450–1600, the Ottomans and Indian Mughals dominated Islamic civilization. Two smaller realms existed in Morocco and Persia, ruled by the Saadid (1509–1659) and Safavid (1501–1722) dynasties, respectively. The Saadid sultans defended themselves successfully against the Ottoman expansion and liberated themselves from the Portuguese occupation of Morocco's Atlantic ports. In 1591, the Saadids sent an army to West Africa in an unsuccessful attempt to revive the gold trade. Moroccan army officers assumed power in Timbuktu, and their descendants, the Ruma, became provincial lords independent of Morocco. Without West African gold, the Saadids in Morocco split into provincial realms and were succeeded in 1659 by the Alaouite dynasty which is still in power today.

The Safavids grew in the mid-1400s from a mixed Kurdish-Turkish mystical brotherhood in northwestern Iran into a Shiite warrior organization that carried out raids against Christians in the Caucasus. In 1501, the leadership of the brotherhood put forward a 14-year-old boy named Ismail as the Hidden Twelfth Imam. According to Shiite doctrine, the Hidden Imam, or Messiah, was expected to arrive and establish a Muslim apocalyptic realm of justice at the end of time, before God's Last Judgment. This realm would replace the "unjust" Sunni

Shipbuilding

With the appearance of empires during the Iron Age, four regional but interconnected shipbuilding traditions—Mediterranean, North Sea, Indian Ocean, and China Sea—emerged.

In the Mediterranean, around 500 BCE, shipwrights began to use nailed planks for their war galleys as well as for cargo transports. In the Roman Empire (ca. 200 BCE–500 CE), nailed planking allowed the development of the roundship (image *a*), a large vessel 120 feet in length with a capacity of 400 tons of cargo for the transport of grain from Egypt to Italy. The roundship and its variations had double planking, multiple masts, and multiple square sails. After 100 BCE, the originally Egyptian triangular (lateen) sail allowed for tacking (zigzagging) against the wind, greatly expanding shipping during the summer sailing season.

The Celtic North Sea tradition adapted to the Mediterranean patterns of the Romans. Shipwrights in Celtic regions shifted to frame-first construction for small boats in the 300s. At the same time, Norsemen, or Vikings, innovated by introducing overlapping (clinkered) plank joining for their seagoing boats. The North Sea innovations, arriving as they did at the end of the western Roman Empire, remained local for nearly half a millennium.

China made major contributions to ship construction. In the Han period (206 BCE–220 CE) there is evidence from clay models for the use of nailed planks in riverboats. One model, dating to the first century CE, shows a central steering rudder at the end of the boat. At the same time, similar stern rudders appeared in the Roman Empire. Who adopted what from whom, if there was any borrowing at all, is still an unanswered question.

Patterns of Shipbuilding. Left to right: (a) Hellenistic-Roman roundship, (b) Chinese junk, (c) Indian Ocean dhow

Ottoman Empire. The Ottomans, however, crushed the Safavid challenge in 1514 at the Battle of Chaldiran, as mentioned above. Ismail dropped his claim to messianic status, and his successors assumed the more modest title of king (Persian *shah*) as the head of state.

The Safavids recruited a standing infantry from among young Christians on lands conquered in the Caucasus. They held fast to Shiism, thereby continuing their opposition to the Sunni Ottomans, and made this form of Islam dominant

Shipbuilding innovations continued after 600 CE. In Tang China, junks with multiple bulkheads (watertight compartments) and layers of planks appeared. The average junk was 140 feet long, had a cargo capacity of 600 tons, and could carry on its three or four decks several hundred mariners and passengers (see image *b*). Junks had multiple masts, and their trapezoidal (lug) and square sails made of matted fibers were strengthened (battened) with poles sewed to the surface. The Middle Eastern, eastern African, and Indian dhow was built with sewed or nailed planks and rigged with lateen and square sails, traveling as far as southern China (see image *c*).

In western Europe, the patterns of Mediterranean and North Sea shipbuilding merged during the thirteenth century. At that time, northern shipwrights developed the cog, a ship of some 60 feet in length and 30 tons in cargo capacity, with square sails and flush planking below and clinkered planking above the waterline. Northern European crusaders traveled during 1150–1300 on cogs via the Atlantic to the Mediterranean. Builders adapted the cog's clinker technique to the roundship tradition that Muslims as well as Eastern and Western Christians had modified in the previous centuries. Genoese clinkered roundships pioneered the Mediterranean–North Sea trade in the early fourteenth century (see image *d*).

Lisbon shipwrights in Portugal developed the caravel around 1430. The caravel was a 60-foot-long ship with a 50-ton freight capacity, a stern rudder, square and lateen sails, and a magnetic compass (of Chinese origin). The caravel and, after 1500, the similarly built but much larger galleon were the main vessels the Portuguese, Spanish, Dutch, and English used during their oceanic voyages from the mid-fifteenth to mid-eighteenth centuries (see image *e*).

Patterns of Shipbuilding (*continued*). From top: (d) Baltic cog, (e) Iberian caravel. These ships illustrate the varieties of shipbuilding traditions that developed over thousands of years.

Questions

- How does the history of shipbuilding demonstrate the ways in which innovations spread from one place to another?

- Do the adaptations in shipbuilding that flowed between cultures that were nominally in conflict with each other provide a different perspective on the way these cultures interacted?

in Iran. They moved the capital from Tabriz to the centrally located Isfahan in 1590, and built a palace, administration, and mosque complex in the city. They also held the monopoly in the production of Caspian Sea silk, a high-quality export product.

Not everyone accepted Shiism, however. An attempt to force the Shiite doctrines on the Afghanis backfired badly when enraged Sunni tribes formed a coalition, defeated the Safavids, and ended their regime in 1722.

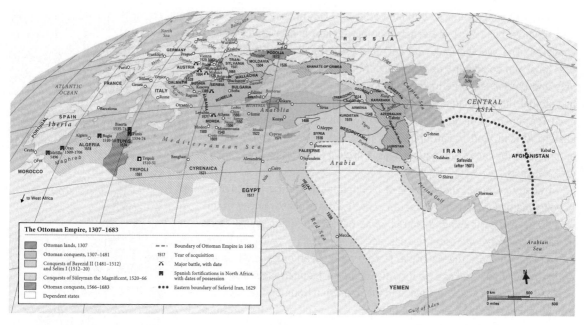

MAP 16.2 The Ottoman Empire, 1307-1683

Rise of the Habsburgs

On the Iberian Peninsula, Castile-Aragon evolved into the center of a vast empire. A daughter of Isabella and Ferdinand married a member of the Habsburg dynastic family, which ruled Flanders, Burgundy, Naples, Sicily, as well as the "Holy Roman Empire of the German Nation," as the collection of German principalities was called. Their son, Charles V, not only inherited Castile–Aragon, now merged and called Spain, and the first four of the above Habsburg territories but also became the ruler of the Aztec and Inca empires in the Americas. In both Austria and the western Mediterranean the Habsburgs were direct neighbors of the Ottomans (see Map 16.3).

In addition, in 1519 the princely and ecclesiastic electors of the Holy Roman Empire elevated Charles to the position of German king and Roman emperor. They did so after having received lavish sums of money from Charles to prevent them from electing the French or English king to the imperial position. In his new role he was now the direct counterpart of Sultan Süleyman in the struggle for dominance in the Christian–Muslim world of Europe, the Middle East, and northern Africa. Both the Habsburgs and the Ottomans renewed the traditional Islamic–Christian imperialism which had characterized the period 629–950 and which had been replaced by the Muslim and Christian commonwealths of 950–1450.

Habsburg Distractions

Charles V faced a daunting task in his effort to prevent the Ottomans from advancing against the Christians in the Balkans and the Mediterranean. Problems in his European territories diverted his attention from what Christians in most parts of Europe perceived as a pervasive Ottoman–Muslim threat. During the first three decades of the sixteenth century, revolts in

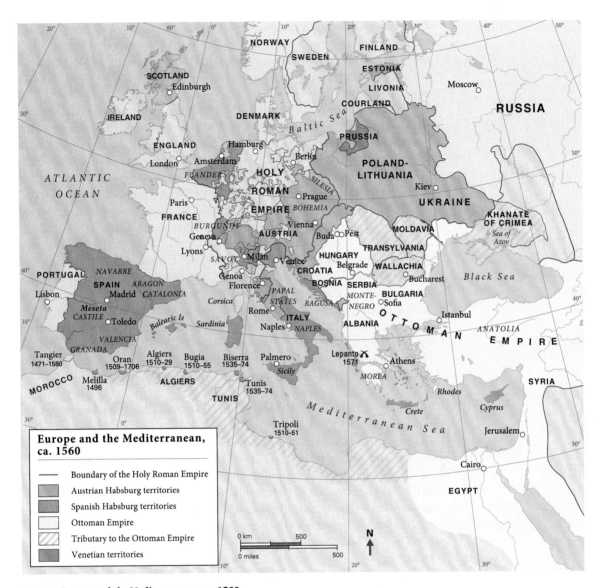

MAP 16.3 Europe and the Mediterranean, ca. 1560

Iberia, the Protestant Reformation in the German states, and renewed war with France commanded Charles's attention.

The emperor's distractions increased further in 1534 when, in an attempt to drive the Habsburgs out of Italy, France forged an alliance with the Ottomans. While this alliance horrified western Europe, it demonstrated that the Ottomans had become crucial players in European politics.

Habsburg and Ottoman Losses   The multiple engagements strained Habsburg resources against the Ottomans, who pressed ahead on the two fronts of the Balkans and North Africa. Although Charles V deputized his younger brother Ferdinand

I to shore up the Balkan defenses, he was unable to send him enough troops. After a series of defeats, Austria had to pay the Ottomans tribute and, eventually, sign a humiliating truce (1562). On the western Mediterranean front, by 1556, at the end of Charles V's reign, only two of eight Habsburg garrisons had survived Ottoman onslaught.

A third frontier of the Muslim–Christian struggle for dominance was the Indian Ocean. After Vasco da Gama had returned from India in 1498, the Portuguese kings sought to break into the Muslim-dominated Indian Ocean trade. In response, the Ottomans protected existing Muslim commercial interests in the Indian Ocean. They blocked Portuguese military support for Ethiopia and strengthened their ally, the sultan of Aceh (AH-chay) on the Indonesian island of Sumatra, by providing him with troops and weapons. War on land and on sea raged in the Indian Ocean through most of the sixteenth century.

In the long run, the Portuguese were successful in destroying the Ottoman fleets sent against them, but smaller convoys of Ottoman galleys continued to harass Portuguese shipping interests. By 1570 the Muslims traded as much via the Red Sea route to the Mediterranean as the Portuguese did by circumnavigating Africa. In addition, the Ottomans now benefited from the trade of coffee, newly produced in Ethiopia and Yemen. Both Portugal and the Ottomans reduced their by now unsustainable military presence in the Indian Ocean, which allowed the Netherlands in the early seventeenth century to overtake both Portugal and the Ottoman Empire in the Indian Ocean spice trade (see Map 16.4).

Habsburg–Ottoman Balance In the 1550s, Charles V decided to ensure the continuation of Habsburg power through a division of his western and eastern territories. Accordingly, he bestowed Spain, Naples, the Netherlands, and the Americas on his son Philip II (r. 1556–1598). The Habsburg possessions of Austria, Bohemia, and the remnant of Hungary not lost to the Ottomans, as well as the Holy Roman Empire (Germany), went to his brother Ferdinand I (r. 1558–1564). Charles hoped that his son and brother would cooperate and help each other militarily against the Ottomans.

When Philip took over the Spanish throne, he realized that most of the Habsburg military was stationed outside Spain, leaving that country vulnerable to attack—especially as the Ottomans had recently conquered Spanish strongholds in North Africa. Fearful of **Morisco** support for an Ottoman invasion of Spain, Philip's administration and the Inquisition renewed their decrees of conversion.

Moriscos: From Latin *maurus* ("Moor"; in medieval usage, also "dark-skinned"); Castilian term referring to North Africans and to Muslims under Spanish rule.

This sparked a revolt among the Moriscos of Granada in 1568–1570, which Philip was able to suppress only after recourse to troops and firearms from Italy. To break up the large concentrations of Granadan Moriscos in the south of Spain, Philip ordered them to be dispersed throughout the peninsula. At the same time, to alleviate the Ottoman naval threat, Philip, the pope, Venice, and Genoa formed a Holy Christian League. The fleet succeeded in 1571 in destroying the entire Ottoman navy at Lepanto (now Nafpaktos), in Ottoman Greece.

The Ottomans, however, rebuilt their navy and captured the strategic port city of Tunis in 1574 from the Spaniards. After this date, Venice was the only naval enemy of the Ottomans. The Ottomans turned their attention to the rival Safavid

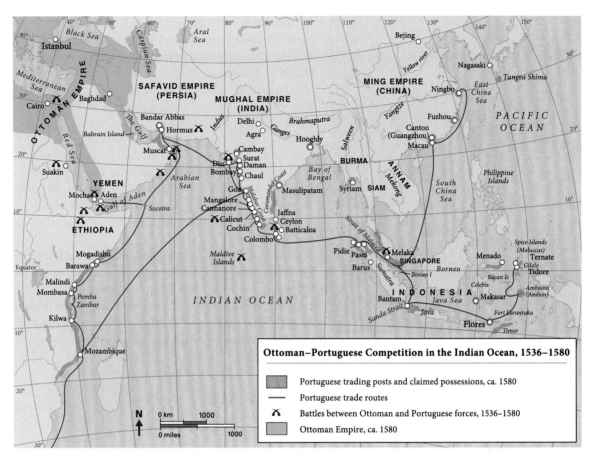

MAP 16.4 **Ottoman–Portuguese Competition in the Indian Ocean, 1536–1580**

Empire, where they exploited a period of dynastic instability for the conquest of territories in the Caucasus (1578–1590). The Catholic Philip II, for his part, was faced with the Protestant war of independence in the Netherlands. This war was so expensive that Philip II had to declare bankruptcy and sue for peace with the Ottomans (1580).

The Limits of Ottoman Power   After their victory over the Safavids, the Ottomans looked again to the west, where a long peace with Ferdinand I in Austria (since 1562) was ready to collapse. A series of raids and counter-raids at the Austrian and Transylvanian borders had inflamed tempers, and in 1593 the Ottomans went on the attack.

Eventually, the Ottomans were not able to defeat the Austrians on the battlefield. In 1606, the Ottomans and Austrian Habsburgs made peace again. With minor modifications in favor of the Austrians, the two sides returned to their earlier borders. The Austrians made one more tribute payment and then let their obligation lapse. Officially, the Ottomans conceded nothing, but in practical terms Austria was no longer a vassal state.

Paolo Veronese, *Battle of*
Lepanto, **altar painting with**
four saints beseeching the
Virgin Mary to grant victory
to the Christians (ca. 1572).
In the sixteenth century, the
entire Mediterranean, from
Gibraltar to Cyprus, was a
naval battleground between
Christians and Muslims. The
Christians won the Battle of
Lepanto thanks to superior
naval tactics. At the end of the
battle "the sea was entirely
covered, not just with masts,
spars, oars, and broken wood,
but with an innumerable
quantity of blood that turned
the water as red as blood."

Expulsion of the Moriscos   Although the peace between the Ottomans and Spanish Habsburgs held, Philip and his successors were aware of the possibility of renewed Ottoman aid to the Moriscos, who continued to resist conversion. The church advocated the expulsion of the Moriscos, arguing that the allegedly high Muslim birthrate was a serious threat.

Fierce resistance against the proposed expulsion, however, rose among the Christian landowners in the southeastern province of Valencia. These landowners benefited from the skills of their Morisco tenant farmers. Weighing the potential Ottoman threat against the possibility of economic damage, the government decided in 1580 in favor of expulsion.

It took until 1609, however, before a compensation deal with the landowners in Valencia was worked out. In the following five years, some 300,000 Moriscos were forcibly expelled from Spain, under often appalling circumstances. As in the case of the Jews a century earlier, Spain's loss was the Ottoman Empire's gain, this time mostly in the form of skilled irrigation farmers.

The Centralizing State: Origins and Interactions

The major technological change in the Middle East and Europe during 1250–1350 was the appearance of firearms. It took until the mid-1400s, however, before cannons and muskets were effective enough to make a difference in warfare. At this time, a pattern emerged whereby rulers created centralized states to finance their shift to firearm-bearing infantries. Consequently, they resumed the policy of conquest and imperialism. Both the Ottomans and the Habsburgs raised immense amounts of silver and gold to spend on cannons, muskets, and ships for achieving world rule.

State Transformation, Money, and Firearms

In the early stages of their realms, the kings of Iberia (1150–1400) and the Ottoman sultans (1300–1400) compensated military commanders for their service with land grants. Once the Iberian and Ottoman rulers had conquered cities and gained control over long-distance trade, however, patterns changed. Rulers began collecting taxes in cash, with which they paid regiments of personal guards to supplement the army of land-grant officers. This centralizing state was the forerunner of the absolutist state of the early seventeenth century.

The Land-Grant System   In the 1300s, Ottoman military lords created personal domains on lands they had conquered and took rents in kind from villagers to finance their dynastic households. Members of their clan or adherents (many of whom were holy warriors and/or adventurers), received other conquered lands, from which they collected rents. As the Ottomans conquered Byzantine cities, they enjoyed the benefits of a **money economy**. They collected taxes in coins from the markets and tollbooths at city gates, as well as from the Christians and Jews subject to the head tax.

After the conquest of the southern Balkans by the Ottoman Empire in the fifteenth and sixteenth centuries, both the land-grant system and the money economy expanded. A military ruling class of grant holders emerged, cavalrymen who lived with their households of retainers in the interior of Anatolia and the Balkans. Most of the time, they were away on campaign with the sultans, leaving managers in charge of the collection of rents. By the early years of the sixteenth century, the landed ruling class of cavalrymen constituted a reserve of warriors for the mobilization of troops each summer.

The Janissaries   The military institution of the **Janissaries**—troops who received salaries from the central treasury—is first documented in 1395. It was based on a practice (called ***devşirme*** [DEV-shirm]) of conscripting young boys from the empire's Christian population. Boys between the ages of 6 and 16 were sent to Constantinople, where they were converted to Islam and trained as future soldiers and administrators. The youth then entered the system of manumitted palace slaves under the orders of the sultan and his ministers.

The practice of *devşirme* contradicted Islamic law, which forbade the enslavement of "peoples of the Book" (Jews, Christians, and Zoroastrians). Its existence, therefore, documents the extent to which the sultans reasserted the Roman–Sasanid–Arab imperial traditions of the ruler making doctrine and law.

Toward the first half of the fifteenth century, the sultans equipped their Janissaries with cannons and matchlock muskets. By this point, firearms had undergone some 150 years of development in the Middle East and North Africa. By the mid-1400s, gigantic siege cannons and slow but reliable matchlock muskets were the standard equipment of Ottoman and other armies, and the sultans relied on indigenous, rather than European, gunsmiths.

Revenues and Money   The maintenance of a salaried standing army and a central administration would have been impossible without precious metals. Therefore, the Ottoman imperial expansion was driven by the need to acquire mineral deposits. During the fifteenth century the Ottomans captured the silver, lead, and iron mines of Serbia and Bosnia. Together with Anatolian copper, iron, and silver mines, the Balkan mines made the Ottomans the owners of the largest precious metal production centers prior to the Habsburg acquisition of the Mexican and Andean mines in the mid-1500s.

The sultans left the Balkan mining and smelting operations in the hands of preconquest Christian entrepreneurs, who were integrated into the Ottoman imperial money economy as tax farmers. **Tax farming** was the preferred method of producing cash revenues for the central administration. The holders of tax farms delivered the profits from the production of minerals to the state, minus the commission they were entitled to subtract for themselves. Thus, tax farmers were crucial members of the ruling class.

The right to mint silver was part of the tax-farm regime, as were the market, city gate, and port duties. The tax-farm regime was dependent on a strong sultan

Money economy: Form of economic organization in which mutual obligations are settled through monetary exchanges; in contrast, a system of land grants obliges the landholders to provide military service, without payment, to the grantee (sultan or king).

Janissaries: Infantry soldiers recruited among the Christian population of the Ottoman Empire and paid from the central treasury; from Turkish *yeniçeri*, "new troops."

Devşirme: The levy on boys in the Ottoman Empire; that is, the obligation of the Christian population to contribute adolescent males to the military and administrative classes.

Tax farming: Governmental auction of the right to collect taxes in a district. The tax farmer advanced these taxes to the treasury and retained a commission.

Boy Levy (*devşirme*) in a Christian Village. This miniature graphically depicts the trauma of conscription, including the wailing of the village women and the assembly of boys waiting to be taken away by implacable representatives of the sultan.

or chief minister, the grand vizier. Without close supervision, this regime could easily become decentralized, which indeed eventually happened in the Ottoman Empire.

Süleyman's Centralizing State   The Ottoman state reached its apogee under Sultan Süleyman I, "the Magnificent." The sultan financed a massive expansion of the military and bureaucracy and formed a centralized state, the purpose of which was to project power and cultural splendor toward its subjects as well as Christian enemies outside the empire.

The bureaucrats were recruited from two population groups. Most top ministers and officers in the fifteenth and sixteenth centuries came from the *devşirme* among the Christians. The empire's other recruits came from colleges to which the Muslim population of the empire had access. Ambitious villagers far from urban centers could gain upward mobility through the colleges. Muslims of Christian parentage made up the top layer of the elite, while Muslims of Islamic descent occupied the middle ranks.

Under Süleyman, the Janissaries comprised musket-equipped troopers, a cavalry, and artillery regiments. Most were stationed in Constantinople, while others served in provincial cities and border fortresses.

Typical military campaigns required sophisticated logistics. Wages, gunpowder, weapons, and foodstuffs were carried on wagons and barges, since soldiers were not permitted to provision themselves from villagers, whether friend or foe. Although the state collected heavy taxes, it had a strong interest in not destroying village productivity.

Charles V's Centralizing State   The centralizing state began in Iberia with the reforms of Isabella and Ferdinand and reached its mature phase under Charles V. From the late fifteenth century onward, Castile and Aragon shared fiscal characteristics with the Ottomans, such as tax farming. In addition, Muslims paid head taxes in cash. Most of the money taxes were also enforced in Flanders, Burgundy, Naples, Sicily, and Austria, after Iberia's incorporation into the Habsburg domain in 1516. These taxes were more substantial than those of Spain.

From 1521 to 1536, the Spanish crown enlarged its money income from looted Aztec and Inca gold and silver. Under Charles V, Habsburg imperial revenues doubled, reaching about the same level as those of the Ottomans. At the height of their struggle for dominance in the Muslim–Christian world, the Habsburgs and the Ottomans expended similar resources in wars with each other.

In one significant respect, however, the two empires differed. The cavalry ruling class of the Ottoman Empire was nonhereditary. By contrast, the Iberian landholder cavalry possessed a legal right to inheritance. When Isabella and Ferdinand embarked on state centralization, they had to wrestle with a powerful, landed aristocracy that had taken over royal jurisdiction and tax prerogatives on their vast lands. The two monarchs took back much of the jurisdiction but were unable to do much about the taxes.

The Habsburgs sought to overcome their lack of power over the aristocracy and the weakness of their Spanish tax base by exploiting the Italian and Flemish cities and the American colonies. But in the long run their finances remained precarious. Spanish aristocrats seldom fulfilled their obligation to unpaid military service. As a result, the kings hired as many Italians, Flemings, and Germans as possible, and at times they deployed these mercenaries to Spain in order to maintain peace there.

Although the Ottoman and Habsburg patterns of centralized state formation bore similarities to patterns in the earlier Roman and Arab Empires, the centralizing states of the period after 1450 were much more potent enterprises because of firearms. They were established polities, evolving into absolutist and eventually national states.

Ottoman Siege of a Christian Fortress. By the middle of the fifteenth century, cannons had revolutionized warfare. Niccolò Machiavelli, ever attuned to new developments, noted in 1519 that "no wall exists, however thick, that artillery cannot destroy in a few days." Machiavelli could have been commenting on the Ottomans, who were masters of siege warfare. Sultan Mehmet II, the conqueror of Constantinople in 1453, founded the Imperial Cannon Foundry shortly thereafter; it would go on to make some of the biggest cannons of the period.

Imperial Courts, Urban Festivities, and the Arts

Ottoman and Habsburg rulers projected the splendor of their states to subjects at home as well as enemies abroad. Although Christian and Muslim artists and artisans belonged to different religious and cultural traditions, their artistic achievements were inspired by the same impulse: to glorify their states through religious expression.

The Ottoman Empire: Palaces, Festivities, and the Arts

The Ottomans built palaces and celebrated public feasts to demonstrate their imperial power and wealth. Many mosques were built during the sixteenth century. Painting and illustration were found only inside the privacy of the Ottoman palace and wealthy households. Theater and music were enjoyed on the popular level, in defiance of religious restrictions.

The Topkapı Palace   When the Ottoman sultans conquered the Byzantine capital Constantinople in 1453, it was dilapidated and depopulated. The sultans initiated large construction projects and populated the city with craftspeople and traders from across their empire. By 1600 the city was again an imposing metropolis, easily the largest city in Europe at that time.

One of the construction projects was a new palace for the sultans, the Topkapı Sarayı, or "Palace of the Gun Gate," begun in 1459. (It was originally called the "Imperial New Palace," receiving its current name in the nineteenth century.) The Topkapı complex included the main administrative school, military barracks, an armory, a hospital, and living quarters, or harem, for the ruling family.

The institution of the harem arose during the reign of Süleyman. At that time, sultans no longer pursued marriage alliances with neighboring Islamic rulers. Instead, they chose slave concubines (often Christian) for the procreation of children. A concubine who bore a son to the reigning sultan acquired privileges.

The head eunuch of the harem guard evolved into a powerful intermediary for diplomatic and military decisions between the sultan's mother, who was confined to the harem, and those she sought to influence. In addition, the sultan's mother arranged marriages of her daughters to high-ranking officials. In the face of the strong patriarchal order of the Ottoman Empire, such women exercised considerable power.

Public Festivities   As in Habsburg Spain, feasts and celebrations were events that displayed the state's largesse. Typical festivities commemorated Muslim holidays. Other feasts were connected with the birthday of the Prophet Muhammad and his journey to heaven and hell. Processions and communal meals commemorated the birthdays of local Muslim saints in many cities. As in Christian Spain, these feasts attracted large crowds.

Wrestlers, ram handlers, and horsemen performed in the Hippodrome, the stadium for public festivities. At the harbor of the Golden Horn, tightrope artists performed high above the water. Court painters recorded the procession and performance scenes in picture albums. The sultans incorporated these albums into their libraries, together with history books recording their military victories against the Habsburgs.

Imperial Hall, Topkapı Palace. The Ottomans never forgot their nomadic roots. Topkapı Palace, completed in 1479 and expanded and redecorated several times, resembles in many ways a vast encampment, with a series of enclosed courtyards. At the center of the palace complex were the harem and the private apartments of the sultan, which included the Imperial Hall, where the sultan would receive members of his family and closest advisors.

Popular Theater   The evenings of the fasting month of Ramadan were filled with festive meals and a special form of entertainment, the Karagöz ("Black Eye") shadow theater. This form of theater came from Egypt, although it probably had Javanese–Chinese roots. For boys, a performance of the Karagöz theater accompanied the ritual of circumcision, a rite of passage from the ancient Near East adopted by Islamic civilization. Circumcision signified the passage from the nurturing care of the mother to the educational discipline of the father.

Mosque Architecture   During the sixteenth century, the architect Sinan (ca. 1492–1588) filled Constantinople and the earlier Ottoman capital Edirne with imperial mosques, defined by their slender minarets. Sultan Süleyman, wealthy officials, and private donors provided the funds. Sinan was able to hire as many as 25,000 laborers, enabling him to build each of his mosques in six years or less.

Sinan's most original contribution to architecture was the replacement of the highly visible and massive four exterior buttresses, which marked the square ground plan of the Hagia Sophia, with up to eight slender pillars as hidden internal supports of the dome. His intention was not massive monumentality but elegant spaciousness.

The Spanish Habsburg Empire: Popular Festivities and the Arts

The culture of the Habsburg Empire was strongly religious, and both state-sponsored spectacles and popular festivities displayed devotion to the Catholic faith. Secular tendencies, however, emerged also as a result of the Renaissance. Originating in Italy and the Netherlands, the Renaissance emphasized pre-Christian Greek and Roman heritages.

Faith, Capital and Palace   Catholicism was the majority religion by the sixteenth century and a powerful unifying force, in spite of the strong linguistic differences among the provinces of the Iberian Peninsula. Charles V resided for a while in a palace in Granada next door to the formerly Muslim Alhambra palace—but Granada was too Moorish and, geographically too far away from the north for many Spanish subjects to be properly awed.

Only a few places in Spain were suited for the location of a central palace and administration. Philip II eventually found such a place near the city of Madrid, which had once been a Muslim provincial capital. There, royal architect Juan Bautista de Toledo (ca. 1515–1567) built the Renaissance-style palace and monastery complex of El Escorial (1563–1584). As a result, Madrid became the seat of the administration and later of the court.

Christian State Festivities   Given the close association between the state and the church, the Spanish crown expressed its glory through the observance of feast days of the Christian calendar. These feasts were the occasion for processions and **passion plays**, during which urban residents affirmed their Catholic faith. During Holy Week, the week preceding Easter, Catholics marched through the streets, carrying heavy crosses or shouldering wooden platforms with statues of Jesus and Mary. The physical rigors of the Holy Week processions were collective reenactments of Jesus's suffering on the Cross.

By contrast, the processions that took place several weeks after Easter were joyous celebrations. Costumed marchers participated in jostling and pushing contests, played music, performed dances, and enacted scenes from the Bible.

The Auto-da-Fé   The investigation or proceeding of faith (Portuguese *auto-da-fé*, "act of faith") was a show trial in which the state, through the Spanish Inquisition, judged a person's commitment to Catholicism. The Inquisition employed thousands of state-appointed church officials to investigate anonymous denunciations of individuals failing to conform to the Catholic faith.

Suspected offenders, such as Jewish or Muslim converts to Catholicism or perceived deviants from Catholicism, had to appear before a tribunal. In secret trials, officials determined the offense and the appropriate punishment. These trials often employed torture. However, scholarship has emphasized that in the great majority of cases the punishments were minor, or the investigations did not lead to convictions.

Passion play: Dramatic representation of the trial, suffering, and death of Jesus Christ; passion plays are still an integral part of Holy Week in many Catholic countries today.

Popular Festivities   Jousts (mock combats between contestants mounted on horseback) were secular, primarily aristocratic events. Contestants rode their horses into the city square and led their horses through a complex series of movements. At the height of the spectacle, contestants galloped past each other, hurling their javelins at one another while protecting themselves with their shields. The joust evolved eventually into exhibitions of dressage ("training"), cultivated by the Austrian Habsburgs, who in 1572 founded the Spanish Court Riding School in Vienna.

Bullfights often followed the jousts. During the Middle Ages, bullfights were aristocratic pastimes that drew spectators from local estates. Bullfighters, armed with detachable metal points on three-foot-long spears, tackled several bulls in a town square. The bullfighter who stuck the largest number of points into the shoulders of the bull was the winner.

Theater, Literature, and Painting   The dramatic enactments of biblical scenes in the passion plays and religious processions were the origin of secular theater in Italy and Spain. Stationary theaters appeared in the main cities of Spain during the sixteenth century. A performance typically began with a musical prelude and a prologue describing the piece, followed by the three acts of a drama or comedy. Many were hugely successful, enjoying the attendance or even sponsorship of courtiers, magistrates, and merchants.

An important writer of the period was Miguel de Cervantes (1547–1616). His masterpiece, *Don Quixote*, describes the adventures of a poverty-stricken knight and his attendant, the peasant Sancho Panza, as they wander around Spain

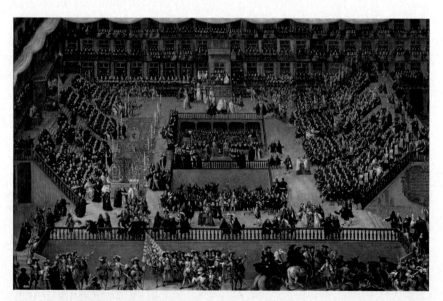

Auto-da-Fé, Madrid. This detail from a 1683 painting by the Italian-born painter Francisco Rizi shows a huge assembly in the Plaza Mayor of Madrid. It captures the solemn spectacle of the trial: in the center, below a raised platform, the accused stand in the docket waiting for their convictions to be pronounced; ecclesiastical and civil authorities follow the proceedings from grandstands. On the left, an altar is visible: The celebration of mass, often lasting for hours, was a common feature of the auto-da-fé.

searching for the life of bygone *Reconquista* chivalry. *Don Quixote* is an example of a new literary form: the novel.

The outstanding painter of Spain during Philip II's reign was El Greco (Domenikos Theotokopoulos, ca. 1546–1614), a native of the island of Crete. El Greco's works reflect Spanish Catholicism, with its emphasis on strict obedience to traditional faith and fervent personal piety. His characteristic style represents a variation of Mannerism (with its perspective exaggerations), which succeeded the Renaissance style in Venice during the later sixteenth century.

Putting It All Together

The Ottoman–Habsburg struggle can be seen as another chapter in the long history of competition that began when the Achaemenid Persian Empire expanded into the Mediterranean and was resisted by the Greeks in the middle of the first millennium BCE. There were obvious religious and cultural differences between the Islamic and Western Christian civilizations as they encountered each other during the Ottoman–Habsburg period. But their commonalities are equally interesting. Both were representatives of the return to imperialism, and in the pursuit of their imperial goals, both adopted the policy of the centralizing state with its firearm infantries and urban money economy. Both found it crucial to project their glory to the population and to sponsor artistic expression. In the long run, however, the imperial ambitions of the Ottomans and Habsburgs exceeded their ability to raise cash. Although firearms and a monetized urban economy made them different from previous empires, they were as unstable as all their imperial predecessors. Eventually, around 1600, they reached the limits of their conquests.

Review and Relate

Thinking Through Patterns

Examine the ways historians approach the big questions of this chapter.

In 1300, the Ottomans renewed the Arab-Islamic tradition of jihad against the Eastern Christian empire of Byzantium, defeating the empire with the conquest of Constantinople in 1453. They also carried the war into the western Mediterranean and Indian Ocean. In Western Christian Iberia, the rekindling of the reconquest was more successful. Invigorated by a merging of the concepts of the Crusade and the *Reconquista*, the Iberians expanded overseas to circumvent the Muslims and trade for Indian spices directly. The so-called Age of Exploration is rooted in the Western traditions of war against Islamic civilization.

> What patterns characterized the Christian and Muslim imperial competition in the period 1300–1600? Which elements distinguished them from each other, and which elements were similar? How did the pattern change over time?

How did the centralizing state in the Middle East and Europe function in the period 1450–1600? How did economics, military power, and imperial objectives interact to create the centralizing state?

Which patterns did cultural expressions follow in the Habsburg and Ottoman Empires? Why did the ruling classes of these empires sponsor these expressions?

In the mid-1400s, the Middle East and Europe returned to the pattern of imperial state formation after a lull during which states had competed against each other within their respective commonwealths. The element which fueled this return was gunpowder weaponry. The use of cannons and handheld firearms became widespread during this time but required major financial outlays on the part of the states. The two empires became states based on a money economy: bureaucracies maintained centralized departments that regulated the collection of taxes and the payroll of soldiers.

The rulers of these empires were concerned to portray themselves, their military, and their bureaucracies as highly successful and just. The state had to be as visible and benevolent as possible. Rulers, therefore, were builders of palaces, churches, or mosques. They celebrated religious and secular festivities with great pomp and encouraged ministers and the nobility to do likewise. In the imperial capitals, they patronized architects, artists, and writers, resulting in an explosion of intellectual and artistic creativity. In this regard, the Ottomans and the Habsburgs followed similar patterns of cultural expression.

Against the Grain

Consider this as a counterpoint to the main patterns examined in this chapter.

Tilting at Windmills

- What explains the lasting literary success of Don Quixote?
- Why has the phrase "tilting at windmills" undergone a change of meaning from the original "fighting imaginary foes" to "taking on a situation against all seeming evidence" in our own time?

Cervantes's *The Ingenious Gentleman Don Quixote of La Mancha* contributed to the rise of the novel as a characteristic European form of literary expression. Cervantes composed his novel in opposition to the dominant literary conventions of his time—as he wrote, to "ridicule the absurdity of those books of chivalry, which have, as it were, fascinated the eyes and judgement of the world, and in particular of the vulgar."

Every episode in this novel parodies one or another absurdity in society. The frame is provided by the fictional figure of Cide Hamete Benengeli, a purportedly perfidious Muslim historian who might have been lying when he chronicled the lives of the knight Don Quixote and his squire Sancho Panza. Don Quixote's joust, or "tilting," against windmills has become a powerful metaphor for rebelling against the overpowering conventions of society.

Don Quixote is today acclaimed as the second-most-printed text after the Bible. Over the past four centuries, each generation has interpreted the text anew. Revolutionary France saw Don Quixote as a doomed visionary; German Romantics, as a hero destined to fail; Communists, as an anti-capitalist rebel before his time; and secular progressives, as an unconventional hero at the dawn of modern free society. For Karl Marx, Don Quixote was the hidalgo who yearned for a return to the feudal aristocracy of the past. Sigmund Freud saw the knight-errant as "tragic in his helplessness while the plot is unraveled." In our own time, Don Quixote has become the quintessential postmodern figure; in the words of Michel Foucault, his "truth is not in the relation of the words to the world but in that slender and constant relation woven between themselves as verbal signs." As a tragic or comic figure, Don Quixote continues to be an irresistible symbol of opposition.

Key Terms

Apocalypse 374	Janissaries 385	Moriscos 382
Corsairs 372	Military orders 373	Passion play 389
Devşirme 385	Money economy 385	Tax farming 385

OXFORD insight study guide
Active Engagement, Deeper Understanding

Learn more with this chapter's digital tools, including the Oxford Insight Study Guide, at http://www.oup.com/he/vonsivers4e. Please see the Further Resources section at the back of the book for additional readings and suggested websites.

Sources for Chapter 16

SOURCE 16.1 Columbus reports on his
first voyage, 1493

Born in Genoa, Italy, Christopher Columbus (1451–1506) spent his early years in maritime ventures and later sailed with the Portuguese fleet. In his desire to acquire wealth and fame, and inspired by Portuguese attempts to gain access to the Spice Islands, Columbus studied several global maps which indicated that it was possible to reach Asia by sailing westward across the Atlantic. Confident that he could fulfill his ambition, Columbus sought funding from the Portuguese king, John II, who denied his request. Columbus then turned to Ferdinand and Isabella, rulers of Spain, who were determined to best Portugal in the race to reach the riches of the Indies. After initially turning him down, Ferdinand and Isabella finally granted Columbus the financial backing to undertake his expedition. After a five-week voyage from the Canary Islands, Columbus landed in the Bahamas, thinking that he had successfully reached Asia. After returning to Spain early in 1493, Columbus penned a letter to Ferdinand and Isabella in which he described his discoveries, along with the proclamation that the Caribbean Islands were now in the possession of Spain.

On the thirty-third day after leaving Cadiz I came into the Indian Sea, where I discovered many islands inhabited by numerous people. I took possession of all of them for our most fortunate King by making public proclamation and unfurling his standard, no one making any resistance. To the first of them I have given the name of our blessed Saviour, whose aid I have reached this and all the rest; but the Indians call it Guanahani. To each of the others also I gave a new name, ordering one to be called Sancta Maria de Concepcion, another Fernandina, another Isabella, another Juana; and so with all the rest. As soon as we reached the island which I have just said was called Juana, I sailed along its coast some considerable distance towards the West, and found it to be so

Source: © 2012 The Gilder Lehrman Institute of American History, www.gilderlehrman.org

large, without any apparent end, that I believed it was not an island, but a continent, a province of Cathay.

. . .

In the island, which I have said before was called Hispana, there are very lofty and beautiful mountains, great farms, groves and fields, most fertile both for cultivation and for pasturage, and well adapted for constructing buildings. The convenience of the harbors in this island, and the excellence of the rivers, in volume and salubrity, surpass human belief, unless one should see them. In it the trees, pasture-lands and fruits differ much from those of Juana. Besides, this Hispana abounds in various kinds of species, gold and metals. The inhabitants of both sexes of this and of all the other islands I have seen, or of which I have any knowledge, always go as naked as they came into the world, except that some of the women cover their private parts with leaves or branches, or a veil of cotton, which they prepare themselves for this purpose. They are all, as I said before, unprovided with any sort of iron, and they are destitute of arms, which are entirely unknown to them, and for which they are not adapted; not on account of any bodily deformity, for they are well made, but because they are timid and full of terror. They carry, however, canes dried in the sun in place of weapons, upon whose roots they fix a wooded shaft, dried and sharpened to a point. But they never dare to make use of these; for it has often happened, when I have sent two or three of my men to some of their villages to speak with the inhabitants, that a crowd of Indians has sallied forth; but when they saw our men approaching, they speedily took to flight, parents abandoning children, and children their parents. This happened not because any loss or injury had been inflicted upon any of them. On the contrary I gave whatever I had, cloth and many other things, to whomsoever I approached, or with whom I could get speech, without any return being made to me; but they are by nature fearful and timid. But when they see that they are safe, and all fear is banished, they are very guileless and honest, and very liberal of all they have

. . .

They do not practice idolatry; on the contrary, they believe that all strength, all power, in short all blessings, are from Heaven, and I have come down from there with these ships and sailors; and in this spirit was I received everywhere, after they had got over their fear. They are neither lazy nor awkward; but, on the contrary, are of an excellent and acute understanding. Those who have sailed these seas give excellent accounts of everything; but they have never seen men wearing clothes, or ships like ours.

I saw no monsters, neither did I hear accounts of any such except in an island called Charis, the second as one crosses over from Spain to India, which is inhabited by a certain race regarded by their neighbors as very ferocious. They eat human flesh, and make use of several kinds of boats by which they cross over to all the Indian islands, and plunder and carry off whatever they can. But they differ in no respect from the others except in wearing their hair long after the fashion of women. They make use of bows and arrows made of reeds, having pointed shafts fastened to the thicker portion, as we have before described. For this reason they are considered to be ferocious, and the other Indians consequently are terribly afraid of them; but I consider them of no more account than the others. They have intercourse with certain women who dwell alone upon the island of Mateurin, the first as one crosses from Spain to India. These women follow none of the usual occupations of their sex; but they use bows and arrows like those of their husbands, which I have described, and protect themselves with plates of copper, which is found in the greatest abundance among them.

Finally, to sum up in a few words the chief results and advantages of our departure and speedy return, I make this promise to our most invincible Sovereigns, that, if I am supported by some little assistance from them, I will give them as much gold as they have need of, and in addition spices, cotton and mastic, which is found only in Chios, and as much aloes-wood, and as many heathen slaves as their majesties may choose to demand; besides these, rhubarb and other kinds of drugs, which I think the men I left in the fort before alluded to, have already discovered, or will do so; as I have delayed nowhere longer than the winds compelled me, except while I was providing for the construction of a fort in the city of Nativity, and for making all things safe. . . .

Therefore let King and Queen and Princes, and their most fortunate realms, and all other Christian provinces, let us all return thanks to our Lord and Saviour Jesus Christ, who has bestowed so great a victory and reward upon us; let there be processions and solemn sacrifices prepared; let the churches be decked with festal boughs; let Christ rejoice upon Earth as he rejoices in Heaven, as he foresees that so many souls of so many people heretofore lost are to be saved; and let us be glad not only for the exaltation of our faith, but also for the increase of temporal prosperity, in which not only Spain but all Christendom is about to share. As these things have been accomplished so have they been briefly narrated. Farewell.

Christopher Colom,
Admiral of the Ocean Fleet
Lisbon, March 14th.

▶ Working
with Sources

1. **How does Columbus describe differences between the "Indians" and Europeans?**

2. **Why did Columbus dash this letter off to Ferdinand and Isabella soon after he returned from his voyage to the Caribbean?**

SOURCE 16.2   # Christopher Columbus, *The Book of Prophecies*

1501–1502

Although he is more famous for his voyages—and for the richly detailed accounts he made of them—Columbus also composed a book of prophetic revelations toward the end of his life, entitled *El Libro de las Profecías*. Written after his third voyage to the Americas, the book traces the development of God's plans for the end of the world, which could be hastened along, particularly by a swift and decisive move to reclaim Jerusalem from Muslim control. When Jerusalem was once more restored to Christian sovereignty, Columbus predicted, Jesus could return to earth, and all of the events foreseen in the Book of Revelation (and in various medieval revelations, as well) could unfold. It is helpful to place the plans for Columbus's original voyage in 1492 against the backdrop of his religious beliefs, as he encourages Ferdinand and Isabella to take their rightful place in God's mystical plan—as well as in Columbus's own cartographic charts.

Letter from the Admiral to the King and Queen [Ferdinand and Isabella]

. . .

Most exalted rulers: At a very early age I began sailing the sea and have continued until now. This profession creates a curiosity about the secrets of the world. I have been a sailor for forty years, and I have personally sailed to all the known regions. I have had commerce and conversation with knowledgeable people of the clergy and the laity. Latins and Greeks, Jews and Moors, and with many others of different religions. Our Lord has favored my occupation and has given me an intelligent mind. He has endowed me with a great talent for seamanship; sufficient ability in astrology, geometry, and arithmetic; and the mental and physical dexterity required to draw spherical maps of cities, rivers and mountains, islands and ports, with everything in its proper place.

During this time I have studied all kinds of texts: cosmography, histories, chronicles, philosophy, and other disciplines. Through these writings, the hand of Our Lord opened my mind to the possibility of sailing to the Indies and gave me the will to attempt the voyage. With this burning ambition I came to your Highnesses. Everyone who heard about my enterprise rejected it with laughter and ridicule. Neither all the sciences that I mentioned previously nor citations drawn from them were of any help to me. Only Your Highnesses had faith and perseverance. Who could doubt that this flash of understanding was the work

Source: Christopher Columbus, *The Book of Prophecies*, ed. Roberto Rusconi, trans. Blair Sullivan, vol. 3 (Berkeley: University of California Press, 1997), 67–69, 75–77.

of the Holy Spirit, as well as my own? The Holy Spirit illuminated his holy and sacred Scripture, encouraging me in a very strong and clear voice from the forty-four books of the Old Testament, the four evangelists, and twenty-three epistles from the blessed apostles, urging me to proceed. Continually, without ceasing a moment, they insisted that I go on. Our Lord wished to make something clearly miraculous of this voyage to the Indies in order to encourage me and others about the holy temple.

. . .

Most of the prophecies of holy Scripture have already been fulfilled. The Scriptures say this and the Holy Church loudly and unceasingly is saying it, and no other witness is necessary. I will, however, speak of one prophecy in particular because it bears on my argument and gives me support and happiness whenever I think about it.

I have greatly sinned. Yet, every time that I have asked, I have been covered by the mercy and compassion of Our Lord. I have found the sweetest consolation in throwing off all my cares in order to contemplate his marvelous presence.

I have already said that for the voyage to the Indies neither intelligence nor mathematics nor world maps were of any use to me; it was the fulfillment of Isaiah's prophecy. This is what I want to record here in order to remind Your Highnesses and so that you can take pleasure from the things I am going to tell you about Jerusalem on the basis of the same authority. If you have faith in this enterprise, you will certainly have the victory.

. . .

I said above that much that has been prophesied remains to be fulfilled, and I say that these are the world's great events, and I say that a sign of this is the acceleration of Our Lord's activities in this world. I know this from the recent preaching of the gospel in so many lands.

The Calabrian abbot Joachim said that whoever was to rebuild the temple on Mount Zion would come from Spain.

The cardinal Pierre d'Ailly wrote at length about the end of the religion of Mohammed and the coming of the Antichrist in his treatise *De concordia astronomicae veritatis et narrationis historicae* [*On the agreement between astronomical truth and historical narrative*]; he discusses, particularly in the last nine chapters, what many astronomers have said about the ten revolutions of Saturn.

▶ Working with Sources

1. How does Columbus appeal to the "crusading" goals of Ferdinand and Isabella, and why?

2. Would this appeal have found favor with the monarchs, given their other actions in Spain in 1492?

SOURCE 16.3 Thomas the Eparch and Joshua Diplovatatzes, "The Fall of Constantinople"

1453

The siege and conquest of Constantinople by the Ottoman Turks under Mehmet II (r. 1451–1481) was one of the turning points of world history. Unfolding over two months between April 5 and May 29, 1453, the siege exposed the inability of the Byzantine emperor Constantine XI to withstand a sustained and massive attack. Outnumbering the defenders 11 to 1, the Ottomans battered Constantinople's walls with heavy cannons and took advantage of the natural weaknesses of the city's geography. This account, told by two survivors and (self-proclaimed) eyewitnesses to the siege and its aftermath, details some of the specific stages of the defeat—and the suffering for Christians that came as a result.

When the Turk then drew near to Pera in the fortified zone, he seized all the boats he could find and bound them to each other so as to form a bridge which permitted the combatants to fight on the water just as they did on land. The Turks had with them thousands of ladders which they placed against the walls, right at the place which they had fired [their cannon] and breached the wall, just as they did at the cemetery of St. Sebold. The Genoese handled this breach; they wanted to protect it with their ships because they had so many. In the army of the Turk the order had been given fifteen days before the attack that each soldier would carry a ladder, whether he was fighting on land or sea. There also arrived galleys full of armed men: it seemed that they were Genoese and that they had come to aid the besieged, but in fact they were Turks and they were slipping into the gates. Just as this was becoming less worrisome and the city seemed secure, there arrived under the flag of the Genoese several ships which repelled the Turks with great losses.

At dawn on Monday, 29 May, they began an attack that lasted all night until Tuesday evening and they conquered the city. The commander of the Genoese, who was leading the defense of the breach, pretended to be wounded and abandoned his battle station, taking with him all his people. When the Turks realized this, they slipped in through the breach. When the emperor of the Greeks saw this, he exclaimed in a loud voice: "My God, I have been betrayed!" and he suddenly appeared with his people, exhorting the others to stand firm and defend themselves. But then the gate was opened and the crush of people

Source: trans. William L. North from the Italian version in A. Pertusi, ed., *La Caduta di Constantinopoli: Le testimonianze dei contemporanei* (Milan: Mondadori, 1976), 234–239, available online at https://d31kydh6n6r5j5.cloudfront.net /uploads/sites/83/2019/06/Thomas_the_Eparch_and_Joshua_Diplovatatzes_for_MARS_website.pdf

became such that the emperor himself and his [men] were killed by the Turks and the traitors.

Then the Turks ran to the Hagia Sophia, and all those whom they had imprisoned there, they killed in the first heat of rage. Those whom they found later, they bound with a cord around their neck and their hands tied behind their backs and led them out of the city. When the Turk learned that the emperor had been killed in Constantinople, he captured the Grand Duke who was governing in the emperor's stead and had the Grand Duke's son beheaded and then the Grand Duke himself. Then he seized one of the Grand Duke's daughters who was quite beautiful and made her lie on the great altar of Hagia Sophia with a crucifix under her head and then raped her. Then the most brutish of the Turks seized the finest noble women, virgins, and nuns of the city and violated them in the presence of the Greeks and in sacrilege of Christianity. Then they destroyed all the sacred objects and the bodies of the saints and burned everything they found, save for the cross, the nail, and the clothing of Christ: no one knows where these relics ended up, no one has found them. They also wanted to desecrate the image of the Virgin of St. Luke by stabbing six hundred people in front of it, one after another, like madmen. Then they took prisoner those who fell into their hands, tied them with a rope around the neck and calculated the value of each one. Women had to redeem themselves with their own bodies, men by fornicating with their hands or some other means. Whoever was able to pay the assessed amount could remain in his faith and whoever refused had to die. The Turk who had become governor of Constantinople, named Suleiman in German, occupied the temple of Hagia Sophia to practice his faith there. For three days the Turks sacked and pillaged the city, and each kept whatever he found—people and goods—and did with them whatever he wished.

. . .

All this was made known by Thomas the Eparch, a count of Constantinople, and Joshua Diplovatatzes. Thutros of Constantinople translated their Greek into "welisch" and Dumita Exswinnilwacz and Matheus Hack of Utrecht translated their welisch into German.

▶ Working with Sources

1. What does this account suggest about the preparedness of the Turks for the sack of Constantinople—and the lack of preparation on the part of the Byzantine defenders?

2. What details indicate that the taking of Constantinople was seen as a "religious" war on the Ottoman side?

SOURCE 16.4

Evliya Çelebi, "A Procession of Artisans at Istanbul"

ca. 1638

Born on the Golden Horn and raised in the sultan's palace in Istanbul, Çelebi traveled throughout Ottoman domains between 1640 and 1680. He published an account of his travels and experiences as the *Seyahatname*, or *Book of Travels*. In the first of his 10 books in the document, Çelebi provides a lengthy description of Istanbul around the year 1638, including a panoramic view of 1,100 artisan and craft guilds. The numbers and diversity of trades represented underscore the extent of Ottoman commerce—as well as the pride of place each of the city's working people claimed as their due.

The numbers in brackets refer to the order of listing in this chapter.

I: Ship-captains [7] vs. Saddlers [30]

Following the bakers [6], the saddlers wished to pass, but the ship-captains and sea-merchants raised a great fuss. When Sultan Murad got wind of the matter, he consulted with the ulema and the guild shaikhs. They all agreed that it made sense for the ship-captains to proceed after the bakers, because it was they who transported the wheat, and the bakers were dependent on them, and also because Noah was their patron saint.

Comment: the saddlers do not reappear until much later, between the tanners [29] and the shoemakers [31].

. . .

III: Egyptian Merchants [9] vs. Butchers [10]

Following the procession of these Mediterranean Sea captains, the butchers were supposed to pass, according to imperial decree. But all the great Egyptian merchants, including the dealers in rice, hemp, Egyptian reed mats, coffee and sugar gathered together and began quarreling with the butchers. Finally they went before the sultan and said: "My padishah, our galleons are charged with transporting rice, lentils, coffee and hemp. They cannot do without us, nor we without them. Why should these bloody and tricky butchers come between us? Plagues have arisen from cities where they shed their blood, and for fear of this their stalls and shambles in other countries are outside of the city walls.

Source: Robert Dankoff, *An Ottoman Mentality: The World of Evliya Çelebi*, 2nd ed. (Leiden, the Netherlands: Brill, 2006), 86–89.

They are a bloody and filthy band of ill-omen. We, on the other hand, always make Istanbul plentiful and cheap with grains of all sorts."

Now the butchers' eyes went bloodshot. "My padishah," they said, "Our patron saint is Butcher Cömerd and our occupation is with sheep, an animal which the Creator has made the object of mercy, and whose flesh He has made lawful food for the strengthening of His servants' bodies. Bread and meat are mentioned as the foremost of God's gifts to mankind: with a small portion of meat, a poor man can subsist for five or six days. We make our living with such a lawful trade, and are known for our generosity (cömerdlik). It is we who make Istanbul plentiful and cheap. As for these merchants and dealers and profiteers: concerning them the Koran says (2:275), 'God has made selling lawful and profiteering unlawful'. They are such a despised group that after bringing their goods from Egypt they store it in magazines in order to create a shortage, thus causing public harm through their hoarding.

. . .

"Egyptian sugar? But in the Koran the rivers of paradise are praised as being made 'of pure honey' (47:15). Now we have honey from Turkey, Athens, Wallachia, Moldavia, each with seventy distinct qualities. Furthermore, if my padishah wished, thousands of quintals of sugar could be produced in Alanya, Antalya, Silifke, Tarsus, Adana, Payas, Antakya, Aleppo, Damascus, Sidon, Beyrut, Tripoli and other such provinces—enough to make it plentiful and cheap throughout the world—so why do we need your sugar?

"As for coffee: it is an innovation; it prevents sleep; it dulls the generative powers; and coffee houses are dens of sedition. When roasted it is burnt; and in the legal compilations known as *Bezzaziye* and *Tatarhaniye* we have the dictum that 'Whatever is carbonized is absolutely forbidden'—this holds even for burnt bread. Spiced sherbet, pure milk, tea, fennel, salep, and almond-cream—all these are more wholesome than coffee."

. . .

To these objections of the butchers, the Egyptian merchants replied:

. . . "It is true that Turkey has no need of sugar and hemp, and that European sugar is also very fine. But tell us this, O band of butchers: what benefit and return do you offer to the public treasury?"

The butchers had nothing to say to this, and the Egyptian merchants continued: "My padishah, the goods arriving in our galleons provide the public treasury an annual revenue of 11,000 purses from customs dues. As a matter of justice ('adalet ederseñiz) we ought to have precedence in the Muhammadan procession, and the butchers ought to come after us." The şeyhülislam Yahya Efendi and Mu'id Ahmed Efendi cited the hadith, "The best of men is he who is useful to mankind," and the sultan gave the Egyptian merchants a noble rescript authorizing them to go first, and the butchers to go second.

▶ **Working with Sources**

1. Why did the order in which they appeared in the procession matter so much to these particular groups?

2. How did appeals to the Quran accentuate or diminish their case to be placed ahead in the procession?

SOURCE 16.5

Ogier Ghiselin de Busbecq, "The Court of Suleiman the Magnificent"

1581

Ghiselin (1522–1592) was a Flemish ambassador who represented the Austrian Habsburgs at the court of Süleyman, "the Magnificent" (1520–1566) in Istanbul. In 1581, he published an account of his time among the Ottomans as *Itinera Constantinopolitanum et Amasianum* (*Travels in Constantinople and Asia Minor*). In this segment of his travel narrative, he draws attention to the personal habits and behaviors of a contemporary emperor—one who saw himself as the heir to the Romans as well as to the other monarchs who had held Constantinople.

The Sultan was seated on a very low ottoman, not more than a foot from the ground, which was covered with a quantity of costly rugs and cushions of exquisite workmanship; near him lay his bow and arrows. His air, as I said, was by no means gracious, and his face wore a stern, though dignified, expression. On entering we were separately conducted into the royal presence by the chamberlains, who grasped our arms.... After having gone through a pretense of kissing his hand, we were conducted backwards to the wall opposite his seat, care being taken that we should never turn our backs on him. The Sultan then listened to what I had to say; but the language I held was not at all to his taste, for the demands of his Majesty breathed a spirit of independence and dignity ... and so he made no answer beyond saying in a tetchy way, "Giusel, giusel," i.e. well, well ...

. . .

I was greatly struck with the silence and order that prevailed in this great crowd. There were no cries, no hum of voices, the usual accompaniments of a motley gathering, neither was there any jostling; without the slightest disturbance each man took his proper place according to his rank. The Agas, as they call their chiefs, were seated, to wit, generals, colonels (*bimbashi*), and captains (*soubashi*). Men of a lower position stood. The most interesting sight in this assembly was a body of several thousand Janissaries, who were

Source: Wayne S. Vucinich, *The Ottoman Empire: Its Record and Legacy* (Princeton, NJ: Van Nostrand, 1965), 127–129.

drawn up in a long line apart from the rest; their array was so steady and motionless that, being at a little distance, it was some time before I could make up my mind as to whether they were human beings or statues; at last I received a hint to salute them, and saw all their heads bending at the same moment to return my bow.

. . .

When the cavalry had ridden past, they were followed by a long procession of Janissaries, but few of whom carried any arms except their regular weapon, the musket. They were dressed in uniforms of almost the same shape and colour, so that you might recognize them to be the slaves. . . . There is only one thing in which they are extravagant, viz., plumes, head-dresses, etc., and veterans who formed the rear guard were specially distinguished by ornaments of this kind. The plumes which they insert in their frontlets might well be mistaken for a walking forest.

▶ **Working with Sources**

1. **Why were order and discipline apparently so important at Suleiman's court?**

2. **Why might Ghiselin have found the Janissaries so particularly impressive?**

SOURCE 16.6   # Janissary Musket

ca. 1750–1800

The Janissaries constitute the most famous and centralized of the Ottomans' military institutions. A feared and respected military force, the Janissaries were Christian-born males who had been seized from their homes as boys, converted to Islam, and then trained as future soldiers and administrators for the Turks. Under the direct orders of the sultan and his viziers, the Janissaries were equipped with the latest military innovations. These units received cannons and matchlock (later flintlock, below) muskets. The muskets continued their evolution in the Janissaries' hands, becoming standard equipment for Ottoman and other armies.

Source: © INTERFOTO/Alamy.

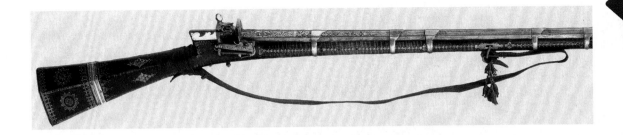

▶ Working with Sources

1. What does the elaborate decoration of this musket suggest about its psychological as well as its practical effects?

2. Was this firearm likely to have been produced by indigenous, rather than European, gunsmiths? Why or why not?

World Period Four

Interactions across the Globe, 1450–1750

The fifteenth century saw a renewal of the imperial impulse in the religious civilizations of the world. A forerunner had been the Mongol empire, which however did not last long; in less than 100 years it was replaced in China by the Ming. The founders of the subsequent new empires were the Mughals in India; the Ottomans, Safavids, and Songhay in the Middle East and Islamic Africa; the Habsburgs in Europe; and the seaborne empires of Portugal and Spain. One byproduct of this new imperial impulse was the discovery of the Americas, which in turn inspired the formulation of the heliocentric universe. The rediscovery of Greek literature in Europe had already set into motion the Renaissance, a broad new approach to understanding the world that provided the spark for the New Science.

China and India, by far the wealthiest and most populous agrarian–urban empires, enjoyed leading positions in the world because they produced everything they needed and wanted. Europe, however, acquired warm-weather crops and minerals through overseas colonial expansion, which would help it to challenge the traditional order.

Chapter 17

The Renaissance, New Sciences, and Religious Wars in Europe

1450–1750

CHAPTER SEVENTEEN PATTERNS

Origins, Interactions, Adaptations During the Middle Ages, a relatively coherent Western Christian religious civilization emerged in Europe. By the middle of the fifteenth century, interactions with Eastern Christianity put in motion the Renaissance, which made European culture highly heterogeneous, with many conflicting political, religious, and social trends. In contrast, the other, more homogeneous religious civilizations in the world rested on deep internal roots and received far fewer outside stimuli for their transformation.

Uniqueness and Similarities The Renaissance, New Science, and Enlightenment are phenomena that helped Europe chart its unique path in world history. These phenomena are not the result of some special genius among Europeans, but rather due to the much humbler historical trajectory of a poor and largely uncultured region that began on the periphery of the Eurasian continent and acculturated itself to the level of a sophisticated, fully diversified religious civilization only thanks to interaction with and adaptation to outside stimuli. Eventually, the tables would turn: for the last few hundred years, Asia, Africa, and Latin America have adapted to the modern stimulus of Western scientific–industrial civilization.

AXIOMATA SIVE LEGES MOTUS

Lex. I.

Corpus omne perseverare in statu suo quiescendi vel movendi uniformiter in directum, nisi quatenus a viribus impressis cogitur statum illum mutare.

Projectilia perseverant in motibus suis nisi quatenus a resisten-

Actioni contrariam semper & æqualem esse reactionem : sive corporum duorum actiones in se mutuo semper esse æquales & in partes contrarias dirigi.

Quicquid premit vel trahit alterum, tantundem ab eo premitur vel trahitur. Siquis lapidem digito premit, premitur & hujus digitus a lapide. Si equus lapidem funi allegatum trahit, retrahetur etiam & equus æqualiter in lapidem: nam funis utrinq; distentus eodem relaxandi se conatu urgebit Equum versus lapidem, ac lapidem versus equum, tantumq; impediet progressum unius quantum promovet progressum alterius. Si corpus aliquod in corpus aliud impingens, motum ejus vi sua quomodocunq; mutaverit, idem quoque vicissim in motu proprio eandem mutationem in partem contrariam vi alterius (ob æqualitatem pressionis mutuæ) subibit. His actionibus æquales fiunt mutationes non velocitatum sed motuum, (scilicet in corporibus non aliunde impeditis :) Mu-

---

One of the most remarkable scientific minds of the seventeenth century was Maria Cunitz (ca. 1607–1664). Under the tutorship of her father, a physician, she became accomplished in six languages, the humanities, and the sciences. During the Thirty Years' War (1618–1648), as Cunitz and her Protestant family sought refuge in a Cistercian monastery, she wrote *Urania propitia* (*Companion to Urania*), in praise of the Greek muse and patron of astronomy. When the family returned home, Cunitz continued to devote her life to science through her careful astronomical observations.

Cunitz's book is a popularization of the astronomical tables of Johannes Kepler (1571–1630), who discovered the elliptical trajectories of the planets. Cunitz's book, published privately in 1650, makes corrections in Kepler's tables and offers simplified calculations of star positions. It was generally well received, although there were a few detractors who found it hard to believe that a woman could succeed in the sciences.

Cunitz lived in a time when Western Christianity had entered the age of early global interaction, from 1450 until 1750. Europe remained institutionally similar to the other parts of the world, especially the Middle East, India, China, and Japan: Rulers throughout Eurasia governed by divine grace; all large states followed patterns of political centralization; and their economies depended on the productivity of agriculture.

Culturally, however, northwestern Europe began to move in a different direction from Islamic, Hindu, Neo-Confucian, and Buddhist civilizations after 1500. New developments in the sciences and philosophy in Europe initiated new cultural patterns. As significant as these patterns were, these new mathematized sciences remained limited to a relatively few educated persons, largely outside the ruling classes. Their ideas diverged substantially from those represented by the Catholic and Protestant ruling classes

CHAPTER OUTLINE

Cultural Transformations: Renaissance, Baroque, and New Sciences

Centralizing States and Religious Upheavals

Putting It All Together

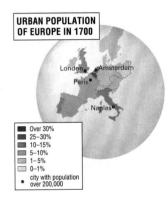

URBAN POPULATION OF EUROPE IN 1700

- Over 30%
- 25–30%
- 10–15%
- 5–10%
- 1–5%
- 0–1%
- • city with population over 200,000

London · Amsterdam
Paris ·
Naples ·

ABOVE: In his *Principia Mathematica*, first published in 1687, Isaac Newton (1643–1727) unified physics and astronomy into a single mathematical system.

Seeing Patterns

❯ What were the reasons for the cultural change that began in Europe with the Renaissance around 1400? In which ways were the subsequent patterns of cultural change different from those in the other religious civilizations of Eurasia?

❯ When and how did the mathematization of the sciences begin, and how did it gain popularity in northwestern Europe? Why is the popularization of the sciences important for understanding the period 1500–1750?

❯ What were the patterns of centralized state formation and transformation in the period 1400–1750? How did the Protestant Reformation and religious wars modify these patterns?

Renaissance: "Rebirth" of culture based on new publications and translations of Greek, Hellenistic, and Roman authors whose writings were previously unknown in Western Christianity.

New Sciences: Mathematized sciences, such as physics, introduced in the 1500s.

and resulted in tensions or even repression of scientists by the authorities. The new scientific and intellectual culture broadened after 1750 and eventually led to the Industrial Revolution.

The European Renaissance, Baroque, and New Sciences began with the appropriation of the Greek and Roman cultural heritage, allegedly absent from the Middle Ages, by an educated elite. However, this elite overestimated the extent of their break from the Middle Ages. Scholars today understand this break as far less radical, with much in culture remaining unchanged. Similarly, the political and social changes of the period 1400–1750 have to be balanced against inherited continuities. While the seeds of a departure of Western Christianity from the general patterns of agrarian–urban society were planted around 1500, the "great divergence" from the agrarian–urban patterns of Islamic, Hindu, and Chinese civilizations began only after 1750.

Cultural Transformations: Renaissance, Baroque, and New Sciences

The **Renaissance** was a period of cultural transformation in the fifteenth century that followed the scholastic Middle Ages in Western Christianity. Its thinkers and artists considered their period a time of "rebirth" (which is the literal meaning of "renaissance" in French). They were powerfully influenced by the writings of Greek and Hellenistic-Roman authors who had been unknown during the scholastic age. In the sixteenth century, the Renaissance gave way to the Baroque in the arts and the **New Sciences**.

The Renaissance and Baroque Arts

An outpouring of learning, scholarship, and art began around 1400 in Italy and spread through northwestern Europe. Thinkers and artists benefited from Greek and Hellenistic-Roman texts that scholars had discovered in Byzantium. The emerging cultures of the Renaissance and Baroque were creative adaptations of those Greek and Hellenistic-Roman writings to the cultural heritage of Western Christianity. This vibrant mixture led to the movement of **Humanism**.

New Manuscripts and Printing   Eastern Christian Byzantium experienced a cultural revival between 1261 and the 1453 Muslim Ottoman conquest of Constantinople. Italian scholars, aware of how much of Greek literature was still absent from Western Christianity, invited Eastern Christian scholars to bring manuscripts to Italy for teaching and translation. Their students became fluent in Greek and translated Hesiod and Homer, Greek plays, Plato and the Neo-Platonists, the still missing works of Aristotle, Hellenistic scientific texts, and the Greek church fathers.

The dissemination of these works was helped by the development of paper. Experimentation in the 1430s with movable metal typeface led to the printing press. A half century later, a printing revolution had taken place in Europe.

Philology and Political Theory   This examination of manuscripts encouraged the study of Greek, Latin, and Hebrew philology. The best-known philologist was the Dutchman Desiderius Erasmus (1466–1536), who published an edition of the Greek and Latin New Testaments in 1516.

Another approach emerged as a central element in political thought. In *The Prince*, Niccolò Machiavelli (1469–1527) argued that what Italy needed was a unifier who possessed what Aristotle discussed in Book 5 of his *Politics*: a person of indomitable spirit (Italian *virtù*) to take the proper steps when political success was to be achieved. Many Renaissance scholars preferred Plato, but Machiavelli remained faithful to Aristotle—an Aristotle later esteemed by the American founding fathers.

The Renaissance Arts   In Italy, a new artistic way of looking at the Roman past and the natural world emerged. The first artists to adopt this perspective were the sculptor Donatello (ca. 1386–1466) and the architect Filippo Brunelleschi (1377–1446), who received their inspiration from Roman imperial statues and ruins. The artistic triumvirate of the high Italian Renaissance was composed of Leonardo da Vinci (1452–1519), Michelangelo (1475–1564), and Raphael (1483–1520). Inspired by the Italian creative outburst, the Renaissance flourished also in Germany, the Netherlands, and France.

For musical composers of the Renaissance, the difficulty was that the music of the Greeks and Romans was completely unknown. A partial solution for this difficulty was found through emphasizing the relationship between the word—that is, rhetoric—and music. In the sixteenth century this emphasis coincided with the Protestant and Catholic demand for liturgical music, such as hymns and masses.

The theater was a relatively late expression of the Renaissance. The popular mystery, passion, and morality plays from the centuries prior to 1400 continued in Catholic countries. In Italy, in the course of the fifteenth century, the *commedia dell'arte* (a secular popular theater) emerged. In England during the sixteenth century, theater troupes were stationary and professional. Sponsored by the aristocracy and the Elizabethan court, the best-known playwright was William Shakespeare (1564–1616).

The Baroque Arts   The Renaissance gave way around 1600 to the Baroque, which dominated the arts until about 1750. Two factors influenced its emergence. First, the Protestant Reformation, Catholic Reformation, and religious wars changed the nature of patronage, on which artists depended. Many Protestant

Humanism: Intellectual movement focusing on human culture, in such fields as philosophy, philology, and literature, and based on the corpus of Greek and Roman texts.

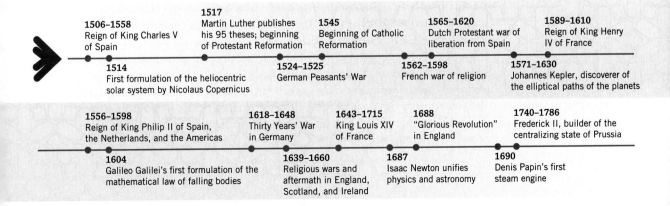

1506–1558
Reign of King Charles V of Spain

1517
Martin Luther publishes his 95 theses; beginning of Protestant Reformation

1545
Beginning of Catholic Reformation

1565–1620
Dutch Protestant war of liberation from Spain

1589–1610
Reign of King Henry IV of France

1514
First formulation of the heliocentric solar system by Nicolaus Copernicus

1524–1525
German Peasants' War

1562–1598
French war of religion

1571–1630
Johannes Kepler, discoverer of the elliptical paths of the planets

1556–1598
Reign of King Philip II of Spain, the Netherlands, and the Americas

1618–1648
Thirty Years' War in Germany

1643–1715
King Louis XIV of France

1688
"Glorious Revolution" in England

1740–1786
Frederick II, builder of the centralizing state of Prussia

1604
Galileo Galilei's first formulation of the mathematical law of falling bodies

1639–1660
Religious wars and aftermath in England, Scotland, and Ireland

1687
Isaac Newton unifies physics and astronomy

1690
Denis Papin's first steam engine

churches, opposed to imagery as incompatible with their view of early Christianity, did not sponsor artists for the adornment of their buildings with religious art.

Second, the predilection for Renaissance balance and restraint gave way to greater spontaneity and dramatic effect. Church and palace architecture shifted to the "baroque" voluptuousness of forms and decorations seen in Bavarian and Austrian Catholic churches, the Versailles Palace, and St. Paul's Cathedral in London, all completed between 1670 and 1750. Baroque composers, as exemplified by the Italian Antonio Vivaldi (1678–1741) and the German Johann Sebastian Bach (1685–1750), benefited from ample church and palace patronage.

The New Sciences

Italian Renaissance scholars were divided between those who continued to adhere to the scholastic Aristotelian scientific method and those (such as Copernicus) who were more interested in newly translated Hellenistic mathematical, astronomical, and geographical texts. In the 1600s, two scientists—Galileo and Newton—abandoned much of the *qualitative* scientific method of Aristotelian scholasticism in favor of the *mathematized* science of physics. In the eighteenth century, Newton's science of a mechanical, deterministic universe became the foundation of modern scientific–industrial society.

Copernicus's Incipient New Science   Nicolaus Copernicus (1473–1543) was born in Toruń, a German-founded city under Polish rule. He studied at the University of Kraków, the only eastern European school to offer courses in astronomy. During the years 1495–1504, he continued his studies at Italian universities. In 1500 he taught mathematics in Rome and perhaps read Greek astronomical texts translated from Arabic. After he graduated with a degree in canon law, Copernicus took an administrative position at the cathedral of Toruń, which allowed him time to pursue astronomical research. One text that Copernicus read, the *Geography* written by the Hellenistic cosmographer Ptolemy, proposed the geographical concept of Earth as a globe composed of a single sphere of intermingled earth and water. This text contradicted the medieval floating theory, according to which the Eurasian-African land mass was one compact body floating on a large surrounding ocean.

Between 1507 and 1514, Copernicus realized that the discovery of the Americas in 1492 provided empirical proof for the theory of the world as a single earth-water sphere, where earth and water were more or less evenly distributed across the surface. It is likely that he saw the new world map by the German cartographer Martin Waldseemüller (ca. 1470–1520), which made him aware of the Americas as hitherto unknown inhabited lands on the other side of the world.

As a result, Copernicus firmly espoused the Ptolemaic theory of the single intermingled water–earth sphere. A globe with well-distributed water and landmasses is a perfect body that moves in perfect circular paths, he argued further. He formulated a hypothesis, according to which the earth is not an exceptional physical object at the center of the universe but a body that has the same appearance and performs the same motions as the other bodies in the planetary system, especially the sun with its similar path. With this revolutionary idea—**heliocentrism**—Copernicus removed the earth from the center of the planetary system and made it revolve around the sun.

Heliocentrism: The discovery that the sun is the center of our solar system.

Renaissance Art. Brunelleschi's cupola for the cathedral of Florence, completed in 1436, was one of the greatest achievements of the early Renaissance (a). Raphael's School of Athens (1509–1510) depicts some 50 philosophers and scientists, with Plato (in red tunic) and Aristotle (blue) in the center of the painting (b).

Galileo's Mathematical Physics   In the decades between the births of Copernicus and Galileo Galilei (1564–1642), mathematics expanded considerably. Euclid's *Elements* was retranslated correctly from the original Greek in 1543. A translation in 1544 of a text on floating and descending bodies by the Hellenistic scholar Archimedes (287–212 BCE) also attracted intense scholarly attention.

In 1604, Galileo combined geometry, algebra, and Archimedean physics to formulate his mathematical "law of falling bodies." While earlier scholars reflected on the logical and/or geometric properties of motion only "according to imagination," Galileo systematically combined imagination with empirical research and experimentation. He thereby established what we now call the (mathematized) "New Sciences."

Running Afoul of the Church   Galileo was one of the first astronomers to use a telescope, which had been recently invented in Flanders. On the basis of his astronomical work, in 1610 he became chief mathematician and philosopher at the court of the Medici, the ruling family of Florence. But his increasing fame also attracted the enmity of the Catholic Church.

As a proponent of Copernican heliocentrism, Galileo seemed to contradict the passage in the Hebrew Bible where God recognized the motion of the sun around the earth. (In Joshua 10:12–13, God stopped the sun's revolution for a day so that the Israelites could win a battle.) In contrast to the more tolerant pope at the time of Copernicus, the Roman Inquisition favored a strictly literal interpretation of this passage. In 1633 Galileo was condemned to house arrest and forced to make a public repudiation of heliocentrism.

The condemnation of Galileo had a chilling effect on scientists in countries where the Catholic Reformation was dominant, such as Italy, Spain, and Portugal. During the seventeenth century, interest in the New Sciences shifted to France,

Waldseemüller's 1507 World Map. The German mapmaker Martin Waldseemüller was the first western Christian to draw a world map which included the newly discovered Americas. He gave them the name "America" after the Italian explorer Amerigo Vespucci (1454–1512), who was the first to state that the Americas were a separate landmass, unconnected to Asia. The single copy of Waldseemüller's map still extant is among the holdings of the US Library of Congress.

Germany, the Netherlands, and England. In these countries, no single church authority was sufficiently dominant to enforce the literal understanding of scripture. As a result, these countries produced mathematicians, astronomers, physicists, and inventors, Catholic as well as Protestant. It was this relative intellectual freedom, not sympathy on the part of religious authorities for the New Sciences, which allowed the latter to flourish, especially in the Netherlands and England.

Iberian Natural Sciences   Southern European countries were still well situated to make substantial scientific contributions, even if not in the New Sciences. Botanists, geographers, ethnographers, physicians, and metallurgists fanned out across the new colonies to research the new plants, diseases, peoples, and mineral resources of the New World, Africa, and Asia. They used the traditional methods of the natural sciences and accumulated a voluminous amount of knowledge. For long periods, the Habsburg monarch kept these discoveries hidden, fearful that colonial competitors would benefit from them. It is only recently that the Iberian contributions to the sciences in the 1500s and 1600s have become more widely known.

Isaac Newton's Mechanics   In the middle of the English struggles between the Protestants and the Catholic/Philo-Catholic Stuart monarchs, Isaac Newton (1643–1727) brought the New Sciences of Copernicus and Galileo to their culmination. As a professor at the University of Cambridge, his primary early contribution was calculus, which he developed at the same time as the German philosopher Gottfried Wilhelm Leibniz (1646–1716). Later in his career, Newton unified the fields of physics and astronomy, establishing the so-called Newtonian synthesis. His *Mathematical Principles of Natural Philosophy*, published in 1687, established a deterministic universe following mathematical rules and formed the basis of science until the early twentieth century, when quantum physics with its conclusion of indeterminacy superseded Newtonianism.

The New Sciences and Their Social Impact

Scientists in the seventeenth century met each other in scientific societies or residential salons. Popularizers introduced the public to the New Sciences. Scientific instruments such as telescopes, microscopes, thermometers, and barometers were constantly improving. Experimentation with barometers, vacuum chambers, and cylinders operating with condensing steam culminated with the invention of the steam engine in England in 1712.

New Science Societies   When the Catholic Reformation drove the New Sciences to northwestern Europe, chartered scientific societies, such as the Royal Society of London (1660) and the Paris Academy of Sciences (1666), were established. These societies co-opted scientists as fellows, held regular meetings, challenged their fellows to answer scientific questions, awarded prizes, and organized expeditions. They also published their findings. Some societies attracted thousands of members representing an important cross section of seventeenth-century urban society in northwest Europe (see Map 17.1).

The New Science triumphed in northwestern Europe in a large, scientifically and technically interested public of experimenters, engineers, instrument makers, artisans, businesspeople, and lay folk. Popularizers lectured to audiences of middle-class amateurs, instrument makers, and craftspeople, especially in England and the Netherlands. Coffeehouses allowed the literate urban public to meet, hear lectures, read the daily newspapers (first appearing in the early seventeenth century), and exchange ideas. Wealthy businessmen endowed public lectures and supported elaborate experiments and expensive laboratory equipment. Male urban literacy is estimated to have exceeded 50 percent in England and the Netherlands during this period, although it remained considerably lower in France, Germany, and Italy.

Women, Social Salons, and the New Science   Women were part of this scientifically inclined public. In the fields of mathematics and astronomy, Sophie Brahe (1556–1643), sister of the Danish astronomer Tycho Brahe (1546–1601), and Maria Cunitz (see the Vignette at the beginning of the chapter) made contributions to the new astronomy of Copernicus and Kepler. According to some estimates, in the second half of the seventeenth century about 14 percent of German astronomers were women. A dozen prominent female astronomers practiced their science privately in Germany, Poland, the Netherlands, France, and England.

Another institution that helped in the popularization of the New Sciences was the salon. As the elegant living room of an urban residence, the salon was a meeting place for the urban social elite to engage in conversations, presentations, and experiments. The culture of the salon emerged first in Paris. Since the Catholic French universities were hostile to many new ideas, educated urban aristocrats and middle-class professionals turned to the salons as places to learn about new scientific developments. Furthermore, French universities and scientific

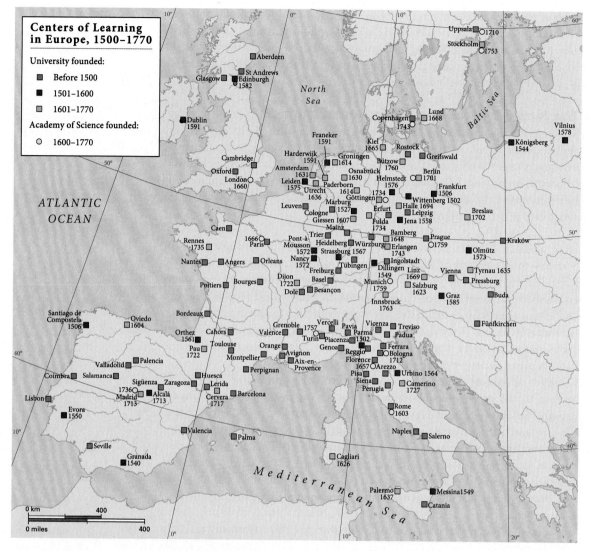

Centers of Learning in Europe, 1500–1770

University founded:
- ■ Before 1500
- ■ 1501–1600
- ■ 1601–1770

Academy of Science founded:
- ○ 1600–1770

MAP 17.1 **Centers of Learning in Europe, 1500–1770**

academies refused to admit women, in contrast to Italian and German institutions. The French salon, therefore, became a bastion of female scholars.

One example of a French woman scientist was Émilie du Châtelet (1706–1749). In a Paris salon she met François-Marie Arouet, known as Voltaire (1694–1778), a writer, skeptic, satirist, and amateur Newtonian. Although Voltaire published prolifically, Châtelet eventually outstripped him in both research and scientific understanding. Her lasting achievement was the translation of Newton's *Mathematical Principles* into French, published in 1759.

Discovery of the Vacuum   Of all the new scientific instruments available at the time, it was the barometer that would prove crucial for the exploration of the properties of the vacuum and condensing steam, eventually leading to the invention of the steam engine. The scientist who laid the groundwork for the barometer was Evangelista Torricelli (1608–1647), an assistant of Galileo. He experimented with mercury-filled glass tubes, demonstrating that atmospheric pressure produced a vacuum inside these tubes.

A few years later, the French mathematician and philosopher Blaise Pascal (1623–1662) used a mercury barometer to demonstrate lower air pressures at higher altitudes. Soon thereafter, scientists discovered the connection between changing atmospheric pressures and the weather. The discovery of the vacuum was an important step toward the practical application of the New Sciences to mechanical engineering in the eighteenth century.

The Steam Engine   The French Huguenot scientist and engineer Denis Papin (ca. 1647–1712) made the first step from the vacuum chamber to the steam engine. In 1690, Papin constructed a cylinder with a piston. Weights, via a cord and two pulleys, held the piston at the top of the cylinder. When heated, water in the bottom of the cylinder turned into steam. When subsequently cooled through the injection of water, the steam condensed, forcing the piston down and lifting the weights up. The Royal Society of London held discussions of his papers, thereby alerting engineers, craftspeople, and entrepreneurs in England to the steam engine as a labor-saving machine. In 1712, the mechanic Thomas Newcomen built the first practical steam engine to pump water from coal mine shafts.

Altogether, it took a little over a century for Europeans to apply the New Sciences to engineering—that is, to the construction of the steam engine. Prior to 1600, mechanical inventions—such as the wheel, the compass, the stern rudder, and the firearm—had been constructed by anonymous tinkerers. By 1700, engineers needed at least a basic understanding of mathematics and such abstract physical phenomena as inertia, gravity, vacuums, and condensing steam in order to build a steam engine or other complex machinery.

Vacuum Power. In 1672, the mayor of Magdeburg, the New Scientist Otto von Guericke, demonstrated the experiment that made him a pioneer in the understanding of the physical properties of the vacuum. In the presence of German emperor Ferdinand III, two teams of horses were unable to pull the two sealed hemispheres apart. Guericke had created a vacuum by pumping out the air from the two sealed copper spheres.

The New Sciences: Philosophical Interpretations

The New Sciences engendered a pattern of radically new intellectual, religious, and political thinking. This thought evolved into a powerful instrument of critique of Christian doctrine and the constitutional order of the absolutist states. Through the new concept of the social contract, these ideas became a potent political force in the course of the 1700s.

Descartes's New Philosophy   The first major New Scientist who started a radical reconsideration of philosophy was the Frenchman René Descartes (1596–1650). In the service of the Dutch and Bavarian courts, he bore witness to the atrocities committed in the name of religious doctrines during the Thirty Years' War. He spent two decades in the Netherlands, studying and teaching the New Sciences. His principal innovation in mathematics was the discovery that geometry could be converted, through algebra, into analytic geometry.

Descartes was shocked by the condemnation of Galileo and decided to abandon all traditional propositions and doctrines of the church. Realizing that the five senses of seeing, hearing, touching, smelling, and tasting were unreliable, he determined that the only reliable body of knowledge was thought, especially mathematical thought. As a person capable of thought, he concluded—bypassing his unreliable senses—that he existed: "I think, therefore I am" (*cogito ergo sum*). A further conclusion from this argument was that he was composed of two radically different substances, a material substance consisting of his body (that is, his senses) and another, immaterial substance consisting of his thinking mind.

Variations on Descartes's New Philosophy   Descartes's radical distinction between body and mind stimulated a lively debate. Was this distinction only conceptual, while reality was experienced as a unified whole? If the dualism was real as well as conceptual, which substance was more fundamental, sensual bodily experience or mental activity, as the creator of the concepts of experience? The answers of three philosophers—Baruch Spinoza, Thomas Hobbes, and John Locke—set the course for two major directions of philosophy during the so-called Enlightenment of the 1700s (see Chapter 23), one Continental European and the other Anglo-American.

For Baruch Spinoza (1632–1677), Descartes's distinction between body and mind was to be understood only in a conceptual sense. He therefore abandoned Descartes's distinction and developed a philosophical system that sought to integrate Galilean nature, the ideas of God, the Good in ethics, and the Just in politics into a unified whole. The Jewish community of Amsterdam, into which he had been born, excommunicated him for heresy, since he seemed to make God immanent in the world.

Both Thomas Hobbes (1588–1679) and John Locke (1632–1704) not only accepted Descartes's radical distinction; they made the body the fundamental reality and the mind a dependent function. Consequently, they focused on the bodily passions, not reason, as the principal human character trait. Hobbes speculated that individuals in the primordial state of nature were engaged in a "war of all against all." To survive, they forged a **social contract** in which they transferred

Social contract: An implicit agreement among the members of a society to cooperate for mutually shared benefits.

all power to a sovereign. Hobbes's book *Leviathan* (1651) can be read as a political theory of absolute rule, but his ideas of a social contract and transfer of power nevertheless move also toward constitutionalism.

Locke focused on the more benign bodily passion of acquisitiveness. Primordial individuals, so he argued, engaged as equals in a social contract for the purpose of erecting a government that protected their properties and established a civil society governed by law. With Hobbes and Locke a line of new thought came to its conclusion, leading from Descartes's two substances to the ideas of absolutism as well as democratic constitutionalism.

Centralizing States and Religious Upheavals

The pattern of the centralizing state transforming the institutional structures of society was characteristic not only of the Ottoman and Habsburg Empires during 1450–1750, but also of other countries of Europe, the Middle East, and India. The financial requirements for such a state required a reorganization of the relationship between rulers, ruling classes, and regional forces. Although the Protestant Reformation and religious wars slowed the pattern of central state formation, two types of states eventually emerged: the French, Russian, and Prussian landed centralizing state and the Dutch and English naval centralizing state.

The Rise of Centralized Kingdoms

The shift from feudal knights to firearm-equipped professional infantries led to states whose rulers sought to strengthen their administrations. Rulers centralized state power, collected taxes, and curbed the decentralizing forces of the nobility, cities, and local institutions. Not all city-states, city-leagues, and religious orders dating to the previous period (600–1450) survived the race to centralization. A winnowing process during 1450–1550 left only a few kingdoms in control of European politics.

The Demographic Curve   Following the demographic disaster of the Black Death, the population of the European states expanded again after 1470 and continued to grow until about 1600, when it entered a half century of stagnation during the coldest and wettest period in recorded history, the Little Ice Age (1550–1750). During 1650–1750, the population rose slowly at a moderate rate from 105 to 140 million. The overall population figures for Europe demonstrate that Western Christianity had risen by 1750 to demographic equivalence to the two leading religious civilizations of India (155 million) and China (225 million).

A Heritage of Decentralization   Bracketed between the two empires of the Ottomans and Habsburgs, Western Christian Europe during the second half of the fifteenth century was comprised of independent or autonomous units,

Mapping the World

In 1400, no accurate map of the world existed anywhere. Prior to the first Portuguese sailing expeditions down the west coast of Africa in the 1420s and 1430s, mariners relied upon local knowledge of winds, waves, and stars to navigate. The Portuguese were the first to use science to sail, adapting scholarship in trigonometry, astronomy, and solar timekeeping developed by Jewish and Muslim scientists in Iberia.

Crucial to this approach was latitude, which required precise calculations of the daily changes in the path of the sun relative to the earth and determination of the exact height of the sun. The invention of the nautical astrolabe in 1497 by the Jewish scientist Abraham Zacuto aided this process. To determine longitude, Jewish scientists in Portugal adapted a method based on the work of the Islamic astronomer al-Biruni (973–1048).

The new maps of the fifteenth century also drew upon an innovation from another part of the world: the compass. Originating in China, the compass was used as a navigational instrument by Muslim sailors during the twelfth century. In the thirteenth century, mapmakers in the Mediterranean began to include compasses on portolans, or nautical charts, enabling sailors to follow their direction on a map.

including the centralizing kingdoms of France and England; the Hanseatic League of trading cities; the Baltic territory ruled by the Catholic crusading order of Teutonic Knights; and the small kingdoms of Denmark, Sweden, Norway, Poland–Lithuania, Bohemia, and Hungary. It furthermore comprised the principalities and cities of Germany, the duchy of Burgundy, the republic of Switzerland, and the city-states of Italy. At the northeastern periphery was the Grand Duchy of Moscow, representing Eastern Christianity after the fall of Byzantium to the Ottomans in 1453. Many of these units competed with each other.

Military and Administrative Capacities   In the course of the sixteenth century, some kingdoms turned their mercenary troops into standing armies and stationed them in star-shaped forts capable of withstanding artillery fire. Habsburg as well as Dutch troops introduced the line infantry in the course of the sixteenth century. Since the line formation required peacetime drills and maneuvers, the regimental system came into use. Soldiers formed permanent regiments and wore standardized multicolored uniforms.

The French-invented flintlock gradually replaced the matchlock musket during 1620–1630. Similarly, during 1660–1700 the French introduced and improved the bayonet. By 1750, armies in the larger European countries were more uniform in their armaments and increased to tens of thousands of soldiers (see Map 17.2).

The military forces were expensive, and taxes expanded during the period 1450–1550. But rulers could not raise taxes without the assent of the ruling classes and cities. Villagers simply moved when taxes became too oppressive. The taxation limits were reached in most European countries in the mid-sixteenth century,

With an accurate science for fixing latitude and improved knowledge for longitude, the science of cartography was transformed in the fifteenth and sixteenth centuries. Any place on earth could be mapped mathematically in relation to any other place, and the direction in which one place lay in relation to another could be plotted using compass lines. By 1500 mapmakers could locate any newly discovered place in the world on a map.

Portolan by Pedro Reinel. Drawn in 1504 by the great Portuguese cartographer Pedro Reinel (ca. 1462–ca. 1542), this nautical chart (portolan) shows compass lines and is the earliest known map to include lines of latitude.

Questions

- How were adaptations from various cultural traditions essential to the transformation of cartography in the fifteenth and sixteenth centuries?

- How are developments in cartography in this time period an example of the shift from descriptive science to mathematical science?

and for the next two centuries rulers could raise finances only to the detriment of their central powers, such as by borrowing from merchants and selling offices. The Netherlands was an exception. Only there did the urban population rise from 10 to 40 percent, willing to pay higher taxes on expanded urban manufactures and commercial suburban farming. The Dutch government also derived revenues from charters granted to overseas trading companies. Given the severe limits on revenue-raising measures in most of Europe, the eighteenth century saw a general deterioration of state finances, which eventually contributed to the American and French Revolutions.

The Protestant Reformation, State Churches, and Independent Congregations

Parallel to the centralism of the kings, the popes restored the central role of the Vatican in the church hierarchy. The popes undertook expensive Vatican construction projects that aroused criticism, especially in Germany, where the leading clergy was strongly identified with Rome. Growing literacy and lay religiosity nurtured a profound theological dissatisfaction, leading to the **Protestant Reformation**. The Reformation began as a movement in the early sixteenth century that demanded a return to the simplicity of early Christianity. The movement quickly engulfed the kingdoms and resulted in religious wars. The divisions mark the culture of Europe even today.

Background to the Reformation   Religious and political changes in the fifteenth century led to the Protestant Reformation. One religious shift was the growth of popular theology, a consequence of the introduction of the printing

Protestant Reformation: Broad movement to reform the Roman Catholic Church, the beginnings of which are usually associated with Martin Luther.

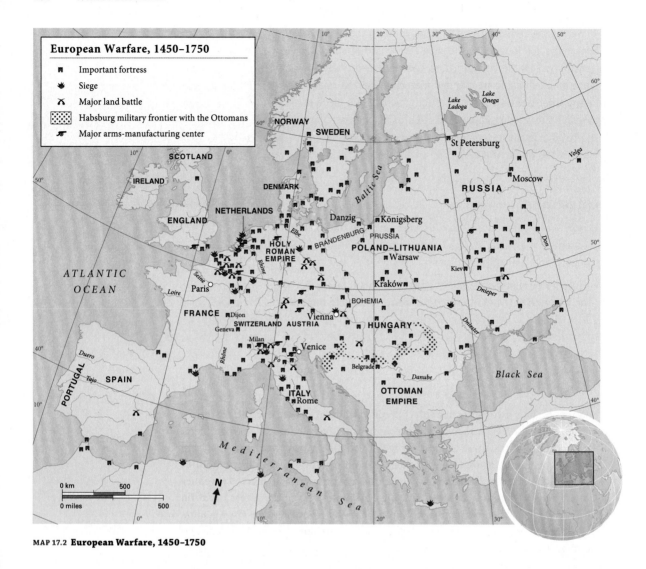

European Warfare, 1450–1750

- ⊞ Important fortress
- ⚘ Siege
- ⚔ Major land battle
- ⊡ Habsburg military frontier with the Ottomans
- ⚒ Major arms-manufacturing center

MAP 17.2 **European Warfare, 1450–1750**

Indulgence: Partial remission of sins after payment of a fine or presentation of a donation. Remission would mean the forgiveness of sins by the Church, but the sinner still remained responsible for his or her sins before God.

press (1454/1455). Devotional tracts catered to the spiritual interests of ordinary people. Many Christians attended Mass daily. Wealthy Christians endowed saint cults and charitable institutions; poor people studied scripture on their own (provided they could read).

A key political change was an increasing inability of the popes to appoint archbishops and bishops outside Italy. The kings of France, Spain, England, and Sweden were transforming their kingdoms into centralized states, reducing the influence of the popes. (The popes' influence remained strong in the politically splintered Germany.) What remained to the popes was the right to collect dues, which they used to finance their expensive administration in Rome. One of the dues was the sale of **indulgences**, which, in popular understanding, were tickets to heaven. Those disturbed by the discrepancy between declining papal power and the remaining financial privileges demanded reforms.

Calvinist preachers went to France and the Netherlands in the mid-1500s. Under the protection of local magistrates, they organized the first independent Calvinist congregations. Calvinist religious self-organization by independent congregations became an alternative to Lutheran state religion.

The Catholic Reformation   The rivalry between Spain and France made it difficult for the popes to address Catholic reforms in order to meet the Protestant challenge. Finally, at the Council of Trent (1545–1563), they abolished payment for indulgences and phased out other church practices considered to be corrupt. These actions launched the **Catholic Reformation**, an effort to gain back dissenting Catholics. Supported by the kings of Spain and France, however, the popes made no changes to the traditional doctrines of faith together with good works, priestly mediation between believer and God, and monasticism. They even revived the papal Inquisition and promulgated a new Index of Prohibited Books.

The popes also furthered the work of the priest Ignatius Loyola (1491–1556). At the head of the Jesuits, Loyola devoted himself to the education of the clergy, the establishment of a network of Catholic schools and colleges, and the conversion of Protestants as well as non-Christians by missionaries to the Americas and eastern Asia. Thanks to Jesuit discipline, Catholics regained self-assurance against the Protestants.

Religious Wars and Political Restoration

The growth of Calvinism led to a civil war in France and a war of liberation from Spanish Catholic rule in the Netherlands in the later sixteenth century. In England, the slow pace of reform in the Anglican Church erupted in the early seventeenth century into a civil war. In Germany, the Catholic–Protestant struggle turned into the Thirty Years' War (1618–1648). The centralizing states evolved into polities based on absolutism, tempered by provincial and local administrative practices.

Civil War in France   During the mid-1500s, Calvinism in France grew mostly in the western cities, where literate merchants and craftspeople were receptive to Protestant publications. Calvinism was an urban denomination; peasants, rooted more deeply in traditional ways of life, did not join in large numbers. Some 10 percent of the population were Huguenots, as the Protestants were called in France. The Huguenots posed a formidable challenge to French Catholicism; and although the government persecuted them, it was impossible to imprison or execute them all.

In many cities, relations between Huguenots and Catholics were uneasy. From time to time, groups of agitators crashed each other's church services. Hostilities escalated after 1560, when the government weakened under a child king and was unable to deal with the increasingly powerful Huguenots. In four western cities, the Huguenots achieved self-government and full freedom of religious practice from the crown. Concerned to find a compromise, in 1572 the now reigning king married his sister to the leader of the Huguenots, King Henry III of Navarre (later King Henry IV of France, 1589–1610), a Protestant

Catholic Reformation: Also known as Counter-Reformation. Reaffirmation of Catholic papal supremacy and the doctrine of faith together with works as preparatory to salvation. Such practices as absenteeism (bishops in Rome instead of their bishoprics) and pluralism (bishops and abbots holding multiple appointments) were abolished.

of the Bourbon family in southwestern France. Henry detested the fanaticism that surrounded him.

Only six days after the wedding, on St. Bartholomew's Day (August 24, 1572), outraged members of the Catholic aristocracy perpetrated a wholesale slaughter of thousands of Huguenots. This massacre, in response to the assassination of a French admiral, occurred with the apparent connivance of the court. For over a decade and a half, civil war raged, in which Spain aided the Catholics and Henry enrolled German and Swiss Protestant mercenaries. A turning point came only when Henry of Navarre became King Henry IV in 1589. It was nine years before he was able to calm the religious fanaticism of the French people. With the Edict of Nantes in 1598, he decreed freedom of religion for Protestants. However, Catholic adherents were deeply offended by the edict as well as by the alleged antipapal policies of Henry IV, and the king was assassinated in 1610. In 1685, King Louis XIV revoked the edict and triggered the emigration of Huguenots to the Netherlands, Germany, England, and North America. At last, France was Catholic again.

The Dutch War of Independence   In the Netherlands, the Spanish overlords were determined to keep the country Catholic. When Charles V resigned in 1556 (effective 1558), his son Philip II (r. 1556–1598) became king of Spain and the Netherlands. Like his father, Philip supported the Catholic Reformation. He asked the Jesuits and the Inquisition to aggressively persecute the Calvinists. Philip also subdivided the bishoprics into smaller units and recruited clergymen in place of members of the nobility.

In response, in 1565 the nobility and Calvinist congregations rose in revolt, triggering what was to become a Protestant war of Dutch liberation from Catholic Spanish overlordship (1565–1620). Philip suppressed the liberation movement, re-imposed Catholicism, and executed thousands of rebels, many of them members of the Dutch aristocracy.

In 1579, rebels renewed the war of liberation. Spain kept fighting the rebellion until acute Spanish financial difficulties prompted the truce of 1609–1621. Although drawn into fighting again during the Thirty Years' War, the Netherlands gained its full independence eventually in 1648.

Civil War in England   The prevalent form of Protestantism in England was Calvinism. During the sixteenth century, the majority of people in England, including Calvinists, belonged to the Anglican Church. English Catholics were a small minority. The percentage of Calvinists was the same as in France before 1685, but the partially reformed Anglican Church under the tolerant queen Elizabeth I (1533–1603) was able to hold them in check.

The Calvinists encompassed moderate and radical tendencies that neutralized each other. Among the radicals were the Puritans, who demanded the abolition of the Anglican clerical hierarchy and a new church order of independent congregations. When Anglican Church reform slowed with the arrival of the Stuart monarchs on the throne of England (1603–1685), unfortunately the balance among the religious tendencies unraveled. As rulers of England, the Stuarts were officially heads of the Anglican state church, but except for the first king, the three successors were either Catholics or Catholic sympathizers. Since they were furthermore rulers of what was called the England of the Three Kingdoms they found it impossible to maneuver among the demands of the English Puritans, Scottish Presbyterians (self-governing regional Calvinists), and Catholic Irish. The issue of how little or how far the Anglican Church had been reformed away from Catholicism and how dominant it should be in the three realms became more and more divisive (see Source 17.1).

In addition, the Stuarts were intent on building a centralized state, highlighting the supremacy of royal over parliamentary power. They collected taxes without the approval of Parliament. Many members of Parliament resented being bypassed. A slight majority in the House of Commons was Puritan, and what they considered the stalled church reform added to their resentment. Eventually, when all tax resources were exhausted, the king had to call Parliament back together. The two sides were unable to come to an agreement, however, and civil war broke out. Since this war was also a conflict among the Three Kingdoms, it had both religious and regional aspects (1639–1651).

Because of widespread pillage and destruction, the indirect effects of the war for the rural population were severe. The **New Model Army**, a professional body of 22,000 troops raised by the Puritan-dominated English Parliament against the royal forces, caused further upheavals by cleansing villages of their "frivolous" local traditions. In the end, Charles was beheaded in 1649 and the monarchy was replaced with a republican theocracy, the "Commonwealth of England."

New Model Army: Army founded by the English parliament in 1645. Infused with Puritan zeal, it was equipped with standardized weapons and professionally trained.

Republic, Restoration, and Revolution   The ruler of this theocracy, Oliver Cromwell (r. 1649–1658), was a Puritan member of the lower nobility and a commander in the New Model Army. After dissolving Parliament, Cromwell handpicked a new parliament but ruled mostly without its consent. Since both Scotland and Ireland were opposed to the English Puritans, Cromwell waged a savage war of submission against the two. The Dutch and Spanish, also opponents of the Puritans, were defeated in naval wars that increased English power in the Atlantic. But fear in Parliament of a permanent centralized state led to a refusal of financial subsidies for the military. After Cromwell's death in 1658, it took just three years to restore the Stuart monarchy and the Anglican state church.

The recalled Stuart kings, however, resumed the policies of centralization. As before, the kings rarely called Parliament together and raised funds without its authorization. But their standing army was intended more to intimidate the parliamentarians than to subjugate them. In the "Glorious Revolution" of 1688, a defiant Parliament deposed the king and made his daughter and her Dutch husband the new co-regents.

The Thirty Years' War in Germany   Continuing religious tensions in Germany erupted into the Thirty Years' War. Rulers of the German principalities had made either Catholicism or Protestantism their state religion, though most tolerated minorities or even admitted them to offices. The Jesuit-educated Ferdinand II (r. 1619–1637), ruler of the Holy Roman Empire, however, refused to appoint Protestants in majority-Protestant Bohemia. In response, Protestant leaders in 1618 renounced Ferdinand's authority and made the Calvinist prince of the Palatinate in the Rhineland their new king.

In a first round of war (1619–1630), Ferdinand and the Catholic princes suppressed the rebellion and advanced toward northern Germany, capturing Lutheran territories for reconversion to Catholicism and defeating Denmark. In 1630, however, the Lutheran king Gustavus II Adolphus (r. 1611–1632) of Sweden intervened. By aiding the German Lutherans, he hoped to consolidate his predominance in the region. Louis XIII (r. 1610–1643) of France granted Sweden financial subsidies, since he was concerned that Ferdinand's victories would further strengthen the Habsburg grip around France. With the politically motivated alliance between Sweden and France, the German Catholic–Protestant war turned into a war for state dominance in Europe.

The Swedes were initially successful but withdrew when Gustavus II Adolphus fell. Ferdinand compromised with the Protestant princes of Germany, by reestablishing the prewar divisions, in order to keep the French out of the war. But Louis XIII entered anyway and occupied Habsburg Alsace. Swedish armies, exploiting the French successes against the Habsburgs, fought their way back into Germany. In 1648, the exhausted Austrian–German Habsburgs agreed to the Peace of Westphalia.

The agreement provided for religious freedom in Germany and ceded Habsburg territories in Alsace to France and the southern side of the Baltic Sea to Sweden. It granted territorial integrity to all European powers. The Spanish

Versailles. Built between 1676 and 1708 on the outskirts of Paris, Versailles emphatically demonstrated the new centralized power of the French monarchy. The main building is a former hunting lodge that Louis XIV decorated with mythological scenes that showed him as the "Sun King." The outer wings housed government offices. Behind the palace, elaborate entertainments were held in the gardens.

Habsburgs continued their war against France until their defeat in 1659, which accelerated the decline of Spain's overseas power. France emerged as the strongest country in Europe, and the Spanish-dominated Caribbean became an area of open rivalry (see Map 17.4).

Absolutism in France? During its period of greatest political dominance, France came under the rule of its longest-reigning monarch, King Louis XIV (r. 1643–1715). He made Versailles—a gigantic palace and gardens near Paris, populated with 10,000 courtiers, attendants, and servants—into a site of almost continuous feasting, entertainment, and intrigue. It was here that Louis, the "Sun King," exercised his "absolute" divine mandate upon his aristocracy and commoners alike.

In practice, the **absolutism** of Louis XIV, as well as absolutism in other European countries, was a mixture of centralized and decentralized forces. On one hand, after the end of the religious wars in 1648, mercenary armies under

Absolutism: Theory of the state in which the unlimited power of the king, ruling under God's divine mandate, was emphasized. In practice, it was neutralized by the nobility and provincial and local communities.

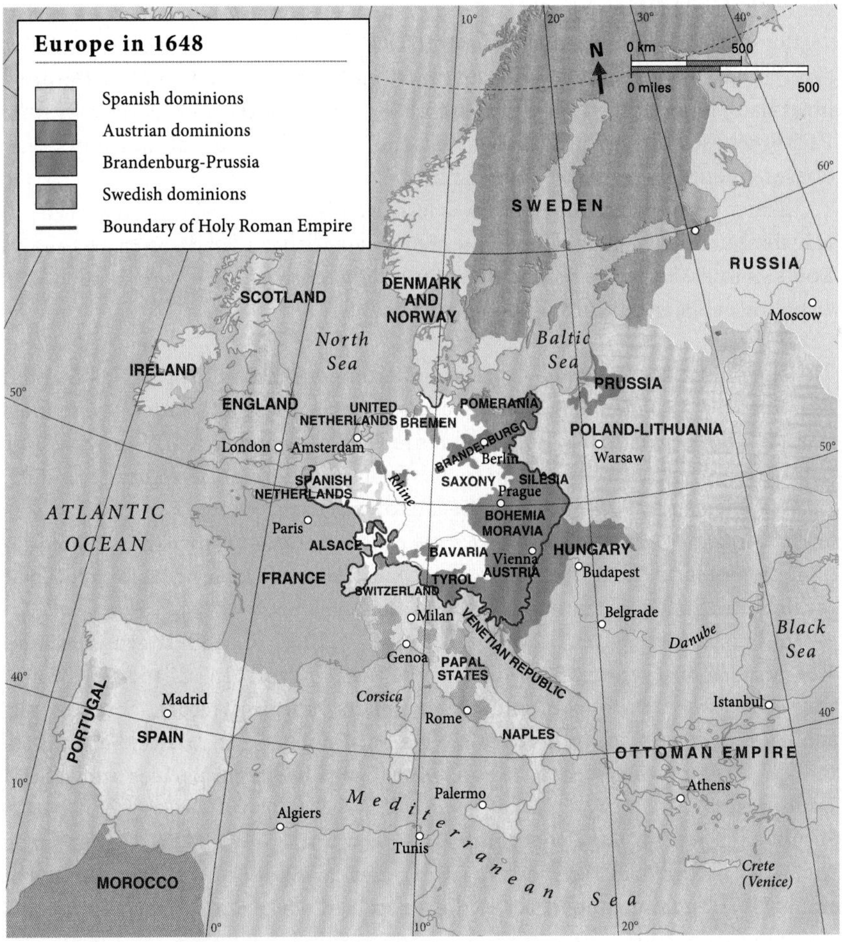

MAP 17.4 **Europe in 1648**

autonomous dukes and counts were replaced by permanent armies or navies under the central command of royal relatives or favorites. The kings no longer called assemblies together to have new taxes approved (in France from 1614 to 1789), and thus many of the nobility's tax privileges disappeared.

On the other hand, kings were aware that true absolutism was possible only if the taxes were collected by centrally salaried employees. However, a centrally paid bureaucracy would have required a central bank with provincial branches, using a credit and debit system. The failed experiment with such a bank in Paris from 1714 to 1720 demonstrated that absolute central control was beyond the powers of the kings.

Instead, the kings had to rely on subcontracting out the collection of taxes to the highest bidders, who then helped themselves to the collection of their incomes. Under Louis XIV anyone who had money or borrowed it from financiers was encouraged to buy an office. The government often forced these officers to grant additional loans to the crown. To retain their loyalty, the government rewarded them with first picks for retaining their offices within the family. They were also privileged to buy landed estates or acquire titles of nobility. By selling offices and titles, the king sought to bind the financial interests of the two nobilities to those of his own.

Louis XIV sent salaried *intendants* to the provinces to ensure that collecting taxes, rendering justice, and policing functioned properly. About half of the provinces had *parlements*—appointed assemblies for the ratification of decrees from Paris—whose officeholders, drawn from the local noble, clerical, and commoner classes, frequently resisted the intendants.

In later years, when Louis XIV was less successful in his wars against the rival Habsburgs and Protestant Dutch, the crown overspent and had to borrow heavily. Louis's successors in the second half of the eighteenth century were saddled with crippling debts, in part brought on by themselves.

The Rise of Russia   The ideological embodiment of absolutism in the Versailles of Louis XIV spawned adaptations across Europe. These adaptations were most visible in eastern Europe, which had far fewer towns and cities. Without a large population of urban commoners to aid them in building the centralized state, rulers there had to make do with the landowning aristocracy. As a result, rulers and aristocracy connived to finance state centralization through an increased exploitation of farmers. In the 1600s, the legal status of farmers deteriorated, their tax liabilities increased, and they became serfs.

Tsar (also spelled czar): Derived from Caesar, title used by the Russian rulers to emphasize their imperial ambitions.

In Russia, **Tsar** Peter I the Great (r. 1682–1725), of the Eastern Christian Romanov dynasty, sought to establish the French-type centralized state. Peter invited western European soldiers, mariners, administrators, craftspeople, scholars, and artists into his service. He built ports on the Baltic Sea and established the new capital of St. Petersburg, with beautiful palaces and official buildings.

The Russian military was completely reorganized by the tsar. Peter made the inherited firearm regiments part of a new army recruited from the traditional Russian landed nobility. Soldiers received education at military schools and academies and were required to provide lifelong service. A census was taken to facilitate the shift from the inherited household tax on the villagers to a new capitation tax collected by military officers. In the process, many farmers now found themselves classified and taxed as serfs, unfree to leave their villages. The result of Peter's reforms was a powerful, expansionary centralizing state (see Map 17.5).

The Rise of Prussia   Like Russia, the principality of Prussia-Brandenburg was underurbanized. When the Lutheran Hohenzollern rulers embarked on the construction of a centralized state in the later seventeenth century, they first broke the tax privileges of the landowning aristocracy and raised taxes themselves through agents. As in Russia, farmers who worked on estates held by landlords were serfs. Since there were few urban middle-class merchants and professionals, the kings enrolled members of the landlord aristocracy in the army and civilian administration.

The Hohenzollern monarchs enlarged the army, employing it during peacetime for drainage and canal projects as well as palace construction in Berlin, the capital. Under Frederick II the Great (r. 1740–1786), Prussia pursued an aggressive foreign policy, seizing Silesia from the Habsburgs in 1742. Frederick also

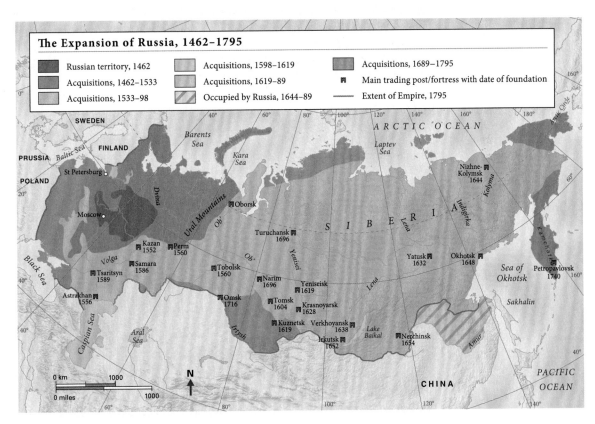

MAP 17.5 **The Expansion of Russia, 1462–1795**

sought to attract immigrants, intensify agriculture, and establish manufacturing. Prussia emerged as a serious competitor of the Habsburgs in the Holy Roman Empire of Germany.

English Constitutionalism   In contrast to Prussia, France, Spain, Austria, and other European states, England had since 1450 a political system ruled by a king or a queen, with a parliament composed of the aristocracy as well as representatives of towns and cities. Only in England did the interests of the nobility and the urban merchants gradually converge: younger sons, unable to inherit the family estate, sought their fortunes in London. English cities allied with the aristocracy in resisting indirect tax increases and forcing the throne to use the revenues of its royal estates to pay soldiers. The efforts of the Stuart kings to create a centralized state based on firearm infantries failed. Instead, the ruling class preferred to build a centralized naval state. After the Glorious Revolution of 1688, England became the world's dominant naval power.

After its victory over the Stuart kings, Parliament consolidated its financial powers through the creation of the Bank of England in 1694. When Mary and William died without children, England continued in 1714 with a king from the principality of Hannover in Germany who was distantly related to the previous royals. Around the same time, England and Scotland united, creating the United Kingdom. Parliament collected taxes and, through its bank, was able to keep its debt service low during the early 1700s. The navy grew twice as large as that of France and was staffed by a well-salaried, disciplined military, while the few land troops were mostly low-paid Hessian-German mercenaries. A two-party system of two aristocracy–merchant alliances emerged. The two

Prussian Military Discipline. The Prussian line infantry made full use in the mid-1700s of flintlock muskets, bayonets, and drilling.

parties were known as the Tories and the Whigs, with the Whigs in power for most of the first half of the eighteenth century.

Putting It All Together

Prior to 1500, all religious civilizations possessed mathematics and qualitative sciences. Trigonometry-based astronomy existed in the Islamic, Hindu, and Christian religious civilizations and was practiced also in China. Physics became the second mathematical science in the early 1500s, but only in Western Christianity. This transformation of the sciences had no practical consequences prior to the invention of the steam engine in the 1700s. Furthermore, the mathematization of physics did little to influence the continued prevalence of qualitative description as the methodology of the other sciences. Most importantly, the rise of the New Sciences should not be confused with the vast changes, called "modernity" after 1800, which propelled the West to world dominance. Although the West began to acquire its scientific and philosophical identity with the introduction of the mathematical sciences in the century between Copernicus and Galileo (1514–1604), the impact of these sciences on the world was felt only after 1800, when they were applied to industry. Once this application gathered momentum in the nineteenth century, Asia and Africa had no choice but to adapt to modern science and industrialization.

Review and Relate

| Thinking Through Patterns

Examine the ways historians approach the big questions of this chapter.

L ocated far from the traditional agrarian–urban centers of Eurasia, Western Christianity adapted its culture in response to outside stimuli coming from Islamic and Eastern Christian civilizations. Without these stimuli, the Renaissance, Baroque, New Science, and Enlightenment would not have developed. In contrast, the Middle East, Byzantium, India, and China, originating within the traditional agrarian–urban centers, received far fewer outside stimuli prior to the scientific–industrial age. Scholars and thinkers in these religious civilizations did not feel the same pressure to change their cultural heritage and adapt as their colleagues in Western Christianity did.

T he discovery of the two new continents of the Americas prompted Nicolaus Copernicus to posit a sun-centered planetary system. Copernicus's new approach to science continued with Galileo Galilei's discovery of the mathematical law of falling bodies in physics and was completed when Isaac Newton unified physics and

> What were the reasons for the cultural change that began in Europe with the Renaissance around 1400? In which ways were the subsequent patterns of cultural change different from those in the other religious civilizations of Eurasia?

> When and how did the New Sciences begin, and how did they gain popularity in

northwestern European society? Why is the popularization of the New Sciences important for understanding the period 1450–1750?

➤ What were the patterns of centralized state formation and transformation in the period 1450–1750? How did the Protestant Reformation and religious wars modify these patterns?

astronomy. The New Sciences became popular in educated urban circles in northwestern Europe, where Catholic and Protestant church authorities were largely divided. In southern Europe, where the Catholic Reformation was powerful and rejected Galileo, the adoption of the New Sciences occurred more slowly. Scientists in northwestern Europe discovered the practical applicability of the New Sciences as they experimented with steam engines, a catalyst for the launching of the scientific–industrial age.

European kingdoms expanded their powers of taxation to the detriment of the nobility. With these funds, they hired and salaried mercenary infantries equipped with firearms, using them to conquer land from their neighbors. The religious wars of the 1500s and 1600s strengthened centralization efforts and hastened the demise of the nobility as an obstacle to the centralized state. In England, Parliament blocked the Stuart kings from building a landed central state and instead pursued the construction of a naval state.

| Against the Grain

Consider this as a counterpoint to the main patterns examined in this chapter.

The Digger Movement

- Was Winstanley hopelessly utopian in his efforts to establish farmer communities on common land in England?

- How have other figures in world history sympathized with the lot of poor and landless farmers and attempted reform (or revolution) on their behalf?

In April 1649, toward the end of the English Civil War and just three months after the execution of King Charles I, a group of farmers and day laborers occupied "common" (public) land south of London to establish a colony. As the farmers and laborers dug up the soil, they came to be called the "Diggers."

Driven off by small landowners who benefited from the use of common land for grazing sheep and cutting timber, a smaller group of Diggers moved on to common land in nearby Cobham in August 1649. This time it was the gentry with their manor rights to the common land who destroyed the Diggers' cottages and fields in the winter of 1650. The Diggers made a much-publicized statement that public land was "the treasure of all people" and should not be reserved for the benefit of anyone—a bold demand that ran counter to the rapidly increasing privatization of land and commercialization of agriculture.

The leader of the group was Gerrard Winstanley (1609–1670), a former cloth merchant in London who had had to abandon his trade in 1643 after he became insolvent. He struggled to regain his solvency in the countryside of Surrey, at one point working as a grazier of cattle. Parts of Surrey had suffered substantial hardship during the Civil War, having been forced to provision and quarter troops. In pamphlets between 1648 and 1650, Winstanley explained the motives and goals of the Diggers, making these affairs relevant, in the religious idiom of Protestantism, for England as a whole. He was the first to identify the problem of the rising numbers of rural landless laborers victimized by the increasing commercialization of agriculture in England—a labor force that continued to increase until the industrializing cities of the later 1700s eventually absorbed them.

Key Terms

Absolutism   415
Catholic Reformation   411
Heliocentrism   398
Humanism   396

Indulgence   408
New Model Army   413
New Sciences   396
Protestant Reformation   407

Renaissance   396
Social contract   402
Tsar   416

Learn more with this chapter's digital tools, including the Oxford Insight Study Guide, at http://www.oup.com/he/vonsivers4e. Please see the Further Resources section at the back of the book for additional readings and suggested websites.

Sources for Chapter 17

SOURCE 17.1 ## Examination of Lady Jane Grey, London

1554

Jane Grey, the granddaughter of Henry VIII's sister Mary, was born in 1537, the same year as Edward VI, the only surviving son of the king who had sought a male heir so desperately. Jane, who like Edward was raised in the Protestant religion Henry had introduced to England, proved a diligent and intellectually gifted teenager. In spite of her youth and gender, Jane corresponded with Protestant authorities on the Continent, but fast-moving events in England precluded further study. When Edward died without an heir in 1553, the throne passed, by prearranged agreement, to his fiercely Catholic half-sister Mary.

However, in order to forestall a Catholic successor—and the dramatic rollback of the Protestant reforms instituted by Henry's and Edward's Church of England— Jane's relatives proclaimed her queen. Her rule lasted a mere nine days. She was imprisoned in the Tower of London by Mary, who was then forced to consider whether Jane's execution was warranted. Shortly before Jane's death, at age 16, Queen Mary sent her own chaplain, Master Feckenham (sometimes rendered as "Fecknam") to try to reconcile Jane to the Catholic faith. The results of this attempt were triumphantly recorded in John Foxe's *Acts and Monuments*, published after the Protestant Queen Elizabeth had triumphed over Mary and the Catholics. Although the conversation recorded here is not a trial transcript—and is a highly partisan account—it does distill some of the central issues that divided Catholics and Protestants in an extremely chaotic and violent period.

> **FECKNAM:** "I am here come to you at this present, sent from the queen [Mary] and her council, to instruct you in the true doctrine of the right faith: although I have so great confidence in you, that I shall have, I trust, little need to travail with you much therein."

Source: "The Examination of Lady Jane Grey (1554)," from Denis R. Janz, ed., *A Reformation Reader: Primary Texts with Introductions*, 2nd ed. (Minneapolis, MN: Fortress Press, 2008), 360–362, taken from *The Acts and Monuments of John Foxe* (London: Seeleys, 1859), 415–417.

JANE: "Forsooth, I heartily thank the queen's highness, which is not unmindful of her humble subject: and I hope, likewise, that you no less will do your duty therein both truly and faithfully, according to that you were sent for."

. . .

FECKNAM: "How many sacraments are there?"

JANE: "Two: the one the sacrament of baptism, and the other the sacrament of the Lord's Supper."

FECKNAM: "No, there are seven."

JANE: "By what Scripture find you that?"

FECKNAM: "Well, we will talk of that hereafter. But what is signified by your two sacraments?"

JANE: "By the sacrament of baptism I am washed with water and regenerated by the Spirit, and that washing is a token to me that I am the child of God. The sacrament of the Lord's Supper, offered unto me, is a sure seal and testimony that I am, by the blood of Christ, which he shed for me on the cross, made partaker of the everlasting kingdom."

FECKNAM: "Why? What do you receive in that sacrament? Do you not receive the very body and blood of Christ?"

JANE: "No, surely, I do not so believe. I think that at the supper I neither receive flesh nor blood, but bread and wine: which bread when it is broken, and the wine when it is drunken, put me in remembrance how that for my sins the body of Christ was broken, and his blood shed on the cross; and with that bread and wine I receive the benefits that come by the breaking of his body, and shedding of his blood, for our sins on the cross."

FECKNAM: "Why, doth not Christ speak these words, 'Take, eat, this is my body?' Require you any plainer words? Doth he not say, it is his body?"

JANE: "I grant, he saith so; and so he saith, 'I am the vine, I am the door'; but he is never the more for that, the door or the vine. Doth not St. Paul say, 'He calleth things that are not, as though they were?' God forbid that I should say, that I eat the very natural body and blood of Christ: for then either I should pluck away my redemption, or else there were two bodies, or two Christs. One body was tormented on the cross, and if they did eat another body, then had he two bodies: or if his body were eaten, then was it not broken upon the cross; or if it were broken upon the cross, it was not eaten of his disciples."

. . .

With these and like such persuasions he would have had her lean to the [Catholic] church, but it would not be. There were many more things whereof they reasoned, but these were the chiefest.

After this, Fecknam took his leave, saying, that he was sorry for her: "For I am sure," quoth he, "that we two shall never meet."

JANE: "True it is," said she, "that we shall never meet, except God turn your heart; for I am assured, unless you repent and turn to God, you are in an evil case. And I pray God, in the bowels of his mercy, to send you his Holy Spirit; for he hath given you his great gift of utterance, if it please him also to open the eyes of your heart."

▶ Working with Sources

1. **What does this source reveal about the religious education of young people in the extended royal household during the final years of Henry VIII and the reign of Edward VI?**

2. **How does the literal interpretation of the Bible enter into this discussion, and why?**

SOURCE 17.2

Emilie du Châtelet, *Discourse on Happiness*

1748

During the Age of Enlightenment, Emilie du Châtelet (1706-1749) was known among philosophes primarily for her translation of Newton's *Mathematical Principles.* A well-educated polymath, she is also remembered for her interest in philosophy; her life-long friend Voltaire remarked that "Her dominant taste was for mathematics and philosophy." Du Châtelet's interest in philosophy is manifested in her *Discourse on Happiness* (*Discours sur le bonheur*), a topic of wide interest discussed in several works of leading male philosophes. What renders Du Châtelet's essay unique, however, are its occasional references to her personal life, its subtle expression of male dominance in the intellectual world, as well as its interests in "illusions" and the value of reason over obeisance to religion.

Would we have a moment of pleasure at the theater if we did not lend ourselves to the illusion that makes us see famous individuals that we know have been dead for a long time, speaking in Alexandrine verse? Truly, what pleasure would one have at any other spectacle where all is illusion if one was not able to abandon oneself to it? Surely there would be much to lose, and those at the opera who only have the pleasure of the music and the dances have a very meager pleasure, one well below that which this enchanting spectacle viewed as a whole provides. I have cited spectacles, because illusion is easier to perceive there. It is, however, involved in all the pleasures of our life, and provides the polish, the gloss of life. Some will perhaps say that illusion does not depend on

Source: Emilie Du Châtelet, *Selected Philosophical and Scientific Writings*, ed. and trans. by Isabelle Bour and Judith P. Zinsser (University of Chicago Press, 2009), 354–364.

us, and that is only too true, up to a point. We cannot give ourselves illusions any more than we can give ourselves tastes, or passions; but we can keep the illusions that we have; we can seek not to destroy them. We can choose not to go behind the set, to see the wheels that make flight, and the other machines of theatrical productions. Such is the artifice that we can use, and that artifice is neither useless nor unproductive.

These are the great machines of happiness, so to speak; but there are yet other, lesser skills that can contribute to our happiness. The first is to be resolute about what one wants to be and about what one wants to do. This is lacking in almost all men; it is, however, the pre-requisite without which there is no happiness at all. Without it, one swims forever in a sea of uncertainties, one destroys in the morning what one made in the evening; life is spent doing stupid things, putting them right, repenting of them. This feeling of repentance is one of the most useless and most disagreeable that our soul can experience. One of the great secrets is to know how to guard against it. As no two things in life are alike, it is almost always useless to see one's errors, or at least to pause a long time to consider them and to reproach oneself with them. In so doing we cover ourselves with confusion in our own eyes for no gain. One must start from where one is, use all one's sagacity to make amends and to find the means to make amends, but there is no point in looking back, and one must always brush from one's mind the memory of one's errors. The ability to benefit from an initial examination, dismiss sad ideas and substitute agreeable ideas, is one of the mainsprings of happiness, and we have this in our power, at least up to a point...

One must have passions to be happy; but they must be made to serve our happiness, and there are some that must absolutely be prevented from entering our soul. I am not speaking here of the passions that are vices, like hatred, vengeance, rage; but ambition, for example, is a passion that I believe one must defend one's soul against, if one wants to be happy. This is not because it does not give enjoyment, for I believe this passion can provide that; it is not because ambition can never be satisfied—that is surely a great good. Rather, it is because ambition, of all the passions, makes our happiness dependent on others. Now the less our happiness depends on others the easier it is for us to be happy. Let us not be afraid to reduce our dependence on others too much, or happiness will always depend on others quite enough. If we value independence, the love of study is, of all the passions, the one that contributes most to our happiness. This love of study holds within it a passion from which a superior soul is never entirely exempt, that of glory. For half the world, glory can only be obtained in this manner, and it is precisely this half whose education made glory inaccessible and made a taste for it impossible.

Undeniably, the love of study is much less necessary to the happiness of men than it is to that of women. Men have infinite resources for their happiness that women lack. They have many means to attain glory, and it is quite certain that the ambition to make their talents useful to their country and to serve their fellow citizens, perhaps by their competency in the art of war, or by their talents for government, or negotiation, is superior to that which one can gain for oneself by study. But women are excluded by definition, from every kind of glory, and when, by chance, one is born with a rather superior soul, only study remains to console her for all the exclusions and all the dependencies to which she finds herself condemned by her place in society... I have said that the love of study is the passion most necessary to our happiness. It is an unfailing resource against misfortunes, it is an inexhaustible source of pleasures, and Cicero is right to say: The pleasures of the senses and those of the heart are, without doubt, above those of study; study is not necessary for happiness: but we may need to feel that we have within us this resource and this support. One may love study and spend whole years, perhaps one's whole life, without studying. Happy is he who spends it thus: for only more lively pleasures cause one to sacrifice a pleasure that one is sure to find and that can be made lively enough to compensate for the loss of others.

I have said that the more our happiness depends on us, the more assured it is; yet the passion that can give us the greatest pleasures and make us happiest, places our happiness entirely in the hands of others. You have already gathered that I am speaking of love. This passion is perhaps the only one that can make us wish to live, and bring us to thank the author of nature, whoever he is, for giving us life. . . The best thing we can do is to persuade ourselves that this happiness is not impossible. However, I do not know if love has ever brought together two people who are so made for each other that they have never known the satiety of delight, nor the cooling of passion caused by a sense of security, nor the indolence and the tedium that arise from the ease and the continuity of a relationship, and whose power of illusion never wanes (for where is illusion more important than in love?); and, last, whose ardor remains the same whether in the enjoyment or in the deprivation of the other's presence, and equally tolerates both unhappiness and pleasure. . .

I have been endowed by God, it is true, with one of these loving and steadfast souls that know neither how to disguise nor how to moderate its passions, that know neither their diminution nor disgust with them, and whose tenacity can resist everything, even the certainty of being no longer loved. But I was happy for ten years because of the love of the man who had completely seduced my soul; and these ten years I spent tête-à-tête with him without a single moment of distaste or hint of melancholy. When age, illness, as well as perhaps the ease of pleasure made his inclination less, for a long time I did not perceive it; I was loving for two, I spent all my time with him, and my heart, free from suspicion, delighted in the pleasure of loving and in the illusion of believing myself loved. True, I have lost this happy state, and this has cost me many tears. Terrible shocks are needed to break such chains. The wound to my heart bled for a long time; I had grounds to complain, and I have pardoned all. I was fair enough to accept that in the whole world, perhaps only my heart possessed the steadfastness that annihilates the power of time; that if age and illness had not entirely extinguished his desire, it would perhaps still have been for me, and that love would have restored him to me; lastly, that his heart, incapable of love, felt for me the most tender affection, and caused him to dedicate his life to me. The certainty that a return of his inclination and his passion was impossible—I know well that such a return is not in nature—imperceptibly led my heart to the peaceful feeling of deep affection; and this sentiment, together with the passion for study, made me happy enough. . .

The great secret for preventing love from making us unhappy is to try never to appear in the wrong with your lover, never to display eagerness when his love is cooling, and always to be a degree cooler than he. This will not bring him back, but nothing could bring him back; there is nothing for us to do then but to forget someone who ceases to love us. If he still loves you, nothing can revive his love and make it as fiery as it was at first, except the fear of losing you and of being less loved. I know that for the susceptible and sincere this secret is difficult to put into practice; however, no effort will be too great, all the more so as it is much more necessary for the susceptible and sincere than for others. Nothing degrades as much as the steps one takes to regain a cold or inconstant heart. This demeans us in the eyes of the one we seek to keep, and in those of other men who might take an interest in us. But, and this is even worse, it makes us unhappy and uselessly torments us. So we must follow this maxim with unwavering courage and never surrender to our own heart on this point. We must attempt, before surrendering to our inclination, to become acquainted with the character of the person to whom we are becoming attached. Reason must be heard when we take counsel with ourselves; not the reason that condemns all types of commitment as contrary to happiness, but that which, in agreeing that one cannot be very happy without loving, wants one to love only in order to be happy, and to conquer an attraction by which it is obvious that one would only suffer unhappiness.

▶ **Discussion Questions**

1. What are du Châtelet's recommendations for attaining happiness?
2. How does du Châtelet explain differences between male and female quests for happiness; and how does she describe her personal experiences with love?

SOURCE 17.3

Sebastian Castellio, *Concerning Whether Heretics Should Be Persecuted*

1554

In October 1553, the extraordinarily gifted Spanish scientist Michael Servetus was executed with the approval and the strong support of John Calvin and his followers in Geneva. The charge was heresy, specifically for denying the existence of the Trinity and the divinity of Christ, and the method of execution—burning at the stake—elicited commentary and protest from across Europe. One of the fullest and most sophisticated protests against this execution was issued by Sebastian Castellio, a professor of Greek language and New Testament theology in the Swiss city of Basel. His book

Source: Sebastian Castellio, *Concerning Heretics, Whether They Are to Be Persecuted and How They Are to Be Treated, A Collection of the Opinions of Learned Men Both Ancient and Modern*, trans. Roland H. Bainton (New York: Octagon, 1965), 132–134.

De Haereticis is a collection of opinions, drawn from Christian writers, from both before and after the Protestant Reformation and across 15 centuries. It is more than an academic exercise, however, as this dedication of the Latin work to a German noble demonstrates.

From the Dedication of the book to Duke Christoph of Württemberg:

Turks: Muslims.

... And just as the **Turks** disagree with the Christians as to the person of Christ, and the Jews with both the Turks and the Christians, and the one condemns the other and holds him for a heretic, so Christians disagree with Christians on many points with regard to the teaching of Christ, and condemn one another and hold each other for heretics. Great controversies and debates occur as to baptism, the Lord's Supper, the invocation of the saints, justification, free will, and other obscure questions, so that Catholics, Lutherans, Zwinglians, Anabaptists, monks, and others condemn and persecute one another more cruelly than the Turks do the Christians. These dissensions arise solely from ignorance of the truth, for if these matters were so obvious and evident as that there is but one God, all Christians would agree among themselves on these points as readily as all nations confess that God is one.

What, then is to be done in such great contentions? We should follow the counsel of Paul, "Let not him that eateth despise him that eateth not ... To his own master he standeth or falleth" [Romans 14:3–4]. Let not the Jews or Turks condemn the Christians, nor let the Christians condemn the Jews or Turks, but rather teach and win them by true religion and justice, and let us, who are Christians, not condemn one another, but, if we are wiser than they, let us also be better and more merciful. This is certain that the better a man knows the truth, the less is he inclined to condemn, as appears in the case of Christ and the apostles. But he who lightly condemns others shows thereby that he knows nothing precisely, because he cannot bear others, for to know is to know how to put into practice. He who does not know how to act mercifully and kindly does not know the nature of mercy and kindness, just as he who cannot blush does not know the nature of shame.

If we were to conduct ourselves in this fashion we should be able to dwell together in concord. Even though in some matters we disagreed, yet should we consent together and forbear one another in love, which is the bond of peace, until we arrive at the unity of the faith [Ephesians 4:2–3]. But now, when we strive with hate and persecutions we go from bad to worse. Nor are we mindful of our office, since we are wholly taken up with condemnation, and the Gospel because of us is made a reproach unto the heathen [Ezekiel 22:4], for when they see us attacking one another with the fury of beasts, and the weak oppressed by the strong, these heathen feel horror and detestation for the Gospel, as if it made men such, and they abominate even Christ himself, as if he commanded men to do such things. We rather degenerate into Turks and Jews than convert them into Christians. Who would wish to be a Christian, when he saw that those who confessed the name of Christ were destroyed by Christians themselves with fire, water, and the sword without mercy and more cruelly treated than brigands and murderers? Who would

Moloch: A Phoenician deity who, according to the Bible, demanded the sacrifice of human children.

Phalaris: Tyrant in pre-Christian Sicily who burned victims alive in a giant bronze bull.

not think Christ a **Moloch**, or some such god, if he wished that men should be immolated to him and burned alive? Who would wish to serve Christ on condition that a difference of opinion on a controversial point with those in authority would be punished by burning alive at the command of Christ himself more cruelly than in the bull of **Phalaris**, even though from the midst of the flames he should call with a loud voice upon Christ, and should cry out that he believed in Him? Imagine Christ, the judge of all, present. Imagine Him pronouncing the sentence and applying the torch. Who would not hold Christ for a Satan? What more could Satan do than burn those who call upon the name of Christ?

▶ **Working with Sources**

1. Was Castellio minimizing the significant theological disputes that had arisen as a result of the Reformation? Were his objections directly applicable to the Servetus case?

2. What did Castellio see as the practical, as well as the theological, consequences of burning those perceived to be "heretics"? Is he convincing on this point?

SOURCE 17.4

Duc de Saint-Simon, "The Daily Habits of Louis XIV at Versailles"

ca. 1715

A noble at Louis XIV's court at Versailles, Louis de Rouvroy, the duc de Saint-Simon (1675–1755), would achieve lasting fame after his death with the publication of his copious, frank, and witty observations of the court. While resident at Versailles for brief periods after 1702 until the king's death in 1715, Saint-Simon paid particular attention to the maneuverings of his fellow aristocrats. He managed to garner the resentment of many of them, especially the king's illegitimate children, "the Bastards," who held a prominent place at court. His accounts of the daily routine of life at Versailles, and the central position of the king who had famously declared "L'état, c'est moi!" are often applied today to spectacles that can also be described as at once grand and a little absurd.

Source: *Memoirs of the Duc de Saint-Simon*, trans. Bayle St. John, ed. W. H. Lewis (New York: Macmillan, 1964), 140–141, 144–145.

At eight o'clock the chief valet de chambre on duty, who alone had slept in the royal chamber, and who had dressed himself, awoke the King. The chief physician, the chief surgeon, and the nurse (as long as she lived), entered at the same time. The latter kissed the King; the others rubbed and often changed his shirt, because he was in the habit of sweating a great deal. At the quarter [hour], the grand chamberlain was called (or, in his absence, the first gentleman of the chamber), and those who had, what was called the *grandes entrées*. The chamberlain (or chief gentleman) drew back the curtains which had been closed again, and presented the holy water from the vase, at the head of the bed. These gentlemen stayed but a moment, and that was the time to speak to the King, if any one had anything to ask of him; in which case the rest stood aside. When, contrary to custom, nobody had aught to say, they were there but for a few moments. He who had opened the curtains and presented the holy water, presented also a prayer-book. Then all passed into the cabinet of the council. A very short religious service being over, the King called, they re-entered. The same officer gave him his dressing-gown; immediately after, other privileged courtiers entered, and then everybody, in time to find the King putting on his shoes and stockings, for he did almost everything himself and with address and grace. Every other day we saw him shave himself; and he had a little short wig in which he always appeared, even in bed, and on medicine days. He often spoke of the chase, and sometimes said a word to somebody. No toilette table was near him; he had simply a mirror held before him.

As soon as he was dressed, he prayed to God, at the side of his bed, where all the clergy present knelt, the cardinals without cushions, all the laity remaining standing; and the captain of the guards came to the balustrade during the prayer, after which the King passed into his cabinet.

He found there, or was followed by all who had the entrée, a very numerous company, for it included everybody in any office. He gave orders to each for the day; thus within half a quarter of an hour it was known what he meant to do; and then all this crowd left directly. The bastards, a few favourites, and the valets alone were left. It was then a good opportunity for talking with the King; for example, about plans of gardens and buildings; and conversation lasted more or less according to the person engaged in it.

. . .

At ten o'clock his supper was served. The captain of the guard announced this to him. A quarter of an hour after the King came to supper, and from the ante-chamber of Madame de Maintenon [his principal mistress] to the table again, any one spoke to him who wished. This supper was always on a grand scale, the royal household (that is, the sons and daughters of France), at table, and a large number of courtiers and ladies present, sitting or standing, and on the evening before the journey to Marly all those ladies who wished to take part in it. That was called presenting yourself for Marly. Men asked in the morning, simply saying to the King, "Sire, Marly." In later years, the King grew tired of this, and a valet wrote up in the gallery the names of those who asked. The ladies continued to present themselves.

. . .

Ruelle: The "little path" between a bed and the wall.

The King, wishing to retire, went and fed his dogs; then said good night, passed into his chamber to the **ruelle** of his bed, where he said his prayers, as in the morning, then undressed. He said good night with an inclination of the head, and whilst everybody was leaving the room stood at the corner of the mantelpiece, where he gave the order to the colonel of the guards alone. Then commenced what was called the *petit coucher,* at which only the specially privileged remained. That was short. They did not leave until he got into bed. It was a moment to speak to him.

▶ **Working with Sources**

1. Why does Saint-Simon pay particular attention to moments of the day during which a courtier could speak directly with the king?

2. What does the combination of religious and secular pursuits in the king's daily habits suggest about life at his court?

SOURCE 17.5

Giorgio Vasari, *The Life of Michelangelo Buonarroti*

1550

Trained as a painter, architect, and goldsmith, Giorgio Vasari (1511–1574) practiced various artistic trades, but is most renowned today as the first art historian. His *Lives of the Most Eminent Painters, Sculptors, and Architects*, first published in 1550, is the principal source of information about the most prominent artists of the European Renaissance. Having studied under the great artist Michelangelo Buonarroti (1475–1564), Vasari was particularly keen to tell his story. In these scenes from his biography of Michelangelo, Vasari draws attention to his master's early training, as well as the prominent roles Lorenzo "il Magnifico" de' Medici and ancient sculpture played in his artistic development.

Source: Giorgio Vasari, *The Lives of the Artists*, trans. Julia Conaway Bondanella and Peter Bondanella (Oxford and New York: Oxford University Press, 1998), 418–420; 427–428.

In those days Lorenzo de' Medici the Magnificent kept Bertoldo the sculptor in his garden near Piazza San Marco, not so much as the custodian or guardian of the many beautiful antiquities he had collected and assembled there at great expense, but rather because he wished above all else to create a school for excellent painters and sculptors ... Thus, Domenico [Ghirlandaio] gave him some of his best young men, including among others Michelangelo and Francesco Granacci; and when they went to the garden, they found that Torrigiani, a young man of the Torrigiani family, was there working on some clay figures in the round that Bertoldo had given him to do.

After Michelangelo saw these figures, he made some himself to rival those of Torrigiani, so that Lorenzo, seeing his high spirit, always had great expectations for him, and, encouraged after only a few days, Michelangelo began copying with a piece of marble the antique head of an old and wrinkled faun with a damaged nose and a laughing mouth, which he found there. Although Michelangelo had never before touched marble or chisels, the imitation turned out so well that Lorenzo was astonished, and when Lorenzo saw that Michelangelo, following his own fantasy rather than the antique head, had carved its mouth open to give it a tongue and to make all its teeth visible, this lord, laughing with pleasure as was his custom, said to him: "But you should have known that old men never have all their teeth and that some of them are always missing." In that simplicity of his, it seemed to Michelangelo, who loved and feared this lord, that Lorenzo was correct; and as soon as Lorenzo left, he immediately broke a tooth on the head and dug out the gum in such a way that it seemed the tooth had fallen out, and anxiously awaited Lorenzo's return, who, after coming back and seeing Michelangelo's simplicity and excellence, laughed about it on more than one occasion, recounting it to his friends as if it were miraculous. . . .

. . .

Around this time it happened that Piero Soderini saw the statue [the *David*, finished in 1504], and it pleased him greatly, but while Michelangelo was giving it the finishing touches, he told Michelangelo that he thought the nose of the figure was too large. Michelangelo, realizing that the Gonfaloniere [a civic official in Florence] was standing under the giant and that his viewpoint did not allow him to see it properly, climbed up the scaffolding to satisfy Soderini (who was behind him nearby), and having quickly grabbed the chisel in his left hand along with a little marble dust that he found on the planks in the scaffolding, Michelangelo began to tap lightly with the chisel, allowing the dust to fall little by little without retouching the nose from the way it was. Then, looking down at the Gonfaloniere who stood there watching, he ordered:

"Look at it now."

"I like it better," replied the Gonfaloniere: "you've made it come alive."

Thus Michelangelo climbed down, and, having contented this lord, he laughed to himself, feeling compassion for those who, in order to make it appear that they understand, do not realize what they are saying; and when the statue was finished and set in its foundation, he uncovered it, and to tell the truth, this work eclipsed all other statues, both modern and ancient, whether Greek or Roman; and it can be said that neither the Marforio in Rome, nor the Tiber and the Nile of the Belvedere, nor the colossal statues of Monte Cavallo can be compared to this David, which Michelangelo completed with so much measure and beauty, and so much skill.

▶ Working with Sources

1. How do these anecdotes illustrate the relationship between artists and their patrons (and funders) during the Renaissance?

2. How did Michelangelo deal with the legacy of artists from Greco-Roman antiquity?

SOURCE 17.6 Galileo Galilei, Letter to the Grand Duchess Christina de' Medici

1615

This famous letter is often cited as an early sign of Galileo's inevitable conflict with church authorities over the Copernican system of planetary motion—and the theory's theological, as well as its scientific, ramifications. Galileo (1564–1642) would be condemned to house arrest in 1632 and forced to make a public repudiation of the heliocentric theory first advanced by Copernicus in the sixteenth century. However, Galileo's connection to the renowned Medici family of Florence was also cause for comment—and caution—from 1610, when he received an appointment and their implicit endorsement.

Constructing a telescope in 1609 (which he proudly claimed could "magnify objects more than 60 times"), Galileo trained it on the moons of Jupiter, which he tracked over several days in 1610. Having named these objects for the Medici family, he rushed these and many other astronomical observations into print in the *Sidereus Nuncius* (*The Starry Messenger*). Inviting other scientists to "apply themselves to examine and determine" these planetary motions, Galileo demonstrated a preference for the Copernican theory and elicited sharp responses, particularly from church officials. In

Source: Galileo Galilei, *The Essential Galileo*, ed. and trans. Maurice A. Finocchiaro (Indianapolis: Hackett, 2008), §4.2.5—4.2.6, 140–144.

1615, the dowager Grand Duchess Christina, mother of his patron, Cosimo II, expressed her own reservations about the implications of the Copernican theory for a passage in the Old Testament. Galileo's response attempts, or seems to attempt, to reconcile experimental science and received religion.

Thus let these people apply themselves to refuting the arguments of Copernicus and of the others, and let them leave its condemnation as erroneous and heretical to the proper authorities; but let them not hope that the very cautious and very wise Fathers and the Infallible One with his absolute wisdom are about to make rash decisions like those into which they would be rushed by their special interests and feelings. For in regard to these and other similar propositions which do not directly involve the faith, no one can doubt that the Supreme Pontiff always has the absolute power of permitting or condemning them; however, no creature has the power of making them be true or false, contrary to what they happen to be by nature and de facto. So it seems more advisable to first become sure about the necessary and immutable truth of the matter, over which no one has control, than to condemn one side when such certainty is lacking; this would imply a loss of freedom of decision and of choice insofar as it would give necessity to things which are presently indifferent, free, and dependent on the will of the supreme authority. In short, if it is inconceivable that a proposition should be declared heretical when one thinks that it may be true, it should be futile for someone to try to bring about the condemnation of the earth's motion and sun's rest unless he first shows it to be impossible and false.

There remains one last thing for us to examine: to what extent it is true that the Joshua passage [Joshua 10:12–13] can be taken without altering the literal meaning of the words, and how it can be that, when the sun obeyed Joshua's order to stop, from this it followed that the day was prolonged by a large amount.

. . .

I think therefore, if I am not mistaken, that one can clearly see that, given the Ptolemaic system, it is necessary to interpret the words in a way different from their literal meaning. Guided by St. Augustine's very useful prescriptions, I should say that the best nonliteral interpretation is not necessarily this, if anyone can find another which is perhaps better and more suitable. So now I want to examine whether the same miracle could be understood in a way more in accordance with what we read in Joshua, if to the Copernican system we add another discovery which I recently made about the solar body. However, I continue to speak with the same reservations—to the effect that I am not so enamored with my own opinions as to want to place them ahead of those of others; nor do I believe it is impossible to put forth interpretations which are better and more in accordance with the Holy Writ.

Let us first assume in accordance with the opinion of the above-mentioned authors, that in the Joshua miracle the whole system of heavenly motions was stopped, so that the stopping of only one would not introduce unnecessarily universal confusion and great turmoil in the whole order of nature.

. . .

Furthermore, what deserves special appreciation, if I am not mistaken, is that with the Copernican system one can very clearly and very easily give a literal meaning to another detail which one reads about the same miracle; that is, that the sun stopped in the middle of heaven. Serious theologians have raised a difficulty about this passage: it seems very probable that, when Joshua asked for the prolongation of the day, the sun was close to setting and not at the meridian; for it was then about the time of the summer solstice, and consequently the days were very long, so that if the sun had been at the meridian then it does not seem likely that it would have been necessary to pray for a lengthening of the day in order to win a battle, since the still remaining time of seven hours or more could very well have been sufficient.

· · ·

We can remove this and every other implausibility, if I am not mistaken, by placing the sun, as the Copernican system does and as it is most necessary to do, in the middle, namely, at the center of the heavenly orbs and of the planetary revolutions; for at any hour of the day, whether at noon or in the afternoon, the day would not have been lengthened and all heavenly turnings stopped by the sun stopping in the middle of the heavens, namely, at the center of the heavens, where it is located. Furthermore, this interpretation agrees all the more with the literal meaning inasmuch as, if one wanted to claim that the sun's stopping occurred at the noon hour, then the proper expression to use would have been to say that it "stood still at the meridian point," or "at the meridian circle," and not "in the middle of the heaven"; in fact, for a spherical body such as heaven, the middle is really and only the center.

▶ Working with Sources

1. **How does Galileo deal with the apparently irreconcilable conclusions of science and the Bible?**

2. **How would you characterize Galileo's tone in his analysis of the verses from the Book of Joshua?**

World Period Four

Interactions across the Globe, 1450–1750

The fifteenth century saw a renewal of the imperial impulse in the religious civilizations of the world. A forerunner had been the Mongol empire, which however did not last long; in less than 100 years it was replaced in China by the Ming. The founders of the subsequent new empires were the Mughals in India; the Ottomans, Safavids, and Songhay in the Middle East and Islamic Africa; the Habsburgs in Europe; and the seaborne empires of Portugal and Spain. One byproduct of this new imperial impulse was the discovery of the Americas, which in turn inspired the formulation of the heliocentric universe. The rediscovery of Greek literature in Europe had already set into motion the Renaissance, a broad new approach to understanding the world that provided the spark for the New Science.

China and India, by far the wealthiest and most populous agrarian–urban empires, enjoyed leading positions in the world because they produced everything they needed and wanted. Europe, however, acquired warm-weather crops and minerals through overseas colonial expansion, which would help it to challenge the traditional order.

 Chapter 18

New Patterns in New Worlds

COLONIALISM AND INDIGENOUS RESPONSES IN THE AMERICAS, 1500–1800

CHAPTER EIGHTEEN PATTERNS

Origins, Interactions, Adaptations The Americas had just reached their agrarian–urban peak with the Aztec and Inca empires when Spanish *conquistadors* arrived from across the Atlantic. After destroying the empires, the Iberians turned the double continent into the colonial warm-weather extension they had previously lacked. A still sparsely populated Iberia, however, could not spare many settlers and, as a result, small minorities governed large labor forces of indigenous Amerindians and slaves imported from Africa to work on sugar, coffee, and cotton plantations, as well as in mines. In North America, Europeans displaced the Amerindian population and drove it into the interior. Over time, urban colonial societies of Hispanics and Anglo-Americans emerged, with their own *creole* culture that distinguished them from Europe.

Uniqueness and Similarities The Spanish and Portuguese colonies evolved along distinct paths, depending on the proportions of settlers, Amerindians, and African slaves in each country. Argentina and Chile had few Amerindians and slaves, but Brazil and many Caribbean islands had huge numbers of African slaves, and large numbers of Amerindians lived in Mexico. Nevertheless, however distinct the colonies were, by 1750 they were all firmly dependent extensions of Europe.

Alonso Ortiz fled from his creditors in Spain in the early 1570s to find a new life in the Americas. In Mexico City, he set up shop as a tanner. Eight Native American employees did the actual labor of stomping the hides in the vats filled with tanning acids. A black slave was the supervisor. Ortiz concentrated on giving instructions and hustling his flourishing business.

Ortiz's situation in Mexico City was not entirely legal, however. He had left his wife and children in Spain, though the law required that families should be united. The authorities rarely enforced this law, but that was no guarantee for Ortiz. Furthermore, he had not yet sent his family any remittances. And then there was still the debt. Ortiz had reasons to be afraid of the law.

To avoid prosecution, Ortiz wrote a letter to his wife. In this letter, he described the comfortable position he had achieved. He announced that his business partner was sending her a sum of money sufficient to begin preparations for her departure from Spain. To his creditors, Ortiz promised to send 100 tanned hides within a year. Evidently aware of her reluctance to join him in Mexico, Ortiz closed his letter with a request to grant him four more years abroad and to do so with a notarized document from her hand. Unfortunately, we do not know her answer.

The Ortiz family drama gives a human face to European colonialism and emigration to the "New World" of the Americas. Like Alonso Ortiz, some 300,000 other Spaniards left the "Old World" (Europe, contiguous with Asia and Africa) between 1500 and 1800. A few hundred letters by emigrants exist, giving us glimpses of their lives in the parts of the Americas conquered by the Spanish and Portuguese in the sixteenth century. These relatively privileged immigrants hoped to build successful enterprises using the labor of Native Americans as well as black slaves imported from Africa. The example of Ortiz shows that even in the socially not very prestigious

CHAPTER OUTLINE

The Colonial Americas: Europe's Warm-Weather Extension

The Making of American Societies: Origins and Transformations

Putting It All Together

THE AMERICAS IN 1750

- Spanish
- Portuguese
- British
- French
- Dutch

ABOVE: In his monumental *Historia de la conquista de México,* written more than 150 years after the events described, Antonio de Solís (1610–1686) depicted the meeting of Moctezuma and Cortés.

423

❯ What is the significance of western Europeans acquiring the Americas as a warm-weather extension of their northern continent?

❯ What was the main pattern of social development in colonial America during the period 1500–1800?

❯ Why and how did European settlers in South and North America strive for self-government, and how successful were they in achieving their goals?

Land-labor grant (*encomienda*): Land grant by the government to an entrepreneur, entitling him to use forced indigenous or imported slave labor on that land for the exploitation of agricultural and mineral resources.

craft of tanning, a man could achieve a measure of comfort by having people of even lower status working for him.

Beginning in the sixteenth century, the Americas became an extension of Europe. European settlers extracted mineral and agricultural resources from these new lands. A pattern emerged in which gold and silver, as well as agricultural products, were intensively exploited. In this role, the Americas became a crucial factor in Europe's changing position in the world. First, Europe acquired precious metals, which its two largest competitors, India and China, lacked. Second, with agricultural commodities pouring in from the Americas, Europe rose to a position of agrarian autonomy similar to that of India and China.

The Colonial Americas: Europe's Warm-Weather Extension

The European extension into the Americas followed Columbus's pursuit of a sea route to India that would circumvent the Muslim dominance of the trade with India and China. The Spaniards financed their imperial expansion as well as their wars against Ottoman and European rivals with American gold and silver, leaving little for domestic investment. A pattern evolved in which Iberian settlers transformed the Americas into mineral-extracting and agrarian colonies based on either cheap or forced labor.

The Conquest of Mexico and Peru

The Spanish conquerors of the Aztec and Inca Empires exploited internal weaknesses in the empires. They eliminated the top of the power structures, paralyzing the decision-making apparatuses long enough for their conquests to succeed. Soon after the conquests, the Old World disease of smallpox ravaged the Native American population and dramatically reduced the indigenous labor force. To make up for this reduction, colonial authorities imported black slaves from Africa. A three-tiered society of European immigrants, Native Americans, and black slaves emerged in the Spanish and Portuguese Americas.

From Trading Posts to Conquest   Columbus had discovered the Caribbean islands under a royal commission which entitled him to build fortified posts and to trade with the indigenous Taínos. Trade relations with the Taínos, however, deteriorated into exploitation, with the Spaniards usurping the traditional entitlements of the Taíno chiefs to the labor of their fellow men. With the help of **land-labor grants** (Spanish *encomiendas*), the Spanish took over from the Taíno chiefs and, through forced labor, amassed quantities of gold. What had begun as trade-post settlement turned into full-blown conquest of land.

The Spaniards conquered the Caribbean islands not only through force. Much more severe in its consequences was the indirect conquest through disease. Smallpox wiped out an estimated 250,000 to 1 million Taínos as well as the Caribs. Isolated from the rest of humankind, Native Americans possessed no immunity against smallpox and other introduced diseases.

Protests, mostly among some members of the clergy, arose against both the labor exploitation and the helplessness of the Taínos against disease. The land-labor grant system finally came to an end after 1542 with the introduction of the *repartimiento* system (see p. 429).

First Mainland Conquests Hernán Cortés (1485–1547), upon arriving on Hispaniola in 1504, advanced from governmental scribe in Hispaniola to mayor of Santiago in Cuba. Thanks to labor grants, he became rich. When the Cuban governor asked him in 1518 to lead an expedition for trade and exploration to the Yucatán Peninsula in Mexico, Cortés enthusiastically agreed. He assembled 300 men, considerably exceeding his contract. The governor tried to stop him, but Cortés departed quickly for the American mainland.

As the Cuban governor had feared, Cortés did not bother with trading posts in Yucatán. The Spanish had learned of the existence of the Aztec Empire, with its immense silver and gold treasures. In a first encounter, Cortés's small Spanish force defeated a much larger indigenous force at Tabasco. The Spaniards' steel weapons and armor proved superior in hand-to-hand combat against the defenders.

Among the gifts presented by the defeated Native Americans in Tabasco was Malinche, an enslaved Nahuatl [NAH-wat(l)]-speaking woman. Malinche quickly learned Spanish and became the consort of Cortés. As a translator, Malinche was nearly as decisive as Cortés in shaping events, given that the latter was ignorant of indigenous affairs. With Tabasco conquered, Cortés quickly moved on; he was afraid that the Cuban governor would otherwise force him to return to Cuba.

Cultural Intermediary. The Tabascans gave Malinche, or Doña Marina, to Hernán Cortés as a form of tribute after they were defeated by the Spanish. Malinche served Cortés as a translator and mistress, playing a central role in Cortés's eventual victory over the Aztecs. She was in many respects the principal face of the Spanish and is always depicted center stage in Native American visual accounts of the conquest.

Conquest of the Aztec Empire On the southeast coast of Mexico, Cortés founded the city of Veracruz. He had his followers elect a town council, which made Cortés their head and chief justice, allowing Cortés to claim legitimacy for his march inland. Marching inland, the Spaniards ran into resistance from indigenous people, suffering their first losses of horses and men. They pressed onward with thousands of Native American allies, most notably the Tlaxcalans [tlash-KAH-lans], traditional enemies of the Aztecs. The support from these indigenous peoples proved essential when Cortés and his army reached the court of the Aztecs.

1492	1516–1556	1521
Christopher Columbus lands in the Caribbean	Reign of Charles V, Habsburg king of Spain and the Americas	Spanish conquest of the Aztec Empire in Mexico

1500 Pedro Álvares Cabral claims Brazil for Portugal
1519–1521 Reign of Cuauhtémoc, last ruler of the Aztec Empire
1532–1533 Reign of Atahualpa, last ruler of the Inca Empire

1533 Spanish conquest of the Inca Empire in Peru
1607 Jamestown, Virginia, first permanent English settlement
1690 Gold discovered in Brazil

1545 Founding of silver mine of Potosí
1608 Quebec City, first permanent French settlement

When Cortés arrived at the city of Tenochtitlán on November 2, 1519, the emperor Moctezuma II (r. 1502–1519) was unsure of how to react to the invaders. To gain time, Moctezuma greeted the Spaniard in person and invited him to his palace. Cortés and his company, now numbering some 600 Spaniards, took up quarters in the palace precincts. After a week of deteriorating discussions, Cortés suddenly put the incredulous emperor under house arrest and made him swear allegiance to Charles V.

However, Cortés was diverted by the need to march back east, where troops from Cuba had arrived to arrest him. After defeating these troops, he pressed the remnants into his own service and returned to Tenochtitlán. During his absence, the Spaniards who had remained in Moctezuma's palace had massacred Aztec nobles. As an infuriated crowd of Tenochtitlán's inhabitants invaded the palace, Moctezuma and some 200 Spaniards died. The rest of the Spanish retreated east to their Tlaxcalan allies. There, after his return, Cortés devised a new plan for capturing Tenochtitlán.

After 10 months of preparations, the Spaniards returned to the Aztec capital. In command now of about 2,000 Spanish soldiers and assisted by some 50,000 Native American troops, Cortés laid siege to the city. After nearly three months, much of the city was in ruins, water and food became scarce, and smallpox began to decimate the population. On August 21, 1521, the Spaniards and their allies stormed the city and looted its gold treasury. They captured the last emperor, Cuauhtémoc [kwaw-TAY-mok] and executed him in 1525, thus ending the Aztec Empire (see Map 18.1).

Conquest by Surprise. The Spanish conqueror Francisco Pizarro captured Emperor Atahualpa in an ambush. Atahualpa promised a roomful of gold in return for his release, but the Spaniards collected the gold and murdered Atahualpa before generals of the Inca army could organize an armed resistance.

Conquest of the Inca Empire A relative of Cortés, Francisco Pizarro (ca. 1475–1541), planned to conquer the Andean empire of the Incas. Pizarro, like Cortés born in Spain but uneducated, had arrived in Hispaniola as part of an expedition in 1513 that went on to discover Panama and the Pacific. He became mayor of Panama City, acquired some wealth, and heard rumors about an empire of gold and silver to the south. After a failed initial expedition, he captured some precious metal from an oceangoing Inca sailing raft. Upon receiving a permit from Charles V to establish a trading post, Pizarro and a team departed in late December 1530.

In the years before Pizarro's expedition, smallpox had ravaged the Inca Empire, killing the emperor and his heir apparent and leading to a protracted war of succession between two surviving sons. When Pizarro entered the Inca Empire, one of those sons, Atahualpa, was encamped with an army of 40,000 men near the town of Cajamarca.

Arriving at Cajamarca, Pizarro arranged an unarmed audience with Atahualpa. On November 16, 1532, Atahualpa came to this audience, surrounded by several thousand unarmed retainers, while Pizarro's soldiers hid nearby. At a signal, these soldiers rushed forward, capturing Atahualpa and massacring his retainers. Not one Spanish soldier was killed.

The ambush paralyzed the Inca Empire at the very top. Atahualpa offered his captors a room full of gold and silver as ransom. In the following two months, Inca administrators delivered immense quantities of precious metals to Pizarro. But

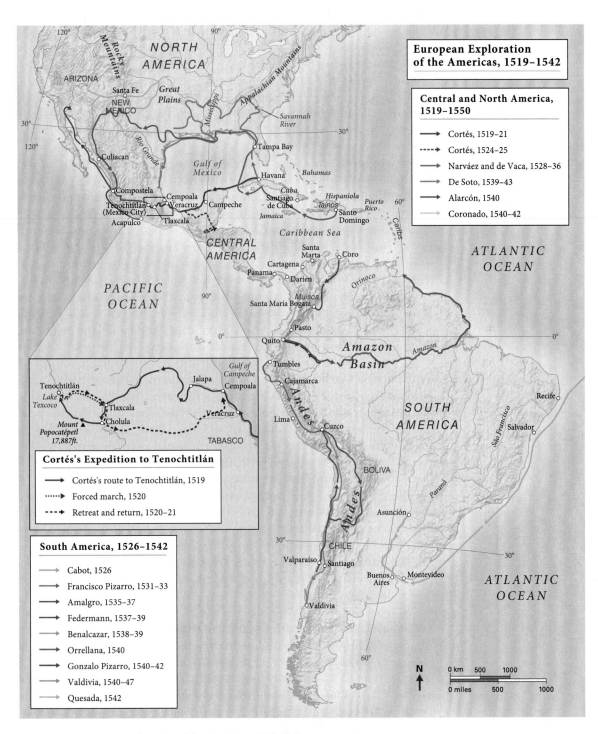

European Exploration of the Americas, 1519–1542

Central and North America, 1519–1550

→	Cortés, 1519–21
┈▶	Cortés, 1524–25
→	Narváez and de Vaca, 1528–36
→	De Soto, 1539–43
→	Alarcón, 1540
→	Coronado, 1540–42

Cortés's Expedition to Tenochtitlán

→	Cortés's route to Tenochtitlán, 1519
┈▶	Forced march, 1520
┈▶	Retreat and return, 1520–21

South America, 1526–1542

→	Cabot, 1526
→	Francisco Pizarro, 1531–33
→	Amalgro, 1535–37
→	Federmann, 1537–39
→	Benalcazar, 1538–39
→	Orrellana, 1540
→	Gonzalo Pizarro, 1540–42
→	Valdivia, 1540–47
→	Quesada, 1542

MAP 18.1 **The European Exploration of the Americas, 1519–1542**

Spanish officers executed Atahualpa anyway on July 26, 1533, hoping to keep the Incas disorganized.

The Spaniards then captured the Incan capital, Cuzco, massacring the inhabitants and stripping the city of its immense gold and silver treasures. In 1535 Pizarro founded a new capital, Lima, which was more conveniently located on the coast. Although Incas in the south rebuilt a kingdom, the Spanish eventually gained full control of the Inca Empire in 1572.

The Portuguese Conquest of Brazil   Navigators from both Spain and Portugal had first sighted the Brazilian coast in 1499–1500, and the Portuguese quickly claimed it for themselves. The majority of Brazil's indigenous population at that time lived in villages based on agriculture, fishing, and hunting.

The Portuguese were interested initially in trade with villagers, mostly for brazilwood, which was used to make a red dye and for which the country of Brazil was named. When French traders appeared, ignoring the Portuguese commercial treaties with the tribes, the Portuguese crown shifted to trading-post settlements. Land grants were made with the obligation to build fortified coastal villages for settlers and to engage in agriculture and friendly trade. By the mid-sixteenth century, inhabitants of some of these villages intermarried with local indigenous chieftain families and established sugarcane plantations.

Explanations for the Spanish Success   The stupendous victories of handfuls of Spaniards over huge empires defies easy explanation. Four factors invite consideration. First, the conquistadors went straight to the top of the imperial pyramid. The emperors expected diplomatic deference, but confronted instead with arrogance and brutality, they were thrown off balance by the Spaniards. Second, in both the Aztec and Inca Empires, individuals and groups contested the hierarchical power structure. The conquistadors either found allies among the subject populations or encountered a divided leadership. Third, European-introduced diseases took a devastating toll. In both empires, smallpox hit at critical moments during or right before the Spanish invasions. Finally, thanks to horses and European steel weapons and armor, small numbers of Spaniards were able to hold large numbers of attacking Aztecs and Incas at bay in hand-to-hand combat. Cannons and matchlock muskets were less important, since they were useless in close encounters.

The Establishment of Colonial Institutions

The Spanish crown established administrative hierarchies in the Americas, with governors at the top and lower ranks of functionaries. Some settler autonomy was permitted through town and city councils, but the crown was determined to make the Americas a territorial extension of the European pattern of centralized state formation. Several hundred thousand settlers found a new life in the Americas. By the early seventeenth century, an elite of Spaniards who had been born in America, called **Creoles** (Spanish *criollos*), first assisted and later replaced most of the administrators sent from Spain (see Map 18.2).

Creoles: American-born descendants of European, primarily Spanish, immigrants.

From Conquest to Colonialism   The riches of Cortés and Pizarro inspired further expeditions into Central and North America, Chile, and the Amazon. These expeditions, however, yielded only modest amounts of gold and earned more from selling captured Native Americans into slavery. In the north, expeditions penetrated as far as Arizona, New Mexico, Texas, Oklahoma, Kansas, and Florida, but encountered only relatively poor villagers and Pueblo towns. No new golden kingdoms beyond the Aztec and Inca Empires were discovered in the Americas.

In the mid-sixteenth century, the conquistadors shifted from looting to the exploitation of Native American labor in mines and in agriculture. Explorers discovered silver in Bolivia (1545) and northern Mexico (1556), gold in Chile (1552), and mercury in Peru (1563).

Indigenous peoples occasionally resisted incorporation into the Spanish colonies. Notably, the Mapuche in southern Chile repulsed all attempts by the Spanish to subdue them. Initially, in 1550–1553 the Spanish succeeded in establishing forts and opening a gold mine, but they failed to gain more than a border strip with an adjacent no-man's-land. In 1612 they agreed to a temporary peace that left the majority of the Mapuche independent.

Another Native American people who successfully resisted the Spanish conquest were the Asháninka in the Peruvian rain forest. The Asháninka exploited hillside salt veins in their region and were traders of goods between the Andes and the rain forest. It was only in 1737 that the Spanish finally succeeded in building a fort in the region—a first step toward projecting colonial power into the rain forest.

Bureaucratic Efficiency   During the first two generations after the conquest, Spain maintained an efficient colonial administration to deliver revenues to Spain. In addition, the viceroyalty of New Spain in Mexico remitted another 25 percent of its revenues to the Philippines, the Pacific province for which it was administratively responsible from 1571 onward. Settlers in New Spain had to pay up to 40 different taxes and dues. The only income tax was the tithe to the church, which the administration collected and, at times, used for its own budgetary purposes. Altogether, however, for the settlers the tax level was lower in the New World than in Spain, and the same was true for the English and French colonists in North America.

In the 1540s the government introduced rotating **labor assignments** (*repartimientos*) to phase out the *encomiendas*. This institution of rotating labor assignments was a continuation of the *mit'a* system, which the Incas had devised as a form of taxation (see Chapter 15). Rotating labor assignments meant that a percentage of villagers had to provide labor to the state. Private entrepreneurs could also contract for indigenous labor assignments, especially in mining regions.

Brazil in 1519. This early map is fairly accurate for the northern coast, but increasingly less accurate as one moves south. First explorations of the south by both Portuguese and Spanish mariners date to 1513–1516. Ferdinand Magellan passed through several places along the southern coast on his journey around the world in 1520–1521. The scenes on the map depict Native Americans cutting and collecting brazilwood, the source of a red dye much in demand by the Portuguese during the early period of colonization.

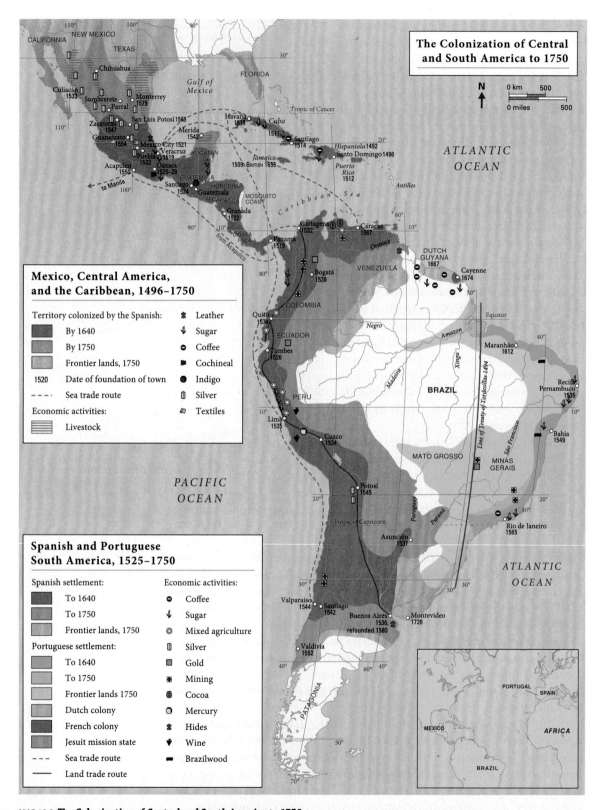

The Colonization of Central and South America to 1750

N

0 km 500
0 miles 500

Mexico, Central America, and the Caribbean, 1496–1750

Territory colonized by the Spanish:

■ By 1640
■ By 1750
■ Frontier lands, 1750
1520 Date of foundation of town
--- Sea trade route
Economic activities:
▤ Livestock

🐃 Leather
↓ Sugar
● Coffee
🦐 Cochineal
● Indigo
▯ Silver
▨ Textiles

Spanish and Portuguese South America, 1525–1750

Spanish settlement:
■ To 1640
■ To 1750
■ Frontier lands, 1750

Portuguese settlement:
■ To 1640
■ To 1750
■ Frontier lands 1750
■ Dutch colony
■ French colony
■ Jesuit mission state
--- Sea trade route
— Land trade route

Economic activities:
● Coffee
↓ Sugar
◎ Mixed agriculture
▯ Silver
▪ Gold
✣ Mining
◐ Cocoa
◑ Mercury
🐃 Hides
⬇ Wine
➖ Brazilwood

MAP 18.2 The Colonization of Central and South America to 1750

In Mexico the *repartimiento* fell out of use in the first half of the seventeenth century due to the toll of smallpox on the Native American population. The replacement for the lost workers was wage labor. In highland Peru, where the effects of smallpox were less severe, the assignment system lasted to the end of the colonial period. Wage labor expanded there as well. Wages for Native Americans and blacks remained everywhere lower than those for Creoles.

The Rise of the Creoles Administrative and fiscal efficiency did not last very long. The wars of the Spanish Habsburg Empire cost more than the crown was able to collect in revenues. In order to make up the financial deficit, the crown began to sell offices in the Americas to the highest bidders. By the end of the century, Creoles had purchased life appointments in city councils as well as other important sinecures that allowed them to collect fees and rents. Local oligarchies emerged, effectively ending participatory politics in Spanish colonial America.

The effects of the change from recruitment by merit to recruitment by wealth on the functioning of the bureaucracy were far-reaching. Creoles advanced on a broad front in the administrative positions, while fewer Spaniards found it attractive to buy positions from abroad. The only opportunities which European Spaniards still found enticing were positions that gave their owners the right to subject the Native Americans to forced purchases of goods, yielding huge profits. By 1700, the consequences of the Spanish crown selling most of its American administrative offices were a decline in the competence of officeholders, the emergence of a Creole elite able to bend the Spanish administration to its will, and a decentralization of the decision-making processes.

Northwest European Interference As Spain's administrative grip on the Americas weakened during the seventeenth century, the need to defend the continents militarily against European interlopers arose. European **privateers**, holding royal charters, harassed Spanish silver shipments and ports in the Caribbean. In the early seventeenth century, the French, English, and Dutch governments occupied the smaller Caribbean islands not claimed by Spain. Privateer and contraband traders stationed on these islands further damaged Spain's monopoly of shipping between Europe and the Caribbean.

Conquests of Spanish islands followed in the second half of the century. England captured Jamaica in 1655, and France colonized western Hispaniola (Saint-Domingue) in 1665. Along the Pacific coast, the galleons of the annual Acapulco–Manila fleet were the targets of English privateers. Over the course of the seventeenth century, Spain allocated one-half to two-thirds of its American revenues to the defense of its annual treasure fleets and Caribbean possessions.

Bourbon Reforms After the death of the last, childless Habsburg king of Spain in 1700, the new French-descended dynasty of the Bourbons made major efforts to regain control over their American possessions. Fortunately, population increases among the settlers as well as the Native Americans offered opportunities to Spanish manufacturers and merchants. By the middle of the eighteenth century, the Bourbon reform program began to show results.

The reforms aimed to improve naval connections and administrative control between the mother country and the colonies. The monopolistic annual

Labor assignment (*repartimiento*): Obligation by villagers to send stipulated numbers of people as laborers to a contractor, who had the right to exploit a mine or other labor-intensive enterprise; the contractors paid the laborers minimal wages and bound them through debt peonage (repayment of money advances) to their businesses.

Privateers: Individuals or ships granted permission to attack enemy shipping and to keep a percentage of the prize money the captured ships brought at auction; in practice, privateers were often indistinguishable from pirates.

armed silver fleet was reduced. Instead, the government authorized more frequent single sailings. Newly formed Spanish companies, receiving exclusive rights at specific ports, reduced contraband trade. Elections took place again for municipal councils. Spanish-born salaried officials replaced many Creole tax and office farmers. The original two viceroyalties were subdivided into four, to improve administrative control. The sale of tobacco and brandy became state monopolies. Silver mining and cotton textile manufacturing were expanded. By the second half of the eighteenth century, Spain had regained a measure of control over its colonies.

As a result, government revenues rose substantially. In the end, however, the reforms remained incomplete. Since the Spanish economy was not also reformed, the changes did not much diminish the English and French dominance of the import market. Spain failed to produce goods at competitive prices for the colonies; thus the level of English and French exports to the Americas remained high.

Early Portuguese Colonialism   In contrast to the Spanish Americas, the Portuguese overseas province of Brazil developed only slowly during the sixteenth century. The first governor-general arrived in 1549. He and his successors (after 1640 called viceroys, as in the Spanish colonies) were members of the high aristocracy, but their positions were salaried and subject to term limits. As the colony grew, the crown created a council in the capital of Lisbon for all Brazilian appointments and established a high court for all judicial affairs in Bahia in northern Brazil. In the early seventeenth century, offices became as open to purchase as in the Spanish colonies, although not on the city council level, where an electoral process survived.

Jesuits converted the Native Americans, whom they transported to Jesuit-administered villages. Colonial cities and Jesuits repeatedly clashed over the slave raids of the "pioneers" (*bandeirantes*) in village territories. Although the Portuguese crown and church had, like the Spanish, forbidden the enslavement of Native Americans, the *bandeirantes* exploited a loophole. The law was interpreted as allowing the enslavement of Native Americans who resisted conversion to Christianity. For a long time, Lisbon and the Jesuits were powerless against this interpretation.

Expansion into the Interior   In the middle of the seventeenth century, the Jesuits and Native Americans pushed many *bandeirantes* west and north, where the latter switched from slave raiding to prospecting for gold. In the far north, however, the raids continued until 1680, when the Portuguese administration finally ended Native American slavery, almost a century and a half after Spain.

As a result of gold discoveries in Minas Gerais in 1690 by *bandeirantes*, the European immigrant population increased rapidly. Brazilians imported slaves from Africa, to work at first in the sugar plantations and, after 1690, in the mines, where their numbers increased to two-thirds of the labor force. The peak of the gold boom came in the 1750s, when the importance of gold was second only to that of sugar among Brazilian exports to Europe.

Early in the gold boom, the crown created the new Ministry of the Navy and Overseas Territories, which greatly expanded the administrative structure in Brazil, and moved the capital from Bahia to Rio de Janeiro in 1736. The ministry in Lisbon ended the sale of offices, increased the efficiency of tax collection, and encouraged Brazilian textile manufacturing to render the province more independent from English imports. By the mid-1700s, Brazil was a flourishing overseas colony of Portugal.

North American Settlements   Efforts at settlement in North America in the sixteenth century were unsuccessful. Only in the early part of the seventeenth century did French, English, and Dutch merchant investors succeed in establishing small communities of settlers on the coast: Jamestown (founded in 1607 in today's Virginia), Quebec (1608, Canada), Plymouth and Boston (1620 and 1630, respectively, in today's Massachusetts), and New Amsterdam (1625, today's New York). Subsistence agriculture and fur, however, were not enough for growth. The settlements struggled through the seventeenth century, sustained either by Catholic missionary efforts or by the Puritans who had escaped persecution in England. Southern places like Jamestown survived because they adopted tobacco as a cash crop for export to Europe. In contrast to Mexico and Peru, the North American settlements were not followed—at least, not at first—by territorial conquests (see Map 18.3).

Native Americans   European arrivals in North America soon began supplementing agriculture with trade, exchanging metal and glass wares, beads, and seashells for furs with the Native American groups of the interior. As a result, smallpox, already a menace during the 1500s in North America, became devastating as contacts intensified.

The introduction of guns contributed an additional lethal factor to trading arrangements, as traders provided Native American trading partners with flintlocks in order to increase the yield of furs. As a result, during the 1600s the Iroquois in the northeast were able to organize themselves into an armed federation, capable of inflicting heavy losses on rival groups as well as on European traders and settlers.

Mine Workers. The discovery of gold and diamonds in Minas Gerais led to a boom but did little to contribute to the long-term health of the Brazilian economy. With the Native American population decimated by disease, African slaves performed the backbreaking work.

Farther south, in Virginia, the Jamestown settlers encountered the Powhatan confederacy. These Native Americans dominated the region between the Chesapeake Bay and the Appalachian Mountains. Initially, the Powhatan supplied Jamestown with foodstuffs and sought to integrate the settlement into their confederation. When this attempt failed, however, the confederacy raided Jamestown twice. But the settlers defeated the Powhatan in 1646, thereafter

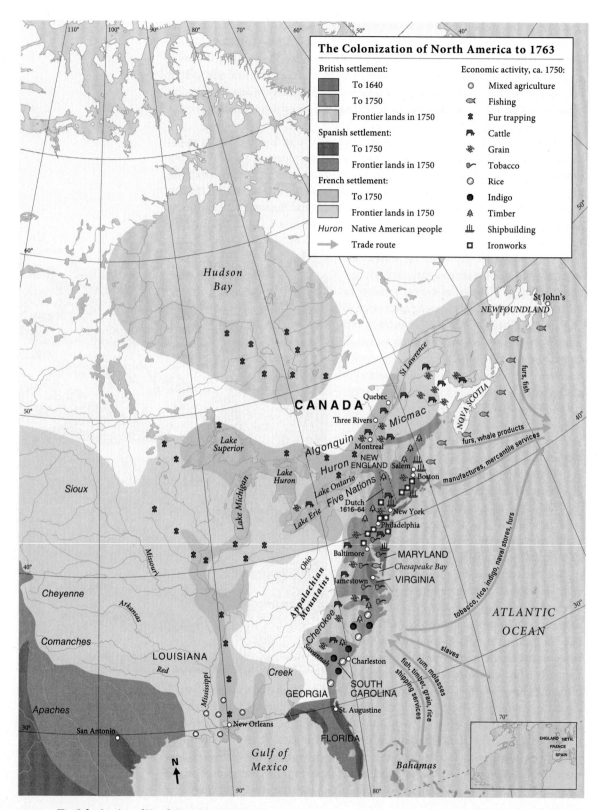

The Colonization of North America to 1763

British settlement:
- To 1640
- To 1750
- Frontier lands in 1750

Spanish settlement:
- To 1750
- Frontier lands in 1750

French settlement:
- To 1750
- Frontier lands in 1750

Huron   Native American people

→   Trade route

Economic activity, ca. 1750:
- Mixed agriculture
- Fishing
- Fur trapping
- Cattle
- Grain
- Tobacco
- Rice
- Indigo
- Timber
- Shipbuilding
- Ironworks

Hudson Bay

St John's
NEWFOUNDLAND

St. Lawrence

CANADA   Quebec

Three Rivers

Micmac

NOVA SCOTIA

furs, fish

furs, whale products

Algonquin

Montreal

NEW ENGLAND   Salem

Boston

manufactures, mercantile services

Lake Superior

Lake Huron

Huron

Five Nations

Lake Ontario

Dutch 1616–64

New York

Lake Erie

Philadelphia

Sioux

Lake Michigan

Missouri

Ohio

Baltimore   MARYLAND

Chesapeake Bay

Appalachian Mountains

Jamestown   VIRGINIA

tobacco, rice, indigo, naval stores, furs

ATLANTIC OCEAN

Cheyenne

Arkansas

Cherokee

Comanches

slaves

Savannah

LOUISIANA

Red

Creek

Charleston

rum, molasses

fish, timber, grain, rice

shipping services

Apaches

Mississippi

GEORGIA   SOUTH CAROLINA

San Antonio

New Orleans

St. Augustine

FLORIDA

N

Gulf of Mexico

Bahamas

ENGLAND   NETH.
FRANCE
SPAIN

MAP 18.3 **The Colonization of North America to 1763**

occupying their lands. The decline of the Powhatan in the later 1600s allowed the English settlers of Virginia to move westward, in contrast to the Puritans in New England, where the Iroquois, although allied with the English against the French, blocked any western expansion.

The Iroquois were determined to maintain their dominance of the fur trade, driving smaller Native American groups westward into the Great Lakes region and Mississippi plains, where these groups settled as refugees. French officials and Jesuit missionaries sought to create an alliance with the refugee peoples, to counterbalance the powerful Iroquois to the east. Many Native Americans converted to Christianity, creating a Creole Christianity similar to that of the Africans of Kongo and the Mexicans after the Spanish conquest of the Aztecs.

Major population movements also occurred further west on the Great Plains, where the Apaches arrived from the Great Basin in the Rockies. They had captured horses that had escaped during the Pueblo uprising of 1680–1695 against Spain. The Comanches, who arrived from the west on horses at the same time, had, in addition, acquired firearms and around 1725 began their expansion at the expense of the Apaches. The Sioux from the northern forests and the Cheyenne from the Great Basin added to the mix of federations on the Great Plains in the early 1700s. Smallpox epidemics did not reach the Plains until the mid-1700s, while in the east the ravages of this epidemic had weakened the Iroquois so much that they concluded a peace with the French in 1701.

French Canada   The involvement of the French in the Great Lakes region with refugees fleeing from the Iroquois was part of a program of expansion into the center of North America, begun in 1663. The governor of Quebec had dispatched explorers, fur traders, and missionaries into the Great Lakes region and the Mississippi valley. The French government then sent farmers, craftspeople, and single women from France to establish settlements. The most successful settlement, called *la Louisiane"* (Louisiana in English, after which the later state was named) in honor of Louis XIV, was at the mouth of the Mississippi, where settlers with African slaves founded sugar plantations. Because immigration was restricted to French subjects and excluded Protestants, Louisiana had far fewer settlers than English North America.

Colonial Assemblies   As immigration to New England picked up, the merchant companies in Europe, which had financed the journeys of the settlers, were initially responsible for the administration of settlement colonies. The first settlers to demand participation in the colonial administration were Virginian tobacco growers, who in 1619 created an early popular assembly. The other English colonies soon followed suit, creating their own assemblies. In contrast to Spain and Portugal, England was initially uninvolved in the governance of the overseas territories.

When England eventually took the governance of the colonies away from the charter merchants and companies in the second half of the seventeenth century, it faced entrenched settler assemblies. Many governors were deputies of aristocrats who never traveled to America. These governors were powerless to prevent the assemblies from appropriating rights to levy taxes and making appointments. The assemblies thus modeled themselves after Parliament in London. As in England,

The Columbian Exchange

Few of us can imagine an Italian kitchen without tomatoes or an Irish meal without potatoes or Chinese or Indian cuisine without chilies, but until fairly recently each of these foods was unknown to the Old World. Likewise, for millennia apples, as well as many other common fruits, were absent from the New World. It was not until the sixteenth century that new patterns of ecology and biology changed the course of millions of years of divergent evolution.

When considering the long list of life forms that moved across the oceans in the Columbian Exchange, the impact of European weeds and grasses on American grasslands, which made it possible for the North American prairie and the South American pampas to support livestock, should not be overlooked. By binding the soil together with their long, tough roots, the "empire of the dandelion" provided the conditions for the grazing of sheep, cattle, and horses, as well as the planting of crops like wheat.

The other silent invader that accompanied the conquistadors was disease. Thousands of years of mutual isolation between the Americas and Afro-Eurasia rendered the immune systems of Native Americans vulnerable to the scourges that European colonists unwittingly brought with them. By some estimates, the native populations of Mesoamerica and the Andes plummeted by 90 percent in the period 1500–1700. In comparison, the contagions the New World reciprocated upon the Old World—syphilis and tuberculosis—did not unleash nearly the same devastation, and the New World origin of these diseases is still debated.

Therefore, the big winner in the Columbian Exchange was western Europe, though the effects of the New World bounty took centuries to be fully discerned. While Asia and Africa also benefited from the Columbian Exchange, the Europeans got a continent endowed with a warm climate in which they could create new and improved versions of their homelands. The Native Americans were nearly wiped out by disease, their lands appropriated, and the survivors either enslaved or marginalized. The precipitous drop in the population of Native Americans, combined with the tropical and semitropical climate of much of the Americas, created the necessary

these assemblies excluded poorer settlers who did not meet the property requirements to vote or stand for elections.

Territorial Expansion   Steady immigration encouraged land speculators in the British colonies to cast their sights beyond the Appalachian Mountains. In 1749, the Ohio Company of Virginia received a royal permit to develop land, together with a protective fort, south of the Ohio River. The French, however, also claimed the Ohio valley. Tensions over the valley soon erupted into open hostility. Initially, the local encounters went badly for the Virginian militia and British army. In 1755, he British and French broadened their clash into a worldwide war for dominance in the colonies and Europe, the Seven Years' War of 1756–1763.

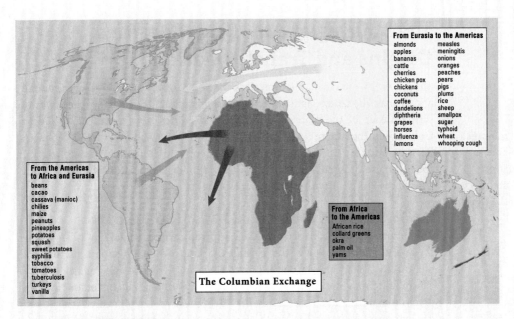

From Eurasia to the Americas

almonds	measles
apples	meningitis
bananas	onions
cattle	oranges
cherries	peaches
chicken pox	pears
chickens	pigs
coconuts	plums
coffee	rice
dandelions	sheep
diphtheria	smallpox
grapes	sugar
horses	typhoid
influenza	wheat
lemons	whooping cough

From the Americas to Africa and Eurasia

beans
cacao
cassava (manioc)
chilies
maize
peanuts
pineapples
potatoes
squash
sweet potatoes
syphilis
tobacco
tomatoes
tuberculosis
turkeys
vanilla

From Africa to the Americas

African rice
collard greens
okra
palm oil
yams

The Columbian Exchange

MAP 18.4 **The Columbian Exchange**

conditions for the Atlantic slave trade. The population losses from this trade were monumental.

Questions

- Can the Columbian Exchange be considered one of the origins of the modern world? How? Why? How does the Columbian Exchange demonstrate the origins, interactions, and adaptations model that is used throughout this book?

- Weigh the positive and negative outcomes of the Columbian Exchange. Is it possible to determine whether the overall effects of the Columbian Exchange on human society and the natural environment were for the better or for the worse?

The Seven Years' War   Both France and Great Britain borrowed heavily to finance the war. England had the superior navy and France the superior army. Since the British navy succeeded in choking off French supplies to its increasingly isolated land troops, Britain won the war overseas. In Europe, Britain's failure to supply the troops of its ally Prussia against the Austrian–French alliance caused the war on that front to end in a draw. Overseas, the British gained most of the French holdings in India, several islands in the Caribbean, all of Canada, and all the land east of the Mississippi. The costs, however, proved to be unmanageable for all concerned. The unpaid debts became the root cause of the American, French, and Haitian constitutional revolutions that began 13 years later.

The Making of American Societies: Origins and Transformations

The patterns which made the Americas an extension of Europe emerged gradually and displayed characteristics specific to each region. On one hand, there was the slow transfer of the plants and animals native to each continent, called the **Columbian Exchange** (see "Patterns Up Close"). On the other hand, Spain and Portugal adopted different strategies of mineral and agricultural exploitation. In spite of these different strategies, however, the settler societies of the two countries in the end displayed similar characteristics.

Columbian Exchange: Exchange of plants, animals, and diseases between the Americas and the rest of the world.

Exploitation of Mineral and Tropical Resources

The pattern of European expansion into subtropical and tropical lands began with the Spanish colonization of the Caribbean islands. When the Spanish crown ran out of gold in the Caribbean, it exported silver from Mexico and Peru to finance a centralizing state. By contrast, Portugal's colony of Brazil did not at first mine for precious metals, and consequently the Portuguese crown pioneered the growing of sugar on plantations. The North American colonies of England and France had, in comparison, little native industry at first. When they moved farther south, however, they adopted the plantation system for indigo and rice.

Silver Mines   Two main mining centers emerged in the Spanish colonies: Potosí in southeastern Peru (today Bolivia) and Zacatecas and Guanajuato in northern Mexico. During the eighteenth century, gold mining in Colombia and Chile rose to importance as well.

Innovations such as the "patio" method (named for the enclosure where the process was carried out), which facilitated the extraction of silver through the use of mercury, and the unrestrained exploitation of indigenous labor made American silver highly competitive in the world market. Conditions among the Native Americans and blacks employed as labor were abominable. Few laborers lasted through more than two forced recruitment (*repartimiento*) cycles before they were incapacitated or dead.

Since the exploitation of the mines was of central importance, for the first century and a half of New World colonization, the Spanish crown organized its other provinces around the needs of the mining centers. The main function of Hispaniola and Cuba in the Caribbean was to feed and protect Havana, the collection point for Mexican and Peruvian silver and the port from where the annual Spanish fleet shipped the American silver across the Atlantic.

A second region, Argentina and Paraguay, was colonized as a bulwark to prevent the Portuguese and Dutch from accessing Peruvian silver. Once established, the two colonies produced goods and foodstuffs to supply the miners in Potosí.

A third colonial region, Venezuela, began as a grain and cattle supply base for Cartagena, the port for the shipment of Colombian gold, and Panama City (on the south coast of Panama) and Portobelo (on the north coast), ports for the transshipment of Peruvian silver from the Pacific to Havana. Thus, three major regions of the Spanish overseas empire in the Americas were mostly peripheral as agricultural producers during the sixteenth century. Only after the middle of the century did they begin to specialize in tropical agricultural goods, and they were exporters only in the eighteenth century.

Wheat Farming and Cattle Ranching   To support the mining centers and administrative cities, the Spanish colonial government encouraged the development of agricultural estates (*haciendas*). Native American tenant farmers were forced to grow wheat and raise livestock for the conquerors, who were now agricultural entrepreneurs. In the latter part of the sixteenth century, the land grants gave way to rotating forced labor as well as wage labor. A landowner class emerged.

Like the conquistadors before, a majority of landowners produced wheat and animals for sale to urban and mining centers. As the Native American population declined in the seventeenth century and the church helped in consolidating the remaining population in large villages, additional land became available for the establishment of estates. From 1631 onward, authorities granted Spanish settler families the right to maintain their estates undivided from generation to generation. Secular and clerical landowning interests supported a powerful upper social stratum of Creoles from the eighteenth century onward.

Plantations and Gold Mining in Brazil   Brazil's economic activities began with brazilwood, followed by sugar plantations, before gold mining rose to prominence in the eighteenth century.

These gold-mining operations were less capital-intensive than the silver mines in Spanish America. Most miners were relatively small operators with a few black slaves as unskilled laborers. Many entrepreneurs were indebted for their slaves to absentee capitalists, with whom they shared the profits. Since prospecting took place on the land of Native Americans, bloody encounters were frequent. Brazil's gold production was a welcome bonanza for Portugal at a time of low agricultural prices.

The Silver Mountain of Potosí. Note the patios in the left foreground and the water-driven crushing mill in the center, which ground the silver-bearing ore into a fine sand that then was moistened, caked, amalgamated with mercury, and dried on the patio. The mine workers' insect-like shapes reinforce the dehumanizing effects of their labor.

Plantations in Spanish and English America   The expansion of plantation farming in the Spanish colonies was a result of the Bourbon reforms. Although sugar, tobacco, and rice had been introduced early into the Caribbean and southern Mexico, it was only in the plantation system of the eighteenth century that these and other crops were produced for export to Europe. The owners of plantations invested in African slave labor, with the result that the slave trade hit full stride beginning around 1750.

English northeast American settlements in Virginia and Carolina exported tobacco and rice beginning in the 1660s. Georgia joined southern Carolina as a major plantation colony in 1750. In the eighteenth century, New England exported timber for shipbuilding and charcoal production in Great Britain. These timber exports illustrate the importance of the Americas as a replacement for dwindling fuel resources across much of northern Europe. Altogether, it was thanks to the Americas that mostly cold and rainy Europe rose into the ranks of the wealthy Indian and Chinese empires.

Social Strata, Castes, and Ethnic Groups

Given the small settler population of the Americas, the temptation to develop a system of forced labor in agriculture and mining was irresistible. Since the Native Americans and African slaves pressed into labor were ethnically so different from the Europeans, however, a social system evolved in which the latter two not only were economically underprivileged but also made up the ethnically nonintegrated lowest rungs of the social ladder. A pattern of legal and customary discrimination evolved which prevented the integration of American ethnicities into settler society.

The Social Elite   The heirs of the Spanish conquistadors and estate owners maintained city residences and employed managers on their agricultural properties. In Brazil, cities emerged more slowly. During the seventeenth century, estate owners intermarried with the Madrid- and Lisbon-appointed administrators, creating the top tier of settler society known as Creoles. They formed a relatively closed society in which descent, intermarriage, landed property, and a government position counted more than money and education.

In the seventeenth and eighteenth centuries, the estate owners farmed predominantly with Native American forced labor. In contrast to the black slave plantation estates of the Caribbean and coastal regions of Spanish and Portuguese America, these farming estates did not export their goods to Europe.

As local producers with little competition, farming and ranching estate owners did not feel market pressures. They exploited their estates with minimal investments and usually drew profits of less than 5 percent of annual revenues. As a result, they were often heavily indebted.

Lower Creoles   The second tier of Creole society consisted of privileged European settlers who, as craftspeople and traders, theoretically worked with their hands. In practice, many of them were owner-operators who employed Native Americans and/or black slaves. Many strove to rise into the ranks of the landowning Creoles.

Wealthy weavers ran textile manufactures mostly concentrated in the cities of Mexico, Peru, Paraguay, and Argentina. On a smaller scale, manufactures also existed for pottery and leather goods. On the whole, the urban manufacturing activities of the popular people, serving the poor in local markets, remained vibrant until well into the nineteenth century, in spite of massive European imports. Prior to the arrival of railroads, the transportation of imports into the interior of the Americas was prohibitively expensive.

Mestizos and Mulattoes The mixed European–Native American and European–African population had the collective name of "caste" (*casta*), something like an ethnic group. The two most important castes were the *mestizos* (Spanish), or *mestiços* (Portuguese), who had Iberian fathers and Native American mothers, and *mulatos*, who had Iberian fathers and black mothers. By 1800 the *castas* as a whole formed the third largest population category in Latin America. In both Spanish and Portuguese America, there were also a small percentage of people descended from Native American and black unions. These intermediate population groups played important neutralizing roles in colonial society, as they had one foot in both the Creole and subordinate social strata (see Figure 18.1).

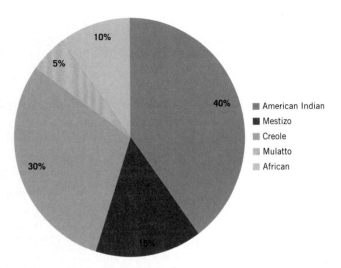

American Indian
Mestizo
Creole
Mulatto
African

Figure 18.1 **Ethnic Composition of Latin America, ca. 1800**

Mestizos and **mulattoes** filled the lower levels of the bureaucracy and the lay hierarchy in the church. They held skilled and supervisory positions in mines and on estates. In addition, in the armed forces mulattoes dominated the ranks of enlisted men; in the defense militias, they even held officer ranks. In Brazil, many mulattoes and black freedmen were farmers. Much of the craft production was in their hands. Many laws kept mestizos and mulattoes in their intermediate social and political positions.

Women The roles played by women depended on their social position. Elite Creole households followed the Mediterranean tradition of secluding women from men. Within the household, Creole women were the owners of substantial dowries and legally stipulated grooms' gifts. Often, they actively managed the investment of their assets. Outside the household, however, even elite women lost all protection. Husbands and fathers could banish daughters or wives to convents for alleged lapses in chastity, or even kill them without punishment. Thus, even elite women were bound by limits set by a patriarchal society.

On the lower rungs of society, gender separation was much less prevalent. Men, women, and children shared labor in the fields and workshops. Girls or wives took in clothes to wash or went out to work as domestics in wealthy households. Older women dominated retail in market stalls. Working families with few assets suffered abandonment by males. Women headed one-third of all households in Mexico City, according to an 1811 census. Among black slaves in the region of São Paulo, 70 percent of women were without formal ties to the men who fathered their children. The most pronounced division in colonial society was that of a patriarchy among the Creoles and a slave society dominated by women, with frequently absent men.

Amerindians (Native Americans) In the immediate aftermath of the conquest, Amerindians could be found at all social levels. Social distinctions, however, disappeared during the first 150 years of Spanish colonialism as disease

Mestizo: The offspring of a Spanish or Portuguese father and a Native American mother.

Mulatto: The offspring of a Spanish or Portuguese father and an African mother.

Illustration from an Indian Land Record. The Spaniards almost completely wiped out the Aztec archives after the conquest of Mexico; surviving examples of Indian manuscripts are thus extremely rare. Although the example shown here, made from the bark of a fig tree, claims to date from the early 1500s, it is part of the so-called Techialoyan land records created in the seventeenth century to substantiate native land claims. These "*títulos primordiales,*" as they were called, were essentially municipal histories that documented in text and pictures local accounts of important events and territorial boundaries.

reduced the Amerindian population by nearly 80 percent. It was only in the twentieth century that population figures reached the preconquest level again in most parts of Latin America.

Apart from European diseases, the Amerindians in the Amazon, Orinoco, and Maracaibo rain forests were the least affected by European colonials during the period 1500–1800. Not only were their lands economically the least promising, but they also defended those lands successfully. In many arid or semiarid regions, such as Patagonia, southern Chile, the Argentine grasslands (pampas), the Paraguayan salt marshes and deserts, and northern Mexican mountains and steppes, the seminomadic Amerindians quickly adopted the European horse and became highly mobile warrior peoples in defense of their mostly independent territories.

The villagers of Mexico, Yucatán, Guatemala, Colombia, Ecuador, and Peru had fewer choices. When smallpox reduced their numbers in the second half of the sixteenth century, authorities razed villages and concentrated the survivors in *pueblos de indios*. Initially, the Amerindians put up strong resistance against these resettlements. From the middle of the seventeenth century, however, the pueblos were self-administering units, with councils (*cabildos*), churches, schools, communal lands, and family parcels.

The councils were important institutions of legal training and social mobility for Amerindians. Initially, the traditional "noble" chiefly families descending from the preconquest Aztec and Inca ruling classes were in control as administrators. The many village functions, however, for which the *cabildos* were responsible allowed commoners to move up into auxiliary roles.

Amerindian villages were closed to settlers, and the only outsiders admitted were Catholic priests. Contact with the Spanish world remained minimal, and acculturation went little beyond official conversion to Catholicism. Thus, even in the heartlands of Spanish America, Amerindian adaptation to the rulers remained limited.

Unfortunately, however, tremendous demographic losses made the Amerindians in the pueblos vulnerable to the loss of their land. Estate owners expanded their holdings, and when the population rebounded, many estates had grown to immense sizes. Villages began to run out of land for their inhabitants. Increasing numbers of Amerindians had to rent land from estate owners or find work on estates as farmhands. They became estranged from their villages, fell into debt peonage, and entered the ranks of the working poor.

New England Society   In the early modern period, the small family farm remained the norm for the majority of New England's population. An acute lack of money and cheap means of transportation hampered the development of market networks in the interior well into the 1770s. The situation was better in the agriculturally more favored colonies in the Mid-Atlantic, especially in Pennsylvania. The number of plantations in the south rose steadily, demanding a substantial increase in numbers of slaves, although world market fluctuations left planters vulnerable. Except for boom periods in the plantation sector, the rural areas remained largely poor.

Real changes occurred during the early eighteenth century in the urban regions of New England. Large port cities emerged which shipped in goods from Europe in return for timber. A wealthy merchant class formed, spawning urban strata of professionals. Primary school education was provided by municipal public schools as well as by some churches, and evening schools for craftspeople also existed. By the middle of the eighteenth century, a majority of men could read and write. Finally, in contrast to Latin America, social ranks in New England were less elaborate.

The Adaptation of the Americas to European Culture

European settlers brought two distinct cultures to the Americas. In the Mid-Atlantic, the Caribbean, and Central and South America, they brought with them the Catholic Reformation, a culture that resisted the New Science and the Enlightenment until the late eighteenth century. In the northeast, colonists implanted dissident Protestantism as well as the Anglicanism of Great Britain and the Presbyterianism of Scotland.

Catholic Missionary Work   Spanish and Portuguese monarchs relied on the Catholic Church for their rule in the new American provinces. A strong motive driving many in the church and society was the belief in the imminent Second Coming of Jesus. This belief was one inspiration for the original Atlantic expansion (see Chapter 16). When the Aztec and Inca Empires fell, members of the Franciscan order, the main proponents of the belief in the imminence of the Second Coming, interpreted it as a sign of the urgent duty to convert the Amerindians to Christianity.

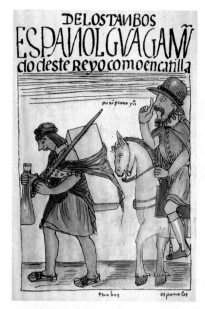

Spanish Cruelty to Incas.
Felipe Guamán Poma de Ayala, a Peruvian claiming noble Inca descent, was a colonial administrator, well educated and an ardent Christian. He is remembered today as a biting critic of the colonial administration and the clergy, whom he accused of mistreating and exploiting the Andean population, as in this colored woodcut print.

Thousands of preaching monks, later followed by the Jesuits, fanned out among the Amerindians. They baptized them, introduced the sacraments, and taught them basic theological concepts. The missionaries learned native languages, translated the catechism and New Testament into those languages, and taught the children of the ruling native families how to read and write.

The role and function of saints formed one element of Catholic Christianity to which Amerindians acculturated early. Good works as God-pleasing human efforts to gain salvation in the afterlife formed another. The veneration of images of the Virgin Mary and pilgrimages to the chapels and churches where they were kept constituted a third element. On the other hand, the Spanish Inquisition also operated in the Spanish and Portuguese colonies, seeking to limit the degree to which Catholicism and traditional religion mingled.

Education and the Arts The Catholic Reformation also influenced the organization of education. The Franciscans and Dominicans had offered education to the children of settlers early on and, in colleges, trained graduates for missionary work. New World universities taught theology, church law, and Native American languages. Under the impact of the Jesuits, universities broadened the curriculum. Although the universities did not teach the New Sciences and Enlightenment of northwestern Europe, there was nevertheless scientific research on tropical diseases, plants, and animals. The extent of this research was long kept secret by the Spanish and Portuguese monarchs from their European competitors.

Furthermore, missionary monks collected and recorded Native American manuscripts and oral traditions, such as the Aztec *Anales de Tula* and the Maya *Popol Vuh*. Others wrote histories and ethnographies of the indigenous peoples.

A number of Amerindian and mestizo chroniclers, historians, and commentators on the early modern state and society are similarly noteworthy. Felipe Guamán Poma de Ayala (ca. 1535–1616), a native Peruvian, is of particular interest. He accompanied his 800-page manuscript, entitled (in English translation) *The First New Chronicle and Good Government*, with some 400 drawings of daily-life activities in the Peruvian villages. Unfortunately, King Philip II of Spain forbade in 1577 the publication of all manuscripts dealing with what he called idolatry and superstition. Many manuscripts lay hidden in archives until modern times.

Protestantism in New England Religious diversity was a defining cultural trait of English settlements in North America. The spectrum of Christian denominations ranged from English and continental European versions of Protestantism to Anglicanism and a minority of Catholics. Dissenters frequently split from the existing denominations, moved into new territory, and founded new settlements.

An early example of religious splintering was the rise of an antinomian ("opposed to the law") group within Puritan-dominated Massachusetts. The preachers and settlers represented in the General Court, as their assembly was called, were committed to the Calvinist balance between "inner" personal grace obtained from God and "outer" works according to the moral law mandated by the Ten Commandments. The antinomian (or Free Grace) group, however, advocated an exclusive commitment to inner grace through spiritual perfection.

Their leader was Anne Hutchinson, an early proponent of women's rights and an inspiring preacher. She was accused of arguing that she could recognize those believers in Calvinist Protestantism who were predestined for salvation and that these believers would be saved even if they had sinned. After a power struggle, the General Court prevailed and forced the antinomians to move to Rhode Island in 1638.

The example of Hutchinson is noteworthy in part because it led to the founding of Harvard College in 1636 by the General Court as an institution combating antinomianism. Harvard was the first institution of higher learning in North America.

Witch Trial. In the course of the 1600s, in the relatively autonomous English colonies of Northeast America, more persons were accused, tried, and convicted of witchcraft than anywhere else. Of the 140 persons coming to trial between 1620 and 1725, 86 percent were women. Three witch panics are recorded: Bermuda, 1651; Hartford, Connecticut, 1652–1665; and Salem, Massachusetts, 1692–1693. This anonymous American woodcut of the early 1600s shows one method used to try someone for witchcraft: The accused would swim or float, if guilty—or sink, if innocent.

New Sciences Research As discussed in Chapter 17, the New Sciences had their most hospitable home in northwestern Europe, where the rivalry between Protestantism and Catholicism had left enough of an authority-free space for the New Sciences to flourish. Under similar circumstances—intense rivalry among denominations—English North America also proved hospitable to the New Sciences. An early practitioner was Benjamin Franklin (1706–1790), who began his career as a printer, journalist, and newspaper editor. Franklin founded the University of Pennsylvania (1740), the first secular university in North America, and the American Philosophical Society (1743), the first scientific society. This hospitality for the New Sciences in North America was in contrast to Latin America, where a uniform Catholic Reformation prevented its rise.

Witch Hunts In the last decade of the seventeenth century, religious intensity was at the root of a witchcraft frenzy that seized New England. Witches, male and female, were believed to be persons exerting a negative influence, or black magic, on their victims. In medieval Europe, the church had kept witchcraft hidden, but in the wake of challenges to church authority, it had become more visible. In the North American colonies, with no overarching religious authority, the visibility of witchcraft was particularly high.

This sensitivity erupted into hysteria in Salem, Massachusetts, in 1692. Tituba, a Native American slave from Barbados, worked in the household of a pastor. She practiced voodoo, the West African–originated, part-African and part-Christian religious practice of influencing others. When young girls in the pastor's household suffered from convulsions, mass hysteria broke out, in which 14 women and five men accused of being witches or accomplices were executed. (Tituba, ironically, survived.) A new governor finally restored order.

Revivalism   Religious fervor expressed itself also in periodic Protestant renewal movements, such as the "Great Awakening" of the 1730s and 1740s. The
main impulse for this revivalist movement came from the brothers John and
Charles Wesley, two Methodist preachers in England who toured Georgia in
1735, and their friend George Whitefield (WHIT-field), who traveled to North
America in 1739 and preached a series of sensational and popular revival sermons.
Preachers from other denominations joined, all exhorting Protestants to literally
"start anew" in their relationship with God. Thus, revivalism, recurring with great
regularity to the present, became a potent force in Protestant America, at opposing purposes with secular founding-father constitutionalism.

Putting It All Together

During the period 1500–1800, the contours of a new pattern in which the
Americas formed a resource-rich extension of Europe took shape. During this
time, China and India continued to be the most populous and wealthiest agrarian–urban regions of the world. In 1500, Europe was struggling to defend itself
against the push of the Ottoman Empire into eastern Europe and the western
Mediterranean. But its successful conquest of Iberia from the Muslims led to the
discovery of the Americas. Possession of the Americas made Europe similar to
China and India in that it now encompassed, in addition to its northerly cold climates, subtropical and tropical regions that produced cash crops as well as precious metals. Over the next 300 years, Europe narrowed the gap between itself
and China and India.

However, because of fierce competition both with the Ottoman Empire and
internally, much of the wealth Europe gained in the Americas was wasted on warfare. The centralizing state, created in part to support war, ran into insurmountable budgetary barriers. Even mercantilism, a logical extension of the centralizing
state, had limited effects. Its centerpiece, state support for the export of manufactures to the American colonies, functioned unevenly. The Spanish and Portuguese
governments, with weak urban infrastructures and low manufacturing capabilities, were unable to enforce this state-supported trade until the eighteenth
century and even then only in very limited ways. France and England practiced
mercantilism more successfully but were able to do so in the Americas only from
the late seventeenth century onward, when their plantation systems began to take
shape. Although the American extension of Europe had the potential of making
Europe self-sufficient, this potential was realized only partially during the colonial period.

Debate continues over the question of the degree of wealth the Americas
added to Europe. On one hand, research has established that the British slave
trade for sugar plantations added at best 1 percent to the British gross domestic
product (GDP). The profits from the production of sugar on the English island of
Jamaica may have added another 4 percent to the British GDP. Without doubt,
private slave-trading and sugar-producing enterprises were immensely profitable
to individuals and groups. However, these profits were smaller if one takes into
account the immense waste of revenues on military ventures—hence the doubts

raised by scholars today about large gains made by Europe through its American colonial acquisitions.

On the other hand, the European extension to the Americas was clearly a momentous event in world history. It might have produced dubious overall profits for Europe, but it definitely encouraged the parting of ways between Europe on one hand and Asia and Africa on the other, once a new scientific–industrial society began to emerge around 1800.

Review and Relate

Thinking Through Patterns

Examine the ways historians approach the big questions of this chapter.

In their role as subtropical and tropical extensions of Europe, the Americas had a considerable impact on Europe's changing position in the world. First, Europe acquired large quantities of precious metals, which its two largest competitors, India and China, lacked. Second, with its new access to warm-weather agricultural products, Europe rose to a position of agrarian autonomy similar to that of India and China. In terms of resources, compared with the principal religious civilizations of India and China, Europe grew between 1550 and 1800 from a position of inferiority to one of near parity.

> What is the significance of western Europeans acquiring the Americas as a warm-weather extension of their northern continent?

Because the numbers of Europeans who emigrated to the Americas was low for most of the colonial period, they never exceeded the numbers of Native Americans or African slaves. The result was a privileged settler society that held superior positions on the top rung of the social hierarchy. In principle, given an initially large indigenous population, labor was cheap but should have become more expensive as diseases reduced the Native Americans. In fact, labor always remained cheap, in part because of forced labor and in part because of racial prejudice.

> What was the main pattern of social development in colonial America during the period 1500–1800?

Two contrasting patterns characterized the way in which European colonies were governed. The Spanish and Portuguese crowns, interested in extracting minerals and warm-weather products from the colonies, were motivated to exercise centralized control over their possessions in the Americas. In contrast, the British crown granted self-government to the Northeast American colonies from the start, in part because the colonies were far less important economically and in part because of a long tradition of self-rule at home. Nevertheless, even though Latin American settlers achieved only partial self-rule in their towns and cities, they destroyed central rule indirectly

> Why and how did European settlers in South and North America strive for self-government, and how successful were they in achieving their goals?

through the purchase of offices. After financial reforms, Spain and Portugal reestablished a degree of central rule through the appointment of officers from the home countries.

| Against the Grain

Consider this as a counterpoint to the main patterns examined in this chapter.

Juana Inés de la Cruz

- Why were the Latin American colonies more socially conservative than Europe?

- Was de la Cruz right to stop her correspondence with the Mexican clergy in 1693?

In the wake of the Protestant and Catholic Reformations of the 1500s, it was no longer unusual for European women to pursue higher education. In the more conservative Latin American colonies of Spain, Juana Inés de la Cruz (1651–1695) was less fortunate, even though her fame as the intellectually most brilliant figure of the seventeenth century in the colonies endured.

De la Cruz was the illegitimate child of a Spanish immigrant father and a Creole mother. She grew up on the hacienda of her maternal grandfather, in whose library she secretly studied Latin, Greek, and Nahuatl, and also composed her first poems. Unable, as a woman, to be admitted to the university in Mexico City, de la Cruz was fortunate to receive further education from the wife of the vice regent of New Spain. In order to continue her studies, she entered a convent in 1668. Here, she continued to study and write hundreds of poems, comedies, religious dramas, and theological texts. Her seminars with courtiers and scholarly visitors were a major attraction.

In 1688, however, she lost her protection at court with the departure of her vice regal supporters for Spain. Her superior, the archbishop of Mexico, was an open misogynist. A crisis came in 1690 when the bishop of Puebla published de la Cruz's critique of a famous sermon of 1650 by the Portuguese Jesuit António Vieira on Jesus's act of washing his disciples' feet, together with his own critique of de la Cruz. De la Cruz viewed Vieira's interpretation as more hierarchical/male and her own interpretation as humbler/female.

A year later, in 1691, de la Cruz wrote a spirited riposte to the bishop's apparently well-meaning advice to her in his critique to be more conscious of her status as a woman. Her message was clear: even though women had to be silent in church, as St. Paul had taught, neither study nor writing was prohibited for women. Before the church could censor her, in 1693 Juana Inés de la Cruz stopped writing. She died two years later.

Key Terms

Columbian Exchange   438
Creoles   428
Labor assignment
  (*repartimiento*)   429

Land-labor grant
  (*encomienda*)   424
Mestizo   441

Mulatto   441
Privateers   431

Learn more with this chapter's digital tools, including the Oxford Insight Study Guide, at http://www.oup.com/he/vonsivers4e. Please see the Further Resources section at the back of the book for additional readings and suggested websites.

Sources for Chapter 18

Scandal at the church: José de Álfaro accuses Doña Theresa Bravo and others of insulting and beating his castiza wife, Joséfa Cadena

1782

In all agrarian–urban societies, honor codes of varying degrees of severity regulated social relations. Precolonial Latin America was no different; with the Creoles at the top of the social hierarchy, this code demanded severe retribution against anyone besmirching the honor of its members, but members of lower-level strata were no less vigilant in the protection of their members. What happened when the honor codes of people from different social strata clashed? The following court case occurred in a Mexican city in 1782. Unfortunately, no settlement of the case is recorded.

The Court Case

17.1 Alcalde Mayor Don Thomás Velasco Receives the Criminal Complaint
Criminal proceedings as a result of the denunciation by José de Álfaro against doña Teresa Bravo, her daughter Teresa, and her sisters Francisca, as well as a woman deposited in their home, and don Diego Fernández, the husband of doña Teresa, for the mistreatment of his wife, Joséfa Cadena. All are *vecinos* [residents] of this town. The presiding judge in this jurisdiction is don Thomas de Velasco, alcalde mayor and commissioner. . .

In the town and *cabecera* [municipality] of San Juan Teotihuacán, on October 16, 1782, before me, Captain don Tomás de Velasco, *alcalde mayor* [regional magistrate] of this jurisdiction for His Majesty, may God protect him, this petition and its contents are presented, in the presence of witnesses and in the absence of a notary.

17.2 The Petition and Criminal Complaint of José de Álfaro
I, José de Álfaro, resident of this town . . . say that on Sunday the thirteenth of this month, my wife, Joséfa Cadena, was coming [out of church] after mass and

Source: Excerpted and adapted from Sonya Lipsett Rivera, "Scandal at the Church: José de Álfaro Accuses Doña Theresa Bravo and Others of Insulting and Beating His Castiza Wife, Joséfa Cadena (Mexico, 1782)," in Richard Boyer and Geoffrey Spurling, eds., *Colonial Lives: Documents in Latin American History, 1550–1850* (Oxford and New York: Oxford University Press, 2000), 216–223, http://chnm.gmu.edu/wwh/p/232.html

passed close to doña Teresa Bravo, the wife of don Diego Fernández, *cobrador de las rentas de alcabalas y pulques* [official in charge of the collection of sales taxes and taxes on pulque]. Doña Teresa, using the pretext that my wife had brushed against her, which was not true, sprung forward, saying to her, "Oh, you black whore, you dare to brush against me." And throwing her to the ground, not only doña Teresa, but also her daughter, her sister, and the woman who was deposited with them and was in their company, hit her [Joséfa] many times. Although don Diego was present, instead of trying to calm them, he said, "Give it to that black whore again." In this way, my wife came out of this attack with marks on her face and a big scratch. She has bruises all over her body because of the beating, and since she is pregnant and now she is bleeding, we are worried about the unfortunate consequences of this encounter and that she might lose not only the baby's life but her own.

In the above related events, doña Teresa and her husband, as well as the other accomplices, insulted my wife and me in a very grave manner, and in all the ways imaginable. To a married woman, no insult is greater than to call her a black whore, since this offends her fidelity and her *calidad* [here: race]. Her honor is publicly known, and she is not a black but rather a *castiza* [three-quarters white, one-quarter Amerindian]. In regards to actions, none is worse than to have hit her all over her body and to have marked her face. What makes all this much worse is that the insults occurred in public and in the presence of a numerous crowd who were leaving mass. Don Diego is a participant in this crime, not only because he did not prevent it as he should have and as would have been easy for him due to the power vested in him as a husband, but also because he encouraged his wife and the others who insulted my wife, to consummate the humiliation. . .

[José de Álfaro] does not know how to sign.

Signed by Licentiate Manuel Cordero

17. 3 [The Alcalde Mayor orders that information on the petition be collected and that two surgeons examine Joséfa Cadena.] *17.4–17. 5* [Two surgeons examined Joséfa Cadena and testified that she had a scar running from her right eyebrow to her hairline apparently caused by fingernails, and while six months' pregnant had suffered injuries to her hips, thighs, and groin and had been hemorrhaging through her vagina since the previous Sunday and so was at risk of miscarriage]. *17.6 [The Alcalde Mayor Orders José de Álfaro to Present His Witnesses.]*

17.7 Testimony of Don Manuel Delfin
On October 18, 1782 . . . José de Álfaro presented as a witness a man from whom I took the oath that he made to God and the holy cross in accordance with the law. He said that his name is Manuel Delfin, that he is married, of Spanish *calidad*, and forty years of age, and is a resident of this *cabecera*. He knows the person who presents him as a witness. And it is true that on Sunday, the thirteenth of the present month, he was leaving early mass in the company of don Diego Fernández . . . they heard shouts and turned around to see that Joséfa Cadena was seated on the ground, in the company of her sister, and that doña Teresa Bravo and her daughter Teresa and her aunt Francisca, as well as a woman deposited with them and many other women who he does not

remember, were mistreating her with words. Joséfa Cadena got up and tried to hit them, and the young Teresa threw her onto the ground. He saw this because he went there to separate them, which he was able to do. But the others continued to mistreat her with very indecorous words and indecent expressions. And Chepa's [a nickname for Joséfa] brother arrived and tried to defend her with indecorous words, and it was then that don Diego Fernández answered them with the same impurity and without stopping. And then near the house of don Diego, the witness revealed that Joséfa had said to doña Teresa that she was a whore and that no one had found a friend under her [Joséfa's] bed. It was then that the fight began. All who participated were hit and scratched, but there was no use of arms . . .

[Ratifies and signs].

▶ **Working with Sources**

1. **What appears to us as a simple legal case of assault actually involves the view of honor on different social levels. Which levels are involved and what are the distinctive definitions of honor on each level?**

2. **Compare premodern and modern definitions of honor with each other. What are the main differences?**

SOURCE 18.2 # Marina de San Miguel's Confessions before the Inquisition, Mexico City

1598–1599

The Inquisition was well established in Spain at the time of Cortés's conquest in the 1520s. A tribunal of the Holy Office of the Inquisition came in the conquistadors' wake, ultimately established at Mexico City in 1571 with authority to regulate Catholic morality throughout "New Spain." Most of the Inquisition trials concerned petty breaches of religious conduct, but others dealt with the much more serious crime of heresy. In November 1598, the Inquisition became alarmed about the rise of a group who believed that the Day of Judgment was at hand. Among the group denounced to the Holy Office was Marina de San Miguel, a Spanish-born woman who held a high status due to her mystical visions. Her confessions reveal the degree to which admissions of "deviance" could be extorted from a victim.

Source: Jacqueline Holler, "The Spiritual and Physical Ecstasies of a Sixteenth-Century Beata: Marina de San Miguel Confesses Before the Mexican Inquisition," in Richard Boyer and Geoffrey Spurling, eds., *Colonial Lives: Documents on Latin American History, 1550–1850* (Oxford and New York: Oxford University Press, 2000), 79–98.

In March 1601, Marina was stripped naked to the waist and paraded upon a mule. Forced to confess her errors, she was sentenced to 100 lashes with a whip. Confined to a plague hospital, she died some time later.

First Confession

In the city of Mexico, Friday, November 20, 1598. The Lord Inquisitor *licenciado* don Alonso de Peralta in his morning audience ordered that a woman be brought before him from one of the secret prisons of this Holy Office. Being present, she swore an oath *en forma devida de derecho* under which she promised to tell the truth here in this audience and in all the others that might be held until the determination of her case, and to keep secret everything that she might see or believe or that might be talked about with her or that might happen concerning this her case.

. . .

She was asked if she knows, presumes, or suspects the cause for her arrest and imprisonment in the prisons of the Holy Office. . .. The inquisitor said that with her illness she must have imagined it. And she says that she wants to go over her memory so that she can tell the truth about everything that she might remember.

With this the audience ceased, because it was past eleven. The above was read and she approved it and signed it. And she was ordered to return to her cell, very admonished to examine her memory as she was offered to do.

. . .

Third Confession

In the city of Mexico, Tuesday, November 24, 1598. . ..

She said that what she has remembered is that in the course of her life some spiritual things have happened to her, which she has talked about to some people. And she believes that they have been the cause of her imprisonment, because they were scandalized by what she told them.

. . .

And then she opened her eyes and began to shake and get up from the bench on which she was seated, saying, "My love, help me God, how strongly you have given me this." And among these words she said to the Lord Inquisitor that when she is given these trances, she should be shaken vigorously to awaken her from her deep dream. Then she returned to being as though sleeping. The inquisitor called her by her name and she did not respond, nor the second time. And the third time she opened her eyes and made faces, and made signs with her hands to her mouth.

. . .

Sixth Confession

In the city of Mexico, Monday, January 25, 1599. . . .

She said that it's like this. . . . She has been condemned to hell, because for fifteen years she has had a sensual temptation of the flesh, which makes her perform dishonest acts with her own hands on her shameful parts. She came to pollution [orgasm] saying dishonest words that provoke lust, calling by their dishonest names many dirty and lascivious things. She was tempted to this by the devil, who appeared to her internally in the form of an Angel of Light, who told her that she should do these things, because they were no sin. This was to make her abandon her scruples. And the devil appeared to her in the form of Christ our Redeemer, in such a way that she might uncover her breasts and have carnal union with him. And thus, for fifteen years, she has had carnal union occasionally from month to month, or every two months. And if it had been more she would accuse herself of that too, because she is only trying to save her soul, with no regard to honor or the world. And the carnal act that the devil as Angel of Light and in the form of Christ had with her was the same as if she had had it with a man. And he kissed her, and she enjoyed it, and she felt a great ardor in her whole body, with particular delight and pleasure.

. . .

Eighth Confession

In the city of Mexico, Wednesday, January 27, 1599. . . .

But all the times she had the copulation with the devil in the form of Christ she doubted whether it was the devil or not, from which doubts one can infer that she did not believe as firmly as she ought to have that such things could not possibly be from Christ. In this she should urgently discharge her conscience. . . .

. . .

[After the *Ninth Confession*:]

In the city of Mexico, Tuesday, Day of the Purification of our Lady, February 2, 1599, the Lord Inquisitor in his afternoon audience ordered Marina de San Miguel brought before him. And once present she was told that if she has remembered anything in her case she should say it, and the truth, under the oath that she has made.

She said no. . . .

▶ **Working with Sources**

1. **What does this document indicate about the working methods of the Inquisition (and their "successes") in Mexico in the 1590s?**

2. **Does the Inquisition seem to have been more concerned about Marina's sexuality than her mystical experiences?**

SOURCE 18.3   Nahuatl Land Sale Documents, Mexico

ca. 1610

After the conquest of the Aztec imperial capital of Tenochtitlán, Spaniards turned their attention to the productive farmland in the surrounding countryside, which was inhabited by Nahuatl-speaking native people. By the late sixteenth century, Spaniards began to expand rapidly into this territory. They acquired estates in a variety of ways, from royal grants to open seizure of property. Nevertheless, the purchase of plots of land from individual Nahuas was also common—although sometimes the sellers came to regret the transaction and petitioned higher authorities for redress of their grievances.

Altepetl: City-state.

Teopixqui: Priest, in Nahuatl.

Tlaxilacalli: Subunit of an *altepetl*

Teniente: Lieutenant.

Here in the ***altepetl*** Santo Domingo Mixcoac, Marquesado del Valle, on the first day of July of the year 1612, I, Joaquín de San Francisco, and my wife, Juana Feliciana, citizens here in the *altepetl* of Santa María Purificación Tlilhuacan, sell to Dr. Diego de León Plaza, ***teopixqui***, one field and house that we have in the ***tlaxilacalli*** Tlilhuacan next to the house of Juan Bautista, Spaniard. Where we are is right in the middle of [in between] their houses. And now we receive [the money] in person. The reason we sell it is that we have no children to whom it might belong. For there is another land and house, but [the land] here we can no longer [work] because it is really in the middle of [land belonging to] Spaniards. [The land] is not *tributario*, for my father, named Juan Altamirano, and my mother, María Catalina, really left it to me. And now I give it to [the doctor] very voluntarily. And now he is personally giving me 130 pesos. Both my wife and I receive it in person before the witnesses. And the tribute will be remedied with [the price]; it will pay it. The land [upon which tribute is owed] is at Colonanco. It is adjacent to the land of Miguel de Santiago and Lucas Pérez. And the witnesses [are] Antonio de Fuentes and señora Inés de Vera and Juana de Vera, Spanish women (and the Nahuas) Juan Josef, Gabriel Francisco, María, Mariana, and Sebastián Juan. And because we do not know how to write, I, Joaquín [de San] Francisco, and my wife asked a witness to set down [a signature] on our behalf [along with the notary?] Juan Vázquez, Spaniard. Witnesses, Antonio de Fuentes, [etc.] Before me, Matías Valeriano, notary. And both of them, he and his wife [Joaquín de San Francisco and Juana Feliciana], received the 140 pesos each three months, [presumably paid in installments?] before the witnesses who were mentioned. Before me, Matías Valeriano, notary.

· · ·

Source: Rebecca Horn, "Spaniards in the Nahua Countryside: Dr. Diego de León Plaza and Nahuatl Land Sale Documents (Mexico, Early Seventeenth Century)," in Richard Boyer and Geoffrey Spurling, eds., *Colonial Lives: Documents on Latin American History, 1550–1850* (Oxford and New York: Oxford University Press, 2000), 102–103, 108–109.

[Letter of complaint to the authorities of Santo Domino Mixcoac, on the behalf of a group of Nahuas, undated:]

We are citizens here in Santo Domingo Mixcoac. We state that we found out that Paula and Juana and María and Catalina and Inés and Anastacia complain about the **teniente** before you [the *corregidor, gobernador, regidores*, etc.]. It is Antonio de Fuentes whom they are accusing because they say he mistreats them. [They say] he robs [people's land].

. . .

And now [the] Spaniard Napolles disputes with the *teniente*. And Napolles goes around to each house exerting pressure on, forcing many people [to say "get rid of the *teniente*"]. [He says:] "Let there be no officer of the justice. I will help you expel the *teniente* because we will be happy if there is no officer of the law on your land." Napolles, Spaniard, keeps a woman at his house and he is forcing her. For this reason [the authorities] arrested him for concubinage. They gave him a fine about which he became very angry and they arrested him. He stole four pigs, the property of a person named Francisco Hernández, Spaniard, and because of that they arrested him. He was scorched [burned] for their relatives accuse them.

. . .

And so now with great concern and with bowing down we implore you [the *corregidor, gobernador,* and *regidores*, etc.] and we ask for justice. Everyone knows how [the blacks and *mestizos*] mistreat us. They don't go to confession. They are already a little afraid and are already living a little better. And we ask for justice. Let them be punished. We who ask it are Juan Joseph, Francisco de San Juan, and Francisco Juan.

▶ Working
with Sources

1. **Why do the documents incorporate Nahuatl terms at some times but not at others?**

2. **How do the documents illustrate the various levels of justice available to native people and to "Spaniards"?**

SOURCE 18.4 *The Jesuit Relations*, French North America

1649

The *Jesuit Relations* are the most important documents attesting to the encounter between Europeans and native North Americans or Amerindians in the seventeenth century. These annual reports of French missionaries from the Society of Jesus document the conversions—or attempted conversions—of the various indigenous peoples in what is today the St. Lawrence River basin and the Great Lakes region. When they arrived on the banks of the St. Lawrence in 1625, French Jesuits were entering a continent still very much under control of First Nations peoples, who were divided by their own ethnic and linguistic differences. Even the catchall terms "Huron" and "Iroquois" masked their nature as confederacies, composed of several distinct nations, who had joined together prior to the arrival of Europeans.

When the Jesuits made headway with one group, they usually lost initiative with the group's rivals—and sometimes found themselves in the midst of a conflict that they could barely understand or appreciate. This section of the *Relations* concerns the torture and murder of Jean Brébeuf, who had lived among the Hurons at various points from the 1620s through the 1640s, observing their culture and systematically attempting to convert them to Catholicism. However, when an Iroquois raiding party invaded his settlement, the depth of the Hurons' Christian commitment—and his own—would be tested.

The sixteenth day of March in the present year, 1649, marked the beginning of our misfortunes—if an event, which no doubt has been the salvation of many of God's elect, can be called a misfortune.

The Iroquois, enemies of the Hurons, arrived by night at the frontier of this country. They numbered about a thousand men, well furnished with weapons, most of them carrying firearms obtained from their allies, the Dutch. We had no knowledge of their approach, although they had started from their country in the autumn, hunting in the forests throughout the winter, and had made a difficult journey of nearly two hundred leagues over the snow in order to take us by surprise. By night, they reconnoitered the condition of the first place upon which they had designs. It was surrounded by a pine stockade fifteen or sixteen feet in height, and a deep ditch with which nature had strongly fortified this place on three sides. There remained only a small space that was weaker than the others.

Source: Paul Ragueneau, "Relation of 1648–49," in Allan Greer, ed., *The Jesuit Relations: Natives and Missionaries in Seventeenth-Century North America* (Boston: Bedford/St. Martin's, 2000), 112–115.

It was at this weak point that the enemy made a breach at daybreak, but so secretly and promptly that he was master of the place before anyone could mount a defense. All were then sleeping deeply, and they had no time to recognize the danger. Thus this village was taken, almost without striking a blow and with only ten Iroquois killed. Part of the Hurons—men, women, and children—were massacred then and there, while the others were made captives and were reserved for cruelties more terrible than death.

. . .

The enemy did not stop there, but followed up his victory, and before sunrise he appeared in arms to attack the town of St. Louis, which was fortified with a fairly good stockade. Most of the women and the children had just gone from it upon hearing the news which had arrived regarding the approach of the Iroquois. The people of greatest courage, about eighty persons, being resolved to defend themselves well, courageously repulsed the first and the second assaults, killing about thirty of the enemy's boldest men, in addition to many wounded. But finally, the larger number prevailed, as the Iroquois used their hatchets to undermine the palisade of stakes and opened a passage for themselves through some considerable breaches.

About nine o'clock in the morning, we perceived from our house at St. Marie the fire which was consuming the cabins of that town, where the enemy, after entering victoriously, had reduced everything to desolation. They cast into the flames the old, the sick, the children who had not been able to escape, and all those who, being too severely wounded, could not have followed them into captivity. At the sight of those flames, and by the color of the smoke which issued from them, we understood sufficiently what was happening, for this town of St. Louis was no more than a league distant from us. Two Christians who escaped the fire arrived about this time and confirmed this.

In this town of St. Louis were at that time two of our fathers, Father Jean de Brébeuf and Father Gabriel Lalemant, who had charge of a cluster of five towns. These formed but one of the eleven missions of which we have spoken above, and we call it the mission of St. Ignace.

Some Christians had begged the fathers to preserve their lives for the glory of God, which would have been as easy for them as for the more than five hundred persons who went away at the first alarm, for there was more than enough time to reach a place of safety. But their zeal could not permit such a thing, and the salvation of their flock was dearer to them than the love of their own lives. They employed the moments left to them as the most precious which they had ever had in the world, and through the heat of the battle their hearts were on fire for the salvation of souls. One was at the breach, baptizing the **catechumens**, and the other was giving absolution to the **neophytes**. Both of them urged the Christians to die in the sentiments of piety with which they consoled them in their miseries. Never was their faith more alive, nor their love for their good fathers and pastors more keenly felt.

An infidel, seeing the desperate situation, spoke of taking flight, but a Christian named Etienne Annaotaha, the most esteemed in the country for his courage and his exploits against the enemy, would never allow it. "What!" he said. "Could we ever abandon these two good fathers, who have exposed their lives

Catechumens: Native converts who had not yet been baptized.

Neophytes: Recently baptized Christians.

for us? Their love for our salvation will be the cause of their death, for there is no longer time for them to flee across the snows. Let us then die with them, and we shall go together to heaven." This man had made a general confession a few days previously, having had a presentiment of the danger awaiting him and saying that he wished that death should find him disposed for Heaven. And indeed he, as well as many other Christians, had abandoned themselves to fervor in a manner so extraordinary that we shall never be sufficiently able to bless the guidance of God over so many predestinated souls. His divine providence continues lovingly to guide them in death as in life.

▶ Working with Sources

1. How well do the Jesuits seem to have understood the conflicts among native peoples in this region?

2. How was Ragueneau's reporting of the battle designed to highlight the "success" of the mission, despite an apparent setback?

Further Resources

Chapter 1

Burroughs, William J. *Climate Change in Prehistory: The End of the Reign of Chaos*. Cambridge: Cambridge University Press, 2005. Very well-researched and up-to-date discussion of climate and human evolution.

Condemi, Silvana, and François Savatier. *A Pocket History of Human Evolution: How We Became Sapiens*. Paris: Flammarion, 2019. A short, up-to-date introduction to the ever-changing story of human evolution by a prominent paleoanthropologist and a science journalist. Includes new research on the Neanderthals and the discovery of the Denisovans.

Finlayson, Clive. *The Smart Neanderthal: Bird Catching, Cave Art, and the Cognitive Revolution*. Oxford and New York: Oxford University Press, 2019. The author is a foremost authority on the rise and disappearance of the Neanderthals and is emphatic on their contributions to emerging human culture in Europe.

Flood, Josephine. *The Original Australians: The Story of the Aboriginal People*. Crows Nest, Australia: Allen and Unwin, 2019. A summary of the research carried out for more than half a century by one of the leading Australian archaeologists on Aboriginal culture.

Johanson, Donald, and Kate Wong. *Lucy: The Quest for Human Origins*. New York: Three Rivers, 2009. Bestseller that made Lucy famous and provided the inspiration for the vignette at the beginning of Chapter 1.

McBrearty, Sally. *Companion to Human Evolution*. San Diego, CA: Cognella, 2014. The author carried out pioneering work, emphasizing the African origins of *H. sapiens* not only as an anatomically but also intellectually modern human being before ever migrating to the rest of the world.

Pääbo, Svante. *Neanderthal Man: In Search of the Lost Genomes*. New York: Basic Books, 2014. Pääbo is the first paleogeneticist to sequence the full genome of a Neanderthal fossil as well as that of a new species of hominin, Dinoseva, discovered in Siberia in 2010.

Tattersall, Ian. *Masters of the Planet: The Search for Human Origins*. New York: Palgrave Macmillan, 2012. A scholarly, well-founded overview for the general reader by one of the leading senior paleoanthropologists.

Von Petzinger, Genevieve. *First Signs: Unlocking the Mysteries of the World's Oldest Symbols*. New York: Atria Books, 2016. Very little is known about the meaning of the prehistoric cave paintings found across the world. Von Petzinger focuses on a set of similar symbols found in many of these caves and attempts to interpret them as predecessors of the much later early writing systems.

WEBSITES

Bradshaw Foundation, http://www.bradshawfoundation.com/. The Bradshaw Foundation has a large website on human evolution and rock art, with many images, and a link to Stephen Oppenheimer's website Journey of Mankind: The Peopling of the World, an important overview of *Homo sapiens* migrations.

Institute of Human Origins, Arizona State University, http://iho.asu.edu/. Arizona State University's Institute of Human Origins runs the popular but scholarly website Becoming Human (http://www.becominghuman.org/).

Chapter 2

Alcock, Susan E., John Bodel, and Richard J. A. Talbert, eds. *Highways, Byways, and Road Systems in the Pre-Modern World*. Chichester: John Wiley & Sons, 2012. Fascinating global survey of methods of transport and communication.

Assmann, Jan. *The Search for God in Ancient Egypt*. Ithaca, NY: Cornell University Press, 2001. Reflective investigation of the dimensions of Egyptian polytheism by a leading Egyptologist.

Bottéro, Jean. *Mesopotamia: Writing, Reasoning, and the Gods*. Chicago: University of Chicago Press, 1992. Classic intellectual history of ancient Mesopotamia.

Cline, Eric H. *1177 B.C.: The Year Civilization Collapsed*. Princeton, NJ: Princeton University Press, 2014. Revisionist study by a scholar of classics and anthropology attempting to understand the sudden irruption of the mysterious "Sea People" into the Near East, conventionally assumed to mark the end of the Bronze Age and the beginning of the Iron Age. This authoritative study replaces Robert Drews, 1993.

Finkelstein, Israel, and Neil Asher Silberman, *The Bible Unearthed: Archaeology's New Vision of Ancient Israel and the Origin of Its Sacred Texts*. New York, London, Toronto, Sydney: The Free Press, 2001. The two authors are the leading archaeologists of Israel. Their research revolutionized our understanding of the ancient Israelites.

Kramer, Samuel Noah. *The Sumerians: Their History, Culture, and Character*. Chicago: University of Chicago Press, 2010. An expanded version of Kramer's earlier work, *History Begins at Sumer* (1988), this is a fascinating presentation of the many "firsts" originating in the world's earliest urban civilization, written by a leading Sumerologist.

Mithen, Steven. *After the Ice: A Global Human History, 20,000–5000 B.C.* Cambridge, MA: Harvard University Press, 2003. Engagingly written story of humans settling, becoming farmers, and founding villages and towns, as seen through the eyes of a modern time traveler.

Svärd, Saana, and Agnès Garcia-Ventura. *Studying Gender in the Ancient Near East*. University Park, PA: Eisenbrauns, 2018. A new book that brings together established and emerging scholars of gender for the exploration of case studies as well as current theories of gender applicable to the ancient Near East.

Van de Mieroop, Marc. *The Ancient Mesopotamian City*. Oxford: Clarendon, 1997. Full examination of Mesopotamian urban institutions, including city assemblies.

WEBSITES

British Museum, *Ancient Egypt*, http://www.ancientegypt .co.uk/menu.html. Pictorial introduction, with short texts.

Livius.org, "Mesopotamia," http://www.livius.org/babylonia .html. A large collection of translated texts and references to philological articles, with portals on Mesopotamia, Egypt, Anatolia, and Greece.

Oriental Institute, University of Chicago. Ancient Mesopotamia, http://mesopotamia.lib.uchicago.edu/. A user-friendly portal to the world-renowned Mesopotamia collection of the Oriental Institute.

Chapter 3

Avari, Burjor. *India: The Ancient Past*. 2nd ed. New York: Routledge, 2016. Recent, accessible scholarship on the subcontinent from pre-Harappan times to the Turco-Afghan invasions. Particularly useful on the transition from the Harappan to the Vedic period and the latest work on the role of Indo-Europeans.

Bryant, Edwin. *The Quest for the Origins of Vedic Culture: The Indo-Aryan Migration Debate*. Oxford and New York: Oxford University Press, 2001. A scholarly yet readable attempt to address the linguistic and archaeological evidence surrounding the thesis of Aryan migration versus the more recent theory of indigenous Vedic development.

Embree, Ainslee T., ed. *Sources of Indian Tradition*, vol. 1, 2nd ed. New York: Columbia University Press, 1988. Though the language is dated in places, this is still the most comprehensive sourcebook of Indian thought available. Recent additions on women and gender make it even more so. Sophisticated yet readable introductions, glosses, and commentary.

Eraly, Abraham. *Gem in the Lotus: The Seeding of Indian Civilization*. London: Weidenfeld & Nicholson, 2004. Readable, comprehensive survey of recent scholarship from prehistory to the reign of Ashoka during the Mauryan dynasty of the fourth and third centuries BCE. Emphasis on transitional period of sixth-century religious innovations, particularly Buddhism.

Kenoyer, Jonathan Mark. *Ancient Cities of the Indus Valley Civilization*. Oxford and New York: Oxford University Press, 1998. Comprehensive work by team leader of Harappan Research Project. Particularly good on Lothal.

Klostermaier, Klaus. *A Survey of Hinduism*, 3rd ed. Albany, NY: SUNY Press, 2007. Comprehensive thematic treatment of major themes of Hinduism from the Vedas to Hinduism's relationship to modern science.

Possehl, Gregory L., ed. *Harappan Civilization: A Recent Perspective*, 2nd ed. New Delhi: Oxford University Press, 1993. Sound and extensive treatment of recent work and issues in Indus Valley archaeology by one of the leading

on-site researchers and a former student of Walter Fairservis. Used to best advantage by experienced students.

Singh, Upinder. *A History of Ancient and Early Medieval India: From the Stone Age to the 12th Century*. New Delhi: Pearson, 2008. Sweeping text by a longtime instructor of Indian history at the University of Delhi. Suitable for undergraduates and current on the latest debates on ancient origins.

Wolpert, Stanley. *A New History of India*, 5th ed. Oxford and New York: Oxford University Press, 2004. Another extremely useful, readable, one-volume history from Neolithic times to the present. Excellent first work for serious students.

WEBSITES

Columbia University Libraries. South and Southeast Asian Studies, www.columbia.edu/cu/lweb/indiv/southasia/cuvl/history .html. Run by Columbia University, this site contains links to "WWW.Virtual Library: Indian History," "Regnal Chronologies," "Internet Indian History Sourcebook," and "Medical History of British India."

Harappa, http://www.harappa.com. Contains a wealth of images of artifacts and other archaeological treasures from the Indus Valley.

Chapter 4

Chang, Kwang-chih. *The Archaeology of Ancient China*, 4th ed. New Haven, CT: Yale University Press, 1986. Sophisticated treatment of archaeology of Shang China. Prime exponent of the view of overlapping periods and territories for the Three Dynasties (Sandai) period. Erudite, yet accessible for experienced students.

Keightly, David N., ed. *The Origins of Chinese Civilization*. Berkeley and Los Angeles: University of California Press, 1983. Symposium volume on a variety of Three Dynasties topics by leading scholars. Some exposure to early Chinese history and archaeology is necessary in order to best appreciate these essays.

Linduff, Katheryn M., and Yan Sun, eds. *Gender and Chinese Archaeology*. Walnut Creek, CA: Altamira, 2004. Re-examines the role of gender in ancient China in the context of a critique of the general lack of gendered research in archaeology as a whole.

Liu, Xiang. *Exemplary Women of Early China: The Lienu zhuan of Liu Xiang*. Edited and translated by Anne Behnke Kinney. New York: Columbia University Press, 2014. One of the few accounts we have of the lives of women during the Three Dynasties period; covers 120 short biographies of Zhou women.

Lowe, Michael, and Edward L. Shaughnessy, eds. *The Cambridge History of Ancient China: From the Origins of Civilization to 221 B.C.* Cambridge, UK: Cambridge University Press, 1999. The opening volume of the Cambridge History of China series, this is the most complete multi-essay collection on all aspects of recent Chinese ancient historical and archaeological work. The place to start for the serious student contemplating in-depth research.

Szonyi, Michael, ed. *A Companion to Chinese History*. Hoboken, NJ: Wiley Blackwell, 2017. Part of "Wiley Blackwell Companions to World History," this work is ideally suited to world history instructors interested in sampling the latest scholarship from American, European, Chinese, and Japanese authors.

Thorp, Robert L. *China in the Early Bronze Age: Shang Civilization*. Philadelphia: University of Pennsylvania Press, 2006. Comprehensive yet accessible survey of recent archaeological work on the period 2070–1046 BCE, including traditional Xia and Shang periods under the heading of China's "bronze age."

Wang, Aihe. *Cosmology and Political Culture in Early China*. Cambridge, UK: Cambridge University Press, 2000. Part of the Cambridge Studies in Chinese History, Literature, and Institutions series. Wang argues that control of cosmology—how the world and universe operate—was a vital key to the wielding of power by the Shang and Zhou rulers. Recommended for serious students.

Wang, Robin. *Images of Women in Chinese Thought and Culture: Writings from the Pre-Qin Period Through the Song Dynasty*. Indianapolis, IN: Hackett Publishing, 2003. Excerpts from classical and more obscure texts on the role and treatment of women in early China. A large and useful section on pre-Confucian texts.

Watson, Burton, trans. *The Tso Chuan: Selections from China's Oldest Narrative History*. New York: Columbia University Press, 1989. Elegant translation by one of the most prolific of scholars working today. Excellent introduction to Zhou period and politics. Appropriate for beginning students, though more useful for those with some prior introduction to the period.

WEBSITES

http://lucian.uchicago.edu/blogs/earlychina/ssec/. This is the site of the journal *Early China*, published by the Society for the Study of Early China. Accessible only to members.

British Museum. Ancient China, http://www.ancientchina.co.uk. This site provides access to the British Museum's ancient Chinese collections and is highly useful for students seeking illustrations of assorted artifacts in a user-friendly environment.

Chapter 5

The Americas

Bellwood, Peter. *First Migrants: Ancient Migration in Global Perspective*. Chichester, UK: John Wiley & Sons, 2013. An intriguing study of prehistoric migration and its role in shaping the emergence of civilization.

Bruhns, Karen Olsen, and Karen E. Stothert. *Women in Ancient America*. Norman: University of Oklahoma Press, 2nd ed. 2014. A comprehensive account of women's roles in daily life, religion, politics, and war in foraging and farming as well as urban societies in the Americas.

Grove, David C. *Discovering the Olmecs: An Unconventional History*. Austin, TX: University of Texas Press, 2014. During his long career, the author became one of the foremost authorities on the Olmecs. His history is "unconventional" because it includes extensive discussions of the personalities of scholars and their excavations of Olmec sites.

Quilter, Jeffrey. *The Ancient Central Andes*. Milton Park and New York: Routledge, 2014. Comprehensive overview of Andean history by an anthropologist with many years of research on South America. The book brings together the results of much of the work done in recent years.

Solis, Ruth Shady, Haas, Jonathan, and Creamer, Winifred. "Dating Caral, a Preceramic Site in the Supe Valley on the Central Coast of Peru," *Science* 292:5517 (2001): 723–726. Pathbreaking early report of early scientific work on Caral Supe and the oldest American cities.

Suarez, Rafael, and Ciprian F. Ardelean, eds. *People and Culture in Ice Age Americas: New Dimensions in Paleoamerican Archaeology*. Salt Lake City, UT: University of Utah Press, 2019. Collection of articles by leading scholars discussing the most recent results (to 2014) of prehistoric American archaeology.

von Hagen, Adriana, and Craig Morris. *The Cities of the Ancient Andes*. New York: Thames & Hudson, 1999. While more geared to later periods, still a useful overview, with illustrations, by specialists on Andean cultures.

Oceania

Carson, Mike T., *First Settlement of Remote Oceania: Earliest Sites in the Mariana Islands*. Heidelberg, Germany: Springer-Verlag, 2014. Study based on new archaeological research by a specialist on Pacific research.

Hunt, Terry, and Carl Lipo. *The Statues that Walked: Unraveling the Mystery of Easter Island*. New York, London, Toronto, Sydney: The Free Press, 2014. Revisionist book by two anthropologists who challenge the societal collapse theory of Easter Island (Rapa Nui) society and offer fascinating new views on the precolonial history of the island.

Kirch, Patrick V. *A Shark Going Inland Is My Chief: The Island Civilization of Ancient Hawai'i*. Berkeley and Los Angeles: University of California Press, 2019. Book on the precolonial civilization of Hawaii by one of the most published specialists on Oceania. Written for nonspecialists wishing to find an introduction to the precolonial Pacific world.

Matsuda, Matt K. *Pacific Worlds: A History of Seas, Peoples, and Cultures*. Cambridge, UK: Cambridge University Press, 2012. General history of the Pacific with an emphasis on the early modern period.

WEBSITES

Foundation for the Advancement of Mesoamerican Studies (FAMSI), http://www.famsi.org/. Collaborates with the Los Angeles County Museum of Art and runs a wide range of scholarly, funding, and educational outreach programs aimed at advancing studies of Mesoamerica.

*Britannica.*http://www.britannica.com/EBchecked/topic/468832/ Polynesian-culture. Good link leading to an 8,000-word essay on leading topics concerning Polynesia and Oceania. In order to access the complete essay the reader must apply for a free trial of the online *Encyclopedia Britannica.*

Chapter 6
Sub-Saharan Africa

Chami, Félix. *The Unity of African Ancient History: 3000 BC to 500 AD.* Dar es Salaam: E&D, 2006. General overview by one of the leading archaeologists of East Africa.

Insoll, Timothy, ed. *Material Explorations in African Archaeology.* Oxford and New York: Oxford University Press, 2015. The first book of its kind to explore the ethnographic and archaeological record of Africa for human and material evidence dealing with topics such as ancestry, monuments, animals, shrines, landscapes, healing, and divination.

McIntosh, Roderick J. *Ancient Middle Niger: Urbanism and the Self-Organizing Landscape.* Cambridge, UK: Cambridge University Press, 2005. Important revisionist work on the origins of urbanism and kingship in West Africa.

Mitchell, Peter, and Paul Lane. *The Oxford Handbook of African Archaeology.* Oxford: Oxford University Press, 2013. A total of 70 essays by specialists on all aspects of human culture in Africa, with an emphasis on foragers, agriculturalists, and early urbanists.

Vansina, Jan. *Paths in the Rainforests: Toward a History of Political Tradition in Equatorial Africa.* Madison: University of Wisconsin Press, 1990. Magisterial presentation of the Bantu dispersal and village life in the rain forest.

Mesoamerica and the Andes

Braswell, Geoffrey E., ed. *The Ancient Maya of Mexico: Reinterpreting the Past of the Northern Lowlands.* Milton Park, UK, and New York: Routledge, 2014. Contains articles on the origins of the ballgame and the Mayan "collapse."

Evans, Susan Tobey. *Ancient Mexico and Central America: Archaeology and Culture History.* London: Thames & Hudson, 2004. Densely but clearly written and detailed, with many sidebars on special topics.

Grube, Nikolai, ed. *Maya: Divine Kings of the Rain Forest.* Cologne, Germany: Könemann, 2001. Lavishly illustrated book with short contributions by many hands.

Martin, Simon. *Ancient Maya Politics: A Political Anthropology of the Classic Period, 150–900 CE.* Cambridge, UK: Cambridge University Press, 2020. Making use of newly deciphered Mayan glyptic inscriptions, Martin explains the coexistence of many Mayan polities without leading to the eventual establishment of an empire; that is, why no Mayan kingdom ever succeeded in forcibly uniting the many coexisting Maya kingdoms into a single unit.

Schele, Linda, and David Freidel. *A Forest of Kings: The Untold Story of the Ancient Maya.* New York: Quill-William Morrow, 1990. Classic study summarizing the results of the decipherment of Maya glyphs, by two pioneers.

Stuart, David. *The Order of Days: Unlocking the Secrets of the Ancient Maya.* New York: Three Rivers Press, 2011. Magisterial summary of our current knowledge of Maya culture.

WEBSITES

Stanford University Libraries, Africa South of the Sahara, https://library.stanford.edu/areas/african-collections: A large, resource-filled website based at Stanford University.

Ancient Wisdom, http://www.ancient-wisdom.com/americaprecolumbian.htm: Basic essays on pre-Columbian peoples and civilizations.

Chapter 7

Boyce, Mary. *A History of Zoroastrianism.* Vol. 1, *The Early Period,* rev. ed. Handbuch der Orientalistik. Leiden, the Netherlands: E. J. Brill, 1989. Standard work by the leading scholar on the subject.

Briant, Pierre. *From Cyrus to Alexander: A History of the Persian Empire.* Winona Lake, IN: Eisenbrauns, 2000. Monumental work; the most detailed and authoritative study of the topic to date.

Dignas, Beate, and Engelbert Winter. *Rome and Persia in Late Antiquity: Neighbours and Rivals.* Cambridge, UK: Cambridge University Press, 2007. Detailed historical investigation of the rivalry between Rome and Persia.

Freeman, Phillip. *Alexander the Great.* New York: Simon & Schuster, 2011. Illuminating study of Alexander the Great intended for a general audience.

Harper, Kyle. *The Fate of Rome: Climate, Disease, and the End of an Empire.* Princeton, NJ: Princeton University Press, 2017. Describes how a combination of climatic changes and the spread of epidemic diseases contributed to the fall of Rome.

Hubbard, Thomas K., ed. *A Companion to Greek and Roman Sexualities.* Chichester, UK: John Wiley & Sons, 2014. Far-ranging and informative collection of essays on all aspects of sexuality in ancient Greece and Rome.

Karanika, Andromache. *Voices at Work: Women, Performance, and Labor in Ancient Greece.* Baltimore: Johns Hopkins University Press, 2014. An analysis of ancient Greek work songs, primarily those of women, and how they were incorporated in assorted literary genres.

Lehoux, Daryn. *What Did the Romans Know? An Inquiry into Science and Worldmaking.* Chicago: University of Chicago Press, 2012. Sophisticated analysis of Roman science in both its derivative and unique aspects.

Mathisen, Ralph. *Ancient Mediterranean Civilizations: From Prehistory to 640 CE,* 2nd ed. Oxford and New York: Oxford University Press, 2014. Revised overview with special emphasis on ethnicity, gender, and slavery.

Shaked, Shaul. *Dualism in Transformation: Varieties of Religion in Sasanian Iran.* London: School of Oriental and African Studies, 1994. Short history of the different religions in Sasanid Persia.

Smith, Mark S. *The Early History of God: Yahweh and the Other Deities in Ancient Israel*. San Francisco: Harper & Row, 1990. Very readable introduction to the problem of early monotheism among Israelites.

WEBSITES

British Museum. Ancient Greece, http://www.ancientgreece.co.uk/menu.html. Open the door to the compelling world of Ancient Greece. The British Museum has compiled a collection of images and information on various aspects of Greek history such as the Acropolis, Athens, daily life, festivals and games, Sparta, war, and gods.

Harvard University. Digital Atlas of Roman and Medieval Civilizations, http://darmc.harvard.edu/icb/icb.do?keyword=k40248&pageid=icb.page188868. Harvard University allows students to tailor searches in order to access specific geopolitical and spatial cartographical representations of the Roman and medieval worlds.

Perseus Digital Library, http://www.perseus.tufts.edu/hopper/. Probably the largest website on Greece and Rome, with immense resources, hosted by Tufts University.

Chapter 8

Auboyer, Jeannine. *Daily Life in Ancient India*. London: Phoenix, 2002. Overview consisting of sections on social structures/religious principles, individual/collective existence, and royal and administrative existence. Multidisciplinary approach appropriate for most undergraduates.

Chakravarti, Uma. *The Social Dimensions of Early Buddhism*. New Delhi: Oxford University Press, 1987. Thorough analysis, with extensive glossary, of the influence of the north Indian economic transition to peasant market farming on the social milieu of early Buddhism.

Diem-Lane, Andrea. *Ahimsa: A Brief Guide to Jainism*. Walnut, CA: MSAC Philosophy Group, 2016. Short, student-friendly guide to Jain concepts, history, and Jainism today.

Doniger, Wendy. *The Hindus: An Alternative History*. New York: Penguin, 2009. Vivid but controversial new interpretation of the history of Hinduism by one of the leading scholars of Indian history. The book's portrayals of Hindu history, particularly in the area between myth and history, have prompted a lawsuit in India, which resulted in the withdrawal of the book there by the publisher in early 2014.

Embree, Ainslee T. *Sources of Indian Tradition*, 2 vols. 2nd ed. New York: Columbia University Press, 1988. The latest edition contains a number of new selections useful for the study of social relations in addition to the older religious material. As with all of the works in this series, the level of writing is sophisticated, though accessible; the overviews are masterly; and the works are ably translated.

Keay, John. *India: A History*. New York: Grove, 2000. Lively, highly detailed narrative history, with a number of useful charts and genealogies of ruling houses. Sympathetic treatment of controversial matters.

Knott, Kim. *Hinduism: A Very Short Introduction*. Oxford and New York: Oxford University Press, 1998. Sound, brief discussion of modern Hinduism and its formative influences. Asks provocative questions such as "What is a religion?" and "Is Hinduism something more than the Western conception of religion?"

Nikam, N. A., and Richard McKeon, eds. and trans. *The Edicts of Asoka*. Chicago: University of Chicago Press, 1959. Slim but useful volume for those interested in reading the entire collection of Ashoka's Pillar, Cave, and Rock Edicts. Short, accessible introduction.

Padoux, Andre. *The Hindu Tantric World: An Overview*. Chicago: University of Chicago Press, 2017. Erudite but accessible entre into the complex and often misunderstood field of Tantric studies. Padoux deals with definitions, ritual, sacred literature and its history down to the present. Best for undergraduates with some grounding in Hinduism.

Willis, Michael. *The Archaeology of Hindu Ritual*. Cambridge, UK: Cambridge University Press, 2009. Best utilized by experienced students, this book uses site archaeology, Sanskrit documents, and studies of ancient astronomy to plot the development of Hinduism under the Guptas and their use of it in statecraft as they created their vision of a universal empire.

Wolpert, Stanley. *A New History of India*, 6th ed. Oxford and New York: Oxford University Press, 2000. The standard introductory work to the long sweep of Indian history. Evenly divided between the period up to and including the Mughals and the modern era. Good coverage of geography and environment, as well as social and gender issues. Good select bibliography arranged by chapter; highly useful glossary of Indian terms.

WEBSITE

Digital Library of India, http://www.dli.ernet.in. This online resource, hosted by the Indian Institute of Science, Bangalore, contains primary and secondary sources not only for history but also for culture, economics, literature, and a host of other subjects.

Chapter 9

Henricks, Robert C., trans. *Lao-Tzu, Te-Tao Ching. A New Translation Based on the Recently Discovered Ma-wang-tui Texts*. New York: Ballantine Books, 1989. Some of the initial work done on the earliest extant Daoist texts, reinterpreting our understanding of philosophical Daoism.

Hinsch, Bret. *Women in Early Imperial China*. Lanham, MD: Rowman & Littlefield, 2002. Broad examination of the place of women, and transition of the place of women, during the crucial early Chinese dynasties.

Huang, Ray. *China: A Macro History*. Armonk, NY: M. E. Sharpe, 1997. Readable, entertaining, and highly useful one-volume history. Particularly good on the complex politics of the post-Han and Song–Yuan periods.

Keay, John. *China: A History*. New York: Basic Books, 2009. Adventurous and well-written general history of China from prehistory to the present. Especially good for students with some previous grounding in the essentials of Chinese history.

Lewis, Mark Edward. *The Early Chinese Empires: Qin and Han*. Cambridge, MA: Harvard University Press, 2007. Detailed exploration of the rise and adaptations of China's initial empires. Better for advanced students.

Qian, Sima. *Records of the Grand Historian*. Translated by Burton Watson. 3 vols., rev. ed. New York: Columbia University Press, 1993. Powerful translation of China's supreme historical work by one of its best interpreters. Includes material from the Qin and Han dynasties. Invaluable source for serious students.

Whitfield, Susan. *Silk, Slaves, and Stupas: Material Culture of the Silk Road*. Oakland: University of California Press, 2018. A work covering the latest scholarship on the people, objects, modes of travel, and societies along the various tracks that made up what later came to be called "The Silk Road."

Yao Xinzhong. *An Introduction to Confucianism*. Cambridge, UK: Cambridge University Press, 2000. Overview of the tradition of the *ru* as it evolved and its status today.

WEBSITES

Asian Topics for Asian Educators. "Defining 'Daoism': A Complex History," http://afe.easia.columbia.edu/cosmos/ort/daoism.htm. Looks at Daoism as a term, its use, and its practice in terms of morality, society, nature, and the self.

Chapter 10

The Arabian Nights. Translated by Husain Haddawy. New York: Norton, 1990. Based on the critical edition by Muhsin Mahdi, which reconstitutes the original thirteenth-century text.

Barry, Michael. *Figurative Art in Medieval Islam and the Riddle of Bihazâd of Herât (1465–1535)*. Paris: Flammarion, 2004.

Chaudhuri, K. N. *Trade and Civilization in the Indian Ocean*. Cambridge, UK: Cambridge University Press, 1985. Discusses the historical evolution of the trade and its various aspects (sea routes, ships, commodities, and capital investments).

Decker, Michael J. *The Byzantine Dark Ages*. London and New York: Bloomsbury Academic, 2016. The period of 600–900 CE is the least documented period in Byzantine history. This wide-ranging new study takes a fresh look at the urban, rural, and economic situation during this period on the basis of the available documentation, from written sources and numismatics to archaeological sites and ceramics.

Fryde, Edmund. *The Early Palaeologan Renaissance (1261–c. 1360)*. Leiden, the Netherlands: E. J. Brill, 2000. Detailed presentation of the main philosophical and scientific figures of Byzantium after the recovery from the Latin interruption.

Herrin, Judith. *Unrivalled Influence: Women and Empire in Byzantium*. Princeton, NJ: Princeton University Press, 2013.

Detailed investigation by a leading Byzantine historian and engaged feminist.

Hoyland, Robert. *In God's Path: The Arab Conquests and the Creation of an Islamic Empire*. Oxford and New York: Oxford University Press, 2014. A new history of Islamic origins, seeking to combine Christian and Islamic sources.

Khalili, Jim al-. *The House of Wisdom: How Arabic Science Saved Ancient Knowledge and Gave Us the Renaissance*. New York: Penguin, 2010. In spite of the somewhat overwrought title, an expertly written introduction to the golden age of Arabic science by a scientist.

Laiou, Angeliki E., and Cécile Morrisson. *The Byzantine Economy*. Cambridge, UK: Cambridge University Press, 2007. Comprehensive and well-researched study of ups and downs in the demography, productive capacity, and long-distance trade of Byzantium.

Lapidus, Ira. *Muslim Cities in the Later Middle Ages*. Cambridge, UK: Cambridge University Press, 1984. Seminal work and still the only study of Muslim urban society, although it should be supplemented by Shlomo D. Goitein's monumental study of Jews, *A Mediterranean Society* (1967–1993).

Rippin, Andrew. *Muslims: Their Religious Beliefs and Practices*, 5th ed. London: Routledge, 2018. One of the best and most accessible introductions to the basic beliefs and practices of Islam, based on the re-evaluation of Islamic origins also presented in this chapter.

Tyerman, Christopher. *God's War: A New History of the Crusades*. Cambridge, MA: Belknap, 2006. Persuasive revisionist history by a leading Crusade historian.

WEBSITES

BBC—Religion: Islam. http://www.bbc.co.uk/religion/religions/islam/. A very basic overview of Islamic civilization. Most websites on Islam and Islamic civilization are apologetic (pro-Muslim or pro-Christian), and earlier scholarly websites are no longer available.

Islamic Awareness. http://www.islamic-awareness.org/. This website, even though Islam-apologetic, is a fountain of early documents relevant for Islamic history.

Chapter 11

Berend, Norma, Przemyslaw Urbanczlyk, and Przemyslaw Wiszewski. *Central Europe in the High Middle Ages: Bohemia, Hungary and Poland, ca. 900–ca. 1300*. New York: Cambridge University Press, 2013. Learned and insightful study that explores frequently overlooked aspects of medieval Europe.

Brown, Peter. *The Rise of Western Christendom: Triumph and Diversity, A.D. 200–1000*, Tenth Anniversary Revised Edition. Chichester, UK: John Wiley & Sons, Inc., 2013. Traces the development of Christian Europe from the perspective of the church.

Grant, Edward. *The Foundation of Modern Science in the Middle Ages*. Cambridge, UK: Cambridge University Press, 1996. Seminal study of the contributions of medieval science to the scientific revolution of the seventeenth century.

Jambroziak, Emilia. *The Cistercian Order in Medieval Europe, 1090–1520*. New York: Routledge, 2013. Presents new perspectives regarding the spread of Cistercians across Europe, with emphasis on their unique administrative policies.

König, Daniel G. *Arabic-Islamic Views of the Latin West: Tracing the Emergence of Medieval Europe*. New York: Oxford University Press, 2015. Challenges the traditional view of Bernard Lewis that Muslims considered Europe a backward and infantile culture.

Lawrence, C. H. *Medieval Monasticism: Forms of Religious Life in Western Europe in the Middle Ages*, 2nd ed. New York: Longman, 1984. Thorough survey of the development of the Western monastic tradition.

McKitterick, Rosamond. *Charlemagne: The Formation of a European Identity*. Cambridge, UK: Cambridge University Press, 2008. An examination of how Charlemagne's policies contributed to the idea of Europe.

Platt, Colin. *King Death: The Black Death and Its Aftermath in Late-Medieval England*. Toronto: University of Toronto Press, 1997. Riveting analysis of the effects of the Black Death on all aspects of society.

Riley-Smith, Jonathan, ed. *The Oxford Illustrated History of the Crusades*. Oxford and New York: Oxford University Press, 1995. A very useful and readable history of the crusading movement.

Turner, Denys. *Thomas Aquinas: A Portrait*. New Haven, CT: Yale University Press, 2013. Up-to-date biography of one of the greatest figures in medieval philosophy.

Wickham, Chris. *Medieval Europe*. New Haven, CT: Yale University Press, 2016. A scintillating and innovative study that presents new interpretations of important turning points in the development of medieval European civilization.

WEBSITES

British Library. Treasures in Full: Magna Carta, http://www.bl.uk/treasures/magnacarta/virtual_curator/vc9.html. An excellent website that makes available a digitized version of Magna Carta. Audio files answer many FAQs about the manuscript and its significance.

Chapter 12

Asif, Manan Ahmed. *A Book of Conquest: The Chachnama and Muslim Origins in South Asia*. Cambridge, MA: Harvard University Press, 2016. Comprehensive study of the pivotal story of deceit and conquest and the contentious legacy surrounding the initial Muslim forays into India.

Chiu-Duke, Josephine. *To Rebuild the Empire: Lu Chih's Confucian Pragmatist Approach to the Mid-Tang Predicament*. Albany, NY: SUNY Press, 2000. Political and philosophical study of one of the Tang era's most important prime ministers and his attempts to retrieve Tang fortunes and actions in the beginning of the period's Confucian revival.

De Bary, William T., and Irene Bloom, eds. *Sources of Chinese Tradition*, 2nd ed., vol. 1. New York: Columbia University Press, 1999. Excellent introduction to major Chinese philosophical schools. Extensive coverage of Buddhism and Neo-Confucianism with accessible, highly informative introductions to the documents themselves.

Ebrey, Patricia Buckley, ed. *The Inner Quarters*. Berkeley and Los Angeles: University of California Press, 1993. Perhaps the best scholarly exploration of the roles of women in Song China.

Hansen, Valerie. *The Open Empire: A History of China to 1600*. New York: W. W. Norton, 2000. A fresh and accessible synthesis of premodern Chinese history.

Lane, George. *A Short History of the Mongols*. London: I.B. Tauris, 2018. An introductory text as part of Tauris' Short Histories, this provides an excellent overview of the latest scholarship on the role of the Mongols in Asian and world history, while challenging commonly held views of the Mongols as simply ruthless conquerors.

Levathes, Louise.. *When China Ruled the Seas: The Treasure Fleet of the Dragon Throne 1405–1433*. New York: Simon & Schuster, 1994. Delightful coverage of the voyages of Zheng He from 1405 to 1433. Particularly good on the aftermath of the voyages.

Robinson, Francis. *Islam and Muslim History in South Asia*. Oxford and New York: Oxford University Press, 2004. Compendium of essays and reviews by the author on a variety of subjects concerning the history and status of Islam in the subcontinent. Of particular interest is his response to Samuel Huntington's famous "clash of civilizations" thesis.

Singh, Patwant. *The Sikhs*. London: John Murray, 1999. Readable popular history of the Sikh experience to the present by an adherent. Especially useful on the years from Guru Nanak to the changes of the early eighteenth century and the transition to a more militant faith.

WEBSITES

Asian Topics in World History. "The Mongols in World History," http://afe.easia.columbia.edu/mongols/. With a timeline spanning 1000–1500, "The Mongols in World History" delivers a concise and colorful history of the Mongols' impact on global history.

Fordham University. Internet Indian History Sourcebook, http://www.fordham.edu/halsall/india/indiasbook.asp. One of the series of online "sourcebooks" by Fordham containing links to important documents, secondary literature, and assorted other web resources.

Fordham University. Internet East Asian History Sourcebook, http://www.fordham.edu/halsall/eastasia/eastasiasbook.asp. As with its counterpart above, this is one in the series of useful online sources and links put together by Fordham, in this case about East Asia, with particular emphasis on the role of China as a center of cultural diffusion.

Chapter 13
General

Holcombe, Charles. *A History of East Asia, From the Origins of Civilization to the Twenty-First Century*. Cambridge, UK: Cambridge University Press, 2011. A top one-volume history of China, Korea, and Japan, with an emphasis on the region's shared past.

Mann, Susan. *East Asia (China, Korea, Japan)*. Washington, DC: American Historical Association, 1999. The second volume in the Women's and Gender History in Global Perspective series. Short, informative work with historiographic overviews and cross-cultural comparisons among the three countries named in the title. Critical annotated bibliographies on the use of standard texts in integrating women and gender into Asian studies.

Neuman, W. Lawrence. *East Asian Societies*. Ann Arbor, MI: Association For Asian Studies, 2014. Part of the AAS's "Key Issues in Asian Studies," this provides a short, accessible introduction to the region for beginning students.

Ramusack, Barbara N., and Sharon Sievers. *Women in Asia*. Bloomington: Indiana University Press, 1999. Part of the series Restoring Women to History. Far-ranging book divided into two parts, "Women in South and Southeast Asia" and "Women in East Asia." Coverage of individual countries, extensive chronologies, valuable bibliographies. Most useful for advanced undergraduates.

Korea

De Bary, William T., ed. *Sources of Korean Tradition*, vol. 1. Introduction to Asian Civilizations. New York: Columbia University Press, 1997. Part of the renowned Columbia series on the great traditions of East Asia. Perhaps the most complete body of accessible sources for undergraduates.

Korean Overseas Information Service. *A Handbook of Korea*. Seoul: KOIS, 1993. Wonderfully complete history, geography, guidebook, and sociology text. Excellent source, but students should keep in mind its provenance and treat some of its historical claims to uniqueness accordingly.

Seth, Michael J. *A Concise History of Korea*. 2nd ed. Lanham, MD: Rowman and Littlefield, 2016. Well-researched and comprehensive history of the Korean peninsula from Neolithic times to 2016. Covers both North and South Korea, though the South comes in for the most detailed treatment.

Japan

De Bary, William T., ed. *Sources of Japanese Tradition*, vol. 1. *Introduction to Asian Civilizations*. 2nd ed. New York: Columbia University Press, 2002. Like the volume above on Korea and the others in this series on India and China, the sources are well selected, the glossaries are sound, and the overviews of the material are masterful. As with the other East Asia volumes, the complexities of the various Buddhist schools are especially well drawn. Students with some previous experience will derive the most benefit from this excellent volume.

Murasaki Shikibu. *The Tale of Genji*. Dennis Washburn, trans. New York: W. W. Norton, 2015. The latest of only four complete translations of this classic into English, it is notable for its clarity, accessibility, literal accuracy to the source material, and literary quality.

Totman, Conrad. *A History of Japan*. Oxford, UK: Blackwell, 2000. Part of Blackwell's History of the World series. A large, well-balanced, and comprehensive history. More than half of the material is on the pre-1867 period, with extensive coverage of social history and demographics.

Vietnam

Steinberg, Joel David, ed. *In Search of Southeast Asia*, rev. ed. Honolulu: University of Hawaii Press, 1987. Extensive coverage of Vietnam within the context of an area study of Southeast Asia. Though weighted toward the modern period, very good coverage of agricultural and religious life in the opening chapters.

Taylor, Keith W. *The Birth of Vietnam*. Berkeley and Los Angeles: University of California Press, 1983. Comprehensive, magisterial volume on early Vietnamese history and historical identity amid the long Chinese occupation. Best for students with some background in Southeast Asian and Chinese history.

WEBSITES

https://www.britishmuseum.org/collection/search?keyword=asian&keyword=studies Department of Prints and Drawings, British Museum,. A comprehensive source for all manner of interests related to Asian studies.

Public Broadcasting Service, Hidden Korea, http://www.pbs.org/hiddenkorea/history.htm. Sound introduction to the geography, people, history and culture of Korea, with links to additional source material.

Chapter 14

Berzock, Kathleen, ed. *Caravans of Gold, Fragments in Time: Art, Culture, and Exchange Across Medieval Saharan Africa*. Princeton, NJ: Princeton University Press, 2019. Richly illustrated catalogue of an exhibit by the Block Museum of Art, Northwestern University, with wide-ranging articles by international scholars.

Birmingham, David, and Phyllis M. Martin, eds. *History of Central Africa*, vol. 1. London: Longman, 1983. The first chapter, by Birmingham, provides an excellent summary of the history of Luba prior to 1450.

Collins, Robert O., and James M. Burns. *A History of Subsaharan Africa*, 2nd ed. Cambridge: Cambridge University Press, 2014. Authoritative history by two well-known Africanists, updated by Burns after the death of Collins.

Crummey, David. *Land and Society in the Christian Kingdom of Ethiopia: From the Thirteenth to the Twentieth Century*. Urbana: University of Illinois Press, 2000. The first book in which the rich land records of the church have been used for a reconstruction of agriculture and land tenure.

Gomez, Michael A. *African Dominion: A New History of Empire in Early and Medieval West Africa*. Princeton, NJ: Princeton University Press, 2018. A detailed new history of West Africa during its imperial period, based on new documents from archives in Timbuktu and Jenné as well as the traditional written sources. The author sets new standards following the previous work by Nehemia Levtzion.

Horton, Mark, and John Middleton. *The Swahili: The Social Landscape of a Mercantile Society.* Oxford, UK: Blackwell, 2000. A study that gives full attention to the larger context of East Africa in which the Swahilis flourished. Middleton is the author of another important study, *The World of the Swahili: An African Mercantile Civilization* (Yale University Press, 1992).

Huffman, Thomas. *Palaces of Stone: Uncovering Ancient Southern African Kingdoms.* Capetown and Johannesburg: Penguin Random House South Africa, 2020. Definitive study of the precolonial southern African kingdoms by their foremost archaeologist.

Ruffini, Giovanni. *Medieval Nubia: A Social and Economic History.* Oxford and New York: Oxford University Press, 2012. Revisionist history based on new sources, arguing for the existence of a sophisticated money economy.

WEBSITES

Heilbrunn Timeline of Art History, Ife (from ca. 350 B.C.): http://www.metmuseum.org/toah/hd/ife/hd_ife.htm. An excellent introductory website hosted by the Metropolitan Museum of Art. It contains many links and presents clear overviews.

Ancient History Encyclopedia, https://www.ancient.eu/article/1383/the-gold-trade-of-ancient--medieval-west-africa/. Focuses on the gold trade, with excellent summaries on the kingdoms and empires.

Chapter 15

Bruhns, Karen Olsen, and Karen E. Stothert. *Women in Ancient America.* Norman: University of Oklahoma Press, 2nd ed. 2014. Comprehensive account of women's role in daily life, religion, politics, and war in forager and agrarian–urban societies.

Carrasco, Davíd. *The Aztecs: A Very Short Introduction.* Oxford and New York: Oxford University Press, 2012. Clear, compressed account by a specialist, containing all essential information.

D'Altroy, Terence. *The Incas.* 2nd ed. Hoboken, NJ: John Wiley and Sons, 2014. Well-organized and comprehensive overview by a leading anthropologist.

Hassig, Ross. *War and Society in Ancient Mesoamerica.* Berkeley and Los Angeles: University of California Press, 1992. Best study of the rising importance of militarism in Mesoamerican city-states, up to the Aztec Empire.

Kelly, John, and James A. Brown. *Cahokia: City of the Cosmos.* Cowley Road, UK, and Casemate Books, Haverton, PA: Oxbow Books Limited, 2020. Archaeological and anthropological study of this important early North American site, assembling the most recent research.

Malpass, Michael A. *Daily Life in the Inca Empire*, 2nd ed. Westport, CT: Greenwood, 2009. Clear, straightforward, and readable account of ordinary people's lives by a specialist.

Smith, Michael E., *The Aztecs*, 3rd ed. Hoboken, NJ: Wiley, 2013. Up-to-date, extensive account of all aspects of Inca history and civilization.

Townsend, Camilla. *Fifth Sun: A New History of the Aztecs.* Oxford and New York: Oxford University Press, 2019. This revisionist study makes full use of the so-called yearly accounts, or annals, composed by Aztecs in Nahuatl in an effort to overcome the one-sided perspective of the Spanish conquerors.

WEBSITE

Aztec history: *Aztec-History*, http://www.aztec-history.com/. Introductory website, easily navigable, with links.

Inca history: *Ancient History Encyclopedia*, https://www.ancient.eu/Inca_Civilization. Informed, well-written summaries.

Chapter 16

Ágoston, Gábor. *Guns for the Sultan: Military Power and the Weapons Industry in the Ottoman Empire.* Cambridge, UK: Cambridge University Press, 2005. Thorough study, which is based on newly accessible Ottoman archival materials and emphasizes the technological prowess of Ottoman gunsmiths.

Casale, Giancarlo. *The Ottoman Age of Exploration.* Oxford and New York: Oxford University Press, 2010. Detailed correction, based on Ottoman and Portuguese archives, of the traditional characterization of the Ottoman Empire as a land-oriented power.

Casey, James. *Early Modern Spain: A Social History.* London: Routledge, 1999. Detailed, well-documented analysis of rural–urban and king–nobility tensions.

Elliott, John Huxtable. *Spain, Europe, and the Wider World: 1500–1800.* New Haven, CT: Yale University Press, 2009. A comprehensive overview, particularly strong on culture during the 1500s.

Fichtner, Paula Sutter. *Terror and Tolerations: The Habsburg Empire Confronts Islam, 1526–1850.* London: Reaktion, 2008. A revisionist perspective of relationships between Habsburgs and Ottomans.

Glete, Jan. *War and the State in Early Modern Europe: Spain, the Dutch Republic, and Sweden as Fiscal–Military States, 1500–1660.* London: Routledge, 2002. A complex but persuasive construction of the forerunner to the absolute state. Unfortunately leaves out the Ottoman Empire.

Murphey, Rhoads. *Ottoman Warfare, 1500–1700.* New Brunswick, NJ: Rutgers University Press, 1999. Author presents a vivid picture of the Janissaries, their discipline, organization, campaigns, and voracious demands for salary increases.

Pamuk, Sevket. *A Monetary History of the Ottoman Empire.* Cambridge, UK: Cambridge University Press, 2000. Superb analysis of Ottoman archival resources on the role and function of American silver in the money economy of the Ottomans.

Phillips, William D., Jr., and Carla Rhan Phillips. *The Worlds of Christopher Columbus.* New York: Cambridge University

Press, 1992. A biographical study of Columbus, emphasizing the establishment of global interconnections resulting from his voyages

Ruiz, Teofilo R. *Spanish Society, 1400–1600*. London: Longman, 2001. Richly detailed social studies rewarding anyone interested in changing class structures, rural–urban movement, and extension of the money market into the countryside.

Subrahmanyam, Sanjay. *The Career and Legend of Vasco da Gama*. Cambridge, UK: Cambridge University Press, 1997. Focuses on the religious motivations of Vasco da Gama and the commercial impact of his journey to India.

WEBSITES

Frontline, "Apocalypse! The Evolution of Apocalyptic Belief and How It Shaped the Western World," PBS, 1995, http://www.pbs.org/wgbh/pages/frontline/shows/apocalypse/. The contribution by Bernard McGinn, University of Chicago, under the heading of "Apocalypticism Explained: Joachim of Fiore," is of particular relevance for the understanding of Christopher Columbus viewing himself as a precursor of Christ's Second Coming.

Islam: Empire of Faith: Timeline, http://www.pbs.org/empires/islam/timeline.html. Comprehensive and informative, this PBS website on the Ottoman Empire examines various facets of this Islamic culture, such as scientific innovations, faith, and leaders.

Chapter 17

Biro, Jacquelin. *On Earth as in Heaven: Cosmography and the Shape of the Earth from Copernicus to Descartes*. Saarbrücken, Germany: VDM Verlag Dr. Müller, 2009. Short study establishing the connection between geography and cosmology in Copernicus. Uses the pathbreaking articles by Thomas Goldberg.

Black, Jeremy. *Kings, Nobles, and Commoners: States and Societies in Early Modern Europe—A Revisionist History*. London: I. B. Tauris, 2004. Available also electronically on ebrary; persuasive thesis, largely accepted by scholars, of a continuity of institutional practices in Europe across the sixteenth and seventeenth centuries, casting doubt on absolutism as being more than a theory.

Cañizares-Esguerra, Jorge. *Nature, Empire, and Nation: Explorations of the History of Science in the Iberian World*. Stanford, CA: Stanford University Press, 2006. A collection of essays that provides new perspectives on the history of science in early modern Iberia.

Geanakoplos, Deno John. *Constantinople and the West: Essays on the Late Byzantine (Palaeologan) and Italian Renaissances and the Byzantine and Roman Churches*. Madison: University of Wisconsin Press, 1989. Fundamental discussion of the extensive transfer of texts and scholars during the 1400s.

Jacob, Margaret C. and Larry Stewart. *Practical Matter: Newton's Science in the Service of Industry and Empire, 1687–1851*. Cambridge, MA: Harvard University Press, 2004.

An interesting and important description of interconnections between Newtonian sciences and eighteenth-century industrial developments.

Margolis, Howard. *It Started with Copernicus: How Turning the World Inside Out Led to the Scientific Revolution*. New York: McGraw-Hill, 2002. Important scholarly study of the connection between the discovery of the Americas and Copernicus's formulation of a sun-centered planetary system.

Nexon, Daniel H. *The Struggle for Power in Early Modern Europe: Religious Conflict, Dynastic Empires and International Change*. Princeton, NJ: Princeton University Press, 2009. Charles Tilly–inspired re-evaluation of the changes occurring in sixteenth- and seventeenth-century Europe.

Park, Katharine, and Lorraine Daston, eds. *The Cambridge History of Science. Vol. 3, Early Modern Science*. Cambridge, UK: Cambridge University Press, 2006. Voluminous coverage of all aspects of science, under the currently paradigmatic thesis that there was no dramatic scientific revolution in Western Christian civilization.

Roper, Lyndal. *Martin Luther: Renegade and Prophet*. New York: Random House, 2017. A brilliant study of Luther's multifaceted and coarse character and personality.

Schiebinger, Londa. *The Mind Has No Sex? Women in the Origins of Modern Science*. Cambridge, MA: Harvard University Press, 1989. A pioneering study presenting biographies and summaries of scientific contributions made by women. Discusses the importance of Maria Cunitz.

Wiesner-Hanks, Merry E. *Early Modern Europe, 1450–1789*. 2nd ed. Cambridge, UK: Cambridge University Press, 2013. Textbook in the Cambridge History of Europe series with a broad coverage of topics.

WEBSITES

Ames Research Center. "Johannes Kepler: His Life, His Laws and Times," http://kepler.nasa.gov/Mission/JohannesKepler/. This NASA website looks at the life and views of Johannes Kepler. It examines his discoveries, his contemporaries, and the events that shaped modern science.

Howard, Sharon. "Early Modern Resources," http://sharonhoward.org/earlymodern.html. Website with many links on the full range of institutional and cultural change.

Chapter 18

Alchon, Suzanne A. *A Pest in the Land: New World Epidemics in a Global Perspective*. Albuquerque: University of New Mexico Press, 2003. A broad overview, making medical history comprehensible.

Behringer, Wolfgang. *Witches and Witch-Hunts: A Global History*. Cambridge, UK: Polity, 2004. A well-grounded overview of the phenomenon of the fear of witches, summarizing the scholarship of the past decades.

Bulmer-Thomas, Victor, John S. Coatsworth, and Roberto Cortés Conde, eds. *The Cambridge Economic History of Latin America. Vol. 1, The Colonial Era and the Short*

Nineteenth Century. Cambridge, UK: Cambridge University Press, 2006. Collection of specialized summary articles on aspects of Iberian colonialism.

Eastman, Scott, *Preaching Spanish Nationalism across the Hispanic Atlantic, 1759–1823*. Baton Rouge: Louisiana State University Press, 2012. Close look at the national reform debates in the Iberian Atlantic world at the close of colonialism.

Ekberg, Carl J. *French Roots in the Illinois Country: The Mississippi Frontier in Colonial Times*. Urbana: University of Illinois Press, 1998. Detailed, deeply researched historical account.

Peloso, Vincent. *Race and Ethnicity in Latin America*. Milton Park and New York: Routledge, 2014. Excellent presentation of the publicly enshrined, complex racial and ethnic identities during colonialism and since independence.

Restall, Matthew, and Kris Lane. *Latin America in Colonial Times*, 2nd ed. Cambridge, UK: Cambridge University Press, 2018. This study offers a new social and cultural focus not only of the European settlers but also of the conquered Amerindian population. Clear and engagingly written narrative.

Richter, Daniel K. *Facing East from Indian Country: A Native History of Early America*. Cambridge, MA: Harvard University Press, 2003. One of the few, and still unsurpassed, scholarly books that seeks to understand early modern North American history from the Native American perspective.

Socolow, Susan M. *The Women of Latin America*. Cambridge, UK: Cambridge University Press, 2nd ed. 2015. Surveys the patriarchal order and the function of women within it.

Stein, Stanley J., and Barbara H. Stein. *Silver, Trade, and War: Spain and America in the Making of Early Modern Europe*. Baltimore: Johns Hopkins University Press, 2000. Covers the significance of American silver reaching as far as China.

Taylor, Alan. *American Colonies*. London: Penguin, 2001. History of the English colonies in New England, written from a broad Atlantic perspective.

WEBSITE

Conquistadors, http://www.pbs.org/conquistadors/. Interactive website that allows you to track the journeys made by the Conquistadors such as Cortés, Pizarro, Orellana, and Cabeza de Vaca. Learn more about their conquests in the Americas and the legacy they left behind them.

Chapter 19

Carney, Judith A. *Black Rice: The African Origins of Rice Cultivation in the Americas*. Cambridge, MA: Harvard University Press, 2001. Study which goes a long way toward correcting the stereotype that black slaves were unskilled laborers, and carefully documents the transfer of rice-growing culture from West Africa to the Americas.

Dubois, Laurent, and Julius S. Scott, eds. *Origins of the Black Atlantic: Rewriting Histories*. New York: Routledge, 2010. Book that focuses on African slaves in the Americas as they had to arrange themselves in their new lives.

Gray, Richard, and David Birmingham, eds. *Pre-Colonial African Trade*. London and New York: Oxford University Press, 1970. Collective work in which contributors emphasize the growth and intensification of trade in the centuries of 1500–1800.

Hall, Gwendolyn Midlo. *Slavery and African Ethnicities in the Americas: Restoring the Links*. Chapel Hill: University of North Carolina Press, 2005. Study that focuses on slaves in the Americas according to their regions of origin in Africa.

Heywood, Linda M., and John K. Thornton. *Central Africans, Atlantic Creoles, and the Foundation of the Americas*. Cambridge, UK: Cambridge University Press, 2007. Pathbreaking investigation of the creation and role of Creole culture in Africa and the Americas.

Iliffe, John. *Africans: The History of a Continent*. 3rd ed. Cambridge, UK: Cambridge University Press, 2015. Standard historical summary by an established African historian.

Kriger, Colleen E. *Cloth in West African History*. Lanham, MD: Altamira, 2006. Detailed investigation of the sophisticated indigenous West African cloth industry.

LaGamma, Alisa. *Kongo: Power and Majesty*. New York: Metropolitan Museum of Art, 2015. Superbly illustrated exhibition catalogue, with articles by leading Africanists.

Lovejoy, Paul E. *Slavery in the Global Diaspora of Africa*. London and New York: Routledge, 2019. Discussion of the impact of the slave trade on migration, social structures, women and children from a West African perspective. The author is one of the foremost authorities on black slavery in Africa and the Americas.

Oliver, Roland, and Anthony Atmore. *Medieval Africa, 1250–1800*. Cambridge, UK: Cambridge University Press, 2001. Revised and updated historical overview, divided into regions and providing detailed regional histories on the emerging kingdoms.

Stapleton, Timothy J. *A Military History of Africa*. Vol. 1, *The Precolonial Period: From Ancient Egypt to the Zulu Kingdom (Earliest Times to ca. 1870)*. Santa Barbara, CA: Praeger, 2013. Summary of the historical evolution of West, East, Central, and South Africa.

Thornton, John. *The Kongolese Saint Anthony: Dona Beatriz Kimpa Vita and the Antonian Movement, 1684–1706*. Cambridge, UK: Cambridge University Press, 1998. Detailed biography of Dona Beatriz, from which the vignette at the beginning of the chapter is borrowed; includes a general overview of the history of Kongo during the civil war.

WEBSITE

Early modern African history: *South African History Online*, https://www.sahistory.org.za/. Website with a broad range of topics.

Chapter 20

Bernier, François. *Travels in the Mogul Empire, A.D. 1656–1668*. Translated by Archibald Constable. Delhi: S. Chand, 1968.

One of many fascinating travel accounts by European diplomats, merchants, and missionaries.

Eaton, Richard M. *Essays on Islam and Indian History*. Oxford and New York: Oxford University Press, 2002. A compendium of the new scholarly consensus on, among other things, the differences between the clerical view of Islamic observance and its actual impact in rural India. Contains both historiography and material on civilizational and cultural issues.

Gommans, J. J. L. *Mughal Warfare: Indian Frontiers and Highroads to Empire 1500–1700*. New York: Routledge, 2002. Sound examination of the Mughal Empire as a centralizing state increasingly reliant on a strong military for border defense and extending its sway. Examination of the structure of Mughal forces and the organization and weapons of the military.

Hunt, Margaret R., and Philip J. Stern, eds. *The English East India Company at the Height of Mughal Expansion: A Soldier's Diary of the 1689 Siege of Bombay with Related Documents*. Boston and New York: Bedford/St. Martin's, 2016. Illuminating look at the interplay of Mughal and European actors during the reign of Aurangzeb through the eyes of James Hilton, an English East India Company soldier, whose diary had previously been unpublished.

Nizami, Khaliq A. *Akbar and Religion*. Delhi: IAD, 1989. Extensive treatment of Akbar's evolving move toward devising his *din-i ilahi* movement, by a leading scholar of Indian religious and intellectual history.

Palat, Ravi. *The Making of an Indian Ocean World-Economy, 1250–1650*. New York: Palgrave Macmillan, 2015. This work seeks to break out of proto-capitalist perspectives of noncapitalist countries and instead sees much of the Indian Ocean system growing from the "paddy fields and bazaars" named in the subtitle, which provided a rich agricultural environment that stimulated "commercialization without capitalism."

Richards, John F. *The Mughal Empire*. Cambridge, UK: Cambridge University Press, 1993. Comprehensive volume in the New Cambridge History of India series. Sophisticated treatment; best suited to advanced students. Extensive glossary and useful bibliographic essay.

Sen, Siddhartha. *Colonizing, Decolonizing, and Globalizing Kolkata: From a Colonial to a Post-Marxist City*. Amsterdam: Amsterdam University Press, 2017. Centered on the urban history of Kolkata (Calcutta) as the nexus of British imperial rule and since independence, it examines areas of contested identity, particularly in the city's architecture and material culture.

Schimmel, Annemarie. *The Empire of the Great Mughals: History, Art, and Culture*. London: Reaktion, 2004. Revised edition of a volume published in German in 2000. Lavish illustrations, wonderfully drawn portraits of key individuals, and extensive treatment of social, family, and gender relations at the Mughal court.

WEBSITE

Association for Asian Studies, http://www. asian-studies.org/ As with other Asian topics, one of the most reliable websites is sponsored by the Association for Asian Studies, the largest professional organization for scholars of Asia.

Chapter 21
China

Crossley, Pamela K. *A Translucent Mirror: History and Identity in Qing Imperial Ideology*. Los Angeles: University of California Press, 1999. Pioneering study of the transformation of Qing self-image to one of leading a universal, multicultural empire.

De Bary, William T., and Irene Bloom, comps. *Sources of Chinese Tradition*, 2 vols., 2nd ed. New York: Columbia University Press, 1999. Thoroughgoing update of the classic sourcebook for Chinese literature and philosophy, with a considerable amount of social, family, and women's works now included.

Mungello, D. E. *The Great Encounter of China and West*. Lanham, MD: Rowman & Littlefield, 1999. Sound historical overview of the period marking the first European maritime expeditions into East Asia and extending to the height of the Canton trade and the beginnings of the opium era.

Pomeranz, Kenneth. *The Great Divergence: China, Europe, and the Making of the Modern World Economy*. Princeton, NJ: Princeton University Press, 2001. Pathbreaking work mounting the strongest argument yet in favor of the balance of economic power remaining in East Asia until the Industrial Revolution was well under way.

Shuo Wang. "Manchu Women in Transition: Gender Relations and Sexuality," in Stephen A. Wadley and Carsten Naeher, eds. *Proceedings of the First North American Conference on Manchu Studies*. Wiesbaden, Germany: Otto Harrassowitz, 2006: 105–130. Pathbreaking study of the role of Manchu women in Qing China in resistance to assimilation and preserving cultural identity.

Spence, Jonathan. *The Memory Palace of Matteo Ricci*. New York: Penguin, 1984. Highly original treatment of Ricci and the beginning of the Jesuit interlude in late Ming and early Qing China that attempts to penetrate Ricci's world through the missionary's own memory techniques.

Japan

De Bary, William T., ed. *Sources of Japanese Tradition*, 2 vols. New York: Columbia University Press, 1964. The Tokugawa era spans volumes 1 and 2, with its inception and political and philosophical foundations thoroughly covered in volume 1 and the Shinto revival of national learning, the later Mito school, and various partisans of national unity in the face of foreign intrusion covered in the beginning of volume 2.

Gordon, Andrew. *A Modern History of Japan from Tokugawa Times to the Present*. Oxford and New York: Oxford University Press, 2009. One of the few treatments of Japanese history that spans both the Tokugawa and the modern eras, rather than making the usual break in either 1853 or 1867/1868. Both the continuity of the past and the novelty of the new era are therefore juxtaposed and highlighted. Most useful for students with a background at least equivalent to that supplied by this text.

Lippit, Yukio, ed. *The Artist in Edo*. Washington, DC: National Gallery of Art and New Haven: Yale University Press, 2018. Compendium volume of essays by Japanese and Western scholars on contemporary issues surrounding the role of art, politics, and aesthetics in Tokugawa Japan. Useful for students with some grounding in the era.

WEBSITE

Zheng He. https://exploration.marinersmuseum.org/subject/zheng-he/. Good capsule history of the Chinese mariner with sources.

Chapter 22

Hardman, John. *Louis XVI*. New Haven: Yale University Press. 1993. An insightful analysis of Louis XVI from the perspective of his inner self—his strange preoccupation with minutiae rather than the impending revolution.

Herb, Guntram H. *Nations and Nationalism: A Global Historical Overview*. Santa Barbara, CA: ABC-Clio, 2008. Contains a large number of articles on the varieties of ethnic nationalism and culture and the proliferation of nationalism in Europe and Latin America.

Israel, Jonathan I. *A Revolution of the Mind: Radical Enlightenment and the Origins of Modern Democracy*. Princeton, NJ: Princeton University Press, 2010. Israel is a pioneer of the contemporary renewal of intellectual history, and his investigations of the Enlightenment tradition are pathbreaking.

Kaiser, Thomas E., and Dale K. Van Kley, eds. *From Deficit to Deluge: The Origins of the French Revolution*. Stanford, CA: Stanford University Press, 2011. Thoughtful re-evaluation of the scholarly field that takes into account the latest interpretations.

Kitchen, Martin. *A History of Modern Germany: 1800 to the Present*. Hoboken, NJ: Wiley-Blackwell, 2011. A broadly conceived historical overview, ranging from politics and economics to culture.

Osterhammel, Jürgen. *The Transformation of the World: A Global History of the Nineteenth Century*. Princeton, NJ: 2015. Celebrated evaluation of the myriads of changes and transformations characterizing the nineteenth century.

Rakove, Jack. *Revolutionaries: A New History of the Invention of America*. Boston: Houghton Mifflin, 2010. A new narrative history focusing on the principal figures in the revolution.

Riall, Lucy. *Risorgimento: The History of Italy from Napoleon to Nation-State*. New York: Palgrave Macmillan, 2009. Historical summary, incorporating the research of the past half-century, presented in a clear overview.

Suchet, John. *Beethoven: The Man Revealed*. New York: Atlantic Monthly Press, 2012. A fascinating biographical study of Beethoven's personal struggles.

West, Elliott. *The Last Indian War: The Nez Perce Story*. Oxford and New York: Oxford University Press, 2009. Vivid story of the end of the US wars for the subjugation of the Native Americans.

Wood, Gordon S. *The American Revolution: A History*. New York: Modern Library, 2002. A short, readable summary reflective of many decades of revisionism in the discussion of the American Revolution.

WEBSITES

Liberty, Equality, Fraternity: Exploring the French Revolution, http://chnm.gmu.edu/revolution/. This website boasts 250 images, 350 text documents, 13 songs, 13 maps, and a timeline all focused on the French Revolution.

Nationalism Project, http://www.nationalismproject.org/. A large website with links to bibliographies, essays, new books, and book reviews.

Chapter 23

Adelman, Jeremy. *Sovereignty and Revolution in the Iberian Atlantic*, Princeton, NJ: Princeton University Press, 2006. A leading study in a group of recent works on the transatlantic character of colonial and postcolonial Latin America.

Bulmer-Thomas, Victor. *The Economic History of Latin America since Independence*, 2nd ed. Cambridge, UK: Cambridge University Press, 2003. A highly analytical and sympathetic investigation of the Latin American export and self-sufficiency economies, calling into question the long-dominant dependency theories of Latin America.

Burkholder, Mark, and Lyman Johnson. *Colonial Latin America*, 6th ed. New York: Oxford University Press, 2008. Overview, with focus on social and cultural history.

Dawson, Alexander. *Latin America since Independence: A History with Primary Sources*. New York: Routledge, 2011. Selection of topics with documentary base; for the nineteenth century, covers the topics of the nation-state, caudillo politics, race, and the policy of growth through commodity exports.

Drake, Paul W. *Between Tyranny and Anarchy: A History of Democracy in Latin America*. Stanford, CA: Stanford University Press, 2009. The author traces the concepts of constitutionalism, autocracy, and voting rights since independence in clear and persuasive strokes.

Dupuy, Alex. *Rethinking the Haitian Revolution: Slavery, Independence, and the Struggle for Recognition*. Lanham, MD, Boulder, CO, New York, and London: Rowman and Littlefield, 2019. Ambitious effort by a sociologist to view the Haitian Revolution within the framework of early modern capitalism and the European, Hegelian-inspired ideology of races.

Girard, Philippe. *Toussaint Louverture: A Revolutionary Life*. New York: Basic Books, 2016. The most recent biography of the pioneer of Haiti's independence, written by the leading biographer of Toussaint.

Hämäläinen, Pekka. *The Comanche Empire*. New Haven, CT: Yale University Press, 2008. A revisionist account that puts the extraordinary importance of the Comanche empire for the history of Mexico and the United States in the nineteenth century into the proper perspective.

Moya, Jose C., ed. *The Oxford Handbook of Latin American History*. Oxford and New York: Oxford University Press, 2011. Important collection of political, social, economic, and cultural essays by leading specialists on nineteenth-century Latin America.

Sabato, Hilda. *Republics of the New World: The Revolutionary Political Experiment in Nineteenth-Century Latin America*. Princeton, NJ: Princeton University Press, 2018. Explores the specifically Latin American conditions for the development of a republican tradition.

Sanders, James E. *Vanguard of the Atlantic World: Creating Modernity, Nation, and Democracy in Nineteenth-Century Latin America*. Durham, NC: Duke University Press, 2014. Ambitious effort to evaluate the Latin American contributions to the creation of the modern state.

Sater, William F. *Andean Tragedy: Fighting the War of the Pacific, 1879–1884*. Lincoln: University of Nebraska Press, 2007. Close examination of this destructive war on the South American west coast.

Skidmore, Thomas. *Brazil: Five Centuries of Change*, 2nd ed. Oxford and New York: Oxford University Press, 2010. Short but magisterial text on the history of Brazil, with a detailed chapter on Brazil's path toward independence in the nineteenth century.

Wright, Thomas C. *Latin America since Independence: Two Centuries of Continuity and Change*. Lanham, MD, Boulder, CO, New York, and London: Rowman and Littlefield, 2017. A clearly written text on the five legacies of authoritarianism, social hierarchy, Catholicism, economic dependency, and landownership.

WEBSITE

Latin American Independence: *Macro History: World History,* http://www.fsmitha.com/h3/h36-2gr.html. Essays on independence from Spain and Portugal.

Chapter 24
China

Cohen, Paul. *Discovering History in China*. New York: Columbia University Press, 1984. Pivotal work on the historiography of American writers on China. Critiques their collective ethnocentrism in attempting to fit Chinese history into Western perspectives and approaches.

Fairbank, John K., and Su-yu Teng. *China's Response to the West*. Cambridge, MA: Harvard University Press, 1954. Though dated in approach, still a vitally important collection of sources in translation for the period from the late eighteenth century till 1923.

Meyer-Fong, Tobie. *What Remains: Coming to Terms with Civil War in 19th Century China*. Stanford, CA: Stanford University Press, 2013. Extensive treatment of individual experiences during the world's bloodiest civil war, the Taiping Rebellion.

Platt, Stephen R. *Autumn in the Heavenly Kingdom*. New York: Knopf, 2012. Reinterpretation of the Taiping era as global

political and economic phenomena involving the curtailing of US cotton exports during its civil war, the effects on the British textile industry, and the loss of Chinese markets during the Taiping Rebellion.

Shan, Patrick Fuliang. *Yuan Shikai: A Reappraisal*. Vancouver: University of British Columbia Press, 2018. While Yuan is best remembered for his failed presidency of the Chinese Republic and last-minute attempt to revive the imperial government, Shan's study gives us a far more nuanced picture of his role as diplomat and military reformer.

Spence, Jonathan D. *The Search for Modern China*. New York: Norton, 1990. Extensive, far-reaching interpretation of the period from China's nineteenth-century decline in the face of Western imperialism, through its revolutionary era, and finally to its recent bid for global preeminence.

Japan

Keene, Donald. *Emperor of Japan: Meiji and His World, 1852–1912*. New York: Columbia University Press, 2002. Masterly treatment of Japan's modernizing emperor and his vast influence on Japan and Asia, by one of the twentieth century's finest translators and scholars of Japan.

Reischauer, Edwin O., and Albert M. Craig. *Japan: Tradition and Transformation*. Boston: Houghton Mifflin, 1989. Somewhat dated but still highly useful introductory text by two of the twentieth century's leading scholars of Japanese history.

Totman, Conrad. *Politics in the Tokugawa Bakufu, 1600–1843*. Berkeley: University of California Press, 1988. Updated edition of Totman's breakthrough 1967 work. It remains one of the few highly detailed and deeply sourced monographs on the inner workings of the Tokugawa shogunate.

Walthall, Anne, and M. William Steele, *Politics and Society in Japan's Meiji Restoration: A Brief History with Documents*. New York: Bedford/St. Martin's, 2016. As with others in this series, a sound introduction for students with little or no background in the subject, accompanied by well-chosen documents.

WEBSITES

Association for Asian Studies, http://www.asian-studies.org/. This website of the Association for Asian Studies has links to sources more suited to advanced term papers and seminar projects.

Education about Asia, http://www.asian-studies.org/eaa/. This site provides the best online sources for modern Chinese and Japanese history.

Sino-Japanese War 1894–5, http://sinojapanesewar.com/. Packed with maps, photographs and movies depicting the conflict between Japan and China at the end of the nineteenth century; students can learn more about causes and consequences of the Sino–Japanese War.

Chapter 25

Brisku, Adrian. *Political Reform in the Ottoman and Russian Empires: A Comparative Approach*. London, Oxford,

New York, New Delhi, and Sydney: Bloomsbury Academic, 2019. Both empires faced the same challenges, that is, to undertake constitutional reforms without undermining the traditional hierarchical order. A clear exposition of these challenges and the efforts made to respond to them.

Gaudin, Corinne. *Ruling Peasants: Village and State in Later Imperial Russia.* DeKalb: Northern Illinois University Press, 2007. A close and sympathetic analysis of rural Russia.

Inalcik, Halil, and Donald Quataert, eds. *An Economic and Social History of the Ottoman Empire. Vol. 2, 1600–1914.* Cambridge, UK: Cambridge University Press, 1994. A pioneering work with contributions by leading Ottoman historians on rural structures, monetary developments, and industrialization efforts.

Kasaba, Resat, ed. *The Cambridge History of Turkey. Vol. 5, Turkey in the Modern World.* Cambridge, UK: Cambridge University Press, 2008. An ambitious effort to assemble the leading authorities on the Ottoman Empire and provide a comprehensive overview.

Lapavitsas, Costas, and Pinar Cakiroglu. *Capitalism in the Ottoman Balkans: Industrialisation and Modernity in Macedonia.* London: I. B. Tauris, 2019. Based on archival sources, this study reveals for the first time the dynamic push toward urbanization and industrial development in this European province of the Ottoman Empire, beginning at the end of the nineteenth century.

Massie, Robert K. *Catherine the Great: Portrait of a Woman.* New York: Random House, 2012. A comprehensive and insightful biography of one of the most fascinating women in history, whose policies, reforms, and personal life changed the course of Russian history.

Nikitenko, Aleksandr. *Up from Serfdom: My Childhood and Youth in Russia, 1804–1824.* Translated by Helen Saltz Jacobson. New Haven, CT: Yale University Press, 2001. Touching autobiography summarized at the beginning of the chapter.

Pamuk, Şevket. *Uneven Centuries: Economic Development of Turkey since 1820.* Princeton, NJ: Princeton University Press, 2018. Study by the leading economic historian of the Ottoman Empire which, for the first time, looks at the larger picture of economic and social change in this important multiethnic empire facing the challenges of Western modernity.

Poe, Marshall T. *Russia's Moment in World History.* Princeton, NJ: Princeton University Press, 2003. A superb scholarly overview of Russian history, written from a broad perspective and taking into account a good number of Western stereotypes about Russia, especially in the nineteenth century.

Rieber, Alfred J. *The Imperial Russian Project: Autocratic Politics, Economic Development, and Social Fragmentation.* Toronto, Buffalo, London: University of Toronto Press, 2018. Essays by the author on three interwoven subjects: the autocratic system of governance, the impact of economic change on the empire, and the fragmentation of society in the nineteenth century.

Uyar, Mesut, and Edward J. Erickson. *A Military History of the Ottomans: From Osman to Atatürk.* Santa Barbara, CA: Praeger Security International, 2009. A detailed, well-documented history of the Ottoman Empire from the perspective of its imperial designs and military forces, by two military officers in academic positions.

Zurcher, Erik J. *The Young Turk Legacy and Nation Building: From the Ottoman Empire to Atatürk's Turkey.* London: I. B. Tauris, 2010. Detailed yet readable account of how the Young Turk movement laid the foundation for Kemal Atatürk's Republic of Turkey.

WEBSITE

Russian Legacy. "Russian Empire (1689–1825)," http://www.russianlegacy.com/en/go_to/history/russian_empire.htm. A website devoted to the Russian Empire, organized as a timeline with links.

Chapter 26

Allen, Robert C. *The British Industrial Revolution in Global Perspective.* Cambridge, UK: Cambridge University Press, 2009. An in-depth analysis, well supported by economic data, not only of why the Industrial Revolution occurred first in Britain but also of how new British technologies carried industrialism around the world.

Dublin, Thomas, ed. *Farm to Factory: Women's Letters, 1830–1860.* New York: Columbia University Press, 1981. A fascinating collection of correspondence written by women who describe their experiences in moving from rural areas of New England to urban centers in search of work in textile factories.

Griffin, Emma. *Liberty's Dawn: A People's History of the Industrial Revolution.* New Haven, CT: Yale University Press, 2013. Riveting study of the impact of the Industrial Revolution on the lives of working men and women in Britain, as told in autobiographies and memoirs.

Headrick, Daniel R. *The Tools of Empire: Technology and European Imperialism in the Nineteenth Century.* Oxford and New York: Oxford University Press, 1981. A fascinating and clearly written analysis of the connections between the development of new technologies and their role in European imperialism.

Hobsbawm, Eric. *The Age of Revolution: 1789–1848.* London: Vintage, 1996. A sophisticated analysis of the Industrial Revolution (one element of the "twin revolution," the other being the French Revolution) that examines the effects of industrialism on social and cultural developments from a Marxist perspective.

Landers, Jane G. *Atlantic Creoles in the Age of Revolutions.* Cambridge: Harvard University Press, 2010. A fastidiously researched presentation of several black men (e.g., Big Prince Whitten) who carved out comfortable lives amid revolution in the Atlantic world.

Lynch, John. *Simón Bolívar: A Life.* New Haven: Yale University Press, 2006. A fresh look at the life and times of the Liberator, particularly his determination to enact reformist measures.

Rosen, William. *The Most Powerful Idea in the World: A Story of Steam, Industry, and Innovation.* Chicago: University of Chicago Press, 2012. Absorbing history of the importance of steam technologies in the development of industrialism.

Roudinesco, Elisabeth, and Catherine Porter. *Freud: In His Time and Ours.* Cambridge, MA: Harvard University Press, 2016. A bold, comprehensive, and innovative analysis of one of the most influential—and complex—figures at the turn of the twentieth century.

Sperber, Jonathan. *Karl Marx: A Nineteenth-Century Life.* New York: W. W. Norton, 2013. A carefully researched biography that contextualizes Marx vis-à-vis the age of early industrialism and in comparison with other luminaries in the turbulent nineteenth century.

WEBSITES

Claude Monet: Life and Paintings, http://www.monetpainting. net/. A visually beautiful website which reproduces many of Monet's masterpieces, it also includes an extensive biographical account of the famous painter's life and works as well as information about his wife Camille, his gardens at Giverny, and a chronology.

Darwin Online, http://darwin-online.org.uk/. This website has reproduced, in full, the works of Charles Darwin. In addition to providing digitized facsimiles of his works, private papers, and manuscripts, it has also added a concise biographical account and numerous images of Darwin throughout his life.

Einstein Archives Online, http://www.alberteinstein.info/. Fantastic and informative website that houses digitized manuscripts of Einstein's work. Also includes a gallery of images.

ThomasEdison.org, http://www.thomasedison.org/. Remarkable website that explores Thomas Edison's impact on modernity through his innovations and inventions. This site also reproduces all of Edison's scientific sketches, which are available to download as PDF files.

Chapter 27

Belich, James. *Replenishing the Earth: The Settler Revolution and the Rise of the Anglo-World, 1783–1939.* Oxford and New York: Oxford University Press, 2009. Important study by an Australian historian, focusing on the British settler colonies.

Chamberlain, M. E. *The Scramble for Africa.* New York: Routledge, 2013. Insightful account of the European colonization of Africa during the period 1870 to 1914.

Ferguson, Niall. *Empire: The Rise and Demise of the British World Order and the Lessons for Global Power.* New York: Perseus, 2002. Controversial but widely acknowledged analysis of the question of whether imperialism deserves its negative reputation or not.

Hobsbawm, Eric. *The Age of Empire, 1875–1914.* New York: Vintage, 1989. Immensely well-informed investigation of the climactic period of the new imperialism at the end of the nineteenth century.

Hochschild, Adam. *King Leopold's Ghost: A Story of Greed, Terror, and Heroism in Colonial Africa.* New York: Houghton Mifflin, 1998. A gripping exposé of Leopold II's brutal tactics in seizing territory and exploiting African labor in the Congo.

Jefferies, Matthew. *Contesting the German Empire, 1871–1918.* Malden, MA: Blackwell, 2008. Up-to-date summary of the German historical debate on the colonial period.

Kiernan, Ben. *Viet Nam: A History from Earliest Times to the Present.* Oxford: Oxford University Press, 2017. Extensive, scholarly, yet accessible to undergraduates, this is currently the most complete history of Vietnam to date. Welcome emphasis on environmental factors as well as French archival and newly declassified American materials.

Vickers, Adrian. *A History of Modern Indonesia,* 2nd ed. Cambridge, UK: Cambridge University Press, 2013. Well-written account of Indonesia growing from heteregenous Dutch colonial islands into a modern nation state.

Singer, Barnett, and John Langdon. *Cultured Force: Makers and Defenders of the French Colonial Empire.* Madison: University of Wisconsin Press, 2004. Study of the principal military figures who helped create the French nineteenth-century empire.

Streets-Salter, Heather, and Trevor R. Getz, *Empires and Colonies in the World: A Global Perspective.* Oxford and New York: Oxford University Press, 2015. Particularly illuminative chapters on the new imperialism in the nineteenth century.

WEBSITES

The Colonization of Africa, http://exhibitions.nypl.org/africanaage/ essay-colonization-of-africa.html. An academically based summary with further essays on African topics.

South Asian History—Colonial India, http://www.lib.berkeley. edu/SSEAL/SouthAsia/india_colonial.html. Very detailed website with primary documents and subtopics of nineteenth-century British India.

Chapter 28

Clark, Christopher. *The Sleepwalkers: How Europe Went to War in 1914.* New York: Harper Perennial, 2014. One of a slew of new investigations into the origins of the war published to mark its centennial; emphasizes the Austrian–Serbian roots of the war.

Cohen, Adam. *Imbeciles: The Supreme Court, American Eugenics, and the Sterilization of Carrie Buck.* New York: Penguin, 2016.

Fritzsche, Peter. *Life and Death in the Third Reich.* Cambridge, MA: Harvard University Press, 2008. Book that seeks to understand the German nation's choice of adapting itself to Nazi rule.

Gelvin, James L. *The Modern Middle East: A History,* 4th ed. Oxford and New York: Oxford University Press, 2015. Contains chapters on Arab nationalism, British and French colonialism, and Turkey and Iran in the interwar period.

Gordon, Andrew. *A Modern History of Japan: From Tokugawa Times to the Present,* 2nd ed. Oxford and New York: Oxford

University Press, 2009. Detailed overview of Japan's interwar period in the middle chapters.

Grasso, June M., J. P. Corrin, and Michael Kort. *Modernization and Revolution in Modern China: From the Opium Wars to the Olympics*, 4th ed. Armonk, NY: M. E. Sharpe, 2009. General overview with a focus on modernization in relation to the strong survival of tradition.

Hung, Chang-Tai. *Mao's New World: Political Culture in the Early People's Republic*. Ithaca, NY: Cornell University Press, 2011. A broad collection of cultural expressions, ranging from dancing to cartoons, utilized to enhance loyalty to the CCP.

Martel, Gordon, ed. *A Companion to Europe 1900–1945*. Malden, MA: Wiley-Blackwell, 2010. Collective work covering a large variety of cultural, social, and political European topics in the interwar period.

Meade, Teresa A. *A History of Modern Latin America: 1800 to the Present*. Malden, MA: Wiley-Routledge, 2010. Topical discussion of the major issues in Latin American history, with chapters on the first half of the twentieth century.

Neiberg, Michael S. *The Treaty of Versailles: A Concise Study*. Oxford and New York: Oxford University Press, 2017. An assessment of the complexities attending the settlement of World War I, along with the consequences of its many flaws and failures.

Service, Robert. *Lenin: A Biography*. Cambridge, MA: Harvard University Press, 2000. An interesting portrait of Lenin's character and personality, highlighting his idiosyncrasies.

Snyder, Timothy. *Bloodlands: Europe between Hitler and Stalin*. New York: Basic Books, 2010. Book that chronicles the horrific destruction left behind by these two dictators.

Wilson, Mark R. *Destructive Creation: American Business and the Winning of World War II*. Philadelphia: University of Pennsylvania Press, 2016. A thoroughly researched revisionist interpretation of the strained relationship between big business and the federal government as America mobilized for, and engaged in, World War II.

WEBSITES

BBC. World War One, http://www.bbc.co.uk/ww1, and World War Two (archived), http://www.bbc.co.uk/history/worldwars/wwtwo/. The BBC's treatment of the causes, course, and consequences of both WWI and WWII from an Allied position.

Marxists Internet Archive. "The Bolsheviks," http://www.marxists.org/subject/bolsheviks/index.htm. A complete review of the Bolshevik party members, including biographies and links to archives which contain their works.

1937 Nanking Massacre, http://www.nanking-massacre.com/Home.html. A disturbing collection of pictures and articles tell the gruesome history of the Rape of Nanjing.

United States Holocaust Memorial Museum. Holocaust Encyclopedia, http://www.ushmm.org/wlc/en/article.php? ModuleId=10005151. The US Holocaust Memorial Museum looks back on one of the darkest times in Western history.

U.S. History, http://www.ushistory.org/us/. Maintained by Independence Hall Association in Philadelphia, this website contains many links to topics discussed in this chapter.

Chapter 29

Baret, Roby Carol. *The Greater Middle East and the Cold War: US Foreign Policy under Eisenhower and Kennedy*. London: I.B. Tauris, 2007. Thoroughly researched analysis of American policies in the Middle East, North Africa, and South Asia.

Birmingham, David. *Kwame Nkrumah: Father of African Nationalism*. Athens: University of Ohio Press, 1998. Short biography by a leading modern African historian.

Conniff, Michael L. *Populism in Latin America*. Tuscaloosa: University of Alabama Press, 1999. The author is a well-published scholar on modern Latin America.

Damrosch, David, David Lawrence Pike, Djelal Kadir, and Ursula K. Heise, eds. *The Longman Anthology of World Literature*. Vol. F, *The Twentieth Century*. New York: Longman/Pearson, 2008. A rich, diverse selection of texts. Alternatively, Norton published a similar, somewhat larger anthology of world literature in 2003.

De Witte, Ludo. *The Assassination of Lumumba*. Translated by Ann Wright and Renée Fenby. London: Verso, 2002. An admirably researched study of the machinations of the Belgian government in protecting its mining interests, with the connivance of CIA director Allen Dulles and President Dwight D. Eisenhower.

Guha, Ramachandra. *India after Gandhi: A History of the World's Largest Democracy*. New York: Harper Collins 2007. Highly readable, popular history with well-sketched biographical treatments of leading individuals, more obscure cultural figures, and ordinary people. Accessible to even beginning students.

Hasegawa, Tsuyoshi. *The Cold War in East Asia, 1945–1991*. Stanford, CA: Stanford University Press, 2011. A new summary, based on archival research by a leading Japanese historian teaching in the United States. New insights on the Soviet entry into World War II against Japan.

Herman, Arthur. *Joseph McCarthy: Reexamining the Life and Legacy of America's Most Hated Senator*. New York: Free Press, 2000. A fascinating study of the Wisconsin senator whose virulent campaign against communism launched decades of fear and reprisals in America during the Cold War era.

Jansen, Jan C., and Jürgen Osterhammel. *Decolonization: A Short History*. Princeton, NJ: Princeton University Press, 2017. Superb, analytical well-grounded summary of the decolonization process and its aftermath in the second half of the twentieth century.

Jankowski, James. *Nasser's Egypt, Arab Nationalism, and the United Arab Republic*. Boulder, CO: Lynne Rienner, 2002. A carefully researched account of the origin, evolution, and eventual collapse of the United Arab Republic.

Meredith, Martin. *The Fate of Africa: A History of the Continent since Independence*. Philadelphia: Perseus, 2011. A revised and up-to-date study of a fundamental analysis of Africa during the modern era.

Wang, Juoyue. *In Sputnik's Shadow: The President's Science Advisory Committee and Cold War in America.* New Brunswick, NJ: Rutgers University Press, 2008. Traces the evolution of the President's Science Advisory Committee following new directions after Russia's successful launching of Sputnik in 1957.

WEBSITES

Economist. "The Suez Crisis: An Affair to Remember," http://www.economist.com/node/7218678. The *Economist* magazine looks back on the Suez Crisis.

NASA. "Yuri Gagarin: First Man in Space," http://www.nasa.gov/mission_pages/shuttle/sts1/gagarin_anniversary.html. In addition to information and video footage regarding Yuri Gagarin's orbit of the earth, students will also find information on America's space history.

The History.com website has a detailed, illustrated subsection on the Berlin Wall: https://www.history.com/topics/cold-war/berlin-wall.

Chapter 30

Ash, Timothy Garton. *The Magic Lantern: The Revolution of '89 Witnessed in Warsaw, Budapest, Berlin, and Prague.* New York: Random House, 1999. A gripping first-hand account of the wave of anticommunist revolutions that rocked Eastern Europe after 1989.

Cooper, James. *Margaret Thatcher and Ronald Reagan: A Very Political Special Relationship.* New York: Palgrave Macmillan, 2012. Insightful observations regarding conjoined policies of Reagan and Thatcher, particularly their economic policies during the 1980s.

Emery, Christian. *US Foreign Policy and the Iranian Revolution: The Cold War Dynamics of Engagement and Strategic Alliance.* New York: Palgrave Macmillan, 2013. Discusses the 1979 Iranian revolution with emphasis on the Carter administration's mishandling of critical developments, resulting in the radicals' overtaking of the Iranian Revolution.

Fanon, Frantz. *The Wretched of the Earth.* New York: Grove, 1961. One of the most provocative and influential treatments of theoretical and practical issues surrounding decolonization. Fanon champions violence as an essential part of the decolonization process and advocates a modified Marxist approach that takes into consideration the nuances of race and the legacies of colonialism.

Frieden, Jeffrey. *Global Capitalism: Its Fall and Rise in the Twentieth Century.* New York: W. W. Norton, 2006. Despite the title, a comprehensive history of global networks from the days of mercantilism to the twenty-first century. Predominant emphasis on twentieth century; highly readable, though the material is best suited for more advanced students.

Gaddis, John Lewis. *The Cold War: A New History.* New York: Penguin, 2005. Though criticized by some scholars for his pro-American positions, America's foremost historian of the Cold War produces here a vivid, at times counterintuitive, view of the Cold War and its global impact. Readable even for beginning students.

Gitlin, Todd. *The Sixties: Years of Hope, Days of Rage,* rev. ed. New York: Bantam, 1993. Lively, provocative account of this pivotal decade by the former radical, now a sociologist. Especially effective at depicting the personalities of the pivotal period 1967–1969.

Goodwin, Doris Kearns. *Lyndon Johnson and the American Dream.* New York: St. Martin's Press, 1991. Insightful and probing study of President Johnson's character and personality, from his early years through his extensive political career.

Harmer, Tanya. *Allende's Chile and the Inter-American Cold War.* Chapel Hill, NC: *University of North Carolina Press, 2014.* A reinterpretation of American determination to overturn Allende's leftist government and its subsequent results.

Liang Heng and Judith Shapiro. *After the Nightmare: A Survivor of the Cultural Revolution Reports on China Today.* New York: Knopf, 1986. Highly readable, poignant first-person accounts of people's experiences during the trauma of China's Cultural Revolution by a former husband-and-wife team. Especially interesting because China was at the beginning of its Four Modernizations when this was written, and the wounds of the Cultural Revolution were still fresh.

Raleigh, Donald J. *Soviet Baby Boomers: An Oral History of Russia's Cold War Generation.* Oxford and New York: Oxford University Press, 2012. A revealing and entertaining account of new social and cultural trends among Russia's youth, as told in a series of interviews.

Smith, Bonnie, ed. *Global Feminisms since 1945.* London: Routledge, 2000. Part of the Rewriting Histories series, this work brings together under the editorship of Smith a host of essays by writers such as Sara Evans, Mary Ann Tetreault, and Miriam Ching Yoon Louie on feminism in Asia, Africa, and Latin America, as well as Europe and the United States. Sections are thematically arranged under such headings as "Nation-Building," "Sources of Activism," "Women's Liberation," and "New Waves in the 1980s and 1990s." Comprehensive and readable, though some background in women's history is recommended.

WEBSITES

Cold War International History Project, https://www.wilsoncenter.org/program/cold-war-international-history-project. Run by the Woodrow Wilson International Center for Scholars. Rich archival materials, including collections on the end of the Cold War, the Soviet invasion of Afghanistan, the Cuban Missile Crisis, and Chinese foreign policy documents.

The "Office of the Historian," a semi-official website of the State Department and associated foreign policy historians offers studies on a variety of 20th-century topics: https://history.state.gov/about.

The United Nations has a detailed website on decolonization: https://www.un.org/en/sections/issues-depth/decolonization/index.html.

Chapter 31

Daniels, Robert V. *The Rise and Fall of Communism in the Soviet Union*. New Haven, CT: Yale University Press, 2010. A magisterial summary of the communist period by a specialist.

Dillon, Michael. *Contemporary China: An Introduction*. New York: Routledge, 2009. Concise yet specific overview of the economy, society, and politics of the country.

Eichengreen, Barry. *Exorbitant Privilege: The Rise and Fall of the Dollar and the Future of the Monetary System*. Oxford and New York: Oxford University Press, 2011. The author is an academic specialist on US monetary policies, writing in an accessible style and presenting a fascinating picture of the role of something as prosaic as greenbacks.

Faust, Aaron M. *The Ba'thification of Iraq: Saddam Hussein's Totalitarianism*. Austin, TX: University of Texas Press, 2015. Based on meticulous research among Ba'th Party documents, this study reveals how Saddam Hussein developed a totalitarian regime in Iraq and why his dictatorship succeeded in gaining the loyalty of millions of Iraqis for nearly 25 years.

Gelvin, James L. *The Arab Uprisings: What Everyone Needs to Know*. Oxford and New York: Oxford University Press, 2012. Concise overview of the Arab Spring events with carefully selected background information.

Houghton, John. *Global Warming: The Complete Briefing*. 5th ed. Cambridge, UK: Cambridge University Press, 2015. One of the most authoritative summaries of all aspects of global warming.

Jacka, Tamara, Andrew Kipnis, and Sally Sargeson. *Contemporary China: Society and Social Change*. Cambridge, UK: Cambridge University Press, 2013. Ambitious sociological–historical study focusing on the many differences within Chinese society and the forces that drive change in contemporary China.

Luong, Hy V. *Postwar Vietnam: Dynamics of a Transforming Society*. Lanham, MD: Institute of Southeast Asian Studies and Rowman & Littlefield, 2003. Important study of reforms geared toward opening up Vietnam's economy and its effects on society, among them a growing divide between urban and rural areas.

Meade, Teresa A. *A History of Modern Latin America: 1800 to the Present*. 2nd ed. Malden, MA: Wiley-Blackwell, 2016. The book is an excellent, comprehensive analysis and has a strong final chapter on recent Latin America.

Saxonberg, Steven. *The Fall: A Comparative Study of the End of Communism in Czechoslovakia, East Germany, Hungary, and Poland*. Amsterdam, The Netherlands: Harwood Academic, 2001. A well-informed overview of the different trajectories by an academic teaching in Prague.

Swanimathan, Jayshankar M. *Indian Economic Superpower: Fact or Fiction?* Singapore: World Scientific Publishing, 2009. A thoughtful evaluation of the pros and cons of economic growth in India, in concise overviews.

WEBSITES

Wikiwand has a website on contemporary history with many tabs on recent events and topics: https://www.wikiwand.com/en/Contemporary_history.

BBC. Nelson Mandela's Life and Times, http://www.bbc.co.uk/news/world-africa-12305154. The BBC News looks back at the life and career of Nelson Mandela.

Sierra Club, http://sierraclub.org/. Balanced and informative environmental websites.

Credits

Source Index

Page numbers of the form S8-7–S8-8 indicate, in this case, a source document in chapter 8 on pages 7–8 in the source documents at the end of chapter 8. If the page number for the source document is followed by (d) this indicates a text source document. If the page number for the source document is followed by (v) this indicates a visual source document.

'Abd al-'Azīz al-Bakrī: on West Africa, S14-7–S14-8 (d)

Abelard, Peter: *The Story of My Misfortunes* by, S11-7–S11-8 (d)

Adelard of Bath: *Questiones naturales* by, S11-3–S11-5 (d)

Admonitions for Women (Nüjie) (Ban Zhao), S9-6–S9-7 (d)

Afonso I (Nzinga Mbemba) of Kongo: letter to King of Portugal, S19-3–S19-5 (d)

Africa: 'Abd al-'Azīz al-Bakrī on, S14-7–S14-8 (d); bananas from, S6-2–S6-3 (d); Ibn Battuta's journey to the East African coast, S14-4–S14-6 (d)

Ahuitzotl: eighth king of Aztec Empire, S15-3–S15-4 (d)

Alexander II: abolition of serfdom by, S25-6–S25-8 (d)

Alexander I: Metternich's secret memorandum to, S22-12–S22-13 (d)

Álfaro, José de: in scandal at the church, S18-2–S18-4 (d)

Allende, Salvador: "Last Words to the Nation" by, S30-11–S30-12 (d)

amulet containing passages from Qur'an worn by Muslim slaves who rioted in Bahia, Brazil, S23-6–S23-8 (d)

Analects (Lunyu) (Confucius), S9-2–S9-3 (d)

ANZAC. *See* Australian and New Zealand Army Corps

Ashley Commission: miners' testimony at, S26-5–S26-6 (d)

Ashoka: Seven Pillar Edicts of, S8-2–S8-4 (d)

Aten: great hymn to, S2-8–S2-9 (d)

Aurangzeb, edicts of, S20-5–S20-6 (d)

Australian and New Zealand Army Corps (ANZAC) at Galliopi, S28-2–S28-4 (d)

Avalokiteshvara: copper head of, Vietnam, S13-9 (v)

Aztec Empire: Ahuitzotl eighth king of, S15-3–S15-4 (d)

Babur, Zahiruddin Muhammad: *The Baburnama* by, S20-2–S20-3 (d)

The Baburnama (Babur), S20-2–S20-3 (d)

Bachellery, Josefina: "The Education of Women" by, S23-2–S23-4 (d)

Bahia, Brazil: amulet containing passages from Qur'an worn by Muslim slaves who rioted in, S23-6–S23-8 (d)

Al-Bakrī, 'Abd al-'Azīz: *Kitāb al-masālik wa-'l-mamālik* by, S14-7–S14-8 (d)

bananas: Africa's earliest, S6-2–S6-3 (d)

Ban Zaho: *Admonitions for Women* by, S9-6–S9-7 (d)

Bhagavad Gita, S3-2–S3-4 (d)

bin Laden, Osama: "Declaration of War against the Americans Occupying the Land of Two Holy Places," S31-2–S31-4 (d)

Black Death: flagellants attempt to ward off in Germany and England, S11-10–S11-11 (d)

Boccaccio, Giovanni: *The Decameron* "Putting the Devil Back in Hell" by, S11-8–S11-10 (d)

Bodhisattva Avalokiteshvara: copper head of, Vietnam, S13-9 (v)

The Book of Lord Shang (Shangjun Shu), S4-5–S4-6 (d)

Book of Mencius (Mengzi) (Mencius), S9-3–S9-4 (d)

The Book of Odes (Shijing), S4-2–S4-3 (d)

The Book of Prophecies (Columbus), S16-5–S16-6 (d)

The Book of Routes and Realms (Kitāb al-masālik wa-'l-mamālik) (al-Bakrī), S14-7–S14-8 (d)

Botswana, Rhino Cave in: python–Shaped ornamented rock from, S1-3 (v)

Bravo, Doña Theresa: in scandal at the church, S18-2–S18-4 (d)

Brazil: amulet containing passages from Qur'an worn by Muslim slaves who rioted in, S23-6–S23-8 (d)

Brihadaranyaka Upanishad, S3-6–S3-7 (d)

Brittain, Vera: *Testament of Youth* by, S28-4–S28-6 (d)

Buddhism, in Korea: *Haedong kosŭng chŏn* on, S13-6–S13-8 (d)

Burke, Edmund: *Reflections on the Revolution in France* by, S22-8–S22-9 (d)

Cadena, Joséfa: in scandal at the church, S18-2–S18-4 (d)

Caral–Supe culture, Peru: quipu from, S5-2 (v)

casta paintings: in Mexico, S19-10–S10-11 (v)

Castello, Sebastian: *Concerning Whether Heretics Should Be Persecuted* by, S17-7–S17-9 (d)

Castro, Fidel: letters between Nikita Khrushchev and on Cuban Missile Crisis, S29-7–S29-10 (d)

Çelebi, Evliya: "A Procession of Artisans at Istanbul" by, S16-9–S16-11 (d)

The Chachnamah, S12-2–S12-3 (d)

Châtelet, Emilie du: *Discourse on Happiness* by, S17-4–S17-7 (d)

Chavin de Huántar, Peru: textile fragment from, S5-3 (v)

China in the Sixteenth Century (Ricci), S21-2–S21-4 (d)

China: Mccartney on possibilities of British commerce, S21-4–S21-6 (d)

Chinese coolie photograph: Peru, S23-9 (v)

Christian Topography (Cosmas Indicopleustes), S6-8–S6-9 (d)

Chronicles of Japan (Nihongi), S13-4–S13-6 (d)

Churchill, Winston: "The Iron Curtain Speech" by, S29-5–S29-7 (d)

Cieza de León, Pedro: on Incan roads, S15-6–S15-7 (d)

climate change: United Nations framework convention on, S31-12–S31-13 (d)

The Cloud Messenger (Kalidasa), S8-9–S8-11 (d)

Code of Manu, S3-8–S3-9 (d)

Columbus, Christopher: *The Book of Prophecies* by, S16-5–S16-6 (d); reports on his first voyage, 1493, S16-2–S16-4 (d)

Concerning Whether Heretics Should Be Persecuted (Castello), S17-7–S17-9 (d)

Confucius: *Analects* of, S9-2–S9-3 (d)

The Conquest of New Spain (Díaz), S15–S15-6 (d)

Constantinople: "The Fall of Constantinople" on, S16-7–S16-8 (d)

Cosmas Indicopleustes (Cosmas the India-Voyager): *Christian Topography* by, S6-8–S6-9 (d)

"The Court of Suleiman the Magnificent" (Ghiselin de Busbecq), S16-11–S16-12 (d)

Crimea annexation: Vladimir Putin address to Duma concerning, S31-04–S31-7 (d)

Cuban Missile Crisis: letters between Fidel Castro and Nikita Khrushchev, S29-7–S29-10 (d)

Cyrus Cylinder, S7-2–S7-3 (d)

"The Daily Habits of Louis XIV at Versailles" (duc de Saint–Simon), S17-9–S17-11 (d)

Darwin, Charles: *The Origin of Species* by, S26-9–S26-11 (d)

de Beauvoir, Simone: *The Second Sex* by, S30-6–S30-8 (d)

The Decameron "Putting the Devil Back in Hell" (Boccaccio), S11-8–S11-10 (d)

Declaration of the Rights of Man and of the Citizen: France, S22-2–S22-3 (d)

The Declaration of the Rights of Woman (de Gouges), S22-4–S22-6 (d)

"Declaration of War against the Americans Occupying the Land of Two Holy Places" (bin Laden), S31-2–S31-4 (d)

de Gouges, Olympe: *The Declaration of the Rights of Woman*, S22-4–S22-6 (d)

de' Medici, Christina: Galileo Galilei: letter to, S17-13–S17-15 (d)

Díaz, Bernal: *The Conquest of New Spain* by, S15–S15-6 (d)

Dickens, Charles: *Hard Times* by, S26-2–S26-3 (d)

Diplovatatzes, Joshua: "The Fall of Constantinople" by, S16-7–S16-8 (d)

Discourse on Happiness (Châtelet), S17-4–S17-7 (d)

Dzudzuana Cave, Republic of Georgia, Caucasus Mountains: flax fibers from, S1-7 (v)

East African coast: Ibn Battuta's journey to, S14-4–S14-6 (d)

East Asia: pottery's origins in, S1-4–S1-6 (v)

edicts: of Aurangzeb, S20-5–S20-6 (d); from Qianlong Emperor to King George III, S21-6–S21-9 (d); Rose Garden, S25-4–S25-6 (d)

"The Education of Women" (Bachellery), S23-2–S23-4 (d)

Edwin Smith Papyrus: three spinal injury cases in, S2-4–S2-5 (d)

Egypt, Middle Kingdom, Twelfth Dynasty: advice from a royal scribe to his apprentice, S2-6–S2-7 (d)

Einhard: *Life of Charlemagne* by, S11-2–S11-3 (d)

El Castio de Huarmey, Peru: skeletons in Wari royal tomb site, S15-2–S15-3 (v)

emerald box: Mughal, S20-7 (v)

England: flagellants attempt to ward off Black Death in, S11-10–S11-11 (d)

Equiano, Olaudah: *The Interesting Narrative of the Life of Olaudah Equiano* by, S19-8–S19-10 (d)

Eredo, Sungbo's Eredo, walls and moats, Nigeria, S14-8–S14-9 (d)

Ethiopia: *The Fetha Nagast* from, S14-2–S14-4 (d)

examination of Lady Jane Grey, London, S17-2–S17-4 (d)

"The Fall of Constantinople" (Thomas the Eparch and Diplovatatzes), S16-7–S16-8 (d)

The Fetha Nagast: Ethiopia, S14-2–S14-4 (d)

feudal contracts and the swearing of fealty, S11-5–S11-6 (d)

flagellants attempt to ward off Black Death in Germany and England, S11-10–S11-11 (d)

flax fibers: Dzudzuana Cave, Republic of Georgia, Caucasus Mountains, S1-7 (v)

"Foundations and Doctrine of Fascism" (Mussolini and Gentile), S28-7–S28-8 (d)

France: *Declaration of the Rights of Man and of the Citizen*, S22-2–S22-3 (d); *Reflections on the Revolution in France* on, S22-8–S22-9 (d)

French North America: *The Jesuit Relations*, S18-9–S18-11 (d)

Fustat: Jewish engagement contract from, S10-8–S10-9 (d)

Galileo Galilei: letter to the Grand Duchess Christina de' Medici, S17-13–S17-15 (d)

Gallipoli: ANZAC troops at, S28-2–S28-4 (d)

Gal'pern Matchbox Factory female workers' strike: Pinsk, S25-8–S25-11 (d)

Gandhi, Indira: "What Educated Women Can Do" by, S29-12–S29-14 (d)

Genghis Khan strikes West, S12-7–S12-9 (d)

Gentile, Giovanni: "Foundations and Doctrine of Fascism" by, S28-7–S28-8 (d)

George III: Qianlong Emperor's edicts to, S21-6–S21-9 (d)

Germany: flagellants attempt to ward off Black Death in, S11-10–S11-11 (d)

Ghiselin de Busbecq, Ogier: "The Court of Suleiman the Magnificent" by, S16-11–S16-12 (d)

Gorbachev, Mikhail: *Perestroika: New Thinking for Our Country and the World* by, S30-2–S30-4 (d)

Great Britain: Lin Zexu's letter to Queen Victoria, S24-2–S24-3 (d); miners' testimony at Ashley Commission, S26-5–S26-6 (d)

Great Hymn to the Aten, S2-8–S2-9 (d)

Great Revolt: in India, S27-2–S27-5 (d)

Grey, Lady Jane; examination of, S17-2–S17-4 (d)

Grotte des Pigeons, Taforalt, Morocco: shell bead jewelry from, S1-2 (v)

Hachiya, Michihiko: *Hiroshima Diary* by, S28-13–S28-15 (d)

Haedong kosŭng chŏn (*The Lives of Eminent Korean Monks*): on Buddhism in Korea, S13-6–S13-8 (d)

Hammurabi: Law Code of, S2-2–S2-3 (d)

Hard Times (Dickens), S26-2–S26-3 (d)

Henan Museum, Guo state, Sanmenxia city: iron sword with jade handle, earliest cast-iron object, S4-6–S4-7 (v)

Hippocrates: *On The Sacred Disease* by, S7-5–S7-8 (d)

Hiroshima Diary (Hachiya), S28-13–S28-15 (d)

Histories (Herodotus), S7-3–S-75 (d)

Hitler, Adolf: *Mein Kampf* by, S28-9–S28-11 (d)

Ho Chi Minh: "The Path Which Led Me to Leninism" by, S29-10–S29-12 (d)

Huskisson, William: death as first casualty of railroad accident, S26-3–S26-4 (d)

Hypatia, Alexandria, Egypt: murder of, S7-13–S7-15 (d)

Ibn 'Abd al-Qadir, Ismail: *The Life of the Sudanese Mahdi* by, S27-5–S27-6 (d)

Ibn Battuta: journey to the East African coast, S14-4–S14-6 (d)

Ibn Munqidh, Usama: *Memoirs of Usama Ibn Munqidh* by, S10-6–S10-8 (d)

iconoclasm controversy: documents related to, S10-4–S10-6 (d)

"I Have a Dream" (King), S30-4–S30-6 (d)

Incan roads: Cieza de León on, S15-6–S15-7 (d)

India: Great Revolt in, S27-2–S27-5 (d)

Inland Niger Delta, S6-4–S6-6 (v)

Inquisition: confessions of Marina de San Miguel before, S18-4–S18-6 (d)

"The Iron Curtain Speech" (Churchill), S29-5–S29-7 (d)

iron sword with jade handle: Henan Museum, Guo state, Sanmenxia city, S4-6–S4-7 (v)

Islamic mystic's highest meditative state, S10-10–S10-11 (d)

Istanbul: "A Procession of Artisans at Istanbul" on, S16-9–S16-11 (d)

Al-Jahiz: "The Story of the Judge and the Fly" by, S10-2–S10-3 (d)

Janissary musket, S16-12–S16-13 (v)

Japan: Meiji Constitution of, S24-6–S24-8 (d); *Nihongi* of, S13-4–S13-6 (d); "Secret Plan for Managing the Country" on, S21-9–S21-11 (d)

Jefferson Day: Roosevelt's undelivered address planned for, S28-11–S28-13 (d)

The Jesuit Relations: French North America, S18-9–S18-11 (d)

Jewish engagement contract from Fustat, S10-8–S10-9 (d)

Kalidasa (*The Cloud Messenger*), S8-9–S8-11 (d)

K'atun, Lady: queen of Piedras Negras, S6-6–S6-8 (v)

Kennewick Man: DNA results showing him as Native American, S5-4–S5-6 (v)

Khrushchev, Nikita: letters between Fidel Castro on Cuban Missile Crisis, S29-7–S29-10 (d)

King, Martin Luther, Jr.: "I Have a Dream" by, S30-4–S30-6 (d)

Kipling, Rudyard: "The White Man's Burden" by, S27-7–S27-9 (d)

Kitāb al-masālik wa-'l-mamālik (The Book of Routes and Realms) (al-Bakri), S14-7–S14-8 (d)

Knossos, Minoan Crete: sketch of palace complex at, S2-7–S2-8 (v)

Kokoro (Soseki), S24-9–S24-11 (d)

Kongo, Afonso I of: letter to King of Portugal, S19-3–S19-5 (d)

Korea, Buddhism in: *Haedong kosŭng chŏn* on, S13-6–S13-8 (d)

"Last Words to the Nation" (Allende), S30-11–S30-12 (d)

Law Code of Hammurabi, S2-2–S2-3 (d)

Letters from the Levant (Montagu), S25-2–S25-4 (d)

Life of Charlemagne (Vita Caroli Magni) (Einhard), S11-2–S11-3 (d)

The Life of Michelangelo Buonarroti (Vasari), S17-11–S17-13 (d)

The Life of the Sudanese Mahdi (Ibn 'Abd al-Qadir), S27-5–S27-6 (d)

Lin Zexu's letter to Queen Victoria of Great Britain, S24-2–S24-3 (d)

Li Si: "Memorial on the Burning of Books" by, S9-4–S9-5 (d)

The Lives of Eminent Korean Monks (Haedong kosŭng chŏn): on Buddhism in Korea, S13-6–S13-8 (d)

London, examination of Lady Jane Grey in, S17-2–S17-4 (d)

Louis XIV: "The Daily Habits of Louis XIV at Versailles" on, S17-9–S17-11 (d)

Maccabees, S7-8–S7-10 (d)

Mandela, Nelson: inauguration speech of, S30-13–S30-15 (d)

Marx, Karl: "Wage Labour and Capital" by, S26-7–S26-9 (d)

Mccartney, George: on China and possibilities of British commerce, S21-4–S21-6 (d)

Meiji Constitution of Empire of Japan, S24-6–S24-8 (d)

Mein Kampf (Hitler), S28-9–S28-11 (d)

Memoirs of Usama Ibn Munqidh (Ibn Munqidh), S10-6–S10-8 (d)

"Memorial on the Burning of Books" (Li Si), S9-4–S9-5 (d)

Mencius: *Book of Mencius* by, S9-3–S9-4 (d)

Meroë, Sudan: relief sculpture from, S6-3–S6-4 (v)

Metternich, Clemens von: secret memorandum to Tsar Alexander I, S22-12–S22-13 (d)

Mexico: casta painting of, S19-10–S10-11 (v); Nahuatl land sale documents in, S18-7–S18-8 (d); scandal at the church: José de Álfaro accuses Doña Theresa Bravo and

others of insulting and beating his Castiza wife, Joséfa Cadena in, S18-2–S18-4 (d)

Mexico City: confessions before the Inquisition in, S18-4-18-6 (d)

Michelangelo Buonarroti: *The Life of Michelangelo Buonarroti* on, S17-11–S17-13 (d)

Middle Kingdom Egypt, Twelfth Dynasty: advice from a royal scribe to his apprentice, S2-6–S2-7 (d)

The The Milindapanha (Questions of King Milinda), S8-4–S8-7 (d)

miners' testimony: Ashley Commission, S26-5–S26-6 (d)

Ming Dynasty: model of ship in flotilla of Zheng He, S12-6–S12-7 (v)

The Mingling of Two Oceans (Shikuh), S20-3–S20-5 (d)

Montagu, Mary Wortley: *Letters from the Levant* by, S25-2–S25-4 (d)

Mughal emerald box, S20-7 (v)

musket: of Janissaries, S16-12–S16-13 (v)

Mussolini, Benito: "Foundations and Doctrine of Fascism" by, S28-7–S28-8 (d)

My Own Story (Pankhurst), S26-11–S26-13 (d)

Nahuatl land sale documents: Mexico, S18-7–S18-8 (d)

Nigeria, Sungbo's Eredo, walls and moats, S14-8–S14-9 (d)

Nihongi (Chronicles of Japan), S13-4–S13-6 (d)

Nkrumah, Kwame, "I Speak of Freedom" by, S29-15–S29-17 (d)

Nüjie (Admonitions for Women) (Ban Zhao), S9-6–S9-7 (d)

Nzinga Mbemba (Afonso I) of Kongo: letter to King of Portugal, S19-3–S19-5 (d)

Obama, Barack: address to American youth, S31-7–S31-11 (d)

On The Sacred Disease (Hippocrates), S7-5–S7-8 (d)

opium trade suppression, S24-4–S24-6 (d)

The Origin of Species (Darwin), S26-9–S26-11 (d)

Ottoman Empire: Rose Garden Edict, S25-4–S25-6 (d)

Paine, Thomas: *Rights of Man* by, S22-10–S22-12 (d)

Pankhurst, Emmeline: *My Own Story* by, S26-11–S26-13 (d)

Paris: United Nations framework convention on climate change in, S31-12–S31-13 (d)

"The Path Which Led Me to Leninism" (Ho Chi Minh), S29-10–S29-12 (d)

Perestroika: New Thinking for Our Country and the World (Gorbachev), S30-2–S30-4 (d)

Peru: Caral–Supe culture: quipu from, S5-2 (v); Chavin de Huántar in: textile fragment from, S5-3 (v); Chinese coolie photograph, S23-9 (v); El Castio de Huarmey in: skeletons in Wari royal tomb site, S15-2–S15-3 (v)

Piedras Negras: Lady K'atun of, S6-6–S6-8 (v)

Pinsk, Russia: Gal'pern Matchbox Factory female workers' strike, S25-8–S25-11 (d)

poetry of Tang Dynasty, S12-4–S12-6 (d)

Pompeii: graffiti from walls of (anon.), S7-11–S7-12 (d)

Portugal, King of: letter from Afonso I of Kongo, S19-3–S19-5 (d)

"A Procession of Artisans at Istanbul" (Çelebi), S16-9–S16-11 (d)

Putin, Vladimir: address to Duma concerning annexation of Crimea, S31-04–S31-7 (d)

Qianlong Emperor: edicts to King George III of, S21-6–S21-9 (d)

Questiones naturales (Adelard of Bath), S11-3–S11-5 (d)

The Questions of King Milinda (The Milindapanha), S8-4–S8-7 (d)

Qur'an: amulet containing passages from worn by Muslim slaves who rioted in Bahia, Brazil, S23-6–S23-8 (d)

railroad: William Huskisson as first casualty of accident, S26-3–S26-4 (d)

A Record of Buddhistic Kingdoms: excerpts from, S8-8–S8-9 (d)

Reflections on the Revolution in France (Burke), S22-8–S22-9 (d)

Republic of Georgia, Dzudzuana Cave in: flax fibers from, S1-7 (v)

Rhino Cave, Botswana: python–Shaped ornamented rock from, S1-3 (v)

Rhode Island: documents on slave ship *Sally*, S19-5–S19-8 (v)

Ricci, Matteo: *China in the Sixteenth Century* by, S21-2–S21-4 (d)

Rights of Man (Paine), S22-10–S22-12 (d)

Roosevelt, Franklin D.: undelivered address planned for Jefferson Day, S28-11–S28-13 (d)

Rose Garden Edict, S25-4–S25-6 (d)

Russia: Alexander II's abolition of serfdom, S25-6–S25-8 (d); Metternich's secret memorandum to Alexander I, S22-12–S22-13 (d); Pinsk in: Gal'pern Matchbox Factory female workers' strike, S25-8–S25-11 (d)

Al–Saadi, Abd al-Rahman: on scholars of Timbuktu, S19-2–S19-3 (d)

Saint–Simon, duc de: "The Daily Habits of Louis XIV at Versailles" by, S17-9–S17-11 (d)

Sally slave ship: documents concerning, Rhode Island, S19-5–S19-8 (v)

San Miguel, Marina de: confessions before the Inquisition, Mexico City, of, S18-4–S18-6 (d)

Sarmiento, Domingo Faustino: *Travels in the United States in 1847* by, S23-4–S23-6 (d)

scandal at the church: José de Álfaro accuses Doña Theresa Bravo and others of insulting and beating his Castiza wife, Joséfa Cadena, S18-2–S18-4 (d)

The Second Sex (de Beauvoir), S30-6–S30-8 (d)

"Secret Plan for Managing the Country" (Toshiaki), S21-9–S21-11 (d)

serfdom abolition: by Alexander II, S25-6–S25-8 (d)

Seven Pillar Edits of King Ashoka, S8-2–S8-4 (d)

The Shangjun Shu (Book of Lord Shang), S4-5–S4-6 (d)

Shao, Duke of: announcement of, S4-3–S4-5 (d)

Shiji: "Memorial on the Burning of Books" from, S9-4–S9-5 (d)

Shijing (The Book of Odes), S4-2–S4-3 (d)

Shikibu, Murasaki: *The Tale of Genji* by, S13-2–S13-3 (d)

Shikuh, Muhammad Dara: *The Mingling of Two Oceans* by, S20-3–S20-5 (d)

slave ship *Sally:* documents concerning, Rhode Island, S19-5–S19-8 (v)

Smith, Edwin, Papyrus, three spinal injury cases in, S2-4–S2-5 (d)

Soseki, Natsume: *Kokoro* by, S24-9–S24-11 (d)

The Story of My Misfortunes (Abelard), S11-7–S11-8 (d)

"The Story of the Judge and the Fly" (Al-Jahiz), S10-2–S10-3 (d)

Sudan: *The Life of the Sudanese Mahdi* (Ibn 'Abd al-Qadir), S27-5–S27-6 (d); Meroë in: relief sculpture from, S6-3–S6-4 (v)

Suleiman the Magnificent: "The Court of Suleiman the Magnificent" on, S16-11–S16-12 (d)

Sungbo's Eredo: walls and moats, Nigeria, S14-8–S14-9 (d)

The Tale of Genji (Shikibu), S13-2–S13-3 (d)

Tang Dynasty: poetry of, S12-4–S12-6 (d)

Testament of Youth (Brittain), S28-4–S28-6 (d)

Thomas the Eparch: "The Fall of Constantinople" by, S16-7–S16-8 (d)

Tiananmen Square protests: coverage of, S30-8–S30-10 (d)

Timbuktu scholars: al–Saadi on, S19-2–S19-3 (d)

"Torture" from *Philosophical Dictionary* (Voltaire), S22-6–S22-7 (d)

Toshiaki, Honda: "Secret Plan for Managing the Country" by, S21-9–S21-11 (d)

"To the Person Sitting in Darkness" (Twain), S27-9–S27-11 (d)

Travels in the United States in 1847 (Sarmiento), S23-4–S23-6 (d)

Twain, Mark: "To the Person Sitting in Darkness" by, S27-9–S27-11 (d)

United Nations: framework convention on climate change of, S31-12–S31-13 (d);

Universal Declaration of Human Rights of, S29-2–S29-5 (d)

United States: *Travels in the United States in 1847* on, S23-4–S23-6 (d)

Universal Declaration of Human Rights: of United Nations, S29-2–S29-5 (d)

Vanuatu, western Pacific: Lapita pot shards from, S5-7 (v)

Varuna: prayer to, S3-5 (d)

Vasari, Giorgio: *The Life of Michelangelo Buonarroti* by, S17-11–S17-13 (d)

Victoria (Queen): Lin Zexu's letter to, S24-2–S24-3 (d)

Vietnam: Bodhisattva Avalokiteshvara copper head from, S13-9 (v)

Vita Caroli Magni (Life of Charlemagne) (Einhard), S11-2–S11-3 (d)

Voltaire: "Torture" from *Philosophical Dictionary* by, S22-6–S22-7 (d)

"Wage Labour and Capital" (Marx), S26-7–S26-9 (d)

Wari royal tomb site: at El Castio de Huarmey, Peru, S15-2–S15-3 (v)

West Africa: 'Abd al-'Azīz al-Bakrī: on, S14-7–S14-8 (d)

"What Educated Women Can Do" (Gandhi), S29-12–S29-14 (d)

"The White Man's Burden" (Kipling), S27-7–S27-9 (d)

Zheng He: Ming Dynasty model of ship in flotilla of, S12-6–S12-7 (v)

Subject Index

Page numbers followed by *f* denote a figure, page numbers followed by *m* denote a map, and page numbers in italics denote a picture.

Abbasids, 261; Byzantium and, 229; Nubia and, 331; Shiite Islam and, 228; in Syria, 225; Umayyads and, 224

Abd al-Malik, 223, 226

Abdülhamit II, 607–8

Abelard, Peter, 268–69

Abhidharma, 185

Abolition of slavery: in Brazil, 555; by Great Britain, 663; in Latin America, 569–70; in US, 541

Aboriginals: of Japan, 313; of Taiwan, 118. *See also* Australian Aboriginals

Abortion, 745; with China's one-child policy, 750

Absolutism: in France, 415–16; Locke and, 405

Abstract expressionism, *716*

Abzu, 49

AC. *See* Alternating current

ACA. *See* Affordable Care Act

Academy of Florence, 248

Academy of Medicine (France), 530

Academy of Sciences (Paris), 401

Aceh, 382, 668

Achaemenids: empire of, 150–52, 151*m*; government of, 152; Greece and, 154–55; Judaism and, 163, 165–66; military of, 151; polytheism of, 152; as Zoroastrians, 152

Acheulian tools, 7, *7*

Acropolis, 154, *155*

Adal, 456

Adelard of Bath, 270

Adena, 115, 116*m*

Admonitions for Women (Ban Zhao), 214

Adriatic Sea, Ottoman Empire and, 376–77

Advanced Research Projects Agency (ARPA), 786

The Aeneid (Virgil), 170, 171, *171*

Aeschylus, 170

Aesthetics, in China, 215

Affordable Care Act (ACA), 776

Afghanistan: Achaemenids and, 151; Great Britain and, 661; Mughals in, 479, 482; Soviet Union and, 737, *737*, 740–41; Sunni Islam in, 379; US and, 770

AFL. *See* American Federation of Labor

Africa: agriculture of, 125–31, 786; Americas and, 134; chiefdoms of, 126; China and, 786; Christianity in, 663; city-states of, 126–28; civilizing mission in, 663; Cold War in, 730–32; colonialism in, 663–67, 663–67*m*, 730; constitutionalism in, 732; economy of, 786; empires in, 473; fossils from, 3; France and, 666–67; Great Britain and, 666–67; history of, 134; Islam in, 785–86; kingdoms of, 125–30, 128*m*, 473; migrations from, 10, 11*m*; nation-states in, 722*m*, 730–32; origins of humanity in, 2–25, *6*; population growth in, 784–85; railroads in, 666–67; rain forests in, 17, 130–31; religion in, 451–52; rock art in, 47; savanna of, 130–31; sculptures in, 344–45, *345*; slaves from, 440, 461*m*, 473; state formation in, 328–49; transformations in, 784–86; witchcraft in, 451. *See also* East Africa; Northeast Africa; Southern Africa; Sub-Saharan Africa; West Africa; *specific countries*

African Americans: Harlem Renaissance of, 683, 686–87; lynchings of, 542; voting rights of, 542

African diaspora, 686–87; culture of, 468–71

African National Congress (ANC), 758, 762–63

African spirituality, 133, 330; in ancient Ghana, 342

Afrikaans Medium Decree, 758

Afrikaners, 459

Afro-Eurasian world commercial system, trade in, 241–42, 242*m*

Agrarian–urban centers (society): in Americas, 108–12; in China, 76–99; in East Africa, 131–34; in eastern Mediterranean, 26–53; in Egypt, 31–41, 32*m*; in Fertile Crescent, 27–31; gender relations in, 9; of *Homo sapiens*, 9; in India, 54–75; in Mesopotamia, 31–41, 32*m*; in Middle East, 26–53; in southern Africa, 131–34; in sub-Saharan Africa, 130–31, 132*m*; in Vietnam, 321–22

Agricultural estates (*haciendas*), 439, 563

Agriculture: in Africa, 125–31, 786; in Aksum, 128; in Amazon, 369; in Americas, 107–17; in China, 720–21; in East Africa, 132–33; in eastern Mediterranean, 29*m*; in Egypt, 39; in Europe, 260–61; in Fertile Crescent, 23, 27, 28–31; in Han dynasty, *210*, 210–11; in India, 66, 725; industrialization and, 626; of Islam, 261; in Japan, 314, 318; in Korea, 306; in Latin America, 568–69; in Middle East, 29*m*, 41; in Ming dynasty, 500–501, 509; of Mughals, 488; in Neolithic Age, 47; in Nubia, 331; in Papua New Guinea, *118*; in Philippines, 670; revolution in, 260–61; in Russia, 616–17; of Sasanids, 228; in Shang dynasty, 89; in Soviet Union, 693, *693*; of Tiwanaku, 355–56; in Vietnam, 323–24, 672; Yellow River and, 96; in Zhou dynasty, 90. *See also* Animal domestication; Plant domestication; *specific crops*

Agrippina the Younger, 159

Aguinaldo, Emilio, 671

Ahadith, 226

Ahimsa (nonviolence), 178, 183–84

Ahmadinejad, Mahmoud, 779

Ahoms, 483

Ahura Mazda, 152, 164

AIM. *See* American Indian Movement

Ainu, 313

Airplanes: invention of, 633; in September 11, 2011 terrorist attack, 770

Akbar, Jalal ud-Din, 480–81, 481*m*, 483, 484–85

Akhenaten, 48, *48*, 52–53

Akkad, 26, 35, 35*m*

Aksum, 128*m*, 128–30, *129*; silk and, 211

Alamo, 561

Alaouite dynasty, in Morocco, 377

Alaska, 10, 18, 19, 105

Albania, 609, 742, 777

Albigensians, 278–79

Alexander I, 614

Alexander II, 617, 623, 691

Alexander the Great, 67, 155, 157*m*; in Babylonia, 175; in India, 175, 176–77

Alexander V, 274

Alexius I Comnenus, 234–36

Algebra, 50, 168, 193, 244

Algeria, France and, 651, 660–61, 730

Alhambra of Granada, 245

Ali, Muhammad, 605, *607*, 662

Allah, 223, 301, 477

Allegory, 477

Allende, Salvador, 759

Alpaca, 108, 111, 142, 356

Alphabet: of Meroë, 127; of Phoenicians, 44, *44*

Altaics, 86, 306; Japan and, 313

Alternating current (AC), 631–33

Alt-Right, 776

Altruism, in Buddhism, 184

Amazon, rain forests of, 116, 369

The Ambassadors (James), 546

Amda Seyon, 335

Amenemhet III, 39

Amenhotep IV, 53

American Civil War, 541, 562

American Federation of Labor (AFL), 683

American Indian Movement (AIM), 744

American Indian Wars, 543

American Philosophical Society, 445

American Revolution, 524–26; constitutionalism and, 547

American System, 643, *643*

Americas, 100–117; Africa and, 134; agrarian–urban centers of, 108–12; agriculture of, 107–17; animal domestication in, 108, *108*; asteroids in, 106; caste system in, 440–43; Catholicism in, 443–44; cattle in, 439; climate change in, 106; colonialism in, 424–37, 428*m*; empires in, 350–69, 353*m*; environment of, 102–5, 104*m*; European culture and, 443–46; foraging in, 105–7; gravesites in, 107; iron in, 146; migrations to, 17–23, 22*m*; in Neolithic Age, 108–9; ocean currents of, 103–5; plantation slavery in, 439–40, 459–68; pyramids of, 101, 109; rock art in, 107, *107*; separate evolution of, 120–21; silver in, 438–39, *439*; slavery in, 463*m*; social classes in, 109, 440–43; spears (points) in, 105–6, 107; sub-Saharan Africa and, 145; wheat in, 439; women in, 441. *See also* Central America; Mesoamerica; North America; South America; *specific countries*

Amerindians. *See* Native Americans

Amida (Buddha of the Pure Land), 215, *320*

Amistad, *566*

Amitabha (Heavenly Buddha of the Western Paradise), 185

Ammonia, 631

Amun-Re, 52

Analects (*Lunyu*) (Confucius), 198, 299

Anales deTula, 444

Anatolia, 42; Achaemenids and, 151; Arabs in, 229; Byzantium and, 226, 229, 231; fire temples of, 165; Greece and, 689; polytheism in, 47–48

Anaximander, 165

ANC. *See* African National Congress

Ancestral worship, in Ming dynasty, 511

Ancient Ghana, 341–42

Andes, 102; chiefdoms of, 141–44, 144*m*; cities in, 109–12, 110*m*; foraging in, 115; human sacrifice in, 366, 366–67; mummies of, 366–67; roads in, 108; Tiwanaku of, 355–56, *356*, 357*m*, 368; trade in, 110; Wari of, 357*m*, 357–58, 368. *See also* Inca

Anglican Church, 412–13

Anglo-Saxons, 253

Angola, 666; civil war in, 757

Aniconism, 245–46

Animal domestication: in Americas, 108, *108*; in Fertile Crescent, 51–52; in Harappa, 60, *61*; in India, 65; in Middle East, 41; in Oceania, 119; in Shang dynasty, 89. *See also* Cattle

Animal Farm (Orwell), *684*

An Lushan, 289

Anne of Bohemia, 274

Anselm, Saint, 268

Anthony of Padua, Saint, 451

Antigonids, 156–57

Antinomian group, 445

Antioch, siege of, 236

Anti-Semitism, Black Death and, 271

Anzick-1 fossil, 20

Apaches, 435

Apartheid, in South Africa, 757–58, *758*, 762–63, 785

Aphorisms of Love (*Kama Sutra*) (Vatsyayana), 69–70, 192

Apocalypse: of Christianity, 166, 373–74; of Zoroastrians, 164

Apocalypticism, 228

Aponte, José Antonio, 567

Appeasement: of Japan, 701; of Nazi Germany, 696

Aquinas, Thomas, Saint, 265, 269, 276

Arabian Nights, 245

Arab-Israeli Wars, 752, 752–54, 753*m*

Arab League, 755

Arabs, 45; in Anatolia, 229; Christianity of, 222; conquests of, 223–24, 224*m*–25*m*; in East Africa, 335; in Egypt, 222; in India, 281; nationalism of, 778; Nubia and, 330, 331; oil embargo of, 754; OPEC of, 738; Sasanids and, 222; in Syria, 222; Zionism and, 688

Arab Spring, 778, 780–83; SNSs in, 786

Arafat, Yasir, 753, 754

Aragon, 372, 374

Archimedes, 168, 399

Architecture: of Harappa, 61; of Islam, 245; of Japan, 314; of Mughals, 494; of Ottoman Empire, 387–89, *388*; of Roman Empire, 171; of Sasanids, 169

Ardashir, 159

Ardi species, 5

Argentina, 551; cattle in, 569; colonialism of, 438; Creoles in, 552–54; Dirty War in, 760; exports of, 788; as nation-state, 552–54; populism in, 719

Aripithecus kaddaba, 4

Aristocratic landlords: in Byzantium, 239–41; of centralizing states, 387; in feudalism, 258; in Japan, 591; in Korea, 311; in Latin America, 552–64

Aristocratic Republic, 558

Aristophanes, 170

Aristotle, 165, *165*, 267; challenges to, 270; Machiavelli and, 397; scholasticism and, 268

Arjuna, 67

Ark of the Covenant, 334

Armenia: Ottoman Empire and, 608; Soviet Union and, 691; Turkey and, 689

Army of the Andes, 553

Arouet, François-Marie, 402

ARPA. *See* Advanced Research Projects Agency

Art Deco, 696

Artha, 69

Arthashastra (Kautilya), 67, 176

Articles of Confederation, 526

Artillery. *See* Cannons

Art of War (Sun Zi), 67

Arts: in Byzantium, 245–47; of Greece, 169–70; of India, 192–93; Islam and, 244; in Japan, 597; of Latin America, 572–73; in Ming dynasty, 511; modernity in, 646–47, *647*, 716; of Mughals, 493–94; of Persia, 168–69; of Renaissance, 396–98, 399; of Roman Empire, 170–71; of romanticism, 545. *See also* Rock art; *specific topics*

Aryans, 695; Harappa and, 63; Indo-Europeans and, 64–65

Asceticism: in Hinduism, 72, *72*; in Jainism, 182–83

Asháninka, 429

Ashante, 663–64

Ashoka, 178*m*, 178–79, *179*, 194

Asia: in Cold War, 724–29; migrations to Australia, 10–14; migrations to Europe from, 14–16; monsoons in, 57; nation-states in, 722*m*, 724–29. *See also* East Asia; Southeast Asia; *specific countries*

Al-Assad, Bashar, 782–83

Assemblies, in Mesopotamia, 32

Assembly line, 643, *643*; for Holocaust, 697

Assur, 43

Assyrians: in Egypt, 126; empire of, 43; Greece and, 170

Asteroids, in Americas, 106

Astrolabe, 406

Astronomy, 168; in China, 215–16; of Mughals, 491–92; in Renaissance, 395, 398–400

Aswan High Dam, 723

Atahualpa, *426*, 426–28

Atatürk (Mustafa Kemal), 689, *689*

Atheism, of Jainism, 184

Athens, 46, 152–54; democracy in, 153, 154, 173; women in, 173

Atlantic system, for slave trade, 466, 466*m*

Atlatl, 107

Atman (self), 72

Atomic bombs, at Hiroshima and Nagasaki, 702, *709*

Atomic physics, 644

Atum, 49

Augustine, 167, 253

Augustus, *158*, 158–59

Aurangzeb, 485–86

Austen, Jane, 545

Australia: geography of, 11–12; Great Britain and, 658–60; human adaptations from Africa in, 7–16; Ice Age in, 12,

17; migration from South Asia, 10–14; migrations to, 658–59; rain forests in, 17; rock art in, 47

Australian Aboriginals, 659; culture of, 12–13; Dreamtime of, 13; foraging by, 12; gender relations of, 12; rock art of, 2, *13*, 13–14; women of, 12

Australopiths (*Australopithecus*), 5

Austria: Habsburgs and, 382; Nazi Germany and, 696; Ottoman Empire and, 382; uprising in, 538

Austria-Hungary, 608; Treaty of Versailles and, 681

Austronesian language, 81

Autarky, 685

Auto-da-fé, 389, *390*

Automobile: assembly line for, *643*; invention of, 632

Avatars, 186–87

Averroes (Ibn Rushd), 244

Avesta, 164

Avicenna (Ibn Sina), 244, 270

Ayllu, 361–62

Azerbaijan, Soviet Union and, 691

Aztec, 145, 351, 358–60, *359m*, *360*, *362*, 364–65, *365m*; *Anales de Tula* of, 444; Spain and, 359, 424–26

Azurduy de Padilla, Juana, 551

Baath Party, 782

Babi movement, 612

Babur, Zahir ud-Din Muhammad, 479, *480*, *480m*

Baby-boom generation, 715, 745

Babylonia, 35, *35m*; Achaemenids and, 151; Alexander the Great in, 175; Assyrians and, 43; Judaism and, 163; laws of, 36–37. *See also* Neo-Babylonia

Babylonian captivity, 45

Bach, Johann Sebastian, 398

Bacon, Roger, 270

Bactria-Margiana Archaeological Complex (BMAC), 60, 61, 65

Badshahi Mosque, 494

Al-Baghdadi, Abu Bakr, 783

Baha'i faith, 612

Bahrain, 781

Bajondillo Cave, 21

Bakufu (tent government), 514

Balban, 284

Balfour Declaration, 688

Balkans: Byzantium and, 229; Islam in, 375–84; Ottoman Empire and, 609; Soviet Union and, 708; in World War I, 678–79

Balmeceda, José, 562

Baltic states, 742

Baluchistan, 58

Bambuk, 342

Bana, 282

Banana, 134

Ban Biao, 214

Bandaranaike, Sirimavo, 707, 724

Bandeirantes, 432

Bandung Conference, 726–27, *727*

Bangladesh, 56; as nation-state, 724

Ban Gu, 214

Banjo, 470

Bank of England, 626

Banks: China and, 588; in Dawes Plan, 695; in Europe, 275; factories and, 571; Great Depression and, 684; in Mexico, 771

Al-Banna, Hasan, 723

Banner system, of Manchus, 503

Banpo Village, 80–81, *81*

Bantus, 131, 132–33, 134

Bantustans, 762

Banu, Nadira, 494

Ban Zhao, 211, 214

Baojia, 298, 509

Barbados, 462, 464

Barometer, 402–3

Baron, 260

Baroque arts, 397–98

Barrel vaults, 169, 268

Baseball, 642

Basho, Matsuo, 518

Basilica, *265*, 268

Ba states, in Zhou dynasty, 88

Bathhouses, in Japan, 516, 517, 596

Battle of Adowa, 666

Battle of Agincourt, 273

Battle of Chaldiran, 378

Battle of Crécy, 273

Battle of Hastings, 259

Battle of Manzikert, 234, 235

Battle of Poitiers, 273

Battle of the Marne, 679

Battle of Tippecanoe, 543

Battle of Tours, 224, 255

Bautista de Toledo, Juan, 389

Bay of Pigs, 714

Beat Generation, 734–35

The Beatles, 734

Beatriz, Dona, 451–52

Becquerel, Antoine, 644

Beethoven, Ludwig van, 545

Being, 165

Belgium: Congo and, 666, 667, 674–75, 731–32; industrialization in, 628

Bell, Alexander Graham, 634

Benedict, Saint, 255

Benedictines, 255, 264

Benin, 458, *458*

Berbers, 223–24; in ancient Ghana, 342

Beringia Land Bridge, 18

Beringia Standstill, 19

Berlin Airlift, 709

Berlin Wall, 714–15, 742

Berlioz, Hector, 545

Bhagavad Gita, 67, 69, 186

Bharat, 67

Biafra, 756

Bible: in Germany, 409; translation of, 274. *See also* Hebrew Bible; New Testament

Big business: industrialization and, 642–43; in Japan, 698

Bilal, 329

Bin Laden, Osama, 770

Bipedalism, of hominins, 4

Birth of a Nation, 471

Al-Biruni, 406

Bismarck, Otto von, *539*, 539–40

Bismarck Archipelago, 118

Black Death (plague), 271–72, *272m*, 273; centralized kingdoms and, 405; in China, 243, 294, 500

Black earth, 616

The Black Man's Burden (Morel), 675

Black pepper, *190*, 190–91

Black Sea: Black Death and, 243; Catherine I "The Great" and, 614; Eastern Christianity and, 232; Ottoman Empire and, 603

Blackshirts, 693

Blanc, Louis, 639–40

Blitzkrieg (lightning war), 696

Blombos Cave, 10, *10m*

Bloody Sunday, 620

Bluefish Caves, 19

BMAC. *See* Bactria-Margiana Archaeological Complex

Board of Overseers, of Sparta, 154

Boccaccio, Giovanni, 276

Bodhisattva, *214*, 215, *320*; sculpture of, *192*

Bodhisattva, 185

Boers, 459, 757

Bohemia, 382

Bolan Pass, 56

Bolívar, Simón, 556–57

Bolivia, 551; as nation-state, 552–54, 556–57; silver in, 429

Bolshevik Revolution, 700

Bolsheviks, 620, 680, 691

Bonaparte, Louis-Napoleon. *See* Napoleon III

Bonaparte, Napoleon. *See* Napoleon Bonaparte

Boniface, Saint, 253

Boniface VIII, 273

Book of Hamza (*Hamzanama*), 493, *494*

Book of History. See Shujing

Book of Kings (*Shahname*) (Firdosi), 168, 245

Book of Mencius (*Mengzi*) (Mencius), 199, 299

The Book of Odes. See Shijing

Book of Sentences (Lombard), 270

The Book of Songs. See Shijing

Borana lunar calendar, 125, 133

Bosnia-Herzegovina: Bulgaria and, 608; Congress of Berlin and, 607; ethnic nationalism in, 679
Boston, 433
Boston Tea Party, 526
Bouazizi, Mohamed, 781, 782
Bourbons, 431–32
Bourgeoisie, 263, 637
Boxer Rebellion, 587–88, 699
Bradshaw paintings (Gwion Gwion), *13*, 13–14
Brahe, Sophie, 401
Brahe, Tycho, 401
Brahma, 186
Brahman, 72, 182
Brahmans, 70
Brazil: abolition of slavery in, 555; Canudos in, 574–75; Catholicism in, 575; coffee in, 556, 569; economy of, 760; exports of, 788; federalism in, 555; gold in, 432–33, *433*, 439; maps of, *429*; as nation-state, 554–56; plantation slavery in, 439, 462; populism in, 719; Portugal and, 428, 432–33, 554–55; slave revolts in, 566–67; Uruguay and, 554
Brazil, Russia, India, and China (BRIC), 766
Breech-loading weapons, 634
Brexit, 776
Brezhnev, Leonid, 738, 739–40
Brezhnev Doctrine, 740
BRIC. *See* Brazil, Russia, India, and China
Bride-price, 322
British East India Company, 507–8, 653; in India, 652–56; opium and, 579; Stamp Act and, 525–26
Brontë, Anne, 545
Brontë, Charlotte, 545
Brontë, Emily, 545
Bronze Age, 33–34; Achaemenids in, 150; in China, 96–97; collapse, 42, 43; India in, 65; in Japan, 314
Bronzes: in Jenné-jeno, 130; of Neolithic China, 81; of Shang dynasty, 77, 86, 93; of Xia dynasty, 83
Brunelleschi, Filippo, 397, 399
Bubonic plague. *See* Black Death
Buddha of the Pure Land (Amida), 215
Buddhism, *186*; Ashoka and, 178–79; caste system and, 190; in China, 214–15; of counterculture, 734; of East Asia, 215; Four Noble Truths of, 184–85; Hinduism and, 180; in India, 189, 194, 281–82; Islam and, 226; in Japan, 315, 319–20, 327; in Korea, 308, *309*, 312–13; Middle Way of, 184; in Ming dynasty, 511; Neo-Confucianism and, 298, 299, 302; *nirvana* and, 184–85; Noble Eightfold Path of, 184–85; spread of, *187m*; in Tang dynasty, 206–7, 287–90, 302; texts of, 185; in Vietnam, 321–22, 324–25; Zen, 215, 320, 327

Buffalo, 543
Buhari, Muhammadu, 727
Bulgaria: Bosnia-Herzegovina and, 608; Congress of Berlin and, 607; democracy in, 742; Ottoman Empire in, 608; in World War I, 679
Bulgars, 229, 231
Bullfights, 389
Bunraku, 518
Bunyoro kingdom, 455
Bureaucracy: of British India, 656–57; of China, 200; of Egypt, 38–39; of France, 416; of Harappa, 61; of Korea, 308; of Ming dynasty, 296; of Mughals, 478, 487–88; of Ottoman Empire, 386; of Song dynasty, 290; of Spanish colonialism, 429–31; of Tang dynasty, 289; of Vietnam, 323; of Zhou dynasty, 90–91
Burial sites. *See* Gravesites
Burma, 672; as nation-state, 724
Burroughs, William, 734
Burundi, 665
Bush, George H. W., 770
Bush, George W., 769, 770
Bushido (Way of the Warrior), 317, 327
Buyids, 336
Bye industries, 263
Byzantium, 231*m*; Anatolia and, 226, 229, 231; aristocratic landlords in, 239–41; arts in, 245–47; Balkans and, 229; Charlemagne and, 257; commonwealth of, *230*, 230–32; Eastern Christianity of, 223, 229–37; Egypt and, 223; iconoclasm in, 229–30; icons of, 246–47, *247*; Manzikert and, 234–35, *235*; military of, 232–33; Ottoman Empire and, 376; philosophy in, 247–48; provincial and central organization of, 239–40, *240*; recentralization of, 241; Renaissance in, 248; Roman Empire as, 223; Seljuk Turks and, 233–34; Zoroastrianism in, 278

Cahokia, 134
Cahuachi, 143
Calakmul, 135, 136
Calculus, 400, 491
Calendar: in Africa, 133; Borana lunar calendar, 125, 133; of Maya, 137; in Mexico, 125; of Mughals, 492; Nazca geoglyphs as, 146; in Russia, 680
Calicoes, 490
Caliphates, 227; Kanem-Bornu as, 454–55
Caliphs, 223, 227
Calligraphy: of China, 94, *95*, 215; of Japan, 316, 317, 518; Zen Buddhism and, 327
Calvin, John, 409
Calvinism, 409–12; in New England, 444–45
Cambodia, 672; Khmer Rouge in, 752
Camel, 32, 106, 222
Canaanites (Phoenicians), 44; alphabet of, *44*

Canada, France and, 435
Canadian Shield, 103
Canary Islands, 372
Cannons (artillery): breech-loading, 634; in colonialism, 658–59; in Iran-Iraq War, 755; of Ming dynasty, 509–10; of Ottoman Empire, 385
Canoes, 17
Canon law, 270
Canon of Medicine (Avicenna), 270
Canterbury Tales (Chaucer), 276
Canton system, of Ming dynasty, 507–8, *508*
Canudos, 574–75
Cao Xueqin, 592
Capet, Hugh, 259
Capetians, 259
Capitalism: in China, 748, 749; colonialism as, 673; critics of, 639; in Europe, 263; in Japan, 593–94; in Russia, 620
Capitalist democracy: Great Depression and, 684; modernity of, 766–74; of US, 766–74
Caral-Supe, 101, 109, 134
Caravel, 379
Carbon footprint, 788
Carburetor, 632
Caribbean: climate of, 103; Columbus to, 375; economy of, 565*m*; foraging in, 116–17; plantation slavery in, 460–62; population growth in, 718*m*; Spain in, 424; sugarcane in, 569; urbanization in, 718*m*
Caribs, 424
Carnation Revolution, 732
Carnegie, Andrew, 643
Carnegie Endowment, 683–84
Carolingians, 255, 277
Carranza, Venustiano, 564
Cartels: of big business, 642; in Japan, 593–94, 698
Carter, Jimmy, 754, 756
Carthage, 156–57
Cascajal stone, 115
Caste system: in Americas, 440–43; of Bunyoro Kingdom, 455; of India, 69, 70–71, 189–90, 286, 783
Castile, 372, 374
Castro, Fidel, 714
Çatal Hüyük, 47
Cataphracts, 151, 156
Catastrophe (Diamond), 122
Categorical imperative, 534
Cathars, 278–79
Catherine II "The Great," 613–14
Catholicism, 167; in Americas, 443–44; in Brazil, 575; in China, 507; in France, 537; French Revolution and, 527; Galileo and, 399–400; in Italy, 693; in Kongo, 459; Ku Klux Klan and, 683; in Latin America, 567–68, 572; in Mexico, 559; Nazi Germany and, 695; in Poland, 712; saints in, 444;

Thirty Years' War and, 413–15; in Vietnam, 672. *See also* Papacy

Catholic Reformation, 411; Baroque arts and, 397; education and, 444; New Sciences and, 401

Cattle: in Americas, 439; in Argentina, 569; in central Africa, 455

Cattle lords, 455

Caudillismo, 566

Caudillo, 556; in Mexico, 559; in Venezuela, 557–58

Cave painting. *See* Rock art

Caves: hominins in, 6–7; *Homo sapiens* in, 8; Neanderthals in, 14–15

Cavour, Camillo di, 539

Ceaușescu, Nicolae, 742

Celibacy, 232

Celluloid, 631

Celts, 253; ships of, 378

Central Africa, 455; chiefdoms and kingdoms of, 340–41; Livingstone in, 663

Central America: colonialism in, 430m; proxy wars in, 759. *See also* Mesoamerica

Central Intelligence Agency (CIA), 711; in Chile, 759; in Congo, 732; in Ghana, 731

Centralized kingdoms, 405–7

Centralizing states: in Europe, 386–87, 392, 420; in Middle East, 392

Cervantes, Miguel de, 390–91, 392–93

Césaire, Aimé, 687

Cesspits, 60

Ceuta, 374

Ceylon. *See* Sri Lanka

Chagatai, 292, 478, 493

Chalcedon (Chalcedonian church), 149–50

Chalcolithic Age (Copper Age), 33

Chalukyas, 180, 283

Chamberlain, Neville, 696, 697

Chan Buddhism. *See* Zen Buddhism

Chandragupta I, 180

Chandragupta Maurya, 175, 176–78, 183

Chaos, 170

Charaka Samhita, 193

Chariots: of Hittites, 42; in India, 65; in Middle East and eastern Mediterranean, 41; in Shang dynasty, 84–85, 86

Charlemagne, empires of, 254, 256m, 256–57, 257; Germany and, 260

Charles I, 420

Charles IV, 272

Charles V, 371, 380–82, 386–87; Protestant Reformation and, 409

Charles VII, 273

Charles X, 537, 651

Chartism, 640

Châtelet, Émilie du, 402

Chattel, slaves as, 460

Chaucer, Geoffrey, 276

Chauvet Cave, 15

Chávez, Hugo, 787

Chavín de Huántar, 110–12, *111*, 134

Chemicals, 631

Cheng (First Emperor), *202*, 202–3, 217

Chernobyl nuclear accident, 742

Chernyshevsky, Nikolai, 623

Cheyenne, 435

Chiang K'ai-shek, 700–701, 720

Chiapas, 254

Chichén Itzá, 354–55, *355*

Chiefdoms: of Africa, 126; of Andes, 141–44, 144m; of central Africa, 340–41; of Mesoamerica, 134–41; in Mexican Basin, 352; of sub-Saharan Africa, 146

Childebert II, 255

Child labor, 640–41; in coal mines, 639, *639*

Chile: copper in, 568; exports of, 788; gold in, 429; as nation-state, 558; populism in, 719; proxy war in, 759

China: aesthetics in, 215; Africa and, 786; agrarian society in, 76–99; agriculture of, 720–21; astronomy in, 215–16; Black Death in, 243, 294, 500; in BRIC, 766; Bronze Age in, 96–97; Buddhism in, 185, 214–15; bureaucracy in, 200; calligraphy of, 94, 95, 215; capitalism in, 748, 749; Catholicism in, 507; climate of, 78–80, 79m, 97; colonialism by, 586–87; communism in, 774–75; Communist Party in, 700, 720–21; Confucianism in, 198–200; coolies from, 570; cotton in, 502; Cultural Revolution in, 738, 748–50; culture of, 82, 96; Daoism in, 200–201; deserts of, 78, 80; economy of, 766, 774, 774–75; empires in, 198–207; environment of, 97; Europe and, 507; exports of, 290; feudalism in, 295; Four Modernizations in, 749–50, 774; France and, 587; geography of, 78–80, 79m; Great Leap Forward in, 720–21; Great Wall of, 2–5, 202, 216, 296; greenhouse gases in, 789; imperial unification of, 196–218; import-substitution industrialization in, 768; India and, 748; Industrial Revolution in, 500; irrigation in, 202; Japan and, 326, 512–13, 513m, 515, 584–85, *586*, 586–87, 700, 701; Korea and, 307–9, 315, 326, 711–12; land reform in, 720; languages in, 81; literature in, 300; migrations from, 571m; modernism in, 577; Mongols in, 275; nationalism in, 700–701; Neo-Confucianism in, 520; in Neolithic Age, 80–82, 97; nomads in, 203–4; nuclear weapons of, 748; one-child policy in, 750; porcelain in, 208, 216, 502, 505, *505*; Portugal and, 507; printing in, 216; Protestantism in, 593; responsibility system of, 749; rice in, 82; roads in, 202; science and technology in, 584–85; ships of, 262, 378; silk in, 80–81, 208, 502; Silk Road in, 203, 210–11; social classes in, 203;

social stratification in, 84; South Africa and, 757; Soviet Union and, 719, 721, 738, 748; steam engine in, *581*; stirrups in, *206*, 206–7; tea from, 290, 317, 320, 502; textile industry in, 627; Thermidorean Reaction by, 748; Three Kingdoms period in, 205; trade by, 502, 502m; treaty ports in, 582m; in UN, 749; Vietnam and, 729, 748, 752; women in, 98–99, 217–18; women's rights in, 747; in World War I, 679; writing in, 202, 204; Yellow River in, 78–83. *See also* Han dynasty; Mandate of Heaven; Ming dynasty; Qin dynasty; Qing dynasty; Shang dynasty; Song dynasty; Tang dynasty; Xia dynasty; Yuan dynasty; Zhou dynasty

Chinampas, 364–65

Chishti, Salim, 482, *483*

Cholas, 180, 283

Choson, 307

Christianity: in Africa, 663; in Aksum, 129; apocalypse of, 166, 373–74; of Arabs, 222; church of, 166–67; in Ethiopia, 333–35, 456; in Granada, 374–75; in Iberia, 372–75; in India, 654, 655; in Indian Ocean, 382; Islam and, 226, 372–84, 391; in Japan, 515; in Kongo, 458–59, *459*; in Mesopotamia, 149–50; of Native Americans, 432, 435; Nietzsche on, 646; in Nigeria, 756; in northeast Africa, 330–35, 347; origins of, 166; in Ottoman Empire, 606; paganism to, 255; in Persia, 160; in Roman Empire, 159–61; as state religions, 249; Sufism and, 243. *See also* Catholicism; Coptic Christianity; Eastern Christianity; Protestantism; Western Christianity

Chromaticism, 647

Chronicles of Japan (*Nihongi*), 321

Chungin, 312

Chu nom (southern characters), 325

Church Fathers, 167, 708

Churchill, Winston, 697

Chushingura (*The Forty-Seven Ronin*) (Monzaemon), 518

CIA. *See* Central Intelligence Agency

Circumcision, 388

Cistercians, 264

Cities, city-states: of Africa, 126–28; of Andes, 109–12, 110m; of East Africa, 133–34, 335–37, 336m; of Greece, 46, 152–55, 153m; of Harappa, 59m, 59–60; of Inca, 362; of Italy, 156; of Mesoamerica, 112–16; of Mesopotamia, 4, 33–34; of Ming dynasty, 297; of Oceania, 121; of Phoenicians, 44; of Sicily, 156; of sub-Saharan Africa, 146; of Swahili, 134, 336, 338m, 665

Citizen Amendment Bill, in India, 783

The City of God (Augustine), 167

"City of Victory" (Vijayanagar), 283

Civil Code, in France, 529

Civilizing mission, in Africa, 663
Civil Rights, Act of 1964, 744
Civil rights movement: student
    demonstrations for, 745–46; in US, 744–45
Civil service (India), 656
Civil wars: American Civil War, 541, 562; in
    Angola, 757; from Arab Spring, 782–82;
    in England, 412–13, 420–21; in France,
    411–12; in Lebanon, 754–55; in Nigeria,
    756; in Rwanda, 770; in Somalia, 785; in
    Soviet Union, 692–93; in Spain, 696; in
    Sudan, 771; in Syria, 778; in Yemen, 765; in
    Yugoslavia, 777
Cixi (Empress Dowager), 290, 303, 585
Clans: in African diaspora, 469; of Andes, 357;
    of Australian Aboriginals, 13; of Aztec, 365;
    in India, 69, 70–71; in Japan, 314, 315; in
    Vietnam, 322, 324; in Xia dynasty, 83
Clarified butter (ghee), 65
Classic of Documents. See Shujing
Classic of Filial Piety (Xiaojing), 214
Classic of the Way and Virtue (Daode Jing), 200
Claudius Ptolemy, 168
Cleisthenes, 153
Clement V, 273
Clement VII, 274
Clermont (steam ship), 627
Client states, of Shang dynasty, 85
Climate: of Caribbean, 103; of China, 78–80,'
    79m, 97; of Japan, 313, 314m; of Korea,
    306, 308m; of Mesoamerica, 103; of North
    America, 103; of South America, 103
Climate change, 790m; in Americas, 106;
    global warming and, 788–90; Harappa and,
    62; hominins and, 4; Neanderthals and, 20;
    in Teotihuacán, 141. See also Ice Age
Clinton, Bill, 769
Clinton, Hillary, 776
Clive, Robert, 652, 653
Cloves, 283
Clovis (Frankish king), 254
Clovis-first debates, 106
Clovis points, 19, 105–6
Coal mines, 626, 639, 640–41
Cochinchina, 672
Code of Manu, 69
Codex Justinianus, 162
Coercive Acts (Intolerable Acts), 526
Coffee: in Brazil, 556, 569; in Latin America,
    569; New Sciences and, 401; Ottoman
    Empire and, 382; in Vietnam, 672
Cold War, 708–33, 710m; in Africa, 730–32;
    Asia in, 724–29; containment in, 708;
    Cuban Missile Crisis in, 715, 738, 750;
    Egypt in, 723–24; end of, 736–63; Hungary
    in, 713, 713; Korea in, 711–12; NAM in,
    707, 724, 726–27; nation-states in, 719–32;
    Palestine and, 721–23; Poland in, 712;
    weapons in, 713–14; Yugoslavia in, 708–9
College of Cardinals, 264, 273, 274

Colombia: democracy in, 718; land reform in,
    719; Marxism in, 787; in NAM, 727; slave
    revolts in, 471
Colonialism: in Africa, 663–67, 663–67m,
    730; in Americas, 424–37, 428m; as
    capitalism, 673; in Central America, 430m;
    by China, 586–87; competition in, 661m;
    in Cuba, 438; in East Africa, 665–66; by
    England, 435–36, 524–25, 525m; in Korea,
    586–87; in Middle East, 660–63; in North
    America, 433–46, 435m, 524–25, 525m; in
    Polynesia, 119; by Portugal, 432–33; 1750-
    1914, 650–75; social Darwinism and, 645;
    in South America, 430m; in Southeast Asia,
    586–87, 667–73, 669m; by Spain, 428–32;
    in West Africa, 663–65
Columbian Exchange, 436–37, 437m, 438;
    China and, 500
Columbus, Christopher, 375, 375
Comanches, 435; Mexico and, 559–60
COMECON. See Council for Mutual
    Economic Assistance
Commanderies, in China, 203
Commedia dell'arte, 397
Committee of Public Safety, in French
    Revolution, 528
Committee of Union and Progress (CUP),
    608–9
Commonwealth of Independent States, 742
Commune, 548–49
Communism: in China, 774–75; in Congo,
    732; in Cuba, 714; in Greece, 708–9;
    Hitler and, 695; Marx and Engels in,
    640; McCarthy and, 712; in sub-
    Saharan Africa, 784; in Vietnam, 750–52,
    775; in Yugoslavia, 777. See also Soviet
    Union
The Communist Manifesto (Marx and Engels),
    640
Communist Party: in China, 700, 720–21;
    in France, 686; in Poland, 742; in Soviet
    Union, 691–92
Companion to Urania (Urania propitia)
    (Cunitz), 395
Compass, 262, 406
Comte, Auguste, 545
CONADEP. See National Commission on the
    Disappearance of Persons
Concert of Europe, 660
Concordat of Worms, 264
Confessions (Augustine), 167
Confucianism: in China, 198–200; in Han
    dynasty, 212–14; Islam and, 226; in Korea,
    308; Legalism and, 200; in Ming dynasty,
    297; in Qin dynasty, 203; in Vietnam, 323.
    See also Neo-Confucianism
Confucius, 96, 97, 198, 217
Congo (Zaire): Belgium and, 666, 667, 674–
    75, 731–32; as nation-state, 731–32. See also
    Democratic Republic of the Congo

Congo Reform Association, 675
Congress of Berlin, 607
Congress of Vienna, 536–37, 537m, 614
Conrad III, 267
Constance of Sicily, 260
Constantine I the Great, 159–60, 171
Constantine XI, 377
Constantinople, 232; Jerusalem and, 236, 237;
    Ottoman Empire and, 376–77; Russia and,
    616, 618; Western Christianity in, 234,
    270–76
Constitutionalism: in Africa, 732; American
    Revolution and, 547; in England, 418–19;
    ethnic nationalism and, 535, 547–48; in
    France, 523; French Revolution and, 547;
    in Haiti, 535; in Latin America, 552–64,
    566–67, 690; Locke and, 405; in Mexico,
    563–64; in Nigeria, 756; in Ottoman
    Empire, 606–7; in Russia, 613
Constitutional monarchy, in France, 527
Consumerism: in US, 681–83; after World
    War II, 715–16
Containment, in Cold War, 708
Continental Association, 526
Continuous-flow production, 643, 643
Contraception, 745
Cook, James, 658
Coolidge, Calvin, 683
Coolies, 570
Cooper's Ferry, 19, 102
Copernicus, Nicolaus, 168, 398
Copper: in Africa, 130; in Chile, 568; of
    Hopewell, 101, 101; of Neolithic China, 81;
    in Tichitt and Oualata, 126; of Toltec, 352
Copper Age (Chalcolithic Age), 33
Coptic Christianity, 167; in Aksum, 129; in
    Ethiopia, 456; in Nubia, 330, 331, 333
Cordilleran ice sheet, 17, 19
Cordilleras, 102
Cordite, 634
Coricancha, 365
Corn, 108, 112, 112–13, 113m, 146; in central
    Africa, 455; in Ming dynasty, 500
Corn Laws, of England, 544
Coronation, 255
Corporate state, 693–94
Corpus Iuris Civilis (Justinian), 269–70
Corsairs, 371
Cortés, Hernán, 425, 425–26
Corvée, 324
Costa Rica: coolies in, 570; democracy in,
    718; populism in, 719
Cottage industries, 626
Cotton: calicoes of, 490; in China, 502;
    coolies and, 570; in East Africa, 665; from
    India, 490, 626; in Nubia, 331
Council for Mutual Economic Assistance
    (COMECON), 709
Council of Constance, 275
Council of Elders, of Sparta, 153–54

Council of Nicaea, 160

Council of Trent, 411

Counterculture, 734–35

The Course of Positive Philosophy (Comte), 545

COVID-19, 681, 766; China and, 775

Creation myths, 49, 170; of Inca, 360

Creed, 232

Creole Christianity, 435

Creoles, 428, 431, 440, 550–75; from African diaspora, 468–70; in Argentina, 552–54; in Kongo, 459; literature of, 573; in Mexico, 558–59, 562–63

Crete, 39–41

Crimea: Catherine II "The Great" and, 614; Russia and, 772

Crimean War, 616, 631, 661

Cro-Magnon, 2

Cromwell, Oliver, 413

Crucifixion, of Jesus of Nazareth, 264–65, *265*

Crusades, 235–37, 236*m*, 266–67; Egypt and, 237; First, 234, 266*m*; Fourth, 234, 237, 248; Jerusalem in, 267; Second, 236; Third, 237, 267

Ctesiphon, 156, 169, *169*

Cuauhtémoc, 426

Cuba: colonialism in, 438; communism in, 714; coolies in, 570; Cortés and, 425; land reform in, 717; slave revolts in, 566–67

Cuban Missile Crisis, 715, 738, 750

Cubism, 646, *647*

Cultivation system, in Indonesia, 668

Cultural nationalism, of Germany, 535–36

Cultural Revolution, in China, 738, 748–50

Culture: of African diaspora, 468–71; of Australian Aboriginals, 12–13; in China, 82, 96; of Enlightenment, 533–35; of Europe, Americas and, 443–46; of Greece, 169–70; of Habsburgs, 392; of Harappa, 60–61; Hellenism, 155, 165; in High Middle Ages, 267–70; of *Homo sapiens*, 3–4; in India, 68–73; of Islam, 243–45, 249; in Japan, 320–21, 597; in Korea, 312–13; of Latin America, 572–73; of Meroë, 127–28; in Middle East, 47–50; in Ming dynasty, 511; of Ottoman Empire, 392; of Persia, 168–69; of Qing dynasty, 592–93; of Renaissance, 394–421; of slaves, 471; of Song dynasty, 290; of Vietnam, 323; after World War II, 715–16. *See also* Arts; Enlightenment; *specific topics*

Cuneiform writing, 34, *34*

Cunitz, Maria, 395, 401

Cunningham, Alexander, 55

CUP. *See* Committee of Union and Progress

Curie, Marie, 644

Cuzco, 144, 360–61, 365, 368, 428

Cyprus: Great Britain and, 662; Minoan kingdoms of, 39–41

Cyrus II the Great, 150–51

Czar (tsar), 416; collapse of, 680

Czechoslovakia: Marshall Plan and, 709; Nazi Germany and, 696; Prague Spring in, 739–40

Da Gama, Vasco, 375, 486, 507

Daimyo, 317, *318,* 320, 327, 514

Dai Viet (Great Viet), 323

Dalai Lama, 505

Dalits, 70

Dante Alighieri, 276

Dao (Way), 198, 299

Daode Jing (*Classic of the Way and Virtue*), 200

Daoism, 200–201; Han dynasty and, 205; Islam and, 226; in Ming dynasty, 511; Neo-Confucianism and, 298, 299, 302

Daoxue, 299

Dapenkeng, 81

Darwin, Charles, 644–45, *645*

Dasas, 63, 70

Daughters of Liberty, 525

Da Vinci, Leonardo, 397

Dawes Plan (US), 695

Death in the Snow (Makovsky), *621*

Decameron (Boccaccio), 276

Deccan Plateau, 56

Decembrist Revolt, 614

Decimal system, of Harappa, 60

Declaration of Independence, 526, 606

Declaration of the Rights of Man and of the Citizen, 527, 606

Decolonization. *See* Nation-states

Decretum (Gratian), 270

De Gaulle, Charles, 728

De Klerk, Frederik Willem, 758

De la Cruz, Juana Inés, 448

Demesne, 259

Democracy, 47; in Athens, 153, 154, 173; in Bulgaria, 742; in India, 725; in Latin America, 718–19. *See also* Capitalist democracy

Democratic Republic of the Congo, 665, 785

Les Demoiselles d'Avignon (Picasso), 646, *647*

Deng Xiaoping, 721, 748, 749

Denisovans, 14

Denmark, Protestant Revolution in, 409, 540

Department of Commerce and Labor, US, 543

Descartes, René, 404, 534

The Descent of Man (Darwin), 645

Description of Africa (al-Wazzan), 371

Deserts: of China, 78, 80; in Ghana, 341; of India, 57; Kalahari, 17, 133

Dessalines, Jean-Jacques, 532

Détente, 738, 739

Deval, Pierre, 651

Devotion, in Hinduism, 180, 185–87

Devşirme, 385, *386*

Dharma: in Buddhism, 178–79; in Vedas, 67, 69; wheel of, 192

Di, 94

Dialectic, 545

Dialectical materialism, 640

Diamond, Jared, 122

Díaz, Porfirio, 562–63

Dickens, Charles, 546

Diderot, Denis, 533; Catherine I the Great and, 613

Diggers, in England, 420–21

Dihar, 281

Dinh Bo Linh, 323

Diocletian, 159

Dionysiac cult, 170

Dionysius Exiguus, 265

Dirigibles, 633

Dirty War, in Argentina, 760

Disease burdens, Neanderthals and, 21

The Divine Comedy (Dante), 276

Divine wind (*kamikaze*), 316

Dmanisi Cave, 6–7

Doctrine of the Mean, 299

Dollar regime, of US, 767, 771

Dome of the Rock, 223

Dominic, Saint, 265

Dominicans, 265; in China, 507

Donatello, 397

Donation of Constantine, 233

Don Quixote (Cervantes), 390–91, *392–93*

Dorgon, 503

The Dream of the Red Chamber (*Hong Lou Meng*) (Cao Xueqin), 592

Dreamtime, 13

Duarte, Eva, 719

Dubček, Alexander, 739–40

DuBois, W. E. B., 686–87

Du Fu, 290

Dulles, Allen, 714

Duma, 621

Dura-Europos, *167*

Durga, 187

Dutch learning, 515, 521

Dutch United East India Company (VOC), 667–68

Dutch West India Company, 459

Dynamite, 634

Early Classic Period, of Maya, 136

Early Dynastic Period, of Egypt, 26, 38

Early humans. *See* Agrarian–urban centers; Neolithic Age; Paleolithic Age

Earthquake detector, *215,* 216

East Africa: agrarian–urban centers of, 131–34; agriculture of, 132–33; city-states in, 133–34, 335–37; colonialism in, 665–66; foraging in, 132; Indonesia and, 133; Islam in, 348; kingdoms in, 335–37; trade by, 242

East Asia: Buddhism of, 215; printing in, 310–11. *See also* China; Japan

Easter, 265

Easter Island (Rapa Nui), 118, 119, *122,* 122–23

Eastern Christianity: Black Sea and, 232; of Bulgars, 231; of Byzantium, 223, 229–37; evolution of, 249–50; height of civilization, 237–43; iconoclasm of, 229–30; Western Christianity and, 233

Eastern Mediterranean: agrarian–urban centers in, 26–53; agriculture of, 29m; chariots in, 41

Eastern Syriac Church, 167

East Germany (German Democratic Republic): Berlin Wall and, 714–15, 742; uprising in, 712

East India Railway, 55

Economy: of Africa, 786; of Brazil, 760; of Caribbean, 565m; of China, 766, 774, 774–75; of Enlightenment, 534; of Europe, 776–77; of Han dynasty, 208–11, 209m; of India, 188–89, 286; of Japan, 318, 515–18, 516m; of Latin America, 564–72, 565m, 574; money, 385; of Mughals, 488–90; of Nazi Germany, 696; of 1970s and 1980s, 747–48; of Ottoman Empire, 609; of Qing dynasty, 591–92; of Russia, 771–72; of Shang dynasty, 89–90; of US, 771, 776–77; of Vietnam, 323–24; of Zhou dynasty, 90–91

Ecuador, 719

Edict of Nantes, 412

Edison, Thomas, 642

Education: Catherine II "The Great" and, 613; Catholic Reformation and, 444

Edward I, 260

Edward III, 272–73

Edwin Smith Papyrus, 50

Egypt: Achaemenids and, 152; agrarian-urban centers in, 31–41, 32m; Arabs in, 222; Arab Spring in, 780–82; Assyrians in, 126; bureaucracy in, 38–39; Byzantium and, 223; in Cold War, 723–24; Coptic Christianity in, 167; creation myth of, 49; Crusades and, 237; Early Dynastic Period in, 26; Free Officers in, 723–24; Great Britain and, 662, 662, 688–89; hieroglyphic writing in, 38, 38–39; Hittites and, 42; India and, 74–75; irrigation in, 32; Islam in, 236, 242; Israel and, 738, 754; Judaism in, 242; kingdoms of, 38–39, 42; land reform in, 723; literature in, 48–49; Mamluks in, 233, 237, 238–39, 239; medical science in, 50; Muslim Brotherhood in, 723, 753; in NAM, 707, 724; Napoleon Bonaparte in, 603; nomads in, 32; Nubia in, 126; Ottoman Empire and, 605, 608; paintings of, 49–50; Philistines and, 44–45; Phoenicians and, 44; polytheism in, 48; pyramids of, 38–39, 39; religion in, 52–53; sharecroppers in, 32; in Six-Day War, 753; Sunni Islam in, 237; temples in, 33; tombs in, 33; women in, 37–38; women's rights in, 747. *See also* Nile River

Eiffel, Alexandre Gustave, 642

Einstein, Albert, 644

Eisai, 320

Eisenhower, Dwight D., 712, 714, 729

Elamo-Dravidian family, 58

El Castillo cave, 15

Electricity: for incandescent light bulb, 642; in second Industrial Revolution, 631–32

Elements (Euclid), 399

El Greco, 390

Eliot, George, 546

Elizabeth I, 412

Elmina, 457

El Mirador, 136, 136

El Niño, 105

El Paraíso, Peru, 109–10

El Salvador, 759

Emancipation Edict (Russia), 617, 623

Emmebaragesi of Kish, 35

Empires: in Africa, 473; in Americas, 350–69, 353m; in China, 198–207; in India, 174–95; of Japan, 590, 590m; of Persia, 155–63; World War I and, 677–81. *See also specific empires*

Empress Dowager (Cixi), 290, 303, 585

Encomiendas (land-labor grants), 424, 425

Encyclopédie (Diderot), 533

Energy: for industrialization, 626–27; in second Industrial Revolution, 631–33

Enfield rifles, 655

Engels, Friedrich, 639, 640

England: American Revolution and, 524–26; Black Death in, 271; Brexit of, 776; Calvinism in, 412–13; civil war in, 412–13, 420–21; colonialism by, 435–36, 524–25, 525m; constitutionalism in, 418–19; Glorious Revolution in, 524, 668; Hundred Years' War and, 272–73, 274; India and, 486–87; Jamaica and, 431; Luddites in, 649; mercantilism of, 462; military of, 413; New Sciences in, 401; opium in, 579–84, 580m; Plantagenet kings of, 259; political reorganization in, 274; privateers of, 465; Protestant Revolution in, 409; Scotland and, 418; in Seven Years' War, 437, 524, 526–27, 652; Three Kingdoms of, 413

Enheduanna, 27

Enlightenment, 524; Catherine II "The Great" and, 613; culture of, 533–35; economy of, 534; ethnic nationalism and, 535–36; French Revolution and, 526; in Germany, 535–36; Haiti and, 532; industrialization and, 626; Jefferson and, 526; literature of, 534; Mexico and, 558; music of, 534; Napoleon Bonaparte and, 529; philosophy of, 533–34; romanticism and, 544–45; after World War II, 716

Entente Cordiale, 667

Enuma Elish, 49, 170

Environment: of Americas, 102–5, 104m; of China, 97; of Fertile Crescent, 28–29,

51; of Ice Age, 17; of Korea, 306, 308m; of Oceania, 118–19. *See also* Climate; Climate change

Equal Rights Amendment (ERA), 746–47

Erasmus, Desiderius, 397

Erdoğan, Recep Tayyip, 780, 781

Eritrea, 666; Italy and, 694

Erligang, 89

Erlitou, 83

El Escorial, 389

Estancias (estates), 554

Estates-General, 259, 527

Estonia, 742

Ethiopia, 130, 333–35, 335m, 667; Christianity in, 333; coffee in, 382; Coptic Christianity in, 456; Italy and, 666, 694; Meroë and, 129; Portugal and, 456–57; Roman Empire and, 163

Ethnic cleansing, in Yugoslavia, 777

Ethnic nationalism: in Bosnia-Herzegovina, 679; constitutionalism and, 547–48; Enlightenment and, 535–36; of Greece, 604–5; in Italy, 538–39; of Zionism, 688

Eubanks, Mary, 113

Eucalyptus, 12

Eucharist, 232, 507

Euclid, 399

Eugenics, 683–84

Eunuchs, of Ottoman Empire harems, 388

Euphrates River, 28, 31; Judaism on, 167; Sasanids and, 228; synagogues on, 167

Eurasia, 148–73; contrasting patterns in, 280–303; human adaptations from Africa in, 7–16; India and, 56; Meroë and, 128; rock art in, 14; Shang dynasty and, 86; trade in, 285m. *See also specific countries*

Euripides, 170, 173

Europe: agricultural revolution in, 260–61; banks in, 275; capitalism in, 263; centralizing states in, 386–87, 392, 420; China and, 507; colonialism by, 119, 424–37, 428m; culture of, Americas and, 443–46; economy of, 776–77; famine in, 271; feudalism in, 257–58, 258f; firearms in, 384; guilds in, 263; High Middle Ages in, 267–70; industrialization in, 625, 630m; Jews and Judaism in, 263; literature in, 276; migrations from Asia, 14–16; migrations in, 636–37, 638m; Napoleon Bonaparte and, 529m; nation-states in, 536–40, 537m, 541m; philosophy in, 276; privateers of, 431; rock art in, 15, 16; ships of, 379; social classes in, 263; trade in, 261–62, 275; urbanization in, 263; World War II in, 696–98, 699m. *See also* Colonialism; Western Christianity; *specific countries*

European Concert, 539, 540

Evans, Mary Ann (George Eliot), 546

Evolution, theory of, 644–45

Ewuare, 458

"The Exaltation of Inanna" (Enheduanna), 27
Existentialism, 716
Explorer I, 714
Exports: from Australia, 659; from China, 290; from Latin America, 568–72, 574, 788; to US, 768; from Vietnam, 775
Extraterritoriality, 581
Ezana, 129

Factories, 639; in China, 508, *508*; industrialization and, 627; in Latin America, 571–72
Factory Act, 640
Falklands War, 760
"The Fall of the House of Usher" (Poe), 545
Family: in India, 190–91; in Japan, 318–19; in Latin America, 572; in Ming dynasty, 297–98; of Mughals, 490–91; in Qing dynasty, 508–9, 592; in Shang dynasty, 89–90
Famine: in Europe, 271; Great Famine, of Ireland, 544; in India, 725; in Japan, 518; in Russia, *617*
Faraday, Michael, 631
Far from the Madding Crowd (Hardy), 646
Fascism, in Italy, 693–94
Fashoda, 666
Fatehpur Sikri, 482
Fatimids, 228, 234, 236; Nubia and, 331
Faust (Goethe), 534
Fayyum, 31, 39
February Revolution, in Russia, 680
Federalism: in Brazil, 555; in Venezuela, 557
Federal Reserve Act, 543
Federal Trade Commission Act, 543
Female infanticide, 298
Feminism, 746*m*, 746–47
Ferdinand I, 381–82
Ferdinand II, 374, 375, 386–87; Thirty Years' War and, 413–14
Ferdinand IV, 262
Fernando VII, 557, 559
Fertile Crescent: agrarian–urban centers in, 27–31; agriculture of, 23, 27, 28–31; animal domestication in, 51–52; environment of, 28–29, 51; foraging in, 27, 28–31; hamlets in, 29–30; plant domestication in, 51–52
Fertilizers, manure, 261
Festivities: of Habsburgs, 390; of Ottoman Empire, 388
Feudalism: in China, 295; in Europe, 257–58, 258*f*; in Zhou dynasty, 88–89. *See also* Serfdom
Fichte, Johann Gottlieb, 536
Film industry: in US, 681; after World War II, 716
Final Solution, 697
Firdosi, 168, 245
Firearms, 384; breech-loading, 634; in colonialism, 658–59; Enfield rifles, 655; flintlock muskets, 406, 433, 658; in Japan,

514–15; matchlock musket, 406; of Ming dynasty, 509–10; of Mughals, 491; of Native Americans, 433, 435, 559; of Ottoman Empire, 386; revolver, 634; rifled musket, 634; samurai and, 514–15
Fire temples, 165
First Balkan War, 266*m*
First Crusade, 233, 264
First Emperor (Cheng, Qin Shi Huangdi), 202, 202–3, 217
The First New Chronicle and Good Government (Poma de Ayala), 444
First Opium War, 580, 588
First War of Independence, in India, 655–56
Flaubert, Gustave, 546
Flemish weavers, 253, 261
Flintlock muskets, 406, 658; of Native Americans, 433, 559
Flores Island, Indonesia, 24–25
Flying buttresses, on Gothic cathedrals, 269
Flying shuttle, 627
Food: from African diaspora, 470; French Revolution and, 527; in Japan, 516
Football Association, in Great Britain, 642
Foot binding, 217, 298, 592
Foraging: in Americas, 105–7; in Andes, 115; by Australian Aboriginals, 12; in Caribbean, 116–17; in East Africa, 132; in Fertile Crescent, 27, 28–31; by *Homo sapiens*, 8; in Mesoamerica, 115
Ford, Henry, 684
Former (Western) Han, 204
Fortunate Edict, 606
The Forty-Seven Ronin (*Chushingura*) (Monzaemon), 518
Fossils, 20; from Africa, 3
Fourier, Charles, 640
Four Modernizations, in China, 749–50, 774
Four Noble Truths, of Buddhism, 184–85
Fourteen Points, of Wilson, 680
Fourth Crusade, 234, 237, 248
Frame Breaking Act (England), 649
France: absolutism in, 415–16; Africa and, 666–67; Algeria and, 651, 660–61, 730; American Revolution and, 527; Calvinism in, 409–11; Canada and, 435; Catholicism in, 537; Catholic Reformation in, 411; China and, 587; civil war in, 411–12; Communist Party in, 686; constitutionalism in, 523; in Crimean War, 616, 631, 661; Estates-General in, 259; Great Depression and, 686; Haiti and, 523–24, 529–32, *530*; Hispaniola and, 431; Hundred Years' War and, 272–73, 274; India and, 486–87; industrialization in, 628; mandates to, 687–88; mercantilism of, 462; Mexico and, 561–62; modernity in, 651; monasteries in, reform of, 264; Nazi Germany and, 696; New Sciences in, 401; Ottoman Empire and, 381, 606; political reorganization in, 274; restoration

monarchy in, 537; Russia and, 614; in Seven Years' War, 437, 524, 526–27, 652; Suez Canal and, 723–24; Third Republic of, 540, 548–49; Thirty Years' War and, 413–15; Triple Intervention by, 590, 619; Tunisia and, 662–63; Vietnam and, 671–73, 729; West Africa and, 664–65; women's suffrage in, 641; World War II in, 696–97. *See also* French Revolution; Paris; World War I
Franciscans, 265, 373; in China, 507
Francis of Assisi, Saint, 265
Franco, Francisco, 696
Franco-Prussian War, 539, 661
Frankish Gaul, 254–55
Frankish inquest, 257
Franz Ferdinand, 681
Frederick I, 260
Frederick II "The Great," 417–18
Freemasons, 534
Free Officers, in Egypt, 723–24
French Revolution, 523, 526–29, *528*; constitutionalism and, 547; guillotine in, 530–31, *531*; Russia and, 614
Freud, Sigmund, 645
FSLN. *See* Sandinista National Liberation Front
Fugitive Slave Act, 471
Fu Hao, 77, 86, 91–92
Fujiwara no Kamatari, 315
Fulton, Robert, 627

Gaia, 170
Galen, 270
Galileo Galilei, 270, 399–400; Descartes and, 404
Gandhi, Indira, 497, 707
Gandhi, Mohandas "Mahatma," 689–90, *690*, 724–25
Ganges River, 56, 64, 74; Mauryas and, 176; Vedas and, 182
Gaozu (Liu Bang), 203
Garibaldi, Giuseppe, 539
Garvey, Marcus, 687
Gasoline, 632
Gatling gun, 634, *635*
Gauchos, 553
Gautama, Siddhartha, 182, 184
Gay Liberation Front (GLF), 745
Gays. *See* Homosexuals
Gaza, 778–79
Geisha, 517
Gender relations: of agrarian–urban society, 9; of Australian Aboriginals, 12; of Han dynasty, 211; of Inca, 365–66; of India, 69–70, 192; of Middle East, 35–38; of Ming dynasty, 298; of Mughals, 490–91; of Tang dynasty, 211. *See also* Women
Genesis, 49, 265
Genghis Khan, 237, 291, 294, 302; Timur and, 478–79

Genji Monagatori (Tale of Genji) (Murasaki Shikibu), 305, 321
Genoa, 372
Genocide: in Cambodia, 752; in East Africa, 665–66; of Jews, 697, 698
Genro, 589
Gentleman (*junzi*), 199
Geoglyphs, of Nazca, 143–44, 146–47
Geometry, 168; Islam and, 244
Georgia (nation-state): Ottoman Empire and, 603; Russia and, 771; Soviet Union and, 691
Georgia (US state), 474–75
Gerbert of Aurillac, 267–68, 270
German Confederation, 538
German Democratic Republic. *See* East Germany
German Southwest Africa, 665
Germany: Bible in, 409; big business in, 642–43; Bismarck and, 539, 539–40; Boxer Rebellion and, 587–88; Charlemagne empire and, 260; Congress of Vienna and, 536–37; cultural nationalism of, 535–36; East Africa and, 665; Enlightenment in, 535–36; hyperinflation in, 694–95, 695; industrialization in, 628; Morocco and, 667; New Sciences in, 401; papal reform and, 264; Soviet Union and, 708; steel from, 631; textile industry in, 665; Thirty Years' War in, 413–15; Triple Intervention by, 590, 619; Weimar Republic in, 694–95; women's suffrage in, 641. *See also* East Germany; Nazi Germany; World War I; World War II
Gestapo, 696
Ghana, 329–30; ancient, 341–42; as nation-state, 730–31. *See also* Ancient Ghana
Ghee (clarified butter), 65
Ghettos, Jews in, 263
Ghost Dance, 543
Gibbet, Halifax, 530
Gibraltar, 262
Gilgamesh, 48–49, 170
Ginsberg, Allen, 734
Glasnost, 740, 741–42
GLF. *See* Gay Liberation Front
Globalization: poor countries and, 772–74; US and, 768–69
Global warming, 788–90
Glorious Revolution (England), 413, 524, 668
Glyphic script, of Maya, 136
Goban Taiheiki (Monzaemon), 518
Göbekli Tepe, 47
Gobi Desert, 78
Go-Daigo, 316
Goethe, Johann Wolfgang von, 534, 535
Gold: Achaemenids and, 152; in Australia, 659, 660; of Aztec, 424; in Brazil, 432–33, 433, 439; at Chavín de Huántar, 110, 111; in Chile, 429; in East Africa, 338–40; in

ancient Ghana, 342; in Iberia, 341; of Inca, 426–28; in Jenné-jeno, 130; in Mali, 342–45; Mauryans and, 179; of Neolithic China, 81; in Nubia, 126; in West Africa, 341, 374, 377, 663
Golden Horde, 292
Golden Horn, 376, 388
Gold standard: China and, 701; of Great Britain, 568; US and, 767
Goodyear, Charles, 631
Gorbachev, Mikhail, 740, 741–42
Gothic cathedrals, 267, 267–68
Gouache, 493
Government: of Achaemenids, 152; Confucianism and, 198–99; Daoism and, 200–201; of East Africa, 337; of Harappa, 60–61; of Inca, 362; of Mughals, 487–88; of Nubia, 331; of Zhou dynasty, 90, 97. *See also* Bureaucracy
Government of India Act, 690
Gowon, Yakubu, 756
Granada: Christianity in, 374–75; Jews of, 375; Morisco of, 382, 384
Gran Colombia, 557
Grand Canal, in China, 205
Grand Secretariat, 296, 504
Grasses: in Australia, 12; teosinte, 108
Grasslands: in Ethiopia, 129; in India, 65; Neanderthals in, 20
Gratian, 270
Gravesites (tombs): in Americas, 107; in Egypt, 33; Egypt's pyramids, 38–39, 39; in Harappa, 62; of *Homo sapiens*, 99–10; in Japan, 315; of Neanderthals, 14; of Nubia, 126; of Olmec, 114; of Qin dynasty, 202, 202; in Shang dynasty, 91–92, 94; in Xia dynasty, 83
Gray, Tom, 3
Great Awakening, 446
Great Britain: abolition of slavery by, 663; Afghanistan and, 661; Africa and, 666–67; Australia and, 658–60; big business in, 642; coal mines in, 626; Concert of Europe and, 660; in Crimean War, 616, 631, 661; Cyprus and, 662; Egypt and, 662, 662, 688–89; in Falklands War, 760; Football Association in, 642; gold standard of, 568; Great Depression and, 685; India and, 652–56, 654m, 655, 655f, 657m, 689–90; industrialization in, 625, 626–27, 629m; Iraq and, 688; Israel and, 722; mandates to, 687–88; nation-states of, 544; Nazi Germany and, 696; in 1970s and 1980s, 747–48; Ottoman Empire and, 605, 662; paganism in, 253; Palestine and, 721–23; Russia and, 661; Sudan and, 662; Suez Canal and, 723–24; textile industry in, 639; Turkey and, 689, 689; urbanism in, 636; West Africa and, 663–64; women's suffrage in, 641; in World War II, 697–98; Zionism and, 688. *See also* England; Scotland; World War I

Great Depression, 684, 684–85; African railroads and, 667; France and, 686; Great Britain and, 685; in Italy, 694; in Latin America, 690–91
Great Enclosure, 340
Greater East Asia Co-Prosperity Sphere, 702
Great Famine (Ireland), 544
Great Game, 661
Great Indian (Thar) Desert, 57
Great Leap Forward, in China, 720–21
Great Learning, 299
Great Plains, Native Americans of, 435
Great Reform (*Taika*), 315
Great Reform Bill (England), 544
Great Viet (Dai Viet), 323
Great Wall of China, 2–5, 202, 216; Korea and, 308; in Ming dynasty, 296
Great War. *See* World War I
Great Zimbabwe, 339–40, 340
Greece: Achaemenids and, 154–55; alphabet of, 44; Anatolia and, 689; arts of, 169–70; city-states of, 152–55, 153m; communism in, 708–9; culture of, 169–70; kingdoms of, 45–47; literature of, 169–70; Middle East and, 155; Ottoman Empire and, 604–5, 608; Persians and, 150–55; philosophy of, 165; political rights in, 46–47; Russia and, 616; sculpture in, 170; Sea People from, 42, 44; Sufism and, 243; women in, 154; in World War I, 679; Yugoslavia and, 708–9
Greenhouse gases, 788–89; in China, 789
Gregory I, 253, 255
Gregory VII, 264
Gregory XI, 273–74
Gromyko, Andrei, 739
Grosseteste, Robert, 270
Guanajuato, 438
Guanches, 372
Guanyin, 214, 215
Guardian Council, in Iran, 755
Guatemala: populism in, 719; Toltec in, 354
Gudit, 333
Guerrero, Vicente, 559
Guilds, in Europe, 263
Guillotin, Joseph Ignace, 530–31
Guillotine, 530–31, 531
Gülen, Fethullah, 780
Gulf of Tonkin Resolution, 750–51
Gulf Stream, 103–5
Gullah, 470
Gumbos, 470
Guncotton, 634
Gunpowder, 292, 292–93; in second Industrial Revolution, 634
Gunpowder empires, 491
Gupta Empire, 161, 179–80, 181m; Huns and, 281
Gustavus II Adolphus, 414
Gu Yanwu, 511

Gwion Gwion (Bradshaw paintings), *13*, 13–14
Gypsies (Roma), 696

H1N1 influenza, 681
Habsburgs: centralizing states of, 386–87; culture of, 392; festivities of, 390; in Italy, 381; Ottoman Empire and, 376–84, 602; Poland and, 614; rise of, 380; in Spain, 380; Thirty Years' War and, 413–15
Haciendas (agricultural estates), 439, 563
Hadar AL 288-1 (Lucy), 3
Hadith, 226
Haiku, 518
Haiti: constitutionalism in, 535; plantation slavery in, 529–30; slave revolts in, 523–24, 529–32, *530*
Hajj (pilgrimage), 226
Hakra-Nara River, 62
Halo, 246, *483*
Hamas, 779
Hamlets: in Chavín de Huántar, 110; in Fertile Crescent, 29–30; of Paracas, 143
Hammurabi, 35, 36–37
Hamzanama (Book of Hamza), 493, *494*
Han dynasty, in China, 88, 203–5, *204m*; agriculture of, *210*, 210–11; Confucianism in, 212–14; economy of, 208–11, *209m*; gender relations in, 211; historians in, 214; India and, 189; Korea and, 307; land reform in, 209; Parthians and, 156; Red Eyebrow Revolt in, 204; science and technology in, 215–16; ships of, 378; unity under, 216; Vietnam and, 323; women in, 211
Han Fei, 200, 202
Hangul, 312
Hanseatic League, 275, 406
Hanshu (*The History of the Former Han*) (Ban Biao and Ban Gu), 214
Hara-kiri (ritual suicide), 317
Harappa, 55, 56–63; animal domestication in, 60, *61*; architecture of, 61; Aryans and, 63; city-states in, *59m*, 59–60; collapse of, 62–63, 74; culture of, 60–61; government in, 60–61; Indo-Europeans and, 63–64; origins of, 73; religion in, 62; trade by, 61; uniformity of, 59–60
Harding, Warren G., 683
Hardy, Thomas, 646
Harems, in Ottoman Empire, 388
Al-Hariri, 240, 243, 245
Harlem Renaissance, 683, 686–87
Harmonious society, in China, 774–75
Harnesses, for horses, 261
Harsha Vardhana, 282–83, *283m*
Harvard College, 445
Hashemites, 688
Hasmonean, 166
Hausa, 756
Hausaland, 455
Haussmann, Georges-Eugène, 642

Havel, Václav, 742
Hawaii, 119
Headmen, 203
Heavenly Buddha of the Western Paradise (Amitabha), 185
Heavenly Kingdom of Great Peace (*taiping tianguo*), 583
Hebrew Bible, 45, 49; Galileo and, 399; iconoclasm and, 230
Hegel, Georg Wilhelm Friedrich, 545, 623; Marx and, 640
Hegemony, in Zhou dynasty, 88–89
Heian period (Japan), 315, 316, *316m*
Hellenism, 155; India and, 193; Islam and, 244; in Palestine, 165
Helots, 154
Henry II, *258*, 259–60
Henry III of Navarre, 411–12
Henry IV, 264
Henry the Navigator, 374, 456
Henry VI, 260
Henry VIII, 409
Heraclitus, 165
Heraclius, 150, 222–23
Herder, Johann Gottfried, 535–36
Herero, 665
Heresy: of Cathars, 278–79; in Western Christianity, 265
Herodians, 166
Herodotus, 166
Hertz, Heinrich Rudolf, 634
Herzl, Theodore, 688
Hesiod, 170
Hezbollah, 778
Hidalgo y Costilla, Miguel, 558–59
Hidden Imam (Messiah), 377
Hidden Twelfth Imam (Ismail), 377
Hideki, Tojo, 702
Hideyoshi, Toyotomi, 499, 503, *512*, 512–13, *513m*
Hierakonopolis, 38
Hieroglyphic writing: in Egypt, 38, 38–39; of Meroë, 127
High Middle Ages, 267–70
Himalaya Mountains, 56; China and, 78
Himyar, 129
Hindenburg, Paul von, 695
Hinduism, 70–73, 282–83; asceticism in, 72, *72*; devotion in, 180, 185–87; Great Britain and, 656–57; of Gupta Empire, 180; in India, 783; Islam and, 226, 301–2; nationalism of, 724–25, 783; property rights in, 191; Sikhism and, 286
Hippies, 745
Hippodrome, 388
Hirobumi, Ito, 577, 594
Hiroshima, 702, *709*
Hispaniola, 431
The History of the Former Han (*Hanshu*) (Ban Biao and Ban Gu), 214
Hitler, Adolf, 695–96, 697; eugenics and, 684

Hittites: Assyrians and, 43; Egypt and, 42; empire of, 41–42; Phoenicians and, 44
Hobbes, Thomas, 404–5, 526
Hobbits, of Flores Island, 24–25
Ho Chi Minh, 729
Hohenzollern, 417–18
Hohlenstein-Stadel cave, 16
Holocaust, 697
Holy Christian League, 382
Holy Roman Empire, 260; Council of Constance and, 275; Habsburgs and, 382; papacy and, 264; Thirty Years' War and, 413
Holy Rule (St. Benedict), 255
Holy war. *See Jihad*
Homer, 170
Homestead Act, 543
Hominids, 3
Hominins: bipedalism of, 4; in caves, 6–7; climate change and, 4; of Flores Island, 24–25; in savanna, 5
Homo erectus, 4, 6–7; hobbits of Flores Island and, 25
Homo floresiensis, 25
Homo neanderthalensis. See Neanderthals
Homo sapiens, 7–8; agrarian–urban society of, 9; in caves, 8; culture of, 3–4; foraging by, 8; migrations of, 10–14, *11m*; rock art of, 24; symbols of, 9–10
Homosexuals: gay rights movement for, *745*, 745; Islam and, 245; Nazi Germany and, 696
Honduras, 573
Hong Lou Meng (*The Dream of the Red Chamber*) (Cao Xueqin), 592
Hongwu (Zhu Yuanzhang), 296, 297, 309
Hong Xiuquan, 582–83
Hong xue (redology), 592
Hoover, Herbert, 683, 684
Hopewell, 101, *101*, 115, *116m*
Hoplites, 151
Horace, 170
Horses: in agricultural revolution, 261; of Comanches, 435; harnesses for, 261; in Middle East, 41; of Mongolia, 84–85; stirrups for, *206*, 206–7. *See also* Chariots
Horus, 38
Hostage crisis, in Iran, 756
Household slavery, 457
House of Commons, 274
House Un-American Activities Committee, 712
Howl and Other Poems (Ginsberg), 734
Huaca, 147
Huainan zi, 213
Huang Zongxi, 511
Hughes, Langston, 686, *687*
Huguenots, 411–12
Hui Neng, 215
Hui of Liang, 197
Huitzilpochtli, 358
Humanism, 396, 397; of Renaissance, 276

Human sacrifice: in Andes, *366*, 366–67; at
  Chavín de Huántar, 111; by Maya, 137,
  139, 141; in Mesoamerica, *366*, 366–67; in
  Shang dynasty, 94
Humayun, 479–80, *482*; Shiite Islam of, 483
Hunas, 180
Hundred days of reform, of Ming dynasty, 587
Hundred Flowers campaign, in China, 720
Hundred Years' War, 272–73, 274
Hungary: in Cold War, 713, *713*; Marshall
  Plan and, 709; nationalism in, 713, *713*,
  777; Ottoman Empire in, 377
Huns, 281
Hunt, Terry, 123
Hunting and gathering. *See* Foraging
Hurricanes, 103, 105
Hurston, Zora Neale, 686
Husák, Gustáv, 740, 742
Husayn, 227
Huss, John, 274, 275, 409
Hussein, Saddam, 755, 769–70
Hussein Dey, 651
Hutchinson, Anne, 445
Hutu, 455, 770
Hu Yaobang, 750
Hydrostatics, 168
Hygiene revolution, 631
Hyperinflation, in Germany, 694–95, *695*
Hysteria, 645

Ibangala, 459
Iberia: Christianity in, 372–75; military orders
  of, 372; natural sciences of, 400. *See also*
  Portugal; Spain
Ibn Battuta of Tangier, 294
Ibn Khaldun, 244
Ibn Qasim, Muhammad, 281
Ibn Rushd (Averroes), 244
Ibn Sina (Avicenna), 244, 270
Ibn Taymiyya, Taqi al-Din, 250–51
Ibn Tughluq, Muhammad ("Muhammad the
  Bloody"), 285
ICBM. *See* Intercontinental ballistic missile
Ice Age, 17–23, *18*; in Australia, 12, 17;
  canoes in, 17; clothing in, 17; environment
  of, 17; Japan and, 313; Middle East in,
  28–29; Neanderthals and, 21
Iconoclasm: in Byzantium, 229–30; of Eastern
  Christianity, 229–30
Icons, of Byzantium, 246–47, *247*
Ieyasu, Tokugawa, 513, 514–15, 520–21,
  588–89
Igbo, 756
Ijebu, 346
Iliad (Homer), 170
Ilkhans, 291–92
Illustrated Gazetteer of the Maritime Countries
  (Wei Yuan), 592
IMF. *See* International Monetary Fund
Immigration. *See* Migrations

Imperialism. *See* Colonialism; Empires
Import-substitution industrialization: in
  Brazil, 556, 760; in China, 768
Impression, Sunrise (Monet), 646
Impressionism, 646
Inca, 144, 351, 360–63, *361m*; gender
  relations of, 365–66; government of, 362;
  quipu of, 109; roads of, 363, *363*; Spain
  and, 426–28, *444*
Incandescent light bulb, 642
Indentured laborers, 462, 464; in Australia,
  658–59
India, *68m*; agrarian society in, 54–75;
  agriculture of, 66, 725; Alexander the Great
  in, 175, 176–77; animal domestication in,
  65; Arabs in, 281; arts of, 192–93; in BRIC,
  766; British East India Company in, 652–56;
  in Bronze Age, 65; Buddhism in, 189, 194,
  281–82; caste system of, 69, 70–71, 189–90,
  286, 783; China and, 748; Christianity in,
  654, 655; civil service in, 656; in Common
  Era, 281; coolies from, 570; cotton from,
  490, 626; culture of, 68–73; da Gama to, 375;
  democracy in, 725; economy of, 188–89,
  286; empires in, 174–95; England and, 486–
  87; family in, 190–91; famine in, 725; First
  War of Independence in, 655–56; France
  and, 486–87; gender relations in, 69–70,
  192; grasslands in, 65; Great Britain and,
  652–56, *654m*, 655, *655f*, *657m*, 689–90;
  Gupta Empire of, 161, 179–80, *181m*, 281;
  industrialization in, 725; Islam in, 283–86,
  301–2, 724, 783; kingdoms of, 67–68, 179;
  literature of, 192–93; Mauryans of, 176–79,
  178m; middle class in, 784; migrations from,
  571m; monsoon system in, 56–57, *57m*,
  725; in NAM, 707, 724, 727; as nation-state,
  724–28; Netherlands and, 486–87; nomads
  in, 179; pepper from, *190*, 190–91; Portugal
  and, 375, 486–87; power in, 66–68; railroads
  in, 55; religion in, 68–73; republicanism
  in, 194–95; rice in, 66; Sasanids and, 168;
  science and technology of, 192–93; self-rule
  for, 689–90; sexuality in, 69–70; silk in, 488;
  Silk Road in, 189; social classes in, 69, 70–71;
  South Africa and, 757; Southeast Asia and,
  189; taxes in, 188, 286; textile industry in,
  627; topography of, 56–57; trade by, 188–89,
  489m, 489–90; urbanization in, 725, 783;
  Vedas of, 64–66; women in, 69–70; women's
  rights in, 747. *See also* Harappa; Hinduism;
  Mughals; North India; South India
Indian National Congress, 656
Indian Ocean: Christianity in, 382; East Africa
  and, 133; Islam in, 382; Ming dynasty and,
  337; Ottoman Empire and, *383m*; Portugal
  and, *383m*
Indian Removal Act, 543
Indigo: in Ming dynasty, 500; in North
  America, 464–65

Individualism, 218
Indo-Aryans, 65
Indo-Europeans: Aryans and, 64–65; Harappa
  and, 63–64; Shang dynasty and, 84
Indonesia: East Africa and, 133; Flores Island,
  24–25; NAM and, 707; as nation-state,
  724; Netherlands and, 667–68
Indulgences, 408, 409, 411
Indus River (Valley): Achaemenids and, 152;
  Hinduism and, 71. *See also* Harappa
Industrialization, 624–49; agriculture and,
  626; big business and, 642–43; critics of,
  639–41; 1871-1914, 628–34; energy for,
  626–27; in Europe, 625, *630m*; factories
  and, 627; global warming and, 788; in Great
  Britain, 625, 626–27, *629m*; in India, 725;
  in Japan, 631; in Latin America, 717–19,
  787–88; leisure and, 642; Luddites and,
  648–49; migrations and, 636–37, *638m*;
  mining and, 639, *639*; modernity and, 646–
  47; in North America, 625–26; origins and
  growth of, 625–34; population growth and,
  635–36, *636m–37m*; in Russia, 618–20,
  631; science and technology and, 644–46;
  1750-1914, 635–43; sewer systems and,
  641–42; social and economic impacts
  of, 635–43; social classes and, 637–39;
  socialism and, 639–40; in Soviet Union,
  693; sports and, 642; in Turkey, 780; in
  US, 628; women and, 641. *See also* Import-
  substitution industrialization
Industrial Revolution, 625; in China, 500;
  Latin America and, 569; second, 628–34
Infanticide: female, in China, 298, 509, 750;
  in Japan, 518
Influenza, 681
Information technology (IT), 768–69
Inland Delta, Niger, 130
Inner Mongolia, 80
Innocent III, 265, 267; Cathars and, 279
*Inquiry into the Nature and Causes of the Wealth
  of Nations* (Smith, A.), 534
Institutionalization, of Mughals, 480
Institutional Revolutionary Party (PRI),
  786–87
Intercontinental ballistic missile (ICBM),
  713–14
Internal combustion engine, 632–33
International Monetary Fund (IMF), 771
The Interpretation of Dreams (Freud), 645
Interstadials, 107
Inti, 360
Intolerable Acts (Coercive Acts), 526
Inuit, 115
Investiture controversy, 264
Ionia, 154
Iran: Baha'is in, 612; fire temples of, 165;
  hostage crisis in, 756; Islamic Revolution
  in, 611, 755–56; Israel and, 779–80;

Mongols in, 237; Ottoman Empire and, 609–12; Qajars in, 609–12; Safavids in, 377, 609–12; Shiite Islam in, 227, 609. *See also* Persians

Iran-Iraq War, 755–56

Iraq: Great Britain and, 688; in Iran-Iraq War, 755–56; Mongols in, 237; Shiite Islam in, 227; US and, 769–70

Ireland, Great Famine of, 544

Iron: in Africa, 130; in Americas, 146; in Greece, 46; in Han dynasty, 208; of Hittites, 41–42; in Meroë, 128; steel and, 630–31; in Zhou dynasty, 95–96

Iron Age, 42; African spirituality in, 133

Iron curtain, 708

Iroquois, 435

Irrigation: in Americas, 109; in China, 202; in Japan, 318; in Mesopotamia and Egypt, 32; in Nazca, 143

Isabella, 374, 375, 386–87

ISIS. *See* Islamic State in Iraq and al-Sham

Islam (Muslims): in Africa, 785–86; agriculture of, 261; in ancient Ghana, 342; architecture of, 245; arts and, 244; in Balkans, 375–84; Christianity and, 372–84, 391; circumcision in, 388; commonwealth of, 228, 228*m*; culture of, 243–45, 249; duties of, 226; in East Africa, 336, 348; in Egypt, 236, 242; in Ethiopia, 334–35, 456; formation of, 222–28; height of civilization, 237–43; Hinduism and, in India, 301–2; in India, 283–86, 301–2, 724, 783; in Indian Ocean, 382; literature and, 245; in Mediterranean, 236; miniatures of, 246–47; in Nigeria, 756; in northeast Africa, 330–35; of Seljuks, 233–34; Sikhism and, 286; slavery and, 385; in Spain, 265; in sub-Saharan Africa, 454–55; Sufism and, 243; theology of, 226; of Umayyads, 223; in West Africa, 348, 664–65. *See also* Byzantium; Mughals; Ottoman Empire; Sharia Law; Shiite Islam; Sunni Islam

Islamic Government (Khomeini), 755

Islamic Revolution (Iran), 611, 755–56

Islamic State in Iraq and al-Sham (ISIS), 783

Islamism, 778

Ismail (Hidden Twelfth Imam), 377

Israel, 721–23; in Arab-Israeli Wars, 752, 752–54, 753*m*; Egypt and, 723, 738, 754; Gaza and, 778–79; Iran and, 779–80; Jordan and, 754; Soviet Union and, 722; Syria and, 738. *See also* Jerusalem

Israelites, 44–45. *See also* Jews and Judaism

Isthmus Declaration, 156–57

IT. *See* Information technology

Italy: Byzantium and, 232; Catholicism in, 693; city-states in, 156; corporate state in, 693–94; East Africa and, 666; Ethiopia and, 694; ethnic nationalism in, 538–39; fascism in, 693–94; Genoa in, 372; Great Depression in, 694; Habsburgs in, 381;

Libya and, 694; New Sciences in, 401; Norman Conquest of, 261; poetry in, 276; in World War I, 679. *See also* Roman Empire

Iturbide, Agustín de, 559

Itzcóatl, 359

Jacobite Church, 167

Jade: Maya and, 135; of Neolithic China, 81; of Olmec, 114, *114*

Jahan, Nur, 490, *491*

Jahangir, 482–83

Jainism, 177, 180; asceticism of, 182–83; caste system and, 190

Jamaica: England and, 431; Rastafarians in, 334; slave revolts in, 471

Jama Masjid, 494

Jambalya, 470

James, Henry, 546

Jamestown, 433, 464

Janapadas, 66, 70

Janissaries, 385, 602, 604

Japan, 313–21, 512–19; aboriginals of, 313; agriculture of, 314, 318; aristocratic landlords in, 591; arts in, 597; bathhouses in, 516, 517, 596; Buddhism in, 185, 315, 319–20, 327; calligraphy of, 316, 317, 518; capitalism in, 593–94; cartels in, 593–94, 698; China and, 326, 512–13, 513*m*, 515, 584–85, *586*, 586–87, 700, 701; Christianity in, 515; climate of, 313, 314*m*; culture of, 319–20, 597; economy of, 318, 515–18, 516*m*; empire of, 590, 590*m*; family in, 318–19; firearms in, 514–15; First Opium War and, 588; food in, 516; industrialization in, 631; Korea and, 326; languages of, 313; literature in, 305, 592, 597; Manchuria and, 577, 700; Meiji in, 515, 588–90, 590*m*, 593–97, 631; military of, 316–17, 698, 700; modernism in, 577; modernity and modernism in, 595*m*; navy of, 587; Neo-Confucianism in, 499, 513, 515, 517; Netherlands and, 515, 521; newspapers in, 592; novel in, 305, 592, 597; paintings in, 305, *305*, 518, *518*; political parties in, 595–96; porcelain in, 516; railroads in, 589, 594, *594*; religion in, 319–20; roads in, 593; in Russo-Japanese War, 620; science and technology in, 584–85, 596–97; seclusion of, 515, 520–21, 588; Shogun in, 316–17; in Sino-Japanese War, *586*, 586–87; Taiwan and, 619; telegraph in, 589, 594; telephone in, 594; theater in, 518, 597; Triple Intervention on, 590, 619; US and, 589; Vietnam and, 326; women in, 318–19, 517; in World War I, 679; in World War II, 702. *See also* World War II

Japan Current, 313

Jati, 69

Jazz, 683, 686

Jebel Irhoud, 7–8

Jefferson, Thomas, 526

Jenné-jeno, *130*, 130–31, 134, 341

Jerusalem, 45; Achaemenids and, 151; Constantinople and, 236, 237; in Crusades, 267; First Crusade and, 233; Henry the Navigator and, 456; Jesus in, 166; Mamluks in, 234, 335; Second Temple at, 164, 165

Jesuits: in Brazil, 432; Catholic Reformation and, 411; in China, 507; in Ethiopia, 456; Iroquois and, 435; papacy and, 507

Jesus of Nazareth, 160, 166; Crucifixion of, 264–65, *265*; divinization of, 167; iconoclasm and, 230; Jews as murderers of, 263; passion plays and, 389; as son of God, 223

Jews and Judaism, 163–64; Achaemenids and, 165–66; in Aksum, 129; in Egypt, 242; on Euphrates River, *167*; in Europe, 263; genocide of, 697, *698*; in ghettos, 263; of Granada, 375; Hitler and, 695; Holocaust of, 697; Ku Klux Klan and, 683; in Mesopotamia, 163; as murderers of Christ, 263; Nazi Germany and, 705–6; in Ottoman Empire, 606; in Palestine, 163, 165–66; in Persia, 160; saviors of, 704–5; Zionism and, 688. *See also* Israel

Ji, Lady, 92

Jihad (holy war), 226; in Arab Spring, 782; of Seljuks, 234; in Somalia, 785

Jinnah, Muhammad Ali, 690

Joan of Arc, 273

Johanson, Donald, 3, *5*

John, King, 260

Johnson, James Weldon, 686

Johnson, Lyndon B., 739, 744; Vietnam War and, 750

John the Baptist, 166

Jordan, 754

Jousts, 389

Juárez, Benito, 561

Judah, 45

Judaism. *See* Jews and Judaism

Julius Caesar, 158

Junzi (gentleman), 199

Jurchens, 291

Justinian I "The Great," 162, 269–70; Plague of, 160–61; silk and, 211

Kabuki, 518, 597

Kahun Papyrus, 50

Kailsantha Temple, *183*

Kalahari Desert, 17, 133

Kali, 187

Kalinga, 178

Kama Sutra (Aphorisms of Love) (Vatsyayana), 69–70, 192

Kamikaze (divine wind), 316

Kana system, 321

Kanchipuram, 283

Kanem-Bornu, 454–55

Kang (heated bed), 80

Kangxi, 504, 511
Kang Youwei, 587
Kanishka, 179
Kannon, *214*, 215, *320*
Kant, Immanuel, 534
Karbala, 227
Karma, 183
Karman, Tawakkol, 765
Karma-samsara, 72–73
Kasa-Vubu, Joseph, 731–32
Kashmir, 725
Katipunan, 670
Kaudinya, 189
Kautilya, 67, 176
Kelp Highway, 19
Kemal, Mustafa. *See* Atatürk
Kennedy, John F., 714, 715, 729; assassination of, 744
Kennedy, Robert, 746
Kennewick Man, 21
Kenya, 145, 665; as nation-state, 731
Kenyatta, Jomo, 731
Kepler, Johannes, 395
Kerma, 126
Kerosene, 632
Kerouac, Jack, 734
Kharijis, 336, 342
Khartoum, 126
Khmer Rouge, 752
Khmers, 189
Khoi, 459
Khomeini, Ayatollah Ruhollah, 611, 755, 756, 779
Khosrow I, 162–63
Khosrow II, 149–50, 222, 223
Khrushchev, Nikita, 708, 713; Cuba and, 714; Cuban Missile Crisis and, 715, 738; Great Leap Forward and, 721; Mao Zedong and, 748; for nationalism, 712; Stalin and, 721, 738
Khubilai Khan, 291, *295*
Khufu, 39
Khurram (Shah Jahan), 483–84
Al-Khwarizmi, Muhammad ibn Musa, 244
Khyber Pass, 56, 78
Kibbutz, 752
Kiev, 232, 234
Kikuchi, Takeo, 677
Kim Jong-un, 792
King, Martin Luther, Jr., 744, 746
Kingdoms: in Africa, 125–30, 473; of Africa, 126–30, 128*m*; of central Africa, 340–41; centralized, 405–7; in East Africa, 335–37; of Egypt, 38–39, 42; of Greece, 45–47; of India, 67–68, 179; of Maya, 354–55, 355; of Mesoamerica, 134–41, 352–55; of Mesopotamia, 34–38, 35*m*; of Minoans, 39–41; of Mycenaeans, 45–47; of north India, 283; in Nubia, 330–33; of Philistines and Israelites, 45; of Phoenicians, 44; in

southern Africa, 337–40; of south India, 180–81; of sub-Saharan Africa, 146, 454*m*; in West Africa, 341–46, 343*m*
King List (Mesopotamia), 34
King's Peace of 386 BCE, 154–55
Kipling, Rudyard, 674
Kofun, 315
Koguryo kingdom (Korea), 308
Kojiki (*Records of Ancient Matters*), 321
Kokoro (Soseki), 597
Kokutai (national polity/essence), 677, 698
Komnenos dynasty, in Byzantium, 241
Kong, 198
Kong fuzi, 198
Kongo, 451–52; Christianity in, 458–59, *459*; slaves from, 459
Korea: agriculture of, 306; aristocratic landlords in, 311; Buddhism in, 308, *309*, 312–13; bureaucracy in, 308; China and, 307–9, 315, 326; climate of, 306, 308*m*; in Cold War, 711–12; colonialism in, 586–87; Confucianism in, 308; culture of, 312–13; environment of, 306, 308*m*; Japan and, 326, 515; land reform in, 310–11; literacy in, 312–13; literature in, 313; marriage in, 312; Neo-Confucianism in, 309–12; printing in, 312–13; Qin dynasty and, 577; religion in, 312–13; silk in, 311; social classes in, 310, 312; taxes in, 308; Three Kingdoms of, 307–8; Vietnam and, 326; women in, 312; writing in, 312; in Yuan dynasty, 292. *See also* North Korea
Koryo kingdom, 308–9, 309*m*
Kosala, 176
Krishna (god), 67, 69, 186; Krishna I (ruler), 180
Kshatriyas, 70
Ku Klux Klan, 683
Kulaks, 692
Kurds, Kurdish: ISIS and, 783; Saladin and, 237
Kuroshio current, 105
Kushans, 179
Kushites, 145
Kuwait, 770
Kyoto Protocol, 789–91

Labor assignments (*repartimiento*), 425, 429; in Mexico, 431
Lady Ji, 92
Lahori, Ustad Ahmad, 494
Laissez-faire, 534
Land bridges, 17
Land Code, of Ottoman Empire, 606
Land grants: in Hittite Empire, 42; in Korea, 310; in Ottoman Empire, 384–85; in Qin dynasty, 201
Land-labor grants (*encomiendas*), 424–25
Land reform: in China, 720; in Colombia, 719; in Cuba, 717; in Egypt, 723; in Han dynasty, 209; in Korea, 310–11

Langland, William, 276
Languages: of Akkad, 35; Austronesian, 81; in China, 81; of East Africa, 131, 132–33; of Hittites, 42; of Japan, 313; in Middle East, 26; Proto-Indo-European, 41; Sino-Tibetan, 81; of Vietnam, 325. *See also* Writing
Laos, 672
Lao Tzu, 200
Lapita, 118–19; from Taiwan, 100
Lascaux Cave, 16, *16*
Last Glacial Maximum (LGM), 18
Last Judgment, 377
Lateen sail, 262
Later (Eastern) Han, 204
Latin America, 550–75; abolition of slavery in, 569–70; agriculture of, 568–69; aristocratic landlords in, 552–64; arts of, 572–73; Catholicism in, 567–68, 572; coffee in, 569; constitutionalism in, 552–64, 566–67, 690; culture of, 572–73; democracy in, 718–19; economy of, 564–72, 565*m*, 574; expansion of, 786–88; exports from, 568–72, 574, 788; factories in, 571–72; family in, 572; Great Depression in, 690–91; industrialization in, 717–19, 787–88; Industrial Revolution and, 569; literature of, 572–73; migrations in, 569–70, *570*; nation-states of, 560*m*; population growth in, 718*m*; populism in, 718–19; proxy wars in, 759–60; urbanization in, 717, 718*m*; women in, 572. *See also* Caribbean; Central America; Mesoamerica; South America; *specific countries*
Latin Christianity, 254–55
Latvia, 742
La Venta, 114, 115
Lawrence, T. E., 687–88
Laws: of Babylonia, 36–37; canon, 270; Corn Laws, of England, 544; in High Middle Ages, 269–70; of Roman Empire, 162. *See also* Sharia Law
League of Nations, 681; Ethiopia and, 694; mandates of, 687–88
Leang Bulu' Sipong 4 cave, 15
Lebanon: civil war in, 754–55; Shiite Islam in, 227
Lebensraum (living space), 680, 695
Le dynasty, in Vietnam, 323, 325
Legalism, Confucianism and, 200, 212
Legge, James, 197
Legionaries, 156–58
Leisure, industrialization and, 642
Le Loi, 323
Lenin, Vladimir Ilyich, 620, 623, 673, 680, 691
Lennon, John, 734
Leo III, 257
Leo IX, 232
Leopold II, 665, 666
Leo Africanus, "the African" (al-Wazzan, al-Hasan Ibn Muhammad), 371
Leo X, 371

Lesbian, Gay, Bisexual, Transgender, and
    Queer (LGBTQ), 745
Letters of marque, 462
Levallois tools, 8
Leviathan (Hobbes), 405
LGBTQ. *See* Lesbian, Gay, Bisexual,
    Transgender, and Queer
LGM. *See* Last Glacial Maximum
Li (ritual), 199, 298–99
Liang Qichao, 587
Li Bai, 290
Liberia, 667, 785
Library of Alexandria, 168
Libya (Tripolitania): Arab Spring in, 781; Italy
    and, 666, 694
Li dynasty, in Vietnam, 323
Life lease (*malikane*), 602
Life of Harsha (Bana), 282
Light bulb, 642
Lightning war (*Blitzkrieg*), 696
Li Hongzhang, 577, 585
Lijia, 509
Lin Biao, 748
Lincoln, Abraham, 541
Linear A, 41
Linear B, 45
Lin Zexu, 580
Lipo, Carl, 123
Li Shimin, 206
Li Si, 202, 203
Literacy: in Japan, 319; in Korea, 312–13;
    Protestant Reformation and, 407
Literature: of China, 300; of Egypt, 48–49;
    of Enlightenment, 534; of Europe, 276; of
    Greece, 169–70; of Habsburgs, 390–91;
    of India, 192–93; Islam and, 245; of
    Japan, 305, 592, 597; of Korea, 313;
    of America, 572–73; of Mesopotamia,
    48–49; of Ming dynasty, 511; modernity
    in, 646; of Mughals, 493; of realism, 546;
    of Renaissance, 396; of Roman Empire,
    170–71; of romanticism, 545; after World
    War II, 716. *See also* Novel; Poetry
Lithuania, 742
Little Ice Age, 271; centralized kingdoms
    and, 405
Liu Bang (Gaozu), 203
Liu Shaoqi, 721, 748
Livia, 159
Living space (*Lebensraum*), 680, 695
Livingstone, David, 663
Llama, 142, 356
Locke, John, 405
Lodi, Ibrahim, 479
Lombard, Peter, 270
London Working Men's Association, 640
Long Depression, 544, 619
Long March, in China, 701–2
Longshan period, in China, 81, 82; Xia dynasty
    and, 83

López, Francisco Solano, 553–54
Lord of Sipán, 142
Lord of the Rings (Tolkien), 25
Lorentz, Hendrik, 644
Lothal, 61–62, 63
Lotus Sutra, 319
Louis, Antoine, 530–31
Louisiana Purchase, 542
Louisiane, 435
Louis-Philippe, 537
Louis the Pious, 257
Louis VII, 267
Louis XIII, 414
Louis XIV, 415–16, 435
Louis XVI, 526–27, 537; execution of, *531*
Louis XVIII, 537
Loyola, Ignatius, 411
Luba kingdom, 340*m*, 340–41
Lucy (Hadar AL 288-1), 3, *5*
Luddites, 648–49
Lumumba, Patrice, 731–32
Lunyu (*Analects*) (Confucius), 198, 299
Lusitania, 680
Luther, Martin, 409, 452
Lynchings, of African Americans, 542

MacArthur, Douglas, 711
Macaulay, Thomas B., 654
Macedonia, 155
Machiavelli, Niccolò, 397
Machine gun, 634, *635*
Maciel, Vicente Mendes, 574–75
Madame Bovary (Flaubert), 546
Madero, Francisco, 563
Magadha, 175
Magellan, Ferdinand, 669
The Magic Flute (Mozart), 534
Maginot Line, 697
Magna Carta, 260
Magnetic compass, 262
Maguey, 140
Magyars, 257
Mahabharata, 67, *67*, 186
Mahajanapadas, 66
Mahal, Mumtaz, 477
Mahapadma Nanda, 176
Maharajas, 66
Mahavira, 177, 182
Mahayana, 185; Vietnam and, 324–25
Mahendra Varman I, 180
Maize, 112–13
Maji-Maji rebellion, 665
Makovsky, Vladimir Yegorovich, *621*
Malacca, Strait of, 515
Malaria, 663
Malaysia, 724
Mali, 342–46, *346*; Songhay Empire and,
    452–53
Malikane (life lease), 602
Malinche, 425, *425*

Malinke, 343–44
Maluka Islands, 667
Mami Wata, 469, *469*
Mamluks, 233; in Egypt, 237, 238–39, *239*;
    in Jerusalem, 335; Mongols and, 237;
    Nubia and, 330; Ottoman Empire and, 377;
    Palestine and, 372
Manchuria: Choson and, 307; Japan and,
    577, 700
Manchus, 292; Qing dynasty and, 503
Mandate of Heaven, in China, 87–88, 98, 315;
    Confucius and, 198; Mencius and, 199
Mandates, of League of Nations, 687–88
Mandela, Nelson, 758, 762, 785, *785*
Manichaeism, 278
Manorialism, 258, 258*f*
Mansabdars, 487–88
Mansa Musa, 345
Manumission, 464
Manure fertilizers, 261
Man'yoshu (*The Ten Thousand Leaves*), 321
Manzikert, 234–35, *235*
Mao Zedong, 701, 720; death of, 748, 749;
    Khrushchev and, 748
Maps: of Brazil, 429; of Renaissance, 406–7;
    of Waldseemüller, *400*
Mapuche, 429
Mapungubwe, 337–38
Maqamat (al-Hariri), 245
Marajó, 116
Marathas, 486
Marathon, 154
Marconi, Guglielmo, 634
Marcus, Siegfried, 632
Marduk, 49, 151
Marie-Antoinette, 528
Marius, 158
Maronites, 754
Maroons, 472
Marriage: of Australian Aboriginals, 12–13; in
    Japan, 319; in Korea, 312; in Mesopotamia,
    37; in Mexico, 572; same-sex, 745; in
    Vietnam, 322
Marshall Plan, 709
Martel, Charles ("the Hammer"), 224, 255
Martial Emperor (Wudi), 156, 203–4
Martin V, 275
Marx, Karl, 623, 639, 640
Marxism, 620; in Colombia, 787; Mussolini
    and, 693; in Soviet Union, 691
Mary (mother of Jesus), 230
Matchlock musket, 406
Mathematical Principles of Natural Philosophy
    (Newton), 401
Mathematics: algebra, 50, 168, 193, 244;
    calculus, 400, 491; geometry, 168, 244; in
    High Middle Ages, 270; of Mughals, 491; in
    Renaissance, 399
Matriarchal clans, 314
Matrilineal clans, 314

Matrilocal clans, 322

Matrilocal marriage, 312

Mauryan Empire (India), 176–79, 178m

Maxim, Hiram, 634, 635

Maximilian, 562, 562

Maya, 354–55, 355; ball game of, 138, 138–39; calendar of, 137; in Caribbean, 117; collapse of, 139; glyphic script of, 136; human sacrifice by, 137, 139, 141; in Mesoamerica, 135m, 135–41; polytheism of, 137, 139; *Popol Vuh* of, 444; social classes of, 137–38; writing of, 136, 139, 140; in Yucatán Peninsula, 135m, 135–41

Mazdak, 162

McCarthy, Joseph, 712

Mccartney, George, 578

McKay, Claude, 686

McMahon-Hussein correspondence, 688

McNamara, Robert, 750

Mean speed theorem, 270

Meat Inspection Act, 543

Mecca, 226, 377

Medea (Euripides), 173

Medes, 150–51

Medical science: in Egypt, 50; in High Middle Ages, 269–70; Islam and, 244

Medici, Giovanni Leone di, 371

Medina, 226

Mediterranean: Islam in, 236; Middle East and, 172; ships in, 378, 378–79, 379; trade on, 261–62, 262m. *See also* Eastern Mediterranean

Megasthenes, 177

Mehmet II, "The Conqueror," 376–77

Mehrgarh, 58

Meiji (Mutsuhito), in Japan, 515, 588–90, 590m, 593–97, 631

Mein Kampf (Hitler), 695, 697

Meluhha, 61

Menander, 179

Mencius, 197, 199, 217

Mengzi (Book of Mencius) (Mencius), 199, 299

Mensheviks, 620

Mercantilism: in Caribbean, 462; Navigation Acts and, 465; in Zhou dynasty, 91

Mercury, in Peru, 429

Meroë, 126, 127–29; Nubia and, 330

Merovingians, 254, 277

Mesoamerica, 353m; chiefdoms of, 134–41; city-states in, 112–16; climate of, 103; foraging in, 115; human sacrifice in, 366, 366–67; kingdoms of, 134–41, 352–55; Maya in, 135m, 135–41, 354–55, 355; pottery in, 109; Toltec in, 352–55. *See also* Aztec

Mesopotamia, 27, 27; Achaemenids and, 152; agrarian–urban centers in, 31–41, 32m; Akkad and, 26; assemblies in, 32; Assyrians and, 43; Christianity in, 149–50; city-states of, 4, 33–34; India and, 74–75; irrigation in, 32; Judaism in, 163; kingdoms of, 34–38, 35m; literature in, 48–49; nomads in, 32; paintings of, 49–50; polytheism in, 48; sharecroppers in, 32; trade in, 32–33; women in, 36–37

Messiah, 223, 224, 377

Mestizos, 441, 558

Metternich, Klemens von, 536

Mexican-American War, 588

Mexican Basin: Aztec of, 358–60, 359m, 360, 364–65, 365m; military in, 352–54; Teotihuacán in, 134, 140–41

Mexican Revolution, 559, 560, 563–64

Mexico: banks in, 771; border wall with, 776; calendar in, 125; Catholicism in, 559; caudillo in, 559; Comanches and, 559–60; constitutionalism in, 563–64; Creoles in, 558–59, 562–63; Díaz and, 562–63; exports of, 788; France and, 561–62; independence of, 559; labor assignments in, 431; marriage in, 572; Native Americans in, 423–24; Oaxaca in, 125; PRI in, 786–87; silver in, 438, 669; Spain and, 424–26; Teotihuacán in, 352–55; uprising in, 558–59; urbanism in, 690; US and, 560–61, 561m, 776. *See also* Mesoamerica

Michael I Cerularius, 232–33

Michelangelo, 397

Microlith, 314

Midden, 108

Middle class: in China, 774; in France, 686; in India, 783–84, 784; industrialization and, 638; in Turkey, 689, 780

Middle East, 777–83; agrarian society in, 29; agrarian–urban centers of, 26–53; agriculture of, 29m, 41; Black Death and, 243; centralizing states in, 392; chariots in, 41; colonialism in, 660–63; culture of, 47–50; firearms in, 384; gender relations in, 35–38; Greece and, 155; horses in, 41; in Ice Age, 28–29; Islamism in, 778; mandates in, 687–88; Mediterranean and, 172; migrations in, 778; monotheism in, 163–67, 172; nation-states in, 722m; Ottoman Empire in, 602; patriarchy in, 35–38; religion in, 47–50; science and technology in, 50; selective breeding in, 30; Seljuk Turks in, 265. *See also specific countries*

Middle Kingdom, of Egypt, 39

Middle Passage, 467

Middle Way, 184

Migrations: African diaspora, 468–71, 686–87; to Australia, 658–59; from China, 571m; in Europe, 636–37, 638m; from India, 571m; industrialization and, 636–37, 638m; in Latin America, 569–70, 570; in Middle East, 778; in South Africa, 757; Zionism and, 688

Military: of Achaemenids, 151; of Aztecs, 360, 362; of Byzantium, 232–33; of centralized kingdoms, 406–7; of England, 413, 418; of France, 527, 528–29; of Greece, 46; of Inca, 362–63; of Japan, 316–17, 698, 700; of Mali, 344–45; of Manchus, 503; in Mexican Basin, 352–54; of Nazi Germany, 696; of North Korea, 792–93; of Nubia, 126; of Ottoman Empire, 386; of Philistines, 45; of Prussia, 418; of Qianlong, 506; of Qin dynasty, 202; of Roman Empire, 156–58; of Russia, 416–17; of Shang dynasty, 77, 90; of Toltecs, 353–54; of US, 769; of Zhou dynasty, 90–91

Military orders, of Iberia, 372

Millet, 134

Milošević, Slobodan, 777

Mines Act of 1842, 641

Ming dynasty, in China, 296–300, 500–510, 501m; agriculture of, 500–501, 509; bureaucracy in, 296; Canton system in, 507–8, 508; cities in, 297; Confucianism in, 297; culture of, 511; decline of, 502–3; in East Africa, 337, 339; family in, 297–98; gender relations in, 298; Grand Secretariat of, 504; Great Wall in, 296; hundred days of reform of, 587; Indian Ocean and, 337; literature in, 511; navy of, 296–97; Neo-Confucianism in, 298–99, 502, 511; religion in, 511–12; rice in, 500; science and technology in, 299, 509–11; social classes in, 297; trade in, 504, 504m, 504–5, 505; tribute system of, 309; women in, 298, 509

Miniatures, of Islamic, 246–47

Mining: in Africa, 130; in Australia, 659; coal, 626, 639, 640–41; in Egypt, 39; in Han dynasty, 208; of Hittites, 41–42; industrialization and, 639, 639; in Latin America, 568; in Mesopotamia, 33; of Minoans, 41. *See also specific metals*

Minoans: kingdoms of, 39–41; paintings of, 49–50

Minutemen, 526

"Minute on Education" (Macaulay), 654

Mit'a, 362

Mithridates II "The Great," 156

Moche Valley, in Peru, 134, 142–43

Moctezuma II, 426

Modernity (modernism): in arts, 646–47, 647, 716; of capitalist democracy, 766–74; in China, 576–99; in France, 651; industrialization and, 646–47; in Japan, 576–99, 595m; in literature, 646; in music, 647; in Ottoman Empire, 603, 622; in philosophy, 646; reactions to, 599; in religion, 646; in Russia, 622; in Soviet Union, 691–92; in US, 681; World War I and, 677–81, 704; after World War II, 716. *See also* Capitalism; Communism; Urbanization

Mo Di, 218

Modi, Narendra, 783

Mohenjo-Daro, 56, 59, 60*m*

Moksha, 182, 184

Moldboard, 261, 299

Molucca Islands, 283

Monasteries, 255; in Ethiopia, 333; in France, reform of, 264; in Japan, 316, 319

Monet, Claude, 646

Money economy, 385

Mongolia: horses of, 84–85; in Yuan dynasty, 292

Mongols, 295*m*; in China, 275; in Iran, 237; in Iraq, 237; in Japan, 316; in Korea, 308–9; Mamluks and, 237; Qing dynasty and, 505; slaves of, 309; Song dynasty and, 291; strengths of, 302; in Vietnam, 243, 323; Yuan dynasty and, 291–95, 309, 478

Monism, 165, 172; Upanishads and, 182

Monochrome painting, 518

Monogamous marriage, of Australian Aboriginals, 12–13

Monopolies: of big business, 642; in Chinese porcelain, 505; in US, 543

Monotheism: Akhenaten and, 53; in Middle East, 163–67, 172; in Roman Empire, 158–60. *See also* Christianity; Islam; Jews and Judaism; Zoroastrians

Monroe Doctrine, 561

Monsoon system: in India, 56–57, 57*m*, 725; in Japan, 313

Montenegro: Congress of Berlin and, 607; Ottoman Empire in, 608

Monzaemon, Chikamatsu, 518

Moquegua, 356

Morel, Edward D., 674–75

Morisco, 382, 384

Morocco: Germany and, 667; Ottoman Empire in, 377–79; women's rights in, 747

Morse, Samuel F. B., 633

Morsi, Muhammad, 781

Mosaics, 166

Mosques, 245; of Mughals, 494; in Ottoman Empire, 388–89

Most-favored nations, 581

Mothers of Plaza de Mayo, 760

Mound building, 115; in Tichitt and Oualata, 126

"Mourning Chen Tao" (Du Fu), 290

Mozambique, 666

Mozart, Wolfgang Amadeus, 534, *534*

Muawiya, 223

Mugabe, Robert, 757

Mughals, 476–97; agriculture of, 488; Akbar and, 480–81, 481*m*, 483, 484–85; architecture of, 494; arts of, 493–94; Aurangzeb and, 485–86; Babur and, 479, *480*, 480*m*; bureaucracy of, 478, 487–88; decline of, 496; economy of, 488–90; family of, 490–91; gender relations of, 490–91; government of, 487–88; history and politics

of, 478–87; in India, 285–86, 286*m*; literature of, 493; Marathas and, 486; mosques of, 494; in north India, 480–81, 481*m*; paintings of, 493–94; religion and, 484–85, *485*, 492–93, 495–96; Revolt of the Sons of, 482; Safavids and, 483; science and technology of, 491–92; Shah Jahan and, 483–84; Shiite Islam of, 483; Sikhism and, 486, 496–97; strengths and weaknesses of, 495; Timur and, 478–79, 479*m*; women of, 490–91

Muhammad (Prophet), 226, 610

"Muhammad The Bloody" (ibn Tughluq, Muhammad), 285

Mujahideen, 737

Mukhtar, Umar, 666

Mulattoes, 441

Mummies: of Andes, 366–67; black pepper for, 190; in Nazca, 143; of Neolithic Age, 108; in Peru, 142, 351; of Shang dynasty, 84

Munich Agreement, 696

Music: of African diaspora, 470; of Enlightenment, 534; modernity in, 647; of Renaissance, 397; of romanticism, 545; of Tang dynasty, 289; after World War II, 716

Muslim Brotherhood, in Egypt, 723, 753

Muslim Student Followers of the Imam's Line, 756

Mussolini, Benito (Il Duce), 693–94

Mutsuhito (Meiji), in Japan, 588–90, 590*m*, 593–97, 631

Myanmar, 56

Mycenaeans, 42, 45–47; Phoenicians and, 44

NAACP, 686

Nabobs, 652–53

Nagarjuna, 192

Nagasaki, 702, *709*

Nagy, Imre, 713

Nahuatl, 352, 425, 559

Naia, 20

Nakbé, 136

NAM. *See* Non-Aligned Movement

Nama, 665

Namibia, 666

Nanak, 286

Napata, 126

Napoleon Bonaparte, 528–29, 529*m*; in Egypt, 603; Haiti and, 532; Ottoman Empire and, 603; in Russia, 613, 614

Napoleon III, 537, 539; Mexico and, 562; Ottoman Empire and, 606; Palestine and, 616; Paris and, 642; Vietnam and, 672

Naram-Sin of Akkad, 35, 43

Narasimha Varman II, 180

Nasser, Gamal Abdel, 707, 723–24

Natapputta, Nigantha, 182

National Commission on the Disappearance of Persons (CONADEP), in Argentina, 760

Nationalism: of Arabs, 778; in China, 700–701; cultural, of Germany, 535–36; of

Hindus, 724–25, 783; in Hungary, 713, *713*, 777; Khrushchev for, 712; in Philippines, 670; in Poland, 712, 777; in Vietnam, 673; World War I and, 645. *See also* Ethnic nationalism; Supremacist nationalism

National Organization of Women (NOW), 746

National polity/essence (*kokutai*), 677, 698

National Rifle Association, 776

National Security Strategy of 2002, of US, 769

National Socialist German Workers' Party. *See* Nazi Germany

Nation-states: in Africa, 722*m*, 730–32; Argentina as, 552–54; in Asia, 722*m*, 724–29; Bolivia as, 552–54, 556–57; Brazil as, 554–56; Chile as, 558; in Cold War, 719–32; Congo as, 731–32; in Europe, 536–40, 537*m*, 541*m*; Ghana as, 730–31; of Great Britain, 544; of Haiti, 532–33; India as, 724–28; Japan as, 589; Kenya as, 731; of Latin America, 560*m*; in Middle East, 722*m*; Paraguay, 552–54; Peru as, 558; Poland as, 740; in Southeast Asia, 728–7729; in sub-Saharan Africa, 732; Uruguay as, 552–54; US as, 540–44, 542*m*; Vietnam as, 729

Native Americans, 21–23; Beringia Standstill and, 19; Christianity of, 432, 435; civil right movement for, 744; foraging by, 105–7; Louisiana Purchase and, 542; in Mexico, 423–24; in North America, 433–35; on reservations, 543; slavery of, 429, 432; social level of, 441–43; tobacco and, 464; in US, 542, 542–43. *See also specific tribes and empires*

NATO. *See* North Atlantic Treaty Organization

Natufians, 29–30, 47

Naturalism, 47

Natural sciences, of Habsburg Empire, 400

Natural selection, 645

Navigation Acts, 465

Navy: of Achaemenids, 151; of England, 418; of Japan, 587; of Ming dynasty, 296–97; of Ottoman Empire, 382–83; of Song dynasty, 292; of Sparta, 154

Nazca, 143–44, 146–47

Nazi Germany: Aryans and, 63; Catholicism and, 695; defiance of, 705–6; eugenics and, 684; Jews and, 705–6; in World War II, 696–98, 704–5. *See also* World War II

Ndongo, 459

Neanderthals (*Homo neanderthalensis*): disappearance of, 20–21; rock art of, 14–15, 20, *20*

Négritude, 687

Nehru, Jawaharlal, 724, 725

Neo-Assyrian Empire, 43

Neo-Babylonia, 45; Achaemenids and, 151; Judaism and, 163

Neo-Confucianism, 302; in China, 520; in Japan, 319, 499, 513, 515, 517; in Korea, 309–12; in Ming dynasty, 298–99, 502, 511; in Song dynasty, 290; tribute mission system of, 521

Neolithic Age (New Stone Age): agriculture of, 47; Americas in, 108–9; China in, 80–82, 97; in Egypt, 31; India in, 58; in Middle East, 30; in Vietnam, 321

NEP. *See* New Economic Policy

Netherlands: Calvinism in, 411, 412; India and, 486–87; Indonesia and, 667–68; Japan and, 515, 521; New Sciences in, 401; privateers of, 465; South Africa and, 459; Spain and, 412

New Amsterdam, 433

Newcomen, Thomas, 403

New Deal, 684–85

New Economic Policy (NEP), in Soviet Union, 692

New England, 443; Calvinism in, 444–45; Protestantism in, 444–46; Puritans in, 435, 444–45; witchcraft in, 445, *445*

New Harmony, 640

New Kingdom, of Egypt, 38, 42, 48

New Lanark, 640

New Model Army, 413

New Sciences (Scientific Revolution), 398–405, 419–20; Enlightenment and, 526; philosophy and, 404–5; social impact of, 401–3

Newspapers: in Japan, 592; photography for, 597

New Stone Age. *See* Neolithic Age

New Testament, 166; Erasmus on, 397; Protestant Reformation and, 409

Newton, Isaac, 400–401, 402; Einstein and, 644

New Zealand, 119

Ngangas, 451

Ngo Dinh Diem, 729, 750

NGOs. *See* Non-governmental organizations

Nguyen dynasty, in Vietnam, 671

Nguyen Van Thieu, 750

Nian Rebellion, 591

Nicaragua, 759

Nicene Creed, 160

Nichiren, 320

Nicholas I, 614–16, 617

Nicholas II, 680

Nietzsche, Friedrich, 646

Niger, 134

Nigeria, 131, 785; civil war in, 756

Nihongi (*Chronicles of Japan*), 321

Nikitenko, Aleksander, 601

Nile River (Valley), 28, 31; Akkad and, 26; Meroë on, 126, 127–29; Nubia in, 330–33

Nineteen Eighty-Four (Orwell), *684*

Nineteenth Amendment, 681

Nirvana, 184–85

Nixon, Richard, 749; dollar regime and, 767; Vietnam War and, 751–52

Nkomo, Joshua, 757

Nkrumah, Kwame, 730–31

Nobel, Alfred Bernhard, 631

Noble Eightfold Path, of Buddhism, 184–85

Nobunaga, Oda, 512–13

Noh, 518, 597

Nomads: in China, 203–4; of East Africa, 131; in India, 179; in Meroë, 129; in Mesopotamia and Egypt, 32; Roman Empire and, 161–63, *162m*; in Tang dynasty, 291

Non-Aligned Movement (NAM), 707, 724, 726–27

Non-governmental organizations (NGOs), 771

Nonproliferation, of nuclear weapons, 738

Nontariff autonomy, 581

Nonviolence (*ahimsa*), 178, 183–84

Norman Conquest: Frankish inquest and, 257; Hundred Years' War and, 272–73; of Italy, 261; of Sicily, 261

Normans, Byzantium and, 232, 234

North Africa: Ottoman Empire in, 602; Spain in, 377

North America: climate of, 103; colonialism in, 433–46, *435m*, 524–25, *525m*; industrialization in, 625–26; Native Americans in, 433–35; revolutions in, 524–26; slavery in, 464–65, *465*. *See also* Canada; Mexico; United States

North Atlantic Treaty Organization (NATO), 711

Northeast Africa: Christianity in, 330–35, 347; Islam in, 330–35; trade in, 331, *332m*

Northern Expedition, 700, 701

North India: British East India Company in, 653–54; kingdoms of, 283; Mughals in, 480–81, *481m*

North Korea: nuclear weapons in, 779, 793; socialism in, 792–93

North Pacific current, 105

Novel: in Japan, 305, 592, 597; in Russia, 623; in Yuan dynasty, 300

NOW. *See* National Organization of Women

Nubia, 126; Arabs and, 330, 331

Nuclear Test Ban Treaty, 715, 738

Nuclear weapons: of China, 748; Cuban Missile Crisis and, 715, 738, 750; at Hiroshima and Nagasaki, 702, 709; ICBMs for, 713–14; Iran and, 779–80; nonproliferation of, 738; of North Korea, 779, 793; SALT II and, 740. *See also* Cold War

Oaxaca, 125

Obama, Barack, 769, 776

Obregón, Álvaro, 564

Obsidian, 8–9; of Maya, 135, 140; of Minoans, 41; of Toltec, 352–53

Ocean currents, of Americas, 103–5

Oceania: city-states in, 121; environment of, 118–19; migrations in, 117–19, *118m*

Ochre, 10, *10m*

Octavian, 157, 158

October Manifesto, 620–21

Office of Strategic Services (OSS), 711

Official nationality, in Russia, 614–15

Ogé, Vincent, 523–24, 531

Oglethorpe, James, 465, 474–75

Ohio Company of Virginia, 436

Oil: in Angola, 757; Arab embargo of, 754; for internal combustion engine, 632; in Iran, 755, 779; OPEC and, 738; price collapse of, 742; in Venezuela, 719, 787

Old Kingdom, of Egypt, *40m*, 53; pyramids of, 38–39, *39*

Oldowan tools, 5, 7, *7*

Old Stone Age (Paleolithic Age), 6

Olmec, *113*, 113–15, 134

Olympic Games, 152–53, 642

One-child policy, in China, 750

On the Origin of Species by Means of Natural Selection (Darwin), 644–45

On the Road (Kerouac), 734

OPEC. *See* Organization of the Petroleum Exporting Countries

Operation Colombo, 759

Opium, 579–84, *580m*, *581*; First Opium War, 580, 588; Second Opium War, 583–84; Taiping Rebellion and, 582–83, *583m*; Treaty of Nanjing and, 580, 581

Oracle bones, 93, 93–94

Oracles, 152; women at, 154

Oral tradition, of Mali, 344

Ordos Desert, 78, 80

Organization of the Petroleum Exporting Countries (OPEC), 738; dollar regime and, 767

The Organization of Work (Blanc), 639

Orrorin femurs, 4

Ortega, Daniel, 759

Orthodox Church, 167

Ortiz, Alonso, 423–24

Orwell, George, *684*

Osman, 376

OSS. *See* Office of Strategic Studies

Otto I of Saxony, 260

Ottoman Empire, *380m*, 602–12; Adriatic Sea and, 376–77; architecture of, 387–89, *388*; Armenia and, 608; Austria and, 382; Balkans and, 609; in Bulgaria, 608; bureaucracy of, 386; Byzantium and, 376; cannons of, 385; centralizing states of, 386–87; Christianity in, 606; coffee and, 382; colonialism by, 660; Constantinople and, 376–77; constitutionalism in, 606–7; in Crimean War, 616, 631, 661; culture of, 392; decentralization in, 603; decline of, 603–9, *604m–5m*; economy of, 609; Egypt and, 605, 608; festivities of, 388;

firearms of, 386; France and, 381; Great Britain and, 605, 662; Greece and, 604–5, 608; Habsburgs and, 376–84, 602; Indian Ocean and, 383*m*; Iran and, 609–12; Jews in, 606; land-grants system of, 384–85; in Middle East, 602; military of, 386; modernity and modernism in, 603, 622; in Montenegro, 608; in Morocco, 377–79; mosques in, 388–89; Napoleon Bonaparte and, 603; Napoleon III and, 606; navy of, 382–83; in North Africa, 602; Parliament of, 607, *608*; in Persia, 377–79; Portugal and, 382; reforms in, 602, 606; Russia and, 614, 616, 618; in Russo-Ottoman War, 616, 618; Safavids and, 377, 383; in Serbia, 608; Sunni Islam of, 377; Syria and, 605; Tanzimat in, 606; tax farming by, 385–86; textile industry in, 609; theater in, 388; Treaty of Versailles and, 681; Tunisia and, 608; World War I and, 677–78

Oualata, 126–27

Owen, Robert, 640

Oxford Calculators, 270

Oyo, 346

Pääbo, Svante, 21

Pachacuti, 361, 362

Pacific Ocean: El Niño in, 105; World War II in, 702, 703*m*. *See also* Oceania

Paekche kingdom (Korea), 308

Paganism: to Christianity, 255; in Great Britain, 253

Pahlavi, Muhammad Reza, 755

Paintings: of Habsburgs, 390–91; icons, in Byzantium, 246–47; of Japan, 305, *305*, 518, *518*; of Mesopotamia, Egypt, and Minoans, 49–50; of Ming dynasty, 511; miniatures, Islamic, 146–47; monochrome, 518; of Mughals, 493–94; of Roman Empire, 171; of romanticism, 545; of Russia, *621*; after World War II, 716, *716*. *See also* Rock art

Pakistan, 56; as nation-state, 724, 725

Palace-states: of Minoans, 39–40; of Mycenaeans, 46

Palaiologos, 241

Paleolithic Age (Old Stone Age), 6; Ice Age and, 17

Palestine, 723*m*; Cold War and, 721–23; Egypt and, 723; Gaza and, 778–79; Great Britain and, 721–23; Judaism in, 163, 165–66; Mamluks and, 372; Napoleon III and, 616; Zionism and, 688

Palestine Liberation Organization (PLO), 753, 754–55, 778, 779

Pali Canon, 185

Pallavas, 180

Pamir Mountains, 78

Panama Canal, 558, 632

Pandyas, 180

Pankhurst, Emmeline, 641, *641*

Pan-Slavism, 617–18; Bosnia-Herzegovina and, 679

Pantheon, 171

Papacy: canon law of, 270; Catholic Reformation and, 411; Jesuits and, 507; Protestant Reformation and, 408; reform of, 264; in Western Christianity, 255; Western Schism of, 273–74, 274*m*. *See also specific popes*

Papal Election Decree, 264

Papal States, 539

Paper, 208, *208*; in China, 502

Papin, Denis, 403

Papua New Guinea, *118*

Paracas, 143–44

Paraguay: colonialism of, 438; as nation-state, 552–54

Pardos, 556

Pargana, 488, 490

Paris: Academy of Sciences in, 410; redesign of, 642; universities in, 267–68

Paris Agreement, 790

Parliament, 260; in England, 274, 413, 544; House of Commons in, 274; of Ottoman Empire, 607, *608*

Parthians: Han dynasty and, 156; Roman Empire and, 156–59

Pascal, Blaise, 403

Passion plays, 389

Pastoral Symphony (Beethoven), 545

Patriarchy: in Middle East, 26, 35–38; Vedas and, 65

Patricians, 336, 337

Paul, Mary, 625

Paul of Tarsus, 166

Pax Mongolica, 275

Pax romana (Roman Peace), 158

Peace of Westphalia, 414

Peace Preservation Law of 1925, in Japan, 698

Peanuts, 500

Pearl Harbor, 702

Pearl River, 78

Peasants' Revolt, 272; Protestant Revolution and, 409

Pedra Furada, 107, *107*

Pedro I, 555

Pedro II, 555

Pedro IV, 452

Pelesets (Philistines), 42, 44–45

Peloponnesian War, 154

Peloponnesus Peninsula, 153

People's Liberation Army, of China, 701

People's War, in China, 700

Pepin III, "The Short," 255, 256

Pepper, *190*, 190–91

Perestroika, 740, 741–42

Periplus of the Erythrean Sea, 189

Perón, Isabel, 760

Perón, Juan, 719, 760

Peronism, 719

Perpetual Peace (Kant), 534

Perry, Matthew C., *588*, 589, 631

Persepolis, 152

Persia: arts of, 168–69; culture of, 168–69; empires of, 155–63; Greece and, 150–55; Ottoman Empire in, 377–79; recovery of, 162–63; religion in, 160; roads of, 152; Roman Empire and, 155–63, 222–23. *See also* Achaemenids; Parthians; Safavids; Sasanids

The Persians (Aeschylus), 170

Peru: Caral-Supe in, 101, 109, 134; coolies in, 570; independence of, 551; mercury in, 429; Moche Valley in, 134, 142–43; in NAM, 727; as nation-state, 558; Nazca of, 143–44, 146–47; Paracas in, 143–44; populism in, 719; rain forests of, 429; Shining Path in, 351; Spain and, 426–28, 557; Tiwanaku of, 355–56, *356*, 357*m*, 368; Wari of, 144, 357*m*, 357–58, 368. *See also* Inca

Peter I "The Great," 416, 613

Petrarch, Francesco, 276

Petronius, 276

Phallic stones, 62

Phan Boi Chau, 673

Pharisees, 166

Philip II, 155, 382, 383, 389, 412, 444

Philip IV, 259, 273

Philippine-American War, 670–71, *671*

Philippines: East Africa and, 133; nationalism in, 670; Spain and, 668–71; in World War II, 702

Philip VI, 272

Philistines (Pelesets), 42, 44–45

Philology, 397

Philosophy: in Byzantium, 247–48; of Enlightenment, 533–34; in Europe, 276; of Greece, 165; modernity in, 646; New Sciences and, 404–5; of realism, 545; of romanticism, 544–45; of Sufism, 244

Phoenicians (Canaanites), 44; alphabet of, *44*

Photography: for newspapers, 597; for realism, *546*

Physics, 168

Phytoliths, 131

Picasso, Pablo, 646, *647*

Pictures of the floating world (*ukiyo-e*), 518–19

Piedmont, 539

Piérola, Nicolás de, 558

Piers Plowman (Langland), 276

Pietism, 535

Pilgrimage (*hajj*), 226

Pillow Talk (Shonagon), 305

Pinochet, Augusto, 759

Pitaka, 185

Pizan, Christine de, 276

Pizarro, Francisco, 426–28

Plague. *See* Black Death

Plague of Justinian, 160–61

Planck, Max, 644

Plantagenet kings, of England, 259

Plantation slavery: in Americas, 439–40, 459–68; in Brazil, 439, 462; in Caribbean, 460–62; in Haiti, 529–30; slave revolts of, 470–71, 472*m*

Plant domestication: in Africa, 131; in Americas, 108; of corn, *112*, 112–13, 113*m*; in Fertile Crescent, 51–52; of rice, 66, 82. *See also specific crops*

The Platform of the Sixth Patriarch (Hui Neng), 215

Plato, 165, 248

PLO. *See* Palestine Liberation Organization

Plow, 260–61

Plymouth, 433

Poe, Edgar Allan, 545

Poetry: Islam and, 245; in Italy, 276; in Japan, 321, 518, 592; in Tang dynasty, 290; for women, 170

Poetry Classic. See Shijing

Pointed arches, on Gothic cathedrals, 269

Poland: Catholicism in, 712; in Cold War, 712; Communist Party in, 742; Marshall Plan and, 709; nationalism in, 712, 777; as nation-state, 740; Russia and, 614, 615; World War II in, 696–97

Politics and political parties: in England, 418–19; in Germany, 694; in Greece, 46–47; of Han dynasty, 203; in India, 689–90; in Japan, 595–96; in Mexico, 690; in Polynesia, 119; in Russia, 620; in Turkey, 780; in Vietnam, 324

Polo, Marco, 294

Pol Pot, 752

Polynesia, 119

Polytheism, 47–48; of Achaemenids, 152; breakdown of, 165; challenges to, 163–65; Judaism and, 166; of Maya, 137, 139; in Roman Empire, 159

Poma de Ayala, Felipe Guamán, 444

Pompeii, 171

Pompey, 158

Poopó, Lake, 356

Pop culture, 683

Popol Vuh, 444

Popular piety, 264–65

Population growth: in Africa, 784–85; in Caribbean, 718*m*; industrialization and, 635–36, 636*m*–37*m*; in Latin America, 718*m*

Populism: in Latin America, 718–19; of Tea Party movement, 776

Porcelain: in China, 208, 216, 502, 504–5, 505; in Europe, 505; in Japan, 516; in Song dynasty, 299, 300

Portugal: apocalypse and, 374; Brazil and, 428, 432–33, 554–55; China and, 507; colonialism by, 432–33; East Africa and, 665; Ethiopia and, 456–57; India and, 375, 486–87; Indian Ocean and, 383*m*;

Japan and, 515; Ottoman Empire and, 382; *Reconquista* in, 372, 374; ships of, 379; slaves of, 456–59, *457*; Spain and, 669; spice trade of, 486; West Africa and, 456, 507

Positivism, 545, 556

Post-colonialism, 766

Postmodernism, 766

Potatoes, 108, 146; in Ming dynasty, 500

Potosí, 438, *439*

Pottery: at Chavín de Huántar, 110; in Jenné-jeno, 130, *130*; of Maya, 136; in Mesoamerica, 109; in Nazca, 143; of Olmec, 114. *See also* Porcelain

Powell, Adam Clayton, 726

Power loom, 627

Powhatan confederacy, 433–35

Prague Spring, 739–40

Predestination, 410

Prehistory. *See* Hominins; Neolithic Age; Paleolithic Age

Presentism, 460

PRI. *See* Institutional Revolutionary Party

Priest-rulers, of Olmec, 114

The Prince (Machiavelli), 397

Printing: in China, 216; in East Asia, 310–11; in Japan, 518–19; in Korea, 312–13; Protestant Reformation and, 407–8; in Renaissance, 396

Privateers, 431, 462, 465

Progressive era, in US, 543

Property rights: in Egypt, 37; in Hinduism, 191; in Mesopotamia, 36

Proskouriakoff, Tatiana, 139

Protestantism: in China, 583 2, 593; in New England, 444–46

Protestant Reformation, 407–11, 410*m*; Baroque arts and, 397

Proto-Indo-European language, 41

Proto-Mediterraneans, 60

Proxy wars, in Latin America, 759

Prussia, 417–18; Bismarck and, 539–40; in Franco-Prussian War, 539, 661; German Federation and, 538; military of, *418*; Poland and, 614

Psychoanalysis, 645

Ptolemaic kings, 166

Ptolemy, 244

Public Debt Administration, of Ottoman Empire, 607

Pueblo, 134, 352, 435

Pueblo Revolt, 559

Pulque, 140, 365

Puquios, 147

Pure Food and Drug Act, 543

Puritans, 413; in New England, 435, 444–45

Puruchuco, 351

Purusha, 70

Pu Songling, 511–12

Putin, Vladimir, 771–72

Pu-Yi, 700

Pygmies, 132

Pyramids: of Americas, 101, 109; of Egypt, 38–39, *39*; of Tenochtitlán, 364; in Teotihuacán, 141

Qaddafi, Muammar el-, 781

Qadesh, 42

Al-Qaeda, 770, 783

Qajars, 609–12

Qi, 298–99

Qianlong, 506, 506*m*, 511

Qin dynasty, in China, 201*m*, 201–3; Confucianism in, 213; First Emperor of, 202, 202–3; gravesites of, 202, *202*; Korea and, 307, 577; unity under, 216; Vietnam and, 322–23; Zhou dynasty and, 201–2

Qing dynasty, in China, 503–12; Boxer Rebellion and, 587–88, 699; culture of, 592–93; economy of, 591–92; family in, 508–9, 592; Manchus and, 503; Mongols and, 505; opium in, 579–84, 580*m*; race for concessions in, 587, *587*; republicanism in, 699–700; science and technology in, 592–93; trade in, 507–8, *508*, 578–80

Qin Shi Huangdi (First Emperor), *202*, 202–3, 217

Quantum Theory, 644

Que, 77

Quetzalcoatl, 141

Queue edict, 503

Quipu, 109, 362

Quotations from Chairman Mao Zedong (Mao Zedong), 748

Quran, 227; in Iran, 755; ISIS and, 783; Muhammad in, 226

Race for concessions, in Qing dynasty, 587, *587*

Racism: from slavery, 474; against Slavs, 697; of South African apartheid, 757–58, 762–63, 785

Radical republicanism, in France, 527, 528

Radioactivity, 644

Radiocarbon dating: of Borana lunar calendar, 125; at Caral-Supe, 101; of spear (points), 19

Railroads: of Africa, 666–67; coolies and, 570; of India, 55; of Industrial Revolution, 627-28, 631; of Japan, 589, 594, *594*; Trans-Siberian, 590, 619; of US, 543, 628

Rain-forest kingdoms, of West Africa, 346

Rain forests: in Africa, 17, 130–31; of Amazon, 116, 369; in Americas, 103; in Australia, 17; Maya and, 136; in Mesoamerica, 354; of Peru, 429

Raj, 656–57

Rajputs, 479

Ramadan, 226

Ramadan War, 753–54
Ramayana, 67, 186
Rapa Nui (Easter Island), 118, 119, *122*, 122–23
Rape of Nanjing, 701–2
Raphael, 397
Al-Rashid, Harun, 257
Rastafarians, 334
Rayon, 631
Raziya, 284
Reagan, Ronald, 747–48
Realism, 545–46, *546*, 548
Reciprocity, 198, 358; of Aztec, 359–60; of Inca, 361–62; of Tiwanaku, 356
Reconquista, 265; in Portugal, 372, 374
Records of Ancient Matters (*Kojiki*), 321
The Records of the Grand Historian (*Shiji*) (Sima Qian), 214, 307
Red Eyebrow Revolt, 204–5
Redology (*hong xue*), 592
Red Sea: Ethiopia and, 335, 456; Meroë and, 129; Nubia and, 331
Re-education, in China, 720
Reformation. *See* Protestant Reformation
Reform War, of Mexico, 561
Regency, 480
Reiche, Maria, 146
Reichstag fire, 695
Reign of Terror, in French Revolution, 528
Relativity Theory, 644
Religion: in Africa, 451–52; in Caribbean, 117; of counterculture, 734; in Egypt, 52–53; in Harappa, 62; of Hittites, 42; in India, 68–73; in Japan, 319–20; in Korea, 312–13; of Meroë, 127; in Mesopotamia, 48; in Middle East, 26, 47–50; in Ming dynasty, 511–12; modernity in, 646; Mughals and, 484–85, *485*, 492–93, 495–96; in Persia, 160; schism in, 183; in Shang dynasty, 92–96; of slaves, 468–69; in Tichitt and Oualata, 126; of Umayyads, 223; in Zhou dynasty, 92–96. *See also* State religions; *specific religions or religion types*
Renaissance: arts of, 396–97, *399*; in Byzantium, 248; culture of, 394–421; *Donation of Constantine* and, 233; Harlem, 683, 686–87; humanism of, 276; maps of, 406–7; music in, 397; science and technology in, 398–405, 419–20; theater in, 397; of twelfth century, 277–78
Renewed imperialism, 651–75
Repartimiento (labor assignments), 425, 429; in Mexico, 431
Republicanism, 47; of Bolívar, 557; in France, 527, 528; in India, 194–95; in Qing dynasty, 699–700; in Roman Empire, 156
Responsibility system, in China, 749
Restoration monarchies, 536–40
Revivalism, 446

Revolt of the Sons, of Mughals, 482
Revolver, 634
Rhapta, 133–34
Rhind Mathematical Papyrus, 50
Rhodes, Cecil, 666
Rhodesia, 757
Ribbed vaults, on Gothic cathedrals, 269
Ricci, Matteo, 507
Rice: in Africa, 134; in Australia, 658; in China, 82; in Eucharist, 507; in India, 66; in Japan, 314, 315; in Ming dynasty, 500; in North America, 464–65; in Vietnam, 323
Richard I, 267
Rifled musket, 634
Rig-Veda, 63, 65, 70, 74
Rikyu, Sen-no, 320
Rio de Oro, 666
Rites Controversy, 507
Ritual (*li*), 199
Ritual pollution, 189
Ritual suicide (*hara-kiri*), 317
Rivera, Diego, 559, *559*
Rizal, José, 670
Roads: of Achaemenids, 152; of Andes, 108; of China, 202; of Inca, 363, *363*; of Japan, 593; of Persia, 152; of Qin dynasty, 202
The Road to Wigan Pier (Orwell), *684*
Roaring Twenties, 681
Rock art: in Africa, 47; in Americas, 107, *107*; in Australia, 47; of Australian Aboriginals, 2, *13*, 13–14; in Blombos Cave, 10, *10m*; of Cro-Magnon, 2; in Eurasia, 14; in Europe, 15, *16*; of *Homo sapiens*, 24; of Neanderthals, 14–15, 20, *20*; on Sulawesi, Indonesia, 15
Rocky Mountains, 102
Roentgen, Wilhelm, 644
Roe v. Wade, 745
Rojdi, 61
Roma (Gypsies), 696
Roman Empire: ancient Ghana and, 341; architecture of, 171; arts of, 170–71; Christianity in, 159–61; imperial beginnings, 156–57; India and, 189; laws of, 162; legionaries of, 156–58; literature of, 170–71; Meroë and, 128; military of, 156–58; monotheism in, 158–60; nomads and, 161–63, *162m*; paintings of, 171; Parthians and, 156–59; Persians and, 155–63, 222–23; polytheism in, 159; recovery of, 162; republicanism in, 156; Sasanids and, 149–50, 159–63, 222; sculpture in, 170–71; ships of, 378; silk and, 211; slaves of, 157–58; triumvirate of, 158; women in, 158–59
Romania: Congress of Berlin and, 607; democracy in, 742; in World War I, 679
Roman Inquisition, 399
Romanov dynasty, in Russia, 416

Roman Peace (*pax romana*), 158
Romanticism, 544–45, 548; modernity in, 646; in music, 647
Roosevelt, Franklin D., 684–85
Roosevelt, Theodore, 558
Rose Garden Edict, 606
Rouhani, Hasan, 779
Rousseau, Jean-Jacques, 533–34
Royal Society of London, 401, 403
Rubber: in Congo, 665; slaves for, 674; in Vietnam, 672; vulcanization of, 631
Rule of alternate attendance (*sankin kotai*), 514
Rumelia, 608
Rumi, Jalal al-Din, 245
Rus, 232, 234
Russia, 612–21; agriculture of, 616–17; in BRIC, 766; colonialism by, 660; Constantinople and, 616, 618; constitutionalism in, 613; in Crimean War, 616, 631, 661; economy of, 771–72; expansion of, 416–17, *417m*, *615m*; famine in, *617*; February Revolution in, 680; first Revolution of, 620–21; France and, 614; French Revolution and, 614; Great Britain and, 661; Greece and, 616; industrialization in, 618–20, 631; modernity and modernism in, 622; Napoleon Bonaparte in, 613, 614; novel in, 623; official nationality in, 614–15; Ottoman Empire and, 614, 616, 618; paintings in, *621*; Poland and, 614, 615; political parties in, 620; reforms in, 616–18; Serbia and, 777; serfdom in, 601, 616–17; Triple Intervention by, 590, 619; Venezuela and, 787. *See also* Soviet Union; World War I
Russian Revolution, first, *621*
Russo-Japanese War, 620
Russo-Ottoman War, 616, 618
Rutherford, Ernest, 644
Rwanda, 665; civil war in, 770

SA. *See* Sturmabteilung
Saadids, 377
Sacco, Nicola, 683
Sacraments, 274
El-Sadat, Anwar, 754
Sadler Report, 640
Safavids: in Iran, 377, 609–12; Mughals and, 483; Ottoman Empire and, 377, 383; Shiite Islam of, 377, 378–79
Sahel, 130, 341
Saints: in Catholicism, 444. *See also specific saints*
Saint-Simon, Henri de, 639–40
Saladin (Salah al-Din), 237, 267
Salem witch trials, 445, *445*
Salons, for New Sciences, 401–2
SALT II, 740

Salt March, 690, *690*

Same-sex marriage, 745

Samudragupta, 180

Samurai, 317, *318*, 514–15; in peacetime, 517–18

Sandinista National Liberation Front (FSLN), 759

Sandrokottos, 175

Sankin kotai (rule of alternate attendance), 514

San Lorenzo, 113–14

San Martín, José de, 552–53, 557

Santa Anna, Antonio López de, 559, 561

Sappho of Lesbos, 170

Sargon of Akkad, 27, 35

Sasanids: agriculture of, 228; Aksum and, 129–30; Arabs and, 222; architecture of, 169; India and, 168, 189; Roman Empire and, 149–50, 159–63, 222; as Zoroastrians, 149–50

Satori, 320, 327

Saul, 45

Savanna: of Africa, 130–31; hominins in, 5

Savery, Thomas, 632

Savior, of Zoroastrians, 164

Schism: in religion, 183; Western Schism, 273–74, *274m*

Schmidt, Tobias, 531

Schoenberg, Arnold, 647

Scholasticism, 268

Schutzstaffel (SS), 696

Science and technology: of China, 584–85; of Han dynasty, 215–16; of High Middle Ages, 270; of India, 192–93; industrialization and, 644–46; of Japan, 584–85, 596–97; at Library of Alexandria, 168; of Middle East, 50; of Ming dynasty, 299, 509–11; of Mughals, 491–92; of Qing dynasty, 592–93; of Renaissance, 398–405, 419–20; of Song dynasty, 290; of Zhou dynasty, 95–96. *See also* New Sciences

Scientific management, 643

Scientific Revolution. *See* New Sciences

Scientific socialism, 640

Scotland: England and, 418; as nation-state, 544; New Lanark in, 640; Protestant Revolution in, 409

Scotus, John Duns, 276

Scramble for Africa, 663–67m

Sculpture: in Africa, 344–45, *345*; of bodhisattva, *192*; in Greece, 170; in Roman Empire, 170–71

SDI. *See* Strategic Defense Initiative

Sea People, from Greece, 42, 44, 46

Sebastião I, 459

Second Crusade, 236

Second Industrial Revolution, 628–34

Second Isaiah (Deutero-Isaiah), 163–64

Second Opium War, 583–84

Second Reform Act (England), 544

Second Temple, 164, 165

Secret History of the Mongols, 294

Securities and Exchange Commission (SEC), 684–85

Selective breeding, 30

Seleucids: Judaism and, 166; Parthians and, 156

Seleucus Nikator, 67, 175, 177

Self (*atman*), 72

Self-rule (*swaraj*), 689–90

Self-strengthening, 577, *584*, 584–85, 591; of Ottoman Empire, 608–9

Seljuk Turks: Byzantium and, 233–34; in Middle East, 265

Senegal, 666

Senghor, Léopold, 687

Sen-no Rikyu, 320

September 11, 2001 terrorist attack, 769, *770*

Serbia: Bosnia-Herzegovina and, 679; Congress of Berlin and, 607; Ottoman Empire in, 377, 608; supremacist nationalism of, 777

Serfdom, in Russia, 601, 616–17

Seveners, 228, 234

Seven Years' War, 437, 524, 526–27; British East India Company and, 652

Sewer systems: of Harappa, 59, 60; industrialization and, 641–42; of Tenochtitlán, 364; of Teotihuacán, 141

Sexuality: in India, 69–70. *See also* Homosexuals

Sexual revolution, 744–45

Shabab, 785

Shahinshahs, 152

Shah Jahan (Khurram), 483–84

Shahname (*Book of Kings*) (Firdosi), 168, 245

Shakas, 180

Shakespeare, William, 397

Shakti, 187

Shamans, 107, *107*; in Caribbean, 117

Shan, 482–83

Shangdi, 93, 94

Shang dynasty, in China, 77, *84*, *85m*; agriculture of, 89; animal domestication in, 89; bronzes of, 86, 93; chariots in, 84–85, *86*; client states of, 85; culture of, 96; economy of, 89–90; family in, 89–90; gravesites in, 91–92, 94; human sacrifice in, 94; religion in, 92–96; *Shujing* on, 82, 84; social classes in, 89–90; trade in, 86; women in, 91–92; writing in, 93–95, *94*; Yellow River and, 77–78

Shanghai Communiqué, 749

Shapur II, 160

Sharecroppers, in Mesopotamia and Egypt, 32

Sharia Law, 227; in India, 486; Islamism and, 785; Sufism and, 244

Shaw, George Bernard, 646

Shi, 91

Shiite Islam, 227–28, 610–11; Hidden Imam of, 377; in Iran, 609, 755; of Mughals, 483; of Safavids, 377, 378–79; Seljuks and, 234

Shiji (*The Records of the Grand Historian*) (Sima Qian), 214, 307

Shijing (*The Book of Odes, Poetry Classic, The Book of Songs*), 92, 96, 98

Shikibu, Murasaki, 305, 321

Shining Path, in Peru, 351

Shinto (way of the gods), 315, 319–20

Ships: of China, 262; in colonialism, 658–59; of Genoa, 372; in Mediterranean, 378, 378–79, *379*; of Portugal, 372; for slave trade, 467, *467*; steam engine for, 627–28; sternpost rudder on, 262. *See also* Navy

Shiraz, 336

Shirin, 149–50

Shiva, 180, 186

Shoguns, 316–17, 512

Shonagon, Sei, 305

Shotoku (Prince), 315

Shudra, 70

Shujing (*Book of History, Classic of Documents*), 82, 83, 84, 87

Shun, 82

Siam. *See* Thailand

Sicily, 236; city-states in, 156; in Holy Roman Empire, 260; Norman Conquest of, 261

Sierra Madre Mountains, 102

Sikhism, 286; Mughals and, 486, 496–97

Silk: in China, 80–81, 208, 502; in India, 488; in Korea, 311; rayon and, 631

Silk Road, 78, 212m–13m, 242, 478; agricultural revolution and, 261; Black Death and, 243; in China, 203, 210–11; in India, 189; Mongols and, 275; Mughals and, 482; Parthians and, 156; in Tang dynasty, 289, 290; Xiongnu on, 203

Silla kingdom, in Korea, 308, 315

Silver: Achaemenids and, 152; in Americas, 438–39, *439*; in Bolivia, 429; at Chavín de Huántar, 110; coolies and, 570; of Inca, 426–28; Mauryans and, 179; in Mexico, 669; tax farming and, 385

Sima Qian, 214, 307

Sima Tan, 214

Single-whip tax system, of Ming dynasty, 502

Sinicization, 203–4, 322–23

Sino-Japanese War, *586*, 586–87

Sino-Soviet Split, 721

Sino-Tibetan language group, 81

Sioux, 435

Sirleaf, Ellen Johnson, 785

Sisi, Abdel Fattah, 782

Six-Day War, 752

Slater, Samuel, 628

Slave revolts: in Brazil, 566–67; in Cuba, 566–67; in Haiti, 523–24, 529–32, *530*; of plantation slavery, 470–71, *472m*

Slaves and slavery: from Africa, 440, 461*m*, 473; in agrarian–urban society, 9; in Americas, 463*m*; as chattel, 460; culture of, *471*; from East Africa, 336; Islam and, 385; from Kongo, 459; in Middle East, 35; of Mongols, 309; music of, 470; of Native Americans, 429, 432; in North America, 464–65, *465*; from Nubia, 331; of Portugal, 456–59, *457*; racism from, 474; religions of, 468–69; of Roman Empire, 157–58; for rubber, 674; ships for, 467, *467*; social class of, 464; from sub-Saharan Africa, 452–59; from West Africa, 663. *See also* Abolition of slavery; Plantation slavery

Slavs: Byzantium and, 376; pan-Slavism and, 617–18, 679; racism against, 697; Varangians and, 232

Sleeping sickness, 132

Smallpox, 424, 426, 431, 435, 442

Smriti, 69

Smith, Adam, 534, 539

Smith, Ian, 757

SNSs. *See* Social networking sites

Soccer, 642

Social classes: in Americas, 109, 440–43; in China, 203; in Europe, 263; in Greece, 46; in Harappa, 61; of Inca, 362; in India, 69, 70–71; industrialization and, 637–39; in Korea, 310, 312; of Maya, 137–38; in Middle East, 35–38; in Ming dynasty, 297; of Neolithic China, 81; in Shang dynasty, 89–90; of slaves, 464; Vedas and, 182; in Xia dynasty, 83; in Zhou dynasty, 91. *See also* Caste system; Middle class

Social contract, 404–5; after World War II, 716

Social Contract (Rousseau), 533–34

Social Darwinism, 645; colonialism and, 674

Socialism: in China, 701; in India, 725, 726–27; industrialization and, 639–40; in Latin American proxy wars, 759; in North Korea, 792–93; scientific, 640; in Sri Lanka, 707; in Venezuela, 787. *See also* Communism

Social networking sites (SNSs), 786, 786–87

Social Security Act, 684

Social stratification: in China, 84; in Jenné-jeno, 130; of Maya, 136

Society of Friends of Blacks, 523

Society of the Harmonious Fists, 588

Soga clan, 315

Solidarity, in Poland, 740, 742

Solomon, 45

Solomonid dynasty, in Ethiopia, 334

Somalia, 666; civil war in, 785; Italy and, 694; *jihad* in, 785

Somoza García, Anastasio, 759

Song dynasty, in China: bureaucracy in, 290; gunpowder in, *292*, 292–93; Mongols and, 291; Neo-Confucianism in, 290; porcelain in, 216, 299, *300*; women in, 218

Songhay Empire, 452–54

Soninke, 341, 342

Sonno joi, 589

Sons of Liberty, 525

Sophocles, 170

Soseki, Natsume, 597

Sot-weed. *See* Tobacco

South Africa, 757–58, *758*, 762–63, 785; Netherlands and, 459

South America: climate of, 103; colonialism in, 430*m*. *See also* Andes; *specific countries*

South Asia, migrations to Australia, 10–14

South Carolina, 464

Southeast Asia, 322*m*; colonialism in, 586–87, 667–73, 669*m*; India and, 189; nation-states in, 728–7729; trade in, 489*m*; in World War II, 702

Southern Africa: agrarian–urban centers of, 131–34; kingdoms in, 337–40

Southern characters (*chu nom*), 325

Southern Cone, 552

South India, kingdoms of, 180–81

Soviet Union: Afghanistan and, 737, *737*, 740–41; agriculture of, 693, *693*; Angola and, 757; Balkans and, 708; China and, 719, 721, 738, 748; civil war in, 692–93; Communist Party in, 691–92; decline of, 738–42, 742*m*; Germany and, 708; industrialization in, 693; Israel and, 722; modernity in, 691–92; Prague Spring and, 739–40; Vietnam and, 729; in World War II, 697. *See also* Cold War

Spain: American Revolution and, 527; Aztec and, 359, 424–26; in Caribbean, 424; Catholic Reformation in, 411; colonialism by, 428–32, 434–28; Gibraltar and, 262; Habsburgs in, 380; Inca and, 426–28, *444*; Islam in, 265; Mexico and, 424–26; Morisco expulsion from, 384; Netherlands and, 412, 667; in North Africa, 377; Peru and, 426–28, 557; Philippines and, 668–71; Portugal and, 669; Pueblo Revolt and, 559; Rio de Oro and, 666

Spanish-American War, 670–71

Spanish Civil War, 696

"Spanish Flu," 681

Spanish Inquisition, 374

Sparta, 46, 47, 152–54

Spartacus, 158

Spears (points): in Americas, 105–6, 107; radiocarbon dating of, 19

Spencer, Herbert, 645

Spice trade, 130; for black pepper, *190*, 190–91; Netherlands and, 667; of Portugal, 486; Spain and, 669

Spinning jenny, 627

Spinning mule, 627

Spinoza, Baruch, 404

Sports, industrialization and, 642

Spring and Autumn Chronicles, 87

Sputnik, 713–14, *714*

Squinches, 169

Sri Lanka (Ceylon): Cholas in, 283; in NAM, 707, 724; as nation-state, 724

Srivijaya, 283

SS. *See Schutzstaffel*

Stagflation, 747

Stalin, Joseph, 697, 708; death of, 712; Khrushchev and, 721, 738; Marshall Plan and, 709; Tito and, 709

Stamp Act, 525–26

Standard of Ur, 27

Standard Oil Company, 642–43

Stanley, Henry Morton, 665

START. *See* Strategic Arms Reduction Talks/Treaty

Star Wars. *See* Strategic Defense Initiative

State religion, 174; in Aksum, 129; Calvinism as, 411; in China, 196, 315; Christianity as, 249; of Italy, 692; monotheism as, 159, 163; of Roman Empire, 327; of Safavids, 493; Zoroastrianism as, 249

Steam engine, 403; in China, *581*; for ships, 627–28; for textile industry, 627

Steel: big business in, 642–43; in second Industrial Revolution, 630

Sterilization, of women, 684

Sternpost rudder, 262

Stirrups, *206*, 206–7

Stoics, 166

Stonewall Inn, 745, *745*

Strait of Gibraltar, 262

Strait of Tiran, 723

Strange Tales from the Make-Do Studio (Pu Songling), 511–12

Strategic Arms Reduction Talks/Treaty (START), 740

Strategic Defense Initiative (SDI, Star Wars), 741

Stream of consciousness, 683

Striation, 306

Stuart monarchs, of England, 412–13

Sturmabteilung (SA), 696

Subaltern, 657

Subatomic particles, 644

Subconscious, 645

Sub-Saharan Africa: agrarian–urban centers of, 130–31, 132*m*; Americas and, 145; chiefdoms of, 146; city-states of, 146; communism in, 784; history of, 134; Islam in, 454–55; kingdoms of, 146, 454*m*; nation-states in, 732; slaves from, 452–59

Sudan: Great Britain and, 662; UN in, 770–71

Suez Canal, 662, 688–89, 723–24

Suffragettes, 641, *641*

Sufism, 482, 493; Sunni Islam and, 243–44, 250–51

Sugarcane: in Australia, 658; in Brazil, 462; in Canary Islands, 372; in Caribbean, 460–62, 569; coolies and, 570; in Ming dynasty, 500; in North America, 464–65

Suger, Abbot, 269

Sui, 205; Tang dynasty and, 287
Suiko, 315, 319
Sukarno, 707
Süleyman I, "The Magnificent," 377, 386
Sultanates, of north India, 286, 286m
Sumer, Sumerian, 34–37, 34, 48
Summa Theologica (Aquinas), 269
Summer of love, 745
Sundiata, 344, 348–49
Sungbo's Eredo, 346
Sunna, 226, 227
Sunni Islam, 227, 610–11; in Afghanistan, 379; in Egypt, 237; ISIS and, 783; of Ottoman Empire, 377; Sufism and, 243–44, 250–51
Sun Yat-sen, 699
Sun Zi, 67
Supremacist nationalism, 693–98, 704; of Serbia, 777
Surinam, 471
Sustainability, 788–90
Swahili, city-states of, 134, 336, 338m, 665
Swaraj (self-rule), 689–90
Swastika, 62
Sweden: Protestant Revolution in, 409; sterilization of women in, 684; Thirty Years' War and, 414
Switzerland: Calvinism in, 409–11; Protestant Revolution in, 409
Sykes-Picot agreement, 688
Syllabary, 305, 321
Sylvester II, 267
Symbols: in Harappa, 62; of *Homo sapiens*, 9–10; modernity in, 646; of Neanderthals, 14
Symphonie fantastique (Berlioz), 545
Synagogues, 166; on Euphrates River, 167
Syria: Abbasids in, 225; Achaemenids and, 151; Arabs in, 222; Arab Spring in, 781–83; Assyrians and, 43; civil war in, 778; Israel and, 738; Jacobite Church in, 167; Judaism in, 163; in Lebanese civil war, 754–55; Ottoman Empire and, 605; in Six-Day War, 753; Treaty of Kadesh and, 42; in United Arab Republic, 724; Syriac Orthodox Church, 149–50

Taejo, 308
Taif Agreement, 755
Taiho Code, 315
Taika (Great Reform), 315
Tailor's Rebellion, 567
Taíno, 117, 424–25
Taiping Rebellion (Qing dynasty), 582–83, 583m
Taiping tianguo (Heavenly Kingdom of Great Peace), 583
Taisho Democracy (Japan), 698
Taiwan: Aboriginals of, 118; Austronesian language on, 81; Japan and, 619; Lapita from, 100; Qing dynasty and, 577
Taj Mahal, 477, 477, 494

Takauji, Ashikaga, 316–17
Taklamakan Desert, 78
Takrur, 342
Tale of Genji (*Genji Monagatori*) (Shikibu), 305, 321
Taliban, 770
Tambo, Oliver, 762
Tamerlane (Timur-i-Lang), 285, 376, 478–79, 479m
Tamils, 180
Tang dynasty, in China, 206–7; Buddhism in, 287–90, 302; bureaucracy in, 289; gender relations in, 211; music in, 289; nomads in, 291; poetry in, 290; porcelain in, 216; ships of, 379; Silk Road in, 289, 290; Sui and, 287; trade in, 290; Vietnam and, 325; women in, 218
Tantra, 187
Tanzania, 134, 665
Tanzimat, 606
Tariffs, 628; in India, 188
Tatars, 614
Tatsukichi, Minobe, 677
Tawantinsuyu, 360
Taxes: of Aksum, 129; American Revolution and, 525–26; of Aztec, 365; of centralized kingdoms, 406–7; of France, 416; French Revolution and, 527; of India, 188, 286, 654; of Korea, 308; of Manchus, 503; of Mauryans, 176, 179; of Ming dynasty, 502; of Mughals, 488; of Nubia, 331; of Roman Empire, 159; of US, 776; of Zhou dynasty, 90–91. *See also* Tariffs
Tax farming, 242, 385–86
Taxila, 175, 176
Tea: ceremony, 320; from China, 290, 317, 320, 502; Stamp Act on, 525–26; in Tang dynasty, 290; in Vietnam, 672
Tea Party movement, 776
Technology. *See* Science and technology
Tecumseh, 542–43
Telegraph, 633–34; in Japan, 589, 594
Telephone, 634; in Japan, 594
Temples: in Egypt, 33; in Greece, 46; of Hinduism, 180; in Jerusalem, 151; of Maya, 136, 136; in Mesopotamia, 48; in Moche Valley, 142; of Nubia, 126; of Roman Empire, 171; in Teotihuacán, 141, 143; of Zoroastrians, 164
Tenements, 639, 640
Ten Hours Act, 641
Tennessee Valley Authority, 684
Tenochtitlán, 359, 364–65, 365m, 368; Cortés in, 426
Tenskwatawa, 542–43
Tent government (*bakufu*), 514
The Ten Thousand Leaves (*Man'yoshu*), 321
Teosinte, 108
Teotihuacán, 134, 140–41, 143, 352–55
Tesla, Nikola, 631–33

Tet Offensive, 751
Texas, 561
Texcoco, Lake, 140
Textile industry: in China, 627; in Germany, 665; in Great Britain, 639; in India, 627; in Ottoman Empire, 609; steam engine for, 627; in US, 625, 628
Thackeray, William Makepeace, 546
Thailand (Siam), 672
Thales, 165
Thar (Great Indian) Desert, 57
Thatcher, Margaret, 747–48
Theater: of Habsburgs, 390–91; in Japan, 518, 597; in Ottoman Empire, 388; in Renaissance, 397; after World War II, 716
Themata, 229
Theogony (Hesiod), 170
Theory of Relativity, 644
Theravada, 185; Vietnam and, 324–25
Thermidorean Reaction, 748
Third Coalition, 614
Third Crusade, 237, 267
Third estate, 527
Third Reich, 696
Third Republic, in France, 540, 548–49
Third Section, 615
Thirty Years' War, 413–15
Three Kingdoms: of China, 205; of England, 413; of Korea, 307–8
Thunberg, Greta, 790
Tiamat, 49
Tiananmen Square, 749, 749, 750
Tiantai, 215
Tibet: in Qing dynasty, 505; in Yuan dynasty, 292
Tichitt, 126–27
Tigris River, 28, 31; Assyrians and, 43; Sasanids and, 228
Tikal, 135, 136
Timbuktu, 345, 377; Songhay Empire and, 453
Timurids, 479, 487
Timur-i-Lang (Tamerlane), 285, 376, 478–79, 479m
Titicaca, Lake, 355–56
Tito, Josip Broz, 708–9, 777
Tituba, 445
Tiwanaku, 355–56, 356, 357m, 368; Wari and, 357–58
Tlaxcala, 359, 425
TNT, 634
Toba, 205
Tobacco, 464; in Ming dynasty, 500
Tocharian, 84
Tokugawa. *See* Ieyasu, Tokugawa
Toledo, 236
Tolkien, J. R. R., 25
Toltec, 352–55
Tombs. *See* Gravesites
Topkapı Palace, 377, 387–88, 388

Tories, 419

Torricelli, Evangelista, 403

Total war, in World War I, *678*, 679

Toumaï skull, 4

Tour de France, 642

Toussaint Louverture, François-Dominique, 532

Trade: in Afro-Eurasian world commercial system, 241–42, *242m*; by Aksum, 128, 130; in Andes, 110; by Athens, 153; by China, 502, *502m*; in Egypt, 39; in Eurasia, *285m*; in Europe, 261–62, 275; in Ghana, 341; global balance of, *768m*; in Greece, 46; by Harappa, 61; by India, 188–89, *489m*, 489–90; in Mali, 342–43; on Mediterranean, 261–62, *262m*; in Mesopotamia, 32–33; in Ming dynasty, *504*, *504m*, 504–5, *505*; by Minoans, 41; in northeast Africa, 331, *332m*; by Olmec, 114; by Phoenicians, 44; by Qing dynasty, 507–8, *508*, 578–80; in Shang dynasty, 86; in Southeast Asia, *489m*; in Tang dynasty, 290; by Toltec, 354; in Vietnam, 324; in Zhou dynasty, 91. *See also* Exports; Silk Road

Trade forts: for African slave trade, 457; of Netherlands and Portugal, 667–68; of Spain, 669

Trade winds, 103–5

Trail of Tears, 543

Tran dynasty, in Vietnam, 323

Transcendence, 163, 172; in Being, 165; Buddhism and, 184; Daoism and, 200; Jainism and, 184; in Sufism, 244; in Upanishads, 182

Trans-Siberian Railroad, 590, 619

Treaty of Brest-Litovsk, 680

Treaty of Kadesh, 42

Treaty of Kanagawa, 589

Treaty of Nanjing, 580, 581

Treaty of Paris, 273

Treaty of Shimonoseki, 577

Treaty of Verdun, 257

Treaty of Versailles, 681, 694

Tres Zapotes, 114

Tribute system: of Ming dynasty, 309; of Neo-Confucianism, 521

Trinitarianism, 223

Tripitaka, 185, 312

Triple Intervention, 590, 619

Tripolitania. *See* Libya

Triumvirate, of Roman Empire, 158

Trotsky, Leon, 691

Truman, Harry S, 702

Truman Doctrine, 708–9

Trump, Donald, 776, 780, 790

Trung Nhi, 323

Trung Trac, 323

Tsar (czar), 416; collapse of, 680

Tsetse fly, 132

Tughluq, Muhammad, "The Bloody," 286

Tulans, 352

Tundra, 18

Tunisia, 156; Arab Spring in, 780–82; France and, 662–63; Ottoman Empire and, 608

Túpac Amaru, 351

Turkana steppe, 5

Turkey, *781*; Great Britain and, 689, *689*; industrialization in, 780

Turkistan, 163

Turks: Abbasids and, 228; Byzantium and, 376. *See also* Ottoman Empire; Seljuk Turks

Turner, Nat, 471

Tutankhamen, *43*, 53

Tutenkhaten, 53

Tuxen, Laurits Regner, *619*

Twelve Tablets, of Roman Empire, 156

Twelve-tone music, 647

Tzompantii, 366–67

Ubaid, 31, 48

Uji, 318

Ukiyo-e (pictures of the floating world), 518–19

Ukraine: Chernobyl nuclear accident in, 742; Russia and, 772; Soviet Union and, 691

Ulama, 227

Umar, Al-Hajj, 664–65

Umayyads, 261; Abbasids and, 224; Byzantium and, 229; religion of, 223

Umma, 226

UN. *See* United Nations

Unction, 255

Union of German Women's Organizations, 641

Union of Soviet Socialist Republics. *See* Soviet Union

United Arab Republic, 724

United Nations (UN), 708; Charter of, 534; China in, 749; Iran and, 779; Iraq and, 770; North Korea and, 792–93; Palestine and, 721–22; peacekeeping by, 770–71

United States (US): abolition of slavery in, 541; Afghanistan and, 770; big business in, 642–43; capitalist democracy of, 766–74; China and, 749; civil rights movement in, 744–45; consumerism in, 681–83; Dawes Plan of, 695; dollar regime of, 767, 771; early years of, 526; economy of, 771, 776–77; exports to, 768; globalization and, 768–69; in Great Depression, 684–85; industrialization in, 628; Iran hostage crisis and, 756; Iraq and, 769–70; ISIS and, 783; IT in, 768–69; Japan and, 589; Korea and, 711–12; in Latin American proxy wars, 759; McCarthyism in, 712; in Mexican-American War, 588; Mexico and, 560–61, *561m*, 776; military of, 769; modernity in, 681; as nation-state, 540–44, *542m*; Native Americans in, *542*, 542–43; in 1970s and

1980s, 747–48; Ottoman Empire and, 606; in Philippine-American War, 670–71, *671*; Progressive era in, 543; railroads in, 543, 628; security commitments of, *772m–73m*; in Spanish-American War, 670–71; taxes in, 776; textile industry in, 625, 628; Vietnam and, 729; in Vietnam War, 750–52, *751m*; women in, 681–83; women's suffrage in, 641; in World War II, 697–98, 702. *See also* Cold War; World War I

United States Steel Corporation, 643

Universal love, 218

Universal Negro Improvement Association, 687

Universities, in High Middle Ages, 267–69

Untouchables, 70

Upanishads, 72, 182

Urania propitia (*Companion to Urania*) (Cunitz), 395

Urban II, 234, 265

Urbanization (urbanism): in Caribbean, *718m*; in East Africa, 336–37; in Europe, 263; in India, 725, 783; industrialization and, 635–36; in Latin America, 717, *718m*; of Maya, 355; in Mexico, 690. *See also* Cities, city-states

Urban VI, 274

Uruguay, 552–54

Uruk, 33

Urukagina of Lagash, 36

US. *See* United States

Usulism, 611

Usury, 410

Utamaro, Kitagawa, 519

Utari, 313

Vacuum, 402–3, *403*

Vaishyas, 70

Valencia, 384

Vanity Fair (Thackeray), 546

Vanzetti, Bartolomeo, 683

Varangians, 231–32, 233, 234–35; as mercenaries, 241

Varnas, 69, 70, 71

Vatsyayana, 69–70, 192

Vedanta, 72

Vedas, 64–67; Hinduism and, 70–73; reformers of, 182–87

Venezuela: caudillo in, 557–58; colonialism of, 438; democracy in, 718, 719; in NAM, 727; oil in, 719, 787; populism in, 719; socialism in, 787

Venus figurines, 15, *15*, 47

Vernacular, 276

Veronese, Paolo, 384

Versailles Palace, 398, *414*

Versailles Treaty, 681, 694, 700

Vesuvius, Mount, 171

Vichy government, 697

Victor Emanuel II, 539

Victoria, Lake, 31, 455

Vietcong, 729, 750, 751

Vietminh, 729

Vietnam: agrarian–urban centers in, 321–22; agriculture of, 323–24; Buddhism in, 321–22, 324–25; China and, 748, 752; communism in, 750–52, 775; culture of, 323; economy of, 323–24; France and, 671–73, 729; Japan and, 326; Korea and, 326; Mongols in, 243; as nation-state, 724, 729; Neolithic Age in, 321; US and, 729; writing in, 325; in Yuan dynasty, 292

Vietnam Restoration League, 673

Vietnam War, 750–52, 751*m*

Vijayanagar ("City of Victory"), 283

Vikings, 257

Villa, Francisco "Pancho," 563–64

Vinaya, 185

Viracocha, 360

Virgil, 170, 171, *171*

Virgin Mary, 444, 494

Vishnu, 180, 186

Visigoths, 223

Vivaldi, Antonio, 398

VOC. *See* Dutch United East India Company

Volga trade route, 242

Voltaire, 402; Catherine I "The Great" and, 613

Voodoo, 445, *468*, 468–69

Voting rights: of African Americans, 542; Chartism and, 640; of women, 641, 681, 689

Voting Rights Act of 1965, 744

Vulcanization of rubber, 631

Wagner, Richard, 647

Waldseemüller, Martin, *400*

Wales, 544

Wałęsa, Lech, 740, 742

Wang Anshi, 290–91

Wang Chong, 216

Wang Mang, 204–5

Wang Yangming, 299, 511

Wari, 144, 357*m*, 357–58, 368

War on Terror, 769

Warring States period, in China, 89, 197; Confucianism in, 213; Xunzi and, 200

Warsaw Pact, 711, 713; Brezhnev Doctrine of, 740

Washington, George, 526

Washington Consensus, 771, 775

Water frame, 627

Watermills, 261

Watt, James, 632

Way (*Dao*), 198, 299

Way of the Warrior (*bushido*), 317, 327

Al-Wazzan, al-Hasan Ibn Muhammad (Leo Africanus ["the African"]), 371

Weapons: in Cold War, 713–14; in second Industrial Revolution, 634. *See also* Cannons; Firearms; Nuclear weapons

Weapons of mass destruction, in Iraq, 770

Weimar Republic, 694–95

Wei Yuan, 592

Well-field system, in Zhou dynasty, 90–91

Wells, 261

Wen Bo, 92

Wesley, Charles, 446

Wesley, John, 446

West Africa: colonialism in, 663–65; gold in, 374, 377; Islam in, 348; kingdoms in, 341–46, 343*m*; Portugal and, 456, 507

Western Christianity: adaptation of, 248, 252–79; centralized kingdoms and, 405; in Constantinople, 234, 270–76; Eastern Christianity and, 233; evolution of, 249–50; expansion of, 370–92; formation of, 254–58; heresy in, 265; papacy in, 255; popular piety in, 264–65; recovery of, 259–63; reform of, 264–67

Western Schism, 273–74, 274*m*

What Is to Be Done? (Chernyshevsky), 623; (Lenin), 623

Wheat: in Americas, 439; in Nubia, 331

Wheel, 108, 121, 146; of *dharma*, 192

Whigs, 419

Whitefield, George, 446

"The White Man's Burden" (Kipling), 674

Wilhelm I, 539

William I, 259, 264

William of Ockham, 276

William of Orange, 668

Wilson, Woodrow, 680

Windmills, 261

Winstanley, Gerrard, 420–21

Wireless telegraph, 634

Witchcraft: in Africa, 133, 451; in New England, 445, *445*

Women: in Americas, 441; in Athens, 173; of Australian Aboriginals, 12; in China, 98–99, 217–18; civil rights for, 744–45, 746*m*, 746–47; in Egypt, 37–38; Equal Rights Amendment (ERA), 746–47; in Greece, 154; in Han dynasty, 211; of Inca, 365–66; in India, 69–70; industrialization and, 641; in Japan, 318–19, 517; in Korea, 312; in Latin America, 572; in Mesopotamia, 36–37; in Ming dynasty, 298, 509; in mining, 639, *639*; of Mughals, 490–91; New Sciences and, 401–2; of Ottoman Empire harems, 388; poetry for, 170; in Roman Empire, 158–59; in Shang dynasty, 91–92; in Song dynasty, 218; sterilization of, 684; in Tang dynasty, 218; in US, 681–83; in

Vietnam, 324; voting rights of, 641, 681, 689; in Zhou dynasty, 92

Women Journalists Without Chains, 765

Women's Social and Political Union, 641

Woodstock Festival, 745

Working class: industrialization and, 639, *640*; in Venezuela, 787

The Works of Mencius (Legge), 197

World Trade Center, 769, *770*

World War I: empires and, 677–81; Gatling guns in, 634; modernity and, 677–81, 704; nationalism and, 645; total war in, 678, 679; Turkey and, 689

World War II: culture after, 715–16; in Europe, 696–98, 699*m*; in France, 696–97; Great Britain in, 697–98; Japan in, 702; Nazi Germany in, 696–98, 704–5; in Pacific Ocean, 702, 703*m*; in Poland, 696–97; Soviet Union in, 697; US in, 697–98, 702

Wounded Knee, 543, 744

Wright, Richard, 726

Wright brothers, 633

Writing: of Achaemenids, 152; in China, 202, 204; cuneiform, 34, *34*; in Harappa, 62; in Korea, 312; of Maya, 136, 139, *140*; of Minoans, 39; of Olmec, 115; of Phoenicians, 44; in Shang dynasty, 93–95, *94*; in Vietnam, 325; in Zhou dynasty, 93–95, *94*. *See also* Calligraphy; Hieroglyphic writing

Writs, 260

Wu (Empress), 290, *290*, 302–3

Wudi (Martial Emperor), 156, 203–4; Vietnam and, 323

Wu Ding, 77, 85, 93

Wu Sangui, 503

Wycliffe, John, 274

Xavier, Francis, 507

Xesspe, Toribio Mejia, 146

Xia dynasty, in China: culture of, 96; *Shujing* on, 82, 83; Yellow River and, 80

Xiang, 197

Xiaojing (*Classic of Filial Piety*), 214

Xiongnu, 179, 202, 203

X-rays, 644

Xuan Zang, 214–15, 282–83

Xunzi, 199–200

Xu Qinxian, 750

Yahweh, 163–64, 166

Yam, 470

Yamato, 314, 315

Yang, 299

Yang Jian, 205

Yangshao period, in Xia dynasty, 83

Yang Zhu, 218

Yangzi River, 78

Yanukovych, Viktor, 772
Yao, 82
Yasht, 160, 164
Yayoi period (Japan), 314
Yellow fever, 663
Yellow River, 78–83; agriculture and, 96;
    Shang dynasty and, 77–78
Yeltsin, Boris, 742
Yemen, 129, 133–34; Arab Spring in, 781;
    civil war in, 765; coffee in, 382; Persia
    and, 163
Yi dynasty, in Korea, 309–11
Yin, 299
Yoga, 72
Yom Kippur War, 753–54
Yongban, 312
Yongle, 296–97
Yongzheng, 504, 507, 511
Yoritomo, Minamoto, 316
Yoruba, 756
Younger Dryas, 30, 106
Young Ottomans, 607
Yu, 80, 82

Yuan dynasty, in China, 291–95; Mongols
    and, 309, 478; novel in, 300
Yuan Shikai, 699–700
Yucatán Peninsula: Maya in, 135*m*, 135–41,
    354–55, 355; Teotihuacán in, 352–55
Yuezhi, 179
Yugoslavia: civil war in, 777; in Cold War,
    708–9; in NAM, 707, 724

Zacatecas, 438
Zacuto, Abraham, 406
Zaghlul, Saad, 689
Zagwe dynasty, in Ethiopia, 333–34
Zaibatsu (cartels), 593–94, 698
Zaire. *See* Congo
Zanzibar, 134, 665
Zapata, Emiliano, *464*, 563–64
Zemstvos, 617
Zen Buddhism, 215, 320, 327
Zeng Guofan, 585
Zengi, Imad al-Din, 236
Zeppelin, Ferdinand von, 633
Zeus, 170

Zhang Heng, 215–16
Zhang Zuolin, 700
Zheng He, 296, 337
Zhou dynasty, in China, 87*m*; agriculture
    of, 90; culture of, 96; economy of, 90–91;
    feudalism in, 88–89; government in, 90,
    97; hegemony in, 88–89; iron in, 95–96;
    Korea and, 307; Qin dynasty and, 201–2;
    religion in, 92–96; science and technology
    of, 95–96; *Shujing* on, 82, 87; social classes
    in, 91; trade in, 91; Vietnam and, 321–22;
    western and eastern, 88; women in, 92;
    writing in, 93–95, *94*
Zhu Xi, 299
Zhu Yuanzhang (Hongwu), 296, 297, 309
Zimbabwe, 349–50, 756–57
Zionism, 688
Zoroastrians, *164*, 164–65; Achaemenids
    as, 152; in Byzantium, 278; Islam and,
    226; Sasanids as, 149–50; as state
    religions, 249; Sufism and, 243; Yasht of,
    160, 164
Zulu, 131, 757